Tulsian's

CORPORATE ACCOUNTING

Tulsian's
CORPORATE ACCOUNTING

CA (Dr.) P.C. TULSIAN

M.Com., Ph.D., FCA, PGDFM

Additional Director (Former)
Board of Studies
The Institute of Chartered Accountants of India, New Delhi
Principal (Former)
Ramjas College
University of Delhi
New Delhi
Recipient of an Award for 'Exemplary Services contributed to the cause of Profession'
by The Institute of Chartered Accountants of India, New Delhi
Also Recipient of an 'Excellence Award' by University of Delhi, New Delhi

CA BHARAT TULSIAN

Chartered Accountant

Alumnus of Sri Ram College of Commerce (SRCC), University of Delhi, New Delhi
Recipient of An Award for the **'Best Article on Foreign Exchange'** *in All India*
by The Institute of Chartered Accountants of India, New Delhi

TUSHAR TULSIAN

MBA (Finance), Indian School of Business (ISB)
Investment Banker (Former), J.P. Morgan

S Chand And Company Limited
(ISO 9001 Certified Company)

S Chand And Company Limited

(ISO 9001 Certified Company)

Head Office: D-92, Sector–2, Noida – 201301, U.P. (India), Ph. 91-120-4682700

Registered Office: A-27, 2nd Floor, Mohan Co-operative Industrial Estate, New Delhi – 110 044, Phone: 011-49731800

www.**schandpublishing.com;** e-mail: **info@schandpublishing.com**

Marketing Offices:

Chennai	:	Ph: 23632120; chennai@schandpublishing.com
Guwahati	:	Ph: 2738811, 2735640; guwahati@schandpublishing.com
Hyderabad	:	Ph: 40186018; hyderabad@schandpublishing.com
Jalandhar	:	Ph: 4645630; jalandhar@schandpublishing.com
Kolkata	:	Ph: 23357458, 23353914; kolkata@schandpublishing.com
Lucknow	:	Ph: 4003633; lucknow@schandpublishing.com
Mumbai	:	Ph: 25000297; mumbai@schandpublishing.com
Patna	:	Ph: 2260011; patna@schandpublishing.com

First Edition 2023
Reprints 2023, 2024
Reprint 2025

ISBN: 978-93-550-1756-7 **Product Code:** H8CAC48ACCN10ENAA23O

PRINTED IN INDIA

By Vikas Publishing House Private Limited, Plot 20/4, Site-IV, Industrial Area Sahibabad, Ghaziabad – 201 010 and Published by S Chand And Company Limited, A-27, 2nd Floor, Mohan Co-operative Industrial Estate, New Delhi – 110 044.

her

Dedicated to
our first two gurus
Late Smt. Shanti Devi Tulsian
&
Late Sh. B. P. Tulsian

Preface

The book adopts a fresh and novel approach to the study of Corporate Accounting for the students of B.Com. under the recommended National Education Policy 2020 (NEP 2020). It has been written in a teach yourself style strictly following a student-friendly approach, and is essentially meant to serve as a tutor at home. Among the important features of this book includes:

PEDAGOGICAL FEATURES

Simple Language	The text is presented in the simplest language "meant to serve beginners".
Heading for each Paragraph	Each paragraph has been arranged under a suitable heading for easy retention of concepts.
Tabular Form	Wherever possible the text matter relating to a particular topic/sub-topic has been presented in a Tabular Form.
Eye-catching Screens	All important equations, formulae, figures and practical steps have been presented in screen format to catch the eye.
Uniform Format of Chapter	Each chapter has been uniformly organised under suitable headings, viz., text supported by suitable illustrations, solved problems.

DISTINCTIVE FEATURES

Important Distinctions	Over 50 distinctions have been provided for a better comparative study.
Exhibits	Over 100 exhibits to acquaint students with various accounting treatment and formats.
Illustrations	Over 300 Illustrations have been provided for a better understanding of the text.
Solved Problems	Over 250 solved problems along with necessary working notes and alternative solution have been provided throughout the text.

Acknowledgements

We wish to express our sincere thanks to several individuals who have been a source of inspiration and support personally and professionally including Dr. R.P. Tulsian, Dr. Renu Gupta, Dr. Vibha Jain, Dr. Sandeep Kumar Goel, Dr. Sandeep Garg, Dr. Shalini Aggarwal, Dr. Sonal Gupta, Dr. Saloni Gupta, Dr. Hem Chand Jain, Dr. K.B. Gupta, Dr. Seema Gupta, Dr. Mukesh Jain, Dr. Naresh Gupta, Dr. Amit Singhal, Dr. Manju Gupta, Dr. Sunita Gupta, Dr. V.P. Bansal, Dr. Sushma Aggarwal, Dr. C.P. Gupta, CA N.D. Gupta, CA Naveen Gupta, CA M.K. Sharda, CA Anil Jindal, CA Madhu Sudan Goyal, CA M.K. Aggarwal, CA Amrit Aggarwal, CA Arun Jain, CA Sunil Aggarwal, CA Vinod Aggarwal, CA Virender Aggarwal, CA S.K. Gupta, CA Ishwar Khemka, CA Prem Bansal, CA Ashish Gupta, CA Kuldeep Bhardwaj, CA Neeraj Chabra, CA Kishore Paul, CA Pradeep Narang, CA R. Devarajan, CA Arnav Chakrabarty, CA Seema Gupta, CA Shilpa Aggarwal, Dr M.P. Meena, Dr Mohinder Paul, CA Sweta Gupta, Dr Balbir Kaur and Dr Rovika Prem.

Special word of thanks is also due to our favourite students CA (Dr) Vishal Pandey, CA (Dr) Pankaj Jain, CA Atul Aggarwal, CA Sunil Bhala, CA Rajesh Jindal, Arushi Jindal, CA Pallavi, CA Antima Jain, CA Piyush Tulsian, CA Swati Tulsian, CA Piyush, CA Prarthana Mittal, CA Aman Mittal, CA Piyush Sharma, CA Mohit Gupta, Sheena Tulsian, CS Hitesh Keshwani, Vinay Karnani, Taanisha Murarka, Priyanshu, Apoorva Gupta, Sahil Sharma, Hiten Bansal, Nikhitha T., Manreen Kaur and many more, who provided incisive comments and useful feedback.

We must conclude that this book would never has been written without the support, encouragement and prodding of our family members. Many thanks to them.

Any criticisms or suggestions for further improvement of the book will be gratefully acknowledged and appreciated.

CA (Dr.) P.C. Tulsian
www.pctulsian.com
pctulsian@gmail.com

CA Bharat Tulsian
bharattulsian88@gmail.com

Tushar Tulsian
tushartulsian@gmail.com

Syllabus

B COM COURSE SYLLABUS
Paper : CORPORATE ACCOUNTING

Time: 3 Hours **Marks:160**

Objective:

The course aims to help learners to acquire conceptual knowledge of financial accounting, to impart skills for recording various kinds of business transactions and to prepare financial statements.

Unit	*Contents*	*Relevant Chapter of the Book*
1.	**Unit 1: Accounting for Share Capital and Debentures**	**1-7**
	Types of shares; Accounting for Share Capital, Issue of Rights and Bonus Shares; ESOPs and Buy-Back of shares; Issue and Redemption of preference Shares and Debentures. Underwriting of Shares and Debentures. [In reference to Relevant Accounting Standards (AS and Ind AS) and Guidance Notes as applicable.]	
2.	**Unit 2: Financial Statements of Companies**	**8-11**
	Preparation of financial statements of corporate entities including one Person Company (excluding calculation of managerial remuneration) as per Division I and II of Schedule III of the Companies Act 2013; Related Parties as per AS-18, Preparation of Statement of Profit and Loss, Balance Sheet, Statement of Equity and Cashflow Statement manually and using appropriate software. Interpreting the ratios calculated as per Schedule III of the Companies Act 2013 [with reference to Relevant Accounting Standards (AS and Ind AS) and the relevant provisions of The Companies Act, 2013, as applicable.]. Calculation of EPS as per AS 20.	
3.	**Unit 3: Valuation of Intangible Assets and Shares**	**12-15**
	Valuation of Intangible Assets and Shares. Value Added Statement, Economic Value Added, Market Value Added, Shareholders Value Added.	
4.	**Unit 4: Amalgamation of Companies and Internal Reconstruction**	**16-17**
	(a) Accounting for Amalgamation of Companies (excluding inter-company holdings) applying AS 14/Ind AS 103. (b) Accounting for Different forms of Internal Reconstruction (excluding drafting of Internal Reconstruction Scheme).	

5.	Unit 5: Corporate Financial Reporting	18-19
	Meaning, need and objectives; Constituents of Annual Report and how it is different from financial statements; Contents of report of the Board of Directors; XBRL Reporting. Drafting of Notes to Accounts. Segment Reporting as per AS-17 , Sustainability Reporting, Triple Bottom Line Reporting, CSR Reporting.	
	Notes: 1. The relevant Accounting Standards (both AS & Ind AS) for all of the above topics should be covered. 2. Any revision of the relevant Indian Accounting Standards/ Accounting Standards would become applicable. 3. The relevant provisions of The Companies Act, 2013, as applicable for all of the above topics should be covered.	
	Practical Exercises: **The learners are required to:** 1. Collect prospectus issued by reputed companies, and examine the matters related to issues of shares. 2. Examine the annual reports of business organisations to find out whether applicable accounting standards (AS and Ind AS) are complied with or not. 3. Collect information from business newspapers, periodicals, print and digital media on the amalgamation of companies and prepare a report. 4. Prepare financial statements using appropriate software. 5. Download company annual reports of reputed companies from the websites and analyse the voluntary and mandatory information contained in these statements.	

Contents

No.	Chapter Name	Page No.
1.	Accounting for Share Capital	1.1—1.82
2.	Accounting for Bonus Issue	2.1—2.16
3.	Redemption of Redeemable Preference Shares	3.1—3.44
4.	Accounting for Buy-Back of Shares	4.1—4.28
5A.	Issue of Debentures	5A.1—5A.46
5B.	Redemption of Debentures	5B.1—5B.84
6.	Underwriting of Shares and Debentures	6.1—6.32
7.	Accounting for Employee Stock Option Plan	7.1—7.40
8.	Financial Statements of a Company	8.1—8.126
9.	AS 20 – Earnings Per Share	9.1—9.24
10.	AS 18 – Related Party Disclosures	10.1—10.12
11.	Cash Flow Statement	11.1—11.118
12.	Valuation of Goodwill	12.1—12.64
13.	Valuation of Brand	13.1—13.20
14.	Valuation of Shares	14.1—14.64
15.	Value Added Statement [Including Economic Value Added, Market Value Added & Shareholders' Value Added]	15.1—15.46
16.	Amalgamation of Companies	16.1—16.96
17.	Internal Reconstruction	17.1—17.90
18.	Corporate Financial Reporting	18.1—18.32
19.	AS 17–Segment Reporting	19.1—19.26

Contents

No.	Chapter Name	Page No.
1.	Accounting for Share Capital	1.1—1.82
2.	Accounting for Bonus Issue	2.1—2.16
3.	Redemption of Redeemable Preference Shares	3.1—3.44
4.	Accounting for Buy-Back of Shares	4.1—4.26
5A.	Issue of Debentures	5A.1—5A.46
5B.	Redemption of Debentures	5B.1—5B.84
6.	Underwriting of Shares and Debentures	6.1—6.32
7.	Accounting for Employee Stock Option Plan	7.1—7.40
8.	Financial Statements of a Company	8.1—8.126
9.	AS 20 – Earnings Per Share	9.1—9.24
10.	AS 18 – Related Party Disclosures	10.1—10.12
11.	Cash Flow Statement	11.1—11.118
12.	Valuation of Goodwill	12.1—12.64
13.	Valuation of Brand	13.1—13.20
14.	Valuation of Shares	14.1—14.64
15.	Value Added Statement [Including Economic Value Added, Market Value Added & Shareholders' Value Added]	15.1—15.46
16.	Amalgamation of Companies	16.1—16.96
17.	Internal Reconstruction	17.1—17.90
18.	Corporate Financial Reporting	18.1—18.32
19.	AS 17–Segment Reporting	19.1—19.26

1 ACCOUNTING FOR SHARE CAPITAL

LEARNING OBJECTIVES

After studying this chapter, you should be able to understand:

- ◇ Meaning, Nature and Characteristics of a Company
- ◇ Private Company and Public Company
- ◇ Meaning and Categories of Share Capital
- ◇ Meaning, Nature and Classes of Shares
- ◇ Important Points in case of an Issue of Shares to the Public
- ◇ Issue of Shares at Par
- ◇ Issue of Shares at a Premium [Sec. 52]
- ◇ Issue of Shares at a Discount [Sec. 53]
- ◇ Under-Subscription
- ◇ Over-Subscription
- ◇ *Pro rata* allotment
- ◇ Calls-In-arrears and Calls-in-advance
- ◇ Issue of Shares for Consideration other than Cash
- ◇ Forfeiture of Shares
- ◇ Re-Issue of Shares
- ◇ Forfeiture and Re-issue of Shares Allotted on Pro-rata basis in Case of Over-Subscription
- ◇ Disclosure of Share Capital in Company's Balance Sheet
- ◇ Private Placement of Shares

With the expansion in the scale of operations and increase in risk involved, non- corporate forms of organizations (i.e., sole proprietorship, partnership firms) found themselves unequal to the task of meeting all the capital requirements and increased risks of the present day large scale business operations. Thus, a relatively new form of business organisation came into vogue and this is called a 'Joint Stock Company' *or* simply, a company.

1.0 MEANING, CHARACTERISTICS AND NATURE OF A COMPANY

Meaning	A company is an incorporated association which is an artificial person created by law, having a corporate and legal personality distinct and separate from its members, perpetual succession and a common seal.

Characteristics	The essential characteristics of a company are as follows: (a) It is an **incorporated (registered) association** (b) It is an **artificial person created by law.** (c) It has a separate legal entity. (d) It has a **perpetual succession**, (i.e. Continued existence) (it can be created and wound up by law only). (e) It has a **common seal**, i.e., official signature of the company.
Nature	A company is a corporate and legal personality distinct and separate from its members.

2.0 REGISTERED *or* INCORPORATED COMPANY

MEANING OF REGISTERED COMPANY

A registered company is one which is registered in accordance with the provisions of the Companies Act of 2013 and also includes the existing companies. By existing company we mean a company formed and registered under any of the previous laws. A registered company comes into existence only when it receives the certificate of incorporation. Registered companies are governed by the provisions of The Companies Act.

A Registered Company may *either* be a private company *or* a public company.

MEANING OF PRIVATE COMPANY

A Private Company means a company which has a minimum paid up capital of ₹ 1,00,000 *or* such higher paid up capital as may be prescribed, and by its articles:

(a) restricts the right to transfer its shares, if any,

(b) except in case of one person company limits the number of its members to 200, and

(c) prohibits any invitation to the public to subscribe for any securities of the company.

Notes:

1. *Since the above-mentioned restrictions must be contained in the articles of a private limited company, it is necessary for a private company to frame its own articles. However, the articles of a private company not having share capital is not required to contain the restriction regarding the transfer of shares.*
2. *A private company may be (a) a company limited by shares, or (b) a company limited by guarantee, or (c) an unlimited company.*
3. *In case a private company is a limited company, then it must add the words 'Private Limited' at the end of its name.*
4. *If a private company does not comply with any of the restrictions contained in the articles, it ceases to enjoy some of the privileges granted to a private company.*
5. *A private company must have at least 2 directors.*

MEANING OF PUBLIC COMPANY

Public company means a company which is

Either

(a) not a private company and has a minimum paid-up capital of ₹ 5,00,000 *or* such higher paid-up capital as may be prescribed; *or*

(b) is a private company which is subsidiary of public company.

Notes:

1. *There is no restriction on the maximum number of members. However, the maximum number of members depends upon the number of shares allotted.*
2. *A public company may be (a) a company limited by shares, or (b) a company limited by guarantee, or (c) an unlimited company.*
3. *In case a public company is a limited company, then it must add the words 'Limited' at the end of its name.*
4. *A public company must have at least 7 members. [Section 12(1)]*
5. *A public company must have at least 3 directors.*

3.0 SHARE CAPITAL

Meaning	Share Capital means the capital raised by the issue of shares. The amounts invested by the shareholders towards the face value of shares are collectively known as 'Share Capital' which is quite distinct from the capital put in by individual shareholders.
Three	The share capital is divided under the following three heads: 1. **Authorised Capital:** An Authorised Capital refers to that capital which is authorised by the Memorandum of Association to be the maximum amount of share capital of the company. This is the maximum limit of the company which it is authorised to raise and beyond which the company cannot raise unless the capital clause in the Memorandum is changed. 2. **Issued Capital:** An Issued Capital refers to the nominal value of that part of authorised capital, which the company issues from time to time for subscription. 3. **Subscribed Capital:** Subscribed Capital refers to the capital which has been subscribed by the members of a company.
Other Terms used under the Act	1. **Unissued Capital:** Unissued Capital refers to that portion of the authorized capital which has not yet been issued. 2. **Uncalled Capital:** Uncalled capital refers to that portion of the issued capital which has not yet been called up by the company. 3. **Reserve Capital:** It refers to that portion of uncalled share capital which shall not be capable of being called up except in the event and for the purposes of the company being wound up (Sec. 65).

ILLUSTRATION 1

Calculate (a) Authorised Capital (b) Issued Capital (c) Unissued Capital (d) Subscribed Capital, (e) Called-up capital, (f) Uncalled Capital (g) Paid-up Capital in each of the following alternative cases:

Case (i) X Ltd. was formed with a capital of ₹ 10,00,000 divided into shares of ₹ 10 each. X offered the entire shares and called up fully on application. The subscribers paid ₹ 10,00,000.

Case (ii) X Ltd. was formed with a capital of ₹ 10,00,000 divided into shares of ₹ 10 each. It offered 90% shares and called up fully on application. The subscribers paid ₹ 9,00,000.

Case (iii) X Ltd. was formed with a capital of ₹ 10,00,000 divided into shares of ₹ 10 each. It offered 90% shares and called up fully on application. The subscribers paid ₹ 8,10,000.

Case (iv) X Ltd. was formed with a capital of ₹ 10,00,000 divided into shares of ₹ 10 each. It offered 90% shares and called up 60% on application. The subscribers paid ₹ 4,86,000.

SOLUTION:

CALCULATION OF VARIOUS TYPES OF CAPITAL

Type of Capital	*Case (i)* (₹)	*Case (ii)* (₹)	*Case (iii)* (₹)	*Case (iv)* (₹)
A. Authorised Capital	10,00,000	10,00,000	10,00,000	10,00,000
B. Issued Capital	10,00,000	9,00,000	9,00,000	9,00,000
C. Unissued Capital [A – B]	NIL	1,00,000	1,00,000	1,00,000
D. Subscribed Capital	10,00,000	9,00,000	8,10,000	4,86,000
E. Called-up Capital	10,00,000	9,00,000	8,10,000	4,86,000
F. Uncalled Capital	NIL	NIL	NIL	3,24,000
G. Paid-up Capital	10,00,000	9,00,000	8,10,000	4,86,000

DISTINCTION BETWEEN AUTHORISED CAPITAL AND ISSUED CAPITAL

Authorised Capital and Issued Capital can be distinguished as follows:

Basis of Distinction	*Authorised Capital*	*Issued Capital*
1. Meaning	It refers to that amount which is stated in the Memorandum of Association as the share capital of the company.	It refers to the nominal value of that part of authorised capital which has been (i) subscribed for by the signatories to the Memorandum of Association and (ii) allotted for cash *or* consideration other than cash.
2. Consideration of future requirements	Its amount is determined after considering **present and future requirements.**	Its amount is determined after considering the **present requirements.**
3. Disclosure in Memorandum of Association	Its amount is **required** to be disclosed in Memorandum of Association.	Its amount is **not required** to be disclosed in the Memorandum of Association.
4. Is it the basis of Stamp Duty?	Stamp Duty is payable on the basis of **authorised capital.**	It is **not the basis** for calculating **stamp duty.**
5. Is it the basis of Company registration fees?	Company registration fee is payable on the **basis** of authorised capital.	Issued capital is **not the basis** for registration fees.
6. Does the change amount to an alteration of Memorandum?	Any change in the amount of authorised capital **amounts** to an alternation of Memorandum of Association.	Any change in the amount of issued capital **does not amount** to an alteration of Memorandum of Association.
7. Whether one can exceed other	It **can exceed** issued capital.	It **cannot exceed** authorised capital.

DISTINCTION BETWEEN RESERVE CAPITAL AND CAPITAL RESERVE

Reserve Capital should not be confused with Capital Reserve which is created out of profits.

Reserve Capital and Capital Reserve can be distinguished as follows:

Basis of Distinction	*Reserve Capital*	*Capital Reserve*
1. Meaning	It refers to those portion of uncalled share capital which shall not be capable of being called up except in the event and for the purpose of the company being wound up. (Sec. 65)	It refers to those amounts which are not regarded as free for distribution by way of divided through Profit and Loss Account.
2. Mandatory *or* Not	It is **not mandatory** to create Reserve Capital.	It is **mandatory** to create Capital Reserve in case of profit on forfeited shares.
3. Disclosure in Balance Sheet	It is **not disclosed** in the company's Balance Sheet.	It is required to be **disclosed** as the 1st item under the head 'Reserves and Surplus' on the liabilities side of the Balance Sheet.
4. Time when it can be used	It can be used during **only at the time of winding up.**	It can be used **during the life of the company.**
5. Realised vs. Unrealised	It refers to the amount which has *neither* **been called up** *nor* **been received.**	It (excluding items like revaluation profit) refers to that amount which has already been **realised.**
6. Can it be used to write off capital losses?	It **cannot be used** to write off capital losses.	It **can be used** to write off capital losses.
7. Can it be used to declare share bonus?	It **cannot be used** to declare a share bonus.	It (excluding items like revaluation profit) **can be used** to declare a share bonus.

4.0 SHARE

Meaning	A 'Share' is one of the units into which the capital of the company is divided. Section 2(84) of the Companies Act, 2013 defines a share as "a share in the share capital of a company, and includes stock except where a distinction between stock and share is expressed *or* implied". *For example*, where a company has a share capital of ₹ 1,00,000 divided into 10,000 units of ₹ 10 each, then each unit of ₹ 10 is called a share of ₹ 10 each and a person who has taken 10 shares of that company is said to have share in the share capital of the company to the extent of ₹ 100. A share may be partly paid up *or* fully paid up. The persons who contribute money through shares are called Shareholders.
Nature	A share is not a sum of money but is an interest measured by a sum of money and is made of various rights and obligations contained in the contract (i.e., Articles of Association). The shares are the movable properties transferable in the manner provided by the Articles of the company.
Disclosure	The amount of authorized capital, together with the number of shares in which it is divided, is stated in the Memorandum of Association but the classes of shares in which the company's capital is to be divided, along with their respective rights and obligations, are determined by the Articles of Association of the company.

Classes	Under the existing provisions of Sec. 43 of the Companies Act, now only two kinds of shares may be issued, viz., Preference shares and Equity shares. **I. Preference Share:** According to Sec. 43, a preference share is one which carries the following two rights: (a) a right to receive dividend at a stipulated rate *or* of a fixed amount before any dividend is paid on equity shares. (b) a right to receive repayment of capital on winding up of the company, before the capital of equity shareholders is returned. In addition to the aforesaid two preferential rights, a preference share may carry some other rights. On the basis of additional rights, preference shares can be classified as follows: 1. **Cumulative Preference Share** is that share on which arrears of dividend accumulate. It implies that in case no dividend is declared in any particular year(s), the arrears of dividend shall be paid in the year in which dividend is declared. The arrears of dividend on cumulative preference shares are shown in the Balance Sheet as a **Commitments**. 2. **Non-cumulative Preference Share** is that share on which arrears of dividend do not accumulate as per the express provision in the Articles of Association. It implies that in case no dividend is declared in any particular year, the right to receive such dividend for that year expires. 3. **Participating Preference Share** is that share which, in addition to two basic preferential rights, also carries one *or* more of the following rights as per Articles: (i) a right to participate in the surplus profits left after paying dividend to equity shareholders at a stipulated rate. (ii) a right to participate in the surplus assets left after the repayment of capital to equity shareholders on the winding up of the company. 4. **Non-participating Preference Share** is that share which is not a participating share. Unless otherwise stated, a preference share is always deemed to be a non-participating preference share. 5. **Convertible Preference Share** is that share which confers on its holder a right of conversion into equity share. 6. **Non-convertible Preference Share** is that share which does not confer on its holder a right of conversion into equity share. Unless otherwise stated, a preference share is always deemed to be a non-convertible one. 7. **Redeemable Preference Share** is that share which is redeemable in accordance with the provisions of Sec. 55. Now, no company limited by shares can issue any preference share which is irredeemable. **II. Equity Share** An equity share is a share which is not a preference share. According to Section 43(a) equity share capital may be (i) with voting rights; *or* (ii) with differential rights as to voting, dividend *or* otherwise in accordance with such rules and subject to such conditions as may be prescribed.

DISTINCTION BETWEEN AN EQUITY SHARE AND PREFERENCE SHARE

An Equity Share and Preference Share can be distinguished as follows:

Basis of Distinction	*An Equity Share*	*A Preference Share*
1. Preferential right as to the payment of dividend	Payment of equity dividend is made **after** the payment of preference dividend.	Payment of preference dividend is made **before** the payment of equity dividend.
2. Preferential right as to the repayment of capital	Repayment of Equity share capital is made **after** the repayment of preference share capital.	Repayment of preference share capital is made **before** the repayment of equity share capital.
3. Fluctuations in the rate of dividend	The rate of equity dividend **may vary** from year to year depending upon the decision of directors and members.	The rate of preference dividend is **fixed.**
4. Arrears of dividend	In case of an equity share, arrears of dividend **cannot accumulate** in any case.	In case of a preference share, arrears of dividend may **accumulate.**
5. Convertibility	It **cannot** be convertible.	It **may be** convertible.
6. Voting Rights	Equity shareholders generally **enjoy** voting rights.	Preference shareholders **do not have** any voting rights **except at their class meetings.**
7. Redeemability	It is **not redeemable** during the life time of the company **unless** the company decides to **buyback** the shares.	It is **redeemable** during the life time of the company.

5.0 IMPORTANT POINTS IN CASE OF AN ISSUE OF SHARES TO THE PUBLIC

Prospectus	When a Public company intends to raise capital by issuing its shares to the public, it invites the public to make an offer to buy its shares through a document called 'Prospectus'. According to Sec. 26, a copy of prospectus is required to be delivered to the Registrar for registration on *or* before the date of publication thereof. Prospectus must be issued with 90 days of its registration.
Compulsory Listing	Every company, intending to offer shares *or* debentures to the public for subscription by the issue of a prospectus must, before such issue, make an application to at least one recognised stock exchange for permission for the shares *or* debentures intending to be so offered to be dealt in the stock exchange [Sec 40]. The name of such stock exchange(s) must be stated in the prospectus.
Applications	1. An application for shares is an offer to take shares made by an applicant. 2. The amount which the applicant is required to pay with the application is called as 'Application Money'. 3. **Minimum Application Money Per Share:** The amount payable on application on each share must be at least 5% of the nominal amount of share. [Sec. 39]. However, as per SEBI Guidelines the minimum Application Moneys to be paid by an applicant along with the application must be (i) at least 25% of the issue price (ii) within the range of ₹ 5,000 to ₹ 7,000.

<table>
<tr><td></td><td>4. Application Money to be Deposited in a Scheduled Bank: All moneys received from applicants for shares shall be deposited and kept deposited in a Scheduled Bank: (i) until the certificate to commence business is obtained; or (ii) where such certificate has already been obtained, until the full amount of minimum subscription has been received by the company.</td></tr>
<tr><td>Allotment</td><td>1. Allotment is an acceptance by the company of the offer made by an applicant. The term 'Allotment' means the appropriation out of the previously unappropriated capital of the company, of a certain number of shares to a person. It is on allotment that shares come into existence.
2. The amount payable on allotment is called 'Allotment Money'.
3. In case of first allotment of shares, no allotment shall be made unless the amount stated in the prospectus as the minimum subscription has been subscribed and the sum payable on application for the stated amount has been received by the company. [Sec 39] As per SEBI Guidelines, in case of non-receipt by the company of 90% of the issued amount from public subscription plus accepted devolvement from underwriters or from other sources in case of under subscribed issues, within 60 days from the date of closure of the issue, the company must refund the subscription amount in full within 78 days without interest and with interest @ 15% p.a. for the delayed period beyond 78 days from the date of closure of the issue.
4. The basis of allotment is decided by the Board of Directors in consultation with the concerned recognised Stock Exchange and as a result, the following courses of action are taken:
(i) In case of Application rejected fully: Letters of Regret along with refund orders are sent.
(ii) In case of Application accepted fully: Letters of Allotment are sent
(iii) In case of Applications accepted partially: Letters of Allotment along with refund orders in respect of excess Application Money not adjusted towards other sums due on shares are sent.</td></tr>
<tr><td>Calls</td><td>1. A call in the strict sense, is a demand by the company for payment of part of the issue price of shares or debentures which has not been paid and the date of whose payment was not specified in the terms of the issue.
2. The remaining amount (i.e. other than Application Money and allotment money) due from shareholders may be demanded in one or more parts which are termed as 'First Call', 'Second Call' and so on. A word 'Final' is added to the last call. For example, in case the second call is the last one, then the Second Call will be termed as 'Second & Final Call'.
3. It may be noted that the instalments of the issue price specified in the terms of issue, are strictly not calls unless the Articles specifically provides therefore.
4. The legal provisions relating to calls are as under:
(i) A call must be made under a resolution of the Board of Directors passed at a meeting of the Board [Sec 179].
(ii) The calls must be made on a uniform basis on all shares falling under the same class. Shares of the same nominal value on which different amounts have been paid up shall not be deemed to fall under the same class. (Sec. 49).</td></tr>
</table>

Calls	(iii) A company may, if so authorised by its articles, accept from any member the whole *or* a part of the amount remaining unpaid on any shares held by him although no part of that amount has been called up. [Sec. 50]. (iv) The call must be made strictly in according with the provisions of the Articles. If the Articles are silent, the provisions laid down in Table 'A" shall be applicable. Table 'A' imposes the following restrictions: (i) The amount of call must not exceed 25% of the nominal value of the shares; (ii) At least 1 month must have elapsed since the date which was fixed for the payment of the last preceding call. (iii) At least 14 days notice specifying the time and place of payment must be given. (v) As per SEBI guidelines, the calls must be structured in such a manner that the entire subscription money is received within 12 months from the date of allotment and if the investor fails to pay call money within 12 months, the subscription money already paid may be forfeited.

6.0 ISSUE OF SHARES

WORTH NOTING POINTS

Consideration	Shares may be issued for Cash *or* for Consideration other than Cash.
Issue Price	Issue Price means the price at which shares are issued. Shares may be issued at par *or* at a premium *or* at a discount.
Payment of Issue Price	Issue Price may be payable *either* in lump sum along with application *or* in instalments at different stages (e.g., partly on application, partly on allotment, partly on call).
Par Value	Par Value means the Nominal *or* Face Value of a share. Each company can decide its own par value say ₹ 1, ₹ 2, ₹ 5, ₹ 10, ₹ 20, ₹ 50, ₹ 100 as per SEBI Guidelines.

ACCOUNTING PROCEDURE FOR THE ISSUE OF SHARES FOR CASH

Step 1: *Record the receipt of Application Money*

Step 2: ***Situation I*: When No. of Shares applied = No. of Shares offered**

Transfer Application Money on the shares allotted to 'Share Capital A/c'.

OR

***Situation II*: When No. of Shares applied < No. of Shares offered**

(a) *If the Minimum Subscription has at least been received.*

Transfer Application Money on the shares allotted to 'Share Capital A/c'.

(b) *If the Minimum Subscription has not been received.*

Refund Application Money to all the applicants.

OR

***Situation III* : When No. of Shares applied > No. of Shares offered**

Transfer Application Money on the shares allotted to 'Share Capital A/c' and Transfer excess Application Money (not exceeding the amount due on allotment) to 'Share Allotment Account' in case of partially accepted applications and Refund Application Money in case of rejected applications and excess Application Money over and above the allotment money in case of partially accepted applications.

Note: *The aforesaid treatment is suggested when question is silent about the treatment of Excess Application Money.*

Step 3: *Make due Allotment Money on shares allotted.*
Step 4: *Record the receipt of Allotment Money.*
Step 5: *Make due the First Call money on shares allotted.*
Step 6: *Record the receipt of First Call Money and so on.*

7.0 ISSUE OF SHARES AT PAR

MEANING OF SHARES ISSUED AT PAR

Shares are said to be issued at par when they are issued at a **price equal to the face value**, i.e., when the issue price is equal to the face value. *For example*, if a share of ₹ 10 is issued at ₹ 10, it is said that the share has been issued at par. The issue price of a share may be payable *either* in lump sum along with the application *or* in instalments.

JOURNAL ENTRIES IF THE ISSUE PRICE IS PAYABLE IN LUMP SUM

Date	*Particulars*	*L.F.*	*Dr. (₹)*	*Cr. (₹)*
1.	**On Receipt of Application Money**			
	Bank A/c Dr.		(With Application Money received)	
	To Share Application & Allotment A/c			
	(Being the Application Money received)			
2.	**On Adjustment of Application Money**			
	Share Application & Allotment A/c Dr.		(With Application Money received)	
	To Share Capital A/c		(With Application Money due on Shares allotted)	
	To Bank A/c		(With Application Money on Rejected Applications)	
	(Being the Application Money adjusted and Surplus refunded)			

JOURNAL ENTRIES IF THE ISSUE PRICE IS PAYABLE IN INSTALMENTS

Date	*Particulars*	*L.F.*	*Dr. (₹)*	*Cr. (₹)*
1.	**On Receipt of Application Money**			
	Bank A/c Dr.		(With Application Money received)	
	To Share Application A/c		[No. of Shares Applied × Application Money Per Share]	
	(Being the Application Money received)			

2.	**On Adjustment of Application Money** Share Application A/c Dr. To Bank A/c To Share Capital A/c (Being the Application Money adjusted and Surplus refunded)			(With Application Money on Rejected Applications) (With Application Money due on Shares allotted) [No. of Shares Allotted × Application Money Per Share]
3.	**On Making Allotment Money due** Share Allotment A/c Dr. To Share Capital A/c (Being the Allotment Money due)			(With Allotment Money due) [No. of Shares Allotted × Allotment Money Per Share]
4.	**On Receipt of Allotment Money** Bank A/c Dr. To Share Allotment A/c (Being the Allotment Money received)			(With Allotment Money received)
5.	**On Making the First Call** Share First Call A/c Dr. To Share Capital A/c (Being the First Call Money due)			(With First Call Money due) [No. of Shares Allotted × I Call Money Per Share]
6.	**On Receipt of the First Call** Bank A/c Dr. To Share First Call A/c (Being the First Call Money received)			(With First Call Money received)

TUTORIAL NOTES

Entries for Second Call, Third call	Similar entries may be made for the second call and third call through Share Second Call Account and Share Third Call Account respectively. In case of last call, the word 'final' is also added to the concerned 'Share Call Account'. In case the entire balance is payable on a single call, usually the term 'Share Call Account' is used.
Cash Book	In case the Cash Book is required to be prepared, all cash and bank transactions will be entered in the cash book and other transactions will be entered in the 'Journal Proper'.
Equity *or* Preference	In order to distinguish one type of share from the other one, the name of the share (i.e., whether Equity or Preference) must be prefixed with the word 'Share' e.g., Preference Share Capital Account, Equity Share Capital Account, Preference Share Application Account.
Share Application & Allotment A/c	Instead of preparing separate Share Application A/c & Share Allotment A/c, entries relating to the application and allotment may be passed through a combined, 'Share Application & Allotment A/c'. In such a case, an entry for transferring the surplus Application Money towards allotment on partially accepted applications, is not required to be passed.

Lump sum Issue Price	In case the issue price is payable in lump sum in one instalment, the entries should be passed through a combined Account namely: 'Share Application and Allotment Account'.
Nature of Share Application A/c	Share Application Account is a personal account of applicants who have applied for shares.
Nature of Share Allotment A/c	Share Allotment Account is a personal account of allottees to whom the shares have been allotted.
Adjustment of Excess Application Money	Unless otherwise stated in the question, the excess Application Money over and above that due on allotment should be refunded to the allottees.

ILLUSTRATION 2 [ISSUE PRICE IS PAYABLE IN INSTALMENTS]

X Ltd. was registered with a capital of ₹. 10,00,000 in shares of ₹ 10 each. It issued a prospectus inviting applications for 10,000 shares payable as follows:

On Application	₹ 4	On Allotment	₹ 3
On First Call	₹ 2	On Second Call	Balance

Applications were received for 10,000 shares. All money was duly received. Pass the necessary Journal entries.

SOLUTION:

JOURNAL

Date	Particulars		L.F.	Dr. (₹)	Cr. (₹)
1.	Bank A/c	Dr.		40,000	
	To Share Application A/c				40,000
	(Being the Application Money received on 10,000 @ ₹ 4 per share)				
2.	Share Application A/c	Dr.		40,000	
	To Share Capital A/c				40,000
	(Being the Application Money adjusted)				
3.	Share Allotment A/c	Dr.		30,000	
	To Share Capital A/c				30,000
	(Being the allotment money due on 10,000 shares @ ₹ 3 per share)				
4.	Bank A/c	Dr.		30,000	
	To Share Allotment A/c				30,000
	(Being the allotment money received)				
5.	Share First Call A/c	Dr.		20,000	
	To Share Capital A/c				20,000
	(Being the 1st Call money due on 10,000 shares @ ₹ 2 per share)				

6.	Bank A/c Dr. To Share 1st Call A/c (Being the share 1st call money received on 10,000 shares @ ₹ 2 per share)		20,000	20,000
7.	Share Second & Final Call A/c Dr. To Share Capital A/c (Being the share second & final call money due on 10,000 shares @ ₹ 1 per share)		10,000	10,000
8.	Bank A/c Dr. To Share Second & Final Call A/c (Being the share second & final call money received on 10,000) @ ₹ 1 per share)		10,000	10,000

ILLUSTRATION 3 [ISSUE PRICE IS PAYABLE IN LUMP SUM]

X Ltd. invited applications for 10,000 Equity Shares of ₹ 10 each issued at par. The whole amount was payable on application. The issue was fully subscribed. Pass the necessary Journal entries.

SOLUTION

JOURNAL

Date	*Particulars*	*L.F.*	*Dr. (₹)*	*Cr. (₹)*
1.	Bank A/c Dr. To Share Application & Allotment A/c (Being the Application Money received)		1,00,000	1,00,000
2.	Share Application & Allotment A/c Dr. To Share Capital A/c (Being the Application Money adjusted)		1,00,000	1,00,000

8.0 ISSUE OF SHARES AT A PREMIUM [SEC. 52]

Meaning	(a) Shares are said to be issued at a premium when they are issued at a price higher than the face value. (b) The excess of issue price over the face value is called as the amount of 'Securities Premium', e.g., if a share of ₹ 10 is issued at ₹ 15, it is said that the share has been issued at a premium of ₹ 5.
Nature	Securities Premium (whether received in cash *or* in kind) is a capital receipt and not a revenue receipt.
Treatment	The premium must be credited to a separate account called **'Securities Premium Account'.**
Demand	1. The amount of securities premium may be demanded along with the Application Money/allotment money/call money. 2. The amount of securities premium may be demanded *either* in lump sum *or* in instalments e.g., partly with Application Money and balance with allotment money.
Consideration	A company may issue securities at premium for cash *or* consideration other than cash.

Not Free Reserve	Securities Premium can not be treated as free reserves except for the purpose of Buy-back of shares.
Disclosure	The balance of Securities Premium Account appears under the head **'Shareholders' Funds'** and sub-head **'Reserves and Surplus'** in the Balance Sheet.
Purposes	(a) According to Sec. 52 of the Companies Act 2013, the Securities Premium may be applied only for the following purposes: 1. To issue fully paid **Bonus Shares** to the members. 2. To **write off Preliminary Expenses** of the company. 3. To **write off the expenses of** *or* the **commission** paid *or* **discount allowed on** any issue of **shares** *or* **debentures** of the company. 4. To provide for the **premium payable on the redemption** of any **Redeemable Preference Shares** *or* of any **Debentures** of the company. 5. To purchase its own shares *or* other securities u/s 68.

EXAMPLE 1

X Ltd. paid up share capital of ₹ 60,00,000 has a balance of ₹ 15,00,000 in Securities Premium Account. The company management does not want to carry over this balance. You are required to suggest the method for utilising this premium money that would achieve the objective of the management and maximize the return to shareholders.

SOLUTION

As per Sec. 52 of the Companies Act Securities premium money can be utilised to issue fully paid Bonus Shares to members. Hence the management should utilise the securities premium of ₹ 15,00,000 by issue of bonus shares to the shareholders in the ratio of 1 : 4 (i.e. one bonus share for every four share held).

EXAMPLE 2

Shubh Limited has the following balances appearing in its Balance Sheet:

Securities Premium	₹ 22,00,000
9% Debentures	₹ 1,20,00,000
Underwriting Commission	₹ 10,00,000

The company decided to redeem its 9% Debentures at a premium of 10%. You are required to suggest the ways in which the company can utilise the securities premium amount.

SOLUTION

(i) Utilize ₹ 10,00,000 to write off underwriting commission.

(ii) Utilize remaining ₹ 12,00,000 to provide for premium on redemption of 9% Debentures.

METHODS OF RECORDING

There are two methods of recording the securities premium:

1. Due Method	Under Due Method (i) an entry is passed for securities premium, when it becomes due and (ii) on receipt of securities premium, the Share Allotment Account is credited with the amount received (including securities premium) on allotment.
2. Receipt Method	Under Receipt Method (i) no entry is passed for securities premium when it becomes due, and (ii) on receipt of securities premium, the 'Securities Premium Account' is credited with the amount of securities premium received. The advantage of this method is that the 'Securities Premium Account' will not be required to be debited in the event of the forfeiture of those shares on which the securities premium money has not been received.

Note: *Due Method of recording 'Securities Premium' has been followed in this book.*

JOURNAL ENTRIES IF THE ISSUE PRICE IS PAYABLE IN LUMP SUM

Date	*Particulars*	*L.F.*	*Dr. (₹)*	*Cr. (₹)*
1.	**On Receipt of Application Money**			
	Bank A/c Dr.		(With Application Money received)	
	To Share Application & Allotment A/c			
	(Being the Application Money received)			
2.	**On Adjustment of Application Money**			
	Share Application & Allotment A/c Dr.		(With Application Money received)	
	To Share Capital A/c		(With Total Face Value due on Shares allotted)]	
	To Securities Premium A/c		(With Premium Money due on Shares allotted)	
	To Bank A/c		(With Application Money on Rejected Applications]	
	(Being the Application Money adjusted and surplus refunded)			

JOURNAL ENTRIES IF THE ISSUE PRICE IS PAYABLE IN LUMP SUM

All entries (except entry No. 3) are same as mentioned in case of issue of shares at par. However, assuming that the premium is demanded along with allotment money, the 3rd entry shall appear as follows:

JOURNAL

Date	*Particulars*	*L.F.*	*Dr. (₹)*	*Cr. (₹)*
	Share Allotment A/c Dr.		(With Total Allotment Money)	
	To Share Capital A/c		(With Face Value on Allotment due)	
	To Securities Premium A/c		(With Premium Money due)	
	(Being the Allotment Money due)			

ILLUSTRATION 4 [ISSUE PRICE IS PAYABLE IN INSTALMENTS]

X Ltd. was registered with a capital of ₹ 10,00,000 in shares of ₹ 10 each. It issued a prospectus inviting applications for 10,000 shares at 40% premium payable as follows:

On Application ₹ 5 (including ₹ 1 Premium), On Allotment ₹ 4 (including ₹ 1 Premium)
On First Call ₹ 3 (including ₹ 1 Premium), On Second Call Balance.

Applications were received for 10,000 shares. All money was duly received. Pass the necessary Journal entries.

SOLUTION:

JOURNAL

Date	*Particulars*	*L.F.*	*Dr. (₹)*	*Cr. (₹)*
1.	Bank A/c Dr. To Share Application A/c (Being the Application Money received on 10,000 @ ₹. 5 per share)		50,000	 50,000
2.	Share Application A/c Dr. To Share Capital A/c To Securities Premium A/c (Being the Application Money adjusted)		50,000	 40,000 10,000
3.	Share Allotment A/c Dr. To Share Capital A/c To Securities Premium A/c (Being the Allotment Money due on 10,000 shares)		40,000	 30,000 10,000
4.	Bank A/c Dr. To Share Allotment A/c (Being the Allotment Money received)		40,000	 40,000
5.	Share First Call A/c Dr. To Share Capital A/c To Securities Premium A/c (Being the 1st Call Money due on 10,000 shares)		30,000	 20,000 10,000
6.	Bank A/c Dr. To Share 1st Call A/c (Being the share 1st call money received on 10,000 shares @ ₹ 2 per share)		30,000	 30,000
7.	Share Second & Final Call A/c Dr. To Share Capital A/c To Securities Premium A/c (Being the Share Second & Final Call Money due on 10,000 shares)		20,000	 10,000 10,000
8.	Bank A/c Dr. To Share Second & Final Call A/c (Being the Share Second & Final Call Money received)		20,000	 20,000

9.0 ISSUE OF SHARES AT A DISCOUNT [SEC. 53]

Meaning	(a) Shares are said to be issued at a discount when they are issued at a price lower than the face value. (b) The excess of the face value over the issue price is called as the amount of discount, e.g., if a share of ₹ 10 is issued at ₹ 9, it is said that the share has been issued at a discount of ₹ 1.
Legal Provision	1. Except the issue of Sweat Equity shares, a company shall not issue shares at a discount. 2. Any share issued by a company at a discounted price shall be void. 3. Where a company contravenes the provisions of this section, the company shall be punishable with fine which shall be at least ₹ 1,00,000 but which may extend to ₹ 5,00,000 and every officer who is in default shall be punishable with imprisonment for a term which may extend to 6 months *or* with fine which shall be at least ₹ 1,00,000 but which may extend to ₹ 5,00,000 *or* with both.

10.0 UNDER-SUBSCRIPTION

MEANING OF UNDER-SUBSCRIPTION

Shares are said to be under-subscribed when the number of shares applied for is *less* than the number of shares offered. *For example*, in case a company has offered 5,000 shares to public but the public applied for 4,500 shares only, it is called a case of under-subscription. In such a case, it must be ensured that the company has received the minimum subscription.

SEBI GUIDELINES

As per SEBI Guidelines, Minimum Subscription is 90% of the issued amount from public subscription *plus* accepted devolvement from underwriters *or* from other sources in case of under subscribed issues. In case of non-receipt minimum subscription within 60 days from the date of closure of the issue, the company must refund the subscription amount in full within 78 days without interest and with interest @ 15% p.a. for the delayed period beyond 78 days from the date of closure of the issue.

ILLUSTRATION 5

Y Ltd. invited applications for 10,000 Equity Shares of ₹ 10 each issued at 40% premium. The whole amount was payable on application. The issue was under subscribed by 1,000 shares. Pass the necessary Journal entries.

SOLUTION

JOURNAL

Date	Particulars		L.F.	Dr. (₹)	Cr. (₹)
1.	Bank A/c	Dr.		1,26,000	
	To Share Application & Allotment A/c				1,26,000
	(Being the Application Money received)				
2.	Share Application & Allotment A/c	Dr.		1,26,000	
	To Share Capital A/c				90,000
	To Securities Premium A/c				36,000
	(Being the Application Money adjusted)				

11.0 OVER-SUBSCRIPTION

MEANING OF OVER-SUBSCRIPTION

Shares are said to be over-subscribed when the numbers of shares applied is more than the number of shares offered. *For example*, in case a company has offered 5,000 shares to public but the public applied for 6,000 only, it is called a case of over-subscription.

DISTINCTION BETWEEN OVER-SUBSCRIPTION AND UNDER-SUBSCRIPTION

Over-subscription and Under-subscription of shares can be distinguished as follows:

Basis of Distinction	***Over-Subscription of Shares***	***Under-Subscription of Shares***
1. No. of Shares applied as compared to No. of shares offered.	In case of over-subscription, number of shares applied for is **more** than the number of shares offered by the company.	In case of under-subscription, number of shares applied for is *less* than the number of shares offered by the company.
2. Acceptance of all Applications	All applications are **not accepted in full.**	All applications are **accepted in full.**
3. Problem of minimum subscription when shares are issued for the first time.	This problem **does not arise** at all.	If the minimum subscription has not been subscribed, all application money may be **required to be returned.**
4. Return of Money if minimum subscription has been received	The company returns the money to the applicants whose applications have *either* been rejected *or* have been accepted partially.	The question of returning the money does not arise at all.

ILLUSTRATION 6

Y Ltd. invited applications for 10,000 Equity Shares of ₹ 10 each issued at 40% premium. The whole amount was payable on application. The issue was over subscribed by 2,000 shares. Pass the necessary Journal Entries.

SOLUTION

JOURNAL

Date	*Particulars*		*L.F.*	*Dr. (₹)*	*Cr. (₹)*
1.	Bank A/c	Dr.		1,68,000	
	To Share Application & Allotment A/c				1,68,000
	(Being the Application Money received)				
2.	Share Application & Allotment A/c	Dr.		1,68,000	
	To Share Capital A/c				1,00,000
	To Securities Premium A/c				40,000
	To Bank A/c				28,000
	(Being the Application Money adjusted and Surplus refunded)				

ALTERNATIVES AVAILABLE IN CASE OF OVER-SUBSCRIPTION

Following three alternatives are available to deal with the situation of oversubscription:

Alternative	*Course of Action*
1. **First Alternative Applications]** **[Rejection of Excess Applications]**	1. Excess Applications are rejected. 2. Shares are allotted in full to the remaining applicants rejected. 3. Application Money on rejected excess applications is refunded.
2. **Second Alternative. [*Pro rata* Allotment]**	1. Shares are allotted on proportionate basis to all the applicants.
3. **Third Alternative** **[Any Combination of above Two Alternatives]**	**Combination 1.** Some Applications are rejected and shares are allotted on proportionate basis to the remaining applicants. **Combination 2.** Some Applications are accepted in full and shares are allotted on proportionate basis to the remaining applicants. **Combination 3.** Some Applications are accepted in full, some applications are rejected in full and shares are allotted on proportionate basis to the remaining applicants.

MEANING OF *PRO RATA* ALLOTMENT

Meaning	*Pro rata* allotment means allotment of *less* number of shares to applicants for more number of shares on proportionate basis.
When required	*Pro rata* allotment is required in case of over-subscription (i.e. when the number of shares applied for is more than the number of shares offered by the company.)
***Pro rata* Ratio**	In case of *Pro rata* Allotment one should always calculate *Pro rata* Ratio (which means the Ratio of Total Number of Shares Applied to the Total Number of Shares Allotted). This *Pro rata* Ratio is used to ascertain: (a) the Number of Shares Allotted to an applicant if Number of Shares Applied by him is given. (b) the Number of Shares Applied by an applicant if Number of Shares Allotted to him is given.

Note: *In pro rata allotment when shares are issued at a premium, excess money received on application will first be adjusted towards the share capital. Any excess thereon will be utilized towards the Securities Premium Reserve.*

ILLUSTRATION 7

As a director of a company you had invited applications for 30,000 equity shares of ₹ 10 each. The total Application Money received @ ₹ 2 per share was ₹ 72,000. Name the kind of subscription. List the three alternatives for allotting these shares.

SOLUTION

Shares applied by the public = $\frac{\text{Total Application Money Received}}{\text{Application Money per Share}}$ = ₹ 72,000/ ₹ 2 = 36,000

It is a case of over subscription since the number of shares applied (i.e., 36,000) is more than the number of shares offered (i.e., 30,000).

Following are the alternatives for allotting these shares:

Alternative	*Course of Action*
1.	Reject applications for 6,000 shares and make full allotment to the remaining applicants of 30,000 shares.
2.	Make *pro rata* allotment to all the applicants in the *pro rata* Ratio of 5:6 (i.e., 30,000/36,000)
3.	Reject applications for 3,000 shares and make *pro rata* allotment to the remaining applicants in the *pro rata* Ratio of 10:11 (i.e., 30,000/33,000)
4.	Allot 3,000 shares in full and make *pro rata* allotment to the remaining applicants in the *pro rata* Ratio of 9:11 (i.e., 27,000/33,000)
5.	Reject applications for 3,000 shares, accept 3,000 shares in full and make *pro rata* allotment to the remaining applicants in the *pro rata* Ratio of 9 :10 (i.e., 27,000/30,000)

STATEMENT SHOWING THE ADJUSTMENT OF APPLICATION MONEY RECEIVED

In case of oversubscription, the following Adjustment Table may be prepared to show the adjustment of Application Money received.

Category	*Shares Applied*	*Shares Allotted*	*Application Money Received*	*Adjustment of Application Money Received*			
				Share Capital	*Share Allotment*	*Calls-in Advance*	*Refund*
I							
II							
III							
IV							
TOTAL							

ILLUSTRATION 8

X Ltd. invited applicants for 2,00,000 shares of ₹ 10 each payable as ₹ 2 on application, ₹ 5 on allotment and ₹ 3 on call. Application for 6,55,000 shares were received and the allotments was made as follows:

Category	*Shares applied*	*Shares allotted*
I	50,000	50,000
II	50,000	40,000
III	35,000	10,000
IV	90,000	20,000
V	1,00,000	20,000
VI	3,30,000	60,000

Required: Prepare the statement showing the adjustment of Application Money received (a) If excess Application Money was adjusted towards sum due on allotment, (b) If excess Application Money was adjusted towards other sums due on shares.

SOLUTION

CASE (A) IF EXCESS APPLICATION MONEY WAS ADJUSTED TOWARDS SUM DUE ON ALLOTMENT

Category	Shares Applied	Shares Allotted	Application Money Received	Adjustment of Application Money Received			
				Share Capital	Share Allotment	Calls-in Advance	Refund
I	50,000	50,000	1,00,000	1,00,000	–	–	–
II	50,000	40,000	1,00,000	80,000	20,000	–	–
III	35,000	10,000	70,000	20,000	50,000	–	–
IV	90,000	20,000	1,80,000	40,000	1,00,000	–	40,000
V	1,00,000	20,000	2,00,000	40,000	1,00,000	–	60,000
VI	3,30,000	60,000	6,60,000	1,20,000	3,00,000	–	2,40,000

CASE (B) IF EXCESS APPLICATION MONEY WAS ADJUSTED TOWARDS OTHER SUMS DUE ON SHARES

Category	Shares Applied	Shares Allotted	Application Money Received	Adjustment of Application Money Received			
				Share Capital	Share Allotment	Calls-in Advance	Refund
I	50,000	50,000	1,00,000	1,00,000	–	–	–
II	50,000	40,000	1,00,000	80,000	20,000	–	–
III	35,000	10,000	70,000	20,000	50,000	–	–
IV	90,000	20,000	1,80,000	40,000	1,00,000	40,000	–
V	1,00,000	20,000	2,00,000	40,000	1,00,000	60,000	–
VI	3,30,000	60,000	6,60,000	1,20,000	3,00,000	1,80,000	60,000

TREATMENT OF EXCESS APPLICATION MONEY ON APPLICATIONS ACCEPTED

Following treatment is suggested to deal with the Excess Application Money on Applications accepted:

Situation	Suggested Treatment
1. **If the Question is silent** **or** **If the Question states:** **"Money overpaid on applications was to be applied towards sum due on allotment."** **or** **"The excess application money received was to be adjusted against allotment only."**	Retain the excess Application Money (received on Applications accepted) only upto the Allotment Money due and Refund the remaining excess Application Money. **Journal Entry to Adjust Application Money** Share Application A/c Dr. [with Application Money received] To Share Capital A/c [with Application Money due on Shares allotted] To Share Allotment A/c [with Application Money adjusted towards allotment] To Bank A/c [with Application Money refunded on rejected applications]

2. If the Question states: "Money overpaid on applications was to be applied towards other sum due on shares."	Retain the excess Application Money (received on Applications accepted) upto the Allotment and Calls Money due and Refund the remaining excess Application Money. **Journal Entry to Adjust Application Money** Share Application A/c Dr. [with Application Money received] To Share Capital A/c [with Application Money due on Shares allotted] To Share Allotment A/c [with Application Money adjusted towards allotment] To Calls-in-Advance A/c [with Application Money adjusted towards Calls] To Bank A/c [With Application Money refunded on rejected applications]

ILLUSTRATION 9

TULSIAN Ltd. invited applications for issuing 1,00,000 Equity shares of ₹ 10 each issued at a premium of ₹ 3 per share payable as follows:

On Application	₹ 5 per share (including premium ₹ 1)
On Allotment	₹ 5 per share (including premium ₹ 1)
On Call	Balance

Applications were received for 2,20,000 shares. Applications for 20,000 shares were rejected and their application money was refunded. Shares were allotted to the remaining applicants as follows:

A. Allotted in full to *Katrina* who had applied for 10,000 shares.

B. Applications for 40,000 shares were allotted 30,000 shares on *pro rata* basis.

C. Allotted balance of the shares on *pro rata* basis to the other applicants.

All allottees paid their dues as per schedule.

Required: Prepare the Statement showing the adjustment of Application Money received. Pass the necessary Journal Entries.

SOLUTION

1. STATEMENT SHOWING THE ADJUSTMENT OF APPLICATION MONEY RECEIVED

Category	*Shares Applied*	*Shares Allotted*	*Application Money Received*	*Adjustment of Application Money Received*			
				Share Capital	*Share Allotment*	*Calls-in Advance*	*Refund*
—	20,000	0	1,00,000	0	0	0	1,00,000
I	10,000	10,000	50,000	50,000	—	—	—
II	40,000	30,000	2,00,000	1,50,000	50,000	—	—
III	1,50,000	60,000	7,50,000	3,00,000	3,00,000	1,50,000	—
Total	2,20,000	1,00,000	11,00,000	5,00,000	3,50,000	1,50,000	1,00,000

2. JOURNAL

Date	Particulars		L.F.	Dr. (₹)	Cr. (₹)
1.	Bank A/c	Dr.		11,00,000	
	To Share Application A/c				11,00,000
	(Being the application money received)				
2.	Share Application A/c	Dr.		11,00,000	
	To Share Capital A/c (1,00,000 × ₹ 4)				4,00,000
	To Securities Premium A/c (1,00,000 × ₹ 1)				1,00,000
	To Share Allotment A/c				3,50,000
	To Bank a/c (20,000 × ₹ 5)				1,00,000
	To Calls-in Advance A/c				1,50,000
	(Being the Application Money adjusted & Surplus refunded)				
3.	Share Allotment A/c (1,00,000 × ₹ 5)	Dr.		5,00,000	
	To Share Capital A/c (1,00,000 × ₹ 4)				4,00,000
	To Securities Premium A/c (1,00,000 × ₹ 1)				1,00,000
	(Being the Allotment Money due)				
4.	Bank A/c	Dr.		1,50,000	
	To Share Allotment A/c				1,50,000
	(Being the remaining Allotment Money received)				
5.	Share First & Final Call A/c (1,00,000 × ₹ 3)	Dr.		3,00,000	
	To Share Capital A/c (1,00,000 × ₹ 2)				2,00,000
	To Securities Premium A/c (1,00,000 × ₹ 1)				1,00,000
	(Being the First & Final Call Money due)				
6.	Bank A/c	Dr.		1,50,000	
	Calls-in-advance A/c	Dr.		1,50,000	
	To Share First & Final Call A/c				3,00,000
	(Being the First and Final Call Money received and Calls in advance adjusted)				

ILLUSTRATION 10

Applications for 40,000 shares were allotted 30,000 shares on pro rata basis. X, was allotted 600 shares and Z, applied for 400 shares. Calculate the Total No. of Shares applied by X and the Total No. of Shares allotted to Z.

SOLUTION

1. Total No. of Shares applied by X = (40,000 × 600 / 30,000) = 800 Shares
2. Total No. of Shares allotted to Z = (30,000 × 400 / 40,000) = 300 Shares

ILLUSTRATION 11

60,000 shares were allotted on *pro rata* basis to the Applicants for 1,50,000 shares. *X*, was allotted 600 shares and *Z*, applied for 400 shares. Calculate the Total No. of Shares applied by X and the Total No. of Shares allotted to Z.

SOLUTION

1. Total No. of Shares applied by X = (150,000 × 600 / 60,000) = 1500 Shares
2. Total No. of Shares allotted to Z = (60,000 × 400 / 150,000) = 240 Shares

ILLUSTRATION 12

TULSIAN Ltd. invited applications for issuing 1,00,000 Equity shares of ₹ 10 each issued at a premium of ₹ 3 per share payable as follows:

On Application	₹ 5 per share (including premium ₹ 1)
On Allotment	₹ 5 per share (including premium ₹ 1)
On Call	Balance

Applications were received for 2,20,000 shares. Applications for 20,000 shares were rejected and their application money was refunded. Shares were allotted to the remaining applicants as follows:

A. Allotted in full to *Katrina* who had applied for 10,000 shares.

B. Applications for 40,000 shares were allotted 30,000 shares on *pro rata* basis.

C. Allotted balance of the shares on *pro rata* basis to the other applicants

Excess application money was utilised in payment of allotment and call. The Call was duly made.

Katrina did not pay any money other than Application Money and *Z*, who applied for 400 shares in Category B paid the call money due along with allotment. All other allottees paid their dues as per schedule.

Required:

(a) Prepare the Statement showing the adjustment of Application Money received,

(b) Calculate the Total No. of Shares allotted to Z,

(c) Calculate the Total Money received at the allotment stage,

(d) Calculate the Total Money received at the Call stage,

(e) Pass the necessary journal entries in the books of Tulsian Ltd. assuming that Calls-in-arrears Account is maintained.

SOLUTION

(A) STATEMENT SHOWING THE ADJUSTMENT OF APPLICATION MONEY RECEIVED

Category	Shares Applied	Shares Allotted	Application Money Received	Adjustment of Application Money Received			
				Share Capital	Share Allotment	Calls-in Advance	Refund
—	20,000	0	1,00,000	0	0	0	1,00,000
I	10,000	10,000	50,000	50,000	—	—	—
II	40,000	30,000	2,00,000	1,50,000	50,000		—
III	1,50,000	60,000	7,50,000	3,00,000	3,00,000	1,50,000	—
Total	2,20,000	1,00,000	11,00,000	5,00,000	3,50,000	1,50,000	1,00,000

(B) Total No. of Shares allotted to Z = (30,000 × 400 / 40,000) = 300 Shares

(C) CALCULATION OF TOTAL MONEY RECEIVED AT THE ALLOTMENT STAGE

Particulars	₹
Total Allotment Money due (1,00,000 × ₹ 5)	5,00,000
Less: Surplus Application Money adjusted as per WN 1	(3,50,000)
Less: Not received from Defaulter (10000 × ₹ 5)	(50,000)
	1,00,000
Add: Calls-in-advance [300 × ₹ 3]	900
	1,00,900

(D) CALCULATION OF TOTAL MONEY RECEIVED AT THE CALL STAGE

Particulars	₹
Total Call Money due (1,00,000 × ₹ 3)	3,00,000
Less: Surplus Application Money adjusted as per WN 1	(1,50,000)
Less: Not received from Defaulter (10000 × ₹ 3)	(30,000)
Less: Calls-in-advance [300 × ₹ 3]	(900)
	1,19,100

(E) JOURNAL

Date	*Particulars*		*L.F.*	*Dr. (₹)*	*Cr. (₹)*
1.	Bank A/c	Dr.		11,00,000	
	To Share Application A/c				11,00,000
	(Being the application money received)				
2.	Share Application A/c	Dr.		11,00,000	
	To Share Capital A/c (1,00,000 × ₹ 4)				4,00,000
	To Securities Premium A/c (1,00,000 × ₹ 1)				1,00,000
	To Share Allotment A/c				3,50,000
	To Bank a/c (20,000 × ₹ 5)				1,00,000
	To Calls-in Advance A/c				1,50,000
	(Being the Application Money adjusted & Surplus refunded)				
3.	Share Allotment A/c (1,00,000 × ₹ 5)	Dr.		5,00,000	
	To Share Capital A/c (1,00,000 × ₹ 4)				4,00,000
	To Securities Premium A/c (1,00,000 × ₹ 1)				1,00,000
	(Being the Allotment Money due)				
4.	Bank A/c [as per WN 4]	Dr.		1,00,900	
	Calls-in-arrears A/c (10,000 × ₹ 5)	Dr.		50,000	
	To Share Allotment A/c				1,50,000
	To Calls-in Advance A/c [300 × ₹ 3]				900
	(Being the Allotment Money received except on 10000 shares and Calls in advance received on 300 shares)				

5.	Share First & Final Call A/c (1,00,000 × ₹ 3) Dr.		3,00,000	
	To Share Capital A/c (1,00,000 × ₹ 2)			2,00,000
	To Securities Premium A/c (1,00,000 × ₹ 1)			1,00,000
	(Being the First & Final Call Money due)			
6.	Bank A/c Dr.		1,19,100	
	Calls-in-advance A/c Dr.		1,50,900	
	Calls-in-arrears A/c (10,000 × ₹ 3) Dr.		30,000	
	To Share First & Final Call A/c			3,00,000
	(Being the First and Final Call Money received except on 10000 shares and Calls in advance adjusted)			

ILLUSTRATION 13

Srijan Ltd. issued ₹ 10,00,000 new capital divided into ₹ 100 shares at a premium of ₹ 20 per share payable, as under:

On Application	₹ 10 per share
On Allotment	₹ 40 per share (Including ₹ 10 premium)
On First and Final Call	Balance

Overpayments on application were to be applied towards sums due on allotment and call. Where no allotment was made, money was to be returned in full. The issue was over-subscribed to the extent of 13,000 shares. Applicants for 12,000 shares were allotted only 2,000 shares and applicants for 3,000 shares were sent letters of regret and application deposits were returned to them. All the money due on allotment and final call was duly received.

Required: Make the necessary entries in the Company's books to record the above transactions.

SOLUTION

JOURNAL

Date	Particulars	L.F.	Dr. (₹)	Cr. (₹)
1.	Bank A/c Dr.		2,30,000	
	To Share Application A/c			2,30,000
	(Being the Application Money received on 23,000 shares @ ₹10 per share)			
2.	Share Application A/c Dr.		2,30,000	
	To Share Capital A/c			1,00,000
	To Share Allotment A/c			80,000
	To Bank A/c			30,000
	To Calls-in Advance A/c			20,000
	(Being the Applications Money adjusted and the Surplus refunded)			
3.	Share Allotment A/c Dr.		4,00,000	
	To Share Capital A/c			3,00,000
	To Securities Premium A/c			1,00,000
	(Being the Allotment Money due)			
4.	Bank A/c Dr.		3,20,000	
	To Share Allotment A/c			3,20,000
	(Being the Allotment money received)			

5.	Share First and Final Call A/c	Dr.	7,00,000	
	To Share Capital A/c			6,00,000
	To Securities Premium A/c			1,00,000
	(Being the Final Call made due)			
6.	Bank A/c	Dr.	6,80,000	
	Calls-in Advance A/c	Dr.	20,000	
	To Share First and Final Call A/c			7,00,000
	(Being the Final Call Money received)			

Working Note:

ADJUSTMENT OF APP. MONEY RECEIVED ON SHARES ALLOTTED ON *PRO RATA* BASIS

A.	Application Money received on shares applied (12,000 × ₹ 10)	₹ 1,20,000
B.	*Less:* Application Money due on shares allotted (2,000 × ₹ 10)	₹20,000
C.	Excess Application Money	₹ 1,00,000
D.	*Less:* Allotment Money due on shares allotted (2,000 × ₹ 40)	(₹ 80,000)
E.	Calls-in Advance received	₹ 20,000

HOW TO CALCULATE THE AMOUNT DUE BUT NOT RECEIVED FROM DEFAULTING SHAREHOLDER TO WHOM SHARES WERE ALLOTTED ON *PRO RATA* BASIS

Step 1: *Calculate the Total Number of Shares applied for (if not given) as under:*

$$\frac{\text{Total no. of Shares applied under prorata category}}{\text{Total no. Shares allotted under prorata category}} \times \text{No. of Shares allotted to defaulter}$$

OR

Calculate the Total Number of Shares allotted (if not given) as under:

$$\frac{\text{Total no. of Shares allotted under prorata category}}{\text{Total no. of Shares applied under prorata category}} \times \text{No. of Shares applied to defaulter}$$

Step 2: *Calculate the Total Application Money received on shares applied by defaulter*

= No. of Shares applied by defaulter × Application Money per share

Step 3: *Calculate the Application Money due on Shares allotted to defaulter*

= No. of Shares Allotted to Defaulter × Application Money per share

Step 4: *Calculate the Excess Application Money*

= Amount as per Step 2 – Amount as per Step 3

Step 5: *Calculate the Allotment or Call Money due on shares allotted*

No. of Shares allotted to Defaulter × Allotment Money/Call Money per share

Step 6: *Calculate the Allotment or Call Money due but not received*

= Amount as per Step 5 – Amount as per Step 4.

HOW TO CALCULATE THE AMOUNT RECEIVED ON ALLOTMENT STAGE

Step 1: *Calculate the Total Allotment Money due*

[= Total No. of Shares Allotted × Allotment Money per share]

Step 2: *Deduct Allotment Money already received on Application stage.*

Step 3: *Deduct Allotment Money not received from Defaulting Shareholders.*

Step 4: *Add: Calls-in-advance (if any) received on Allotment stage.*

Step 5: *Calculate the Amount Received On Allotment Stage*

= Step 1 – Step 2 – Step 3 + Step 4

ILLUSTRATION 14

BT Ltd issued a prospectus inviting applications for 20,000 shares of ₹ 10 each at a premium of ₹ 2 per share payable as follows: on Application ₹ 2, on Allotment ₹ 5 (including premium), on First Call ₹ 3, on Second & Final Call ₹ 2.

Applications were received for 30,000 shares and *pro rata* allotment was made on the applications for 24,000 shares. It was decided to utilise excess Application Money towards the amount due on allotment. Ramesh to whom 400 shares were allotted failed to pay the allotment money and Mohan, the holder of 600 shares failed to pay the two calls.

Required: Pass the necessary journal entries.

SOLUTION

JOURNAL OF BT LTD.

Date	*Particulars*		*L.F.*	*Dr. (₹)*	*Cr. (₹)*
1.	Bank A/c (30,000 × ₹ 2)	Dr.		60,000	
	To Share Application A/c				60,000
	(Being the Application Money received on 30,000 shares)				
2.	Share Application A/c (30,000 × ₹ 2)	Dr.		60,000	
	To Share Capital A/c (20,000 × ₹ 2)				40,000
	To Bank A/c (6,000 × ₹ 2)				12,000
	To Share Allotment A/c (4,000 × ₹ 2)				8,000
	(Being the Application Money adjusted & Surplus refunded)				
3.	Share Allotment A/c (20,000 × ₹ 5)	Dr.		1,00,000	
	To Share Capital A/c (20,000 × ₹ 3)				60,000
	To Securities Premium A/c (20,000 × ₹ 2)				40,000
	(Being the Allotment Money due)				
4.	Bank A/c (₹ 1,00,000 – ₹ 8,000 – ₹ 1,840)	Dr.		90,160	
	To Share Allotment A/c				90,160
	(Being the remaining Allotment Money received on 19,600 shares) [See Working Note 2 & 3]				
5.	Share First Call A/c (20,000 × ₹ 3)	Dr.		60,000	
	To Share Capital A/c (20,000 × ₹ 3)				60,000
	(Being the First Call Money due)				
6.	Bank A/c (19,000 × ₹ 3)	Dr.		57,000	
	To Share First Call A/c				57,000
	(Being the First Call Money received on 19,000 shares)				
7.	Share Second & Final Call A/c (20,000 × ₹ 2)	Dr.		40,000	
	To Share Capital A/c				40,000
	(Being the Second & Final Call due)				

8.	Bank A/c (19,000 × ₹ 2) Dr.	38,000	
	To Share Second & Final Call A/c		38,000
	(Being the Second & Final Call received on 19,000 shares)		

WORKING NOTES:

1. **Total No. of Shares applied by Ramesh** = (400 × 24,000/20,000) = 480

2. CALCULATION OF THE AMOUNT DUE BUT NOT RECEIVED ON ALLOTMENT FROM RAMESH

	Particulars	₹
A.	Application Money received on shares applied (480 × ₹ 2)	960
B.	*Less:* Application Money due on shares allotted (400 × ₹ 2)	800
C.	Excess Application Money [A – B]	160
D.	Allotment Money due on shares allotted (400 × ₹ 5)	2,000
E.	Allotment Money due but not received (₹ 2,000 – ₹ 160)	1,840

3. CALCULATION OF ALLOTMENT MONEY RECEIVED LATER ON

	Particulars	₹
A.	Total Allotment Money Due (20,000 × ₹ 5)	1,00,000
B.	*Less:* Allotment Money Already received on application stage (4,000 × ₹ 2)	(8,000)
C.	*Less:* Allotment Money not received [as per Note (2)]	(1,840)
		90,160

ILLUSTRATION 15

TULSIAN Ltd. invited applications for issuing 1,00,000 Equity shares of ₹ 10 each issued at a premium of ₹ 3 per share payable as follows:

On Application	₹ 5 per share(including premium ₹ 1)
On Allotment	₹ 5 per share(including premium ₹ 1)
On Call	Balance

Applications were received for 2,20,000 shares. Applications for 20,000 shares were rejected and their application money was refunded. Shares were allotted to the remaining applicants as follows:

A. Allotted in full to *Katrina* who had applied for 10,000 shares.

B. Applications for 40,000 shares were allotted 30,000 shares on *pro rata* basis.

C. Allotted balance of the shares on *pro rata* basis to the other applicants

Excess application money was utilised in payment of allotment and call. The Call was duly made.

X, who was allotted 600 shares in Category B did not pay any money other than Application Money and *Y*, who applied for 1500 shares in Category C failed to pay the call money. *Z*, who applied for 400 shares in Category B paid the call money due along with allotment. All other allottees paid their dues as per schedule.

Required:

(a) Prepare the Statement showing the adjustment of Application Money received

(b) Calculate the Total No. of Shares applied by X

(c) Calculate the Total No. of Shares allotted to Z

(d) Calculate the Allotment money due but not received from X

(e) Calculate the Total Money received at the allotment stage

(f) Calculate the Total No. of Shares allotted to Y

(g) Calculate the Call money due but not received from Y

(h) Calculate the Total Money received at the Call stage

(i) Pass the necessary journal entries in the books of Tulsian Ltd. assuming that Calls-in-arrears Account is maintained.

SOLUTION

(A) STATEMENT SHOWING THE ADJUSTMENT OF APPLICATION MONEY RECEIVED

Category	Shares Applied	Shares Allotted	Application Money Received	Adjustment of Application Money Received			
				Share Capital	Share Allotment	Calls-in Advance	Refund
—	20,000	0	1,00,000	0	0	0	1,00,000
I	10,000	10,000	50,000	50,000	—	—	—
II	40,000	30,000	2,00,000	1,50,000	50,000	—	—
III	1,50,000	60,000	7,50,000	3,00,000	3,00,000	1,50,000	—
Total	2,20,000	1,00,000	11,00,000	5,00,000	3,50,000	1,50,000	1,00,000

(B) Total No. of Shares applied by X = (40,000 × 600 / 30,000) = 800 Shares

(C) Total No. of Shares allotted to Z = (30,000 × 400 / 40,000) = 300 Shares

(D) CALCULATION OF ALLOTMENT MONEY DUE BUT NOT RECEIVED

Particulars	₹
Application Money received from defaulter (800 × ₹ 5)	4,000
Less: Application Money adjusted (600 × ₹ 5)	(3,000)
Excess Application Money	1,000
Allotment Money due (600 × ₹ 5)	3,000
Amount due but not received on allotment	**2,000**

(E) CALCULATION OF TOTAL MONEY RECEIVED AT THE ALLOTMENT STAGE

Particulars	₹
Total Allotment Money due (1,00,000 × ₹ 5)	5,00,000
Less: Surplus Application Money adjusted as per WN A	(3,50,000)
Less: Not received from Defaulter as per WN D	(2,000)
	1,48,000
Add: Calls-in-advance [300 × ₹ 3]	900
	1,48,900

(F) Total No. of Shares allotted to Y = (60,000 × 1500 / 1,50,000) = 600 Shares

(G) CALCULATION OF CALL MONEY DUE BUT NOT RECEIVED FROM Y

Particulars	₹
Application Money received from defaulter (1,500 × ₹ 5)	7,500
Less: Application Money adjusted (600 × ₹ 5)	3,000
Excess Application Money	4,500
Less: Excess Application Money adjusted on allotment (600 × ₹ 5)	(3,000)
Excess Application Money adjusted on Call	(1,500)
Call Money due (600 × ₹ 3)	1,800
Amount due but not received on Call	**300**

(H) CALCULATION OF CALL MONEY RECEIVED LATER ON

Particulars	₹
Total Call Money due (1,00,000 × ₹ 3)	3,00,000
Less: Surplus Application Money adjusted as per A	(1,50,000)
Less: Not received from Y as per G	(300)
Less: Calls-in-advance [300 × ₹ 3]	(900)
Less: Not received from X [600 × ₹ 3]	(1,800)
	1,47,000

(I) JOURNAL

Date	*Particulars*		*L.F.*	*Dr. (₹)*	*Cr. (₹)*
1.	Bank A/c	Dr.		11,00,000	
	To Share Application A/c				11,00,000
	(Being the application money received)				
2.	Share Application A/c	Dr.		11,00,000	
	To Share Capital A/c (1,00,000 × ₹ 4)				4,00,000
	To Securities Premium A/c (1,00,000 × ₹ 1)				1,00,000
	To Share Allotment A/c				3,50,000
	To Bank a/c (20,000 × ₹ 5)				1,00,000
	To Calls-in Advance A/c				1,50,000
	(Being the Application Money adjusted & Surplus refunded)				
3.	Share Allotment A/c(1,00,000 × ₹ 5)	Dr.		5,00,000	
	To Share Capital A/c (1,00,000 × ₹ 4)				4,00,000
	To Securities Premium A/c(1,00,000 × ₹ 1)				1,00,000
	(Being the Allotment Money due)				
4.	Bank A/c [as per WN 4]	Dr.		1,48,900	
	Calls-in-arrears A/c [as per WN 3]	Dr.		2,000	
	To Share Allotment A/c				1,50,000
	To Calls-in Advance A/c [300 × ₹ 3]				900
	(Being the Allotment Money received except on 600 shares and Calls in advance received on 300 shares)				

5.	Share First & Final Call A/c(1,00,000 × ₹ 3)	Dr.		3,00,000	
	To Share Capital A/c(1,00,000 × ₹ 2)				2,00,000
	To Securities Premium A/c(1,00,000 × ₹ 1)				1,00,000
	(Being the First & Final Call Money due)				
6.	Bank A/c	Dr.		1,47,000	
	Calls-in-advance A/c	Dr.		1,50,900	
	Calls-in-arrears A/c [₹1,800 + ₹ 300]	Dr.		2,100	
	To Share First & Final Call A/c				3,00,000
	(Being the First and Final Call Money received except on 1200 shares and Calls in advance adjusted)				

12.0 CALLS-IN-ARREARS AND CALLS-IN-ADVANCE

Meaning	Calls-in-arrears refer to the amount called up by the company which has not yet been received from the shareholders till the last day fixed for the payment thereof. The total of the unpaid amounts on account of one *or* more instalments may *or* may not be transferred to Calls-in-arrears Account *or* Calls Unpaid Account.
Nature	Calls-in-arrears Account is an Asset Account which represents the Called up Amount not received from some shareholders.
Disclosure	The amount of Calls-in-arrears is shown in the **Notes to Accounts 'Share Capital'** to the Balance Sheet.
Rate of Interest	The directors can charge interest on calls-in-arrears at a rate specified in the Articles from the last date fixed for payment to the date of actual payment. But if the Articles are silent, **Table F** shall be applicable which empowers the Board of Directors to charge interest at a rate **not exceeding 10% p.a.** However, the directors have the authority to waive the payment of interest on calls-in-arrears at their discretion.

JOURNAL ENTRIES RELATING TO CALLS-IN-ARREARS

Date	*Particulars*		*L.F.*	*Dr. (₹)*	*Cr. (₹)*
1.	**On Non-receipt of Call till the day fixed**				
	Calls-in-arrears A/c	Dr.		(With Called-up amount not received)	
	To Relevant Call A/c				
2.	**On Receipt of Calls-in-arrears at a subsequent date**				
	Bank A/c	Dr.		(With the Calls-in-arrears received)	
	To Calls-in-arrears A/c				
3.	**On Making due the interest on Calls-in-arrears**				
	Sundry Members' A/c	Dr.		(With Interest due)	
	To Interest on Calls-in-arrears A/c				
4.	**On Receipt of Interest on Calls-in-arrears**				
	Bank A/c	Dr.		(With Interest received)	
	To Sundry Members' A/c				
5.	**On Transfer of Interest on Calls in arrears A/c to Profit & Loss A/c at the end of the accounting period**				
	Interest on Calls-in-arrears A/c	Dr.		(With Interest)	
	To Profit and Loss A/c				

13.0 CALLS-IN-ADVANCE

Meaning	Calls-in-advance refer to the Uncalled up amount received in advance from some shareholders. A company may accept calls-in-advance only if Articles authorise to do so.
Nature	Calls-in-advance Account is a Liability Account which represents the Uncalled amount received in advance from some shareholders.
Disclosure	The balance in Calls-in-advance Account is shown under the head **'Current Liabilities'** and sub-head **'Other current Liabilities'**.
Rate of Interest	The Board must pay interest on calls-in-advance at a rate specified in the Articles from the date of its receipt to the date when the call becomes due. But if the Articles are silent, **Table 'F'** shall be applicable which gives option to Board of Directors to pay interest on calls-in-advance at a rate **not exceeding 12% p.a.**

JOURNAL ENTRIES RELATING TO CALLS-IN-ADVANCE

Date	*Particulars*	*L.F.*	*Dr. (₹)*	*Cr. (₹)*
1.	**On Receipt of Calls-in-Advance** Bank A/c Dr. To Calls in-Advance A/c		(With the Uncalled up amount received in advance)	
2.	**On Adjustment of Calls-in-Advance when such amount is called up** Calls-in-Advance A/c Dr. To Relevant Call A/c		(With Calls-in-Advance adjusted)	
3.	**On Making due the Interest on Calls-in Advance** Interest on Calls-in-Advance A/c Dr. To Sundry Members' A/c		(With the Interest payable)	
4.	**On Payment of Interest on Calls-in Advance** Sundry Members' A/c Dr. To Bank A/c		(With Interest paid)	
5.	**On T/f of Interest on Calls-in-Advance A/c to P&L A/c at the end of the accounting period** Profit and Loss A/c Dr. To Interest on Calls-in-Advance A/c		(With Interest)	

TUTORIAL NOTES

1. *Interest on Calls-in-advance is a charge against the profit and hence is to be paid whether there are profits or not.*
2. *Outstanding Interest on Calls-in-advance appears under the head 'Current liabilities' and sub-head Other Current Liabilities in the Balance Sheet.*

14.0 DISTINCTION BETWEEN CALLS-IN-ARREARS & CALLS-IN-ADVANCE

Calls-in-arrears differ from Calls-in-advance in the following respects:

Basis of Distinction	*Calls-in-arrears*	*Calls-in-advance*
1. Meaning	It refers to the Called up amount not yet received from some shareholders till the last day fixed for payment thereof.	It refers to the Uncalled up amount received in advance from some shareholders.
2. Authority under Articles	There is **no question** of any authority under Articles.	A company may accept Calls-in-advance only if Articles permit.
3. Interest	Interest is **charged** on Calls-in-arrears.	Interest is **allowed** on Calls-in-advance.
4. Maximum Rate of Interest	The maximum rate of interest as per **Table F** is **10%** p.a.	The maximum rate of interest as per **Table F** is **12%** p.a.
5. Disclosure	The amount of Calls-in-arrears is shown in the **Notes to Accounts 'Share Capital'** to the Balance Sheet.	The amount of Calls-in-advance is shown under the head **'Current Liabilities'** and sub-head **'Other Current Liabilities'.**

ILLUSTRATION 16

Bharat Tushar Ltd. offered 20,000 shares of ₹ 10 each at a premium of 10% payable as follows: On Application ₹ 2 (1st Jan.), On Allotment ₹ 4 (including premium) (1st April), on First Call ₹ 3 (1st June), on Second & Final Call ₹ 2 (1st Aug).

Applications were received for 18,000 shares and the directors made allotment. One shareholder to whom 400 shares were allotted paid the entire balance on his share holdings with allotment money and another shareholder did not pay allotment and 1st call money on his 600 shares but which he paid with final call.

Required: Calculate the amount of interest paid and received on Calls-in-advance and Calls in arrears respectively on 1st Aug. Also give Journal entries to record the above transactions assuming that Calls-in-arrears Account is maintained.

SOLUTION

CALCULATION OF INTEREST ON CALLS-IN-ADVANCE

On ₹ 1200 (i.e. 400 × ₹ 3) for 2 months @ 12 % p.a.	₹ 24
On ₹ 800 (i.e. 400 × ₹ 2) for 4 months @ 12 % p.a.	₹ 32
	₹ 56

CALCULATION OF INTEREST ON CALLS-IN-ARREARS

On ₹ 2,400 (i.e. 600 × ₹ 4) for 4 months @ 10% p.a.	₹ 80
On ₹ 1,800 (i.e. 600 × ₹ 3) for 2 months @ 10% p.a.	₹ 30
	₹ 110

JOURNAL OF BHARAT TUSHAR LTD.

Date	Particulars		L.F.	Dr. (₹)	Cr. (₹)
Jan. 1.	Bank A/c [18,000 × ₹ 2]	Dr.		36,000	
	To Share Application A/c				36,000
	(Being the Application Money received on 18,000 shares)				
Apr. 1.	Share Application A/c	Dr.		36,000	
	To Share Capital A/c				36,000
	(Being the Application Money adjusted)				
	Share Allotment A/c [18000 × ₹ 4]	Dr.		72,000	
	To Share Capital A/c [18,000 × ₹ 3]				54,000
	To Securities Premium A/c [18,000 + ₹ 1]				18,000
	(Being the Allotment Money due)				
	Bank A/c [(17,400 × ₹ 4) + (400 × ₹ 5)]	Dr.		71,600	
	Calls-in-arrears A/c [600 × ₹ 4]	Dr.		2,400	
	To Share Allotment A/c [18,000 × ₹ 4]				72,000
	To Call-in-advance A/c [400 × ₹ 5]				2,000
	(Being the allotment money received on 17,400 shares & Calls-in-advance on 400 shares)				
June 1	Share First Call A/c [18,000 × ₹ 3]	Dr.		54,000	
	To Share Capital A/c				54,000
	(Being the First Call Money due on 18,000 shares)				
	Bank A/c [17,000 × ₹ 3]	Dr.		51,000	
	Calls-in-advance A/c [400 × ₹ 3]	Dr.		1,200	
	Calls-in-arrears A/c [600 × ₹ 3]	Dr.		1,800	
	To Share First Call A/c				54,000
	(Being the First Call Money received except on 600 shares, Call-in-advance on 400 shares adjusted)				
August 1	Share Second & Final Call A/c [18,000 × ₹ 2]	Dr.		36,000	
	To Share Capital A/c				36,000
	(Being the Second & Final Call Money due)				
	Bank A/c [(17,600 × ₹ 2) + (600 × ₹ 7)]	Dr.		39,400	
	Calls-in-advance A/c [400 × ₹ 2]	Dr.		800	
	To Share Second & Final Call A/c				36,000
	To Calls-in-arrears A/c [600 × ₹ 3]				4,200
	(Being the Second & Final Call Money received along with Calls-in-arrears and Call-in-advance on 400 shares adjusted)				
	Sundry Members' A/c	Dr.		110	
	To Interest on Calls-in-arrears A/c				110
	(Being the Interest on Calls-in-arrears due)				
	Bank A/c	Dr.		110	
	To Sundry Members' A/c				110
	(Being the Interest on Calls-in-arrears received)				

	Interest on Calls-in-Advance A/c Dr.		56	
	To Sundry Members' A/c			56
	(Being Interest on Calls in-advance)			
	Sundry Members' A/c Dr.		56	
	To Bank A/c			56
	(Being the Interest on Calls-in-advance paid)			

Note: At the end of accounting period Interest Accounts will be transferred to Profit & Loss A/c.

ILLUSTRATION 17

X Ltd. issued to the public for subscription 40,000 shares of ₹ 10 each at par payable as ₹ 2 each on Application, Allotment and First Call and the balance on the Final Call. Applications were received for 60,000 Shares and allotment was made *pro rata* to 80% of applicants. R to whom 1,600 shares were allotted paid only the Application Money and S who had applied for 2,400 shares paid the entire call money due along with the allotment. Pass the necessary Journal entries to record the above transactions assuming that Calls-in-arrears Account is maintained.

SOLUTION

JOURNAL

Date	Particulars	L.F.	Dr. (₹)	Cr. (₹)
	Bank A/c [60,000 × ₹ 2] Dr.		1,20,000	
	To Share Application A/c			1,20,000
	(Being the Application Money received on 60,000 shares)			
	Share Application A/c Dr.		1,20,000	
	To Share Capital A/c (40,000 × ₹ 2)			80,000
	To Bank A/c (12,000 × ₹ 2)			24,000
	To Share Allotment A/c (8,000 × ₹ 2)			16,000
	(Being the Application Money adjusted & Surplus Refunded)			
	Share Allotment A/c (40,000 × ₹ 2) Dr.		80,000	
	To Share Capital A/c			80,000
	(Being the allotment money due on 40,000 shares)			
	Bank A/c Dr.		73,440	
	Calls-in-Arrears A/c Dr.		2,560	
	To Share Allotment A/c			64,000
	To Calls-in-Advance A/c			12,000
	(Being the allotment money received except for 1,600 shares of R along with calls money in advance for 2,000 shares of S) [Refer to WN 1, 2, 3]			
	Share First Call A/c [40,000 × ₹ 2] Dr.		80,000	
	To Share Capital A/c			80,000
	(Being the first call money due on 40,000 shares)			
	Bank A/c Dr.		72,800	
	Calls-in-Arrears A/c Dr.		3,200	

	Calls-in-Advance A/c Dr. To Share First Call A/c (Being the First Call Money received except on 1,600 shares and Calls-in-Advance adjusted for 2,000 shares)		4,000	80,000
	Share Final Call A/c Dr. To Share Capital A/c (Being the final call money due on 40,000 shares)		1,20,000	1,20,000
	Bank A/c [Balancing Figure] Dr. Calls-in-Arrear A/c [1,600 × ₹ 4] Dr. Calls-in Advance A/c [2,000 × ₹ 4] Dr. To Share Final Call A/c (Being the final call money received except for 1,600 shares of R and Calls-in-Advance adjusted for 2,000 shares of S)		1,45,600 6,400 8,000	1,60,000

Working Notes:

1. CALCULATION OF ALLOTMENT MONEY DUE BUT NOT RECEIVED FROM R.

Shares applied by R = (48,000/40,000) × 1,600 = 1,920 Shares.	
Application Money received R = (1,920 × ₹ 2)	₹ 3,840
Less: Application Money due (1,600 × ₹ 2)	3,200
Excess Application Money	640
Allotment Money due (1,600 × ₹ 2)	3,200
Allotment Money due but not received from R.	2,560

2. CALCULATION OF CALLS-IN-ADVANCE RECEIVED FROM S:

(a) No. of Shares allotted to S = (40,000/48,000) × 2,400 = 2,000 Shares.

(b) Calls-in-Advance = 2,000 × ₹ 6 = ₹ 12,000

3. ALLOTMENT MONEY RECEIVED LATER ON

Total Amount due on Allotment (40,000 × ₹ 2)	80,000
Less: Excess Application Money adjusted	(16,000)
Less: Allotment Money not received from R	(2,560)
Add: Calls-in-Advance from S	12,000
	73,440

ILLUSTRATION 18

Petromax Ltd. issued 50,000 shares of ₹ 10 each at a premium of ₹ 2 per share payable as ₹ 3 on application, ₹ 5 including premium on allotment and the balance in equal instalments over two calls. Applications were received for 92,000 shares and the allotment was done as under:

A. Applicants of 40,000 shares : Allotted 30,000 Shares

B. Applicants of 40,000 shares : Allotted 20,000 Shares

C. Applicants of 12,000 shares : Nil

Suresh, who had applied for 2,000 shares (Category A) did not pay any money other than Application Money. *Chander*, who was allotted 800 shares (Category B) paid the calls money due along with allotment. All other allottees paid their dues as per schedule.

Required: Pass the necessary Journal entries in the books of Petromax Ltd. to record the above assuming that Calls-in-arrears Account is maintained.

SOLUTION

JOURNAL

Date	Particulars		L.F.	Dr. (₹)	Cr. (₹)
	Bank A/c [92,000 × ₹ 3]	Dr.		2,76,000	
	To Share Application A/c				2,76,000
	(Being the Application Money received on 92,000 shares @ ₹ 3 per share)				
	Share Application A/c	Dr.		2,76,000	
	To Share Capital A/c (50,000 × ₹ 3)				1,50,000
	To Bank A/c (12,000 × ₹ 3)				36,000
	To Share Allotment A/c (30,000 × ₹ 3)				90,000
	(Being the Application Money adjusted)				
	Share Allotment A/c (50,000 × ₹ 5)	Dr.		2,50,000	
	To Share Capital A/c (50,000 × ₹ 3)				1,50,000
	To Securities Premium A/c (50,000 × ₹ 2)				1,00,000
	(Being the Allotment Money due on 50,000 shares)				
	Bank A/c	Dr.		1,57,200	
	Calls-in-Arrears A/c	Dr.		6,000	
	To Share Allotment A/c [₹ 2,50,000 – ₹ 90,000]				1,60,000
	To Calls-in-Advance A/c [800 × ₹ 4]				3,200
	(Being the Allotment Money received except on 1,500 shares and Calls in advance received on 800 shares) [Refer to WN: 1, 2, 3, 4]				
	Share First Call A/c (50,000 × ₹ 2)	Dr.		1,00,000	
	To Share Capital A/c				1,00,000
	(Being the First Call Money due on 50,000 shares)				
	Bank A/c [Balance Figure]	Dr.		95,400	
	Calls-in-Advance A/c (800 × ₹ 2)	Dr.		1,600	
	Calls-in-Arrears A/c (1,500 × ₹ 2)	Dr.		3,000	
	To Share First call A/c				1,00,000
	(Being the first call money received except on 1,500 shares and Calls-in-Advance adjusted on 800 shares)				
	Share Final Call A/c [50,000 × ₹ 2]	Dr.		1,00,000	
	To Share Capital A/c				1,00,000
	(Being the Final Call Money due on 50,000 shares)				
	Bank A/c	Dr.		95,400	
	Calls-in-Advance A/c	Dr.		1,600	
	Calls-in-Arrears A/c	Dr.		3,000	
	To Share Final call A/c				1,00,000
	(Being the Final Call Money received except on 1,500 Shares and Calls-in-Advance adjusted on 800 shares)				

Working Notes:

1. CALCULATION OF ALLOTMENT MONEY DUE BUT NOT RECEIVED FROM SURESH.

Number of shares allotted = 30,000/40,000 × 2,000 = 1,500 Shares	
Application Money received [(2,000 × ₹ 3]	6,000
Application Money due [1,500 × ₹ 3]	4,500
Excess Application Money adjusted on allotment. [₹ 6,000 – ₹ 4,500]	1,500
Money due from Suresh on allotment [1,500 × ₹ 5]	7,500
Allotment Money due not received [7,500 – 1,500]	6,000

2. CALCULATION OF ALLOTMENT MONEY RECEIVED LATER ON

Total Allotment Money due (50,000 × ₹ 5)	2,50,000
Less: Excess Application Money adjusted at application stage	(90,000)
Less: Allotment Money not received from Suresh	6,000
	1,54,000

3. Calls-in-Advance on 800 shares = 800 × ₹ 4 = ₹ 3,200

4. Total Money received at the Time of Allotment = ₹ 1,54,000 + ₹ 3,200 = ₹ 1,57,200.

15.0 ISSUE OF SHARES FOR CONSIDERATION OTHER THAN CASH

MEANING OF ISSUE OF SHARES FOR CONSIDERATION OTHER THAN CASH

When the company purchases some assets (including services), instead of making the payment to the supplier in the form of cash, it issues its fully paid shares, such issue of shares is called as the issue of shares for consideration other than cash. Such shares can be issued at par, premium *or* at a discount.

PURCHASE CONSIDERATION

Purchase Consideration is the amount paid by purchasing company in consideration for purchase of assets/business from another enterprise. Unless otherwise stated, Purchase consideration on Net Assets basis is arrived at as follows:

Purchase Consideration

= Agreed Value of All Assets taken over – Agreed Amount of Liabilities assumed

For Example, X Ltd. has acquired from Y Assets worth ₹ 20,00,000 and Liabilities of ₹ 6,00,000. In this case, Purchase Consideration is ₹ 14,00,000 (i.e. ₹ 20,00,000 – ₹ 6,00,000.)

TREATMENT OF DIFFERENCE BETWEEN PURCHASE CONSIDERATION AND NET ASSETS ACQUIRED

Case	*Accounting Treatment*
If Purchase Consideration > Net Assets	The excess of Purchase Consideration over Net Assets acquired should be debited to **'Goodwill Account'**.
If Net Assets > Purchase Consideration	The excess of Net Assets acquired over Purchase Consideration should be credited to **'Capital Reserve Account'**.

DISCLOSURE

Number and Class of Shares issued for consideration other than Cash are disclosed in Notes to Accounts 'Share Capital' in the Balance Sheet of a company.

JOURNAL ENTRIES

Date	Particulars		L.F.	Dr. (₹)	Cr. (₹)
1.	**On Purchase of Business/Assets**				
	Sundry Assets	Dr.		(With the Agreed Values of Assets taken over)	
	*Goodwill A/c	Dr.		(With Excess of Purchase Consideration over the Value of Net Assets)	
	To Sundry Liabilities			(With the Agreed Amount of Liabilities taken over)	
	To Vendor's A/c			(With Purchase consideration Payable)	
	To *Capital Reserve A/c			(With Excess of Value of Net Assets over the Purchase Consideration)	
	(Being the purchase of Assets/Business) *Either Goodwill *or* Capital Reserve				
2.	**On Part Payment to Vendor**				
	Vendor's A/c	Dr.		[With Part Payment]	
	To Cash A/c			[With Cash Payment]	
	To Bank A/c			[With Cheque/Bank Draft]	
	To Bills Payable A/c			[With Promissory Note]	
	(Being the Part Payment made to Vendor)				
3.	**On Issue of Shares**				
(a)	**If Shares are issued to Vendor at Par:**				
	Vendor's A/c	Dr.		(With Balance Purchase Consideration)	
	To Share Capital A/c				
(b)	**If Shares are issued to Vendor at Premium:**				
	Vendor's A/c	Dr.		(With Balance Purchase Consideration)	
	To Share Capital A/c			(With the Nominal Value)	
	To Securities Premium A/c			(With Premium on Issue)	

ILLUSTRATION 19

On April 1, X Ltd. took over the Assets of ₹ 6,80,000 and Creditors of ₹ 80,000 of Y Ltd. payable 10% by a cheque and the balance by the issue of fully paid Equity Shares of ₹ 100 each. Pass the necessary Journal Entries in the books of the company on April 1 if such Shares are issued

(a) at par

(b) at a premium of 20%.

SOLUTION

JOURNAL OF X LTD.

Date	Particulars	L.F.	Dr. (₹)	Cr. (₹)
April 1	**Entry 1 in all cases**		6,80,000	
	Sundry Assets A/c Dr.			
	To Sundry Creditors			80,000
	To Y Ltd.			6,00,000
	(Being the purchase of Business from Y Ltd.)			
April 1	**Case (a)**			
	Y Ltd. Dr.		6,00,000	
	To Bank A/c [₹ 6,00,000 X 10/100]			60,000
	To Equity Share Capital A/c			5,40,000
	(Being 10% by a cheque and the balance the issue of 5,400 shares at par to Y Ltd.)			
	[No. of Shares to be issued = ₹ 5,40,000 / ₹ 100 = 5,400]			
April 1	**Case (b)**			
	Y Ltd. Dr.		6,00,000	
	To Bank A/c [₹ 6,00,000 X 10/100]			60,000
	To Equity Share Capital A/c			4,50,000
	To Securities Premium A/c			90,000
	(Being 10% by a cheque and the balance the issue of 4,500 shares at 20% premium to Y Ltd.)			
	[No. of Shares to be issued = ₹ 5,40,000 / ₹ 120 = 4,500]			

ILLUSTRATION 20

On April 1,X Ltd. purchased a running business from Y Ltd. for ₹ 10,40,000 payable as to 25% by a cheque and the balance by an issue of fully paid Equity Shares of ₹ 100 each at a premium of 4%. The assets and liabilities consisted of the following:

Building ₹ 6,00,000, Plant and Machinery ₹ 1,00,000, Inventories ₹ 2,00,000, Trade Receivables ₹ 1,80,000, Trade Payables ₹ 80,000.

Pass the necessary journal entries in the books of X Ltd on April 1.

SOLUTION

JOURNAL OF X LTD.

Date	Particulars	L.F.	Dr. (₹)	Cr. (₹)
April 1	Building Dr.		6,00,000	
	Plant and Machinery Dr.		1,00,000	
	Inventories Dr.		2,00,000	
	Trade Receivables Dr.		1,80,000	
	Goodwill A/c *[Balancing Figure]* Dr.		40,000	

	To Trade Payables			80,000
	To Y Ltd.			10,40,000
	(Being the purchase of Business from Y Ltd.)			
April 1	Y Ltd. Dr.		10,40,000	
	To Bank A/c [10,40,000 × 25%]			**2,60, 000**
	To Equity Share Capital A/c			7,50,000
	To Securities Premium A/c [₹ 7,50,000 × 4%]			30,000
	(Being 25% by a cheque and the balance by an issue of 7,500 shares at 20% premium to Y Ltd.)			
	[No. of Shares to be issued = ₹ 7,80,000 / ₹ 104 = 7,500]			

ILLUSTRATION 21

On April 1,X Ltd. purchased a running business from Y Ltd. for ₹ 9,60,000 payable as to 25% by a cheque and the balance by an issue of fully paid Equity Shares of ₹ 100 each at a premium of 20%. The assets and liabilities consisted of the following:

Building ₹ 6,00,000, Plant and Machinery ₹ 1,00,000, Inventories ₹ 2,00,000, Trade Receivables ₹ 1,80,000, Trade Payables ₹ 80,000.

Pass the necessary journal entries in the books of X Ltd on April 1.

SOLUTION

JOURNAL OF X LTD.

Date	*Particulars*	*L.F.*	*Dr. (₹)*	*Cr. (₹)*
April 1	Building Dr.		6,00,000	
	Plant and Machinery Dr.		1,00,000	
	Inventories Dr.		2,00,000	
	Trade Receivables Dr.		1,80,000	
	To Trade Payables			80,000
	To Y Ltd.			9,60,000
	To Capital Reserve A/c *[Balancing Figure]*			40,000
	(Being the purchase of Business from Y Ltd.)			
April 1	Y Ltd. Dr.		9,60,000	
	To Bank A/c [₹ 9,60,000 × 25%]			**2,40, 000**
	To Equity Share Capital A/c			6,00,000
	To Securities Premium A/c [₹ 6,00,000 × 20%]			1,20,000
	(Being 25% by a cheque and the balance by an issue of 6,000 shares at 20% premium to Y Ltd.)			
	[No. of Shares to be issued = ₹ 7,20,000 / ₹ 120 = 6,000]			

ILLUSTRATION 22

X Ltd. issued 2,000 shares of ₹ 10 each credited as fully paid to the promoters for their services and issued 1,000 shares of ₹ 10 each credited as fully paid to the underwriters for their underwriting services. Journalise these transactions.

SOLUTION

JOURNAL OF X LTD.

Date	Particulars		L.F.	Dr. (₹)	Cr. (₹)
1.	Incorporation Costs A/c	Dr.		20,000	
	To Share Capital A/c				20,000
	(Being the issue of 2,000 shares of ₹ 10 each at par to promoters as per Board's Resolution dated...)				
2.	Underwriting Commission A/c	Dr.		10,000	
	To Underwriter's A/c				10,000
	(Being the underwriting commission due on shares)				
3.	Underwriter's A/c	Dr.		10,000	
	To Share Capital A/c				10,000
	(Being the issue of 1,000 shares of ₹ 10 each at par to underwriters as per the Board's Resolution dated...)				

16.0 FORFEITURE OF SHARES

FORFEITURE OF SHARES

Meaning	Forfeiture of shares means the cancellation of allotment to defaulting shareholders and to treat the amount already received on such shares as forfeited to the company. Thus, forfeiture of shares is at the instance of company.
Authority	When a shareholder fails to pay one *or* more instalments (viz., allotment money and/or call money) due on the shares held by him, the company has the authority to forfeit such shares by strictly following the procedure specified in its Articles of Association.
SEBI Guidelines	According to SEBI Guidelines, the subscription money must be received within twelve months from the date of allotment. If the investor fails to pay the call money within twelve months, the subscription money already paid may be forfeited.
Property	Forfeited shares become the property of the company.

SURRENDER OF SHARES

Meaning	Surrender of shares is a voluntary return of shares for the purposes of cancellation. Surrender of Shares is at the instance of Shareholder.
Authority	The directors can accept the surrender of shares only when the Articles authorise them to do so.
Lawful	Surrender is lawful only in two cases viz. a) where it is done as a short cut to forfeiture to avoid the formalities for a valid forfeiture & b) Where shares are surrendered in exchange for new shares of the same nominal value (but with different rights).
Void	A surrender will be void if it amounts to purchase of the shares by the company *or* if it is accepted for the purpose of relieving a member from his liabilities.
Accounting Treatment	So far as accounting treatment is concerned, the Surrender of Shares is considered similar to the Forfeiture of Shares. Surrendered Shares may be reissued in the same way as Forfeited Shares.

ACCOUNTING TREATMENT OF FORFEITURE OF SHARES

Generally speaking, accounting treatment on forfeiture is to reverse all the entries (except those relating to Securities Premium received) already passed till the stage of forfeiture and to treat the amount already received (excluding Securities Premium) as forfeited to the company. The accounting treatment to record the forfeiture of shares in various cases is summarised as follows:

17.0 FORFEITURE OF SHARES WHICH WERE ISSUED AT PAR

A/C TO BE DEBITED

Debit 'Share Capital Account' with the amount called up on such shares till the stage of forfeiture.

A/CS TO BE CREDITED

1. Credit Share Allotment Account and/or Share Call(s) Account (or Calls-in-arrears Account, if any, maintained) with the amount due but not received on such shares.
2. Credit 'Forfeited Shares Account' with the amount received on such shares.

JOURNAL ENTRY

Date	Particulars	L.F.	Dr. (₹)	Cr. (₹)
	Share Capital A/c Dr.		(With the amount called up on shares forfeited)	
	To Forfeited Shares A/c			(With the amount already received)
	To Share Allotment A/c			(With the amount due but not received on allotment)
	To Share Call A/c			(With the amount due but not received on Call)
	(Being ... shares forfeited for non-payment of...)			

Notes:

1. *In case "Calls-in-Arrears" account is maintained by the company, "Calls-in-Arrears" account would be credited in the above entry instead of 'Share Allotment' and/or 'Share Call/Calls' accounts.*
2. *Always use Calls-in-arrears Account if the nature of the amount called up but not received is not clear in the question.*

DISCLOSURE

The balance of the Forfeited Shares Account is shown in **Notes to Accounts 'Share Capital'** to the Balance Sheet till the Forfeited Shares are reissued.

ILLUSTRATION 23

X Ltd. issued 2,000 shares of ₹ 10 each at par payable as under: On application ₹ 2 per share, on allotment ₹ 3 per share. On first call ₹ 3 per share, on second call ₹ 2 per share. Mr. X was allotted 40 shares. Mr. X failed to pay allotment money and on his subsequent failure to pay the first call, his shares were forfeited. Pass the necessary journal entry relating to the forfeiture of shares.

SOLUTION

JOURNAL

Date	Particulars	L.F.	Dr. (₹)	Cr. (₹)
	Share Capital A/c (40 × ₹ 8) Dr.		320	
	To Share Allotment A/c (40 × ₹ 3)			120
	To Share First Call A/c / Calls-in-arrears A/c (40 × ₹ 3)			120
	To Forfeited Shares A/c (40 × ₹ 2)			80
	(Being 40 shares forfeited for non-payment of allotment money and first call money)			

ILLUSTRATION 24

X Ltd. forfeited 40 shares of ₹ 10 each (₹ 8 called up) issued at par to Mr. X on which he had paid ₹ 2 per share. Journalise.

SOLUTION

JOURNAL

Date	Particulars	L.F.	Dr. (₹)	Cr. (₹)
	Share Capital A/c (40 × ₹ 8) Dr.		320	
	To Calls-in-arrears A/c (40 × ₹ 6)			240
	To Forfeited Shares A/c (40 × ₹ 2)			80
	(Being 40 shares forfeited for non-payment of called up amount)			

ILLUSTRATION 25

Paliwal Exports Ltd. with a share capital of ₹ 1,00,000 divided into 2,000 shares of ₹ 50 each offers the shares to the public as under:

₹ 10 per share payable on application; ₹ 10 per share payable on allotment; ₹ 15 per share payable on 1st call; and ₹ 15 per share payable on second call.

Shareholder 'A' who holds 30 shares has paid only the Application Money.

Shareholder 'B' who holds 20 shares has paid Application Money on 20 shares and allotment money on only 10 shares. He has not paid only other calls.

Shareholder 'C' who holds 18 shares has paid only the application and allotment money.

Shareholder 'D' who holds 5 shares has paid application, allotment and first call money.

Shareholder 'E' who holds 3 shares has paid application, allotment and first call money in full and second call money on only 2 shares.

The company forfeits the shares of the above shareholders who have not paid the arrears.

Required: Journalise the above transactions including entries relating to Bank in the books of Paliwal Exports Ltd.

SOLUTION

JOURNAL OF PALIWAL EXPORTS LTD.

Date	Particulars		L.F.	Dr. (₹)	Cr. (₹)
	Bank A/c	Dr.		20,000	
	To Share Application A/c				20,000
	(Being the Application Money received on 2,000 shares)				
	Shares Application A/c	Dr.		20,000	
	To Share Capital A/c				20,000
	(Being the transfer of Application Money on 2,000 shares to Share Capital A/c)				
	Share Allotment A/c	Dr.		20,000	
	To Share Capital A/c				20,000
	(Being the allotment money due)				
	Bank A/c	Dr.		19,600	
	To Share Allotment A/c				19,600
	(Being the allotment money received on 1,960 shares)				
	Share First Call A/c	Dr.		30,000	
	To Share Capital A/c				30,000
	(Being the first call money due)				
	Bank A/c	Dr.		28,980	
	To Share First Call A/c				28,980
	(Being the first call money received on 1,932 shares)				
	Share Second & Final Call A/c	Dr.		30,000	
	To Share Capital A/c				30,000
	(Being the second & final call money due)				
	Bank A/c	Dr.		28,890	
	To Share Second & Final Call A/c				28,890
	(Being the second & final call received on 1,926 shares)				
	Share Capital A/c	Dr.		3,700	
	To Forfeited Shares A/c				1,170
	To Share Allotment A/c				400
	To Share First Call A/c				1,020
	To Share Second & Final Call A/c				1,110
	(Being 74 shares forfeited as per Board's Resolution dated....)				

ILLUSTRATION 26

A Ltd. has an authorised capital of ₹ 2,00,000 divided into shares of ₹ 10 each. Of these, 6,000 shares were issued as fully paid in payment of building purchased from B Ltd. 8,000 shares were subscribed for by the public and during the first year ₹ 5 per share was called up payable ₹ 2 on application, ₹ 1 on allotment, ₹ 1 on the first call and ₹ 1 on second call. The amounts received in respect of these shares were as follows:-

On 6,000 Shares	Full amount called
On 1,250 Shares	₹ 4 Per Share
On 500 Shares	₹ 3 Per Share
On 250 Shares	₹ 2 Per Share

The directors forfeited the 750 shares, on which *less* than ₹ 4 per share had been paid. Pass Journal Entries recording the above transactions (including cash transactions).

SOLUTION

JOURNAL OF A LTD.

Date	*Particulars*		*L.F.*	*Dr. (₹)*	*Cr. (₹)*
	Building A/c	Dr.		60,000	
	To B Ltd.				60,000
	(Being the purchase of building from B Ltd. as per agreement dated....)				
	B Ltd.	Dr.		60,000	
	To Share Capital A/c				60,000
	(Being the issue of 4,000 shares at par)				
	Bank A/c	Dr.		16,000	
	To Share Application A/c				16,000
	(Being the Application Money received)				
	Share Application A/c	Dr.		16,000	
	To Share Capital A/c				16,000
	(Being the Application Money adjusted)				
	Share Allotment A/c	Dr.		8,000	
	To Share Capital A/c				8,000
	(Being the allotment money due)				
	Bank A/c	Dr.		7,750	
	To Share Allotment A/c				7,750
	(Being the allotment money received on 7,750 shares)				
	Share First Call A/c	Dr.		8,000	
	To Share Capital A/c				8,000
	(Being the first call due)				
	Bank A/c	Dr.		7,250	
	To Share First Call A/c				7,250
	(Being the first call received on 7,250 shares)				
	Share Second Call A/c	Dr.		8,000	
	To Share Capital A/c				8,000
	(Being the second call due)				
	Bank A/c	Dr.		6,000	
	To Share Second Call A/c				6,000
	(Being the second call received on 6,000 shares)				

	Share Capital A/c Dr.		3,750	
	To Forfeited Shares A/c			2,000
	To Share Allotment A/c			250
	To Share First Call A/c			750
	To Share Second Call A/c			750
	(Being 750 shares forfeited as per Board's Resolution dated...)			

18.0 FORFEITURE OF SHARES WHICH WERE ISSUED AT A PREMIUM

A/cs to be Debited	1. Debit 'Share Capital Account' with the amount called up (excluding Securities Premium) on such shares till the stage of forfeiture; 2. Debit 'Securities Premium Account' **with the amount of premium due but not received on such shares** (**Note:** This treatment is required only when an entry has already been passed for Securities Premium when it becomes due)
A/cs to be Credited	1. Credit Share Allotment Account and/or Share Call(s) Account (or Calls-in-arrears Account, if any, maintained) with the amount due but not received (excluding Securities Premium, if any received) on such shares. 2. Credit 'Forfeited Shares Account' with the amount received **(excluding Securities Premium, if any, already received)**

JOURNAL ENTRY

Date	*Particulars*	*L.F.*	*Dr. (₹)*	*Cr. (₹)*
	Share Capital A/c Dr.		(With the Called up amount on shares forfeited)	
	Securities Premium A/c Dr.		(With the Securities of Premium not received)	
	To Forfeited Shares A/c			(With the amount already received excluding Securities Premium)
	To Share Allotment A/c			(With the amount due but not received on Allotment)
	To Share Call A/c			(With the amount due but not paid on Call)
	(Being...shares forfeited for non-payment of....)			

Notes:

1. In case "Calls-in-Arrears" account is maintained by the company, "Calls-in-Arrears" account would be credited in the above entry instead of 'Share Allotment' and/or 'Share Call/Calls' accounts.
2. Always use Calls-in-arrears Account if the nature of the amount called up but not received is not clear in the question.

ILLUSTRATION 27

X Ltd. issued 2,000 equity shares of ₹ 10 each at a premium of ₹ 4 per share payable as under: On application ₹ 3 per share (including ₹ 1 premium), on allotment ₹ 4 per share (including ₹ 1 premium), on first call ₹ 4 per share (including ₹ 1 premium), on second call Balance. Mr. X was allotted 40 shares. Mr. X failed to pay allotment money and on his subsequent failure to pay the first call, his shares were forfeited. Pass the necessary journal entry relating to the forfeiture of shares.

SOLUTION

JOURNAL

Date	Particulars	L.F.	Dr. (₹)	Cr. (₹)
	Share Capital A/c (40 × ₹ 8) Dr.		320	
	Securities Premium A/c (40 × ₹ 2) Dr.		80	
	To Share Allotment A/c (40 × ₹ 4)			160
	To Share First Call A/c / Calls-in-arrears A/c (40 × ₹ 4)			160
	To Forfeited Shares A/c (40 × ₹ 2)			80
	(Being 40 shares forfeited for non-payment of allotment money and first call money)			

ILLUSTRATION 28

X Ltd. forfeited 40 shares of ₹ 10 each (₹ 8 called up) issued at 40% premium (payable on final call) to Mr. X on which he had paid ₹ 2 per share. Journalise.

SOLUTION

JOURNAL

Date	Particulars	L.F.	Dr. (₹)	Cr. (₹)
	Share Capital A/c (40 × ₹ 8) Dr.		320	
	To Calls-in-arrears A/c (40 × ₹ 6)			240
	To Forfeited Shares A/c (40 × ₹ 2)			80
	(Being 40 shares forfeited for non-payment of called up amount)			

19.0 RE-ISSUE OF SHARES

MEANING OF RE-ISSUE OF SHARES

Reissue of shares is merely a sale of Forfeited Shares and not an allotment of shares. The forfeited shares can be reissued as per the provisions of the Articles of the company.

RE-ISSUE PRICE OF FORFEITED SHARES

The forfeited shares can be re-issued at par, premium *or* discount.

MINIMUM RE-ISSUE PRICE

The Re-issue Price of forfeited shares must be at least equal to the difference between the Paid up Value of Re-issued Shares and the Amount Forfeited on Re-issued Shares.

In other words, Re-issue Price must not be *less* than the amount unpaid on Forfeited Shares.

MAXIMUM AMOUNT OF DISCOUNT WHICH MAY BE ALLOWED ON RE-ISSUE

Case	*Maximum Permissible Discount On Re-issue*
(a) When the Forfeited Shares were originally issued at par *or* at a premium.	The amount credited to Forfeited Share Account.
(b) When the Forfeited Shares were originally issued at a discount	The amount credited to 'Forfeited Share Account *plus* the amount of original discount.

ACCOUNTS TO BE DEBITED

1. Debit 'Bank Account' with the amount received on shares re-issued.

   Amount = No. of Shares re-issued × Re-issue Price per share

2. Debit 'Discount on Issue of Shares Account' with the amount of discount originally allowed on such shares In case shares were originally issued at a discount.
3. Debit Forfeited Shares Account with the excess of re-issue discount over original discount (if any) allowed on shares re-issued. Such amount is calculated as under:

   = No. of Shares re-issued × [Paid-up Value per share – Re-issue Price per share – Original Discount per share (if any)]

ACCOUNTS TO BE CREDITED

1. Credit Share Capital Account with the paid-up value of shares re-issued.

   Amount = No. of Shares re-issued × Paid-up Value per share

2. Credit 'Securities Premium Account' with Excess of Re-issue Price over Paid-up Value.

TUTORIAL NOTE

Neither 'Discount on Issue of Shares A/c' nor 'Forfeited Shares A/c' is debited when the Forfeited Shares are re-issued at a premium (i.e. Excess of Re-issue Price over Paid up Value)

JOURNAL ENTRY ON RE-ISSUE OF SHARES WHICH WERE ORIGINALLY ISSUED AT PAR OR AT A PREMIUM

Date	*Particulars*	*L.F.*	*Dr. (₹)*	*Cr. (₹)*
	Bank A/c Dr.		(With the amount received on re-issue)	
	Forfeited Shares A/c Dr.		(With the discount allowed on re-issue)	
	To Share Capital A/c		(With the amount credited as paid-up)	

JOURNAL ENTRY ON RE-ISSUE OF FORFEITED SHARES AT A PREMIUM

Date	*Particulars*	*L.F.*	*Dr. (₹)*	*Cr. (₹)*
	Bank A/c Dr.		(With Re-issue Price)	
	To Share Capital A/c		[With Paid Up value]	
	To Securities Premium A/c		[With Excess of Re-issue Price over paid up value]	

JOURNAL ENTRY ON TRANSFER OF PROFIT ON RE-ISSUE

Date	Particulars		L.F.	Dr. (₹)	Cr. (₹)
	Forfeited Shares A/c To Capital Reserve A/c	Dr.		(with Profit on Re-issue)	

CALCULATION OF PROFIT ON RE-ISSUE OF SHARES

	Particulars	Defaulter 1	Defaulter 2
A.	Amount forfeited on Shares re-issued $\left[\left(\frac{\text{Total amount forfeited}}{\text{No. of shares forfeited}}\right) \times \text{No. of Shares re-issued}\right]$	xxx	xxx
B.	*Less:* Re-issue Discount (other than original discount, if any)	xxx	xxx
C.	Profit on re-issue to be t/f to Capital Reserve [A – B]	xxx	xxx

TREATMENT OF BALANCE OF FORFEITED SHARES ACCOUNT

(a) If all the Forfeited Shares have been re-issued	The credit balance left on the Forfeited Shares Account is transferred to Capital Reserve Account by passing the following entry: Forfeited Shares A/c Dr. To Capital Reserve A/c
(b) If some of the Forfeited Shares have been re-issued	The profit on re-issue of shares is **transferred to Capital Reserve Account** and the balance on the Forfeited Shares Account relating to shares not yet re-issued is carried forward and is shown in **Notes to Account 'Share Capital'** in the Balance Sheet.

RE-ISSUE OF SHARES WHICH WERE ORIGINALLY ISSUED AT A PREMIUM

ILLUSTRATION 29

P Ltd. forfeited 50 shares of ₹ 100 each issued at 10% premium for non-payment of allotment money of ₹ 30 per share (including premium) and first call of ₹ 30 per share. The second & final call of ₹ 20 per share was not yet called.

(i) State whether these shares can be reissued.

(ii) State whether these shares can be reissued at premium only.

(iii) State with reason whether these shares can be reissued as ₹ 80 paid up for the ₹ 40 per share.

(iv) If 20 of these shares were re-issued as ₹ 80 paid-up for ₹ 70 per share. Pass Journal Entries regarding forfeiture and re-issue of shares and prepare Forfeited Shares Account.

SOLUTION

(i) Yes. The forfeited shares can be reissued as per the provisions of the Articles of the company.

(ii) No. The forfeited shares can be reissued at par, premium *or* discount.

(iii) **No. Reason:** The maximum permissible discount on re-issue is the amount forfeited on Re-issued shares (i.e. ₹ 30). In the given case, re-issue discount is ₹ 40 which is not permissible.

(IV) JOURNAL

Date	Particulars		L.F.	Dr. (₹)	Cr. (₹)
1.	**On Forfeiture of 50 shares**				
	Share Capital A/c (50 × ₹ 80)	Dr.		4,000	
	Securities Premium A/c [50 × ₹ 10]	Dr.		500	
	To Share Allotment A/c (50 × ₹ 30)				1,500
	To Share First Call A/c / Calls-in-arrears A/c (50 × ₹ 30)				1,500
	To Forfeited Shares A/c (50 × ₹ 30)				1,500
	(Being 50 shares forfeited for non-payment of first call money)				
2.	**On Re-Issue of 20 shares**				
	Bank A/c (20 × ₹ 70)	Dr.		1,400	
	Forfeited Shares A/c (20 × ₹ 10)	Dr.		200	
	To Share Capital A/c (20 × ₹ 80)				1,600
	(Being 20 shares re-issued as ₹ 80 paid-up for ₹ 90 per share)				
3.	Forfeited Shares A/c [(20 × ₹ 30) – ₹ 200]	Dr.		400	
	To Capital Reserve A/c				400
	(Being the transfer of profit on re-issue of 20 shares)				

Dr. **FORFEITED SHARES ACCOUNT** Cr.

Particulars	₹	Particulars	₹
To Share Capital A/c	200	By Share Capital A/c	1,500
To Capital Reserve A/c	400		
To Balance c/d	900		
	1,500		1,500

ILLUSTRATION 30

Bharat Ltd. forfeited 600 shares of ₹ 10 each issued at a premium of 30% to *W* who had paid an application money of ₹ 5 (including ₹ 1 premium), for non-payment of allotment money of ₹ 5 (including ₹ 1 premium). At different intervals of time,out of these 100 shares were re-issued to *X* as ₹ 8 called up for ₹ 7 per share, 100 shares were re-issued to *Y* as ₹ 8 paid up for ₹ 9 per share and 400 shares were re-issued to *Z,* credited as fully paid for ₹ 9 per share. Record the journal entries for forfeiture and reissue of shares.

SOLUTION

JOURNAL OF BHARAT LTD

Date	Particulars		L.F.	Dr. (₹)	Cr. (₹)
	On Forfeiture of 600 Shares				
1.	Share Capital A/c (600 × ₹ 8)	Dr.		4,800	
	Securities Premium A/c (600 × ₹ 1)	Dr.		600	
	To Share Allotment A/c (600 × ₹ 5)				3,000
	To Forfeited Shares A/c (600 × ₹ 4)				2,400
	(Being 600 shares forfeited for non-payment of Allotment money				

	On Re-issue of 100 Shares as ₹ 8 paid-up for ₹ 7 per share			
2.	Bank A/c (100 × ₹ 7) Dr.		700	
	Forfeited Shares A/c (100 × ₹ 1) Dr.		100	
	To Share Capital A/c (100 × ₹ 8)			800
	(Being 100 shares re-issued as ₹ 8 paid-up for ₹ 7 per share)			
3.	Forfeited Shares A/c [(₹ 2,400 × 100/600) – ₹ 100] Dr.		300	
	To Capital Reserve A/c			300
	(Being the transfer of profit on re-issue)			
	On Re-issue of 100 Shares as ₹ 8 paid-up for ₹ 9 per share			
4.	Bank A/c (100 × ₹ 9) Dr.		900	
	To Share Capital A/c (100 × ₹ 8)			800
	To Securities Premium A/c (100 × ₹ 1)			100
	(Being 100 shares re-issued as ₹ 8 paid-up for ₹ 9 per share)			
5.	Forfeited Shares A/c (₹ 2,400 × 100/600) Dr.		400	
	To Capital Reserve A/c			400
	(Being the transfer of profit on re-issue)			
	On Re-issue of 400 Shares			
6.	Bank A/c (400 × ₹ 9) Dr.		3,600	
	Forfeited Shares A/c (400 × ₹ 1) Dr.		400	
	To Share Capital A/c (400 × ₹ 10)			4,000
	(Being 400 shares re-issued as fully paid-up for ₹ 9 per share)			
7.	Forfeited Shares A/c [(₹ 2,400 × 400/600) – ₹ 400] Dr.		1,200	
	To Capital Reserve A/c			1,200
	(Being the transfer of profit on re-issue)			

ILLUSTRATION 31

Tushar Ltd. forfeited 600 shares of ₹ 10 each issued at a premium of 30% to *W* for non-payment of first and final call money of ₹ 3 (including ₹ 1 premium). At different intervals of time,out of these 400 shares were re-issued to *Z*,credited as fully paid for ₹ 9 per share and 100 shares were re-issued to *X* as ₹ 10 paid up for ₹ 11 per share. Record the journal entries for forfeiture and reissue of shares.

SOLUTION

JOURNAL OF TUSHAR LTD

Date	*Particulars*	*L.F.*	*Dr. (₹)*	*Cr. (₹)*
	On Forfeiture of 600 Shares			
1.	Share Capital A/c (600 × ₹ 10) Dr.		6,000	
	Securities Premium A/c (600 × ₹ 1) Dr.		600	
	To Calls-in-arrears A/c (600 × ₹ 3)			1,800
	To Forfeited Shares A/c (600 × ₹ 8)			4,800
	(Being 600 shares forfeited for non-payment of call money)			
	On Re-issue of 400 Shares			
2.	Bank A/c (400 × ₹ 9) Dr.		3,600	
	Forfeited Shares A/c (400 × ₹ 1) Dr.		400	
	To Share Capital A/c (400 × ₹ 10)			4,000
	(Being 400 shares re-issued as fully paid-up for ₹ 9 per share)			

3.	Forfeited Shares A/c [(₹ 4,800 × 400/600) – ₹ 400] Dr. To Capital Reserve A/c (Being the transfer of profit on re-issue)		2,800	2,800
	On Re-issue of 100 Shares			
4.	Bank A/c (100 × ₹ 11) Dr. To Share Capital A/c (100 × ₹ 10) To Securities Premium A/c (100 × ₹ 1) (Being 100 shares re-issued as fully paid-up for ₹ 11 per share)		1,100	1,000 100
5.	Forfeited Shares A/c (₹ 4,800 × 100/600) Dr. To Capital Reserve A/c (Being the transfer of profit on re-issue)		800	800

RE-ISSUE OF SHARES WHICH WERE ORIGINALLY ISSUED AT A DISCOUNT

JOURNAL ENTRY ON RE-ISSUE OF FORFEITED SHARES WHICH WERE ORIGINALLY ISSUED AT A DISCOUNT

Date	Particulars	L.F.	Dr. (₹)	Cr. (₹)
	Bank A/c Dr.		(With the amount received on re-issue)	
	Forfeited Shares A/c Dr.		(With the excess of Re-issue Discount over the Original Discount)	
	To Share Capital A/c		(With the amount credited as Paid-up)	

JOURNAL ENTRY ON RE-ISSUE OF FORFEITED SHARES AT A PREMIUM

Date	Particulars	L.F.	Dr. (₹)	Cr. (₹)
	Bank A/c Dr. To Share Capital A/c To Securities Premium A/c		(With Re-issue Price) [With Paid Up value] [With Excess of Re-issue Price over Paid up value]	

ILLUSTRATION 32

Cloud & Rain Ltd. invited applications for 20,000 Equity shares of ₹ 10 each payable as under:

On applications ₹ 2 per share, on Allotment ₹ 2 per share, on First call ₹ 3 per share, on Final call ₹ 3 per share

The entire issue was subscribed for and paid with the following exceptions:

(i) P, who was allotted 200 shares, failed to pay the money due on allotment and calls.
(ii) Q, who held 150 shares, did not pay the first call and second call.
(iii) R, who held 50 shares, did not pay the amount on second call.

The Board of Directors passed a Resolution forfeiting all the shares of P, Q and R. These shares were subsequently re-issued as fully paid at a discount of 20%.

Required: Pass Journal entries to record transactions in books of Cloud & Rain Ltd.

SOLUTION

JOURNAL OF CLOUD & RAIN LTD.

Date	Particulars		L.F.	Dr. (₹)	Cr. (₹)
1.	Bank A/c	Dr.		40,000	
	To Share Application A/c				40,000
	(Being the Application Money received on 20,000 shares)				
2.	Share Application A/c	Dr.		40,000	
	To Share Capital A/c				40,000
	(Being the Application Money transferred to Share Capital Account)				
3.	Share Allotment A/c	Dr.		40,000	
	To Share Capital A/c				40,000
	(Being the allotment money due on 20,000 shares @ ₹ 2 per share)				
4.	Bank A/c	Dr.		39,600	
	To Share Allotment A/c				39,600
	(Being the allotment money received on 19,800 shares)				
5.	Share 1st Call A/c	Dr.		60,000	
	To Share Capital A/c				60,000
	(Being 1st call money due on 20,000 shares ₹ 3 per share)				
6.	Bank A/c	Dr.		58,950	
	To Share 1st Call A/c				58,950
	(Being, 1st call money received on 19,650 shares)				
7.	Share 2nd & Final Call A/c	Dr.		60,000	
	To Share Capital A/c				60,000
	(Being 2nd and final call money due on 20,000 shares @ ₹ 3 per share)				
8.	Bank A/c	Dr.		58,800	
	To Share 2nd & Final Call A/c				58,800
	(Being 2nd and final call money received on 19,600 shares)				
	Share Capital A/c	Dr.		4,000	
	To Forfeited Shares A/c				1,350
	To Share Allotment A/c				400
	To Share 1st Call A/c				1,050
	To Share 2nd and Final Call A/c				1,200
	(Being 400 shares forfeited)				
	Bank A/c	Dr.		3,200	
	Forfeited Shares A/c	Dr.		800	
	To Share Capital A/c				4,000
	(Being 400 shares re-issued at ₹ 8 per share)				

	Forfeited Shares A/c . . . Dr.		550	
	To Capital Reserve A/c			550
	(Being the transfer of profit on re-issue of 400 forfeited shares to Capital Reserve)			

20.0 FORFEITURE AND RE-ISSUE OF SHARES ALLOTTED ON *Pro rata* BASIS IN CASE OF OVER-SUBSCRIPTION

In case an applicant has been allotted *less* than the number of shares applied for and the excess Application Money has been adjusted towards other sum due on shares allotted, such amount so adjusted should be deducted from the amount due on the allotment/call against which the excess Application Money was adjusted, to arrive at the net amount due but not paid by the shareholder. In such a case, the procedure given below may be followed to ascertain the amount due but not paid:

HOW TO CALCULATE THE AMOUNT DUE BUT NOT RECEIVED FROM DEFAULTER

Step 1: *Calculate the Total Number of Shares Applied for (if not given) as under:*

$$\frac{\text{Total no. of Shares applied under prorata category}}{\text{Total no. of Shares allotted under prorata category}} \times \text{No. of Shares allotted to defaulter}$$

OR

Calculate the Total Number of Shares allotted (if not given) as under:

$$\frac{\text{Total no. of Shares allotted under prorata category}}{\text{Total no. of Shares applied under prorata category}} \times \text{No. of Shares applied to defaulter}$$

Step 2: *Calculate the Total Application Money received on shares applied by defaulter*

= No. of Shares applied by defaulter × Application Money per share

Step 3: *Calculate the Application Money due on Shares allotted to defaulter*

= No. of Shares Allotted to Defaulter × Application Money per share

Step 4: *Calculate the Excess Application Money*

= Amount as per Step 2 – Amount as per Step 3

Step 5: *Calculate the Allotment or Call Money due on shares allotted*

No. of Shares allotted to Defaulter × Allotment Money/Call Money per share

Step 6: *Calculate the Allotment or Call Money due but not received*

= Amount as per Step 5 – Amount as per Step 4.

ILLUSTRATION 33

Bharat Ltd. forfeited 600 shares of ₹ 10 each issued at a premium of 30% to *W* who had applied for 1140 shares and paid an application money of ₹ 5 (including ₹ 1 premium), for non-payment of allotment money of ₹ 5 (including ₹ 1 premium). At different intervals of time,out of these 100 shares were re-issued to *X* as ₹ 8 called up for ₹ 7 per share, 100 shares were re-issued to *Y* as ₹ 8 paid up for ₹ 9 per share and 400 shares were re-issued to *Z*,credited as fully paid for ₹ 9 per share. Record the journal entries for forfeiture and reissue of shares and prepare Forfeited Shares Account assuming that the company follows the policy of adjusting excess Application Money towards other sums due on shares.

SOLUTION

JOURNAL OF BHARAT LTD

Date	Particulars	L.F.	Dr. (₹)	Cr. (₹)
	On Forfeiture of 600 Shares			
1.	Share Capital A/c (600 × ₹ 8) Dr.		4,800	
	Securities Premium A/c (₹ 3,000 – ₹ 2,700) Dr.		300	
	To Share Allotment A/c			300
	To Forfeited Shares A/c (₹ 5,700 – ₹ 600 – ₹ 300)			4,800
	(Being 600 shares forfeited for non-payment of Allotment money			
	On Re-issue of 100 Shares as ₹ 8 paid-up for ₹ 7 per share			
2.	Bank A/c (100 × ₹ 7) Dr.		700	
	Forfeited Shares A/c (100 × ₹ 1) Dr.		100	
	To Share Capital A/c (100 × ₹ 8)			800
	(Being 100 shares re-issued as ₹ 8 paid-up for ₹ 7 per share)			
3.	Forfeited Shares A/c [(₹ 4,800 × 100/600) – ₹ 100] Dr.		700	
	To Capital Reserve A/c			700
	(Being the transfer of profit on re-issue)			
	On Re-issue of 100 Shares as ₹ 8 paid-up for ₹ 9 per share			
4.	Bank A/c (100 × ₹ 9) Dr.		900	
	To Share Capital A/c (100 × ₹ 8)			800
	To Securities Premium A/c (100 × ₹ 1)			100
	(Being 100 shares re-issued as ₹ 8 paid-up for ₹ 9 per share)			
5.	Forfeited Shares A/c (₹ 4,800 × 100/600) Dr.		800	
	To Capital Reserve A/c			800
	(Being the transfer of profit on re-issue)			
	On Re-issue of 400 Shares			
6.	Bank A/c (400 × ₹ 9) Dr.		3,600	
	Forfeited Shares A/c (400 × ₹ 1) Dr.		400	
	To Share Capital A/c (400 × ₹ 10)			4,000
	(Being 400 shares re-issued as fully paid-up for ₹ 9 per share)			
7.	Forfeited Shares A/c [(₹ 4,800 × 400/600) – ₹ 400] Dr.		2,800	
	To Capital Reserve A/c			2,800
	(Being the transfer of profit on re-issue)			

Dr. **FORFEITED SHARES ACCOUNT** *Cr.*

Particulars	₹	Particulars	₹
To Share Capital A/c	100	By Share Capital A/c	4,800
To Capital Reserve A/c	700		
To Capital Reserve A/c	800		
To Share Capital A/c	400		
To Capital Reserve A/c	2,800		
To Balance c/d	0		
	4,800		4,800

CALCULATION OF ALLOTMENT MONEY DUE BUT NOT RECEIVED

Particulars	₹
Application Money received from defaulter (1140 × ₹ 5)	5,700
Less: Application Money adjusted (600 × ₹ 5)	(3,000)
Excess Application Money	2,700
Allotment Money due (600 × ₹ 5)	3,000
Amount due but not received on Allotment towards Securities Premium	300

ILLUSTRATION 34

Tushar Ltd. forfeited 600 shares of ₹ 10 each issued at a premium of 30% to *W* who had applied for 1500 shares and paid an application money of ₹ 5 (including ₹ 1 premium), for non-payment of first and final call money of ₹ 3 (including ₹ 1 premium). At different intervals of time, out of these 400 shares were re-issued to *Z*, credited as fully paid for ₹ 9 per share and 100 shares were re-issued to *X* as ₹ 10 paid up for ₹ 11 per share. Record the journal entries for forfeiture and reissue of shares and prepare Forfeited Shares Account assuming that the company follows the policy of adjusting excess Application Money towards other sums due on shares.

SOLUTION

JOURNAL OF TUSHAR LTD

Date	*Particulars*		*L.F.*	*Dr. (₹)*	*Cr. (₹)*
	On Forfeiture of 600 Shares				
1.	Share Capital A/c (600 × ₹ 10)	Dr.		6,000	
	Securities Premium A/c (₹ 1800 – ₹ 1500)	Dr.		300	
	To Calls-in-arrears A/c				300
	To Forfeited Shares A/c [₹ 7,500 – ₹ 600 – ₹ 600 – ₹ 300]				6,000
	(Being 600 shares forfeited for non-payment of call money)				
	On Re-issue of 400 Shares				
2.	Bank A/c (400 × ₹ 9)	Dr.		3,600	
	Forfeited Shares A/c (400 × ₹ 1)	Dr.		400	
	To Share Capital A/c (400 × ₹ 10)				4,000
	(Being 400 shares re-issued as fully paid-up for ₹9 per share)				
3.	Forfeited Shares A/c [(₹ 6,000 × 400/600) – ₹ 400]	Dr.		3,600	
	To Capital Reserve A/c				3,600
	(Being the transfer of profit on re-issue)				
	On Re-issue of 100 Shares				
4.	Bank A/c (100 × ₹ 11)	Dr.		1,100	
	To Share Capital A/c (100 × ₹ 10)				1,000
	To Securities Premium A/c (100 × ₹ 1)				100
	(Being 100 shares re-issued as fully paid-up for ₹ 11 per share)				
5.	Forfeited Shares A/c (₹ 6,000 × 100/600)	Dr.		1,000	
	To Capital Reserve A/c				1,000
	(Being the transfer of profit on re-issue)				

Dr. **FORFEITED SHARES ACCOUNT** Cr.

Particulars	₹	Particulars	₹
To Share Capital A/c	400	By Share Capital A/c	6,000
To Capital Reserve A/c	3,600		
To Capital Reserve A/c	1,000		
To Balance c/d	1,000		
	6,000		6,000

CALCULATION OF CALL MONEY DUE BUT NOT RECEIVED

Particulars	₹
Application Money received from defaulter (1,500 × ₹ 5)	7,500
Less: Application & Allotment Money adjusted (600 × ₹ 10)	6,000
Excess Application Money	1,500
Excess Application Money adjusted on Call	(1,500)
Call Money due (600 × ₹ 3)	1,800
Amount due but not received on Call towards Securities Premium	300

21.0 HOW TO DISCLOSE 'SHARE CAPITAL' IN THE COMPANY'S BALANCE SHEET

Share Capital is disclosed in the company's Balance Sheet as follows:

AN EXTRACT OF BALANCE SHEET OF ....LTD AS AT ....

Particulars	Note No	Current Year ₹	Previous Year ₹
Equity & Liabilities			
I. Shareholders' Funds			
Share Capital			

Notes to Accounts:

NOTE 1: SHARE CAPITAL

Particulars	₹	₹
Authorised Capital		
..... Shares of ₹ ... each		xxx
Issued Capital		
..... Shares of ₹ ... each		xxx
Subscribed Capital and fully paid		
..... Shares of ₹ ... each, ₹ ... per share paid up	xxx	
***Subscribed Capital but not fully paid**		
..... Shares of ₹ ... each, ₹ ... per share paid up	xxx	
Add: Forfeited Shares	xxx	xxx

Notes:

1. For the period of 5 years immediately preceding the date as at which the Balance Sheet is prepared
   (a) Aggregate Number and Class of **Shares** allotted as fully paid up pursuant to a contract **without payments being received in cash**
   (b) Aggregate Number and Class of **Shares** allotted as fully paid up by way of **Bonus Shares**
   (c) Aggregate Number and Class of **Shares bought back**
2. Calls Unpaid on Shares by Directors & Officers ₹ xxx
3. Forfeited Shares (amount originally paid up) ₹ xxx
4. Reconciliation of the No of shares outstanding at the beginning and at the end of the reporting period
5. Shares in the company held by each shareholder holding more than 5% shares specifying the number of shares h
6. Shares Reserved for issue under options and contracts/commitments for the sale of shares/disinvestment, including the terms and amounts

***Note:** *Subscribed and Paid up Share Capital will include Unpaid Amount on Shares subscribed by Subscribers to Memorandum of Association and such Unpaid Amount will be disclosed under the head 'Current Assets' and sub-head 'Other Current Assets'.*

ILLUSTRATION 35 [DISCLOSURE OF SHARE CAPITAL]

Tulsian Ltd. was formed with a capital of ₹ 70,00,000 divided into 7,00,000 equity shares of ₹ 10 each. The company allotted 10,000 equity shares of ₹ 10 each as fully paid to the signatories to the Memorandum of Association and 5,000 equity shares of ₹ 10 each as fully paid to the vendors against the purchase of building and offered 5,50,000 equity shares of ₹ 10 each at a premium of 10%. The issue price was payable as under:

On Application ₹ 5, on Allotment ₹ 4 (including premium), on Call Balance

The company did not make the call during the year. The public applied for 5,00,000 equity shares. All money were duly received except the allotment money on 1000 shares which were forfeited.

Prepare an extract of Balance Sheet as per Schedule III to The Companies Act 2013 disclosing the above information. Also prepare 'notes to accounts' for the same.

SOLUTION

AN EXTRACT OF BALANCE SHEET OF TULSIAN LTD AS AT ...

Particulars	*Note No*	*Current Year* ₹	*Previous Year* ₹
Equity & Liabilities			
I. Shareholders' Funds			
Share Capital	1	41,47,000	
Reserves & Surplus (Premium)		4,99,000	

Notes To Accounts:

NOTE 1: SHARE CAPITAL

Particulars	₹
Authorised Capital:	
7,00,000 Equity Shares of ₹ 10 each	70,00,000
Issued Capital:	
5,65,000 Equity Shares of ₹ 10 each	56,50,000
Subscribed Capital and fully paid	
15,000 Equity Shares of ₹ 10 each	1,50,000
(Allotted as fully paid up pursuant to a contract without payments being received in cash.)	
Subscribed Capital but not fully paid	
4,99,000 Equity Shares of ₹ 10 each ₹ 8 paid up	39,92,000
Add: Forfeited Shares (1,000 × ₹ 5)	5,000
	41,47,000

22.0 PRIVATE PLACEMENT OF SHARES

Meaning	(a) According to Section 42 private placement of shares implies issue and allotment of shares to a selected group of persons. In other words, an issue, which is not a public issue but offered to a select group of persons, is called 'Private Placement of Shares'. (b) All SEBI Guidelines concerning preferential issue are applicable to private placement of shares as well. (c) In order to make of shares through the private placement route, a company must pass a special Resolution to this effect. Where no special resolution is passed, the company must pass ordinary resolution and obtain the consent of the Central Government stating that the proposal is most beneficial to the company.
Accounting Treatment	Accounting entries relating to the private placement of securities are similar to those discussed at the time of application and allotment.

23.0 RIGHT SHARES [SEC. 62]

Meaning	As per Sec. 62 in case of further issue of shares, further shares must be offered to the existing shareholders in proportion to their existing shareholdings at that date. Such shares are called 'Rights Shares'.
When Available	Such right is available when it is proposed to increase the subscribed capital of the company by allotment of further shares at any time after the expiry of 2 years from the formation of a company *or* after the expiry of 1 year from the first allotment of shares, whichever is earlier.
Option available	The existing shareholder to whom the offer is made, may: 1. Accept the offer in full *or* in part 2. Reject the offer in full 3. Renounce the right in full *or* in part

Value of Right	The computation of Value of Right consists of the following two steps: **Step 1:** ***Calculate Average Price of a share*** $= \frac{\text{Market Price of the Existing Shares + issue price of proportionate Right Shares}}{\text{No. of Existing shares + No. of Right Shares}}$ **Step 2:** ***Calculate Value of Right*** Value of Right = Market Price of a Share-Average Price of a Share
Accounting Treatment	Accounting treatment of right issue of shares is similar to the treatment discussed under application and allotment.

EXAMPLE

X Ltd. offers new shares of ₹ 100 each at 10% premium to the existing shareholders in the ratio of two shares for every five shares held. The Market Price of share is ₹ 124. Calculate the Value of Right.

SOLUTION

Step 1: Average Price = (₹124 × 5) + (₹110 × 2)/ 5 × 2 = ₹ 120

Step 2: Value of Right = ₹ 124 – ₹ 120 = ₹ 4.00

24.0 PREFERENTIAL ALLOTMENT

Meaning	A preferential allotment is one that is made at a pre-determined price to the pre-identified people who wish to take a strategic stake in the company such as promoters, venture capitalists, financial institutions, buyers of companies' products *or* its suppliers.
Guidelines	Some of the guidelines in this regard are as follows: 1. **Lock-in-Period :** The allottees will not sell their securities in the open market for a minimum period of three years from the date of allotment. This period is known as the lock in period. This period is applicable in case of promoters' contribution. However in case of pre-issue of share capital of an unlisted company, the lock-in-period is one year from the date of commencement of commercial production *or* the date of allotment in the public issue, whichever is earlier.
Guidelines	2. **Special Resolution :** The preferential allotment can take place only if three-fourths of the shareholders agree to the issue on preferential basis. 3. **Minimum Issue Price :** The minimum price of such an issue has to be an average of highs and lows of the 26 weeks preceding the date on which the board resolves to make the preferential allotment. 4. **Open Offer :** If the preferential allotments are made over and above 15 per cent of the equity, an open offer is mandated by the SEBI.

25.0 SWEAT EQUITY SHARES [SEC. 54]

Meaning	Sweat equity shares means equity shares issued by the company to employees *or* directors at a discount *or* for consideration other than cash for providing know-how *or* making available right in the nature of intellectual property rights *or* value additions, by whatever name called. [Sec. 2 (88)]

Five Conditions	According to Section 54, a company may issue Sweat Equity Shares if the following conditions are fulfilled, namely: 1. the shares must belong to a **class of shares already issued;** 2. the issue must be authorised by a **special resolution** passed by the company in the general meeting. 3. the resolution must specify the number of shares, current market price, consideration, if any, and the class *or* classes of directors *or* employees to whom such equity shares are to be issued. 4. **at least 1 year must have completed** since the date on which the company was entitled to commence business; 5. the sweat equity shares of a company whose equity shares are listed on a recognised stock exchange must be issued **as per the regulations made by the SEBI.** Provided that in the case of a company whose equity shares are not listed on any recognised stock exchange, the Sweat Equity Shares are issued as per the guidelines prescribed.

26.0 BUY-BACK OF SHARES

Meaning	The term 'Buy-back of Shares' implies the act of purchasing its own shares by a company.
Three Sources of Funds [Sec. 68]	A company may purchase its own shares *or* other specified securities out of : 1. its Free Reserves; or 2. the Securities Premium Account; or 3. the Proceeds of any Shares *or* other Specified Securities;

ISSUE, FORFEITURE & RE-ISSUE

ILLUSTRATION 36

Bharat Ltd issued a prospectus inviting applications for 20,000 shares of ₹ 10 each at a premium of ₹ 2 per share payable as follows: on Application ₹ 2, on Allotment ₹ 5 (including premium), on First Call ₹ 3, on Second & Final Call ₹ 2.

Applications were received for 30,000 shares and *pro rata* allotment was made on the applications for 24,000 shares. It was decided to utilise excess Application Money towards the amount due on allotment. Ramesh to whom 400 shares were allotted failed to pay the allotment money and Mohan, the holder of 600 shares failed to pay the two calls. These were subsequently forfeited after the second call was made. Of the shares forfeited, 800 shares were sold to Krishan credited as full paid for ₹ 9 per share, the whole of Ramesh's shares being included.

Required: Pass the necessary Journal Entries.

SOLUTION

JOURNAL OF BHARAT LTD.

Date	*Particulars*		*L.F.*	*Dr. (₹)*	*Cr. (₹)*
1.	Bank A/c (30,000 × ₹ 2)	Dr.		60,000	
	To Share Application A/c				60,000
	(Being the Application Money received on 30,000 shares)				

2.	Share Application A/c (30,000 × ₹ 2)	Dr.	60,000	
	To Share Capital A/c (20,000 × ₹ 2)			40,000
	To Bank A/c (6,000 × ₹ 2)			12,000
	To Share Allotment A/c (4,000 × ₹ 2)			8,000
	(Being the Application Money adjusted & Surplus refunded)			
3.	Share Allotment A/c (20,000 × ₹ 5)	Dr.	1,00,000	
	To Share Capital A/c (20,000 × ₹ 3)			60,000
	To Securities Premium A/c (20,000 × ₹ 2)			40,000
	(Being the Allotment Money due)			
4.	Bank A/c (₹ 1,00,000 – ₹ 8,000 – ₹ 1,840)	Dr.	90,160	
	To Share Allotment A/c			90,160
	(Being the remaining Allotment Money received on 19,600 shares) [See Working Note 2 & 3]			
5.	Share First Call A/c (20,000 × ₹ 3)	Dr.	60,000	
	To Share Capital A/c (20,000 × ₹ 3)			60,000
	(Being the First Call Money due)			
6.	Bank A/c (19,000 × ₹ 3)	Dr.	57,000	
	To Share First Call A/c			57,000
	(Being the First Call Money received on 19,000 shares)			
7.	Share Second & Final Call A/c (20,000 × ₹ 2)	Dr.	40,000	
	To Share Capital A/c			40,000
	(Being the Second & Final Call due)			
8.	Bank A/c (19,000 × ₹ 2)	Dr.	38,000	
	To Share Second & Final Call A/c			38,000
	(Being the Second & Final call received on 19,000 shares)			
9.	Share Capital A/c (1,000 × ₹ 10)	Dr.	10,000	
	Securities Premium A/c (400 × ₹ 2)	Dr.	800	
	To Share Allotment A/c (₹ 2,000 – ₹ 160)			1,840
	To Share 1st Call A/c (1,000 × ₹ 3)			3,000
	To Share Second & Final Call A/c (1,000 × ₹ 2)			2,000
	To Forfeited Shares A/c (₹ 960 + ₹ 3,000)			3,960
	(Being 400 shares forfeited for non-payment of allotment money & the calls money and 600 shares for non-payment of two calls money)			
10.	Bank A/c (800 × ₹ 9)	Dr.	7,200	
	Forfeited Shares A/c (800 × ₹ 1)	Dr.	800	
	To Share Capital A/c (800 × ₹ 10)			8,000
	(Being the re-issue of 800 shares @ ₹ 9 as fully paid up)			

11.	Forfeited Shares A/c (₹ 560 + ₹ 1,600) Dr.	2,160	
	To Capital Preserve A/c		2,160
	(Being the transfer of profit on re-issue)		

Working Notes:

1. **Total No. of Shares applied by Ramesh** = (400 × 24,000/20,000) = 480

2. CALCULATION OF THE AMOUNT DUE BUT NOT RECEIVED ON ALLOTMENT FROM RAMESH

	Particulars	₹
A.	Application Money received on shares applied (480 × ₹ 2)	960
B.	*Less:* Application Money due on shares allotted (400 × ₹ 2)	800
C.	Excess Application Money [A – B]	160
D.	Allotment Money due on shares allotted (400 × ₹ 5)	2,000
E.	Allotment Money due but not received (₹ 2,000– ₹ 160)	1,840

3. CALCULATION OF ALLOTMENT MONEY RECEIVED LATER ON

	Particulars	₹
A.	Total Allotment Money Due (20,000 × ₹ 5)	1,00,000
B.	*Less:* Allotment Money Already received on application stage (4,000 × ₹ 2)	(8,000)
C.	*Less:* Allotment Money not received [as per Note (2)]	(1,840)
		90,160

4. CALCULATION OF AMOUNT TO BE FORFEITED

	Particulars	*Ramesh*	*Mohan*
A.	Amount Received	960	4,200
B.	*Less:* Premium Received (600 × 2)		1,200
C.	Amount to be forfeited [A – B]	960	3,000

5. CALCULATION OF PROFIT ON RE-ISSUE TO BE TRANSFERRED TO CAPITAL RESERVE

	Particulars	*Ramesh*	*Mohan*
A.	Amount forfeited on Re-issued Shares	960	2,000 [3000 × 400/600]
B.	*Less:* Re-issue Discount	400	400
C.	Profit on Re-issue to be t/f to Capital Reserve	560	1,600

6. *Since the question is silent as to the utilization of ₹ 160 (received for Ramesh) between Share Capital and Securities Premium, it has been assumed that the entire excess of ₹ 160 is exclusively for Share Capital and hence credited to Forfeited Shares A/c in full.*

ILLUSTRATION 37

Tushar Ltd issued a prospectus inviting applications for 20,000 shares of ₹ 10 each at a premium of ₹ 2 per share payable as follows: on Application ₹ 2, on Allotment ₹ 5 (including premium), on First Call ₹ 3, on Second & Final Call ₹ 2.

Applications were received for 30,000 shares and *pro rata* allotment was made on the applications for 24,000 shares. It was decided to utilise excess Application Money towards the amount due on allotment. Ramesh who applied for 480 shares, failed to pay the allotment money and on his subsequent failure to pay the first call, his shares were forfeited. Mohan, the holder of 600 shares, failed to pay the two calls and on his such failure, his shares were forfeited. Of the shares forfeited, 800 shares were sold to Krishan credited as fully paid for ₹ 9 per share, the whole of Ramesh's shares being included.

Required: Pass the necessary Journal Entries.

SOLUTION

JOURNAL OF TUSHAR LTD.

Date	*Particulars*		*L.F.*	*Dr. (₹)*	*Cr. (₹)*
1.	Bank A/c (30,000 × ₹ 2)	Dr.		60,000	
	To Share Application A/c				60,000
	(Being the Application Money received on 30,000 shares)				
2.	Share Application A/c (30,000 × ₹ 2)	Dr.		60,000	
	To Share Capital A/c (20,000 × ₹ 2)				40,000
	To Bank A/c (6,000 × ₹ 2)				12,000
	To Share Allotment A/c (4,000 × ₹ 2)				8,000
	(Being the Application Money adjusted & Surplus refunded)				
3.	Share Allotment A/c (20,000 × ₹ 5)	Dr.		1,00,000	
	To Share Capital A/c (20,000 × ₹ 3)				60,000
	To Securities Premium A/c (20,000 × ₹ 2)				40,000
	(Being the allotment money due)				
4.	Bank A/c (₹ 1,00,000 – ₹ 8,000 – ₹ 1,840)	Dr.		90,160	
	To Share Allotment A/c				90,160
	(Being the remaining allotment money received on 19,600 shares)[See Working Notes 1, 2, 3]				
5.	Share First Call A/c (20,000 × ₹ 3)	Dr.		60,000	
	To Share Capital A/c (20,000 × ₹ 3)				60,000
	(Being the First Call Money due)				
6.	Bank A/c (19,000 × ₹ 3)	Dr.		57,000	
	To Share First Call A/c				57,000
	(Being the First Call Money received on 19,000 shares @ ₹ 3 Per share				
7.	Share Capital A/c (400 × ₹ 8)	Dr.		3,200	
	Securities Premium A/c (400 × ₹ 2)	Dr.		800	
	To Share Allotment A/c (₹ 2,000 – ₹ 160)				1,840
	To Share First Call A/c (400 × ₹ 3)				1,200
	To Forfeited Shares A/c (480 × ₹ 2)				960

	(Being 600 shares forfeited for non-payment of allotment money and the First Call Money)			
8.	Share Second & Final Call A/c (19,600 × ₹ 2) Dr.		39,200	
	To Share Capital A/c			39,200
	(Being the second and final call due on 19,600 shares)			
9.	Bank A/c (19,000 × ₹ 2) Dr.		38,000	
	To Share Second and Final Call A/c			38,000
	(Being the second and final call received on 19,000 shares)			
10.	Share Capital A/c (600 × ₹ 10) Dr.		6,000	
	To Share First Call A/c (600 × ₹ 3)			1,800
	To Share Second and Final Call A/c (600 × ₹ 2)			1,200
	To Forfeited Shares A/c (600 × ₹ 5)			3,000
	(Being 600 shares forfeited for non-payment of the first call and final call)			
11.	Bank A/c (800 × ₹ 9) Dr.		7,200	
	Forfeited Shares A/c (800 × ₹ 1) Dr.		800	
	To Share Capital A/c (800 × ₹ 10)			8,000
	(Being the re-issue of 800 shares @ ₹ 9 as fully paid up)			
12.	Forfeited Shares A/c (₹ 560 + ₹ 1,600) Dr.		2,160	
	To Capital Reserve A/c			2,160
	(Being the transfer of profit on re-issue)			

Working Notes:

1. No. of Shares allotted to Ramesh = 480 × (20,000/24,000) = 400
2. To 5 same as in Previous Problem.

ILLUSTRATION 38

Bharat Tushar Ltd issued a prospectus inviting applications for 20,000 shares of ₹ 10 each at a premium of ₹ 2 per share payable as follows: on Application ₹ 2, on Allotment ₹ 5 (including premium), on first call ₹ 3, on second & final call ₹ 2.

Applications were received for 30,000 shares and *pro rata* allotment was made on the applications for 24,000 shares. It was decided to utilise excess Application Money towards the amount due on allotment. Ramesh to whom 400 shares were allotted failed to pay the allotment money and on his subsequent failure to pay the first call, his shares were forfeited.

Mohan who applied for 720 shares, failed to pay the two calls and on his such failure, his shares were forfeited. Of the shares forfeited, 800 shares were sold to Krishan credited as fully paid for ₹ 11 per share, the whole of Mohan's shares being included.

Required: Pass the necessary Journal Entries.

SOLUTION

JOURNAL OF BHARAT TUSHAR LTD.

Date	*Particulars*	*L.F.*	*Dr. (₹)*	*Cr. (₹)*
1-10	**First 10 Entries upto Second Forfeiture are Same as in Previous Problem**			
11.	Bank A/c (800 × ₹ 11) Dr.		8,800	
	To Share Capital A/c (800 × ₹ 10)			8,000

	To Securities Premium A/c (800 × ₹ 1)			800
	(Being the issue of 800 shares of ₹ 11 as fully paid-up)			
12.	Forfeited Shares A/c (₹ 480 + ₹ 3,000) Dr.		3,480	
	To Capital Reserve A/c			3,480
	(Being the transfer of profit on re-issue)			

Working Notes:

1. to (4) same as in Illustration 36

5. CALCULATION OF PROFIT ON RE-ISSUE TO BE T/F TO CAPITAL RESERVE

Particulars	*Ramesh*	*Mohan*
A. Amount Forfeited on Re-issued shares	480	3,000 [₹ 960 × 200/400]
B. *Less:* Re-issue Discount	—	—
C. Profit on Re-issue to be t/f to Capital Reserve [A – B]	480	3,000

ILLUSTRATION 39

SRCC Ltd. offered 40,000 shares of ₹ 10 each at 20% premium payable as follows:

On application ₹ 6 (including ₹ 1 premium) and balance on allotment. Public has applied for 65,000 shares. Shares were allotted on *pro rata* to the applicants of 50,000 shares. Money overpaid on applications was employed on account of sum due on allotment. All the shareholders have paid the amount up to allotment except Mohan, the allottee of 8,000 shares. His shares were forfeited. 40% of the forfeited shares were reissued at ₹ 11 per share as fully paid up. Pass the necessary journal entries.

SOLUTION

JOURNAL OF SRCC LTD.

Date	*Particulars*	*L.F.*	*Dr. (₹)*	*Cr. (₹)*
1.	Bank A/c (65,000 × ₹ 6) Dr.		3,90,000	
	To Share Application A/c			3,90,000
	(Being the application money received on 65,000 shares)			
2.	Share Application A/c (65,000 × ₹ 6) Dr.		3,90,000	
	To Share Capital A/c (40,000 × ₹ 5)			2,00,000
	To Securities Premium A/c (40,000 × ₹ 1)			40,000
	To Bank A/c (15,000 × ₹ 6)			90,000
	To Share Allotment A/c (10,000 × ₹ 6)			60,000
	(Being the application money adjusted & surplus refunded)			
3.	Share Allotment A/c (40,000 × ₹ 6) Dr.		2,40,000	
	To Share Capital A/c (40,000 × ₹ 5)			2,00,000
	To Securities Premium A/c (40,000 × ₹ 1)			40,000
	(Being the allotment money due)			
4.	Bank A/c Dr.		1,44,000	
	To Share Allotment A/c			1,44,000
	(Being the remaining allotment money received on 32,000 shares) [See working note (ii) & (iii)]			

5.	Share Capital A/c (8,000 × ₹ 10)	Dr.	80,000	
	Securities Premium A/c (8,000 × ₹ 1)	Dr.	8,000	
	To Share Allotment A/c [(8,000 × ₹ 6) – ₹ 12,000]			36,000
	To Forfeited Shares A/c (₹ 60,000 – ₹8,000)			52,000
	(Being 8,000 shares forfeited for non-payment of full allotment money)			
6.	Bank A/c (3,200 × ₹ 11)	Dr.	35,200	
	To Share Capital A/c (3,200 × ₹ 10)			32,000
	To Securities Premium A/c (3,200 × ₹ 1)			3,200
	(Being the re-issue of 3,200 shares @ for 11 as fully paid up)			
7.	Forfeited Shares A/c (₹ 52,000 x 3,200/8000)	Dr.	20,800	
	To Capital Reserve A/c			20,800
	(Being the transfer of profit on re-issue)			

Working Notes:

1. **Total No. of Shares applied by Mohan** = 8,000 × 50,000/40,000 = 10,000

2. AMOUNT DUE BUT NOT RECEIVED ON ALLOTMENT FROM MOHAN

Particulars	₹
A. Application money received on shares applied (₹ 10,000 × ₹ 6)	60,000
B. *Less:* Application Money due on shares allotted (8,000 × ₹ 6)	(48,000)
C. Excess Application Money [A – B]	12,000
D. Allotment Money due on shares allotted (8,000 × ₹ 6)	48,000
E. Allotment Money due but not received (₹ 48,000 – ₹ 12,000)	36,000

3. CALCULATION OF ALLOTMENT MONEY RECEIVED LATER ON

Particulars	₹
A. Total allotment money due (40,000 × ₹ 6)	2,40,000
B. *Less:* Allotment Money Already received on application stage (10,000 × ₹ 6)	(60,000)
C. *Less:* Allotment Money not received [as per note (ii)]	(36,000)
	1,44,000

4. CALCULATION OF AMOUNT TO BE FORFEITED

Particulars	₹
A. Amount Received	60,000
B. *Less:* Premium Received (8,000 × ₹ 1)	(8,000)
C. Amount to be forfeited [A – B]	52,000

ILLUSTRATION 40

Sangita Ltd. Invited applications for issuing into 60,000 shares of ₹ 10 each payable as ₹ 2 per share on application, ₹ 3 per share on allotment and the balance on First and Final Call. Applications for 92,000 shares were received on which the directors allotted as follows:

Applications for 40,000 shares - Full,

Applications for 50,000 shares - 40 per cent,

Applications for 2,000 shares - Nil

₹ 1,08,000 was realised on account of allotment money (excluding the amount carried from Application Money) and ₹ 2,50,000 on account of call. The directors decided to forfeit shares of those applicants to whom full allotment was made and on which allotment money was overdue.

Required: Pass Journal entries in the company's books.

SOLUTION

JOURNAL

Date	Particulars		L.F.	Dr. (₹)	Cr. (₹)
1.	Bank A/c	Dr.		1,84,000	
	To Share Application A/c				1,84,000
	(Being the Application Money received)				
2.	Share Application A/c	Dr.		1,84,000	
	To Share Capital A/c [60,000 × ₹ 2]				1,20,000
	To Bank A/c [2,000 × ₹ 2]				4,000
	To Share Allotment A/c [30,000 × ₹ 2]				60,000
	(Being the Application Money adjusted and surplus refunded)				
3.	Share Allotment A/c [60,000 × ₹ 3]	Dr.		1,80,000	
	To Share Capital A/c				1,80,000
	(Being the Allotment Money due)				
4.	Bank A/c	Dr.		1,08,000	
	To Share Allotment A/c				1,08,000
	(Being the Allotment Money received)				
5.	Share First & Final Call A/c [60,000 × ₹ 5]	Dr.		3,00,000	
	To Share Capital A/c				3,00,000
	(Being the First Call Money due)				
6.	Bank A/c	Dr.		2,50,000	
	To Share First & Final Call A/c				2,50,000
	(Being the First Call Money received)				
7.	Share Capital A/c [4,000 × ₹ 10]	Dr.		40,000	
	To Share Allotment A/c [4,000 × ₹ 3]				12,000
	To Share First & Final Call A/c [4,000 × ₹ 5]				20,000
	To Forfeited Shares A/c [4,000 × ₹ 2]				8,000
	(Being 300 shares forfeited for non-payment of Allotment Money and the call money)				

Notes:

$$\text{No. of Shares Forfeited} = \frac{\text{Allotment Money Not Received}}{\text{Allotment Money per Share}} = \frac{(₹\,180{,}000\ ₹\,60{,}000)\ ₹\,108{,}000}{₹\,3}$$

= 4000 Shares

ILLUSTRATION 41

TULSIAN Ltd. invited applications for issuing 1,00,000 Equity shares of ₹ 10 each issued at a premium of ₹ 3 per share payable as follows:

On Application	₹ 5 per share(including premium ₹ 1)
On Allotment	₹ 5 per share(including premium ₹ 1)
On Call	Balance

Applications were received for 2,20,000 shares. Applications for 20,000 shares were rejected and their application money was refunded. Shares were allotted to the remaining applicants as follows:

A. Allotted in full to *Katrina* who had applied for 10,000 shares.

B. Applications for 40,000 shares were allotted 30,000 shares on *pro rata* basis.

C. Allotted balance of the shares on *pro rata* basis to the other applicants

Excess application money was utilised in payment of allotment and call. The Call was duly made.

X, who was allotted 600 shares in Category B did not pay any money other than Application Money and *Y*, who applied for 1500 shares in Category C failed to pay the call money. *Z*, who applied for 400 shares in Category B paid the calls money due along with allotment. All other allottees paid their dues as per schedule. The directors decided to forfeit the shares on which money was overdue. Of the shares forfeited, 900 shares were re-issued to *W*,credited as fully paid for ₹ 9 per share, the whole of *Y*'s shares being included.

Required:

(a) Prepare the Statement showing the adjustment of Application Money received

(b) Calculate the Total No. of Shares applied by X

(c) Calculate the Total No. of Shares allotted to Z

(d) Calculate the Allotment money due but not received from X

(e) Calculate the Total Money received at the allotment stage

(f) Calculate the Total No. of Shares allotted to Y

(g) Calculate the Call money due but not received from Y

(h) Calculate the Total Money received at the Call stage

(i) Calculate the Amount to be forfeited

(j) Calculate the Profit on Re-issue to be t/f to Capital Reserve.

(k) Pass the necessary journal entries in the books of Tulsian Ltd. assuming that Calls-in-arrears Account is maintained.

SOLUTION

(A) STATEMENT SHOWING THE ADJUSTMENT OF APPLICATION MONEY RECEIVED

Category	*Shares Applied*	*Shares Allotted*	*Application Money Received*	*Adjustment of Application Money Received*			
				Share Capital	*Share Allotment*	*Calls-in Advance*	*Refund*
—	20,000	0	1,00,000	0	0	0	1,00,000
A	10,000	10,000	50,000	50,000	—	—	—
B	40,000	30,000	2,00,000	1,50,000	50,000	—	—
C	1,50,000	60,000	7,50,000	3,00,000	3,00,000	1,50,000	—
Total	2,20,000	1,00,000	11,00,000	5,00,000	3,50,000	1,50,000	1,00,000

(B) Total No. of Shares applied by X = (40,000 × 600 / 30,000) = 800 Shares

(C) Total No. of Shares allotted to Z = (30,000 × 400 / 40,000) = 300 Shares

(D) CALCULATION OF ALLOTMENT MONEY DUE BUT NOT RECEIVED

Particulars	₹
Application Money received from defaulter (800 × ₹ 5)	4,000
Less: Application Money adjusted (600 × ₹ 5)	(3,000)
Excess Application Money	1,000
Allotment Money due (600 × ₹ 5)	3,000
Amount due but not received on allotment	**2,000**

(E) CALCULATION OF TOTAL MONEY RECEIVED AT THE ALLOTMENT STAGE

Particulars	₹
Total Allotment Money due (1,00,000 × ₹ 5)	5,00,000
Less: Surplus Application Money adjusted as per WN A	(3,50,000)
Less: Not received from Defaulter as per WN D	(2,000)
	1,48,000
Add: Calls-in-advance [300 × ₹ 3]	900
	1,48,900

(F) Total No. of Shares allotted to Y = (60,000 × 1500 / 1,50,000) = 600 Shares

(G) CALCULATION OF CALL MONEY DUE BUT NOT RECEIVED

Particulars	₹
Application Money received from defaulter (1,500 × ₹ 5)	7,500
Less: Application Money adjusted (600 × ₹ 5)	3,000
Excess Application Money	4,500
Less: Excess Application Money adjusted on allotment (600 × ₹ 5)	(3,000)
Excess Application Money adjusted on Call	(1,500)
Call Money due (600 × ₹ 3)	1,800
Amount due but not received on Call	**300**

(H) CALCULATION OF CALL MONEY RECEIVED LATER ON

Particulars	₹
Total Call Money due (1,00,000 × ₹ 3)	3,00,000
Less: Surplus Application Money adjusted as per A	(1,50,000)
Less: Not received from Y as per G	(300)
Less: Calls-in-advance [300 × ₹ 3]	(900)
Less: Not received from X	**1,800**
	1,47,000

(I) CALCULATION OF AMOUNT TO BE FORFEITED

Particulars		X	Y
A.	Amount Received	4,000	7,500
B.	*Less:* Premium Received	600	1,500
C.	Amount to be forfeited [A – B]	3,400	6,000

(J) CALCULATION OF PROFIT ON RE-ISSUE TO BE TRANSFERRED TO CAPITAL RESERVE

Particulars		X	Y
A.	Amount forfeited on Re-issued Shares	1,700 [3400 × 300/600]	6,000
B.	*Less:* Re-issue Discount	300	600
C.	Profit on Re-issue to be t/f to Capital Reserve	1,400	5,400

(K) JOURNAL

Date	Particulars		L.F.	Dr. (₹)	Cr. (₹)
1.	Bank A/c	Dr.		11,00,000	
	To Share Application A/c				11,00,000
	(Being the application money received)				
2.	Share Application A/c	Dr.		11,00,000	
	To Share Capital A/c (1,00,000 × ₹ 4)				4,00,000
	To Securities Premium A/c (1,00,000 × ₹ 1)				1,00,000
	To Share Allotment A/c				3,50,000
	To Bank a/c (20,000 × ₹ 5)				1,00,000
	To Calls-in Advance A/c				1,50,000
	(Being the Application Money adjusted & Surplus refunded)				
3.	Share Allotment A/c(1,00,000 × ₹ 5)	Dr.		5,00,000	
	To Share Capital A/c (1,00,000 × ₹ 4)				4,00,000
	To Securities Premium A/c(1,00,000 × ₹ 1)				1,00,000
	(Being the Allotment Money due)				
4.	Bank A/c [as per WN 4]	Dr.		1,48,900	
	Calls-in-arrears A/c [as per WN 3]	Dr.		2,000	

	To Share Allotment A/c			1,50,000
	To Calls-in Advance A/c [300 × ₹ 3]			900
	(Being the Allotment Money received except on 600 shares and Calls in advance received on 300 shares)			
5.	Share First & Final Call A/c (1,00,000 × ₹ 3)	Dr.	3,00,000	
	To Share Capital A/c(1,00,000 × ₹ 2)			2,00,000
	To Securities Premium A/c(1,00,000 × ₹ 1)			1,00,000
	(Being the First & Final Call Money due)			
6.	Bank A/c	Dr.	1,47,000	
	Calls-in-advance A/c	Dr.	1,50,900	
	Calls-in-arrears A/c [₹1,800 + ₹ 300]	Dr.	2,100	
	To Share First & Final Call A/c			3,00,000
	(Being the First and Final Call Money received except on 1200 shares and Calls in advance adjusted)			
7	Share Capital A/c (600 × ₹ 10)	Dr.	6,000	
	Securities Premium A/c (600 × ₹ 2)	Dr.	1,200	
	To Calls-in-arrears A/c [₹ 2,000 + (600 × ₹ 3)]			3,800
	To Forfeited Shares A/c [₹ 4,000 – ₹ 600]			3,400
	(Being 600 shares of X forfeited for non-payment of allotment & call money)			
8	Share Capital A/c (600 × ₹ 10)	Dr.	6,000	
	Securities Premium A/c (₹ 1,800 – ₹1,500)	Dr.	300	
	To Calls-in-arrears A/c			300
	To Forfeited Shares A/c [₹ 7,500 – ₹ 600 – ₹ 600 – ₹ 300]			6,000
	(Being 600 shares of Y forfeited for non-payment of call money)			
9	Bank A/c (900 × ₹ 9)	Dr.	8,100	
	Forfeited Shares A/c (900 × ₹ 1)	Dr.	900	
	To Share Capital A/c			9,000
	(Being 900 forfeited shares reissued @ ₹ 9 per share as fully paid-up)			
10	Forfeited Shares A/c [(₹6,000 +₹ 1,700) – ₹ 900]	Dr.	6,800	
	To Capital Reserve A/c			6,800
	(Being the Profit on re-issue t/f to Capital Reserve)			

ILLUSTRATION 42

TULSIAN Ltd. invited applications for issuing 1,00,000 Equity shares of ₹ 10 each issued at a premium of ₹ 3 per share payable as follows:

On Application	₹ 5 per share(including premium ₹ 1)
On Allotment	₹ 5 per share(including premium ₹ 1)
On Call	Balance

Total Application money received ₹ 11,00,000. Applications for 20,000 shares were rejected and their application money was refunded. Shares were allotted to the remaining applicants as follows:

A. Allotted in full to *Katrina* who had applied for 10,000 shares.

B. Applications for 40,000 shares were allotted 30,000 shares on *pro rata* basis.

C. Allotted balance of the shares on *pro rata* basis to the other applicants

Excess application money was utilised in payment of allotment and call. The Call was duly made.

X, who was allotted 600 shares in Category B did not pay any money other than Application Money and his shares were forfeited immediately after allotment. *Y*, who applied for 1500 shares in Category C failed to pay the call money and on his such failure, his shares were forfeited..*Z*, who applied for 400 shares in Category B paid the call money due along with allotment. All other allottees paid their dues as per schedule. Of the shares forfeited, 900 shares were re-issued to *W*,credited as fully paid for ₹ 9 per share, the whole of *Y*'s shares being included.

Required:

(a) Prepare the Statement showing the adjustment of Application Money received

(b) Calculate the Total No. of Shares applied by X

(c) Calculate the Total No. of Shares allotted to Z

(d) Calculate the Allotment money due but not received from X

(e) Calculate the Total Money received at the allotment stage

(f) Calculate the Total No. of Shares allotted to Y

(g) Calculate the Call money due but not received from Y

(h) Calculate the Total Money received at the Call stage

(i) Calculate the Amount to be forfeited

(j) Calculate the Profit on Re-issue to be t/f to Capital Reserve.

(k) Pass the necessary journal entries in the books of Tulsian Ltd. assuming that Calls-in-arrears Account is maintained.

SOLUTION

Total No. of Shares applied = ₹ 11,00,000/ ₹ 5 = 2,20,000

(A) STATEMENT SHOWING THE ADJUSTMENT OF APPLICATION MONEY RECEIVED

Category	*Shares Applied*	*Shares Allotted*	*Application Money Received*	*Adjustment of Application Money Received*			
				Share Capital	*Share Allotment*	*Calls-in Advance*	*Refund*
—	20,000	0	1,00,000	0	0	0	1,00,000
A	10,000	10,000	50,000	50,000	—	—	—
B	40,000	30,000	2,00,000	1,50,000	50,000	—	—
C	1,50,000	60,000	7,50,000	3,00,000	3,00,000	1,50,000	—
Total	2,20,000	1,00,000	11,00,000	5,00,000	3,50,000	1,50,000	1,00,000

(B) Total No. of Shares applied by X = (40,000 × 600 / 30,000) = 800 Shares

(C) Total No. of Shares allotted to Z = (30,000 × 400 / 40,000) = 300 Shares

(D) CALCULATION OF ALLOTMENT MONEY DUE BUT NOT RECEIVED

Particulars	₹
Application Money received from defaulter (800 × ₹ 5)	4,000
Less: Application Money adjusted (600 × ₹ 5)	(3,000)
Excess Application Money	1,000
Allotment Money due (600 × ₹ 5)	3,000
Amount due but not received on allotment	**2,000**

(E) CALCULATION OF TOTAL MONEY RECEIVED AT THE ALLOTMENT STAGE

Particulars	₹
Total Allotment Money due (1,00,000 × ₹ 5)	5,00,000
Less: Surplus Application Money adjusted as per WN A	(3,50,000)
Less: Not received from Defaulter as per WN D	(2,000)
	1,48,000
Add: Calls-in-advance [300 × ₹ 3]	900
	1,48,900

(F) Total No. of Shares allotted to Y = (60,000 × 1500 / 1,50,000) = 600 Shares

(G) CALCULATION OF CALL MONEY DUE BUT NOT RECEIVED

Particulars	₹
Application Money received from defaulter (1,500 × ₹ 5)	7,500
Less: Application Money adjusted (600 × ₹ 5)	3,000
Excess Application Money	4,500
Less: Excess Application Money adjusted on allotment (600 × ₹ 5)	(3,000)
Excess Application Money adjusted on Call	(1,500)
Call Money due (600 × ₹ 3)	1,800
Amount due but not received on Call	**300**

(H) CALCULATION OF CALL MONEY RECEIVED LATER ON

Particulars	₹
Total Call Money due [99,400 × ₹ 3]	2,98,200
Less: Surplus Application Money adjusted as per A	(1,50,000)
Less: Not received from Defaulter as per G	(300)
Less: Calls-in-advance [300 × ₹ 3]	(900)
	1,47,000

(J) CALCULATION OF PROFIT ON RE-ISSUE TO BE TRANSFERRED TO CAPITAL RESERVE

	Particulars	*X*	*Y*
A.	Amount forfeited on Re-issued Shares	1,700 [3400 × 300/600]	6,000
B.	*Less:* Re-issue Discount	300	600
C.	Profit on Re-issue to be t/f to Capital Reserve	1,400	5,400

(K) JOURNAL

Date	Particulars		L.F.	Dr. (₹)	Cr. (₹)
1.	Bank A/c	Dr.		11,00,000	
	To Share Application A/c				11,00,000
	(Being the application money received)				
2.	Share Application A/c	Dr.		11,00,000	
	To Share Capital A/c (1,00,000 × ₹ 4)				4,00,000
	To Securities Premium A/c (1,00,000 × ₹ 1)				1,00,000
	To Share Allotment A/c				3,50,000
	To Bank a/c (20,000 × ₹ 5)				1,00,000
	To Calls-in Advance A/c				1,50,000
	(Being the Application Money adjusted & Surplus refunded)				
3.	Share Allotment A/c(1,00,000 × ₹ 5)	Dr.		5,00,000	
	To Share Capital A/c (1,00,000 × ₹ 4)				4,00,000
	To Securities Premium A/c(1,00,000 × ₹ 1)				1,00,000
	(Being the Allotment Money due)				
4.	Bank A/c [as per WN 4]	Dr.		1,48,900	
	Calls-in-arrears A/c [as per WN 3]	Dr.		2,000	
	To Share Allotment A/c				1,50,000
	To Calls-in Advance A/c [300 × ₹ 3]				900
	(Being the Allotment Money received except on 600 shares and Calls in advance received on 300 shares)				
5	Share Capital A/c (600 × ₹ 8)	Dr.		4,800	
	Securities Premium A/c (600 × ₹ 1)	Dr.		600	
	To Calls-in-arrears A/c				2000
	To Forfeited Shares A/c [₹ 4,000 – ₹ 600]				3,400
	(Being 600 shares of X forfeited for non-payment of allotment money)				
6.	Share First & Final Call A/c [99,400 × ₹ 3]	Dr.		2,98,200	
	To Share Capital A/c [99,400 × ₹ 2]				1,98,800
	To Securities Premium A/c [99,400 × ₹ 1]				99,400
	(Being the First & Final Call Money due)				
7.	Bank A/c	Dr.		1,47,000	
	Calls-in-advance A/c	Dr.		1,50,900	
	Calls-in-arrears A/c	Dr.		300	
	To Share First & Final Call A/c				2,98,200
	(Being the First and Final Call Money received except on 600 shares and Calls in advance adjusted)				
8	Share Capital A/c (600 × ₹ 10)	Dr.		6,000	
	Securities Premium A/c (₹ 1,800 – ₹1,500)	Dr.		300	
	To Calls-in-arrears A/c				300

	To Forfeited Shares A/c [₹ 7,500 – ₹ 600 – ₹ 600 – ₹ 300] (Being 600 shares of Y forfeited for non-payment of call money)			6,000
9	Bank A/c (900 × ₹ 9) Forfeited Shares A/c (900 × ₹ 1) To Share Capital A/c (Being 900 forfeited shares reissued @ ₹ 9 per share as fully paid-up)	Dr. Dr.	8,100 900	9,000
10	Forfeited Shares A/c [(₹6,000 +₹ 1,700) – ₹ 900] To Capital Reserve A/c (Being the Profit on re-issue t/f to Capital Reserve)	Dr.	6,800	6,800

VERY SHORT ANSWER TYPE QUESTIONS

1. Briefly explain the following:
   (a) Company
   (b) Share
   (c) Minimum Subscription
   (d) An Initial Public Offer (IPO)
   (e) Issue of shares for consideration other than cash
   (f) Pro-rata Allotment
   (g) Private Placement of shares
   (h) Preferential Allotment
   (i) Right Shares
   (j) Sweat Shares
2. Enumerate the following:
   (a) Purposes for which Securities Premium can be used According to Sec. 52 of the Companies Act 2013
   (b) Two Conditions for the issue of Sweat Shares
3. State one basic difference between the following:
   (a) Private Company and a Public Company.
   (b) An Equity Share and Preference Share
   (c) A Cumulative Preference Share and A Non-cumulative Preference Share
   (d) A Participating Preference Share and A Non-participating Preference Share
   (e) A Convertible Preference Share and A Non-convertible Preference Share
   (f) An Authorised Capital and An Issued Capital
   (g) An Issued Capital and Subscribed Capital
   (h) An Unissued Capital and An Uncalled Capital
   (i) Reserve Capital and Capital Reserve
   (j) Forfeiture of Shares and Surrender of Shares.
   (k) Under-subscription of Shares and Over-subscription of Shares
   (l) Calls-in-advance and Calls-in-arrears
   (m) Issue of shares and Reissue of shares

4. Name the head and sub-head under which the following appear in the Balance Sheet:
   (a) Share Capital
   (b) Shares issued for consideration other than cash
   (c) Calls-in-Advance
   (d) Call-in-arrears
   (c) Forfeited Shares Account
5. State the Capital which is stated in the Memorandum of Association.
6. Name that part of capital which is called up only on winding up.
7. Which shares can be issued at discount?
8. What is the maximum rate of interest which the Board of directors of a company can normally pay on Calls-in-advance if the Articles are silent on the matter of such interest?
9. What is the maximum rate of interest which the Board of directors of a company can charge on 'Calls-in-arrears' if the Articles are silent on the matter of such interest?
10. Why 'Securities Premium Account' is not debited at the time of forfeiture of shares which were originally issued at a premium and premium has already been received.
11. At the time of issue of shares if all cash transactions are entered in the Cash Book, where will the non-cash transactions be recorded?
12. X Ltd. with paid up share capital of ₹ 60,00,000 has a balance of ₹ 15,00,000 in Securities Premium Account. The company management does not want to carry over this balance You are required to suggest the method for utilising this premium money that would achieve the objective of the management and maximize the return to shareholders.

SHORT ANSWER TYPE PRACTICAL QUESTIONS

1. Record the journal entries for forfeiture and reissue of shares in the following cases:
   (a) X Ltd. forfeited 20 shares of ₹ 10 each, ₹ 7 called up on which the shareholder had paid application and allotment money of ₹ 5 per share. Out of these, 15 shares were re-issued to Naresh as ₹ 7 per share paid up for ₹ 8 per share.
   (b) Y Ltd. forfeited 90 shares of ₹ 10 each, ₹ 8 called up issued at a premium of ₹ 2 per share to 'R' for non-payment of allotment money of ₹ 5 per share (including premium). Out of these, 80 shares were re-issued to Sanjay as ₹ 8 called up for ₹ 10 per share.

   [**Ans.** (a) CR ₹ 75, (b) CR ₹ 400]

2. Give Necessary journal entries for the forfeiture and re-issue of shares:
   (a) X Ltd. forfeited 300 shares of ₹ 10 each fully called up, held by Ramesh for non-payment of allotment money of ₹ 3 per share and final call of ₹ 4 per share. He paid the application money of ₹ 3 per share. These shares were re-issued to Suresh for ₹ 8 per shares.
   (b) X Ltd. forfeited 200 shares of ₹ 10 each (₹ 7 called up) on which Naresh had paid application and allotment money of ₹ 5 per share. Out of these, 150 shares were re-issued to Mahesh as fully paid up for ₹ 6 per share.
   (c) X Ltd. forfeited 100 shares of ₹ 10 each (₹ 6 called up) issued at a discount of 10% to Dimple on which she paid ₹ 2 per share. Out of these, 80 shares were re-issued to Simple at ₹ 8 per share and called up for ₹ 6 per share.

   [**Ans.** (a) CR ₹ 300, (b) CR ₹ 150, (c) CR ₹ 80]

LONG ANSWER TYPE PRACTICAL QUESTIONS

1. Windfall & Storm Ltd. issued applications for 1,00,000 equity shares of ₹ 10 each, at a premium of ₹ 4 per share. The amount was payable as follows:

   On application ₹ 6 (including ₹ 2 premium), on Allotment ₹ 6 (including ₹ 2 premium), Balance on first and final call.

   Applications for 1,50,000 shares were received. Allotment was made to all the applicants on pro-rata basis. Subodh to whom 200 shares were allotted, failed to pay allotment and call money. Vikram to whom 100 shares were allotted, failed to pay the call money. These shares were forfeited and afterwards re-issued @ ₹ 8 per share fully paid-up. Pass the necessary journal entries.

   [**Ans.** Forfeited Shares A/c credited ₹ 2,200, CR ₹ 1,600]

2. Sun & Moon Ltd. invited applications for issuing 2,00,000 equity shares of ₹ 10 each. The amount was payable as follows:

On Application	₹ 3 per share
On Allotment	₹ 5 per share
On First and Final call	₹ 2 per share

   Application for 3,00,000 shares were received and pro-rata allotment was made to all the applicants on the following basis:

   Applications for 2,00,000 shares were allotted 1,50,000 shares on *pro rata* basis.

   Applications for 1,00,000 shares were allotted 50,000 shares on *pro rata* basis.

   Bajaj, who was allotted 3,000 shares out of the group applying for 2,00,000 shares, failed to pay the allotment money. His shares were forfeited immediately after allotment.

   Sharma who had applied for 2,000 shares out of the group applying for 1,00,000 shares failed to pay the first and final call. His shares were also forfeited.

   Out of the forfeited shares 3,500 shares were re-issued as fully paid up @ ₹ 8 per share. The re-issued shares included all the forfeited shares of Bajaj.

   Required: Pass the necessary journal entries to record the above transactions.

   [**Ans.** Forfeited Shares A/c credited ₹ 18,000, CR ₹ 9,000]

3. Star & Sky Ltd. invited applications for 1,00,000 Equity Shares of ₹ 10 each. The shares were issued at a premium of ₹ 5 per share. The amount was payable as follows:

   On application and Allotment ₹ 8 per share (including premium ₹ 3). Balance on the first and final call.

   Applications for 1,50,000 shares were received. Applications for 10,000 shares were rejected and pro-rata allotment was made to the remaining applicants on the following basis:

   (i) Applications for 80,000 shares were allotted 60,000 shares; and

   (ii) Applications for 60,000 shares were allotted 40,000 shares.

   X, who belonged to the first category and was allotted 300 shares, failed to pay the call money. Y who belonged to the second category and was allotted 200 shares also failed to pay the call money, their shares were forfeited. The forfeited shares were re-issued @ ₹ 12 per share fully paid up.

   Required: Prepare Cash Book and pass necessary Journal entries.

   [**Ans.** Forfeited Shares A/c credited ₹ 4,100, CR ₹ 4,100]

4. Shakti Ltd. invited application for issuing 1,00,000 Equity shares of ₹ 10 each. The amount was payable as follows:

(i) On Application	₹ 3 per share
(ii) On Allotment	₹ 2 per share
(iii) On First and Final Call	Balance

Applications were received for 2,20,000 shares. Applications for 20,000 shares were rejected and their application money was refunded. Shares were allotted to the remaining applicants as follows:

I. Allotted 50% shares to Raman who had applied for 40,000 shares.

II. Allotted in full to Akbar who had applied for 20,000 shares.

III. Allotted balance of the shares on *pro rata* basis to the other applicants.

Excess application money was utilised in payment of allotment and final call. All calls were made and were duly received except the first and final call on 600 shares allotted to an applicant in III category. His shares were forfeited. The forfeited shares were reissued for ₹ 9 per share fully paid up. Pass the necessary Journal entries in the books of Shakti Ltd.

[**Ans.** Forfeited Shares A/c credited ₹ 4,200, CR ₹ 3,600]

5. Piyush Limited is a company with an authorized share capital of ₹2,00,00,000 in equity shares of ₹ 10 each, of which 15,00,000 shares had been issued and fully paid on 30th June. The company proposed to make a further issue of 1,30,000 shares of ₹ 10 each at a price of ₹12 each, the arrangements for payment being:

(i) ₹ 2 per share payable on application, to be received by 1st July.

(ii) Allotment to be made on 10th July and a further ₹ 5 per share (including the premium) to be payable.

(iii) The final call for the balance to be made, and the money received by 30th April.

Applications were received for 4,20,000 shares and were dealt with as follows:

I. Applicants for 20,000 shares received allotment in full;

II. Applicants for 1,00,000 shares received an allotment of one share for every two applied for; no money was returned to these applicants, the surplus on application being used to reduce the amount due on allotment.

III. Applicants for 3,00,000 shares received an allotment of one share for every five shares applied for; the money due on allotment was retained by the company, the excess being returned to the applicants; and

IV. The money due on final call was received on the due date.

Required: record these transactions (including cash items) in the journal of Piyush Ltd.

[**Ans.** Refund ₹ 1,80,000, Balance Allotment Money received ₹ 2,50,000]

6. B Limited issued 50,000 equity shares of ₹ 10 each payable as ₹ 3 per share on application, ₹ 5 per share (including ₹ 2 as premium) on allotment and ₹ 4 per share on call. All these shares were subscribed. Money due on all shares was fully received except from X, holding 1000 shares who failed to pay the allotment and call money and Y, holding 2000 shares, failed to pay the call money. All those 3,000 shares were forfeited. Out of forfeited shares, 2,500 shares (including whole of X's shares) were subsequently re-issued to Z as fully paid up at a discount of ₹ 2 per share.

Pass necessary journal entries in the books of B limited. Also prepare Balance Sheet and notes to accounts of the company.

[**Ans.** Forfeited Shares A/c credited ₹ 15,000, CR ₹ 7,000]

7. X Limited invited applications for issuing 75,000 equity shares of ₹ 10 each at a premium of ₹ 5 per share. The total amount was payable as follows:

- ₹ 9 per share (including premium) on application and allotment
- Balance on the First and Final Call

Applications for 3,00,000 equity shares were received. Applications for 2,00,000 equity shares were rejected and money refunded. Shares were allotted on pro-rata basis to the remaining applicants. The first and final call was made. The amount was duly received except on 1,500 shares applied by Mr. Raj. His shares were forfeited. The forfeited shares were re-issued at a discount of ₹ 4 per share.

Pass necessary journal entries· for the above transactions in the books of X Limited.

[**Ans.** Forfeited Shares A/c credited ₹ 7,875, CR ₹ 3,375]

8. Fashion Garments Ltd invited applications for issuing 10,000 Equity Shares of ₹ 10 each. The amount was payable as follows:

(i) On Application ₹ 1 per share
(ii) On Allotment ₹ 2 per share
(iii) On First call ₹ 3 per share
(iv) On Second and final Call ₹ 4 per share

The issue was fully subscribed. Ram to whom 100 shares were allotted, failed to pay the allotment money and his shares were forfeited immediately after the allotment. Shyam to whom 150 shares were allotted, failed to pay the first call. His shares were also forfeited after the first call. Afterwards the second and final call was made. Mohan to whom 50 shares were allotted failed to pay the second and final call. His shares were also forfeited. Al the forfeited shares were re-issued at ₹ 9 per share fully paid-up.

Pass necessary Journal entries in the books of Fashion Garments Ltd.

[**Ans.** Forfeited Shares A/c credited ₹ 850, CR ₹ 550]

2 ACCOUNTING FOR BONUS ISSUE

LEARNING OBJECTIVES

After studying this chapter, you should be able to understand:

◇ Meaning of Capitalisation of Profits and Bonus Shares
◇ How to Capitalise Profits or Reserves?
◇ Three Sources for Fully Paid-up Bonus Shares [Sec 63(1)]
◇ Distinction between Bonus Shares and Right Shares
◇ Conditions for Issue of Bonus Shares
◇ SEBI Guidelines on Bonus Issues
◇ Accounting Treatment of Bonus Issue

1.0 MEANING OF CAPITALISATION OF PROFITS AND BONUS SHARES

Capitalisation of profits refers to the process of converting profits *or* reserves into paid up capital. A bonus share is a free share issued without any consideration to an existing shareholder in the ratio of number of shares held by that shareholder. Issue of Bonus share, decreases the Reserve & Surplus, increases the issued capital but does not bring any change in cash flow and Net worth of the company.

2.0 HOW TO CAPITALIZE PROFITS *or* RESERVES?

A company may capitalise its profits *or* reserves by issuing fully paid bonus shares to the existing members.

3.0 THREE SOURCES FOR FULLY PAID-UP BONUS SHARES [SEC 63]

As per Sec 63(1), a company may issue fully paid-up bonus shares to its members out of:

(i) Its Free Reserves
(ii) The Securities Premium Account; or
(iii) Tho Capital Redemption Reserve Accounl.

Notes:

1. **Not out of Revaluation Reserves:** No issue of bonus shares shall be made by capitalising reserves created by the Revaluation of Assets.
2. **Meaning of Free Reserves:** As per Sec 2(43) of the Companies Act, 2013, "Free Reserves" mean such reserves which, as per the latest audited balance sheet of a company, are available for distribution as dividend.

3. **Items not treated as Free Reserves:**

(i) Any amount representing unrealised gains, notional gains *or* revaluation of assets, where shown as a reserve *or* otherwise, *or*

(ii) Any change in carrying amount of an asset *or* of a liability recognised in equity, including surplus in Profit and Loss Account on measurement of the Asset *or* the Liability at Fair Value.

4.0 DISTINCTION BETWEEN BONUS SHARES AND RIGHT SHARES

Basis of Distinction	*Bonus Shares*	*Right Shares*
1. Manner of Issue	These are issued by Capitalizing the accumulated profits *or* reserves.	These are issued by issuing new share capital. In case of further issue of shares, further shares must be offered to the existing shareholders in proportion to their existing shareholders at that date. Such shares are called 'Rights Shares.'Such right is available when it is proposed to increase the subscribed capital of the company by allotment of further shares at any time after the expiry of 2 years from the formation of a company *or* after the expiry of 1 year from the first allotment of shares, whichever is earlier.
2. Consideration	These are issued without any consideration.	These are issued for cash.
3. T/f of Right to Receive	Right to receive bonus shares can not be transferred to another person.	Right to subscribe for right shares can be transferred to another person.
4. Apply	Shareholders are not required to apply for bonus shares.	Shareholders are required to apply to subscribe for right shares.
5. Option	Shareholders have no option to receive bonus shares *less* than/more than those offered.	Shareholders have an option to apply for right shares *less* than/more than those offered.
6. Cash Inflow	There is no cash inflow.	There is cash inflow.
7. Debt-Equity Ratio	Not affected	Decreases

5.0 SIMILARITIES BETWEEN BONUS SHARES AND RIGHT SHARES

In case of issue of both bonus shares and right shares,Number of shares increases but EPS deceases.

6.0 CONDITIONS FOR ISSUE OF FULLY PAID-UP BONUS SHARES [SEC 63(2)]

1. **Authorised by Articles:** A company can issue bonus shares if its Articles expressly authorise to do so.

2. **Board's Resolution:** A resolution is to be passed by the Board of Directors recommending its decision to issue bonus shares.
3. **Member's Resolution:** A resolution is to be passed by the members in the general meeting to approve the Board's resolution recommending the issue of bonus shares.

   Members' resolution must state:

   (a) an intention to capitalize the profits *or* reserves, and

   (b) the amount of profits *or* reserves to be capitalized.
4. **No Default in Payment of Interest/Principle:** The company has not defaulted in payment of interest *or* principal in respect of fixed deposits *or* debt securities issued by it.
5. **No Default in Payment of Statutory dues:** The company has not defaulted in respect of payment of statutory dues of the employees such as contribution to provident fund, gratuity and bonus.
6. **No O/s Partly-Paid-Up Shares:** The partly-paid shares, if any, outstanding on the date of allotment are made fully paid-up.
7. **Compliance with Prescribed Conditions:** A Company must comply with Prescribed Conditions.
8. **Not in lieu of Dividend:** The bonus shares shall not be issued in lieu of dividend.

Rule 14: Once the decision to make a bonus issue is announced, the same can not be withdrawn.

7.0 SEBI GUIDELINES ON BONUS ISSUES

A listed company proposing to issue bonus shares shall comply with the following:

1.(a) The articles of association of the company must contain a provision for capitalisation of reserves, etc.

(b) If there is no such provision in the articles the company must pass a resolution at its general body meeting making provision in the articles of association for capitalisation.

2. The company has not defaulted in payment of interest *or* principal in respect of fixed deposits and interest on existing debentures *or* principal on redemption
3. The company has not defaulted in respect of payment of statutory dues of the employees such as contribution to provident fund, gratuity, bonus etc.
4. **The partly-paid shares, if any, outstanding on the date of allotment are made fully paid-up.**
5. **No-company can issue bonus shares to its members without extending similar benefit to convertible debentures holders. Pending such conversion, Bonus Shares in proportion to such convertible part of FCDs/PCDs should be reserved.**

   The shares so reserved may be issued at the time of conversion(s) of such debentures on the same terms on which the bonus issues were made.
6. **The bonus issue shall be made out of free reserves built out of the genuine profits or securities premium collected in cash only.**
7. Reserves created by revaluation of fixed assets shall not be capitalised.
8. The declaration of bonus issue, in lieu of dividend, shall not be made.
9. A company which announces its bonus issue after the approval of the Board of directors must implement the proposal within a period of 15 days from the date of such approval (if Shareholders' approval is not required) *or* 2 months (if Shareholders' approval is required).
10. Once the decision to make a bonus issue is announced, the same can not be withdrawn.

Note: *An unlisted company can utilise Securities Premium not realised in cash for issue of Bonus Shares but a listed company can not do so.*

Is a person who buys shares next day after the date of announcement of bonus by The Board of Directors entitled to Bonus Shares?

Yes.

Reason:

A person who buys shares after the date of announcement of bonus by The Board of Directors but before the EX-BONUS DATE is entitled to Bonus Shares. In other words, A person who buys shares on/after the EX-BONUS DATE is not entitled to Bonus Shares.

8.0 ACCOUNTING TREATMENT OF BONUS ISSUE

The various accounting entries relating to bonus issue are given below:

1.	**On Making the final call due on partly paid Equity Shares**	
	Equity Share Final Call A/c	Dr.
	To Equity Share Capital A/c	
2.	**On Receipt of final call on partly paid Equity Shares**	
	Bank A/c	Dr.
	To Equity Share Final Call A/c	
3.	**On Declaration of Bonus Shares**	
	Capital Redemption Reserve A/c	Dr.
	Securities Premium A/c (realised in cash only)	Dr.
	Capital Reserve (realised in cash only)	Dr.
	General Reserve A/c	Dr.
	Profit & Loss A/c	Dr.
	To Bonus to Shareholders A/c	
4.	**On issue of fully paid Bonus shares**	
	Bonus to Shareholders A/c	Dr.
	To Equity Share Capital A/c	

Note: While accounting for Bonus Shares there should be minimum reduction in free reserves.

For this purpose, first the most restricted Reserve, then less restricted Reserve and so on should be used.

ILLUSTRATION 1

Following items appear in the Trial Balance of Tulsian 1 Ltd.(Listed) as at 31st March 2023:

1.	40,000 Equity Shares of ₹ 10 each, ₹ 7.50 paid up	₹ 3,00,000
2.	60,000 Equity Shares of ₹ 10 each	₹ 6,00,000
3.	Capital Redemption Reserve	₹ 1,30,000
4.	Plant Revaluation Reserve	₹ 10,000

5.	Securities Premium A/c (including ₹ 40,000 on issue of Shares against the purchase of business and ₹ 3,00,000 on issue of Shares on conversion of Debentures into Equity Shares)	₹ 4,75,000
6.	General Reserve	₹ 1,00,000
7.	Profit & Loss Account	₹ 90,000
8.	Capital Reserve (including ₹ 25,000 being Profit on Sale of Machinery)	₹ 75,000

On 1st April,2023, the Company made final call on Equity shares and received the same on 30th April,2023,.On 1st May,2023,the Company decided to issue bonus shares to equity shareholders at the rate of 2 shares for every 5 shares held and for this purpose, it decided that there should be minimum reduction in free reserves.

Required: Pass the necessary journal entries upto 1st May,2023.

SOLUTION

JOURNAL

Date	*Particulars*	*L.F.*	*Dr. (₹)*	*Cr. (₹)*
01.04.2023	Equity Share Final Call A/c Dr.		1,00,000	
	To Equity Share Capital A/c			1,00,000
	(Being the final call of ₹ 2.50 each on 40,000 equity shares to make them fully paid up)			
30.04.2023	Bank A/c Dr.		1,00,000	
	To Equity Share Final Call A/c			1,00,000
	(Being the amount due on final 1 call adjusted against transfer from Capital Reserve & General Reserves to Bonus to Shareholders A/c)			
01.05.2023	Capital Redemption Reserve A/c Dr.		1,30,000	
	Securities Premium A/c Dr.		1,35,000	
	Capital Reserve A/c Dr.		25,000	
	General Reserve A/c Dr.		1,00,000	
	Profit & Loss A/c Dr.		10,000	
	To Bonus to Shareholders A/c			4,00,000
	(Being the bonus declared by issuing 2 bonus shares for every 5 shares held as per general body's resolution dated...)			
01.05.2023	Bonus to Shareholders A/c Dr.		4,00,000	
	To Equity Share Capital A/c			4,00,000
	(Being the issue of 40,000 shares of ₹ 10 each by way of bonus)(100000 x 2/5)			

Notes:

(i) Securities Premium and Capital Reserve realised in cash can be utilized for bonus issue.

(ii) Plant Revaluation Reserve can not be utilized to issue bonus shares.

ILLUSTRATION 2

Following items appear in the Trial Balance of Tulsian 2 Ltd. (Listed) as at 31st March 2023:

1. 40,000 Equity Shares of ₹ 10 each, ₹ 7.50 paid up	₹ 3,00,000
2. 60,000 Equity Shares of ₹ 10 each	₹ 6,00,000
3. Capital Redemption Reserve	₹ 1,30,000
4. Plant Revaluation Reserve	₹ 10,000
5. Securities Premium A/c (including ₹ 40,000 on issue of Shares against the purchase of business and ₹ 3,00,000 on issue of Shares on conversion of Debentures into Equity Shares)	₹ 4,75,000
6. General Reserve	₹ 1,00,000
7. Profit & Loss Account	₹ 90,000
8. Capital Reserve (including ₹ 25,000 being Profit on Sale of Machinery)	₹ 75,000
12% Partly Convertible Debentures @ ₹ 100 each [20% of 12% Debentures are convertible into equity shares of ₹ 10 each at ₹ 15 on 1st July 2023].	7,50,000

On 1st April, 2023, the Company made final call on Equity shares and received the same on 30th April, 2023,.On 1st May,2023,the Company decided to issue bonus shares to equity shareholders at the rate of 2 shares for every 5 shares held and for this purpose, it decided that there should be minimum reduction in free reserves.

Required: Pass the necessary journal entries upto 1st May,2023.

SOLUTION

JOURNAL

Date	*Particulars*	*L.F.*	*Dr. (₹)*	*Cr. (₹)*
01.04.2023	Equity Share Final Call A/c Dr.		1,00,000	
	To Equity Share Capital A/c			1,00,000
	(Being the final call of ₹ 2.50 each on 40,000 equity shares to make them fully paid up)			
30.04.2023	Bank A/c Dr.		1,00,000	
	To Equity Share Final Call A/c			1,00,000
	(Being the amount due on final call adjusted against transfer from Capital Reserve & General Reserves to Bonus to Shareholders A/c)			
01.05.2023	Capital Redemption Reserve A/c Dr.		1,30,000	
	Securities Premium A/c Dr.		1,35,000	
	Capital Reserve A/c Dr.		25,000	
	General Reserve A/c Dr.		1,00,000	
	Profit & Loss A/c Dr.		40,000	
	To Bonus to Shareholders A/c			4,00,000
	To Bonus to PCD A/c			40,000
	(Being the 40000 bonus shares for 100000 Equity Shareholders in the ratio of 2:5 and 4000 bonus shares for convertible portion of PCD i.e. [(20% of 7,50,000)/ ₹15] × 2/5)] as per general body's resolution dated...)			

01.05.2023	Bonus to Shareholders A/c To Equity Share Capital A/c (Being the issue of 40,000 shares of ₹ 10 each by way of bonus)(100000 x 2/5)	Dr.	4,00,000	4,00,000

Notes:

(i) Securities Premium and Capital Reserve realised in cash can be utilized for bonus issue.

(ii) Plant Revaluation Reserve can not be utilized to issue bonus shares.

(iii) As per SEBI guidelines,no-company can issue bonus shares to its members without extending similar benefit to convertible debentures holders. Pending such conversion, Bonus Shares in proportion to such convertible part of FCDs/PCDs should be reserved. The shares so reserved may be issued at the time of conversion(s) of such debentures on the same terms on which the bonus issues were made.

(iv) Bonus to fully paid equity shares=[(100000 × 2/5) × ₹ 10] = ₹ 4,00,000.

No of equity shares to be issued on conversion of Debentures = [750000 × 20%]/₹ 15]=10000

Bonus for Partly Convertible Debentures=[(10000 × 2/5 × ₹ 10]= ₹ 40,000

Total amount of Bonus =₹ 4,40,000

ILLUSTRATION 3

Following items appear in the Trial Balance of BHARAT TUSHAR Ltd. (Listed) as at 31st March 2023:

1.	40,000 Equity Shares of ₹ 10 each, ₹ 7.50 paid up	₹ 3,00,000
2.	60,000 Equity Shares of ₹ 10 each	₹ 6,00,000
3.	Capital Redemption Reserve	₹ 1,30,000
4.	Plant Revaluation Reserve	₹ 10,000
5.	Securities Premium A/c (including ₹ 40,000 on issue of Shares against the purchase of business and ₹ 3,00,000 on issue of Shares on conversion of Debentures into Equity Shares)	₹ 4,75,000
6.	General Reserve	₹ 1,00,000
7.	Profit & Loss Account	₹ 90,000
8.	Capital Reserve (including ₹ 25,000 being Profit on Sale of Machinery)	₹ 75,000
50,000,12% Debentures of ₹ 100 redeemable at a premium of 5% and terms of issue also confer option to the debenture holders to convert 50% of their holding into equity shares of ₹ 10 each at a predetermined price of ₹ 15 per share on 1st July 2023 but option form was to be submitted by 31st March 2023: Holders of 30,000 debentures did not exercise the option.		

On 1st April,2023, the Company made final call on Equity shares and received the same on 30th April,2023,.On 1st May,2023,the Company decided to issue bonus shares to equity shareholders at the rate of 2 shares for every 5 shares held and for this purpose, it decided that there should be minimum reduction in free reserves.

Required: Calculate the Total amount of Bonus Issue.

SOLUTION

Bonus to fully paid equity shares = [(100000 × 2/5) × ₹ 10] = ₹ 4,00,000.

No of equity shares to be issued on conversion of Debentures = {[(50000 - 30000) × ₹ 105 × 50%]/₹ 15} = 70000

Bonus for Partly Convertible Debentures = [(70000 × 2/5) × ₹ 10]= ₹ 2,80,000
Total amount of Bonus = ₹ 6,80,000

Notes:

(i) Securities Premium and Capital Reserve realised in cash can be utilized for bonus issue.

(ii) Plant Revaluation Reserve can not be utilized to issue bonus shares.

(iii) As per SEBI guidelines,no-company can issue bonus shares to its members without extending similar benefit to convertible debentures holders. Pending such conversion, Bonus Shares in proportion to such convertible part of FCDs/PCDs should be reserved. The shares so reserved may be issued at the time of conversion(s) of such debentures on the same terms on which the bonus issues were made.

SOLVED PROBLEMS

PROBLEM 1

Following is the extract of the Balance Sheet of CAS Ltd. as at 31st March, 2023:

Particulars	₹
Authorised Capital	
10,000 12% Preference shares of ₹ 10 each	1,00,000
1,00,000 Equity shares of ₹ 10 each	10,00,000
	11,00,000
Issued and Subscribed Capital:	
8,000 12% Preference shares of ₹ 10 each fully paid	80,000
90,000 Equity shares of ₹ 10 each, ₹ 8 paid up	7,20,000
Reserves and Surplus:	
Capital Redemption Reserve	20,000
General Reserve	1,20,000
Capital Reserve	75,000
Securities Premium	25,000
Profit and Loss Account	1,80,000
Secured Loans:	
12% Partly Convertible Debentures @ ₹ 100 each	5,00,000

On 1st April, 2023 the Company has made final call @ 2 each on 90,000 equity shares. The call money was received by 20th April, 2023. Thereafter the company decided to capitalise its reserves by way of bonus at the rate of one share for every four shares held. Securities premium of ₹ 25,000 includes a premium of ₹ 5,000 for shares issued to vendors pursuant to a scheme of amalgamation. Capital reserves include ₹ 40,0000, being profit on sales of plant and machinery. 20% of 12% Debentures are convertible into equity shares of ₹ 10 each fully paid on 1st July 2023.

Required: Pass the necessary entries in the books of the company and prepare an extract of the Balance Sheet immediately after bonus issue but before conversion of debentures.

SOLUTION

JOURNAL OF CAS LTD.

Date	Particulars		L.F.	Dr. (₹)	Cr. (₹)
April 1	Equity Share Final Call A/c	Dr.		1,80,000	
	To Equity Share Capital A/c				1,80,000
	(Being the Final call of ₹ 2 per share on 90,000 equity shares due as per Board's Resolution dated...)				
April 20	Bank A/c	Dr.		1,80,000	
	To Equity Share Final Call A/c				1,80,000
	(Being the Final Call money on 90,000 equity shares received)				
	Capital Redemption Reserve A/c	Dr.		20,000	
	Capital Reserve A/c [Realized in cash]	Dr.		40,000	
	Securities Premium A/c [25,000 – 5,000]	Dr.		20,000	
	General Reserve A/c	Dr.		1,20,000	
	Profit and Loss A/c	Dr.		50,000	
	To Bonus to Shareholders A/c				2,25,000
	To Bonus to PCD A/c				25,000
	(Being the Bonus issue @ one share for every four shares held by utilising various reserves as per Board's Resolution dated...)				
	Bonus to Shareholders A/c	Dr.		2,25,000	
	To Equity Share Capital A/c				2,25,000
	(Being the Capitalisation of profits)				

AN EXTRACT OF BALANCE SHEET AS AT 30TH APRIL, 2023 (AFTER BONUS ISSUE)

Particulars	Note No.	₹
I. EQUITY AND LIABILITIES		
(1) Shareholders' Funds		
(a) Share Capital	1	12,05,000
(b) Reserves and Surplus	2	1,95,000
(2) Non-Current Liabilities		
(a) Long-term borrowings	3	5,00,000
Total		19,00,000

Notes to Accounts:

Particulars	₹
1. Share Capital	
Authorised Share Capital	
1,25,000 Equity Shares of ₹ 10 each	12,50,000
10,000, 12% Preference Shares of ₹ 10 each	1,00,000
	13,50,000
Issued, Subscribed and fully paid Share Capital	
1,12,500 Equity Shares of ₹ 10 each, fully paid	11,25,000
(Out of above, 22,500 equity shares @ ₹ 10 each were issued by way of bonus)	

	8,000 12% Preference Shares of ₹ 10 each	80,000
	Total	12,05,000
2.	**Reserves and Surplus**	
	Capital Reserves [75,000 – 40,000]	35,000
	Securities Premium Reserves [25,000 – 20,000]	5,000
	Surplus (Profit & Loss Account) [1,80,000 – 50,000]	1,30,000
	Bonus to PCD A/c	25,000
	Total	1,95,000
3.	**Long-term borrowings**	
	Secured	
	Secured 12% Convertible Debentures @ ₹ 100 each (out of above 20% Debentures to be converted into Equity shares @ ₹ 10 each on 1st July, 2023)	5,00,000
	Total	5,00,000

Working Notes:

(i) Capital Reserve realised in cash can be utilised for issue of fully paid bonus shares.

(ii) As per SEBI guidelines, securities premium collected in cash can only be utilised for bonus issue.

(iii) As per SEBI guidelines, no-company can issue bonus shares to its shareholders without extending similar benefit to convertible debentures holders. Pending such conversion, necessary number of shares should be earmarked for convertible debentures holders. Therefore, convertible debenture holders are also entitled to the bonus shares in the same ratio as the equity shareholders.

(iv) It is assumed that the company will pass necessary resolution at its general body meeting for increasing the authorised capital by ₹ 2,50,000.

Issue of Bonus Shares to equity shareholders [22,500 × ₹ 10]	2,25,000
Issue of Bonus Shares to be issued to Debenture holders after conversion [(20% of 5,00,000)/₹ 10] × 1/4 × ₹ 10]	25,000
	2,50,000

PROBLEM 2

Following is the Balance Sheet of Happy Limited as at March 31, 2023:

BALANCE SHEET AS AT 31-3-2023

Particulars	₹
Authorised Share Capital:	
2,00,000 Equity shares of ₹ 10 each	20,00,000
Issued and Subscribed Share Capital:	
2,00,000 Equity shares of ₹ 10 each, ₹ 7 paid up	14,00,000
Reserves and Surplus:	
Capital reserve (Profit on sale of Fixed Assets)	1,30,000
Securities Premium (Includes ₹ 20,000 received otherwise than in cash)	90,000
General reserve	2,40,000

Profit & Loss A/c	5,20,000
Secured loans:	
12% Fully Convertible Debentures @ ₹ 100 each	4,00,000
Current Liabilities	2,20,000
Property,Plant & Equipment	20,00,000
Investments	4,40,000
Current Assets	5,60,000

On April 01, 2023, company has made final call @ ₹ 3 on 2,00,000 equity shares and received complete call money by April 30, 2023. The company wants to issue bonus shares to its shareholders @ one share for every four shares held. 12% Debentures are convertible into equity shares of ₹ 10 each fully paid on June 01, 2023. Necessary resolutions were passed and requisite legal requirements were complied with. For issue of bonus shares it was decided that reserves and surplus, other than Profit and Loss Account, should be first capitalized.

Required: Prepare Balance Sheet as on May 15, 2023, date on which all the formalities related to the issue of bonus shares completed. For the purpose of preparation of Balance Sheet, assume that, Balance Sheet items as on March 31, 2023, which are not effected by issue of bonus shares as above, remains unchanged as on May 15, 2023. Also pass necessary Journal Entries in the books of the company related to issue of bonus shares, for the period from April 01, 2023 to May 15, 2023.

SOLUTION

BALANCE SHEET OF HAPPY LTD. AS AT 15.5.2023

Particulars	***Note No***	***₹ (lacs)***
I. Equity and Liabilities		
(1) Shareholders' Funds		
(a) Share Capital (10 each)	1	25,00,000
(b) Reserves and Surplus	2	4,80,000
(2) Non-Current Liabilities [12% Debentures]		4,00,000
(3) Current Liabilities		2,20,000
Total		36,00,000
II. Assets		
(1) Non-Current Assets		
(a) Property,Plant & Equipment		
Tangible Assets		20,00,000
(b) Non-Current Investments		4,40,000
(2) Current Assets [5,60,000 + 6,00,000]		11,60,000
Total		36,00,000

Notes To Accounts:

Particulars	***₹ (lacs)***
1. Share Capital	
2,50,000 Equity Shares of ₹ 10 each (Of the above 50,000 Shares were issued by way of bonus for consideration otherwise than cash)	25,00,000

2. **Reserves and Surplus**	
Debentures Redemption Reserve	
Profit & Loss Account [5,20,000 – 1,60,000]	3,60,000
Securities Premium	20,000
Bonus to FCD A/c	1,00,000
Total	4,80,000

JOURNAL

Date	Particulars		Dr. (₹)	Cr. (₹)
01.04.2023	Equity Share Final Call A/c	Dr.	6,00,000	
	To Equity Share Capital A/c			6,00,000
	(Being final call of ₹ 3 per share on 2,00,000 equity shares made)			
30.04.2023	Bank A/c	Dr.	6,00,000	
	To Equity Share Final Call A/c			6,00,000
	(Being final call money on 2,00,000 equity shares received)			
15.05.2023	Capital Reserve A/c	Dr.	1,30,000	
	Securities Premium A/c (90,000 – 20, 000)	Dr.	70,000	
	General Reserve A/c	Dr.	2,40,000	
	Profit & Loss A/c	Dr.	1,60,000	
	To Bonus to Shareholders A/c			5,00,000
	To Bonus to FCD A/c			1,00,000
	(Being bonus issue @ one share for every four shares held, by utilizing various reserves)			
15.05.2023	Bonus to Shareholders A/c	Dr.	5,00,000	
	To Equity Share Capital A/c			5,00,000
	(Being capitalization of reserves and profits)			

Working Notes:

(I) AUTHORISED SHARE CAPITAL

Particulars	Number of shares
Existing number of authorised share capital	2,00,000
Add: Issue of bonus shares to existing equity shareholders	50,000
Add: Shares required for conversion of debentures	40,000
Add: Bonus shares to be issued to debenture holders after conversion	10,000
Total authorised share capital as on May 15, 2023 should be	3,00,000

(ii) As per SEBI guidelines, no company can issue bonus shares to its shareholders without extending similar benefit to convertible debenture holders. Pending such conversion, necessary number of shares should be earmarked for convertible debenture holders. Therefore, convertible debenture holders are also entitled to the bonus shares in the same ratio as the equity shareholders on conversion.

(iii) As per SEBI guidelines, securities premium collected in cash can only be utilised for bonus issue.

VERY SHORT ANSWER TYPE QUESTIONS

1. Briefly explain the following:

(a) Capitalisation of Profits and Bonus Shares

(b) Bonus Shares

(c) Free Reserves

2. Enumerate Three Sources for Fully Paid-up Bonus Shares.

3. Write four differences between the Bonus Shares and Right Shares.

4. Write two similarities between Bonus Shares and Right Shares.

5. Write the Conditions for Issue of Bonus Shares as per Sec 63(2) of The Companies Act,2013.

6. Write SEBI Guidelines on Bonus Issues.

ANALYTICAL QUESTIONS

1. Can a listed company utilise Securities Premium not realised in cash for issue of Bonus Shares?

2. Can a listed company issue bonus shares to its members without extending similar benefit to convertible debentures holders?

3. Once the decision to make a bonus issue is announced, can the same be withdrawn?

4. Is a person who buys shares next day after the date of announcement of bonus by The Board of Directors entitled to Bonus Shares?

PRACTICAL QUESTIONS

1. Following items appear in the Trial Balance of Tulsian 1 Ltd.(Listed) as at 31st March 2023:

1.	80,000 Equity Shares of ₹ 10 each, ₹ 7.50 paid up	₹ 6,00,000
2.	120,000 Equity Shares of ₹ 10 each	₹ 12,00,000
3.	Capital Redemption Reserve	₹ 2,60,000
4.	Plant Revaluation Reserve	₹ 20,000
5.	Securities Premium A/c (including ₹ 80,000 on issue of Shares against the purchase of business and ₹ 6,00,000 on issue of Shares on conversion of Debentures into Equity Shares)	₹ 9,50,000
6.	General Reserve	₹ 2,00,000
7.	Profit & Loss Account	₹ 1,80,000
8.	Capital Reserve (including ₹ 50,000 being Profit on Sale of Machinery)	₹ 1,50,000

On 1st April,2023, the Company made final call on Equity shares and received the same on 30th April,2023,.On 1st May,2023,the Company decided to issue bonus shares to equity shareholders at the rate of 2 shares for every 5 shares held and for this purpose, it decided that there should be minimum reduction in free reserves.

Required: Pass the necessary journal entries upto 1st May,2023.

[**Ans** Bonus ₹ 8,00,000]

2. Following items appear in the Trial Balance of Tulsian 2 Ltd. (Listed) as at 31st March 2023:

1. 80,000 Equity Shares of ₹ 10 each, ₹ 7.50 paid up	₹ 6,00,000
2. 120,000 Equity Shares of ₹ 10 each	₹ 12,00,000
3. Capital Redemption Reserve	₹ 2,60,000
4. Plant Revaluation Reserve	₹ 20,000
5. Securities Premium A/c (including ₹ 80,000 on issue of Shares against the purchase of business and ₹ 6,00,000 on issue of Shares on conversion of Debentures into Equity Shares)	₹ 9,50,000
6. General Reserve	₹ 2,00,000
7. Profit & Loss Account	₹ 1,80,000
8. Capital Reserve (including ₹ 50,000 being Profit on Sale of Machinery)	₹ 1,50,000
12% Partly Convertible Debentures @ ₹ 100 each [20% of 12% Debentures are convertible into equity shares of ₹ 10 each at ₹ 15 on 1st July 2023].	15,00,000

On 1st April, 2023, the Company made final call on Equity shares and received the same on 30th April, 2023. On 1st May, 2023, the Company decided to issue bonus shares to equity shareholders at the rate of 2 shares for every 5 shares held and for this purpose, it decided that there should be minimum reduction in free reserves.

Required: Pass the necessary journal entries upto 1st May,2023.

[**Ans** Bonus to Shareholders ₹ 8,00,000, Bonus to PCD ₹ 80,000]

3. Following items appear in the Trial Balance of BHARAT TUSHAR Ltd. (Listed) as at 31st March 2023:

1. 80,000 Equity Shares of ₹ 10 each, ₹ 7.50 paid up	₹ 6,00,000
2. 120,000 Equity Shares of ₹ 10 each	₹ 12,00,000
3. Capital Redemption Reserve	₹ 2,60,000
4. Plant Revaluation Reserve	₹ 20,000
5. Securities Premium A/c (including ₹ 80,000 on issue of Shares against the purchase of business and ₹ 6,00,000 on issue of Shares on conversion of Debentures into Equity Shares)	₹ 9,50,000
6. General Reserve	₹ 2,00,000
7. Profit & Loss Account	₹ 1,80,000
8. Capital Reserve (including ₹ 50,000 being Profit on Sale of Machinery)	₹ 1,50,000
100,000,12% Debentures of ₹ 100 redeemable at a premium of 5% and terms of issue also confer option to the debenture holders to convert 50% of their holding into equity shares of ₹ 10 each at a predetermined price of ₹ 15 per share on 1st July 2023 but option form was to be submitted by 31st March 2023: Holders of 60,000 debentures did not exercise the option.	

On 1st April, 2023, the Company made final call on Equity shares and received the same on 30th April, 2023. On 1st May, 2023, the Company decided to issue bonus shares to equity shareholders at the rate of 2 shares for every 5 shares held and for this purpose, it decided that there should be minimum reduction in free reserves.

Required: Calculate the Total amount of Bonus Issue.

[**Ans** Bonus to Shareholders ₹ 8,00,000, Bonus to PCD ₹ 5,60,000,
Total amount of Bonus Issue ₹ 13,60,000]

4. Following are the balances appear in the trial balance of CEEA Ltd. as at 31st March. 2023.

Particulars	(₹)
10,000; 10% Preference Shares of ₹10 each fully paid	1,00,000
1,00,000 Equity Shares of ₹10 each ₹8 paid up	8,00,000
Reserves and Surplus:	
General Reserve	2,40,000
Securities Premium (collected in cash)	25,000
Profit and Loss Account	1,20,000

On 1st April, 2023 the company has made final call @ ₹ 2 each on 1,00,000 Equity Shares. The call money was received by 15th April, 2023. Thereafter the company decided to issue bonus shares to equity shareholders at the rate of 1 share for every 5 shares held and for this purpose, it decided that there should be minimum reduction in free reserves. Pass Journal entries. [**Ans** Bonus ₹ 2,00,000]

5. Following is the extract of Balance Sheet of Prem Ltd. as at 31st March, 2023 :

Particulars	₹
Authorized capital:	
3,00,000 equity shares of ₹10 each	30,00,000
25,000,10% preference shares of ₹10 each	2,50,000
	32,50,000
Issued and subscribed capital:	
2,70,000 equity shares of ₹ 10 each fully paid up	27,00,000
24,000, 10% preference shares of ₹ 10 each fully paid up	2,40,000
	29,40,000
Reserves and surplus:	
General reserve	3,60,000
Capital redemption reserve	1,20,000
Securities premium (collected in cash)	75,000
Profit and loss account	6,00,000
	11,55,000

On 1st April, 2023, the company decided to capitalize its reserves by way of bonus at the rate of two shares for every five shares held.

Show necessary journal entries in the books of the company and prepare the extract of the balance sheet after bonus issue. [**Ans** Bonus ₹ 10,80,000]

6. Following items appear in the Trail Balance of Star Ltd. as on 31st March, 2023:

Particulars	₹
80,000 Equity Shares of ₹10 each, ₹ 8 paid-up	6,40,000
Capital Reserve (including ₹15,000 being profit on sale of Machinery)	1,10,000
Revaluation Reserve	80,000
Capital Redemption Reserve	75,000
Securities Premium	60,000
General Reserve	2,10,000
Profit & Loss Account (Cr. Balance)	1,00,000

On 1st April,2023, the Company has made final call on Equity shares @₹ 2 per share. The entire money was received in the month of April, 2023.

On 1st June, 2023, the Company decided to issue to Equity shareholders bonus shares at the rate of 2 shares for every 5 shares held and for this purpose, it was decided that there should be minimum reduction in free reserves.

Pass necessary journal entries in the Books of Star Ltd. **[Ans** Bonus ₹ 3,20,000]

7. Following is the extract of the Balance Sheet of K Ltd (listed company) as at 31st March, 2023

	₹
Authorized capital:	
3,00,000 Equity shares of ₹ 10 each	30,00,000
	30,00,000
Issued and Subscribed capital:	
2,00,000 Equity shares of ₹ 10 each, ₹ 8 paid up	16,00,000
Reserves and surplus:	
General Reserve	3,60,000
Capital Redemption Reserve	1,20,000
Securities premium (not realised in cash)	75,000
Profit and Loss Account	6,00,000

On 1st April, 2023, the Company has made final call @ ₹ 2 each on 2,00,000 equity shares. The call money was received by 25th April, 2023. Thereafter, the company decided to capitalize its reserves by way of bonus at the rate of one share for every four shares held.

Show necessary entries in the books of the company and prepare the extract of the Balance Sheet immediately after bonus issue. **[Ans** Bonus ₹ 5,00,000]

8. Following is the extract of the Balance Sheet of CAS Ltd. as at 31st March, 2023:

Particulars	₹
Authorised Capital	
10,000 12% Preference shares of ₹ 10 each	1,00,000
1,00,000 Equity shares of ₹ 10 each	10,00,000
	11,00,000
Issued and Subscribed Capital:	
8,000 12% Preference shares of ₹ 10 each fully paid	80,000
90,000 Equity shares of ₹ 10 each, ₹ 8 paid up	7,20,000
Reserves and Surplus:	
Capital Redemption Reserve	20,000
General Reserve	1,20,000
Capital Reserve	75,000
Securities Premium	25,000
Profit and Loss Account	1,80,000
Secured Loans:	
12% Partly Convertible Debentures @ ₹ 100 each	5,00,000

On 1st April, 2023 the Company has made final call @ 2 each on 90,000 equity shares. The call money was received by 20th April, 2023. Thereafter the company decided to capitalise its reserves by way of bonus at the rate of one share for every four shares held. Securities premium of ₹ 25,000 includes a premium of ₹ 5,000 for shares issued to vendors pursuant to a scheme of amalgamation. Capital reserves include ₹ 40,0000, being profit on sales of plant and machinery. 20% of 12% Debentures are convertible into equity shares of ₹ 10 each fully paid on 1st June 2023.

Required: Show necessary entries in the books of the company and prepare the extract of the Balance Sheet immediately after bonus issue but before conversion of debentures. Are the convertible debenture holders entitled to bonus shares?

[Ans Bonus to Shareholders ₹ 2,25,000, Bonus to PCD after conversion ₹ 25,000, Total amount of Bonus Issue ₹ 2,50,000]

3 REDEMPTION OF REDEEMABLE PREFERENCE SHARES

LEARNING OBJECTIVES

After studying this chapter, you should be able to understand:

◇ What are the Restrictions on the Redemption of Redeemable Preference Shares?

◇ How to Determine the Amount of Minimum Fresh Issue of New Shares?

◇ Accounting Entries on Redemption of Red. Pref. Shares

1.0 WHICH COMPANY CAN ISSUE?

A company limited by shares may, if authorized by its Articles, issue redeemable preference shares.

2.0 CAN A COMPANY ISSUE IRREDEEMABLE PREFERENCE SHARES?

No company limited by shares shall issue irredeemable preference shares. [Section 55(1)].

3.0 WHAT CAN BE THE MAXIMUM PERIOD OF REDEMPTION?

After the commencement of The Companies Act 2013, no company limited by shares shall issue any preference share which is redeemable after the expiry of a period of 20 years from the date of issue. [Section 55(1)]. However, In case of Infrastructure Companies maximum period of Redemption may exceed 20 years

4.0 CONDITIONS FOR THE REDEMPTION OF RED. PREF. SHARES

As per [Section 55(1)], the redemption of preference shares is subject to the following restrictions:

1. **Fully paid:** Such shares can be redeemed only if these are fully paid.
2. **Two Sources of Redeeming such shares:** Such shares can be redeemed only out of the following two sources:

   (a) **Divisible Profits**, i.e., Profits available for distribution as dividend. Some of the examples of Divisible Profits are as under:

      1. General Reserve
      2. Reserve Fund
      3. Dividend Equalisation Fund
      4. Insurance Fund
      5. Workman's Compensation Fund
      6. Workman's Accident Fund
      7. Profit and Loss Account

(b) **Proceeds of fresh issue of shares** (whether Equity or Preference) made for the purpose of redemption.

What constitute the proceeds is explained as follows:

In case of Fresh Issue of shares	What constitute proceeds
(a) A Par (b) At Premium	Nominal value of shares issued Nominal value of shares issued

Tutorial Note: *These shares can be Equity shares or Preference shares.*

3. **Sources of Providing Premium if any, payable on redemption of Preference Shares.**

Case	Sources of providing Premium if any, payable on redemption of Preference Shares before such shares are redeemed.
1. In case of such class of companies, as may be prescribed and whose financial statements comply with the accounting standards prescribed for such class of companies u/s 133 which issued preference shares after the commencement of this Act	Profits (whether divisible or not), e.g. Capital Reserve realised in cash
2. In other cases	(a) Securities Premium Account. (b) Profits (whether divisible or not), e.g. Capital Reserve realised in cash

4. **T/F to CRR A/c:** Where any such shares are redeemed out of divisible profits, an amount equivalent to the nominal value of the shares so redeemed, must be transferred out of divisible profits to Capital Redemption Reserve Account.
5. **Utilization of CRR:** The Capital Redemption Reserve Account may be applied by the company in issuing fully paid bonus shares to the members of the company.

6. Unredeemed Preference Shares: Where a company is not in a position to redeem any preference shares or to pay dividend, if any,on such shares in accordance with the terms of issue (such shares hereinafter referred to as unredeemed preference shares), it may, with the consent of the holders of 3/4th in value of such preference shares and with the approval of the Tribunal on a petition made by it in this behalf, issue further redeemable preference shares equal to the amount due(including the dividend thereon) in respect of the unredeemed preference shares, and on the issue of such further redeemable preference shares, the unredeemed preference shares shall be deemed to have been redeemed:

Provided that the Tribunal shall, while giving approval u/s 55(3), order the redemption forthwith of preference shares held by such persons who have not consented to the issue of further redeemable preference shares.

ILLUSTRATION 1

X Ltd. decides to redeem 13000,15% Red. Pref. Shares of ₹ 100 each at a premium of 10%. It has a General Reserve of ₹ 9,20,000, Profit & Loss A/c balance of ₹ 7,10,000, a Securities Premium of ₹ 2,25,000. It is decided to issue 880, 15% Debentures of ₹ 100 each at par, 100, 12% Pref. Shares of ₹ 100 each at a premium of 20% and 50,000 Equity Shares of ₹ 10 each a premium of 25% for the purpose of redemption of Pref. Calculate the amount to be transferred to Capital Redemption Reserve Account.

SOLUTION

Divisible Profits to be utilized & to be t/f to CRR

= Nominal Value of Pref. Shares to be redeemed – Proceeds of a Fresh Issue of Shares

= ₹ 13,00,000 – [(100 × ₹ 100) + (50000 × ₹ 10)] = ₹ 7,90,000

5.0 HOW TO DETERMINE THE AMOUNT OF MINIMUM FRESH ISSUE OF NEW SHARES?

Calculate Minimum No. of New Shares to comply with Legal Condition of Sec 55

A. Nominal Value of RPS		XXX
B. Less: Divisible Profits available for redemption(say)		
General Reserve	XXX	
+Profit & Loss A/c	XXX	
-Premium Payable on redemption	(XXX)	
-Minimum Balance to be kept(if so desired)	(XXX)	
-Loss on sale of Investments (if unadjusted)	(XXX)	(XXX)
C. Less: Nominal Value of New Shares(not Debentures),if any,issued for Redemption		(XXX)
D. Minimum Nominal Value of Fresh issue of Shares to be issued [A-B-C]		XXX
E. Nominal Value of a New Share		XX
F. Minimum No. of New Shares to comply with legal condition of Sec 55 [D/E]		XXX

Calculate Minimum No. of New Shares to comply with Liquidity Condition (if any)

A. Total Funds required for Redemption[Nominal Value of RPS + Premium Payable on redemption]		XXX
B. Less: Funds available for Redemption (say)		
Cash & Bank Balance given	XXX	
+Final Call on Red. Pref. Shares	XXX	
+ Sale Proceeds of Investments	XXX	
+ Issue Proceeds of **New Shares if any,issued**	XXX	
+ Issue Proceeds of **New Debentures if any,issued**	XXX	
-Minimum Balance to be retained	(XXX)	(XXX)
C. Minimum Issue Proceeds of Fresh issue of Shares to be issued [A-B]		XXX
D. Issue Price of a New Share		XX
E. Minimum No. of New Shares to comply with Liquidity condition [C/D]		XXX

TAKE HIGHER No. of New Shares out of New Shares as per Legal Condition and Liquidity Condition (if any)

ILLUSTRATION 2

X Ltd. decides to redeem 13000,15% Red. Pref. Shares of ₹ 100 each at a premium of 10%. It has a General Reserve of ₹ 9,20,000, Profit & Loss A/c balance of ₹ 7,10,000, a Securities Premium of ₹ 2,25,000. Calculate the minimum number of equity shares of ₹ 10 each to be issued at 25% premium for the purpose of redemption in each of the following cases:

(i) If no other information is given

(ii) If **Investments having book value of** ₹ 8,00,000 are sold for ₹ 6,00,000.

(iii) If the company has to maintain a minimum balance of ₹ 5,00,000 in the Profit & Loss A/c

(iv) If **Investments having book value of** ₹ 8,00,000 are sold for ₹ 6,00,000 and the company has to maintain a minimum balance of ₹ 5,00,000 in the Profit & Loss A/c

SOLUTION All figures (except in row E & F) are in lakh.

Minimum No. of New Shares to comply with Legal Condition of Sec 55

	Case (i)	Case (ii)	Case (iii)	Case (iv)
A. Nominal Value of RPS	₹ 13.00	₹ 13.00	₹ 13.00	₹ 13.00
B. Less: Divisible Profits available for redemption(say)				
General Reserve	₹ 9.20	₹ 9.20	₹ 9.20	₹ 9.20
+Profit & Loss A/c	₹ 7.10	₹ 7.10	₹ 7.10	₹ 7.10
-Premium Payable on redemption	(₹ 1.30)	(₹ 1.30)	(₹ 1.30)	(₹ 1.30)
-Minimum Balance to be kept(if so desired)	(₹ 0)	(₹ 0)	(₹ 5.00)	(₹ 5.00)
-Loss on sale of Investments (if unadjusted)	(₹ 0)	(₹ 2.00)	(₹ 0)	(₹ 2.00)
Total Divisible Profits available for redemption	₹ 15.00	₹ 13.00	₹ 10.00	₹ 8.00
C. Less: Nominal Value of New Shares(not Debentures), if any,issued for Redemption	0	0	0	0
D. Minimum Nominal Value of Fresh issue of Shares to be issued [A-B-C]	Since D P exceed the NV of RPS,there is no need for issue of New Shares.	Since D P equal to the NV of RPS,there is no need for issue of New Shares.	₹ 3.00	₹ 5.00
E. Nominal Value of a New Share			₹ 10	₹ 10
F. Minimum No. of New Shares to comply with legal condition of Sec 55 [D/E]			30,000	50,000

ILLUSTRATION 3

X Ltd. decides to redeem 13000,15% Red. Pref. Shares of ₹ 100 each at a premium of 10%. It has a General Reserve of ₹ 9,20,000, Profit & Loss A/c balance of ₹ 7,10,000, a Securities Premium of ₹ 2,25,000. It is decided to issue 880, 15% Debentures of ₹ 100 each at par and 100, 12% Pref. Shares of ₹ 100 each at a premium of 20% for the purpose of redemption of Pref. Shares. Calculate the minimum number of equity shares of ₹ 10 each to be issued at 25% premium for the purpose of redemption in each of the following cases:

(i) If the company has to maintain a minimum balance of ₹ 5,00,000 in the Profit & Loss A/c

(ii) If **Investments having book value of** ₹ 8,00,000 are sold for ₹ 6,00,000 and the company has to maintain a minimum balance of ₹ 5,00,000 in the Profit & Loss A/c

SOLUTION **All figures (except in row E & F) are in lakh.**

Minimum No. of New Shares to comply with Legal Condition of Sec 55 ₹ in lakh

	Case (i)	**Case (ii)**
A. Nominal Value of RPS	₹ 13.00	₹ 13.00
B. Less: Divisible Profits available for redemption(say)		
General Reserve	₹ 9.20	₹ 9.20
+Profit & Loss A/c	₹ 7.10	₹ 7.10
-Premium Payable on redemption	(₹ 1.30)	(₹ 1.30)
-Minimum Balance to be kept(if so desired)	(₹ 5.00)	(₹ 5.00)
-Loss on sale of Investments (if unadjusted)	(₹ 0)	(₹ 2.00)
Total Divisible Profits available for redemption	₹ 10.00	₹ 8.00
C. Less: Nominal Value of New Shares(not Debentures),if any,issued for Redemption	0.10	0.10
D. Minimum Nominal Value of Fresh issue of Shares to be issued [A-B-C]	₹ 2.90	₹ 4.90
E. Nominal Value of a New Share	₹ 10	₹ 10
F. Minimum No. of New Shares to comply with legal condition of Sec 55 [D/E]	29,000	49,000

ILLUSTRATION 4

X Ltd. decides to redeem 13000,15% Red. Pref. Shares of ₹ 100 each at a premium of 10%. It has a General Reserve of ₹ 9,20,000, Profit & Loss A/c balance of ₹ 7,10,000, a Securities Premium of ₹ 2,25,000, Bank Balance of ₹ 6,30,000 and Investments [Face Value ₹ 10,00,000] of ₹ 20,00,000.40% of Investments are sold at 150% of Face Value. It is decided to issue 880, 15% Debentures of ₹ 100 each at par and 100, 12% Pref. Shares of ₹ 100 each at a premium of 20% for the purpose of redemption of Pref. Shares. Calculate the minimum number of equity shares of ₹ 10 each to be issued at 25% premium for the purpose of redemption if the company has to maintain a minimum balance of ₹ 5,00,000 in the Profit & Loss Account.

SOLUTION

1. Sale Proceeds of Investments = ₹ 4,00,000 × 150/100 = ₹ 6,00,000
2. Book Value of Investments = ₹ 20,00,000 × 40% = ₹ 8,00,000
3. Loss on Sale of Investments = ₹ 6,00,000 – ₹ 8,00,000 = ₹ 2,00,000

All figures (except in row E & F) are in lakh.

Minimum No. of New Shares to comply with Legal Condition of Sec 55 ₹ in lakh

A. Nominal Value of RPS	₹ 13.00
B. Less: Divisible Profits available for redemption(say)	
General Reserve	₹ 9.20
+Profit & Loss A/c	₹ 7.10
-Premium Payable on redemption	(₹ 1.30)
-Minimum Balance to be kept(if so desired)	(₹ 5.00)
-Loss on sale of Investments (if unadjusted)	(₹ 2.00)

Total Divisible Profits available for redemption	₹ 8.00
C. Less: Nominal Value of New Shares(not Debentures),if any,issued for Redemption	0.10
D. Minimum Nominal Value of Fresh issue of Shares to be issued [A-B-C]	₹ 4.90
E. Nominal Value of a New Share	₹ 10
F. Minimum No. of New Shares to comply with legal condition of Sec 55 [D/E]	49,000

ILLUSTRATION 5

X Ltd. decides to redeem 13000,15% Red. Pref. Shares of ₹ 100 each at a premium of 10%. It has a General Reserve of ₹ 9,20,000, Profit & Loss A/c balance of ₹ 7,10,000, a Securities Premium of ₹ 2,25,000, Bank Balance of ₹ 6,30,000 and Investments [Face value ₹ 10,00,000] of ₹ 20,00,000.40% of Investments are sold at 150% of Face Value. Calculate the minimum number of equity shares of ₹ 10 each to be issued at 25% premium for the purpose of redemption if the company has to maintain a minimum balance of ₹ 5,00,000 in Bank Account and of ₹ 5,00,000 in the Profit & Loss Account.

SOLUTION

1. Sale Proceeds of Investments = ₹ 4,00,000 × 150/100 = ₹ 6,00,000
2. Book Value of Investments = ₹ 20,00,000 × 40% = ₹ 8,00,000
3. Loss on Sale of Investments = ₹ 6,00,000 – ₹ 8,00,000 = ₹ 2,00,000

All figures (except in row E & F) are in lakh.

Minimum No. of New Shares to comply with Legal Condition of Sec 55 [₹ in lakh]

A. Nominal Value of RPS	₹ 13.00
B. Less: Divisible Profits available for redemption(say)	
General Reserve	₹ 9.20
+Profit & Loss A/c	₹ 7.10
-Premium Payable on redemption	(₹ 1.30)
-Minimum Balance to be kept(if so desired)	(₹ 5.00)
-Loss on sale of Investments (if unadjusted)	(₹ 2.00)
Total Divisible Profits available for redemption	₹ 8.00
C. Less: Nominal Value of New Shares(not Debentures),if any,issued for Redemption	0
D. Minimum Nominal Value of Fresh issue of Shares to be issued [A-B-C]	₹ 5.00
E. Nominal Value of a New Share	₹ 10
F. Minimum No. of New Shares to comply with legal condition of Sec 55 [D/E]	50,000

All figures (except in row D & E) are in lakh.

Calculate Minimum No. of New Shares to comply with Liquidity Condition

A. Total Funds required for Redemption[Nominal Value of RPS + Premium Payable on redemption]		₹ 14.30
B. Less: Funds available for Redemption (say)		
Cash & Bank Balance given	₹ 6.30	
+Final Call on Red. Pref. Shares		
+ Sale Proceeds of Investments	₹ 6.00	

+ Issue Proceeds of **New Shares if any,issued**	0	
+ Issue Proceeds of **New Debentures if any,issued**	0	
-Minimum Balance to be retained	(₹ 5.00)	₹ 7.30
C. Minimum Issue Proceeds of Fresh issue of Shares to be issued [A-B]		₹ 7.00
D. Issue Price of a New Share		₹ 12.50
E. Minimum No. of New Shares to comply with Liquidity condition [C/D]		56,000

TAKE HIGHER No. of New Shares out of 50000 & 56000..Hence, 56000 New Shares are required to be issued to comply with both the conditions.

ILLUSTRATION 6

X Ltd. decides to redeem 13000,15% Red. Pref. Shares of ₹ 100 each at a premium of 10%. It has a General Reserve of ₹ 9,20,000, Profit & Loss A/c balance of ₹ 7,10,000, a Securities Premium of ₹ 2,25,000, Bank Balance of ₹ 6,30,000 and Investments [Face value ₹ 10,00,000] of ₹ 20,00,000.40% of Investments are sold at 150% of Face Value. It is decided to issue 880, 15% Debentures of ₹ 100 each at par and 100, 12% Pref. Shares of ₹ 100 each at a premium of 20% for the purpose of redemption of Pref. Shares. Calculate the minimum number of equity shares of ₹ 10 each to be issued at 25% premium for the purpose of redemption if the company has to maintain a minimum balance of ₹ 5,00,000 in Bank Account and of ₹ 5,00,000 in the Profit & Loss Account.

SOLUTION

1. Sale Proceeds of Investments = ₹ 4,00,000 × 150/100 = ₹ 6,00,000
2. Book Value of Investments = ₹ 20,00,000 × 40% = ₹ 8,00,000
3. Loss on Sale of Investments = ₹ 6,00,000 – ₹ 8,00,000 = ₹ 2,00,000

All figures (except in row E & F) are in lakh.

Minimum No. of New Shares to comply with Legal Condition of Sec 55 [₹ in lakh]

A. Nominal Value of RPS	₹ 13.00
B. Less: Divisible Profits available for redemption(say)	
General Reserve	₹ 9.20
+Profit & Loss A/c	₹ 7.10
-Premium Payable on redemption	(₹ 1.30)
-Minimum Balance to be kept(if so desired)	(₹ 5.00)
-Loss on sale of Investments (if unadjusted)	(₹ 2.00)
Total Divisible Profits available for redemption	₹ 8.00
C. Less: Nominal Value of New Shares(not Debentures),if any,issued for Redemption	₹ 0.10
D. Minimum Nominal Value of Fresh issue of Shares to be issued [A-B-C]	₹ 4.90
E. Nominal Value of a New Share	₹ 10
F. Minimum No. of New Shares to comply with legal condition of Sec 55 [D/E]	49,000

All figures (except in row D & E) are in lakh.

Minimum No. of New Shares to comply with Liquidity Condition

A. Total Funds required for Redemption[Nominal Value of RPS + Premium Payable on redemption]		₹ 14.30
B. Less: Funds available for Redemption (say)		
Cash & Bank Balance given	₹ 6.30	
+Final Call on Red. Pref. Shares		
+ Sale Proceeds of Investments	₹ 6.00	
+ Issue Proceeds of **New Shares if any,issued**	₹ 0.12	
+ Issue Proceeds of **New Debentures if any,issued**	₹ 0.88	
-Minimum Balance to be retained	(₹ 5.00)	₹ 8.30
C. Minimum Issue Proceeds of Fresh issue of Shares to be issued [A-B]		₹ 6.00
D. Issue Price of a New Share		₹ 12.50
E. Minimum No. of New Shares to comply with Liquidity condition [C/D]		48,000

TAKE HIGHER No. of New Shares out of 49000 & 48000. Hence, 49000 New Shares are required to be issued to comply with both the conditions.

6.0 JOURNAL ENTRIES TO BE PASSED ON THE REDEMPTION OF PREFERENCE SHARES

(a) For making partly paid up Red. Pref. Shares fully paid up	**(i) On Making Final Call** Redeemable Preference Share Final Call A/c Dr. To Red. Pref. Share Capital A/c **(ii) On Receipt of Final Call** Bank A/c Dr. To Redeemable Preference Share Final Call A/c
(b) For realizing Investments to provide cash for redemption	Bank A/c Dr. *[Sale Proceeds]* Profit & Loss A/c Dr. *[Loss]* To Investments A/c *[Book Value]* To Profit & Loss A/c *[Profit]*
(c) For a fresh issue of shares	**(a) On receipt of Application Money** Bank A/c Dr. To Share Application & Allotment A/c **(b) On Account** **(i) If the shares are issued at par** Share Application & Allotment A/c Dr. To Share Capital A/c **(ii) If the shares are issued at premium** Share Application & Allotment A/c Dr. To Share Capital A/c To Securities Premium A/c

(d) For making provision for premium (if any) payable on redemption of preference shares	General Reserve/P& L A/c Dr. To Premium payable on Redemption of Pref. Shares A/c [In relation to fully paid up RPS] To Pref. Share Redemption Suspense A/c [In relation to partly paid up RPS]
(e) For transfer of Nominal Value of RPS redeemed out of divisible Profits to Capital Redemption Reserve Account	P&L A/c/ General Reserve A/c Dr. To Capital Redemption Reserve A/c [In relation to fully paid up RPS] To Pref. Share Redemption Suspense A/c [In relation to partly paid up RPS]
(f) For making money due to Fully paid Redeemable Preference Share Holders	Redeemable Preference Share Capital A/c Dr. Premium on Redemption of Red. Pref. Shares A/c Dr. To Redeemable Preference Share Holders A/c (**Note:** *This entry should be passed in relation to all fully paid preference shares whether or not the holders thereof were traceable*)
(g) For making payment to Fully paid Redeemable Preference Shareholders (other than those who were not traceable)	Redeemable Preference Shareholders A/c Dr. To Bank A/c (**Note:** *This entry should be passed in relation to only those fully paid pref. share holders who were traceable and the balance of Red. Pref. Share holders' Account will appear under the head Current Liabilities in the Balance Sheet*)
(H) On issue of fully paid bonus shares	
(i) *On declaration of Bonus to fully paid Equity Shareholders*	Capital Redemption Reserve A/c Dr. Securities Premium A/c (realised in cash only) Dr. Capital Reserves A/c (realised in cash only) Dr. General Reserve A/c Dr. Profit & Loss A/c Dr. To Bonus to Shareholders A/c
(ii) *On issue of fully paid Bonus shares*	Bonus to Shareholders A/c Dr. To Share Capital A/c

Tutorial Notes: *In case there are calls–in–arrears on some of the Redeemable Preference Shares, then*

1. The premium, if any payable on such Red. Pref. Shares should be credited to Preference Share Redemption Suspense Account.
2. The amount to be transferred to Capital Redemption Reserve Account in relation to such Red. Pref. Shares should be credited to Preference Share Redemption Suspense Account.
3. Preference Share Redemption Suspense Account shall appear under the head 'Current Liabilities' in the Balance Sheet.

ILLUSTRATION 7

Given below are the extracts of Balance Sheet of Tulsian Ltd.(Listed) as at 31st March 2023:

Particulars	₹
Authorised Capital	
13000, 15% Redeemable Preference Shares of ₹ 100 each	13,00,000
4,50,000 Equity shares of ₹ 10 each	45,00,000
Issued and Subscribed Capital	
13000, 15% Redeemable Preference Shares of ₹ 100 each, ₹ 80 per share paid up(issued on 1st April,2015)	10,40,000
4,50,000 Equity Shares of ₹ 10 each, ₹ 8 per share paid up	36,00,000
Plant Revaluation Reserve	5,05,000
General Reserve	9,20,000
Securities Premium (including ₹ 1,00,000 on issue of Shares against the purchase of business)	2,25,000
Profit & Loss Account	7,10,000
Current Liabilities	20,00,000
Property,Plant & Equipment and Intangible Assets	63,70,000
Non–Current Investments [Face value ₹ 10,00,000]	20,00,000
Bank Balance	6,30,000

On 1st April 2023, the Board of Directors decided to make a final call of ₹ 20 on Redeemable Preference Shares and to redeem the same at a premium of 10% on 1st June, 2023. The investments of the face value of ₹ 4,00,000 are sold at the market price which was 150% of the face value.

It is decided to redeem the preference shares partly out of accumulated profits and reserves and partly out of a fresh issue of 50,000 Equity Shares of ₹ 10 each at a premium of 25%. On 1st June,2023 all payments were made on redemption.

On 1st July 2023, the Board decided to issue fully paid bonus shares to the equity shareholders in the ratio of one for five after making final call on equity shares.

Required: Pass the necessary journal entries and prepare the Balance Sheet after giving effect to Board's decisions upto 1st July 2023. Also state the amount by which Authorised Capital is required to be increased by passing the necessary resolution at general body meeting of the company.

SOLUTION

JOURNAL OF TULSIAN LTD.

Date 2023	***Particulars***		***L.F.***	***Dr. (₹)***	***Cr. (₹)***
Apr 1	15% Red. Pref. Share Final Call A/c	Dr.		2,60,000	
	To 15% Red. Pref. Share Capital A/c				2,60,000
	(Being the Final Call on Red. Pref. Shares)				
	Bank A/c	Dr.		2,60,000	
	To 15% Red. Pref. Share Final Call A/c				2,60,000

	(Being the Final Call received on Red. Pref. Shares)			
	Bank A/c	Dr.	6,00,000	
	Profit & Loss A/c	Dr.	2,00,000	
	To Investments			8,00,000
	(Being the Investments of the face value of ₹ 4,00,000 sold at a loss of ₹ 2,00,000 being the difference between the book value and the sale proceeds) Book Value = ₹ 20,00,000 × ₹ 4,00,000/ ₹ 10,00,000 = ₹ 8,00,000 Sale Proceeds = ₹ 4,00,000 × 150/100 = ₹ 6,00,000]			
	Bank A/c	Dr.	6,25,000	
	To Equity Share Capital A/c			5,00,000
	To Securities Premium A/c			1,25,000
	(Being 50,000 Equity Shares of ₹ 10 each issued at 25% premium)			
	General Reserve A/c	Dr.	1,30,000	
	To Premium payable on Redemption A/c			1,30,000
	(Being the Premium payable on Redemption of **fully paid RPS** t/f to Premium payable on Redemption A/c)			
	General Reserve	Dr.	7,90,000	
	Profit & Loss A/c	Dr.	10,000	
	To Capital Redemption Reserve A/c			8,00,000
	(Being an amount equal to the nominal value of **fully paid RPS** redeemed out of divisible profits, t/f to Capital Redemption Reserve A/c)			
	15% Red. Pref. Share Capital A/c	Dr.	13,00,000	
	Premium payable on Redemption A/c	Dr.	1,30,000	
	To Red. Pref. Shareholders A/c			14,30,000
	(Being the amount due to **fully paid RPS** on redemption)			
Jun 1	Red. Pref. Shareholders A/c	Dr.	14,30,000	
	To Bank A/c			14,30,000
	(Being the payment made to all **fully paid RPS**)			
Jul 1	Equity Share Final Call A/c	Dr.	9,00,000	
	To Equity Share Capital A/c			9,00,000
	(Being the Final Call made due on Equity Shares)			
	Bank A/c	Dr.	9,00,000	
	To Equity Share Final Call A/c			9,00,000
	(Being the Final Call received on Equity Shares)			

	Capital Redemption Reserve A/c Dr.		8,00,000	
	Securities Premium A/c Dr.		2,00,000	
	To Bonus to Equity Shareholders' A/c			10,00,000
	(Being the Bonus to Equity Shareholders declared for issuing fully paid Shares in the ratio of 1 for 5. Hence no. of Bonus Shares 100000 i.e.(500000 × 1/5)]			
	Bonus to Equity Shareholders' A/c Dr.		10,00,000	
	To Equity Share Capital A/c			10,00,000
	(Being 100000 Equity Shares of ₹ 10 each fully paid issued as Bonus Shares)			

BALANCE SHEET OF TULSIAN LTD. AS AT 1ST JULY 2023 (AFTER BONUS ISSUE)

Particulars	**Notes**	₹
I. EQUITY AND LIABILITIES		
(1) Shareholders' Funds		
(a) Share Capital	1	60,00,000
(b) Reserves and Surplus	2	11,55,000
(2) Non–Current Liabilities		
(3) Current Liabilities		20,00,000
Total		**91,55,000**
II. ASSETS		
(1) Non–Current Assets		
Property, Plant & Equipment and Intangible Assets		63,70,000
Non–Current Investments (Face Value ₹ 6,00,000)		12,00,000
(2) Current Assets		
Cash & Cash Equivalents		15,85,000
Total		**91,55,000**

Notes to Accounts:

Particulars	₹
1. Share Capital	
6,00,000, Equity Share Capital of ₹ 10 each fully paid up	60,00,000
(Out of above, 1,00,000 equity shares @ ₹ 10 each were issued by way of bonus)	
	60,00,000
2. Reserves And Surplus	
Securities Premium (including ₹ 1,00,000 on issue of Shares against the purchase of business)	1,50,000
Plant Revaluation Reserve	5,05,000
General Reserve	–

Profit & Loss Account	5,00,000
	11,55,000

Working Notes:

1. Divisible Profits to be utilized & to be t/f to CRR

 = Nominal value of Red. Pref. Shares – Proceeds of fresh issue of new shares

 = ₹ 13,00,000 – (50000 × ₹ 10) = ₹ 8,00,000

Dr. **2. BANK ACCOUNT** *Cr.*

Particulars	₹	*Particulars*	₹
To Balance b/d	6,30,000	By 15% Red. Pref. Shareholders A/c	14,30,000
To 15% Red. Pref. Share Final Call A/c	2,60,000	By Balance c/d	15,85,000
To Investments	6,00,000		
To Equity Share Capital A/c	5,00,000		
To Securities Premium A/c	1,25,000		
To Equity Share Capital A/c	9,00,000		
	30,15,000		30,15,000

3. Securities Premium and Capital Reserve realised in cash can be utilized for bonus issue.
4. Plant Revaluation Reserve can not be utilized to issue bonus shares.
5. **AUTHORISED SHARE CAPITAL**

Particulars	₹
Nominal Value of Existing Equity Shares	45,00,000
Nominal Value of New Equity Shares	5,00,000
Add: Nominal Value of bonus shares issued to existing equity shareholders	10,00,000
Total Authorised Share Capital as on July 1, 2023 should be	60,00,000
Total Authorised Share Capital at present	58,00,000
Increase in Authorised Share Capital required by passing the necessary resolution at general body meeting of the company	2,00,000

ILLUSTRATION 8

Given below are the extracts of Balance Sheet of Tulsian Ltd.(Listed) as at 31st March 2023:

Particulars	₹
Authorised Capital	
13000, 15% Redeemable Preference Shares of ₹ 100 each	13,00,000
4,50,000 Equity shares of ₹ 10 each	45,00,000
Issued and Subscribed Capital	
13000, 15% Redeemable Preference Shares of ₹ 100 each, ₹ 80 per share paid up(issued on 1st April,2015)	10,40,000
4,50,000 Equity Shares of ₹ 10 each, ₹ 8 per share paid up	36,00,000

Plant Revaluation Reserve	5,05,000
General Reserve	9,20,000
Securities Premium (including ₹ 1,00,000 on issue of Shares against the purchase of business)	2,25,000
Profit & Loss Account	7,10,000
Current Liabilities	20,00,000
Property,Plant & Equipment and Intangible Assets	63,70,000
Non–Current Investments [Face value ₹ 10,00,000]	20,00,000
Bank Balance	6,30,000

On 1st April 2023, the Board of Directors decided to make a final call of ₹ 20 on Redeemable Preference Shares and to redeem the same at a premium of 10% on 1st June, 2023. The investments of the face value of ₹ 4,00,000 are sold at the market price which was 150% of the face value.

It is decided to issue sufficient number of Equity Shares of ₹ 10 each at a premium of 25% for the purpose of redemption. The company has to maintain a minimum balance of ₹ 5,00,000 in Bank Account and of ₹ 5,00,000 in the Profit & Loss Account. On 1st June,2023 all payments were made on redemption.

On 1st July 2023, the Board decided to issue fully paid bonus shares to the equity shareholders in the ratio of one for five after making final call on equity shares.

Required: Pass the necessary journal entries and prepare the Balance Sheet after giving effect to Board's decisions upto 1st July 2023. Also state the amount by which Authorised Capital is required to be increased by passing the necessary resolution at general body meeting of the company.

SOLUTION

JOURNAL OF TULSIAN LTD.

Date 2023	*Particulars*	*L.F.*	*Dr. (₹)*	*Cr. (₹)*
Apr 1	15% Red. Pref. Share Final Call A/c Dr.		2,60,000	
	To 15% Red. Pref. Share Capital A/c			2,60,000
	(Being the Final Call on Red. Pref. Shares)			
	Bank A/c Dr.		2,60,000	
	To 15% Red. Pref. Share Final Call A/c			2,60,000
	(Being the Final Call received on Red. Pref. Shares)			
	Bank A/c Dr.		6,00,000	
	Profit & Loss A/c Dr.		2,00,000	
	To Investments			8,00,000
	(Being the Investments of the face value of ₹ 4,00,000 sold at a loss of ₹ 2,00,000 being the difference between the book value and the sale proceeds) Book Value = ₹ 20,00,000 × ₹ 4,00,000/ ₹ 10,00,000 = ₹ 8,00,000 Sale Proceeds = ₹ 4,00,000 × 150/100 = ₹ 6,00,000]			

Date	Particulars		Dr. (₹)	Cr. (₹)
	Bank A/c	Dr.	6,25,000	
	To Equity Share Capital A/c			5,00,000
	To Securities Premium A/c			1,25,000
	(Being 50,000 Equity Shares of ₹ 10 each issued at 25% premium)			
	General Reserve A/c	Dr.	1,30,000	
	To Premium payable on Redemption A/c			1,30,000
	(Being the Premium payable on Redemption of **fully paid RPS** t/f to Premium payable on Redemption A/c)			
	General Reserve	Dr.	7,90,000	
	Profit & Loss A/c	Dr.	10,000	
	To Capital Redemption Reserve A/c			8,00,000
	(Being an amount equal to the nominal value of **fully paid RPS** redeemed out of divisible profits, t/f to Capital Redemption Reserve A/c)			
	15% Red. Pref. Share Capital A/c	Dr.	13,00,000	
	Premium payable on Redemption A/c	Dr.	1,30,000	
	To Red. Pref. Shareholders A/c			14,30,000
	(Being the amount due to **fully paid RPS** on redemption)			
Jun 1	Red. Pref. Shareholders A/c	Dr.	14,30,000	
	To Bank A/c			14,30,000
	(Being the payment made to all **fully paid RPS**)			
Jul 1	Equity Share Final Call A/c	Dr.	9,00,000	
	To Equity Share Capital A/c			9,00,000
	(Being the Final Call made due on Equity Shares)			
	Bank A/c	Dr.	9,00,000	
	To Equity Share Final Call A/c			9,00,000
	(Being the Final Call received on Equity Shares)			
	Capital Redemption Reserve A/c	Dr.	8,00,000	
	Securities Premium A/c	Dr.	2,00,000	
	To Bonus to Equity Shareholders' A/c			10,00,000
	(Being the Bonus to Equity Shareholders declared for issuing fully paid Shares in the ratio of 1 for 5. Hence no. of Bonus Shares 100000 i.e.(500000 × 1/5)]			
	Bonus to Equity Shareholders' A/c	Dr.	10,00,000	
	To Equity Share Capital A/c			10,00,000
	(Being 100000 Equity Shares of ₹ 10 each fully paid issued as Bonus Shares)			

BALANCE SHEET OF TULSIAN LTD. AS AT 1ST JULY 2023 (AFTER BONUS ISSUE)

Particulars	*Notes*	₹
I. EQUITY AND LIABILITIES		
(1) Shareholders' Funds		
(a) Share Capital	1	60,00,000
(b) Reserves and Surplus	2	11,55,000
(2) Non–Current Liabilities		
(3) Current Liabilities		20,00,000
Total		**91,55,000**
II. ASSETS		
(1) Non–Current Assets		
Property,Plant & Equipment and Intangible Assets		63,70,000
Non–Current Investments (Face Value ₹ 6,00,000)		12,00,000
(2) Current Assets		
Cash & Cash Equivalents		15,85,000
Total		**91,55,000**

Notes to Accounts:

Particulars	₹
1. Share Capital	
6,00,000, Equity Share Capital of ₹ 10 each fully paid up (Out of above, 1,00,000 equity shares @ ₹ 10 each were issued by way of bonus)	60,00,000
	60,00,000
2. Reserves And Surplus	
Securities Premium (including ₹ 1,00,000 on issue of Shares against the purchase of business)	1,50,000
Plant Revaluation Reserve	5,05,000
General Reserve	–
Profit & Loss Account	5,00,000
	11,55,000

Working Notes:

1. Sale Proceeds of Investments = ₹ 4,00,000 × 150/100 = ₹ 6,00,000
2. Book Value of Investments = ₹ 20,00,000 × 40% = ₹ 8,00,000
3. Loss on Sale of Investments = ₹ 6,00,000 – ₹ 8,00,000 = ₹ 2,00,000

4. Calculate Minimum No. of New Shares to comply with Legal Condition of Sec 55

All figures (except in row E & F) are in lakh.

A. Nominal Value of RPS	₹ 13.00
B. Less: Divisible Profits available for redemption(say)	
General Reserve	₹ 9.20
+Profit & Loss A/c	₹ 7.10
-Premium Payable on redemption	(₹ 1.30)
-Minimum Balance to be kept(if so desired)	(₹ 5.00)
-Loss on sale of Investments (if unadjusted)	(₹ 2.00)
Total Divisible Profits available for redemption	₹ 8.00
C. Less: Nominal Value of New Shares(not Debentures),if any,issued for Redemption	0
D. Minimum Nominal Value of Fresh issue of Shares to be issued [A-B-C]	₹ 5.00
E. Nominal Value of a New Share	₹ 10
F. Minimum No. of New Shares to comply with legal condition of Sec 55 [D/E]	50,000

All figures (except in row D & E) are in lakh.

5. Calculate Minimum No. of New Shares to comply with Liquidity Condition [₹ in lakh]

A. Total Funds required for Redemption[Nominal Value of RPS + Premium Payable on redemption]		₹ 14.30
B. Less: Funds available for Redemption (say)		
Cash & Bank Balance given	₹ 6.30	
+Final Call on Red. Pref. Shares	₹ 2.60	
+ Sale Proceeds of Investments	₹ 6.00	
+ Issue Proceeds of **New Shares if any,issued**	0	
+ Issue Proceeds of **New Debentures if any,issued**	0	
-Minimum Balance to be retained	(₹ 5.00)	₹ 9.90
C. Minimum Issue Proceeds of Fresh issue of Shares to be issued [A-B]		₹ 4.40
D. Issue Price of a New Share		₹ 12.50
E. Minimum No. of New Shares to comply with Liquidity condition [C/D]		35,200

6. TAKE HIGHER No. of New Shares out of 50000 & 35200. Hence, 50000 New Shares are required to be issued to comply with both the conditions.
7. Securities Premium and Capital Reserve realised in cash can be utilized for bonus issue.
8. Plant Revaluation Reserve can not be utilized to issue bonus shares.
9. **AUTHORISED SHARE CAPITAL**

Particulars	₹
Nominal Value of Existing Equity Shares	45,00,000
Nominal Value of New Equity Shares	5,00,000

Add: Nominal Value of bonus shares issued to existing equity shareholders	10,00,000
Total Authorised Share Capital as on July 1, 2023 should be	60,00,000
Total Authorised Share Capital at present	58,00,000
Increase in Authorised Share Capital required by passing the necessary resolution at general body meeting of the company	2,00,000

ILLUSTRATION 9

Given below are the extracts of Balance Sheet of Tulsian Ltd.(Listed) as at 31st March 2023:

Particulars	₹
Authorised Capital	
13000, 15% Redeemable Preference Shares of ₹ 100 each	13,00,000
4,50,000 Equity shares of ₹ 10 each	45,00,000
Issued and Subscribed Capital	
13000, 15% Redeemable Preference Shares of ₹ 100 each, ₹ 80 per share paid up (issued on 1st April,2015)	10,40,000
4,50,000 Equity Shares of ₹ 10 each, ₹ 8 per share paid up	36,00,000
Plant Revaluation Reserve	5,05,000
General Reserve	9,20,000
Securities Premium (including ₹ 1,00,000 on issue of Shares against the purchase of business)	2,25,000
Profit & Loss Account	7,10,000
Current Liabilities	20,00,000
Property,Plant & Equipment and Intangible Assets	63,70,000
Non–Current Investments [Face value ₹ 10,00,000]	20,00,000
Bank Balance	6,30,000

On 1st April 2023, the Board of Directors decided to make a final call of ₹ 20 on Redeemable Preference Shares and to redeem the same at a premium of 10% on 1st June, 2023. The investments of the face value of ₹ 4,00,000 are sold at the market price which was 150% of the face value. The final call was received from all except from holders of 200 Redeemable Preference Shares.

It is decided to issue sufficient number of Equity Shares of ₹ 10 each at a premium of 25% for the purpose of redemption. The company has to maintain a minimum balance of ₹ 5,00,000 in Bank Account and of ₹ 5,00,000 in the Profit & Loss Account. On 1st June,2023 all payments were made on redemption except to holders of 50 shares who could not be traced.

On 1st July 2023, the Board decided to issue fully paid bonus shares to the equity shareholders in the ratio of one for five after making final call on equity shares.

Required: Pass the necessary journal entries and prepare the Balance Sheet after giving effect to Board's decisions upto 1st July 2023. Also state the amount by which Authorised Capital is required to be increased by passing the necessary resolution at general body meeting of the company.

SOLUTION

JOURNAL OF TULSIAN LTD.

Date 2023	Particulars	L.F.	Dr. (₹)	Cr. (₹)
Apr 1	15% Red. Pref. Share Final Call A/c Dr.		2,60,000	
	To 15% Red. Pref. Share Capital A/c			2,60,000
	(Being the Final Call made on Red. Pref. Shares)			
	Bank A/c Dr.		2,56,000	
	Calls in–arrears A/c Dr		4,000	
	To 15% Red. Pref. Share Final Call A/c			2,60,000
	(Being the Final Call received on Red. Pref. Shares except from holders of 200 Shares)			
	Bank A/c Dr.		6,00,000	
	Profit & Loss A/c Dr.		2,00,000	
	To Investments			8,00,000
	(Being the Investments of the face value of ₹ 4,00,000 sold at a loss of ₹ 2,00,000 being the difference between the book value and the sale proceeds) Book Value = ₹ 20,00,000 × ₹ 4,00,000/ ₹ 10,00,000 = ₹ 8,00,000 Sale Proceeds = ₹ 4,00,000 × 150/100 = ₹ 6,00,000]			
	Bank A/c Dr.		6,25,000	
	To Equity Share Capital A/c			5,00,000
	To Securities Premium A/c			1,25,000
	(Being 50,000 Equity Shares of ₹ 10 each issued at 25% premium)			
	General Reserve A/c Dr.		1,30,000	
	To Premium payable on Redemption A/c			1,28,000
	To Preference Shares Redemption Suspense A/c			2,000
	(Being the Premium payable on Redemption of **fully paid RPS** t/f to Premium payable on Redemption A/c and Premium payable on Redemption of partly paid RPS t/f to Preference Shares Redemption Suspense A/c)			
	General Reserve Dr.		7,90,000	
	Profit & Loss A/c Dr.		10,000	
	To Capital Redemption Reserve A/c			7,80,000
	To Preference Shares Redemption Suspense A/c			20,000
	(Being an amount equal to the nominal value of **fully paid RPS** redeemed out of divisible profits, t/f to Capital Redemption Reserve A/c and an amount equal to the nominal value of partly paid Red. Pref. Shares to be redeemed out of divisible profits, t/f to Preference Shares Redemption Suspense A/c)			

Date	Particulars		L.F.	Dr. (₹)	Cr. (₹)
	15% Red. Pref. Share Capital A/c	Dr.		12,80,000	
	Premium payable on Redemption A/c	Dr.		1,28,000	
	To Red. Pref. Shareholders A/c				14,08,000
	(Being the amount due to **fully paid RPS** on redemption)				
Jun 1	Red. Pref. Shareholders A/c	Dr.		14,02,500	
	To Bank A/c				14,02,500
	(Being the payment made to all **fully paid RPS** except to the holders of 50 shares)				
Jul 1	Equity Share Final Call A/c	Dr.		9,00,000	
	To Equity Share Capital A/c				9,00,000
	(Being the Final Call made due on Equity Shares)				
	Bank A/c	Dr.		9,00,000	
	To Equity Share Final Call A/c				9,00,000
	(Being the Final Call received on Equity Shares)				
	Capital Redemption Reserve A/c	Dr.		7,80,000	
	Securities Premium A/c	Dr.		2,20,000	
	To Bonus to Equity Shareholders' A/c				10,00,000
	(Being the Bonus to Equity Shareholders declared for issuing fully paid Shares in the ratio of 1 for 5. Hence no. of Bonus Shares 100000 i.e.(500000 × 1/5)]				
	Bonus to Equity Shareholders' A/c	Dr.		10,00,000	
	To Equity Share Capital A/c				10,00,000
	(Being 100000 Equity Shares of ₹ 10 each fully paid issued as Bonus Shares)				

BALANCE SHEET OF TULSIAN LTD. AS AT 1ST JULY 2023 (AFTER BONUS ISSUE)

Particulars		**Notes**	₹
I. EQUITY AND LIABILITIES			
(1) Shareholders' Funds			
(a) Share Capital		1	60,16,000
(b) Reserves and Surplus		2	11,35,000
(2) Non–Current Liabilities			
(3) Current Liabilities	20,00,000		
Preference Shares Redemption Suspense A/c	22,000		
Red. Pref. Shareholders A/c	5,500		20,27,500
Total			**91,78,500**
II. ASSETS			
(1) Non–Current Assets			
Property, Plant & Equipment and Intangible Assets			63,70,000

	Non–Current Investments (Face Value ₹ 6,00,000)	12,00,000
(2)	**Current Assets**	
	Cash & Cash Equivalents	16,08,500
	Total	**91,78,500**

Notes to Accounts:

Particulars		₹
1. Share Capital		
200 ,15% Redeemable Preference Shares of ₹ 100 each	20,000	
Less: Calls in–arrears @ ₹ 20 Per Share	4,000	16,000
6,00,000, Equity Share Capital of ₹ 10 each fully paid up		60,00,000
(Out of above, 1,00,000 equity shares @ ₹ 10 each were issued by way of bonus)		
		60,16,000
2. Reserves And Surplus		
Securities Premium (including ₹ 1,00,000 on issue of Shares against the purchase of business)		1,30,000
Plant Revaluation Reserve		5,05,000
General Reserve		
Profit & Loss Account		5,00,000
		11,35,000

Working Notes:

1. Sale Proceeds of Investments = ₹ 4,00,000 × 150/100 = ₹ 6,00,000
2. Book Value of Investments = ₹ 20,00,000 × 40% = ₹ 8,00,000
3. Loss on Sale of Investments = ₹ 6,00,000 – ₹ 8,00,000 = ₹ 2,00,000

4. Calculate Minimum No. of New Shares to comply with Legal Condition of Sec 55

All figures (except in row E & F) are in lakh.

A. Nominal Value of RPS	₹ 13.00
B. Less: Divisible Profits available for redemption(say)	
General Reserve	₹ 9.20
+Profit & Loss A/c	₹ 7.10
-Premium Payable on redemption	(₹ 1.30)
-Minimum Balance to be kept(if so desired)	(₹ 5.00)
-Loss on sale of Investments (if unadjusted)	(₹ 2.00)
Total Divisible Profits available for redemption	₹ 8.00
C. Less: Nominal Value of New Shares(not Debentures),if any,issued for Redemption	0
D. Minimum Nominal Value of Fresh issue of Shares to be issued [A-B-C]	₹ 5.00
E. Nominal Value of a New Share	₹ 10
F. Minimum No. of New Shares to comply with legal condition of Sec 55 [D/E]	50,000

All figures (except in row D &E) are in lakh.

5. Calculate Minimum No. of New Shares to comply with Liquidity Condition [₹ in lakh]

A. Total Funds required for Redemption[Nominal Value of RPS + Premium Payable on redemption]		₹ 14.30
B. Less: Funds available for Redemption (say)		
Cash & Bank Balance given	₹ 6.30	
+Final Call on Red. Pref. Shares	₹ 2.56	
+ Sale Proceeds of Investments	₹ 6.00	
+ Issue Proceeds of **New Shares if any,issued**	0	
+ Issue Proceeds of **New Debentures if any,issued**	0	
-Minimum Balance to be retained	(₹ 5.00)	₹ 9.86
C. Minimum Issue Proceeds of Fresh issue of Shares to be issued [A-B]		₹ 4.44
D. Issue Price of a New Share		₹ 12.50
E. Minimum No. of New Shares to comply with Liquidity condition [C/D]		35,520

6. TAKE HIGHER No. of New Shares out of 50000 & 35520. Hence, 50000 New Shares are required to be issued to comply with both the conditions.
7. Securities Premium and Capital Reserve realised in cash can be utilized for bonus issue.
8. Plant Revaluation Reserve can not be utilized to issue bonus shares.
9. **AUTHORISED SHARE CAPITAL**

Particulars	₹
Nominal Value of Existing Equity Shares	45,00,000
Nominal Value of New Equity Shares	5,00,000
Add: Nominal Value of bonus shares issued to existing equity shareholders	10,00,000
Nominal Value of 200 ,15% Redeemable Preference Shares of ₹ 100 each	20,000
Total Authorised Share Capital as on July 1, 2023 should be	60,20,000
Total Authorised Share Capital at present	58,00,000
Increase in Authorised Share Capital required by passing the necessary resolution at general body meeting of the company	2,20,000

ILLUSTRATION 10

Given below are the extracts of Balance Sheet of BHARAT TUSHAR Ltd.(Listed) as at 31st March 2023:

Particulars	₹
Authorised Capital	
13000, 15% Redeemable Preference Shares of ₹ 100 each	13,00,000
4,50,000 Equity shares of ₹ 10 each	45,00,000
Issued and Subscribed Capital	
13000, 15% Redeemable Preference Shares of ₹ 100 each, ₹ 80 per share paid up(issued on 1st April,2015)	10,40,000
4,50,000 Equity Shares of ₹ 10 each, ₹ 8 per share paid up	36,00,000
Plant Revaluation Reserve	4,95,000
General Reserve	9,20,000

Securities Premium (including ₹ 1,00,000 on issue of Shares against the purchase of business)	2,25,000
Profit & Loss Account	7,20,000
12% Partly Convertible Debentures @ ₹ 100 each [20% of 12% Debentures are convertible into equity shares of ₹ 10 each at ₹ 15 each fully paid on 1st Oct 2023].	7,50,000
Current Liabilities	12,50,000
Property,Plant & Equipment and Intangible Assets	63,70,000
Non–Current Investments [Face value ₹ 10,00,000]	20,00,000
Bank Balance	6,30,000

On 1st April 2023, the Board of Directors decided to make a final call of ₹ 20 on Redeemable Preference Shares and to redeem the same at a premium of 10% on 1st June, 2023. The investments of the face value of ₹ 4,00,000 are sold at the market price which was 150% of the face value. The final call was received from all except from holders of 200 Redeemable Preference Shares.

It is decided to issue 880, 15% Debentures of ₹ 100 each at par, 100, 12% Pref. Shares of ₹ 100 each at a premium of 20% and sufficient number of Equity Shares of ₹ 10 each at a premium of 25% for the purpose of redemption. The company has to maintain a minimum balance of ₹ 5,00,000 in Bank Account and of ₹ 5,00,000 in the Profit & Loss Account. On 1st June,2023 all payments were made on redemption except to holders of 50 shares who could not be traced.

On 1st July 2023, the Board decided to issue fully paid bonus shares to the equity shareholders in the ratio of one for five after making final call on equity shares.

Required: Pass the necessary journal entries and prepare the Balance Sheet after giving effect to Board's decisions upto 1st July 2023. Also state the amount by which Authorised Capital is required to be increased by passing the necessary resolution at general body meeting of the company.

SOLUTION

JOURNAL OF BHARAT TUSHAR LTD.

Date 2023	*Particulars*		*L.F.*	*Dr. (₹)*	*Cr. (₹)*
Apr 1	15% Red. Pref. Share Final Call A/c	Dr.		2,60,000	
	To 15% Red. Pref. Share Capital A/c				2,60,000
	(Being the Final Call made on Red. Pref. Shares)				
	Bank A/c	Dr.		2,56,000	
	Calls in–arrears A/c	Dr		4,000	
	To 15% Red. Pref. Share Final Call A/c				2,60,000
	(Being the Final Call received on Red. Pref. Shares except from holders of 200 Shares)				
	Bank A/c	Dr.		6,00,000	
	Profit & Loss A/c	Dr.		2,00,000	
	To Investments				8,00,000

	(Being the Investments of the face value of ₹ 4,00,000 sold at a loss of ₹ 2,00,000 being the difference between the book value and the sale proceeds) Book Value = ₹ 20,00,000 × ₹ 4,00,000/ ₹ 10,00,000 = ₹ 8,00,000 Sale Proceeds = ₹ 4,00,000 × 150/100 = ₹ 6,00,000]		
	Bank A/c Dr. To 15% Debentures Application and Allotment A/c (Application money received for 880 Debentures of ₹ 100 each)	88,000	 88,000
	15% Debentures Application and Allotment A/c Dr. To 15% Debentures Account (Allotment of 880 Debentures of ₹ 100 each)	88,000	 88,000
	Bank A/c Dr. To 12% Pref. Share Application and Allotment A/c (Application money received for 100 12% Pref. shares of ₹ 100 each at 20% premium)	12,000	 12,000
	12% Pref. Share Application and Allotment A/c Dr. To 12% Pref. Share Capital Account To Securities Premium A/c (Allotment of 100 Pref. shares of ₹ 100 each at 20% premium.)	12,000	 10,000 2,000
	Bank A/c Dr. To Equity Share Application and Allotment A/c (Application money received for 50,000 Equity Shares of ₹ 10 each issued at 25% premium)	6,25,000	 6,25,000
	Equity Share Application and Allotment A/c Dr. To Equity Share Capital A/c To Securities Premium A/c (Allotment of 50,000 Equity Shares of ₹ 10 each issued at 25% premium)	6,25,000	 5,00,000 1,25,000
	General Reserve A/c Dr. To Premium payable on Redemption A/c To Preference Shares Redemption Suspense A/c (Being the Premium payable on Redemption of **fully paid RPS** t/f to Premium payable on Redemption A/c and Premium payable on Redemption of partly paid RPS t/f to Preference Shares Redemption Suspense A/c)	1,30,000	 1,28,000 2,000
	General Reserve Dr. Profit & Loss A/c Dr. To Capital Redemption Reserve A/c	7,90,000 10,000	 7,80,000

	To Preference Shares Redemption Suspense A/c (Being an amount equal to the nominal value of **fully paid RPS** redeemed out of divisible profits, t/f to Capital Redemption Reserve A/c and an amount equal to the nominal value of partly paid Red. Pref. Shares to be redeemed out of divisible profits, t/f to Preference Shares Redemption Suspense A/c)		20,000
	15% Red. Pref. Share Capital A/c Dr. Premium payable on Redemption A/c Dr. To Red. Pref. Shareholders A/c (Being the amount due to **fully paid RPS** on redemption)	12,80,000 1,28,000	14,08,000
Jun 1	Red. Pref. Shareholders A/c Dr. To Bank A/c (Being the payment made to all **fully paid RPS** except to the holders of 50 shares)	14,02,500	14,02,500
Jul 1	Equity Share Final Call A/c Dr. To Equity Share Capital A/c (Being the Final Call made due on Equity Shares)	9,00,000	9,00,000
	Bank A/c Dr. To Equity Share Final Call A/c (Being the Final Call received on Equity Shares)	9,00,000	9,00,000
	Capital Redemption Reserve A/c Dr. Securities Premium A/c Dr. To Bonus to Equity Shareholders' A/c To Bonus to PCD A/c (Being the Bonus to Equity Shareholders declared for issuing fully paid Shares in the ratio of 1 for 5. Hence no. of Bonus Shares 102000 i.e.(500000 × 1/5) + (10000 × 1/5)]	7,80,000 2,40,000	10,00,000 20,000
	Bonus to Equity Shareholders' A/c Dr. To Equity Share Capital A/c (Being 100000 Equity Shares of ₹ 10 each fully paid issued as Bonus Shares)	10,00,000	10,00,000

BALANCE SHEET OF BHARAT TUSHAR LTD. AS AT 1ST JULY 2023 (AFTER BONUS ISSUE)

Particulars	*Notes*	₹
I. EQUITY AND LIABILITIES		
(1) Shareholders' Funds		
(a) Share Capital	1	60,26,000
(b) Reserves and Surplus	2	11,37,000
(2) Non–Current Liabilities[Long-term Borrowings].		8,38,000

(3) Current Liabilities	12,50,000	
Preference Shares Redemption Suspense A/c	22,000	
Red. Pref. Shareholders A/c	5,500	12,77,500
Total		**92,78,500**
II. ASSETS		
(1) Non–Current Assets		
Property,Plant & Equipment and Intangible Assets		63,70,000
Non–Current Investments (Face Value ₹ 6,00,000)		12,00,000
(2) Current Assets		
Cash & Cash Equivalents		17,08,500
Total		**92,78,500**

Notes to Accounts:

Particulars		₹
1. Share Capital		
200 ,15% Redeemable Preference Shares of ₹ 100 each	20,000	
Less: Calls in–arrears @ ₹ 20 Per Share	4,000	16,000
100 ,12% Redeemable Preference Shares of ₹ 100 each		10,000
6,00,000, Equity Share Capital of ₹ 10 each fully paid up (Out of above, 1,00,000 equity shares @ ₹ 10 each were issued by way of bonus)		60,00,000
		60,26,000
2. Reserves And Surplus		
Securities Premium (including ₹ 1,00,000 on issue of Shares against the purchase of business)		1,12,000
Plant Revaluation Reserve		4,95,000
Profit & Loss Account		5,10,000
Bonus to PCD A/c		20,000
		11,37,000
3. Long-term Borrowings		
12% Partly Convertible Debentures of ₹ 100 each [20% of 12% Debentures are convertible into equity shares of ₹ 10 each fully paid on 1st Oct 2023		7,50,000
15% Debentures of ₹ 100 each		88,000
		8,38,000

Working Notes:

1. Sale Proceeds of Investments = ₹ 4,00,000 × 150/100 = ₹ 6,00,000
2. Book Value of Investments = ₹ 20,00,000 × 40% = ₹ 8,00,000
3. Loss on Sale of Investments = ₹ 6,00,000 – ₹ 8,00,000 = ₹ 2,00,000

4. Calculate Minimum No. of New Shares to comply with Legal Condition of Sec 55

All figures (except in row E & F) are in lakh.

A. Nominal Value of RPS	₹ 13.00
B. Less: Divisible Profits available for redemption(say)	
General Reserve	₹ 9.20
+Profit & Loss A/c	₹ 7.20
-Premium Payable on redemption	(₹ 1.30)
-Minimum Balance to be kept(if so desired)	(₹ 5.00)
-Loss on sale of Investments (if unadjusted)	(₹ 2.00)
Total Divisible Profits available for redemption	₹ 8.10
C. Less: Nominal Value of New Shares(not Debentures),if any,issued for Redemption	₹ 0.10
D. Minimum Nominal Value of Fresh issue of Shares to be issued [A-B-C]	₹5.00
E. Nominal Value of a New Share	₹ 10
F. Minimum No. of New Shares to comply with legal condition of Sec 55 [D/E]	50,000

5. Calculate Minimum No. of New Shares to comply with Liquidity Condition

All figures (except in row D & E) are in lakh.

A. Total Funds required for Redemption[Nominal Value of RPS + Premium Payable on redemption]		₹ 14.30
B. Less: Funds available for Redemption (say)		
Cash & Bank Balance given	₹ 6.30	
+Final Call on Red. Pref. Shares	₹ 2.56	
+ Sale Proceeds of Investments	₹ 6.00	
+ Issue Proceeds of **New Shares if any,issued**	₹ 0.12	
+ Issue Proceeds of **New Debentures if any,issued**	₹ 0.88	
-Minimum Balance to be retained	(₹ 5.00)	₹ 8.86
C. Minimum Issue Proceeds of Fresh issue of Shares to be issued [A-B]		₹ 5.44
D. Issue Price of a New Share		₹ 12.50
E. Minimum No. of New Shares to comply with Liquidity condition [C/D]		43,520

6. TAKE HIGHER No. of New Shares out of 50000 & 43520. Hence, 50000 New Shares are required to be issued to comply with both the conditions.
7. Securities Premium and Capital Reserve realised in cash can be utilized for bonus issue.
8. Plant Revaluation Reserve can not be utilized to issue bonus shares.
9. As per SEBI guidelines,no–company can issue bonus shares to its members without extending similar benefit to convertible debentures holders. Pending such conversion, Bonus Shares in proportion to such convertible part of FCDs/PCDs should be reserved. The shares so reserved may be issued at the time of conversion(s) of such debentures on the same terms on which the bonus issues were made.
10. Bonus to fully paid equity shares=[(500000 × 1/5) × ₹ 10] = ₹ 10,00,000.

    No of equity shares to be issued on conversion of Debentures = [750000 × 20%]/₹ 15]=10000

Bonus for Partly Convertible Debentures = [(10000 × 1/5 × ₹ 10] = ₹ 20,000

Total amount of Bonus = ₹ 10,20,000

(11) AUTHORISED SHARE CAPITAL

Particulars	₹
Nominal Value of Existing Equity Shares	45,00,000
Nominal Value of New Equity Shares	5,00,000
Nominal Value of Pref. Equity Shares	10,000
Add: Nominal Value of bonus shares issued to existing equity shareholders	10,00,000
Add: Nominal Value of Shares required for conversion of debentures	1,00,000
Add: Nominal Value of Bonus shares to be issued to debentureholders after conversion	20,000
Nominal Value of 200 ,15% Redeemable Preference Shares of ₹ 100 each	20,000
Total Authorised Share Capital as on July 1, 2023 should be	61,50,000
Total Authorised Share Capital at present	58,00,000
Increase in Authorised Share Capital required by passing the necessary resolution at general body meeting of the company	3,50,000

SOLVED PROBLEMS

PROBLEM 1

Given below are the extracts of Balance Sheet of X Ltd (listed company)as at 31st March, 2023:

Particulars	₹
650 15% Red. Pref. Shares of ₹ 100 each (redeemable at a premium of 7½% on April 1, 2023) (issued on April 1,2015)	65,000
4,500 Equity Shares of ₹ 50 each	2,25,000
Securities Premium	5,000
Profit & Loss A/c	52,875
Trade Payables	51,500
Property,Plant,Equipment and Intangible Assets	3,45,000
Non–Current Investments	18,500
Balance at Bank	35,875

In order to facilitate the redemption of the Preference Shares, the Company decided:

(a) to sell all the investments for ₹ 16,000,

(b) to finance part of the redemption from company funds, subject to leaving a balance of ₹ 12,000 in the Profit and Loss Account, and

(c) to issue sufficient Equity Shares of ₹ 50 cash at a premium of ₹ 13 per share to raise the balance of funds required.

The Preference Shares were redeemed on the due date and the issue of Equity Shares was fully subscribed. Pass the necessary Journal entries to record the above transactions.

SOLUTION

JOURNAL

Date	*Particulars*		*L.F.*	*Dr. (₹)*	*Cr. (₹)*
	Bank A/c	Dr.		16,000	
	Profit & Loss A/c	Dr.		2,500	
	To Investments A/c				18,500
	(Sale of investments for ₹ 16,000–loss on sale debited to Profit & Loss A/c)				
	Bank A/c	Dr.		39,690	
	To Equity Share Application and Allotment A/c				39,690
	(Application money received for 630 equity shares of ₹ 50 each at a premium of ₹ 13 per share)				
	Equity Share Application and Allotment A/c	Dr.		39,690	
	To Equity Share Capital Account				31,500
	To Securities Premium A/c				8,190
	(Allotment of 630 equity shares of ₹ 50 each at a premium ₹ 13 per share vide Board Resolution dated...)				
	Profit & Loss A/c	Dr.		38,375	
	To Capital Redemption Reserve A/c				33,500
	To Premium on Redemption A/c				4,875
	(T/f out of profits an amount equal to nominal value of shares redeemed other wise than out of proceeds of the fresh issue & Premium payable on redemption of preference shares charged to Profit & Loss A/c)				
	15% Red. Preference Share Capital A/c	Dr.		65,000	
	Premium on Redemption A/c	Dr.		4,875	
	To Preference Shares holders' A/c				69,875
	(Amount payable on redemption of 650 transferred to Preference Shares Holders A/c)				
	Preference Shareholders' A/c	Dr.		69,875	
	To Bank A/c				69,875
	(Payment to preference shareholders on redemption at a premium of 7½%).				

Working Notes:

1. Divisible Profits to be t/f to CRR = Profit & Loss A/c – Loss on Investments – Premium on RPS – Amount to be retained = ₹ 52,875 – ₹ 2,500 – ₹ 4,875 – ₹ 12,000 = ₹ 33,500
2. Nominal Amount of Equity Shares to be issued (₹ 65,000 – ₹ 33,500) = ₹ 31,500

Dr. **3. BANK ACCOUNT** *Cr.*

Particulars	₹	*Particulars*	₹
To Balance b/d	35,875	By Preference Shares holders A/c	69,875
To Investments	16,000	By Balance c/d	21,690
To Share Application & Allotment A/c	39,690		
	91,565		91,565

PROBLEM 2

The Summarized Balance Sheet of Clean Ltd. as on 31st March, 2023 is as follows:

Particulars	₹
EQUITY AND LIABILITIES	
1. Shareholder's funds:	
(a) Share Capital	5,80,000
(b) Reserves and Surplus	96,000
2. Current Liabilities:	
Trade Payables	1,13,000
Total	7,89,000
ASSETS:	
1. Non-Current Assets	
(a) Property, Plant and Equipment	
Tangible Assets	6,90,000
(b) Non-current investments	37,000
2. Current Assets	
Cash and cash equivalents (Bank)	62,000
Total	7,89,000

The Share Capital of the company consists of ₹ 50 each Equity shares of ₹ 4,50,000 and ₹ 100 each 8% Redeemable Preference Shares of ₹ 1,30,000 (issued on 1.4.2017).Reserves and Surplus comprises statement of profit and loss only. In order to facilitate the redemption of preference shares at a premium of 10%, the Company decided:

(a) to sell all the investments for ₹ 30,000

(b) to finance part of redemption from company funds, subject to, leaving a Bank balance of ₹ 24,000.

(c) to issue minimum equity shares of ₹ 50 each at a premium of ₹ 10 per share to raise the balance of funds required.

You are required to

(1) Pass Journal Entries to record the above transactions.

(2) Prepare Balance Sheet after completion of the above transactions.

SOLUTION

Journal

Date	Particulars		Dr. (₹)	Cr. (₹)
1	Bank A/c	Dr.	75,000	
	To Share Application A/c			75,000
	(For application money received on 1,250 shares @ ₹ 60 per share)			
2	Share Application A/c	Dr.	75,000	
	To Equity Share Capital A/c			62,500
	To Securities Premium A/c			12,500
	(For disposition of application money received)			
3	Preference Share Capital A/c	Dr.	1,30,000	
	Premium on Redemption of Preference Shares A/c	Dr.	13,000	
	To Preference Shareholders A/c			1,43,000
	(For amount payable on redemption of preference shares)			
4	Profit and Loss A/c	Dr.	13,000	
	To Premium on Redemption of Preference Shares A/c			13,000
	(For writing off premium on redemption out of profits)			
5	Bank A/c	Dr.	30,000	
	Profit and Loss A/c (loss on sale) A/c	Dr.	7,000	
	To Investment A/c			37,000
	(For sale of investments at a loss of ₹ 3,500)			
6	Preference Shareholders A/c	Dr.	1,43,000	
	To Bank			1,43,000
	(Being amount paid to Preference shareholders)			
	Profit and Loss A/c	Dr.	67,500	
	To Capital Redemption Reserve A/c			67,500
	(For transfer to CRR out of divisible profits an amount equivalent to excess of nominal value of preference shares over proceeds (face value of equity shares) i.e., ₹ 1,30,000 – ₹ 62,500)			

Balance Sheet of Clean Ltd. (after redemption)

Particulars	Notes No.	₹
EQUITY AND LIABILITIES		
1. Shareholder's funds:		
(a) Share Capital	1	5,12,500
(b) Reserves and Surplus	2	88,500

2. Current Liabilities:		
Trade Payables		1,13,000
Total		7,14,000
ASSETS:		
1. Non-Current Assets		
(a) Property, Plant and Equipment		
Tangible Assets		6,90,000
2. Current Assets		
Cash and cash equivalents (Bank)	3	24,000
Total		7,14,000

Notes to accounts

	Particulars	₹
1.	Share Capital	
	Equity share capital ₹ (4,50,000 + 62,500)	5,12,500
2.	Reserves and Surplus	
	Capital Redemption Reserve	67,500
	Profit and Loss Account ₹ (96,000 – 13,000 – 7,000 – 67,500)	8,500
	Security Premium	12,500
		88,500
3.	Cash and cash equivalents	
	Balances with banks ₹ (62,000 + 75,000 + 30,000 – 1,43,000)	24,000

Working Note: Calculation of Number of Shares:

	₹
Amount payable on redemption (1,30,000 + 10% Premium)	1,43,000
Less: Sale price of investment	(30,000)
	1,13,000
Less: Available bank balance (62,000 – 24,000)	(38,000)
Funds required from fresh issue	75,000
No. of shares = 75,000/60	= 1,250 shares

PROBLEM 3

Given below are the extracts of Balance Sheet of X Ltd (listed company)as at 31st March, 2023:

Particulars	₹	₹
20,000 12% preference shares of ₹ 50 each fully called–up (issued on April 1,2015)	10,00,000	
Less: Calls unpaid @ ₹ 10 per share	20,000	9,80,000
1,00,000 equity shares of ₹ 10 each; ₹ 7.50 per share called–up	7,50,000	
Less: Calls unpaid	7,500	7,42,500
Securities Premium		50,000

General reserve		6,00,000
Calls in advance (final call on equity shares)		2,500
Property,Plant,Equipment and Intangible Assets		12,25,000
Non–Current Investment		2,00,000
Cash and bank balance		9,50,000

On 1st April, 2023 the Board of directors decide that:

(a) The fully paid preference shares are to be redeemed at a premium of 5% and for that purpose 50,000 equity shares of ₹ 10 each are to be issued at par.

(b) The 1,000 equity shares owned by A, an existing shareholder, who has failed to pay the allotment money and the 1st call money @ ₹ 2.50 each share are to be forfeited in the month of June.

(c) The final call of ₹ 2.50 per shares is to be made in the month of July.

All the above decisions are duly complied with according to the time schedule. The amount due on the issue of fresh equity share and on final call are also duly received except from B who had failed to pay the 1st call money for his 1,000 shares holding, has again failed to pay the final call also. These shares of B have been forfeited, in the month of August. Of the total shares forfeited, 1,500 shares are sold to X in September, credited as fully paid for ₹ 9 per share, the whole of A's shares being included. Pass the necessary journal entries.

SOLUTION

JOURNAL

Date	Particulars		L.F.	Dr. (₹)	Cr. (₹)
1.4.2023	Bank A/c	Dr.		5,00,000	
	To Equity Share Application & Allotment A/c				5,00,000
	(Being the application money received)				
1.4.2023	Equity Share Application & Allotment A/c	Dr.		5,00,000	
	To Equity Share Capital A/c				5,00,000
	(Being the Issue of equity shares)				
1.4.2023	General Reserve A/c	Dr.		50,000	
	To Premium on Redemption of Pref. Shares A/c				45,000
	To Pref. Share Redemption Suspense A/c				5,000
	(Being the securities Premium transferred)				
1.4.2023	General Reserve A/c	Dr.		5,00,000	
	To Capital Redemption Reserve A/c				4,00,000
	To Pref. Share Redemption Suspense A/c				1,00,000
	(Being the t/f of the required amount from GR A/c)				
1.4.2023	Pref. Share Capital A/c	Dr.		9,00,000	
	Premium on Redemption of Pref. Shares A/c	Dr.		45,000	
	To Pref. Shareholders' A/c				9,45,000
	(Being the amount payable to fully paid RPS)				

1.4.2023	Pref. Shareholders' A/c Dr.		9,45,000	
	To Bank A/c			9,45,000
	(Being the amount paid to Pref. Shareholders)			
1.6.2023	Equity Share Capital A/c Dr.		7,500	
	To Forfeited Shares A/c			2,500
	To Calls in Arrear A/c			5,000
	(Being A's Shares forfeited)			
1.7.2023	Equity Share Final Call A/c Dr.		2,47,500	
	To Equity Share Capital A/c			2,47,500
	(Being the amount due on final call i.e. 99,000 shares @ ₹ 2.50)			
1.7.2023	Bank A/c Dr.		2,42,500	
	Calls in Arrear A/c Dr.		2,500	
	Calls in Advance A/c Dr.		2,500	
	To Equity Share Final call A/c			2,47,500
	(Being the amount received on final call)			
1.8.2023	Equity Share Capital A/c Dr.		10,000	
	To Forfeited Shares A/c			5,000
	To Calls in Arrear A/c			5,000
	(Being B's Shares forfeited)			
1.9.2023	Bank A/c Dr.		13,500	
	Forfeited Shares A/c		1,500	
	To Equity Share Capital A/c			15,000
	(Being the 1,500 Shares re–issued @ ₹ 9)			
1.9.2023	Forfeited Shares A/c Dr.		3,500	
	To Capital Reserve A/c			3,500
	(Being the t/f of Profit on reissue of forfeited shares)			

Working Notes:

Dr. **FORFEITED SHARES ACCOUNT** *Cr.*

Particulars	₹	***Particulars***	₹
To Equity Share Capital A/c	1,500	By Equity Share Capital A/c	
To Capital Reserve A/c (b.f.)	3,500	(A 's Shares)	2,500
To Balance c/d (500 Shares @ ₹ 5)	2,500	By Equity Share Capital A/c	
		(B's Shares)	5,000
	7,500		7,500

Dr. **BANK ACCOUNT** *Cr.*

Particulars	₹	***Particulars***	₹
To Balance b/d	9,50,000	By Pref. Shareholders	9,45,000
To Equity Share Capital A/c	5,00,000	By Balance c/d	7,61,000

To Equity Share Final Call A/c	2,42,500	
To Equity Share Capital A/c	13,500	
	17,06,000	17,06,000

Note: An adequate provision has been made on 2000 Red Pref. Shares on which calls are in arrears, by transferring the requisite amount of profits to Preference Shares Redemption Suspense account.

PROBLEM 4

Given below are the extracts of Balance Sheet of X Ltd (listed company)as at 31st March, 2023:

Particulars	₹
50,000 Equity Shares of ₹ 10 each, ₹ 8 paid up	4,00,000
5,000, 13% Red. Pref. Shares of ₹ 100 each (issued on April 1,2015)	5,00,000
Securities Premium	98,000
General Reserve	37,500
Profit & Loss A/c	1,64,500
Current Liabilities	3,00,000
Property,Plant,Equipment and Intangible Assets	6,00,000
Non-Current Investments [Face Value ₹1,25,000]	2,00,000
Cash at Bank	3,00,000
Other Current Assets	4,00,000

The Company resolved:

(a) To make final call on partly paid–up equity shares on 1st April, 2023.

(b) To redeem the preference shares on 30th April at a premium of 7½% and for this purpose to issue 3,000 12% preference shares of ₹ 100 each at a premium of 10% payable in full on application.

The resolutions were carried into effect. For the purpose of the above redemption, on 29th April, the company sold its one of the Property having book value of ₹ 3,00,000 for ₹ 3,82,500 and all the investments @208% of Face Value. On 31st May, all payments were made on redemption except to holders of 200 shares who could not be traced.

On 30th June, the directors issued fully paid bonus shares to the then shareholders at the rate of 3 for 5 held.

Required: Pass necessary Journal Entries in the books of the company to record the above transactions.

SOLUTION

JOURNAL

Date	*Particulars*	*L.F.*	*Dr. (₹)*	*Cr. (₹)*
1.4.2023	Equity Share Final Call A/c Dr.		1,00,000	
	To Equity Share Capital A/c			1,00,000
	(Being the final call made due on Equity shares as per Board's Resolution dated...)			

Date	Particulars		Dr. (₹)	Cr. (₹)
1.4.2023	Bank A/c	Dr.	1,00,000	
	To Equity Share Final Call A/c			1,00,000
	(Being the final call received)			
29.4.2023	Bank A/c	Dr.	3,82,500	
	To Property,Plant,Equipment and Intangible Assets A/c			3,00,000
	To Profit & Loss A/c			82,500
	(Being the sale of Property)			
29.4.2023	Bank A/c	Dr.	2,60,000	
	To Investments A/c			2,00,000
	To Profit & Loss A/c			60,000
	(Being the investments sold)			
30.4.2023	Bank A/c	Dr.	3,30,000	
	To Pref. Share Application & Allotment A/c			3,30,000
	(Being the receipt of application money)			
30.4.2023	Pref. Share Application & Allotment A/c	Dr.	3,30,000	
	To 12% Preference Share Capital A/c			3,00,000
	To Securities Premium A/c			30,000
	(Being the amount received on issue of 3,000 12% preference shares of ₹ 100 each at a premium of 10% for the purpose of redemption of shares as per Board's Resolution dated...)			
	General Reserve A/c	Dr.	37,500	
	To Premium on Redemption of Pref. Shares A/c			37,500
	(Being the premium on redemption of share @7½% provided out of General Reserve)			
30.4.2023	Profit & Loss A/c	Dr.	2,00,000	
	To Capital Redemption Reserve A/c			2,00,000
	(Being the amount transferred out of Profit & Loss A/c to Capital Redemption Reserve Account of an amount equal to nominal value of preference shares redeemed otherwise than out of the proceeds of fresh shares issued as per The Companies Act)			
30.4.2023	13% Redeemable Pref. Share Capital A/c	Dr.	5,00,000	
	Premium on Redemption of Preference Shares A/c	Dr.	37,500	
	To Red. Preference Shareholders' A/c			5,37,500
	(Being the amount due on redemption)			
31.5.2023	Red. Preference Shareholders' A/c	Dr.	5,16,000	
	To Bank A/c			5,16,000
	(Being the amount due on redemption paid in full except to holders of 200 shares)			

30.6.2023	Capital Redemption Reserve A/c Dr. Securities Premium A/c Dr. To Bonus to Shareholders A/c (Being the bonus declared as per shareholders' Resolution dated... for issuing fully paid shares)		2,00,000 1,15,000	 3,15,000
30.6.2023	Bonus to Shareholders A/c Dr. To Equity Share Capital A/c (Being the issue of 30,000 fully paid shares of ₹ 10 each as bonus shares in the ratio of 3 for 5 as per Board's Resolution dated...)		3,00,000	 3,00,000

PROBLEM 5

Given below are the extracts of Balance Sheet of X Ltd (listed company)as at 31st March, 2023:

Redeemable Preference Share Capital(of ₹ 100 each) (issued on April 1,2015)	₹ 5,00,000
Less: Calls–in–arrears (Red. Pref. Shares) @ ₹ 20	₹ 10,000
	₹ 4,90,000
General Reserve	3,90,000
Securities Premium	40,000

It is ascertained that: Preference Shares are due for immediate redemption at a premium of 10%. Calls–in–arrears are on account shares held by four members whose whereabouts are not known.

Balance of General Reserve to be fully utilised for the purposes of redemption and the shortfall to be made good by issue of equity shares of ₹ 10 each at par.

The redemption of preference shares was duly carried out.

Required: Pass the Journal entries and the relevant extracts from the liabilities side of the Balance Sheet as they would appear after the redemption is carried out.

SOLUTION

JOURNAL

Date	*Particulars*	*L.F.*	*Dr. (₹)*	*Cr. (₹)*
	General Reserve Dr. To Premium on Redemption of Pref. Shares A/c To Preference Shares Redemption Suspense A/c [Being the premium payable on redemption of preference shares. Premium on redemption of 500 Shares (@ 10 per share) on which calls are in arrears, transferred to Pref. Shares Redemption Suspense A/c)		50,000	 45,000 5,000
	General Reserve A/c Dr. To Capital Redemption Reserve A/c To Preference Shares Redemption Suspense A/c		3,40,000	 2,90,000 50,000

	(Being the creation of Capital Redemption Reserve on redemption of preference shares, amount due on preference shares partly paid–up transferred to Preference Shares Redemption Suspense Account)			
	Bank A/c [5,00,000 -3,40,000] Dr. To Equity Share Application & Allotment A/c (Being the application money received)		1,60,000	1,60,000
	Equity Share Application & Allotment A/c Dr. To Equity Share Capital A/c (Being the 16,000 equity shares of ₹ 10 each issued at par to raise ₹ 1,60,000, required for red. of pref. shares)		1,60,000	1,60,000
	Preference Share Capital A/c Dr. Premium on Redemption of Preference Shares A/c Dr. To Preference Shareholders' A/c (Being the amount due to Pref. Shareholders on redemption)		4,50,000 45,000	4,95,000
	Preference Shareholders' A/c Dr. To Bank A/c (Being the Payment made to the pref. shareholders)		4,95,000	4,95,000

AN EXTRACT OF BALANCE SHEET [AFTER THE REDEMPTION]

Liabilities	₹	₹
Share Capital:		
16,000 Equity Shares of ₹ 10 each fully paid		1,60,000
500 Redeemable Preference Shares of ₹ 100 each fully called up	50,000	
Less: Calls in arrears	(10,000)	40,000
Reserve & Surplus:		
Securities Premium		40,000
Capital Redemption Reserve		2,90,000
Current Liabilities		
Preference Shares Redemption Suspense Account		55,000

VERY SHORT ANSWER TYPE QUESTIONS

1. Briefly explain the following:
   (a) Divisible Profits
   (b) Proceeds of fresh issue of shares
2. Enumerate the following:
   (a) Sources of redemption of Red. Pref. Shares.
   (b) Sources of providing premium payable on redemption
   (c) Two examples of Divisible Profits

3. Write the Conditions for redemption of Red. Pref. Shares. as per Sec 55(1) of The Companies Act,2013.
4. When and what amount is required to be Transferred to Capital Redemption Reserve Account in case of redemption of Red. Pref. Shares?
5. For what purpose the balance of Capital Redemption Reserve Account can be utilised?
6. What can be the Maximum Period of Redemption in case of Infrastructure Companies?
7. What can be the Maximum Period of Redemption in case of Companies other than Infrastructure Companies?
8. Can Securities Premium be used for providing Premium on Redemption of Preference Shares?
9. Can Debentures issued be considered as proceeds for Redemption of Preference Shares?

SHORT ANSWER TYPE PRACTICAL QUESTIONS

1. X Ltd. decides to redeem 26000,15% Red. Pref. Shares of ₹ 100 each at a premium of 10%. It has a General Reserve of ₹ 18,40,000, Profit & Loss A/c balance of ₹ 14,20,000, a Securities Premium of ₹ 4,50,000. It is decided to issue 1760, 15% Debentures of ₹ 100 each at par, 200, 12% Pref. Shares of ₹ 100 each at a premium of 20% and 100,000 Equity Shares of ₹ 10 each a premium of 25% for the purpose of redemption of Pref. Calculate the amount to be transferred to Capital Redemption Reserve Account.

   [Ans ₹ 15,80,000]

2. X Ltd. decides to redeem 26000,15% Red. Pref. Shares of ₹ 100 each at a premium of 10%. It has a General Reserve of ₹ 18,40,000, Profit & Loss A/c balance of ₹ 14,20,000, a Securities Premium of ₹ 4,50,000. Calculate the minimum number of equity shares of ₹ 10 each to be issued at 25% premium for the purpose of redemption in each of the following cases:
   (i) If no other information is given
   (ii) If Investments having book value of ₹ 16,00,000 are sold for ₹ 12,00,000.
   (iii) If the company has to maintain a minimum balance of ₹ 10,00,000 in the Profit & Loss A/c
   (iv) If Investments having book value of ₹ 16,00,000 are sold for ₹ 12,00,000 and the company has to maintain a minimum balance of ₹ 10,00,000 in the Profit & Loss A/c

   [Ans No of Equity Shares to be issued (i) 0 (ii) 0 (iii) 60000 (iv) 100000]

3. X Ltd. decides to redeem 26000,15% Red. Pref. Shares of ₹ 100 each at a premium of 10%. It has a General Reserve of ₹ 18,40,000, Profit & Loss A/c balance of ₹ 14,20,000, a Securities Premium of ₹ 4,50,000. It is decided to issue 1760, 15% Debentures of ₹ 100 each at par and 200, 12% Pref. Shares of ₹ 100 each at a premium of 20% for the purpose of redemption of Pref. Shares. Calculate the minimum number of equity shares of ₹ 10 each to be issued at 25% premium for the purpose of redemption in each of the following cases:
   (i) If the company has to maintain a minimum balance of ₹ 10,00,000 in the Profit & Loss A/c
   (ii) If Investments having book value of ₹ 16,00,000 are sold for ₹ 12,00,000 and the company has to maintain a minimum balance of ₹ 10,00,000 in the Profit & Loss A/c

   [Ans No of Equity Shares to be issued (i) 58000 (ii) 98000]

4. X Ltd. decides to redeem 26000,15% Red. Pref. Shares of ₹ 100 each at a premium of 10%. It has a General Reserve of ₹ 18,40,000, Profit & Loss A/c balance of ₹ 14,20,000, a Securities Premium of ₹4,50,000, Bank Balance of ₹ 12,60,000 and Investments [Face

value ₹ 20,00,000] of ₹ 40,00,000.40% of Investments are sold at 150% of Face Value. It is decided to issue 1760, 15% Debentures of ₹ 100 each at par and 200, 12% Pref. Shares of ₹ 100 each at a premium of 20% for the purpose of redemption of Pref. Shares. Calculate the minimum number of equity shares of ₹ 10 each to be issued at 25% premium for the purpose of redemption if the company has to maintain a minimum balance of ₹ 10,00,000 in the Profit & Loss Account.

[Ans No of Equity Shares to be issued 98000]

5. X Ltd. decides to redeem 26000,15% Red. Pref. Shares of ₹ 100 each at a premium of 10%. It has a General Reserve of ₹ 18,40,000, Profit & Loss A/c balance of ₹ 14,20,000, a Securities Premium of ₹ 4,50,000, Bank Balance of ₹ 12,60,000 and Investments [Face value ₹ 20,00,000] of ₹ 40,00,000.40% of Investments are sold at 150% of Face Value. Calculate the minimum number of equity shares of ₹ 10 each to be issued at 25% premium for the purpose of redemption if the company has to maintain a minimum balance of ₹ 10,00,000 in Bank Account and of ₹ 10,00,000 in the Profit & Loss Account.

[Ans No of Equity Shares to be issued 112000]

6. X Ltd. decides to redeem 26000,15% Red. Pref. Shares of ₹ 100 each at a premium of 10%. It has a General Reserve of ₹ 18,40,000, Profit & Loss A/c balance of ₹ 14,20,000, a Securities Premium of ₹ 4,50,000, Bank Balance of ₹ 12,60,000 and Investments [Face value ₹ 20,00,000] of ₹ 40,00,000.40% of Investments are sold at 150% of Face Value. It is decided to issue 1760, 15% Debentures of ₹ 100 each at par and 200, 12% Pref. Shares of ₹ 100 each at a premium of 20% for the purpose of redemption of Pref. Shares. Calculate the minimum number of equity shares of ₹ 10 each to be issued at 25% premium for the purpose of redemption if the company has to maintain a minimum balance of ₹ 10,00,000 in Bank Account and of ₹ 10,00,000 in the Profit & Loss Account.

[Ans No of Equity Shares to be issued 98000]

LONG ANSWER TYPE PRACTICAL QUESTIONS

1. CEED Limited had 5,000, 10% Redeemable Preference Shares of ₹ 100 each, fully paid up. The company had to redeem these shares at a premium of 10%.It was decided by the company to issue the following:

(i) 40,000 Equity Shares of ₹ 10 each at par

(ii) 2,000, 12% Debentures of ₹100 each.

The issue was fully subscribed and all accounts were received in full. The payment was duly made. The company had sufficient profits. Show journal entries in the books of the company.

[Ans. T/f to CRR ₹ 1,00,000]

2. The Books of CEEA Ltd. shows the following Balances as on 31st December, 2022:

	Amount (₹)
6,00,000 Equity shares of ₹ 10 each fully paid up	60,00,000
30,000, 10% Preference shares of ₹ 100 each, ₹ 80 paid up	24,00,000
Securities Premium	6,00,000
Capital Redemption Reserve	18,00,000
General Reserve	35,00,000

Under the terms of issue, the Preference Shares are redeemable on 31st March, 2023 at a premium of 10%. In order to finance the redemption, the Board of Directors decided to make a fresh issue of 1,50,000 Equity shares of ₹10 each at a premium of 20%, ₹ 2 being payable on application, ₹ 7 (including premium) on allotment and the balance on 1st January, 2024. The issue was fully subscribed and allotment made on 1st March, 2023. The money due on allotment was received by 20th March, 2023.

The preference shares were redeemed after fulfilling the necessary conditions of Section 55 of the Companies Act, 2013.

You are required to pass the necessary Journal Entries and also show how the relevant items will appear in the Balance Sheet of the company after the redemption carried out on 31st March, 2023.

[**Ans.** T/f to CRR ₹ 19,50,000,Hint. proceeds of fresh issue of shares = ₹ 3,00,000 application money+ ₹ 7,50,000 received on allotment towards share capital]

3. Given below are the extracts of Balance Sheet as at 31st March, 2023:

Particulars	₹
50,000 Equity Shares of ₹ 10 each, ₹ 8 paid up	4,00,000
5,000, 13% Red. Pref. Shares of ₹ 100 each	5,00,000
Securities Premium	98,000
General Reserve	90,000
Profit & Loss A/c	1,12,000
Current Liabilities	3,00,000
Tangible Fixed Assets	6,00,000
Non-Current Investments[Face Value ₹1,25,000]	2,00,000
Cash at Bank	3,00,000
Other Current Assets	4,00,000

The Company resolved:

(a) To make final call on equity shares into fully paid-up.

(b) To redeem the preference shares on 30th April at a premium of 7½% and for this purpose to issue 3,000 12% preference shares of ₹ 100 each at a premium of 10% payable in full on application.

The resolutions were carried into effect. For the purpose of the above redemption, on 29th April, the company sold its fixed assets having book value of ₹ 3,00,000 for ₹ 3,82,500 and all the investments @208%. On 31st May, all payments were made on redemption except to holders of 200 shares who could not be traced.

On 30th June, the directors issued fully paid bonus shares to the then shareholders at the rate of 3 for 5 held at a premium of 5%.

Required: Pass necessary Journal Entries in the books of the company to record the above transactions.

[**Ans.** T/f to CRR ₹ 2,00,000, Bonus ₹ 3,15,000]

4. The Summarized Balance Sheet of CEEC Ltd. as on 31st March, 2023 is as follows:

Particulars	₹
EQUITY AND LIABILITIES	
1. Shareholder's funds:	
(a) Share Capital	5,80,000
(b) Reserves and Surplus	96,000

2. Current Liabilities:	
Trade Payables	1,13,000
Total	7,89,000
ASSETS:	
1. Non-Current Assets	
(a) Property, Plant and Equipment	
Tangible Assets	6,90,000
(b) Non-current investments	37,000
2. Current Assets	
Cash and cash equivalents (Bank)	62,000
Total	7,89,000

The Share Capital of the company consists of ₹ 50 each Equity shares of ₹ 4,50,000 and ₹ 100 each 8% Redeemable Preference Shares of ₹ 1,30,000 (issued on 1.4.2018).Reserves and Surplus comprises statement of profit and loss only. In order to facilitate the redemption of preference shares at a premium of 10%, the Company decided:

(a) to sell all the investments for ₹ 30,000

(b) to finance part of redemption from company funds, subject to, leaving a Bank balance of ₹ 24,000.

(c) to issue minimum equity shares of ₹ 50 each at a premium of ₹ 10 per share to raise the balance of funds required.

You are required to

(1) Pass Journal Entries to record the above transactions.

(2) Prepare Balance Sheet after completion of the above transactions.

[**Ans.** No of New Shares to be issued 1250,T/f to CRR ₹ 67,500]

5. The Capital structure of a company CEEB Ltd., consists of 30,000 Equity Shares of ₹ 10 each fully paid up and 2,000 9% Redeemable Preference Shares of ₹ 100 each fully paid up as on 31.03.2023. the other particulars as at 31.03.2023 are as follows:

	(₹)
General Reserve	1,20,000
Profit &Loss Account	60,000
Investment Allowance Reserve (not free for distribution as dividend)	15,000
Cash at bank	1,95,000

Preference Shares are to be redeemed at a premium of 10%. For the purpose of redemption, the directors are empowered to make fresh issue of Equity Shares at per after utilizing the undistributed reserve & surplus, subject to the conditions that a sum of ₹ 40,000 shall be retained in General Reserve and which should not be utilized.

Company also sold investment of 4500 Equity Shares in G Ltd., costing ₹ 45,000 at ₹ 9 per share.

Pass Journal entries to give effect to the above arrangements and also show how the relevant items will appear in the Balance Sheet as at 31.03.2023 of BK Ltd., after the redemption is carried out.

[**Ans.** No of New Shares to be issued 8450,T/f to CRR ₹ 1,15,500]

6. Given below are the extracts of Balance Sheet of Tulsian Ltd. as at 31st March 2023:

Particulars	₹
15% 1300 Redeemable Preference Shares of ₹ 100 each, ₹ 80 per share paid up	1,04,000
45,000 Equity shares of ₹ 10 each, ₹ 9.50 per share paid up	4,27,500
Revaluation Reserve	90,000
Capital Reserve (Realised in Cash)	1,000
General Reserve	80,000
Securities Premium	1,000
Profit & Loss Account	81,000
Current Liabilities	2,15,500
Fixed Assets	7,43,000
Non-Current Investments [Face value ₹ 1,00,000]	2,00,000
Bank Balance	57,000

On 1st April 2023, the Board of Directors decided to make a final call of ₹ 20 on Redeemable Preference Shares and to redeem the same at a premium of 10% on 1st June 2023. The investments of the face value of ₹ 40,000 are sold at the market price which was 150% of the face value.

It is decided to issue sufficient number of Equity Shares of ₹ 10 each at a premium of 25% after leaving a balance of ₹ 1,00,000 in Bank Account. On 1st July 2023, the Board decided to make final call and then issue fully paid bonus shares to the equity shareholders in the ratio of one for five.

Required: Pass the necessary journal entries and the Balance Sheet after giving effect to Board's decisions:

[**Ans.** No of New Shares to be issued 8,000,T/f to CRR ₹ 50,000, Bonus ₹ 1,06,000]

7. Given below are the extracts of Balance Sheet of Tulsian Ltd. as at 31st March 2023:

Particulars	₹
30,000 Equity shares of ₹ 10 each	3,00,000
5,000 Redeemable 8% Preference shares of ₹ 100 each	5,00,000
Securities Premium	6,00,000
General Reserve	6,50,000
Profit & Loss A/c	1,80,000
2500, 9% Debentures of ₹ 100 each	2,50,000
Sundry Creditors	1,70,000
Fixed Assets (net)	7,80,000
Investments (Market Value ₹ 6,80,000)	4,90,000
Deferred Tax Assets	3,40,000
Sundry Debtors	6,20,000
Cash & Bank balance	2,80,000
Preliminary expenses	1,40,000

In Annual General Meeting held on 20th June the company passed the following resolutions:

(i) To split equity share ₹ 10 each into 5 equity shares of ₹ 2 each from 1st July.

(ii) To redeem 8% Preference Shares at a premium of 5%.

(iii) To redeem 9% Debentures by making offer to debenture holders to convert their holdings into equity shares at ₹ 10 per share *or* accept cash on redemption.

(iv) To issue fully paid bonus shares in the ratio of one equity share for every 3 shares held on record date.

On 10th July investments were sold for ₹ 5,55,000 and preference shares were redeemed. 40% of Debentureholder exercised their option to accept cash & their claims were settled on 1st Aug.

The company fixed 5th September as record date and bonus issue was concluded by 12th September. You are requested to journalize the above transactions including cash transactions and prepare Balance Sheet as at 30th September.

[**Ans.** T/f to CRR ₹ 5,00,000, Bonus ₹ 1,10,000]

4 ACCOUNTING FOR BUY-BACK OF SHARES

LEARNING OBJECTIVES

After studying this chapter, you should be able to understand:

- ◇ Meaning of Buy-back of Shares
- ◇ Three Sources of Funds for Buy-back
- ◇ Conditions for Buy-back
- ◇ Accounting Entries for Buy-back

1.0 MEANING OF BUY-BACK OF SHARES

The term buy-back of shares implies the act of purchasing its own shares by a company.

2.0 THREE SOURCES OF FUNDS FOR BUY-BACK [SEC. 68(1)]

A company may purchase its own shares *or* other specified securities out of:

(i) its Free Reserves; or

(ii) the Securities Premium Account; or

(iii) the proceeds of any shares *or* other specified securities;

Provided that no buy-back of any kind of shares *or* other specified securities shall be made out of the proceeds of an earlier issue of the same kind of shares *or* same kind of other specified securities.

3.0 CONDITIONS FOR BUY-BACK [SEC 68]

PROCEDURAL CONDITIONS

1. **Authorised by Articles:** The buy-back must be authorized by the Articles
2. **Special Resolution/Board's Resolution:** The **special resolution** must be passed in the General Meeting of shareholders.

   OR

   The Board must pass a resolution at its meeting where the buy-back does not exceed 10% of the total equity paid up capital and free reserves of the company.
3. **Fully Paid Shares:** All the shares for buy-back must be fully paid-up.
4. **Time Limit :**The buy-back must be completed within 12 months from the date of passing the Special Resolution/Board's Resolution.
5. **From Whom:** The buy-back can be:

   (a) from the existing shareholders *or* security holders on a proportionate basis;

   (b) from the open market;

(c) by purchasing the securities issued to employees of the company pursuant to a scheme of stock option *or* sweat equity.

6. **Declaration of Solvency:** The company must file **Declaration of Solvency** with the Registrar and SEBI in the form of an affidavit signed by at least two directors of the company. The affidavit must state that the Board has made full inquiry into the affairs of the company as a result of which they have formed an option that the company is capable of meeting its liabilities and will not render insolvent within a period of one year from the date of declaration adopted by the Board.

7. **Destroy:** Company shall extinguish and physically destroy the shares *or* securities so bought back within 7 days of the last date of completion of buy-back.

8. **Restriction on further issue within 6 months:** Where a company completes a buy-back of its shares *or* other specified securities, it shall not make a further issue of the same king of shares *or* other securities including allotment of new shares *or* other specified securities within a period of 6 months except by way of:

   (a) a bonus issue or

   (b) in the discharge of subsisting obligations such as conversion of warrants, stock option schemes, sweat equality *or* conversion of preference shares *or* debentures into equity shares.

9. **As per SEBI Guidelines:** In case of listed shares buy-back must be as per SEBI Guidelines and In case of unlisted shares buy-back must be as per Share Capital & Debentures Rules 2014.

   SEBI's Regulations for listed shares:

   (i) No offer of buy-back for at least 15% of the paid up capital and free reserves of the company shall be made from the open market.

   (ii) A company shall not make any offer of buy-back within a period 1 year reckoned from the date of closure of the preceding offer of buy-back, if any.

   (iii) The company shall ensure that at least 50% of the amount earmarked for buy-back is utilized for buying-back shares *or* other specified securities.

ACCOUNTING TREATMENT CONDITION [SEC 69(1)]

10. **Transfer of Certain Sums to Capital Redemption Reserve Account:** Where a company purchases its own shares out of free reserves *or* Securities Premium, then a sum equal to the nominal value of the shares so purchased shall be transferred to the Capital Redemption Reserve (CRR) Account and details of such transfer must be disclosed in the Balance Sheet. The CRR can be utilized to issue fully paid bonus shares to members.

THREE TESTS CONDITIONS

11. **Maximum Limit of Amount of Equity Shares to be bought back:** The buy-back of the shares must **not exceed 25% of total paid-up capital and free reserves.**

12. **Maximum Limit of Number of Equity Shares to be bought back in any Financial Year:** The buy-back of equity shares in any financial year must not exceed **25% of its total paid up equity capital.**

13. **Maximum Debt-Equity Ratio:** The debt-equity ratio must **not be more than 2:1** after such buy-back. Here,

    Debt (after buy-back) = Secured + Unsecured Debt,

    Equity (after buy-back) = Capital + Free Reserves

Note: For the purposes of Section 68, Free Reserves mean Free Reserves available for free distribution as dividend and include the Balance of Securities Premium A/c.

4.0 HOW TO CALCULATE THE MAXIMUM NO. OF SHARES THAT CAN BE BOUGHT BACK

Step 1: *Calculate the Maximum No. of Equity Shares that can be bought back as per following 3 tests.*	
Test	**Max. No. of shares that can be bought back**
1. Outstanding Share Test	= 25% of Total Outstanding Equity Shares
2. Resources Test	= 25% of **(Paid up Capital + Free Reserves)/ Buy back price per share**
3. Debt – Equity Ratio Test	**3A. If buy-back is NOT out of Free Reserves** **=[Present Equity – (Debt Funds/2)] / Buy back Price per Share** **3B. If buy-back is out of Free Reserves** **=[Present Equity – (Debt Funds/2)] / (Buy back Price per Share + Face Value)**
Step 2: *Max. No. of Equity Shares that can be bought back = Least in above 3 Tests*	

5.0 ACCOUNTING ENTRIES

The various journal entries to be passed on buy back are given as follows:

1. To make partly paid Equity Shares Fully paid up		
(a) ***On making final call***		
Equity Share Final Call A/c	Dr.	
To Equity Share Capital A/c		
(b) ***On Receipt of Final Call***		
Bank A/c	Dr.	
To Equity Share Final Call A/c		
2. To realize Investments to provide Cash for buy back		
Bank A/c	Dr.	*[With Sale Proceeds]*
Profit & Loss A/c	Dr.	*[With Loss]*
To Investments A/c		*[With Book value]*
To Profit & Loss A/c		*[With Profit]*
3. To issue fresh other kind of Shares *or* **Securities (say Preference Shares/ Debentures)**		
(a) ***On receipt of Application Money***		
Bank A/c	Dr.	
To Pref. Share Application & Allotment A/c		

(b) ***On Allotment***		
(i) *If at par*		
Pref-share Application & Allotment A/c	Dr.	
To Pref. Share Capital A/c		
(ii) *If at Premium*		
Pref. Share Application & Allotment A/c	Dr.	
To Pref. Share Capital A/c		
To Securities Premium A/c		
4. To make the amount due on buy-back		
Equity Share Capital A/c	Dr.	[With Nominal Value]
Premium payable on Buy Back A/c	Dr.	[With Premium payable]
To Equity Shares Buy Back A/c		[With Total]
5. To make the payment on buy-back		
Equity Shares Buy Back A/c	Dr.	*[With Amount paid]*
To Bank A/c		
6. To adjust the Premium payable on buy-back		
Securities Premium A/c	Dr.	[With Premium]
Revenue Reserve A/c/ Profit & Loss A/c	Dr.	[With Balance if SP is not sufficient]
To Premium payable on Buy Back A/c		[With Total]
7. To transfer Free Reserves to Capital Redemption Reserve Account equal to the Nominal Value of Equity Shares bought back out of Free Reserves		
Revenue Reserve	Dr.	
Profit & Loss A/c	Dr.	
To Capital Redemption Reserve A/c		
Tutorial Note: Capital Redemption Reserve can be utilized only for issuing fully paid bonus shares to members.		

ILLUSTRATION 1 [Calculation of Max. No. of Equity Shares that can be Bought]

Tulsian Ltd. provides you the following information as on 31.03.2023: *₹ in Crores*

(a)	Equity Shares of ₹ 10 each fully paid	330
(b)	10% Red Pref. Shares of ₹ 100 each fully paid	70
(c)	Securities Premium	90
(d)	General Reserve	240
(e)	Profit and Loss A/c	20
(f)	Infrastructure Development Reserve (Statutory Reserve)	100
(g)	Capital Redemption Reserve	50
(h)	Plant Revaluation Reserve	30

(i)	Secured Loans	1000
(j)	Current Liabilities	200

The company has offered buy back price of ₹ 30 per equity share.

Required: Calculate the Maximum permissible number of Equity Shares that can be bought back if the company also has Unsecured Loans of (a) ₹ 800 crores; (b) 200 crores (c) ₹ 500 crores.

SOLUTION

Step 1: Application of 3 Tests

(a) Shares Outstanding Test:

Max. No. of Shares that can be bought back = 25% of 33 = 8.25 crores

(b) Resources Test:

Max. Number of shares that can be bought back

= [25% of (Paid up Capital + Free Reserves)/Buy Back Price per Share]

= [25%(₹ 400 + 350)]/₹ 30 = 6.25 crores

(C) DEBT EQUITY RATIO TEST

*Particulars**	*Situation 1*	*Situation 2*	*Situation 3*
(a) Loan Funds (₹ in crores)	1,800	1,200	1,500
(b) Minimum Equity to be maintained after buy back in the ratio of 2 : 1 (₹ in crores)	900	600	750
(c) Present Equity Shareholders Funds (₹ in crores)	750	750	750
(d) Future Equity Shareholder's Funds	N.A.	712.50 [750–37.5]	N.A.
(e) Maximum permitted buy back of Equity (₹ in crores) [(b) – (c)]	Nil	112.50	Nil
(f) Maximum number of shares that can be bought back @ ₹ 30 per share (shares in crores) [(e)/₹ 30]	Nil	3.75	Nil

Step 2: Max No of Equity Shares that can be bought back

= Least of 8.25 or 6.25 or 3.75

= Max. 3.75 crores Shares can be bought back

Notes:

(i) *Infrastructure Development Reserve, Capital Redemption Reserve and Plant Revaluation Reserve are not free reserves.*

(ii) *For Debt-Equity Ratio, both Secured and Unsecured Loans are considered.*

(iii) Let X = Amount to be t/f to CRR; Y = Maximum permitted buyback of Equity

Y = 750 – X – 600 ...Eq. I

X = (Y/30) × 10 = Y/3 ...Eq. II

by Solving both the Equations

X = ₹ 37.5 crores, Y = ₹ 150 – ₹ 37.5 = ₹ 112.50 crores

ALTERNATIVE METHOD TO CALCULATE MAX NO OF EQUITY SHARES THAT CAN BE BOUGHT BACK

= [Present Equity – (Debt Funds/2)] / (Buy back Price per Share + Face Value)

= [750 – (1200/2)]/(₹ 30 + ₹ 10)= 3.75 crores Shares

ILLUSTRATION 2 [Buy-Back of Shares at Premium out of Free Reserves]

Bharat Ltd. provides you the following information:

1. Issued Capital	:	2,00,000 Equity Shares of ₹ 10 each	
2. Reserves & Surplus	:	Capital Reserve	₹ 10,00,000
		Securities Premium	₹ 18,00,000
		Revenue Reserve	₹ 30,00,000
		Profit & Loss A/c	₹ 40,00,000

3. **Resolution passed to buy back:** 25% of its Equity Shares @ ₹ 50 per share.

Required: Pass journal entries to record the above transactions assuming that the company achieved the target of buy-back.

SOLUTION

JOURNAL

Date	Particulars		L.F.	Dr. (₹)	Cr. (₹)
1.	Equity Share Capital A/c	Dr.		5,00,000	
	Premium payable on Buy Back A/c	Dr.		20,00,000	
	To Equity Share Buyback A/c				25,00,000
	(Being the amount due on Buy Back)				
2.	Equity Shares Buy Back A/c	Dr.		25,00,000	
	To Bank A/c				25,00,000
	(Being the payment made on buy-back)				
3.	Securities Premium A/c	Dr.		18,00,000	
	Revenue Reserve A/c	Dr.		2,00,000	
	To Premium payable on Buy Back A/c				25,00,000
	(Being the adjustment of Premium payable on Buy Back)				
4.	Revenue Reserve A/c	Dr.		5,00,000	
	To Capital Redemption Reserve A/c				5,00,000
	(Being the amount equal to nominal value of equity shares bought back out of free reserves t/f to CRR)				

ILLUSTRATION 3 [Buy-Back of Shares Partly out of Proceeds and Partly out of Free Reserves]

Tushar Ltd. provides you the following information:

1. Issued Capital	:	2,00,000 Equity Shares of ₹ 10 each
		2,000, 10% Pref. Shares of ₹ 100 each (Issued two months back for the purpose of buy-back)
2. Reserves & Surplus	:	Capital Reserve ₹ 10,00,000
		Securities Premium ₹ 18,00,000
		Revenue Reserve ₹ 30,00,000
		Profit & Loss A/c ₹ 40,00,000

3. Resolution passed to buy back: 25% of its Equity Shares @ ₹ 50 per share.

Required: Pass journal entries to record the above transactions assuming that the company achieved the target of buy-back.

SOLUTION

JOURNAL

Date	*Particulars*		*L.F.*	*Dr. (₹)*	*Cr. (₹)*
1.	Equity Share Capital A/c	Dr.		5,00,000	
	Premium payable on Buy Back A/c	Dr.		20,00,000	
	To Equity Share Buyback A/c				25,00,000
	(Being the amount due on Buy Back)				
2.	Equity Shares Buy Back A/c	Dr.		25,00,000	
	To Bank A/c				25,00,000
	(Being the payment made on buy-back)				
3.	Securities Premium A/c	Dr.		18,00,000	
	Revenue Reserve A/c	Dr.		2,00,000	
	To Premium payable on Buy Back A/c				25,00,000
	(Being the adjustment of Premium payable on Buy Back)				
4.	Revenue Reserve A/c [5,00,000 - 2,00,000]	Dr.		3,00,000	
	To Capital Redemption Reserve A/c				3,00,000
	(Being the amount equal to nominal value of equity shares bought back out of free reserves t/f to CRR)				

ILLUSTRATION 4

From the following information calculate the maximum number of shares that can be bought back and pass the necessary journal entries in the books of BHARAT TUSHAR Ltd.:

(a) 10% Redeemable Pref. shares of ₹ 10 each fully paid up	₹	100 lacs
(b) Equity Shares of ₹ 10 each fully paid up	₹	300 lacs
(c) Securities Premium	₹	50 lacs

(d) General Reserve	₹ 250 lacs
(e) Profit & Loss Account	₹ 300 lacs
(f) Capital Redemption Reserve	₹ 20 lacs
(g) Plant Revaluation Reserve	₹ 500 lacs
(h) Capital Reserve	₹ 600 lacs
(i) Export Reserve (Statutory Reserve)	₹ 700 lacs
(j) Secured Loans	₹ 1000 lacs
(k) Unsecured Loans	₹ 640 lacs
(l) Current Liabilities	₹ 100 lacs
(m) Market Price per share ₹ 40	
(n) Buy Back Price offer 25% over the Market Price.	
(o) Investments [Face Value ₹ 200 lacs]	₹ 400 lacs
Sufficient Investments were realized at market price which was 125% of the face value.	
(p) Later the company issued one fully paid up Equity Share of ₹ 10 each by way of bonus shares for every four equity shares held.	

SOLUTION

1. **Outstanding Shares Test:** Max. No. of shares than can be bought back
   = 25% of O/s shares = 25% of 30 lacs = 7.5 lacs
2. **Resources Test:** Max. No. of shares that can be bought back
   = (25% of Paid up Share Capital + Free Reserves)/Buy back price per share
   = 25% (₹ 400 + ₹ 50 + ₹ 250 + ₹ 300)/ (40 + 25%) = 5 lacs
3. **Debt-Equity Test:**

Note: Let X = Amount to be t/f to CRR; Y = Maximum permitted buyback of Equity

Minimum Equity to be maintained = Debt/2 = 1640/2 = 820

Max. Loss on Sale of Sufficient Investments = Y × 150/250

X = (Y/50) × 10 = Y/5 ...Eq. I

Y = 1,000 – 820 – X – Y × 150/250 ...Eq. II

Putting Equation I in Equation II

Y = 180 – Y/5 – 3/5 Y

Y = 180 – 4Y/5

Y + 4Y/5 = 180

Y = 900/9 = ₹ 100 lacs

X = ₹ 100/5 = ₹ 20 lacs

Max. No of shares that can be bought back = ₹ 100/₹ 50 = 2 lacs

Hence, 2 lacs shares being the least in 3 tests can at the most be bought back.

JOURNAL OF TULSIAN LTD. [₹ in lacs]

Data	Particulars		Dr. (₹)	Cr. (₹)
1	Bank A/c [₹ 80 lakh × 125%] Dr.		100	
	Profit & Loss A/c Dr.		60	
	To Investments A/c			160
	(Being the Investments (Face Value of 80 Lacs) of Book value of ₹ 160 lacs sold at 125% of face value			
	Book value = ₹ 400 × ₹ 80/₹ 200 = ₹ 160 lacs			
	Sale Proceeds = ₹ 80 lacs × 125% = ₹ 100 lacs			
2.	Equity Share Capital A/c Dr.		20	
	Premium payable on Buy Back A/c Dr.		80	
	To Equity Share Buyback A/c			100
	(Being the amount due on Buy Back)			
3.	Equity Shares Buy Back A/c Dr.		100	
	To Bank A/c			100
	(Being the payment made on buy-back)			
4.	Securities Premium A/c Dr.		50	
	Revenue Reserve A/c Dr.		30	
	To Premium payable on Buy Back A/c			80
	(Being the adjustment of Premium payable on Buy Back)			
5	General Reserve Dr.		20	
	To Capital Redemption Reserve A/c			20
	(Being the amount equal to nominal value of Equity Shares bought back out of free reserves t/f to CRR)			
6	Capital Redemption Reserve A/c Dr.		40	
	General Reserve A/c Dr.		30	
	To Bonus to Equity Share holders A/c			70
	(Being the utilization CRR and GR to issue 1 bonus share for every 4 shares held)			
7.	Bonus to Equity Shareholders A/c Dr.		70	
	To Equity Share Capital A/c			70
	(Being the issue of one bonus share for every 4 equity share hold)			

SOLVED PROBLEMS

PROBLEM 1

ACS Limited furnishes the extracts of the Balance Sheet as at 31 March 2023:

Particulars	***₹ (in crores)***
13% Preference Shares of ₹ 100 each fully paid	75
Equity Shares of ₹ 10 each fully paid	50
Capital Reserve	50
Revenue Reserve	250
Current Liabilities	140
	565
Property, Plant and Equipment	150
Investments	120
Current Assets	295
	565

The company purchased its own 100 lakh equity shares of ₹ 10 each at ₹ 25 per share on 1 April 2023 out of free reserves. The company also redeemed preference shares on same date. The payments for the above were made out of bank account which forms part of current assets.

Required: Pass necessary journal entries and prepare the Balance Sheet.

SOLUTION

JOURNAL *(₹ in Crores)*

Date	*Particulars*		*L.F.*	*Dr. (₹)*	*Cr. (₹)*
1.	Equity Share Capital A/c	Dr.		10	
	Premium payable on Buy Back A/c	Dr.		15	
	To Equity Share Buyback A/c				25
	(Being the amount due on Buy Back)				
2.	Equity Shares Buy Back A/c	Dr.		25	
	To Bank A/c				25
	(Being the payment made on buy-back)				
3.	Revenue Reserve A/c	Dr.		15	
	To Premium payable on Buy Back A/c				15
	(Being the adjustment of Premium payable on Buy Back)				
4.	Revenue Reserve A/c [10 (Equity)+ 75 (Pref)]	Dr.		85	
	To Capital Redemption Reserve A/c				85
	(Being the transfer of Revenue Reserve to CRR)				
5.	13% Preference Share Capital A/c	Dr.		75	
	To Preference Shareholders A/c				75

	(Being the amount due to preference shareholders on redemption of preference shares)			
6.	Preference Shareholders' A/c	Dr.	75	
	To Bank A/c			75
	(Being the payment made to preference shareholders)			

BALANCE SHEET OF ACS LTD. AS AT 01.04.2023

Particulars	*Note No*	*₹ (lacs)*
I. Equity and Liabilities		
(1) Shareholders' Funds		
(a) Share Capital (₹ 10 each) [50 – 10]		40
(b) Reserves and Surplus	1	285
(2) Non-Current Liabilities		
(3) Current Liabilities		140
Total		465
II. Assets		
(1) Non-Current Assets		
(a) Property, Plant and Equipment		150
(b) Non-Current Investments		120
(2) Current Assets [295 – 100]		195
Total		465

Notes To Accounts:

Particulars	*₹ (lacs)*
1. Reserves and Surplus	
Revenue Reserve [250 – 15 – 85]	150
Capital Reserve	50
Capital Redemption Reserve	85
Total	285

PROBLEM 2

Given below are the extracts from the Balance Sheet of FCS Limited as at 1st March 2023:

Particulars	*(₹ in lakhs)*
Equity Share Capital (Fully paid up shares of ₹ 10 each)	2,400
Securities Premium	350
General Reserve	930
Profit and Loss Account	340
Current Liabilities	2,740
Property, Plant and Equipment	4,052

Investments [Face Value ₹ 200 lacs]	148
Current Assets (including Cash and Bank ₹ 740 lacs)	2,460

On 1 April 2023 the company announced the buy-back of 25% of its equity shares @ 15 per share. For this purpose, it sold all of its investments @ 75% and issued 2,00,000, 14% preferences shares of ₹ 100 each at par, the entire amount being payable with application.

The issue was fully subscribed. The company achieved the target of buy-back. Later the company issued one fully paid up equity share of ₹ 10 by way of bonus shares for every four equity shares held by the equity shareholders.

Required: Pass journal entries for all transactions including cash transactions.

SOLUTION

JOURNAL *(₹ in Lakhs)*

Date	Particulars		L.F.	Dr. (₹)	Cr. (₹)
1.	Bank A/c	Dr.		150	
	To Investments A/c				150
	(Being the sale of investments)				
2.	Investments A/c	Dr.		2	
	To Profit and Loss A/c				2
	(Being the t/f of Profit on sale of Investments)				
3.	Bank A/c	Dr.		200	
	To 14% Preference Share Application & Allotment A/c				200
	(Being the Application money received)				
4.	14% Preference Share Application & Allotment A/c	Dr.		200	
	To 14% Preference Share Capital A/c				200
	(Being the Allotment of Shares)				
5.	Equity Share Capital A/c	Dr.		600	
	Premium payable on Buy Back A/c	Dr.		300	
	To Equity Share Buyback A/c				900
	(Being the amount due on Buy Back)				
6.	Equity Shares Buy Back A/c	Dr.		900	
	To Bank A/c				900
	(Being the payment made on buy-back)				
7.	Securities Premium A/c	Dr.		300	
	To Premium payable on Buy Back A/c				300
	(Being the adjustment of Premium payable on Buy Back)				
8.	Securities Premium A/c [350 - 300]	Dr.		50	
	General Reserve A/c [600 - 200 - 50]	Dr.		350	
	To Capital Redemption Reserve A/c				400

	(Being the Buy-back out of general reserves to the extent not covered by fresh issue of share capital)		
9.	Capital Redemption Reserve A/c Dr. General Reserve A/c Dr. To Bonus Issue A/c (Being the utilisation of capital redemption reserve and General Reserve to issue one bonus share for every four shares held)	400 50	 450
10.	Bonus Issue A/c Dr. To Equity Share Capital a/c (Being the Issue of one bonus share for every four equity shares)	450	 450

Note: Amount of Bonus Issue = 25% of (2400 – 25% of 2400) = 450 lakhs

PROBLEM 3

Given below are the extracts from the Balance Sheet of CANH Ltd. as on 31.3.2023:

Particulars	***(₹ in '000)***
Equity Shares of ₹ 10 each	800
Securities Premium	100
General Reserve	780
Profit and Loss Account	120
Current Liabilities	2,320
Property, Plant and Equipment	2,700
Non-trade Investments	300
Current Assets (including Cash and Bank ₹1,60,000)	1120

CANH Ltd. buy back 16,000 shares of ₹ 20 per share. For this purpose, the Company sold its all non-trade investments for ₹ 3,20,000. Pass Journal Entries with full narrations effecting the buy back.

SOLUTION

JOURNAL OF CANH LTD.

Date	***Particulars***	***Dr. (₹)***	***Cr. (₹)***
1.	Bank A/c Dr. To Non-trade Investments To Profit & Loss A/c (Being the entry for sale of Non-trade Investments)	3,20,000	 3,00,000 20,000
2.	Equity Share Capital A/c Dr. Premium payable on Buy Back A/c Dr. To Equity Share Buy Back A/c (Being the amount due on Buy Back)	1,60,000 1,60,000	 3,20,000

3.	Equity Shares Buy Back A/c	Dr.	3,20,000	
	To Bank A/c			3,20,000
	(Being the payment made on buy-back)			
4.	Securities Premium A/c	Dr.	1,00,000	
	General Reserve A/c	Dr.	60,000	
	To Premium payable on Buy Back A/c			1,60,000
	(Being the adjustment of Premium payable on Buy Back)			
5.	General Reserve	Dr.	1,60,000	
	To Capital Redemption Reserve A/c			1,60,000
	(Being the entry for t/f of General Reserve to Capital Redemption Reserve to the extent of face value of equity shares bought back)			

PROBLEM 4

CAS Ltd. furnishes you with the extracts of Balance Sheet as at 31st March, 2023

(₹ in crores)

12% Redeemable Preference Shares of ₹ 100 each fully paid		75
Equity shares of ₹ 10 each fully paid		25
Capital reserve		15
Securities Premium		25
Revenue Reserves		260
Current Liabilities		40
		440
Funds employed in:		
Property, Plant and Equipment: Cost	100	
Less: Provision for depreciation	100	nil
Investment at cost (market value ₹ 400 Cr.)		100
Current Assets		340
		440

The company redeemed preference shares on 1st April, 2023. It also bought back 50 lakh equity shares of ₹ 10 each at ₹ 50 per share. The payments for the above were made out of the huge bank balances, which appeared as part of current assets.

You are asked to:

(i) Pass journal entries to record the above.

(ii) Prepare Balance Sheet.

(iii) Value equity share on net asset basis.

SOLUTION

JOURNAL OF CAS LTD. *(₹ in lakhs)*

	Particulars	*Dr. (₹)*	*Cr. (₹)*
	Redeemable Preference Share Capital A/c Dr. To Red. Pref. Shareholders A/c (Being redemption of 12% preference shares pursuant to capital re-organisation)	75	75
	Redeemable Preference Shareholders A/c Dr. To Bank A/c (Being the payment made to Red. Pref. Share holders)	75	75
	Revenue Reserves A/c Dr. To Capital Redemption Reserve A/c (Being amount equal to par value of preference shares redeemed out of profits, transferred to capital redemption reserve)	75	75
	Equity Share Capital A/c Dr. Premium payable on Buy Back A/c Dr. To Equity Share Buyback A/c (Being the amount due on Buy Back)	5 20	25
	Equity Shares Buy Back A/c Dr. To Bank A/c (Being the payment made on buy-back)	25	25
	Securities Premium A/c Dr. To Premium payable on Buy Back A/c (Being the adjustment of Premium payable on Buy Back)	20	20
	Securities Premium A/c Dr. To Capital Redemption Reserve A/c (Being transfer of free reserves to capital redemption reserve to the extent of nominal value of capital redeemed through free reserves)	5	5

BALANCE SHEET OF CAS LTD. AS AT 01.04.2023

Particulars	*Note No*	*₹ (lacs)*
I. Equity and Liabilities		
(1) Shareholders' Funds		
(a) Share Capital (₹ 10 each) [25 – 5]		20
(b) Reserves and Surplus	1	280
(2) Non-Current Liabilities [Debentures]		
(3) Current Liabilities		40
Total		340

II. Assets		
(1) Non-Current Assets		
(a) Property, Plant and Equipment [100 – 100]		0
(b) Non-Current Investments [Market Value ₹ 400 crores]		100
(2) Current Assets [340 – 75 – 25]		240
Total		340

Notes To Accounts:

Particulars	***₹ (lacs)***
1. Reserves and Surplus	
Revenue Reserve [260 – 75]	185
Capital Reserve	15
Capital Redemption Reserve	80
Securities Premium [25 – 25]	0
Total	280

NET ASSET VALUE OF AN EQUITY SHARE *(₹ in crores)*

Investments (at market value)	400
Net current assets	200
Net assets available to equity shareholders	600
No. of equity shares = 2 crores	
Value of an equity share = 600 crores/2crores = ₹ 300 crores	

PROBLEM 5

CAMJ Ltd. has the following Capital Structure as on 31.03.2023:

Particulars	***(₹ in crores)***	
(1) Equity Share Capital (Shares of ₹ 10 each fully paid)	—	330
(2) Reserves and Surplus		
General Reserve	240	—
Securities Premium Account	90	—
Profit & Loss Account	90	—
Infrastructure Development Reserve	180	600
(3) Loan Funds		1,800

The Share holders CAMJ Ltd., on the recommendation of their Board of Directors, have approved on 1.04.2023 a proposal to buy back the maximum permissible number of Equity shares considering the large surplus funds available at the disposal of the company.

The prevailing market value of the company's shares is ₹ 25 per share and in order to induce the existing shareholders to offer their shares for buy back, ft was decided to offer a price of 20% over market

You are also informed that the Infrastructure Reserve is created to comply with Income-tax Act requirements.

You are required to compute the maximum number of shares that can be bought back in the light of the above information and also under a situation where the loan funds of the company were either ₹ 1,200 crores *or* ₹ 1,500 crores.

Assuming that the entire back is completed by 30.04.2023, Show the accounting entries in the company's books in each situation. Narrations should form part of your answer.

SOLUTION

(A) STATEMENT DETERMINING THE MAX. NUMBER OF SHARES TO BE BOUGHT BACK

*Particulars**	*Situation 1 (Loan 1800)*	*Situation 2 (Loan 1200)*	*Situation 3 (Loan 1500)*
Shares Outstanding Test	8.25	8.25	8.25
Resources Test	6.25	6.25	6.25
Debt Equity Ratio Test	Nil	3.75	Nil
Maximum number of share that can be bought back [least of above]	Nil	3.75	Nil

JOURNAL ENTRIES FOR BUY BACK (APPLICABLE ONLY FOR SITUATION 2) *₹ in crores*

Date	Particulars		Dr. (₹)	Cr. (₹)
1.	Equity Share Capital A/c	Dr.	37.50	
	Premium payable on Buy Back A/c	Dr.	75.00	
	To Equity Share Buyback A/c			112.50
	(Being the amount due on Buy Back)			
2.	Equity Shares Buy Back A/c	Dr.	112.50	
	To Bank A/c			112.50
	(Being the payment made on buy-back)			
3.	Securities Premium A/c	Dr.	75.00	
	To Premium payable on Buy Back A/c			75.00
	(Being the adjustment of Premium payable on Buy Back)			
4	Securities Premium A/c	Dr.	15.00	
	General Reserve A/c	Dr.	22.50	
	To Capital Redemption Reserve A/c			37.50
	(Being transfer of free reserves to capital redemption reserve to the extent of nominal value of capital redeemed through free reserves)			

Note: Under Situations 1 & 3 the company does not qualify for buy back of shares as per the provisions of Section 68 of The Companies Act, 2013.

Working Notes:

(i) Shares Outstanding Test:

Max. No. of Shares that can be bought back = 25% of 33 = 8.25 crores

(ii) Resources Test:

Max. Number of shares that can be bought back

= [25% of (Paid up Capitals + Free Reserves)/Buy Back Price per share

= [25%(₹ 330 + 420)]/₹ 30 = 6.25 crores

*Particulars**	*Situation 1*	*Situation 2*	*Situation 3*
(a) Loan Funds (₹ in crores)	1,800	1,200	1,500
(b) Minimum Equity to be maintained after buy back in the ratio of 2 : 1 (₹ in crores)	900	600	750
(c) Present Equity Shareholders Funds (₹ in crores)	750	750	750
(d) Future Equity Shareholder's Funds	N.A.	712.50 [750–37.5]	N.A.
(e) Maximum permitted buy back of Equity (₹ in crores) [(b) – (c)]	Nil	112.50	Nil
(f) Maximum number of shares that can be bought back @ ₹ 30 per share (shares in crores) [(d)/₹ 30]	Nil	3.75	Nil

Note: *Infrastructure Development Reserve and Capital Redemption Reserve are not free reserves.*

Step 2: Max No of Equity Shares that can be bought back

= Least of 8.25 or 6.25 or 3.75

= Max. 3.75 crores Shares can be bought back

Notes: Let X = Amount to be t/f to CRR; Y = Maximum permitted buyback of Equity

Y = 750 – X – 600 ...Eq. I

X = (Y/30) × 10 = Y/3 ...Eq. II

by Solving both the Equations

X = ₹ 37.5 crores, Y = ₹ 150 – ₹ 37.5 = ₹ 112.50 crores

ALTERNATIVE METHOD TO CALCULATE MAX NO OF EQUITY SHARES THAT CAN BE BOUGHT BACK

= [Present Equity – (Debt Funds/2)] / (Buy back Price per Share + Face Value)

= [750 – (1200/2)]/(₹ 30 + ₹ 10)= 3.75 crores Shares

PROBLEM 6**

CEE ALOYVERA Ltd. furnishes the following summarised Balance Sheet on 31st March 2023.

(₹ in Lakhs)

	Amount
Equity and Liabilities:	
Shareholders' fund	
Share Capital	
Equity Shares of ₹ 10 each fully paid up	780
6% Redeemable Preference shares of ₹ 50 each fully Paid up	240
Reserves and Surplus	
Capital Reserves	58
General Reserve	289.75
Securities Premium	387.25

Profit & Loss	148
Revaluation Reserve	34
Infrastructure Development Reserve	16
Non-current liabilities	
7% Debentures	268
Unsecured Loans	36
Current Liabilities	395
	2652
Assets:	
Non-current Assets	
Plant and Equipment less depreciation	725
Investment at cost	720
Current Assets	1207
	2652

Other Information:

(1) The company redeemed preference shares at a premium of 10% on 1st April,2023.

(2) It also offered to buy back the maximum permissible number of equity shares of ₹ 10 each at ₹ 30 per share on 2nd April 2023.

(3) The payment for the above was made out of available bank balance, which appeared as a part of the current assets.

(4) The company had investment in own debentures costing ₹ 60 lakhs (face value ₹ 75 lakhs). These debentures were cancelled on 2nd April 2023.

(5) On 4th April 2023 company issued one fully paid-up equity share of ₹ 10 each by way of bonus for every five equity shares held by the shareholders.

You are required to:

(a) Calculate maximum possible number of equity shares that can be bought back as per the Companies Act, 2013 and

(b) Record the Journal Entries for the above-mentioned information.

SOLUTION

(i) Calculation of maximum number of shares to be bought back

Number of shares (in lakhs)

Particulars	*When loan fund is ₹ 304 lakhs*
Shares Outstanding Test (W.N.1)	19.5
Resources Test (W.N.2)	11.175
Debt Equity Ratio Test (W.N.3)	29.725
Maximum number of shares that can be bought back [least of the above]	11.175

Thus, the company can buy 11,17,500 Equity shares at ₹ 30 each.

Working Notes:

1. Shares Outstanding Test

Particulars	*(Shares in lakh)*
Number of shares outstanding	78
25% of the shares outstanding	19.5

2. Resources Test

Particulars	
Paid up capital (₹ in lakh)	780
Free reserves (₹ in lakh) (289.75+387.25+148-24-240*)	561
Shareholders' Funds (₹ in lakh)	1341
25% of Shareholders fund (₹ in lakh)	335.25
Buy-back price per share	30
Number of shares that can be bought back	11.175
*Amount transferred to CRR is excluded from free reserves. Premium on redemption also reduced.	

3. Debt Equity Ratio Test: Loans cannot be in excess of twice the Equity Funds post Buy-Back

	Particulars	*₹ In lakh*
(a)	Loan funds (₹)	304
(b)	Minimum equity to be maintained after buyback in the ratio of 2:1 (₹) (a/2)	152
(c)	Present equity shareholders fund (₹)	1341
(d)	Future equity shareholders fund (₹) (see W.N.4)	1043.75 (1341-297.25)
(e)	Maximum permitted buy-back of Equity (₹) [(d) – (b)]	891.75
(f)	Maximum number of shares that can be bought back @ ₹ 30 per share	29.725
	As per the provisions of the Companies Act, 2013, company	Qualifies

4. Amount transferred to CRR and maximum equity to be bought back will be calculated by simultaneous equation method

Suppose amount transferred to CRR account is 'x' and maximum permitted buy - back of equity is 'y' Then

Equation 1: (Present Equity- Transfer to CRR) - Minimum Equity to be maintained = Maximum Permitted Buy-Back

= (1341 – x) – 152 = y

= 1189 – x =y (1)

Equation 2: Maximum Permitted Buy-Back × Nominal Value Per Share/Offer Price Per Share y/30 × 10 = x or 3x = y (2)

by solving the above two equations we get

x = ₹ 297.25 and y = ₹ 891.75

(ii) Journal Entries for Buy Back **(₹ in lakhs)**

Date	Particulars		Debit	Credit
2023 1st April	6% Redeemable preference share capital A/c	Dr.	240	
	Premium on redemption of preference shares A/c	Dr.	24	
	To Preference shareholders A/c			264
	(Being preference share capital transferred to shareholders account)			
	Preference shareholders A/c	Dr.	264	
	To Bank A/c			264
	(Being payment made to shareholders)			
	Revenue Reserve A/c	Dr.	264	
	To Capital Redemption Reserve A/c			240
	To Premium payable on Redemption of Pref. Shares			24
	(Being creation of CRR to the extent of the face value of pref shares redeemed and Premium payable thereon)			
	Equity Shares buy back A/c	Dr.	335.25	
	To Bank A/c			335.25
	(Being 11.175 lakhs equity shares bought back @ ₹30 per share)			
	Equity Share Capital A/c	Dr.	111.75	
	Premium payable on buy- back A/c	Dr.	223.50	
	To Equity Shares buy back A/c			335.25
	(Being cancellation of shares bought back)			
	Securities Premium A/c	Dr.	335.25	
	To Capital Redemption Reserve A/c			111.75
	To Premium payable on buy- back A/c			223.50
2nd April	(Being creation of CRR to the extent of the face value of equity shares bought back and Premium payable thereon)			
	Debentures A/c	Dr.	75	
	To Investment (own debentures) A/c			60
	To Profit on cancellation of own Debentures A/c			15

	(Being cancellation of own debentures costing ₹ 60 lakhs, face value being ₹ 75 lakhs and the balance being profit on cancellation of debentures)			
4th April	Capital Redemption Reserve	Dr.	133.65	
	To Bonus Shares A/c			133.65
	(Being issue of one bonus equity share for every five equity shares held)			
	Bonus shares A/c	Dr.	133.65	
	To Equity share capital A/c			133.65
	(Being bonus shares issued)			

Working Note: Bonus Share to be issued = 66.825 (78 - 11.175) lakh shares divided by 5 = 13.365 lakh shares.

VERY SHORT ANSWER TYPE QUESTIONS

1. Briefly explain the following:
   (a) Buy-back of shares
   (b) Free Reserves as per Sec 68(1) of The Companies Act,2013
2. Enumerate the following:
   (a) Sources of Funds for Buy-back of shares.
   (b) Sources of providing premium payable on redemption
   (c) Three tests to be satisfied before buy back of shares
3. Write the Conditions for Buy-back of shares as per Sec 68(1) of The Companies Act,2013.
4. When and what amount is required to be transferred to Capital Redemption Reserve Account in case of Buy-back of shares?
5. For what purpose the balance of Capital Redemption Reserve Account can be utilised?
6. What is the Maximum Limit of Amount of Equity Shares to be bought back?
7. What is the Maximum Limit of Number of Equity Shares to be bought back in any Financial Year?
8. What is the Maximum Limit of Debt-Equity Ratio in case of Buy-back of shares?
9. Can transfer from Securities Premium to Capital Redemption Reserve A/c be made in case of Buy-back of shares?

SHORT ANSWER TYPE PRACTICAL QUESTIONS

1. X Ltd. decides to buy-back 50,000 Equity Shares of ₹ 10 each at ₹ 50 per share. It has a Revenue Reserve of ₹ 3,00,000 and a Securities Premium of ₹ 22,00,000. Calculate the amount required to be transferred to Capital Redemption Reserve A/c.

   [**Ans.** T/f to CRR ₹ 5,00,000]

2. X Ltd. decides to buy-back 50,000 Equity Shares of ₹ 10 each at ₹ 50 per share. It has a Revenue Reserve of ₹ 3,00,000 and a Securities Premium of ₹ 22,00,000. It issued two months back 1,000, 10% Red. Pref. Shares of ₹ 100 each at ₹ 200 per share for the purpose of buy-back of Equity Shares. Pass a Journal Entry for transfer to Capital Redemption Reserve Account.

   [**Ans.** T/f to CRR ₹ 4,00,000]

3. Following is the summarized Balance Sheet of CEES Ltd. as on 31st March, 2023.

Liabilities	***In ₹***
Share Capital	
Equity Shares of ₹ 10 each fully paid up	17,00,000
Reserves & Surplus	
Revenue Reserve	23,50,000
Securities Premium	2,50,000
Profit & Loss Account	2,00,000
Infrastructure Development Reserve	1,50,000
Secured Loan	
9% Debentures	22,50,000
Unsecured Loan	8,50,000
Current Maturities of Long term borrowings	15,50,000
	93,00,000
Assets	
Fixed Assets	
Tangible Assets	58,50,000
Current Assets	
Current Assets	34,50,000
	93,00,000

The company wants to buy back 35,000 equity shares of ₹ 10 each fully paid up on 1st April, 2023 at ₹ 30 per share.

Buy Back of shares is fully authorised by its articles and necessary resolutions have been passed by the company towards this. The payment for buy back of shares will be made by the company out of sufficient bank balance available as part of the Current Assets.

Comment with calculations, whether the Buy Back of shares by the company is within the provisions of the Companies Act, 2013.

[Ans. Max. 37,500, Shares can be bought back, T/f to CRR ₹ 3,50,000]

LONG ANSWER TYPE PRACTICAL QUESTIONS

1. The Directors of Umang Ltd. passed a resolution to buyback 5,00,000 of its fully paid equity shares of ₹ 10 each at ₹ 15 per share. This buyback is in compliance with the provisions of the Companies Act, 2013. For this purpose, the company

(i) Sold its investments of ₹ 30,00,000 for ₹ 25,00,000.

(ii) Issued 20,000, 12% preference shares of ₹ 100 each at par, the entire amount being payable with application.

(iii) Used ₹ 15,00,000 of its Securities Premium Account apart from its adequate balance in General Reserve to fulfill the legal requirements regarding buy-back.

(iv) The company has necessary cash balance for the payment to shareholders.

You are required to pass necessary Journal Entries (including narration) regarding buyback of shares in the books of Umang Ltd.

[**Ans.** T/f to CRR ₹ 30,00,000]

2. The summarized Balance Sheet of SM Limited as on 31st March, 2023 was as follows:

		Particulars	Amount in ₹	Amount in ₹
1.		**Equity and liabilities**		
	a.	Shareholder's fund		
		Share capital		
		(60,000 Equity Shares of ₹ 10 Each)		6,00,000
		Reserve & Surplus		
		Security premium	70,000	
		General reserve	63,000	
		Profit and Loss	1,40,000	2,73,000
	b.	Non-current liability		
		9% debentures (secured)		3,00,000
	c.	Current Liabilities		
		Term loan		40,000
		Creditors		65,000
		Provision for taxation		15,000
				12,93,000
2.		**Assets**		
	a.	**Non-current assets**		
		Property plant and equipment		6,00,000
	b.	**Non-current investment**		1,50,000
	c.	**Current assets**		
		Stock	2,00,000	
		Debtors	2,60,000	
		Bank	83,000	5,43,000
				12,93,000

The shareholders adopted the resolution on 31st March, 2023 to:

(i) Buy back 25% of the paid up capital @ ₹ 15 each.

(ii) Issue 10% debentures of ₹ 60,000 at a premium of 10% to finance the buyback of shares.

(iii) Maintain a balance of ₹ 20,000 in General Reserve.

(iv) Sell investments worth ₹ 1,00,000 for ₹ 80,000.

(v) Buy back expenses were ₹ 2,000.

You are required to pass necessary journal entries to record the above transactions and prepare Ledger of Bank Account.

[**Ans.** T/f to CRR ₹ 1,50,000]

3. PAY Limited furnishes you with the following summarized Balance Sheet as at 31st March, 2023:

		(₹ in Lakhs)
Liabilities		
Share Capital:		
Authorised		300
Issued:		
11% Redeemable preference shares of ₹ 100 each fully paid	125	
Equity shares of ₹ 10 each fully paid	175	300
Reserves and surplus:		
Capital reserve	35	
Securities Premium	105	
Revenue reserves	460	
Profit and loss account	50	650
Current liabilities and provisions		50
		1000
Assets		
Fixed assets: cost	100	
Less: Accumulated depreciation	(90)	10
Non-current investments at cost (Market value ₹ 400 Lakhs)		200
Current assets		790
		1000

(i) The company redeemed preference shares at a premium of 4% on 1st April, 2023.

(ii) It also bought back 2.5 lakhs equity shares of ₹ 10 each at ₹ 40 per share. The payments for the above were made out of the bank balances, which appeared as a part of current assets.

You are asked to: Pass journal entries to record the above and Prepare balance sheet as at 01.04.2023.

[**Ans.** T/f to CRR ₹ 150 lakhs]

4. X Ltd. furnishes the following summarized Balance Sheet as at 31-03-2023.

Liabilities	*(in ₹)*	*(in ₹)*
Share Capital		
Equity Share Capital of ₹ 20 each fully paid up	50,00,000	
10,000, 10% Preference Shares of ₹ 100 each fully paid up	10,00,000	60,00,000
Reserves & Surplus		
Capital Reserve	1,00,000	
Security Premium	12,00,000	
Revenue Reserve	5,00,000	
Profit and Loss	20,00,000	
Dividend Equalization Fund	5,50,000	43,50,000
Non-Current Liabilities		
12% Debenture		12,50,000
Current Liabilities and Provisions		5,50,000
Total		1,21,50,000
Assets		
Fixed Assets		
Tangible Assets		1,00,75,000
Current Assets		
Investment	3,00,000	
Inventory	2,00,000	
Cash and Bank	15,75,000	20,75,000
Total		1,21,50,000

The shareholders adopted the resolution on the date of the above mentioned Balance Sheet to:

(1) Buy back 25% of the paid up Equity Share capital and it was decided to offer a price of 20% over market price. The prevailing market value of the company's share is ₹ 30 per share.

(2) To finance the buy-back of shares, company:

(a) Issues 3000, 14% debentures of ₹ 100 each at a premium of 20%.

(b) Issues 2500, 10% preference shares of ₹ 100 each.

(3) Sell investment worth ₹ 1,00,000 for ₹ 1,50,000.

(4) Maintain a balance of ₹ 2,00,000 in Revenue Reserve.

(5) Later the company issue three fully paid up equity share of ₹ 20 each by way of bonus share for every 15 equity share held by the equity shareholders.

You are required to pass the necessary journal entries to record the above transactions and prepare Balance Sheet after buy back.

[**Ans.** T/f to CRR ₹ 10,00,000, No. of bonus shares = 37,500]

5. A company provides the following 2 possible Capital Structures as on 31st March, 2023:

Particulars	*Situation 1 (₹)*	*Situation 2 (₹)*
Equity Share Capital (Shares of ₹ 10 each, fully paid up)	30,00,000	30,00,000
Reserves & Surplus:		
General Reserve	12,00,000	12,00,000
Securities Premium	6,00,000	6,00,000
Profit & Loss	2,10,000	2,10,000
Statutory Reserve	4,20,000	4,20,000
Loan Funds	25,00,000	1,20,00,000

The company is planning to offer buy back of Equity Share at a price of ₹ 30 per equity share.

You are required to calculate maximum permissible number of equity shares that can be bought back in both the situations as per Companies Act, 2013 and are also required to pass necessary Journal Entries in the situation where the buyback is possible.

[**Ans. Situation 1** Max. 41,750 Shares can be bought back, T/f to CRR ₹ 4,17,500 **Situation 2** No Shares can be bought back]

6. Following is the summarized Balance Sheet of CEEC Ltd. as on 31st March, 2023:

Liabilities	₹
Equity shares of ₹ 10 each fully paid up	12,50,000
Bonus Shares	1,00,000
Share Option Outstanding Account	4,00,000
Revenue Reserve	15,00,000
Securities Premium	2,50,000
Profit &,Loss Account	1,25,000
Capital Reserve	1,00,000
Revaluation Reserve	1,00,000
12% Debentures (Secured)	18,75,000
Advance from related parties (Unsecured)	10,00,000
Long term borrowings	19,50,000
	86,50,000
Assets	₹
Fixed Assets	46,50,000
Current Assets	40,00,000
	86,50,000

The Company wants to buy back 25,000 equity shares of ₹ 10 each, on 1st April, 2023 at ₹ 20 per share. Buy back of shares is duly authorised by its Articles and necessary resolution has been passed by the Company towards this. The payment for buy back of shares will be made by the Company out of sufficient bank balance available shown as part of Current Assets.

Comment with your calculations, whether buy back of shares by the Company is within the provisions of the Companies Act, 2013. If yes, pass necessary journal entries towards buy back of shares and prepare the Balance Sheet after buy back of shares.

[**Ans.** Max. 27,083, Shares can be bought back, T/f to CRR ₹ 2,50,000]

ISSUE OF DEBENTURES

LEARNING OBJECTIVES

After studying this chapter, you should be able to understand:

- Meaning and Nature of Debenture
- Distinction Between a Share and a Debenture
- Types of Debentures
- Debenture Trust Deed
- Issue of Debentures for Cash
- Issue of Debentures for Consideration other than Cash
- Issue of Debentures as Collateral Security
- Interest on Debentures

1.0 MEANING AND NATURE OF DEBENTURE

Meaning	Debenture is a written instrument acknowledging a debt and containing provisions as regards the repayment of principal and the payment of interest at a fixed rate. According to Sec. 2(30) of the Companies Act, 2013, Debenture includes Debentures, Stock, Bonds and any Other Securities of a company whether constituting a charge on the assets of the company or not.
Nature	Debenture represents a debt.
Characteristics	The characteristics of a debenture are as follows: 1. It is an acknowledgement of indebtedness by the company to its holder for the amount stated in it. 2. It is issued under the common seal of the company. 3. It provides for a fixed rate of interest. 4. It provides for repayment of principal sum at the fixed date or dates except in case of perpetual (or irredeemable) debentures. 5. It may or may not be secured. 6. It is expressed to be one of a series of like debentures except where single debenture is issued to one person.

2.0 DISTINCTION BETWEEN A SHARE AND A DEBENTURE

A Share and A Debenture can be distinguished as follows:

Basis of Distinction	*A Share*	*A Debenture*
1. Capital vs. Loan	Share is a part of owned **capital.**	Debenture constitutes a **loan.**
2. Reward for Investment	Reward is the payment of **dividend.**	Reward is the payment of **interest.**
3. Fluctuations in the rate of interest and dividend	The rate of dividend **may vary** from year to year depending upon the profit decisions of directors and members.	The rate of interest is **fixed except** in case of Debentures carrying Floating Rate of Interest.
4. Charge vs. Appropriation	Payment of dividend is an **appropriation** out of profit and this cannot be made if there is not profit.	Payment of interest is a **charge** against profits and is to be made even if there is no profit.
5. Priority as to payment of interest/dividend	Payment of **dividend gets no priority** over the payment of interest.	Payment of **interest gets priority** over the payment of dividend.
6. Priority as to repayment of principal during winding up	**Payment** of share capital is made **after** the repayment of **debentures.**	**Payment** of debentures is made **before** the payment of **share capital.**
7. Secured by charge	Shares are **not secured** by any charge.	Non-Convertible Debentures redeemable on or after 18 months are **secured** by a charge.
8. Restriction on issue discount	**Sec. 53 prohibits the** issue of shares at discount.	**No restriction** is imposed on the issue of debentures at discount.
9. Voting Rights	Shareholders generally **enjoy** voting rights.	Debenture-holders **do not** have any voting rights (except at their class-meetings).
10. Convertibility	Equity shares can **never** be **convertible.**	Debentures **can be convertible.**
11. Trust Deed	Trust Deed is **required** to be executed.	Debenture Trust Deed is **required** to be executed.

3.0 TYPES OF DEBENTURES

Debentures can be classified as follows:

1. From the point of view of Security
2. From the point of view of Tenure of Redemption
3. From the point of view of Mode of Redemption

4. From the point of view of Coupon Rate
5. From the point of view of Registration

FROM THE POINT OF VIEW OF SECURITY

1. Unsecured Debentures	These are the Debentures which are not secured on any asset.
2. Fully Secured Debentures	These are the Debentures which are secured either by a fixed charge (i.e., on a particular asset) or by a floating charge (i.e., on the floating assets of the company in general) **Note:** *Charge is one of the form in which a title to property is transferred by way of security for money borrowed. "Charge" includes a Mortgage (i.e., Transfer of Interest in specific Immovable Property). The charge may be fixed charge or floating charge.*
(a) having Fixed Charge	A fixed charge is created against specific assets of the enterprise which are held by the enterprise for use in operations and are not meant for sale.
(b) having Floating Charge	A floating charge is a charge upon a class of assets (e.g., Stock-in trade, Trade Debtors) (both present and future) which are changing from time to time in the ordinary course of business. This implies that Creditors holding a floating charge will have a priority as to repayment over Unsecured Creditors.
3. Partly Secured Debentures	In case of Partly Secured Debentures/bond, specific assets are given by way of charge but their value is less than the amount owed by the company.
First Mortgage Debentures	These are the Debentures which have a **first claim** on the assets charged.
Second Mortgage Debentures	These are the Debentures which have a **second claim** on the assets charged.

FROM THE POINT OF VIEW OF TENURE OF REDEMPTION

1. Redeemable Debentures	These are the Debentures which are repayable after a specified period in lumpsum or by instalments during the life time of the company.
2. Irredeemable Debentures	These are the Debentures which are not redeemable during the life time of the company.

FROM THE POINT OF VIEW OF MODE OF REDEMPTION

1. Convertible Debentures (CD)	These are the Debentures which are convertible into equity shares or other securities either at the option of debenture holders or at the option of the company as the case may be. Convertible debentures are of two types.
(a) Fully Convertible Debentures (FCD)	These are the Debentures where the full amount is convertible into shares or other securities at agreed terms and conditions. Where the conversion is to be made at or after 18 months from the date of allotment but before 36 months, the conversion is optional on the part of debenture holders as per SEBI Guidelines.

(b) Partly Convertible Debentures (PCD)	These are the Debentures where only a portion of the amount of debenture is convertible into shares or other securities at a specified time and remaining part of debenture is redeemable on agreed terms. The portion of debenture which is fully convertible into shares is termed as FCD (i.e., Fully Convertible Debenture) portion and the remaining portion which is not convertible into shares is termed as NCD (i.e., Non-convertible Debenture) portion or popularly known as Khokha in Stock Market.
2. Non-convertible Debentures (NCD)	The Debentures which are not convertible into shares or any other securities are called Non-convertible Debentures.

FROM THE POINT OF VIEW OF COUPON RATE

1. Debentures carrying Fixed Rate of Interest	These Debentures carry a specified fixed rate of interest which is called as coupon rate. For example, 15% Debentures.
2. Debentures carrying Floating Rate of Interest	These Debentures carry a floating rate of interest. The floating interest rate is usually tagged with the Bank Rate and yield on treasury bond plus a reward for risk. Since the bank rate [i.e. Prime Lending Rate (PLR)] and yield on treasury securities keep on fluctuating over a period of time, any change is compensated in the risk premium. The rate of interest in such a case is quoted as "PLR + 50 basis points. In this case, if we assume a PLR of 9%, the rate of interest would be 9.5%. The + basis points is determined in relation to risk involved.
3. A Zero Coupon Bond	A Zero Coupon Bond is one which does not carry a specified rate of interest. In order to compensate the investors, such bonds are then issued at a substantial discount. The difference between the Maturity Value and Issue Price is the total amount of interest related to the duration of the bond.

FROM THE POINT OF VIEW OF REGISTRATION

1. Registered Debentures	These are the Debentures which are payable to the persons whose names appear in the Register of Debenture-holders. These can be transferred only by executing a transfer deed. Interest is paid to the registered holder.
2. Bearer Debentures	These are the Debentures which are payable to the bearer thereof. These can be transferred merely by delivery. Interest is paid to the person who produces the interest coupon attached to such debentures.

DISTINCTION BETWEEN REGISTERED DEBENTURES & BEARER DEBENTURES

Basis of Distinction	Registered Debentures	Bearer Debentures
1. Payable	These are payable to the persons whose name appears in the Register of Debentureholders.	These are payable to the bearer thereof.

2. Transferable	These can be transferred only by executing a transfer deed.	These can be transferred merely by delivery.
3. Interest	Interest is paid to the registered holder.	Interest is paid to the person who produces the interest coupon attached to such debentures.

DISTINCTION BETWEEN CONVERTIBLE & NON-CONVERTIBLE DEBENTURES

Convertible Debentures	Non-convertible Debentures
These are the Debentures where the full amount is convertible into shares or other securities at agreed terms and conditions.	These are the Debentures which are not convertible into shares or any other securities.
Debenture Redemption Reserve is not required to be created.	Debenture Redemption Reserve is required to be created.

DISTINCTION BETWEEN FIXED CHARGE & FLOATING CHARGE DEBENTURES

Fixed Charge Debentures	Floating Charge Debentures
1. These are secured against specific assets of the enterprise which are held by the enterprise for use in operations and are not meant for sale.	1. These are secured upon a class of assets (e.g., Stock-in trade, Trade Debtors) (both present and future) which are changing from time to time in the ordinary course of business.
2. Fixed Charge Debentures have priority as to repayment over Floating Charge Debentures.	2. Floating Charge Debentures have a priority as to repayment over Unsecured Creditors.

DISTINCTION BETWEEN FULLY & PARTLY CONVERTIBLE DEBENTURES

Fully Convertible Debentures differ from the Partly Convertible Debentures in the following respects:

Basis of Distinction	Fully Convertible Debentures	Partly Convertible Debentures
1. Classification for computing debt equity ratio	They are fully classified **as equity** for computing debt equity ratio.	**Convertible** portion is classified as **'equity'** and non-convertible portion **as 'debt'**.
2. Impact on Debt Equity Ratio	These result in **lower** debt equity ratio.	These result in relatively **higher** debt equity ratio.
3. Capital Base	These result in **higher** equity capital on conversion of debentures.	These result in relatively **lower** equity capital on conversion of debentures.
4. Suitability	These are better suited for companies without established track record.	These are better suited for companies with established track record.
5. Servicing of equity	These involve **higher** burden of servicing of equity.	These involve relatively **lesser** burden of equity servicing.

6. Debenture Redemption Reserve (DRR)	DRR is **not required** to be created.	DRR is **required** to be created for 50% of the face value of the non-convertible portion.
7. Buy-back arrangements	**No** buy-back arrangement is required	Buy back arrangement **may be** made for non-convertible portion.

MEANING OF PARI PASSU CLAUSE

1. When debentures are described as ranking pari passu it means all the debentures of a particular series will rank together without any priority of one over the other as regards the charge created. The effect of such a clause is that the debentures of that series are to be discharged ratably in the event of insufficient funds.
2. When there is no pari passu clause, a debenture will rank for priority for the purposes of repayment etc. according to the date of issue and if all of them were issued on the same date, then according to their respective numbers.
3. A company cannot, however, create a new series of debentures to rank pari passu with an old series, unless the power to do so is expressly reserved and contained in the debentures trust deed of the prior series.

4.0 DEBENTURE TRUST DEED

Debenture Trust Deed is a document created by the company whereby trustees are appointed to protect the interest of debenture holders before they are offered for public subscription. Debenture Trust deed is required to be prepared before the issue of prospectus or letter of offer to the public for subscription of debentures.

5.0 ISSUE OF DEBENTURES FOR CASH

Consideration	Debentures may be issued for Cash or for Consideration other than Cash.
Issue Price	Issue Price means price at which Debentures are issued. Debentures may be issued at Par, Premium or Discount.
Payment of issue Price	Issue Price may be payable either in lumpsum or in instalments at different stages.
Par value	Par Value = Nominal Value = Face Value of Debenture
Over Subscription	Debentures are said to over subscribed when No. of Debentures applied (6000) is **more than** the No. of Debentures **offered** (5000).
Under Subscription	Debentures are said to be under subscribed when No. of Debentures applied (4500) is **less than** No. of Debentures **offered** (5000).
Nature of Debenture Application A/c	Debenture Application Account is **Personal** Account of applicants who have applied for Debentures.
Nature of Debenture Allotment A/c	Debenture Allotment Account is **Personal** Account of allotees to whom Debentures have been allotted.
Nature of Debenture A/c	Debenture Account is **Personal** Account of Debentureholders.

Adjustment of Excess Application Money	Unless otherwise stated in question the excess application money over and above that due on allotment should be refunded to allottees.
Entry When issue Price is payable in lump sum	In case Issue Price is payable in lump sum in single instalment, entry should be passed using **'Debenture Application & Allotment A/c.'**
Redemption	Redemption of Debentures means discharge of liability on account of debentures by repayment made to the debentureholders.
Redemption Price	Practically speaking, Debentures may be redeemed at par or premium.
Accounting	The pattern of accounting entries on the issue of debentures is basically similar to the one on the issue of shares. The only differences are: (a) The term 'Debentures' is substituted for the word Share' (b) The percentage of interest is prefixed to the term 'Debentures' (say 15% Debentures) (c) The terms and conditions of redemption of debentures are to be considered.
Different Cases	Depending upon the terms and conditions of Issue and Redemption of Debentures, practically speaking there may be the following six cases:

Case No.	*Conditions of Issue*	*Conditions of Redemption*
I.	Issue at Par (e.g. at ₹ 100)	Redemption at Par (e.g. at ₹ 100)
II.	Issue at Premium (e.g. at ₹ 105)	Redemption at Par (e.g. at ₹ 100)
III.	Issue at Discount (e.g. at ₹ 90)	Redemption at Par (e.g. at ₹ 100)
IV.	Issue at Par (e.g. at ₹ 100)	Redemption at Premium (e.g. at ₹ 110)
V.	Issue at Discount (e.g. at ₹ 90)	Redemption at Premium (e.g. at ₹ 110)
VI.	Issue at Premium (e.g. at ₹ 105)	Redemption at Premium (e.g. at ₹ 110)

6.0 DEBENTURES ISSUED AT PAR AND REDEEMABLE AT PAR

MEANING

(a) Debentures are said to have been issued at par when the Issue Price is equal to the Face Value.

(b) Debentures are said to be redeemable at par when the Redeemable Value is equal to the Face Value.

Example: An issue of a Debenture of ₹ 100 at ₹ 100 and redeemable at ₹ 100.

JOURNAL ENTRIES IF THE ISSUE PRICE IS PAYABLE IN LUMPSUM

Date	Particulars	L.F.	Dr. (₹)	Cr.(₹)
1.	**On Receipt of Application money** Bank A/c Dr. To Debenture Application & Allotment A/c (Being the Application Money received)			
2.	**On Adjustment of Application Money** Debenture Application & Allotment A/c Dr. To X% Debentures A/c (Being the issue of ....% Debentures of the ₹ each at par)			

JOURNAL ENTRIES IF THE ISSUE PRICE IS PAYABLE IN INSTALMENTS

Date	Particulars	L.F.	Dr. (₹)	Cr.(₹)
1.	**On Receipt of Application Money** Bank A/c Dr. To Debenture Application A/c (Being the Application Money received)			
2.	**On Acceptance of Applications** Debenture Application A/c Dr. To X% Debentures A/c (Being the Application Money adjusted)			
3.	**On Making Allotment Money due** Debenture Allotment A/c Dr. To X% Debentures A/c (Being the Allotment Money due)			
4.	**On Receipt of Allotment Money** Bank A/c Dr. To Debenture Allotment A/c (Being the Allotment Money received)			
5.	**On Making the First Call Due** Debenture First Call A/c Dr. To X% Debentures A/c (Being the First Call Money due)			
6.	**On Receipt of the First Call** Bank A/c Dr. To Debenture First Call A/c (Being the First Call Money received)			

TUTORIAL NOTES

1. *Similar entries may be made for the Second Call and Third Call through Debenture Second Call Account & Debenture Third Call Account respectively. In case of last Call, the word 'Final' is also added to the concerned 'Debenture Call Account'. In case, the entire balance is payable on a single call, usually the term 'Debenture Call Account' is used.*
2. *In case the Cash Book is required to be prepared, all cash and bank transactions will be entered in the 'Cash Book' and other transactions will be entered in the 'Journal Proper'.*

3. *Instead of preparing separate 'Debenture Application A/c' and 'Debenture Allotment A/c', entries relating to the application and allotment may be passed through a combined 'Debenture Application and Allotment A/c'. In such a case, an entry for transferring the surplus application money towards allotment on partially accepted applications, is not required to be passed.*

ILLUSTRATION 1 [PAYMENT OF ISSUE PRICE IN LUMP SUM]

A Ltd. issues at par 20,000, 12% Debentures of ₹ 100 each redeemable at par after 4 years. Journalise.

SOLUTION

JOURNAL

Date	Particulars		L.F.	Dr. (₹)	Cr.(₹)
	Bank A/c	Dr.		20,00,000	
	To Debenture Application & Allotment A/c				20,00,000
	(Being the Application Money received)				
	Debenture Application & Allotment A/c	Dr.		20,00,000	
	To 12% Debentures A/c				20,00,000
	(Being the issue of 20,000 12% Debentures of ₹ 100 each at par)				

ILLUSTRATION 2 [PAYMENT OF ISSUE PRICE IN INSTALMENTS]

X Ltd. issued 10,000, 12% Debentures of ₹ 100 each at par, redeemable at par after 5 years, payable as ₹ 60 on application and the balance on allotment. The debentures were fully subscribed and all money was duly received. Journalise these transactions.

SOLUTION

JOURNAL

Date	Particulars		L.F.	Dr. (₹)	Cr.(₹)
	Bank A/c	Dr.		6,00,000	
	To Debenture Application A/c				6,00,000
	(Being the Application Money received)				
	Debenture Application A/c	Dr.		6,00,000	
	To 12% Debentures A/c				6,00,000
	(Being the Application Money adjusted)				
	Debenture Allotment A/c	Dr.		4,00,000	
	To 12% Debentures A/c				4,00,000
	(Being the Allotment Money due)				
	Bank A/c	Dr.		4,00,000	
	To Debenture Allotment A/c				4,00,000
	(Being the Allotment Money received)				

7.0 DEBENTURES ISSUED AT A PREMIUM BUT REDEEMABLE AT PAR

MEANING

Debentures are said to have been issued at premium but redeemable at par when the Issue Price is more than the Face Value but Redeemable Value is equal to Face Value. Example: An Issue of a Debenture of ₹ 100 at ₹ 110 and redeemable at ₹ 100.

SECURITIES PREMIUM

1. Demand	(a) The Securities Premium may be demanded either in lumpsum or in instalments (b) The Securities Premium may be demanded along with Application Money or Allotment Money or Call Money.
2. Treatment	The amount of premium is credited to a separate account called 'Securities Premium Account'.
3. Disclosure	Securities Premium Account appears under the head 'Shareholders' Funds and sub-head 'Reserves & Surplus' in the company's Balance Sheet.

JOURNAL ENTRIES IF THE ISSUE PRICE IS PAYABLE IN LUMPSUM

Date	*Particulars*	*L.F.*	*Dr. (₹)*	*Cr.(₹)*
1.	**On Receipt of Application Money**			
	Bank A/c Dr.			
	To Debenture Application & Allotment A/c			
	(Being the Application Money received)			
2.	**On Adjustment of Application Money**			
	Debenture Application & Allotment A/c Dr.			
	To X% Debentures A/c			
	To Securities Premium A/c			
	(Being the issue of % Debenture of ₹ each at a premium of .....)			

JOURNAL ENTRIES IF THE ISSUE PRICE IS PAYABLE IN INSTALMENTS

All entries (except entry No. 3) are same as mentioned in case of issue of Debentures at par. However, assuming that the premium is demanded along with allotment money, the 3rd entry will appear as follows:

Date	*Particulars*	*L.F.*	*Dr. (₹)*	*Cr.(₹)*
3.	**On Making Allotment Money due**			
	Debenture Allotment A/c Dr.			
	To X% Debentures A/c			
	To Securities Premium A/c			
	(Being the Allotment Money due)			

ILLUSTRATION 3 [PAYMENT OF ISSUE PRICE IN LUMPSUM]

B Ltd. issues 40,000, 12% Debentures of ₹ 100 each at a premium of 5% redeemable at par after 4 years. Journalise.

SOLUTION

JOURNAL

Date	Particulars		L.F.	Dr. (₹)	Cr.(₹)
	Bank A/c	Dr.		42,00,000	
	To Debenture Application & Allotment A/c				42,00,000
	(Being the Application Money received)				
	Debenture Application & Allotment A/c	Dr.		42,00,000	
	To 12% Debentures A/c				40,00,000
	To Securities Premium A/c				2,00,000
	(Being the issue of 40,000, 12% Debentures of ₹ 100 each, at a premium of 5%)				

ILLUSTRATION 4 [PAYMENT OF ISSUE PRICE IN INSTALMENTS]

X Ltd. issued 10,000, 12% Debentures of ₹ 100 each at 6% premium, redeemable at par after 5 years, payable as ₹ 66 on application (including Premium) and the balance on allotment. Debentures were fully subscribed and all money was duly received. Journalise these transactions.

SOLUTION

JOURNAL

Date	Particulars		L.F.	Dr. (₹)	Cr.(₹)
	Bank A/c	Dr.		6,60,000	
	To Debentures Application A/c				6,60,000
	(Being the Application Money received)				
	Debentures Application A/c	Dr.		6,60,000	
	To 12% Debentures a/c				6,00,000
	To Securities Premium A/c				60,000
	(Being the Application Money adjusted)				
	Debenture Allotment A/c	Dr.		4,00,000	
	To 12% Debentures A/c				4,00,000
	(Being the Allotment Money due)				
	Bank A/c	Dr.		4,00,000	
	To Debentures Allotment A/c				4,00,000
	(Being the Allotment Money received)				

8.0 DEBENTURES ISSUED AT A DISCOUNT BUT REDEEMABLE AT PAR

MEANING

Debentures are said to have been issued at discount but redeemable at par when **the Issue Price is less than the Face Value but Redeemable Value is equal to Face Value. Example:** An issue of a Debenture of ₹ 100 at ₹ 90 and redeemable at ₹ 100.

DISCOUNT ON ISSUE OF DEBENTURES

1. Treatment	The amount of discount is debited to a separate account called **'Discount on issue of Debentures Account'**, which represents a capital loss.
2. Writing off	Discount should be written off as far as possible to Securities Premium Account or Profit & Loss Account during the life of debentures before the redemption of debentures.
3. Disclosure of unwritten off Discount	(i) Under the head **'Non-Current Assets'** and sub-head **'Other Non-Current Assets' if it is to be written off after 12 months** from the Balance Sheet ***Date*** or after the Operating Cycle Period. (ii) Under the head **'Current Assets'** and sub-head **'Other Current Assets' if it is to be written off within 12 months** from Balance Sheet ***Date*** or within the Operating Cycle Period.
4. When Debited	(a) Discount on issue of Debentures is debited while making allotment money due. (b) The amount demanded on allotment is generally presumed as net of discount.

JOURNAL ENTRIES IF THE ISSUE PRICE IS PAYABLE IN LUMPSUM

Date	*Particulars*		*L.F.*	*Dr. (₹)*	*Cr.(₹)*
1.	**On Receipt of Application Money**				
	Bank A/c	Dr.			
	To Debenture Application & Allotment A/c				
	(Being the Application Money received)				
2.	**On Adjustment of Application Money**				
	Debenture Application & Allotment A/c	Dr.			
	Discount on Issue of Debentures A/c	Dr.			
	To X% Debentures A/c				
	(Being the issue of ...... % Debentures of ₹ ...... each at a discount of ......)				

JOURNAL ENTRIES IF THE ISSUE PRICE IS PAYABLE IN INSTALMENTS

All entries (except entry No. 3) are same as mentioned in case of issue of Debentures at par.

Date	*Particulars*		*L.F.*	*Dr. (₹)*	*Cr.(₹)*
3.	**On Making Allotment Money due**				
	Debenture Allotment A/c	Dr.			
	Discount on Issue of Debentures A/c	Dr.			
	To X% Debentures A/c				
	(Being the Allotment Money due)				

Tutorial Note: *The amount demanded on allotment should be presumed as net of discount.*

ILLUSTRATION 5 [PAYMENT OF ISSUE PRICE IN LUMP SUM]

C Ltd. issues 30,000, 12% Debentures of ₹ 100 each at a discount of 5% redeemable at par after 4 years. Journalise.

SOLUTION

JOURNAL

Date	Particulars	L.F.	Dr. (₹)	Cr.(₹)
	Bank A/c Dr.		28,50,000	
	To Debenture Application & Allotment A/c			28,50,000
	(Being the Application money received)			
	Debenture Application & Allotment A/c Dr.		28,50,000	
	Discount on issue of Debentures A/c Dr.		1,50,000	
	To 12% Debentures A/c			30,00,000
	(Being the issue of 30,000 12% Debentures of ₹ 100 each at a discount of 5%)			

ILLUSTRATION 6 [PAYMENT OF ISSUE PRICE IN INSTALMENTS]

X Ltd. issued 10,000, 12% Debentures of ₹ 100 each at 6% discount, redeemable at par after 5 years, payable as ₹ 60 on application and the balance on allotment. Debentures were fully subscribed and all money was duly received. Journalise these transactions.

SOLUTION

JOURNAL

Date	Particulars	L.F.	Dr. (₹)	Cr.(₹)
	Bank A/c Dr.		6,00,000	
	To Debenture Application A/c			6,00,000
	(Being the Application Money received)			
	Debenture Application A/c Dr.		6,00,000	
	To 12% Debentures A/c			6,00,000
	(Being the Application Money adjusted)			
	Debenture Allotment A/c Dr.		3,40,000	
	Discount on Issue of Debentures A/c Dr.		60,000	
	To 12% Debentures A/c			4,00,000
	(Being the Allotment Money due)			
	Bank A/c Dr.		3,40,000	
	To Debenture Allotment A/c			3,40,000
	(Being the Allotment Money received)			

9.0 DEBENTURES ISSUED AT PAR BUT REDEEMABLE AT PREMIUM

MEANING

Debentures are said to have been issued at par but redeemable at premium when the Issue Price is equal to the Face Value but the Redeemable Value is more than the Face Value.

Example: An issue of a Debenture of ₹ 100 at ₹ 100 but redeemable at ₹ 106.

LOSS ON ISSUE OF DEBENTURES

1. Meaning	The difference between the Redeemable Value and the Face Value is treated as the anticipated loss to be incurred at the time of redemption of debentures according to Prudence Principle. For example, In an issue of a Debenture of ₹ 100 at ₹ 100 but redeemable at ₹ 106, ₹ 6 (i.e. ₹ 106 – ₹ 100) is treated as the loss on issue of debentures.
2. Treatment	The amount of loss on issue of debentures is debited to a separate account called **'Loss on Issue of Debentures Account'.**
3. Writing Off	Loss on issue of debentures should be written off as far as possible to *Securities Premium Account or Profit or Loss Account* during the life of the debentures before the redemption of debentures.
4. Disclosure	(i) Under the head **'Non-Current Assets'** and sub-head **'Other Non-Current Assets' if it is to be written off after 12 months** from the Balance Sheet ***Date*** or after the Operating Cycle Period. (ii) Under the head **'Current Assets'** and sub-head **'Other Current Assets' if it is to be written off within 12 months** from Balance Sheet ***Date*** or within the Operating Cycle Period.
5. When Debited	Loss on Issue of Debentures is debited while making the Allotment money due.

PREMIUM ON REDEMPTION OF DEBENTURES

1. Treatment	The amount of premium payable on redemption of debentures is credited to a separate account called **'Premium on Redemption of Debentures Account'.**
2. Nature	This account is a **personal account** which represents a liability of the company in respect of premium payable on redemption.
3. Disclosure	(i) Under the head **'Non-Current Liabilities'** and sub-head **'Other Long-term Liabilities' if Debentures are shown as 'Long-term Borrowings'** (ii) Under the head **'Current Liabilities'** and sub-head **'Other Current Liabilities' if Debentures are shown as 'Current Maturities of Long-term Debts'**

JOURNAL ENTRIES IF THE ISSUE PRICE IS PAYABLE IN LUMPSUM

Date	*Particulars*	*L.F.*	*Dr. (₹)*	*Cr.(₹)*
1.	**On Receipt of Application Money**			
	Bank A/c Dr.			
	To Debenture Application & Allotment A/c			
	(Being the Application Money received)			
2.	**On Adjustment of Application Money**			
	Debenture Application & Allotment A/c Dr.			
	Loss on Issue of Debentures A/c Dr.		(With Premium Payable)	
	To X% Debentures A/c		(With Nominal Value)	

	To Premium on Redemption of Debentures A/c		(With Premium Payable)	
	(Being the issue of ...... % Debentures of ₹ ...... each at par redeemable at premium of ......)			

JOURNAL ENTRIES IF THE ISSUE PRICE IS PAYABLE IN INSTALMENTS

All entries (except entry No. 3) are same as mentioned in case of issue of Debentures at par.

Date	*Particulars*	*L.F.*	*Dr. (₹)*	*Cr.(₹)*
3.	**On Making Allotment Money due**			
	Debenture Allotment A/c Dr.			
	(With the Allotment Money due)			
	Loss on Issue of Debentures A/c Dr.			
	(With Premium Payable on redemption)			
	To X% Debentures A/c (With Nominal Value)			
	To Premium on Redemption of Debentures A/c			
	(With Premium Payable on redemption)			
	(Being the Allotment Money due)			

ILLUSTRATION 7 [PAYMENT OF ISSUE PRICE IN LUMPSUM]

D Ltd. issues ₹ 50,000, 12% Debentures of ₹ 100 each at par but redeemable at 105% after 4 years. Journalise.

SOLUTION

JOURNAL

Date	*Particulars*	*L.F.*	*Dr. (₹)*	*Cr.(₹)*
	Bank A/c Dr.		50,000	
	To Debenture Application & Allotment A/c			50,000
	(Being the Application Money received)			
	Debenture Application & Allotment A/c Dr.		50,000	
	Loss on Issue of Debentures A/c Dr.		2,500	
	To 12% Debentures A/c			50,000
	To Premium on Redemption of Debentures A/c			2,500
	(Being the issue of ₹ 50,000, 12% Debentures of ₹ 100 each at par redeemable at 105%)			

ILLUSTRATION 8 [PAYMENT OF ISSUE PRICE IN INSTALMENTS]

X Ltd. issued 10,000, 12% Debentures of ₹ 100 each at par, redeemable at 6% premium after 5 years, payable as ₹ 60 on application and the balance on allotment. The debentures were fully subscribed and all money was duly received. Journalise these transactions.

SOLUTION

JOURNAL

Date	Particulars	L.F.	Dr. (₹)	Cr.(₹)
	Bank A/c Dr. To Debenture Application A/c (Being the Application Money received)		6,00,000	6,00,000
	Debenture Application A/c Dr. To 12% Debentures A/c (Being the Application Money adjusted)		6,00,000	6,00,000
	Debenture Allotment A/c Dr. Loss on Issue of Debentures A/c Dr. To 12% Debentures A/c To Premium on Redemption of Debentures A/c (Being the Allotment Money due)		4,00,000 60,000	4,00,000 60,000
	Bank A/c Dr. To Debenture Allotment A/c (Being the Allotment Money received)		4,00,000	4,00,000

10.0 DEBENTURES ISSUED AT DISCOUNT BUT REDEEMABLE AT PREMIUM

MEANING

Debentures are said to have been issued at discount but redeemable at premium when the Issue Price is less than the Face Value but the Redeemable Value is more than the Face Value.

Example: An issue of a Debenture of ₹ 100 at ₹ 94 but redeemable at ₹ 106.

LOSS ON ISSUE OF DEBENTURES

1. Meaning	From the accounting point of view, Loss on issue of Debentures represents the total of the following two losses: (a) Actual Loss incurred at the time of issue of Debentures by way of Discount. (b) Anticipated Loss to be incurred at the time of Redemption by way of Premium payable on Redemption as per Prudence Principle. For example, In an issue of a Debenture of ₹ 100 at ₹ 94 but redeemable at ₹ 106, ₹ 12 (i.e. ₹ 106 – ₹ 94) is treated as the loss on issue of debentures.
2. Treatment	The amount of loss on issue of debentures is debited to a separate account called **'Loss on Issue of Debentures Account'.**
3. Writing Off	Loss on issue of debentures should be written off as far as possible to *Securities Premium Account or Profit or Loss Account* during the life of the debentures before the redemption of debentures.
4. Disclosure	(i) Under the head **'Non-Current Assets'** and sub-head **'Other Non-Current Assets' if it is to be written off after 12 months** from the Balance Sheet ***Date*** or after the Operating Cycle Period. (ii) Under the head **'Current Assets'** and sub-head **'Other Current Assets' if it is to be written off within 12 months** from Balance Sheet ***Date*** or within the Operating Cycle Period.

5. When Debited	Loss on Issue of Debentures is debited while making the Allotment Money Due.

JOURNAL ENTRIES IF THE ISSUE PRICE IS PAYABLE IN LUMPSUM

Date	*Particulars*	*L.F.*	*Dr. (₹)*	*Cr.(₹)*
1.	**On Receipt of Application Money** Bank A/c Dr. To Debenture Application & Allotment A/c (Being the Application Money received)			
2.	**On Adjustment of Application Money** Debenture Application & Allotment A/c Dr. *(With Application Money received)* Loss on Issue of Debentures A/c Dr. *(With Discount allowed on issue plus Premium on Redemption)* To X% Debentures A/c *(With Nominal Value of Debentures allotted)* To Premium on Redemption of Debentures A/c *(With Premium Payable on redemption)* (Being the issue of ......% Debentures of ₹ ...... each at ......% Discount and redeemable at ......% Premium)			

JOURNAL ENTRIES IF THE ISSUE PRICE IS PAYABLE IN INSTALMENTS

All entries (except entry No. 3) are same as mentioned in case of Issue of Debentures at discount.

Date	*Particulars*	*L.F.*	*Dr. (₹)*	*Cr.(₹)*
3.	**On Making Allotment Money due** Debenture Allotment A/c Dr. *(With the Allotment Money due)* Loss on Issue of Debentures A/c Dr. *(With Discount allowed on issue plus Premium on Redemption)* To X% Debentures A/c *(With Nominal Value of Debentures allotted)* To Premium on Redemption of Debentures A/c *(With Premium Payable on redemption)* (Being the Allotment Money due)			

ILLUSTRATION 9 [PAYMENT OF ISSUE PRICE IN LUMP SUM]

E Ltd. issues ₹ 60,000, 12% Debentures of ₹ 100 each at a discount of 5% redeemable at a premium of 10% after 4 years. Journalise.

SOLUTION

JOURNAL

Date	Particulars	L.F.	Dr. (₹)	Cr.(₹)
	Bank A/c Dr.		57,000	
	To Debenture Application & Allotment A/c			57,000
	(Being the Application money received)			
	Debenture Application & Allotment A/c Dr.		57,000	
	Loss on Issue of Debentures A/c [3,000 + 6,000] Dr.		9,000	
	To 12% Debentures A/c			60,000
	To Premium on Redemption of Debentures A/c			6,000
	(Being the issue of ₹ 60,000 12% Debentures at a discount of 5% and repayable at a premium of 10%)			

ILLUSTRATION 10 [PAYMENT OF ISSUE PRICE IN INSTALMENTS]

X Ltd. issued 10,000, 12% Debentures of ₹ 100 each at 6% discount, redeemable at 10% premium after 5 years, payable as ₹ 60 on application and the balance on allotment. The issue was over-subscribed by 1,000 debentures and allotment was made on *prorata* basis. All money was duly received. Journalise these transactions.

SOLUTION

JOURNAL

Date	Particulars	L.F.	Dr. (₹)	Cr.(₹)
	Bank A/c Dr.		6,60,000	
	To Debenture Application A/c			6,60,000
	(Being the Application Money received)			
	Debenture Application A/c Dr.		6,60,000	
	To 12% Debentures A/c			6,00,000
	To Debenture Allotment A/c			60,000
	(Being the Application Money adjusted)			
	Debenture Allotment A/c Dr.		3,40,000	
	Loss on Issue of Debentures A/c [60,000 + 1,00,000] Dr.		1,60,000	
	To 12% Debentures A/c			4,00,000
	To Premium on Redemption of Debentures A/c			1,00,000
	(Being the Allotment Money due)			
	Bank A/c Dr.		2,80,000	
	To Debenture Allotment A/c			2,80,000
	(Being the Allotment Money received)			

11.0 DEBENTURES ISSUED AT PREMIUM AND REDEEMABLE AT PREMIUM

MEANING

Debentures are said to have been issued at premium and redeemable at premium when both the Issue Price and the Redeemable Value are more than the Face Value.

Example: An issue of a Debenture of ₹ 100 at ₹ 105 and redeemable at ₹ 106.

LOSS ON ISSUE OF DEBENTURES

1. Meaning	The difference between the Redeemable Value and the Face Value is treated as the anticipated to be incurred at the time of redemption of debentures according to Prudence Principle. For example, In an issue of a Debenture of ₹ 100 at ₹ 106 and redeemable at ₹ 106, ₹ 6 (i.e. ₹ 106 – ₹ 100) is treated as the loss on issue of debentures.
2. Treatment	The amount of loss on issue of debentures is debited to a separate account called **'Loss on Issue of Debentures Account'.**
3. Writing Off	Loss on issue of Debentures should be written off as far as possible to Securities Premium Account or Profit or Loss Account during the life of the debentures before the redemption of debentures.
4. Disclosure	(i) Under the head **'Non-Current Assets'** and sub-head **'Other Non-Current Assets' if it is to be written off after 12 months** from the Balance Sheet ***Date*** or after the Operating Cycle Period. (ii) Under the head **'Current Assets'** and sub-head **'Other Current Assets' if it is to be written off within 12 months** from Balance Sheet ***Date*** or within the Operating Cycle Period.
5. When Debited	Loss on issue of Debentures is debited while making the Allotment Money due.

PREMIUM ON REDEMPTION OF DEBENTURES

1. Treatment	The amount of premium payable on redemption of debentures is credited to a separate account called **'Premium on Redemption of Debentures Account'.**
2. Nature	**Premium on Redemption of Debentures Account** is a **personal account** which represents a liability of the company in respect of premium payable on redemption.

JOURNAL ENTRIES IF THE ISSUE PRICE IS PAYABLE IN LUMPSUM

Date	*Particulars*	*L.F.*	*Dr. (₹)*	*Cr.(₹)*
1.	**On Receipt of Application Money**			
	Bank A/c Dr.			
	To Debenture Application & Allotment A/c			
	(Being the Application Money received)			
2.	**On Adjustment of Application Money**			
	Debenture Application & Allotment A/c Dr.			
	(With Application Money received)			
	Loss on Issue of Debentures A/c Dr.			
	(With Premium Payable on redemption)			

	To X% Debentures A/c *(With Nominal Value of Debentures allotted)* To Premium on Redemption of Debentures A/c *(With Premium Payable on redemption)* To Securities Premium A/c *(With Premium on Issue)* (Being the issue of ......% Debentures of ₹ ...... each at a premium of ...... and redeemable at a premium of ......)			

JOURNAL ENTRIES IF THE ISSUE PRICE IS PAYABLE IN INSTALMENTS

All entries (except entry No. 3) are same as mentioned in case of issue of Debentures at par. However, assuming that the premium is demanded along with allotment money, the 3rd entry shall appear as follows:

Date	Particulars	L.F.	Dr. (₹)	Cr.(₹)
3.	**On Making Allotment Money due** Debenture Allotment A/c Dr. *(With the Allotment Money due)* Loss on Issue of Debentures A/c Dr. *(With Premium Payable on redemption)* To X% Debentures A/c *(With Nominal Value of Debentures allotted)* To Premium on Redemption of Debentures A/c *(With Premium Payable on redemption)* To Securities Premium A/c *(With Premium on Issue)* (Being the Allotment Money due)			

ILLUSTRATION 11 [PAYMENT OF ISSUE PRICE IN LUMP SUM]

F Ltd. issues ₹ 70,000, 12% Debentures of ₹ 50 each at a premium of 5% redeemable at a premium of ₹ 10 per Debenture after 4 years. Journalise.

SOLUTION

JOURNAL

Date	Particulars	L.F.	Dr. (₹)	Cr.(₹)
	Bank A/c Dr.		73,500	
	To Debenture Application & Allotment A/c			73,500
	(Being the Debenture Application Money received)			
	Debenture Application & Allotment A/c Dr.		73,500	
	Loss on Issue of Debentures A/c Dr.		14,000	
	To 12% Debentures A/c			70,000
	To Securities Premium A/c			3,500
	To Premium on Redemption of Debentures A/c			14,000

	(Being the issue of ₹ 1,400, 12% Debentures of ₹ 50 each at a premium of 5% and redeemable at a premium of ₹ 10 per Debenture)			

ILLUSTRATION 12 [PAYMENT OF ISSUE PRICE IN INSTALMENTS]

X Ltd. issued 10,000, 12% Debentures of ₹ 100 each at 6% premium, redeemable at 10% premium after 5 years, payable as ₹ 60 on application and the balance on allotment (including premium). The Debentures were over–subscribed by 1,000 Debentures and allotment was made on prorata basis. All money was duly received. Journalise these transactions.

SOLUTION

JOURNAL

Date	Particulars		L.F.	Dr. (₹)	Cr.(₹)
	Bank A/c	Dr.		6,60,000	
	To Debenture Application A/c				6,60,000
	(Being the Application Money received)				
	Debenture Application A/c	Dr.		6,60,000	
	To 12% Debentures A/c				6,00,000
	To Debentures Allotment A/c				60,000
	(Being the Application Money adjusted)				
	Debenture Allotment A/c	Dr.		4,60,000	
	Loss on Issue of Debentures A/c	Dr.		1,00,000	
	To 12% Debentures A/c				4,00,000
	To Securities Premium A/c				60,000
	To Premium on Redemption of Debentures A/c				1,00,000
	(Being the Allotment Money due)				
	Bank A/c	Dr.		4,00,000	
	To Debenture Allotment A/c				4,00,000
	(Being the Allotment Money received)				

ILLUSTRATION 13

Pass Journal Entries in each of the following alternative cases assuming the face value of a debenture being ₹ 100.

(a) A 12% Debenture issued at ₹ 100 repayable at ₹ 100.

(b) A 12% Debenture issued at ₹ 95 repayable at ₹ 100.

(c) A 12% Debenture issued at ₹ 100 repayable at ₹ 105.

(d) A 12% Debenture issued at ₹ 95 repayable at ₹ 105.

(e) A 12% Debenture issued at ₹ 105 repayable at ₹ 110.

(f) A 12% Debenture issued at ₹ 90 repayable at ₹ 95.

SOLUTION

JOURNAL

Date	Particulars		L.F.	Dr. (₹)	Cr.(₹)
(a)	Bank A/c	Dr.		100	
	To Debenture Application & Allotment A/c				100
	(Being the receipt of Debenture Application Money)				
	Debenture Application & Allotment A/c	Dr.		100	
	To 12% Debentures A/c				100
	(Being the issue of debentures at par)				
(b)	Bank A/c	Dr.		95	
	To Debenture Application & Allotment A/c				95
	(Being the receipt of Debenture Application Money)				
	Debenture Application & Allotment A/c	Dr.		95	
	Discount on Issue of Debentures A/c	Dr.		5	
	To 12% Debentures A/c				100
	(Being the issue of debentures at 5% discount)				
(c)	Bank A/c	Dr.		100	
	To Debenture Application & Allotment A/c				100
	(Being the receipt of Debenture Application Money)				
	Debenture Application & Allotment A/c	Dr.		100	
	Loss on Issue of Debentures A/c	Dr.		5	
	To 12% Debentures A/c				100
	To Premium on Redemption of Debentures A/c				5
	(Being the issue of debentures at par but redeemable at 5% premium)				
(d)	Bank A/c	Dr.		95	
	To Debenture Application & Allotment A/c				95
	(Being the receipt of Debenture Application Money)				
	Debenture Application & Allotment A/c	Dr.		95	
	Loss on Issue of Debentures A/c [₹ 5 + ₹ 5]	Dr.		10	
	To 12% Debentures A/c				100
	To Premium on Redemption of Debentures A/c				5
	(Being the issue of debenture at 5% discount which are redeemable at 5% premium)				
(e)	Bank A/c	Dr.		105	
	To Debenture Application & Allotment A/c				105
	(Being the receipt of Debenture Application Money)				
	Debenture Application & Allotment A/c	Dr.		105	
	Loss on Issue of Debentures A/c	Dr.		10	
	To 12% Debentures A/c				100
	To Securities Premium A/c				5

	To Premium on Redemption of Debentures A/c (Being the issue of debenture at 5% premium but redeemable at 10% premium)			10
(f)	Bank A/c Dr. To Debenture Application & Allotment A/c (Being the receipt of Debenture Application Money)		90	90
	Debenture Application & Allotment A/c Dr. Discount on Issue of Debentures A/c Dr. To 12% Debentures A/c (Being the issue of debenture at 10% discount)		90 10	100

Note: *According to prudence and realisation concepts, the latter discount (which is to materialise on redemption) being an unrealised gain, should not be taken into account at the time of issue and allotment of debentures. Practically speaking, this case is not found in practice.*

12.0 ISSUE OF DEBENTURES FOR CONSIDERATION OTHER THAN CASH

MEANING

When the company purchases some assets (including services) and instead of making the payment to the supplier in the form of cash, issues its fully paid debentures, such issue of debentures is called as the issue of debentures for consideration other than cash. Such debentures can be issued at par, at premium or at a discount.

PURCHASE CONSIDERATION

Purchase consideration is the amount paid by purchasing company in consideration for purchase of assets/business from another enterprise. Unless otherwise stated, Purchase consideration is arrived at as follows:

Purchase Consideration = Agreed Value of All Assets taken over – Agreed amount of Liabilities assumed.

For Example, X Ltd. has acquired from Y assets worth ₹ 20,00,000 and liabilities of ₹ 6,00,000. in this case, purchase consideration on Net Assets basis is ₹ 14,00,000 (i.e. ₹ 20,00,000—₹ 6,00,000).

TREATMENT OF DIFFERENCE

Case	Accounting Treatment
If Purchase Consideration > Net Assets	The excess of Purchase Consideration over Net Assets acquired should be debited to **Goodwill Account.**
If Net Assets > Purchase Consideration	The excess of net assets acquired over Purchase Consideration should be credited to **Capital Reserve Account.**

JOURNAL ENTRIES

Date	*Particulars*	*L.F.*	*Dr. (₹)*	*Cr.(₹)*
1.	**On Purchase of Business/Assets** Sundry Assets Dr. *(with the Agreed Value of Assets taken over)* *Goodwill A/c Dr. *(with Excess of Purchase Consideration over the Value of Net Assets)*			

	To Sundry Liabilities *(with the Agreed Amount of Liabilities taken over)* To Vendor's A/c *(with Purchase Consideration)* To *Capital Reserve A/c *(with Excess of Value of Net Assets over the Purchase Consideration)* (Being the purchase of Business/Asset from ……) *Either Goodwill or Capital Reserve.			
2.	**On Making Part Payment** Vendor's A/c *(with Part Payment)* Dr. To Cash A/c *(with Cash)* To Bank A/c *(with Cheque/Draft)* To Bills Payable A/c *(with Promissory Note)* (Being the part payment to ……)			
3.	**On Issue of Debentures** (i) **At Par** Vendor's A/c *(with Purchase Consideration)* Dr. To X% Debentures A/c *(with Nominal Value)* (Being the issue of ……% Debentures of ₹ …… each at par to ……)			
	(ii) **At a Premium** Vendor's A/c *(with Purchase Consideration)* Dr. To X% Debentures A/c *(with the Nominal Value)* To Securities Premium A/c *(with Premium)* (Being the issue of ……% Debentures of ₹ …… each at a premium of …… to ……)			
	(iii) **At a Discount** Vendor's A/c *(with Purchase Consideration)* Dr. Discount on Issue of Debentures A/c Dr. To X% Debentures A/c *(with Nominal Value)* (Being the issue of …… % Debentures of ₹ …… each at a discount of ₹ ……)			

DISCLOSURE

Debentures issued for consideration other than Cash appear under the head **'Non-Current Liabilities'** and sub-head **'Long-term Borrowings'** in the Balance Sheet.

ILLUSTRATION 14

On April 1, X Ltd. took over the Assets of ₹ 6,80,000 and Creditors of ₹ 80,000 of Y Ltd. payable 10% by a cheque and the balance by the issue of fully paid 15% Debentures of ₹ 100 each. Pass the necessary Journal Entries in the books of the company on April 1, if such Debentures are issued

(a) at par (b) at a premium of 20%. (c) at a discount of 10%.

SOLUTION

JOURNAL OF X LTD.

Date	Particulars		L.F.	Dr. (₹)	Cr.(₹)
April 1	**Entry 1 & 2 in all cases**				
1.	Sundry Assets A/c	Dr.		6,80,000	
	To Sundry Creditors				80,000
	To Y Ltd.				6,00,000
	(Being the purchase of Business from Y Ltd.)				
2.	Y Ltd.	Dr		60,000	
	To Bank A/c				60,000
	(Being the part payment made to Vendor by a cheque)				
3.	**Case (a)**				
	Y Ltd.	Dr.		5,40,000	
	To 15% Debentures A/c				5,40,000
	(Being the issue of 5,400 Debentures at par to Y Ltd.) [No. of Debentures to be issued = ₹ 5,40,000/₹ 100 = 5,400]				
3.	**Case (b)**				
	Y Ltd.	Dr.		5,40,000	
	To 15% Debentures A/c				4,50,000
	To Securities Premium A/c				90,000
	(Being the issue of 4,500 Debentures at 20% premium to Y Ltd.) [No. of Debentures to be issued = ₹ 5,40,000/₹ 120 = 4,500]				
3.	**Case (c)**				
	Y Ltd.	Dr.		5,40,000	
	Discount on Issue of Shares A/c	Dr.		60,000	
	To 15% Debentures A/c				6,00,000
	(Being the issue of 6,000 Debentures at a discount of 10% to Y Ltd.) [No. of Debentures to be issued = ₹ 5,40,000/₹ 90 = 6,000]				

ILLUSTRATION 15

On April 1,X Ltd. purchased a running business from Y Ltd. for ₹ 10,40,000 payable as to 25% by a cheque and the balance by an issue of 12% Debentures of ₹ 500 each at a premium of 4 % redeemable at a premium of ₹ 30 per Debenture in three equal installments starting from the end of third year. The assets and liabilities consisted of the following:

Building ₹ 6,00,000, Plant and Machinery ₹ 1,00,000, Inventories ₹ 2,00,000, Trade Receivables ₹ 1,80,000, Trade Payables ₹ 80,000.

Pass the necessary journal entries in the books of X Ltd on April 1.

SOLUTION

JOURNAL

Date	Particulars		L.F.	Dr. (₹)	Cr. (₹)
April 1	Building	Dr.		6,00,000	
	Plant and Machinery	Dr.		1,00,000	
	Inventories	Dr.		2,00,000	
	Trade Receivables	Dr.		1,80,000	
	Goodwill A/c[Balancing Figure]	Dr.		**40,000**	
	To Trade Payables				80,000
	To Y Ltd.				10,40,000
	(Being the purchase of Business from Y Ltd.)				
	Y Ltd.	Dr.		10,40,000	
	Loss on issue of Debentures A/c	Dr.		45,000	
	To Bank A/c [10,40,000 × 25%]				2,60,000
	To 12% Debentures A/c				7,50,000
	To Securities Premium A/c [₹ 7,50,000 × 4%]				30,000
	To Premium on Redemption of Debentures A/c				45,000
	(Being 25% by a cheque and the balance by an issue of 1500 Debentures at a premium of 4% redeemable at premium of ₹ 30 per Debenture).				
	[No. of Debentures to be issued = ₹ 7,80,000 /₹ 520 = 1,500]				

ILLUSTRATION 16

On April 1 ,X Ltd. purchased a running business from Y Ltd. for ₹ 9,60,000 payable as to 25% by a cheque and the balance by an issue of 12% Debentures of ₹ 100 each at a discount of 4 % redeemable at a premium of 6% in three equal installments starting from the end of third year. The assets and liabilities consisted of the following:

Building ₹ 6,00,000, Plant and Machinery ₹ 1,00,000, Inventories ₹ 2,00,000, Trade Receivables ₹ 1,80,000, Trade Payables ₹ 80,000.

Pass the necessary journal entries in the books of X Ltd on April 1.

SOLUTION

JOURNAL

Date	Particulars		L.F.	Dr. (₹)	Cr. (₹)
April 1	Building	Dr.		6,00,000	
	Plant and Machinery	Dr.		1,00,000	
	Inventories	Dr.		2,00,000	
	Trade Receivables	Dr.		1,80,000	
	To Trade Payables				80,000
	To Y Ltd.				9,60,000

	To Capital Reserve A/c *[Balancing Figure]*			**40,000**
	(Being the purchase of Business from Y Ltd.)			
	Y Ltd. Dr.		9,60,000	
	Loss on issue of Debentures A/c Dr.		75,000	
	To Bank A/c [9,60,000 × 25%]			2,40,000
	To 12% Debentures A/c			7,50,000
	To Premium on redemption of Debentures A/c			45,000
	(Being 25% by a cheque and the balance by an issue of 7500 Debentures @ ₹ 100 each at a discount of 4% redeemable at a premium of 6%)			
	[No.of Debentures to be issued = ₹ 7,20,000 /₹ 96 =7500]			

ILLUSTRATION 17

X Ltd. issued 2,000, 15% Debentures of ₹ 100 each credited as fully paid to the promoters for their services and issued 1,000, 15% Debentures of ₹ 100 each credited as fully paid to the underwriters for their underwriting services. Journalise these transactions.

SOLUTION

JOURNAL

Date	*Particulars*	*L.F.*	*Dr. (₹)*	*Cr.(₹)*
1.	Incorporation Costs A/c Dr.		2,00,000	
	To 15% Debentures A/c			2,00,000
	(Being the issue of 2,000 Debentures of ₹ 100 each at par to promoters as per Board's Resolution dated...)			
2.	Underwriting Commission A/c Dr.		1,00,000	
	To Underwriter's A/c			1,00,000
	(Being the underwriting commission due on shares)			
3.	Underwriter's A/c Dr.		1,00,000	
	To 15% Debentures A/c			1,00,000
	(Being the issue of 1,000 Debentures of ₹ 100 each at par to underwriters as per the Board's Resolution dated...)			

13.0 ISSUE OF DEBENTURES AS COLLATERAL SECURITY

MEANING OF DEBENTURES ISSUED AS COLLATERAL SECURITY

The issue of debentures as a collateral security means the issue of debentures as a secondary security against the loan in addition to prime or principal security. It implies stand-by or additional security to obtain secured loan. When the lender is of the view that the primary security is not enough to cover the risk, he/she may ask for further security and the borrower may issue bonds/ debentures by way of additional security in favour of lender known as collateral security.

FEATURES OF DEBENTURES ISSUED AS COLLATERAL SECURITY

1. No interest is payable on such debentures.
2. Such Debentures do not carry any voting rights.
3. Such debentures may either be presented for redemption or sold in the market if the realisable value of primary security is insufficient to cover the outstanding loan amount. However, if the lender has any surplus from sale of security after meeting his dues, he is under obligation to return the same to the borrower.

TREATMENT OF DEBENTURES ISSUED AS COLLATERAL SECURITY

There are two methods of dealing with such debentures as follows:

1. First Method or No Accounting Entry Method — Since no immediate liability is created by the company, no journal entries are passed. The existence of such debentures is disclosed **by way of a Note** in the Balance Sheet under the specific loan account. It creates a **Contingent Liability**. The disclosure of issue of debentures as collateral security in the Balance Sheet of the borrower is shown below:

AN EXTRACT OF BALANCE SHEET AS AT ....

Particulars	*Note No.*	₹
Equity and Liabilities		
Non-Current Liabilities:		
Long-term Borrowings	1	

Note to Accounts:

	Particulars	₹
1.	**Long-term Borrowings**	
	Long-term Loan from Bank (Secured by Assets and X% Debentures of ₹ ... each as Collateral security)	

2. Second Method or An Accounting Entry Method

One accounting entry is passed at the time of issue of such debentures and this entry is cancelled at the time of repayment of loan.

Date	*Particulars*	*L.F.*	*Dr. (₹)*	*Cr.(₹)*
(i)	**On Issue of Debentures as Collateral Security:**			
	Debenture Suspense A/c Dr.			
	To Debentures A/c			
(ii)	**On Release of such Debentures:**			
	Debentures A/c Dr.			
	To Debentures Suspense A/c			

ILLUSTRATION 18

X Ltd. secured a loan of ₹ 8,00,000 from the ICICI Bank on mortgage of Land & Building and issue of 10,000, 15% Debentures of ₹ 100 each as collateral security. How will you treat the issue of such debentures?

SOLUTION

(a) First Method

AN EXTRACT OF BALANCE SHEET OF X LTD. AS AT ....

Particulars	Note No.	₹
Equity and Liabilities		
Non-Current Liabilities:		
Long-term Borrowings	1	8,00,000

Note to Accounts:

Particulars	₹
1. **Long-term Borrowings**	
Long-term Loan from ICICI Bank (Secured by Land & Building and the issue of 10,000, 15% Debentures of ₹ 100 each as collateral security)	8,00,000

(b) Second Method

JOURNAL OF X LTD.

Date	Particulars	L.F.	Dr. (₹)	Cr.(₹)
	Debentures Suspense A/c Dr.		10,00,000	
	To 15% Debentures A/c			10,00,000
	(Being the issue of 10,000, 15% Debentures of ₹ 100 each as collateral security for a loan from a bank as per Board's Resolution dated...)			

AN EXTRACT OF BALANCE SHEET OF X LTD. AS AT ....

Particulars	Note No.	₹
Equity and Liabilities		
Non-Current Liabilities:		
Long-term Borrowings	1	8,00,000

Note to Accounts:

Particulars		₹
1. **Long-term Borrowings**		
Loan from ICICI Bank (Secured by Land & building and the issue of 10,000, 15% Debentures of ₹ 100 each as collateral security)		8,00,000
10,000, 15% Debentures of ₹ 100 each (issued as collateral security)	10,00,000	
Less: Debenture Suspense Account	10,00,000	Nil
		8,00,000

ILLUSTRATION 19

A Ltd. issued 5,000, 9% Debentures of ₹ 100 each at par and also raised a loan of ₹ 80,000 from bank, collaterally secured by ₹ 1,00,000, 9% Debentures. How will you show Debentures in the Balance Sheet of the company assuming that the company has recorded the issue of Debentures as collateral in the books? Also journalise the issue of debentures

SOLUTION

JOURNAL OF A LTD.

[₹ in lakhs]

Date	*Particulars*		*L.F.*	*Dr. (₹)*	*Cr.(₹)*
	Bank A/c	Dr.		5,00,000	
	To Debenture Application & Allotment A/c				5,00,000
	(Being the Application Money received)				
	Debenture Application & Allotment A/c	Dr.		5,00,000	
	To 9% Debentures A/c				5,00,000
	(Being the issue of 5,000, 9% Debentures of ₹ 100 each at par)				
	Debentures Suspense A/c	Dr.		1,00,000	
	To 9% Debentures A/c				1,00,000
	(Being the issue of 1,000, 9% debentures of ₹ 100 each as collateral security for a loan from a bank as per Board's resolution dated...)				

AN EXTRACT OF BALANCE SHEET OF X LTD. AS AT ....

Particulars	*Note No.*	₹
Equity and Liabilities		
Non-Current Liabilities:		
Long-term Borrowings	1	5,80,000

Note to Accounts:

Particulars		₹
1. Long-term Borrowings		
5,000 9% Debentures of ₹ 100 each		5,00,000
Loan from Bank		80,000
(Secured by the issue of 1,000, 9% Debentures of ₹ 100 each as collateral security)		
1,000 9% Debentures of ₹ 100 each (issued as collateral security)	1,00,000	
Less: Debenture Suspense Account	1,00,000	Nil
		5,80,000

14.0 TREATMENT OF DISCOUNT ON ISSUE OF DEBENTURES

MEANING OF DISCOUNT ON ISSUE OF DEBENTURES

Discount on Issue of Debentures (being the Excess of Face Value over Issue Price) represents capital loss. It should be written off as far as possible to Securities Premium Account *or* Profit & Loss Account during the life of debentures before the redemption of Debentures.

JOURNAL ENTRY TO WRITE OFF DISCOUNT

Date	*Particulars*		*L.F.*	*Dr. (₹)*	*Cr.(₹)*
	Securities Premium A/c	Dr.			
	(Amount w/o out of Securities Premium)				
	Profit & Loss A/c *(Amount w/o out of profits)*	Dr.			
	To Discount on Issue of Debentures A/c				
	(Being a portion of discount on issue of Debentures w/o)				

DISCLOSURE OF UNWRITTEN OFF DISCOUNT

The unwritten off balance, if any, of Discount on issue of Debentures Account appears under the head 'Non-Current Assets' and sub-head 'Other Non-Current Assets' in the Company's Balance Sheet.

How to write off Discount when the Debentures are to be redeemed in Lump sum

In such a case, the total amount of discount on issue of debentures is spread equally over the period after which the debentures will be redeemed.

Amount of Discount to be written off annually

$$= \frac{\text{Total Amount of Discount}}{\text{No. of Years after which debentures will be redeemed}}$$

HOW TO WRITE OFF DISCOUNT WHEN THE DEBENTURES ARE TO BE REDEEMED IN INSTALMENTS

In such a case, the total amount of discount on issue of debentures should be written off in the ratio in which the effective amount of debentures has been used each year. The calculation of the amount of discount to be written off each year involves the following practical steps:

Step 1: *Calculate the Face Value of Debentures outstanding in the beginning of each period.*
Step 2: *Calculate the period for which the Face Value of Debentures has been used.*
Step 3: *Calculate the product by multiplying the Face Value of Debentures outstanding by the period of use.*
Step 4: *Calculate the Ratio of various products calculated as per Step 3.*
Step 5: *Distribute the Total Amount of Discount in the ratio of various products.*

TABLE STATEMENT SHOWING THE DEBENTURES DISCOUNT TO BE WRITTEN OFF EACH YEAR

Period ended	*Face value of Debentures Outstanding in the beginning of period*	*Period of use*	*Product*	*Ratio of Products*	*Amount of Discount to be w/o*
A	B	C	D = B × C	E	Total Discount × E_n / Total E
				E_1	Total Discount × E_1/ Total E
				E_2	Total Discount × E_2/Total E
				E_3	Total Discount × E_3/Total E
				E_4	Total Discount × E_4 /Total E
				Total E	

TUTORIAL NOTES

1. *The Companies can write off any higher amount of discount out of available Securities Premium or Profits.*
2. *If the balance of 'Securities Premium Account' is available and is used to write off some portion of Discount on Issue of Debentures, then only the balance of 'Discount on Issue of Debentures Account' is to be written off during the life of debentures.*

ILLUSTRATION 20

On 01.04.2020, A Ltd. issued 1,000, 15% Debentures of ₹ 100 each at a discount of 10% redeemable at par. Show the 'Discount on Issue of Debentures A/c' if (a) such debentures are redeemable after 4 years, and (b) such debentures are redeemable by equal annual drawings in 4 years. A Ltd. follows financial year as its accounting year.

SOLUTION

(a) When Debentures are redeemable after 4 years:

A.	Total Discount allowed (₹ 1,00,000 × 10/100)	= ₹ 10,000
B.	Period for which Debentures are held	= 4 Years
C.	Amount of discount to be written off to P & L A/c every year (A/B)	= ₹ 2,500

Dr. **DISCOUNT ON ISSUE OF DEBENTURES ACCOUNT** *Cr.*

Date	*Particulars*	₹	*Date*	*Particulars*	₹
01.04.2020	To 15% Debentures A/c	10,000	31.03.2021	By P & L A/c	2,500
				By Balance c/d	7,500
		10,000			10,000
01.04.2021	To Balance b/d	7,500	31.03.2022	By P & L A/c	2,500
				By Balance c/d	5,000
		7,500			7,500
01.04.2022	To Balance b/d	5,000	31.03.2023	By P & L A/c	2,500
				By Balance c/d	2,500
		5,000			5,000
01.04.2023	To Balance b/d	2,500	31.03.2024	By P & L A/c	2,500

(b) When Debentures are redeemable by equal annual drawings in 4 years:

STATEMENT SHOWING THE DEBENTURE DISCOUNT TO BE WRITTEN OFF EACH YEAR

Year ended on A	*Face Value of Deb. used B*	*Period of Use C*	*Product D = B × C*	*Ratio E*	*Amount of Discount to be w/o 10,000 × E/10*
31.03.2021	1,00,000	12 months	12,00,000	4	4,000
31.03.2022	75,000	12 months	9,00,000	3	3,000
31.03.2023	50,000	12 months	6,00,000	2	2,000
31.03.2024	25,000	12 months	3,00,000	1	1,000
				10	10,000

Dr. **DISCOUNT ON ISSUE OF DEBENTURES ACCOUNT** *Cr.*

Date	*Particulars*	₹	*Date*	*Particulars*	₹
01.04.2020	To 15% Debentures A/c	10,000	31.03.2021	By P & L A/c	4,000
				By Balance c/d	6,000
		10,000			10,000
01.04.2021	To Balance b/d	6,000	31.03.2022	By P & L A/c	3,000
				By Balance c/d	3,000

		6,000			6,000
01.04.2022	To Balance b/d	3,000	31.03.2023	By P & L A/c By Balance c/d	2,000 1,000
		3,000			3,000
01.04.2023	To Balance b/d	1,000	31.03.2024	By P & L A/c	1,000

ILLUSTRATION 21

On 1.4.2020, X Ltd. issued ₹ 1,00,000 15% Debentures of ₹ 100 each at 94% red. at par as follows:

Year end	*2*	*3*	*4*	*5*
Nominal Value of Debentures to be redeemed	10%	20%	30%	40%

Required: Calculate the amount of discount to be written off each year assuming that the company closes its accounts on financial year basis.

SOLUTION

Total Discount to be w/o = ₹ 1,00,000 × 6/100 = ₹ 6,000

STATEMENT SHOWING THE DEBENTURE DISCOUNT TO BE W/O EACH YEAR

Year ended on *A*	*Face Value of Debentures outstanding (₹)* *B*	*Proportion* *C*	*Amount of Discount to be w/o* *D = ₹ 6,000 × C/40*
31.03.2021	1,00,000	10	₹ 6,000 × 10/40 = 1,500
31.03.2022	1,00,000	10	₹ 6,000 × 10/40 = 1,500
31.03.2023	90,000	9	₹ 6,000 × 9/40 = 1,350
31.03.2024	70,000	7	₹ 6,000 × 7/40 = 1,050
31.03.2025	40,000	4	₹ 6,000 × 4/40 = 600
		40	6,000

ILLUSTRATION 22

F Ltd. issued 12% Debentures of ₹ 100 each valued at ₹ 3,00,000 at a discount of 4%, repayable at par in equal proportions at the end of the 2nd, 4th and 6th year. Calculate the amount of discount to be written off at the end of each year and prepare 'Discount on issue of Debentures Account'.

SOLUTION

Total Discount to be written off = ₹ 3,00,000 × 4/100 = ₹ 12,000

CALCULATION OF AMOUNT OF DISCOUNT WRITTEN OFF EACH YEAR

Year	*O/s Debentures (₹)*	*Ratio*	*Discount written off*
I	3,00,000	3	12,000 × 3/12 = ₹ 3,000
II	3,00,000	3	12,000 × 3/12 = ₹ 3,000
III	2,00,000	2	12,000 × 2/12 = ₹ 2,000
IV	2,00,000	2	12,000 × 2/12 = ₹ 2,000
V	1,00,000	1	12,000 × 1/12 = ₹ 1,000

VI	1,00,000	1	12,000 × 1/12 = ₹ 1,000
		12	12,000

Dr. **DISCOUNT ON ISSUE OF DEBENTURES ACCOUNT** Cr.

Date	Particulars	₹	Date	Particulars	₹
I	To 12% Debentures A/c	12,000	I	By Profit & Loss A/c	3,000
				By Balance c/d	9,000
		12,000			12,000
II	To Balance c/d	9,000	II	By Profit & Loss A/c	3,000
				By Balance c/d	6,000
		9,000			9,000
III	To Balance b/d	6,000	III	By Profit & Loss A/c	2,000
				By Balance c/d	4,000
		6,000			6,000
IV	To Balance b/d	4,000	IV	By Profit & Loss A/c	2,000
				By Balance c/d	3,000
		4,000			4,000
V	To Balance b/d	2,000	V	By Profit & Loss A/c	1,000
				By Balance c/d	1,000
		2,000			2,000
VI	To Balance b/d	1,000	VI	By Profit & Loss A/c	1,000

ILLUSTRATION 23

Y Ltd. issued 1 lakh, 8% Debentures of ₹ 100 each at a discount of 6% on April 1, 2020 redeemable as follows:

40,000 Debentures on March 31, 2022, 20,000 Debentures on March 31, 2023 and remaining Debentures on March 31, 2024.

Required: Calculate the amount of discount to be written off in each of the years till the Debenture are paid. Also prepare Discount on Issue of Debenture Account.

SOLUTION

Total Discount to be w/o = ₹ 100,00,000 × 6/100

= ₹ 6,00,000

CALCULATION OF DISCOUNT ON ISSUE OF DEBENTURES TO BE W/O EACH YEAR

Year ended on A	*Face Value of Debentures outstanding (₹)* B	*Proportion* C	*Amount of Discount to be w/o D = ₹ 6,00,000 × C/30* D
31.03.2021	1,00,00,000	10	6,00,000 × 10/30 = 2,00,000
31.03.2022	1,00,00,000	10	6,00,000 × 10/30 = 2,00,000
31.03.2023	60,00,000	6	6,00,000 × 6/30 = 1,20,000
31.03.2024	40,00,000	4	6,00,000 × 4/30 = 80,000

Dr. **DISCOUNT ON ISSUE OF DEBENTURES ACCOUNT** Cr.

Date	Particulars	₹	Date	Particulars	₹
01.04.2020	To 5% Debentures	6,00,000	31.03.2021	By Profit & Loss A/c	2,00,000
				By Balance c/f	4,00,000
		6,00,000			6,00,000
01.04.2021	To Balance b/f	4,00,000	31.03.2022	By Profit & Loss A/c	2,00,000
				By Balance c/f	2,00,000
		4,00,000			4,00,000
01.04.2022	To Balance b/f	2,00,000	31.03.2023	By Profit & Loss A/c	1,20,000
				By Balance c/f	80,000
		2,00,000			2,00,000
01.04.2023	To Balance b/f	80,000	31.03.2024	By Profit & Loss A/c	80,000

ILLUSTRATION 24

X Ltd issued 12,000, 10% Debentures of ₹ 100 each at a discount of ₹ 50,000 on April 1, 2020. Debentures are repayable in five equal installments starting from the end of third year. Calculate the amount of discount to be written off and record the transaction in the books of X Ltd.

SOLUTION

JOURNAL OF X LTD.

Date	Particulars		L.F.	Dr. (₹)	Cr.(₹)
01.04.2020	Bank A/c	Dr.		11,50,000	
	To Debentures Application & Allotment A/c				11,50,000
	(Being the Application Money received)				
	Debenture Application & Allotment A/c	Dr.		11,50,000	
	Discount on Issue of Debentures A/c	Dr.		50,000	
	To 10% Debentures A/c				12,00,000
	(Being the Application Money Adjusted)				
	Profit and Loss A/c	Dr.		10,000	
	To Discount on issue of Debentures A/c				10,000
	(Being the discount written off)				
31.03.2022	Profit and Loss A/c	Dr.		10,000	
	To Discount on issue of Debentures A/c				10,000
	(Being the discount written off)				
31.03.2023	Profit and Loss A/c	Dr.		10,000	
	To Discount on issue of Debentures A/c				10,000
	(Being the discount written off)				
31.03.2024	Profit and Loss A/c	Dr.		8,000	
	To Discount on issue of Debentures A/c				8,000
	(Being the discount written off)				

31.03.2025	Profit and Loss A/c Dr.		6,000	
	To Discount on issue of Debentures A/c			6,000
	(Being the discount written off)			
31.03.2026	Profit and Loss A/c Dr.		4,000	
	To Discount on issue of Debentures A/c			4,000
	(Being the discount written off)			
31.03.2027	Profit and Loss A/c Dr.		2,000	
	To Discount on issue of Debentures A/c			2,000
	(Being the discount written off)			

Working Note:

DISCOUNT ON ISSUE OF DEBENTURES TO BE CHARGED TO P & L A/C EACH YEAR

Date A	*Amount of Debentures outstanding (₹)* B	*Proportion* C	*Discount to be w/o D = ₹ 50,000 × C/25* D
31.03.2021	120,00,000	5	5/25 × ₹ 50,000 = ₹ 10,000
31.03.2022	120,00,000	5	5/25 × ₹ 50,000 = ₹ 10,000
31.03.2023	120,00,000	5	5/25 × ₹ 50,000 = ₹ 10,000
31.03.2024	96,00,000	4	4/25 × ₹ 50,000 = ₹ 8,000
31.03.2025	72,00,000	3	3/25 × ₹ 50,000 = ₹ 6,000
31.03.2026	48,00,000	2	2/25 × ₹ 50,000 = ₹ 4,000
31.03.2027	24,00,000	1	1/25 × ₹ 50,000 = ₹ 2,000
		25	50,000

ILLUSTRATION 25

Y Ltd. issued Debentures @ 94% for ₹ 1,00,000 on 1st Jan., 2020 repayable by five equal annual drawings of ₹ 20,000 each.

Required: Calculate the amount of discount to be written off each year assuming that the company closes its accounts on 31st March each year.

SOLUTION

Total Discount to be w/o = ₹ 1,00,000 × 6/100 = ₹ 6,000

STATEMENT SHOWING THE DEBENTURE DISCOUNT TO BE WRITTEN OFF EACH YEAR

Period A	*Face Value of Deb. (in lakhs)* B	*Period of Use (month)* C	*Product D = B × C* D	*Ratio* E	*Amount of Discount to be w/o ₹ 6,000 × E/60*	*Amount of Discount to be w/o Each Year*
1.1.2020 – 31.03.2020	1.00	3	3.00	5	500	500
1.4.2020 – 31.12.2020	1.00	9	9.00	15	1,500	
1.1.2021 – 31.03.2021	0.80	3	2.40	4	400	1,900
1.4.2021 – 31.12.2021	0.80	9	7.20	12	1,200	

1.1.2022 – 31.03.2022	0.60	3	1.80	3	300	1,500
1.4.2022 – 31.12.2022	0.60	9	5.40	9	900	
1.1.2023 – 31.03.2023	0.40	3	1.20	2	200	1,100
1.4.2023 – 31.12.2023	0.40	9	3.60	6	600	
1.1.2024 – 31.03.2024	0.20	3	0.60	1	100	700
1.4.2024 – 31.12.2024	0.20	9	1.80	3	300	300

15.0 TREATMENT OF LOSS ON ISSUE OF DEBENTURES

MEANING OF LOSS ON ISSUE OF DEBENTURES

From the accounting point of view, Loss on issue of Debentures represents the total of the following two losses:

1. Actual Loss incurred at the time of issue of Debentures by way of Discount.
2. Anticipated Loss to be incurred at the time of Redemption by way of Premium payable on Redemption as per Prudence Principle.

ACCOUNTING TREATMENT

Loss on issue of debentures is treated in the accounts in the same manner as the Discount on Issue of Debentures.

ILLUSTRATION 26

On 01.04.2020 *X* Ltd. issued 500, 15% Debentures of ₹ 100 each, at a discount of 10% redeemable at a premium of 10%.

Required: Show the 'Loss on Issue of Debentures A/c', if (i) such debentures are redeemable after 4 years, and (ii) such debentures are redeemable by equal annual drawings in 4 years. *X* Ltd. follows financial year as its accounting year.

SOLUTION

(A) WHEN THE DEBENTURES ARE REDEEMABLE AFTER 4 YEARS

A. Discount allowed = ₹ 50,000 × 10/100	= ₹ 5,000
B. Premium on Redemption = ₹ 50,000 × 10/100	= ₹ 5,000
C. Total Loss [A + B]	= ₹ 10,000
D. Redemption Period	= 4 Years
E. Amount of loss to be written off to P & L A/c every year (C/D)	= ₹ 2,500

Dr. **LOSS ON ISSUE OF DEBENTURES ACCOUNT** *Cr.*

Date	Particulars	₹	Date	Particulars	₹
01.04.2020	To 15% Debentures A/c	5,000	31.03.2021	By P & L A/c	2,500
	To premium on Red. of Debentures A/c	5,000		By Balance c/d	7,500
		10,000			10,000
01.04.2021	To Balance b/d	7,500	31.03.2022	By P & L A/c	2,500
				By Balance c/d	5,000
		7,500			7,500

01.04.2022	To Balance b/d	5,000	31.03.2023	By P & L A/c By Balance c/d	2,500 2,500
		5,000			5,000
01.04.2023	To Balance b/d	2,500	31.03.2024	By P & L A/c	2,500

(B) WHEN THE DEBENTURES ARE RED. BY EQUAL ANNUAL DRAWINGS IN 4 YEARS:

Year ended on A	Face Value of Deb. used (in lacs) B	Period of Use (Month) C	Product D = B × C D	Ratio E	Amount of Loss to be w/o ₹ 10,000 × E/10
31.03.2021	50,000	12 months	6,00,000	4	4,000
31.03.2022	37,500	12 months	4,50,000	3	3,000
31.03.2023	25,000	12 months	3,00,000	2	2,000
31.03.2024	12,500	12 months	1,50,000	1	1,000
				10	10,000

Dr. **LOSS ON ISSUE OF DEBENTURES ACCOUNT** *Cr.*

Date	Particulars	₹	Date	Particulars	₹
01.04.2020	To 15% Debentures A/c To premium on Red. of Debentures A/c	5,000 5,000	31.03.2021	By P & L A/c By Balance c/d	4,000 6,000
		10,000			10,000
01.04.2021	To Balance b/d	6,000	31.03.2022	By P & L A/c By Balance c/d	3,000 3,000
		6,000			6,000
01.04.2022	To Balance b/d	3,000	31.03.2023	By P & L A/c By Balance c/d	2,000 1,000
		3,000			3,000
01.04.2023	To Balance b/d	1,000	31.03.2024	By P & L A/c	1,000

ILLUSTRATION 27

On April 1, 2020, X Ltd issued 5,000, 8% Debentures of ₹ 100 each at a discount of 4% redeemable after 5 years at a premium of 6%.

Required: Pass the necessary journal entries for issue of Debentures and writing off Loss on Issue Debentures Account. Also prepare Loss on Issue of Debentures Account.

SOLUTION

A. Discount Allowed = ₹ 5,00,000 × 4/100	= ₹ 20,000
B. Premium on Redemption = ₹ 5,00,000 × 6/100	= ₹ 30,000
C. Total Loss	= ₹ 50,000
D. Redemption Period	= 5 years
E. Amount of Loss to be w/o to P & L A/c each year	= ₹ 50,000/5 = ₹ 10,000

JOURNAL OF X LTD.

Date	Particulars		L.F.	Dr. (₹)	Cr.(₹)
01.04.2020	Bank A/c	Dr.		4,80,000	
	To Debenture Application & Allotment A/c				4,80,000
	(Being the receipt of Application Money)				
01.04.2020	Debenture Application & Allotment A/c	Dr.		4,80,000	
	Loss on Issue of Debentures A/c	Dr.		50,000	
	To 8% Debentures A/c				5,00,000
	To Premium on Redemption of Debentures A/c				30,000
	(Being 5,000, 8% Debentures issued at discount redeemable at premium)				
31.03.2021	Profit & Loss A/c	Dr.		10,000	
	To Loss on Issue of Debentures A/c				10,000
	(Being the Loss on issue of debenture written off)				
31.03.2022	Profit & Loss A/c	Dr.		10,000	
	To Loss on Issue of Debentures A/c				10,000
	(Being the loss on issue of debenture written off)				
31.03.2023	Profit & Loss A/c	Dr.		10,000	
	To Loss on Issue of Debenture A/c				10,000
	(Being the loss on issue of debenture written off)				
31.03.2024	Profit & Loss A/c	Dr.		10,000	
	To Loss on Issue of Debenture A/c				10,000
	(Being the loss on issue of debenture written off)				
31.03.2025	Profit & Loss A/c	Dr.		10,000	
	To Loss on Issue of Debenture A/c				10,000
	(Being the loss on issue of debenture written off)				

Dr. **LOSS ON ISSUE OF DEBENTURES ACCOUNT** Cr.

Date	Particulars	₹	Date	Particulars	₹
01.04.2020	To 8% Debentures	20,000	31.03.2021	By Profit & Loss A/c	10,000
	To Premium on Red.			By Balance c/f	40,000
	of Debentures A/c	30,000			
		50,000			50,000
01.04.2021	To Balance b/f	40,000	31.03.2022	By Profit & Loss A/c	10,000
				To Balance c/f	30,000
		40,000			40,000
01.04.2022	To Balance b/f	30,000	31.03.2023	By Profit & Loss A/c	10,000
				By Balance c/f	20,000
		30,000			30,000
01.04.2023	To balance b/f	20,000	31.03.2024	By Profit & Loss A/c	10,000
				By Balance c/f	10,000

		20,000			20,000
01.04.2024	To Balance b/f	10,000	31.03.2025	By Profit & Loss A/c	10,000

16.0 INTEREST ON DEBENTURES

Meaning	Interest on Debentures is the cost of serving the money raised by the issue of Debentures.
Nature	Interest on Debentures is a charge against the profits of the company and is payable irrespective of the fact whether there are profits or not.
How to Calculate	Interest on Debentures is calculated on the face value and not on the issue price.
TDS (Tax deducted at Source)	The company is also required to deduct income-tax at the prescribed rate from the gross amount of interest in certain cases. The amount of tax so deducted is required to be deposited within the prescribed time limit.
Journal Entries	The following entries are required to be passed:

Case	Journal Entry
(a) For making Interest due	Interest on Debentures A/c Dr. To Debenture-holders A/c To TDS from Deb. Interest A/c (Being the Interest due for...months & T.D.S. @ %)
(b) For making Payment of Interest	Debenture-holder's A/c Dr. To Bank A/c (Being the Payment of Interest)
(c) For payment of T.D.S. (Tax Deducted at Source)	TDS from Deb. Interest A/c Dr. To Bank A/c (Being the Payment of TDS)
(d) For transfer of Debenture interest	Profit & Loss A/c Dr. To Interest on Debentures A/c (Being the t/f of Debenture Interest)

TUTORIAL NOTES

1. *No interest is payable on Debentures issued as collateral security.*
2. *Interest accrued (whether due or not) on Debentures appears under the head 'Current Liabilities' and sub-head 'Other Current Liabilities'.*
3. *Interest on Debentures appears in the Statement of Profit and Loss in the Expense Part under the head 'Finance Costs'*

For Example, X Ltd. issued 1,000, 12% Debentures of ₹ 100 each on 1st July 2019 (Interest dates being 30th June and 31st Dec.). Accounting year is April to March, No interest has been paid till 31st March 2020. In this case, Interest from 1st July 2019 to 31st Dec. 2019 is called 'Interest accrued and due or simply 'Outstanding Interest'. Interest from 1st Jan 2020 to 31st March 2020 is called 'Interest Accrued but not due' or simply 'Accrued Interest'.

ILLUSTRATION 28

Y Ltd. issued 1000, 15% Debentures of ₹ 100 each on 1st April, 2020 at a discount of 10% redeemable at a premium of 10% after 4 years.

Required: Pass Journal entries for the period ended 31st March, 2021 assuming that the Interest is payable half yearly on 30th September and 31st March (assume the rate of Tax deducted at source being 10% and Y Ltd. follows financial year as its accounting year, Loss on Issue of Debentures to be written off equally over 4 years).

SOLUTION

JOURNAL OF Y LTD.

Date	*Particulars*		*L.F.*	*Dr. (₹)*	*Cr.(₹)*
01.04.2020	Bank A/c	Dr.		90,000	
	To Debenture Application & Allotment A/c				90,000
	(Being the Application money received)				
	Debenture Application & Allotment A/c	Dr.		90,000	
	Loss on Issue of Debentures A/c	Dr.		20,000	
	To 15% Debentures A/c				1,00,000
	To Premium on Redemption of Debentures A/c				10,000
	(Being the issue of 1000, 15% Debentures of ₹ 100 each at 10% discount & redeemable at 10% premium)				
30.09.2020	Interest on Debentures A/c	Dr.		7,500	
	[1000 × ₹ 100 × 15% × 6/12]				
	To Debentureholders' A/c (₹ 7,500 × 90%]				6,750
	To TDS From Deb. Int. A/c [₹ 7,500 × 10%]				750
	(Being the Interest due for 6 months & T.D.S. @ 10%)				
30.09.2020	Debentureholders' A/c	Dr.		6,750	
	To Bank A/c				6,750
	(Being the payment of Interest)				
30.09.2020	TDS from Deb. Interest A/c	Dr.		750	
	To Bank A/c				750
	(Being the payment of T.D.S.)				
31.03.2021	Interest on Debentures A/c	Dr.		7,500	
	[1000 × ₹ 100 × 15% × 6/12]				
	To Debenture-holders A/c [₹ 7,500 × 90%]				6,750
	To TDS From Deb. Interest A/c [₹ 7,500 × 10%]				750
	(Being the Interest due for 6 months)				
31.03.2021	Debentureholders' A/c	Dr.		6,750	
	To Bank A/c				6,750
	(Being the payment of Interest)				
31.03.2021	TDS from Deb. Interest A/c	Dr.		750	
	To Bank A/c				750
	(Being the payment of T.D.S.)				

31.03.2021	Profit & Loss A/c [₹ 7,500 + ₹ 7,500]	Dr.		15,000	
	To Interest on Debentures A/c				15,000
	(Being the transfer of Debentures Interest to P & L A/c)				
31.03.2021	Profit & Loss A/c [(₹ 10,000 + ₹ 10,000)/4]	Dr.		5,000	
	To Loss on Issue of Debentures A/c				5,000
	(Being the loss on issue of Debentures written off)				

Note: Loss on Issue of Debentures to be written off equally over 4 years = ₹ 20,000/4 = ₹ 5,000.

VERY SHORT ANSWER TYPE QUESTIONS

1. Briefly explain the following:
   (a) Debenture
   (b) Debentures for consideration other than cash
   (c) Debentures issued as Collateral Security
2. Enumerate the following:
   (a) Two characteristics of Debentures
   (b) Sources of providing premium payable on redemption
   (c) Two types of Debentures from the point of view of Security
   (d) Two types of Debentures from the point of view of Tenure
   (e) Two types of Debentures from the point of view of Mode of Redemption
   (f) Two types of Debentures from the point of view of Coupon Rate
   (g) Two types of Debentures from the point of view of Registration
3. State one basic difference between the following:
   (a) A Share and A Debenture
   (b) Share Capital and Loan Capital
   (c) Secured Debentures and Unsecured Debentures
   (d) Redeemable Debentures and Irredeemable Debentures
   (e) Convertible Debentures and Non-convertible Debentures
   (f) Fully Convertible Debentures (FCD) and Partly Convertible Debentures (PCD)
   (g) Registered Debentures and Bearer Debentures
   (h) Fixed Charge Debentures and Floating Charge Debentures
   (i) First Charge and Second Charge Debentures
4. Name the head and sub-head under which the following appear in the Balance Sheet:
   (a) Premium on Redemption of Debentures Account
   (b) Debentures issued for consideration other than cash
   (c) Debenture Suspense Account
5. State the Nature of the following:
   (a) Debenture Account
   (b) Premium on Redemption of Debentures Account
   (c) Interest on Debentures

6. State the accounting treatment of the following:
   (a) Premium Payable on Redemption of Debentures
   (b) Debentures issued as Collateral Security
7. Name the account to which the amount of premium received on issue of debentures is to be credited.
8. For what purposes, can the premium received on issue of debentures be utilized?
9. Is there any restriction on Issue of Debentures at a discount?
10. Is interest payable on Debentures issued as collateral security?
11. Is the Interest on Debentures calculated at the fixed percentage on the issue price?
12. State with reason whether Interest on Debentures is paid before any dividend is paid to shareholders.

PRACTICAL QUESTIONS

PROBLEM 1

1. Show by means of journal entries how you would record the following issues. Also show how they would appear in the respective Balance Sheets.
   (a) S Ltd. issues ₹ 1,00,000, 12% Debentures of ₹ 100 each at a discount of 9% redeemable at par.
   (b) T Ltd. issues ₹ 1,00,000, 12% Debentures of ₹ 100 each at a discount of 5% redeemable at a premium of 7%.
   (c) U Ltd. issues 1,00,000, 12% Debentures of ₹ 100 each at a premium of 5% redeemable at 110%.
   (d) V Ltd. purchased plant & machinery for ₹ 2,00,000 payable as to 32.5% by cheque and the balance by an issue of 1,500, 12% Debentures of ₹ 100 each.
   (e) W Ltd. purchased land & building for ₹ 6,00,000 payable as to 10% by cheque and the balance by the issue of 4,500, 12% Debentures of ₹ 100 each.
   (f) X Ltd. issued 300, 12% Debentures of ₹ 100 each as a Collateral security to a bank who has advanced a loan of ₹ 25,000 to the company for a period of 5 years
   (g) Y Ltd. issued ₹ 25,000. 12% Debentures of ₹ 100 each to a Creditor for ₹ 20,000 Capital expenditure in satisfaction of his claim.
   (h) Z Ltd. issued ₹ 20,000, 12% Debentures of ₹ 100 each to a vendor who supplied a machine costing ₹ 25,000.
2. X Ltd. took over the Assets of ₹ 3,60,000 and Creditors of ₹ 42,000 of Y & Co. for an agreed amount of ₹ 3,30,000 by the issue of fully paid 12% Debentures of ₹ 100 each at a premium of 10%. These Debentures are redeemable at a premium of 5% after 3 years. Pass the necessary journal entries in the books of X Ltd.

   [**Ans.** Goodwill ₹ 12,000, No. of Debentures to be issued 3,000]
3. X Ltd. took over the Assets of ₹ 4,20,000 and Creditors of ₹ 48,000 of Y Ltd. for a sum of ₹ 3,60,000 payable 10% by a cheque and the balance by the issue of fully paid 15% Debentures of ₹ 100 each at a discount of 10% and redeemable at a premium of 5% after 3 years. Pass the necessary journal entries in the books of X Ltd.

   [**Ans.** Capital Reserve ₹ 12,000, No. of Debentures to be issued 3,600]

4. Tulsian's Ltd., issued 25,000; 10% Debentures of ₹ 100 each. Give the Journal entries and the Balance Sheet in each of the following cases when:
   (i) the debentures were issued at a premium of 20%.
   (ii) the debentures were issued as a collateral security to Bank against a loan of ₹ 20,00,000.
   (iii) the debentures were issued to a supplier of machinery costing ₹ 28,00,000 as his full and final payment.

[**Ans.** (ii) No Entry but only disclosures in Note to B/S]

5. A Ltd. took over the fixed assets of ₹ 12,00,000 and current liabilities of ₹ 1,60,000 of B Ltd. for an agreed purchase consideration of ₹ 10,80,000 to be satisfied by the issue of 15% Debentures of ₹ 100 each. Prepare journal and Balance Sheet of A Ltd. assuming that—
   (a) Such Debentures are issued at par;
   (b) Such Debentures are issued at 20% premium;
   (c) Such Debentures are issued at 10% discount. [**Ans.:** Goodwill ₹ 40,000]

6. On Ist April, 2015, XYZ Ltd. issued 1,00,000, 13% Debentures of ₹ 100 each at a discount of 6%, redeemable at par as follows:

Year-end	1	2	3	4
Face Value of Debentures	10%	20%	30%	40%

Calculate the amount of discount to be written off each year assuming that the company closes its accounts on 31st March each year.

[**Ans.:** (B) Amt of Discount to be W/O ₹ 2,00,000, 1,80,000, 1,40,000, 80,000]

7. J Ltd. issued ₹ 20,00,000, 15% Debentures at 8% discount. Debentures are to be redeemed in the following manner:

Year-end	2	3	4	5
Face Value of Debentures	₹ 2,00,000	₹ 4,00,000	₹ 6,00,000	₹ 8,00,000

Give Journal entry for issue of debentures and Discount on issue of debenture Account for 5 years.

[**Ans.** Amount of discount to be written off: ₹ 40,000, ₹ 40,000, ₹ 36,000, ₹ 28,000, ₹ 16,000]

8. Tushar Tulsian Ltd. (1) issued ₹ 1,00,000, 12% Debentures of ₹ 100 each @ 94% on 1st April, 2015 redeemable by five equal annual drawings of ₹ 20,000 each. The company closes its accounts on 31st March each year. Calculate the amount of discount to be written off each year if the redemption commences from 31st March 2016.

[**Ans.:** Amount of Discount to be w/o: ₹ 2,000, ₹ 1,600, ₹ 1,200, ₹ 800, ₹ 400]

9. Tushar Tulsian Ltd. (2) issued ₹ 1,00,000, 12% Debentures of ₹ 100 each @ 94% on 1st April, 2015 redeemable by five equal annual drawings of ₹ 20,000 each. The company closes its accounts on 31st March each year. Calculate the amount of discount to be written off each year if the redemption commences from 31st March 2017.

[**Ans.:** Amount of Discount to be w/o ₹ 1,500, ₹ 1,500, ₹ 1,200, ₹ 900, ₹ 600, ₹ 300]

10. Tushar Tulsian Ltd. (3) issued ₹ 1,00,000, 12% Debentures of ₹ 100 each @ 94% on 1st April, 2015 redeemable by five equal annual drawings of ₹ 20,000 each. The company closes its accounts on 31st March each year. Calculate the amount of discount to be written off each year if the redemption commences from 31st March 2018.

[**Ans.:** Amount of Discount to be w/o ₹ 1,200, ₹ 1,200, ₹ 1,200, ₹ 960, ₹ 720, ₹ 480, ₹ 240]

11. K Ltd. issued 12% Debentures of the face value of ₹ 3,00,000 at a discount of 5% repayable at par in equal proportions at the end of 5th, 10th and 15th years Show the amount of discount to be written off at the end of each years.

[**Ans.:** Amount of discount to be written off for first five years ₹ 1,500, for next five years ₹ 1,000, for next five years ₹ 500]

12. Madhuri Dixit Ltd. issued 5,000, 12% Debentures of ₹ 100 each at a discount of 5% repayable after 5 years at a premium of 5%. Give journal entry for the issue of such debentures and loss on issue of debentures account for 5 years.

[**Ans.:** Amount of loss on issue of debentures to be written off each year ₹ 10,000]

13. X Ltd. issued ₹ 50,00,000, 8% Debentures of ₹ 100 at a discount of 6% on 1st April 2015 redeemable at premium of 4% by draw of lots as follows:

₹ 20,00,000 Debentures on March 31, 2018.

₹ 10,00,000 Debentures on March 31, 2019.

₹ 20,00,000 Debentures on March 31, 2020.

Required: Compute the amount of loss to be written off in each year till debenture are paid. Also prepare loss on issue of debenture account.

[**Ans.:** ₹ 125 lakhs, ₹ 125 lakhs, ₹ 125 lakhs, ₹ 75 lakhs, ₹ 50 lakhs]

14. X Ltd. took over the Assets of ₹ 11,60,000 and Creditors of ₹ 80,000 of Y Ltd. for ₹ 10,40,000 payable as to 25% by a cheque and the balance by an issue of 12% Debentures of ₹ 100 each. Pass the necessary journal entries in the books of X Ltd. if:

(a) the Debentures are issued at par and are redeemable at 6% premium

(b) the Debentures are issued at 4% premium and are redeemable at 6% premium

(c) the Debentures are issued at a discount of 4 % and are redeemable at a premium of ₹ ₹ 5.76 per Debenture.

[**Ans** Capital Reserve ₹ 40,000, No. of Debentures to be issued (a)7800 (b)7500 (c)8125]

15. X Ltd. took over the Assets of ₹ 10,80,000 and Creditors of ₹ 80,000 of Y Ltd. for ₹ 10,40,000 payable as to 25% by a cheque and the balance by an issue of 12% Debentures of ₹ 500 each. Pass the necessary journal entries in the books of X Ltd. if:

(a) the Debentures are issued at par and are redeemable at 6% premium

(b) the Debentures are issued at 4% premium and are redeemable at 6% premium

(c) the Debentures are issued at a discount of 4 % and are redeemable at a premium of ₹ 30 per Debenture.

[**Ans** Goodwill ₹ 40,000, No. of Debentures to be issued (a)1560 (b)1500 (c)1625]

16. On 01.04.2020 ,Tushar Tulsian Ltd. purchased a running business from Y Ltd. for ₹ 9,60,000 payable as to 25% by a cheque and the balance by an issue of 12% Debentures of ₹ 100 each at a discount of 4 % redeemable at a premium of 6% in three equal installments starting from the end of third year. The assets and liabilities consisted of the following:

Building ₹ 6,00,000, Plant and Machinery ₹ 1,00,000, Inventories ₹ 2,00,000, Trade Receivables ₹ 1,80,000, Trade Payables ₹ 80,000.

Interest is payable half yearly on 30th September and 31st March. Pass the necessary Journal Entries in the books of Tushar Tulsian Ltd for the first year (assume the rate of Tax deducted at source being 10%).

[**Ans** Capital Reserve ₹ 40,000, No. of Debentures to be issued 7500, Loss on Issue of Debentures to be w/o:Yr I ₹ 18,750, Yr II ₹ 18,750, Yr III ₹ 18,750, Yr IV ₹ 12,500,Yr V ₹ 6,250]

17. On April 1,2020, Bharat Tulsian Ltd. purchased a running business from Y Ltd. for ₹ 10,40,000 payable as to 25% by a cheque and the balance by an issue of 12% Debentures of ₹ 500 each at a premium of 4 % redeemable at a premium of ₹ 30 per Debenture in three equal installments starting from the end of third year. The assets and liabilities consisted of the following:

Building ₹ 6,00,000, Plant and Machinery ₹ 1,00,000, Inventories ₹ 2,00,000, Trade Receivables ₹ 1,80,000, Trade Payables ₹ 80,000.

Interest is payable half yearly on 30th September and 31st March. Pass the necessary Journal Entries in the books of Bharat Tulsian Ltd for the first year (assume the rate of Tax deducted at source being 10%).

[**Ans** Goodwill ₹ 40,000, No. of Debentures to be issued 1500, Loss written off out of Securities Premium ₹ 30,000,Balance Loss on Issue of Debentures to be w/o: Yr I ₹ 3,750, Yr II ₹ 3,750, Yr III ₹ 3,750, Yr IV ₹ 2,500,Yr V ₹ 1,250]

5B REDEMPTION OF DEBENTURES

LEARNING OBJECTIVES

After studying this chapter, you should be able to understand:

- Meaning of Redemption of Debentures
- Methods of Redemption of Debentures
- Sources of Redemption of Debentures
- Redemption out of Capital
- Redemption out of Profits
- Redemption by Conversion
- Financing of Redemption of Debentures
- Sinking Fund Method or Debentures Redemption Fund Method
- Redemption by Purchase in the Open Market

1.0 MEANING OF REDEMPTION OF DEBENTURES

Redemption of debentures means discharge of liability on account of Debentures by making repayment to the Debentureholders.

2.0 METHODS OF REDEMPTION OF DEBENTURES

The various methods of redemption of Debentures are as follows:

1. BY PAYMENT IN LUMP SUM

Under this method, the payment of entire Debenture debt is made in one lot at the expiry of a specified period (i.e., at maturity) *or* even before the expiry of the specified period after passing the necessary resolution at the meeting of the debenture-holders. ***For Example***, Reliance Petroleum has made the payment of TOCD (i.e., Triple Option Convertible Debentures) before the expiry of the specified period.

2. BY PAYMENT IN INSTALMENTS

Under this method, the payment of specified portion of Debentures debt is made in instalments at specified dates. ***For Example***, a Debenture of ₹ 100 may be discharged as given below:

20% or ₹ 20 on 1.4.2024, 20% or ₹ 20 on 1.4.2025, 30% or ₹ 30 on 1.4.2026, 30% or ₹ 30 on 1.4.2027

3. REDEMPTION BY PURCHASE IN THE OPEN MARKET

When a company purchases its own debentures in the open market for the purposes of cancellation, such an act of purchasing and cancelling the debentures constitutes redemption by purchase in the open market.

3.0 SOURCES OF REDEMPTION OF DEBENTURES

The various sources out of which the Debentures may be redeemed are as follows:

1. Redemption out of Capital
2. Redemption out of Profits
3. Redemption by Conversion

4.0 REDEMPTION OUT OF CAPITAL

MEANING OF REDEMPTION OUT OF CAPITAL

When adequate profits are not transferred from Profit & Loss Appropriation Account to the Debenture Redemption Reserve Account before the redemption of debentures, such redemption is said to be out of capital.

JOURNAL ENTRIES

Date	*Particulars*	*L.F.*	*Dr. (₹)*	*Dr. (₹)*
	1. For the Amount due to Debentureholders on redemption (a) ***If the Debentures are to be redeemed at par*** Debentures A/c [With Nominal Value] Dr. To Debenture-holders' A/c (Being the Amount due on redemption)			
	(b) ***If the Debentures are to be redeemed at a premium*** Debentures A/c [With Nominal Value] Dr. Premium on Redemption of Debentures A/c Dr. *[With Premium]* To Debenture-holders' A/c [With Total] (Being the Amount due on redemption)			
	2. For Payment to Debentureholders Debenture-holders' A/c (With Payment) Dr. To Bank A/c (Being the Payment made to Debentureholders)			

5.0 REDEMPTION OUT OF PROFITS

MEANING OF REDEMPTION OUT OF PROFITS

When adequate profits are transferred from Profit & Loss Appropriation Account to the Debenture Redemption Reserve Account before the redemption of debentures, such redemption is said to be out of profits.

DEBENTURE REDEMPTION RESERVE [DRR] [RULE 18(7)]

Meaning	DRR is a reserve created out of profits for the purpose of redemption of debentures.
For Listed Co	As per Rule 18(7) of The Companies Act, 2013, a listed company is **not required** to transfer **adequate amounts out of its profits every year** to Debenture Redemption Reserve.
For Unlisted Co[Other than NBFCs registered with RBI,HFCs registered with National Housing Bank]	As per Rule 18(7) of The Companies Act, 2013, a company is required to transfer **adequate amounts out of its profits every year** to Debenture Redemption Reserve until such debentures are redeemed. Debenture Redemption Reserve Account must have a credit balance of **at least an amount equal to 10% of the value of Debentures issued** at the time of redemption of debentures. ***For Example****: X Ltd issued Debentures of ₹ 2 crores with the condition to start redemption in the third year. In such a case, before the debenture redemption begins in 3rd year, the Debenture Redemption Reserve Account must have a balance of at least equal to 2 crores × 10% = 0.20 crore.*
When to Create	Debenture Redemption Reserve must be created **before the redemption starts.**
Applicability	DRR is required to be created only in case of **Non-convertible Debentures (NCD) and Non-convertible portion of Partly Convertible Debentures (PCD).**
Utilisation	The amounts credited to the Debenture Redemption Reserve must be utilised **for the purpose of redemption of debentures.**
Disclosure	Debenture Redemption Reserve Account appears under the head **"Shareholders' Funds"** and Sub-head **'Reserves & Surplus'** in the Balance Sheet.
Closure	On **redemption of the debentures,** DRR proportionate to **Debentures redeemed** is transferred to General Reserve.
Not Mandatory as per Rule 18 (7)	**Creation of Debenture Redemption Reserve is not mandatory–** 1. For Fully Convertible Debentures 2. For Debentures issued by All India Financial Institutions regulated by RBI. 3. For Debentures issued by Banking Companies 4. For Debentures issued by NBFCs registered with RBI on private placement basis.
Not Mandatory as per SEBI	**Creation of Debenture Redemption Reserve is not mandatory–** 1. For Debentures with a maturity period of 18 months *or* less. 2. For Infrastructure Companies (i.e., companies engaged in the business of developing, maintaining and operating infrastructure facilities)

MINIMUM DEBENTURE REDEMPTION RESERVE INVESTMENTS [RULE 18(7)(C)]

Every company required to create/maintain DRR shall **before the 30th day of April** of each year, deposit *or* invest (as the case may be) **at least 15% of the amount of its debentures maturing during the year** ending on the 31st day of March next following in any one *or* more of the following methods, namely:

(a) In Deposits with any Scheduled Bank, free from charge *or* lien;

(b) In Unencumbered Securities of the Central Government *or* of any State Government;

(c) In Unencumbered Securities mentioned under Section 20 (a) to (d) and (ee) of the Indian Trusts Act, 1882;

(d) In Unencumbered Bonds issued by any other company which is notified under Section 20 (f) of the Indian Trusts Act, 1882;

JOURNAL ENTRIES

Date	*Particulars*	*L.F.*	*Dr. (₹)*	*Cr.(₹)*
1.	**For Creation of Debenture Redemption Reserve** Profit & Loss Appropriation A/c *[With DRR created]* Dr. To Debentures Redemption Reserve A/c (Being the DRR created as per Rule 18 (7))			
2.	**For the Purchase of DRR Investments** Debenture Redemption Reserve Investments A/c Dr. To Bank A/c (Being the DRR Investments made equal to 15% of Debentures Maturing)			
3.	**For the Sale of DRR Investments** Bank A/c Dr. To Debenture Redemption Reserve Investments A/c (Being the DRR Investments realised)			
4.	**For the Amt. due to Debentureholders on redemption** Debentures A/c *[With Nominal Value]* Dr. Premium on Redemption of Debentures A/c Dr. *[With Premium if any ,payable]* To Debenture-holders' A/c [With Total] (Being the Amount due on redemption)			
5.	**For Payment to Debentureholders** Debentureholders' A/c *[With Payment]* Dr. To Bank A/c (Being the Payment made to Debentureholders)			
6.	**For T/F of DRR on redemption of Debentures** Debentures Redemption Reserve A/c Dr. *[With DRR T/F]* To General Reserve (Being the t/f of DRR to General Reserve)			

ILLUSTRATION 1

X Ltd. (Unlisted) issued 10,000 10% Debentures of ₹ 100 each at a premium of 8% on 1st April, 2022 redeemable on 31st Aug. 2023. How much amount of Debenture Redemption Reserve is to be created before redemption of debentures?

SOLUTION

As per SEBI Guidelines, No Debenture Redemption Reserve is required to be created since maturity period of debentures does not exceed 18 months but as per Rule 18(7) of The Companies Act, 2013, atleast ₹ 1,00,000 (i.e., 10% of ₹ 10,00,000) must be transferred to Debenture Redemption Reserve.

ILLUSTRATION 2

On 01.04.2023, Y Ltd. (Unlisted) issued 2,000, 15% Convertible Debentures of ₹ 100 each at a discount of 5% redeemable at par after 4 years by converting their holdings into equity shares of ₹ 100 each at a premium of 25%. How much amount of Debenture Redemption Reserve is to be created before redemption of debentures?

SOLUTION

No Debenture Redemption Reserve is required to be created in a case of Fully Convertible Debentures.

ILLUSTRATION 3

On 1st April, 2020, X Ltd. (Unlisted Co other than NBFC & HFC) invited applications for issuing 5,000 10% debentures of ₹ 1,000 each at a discount of 6%. These debentures were repayable at the end of 3rd year at a premium of 10%. Applications for 6,000 debentures were received and the debentures were allotted on *prorata* basis to all the applicants. Excess money received with applications was refunded. The directors decided to transfer the minimum required amount to Debenture Redemption Reserve on 31.3.2022. On 1.4.2022, the company invested the minimum required amount in 9% bank fixed deposit as per the provisions of the Companies Act, 2013. Tax was deducted at source by bank on interest @ 10% p.a. Pass the necessary journal entries upto 31st March,2023 without providing for the Interest and Loss on issue of Debentures.

SOLUTION

JOURNAL

Date	Particulars		LF	Dr. (₹)	Cr. (₹)
2020	Bank A/c	Dr.		56,40,000	
Apr 1	To Debenture Application & Allotment A/c				56,40,000
	(Being application money received on 6,000 debentures)				
Apr 1	Debenture Application & Allotment A/c	Dr.		56,40,000	
	Loss on Issue of Debentures A/c	Dr.		8,00,000	
	To 10% Debentures A/c				50,00,000
	To Premium on Redemption of Debentures A/c				5,00,000
	To Bank A/c				9,40,000
	(Being transfer of application money to debenture account issued at discount of 6%, redeemable at premium of 10%, balance refunded)				
2022	Profit and Loss A/c	Dr.		5,00,000	
Mar 31	To Debenture Redemption Reserve A/c				5,00,000

	(Being Debenture Redemption Reserve created equal to 10% of the face value of debentures)			
2022 Apr 1	Debenture Redemption Investments A/c Dr		7,50,000	
	To Bank A/c			7,50,000
	(Being Debenture Redemption Investments purchased equal to 15% of face value of debentures)			
2023 Mar 31	Bank A/c Dr.		60,750	
	TDS Collected/TDS receivable A/c Dr.		6,750	
	To Interest on Debenture Redemption Investments A/c			67,500
	(Being interest received on Debenture Redemption Investments and tax deducted at source @ 10%)			
"	Bank A/c Dr.		7,50,000	
	To Debenture Redemption Investments A/c			7,50,000
	(Being Debenture Redemption Investments sold)			
"	10% Debentures A/c Dr.		50,00,000	
	Premium on Redemption of Debentures A/c Dr.		5,00,000	
	To Debenture holders A/c			55,00,000
	(Being Debentures due for redemption at a premium of 10%)			
"	Debenture holders A/c Dr.		55,00,000	
	To Bank A/c			55,00,000
	(Being Debenture holders paid)			
"	Debenture Redemption Reserve A/c Dr.		5,00,000	
	To General Reserve A/c			5,00,000
	(Being Debenture Redemption Reserve transferred to general reserve)			

ILLUSTRATION 4

On April 1,2020, TULSIAN Ltd. (Unlisted Co other than NBFC & HFC) invited applications for issuing ₹ 7,50,000,12% Debentures of ₹ 500 each at a premium of 4% redeemable at a premium of ₹ 60 per Debenture in two equal annual instalments starting from the end of third year. Applications for 2,000 Debentures were received and the Debentures were allotted on *prorata* basis to all the applicants. Excess money received with applications was refunded. The directors decided to transfer the minimum required amount to Debenture Redemption Reserve and to invest the minimum required amount in 10% bank fixed deposit as per the provisions of The Companies Act, 2013. Tax was deducted at source by bank on interest @ 10% p.a. Interest is payable on 31st March and is subject to the rate of Tax deducted at source being 10%. Pass the necessary journal entries upto 31.03.2023 ignoring the entries for writing off of Loss on issue of Debentures.

SOLUTION

JOURNAL

Date	Particulars	LF	Dr. (₹)	Cr. (₹)
01.04.2020	Bank A/c Dr.		10,40,000	
	To Debenture Application & Allotment A/c			10,40,000
	(Being application money received on 2,000 debentures)			
01.04.2020	Debenture Application & Allotment A/c Dr.		10,40,000	
	Loss on issue of Debentures A/c Dr.		90,000	
	To Bank A/c [500 × ₹ 520]			2,60,000
	To 12% Debentures A/c			7,50,000
	To Securities Premium A/c [(₹ 7,50,000 × 4%]			30,000
	To Premium on Redemption of Debentures A/c[1500 × ₹ 60]			90,000
	(Being issue of 1500 Debentures at 4% premium redeemable at a premium of ₹ 60 per Debenture and balance refunded)).			
31.03.2021	Interest on Debentures A/c Dr.		90,000	
	[7500 × ₹ 100 × 12%]			
	To Debenture holders' A/c (₹ 90,000 × 90%]			81,000
	To TDS from Deb. Int. A/c [₹ 90,000 × 10%]			9,000
	(Being the Interest due & T.D.S. @ 10%)			
	Debenture holders A/c Dr.		81,000	
	To Bank A/c			81,000
	(Being the Interest paid to Debenture holders)			
31.03.2022	Interest on Debentures A/c Dr.		90,000	
	[7500 × ₹ 100 × 12%]			
	To Debenture holders' A/c (₹ 90,000 × 90%]			81,000
	To TDS from Deb. Int. A/c [₹ 90,000 × 10%]			9,000
	(Being the Interest due & T.D.S. @ 10%)			
	Debenture holders A/c Dr.		81,000	
	To Bank A/c			81,000
	(Being the Interest paid to Debenture holders)			
31.03.2022	Profit and Loss A/c Dr.		75,000	
	To Debenture Redemption Reserve A/c			75,000
	(Being Debenture Redemption Reserve created equal to 10% of the face value of debentures)			
01.04.2022	Debenture Redemption Investments A/c Dr		56,250	
	To Bank A/c			56,250
	(Being Debenture Redemption Investments purchased equal to 15% of face value of debentures to be redeemed)			
31.03.2023	Bank A/c Dr.		5,062.50	
	TDS Collected/TDS receivable A/c Dr.		562.50	

	To Interest on Debenture Redemption Investments A/c (Being interest received on Debenture Redemption Investments and tax deducted at source @ 10%)			5,625
	Bank A/c Dr. To Debenture Redemption Investments A/c (Being Debenture Redemption Investments sold)		56,250	56,250
	12% Debentures A/c Dr. Premium on Redemption of Debentures A/c Dr. To Debenture holders A/c (Being Debentures due for redemption at a premium of ₹ 60)		3,75,000 45,000	4,20,000
	Debenture holders A/c Dr. To Bank A/c (Being Debenture holders paid)		4,20,000	4,20,000
	Debenture Redemption Reserve A/c Dr. To General Reserve A/c (Being the transfer of Proportionate amount of DRR to GR)		37,500	37,500
31.03.2023	Interest on Debentures A/c Dr. [7500 × ₹ 100 × 12%] To Debenture holders' A/c (₹ 90,000 × 90%] To TDS from Deb. Int. A/c [₹ 90,000 × 10%] (Being the Interest due & T.D.S. @ 10%)		90,000	81,000 9,000
	Debenture holders A/c Dr. To Bank A/c (Being the Interest paid to Debenture holders)		81,000	81,000

ILLUSTRATION 5

On April 1,2020, TULSIAN Ltd. (Unlisted Co other than NBFC & HFC) acquired Building at ₹ 12,00,000, Plant and Machinery at ₹ 2,00,000, Inventories at ₹ 4,00,000, Trade Receivables at ₹ 3,60,000 and Trade Payables at ₹ 1,60,000 from Y Ltd. for ₹ 20,80,000 payable as to 25% by a cheque and 50% of the balance by an issue of Shares of ₹ 500 each at a premium of ₹ 20 per Share and the remaining by an issue of 12% Debentures of ₹ 500 each at a premium of 4% redeemable at a premium of ₹ 60 per Debenture in two equal annual instalments starting from the end of third year. The directors decided to transfer the minimum required amount to Debenture Redemption Reserve and to invest the minimum required amount in 10% bank fixed deposit as per the provisions of The Companies Act, 2013. Tax was deducted at source by bank on interest @ 10% p.a. Interest is payable on 31st March and is subject to the rate of Tax deducted at source being 10%.On 31st March, 2023 the company obtained a loan of ₹ 8,00,000 from State Bank of India @ 10 % interest and issued ₹ 10,00,000, 10 % Debentures of ₹ 100 each, in favour of State Bank of India as collateral security and decided to record the issue of such Debentures by passing a journal entry. Pass the necessary journal entries upto 31.03.2023 ignoring the entries for writing off of Loss on issue of Debentures.

SOLUTION

JOURNAL

Date	Particulars		LF	Dr. (₹)	Cr. (₹)
01.04.2020	Building	Dr.		12,00,000	
	Plant and Machinery	Dr.		2,00,000	
	Inventories	Dr.		4,00,000	
	Trade Receivables	Dr.		3,60,000	
	Goodwill A/c [Balancing Figure]	Dr.		**80,000**	
	To Trade Payables				1,60,000
	To Y Ltd.				20,80,000
	(Being the purchase of Business from Y Ltd.)				
01.04.2020	Y Ltd.	Dr.		20,80,000	
	Loss on issue of Debentures A/c	Dr.		90,000	
	To Bank A/c [₹ 20,80,000 × 25%]				5,20,000
	To 12% Debentures A/c				7,50,000
	To Share Capital A/c				7,50,000
	To Securities Premium A/c [(1500 × 20) + (₹ 7,50,000 × 4%]				60,000
	To Premium on Redemption of Debentures A/c				90,000
	(Being issue of 1500 Debentures at 4% premium redeemable at a premium of ₹ 60 per Debenture and 1500 Shares at 4% premium).				
	[No. of Debentures/Shares to be issued = ₹ 7,80,000 /₹ 520 = 1,500]				
31.03.2021	Interest on Debentures A/c	Dr.		90,000	
	[7500 × ₹ 100 × 12%]				
	To Debenture holders' A/c (₹ 90,000 × 90%]				81,000
	To TDS from Deb. Int. A/c [₹ 90,000 × 10%]				9,000
	(Being the Interest due & T.D.S. @ 10%)				
	Debenture holders A/c	Dr.		81,000	
	To Bank A/c				81,000
	(Being the Interest paid to Debenture holders)				
31.03.2022	Interest on Debentures A/c	Dr.		90,000	
	[7500 × ₹ 100 × 12%]				
	To Debenture holders' A/c (₹ 90,000 × 90%]				81,000
	To TDS from Deb. Int. A/c [₹ 90,000 × 10%]				9,000
	(Being the Interest due & T.D.S. @ 10%)				
	Debenture holders A/c	Dr.		81,000	
	To Bank A/c				81,000
	(Being the Interest paid to Debenture holders)				
31.03.2022	Profit and Loss A/c	Dr.		75,000	
	To Debenture Redemption Reserve A/c				75,000

	(Being Debenture Redemption Reserve created equal to 10% of the face value of debentures)		
01.04.2022	Debenture Redemption Investments A/c Dr	56,250	
	To Bank A/c		56,250
	(Being Debenture Redemption Investments purchased equal to 15% of face value of debentures to be redeemed)		
31.03.2023	Bank A/c Dr.	5,062.50	
	TDS Collected/TDS receivable A/c Dr.	562.50	
	To Interest on Debenture Redemption Investments A/c		5,625
	(Being interest received on Debenture Redemption Investments and tax deducted at source @ 10%)		
	Bank A/c Dr.	56,250	
	To Debenture Redemption Investments A/c		56,250
	(Being Debenture Redemption Investments sold)		
	12% Debentures A/c Dr.	3,75,000	
	Premium on Redemption of Debentures A/c Dr.	45,000	
	To Debenture holders A/c		4,20,000
	(Being Debentures due for redemption at a premium of ₹ 60)		
	Debenture holders A/c Dr.	4,20,000	
	To Bank A/c		4,20,000
	(Being Debenture holders paid)		
	Debenture Redemption Reserve A/c Dr.	37,500	
	To General Reserve A/c		37,500
	(Being the transfer of Proportionate amount of DRR to GR)		
31.03.2023	Interest on Debentures A/c Dr.	90,000	
	[7500 × ₹ 100 × 12%]		
	To Debenture holders' A/c (₹ 90,000 × 90%]		81,000
	To TDS from Deb. Int. A/c [₹ 90,000 × 10%]		9,000
	(Being the Interest due & T.D.S. @ 10%)		
	Debenture holders A/c Dr.	81,000	
	To Bank A/c		81,000
	(Being the Interest paid to Debenture holders)		
	Bank A/c Dr.	8,00,000	
	To Loan from SBI A/c		8,00,000
	(Being Loan taken from SBI)		
	Debenture Suspense A/c Dr	10,00,000	
	To 10% Debentures A/c		10,00,000
	(Being 10,000 10% Debentures of ₹ 100 issued as collateral security)		

6.0 REDEMPTION BY CONVERSION

MEANING OF REDEMPTION BY CONVERSION

Redemption by conversion means redeeming the debentures by converting them into new class of debentures *or* shares. However, the debenture-holders would exercise their right of conversion only when they find it beneficial from their viewpoint *or* as agreed as per terms of issue. The new shares *or* debentures can be issued at par, premium *or* discount. There is no requirement of creating Debenture Redemption Reserve in case of redemption of debentures by conversion.

CONVERSION OF DEBENTURES WHICH WERE ORIGINALLY ISSUED AT PAR OR PREMIUM

JOURNAL ENTRY FOR AMOUNT DUE ON REDEMPTION

Date	*Particulars*	*L.F.*	*Dr. (₹)*	*Cr.(₹)*
	Debentures A/c [with Nominal Value] Dr. Premium on Redemption of Debentures A/c Dr. *[with Premium, if any payable on redemption]* To Debenture-holders' A/c [with Amount Due] (Being the amount due to Debenture-holders on red.)			

JOURNAL ENTRY FOR CONVERSION

Date	*Particulars*	*L.F.*	*Dr. (₹)*	*Cr.(₹)*
(i)	**If New Shares/Debentures are issued at par** Debenture-holders' A/c *[with Amount Due]* Dr. To Share Capital A/c/New Debentures A/c *[with Nominal Value]* (Being the issue of .... shares/debentures of ₹ .... each at par)			
(ii)	**If New Shares/Debentures are issued at a Premium** Debenture-holders' A/c *[with Amount Due]* Dr. To Share Capital/New Debentures A/c *[with Nominal Value]* To Securities Premium A/c *[with Premium on Issue]* (Being the issue of ... Shares/Debentures of the ... each at a premium of ...)			
(iii)	**If New Debentures are issued at a discount** Debenture-holders' A/c [with Amount Due] Dr. Discount on Issue of Debentures A/c Dr. *[with Discount on Issue]* To New Debentures A/c [with Nominal Value] (Being the issue of ... debentures of ₹ .... each at a discount of ...)			

TUTORIAL NOTES

1. *At the time of conversion of Convertible Debentures into new shares or debentures, Debenture Redemption Reserve is not required to be created.*
2. *The debenture-holders **can not demand the conversion of the unpaid interest** into shares unless such right is given expressly.*
3. *An issue of Shares at discount is void as per Sec 53 of The Companies Act, 2013.*

ILLUSTRATION 7

1000, 14% Convertible Debentures of ₹ 100 each issued at par and redeemable at 10% premium after 4 years by conversion into Equity Shares of ₹ 10 each. Journalise the issue and redemption of debentures if Equity Shares are issued (a) at par (b) at 25% premium (c) at ₹ 8 paid-up.*[Ignore Interest on Debentures and writing off of Loss on Issue of Debentures has yet been written off].*

SOLUTION

JOURNAL

Date	Particulars		L.F.	Dr. (₹)	Cr.(₹)
	Same Entry on Issue in all cases				
	Bank A/c	Dr.		1,00,000	
	To Debentures Application & Allotment A/c				1,00,000
	(Being the receipt of application money)				
	Debentures Application & Allotment A/c	Dr.		1,00,000	
	Loss on Issue of Debentures A/c	Dr.		10,000	
	To 14% Debentures A/c				1,00,000
	To Premium on Redemption of Debentures A/c				10,000
	(Being the issue of Debentures)				
	Same Entry for amount due to Debentureholders on Redemption in all cases				
	14% Debentures A/c	Dr.		1,00,000	
	Debentures Redemption Premium A/c	Dr.		10,000	
	To Debenture-holders' A/c				1,10,000
	(Being the amount due to debentureholders on conversion of 1,000,14% Debentures)				
	Entry on Issue of Equity Shares in Case (a)				
	Debenture-holders' A/c	Dr.		1,10,000	
	To Equity Share Capital A/c				1,10,000
	(Being the issue of 11000, Equity Shares of ₹ 10 each at par on conversion of 1,000,14% Debentures)				
	Entry on Issue of Equity Shares in Case (b)				
	Debenture-holders' A/c	Dr.		1,10,000	
	To Equity Share Capital A/c				88,000
	To Securities Premium A/c				22,000

	(Being the issue of 8800, Equity Shares of ₹ 10 each at 25% Premium on conversion of 1,000,14% Debentures)			
	Entry on Issue of Equity Shares in Case (c)			
	Debenture-holders' A/c Dr.		1,10,000	
	To Equity Share Capital A/c			1,10,000
	(Being the issue of 13750, Equity Shares of ₹ 10 each at ₹ 8 paid-up on conversion of 1,000,14% Debentures)			

7.0 CONVERSION OF DEBENTURES WHICH WERE ORIGINALLY ISSUED AT A DISCOUNT, INTO NEW DEBENTURES

In case of **Conversion of Debentures (which were originally issued at a discount) into New Debentures,** the **'Discount on Issue of Debentures Account' need not be credited** because there is no violation of Section 53 of The Companies Act, 1956.

JOURNAL ENTRY FOR AMOUNT DUE ON REDEMPTION

Date	*Particulars*	*L.F.*	*Dr. (₹)*	*Cr.(₹)*
	Debentures A/c *[with Nominal Value]* Dr. Premium on Redemption of Debentures A/c Dr. *[with Premium, if any payable on redemption]* To Debenture-holders' A/c [with Amount Due] (Being the Amount due to Debenture-holders on redemption)			

JOURNAL ENTRY FOR CONVERSION

Date	*Particulars*	*L.F.*	*Dr. (₹)*	*Cr.(₹)*
(i)	**If New Debentures are issued at par** Debenture-holders' A/c *[with Amount Due]* Dr. To New Debentures A/c *[with Nominal Value]* (Being the issue of ....Debentures of ₹ .... each at par)			
(ii)	**If New Debentures are issued at a Premium** Debenture-holders' A/c *[with Amount Due]* Dr. To New Debentures A/c *[with Nominal Value]* To Securities Premium A/c *[with Premium on Issue]* (Being the issue of ... Debentures of the ... each at a premium of ...)			
(iii)	**If New Debentures are issued at a discount** Debenture-holders' A/c *[with Amount Due]* Dr. Discount on Issue of Debentures A/c Dr. *[with Discount on Issue]* To New Debentures A/c *[with Nominal Value]* (Being the issue of ... Debentures of ₹ ... each at a discount of ...)			

Note: *An issue of Debentures at discount is not void as per The Companies Act, 2013.*

ILLUSTRATION 8

1000, 14% Convertible Debentures of ₹ 100 each issued at a discount of 5% and redeemable at 10% premium after 4 years by conversion into 15% Debentures of ₹ 100 each. Journalise the issue and redemption of debentures if 15% Debentures are issued (a) at par (b) at 25% premium (c) at ₹ 80 paid-up.*[Ignore Interest on Debentures and writing off of Loss on Issue of Debentures has yet been written off].*

SOLUTION

JOURNAL

Date	Particulars		L.F.	Dr. (₹)	Cr.(₹)
	Same Entry on Issue in all cases				
	Bank A/c	Dr.		95,000	
	To Debentures Application & Allotment A/c				95,000
	(Being the receipt of application money)				
	Debentures Application & Allotment A/c	Dr.		95,000	
	Loss on Issue of Debentures A/c	Dr.		15,000	
	To 14% Debentures A/c				1,00,000
	To Premium on Redemption of Debentures A/c				10,000
	(Being the issue of Debentures)				
	Same Entry for amount due to Debentureholders on Redemption in all cases				
	14% Debentures A/c	Dr.		1,00,000	
	Debentures Redemption Premium A/c	Dr.		10,000	
	To Debenture-holders' A/c				1,10,000
	(Being the amount due to debentureholders on conversion of 1,000,14% Debentures)				
	Entry on Issue of Equity Shares in Case (a)				
	Debenture-holders' A/c	Dr.		1,10,000	
	To 15% Debentures A/c				1,10,000
	(Being the issue of 1100 Debentures of ₹ 100 each at par on conversion of 1,000 Debentures)				
	Entry on Issue of Equity Shares in Case (b)				
	Debenture-holders' A/c	Dr.		1,10,000	
	To 15% Debentures A/c				88,000
	To Securities Premium A/c				22,000
	(Being the issue of 880 Debentures of ₹ 100 each at 25% Premium on conversion of 1,000 Debentures)				
	Entry on Issue of Equity Shares in Case (c)				
	Debenture-holders' A/c	Dr.		1,10,000	
	To 15% Debentures A/c				1,10,000
	(Being the issue of 1375 Debentures of ₹ 100 each at ₹ 80 paid up on conversion of 1,000 Debentures)				

8.0 CONVERSION OF DEBENTURES WHICH WERE ORIGINALLY ISSUED AT A DISCOUNT INTO SHARES

(A) CONVERSION BEFORE MATURITY

In case of conversion of Debentures (which were originally Issued at a discount) into shares, the actual amount realised (i.e., net of discount) from debentures at the time of issue, should be used as the basis for determining the number of shares to be issued otherwise it would amount to an issue of shares at discount which is void as per Sec. 53 of the Companies Act, 2013. Thus, at the time of making due the amount payable to debenture-holders in such a case, **Discount on issue of Debentures Account (Loss on issue of Debentures Account in case of Redemption at Premium)** should be credited with the amount of Discount/Loss which has not yet been written off and Profit & Loss Account should be credited with the amount of Discount/Loss which has already been written off.

(B) CONVERSION AT MATURITY

In case of conversion at maturity the debentures may be converted into the shares on the basis of the nominal value of the debentures and the provisions of Section 53 cannot be regarded as being violated.

JOURNAL ENTRY FOR AMOUNT DUE ON REDEMPTION AT PAR

Date	*Particulars*	*L.F.*	*Dr. (₹)*	*Cr.(₹)*
	Debentures A/c *[with Nominal Value]* Dr. To Discount on Issue of Debentures A/c *[with Discount not yet w/o]* To Profit & Loss A/c *[with Discount already w/o]* To Debenture-holders' A/c *[with Net Amount Due]* (Being the amount due to debenture-holders on redemption)			

JOURNAL ENTRY FOR AMOUNT DUE ON REDEMPTION AT PREMIUM

Date	*Particulars*	*L.F.*	*Dr. (₹)*	*Cr.(₹)*
	Debentures A/c *[with Nominal Value]* Dr. Premium on Redemption of Debentures A/c Dr. *[with Premium Payable]* To Loss on Issue of Debentures A/c *[with Loss on Issue not yet w/o]* To Profit & Loss A/c [with Loss on Issue already w/o] To Debentures-holders' A/c *[with Net Amount Due]* (Being the amount due to debenture-holders on redemption)			

JOURNAL ENTRY FOR CONVERSION

Date	*Particulars*	*L.F.*	*Dr. (₹)*	*Cr.(₹)*
(i)	**If New Shares are issued at Par** Debenture-holders' A/c *[with Amount Due]* Dr. To Share Capital A/c *[with Nominal Value]*			

	(Being the issue of .... Shares of ₹ .... each at par)			
(ii)	**If New Shares are issued at a Premium**			
	Debenture-holders' A/c *[with Amount Due]* Dr.			
	To Share Capital A/c *[with Nominal Value]*			
	To Securities Premium A/c *[with Premium on Issue]*			
	(Being the issue of ...Shares of the ... each at a premium of ...)			

TUTORIAL NOTES

1. *An issue of Shares at discount is void as per Sec 53 of The Companies Act, 2021.*
2. *At the time of conversion of Convertible Debentures into new shares or debentures, Debenture Redemption Reserve is not required to be created.*
3. *The Debenture-holders can not demand the conversion of the unpaid interest into shares unless such right is given expressly.*
4. *In case of Conversion of debentures (which were originally issued at a discount) into New Shares,*
   (a) *if the information about the original period of redemption and actual period of conversion before maturity is given, 'Discount' on issue of Debentures Account' should be credited with the amount of discount which has not yet been written off and Profit & Loss Account should be credited with the amount of discount which has already been written off.*
   (b) *if the information about the original period of redemption and actual period of conversion before maturity is not given 'Discount on Issue of Debentures Account' should be credited with the amount of discount originally allowed by giving a following Note:*
   "It has been assumed no portion of 'Discount on Issue of debentures has yet been written off."

ILLUSTRATION 9

1000, 14% Convertible Debentures of ₹ 100 each issued at a discount of 5% and redeemable at 10% premium after 4 years by conversion into Equity Shares of ₹ 10 each. Journalise the issue and redemption of debentures if Equity Shares are issued (a) at par (b) at 25% premium (c) at ₹ 8 paid-up.*[Ignore Interest on Debentures and writing off of Loss on Issue of Debentures].*

SOLUTION

JOURNAL

Date	*Particulars*	*L.F.*	*Dr. (₹)*	*Cr.(₹)*
	Same Entry on Issue in all cases			
	Bank A/c Dr.		95,000	
	To Debentures Application & Allotment A/c			95,000
	(Being the receipt of application money)			
	Debentures Application & Allotment A/c Dr.		95,000	
	Loss on Issue of Debentures A/c Dr.		15,000	

	To 14% Debentures A/c			1,00,000
	To Premium on Redemption of Debentures A/c			10,000
	(Being the issue of Debentures)			
	Same Entry for amount due to Debentureholders on Redemption in all cases			
	14% Debentures A/c	Dr.	1,00,000	
	Debentures Redemption Premium A/c	Dr.	10,000	
	To Loss on Issue of Debentures A/c			15,000
	To Debenture-holders' A/c			95,000
	(Being the amount due to debenture-holders on conversion of 1,000,14% Debentures)			
	Entry on Issue of Equity Shares in Case (a)			
	Debenture-holders' A/c	Dr.	95,000	
	To Equity Share Capital A/c			95,000
	(Being the issue of 9,500, Equity Shares of ₹ 10 each at par on conversion of 1,000,14% Debentures)			
	Entry on Issue of Equity Shares in Case (b)			
	Debenture-holders' A/c	Dr.	95,000	
	To Equity Share Capital A/c			76,000
	To Securities Premium A/c			19,000
	(Being the issue of 7,600 Equity Shares of ₹ 10 each at a premium of 25% on conversion of 1,000, 14% Debentures)			
	Entry on Issue of Equity Shares in Case (c)			
	Debenture-holders' A/c	Dr.	95,000	
	To Equity Share Capital A/c			95,000
	(Being the issue of 11875 Equity Shares of ₹ 10 each ₹ 8 paid up on conversion of 1,000, 14% Debentures)			

Note: *It has been assumed that no portion of 'Loss on Issue of Debentures* ***has*** *yet been written off.*

ILLUSTRATION 10

On 1st April, 2021, a company issued 1,000, 12% debentures of ₹ 500 each at ₹ 450 each. Debenture-holders were given an option to get their debentures converted into equity shares of ₹ 100 each at a premium of ₹ 50 per share. On 31st March, 2023, one year's interest had accrued on these debentures which was not paid. A holder of 100 debentures informed that he wanted to exercise the option for conversion of debentures into equity shares. The company, therefore, accepted his request and redeemed these 100 debentures by issuing him equity shares. The interest, however, on these 100 debentures was paid to the debentureholder. Pass the necessary journal entries.

SOLUTION

JOURNAL

Date	Particulars		L.F.	Dr. (₹)	Cr.(₹)
01.04.2021	Bank A/c	Dr.		4,50,000	
	To Debentures Application & Allotment A/c	Dr.		4,50,000	
	(Being the receipt of application money)				
01.04.2021	Debentures Application & Allotment A/c	Dr.		4,50,000	
	Discount on Issue of Debentures A/c	Dr.		50,000	
	To 12% Debentures A/c				5,00,000
	(Being the Debentures issued at 10% discount)				
31.03.2023	Interest on Debentures A/c	Dr.		60,000	
	To Interest on debentures accrued & due A/c				60,000
	(Being the Interest due on debentures)				
31.03.2023	12% Debentures A/c	Dr.		50,000	
	To Discount on issue of Debentures A/c				5,000
	To Debentureholders' A/c				45,000
	(Being the amount due to debenture-holders)				
	Debentureholders' A/c	Dr.		45,000	
	To Equity Share Capital A/c				30,000
	To Securities Premium A/c				15,000
	(Being the issue of 300 Equity Shares of ₹ 100 each at a premium of 50%)(₹ *45,000/*₹ *150*)				
	Interest on Debentures accrued & due A/c	Dr.		6,000	
	To Bank A/c				6,000
	(Being the Interest paid to a holder of 100 Debentures)				

Note: *It has been assumed that no portion of 'Discount on Issue of Debentures has yet been written off.*

ILLUSTRATION 11

BHARAT Ltd. issued 2000, 14% Debentures of ₹ 100 each at a discount of 5% and redeemable at 10% premium after 4 years. It redeemed 50% Debentures by converting into equity shares of ₹ 10 each issued at par and the balance by converting into 15% Debentures of ₹ 50 each at a premium of ₹ 12.50 per Debenture before maturity. Journalise the issue and redemption of debentures.

SOLUTION

JOURNAL

Date	Particulars		L.F.	Dr. (₹)	Cr.(₹)
	On Issue				
	Bank A/c	Dr.		1,90,000	
	To Debentures Application & Allotment A/c				1,90,000
	(Being the receipt of application money)				

	Debentures Application & Allotment A/c Dr.		1,90,000	
	Loss on Issue of Debentures A/c Dr.		30,000	
	To 14% Debentures A/c			2,00,000
	To Premium on Redemption of Debentures A/c			20,000
	(Being the issue of Debentures at 5% Discount and redeemable at 10% Premium)			
	On Redemption			
	14% Debentures A/c Dr.		1,00,000	
	Premium on Redemption of Debentures A/c Dr.		10,000	
	To Loss on Issue of Debentures A/c			15,000
	To Debenture-holders' A/c			95,000
	(Being the amount due to debenture-holders on conversion of 1,000,14% Debentures)			
	Debenture-holders' A/c Dr.		95,000	
	To Equity Share Capital A/c			95,000
	(Being the issue of 9,500 Equity Shares of ₹ 10 each at par on conversion of 1,000, 14% Debentures)			
	14% Debentures A/c Dr.		1,00,000	
	Premium on Redemption of Debentures A/c Dr.		10,000	
	To Debenture-holders' A/c			1,10,000
	(Being the amount due on redemption)			
	Debenture-holders' A/c Dr.		1,10,000	
	To 15% Debentures A/c			88,000
	To Securities Premium A/c			22,000
	(Being the issue of 1760 Debentures of ₹ 50 each at 25% Premium on conversion of 1,000 Debentures)			

Notes:

1. *No. of Shares to be issued = ₹ 95,000/₹ 10 = 9,500*
2. *No. of Debentures to be issued = ₹ 1,10,000/₹ 62.50 = 1760*
3. *It has been assumed that no portion of 'Loss on Issue of Debentures* ***has*** *yet been written off.*
4. *In case of Conversion of debentures (which were originally issued at a discount) into new debentures, the 'Discount on Issue of Debentures Account' need not be credited because there is no violation of Sec 53 of The Companies Act, 2013.*

ILLUSTRATION 12

Tulsian Ltd. (Unlisted Co other than NBFC & HFC) has to redeem its outstanding ₹ 5,00,000, 12% Debentures of ₹ 100 each. It redeemed 40% Debentures in cash and the balance at a premium of 20% by converting into 15% Debentures of ₹ 50 each at a Discount of ₹ 2 per Debenture.

Required: Pass the necessary journal entries at the time of redemption of debentures.

SOLUTION

JOURNAL

Date	Particulars		L.F.	Dr. (₹)	Cr.(₹)
	12% Debentures A/c	Dr.		5,00,000	
	Premium on Redemption of Debentures A/c [₹ 3,00,000 × 20%]	Dr.		60,000	
	To Debentureholders' A/c				5,60,000
	(Being the amount due on redemption)				
	Debentureholders' A/c	Dr.		3,60,000	
	Discount on Issue of Debentures A/c	Dr.		15,000	
	To 15% Debentures A/c				3,75,000
	(Being the issue of 7500 Debentures of ₹ 50 each at discount of ₹ 2)				
	Profit & Loss A/c	Dr.		20,000	
	To Debenture Redemption Reserve A/c				20,000
	(Being the transfer of profit equal to 10% of Nominal Value of Deb. Redeemed in cash to DRR as per Rule 18(7))				
	Debenture Redemption Reserve Investments A/c	Dr.		30,000	
	To Bank A/c				30,000
	(Being the DRR Investments made equal to 15%)				
	Bank A/c	Dr.		30,000	
	To Debenture Redemption Reserve Investments A/c				30,000
	(Being the DRR Investments realised)				
	Debentureholders' A/c	Dr.		2,00,000	
	To Bank A/c				2,00,000
	(Being the payment made to Debenture-holders)				
	Debenture Redemption Reserve A/c	Dr.		20,000	
	To General Reserve				20,000
	(Being the transfer of DRR to General Reserve)				

Notes:

1. *No. of 15% Debentures to be issued = [(3000 × ₹ 100) + (₹ 3,00,000 × 20%)]/₹ 48 = 7500*
2. *Cash paid on Redemption = [(2000 × ₹ 100)] = ₹ 2,00,000*

ILLUSTRATION 13

Tulsian Ltd. (Unlisted Co other than NBFC & HFC) served notice of its intention to redeem its outstanding ₹ 3,00,000, 15% Debentures of ₹ 100 each at ₹110 and offered the holders the following options:

(a) To convert their holdings into 12% Cumulative Preference Shares of ₹ 20 each at 110%.

(b) To convert their holdings into 15% Debentures at 96%.

(c) To have their holdings redeemed in cash unless otherwise opted.

Holders of 1,800 Debentures opted for (a) and Holders of 480 Debentures opted for (b).

Required: Pass the necessary journal entries.

SOLUTION

JOURNAL

Date	*Particulars*		*L.F.*	*Dr. (₹)*	*Cr.(₹)*
	15% Debentures A/c	Dr.		3,00,000	
	Premium on Redemption of Debentures A/c	Dr.		30,000	
	To Debentureholders' A/c				3,30,000
	(Being the amount due on redemption)				
	Option (i) (a):				
	Debentureholders' A/c	Dr.		1,98,000	
	To 12% Cumulative Preference Share Capital A/c				1,80,000
	To Securities Premium A/c				18,000
	(Being the issue of 9,000 Cum Pref Shares at 10% premium)				
	Option (i) (b):				
	Debentureholders' A/c	Dr.		52,800	
	Discount on Issue of Debentures A/c	Dr.		2,200	
	To 15% Debentures A/c				55,000
	(Being the issue of 550 Debentures at 4% discount)]				
	Option (ii):				
	Profit & Loss Appropriation A/c	Dr.		7,200	
	To Debenture Redemption Reserve A/c				7,200
	(Being the transfer of profit equal to 10% of Nominal Value of Deb. Redeemed in cash to Debenture Redemption Reserve A/c as per Rule 18(7))				
	Debenture Redemption Reserve Investments A/c	Dr.		10,800	
	To Bank A/c				10,800
	(Being the DRR Investments made equal to 15%)				
	Bank A/c	Dr.		10,800	
	To Debenture Redemption Reserve Investments A/c				10,800
	(Being the DRR Investments realised)				
	Debentureholders' A/c	Dr.		79,200	
	To Bank A/c				79,200
	(Being the payment made to Debenture-holders)				
	Debenture Redemption Reserve A/c	Dr.		7,200	
	To General Reserve				7,200
	(Being the transfer of DRR to General Reserve)				

Notes:

1. *No. of Preference Shares to be issued = [(1800 × ₹ 100) + (₹ 1,80,000 × 10%)]/₹ 22 = 9,000*
2. *No. of 15% Debentures to be issued = [(480 × ₹ 100) + (₹ 48,000 × 10%)]/₹ 96 = 550*
3. *Cash paid on Redemption = [(720 × ₹ 100) + (₹ 72,000 × 10%)] = ₹ 79,200*
4. *No portion of discount on issue of new debentures has been written off in the absence of any information regarding the period of issue & redemption.*
5. *It has been assumed that the balance in P & L Account is sufficient to carry out the aforesaid adjustments.*

ILLUSTRATION 14

Suresh Ltd. (Unlisted Co other than NBFC & HFC) took over the Assets of ₹ 6,00,000 and Creditors of ₹ 70,000 of P & Co. for an agreed amount of ₹ 5,50,000 by the issue of fully paid 12% Debentures of ₹ 100 each at a premium of 10%.These Debentures are redeemable at a premium of 5% after 3 years. Pass the necessary journal entries both at the time of Issue and Redemption of Debentures without providing for the Interest and Loss on issue of Debentures.

SOLUTION

JOURNAL OF SURESH LTD.

Date	Particulars		L.F.	Dr. (₹)	Cr.(₹)
1.	Sundry Assets A/c	Dr.		6,00,000	
	Goodwill [Balancing Figure]	Dr.		**20,000**	
	To Sundry Creditors				70,000
	To P & Co.				5,50,000
	(Being the purchase of Business from P & Co.)				
2.	P & Co.	Dr.		5,50,000	
	Loss on Issue of Debentures A/c	Dr.		25,000	
	To 12% Debentures A/c				5,00,000
	To Securities Premium A/c				50,000
	To Premium on Redemption of Debentures A/c				25,000
	(Being the issue of 5000, 12% Debentures at a premium of 10% and repayable at a premium of 5%)				
	Profit & Loss Appropriation A/c	Dr.		50,000	
	To Debenture Redemption Reserve A/c				50,000
	[Being the creation of DRR as per Rule 18(7)]				
	Debenture Redemption Reserve Investments A/c	Dr.		75,000	
	To Bank A/c				75,000
	(Being the DRR Investments made equal to 15%)				
	Bank A/c	Dr.		75,000	
	To Debenture Redemption Reserve Investments A/c				75,000
	(Being the DRR Investments realised)				
	12% Debentures A/c	Dr.		5,00,000	
	Premium on Redemption of Debentures A/c	Dr.		25,000	

	To Debentureholders' A/c (Being the amount due on redemption)			5,25,000
	Debentureholders' A/c Dr. To Bank A/c (Being the payment made to Debentureholders)		5,25,000	5,25,000
	Debenture Redemption Reserve A/c Dr. To General Reserve (Being the transfer of DRR to General Reserve)		50,000	50,000

Note: *No. of Debentures to be issued = ₹ 5,50,000/₹ 110 = 5,000*

ILLUSTRATION 15

X Ltd. (Unlisted Co other than NBFC & HFC) took over the Assets of ₹ 7,00,000 and Creditors of ₹ 80,000 of Y Ltd. for a sum of ₹ 6,00,000 payable 10% by a cheque and the balance by the issue of fully paid 15% Debentures of ₹ 100 each at a discount of 10%.These Debentures are redeemable at a premium of 5% after 3 years.

Required: Pass the necessary journal entries both at the time of Issue and Redemption of Debentures without providing for the Interest and Loss on issue of Debentures.

SOLUTION

JOURNAL OF X LTD.

Date	Particulars	L.F.	Dr. (₹)	Cr.(₹)
1.	Sundry Assets A/c Dr. To Sundry Creditors To Y Ltd. To **Capital Reserve A/c** (Balancing Figure) (Being the purchase of Business from Y Ltd.)		7,00,000	80,000 6,00,000 **20,000**
2.	Y Ltd. Dr. To Bank A/c (Being the payment made to Vendor by a cheque)		60,000	60,000
3.	Y Ltd. Dr. Loss on Issue of Shares A/c [₹ 60,000 + ₹ 30,000] Dr. To 15% Debentures A/c To Premium on Redemption of Debentures A/c (Being the issue of 6000, 15% Debentures at a discount of 10% and repayable at a premium of 5%)		5,40,000 90,000	6,00,000 30,000
4.	Profit & Loss Appropriation A/c Dr. To Debenture Redemption Reserve A/c [Being the creation of DRR as per Rule 18(7)]		60,000	60,000
5.	Debenture Redemption Reserve Investments A/c Dr. To Bank A/c (Being the DRR Investments made equal to 15%)		90,000	90,000

6.	Bank A/c Dr. To Debenture Redemption Reserve Investments A/c (Being the DRR Investments realised)		90,000	90,000
7.	15% Debentures A/c Dr. Premium on Redemption of Debentures A/c Dr. To Debentureholders' A/c (Being the amount due on redemption)		6,00,000 30,000	6,30,000
8.	Debentureholders' A/c Dr. To Bank A/c (Being the payment made to Debentureholders)		6,30,000	6,30,000
9.	Debenture Redemption Reserve A/c Dr. To General Reserve (Being the transfer of DRR to General Reserve)		60,000	60,000

Note: *No. of Debentures to be issued = ₹ 5,40,000/₹ 90 = 6,000*

ILLUSTRATION 16 [COMPREHENSIVE REVISIONAL ILLUSTRATION]

Bharat Tushar Ltd.(Unlisted Co other than NBFC & HFC) took over the Assets of ₹ 7,00,000 and Creditors of ₹ 80,000 of Y Ltd. for a sum of ₹ 6,00,000 payable 10% by a cheque and the balance by the issue of fully paid 15% Debentures of ₹ 100 each at a discount of 10% and redeemable at a premium of 5%. 25% of these Debentures were redeemed by converting into Equity Shares of ₹ 10 each issued at a premium of 25% and 25% of these Debentures were redeemed by converting into 16% Debentures of ₹ 50 each at a discount of ₹ 5 per Debenture before maturity and the balance redeemed for Cash.

Required: Pass the necessary journal entries both at the time of Issue and Redemption of Debentures without providing for the Interest and Loss on issue of Debentures.

SOLUTION

JOURNAL OF BHARAT TUSHAR LTD.

Date	*Particulars*	*L.F.*	*Dr. (₹)*	*Cr.(₹)*
1.	Sundry Assets A/c Dr. To Sundry Creditors To Y Ltd. To **Capital Reserve A/c** [Balancing figure] (Being the purchase of Business from Y Ltd.)		7,00,000	80,000 6,00,000 **20,000**
2.	Y Ltd. Dr. To Bank A/c (Being the payment made to Vendor by a cheque)		60,000	60,000
3.	Y Ltd. Dr. Loss on Issue of Shares A/c Dr. To 15% Debentures A/c To Premium on Redemption of Debentures A/c		5,40,000 90,000	6,00,000 30,000

	(Being the issue of 6000, 15% Debentures at a discount of 10% and repayable at a premium of 5%)			
4.	Profit & Loss A/c	Dr.	30,000	
	To Debenture Redemption Reserve A/c			30,000
	[Being the creation of DRR as per Rule 18(7)]			
5.	Debenture Redemption Reserve Investments A/c	Dr.	45,000	
	To Bank A/c			45,000
	(Being the DRR Investments made equal to 15%)			
6.	Bank A/c	Dr.	45,000	
	To Debenture Redemption Reserve Investments A/c			45,000
	(Being the DRR Investments realised)			
7.	15% Debentures A/c	Dr.	3,00,000	
	Premium on Redemption of Debentures A/c	Dr.	15,000	
	To Debentureholders' A/c			3,15,000
	(Being the amount due on redemption)			
8.	Debentureholders' A/c	Dr.	3,15,000	
	To Bank A/c			3,15,000
	(Being the payment made to Debentureholders)			
9.	Debenture Redemption Reserve A/c	Dr.	30,000	
	To General Reserve			30,000
	(Being the transfer of DRR to General Reserve)			
10.	15% Debentures A/c	Dr.	1,50,000	
	Premium on Redemption of Debentures A/c	Dr.	7,500	
	To Loss on Issue of Debentures A/c			22,500
	To Debenture-holders' A/c			1,35,000
	(Being the amount due to debenture-holders on conversion of 1,500,15% Debentures)			
11.	Debenture-holders' A/c	Dr.	1,35,000	
	To Equity Share Capital A/c			1,08,000
	To Securities Premium A/c			27,000
	(Being the issue of 10,800 Equity Shares of ₹ 10 each at 25% Premium on conversion of 1,500, 15% Debentures)			
12.	15% Debentures A/c	Dr.	1,50,000	
	Premium on Redemption of Debentures A/c	Dr.	7,500	
	To Debenture-holders' A/c			1,57,500
	(Being the amount due on redemption of 1,500, 15% Debentures)			
13.	Debenture-holders' A/c	Dr.	1,57,500	
	Discount on Issue of Debentures A/c	Dr.	17,500	
	To 16% Debentures A/c			1,75,000

	(Being the issue of 3500 Debentures of ₹ 50 each at a discount of ₹ 5 per Debenture on conversion of 1,500 Debentures)		

Notes:

1. *No. of 15% Debentures to be issued = ₹ 5,40,000/₹ 90 = 6,000*
2. *No. of Shares to be issued on redemption = ₹ 1,35,000/₹ 12.50 = 10,800*
3. *No. of 16% Debentures to be issued on redemption = ₹ 1,57,500/₹ 45 = 3500*
4. *It has been assumed that no portion of 'Loss on Issue of Debentures has yet been written off.*
5. *In case of Conversion of debentures (which were originally issued at a discount) into new debentures, the 'Discount on Issue of Debentures Account' need not be credited because there is no violation of any of provision of Sec 53 of The Companies Act, 2013.*

9.0 FINANCING OF REDEMPTION OF DEBENTURES

To ensure the availability of sufficient cash to redeem the debentures at the end of specified period, a part of divisible profits is set aside and is invested outside the business. For investing the funds outside the business, the company may adopt any one of the following methods:

(a) Sinking Fund Method *or* Debenture Redemption Fund Method

(b) Insurance Policy Method

10.0 SINKING FUND METHOD OR DEBENTURE REDEMPTION FUND METHOD

PRACTICAL STEPS INVOLVED IN THE WORKING OF DEBENTURE REDEMPTION FUND METHOD

Step 1: Calculate the amount of profit to be set aside with the help of Sinking Fund Table

Step 2: Set aside the amount of profit at the end of each year

Step 3: Purchase the Investments at the end of each year (except last year)

Step 4: Receive the interest on investments at the end of each year

Step 5: Repeat Step 2 for each year, Repeat Step 3 for each year except last year, Repeat Step 4 for each year

Step 6: Realise the investments in the year of redemption

Step 7: Transfer profit/loss on sale of Investment to Debenture Redemption Fund Account.

Step 8: Make due the amount payable to Debenture-holders

Step 9: Make payment to Debenture-holders

Step 10: Transfer unwritten off amount of Loss on Issue of Debentures equivalent to Premium payable on redemption of Debentures, (if any), to the debit of Debenture Redemption Reserve Account.

Step 11: Transfer the balance left in Debenture Redemption Reserve Account to General Reserve after all the debentures have been redeemed

JOURNAL ENTRIES

I. At the end of First Year

1. ***For the transfer of profit to DRR***

   Profit & Loss Appropriation A/c Dr. *(With the amount of profit set aside)*

   To Debenture Redemption Reserve A/c

2. ***For Purchase of Investments***

   Debenture Redemption Fund Investment A/c Dr. *(With the amount of investment made)*

   To Bank A/c

II. At the end of Second year and subsequent years other than the last year

3. ***For Receiving the Interest on Investments***

   Bank A/c Dr. *(With the amount of interest received)*

   To Interest on Debenture Redemption Fund Investment A/c

4. ***For the transfer of Interest on Deb. Red. Fund Investment to DRF A/c***

   Interest on Deb. Red. Fund Investment A/c Dr.

   To Debenture Redemption Reserve A/c

5. ***For transfer of profit to DRR***

   Profit and Loss Appropriation A/c Dr. *(With the amount of profit set aside)*

   To Debenture Redemption Reserve A/c

6. ***For Purchase of Investments***

   Debenture Redemption Fund Investment A/c Dr. *(With the amount of investments made)*

   To Bank A/c

III. At the end of last year

7. ***For Receiving the Interest on Investments made***

   Bank A/c Dr. (With the amount of interest received)

   To Interest on Debenture Redemption Fund Investment A/c

8. ***For the transfer of Interest on Deb. Red. Fund Investment to DRF A/c***

   Interest on Deb. Red. Fund Investment A/c Dr.

   To Debenture Redemption Reserve A/c

9. ***For the transfer of profit to DRR***

   Profit and Loss Appropriation A/c Dr. (With the amount of profit set aside)

   To Debenture Redemption Reserve A/c

10. ***For Sale of Investments***

    Bank A/c Dr. (With the sale proceeds)

    To Debenture Redemption Fund Investment A/c

11. ***For the t/f of profit/loss on realisation of Debenture Redemption Fund Investments***

    (a) ***In case of Profit***

    Debenture Redemption Fund Investment A/c Dr. (With the amount of profit)

    To Debenture Redemption Reserve A/c

    (b) ***In case of Loss reverse of the above entry is passed.***

12. ***For Making due the amount payable to Debenture holders***

(a) ***If the Debentures are to be redeemed at par***

Debentures A/c Dr. *(With the amount due)*

To Debenture-holders' A/c

(b) ***If the Debentures are to be redeemed at a premium***

Debentures A/c Dr. *(With Nominal value)*

Debentures Redemption Premium A/c Dr. *(With Premium payable)*

To Debenture-holders' A/c *(With Total)*

13. ***For Redemption***

Debenture-holders' A/c Dr. *(With the amount paid)*

To Bank A/c

14. ***For the transfer of Unwritten off amount of Loss on Issue of Debentures equivalent to the Premium payable on Redemption of Debentures (if any)***

Debenture Redemption Reserve A/c Dr. *(With the amount of*

To Loss on Issue of Debentures A/c *Premium on redemption)*

15. ***For the closure of the Debenture Redemption Reserve Account after all the debentures have been redeemed***

Debenture Redemption Reserve A/c Dr. *[With total]*

To Capital Reserve *[With Profit on Sale of DRRI]*

To General Reserve *[With Balance]*

TUTORIAL NOTES

1. ***Disclosure of Debenture Redemption Reserve Account*** — *Debenture Redemption Reserve A/c shall appear under the head **'Reserves and Surplus'** on the liabilities side of the Balance Sheet till the redemption of the debentures.*
2. ***Disclosure of Debenture Redemption Fund Investment Account*** — *Debenture Redemption Fund Investment A/c shall appear under the head **'Non-Current Investments'** on the assets side of the Balance Sheet till the realisation of the investments.*
3. *In case of redemption of debentures by draw of lots, withdrawal from Debenture Redemption Reserve can be made after Redemption of 10% of the debentures.*

HOW TO CALCULATE THE AMOUNT OF PROFIT TO BE SET ASIDE

The amount of profit to be set aside is to be calculated as follows:

(a) ***If the debentures are to be redeemed at par***

Amount of Profit to be set aside

= Nominal value of Debentures to be redeemed × Present value of ₹ 1 for given number of years at a given rate of interest i.e. $\left[\dfrac{r}{(1+r)^n - 1}\right]$

or = $\dfrac{\text{Nominal value of Debentures to be redeemed}}{\text{Present value of ₹1 for given number of years at a given rate of interest i.e. } \dfrac{r}{(1+r)^n - 1}}$

Example: The 4,420, 15% Debentures of ₹ 100 each issued at par are to be redeemed at par after 4 years. Investments are expected to realise 10% p.a. The table shows that ₹ 0.215470803 invested at the end of each year at 10% compound interest will amount to ₹ 1 at the end of 4 years and ₹ 1 p.a. at 10% interest amounts to ₹ 4.641 in 4 years.

SOLUTION

Amount of Profit to set aside = ₹ 4,42,000 × 0.215470803 = ₹ 95,238.09

or, Amount of Profit to be set aside = ₹ 4,42,000/4.641 = ₹ 95,238.09

(b) ***If the debentures are to be redeemed at a premium***

Amount of Profit

= Nominal value of Debentures *plus* Premium on redemption × Present value of ₹ 1 at a given rate of interest

Example: If the aforesaid debentures are to be redeemed at a premium of 5%, then the amount of profits to be set aside will be calculated as follows:

Amount of profit to be set aside

= (₹ 4,42,000 + ₹ 22,100) × (0.215470803) = ₹ 1,00,000

or = (₹ 4,42,000 + ₹ 22,100)/4.641 = ₹ 1,00,000

HOW TO CALCULATE THE AMOUNT OF INVESTMENTS TO BE MADE

The amount of investments to be made may be calculated as follows:

(a) In case the Investments are to be made in multiples of some specific denomination (say ₹ 10, ₹ 20) only, then only that amount which is fully divisible by the given denomination should be invested, e.g., if the amount available for investment is ₹ 95,238.09 and the investments are to be made in the multiple of ₹ 100 only, then only ₹ 95,200 will be invested and the balance of ₹ 38.09 will be kept separately in Debenture Redemption Fund Cash A/c which shall be considered at the time of making the investments during the next period.

(b) In other cases where no specific direction has been given, the amount of profit set aside **(in case of Non-cumulative Debenture Redemption Reserve)** *or* the amount of profit set aside together with the amount of interest received on DRF investments **(in case of Cumulative Debenture Redemption Reserve)** should be invested fully.

Debenture Redemption Fund may be *either* **cumulative or non-cumulative.**

(i) In case of ***Cumulative Debenture Redemption Reserve***, Interest on Debenture Redemption Fund Investments is credited to Debenture Redemption Reserve A/c and interest is reinvested.

(ii) In case of ***Non-cumulative Debenture Redemption Reserve***, Interest on Debenture Redemption Fund Investments is credited to P & L A/c and interest is not reinvested.

Tutorial Note: *No investment should be made in the last year since there is no logic behind first making investments in the last year and then immediately realising the same.*

HOW TO CALCULATE THE AMOUNT OF INTEREST ON DEBENTURE REDEMPTION FUND INVESTMENTS

In general, the amount of interest on Debenture Redemption Fund Investments is calculated on the Opening Balance of Debenture Redemption Fund Investment Account. Following tables may be helpful for this purpose:

Table I showing the Calculation of the Amount of Investments to be made and Interest to be received [when Investments are to be made equal to the Entire Profits set aside]

[*For Example*, Interest Rate = 10%, Profits to be set aside = ₹ 1,00,000, Year of Realisation of Investments — 4th year]

Year	*Opening Balance*	*Interest*	*Savings or Profits set aside*	*Investments*	*Closing Balance*
A	*B*	*C = B x 10/100*	*D*	*E = C + D*	*F = B + E*
20X1-X2	—	—	1,00,000	1,00,000	1,00,000
20X2-X3	1,00,000	10,000	1,00,000	1,10,000	2,10,000
20X3-X4	2,10,000	21,000	1,00,000	1,21,000	3,31,000
20X4-X5	3,31,000	33,100	1,00,000		—

Table II showing the Calculation of the Amount of Investments to be made and Interest to be received [when Investments are to be made equal to the nearest multiple of particular denomination say ₹ 10, ₹ 100 etc.]

[*For Example*, Interest Rate = 10%, Profits to be set aside = ₹ 23,701.79, Investments to be made in the nearest multiple of ₹ 100, Year of Realisation of Investments — 4th year]

Year	*Opening Balance*	*Interest*	*Savings or Profits set aside*	*Investments*	*Closing Balance*
A	*B*	*C = B x 10/100*	*D*	*E = C + D*	*F = B + E*
20X1		—	23,701.79	23,700	23,700
20X2	23,700	2,370	23,701.79	26,100	49,800
20X3	49,800	4,980	23,701.79	28,700	78,500
20X4	78,500	7,850	23,701.79	—	

ILLUSTRATION 17

On 1st April 2019 Tulsian Ltd. issued 4,420, 12% Debentures of ₹ 100 each at a discount of 10% redeemable at a premium of 5% after 4 years. It was decided to institute a Sinking Fund for the purposes of accumulating sufficient funds to redeem the Debentures and to invest in some readily convertible securities yielding 10% interest p.a. Reference to the table shows that ₹ 1.00 p.a. at 10% compound interest amounts to ₹ 4.641 in 4 years. Investments are to be made in the Bonds of ₹ 100 each available at par.

On 31st March 2023, the investments realised ₹ 3,40,000 and debentures were redeemed. The bank balance as on that date was ₹ 1,00,000.

Required: Give the necessary journal entries and prepare Debenture Redemption Reserve Account and Debentures Redemption Fund Investments Account for 4 years. [Ignore Interest on Debentures and writing off of Discount on Issue of Debentures]

SOLUTION

JOURNAL OF TULSIAN LTD.

Date	*Particulars*		*L.F.*	*Dr. (₹)*	*Cr.(₹)*
01.04.2019	Bank A/c	Dr.		3,97,800	
	To Debentures Application A/c				3,97,800
	(Being the receipt of application money)				

	Debenture Application A/c Dr.		3,97,800	
	Loss on Issue of Debentures A/c Dr.		66,300	
	To 12% Debentures A/c			4,42,000
	To Debentures Redemption Premium A/c			22,100
	(Being the issue of 4,420, 12% Debentures of ₹ 100 each at 10% Discount & redeemable at 5% premium)			
31.03.2020	Profit & Loss Appropriation A/c Dr.		1,00,000	
	To Debenture Redemption Reserve A/c			1,00,000
	(Being the transfer of profit to DRR A/c to provide for redemption of debentures)			
	Debenture Redemption Fund Investment A/c Dr.		1,00,000	
	To Bank A/c			1,00,000
	(Being the investments made in the multiples of ₹ 100)			
31.03.2021	Bank A/c Dr.		10,000	
	To Interest on DRFI A/c			10,000
	(Being the receipt of interest on investments)			
	Interest on DRFI A/c Dr.		10,000	
	To Debenture Redemption Reserve A/c			10,000
	(Being the transfer of Interest on DRFI to DRR A/c)			
	Profit & Loss Appropriation A/c Dr.		1,00,000	
	To Debenture Redemption Reserve A/c			1,00,000
	(Being the transfer to profit to DRR A/c to provide for redemption of debentures)			
	Debenture Redemption Fund Investment A/c	Dr.		1,10,000
	To Bank A/c			1,10,000
	(Being the Investment made in the multiples of ₹ 100)			
31.03.2022	Bank A/c Dr.		21,000	
	To Interest on DRFI A/c			21,000
	(Being the receipt of interest on DRFI)			
	Interest on DRFI A/c Dr.		21,000	
	To Debenture Redemption Reserve A/c			21,000
	(Being the transfer of Interest on DRFI to DRR A/c)			
	Profit & Loss Appropriation A/c Dr.		1,00,000	
	To Debenture Redemption Reserve A/c			1,00,000
	(Being the transfer of profit to DRR A/c to provide for the redemption of debentures)			
	Debenture Redemption Fund Investment A/c Dr.		1,21,000	
	To Bank A/c			1,21,000
	(Being the investments made in the multiples of ₹ 100)			
31.03.2023	Bank A/c Dr.		33,100	
	To Interest on DRFI A/c			33,100
	(Being the receipt of interest on DRFI)			

Date	Particulars		Dr. (₹)	Cr. (₹)
	Interest on DRFI A/c	Dr.	33,100	
	To Debenture Redemption Reserve A/c			33,100
	(Being the transfer of Interest on DRFI to DRR A/c)			
	Profit & Loss Appropriation A/c	Dr.	1,00,000	
	To Debenture Redemption Reserve A/c			1,00,000
	(Being the transfer of profit to DRR A/c to provide for the redemption of debentures)			
	Bank A/c	Dr.	3,40,000	
	To Debenture Redemption Fund Investment A/c			3,40,000
	(Being the realisation of Investments)			
	Debenture Redemption Fund Investment A/c	Dr.	9,000	
	To Debenture Redemption Reserve A/c			9,000
	(Being the transfer of profit on sale of Investment)			
	15% Debentures A/c	Dr.	4,42,000	
	Debentures Redemption Premium A/c	Dr.	22,100	
	To Debenture-holders' A/c			4,64,100
	(Being the amount due on redemption)			
	Debenture-holders' A/c	Dr.	4,64,100	
	To Bank A/c			4,64,100
	(Being the payment made to Debenture-holders)			
	Debenture Redemption Reserve A/c	Dr.	22,100	
	To Loss on Issue of Debentures A/c			22,100
	(Being the transfer of loss on issue of debentures equal to the amount of premium payable on redemption)			
	Debenture Redemption Reserve A/c	Dr.	4,51,000	
	To Capital Reserve A/c			9,000
	To General Reserve A/c			4,42,000
	(Being the transfer of the Profit to CR and balance in DRR A/c to General Reserve)			

Dr. **DEBENTURES REDEMPTION RESERVE ACCOUNT** *Cr.*

Date	Particulars	₹	Date	Particulars	₹
31.03.2020	To Balance c/d	1,00,000	31.03.2020	By P & L App. A/c	1,00,000
31.03.2021	To Balance c/d	2,10,000	01.04.2020	By Balance b/d	1,00,000
			31.03.2021	By Interest on DRFI A/c	10,000
				By P & L App. A/c	1,00,000
		2,10,000			2,10,000
31.03.2022	To Balance c/d	3,31,000	31.04.2021	By Balance b/d	2,10,000
			31.03.2022	By Interest on DRFI A/c	21,000
				By P & L App. A/c	1,00,000
		3,31,000			3,31,000
31.03.2023	To Loss on Issue		01.04.2022	By Balance b/d	3,31,000

	of Debentures A/c (premium)	22,100	31.04.2023	By Interest on DRFI A/c	33,100
	To Capital Reserve A/c	9,000		By P & L App. A/c	1,00,000
	To General Reserve A/c	4,42,000		By Debenture Red. Fund Investment A/c (Profit)	9,000
		4,73,100			4,73,100

Dr. **DEBENTURES REDEMPTION FUND INVESTMENT (DRFI) ACCOUNT** Cr.

Date	Particulars	₹	Date	Particulars	₹
31.03.2020	To Bank A/c	1,00,000	31.03.2020	By Balance c/d	1,00,000
01.04.2020	To Balance b/d	1,00,000	31.03.2021	By Balance c/d	2,10,000
31.03.2021	To Bank A/c	1,10,000			
		2,10,000			2,10,000
01.04.2021	To Balance b/d	2,10,000	31.03.2022	By Balance c/d	3,31,000
31.03.2022	To Bank A/c	1,21,000			
		3,31,000			3,31,000
01.04.2022	To Balance b/d	3,31,000	31.03.2023	By Bank A/c (Sales)	3,40,000
31.03.2023	To Debenture Redem. Reserve A/c (Profit)	9,000			
		3,40,000			3,40,000

Working Notes:

(I) CALCULATION OF THE AMOUNT OF PROFIT SET ASIDE

	Particulars	₹
A	Face Value of Debentures	4,42,000
B	Premium Payable on Redemption	22,100
C	Total Amount to be redeemed (A + B)	4,64,100
D	Value of annuity per ₹ 1	4.641
E	Annual amount of Profits to be set aside (C/D)	1,00,000

(II) CALCULATION OF THE AMOUNT OF INVESTMENTS AND INTEREST

Year A	Opening Balance B	Interest C = B × 10/100	Savings D	Investments E = C + D	Closing Balance F = B + E
2019-2020	—	—	1,00,000	1,00,000	1,00,000
2020-2021	1,00,000	10,000	1,00,000	1,10,000	2,10,000
2021-2022	2,10,000	21,000	1,00,000	1,21,000	3,31,000
2022-2023	3,31,000	33,100	1,00,000	—	—

ILLUSTRATION 18

Calculate the Profit *or* Loss on sale of Debenture Redemption Reserve Investments in each of the following alternative cases:

Case (a)	Debenture Redemption Reserve	₹ 1,80,000
	(represented by ₹ 2,00,000, 10% Govt. Stock)	
	Investments were sold at 83%	
Case (b)	Debenture Redemption Reserve	₹ 1,80,000
	(represented by ₹ 2,00,000, 10% Govt. Stock)	
	Investment were sold at 95%	
Case (c)	Debenture Redemption Reserve	₹ 1,80,000
	(represented by ₹ 1,50,000, 10% Govt. Stock purchased at 80% and ₹ 50,000, 10% Govt. Paper)	
	Investments were sold as follows:	
	10% Govt. Stock at 90%	
	10% Govt. Paper at 110%	
Case (d)	Debenture Redemption Reserve	₹ 1,80,000
	(represented by ₹ 1,50,000 own Debentures purchased at 80% and ₹ 50,000, 10% Govt. Paper)	
	10% Govt. Paper realised 110%	
Case (e)	Debenture Redemption Reserve	₹ 1,80,000
	(represented by ₹ 2,00,000, 10% Govt. Stock)	
	₹ 1,50,000, 10% Govt. Stock realised 83% for redemption of a part of debentures.	

SOLUTION

CALCULATION OF PROFIT OR LOSS ON SALE OF DRR INVESTMENTS

A *Case*	*B* *Face Value*	*C* *Cost/Book Value*	*D* *Sale Proceeds*	*E = D – C* *Profit (Loss)*
(a)	2,00,000	1,80,000	1,66,000	(14,000)
(b)	2,00,000	1,80,000	1,90,000	10,000
(c) (i)	1,50,000	1,20,000	1,35,000	15,000
(c) (ii)	50,000	60,000 [₹ 1,80,000 – ₹ 1,20,000]	55,000	(5,000)
(d) (i)	1,50,000	1,20,000	1,50,000	30,000
(d) (ii)	50,000	60,000 [₹ 1,80,000 – ₹ 1,20,000]	55,000	(5,000)
(e)	1,50,000	1,35,000 [1,50,000/2,00,000 × 1,80,000]	1,24,500	(10,500)

ILLUSTRATION 19A [WHEN ALL THE DEBENTURES ARE REDEEMED]

The following balances appeared in the books of X Ltd. as on 1st Jan. 2023.

9% Debentures	₹ 2,50,000
10% Debentures Redemption Reserve (represented by ₹ 2,00,000, 10% Govt Stock)	₹ 1,80,000

The annual contribution to the Debenture Redemption Reserve was ₹ 50,000 made on 31st Dec. each year. On 31st Dec. 2023, Balance at Bank before the receipt of interest was ₹ 70,000. On the date all the investments were sold at 95% and the debentures were duly redeemed.

Required: (a) Pass the Journal entries for the year ending 31st Dec. 2023 (b) Prepare (i) Debentures Redemption Reserve A/c, (ii) Debenture Redemption Reserve Investment A/c (iii) 9% Debentures A/c (iv) Debentureholders' A/c and (v) Bank A/c

SOLUTION

(A) JOURNAL

Date	*Particulars*		*L.F.*	*Dr. (₹)*	*Cr.(₹)*
31.12.2023	Bank A/c To Interest on DRRI A/c (Being the receipt of interest on DRRI)	Dr.		20,000	20,000
	Interest on DRRI A/c To Debenture Redemption Reserve A/c (Being the transfer of Interest on DRRI to DRR A/c)	Dr.		20,000	20,000
	Profit & Loss Appropriation A/c To Debenture Redemption Reserve A/c (Being the transfer of profit to DRR A/c to provide for the redemption of debentures)	Dr.		50,000	50,000
	Bank A/c To Debenture Redemption Reserve Investment A/c (Being the realisation of Investments)	Dr.		1,90,000	1,90,000
	Debenture Redemption Reserve Investment A/c To Debenture Redemption Reserve A/c (Being the transfer of profit on sale of Investments)	Dr.		10,000	10,000
	9% Debentures A/c To Debenture-holders' A/c (Being the amount due on redemption)	Dr.		2,50,000	2,50,000
	Debenture-holders' A/c To Bank A/c (Being the payment made to Debenture-holders)	Dr.		2,50,000	2,50,000
	Debenture Redemption Reserve A/c To Capital Reserve A/c To General Reserve A/c	Dr.		2,60,000	10,000 2,50,000

	(Being the transfer of Profit to CR A/c & the balance in DRR A/c to General Reserve)			

Ledger Accounts:

Dr. **DEBENTURES REDEMPTION RESERVE ACCOUNT** *Cr.*

Date	*Particulars*	₹	*Date*	*Particulars*	₹
31.12.2023	To Capital Reserve A/c	10,000	01.01.2023	By Balance b/d	1,80,000
	To General Reserve A/c	2,50,000	31.12.2023	By Interest on DRRI A/c (Int. @ 10% on ₹2,00,000)	20,000
			31.12.2023	By P&L Appropriation A/c	50,000
				By DRRI A/c (Profit)	10,000
		2,60,000			2,60,000

Dr. **DEBENTURE REDEMPTION RESERVE INVESTMENT ACCOUNT** *Cr.*

Date	*Particulars*	₹	*Date*	*Particulars*	₹
01.01.2023	To Balance b/d (Face value ₹2,00,000)	1,80,000	31.12.2023	By Bank A/c (95% of ₹ 2,00,000)	1,90,000
31.12.2023	To DRR A/c (Profit)	10,000			
		1,90,000			1,90,000

Dr. **9% DEBENTURES ACCOUNT** *Cr.*

Date	*Particulars*	₹	*Date*	*Particulars*	₹
31.12.2023	To Debentureholders' A/c	2,50,000	01.01.2023	By Balance b/d	2,50,000
		2,50,000			2,50,000

Dr. **DEBENTURE-HOLDERS' ACCOUNT** *Cr.*

Date	*Particulars*	₹	*Date*	*Particulars*	₹
31.12.2023	To Bank A/c	2,50,000	31.12.2023	By 12% Debentures A/c	2,50,000

Dr. **BANK ACCOUNT** *Cr.*

Date	*Particulars*	₹	*Date*	*Particulars*	₹
31.12.2023	To Balance b/d	70,000	31.12.2023	By Debentures-holders' A/c	2,50,000
31.12.2023	To Interest on DRRI A/c	20,000		By Balance c/d	30,000
31.12.2023	To Debenture Redemption Reserve Investment A/c	1,90,000			
		2,80,000			2,80,000

ILLUSTRATION 19B

Prepare Bank Account in Illustration 19A if the balance at Bank after the receipt of interest was ₹ 70,000.

SOLUTION

Dr. **BANK ACCOUNT** Cr.

Date	Particulars	₹	Date	Particulars	₹
31.12.2023	To Balance b/d	70,000	31.12.2023	By Debentures-holders' A/c	2,50,000
31.12.2023	To Interest on DRRI A/c	—		By Balance c/d	10,000
31.12.2023	To Debenture Redemption Reserve Investment A/c	1,90,000			
		2,60,000			2,60,000

ILLUSTRATION 20 [WHEN A PART OF DEBENTURES IS REDEEMED]

On 1.1.2023 the Debentures Redemption Reserve of a company showed a balance of ₹ 1,80,000 represented by ₹ 2,00,000, 10% Govt. Stock. On that date the outstanding 9% debentures of the company were ₹ 2,50,000. The annual contribution to Debenture Redemption Reserve was ₹ 50,000.

On 31st Dec. 2023, the company decided to redeem Debentures of ₹ 1,20,000. For this purpose ₹ 1,50,000 10% Govt. Stock was sold at 83% and debentures were duly redeemed. On 31st Dec. the bank balance before the receipt of interest on investments was ₹ 70,000.

Required: (a) Debentures Redemption Reserve A/c, (b) Debentures Redemption Reserve Investment A/c, (c) Debentures A/c, (d) Debentureholders' A/c and (e) Bank Account.

SOLUTION

Dr. **DEBENTURES REDEMPTION RESERVE ACCOUNT** Cr.

Date	Particulars	₹	Date	Particulars	₹
31.12.2023	To Debenture Redem. Reserve Investment A/c (Loss on sale)	10,500	01.01.2023	By Balance b/d	1,80,000
			31.12.2023	By Interest on DRRI A/c (Int. @ 10% on ₹ 2,00,000)	20,000
	To Balance c/d	2,39,500	31.12.2023	By P&L Appropriation A/c	50,000
		2,50,000			2,50,000

Dr. **DEBENTURE REDEMPTION RESERVE INVESTMENT ACCOUNT** Cr.

Date	Particulars	₹	Date	Particulars	₹
01.01.2023	To Balance b/d (Face value 2,00,000)	1,80,000	31.12.2023	By Bank A/c (83% of ₹ 1,50,000)	1,24,500
			31.12.2023	By Debenture Redemption Reserve A/c	10,500
				By Balance c/d	45,000
		1,80,000			1,80,000

Dr. **9% DEBENTURES ACCOUNT** Cr.

Date	Particulars	₹	Date	Particulars	₹
31.12.2023	To Debentureholders' A/c	1,20,000	01.01.2023	By Balance b/d	2,50,000
	To Balance c/d	1,30,000			
		2,50,000			2,50,000

Dr. **DEBENTURE-HOLDERS' ACCOUNT** Cr.

Date	Particulars	₹	Date	Particulars	₹
31.12.2023	To Bank A/c	1,20,000	31.12.2023	By 12% Debentures A/c	1,20,000

Dr. **BANK ACCOUNT** Cr.

Date	Particulars	₹	Date	Particulars	₹
31.12.2023	To Balance b/d	70,000	31.12.2023	By Debentures-holders' A/c	1,20,000
31.12.2023	To Interest on DRRI A/c	20,000		By Balance c/d	94,500
31.12.2023	To Debenture Redemption Reserve Investment A/c	1,24,500			
		2,14,500			2,14,500

ILLUSTRATION 21

XYZ Ltd. had 16,000, 12% Debentures of 100 each outstanding as on 1st April, 2022, redeemable on 31st March, 2023. On that day, Debenture Redemption fund was ₹ 14,98,000 represented by 2,000 own debentures purchased at the average price of ₹ 99 and 9% Stocks face value of ₹ 13,20,000. The annual instalment was ₹ 56,800.

On 31st March, 2023 the investments were realized at ₹ 98 and the debentures were redeemed. You are required to write up the following accounts for the year ending 31st March 2023:

(a) 12% Debentures Account

(b) Debenture Redemption Fund Account.

SOLUTION

Dr. **(I) 12% DEBENTURES ACCOUNT** Cr.

Particulars	₹	Particulars	₹
To Own Debentures A/c	2,00,000	By Balance b/d	16,00,000
To Bank A/c	14,00,000		
	16,00,000		**16,00,000**

Dr. **(II) DEBENTURE REDEMPTION FUND ACCOUNT** Cr.

Particulars	₹	Particulars	₹
To 9% Stock A/c (loss)	6,400	By Balance b/d	14,98,000
To General Reserve A/c (b.f.)	16,93,200	By Profit and loss A/c	56,800

		By Interest on Sinking Fund A/c	1,42,800
		By Own Debentures A/c	2,000
	16,99,600		**16,99,600**

Working Notes:

(III) AMOUNT OF STOCK AS ON 1ST APRIL, 2022

Sinking Fund Balance as on 1st April, 2022	₹14,98,000
Less: Own debentures	₹ (1,98,000)
	₹ 13,00,000

(ii) Sales Value of 9% Stock = (₹ 13,20,000/ ₹ 100) × ₹ 98 = ₹ 12, 93,600

(iii) Interest credited to Sinking Fund = (₹ 13,20,000 × 9%) + (₹ 2,00,000 × 12%)= ₹ 1,42,800

Dr. **(IV) OWN DEBENTURES ACCOUNT** *Cr.*

Particulars	₹	*Particulars*	₹
To Balance b/d	1,98,000	By 12% Debentures A/c	2,00,000
To Sinking Fund A/c	2,000		
	2,00,000		**2,00,000**

Dr. **(V) 9% STOCK ACCOUNT** *Cr.*

Particulars	₹	*Particulars*	₹
To Balance (Face value 13,20,000)	13,00,000	By Bank A/c	12,93,600
		By Sinking Fund A/c (loss on sales)	6,400
	13,00,000		**13,00,000**

11.0 REDEMPTION OF DEBENTURES BY PURCHASE IN THE OPEN MARKET

MEANING OF REDEMPTION OF DEBENTURES BY PURCHASE IN THE OPEN MARKET

When a company purchases its own debentures in the open market for the purposes of immediate cancellation, such an act of purchasing and cancelling the debentures constitutes redemption by purchase in the open market.

REDEMPTION OF DEBENTURES BY PURCHASE IN THE OPEN MARKET

This method of redemption is advantageous for several reasons as follows:

1. **Saving equal to the amount of discount:** Purchasing the debentures in the open market when they are available at a discount, would enable the company to save money equal to the amount of discount which would have been required to be paid by it in case the debentures are redeemed in the ordinary course.
2. **Reduction in interest burden:** Purchasing the debentures in the open market would also enable the company to reduce the interest burden on debentures purchased in the market and cancelled.
3. **Saving equal to premium payable on redemption:** Purchasing the debentures in the open market would also enable the company to save money equal to the premium which otherwise would have been payable on regular redemption in case of debentures redeemable at premium.

DIVISION OF TOTAL PURCHASE AMOUNT INTO PRINCIPLE AND INTEREST

On Purchase of Debentures in the open market,the company is required to pay to the Seller the following two payments:

1. the payment made towards Principal.
2. the payment made towards Interest accrued from the last due date of interest to the date of purchase.

CUM INTEREST PRICE QUOTATION AND EX-INTEREST PRICE QUOTATION

There are two ways of expressing the price quotations:

1. **Cum Interest Price:** If the interest accrued from the last due date of interest to the date of transaction is **included** in the price quoted, it is called Cum-Interest price which is the total amount paid for the purchase of debentures. Thus,

   Cum-Interest Price = Payment towards Principal + Payment towards Interest accrued from the last due date of interest to the date of transaction.

2. **Ex-Interest Price:** If the interest accrued from the last due date of interest to the date of transaction is not included in the price quoted, it is called Ex-interest price.

   Ex-Interest Price = Payment towards Principal

The payment towards Principal, payment towards Interest and total amount paid for the purchase of Debentures may be calculated with the help of following table:

Price Quotation *A*	*Payment towards Interest* *B*	*Payment towards Principal* *C*	*Total Amount Paid* *D = B + C*
I. Cum-Interest	I = [Nominal Value × Rate/100 × Period/12]	C = Cum-Interest Price -Interest	Cum-Interest Price
II. Ex-Interest	I = [Nominal Value × Rate/100 × Period/12]	C = Ex-Interest Price	Ex-Interest Price + Interest

TUTORIAL NOTES

1. *Brokerage (if any payable) is always calculated with reference to the quotation price (whether cum-interest or ex-interest) of the transaction.*
2. *Interest is always calculated with reference to the face value (or nominal value) of the debentures.*
3. *Unless otherwise stated, the price quotation will be treated as 'Cum-interest' quotation in case of debentures issued by companies.*

ILLUSTRATION 22 [IN CASE OF EX-INTEREST QUOTATION]

Calculate the Total amount paid for the purchase of debentures in each of the following alternative cases:

Case (a) On 1st Jan, X Ltd. purchased 300, 12% Debentures of ₹ 100 each at ₹ 93 ex-interest. The interest is payable half yearly on 30th June and 31st December.

Case (b) On 1st May, X Ltd. purchased 300, 12% Debentures of ₹ 100 each at ₹ 93 ex-interest. The interest is payable half yearly on 30th June and 31st December.

Case (c) On 30th June, X Ltd. purchased 300, 12% Debentures of ₹ 100 each at ₹ 93 ex-interest. The interest is payable half yearly on 30th June and 31st December.

SOLUTION

CALCULATION OF TOTAL AMOUNT PAID

Case *A*	*Interest Accrued from last due date to the date of purchase* *B*	*Ex-Interest Amount or Real Price* *C*	*Total Amount Paid* *D = B + C*
(a)	₹ 30,000 × 12/100 × 0/12 = 0	300 × ₹ 93 = 27,900	₹ 27,900 + 0 = 27,900
(b)	₹ 30,000 × 12/100 × 4/12 = ₹ 1,200	300 × ₹ 93 = 27,900	27,900 + 1,200 = ₹ 29,100
(c)	₹ 30,000 × 12/100 × 6/12 = ₹ 1,800	300 × ₹ 93 = 27,900	27,900 + 1,800 = ₹ 29,700

ILLUSTRATION 23 [IN CASE OF CUM-INTEREST QUOTATION]

Calculate the Payment towards Principal made for the purchase of debentures in each of the following alternative cases:

Case (a) On 1st Jan, X Ltd. purchased 300, 12% Debentures of ₹ 100 each at ₹ 93 Cum-interest. The interest is payable half yearly on 30th June and 31st December.

Case (b) On 1st May, X Ltd. purchased 300, 12% Debentures of ₹ 100 each at ₹ 93 Cum-interest. The interest is payable half yearly on 30th June and 31st December.

Case (c) On 30th June, X Ltd. purchased 300, 12% Debentures of ₹ 100 each at ₹ 93 Cum-interest. The interest is payable half yearly on 30th June and 31st December.

SOLUTION

CALCULATION OF PAYMENT TOWARDS PRINCIPAL

Case *A*	*Interest Accrued from last due date to the date of purchase* *B*	*Cum-Interest Amount or Total Amount Paid* *C*	*Real Price or Ex-Interest Amount* *D = C − B*
(a)	₹ 30,000 ×12/100 × 0/12 = 0	300 × ₹ 93 = 27,900	₹ 27,900 – 0 = 27,900
(b)	₹ 30,000 × 12/100 × 4/12 = ₹ 1,200	300 × ₹ 93 = 27,900	27,900 – 1,200 = ₹ 26,700
(c)	₹ 30,000 × 12/100 × 6/12 = ₹ 1,800	300 × ₹ 93 = 27,900	27,900 – 1,800 = ₹ 26,100

JOURNAL ENTRIES ON PURCHASE OF DEBENTURES IN THE OPEN MARKET FOR IMMEDIATE CANCELLATION

1. **On Purchase of own debentures**

Own Debentures A/c	Dr.	*[Ex-interest price or Real price]*
Interest on Debentures A/c	Dr.	*[Interest accrued]*
To Bank A/c		*[Total Amount paid]*

2. **On cancellation of debentures**

X% Debentures A/c	Dr.	*[Nominal value of debentures)*
To Own Debentures A/c		*[Ex-interest price]*
To Capital Reserve A/c		*[Nominal value – Ex-Interest Price]*

3. **On providing for Interest on Remaining Debentures**

Interest on Debentures A/c	Dr.	
To Debentureholders' A/c		

4. **On payment of Interest on Debentures**
Debentureholders' A/c Dr.
To Bank A/c

5. **On Transfer of Interest on Debentures**
Profit & Loss A/c Dr.
To Interest on Debentures A/c

ILLUSTRATION 24

On 1st April. 2022, Tulsian Ltd.(Listed) had 1,000, 12% Debentures of ₹ 100 each. Interest on debentures is payable half yearly on 30th Sept. and on 31st Mar. On 1st Aug. 2022, the company purchased 300 Own Debentures at ₹ 93 ex-interest for immediate cancellation.

Required: Record the necessary journal entries on 1st Aug and 30th Sept., 2022.

SOLUTION

JOURNAL OF TULSIAN LTD.(LISTED)

Date	Particulars	L.F.	Dr. (₹)	Cr. (₹)
01.08.2022	Own Debentures A/c Dr.		27,900	
	Interest on Debentures A/c Dr.		1,200	
	To Bank A/c			29,100
	(Being the purchase of 300 Own Debentures @ ₹ 93 Ex-Interest)			
	12% Debentures A/c Dr.		30,000	
	To Own Debentures A/c			27,900
	To Capital Reserve A/c			2,100
	(Being the transfer of gain on cancellation of debentures to Capital Reserve)			
30.09.2022	Interest on Debentures A/c Dr.		4,200	
	To Debentureholders' A/c			4,200
	(Being the interest due on debentures)			
	Debentureholders' A/c Dr.		4,200	
	To Bank A/c			4,200
	(Being the interest paid)			

Working Notes:

1. Interest accrued on debentures purchased from the last due date to the date of purchase
= ₹ 30,000 × 12/100 × 4/12 = 1,200

2. Total amount paid = Ex-interest Amount + Interest Accrued
= (300 × ₹ 93) + ₹ 1,200 = ₹ 29,100

3. Gain on Cancellation = Nominal Value – Ex-Interest Amount
= ₹ 30,000 – ₹ 27,900 = ₹ 2,100

ILLUSTRATION 25

On 1st April. 2022, Tulsian Ltd. (Listed) had 1,000, 12% Debentures of ₹ 100 each. Interest on Debentures is payable half yearly on 30th Sept. and on 31st Mar. On 1st Aug. 2022, the company purchased 300 Own Debentures at ₹ 97 Cum-interest for immediate cancellation.

Required: Record the necessary journal entries on 1st Aug and 30th Sept., 2022.

SOLUTION

JOURNAL OF TULSIAN LTD.(LISTED)

Date	***Particulars***	***L.F.***	***Dr. (₹)***	***Cr. (₹)***
01.08.2022	Own Debentures A/c Dr.		27,900	
	Interest on Debentures A/c Dr.		1,200	
	To Bank A/c			29,100
	(Being the purchase of 300 Own Debentures @ ₹ 97 Cum-Interest)			
	12% Debentures A/c Dr.		30,000	
	To Own Debentures A/c			27,900
	To Capital Reserve A/c			2,100
	(Being the t/f of gain on cancellation of debentures)			
30.09.2022	Interest on Debentures A/c Dr.		4,200	
	To Debentureholders' A/c			4,200
	(Being the interest due on debentures)			
	Debentureholders' A/c Dr.		4,200	
	To Bank A/c			4,200
	(Being the interest paid)			

Working Notes:

1. Interest accrued on debentures purchased from the last due date to the date of purchase
   = ₹ 30,000 × 12/100 × 4/12 = ₹ 1,200
2. Total Amount paid = Cum-interest Amount = 300 × ₹ 97 = ₹ 29,100
3. Ex-interest Amount paid = Cum-interest Amount – Interest Accrued
   = ₹ 29,100 – ₹ 1,200 = ₹ 27,900
4. Gain on Cancellation = Nominal Value – Ex-Interest Amount = ₹ 30,000 – ₹ 27,900
   = ₹ 2,100
5. It is assumed that the company has sufficient amount in the Debenture Redemption Reserve, hence no further entry has been passed in this regard.

ILLUSTRATION 26

On 1.4.2022, X Ltd. (Listed) had 1,000 12% Debentures of ₹ 100 each and Debentures Redemption Reserve ₹ 20,000. In accordance with the powers in the deed, the following debentures were purchased in the open market during the year ended 31st Mar. 2023 for immediate cancellation:

1st Aug 300 Debentures @ ₹ 97 cum-Interest

1st Nov. ₹ 20,000 nominal purchased for ₹ 19,350 Ex-Interest

Interest on debentures is payable half-yearly on 30th Sept and on 31st Mar.

Required: Pass the necessary journal entries.

SOLUTION

JOURNAL OF X LTD.(LISTED)

Date	Particulars	L.F.	Dr. (₹)	Cr. (₹)
01.08.2022	Own Debentures A/c Dr.		27,900	
	Interest on Debentures A/c Dr.		1,200	
	To Bank A/c			29,100
	(Being the purchase of 300 debentures @ ₹ 97 cum-interest for cancellation)			
01.08.2022	12% Debentures A/c Dr.		30,000	
	To Own Debentures A/c			27,900
	To Capital Reserve A/c			2,100
	(Being the transfer of gain on cancellation of debentures)			
30.09.2022	Interest on Debentures A/c Dr.		4,200	
	To Debentureholders' A/c			4,200
	(Being the interest due on ₹ 70,000 @ 12% p.a. for 6 months)			
	Debentureholders' A/c Dr.		4,200	
	To Bank A/c			4,200
	(Being the interest paid on Debentures)			
01.11.2022	Own Debentures A/c Dr.		19,350	
	Interest on Debentures A/c Dr.		200	
	To Bank A/c			19,550
	(Being the purchase of 200 debentures for ₹ 19,350 Ex-interest for cancellation)			
01.11.2022	12% Debentures A/c Dr.		20,000	
	To Own Debentures A/c			19,350
	To Capital Reserve A/c			650
	(Being the t/f of gain on cancellation of debentures)			
31.03.2023	Interest on Debentures A/c Dr.		3,000	
	To Debentureholders' A/c			3,000
	(Being the interest due on ₹ 50,000 @ 12% p.a. for 6 months)			
	Debentureholders' A/c Dr.		3,000	
	To Bank A/c			3,000
	(Being the interest paid on Debentures)			

31.03.2023	Profit & Loss A/c Dr. To Interest on Debentures A/c (Being the transfer of debenture interest to P&L A/c)		8,600	8,600

ACCOUNTING ENTRIES WHEN SINKING FUND EXISTS AND OWN DEBENTURES ARE PURCHASED FOR IMMEDIATE CANCELLATION

1. **On Sale of Debentures Redemption Fund Investments**

Bank A/c	Dr. *[Total Amount Received]*
To Debenture Redemption fund Investment A/c	*[Ex-Interest Amount]*
To Interest on Debenture Red. Fund Investment A/c	*[Accrued Interest]*

2. **On Transfer of Profit on sale of DRFI (other than own Deb.)**
   Deb Red. Fund Investment A/c Dr. *[With Profit]*
   To Debenture Redemption Fund A/c
3. **On Purchase of Own Debentures for immediate cancellation**
   Debentures A/c Dr. *[Nominal value]*
   Interest on Debentures A/c Dr. *[Interest accrued]*
   To Bank A/c *[Total Amount paid]*
   To Capital Reserve A/c *[Nominal value – Ex-Interest Price]*
4. **On Providing for Interest on Remaining Debentures**
   Interest on Debentures A/c Dr.
   To Debentureholders' A/c
5. **On Payment of interest on Debentures**
   Debentureholders' A/c Dr.
   To Bank A/c
6. **On Transfer of Interest on Debentures**
   Profit & Loss A/c Dr.
   To Interest on Debentures A/c
7. **On Receipt of Interest on DRFI (other than own Debentures)**
   Bank A/c Dr.
   To Interest on DRFI
8. **On Transfer of Interest on DRFI**
   Interest on DRFI A/c Dr.
   To Debenture Redemption fund A/c

ILLUSTRATION 27 PROFIT/LOSS ON SALE OF DEBENTURE REDEMPTION FUND INVESTMENTS

The following balances appeared in the books X Ltd.(Listed) as on 1st Jan. 2023

1. 6% Debentures (Face value ₹ 100 each) ₹ 2,00,000
2. Debenture Redemption Fund Account ₹ 1,00,000

3. Debenture Redemption Fund Investment represented by ₹ 50,000 own debentures purchased, @ ₹ 90 and the remaining amount by ₹ 60,000, 6% Govt. Securities.

On 1.5.2023, the company sold the Govt. Securities of the face value ₹ 20,000 @ ₹ 95 Ex-Interest and applied the proceeds realised in purchasing 200 own debentures.

Required: Journalise the sale and purchase transactions in each of the following alternative cases:

Case (a) The Interest on Debentures is payable on 30th June and 31st December & Interest on 6% Govt. Securities is receivable in the same dates.

Case (b) The Interest on Debentures is payable on 30th June and 31st Dec. & the interest on Govt. Securities is receivable on 31st March & 30 September.

SOLUTION

(a) JOURNAL OF X LTD.(LISTED)

Date	*Particulars*		*L.F.*	*Dr. (₹)*	*Cr. (₹)*
2023					
May 1	Bank A/c	Dr.		19,400	
	To Debenture Red. Fund Invsts. A/c (Govt. Security)				19,000
	To Interest on DRFI A/c				400
	(Being Sale of Govt. Securities ₹ 20,000 @ ₹ 95 ex. Interest).				
	Debenture Redemption Fund Investment A/c	Dr.		667	
	To Debenture Redemption Fund A/c				667
	(Being the transfer of Profit on Sale of Govt. Securities)				
	DRFI (own Debentures) A/c	Dr.		19,000	
	Debenture Interest A/c	Dr.		400	
	To Bank A/c				19,400
	(Being Purchase of own Deb. ₹ 20,000 @ ₹ 97 cum interest)				

Working Notes:

1. CALCULATION OF THE BOOK VALUE OF GOVT. SECURITIES SOLD

	Particulars	₹
A	Book Value of Total Investments	1,00,000
B	*Less:* Book Value of Own Debentures (₹ 50,000 × 90/100)	45,000
C	Book Value of Total Govt. Securities (Face Value ₹ 60,000)	55,000
D	Book Value of Govt. Securities Sold (₹ 55,000 × ₹ 20,000/₹ 60,000)	18,333

2. CALCULATION OF TOTAL SALES PROCEEDS OF SALE OF GOVT. SECURITY

	Particulars	₹
A	Ex-Sale Proceeds (₹ 20,000 × 95/100)	19,000
B	*Add:* Interest Accrued on ₹ 20,000 for 4 months (₹ 20,000 × 4/12 × 6/100)	400
C	Cum-Sale Proceeds (A + B)	19,400

3. CALCULATION OF PROFIT ON SALE OF GOVT SECURITIES

	Particulars	₹
A	Ex-Sale Proceeds	19,000
B	*Less:* Book Value of Govt. Securities Sold	18,333
C	Profit on Sale (A – B)	667

4. CALCULATION OF ACTUAL COST OF OWN DEBENTURES PURCHASED ON 1ST MAY

	Particulars	₹
A	Cum-Purchase Price Paid for 200 own Debentures	19,400
B	*Less:* Interest Accrued on ₹ 20,000 own Debentures for 4 months (₹ 20,000 × 4/12 × 6/100)	400
C	Actual Cost Price of Debentures Purchased (A–B)	19,000

(b) JOURNAL OF X LTD.(LISTED)

Date	Particulars	L.F.	Dr. (₹)	Cr. (₹)
2023				
May 01	Bank A/c Dr.		19,100	
	To Debenture Red. Fund Invsts. (Govt. securities) A/c			19,000
	To Interest on DRFI A/c			100
	(Being the sale of Govt. Securities of ₹ 20,000 @ ₹ 95 Ex-Interest)			
	Debenture Redemption Fund Investment A/c Dr.		667	
	To Debentures Redemption Fund A/c			667
	(Being the transfer of profit in sale of Govt. Securities)			
	Debenture Redemption Fund Investments (own Debentures) A/c Dr.		18,700	
	Debenture Interest A/c Dr.		400	
	To Bank A/c			19,100
	(Being the purchase of 200 own Debentures @ ₹ 95.5 cum-interest)			

Working Notes:

1. CALCULATION OF THE BOOK VALUE OF GOVT. SECURITIES SOLD

	Particulars	₹
A	Book Value of Total Investments	1,00,000
B	*Less:* Book Value of own Debenture (₹ 50,000 × 90/100)	45,000
C	Book Value of Total Govt. Securities (Fact Value ₹ 60,000)	55,000
D	Book Value of Govt. Securities Sold (₹ 55,000 × ₹ 20,000/₹ 60,000)	18,333

2. CALCULATION OF TOTAL SALE PROCEEDS OR SALE OF GOVT. SECURITIES

	Particulars	₹
A	Ex-Sale Proceeds on a/c of Cost (₹ 20,000 × 95/100)	19,000
B	*Add:* Interest Accrued on ₹ 20,000 for 1 month (₹ 20,000 × 1/2 × 6/100)	100
C	Cum-Sale Proceeds (A + B)	19,100

3. CALCULATION OF PROFIT ON SALE OF GOVT-SECURITIES

	Particulars	₹
A	Ex-Sale Proceeds	19,000
B	*Less:* Book Value of Govt Securities Sold	18,333
C	Profit on Sale (A — B)	667

4. CALCULATION OF ACTUAL COST OF OWN DEBENTURES PURCHASED ON 1ST MAY

	Particulars	₹
A	Cum Purchase Price Paid for 200 Debentures	19,100
B	*Less:* Interest Accrued on ₹ 20,000 Own Debentures Purchased for 4 months (₹ 20,000 × 4/12 × 6/100)	400
C	Actual Cost Price of Debentures purchased (A — B)	18,700

ILLUSTRATION 28

The following balances appeared in the books of CSS Ltd. (Listed) as on 1.1.2023

12% Debentures (face Value ₹ 100)	₹ 1,00,000
Debenture Redemption Fund	₹ 37,500
Debenture Redemption Fund Investment A/c (represents 8% Govt. Securities of the face value of ₹ 45,000)	₹ 37,500

On 1.3.2023, this Company purchased 125 debentures in the market @ ₹ 93 Ex. out of funds raised by selling 8% Govt. Securities of the face value of ₹ 13,500. On 31.12.2023, ₹ 10,400 was appropriated for the Sinking Fund which together with the interest received on Sinking fund during the year was invested in 8% Govt. securities of the face value of ₹ 14,000. The Interest on debenture was payable on 30th June and 31st December and interest on 8% Govt. Securities was receivable on the same dates.

Required: Give the necessary journal Entries & ledger accounts assuming that the own debentures purchased in the market were cancelled immediately.

SOLUTION

JOURNAL

Date	Particulars		L.F.	Dr. (₹)	Cr. (₹)
2023					
Mar. 01	Bank A/c	Dr.		11,875	
	To Debenture Redemption Fund Investment A/c				11,695
	To Interest on Deb. Red. Fund Investment A/c				180

	(Being DRF Investments realised for ₹ 11,875 cum interest)			
	Debenture Redemption Fund Investment A/c Dr. To Debenture Redemption Fund A/c (Being the transfer of Profit on Sale of DRF Investments to DRF A/c)		445	445
	12% Debentures A/c Dr. Debenture Interest A/c Dr. To Bank A/c To Capital Reserve A/c (Being 125 Debentures cancelled)		12,500 250	11,875 875
June 30	Debenture Interest A/c Dr. To Bank A/c (Being Interest Paid on ₹ 87,500 @ 12% for 6 months)		5,250	5,250
	Bank A/c Dr. To Interest on DRFI A/c (Being interest on ₹ 31,500 @ 8% p.a for 6 month)		1,260	1,260
Dec. 31	Debenture Interest Dr. To Bank A/c (Being Interest Paid on ₹ 87,500 @ 12% for 6 months)		5,250	5,250
	Bank A/c Dr. To Interest on DRFI A/c (Being interest on ₹ 31,500 @ 8% p.a for 6 months)		1,260	1,260
	Profit & Loss A/c Dr. To Debenture Interest A/c (Being the transfer of Deb. Interest to P & L A/c)		10,750	10,750
	Interest on DRFI A/c Dr. To DRF A/c (Being the transfer of Interest on DRFI to DRF A/c)		2,700	2,700
	P & L Appropriation A/c Dr. To DRF A/c (Being the transfer of annual profit to DRF A/c)		10,400	10,400
	DRF Investments A/c Dr. To Bank A/c (Being investments made)		13,100	13,100

Ledger Accounts:

Dr. **12% DEBENTURES ACCOUNT** Cr.

Date	Particulars	₹	Date	Particulars	₹
2023			2023		
Mar. 01	To Bank A/c	11,625	Jan 01	By Balance b/d	1,00,000
	To Capital Reserve A/c	875			
Dec. 31	By Balance c/d	87,500			
		1,00,000			1,00,000

Dr. **DEBENTURE REDEMPTION FUND ACCOUNT** Cr.

Date	Particulars	₹	Date	Particulars	₹
2023			2023		
Dec 31	To Balance c/d	51,045	Jan. 01	By Balance b/d	37,500
			Mar. 01	By DRFI A/c	445
			Dec. 31	By Interest on DRFI A/c	2,700
				By P & L Appr. A/c	10,400
		51,045			51,045

Dr. **DEBENTURE REDEMPTION FUND INVESTMENTS ACCOUNT** Cr.

Date	Particulars	₹	Date	Particulars	₹
2023			2023		
Jan. 01	To Balance b/d	37,500	Mar. 01	By Bank A/c	11,695
	(Face Value ₹ 45,000)			(Face Value ₹ 13,500)	
Mar. 01	To DRF A/c	445	Dec. 31	By balance c/d	39,350
Dec. 31	To Bank A/c	13,100		(Face Value ₹ 40,500)	
	(Face Value ₹ 14,000)				
		51,045			51,045

Dr. **DEBENTURE INTEREST ACCOUNT** Cr.

Date	Particulars	₹	Date	Particulars	₹
2023			2023		
Mar. 01	To Bank A/c	250	Dec. 31	By P & L A/c	10,750
June 30	To Bank A/c	5,250			
Dec. 31	To Bank A/c	5,250			
		10,750			10,750

Working Notes:

1. CALCULATION OF TOTAL PAYMENT MADE FOR THE PURCHASE OF 125 DEBENTURES

	Particulars	₹
A	Cost of 125 debentures @ ₹ 93	11,625
B	Interest on ₹ 12,500 @ 12% for 2 months	250
C	Total Payment made (A + B)	11,875

2. CALCULATION OF THE PROFIT ON SALE OF 8% GOVT. SECURITIES

	Particulars	₹
A	Total proceeds Received	11,875
B	*Less:* Interest on ₹ 13,500 @ 8% for 2 months	180
C	Net proceeds of Investments (A – B)	11,695
D	Book value of 8% Govt. Securities sold (₹ 37,500 × ₹ 13,500/₹ 45,000)	11,250
E	Profit on Sale of Investment (C – D)	445

Note: *Unless otherwise stated, price equation is assumed to cum-interest as in case of Sale of Govt. Securities.*

COMPREHENSIVE ILLUSTRATIONS

COMPREHENSIVE ILLUSTRATION 1

On 1st April, 2020,Bharat Tushar Ltd. (listed Co) issued 6,000, 12% Debentures of ₹ 100 each at a discount of 10% and redeemable at a premium of 5% as follows:

25% by converting into Equity Shares of ₹ 10 each issued at a premium of 25% , 25% by converting into 13% Debentures of ₹ 50 each at a discount of ₹ 5 per Debenture and the balance for Cash either by purchase in the open market(if available below par) *or* by drawing a lot.

Interest on Debentures is payable half-yearly on 30th Sept and on 31st Mar. During 2022-2023,the company took the following actions:

Date	*Action*
1st Aug	Purchased 1800 Debentures @ ₹ 97 cum-Interest in the open market for immediate cancellation.
1st Oct.	Converted 25% Debentures into Equity Shares of ₹ 10 each issued at a premium of 25%.
1st Nov.	₹ 60,000 nominal purchased for ₹ 58,050 Ex-Interest in the open market for immediate cancellation.
31st Mar.	Converted 25% Debentures into 13% Debentures of ₹ 50 each at a discount of ₹ 5 per Debenture.

Required: Pass the necessary journal entries for the Redemption of Debentures, Interest on Debentures and Loss on issue of Debentures assuming that no portion of the Loss on issue of Debentures was written off prior to current year.

SOLUTION

JOURNAL OF BHARAT TUSHAR LTD.

Date	*Particulars*		*L.F.*	*Dr. (₹)*	*Cr. (₹)*
01.08.2022	Own Debentures A/c	Dr.		1,67,400	
	Interest on Debentures A/c [180000 × 12% × 4/12]	Dr.		7,200	
	To Bank A/c				1,74,600
	(Being the purchase of 1800 Debentures @ ₹ 97 cum-interest for cancellation)				
01.08.2022	12% Debentures A/c	Dr.		1,80,000	
	To Own Debentures A/c				1,67,400

	To Capital Reserve A/c			12,600
	(Being the transfer of gain on cancellation of debentures)			
30.09.2022	Interest on Debentures A/c [420000 × 12% × 6/12] Dr.		25,200	
	To Debentureholders' A/c			25,200
	(Being the interest due on 4200 Debentures)			
30.09.2022	Debentureholders' A/c Dr.		25,200	
	To Bank A/c			25,200
	(Being the interest paid on Debentures)			
01.10.2022	12% Debentures A/c Dr.		1,50,000	
	Premium on Redemption of Debentures A/c Dr.		7,500	
	To Loss on Issue of Debentures A/c[Dis. + Premium]			22,500
	To Debenture-holders' A/c			1,35,000
	(Being the amount due to debenture-holders on conversion of 1,500,12% Debentures)			
01.10.2022	Debenture-holders' A/c Dr.		1,35,000	
	To Equity Share Capital A/c			1,08,000
	To Securities Premium A/c			27,000
	(Being the issue of 10,800 Equity Shares of ₹ 10 each at 25% Premium on conversion of 1,500, 15% Debentures) [*₹ 1,35,000/₹ 12.50 = 10,800*]			
01.11.2022	Own Debentures A/c Dr.		58,050	
	Interest on Debentures A/c [60000 × 12% × 1/12] Dr.		600	
	To Bank A/c			58,650
	(Being the purchase of 600 debentures for ₹ 58,050 Ex-interest for cancellation)			
01.11.2022	12% Debentures A/c Dr.		60,000	
	To Own Debentures A/c			58,050
	To Capital Reserve A/c			1,950
	(Being the t/f of gain on cancellation of debentures)			
31.03.2023	12% Debentures A/c Dr.		1,50,000	
	Premium on Redemption of Debentures A/c Dr.		7,500	
	To Debenture-holders' A/c			1,57,500
	(Being the amount due on redemption of 1,500, 12% Debentures)			
31.03.2023	Debenture-holders' A/c Dr.		1,57,500	
	Discount on Issue of 13% Debentures A/c Dr.		17,500	
	To 13% Debentures A/c			1,75,000
	(Being the issue of 3500,13% Debentures of ₹ 50 each at a discount of ₹ 5 per Debenture on conversion of 1,500 Debentures) [*₹ 1,57,500/₹ 45 = 3500*]			
31.03.2023	12% Debentures A/c Dr.		60,000	
	Premium on Redemption of Debentures A/c Dr.		3,000	

	To Debentureholders' A/c (Being the amount due on redemption of 600 Debentures)		63,000
31.03.2023	Debentureholders' A/c Dr. To Bank A/c (Being the payment made to Debentureholders)	63,000	63,000
31.03.2023	Interest on Debentures A/c [210000 × 12% × 6/12] Dr. To Debentureholders' A/c (Being the interest due on 2100 Debentures)	12,600	12,600
	Debentureholders' A/c Dr. To Bank A/c (Being the interest paid on Debentures)	12,600	12,600
31.03.2023	Profit & Loss A/c Dr. To Interest on Debentures A/c (Being the transfer of debenture interest to P&L A/c)	45,600	45,600
31.03.2023	Profit & Loss A/c Dr. Premium on Redemption of Debentures A/c Dr. To Loss on Issue of Debentures A/c To Discount on Issue of Debentures A/c (Being the Premium on Redemption of Debentures purchased in the open market cancelled & the balance Loss on Issue of Debentures and Discount w/o)	55,500 12,000	67,500 17,500

Notes:

1. In case of Conversion of Debentures (which were originally issued at a discount) into new shares, the 'Discount/Loss on Issue of Debentures Account' should be credited otherwise it would amount to an issue of shares at discount which is void as per Sec. 53 of the Companies Act, 2013.
2. In case of Conversion of Debentures (which were originally issued at a discount) into new debentures, the 'Discount/Loss on Issue of Debentures Account' need not be credited because there is no violation of Sec 53 of The Companies Act, 2013.

COMPREHENSIVE ILLUSTRATION 2

AMLA GILOY & TULSI Ltd (Listed) provides you the following relevant information as at 31st March, 2023:

Particulars	***(₹ in lakh)***
10% Redeemable Pref. shares of ₹ 10 each fully paid up	100
Equity Shares of ₹ 10 each fully paid up	300
Securities Premium (including ₹ 10,00,000 on issue of Shares against the purchase of business)	130
General Reserve	170
Profit & Loss Account	60
Capital Redemption Reserve	20

Plant Revaluation Reserve	500
Debenture Redemption Reserve	25.50
12% Debentures (of ₹ 100 each)	83
General Investments [Face Value ₹ 200 lakh]	400
Investments in 33000 Own Debentures	30
Debenture Redemption Reserve Investments [Face Value ₹ 15 lakh]	20
Cash at Bank	300

On 1st April,2023,the company decided: (a)To buy back 2 lakh equity shares at ₹ 50. For this purpose, 40% of General Investments were realized at market price which was 125% of the face value. (b)To redeem the Pref. shares at a premium of 10%. (c) To cancel Investments in Own Debentures and to redeem the Debentures at a premium of 5%. Debenture Redemption Reserve Investments realized 20% more than face value. Later on the company issued three fully paid up Equity Shares of ₹ 10 each by way of bonus shares for every five equity shares held. The company desired to have minimum reduction in free reserves.

Required: Pass the necessary Journal Entries relating to part (a), (b), (c) and bonus shares.

SOLUTION

JOURNAL OF AMLA GILOY & TULSI Ltd *[₹ in lakh]*

Data	*Particulars*		*Dr. (₹)*	*Cr. (₹)*
1	Bank A/c [₹ 80 lakh × 125%]	Dr.	100	
	Profit & Loss A/c	Dr.	60	
	To Investments A/c			160
	(Being the Investments (Face Value of 80 Lakh) of Book value of ₹ 160 lakh sold at 125% of face value			
	Book value = ₹ 400 × ₹ 80/ ₹ 200 = ₹ 160 lakh			
	Sale Proceeds = ₹ 80 lakh × 125% = ₹ 100 lakh			
2.	Equity Share Capital A/c	Dr.	20	
	Premium payable on Buy Back A/c	Dr.	80	
	To Equity Share Buyback A/c			100
	(Being the amount due on Buy Back)			
3.	Equity Shares Buy Back A/c	Dr.	100	
	To Bank A/c			100
	(Being the payment made on buy-back)			
4.	Securities Premium A/c	Dr.	100	
	To Premium payable on Buy Back A/c			80
	To Capital Redemption Reserve A/c			20
	(Being Premium payable on Buy Back w/o and the amount equal to nominal value of Equity Shares bought back out of free reserves t/f to CRR)			
5.	10% Red. Preference Share Capital A/c	Dr	100	
	Premium on redemption of Preference Shares A/c	Dr.	10	
	To Preference Shareholders A/c			110
	(Being the amount due to Preference Shareholders)			

6.	Preference Shareholders A/c Dr. To Bank A/c (Being the payment made to Preference Shareholders)	110	110
7.	General Reserve A/c Dr. To Premium on Redemption of Pref. Shares A/c To Capital Redemption Reserve A/c (Being premium on redemption of RPS w/o and the face value of RPS redeemed out of divisible profits t/f to CRR)	110	100 10
8.	12% Debentures A/c Dr. To Investments (Own Debentures) A/c To Capital Reserve A/c (Being the cancellation of own debentures and t/f of profit to Capital Reserve)	33	30 3
9.	12% Debentures A/c Premium on redemption of Debentures A/c To Debentureholders A/c (Being the amount due to Debentureholders)	50.0 2.5	52.5
10.	Debenture-holders' A/c Dr. To Bank A/c (Being the payment made to Debentureholders)	52.5	52.5
11.	Bank A/c Dr. Debenture Redemption Reserve A/c Dr To Debenture Redemption Reserve Investment A/c (Being the realisation of Investments & t/f of loss on sale)	18 2	20
12.	Debenture Redemption Reserve A/c Dr. To Premium on Redemption of Debentures A/c To General Reserve (Being premium on redemption of Debentures t/f to DRR and t/f of DRR to GR) [25.5-2-2.5]	23.5	2.5 21
13.	Capital Redemption Reserve A/c Dr. Securities Premium A/c Dr. General Reserve A/c Dr. To Bonus to Equity Share holders A/c (Being the utilization CRR to issue 3 bonus shares for every 5 shares held)[(30-2)x 3/5]=16.8	140 20 8	168
14.	Bonus to Equity Shareholders A/c Dr. To Equity Share Capital A/c (Being the issue of 3 bonus shares for every 5 equity shares held)	168	168

COMPREHENSIVE ILLUSTRATION 3

NEEM & TULSI Ltd (Listed) provides you the following relevant information as at 31st March ,2023:

Particulars	*(₹ in lakh)*
10% Redeemable Pref. shares of ₹ 10 each fully paid up	100.00
Equity Shares of ₹ 10 each fully paid up	260.00
Equity Shares of ₹ 10 each, ₹ 8 paid up	40.00
Securities Premium (including ₹ 10,00,000 on issue of Shares against the purchase of business)	130.00
Capital Reserve (including ₹ 2,50,000 being Profit on Sale of Machinery)	7.50
General Reserve	116.00
Profit & Loss Account	60.00
Capital Redemption Reserve	1.00
Plant Revaluation Reserve	10.00
Debenture Redemption Reserve	25.50
12% Debentures (of ₹ 100 each)	50.00
General Investments [Face Value ₹ 200 lakh]	400.00
Debenture Redemption Reserve Investments [Face Value ₹ 15 lakh]	20.00
Other Assets [including Cash at Bank ₹ 122 lakh]	380.00

On 1st April, 2023, the company decided: (a)To buy back 2 lakh fully paid equity shares @ ₹ 50. For this purpose, 40% of General Investments were realized at market price which was 125% of the face value. (b) To redeem the Pref. shares at a premium of 10%. (c) To redeem the Debentures at a premium of 5% and also confer option to the debenture holders to convert 50% of their holding into equity shares at a predetermined price of ₹ 15 per share and balance payment to be made in cash. Holders of 30,000 debentures opted to get their debentures redeemed in cash only while the rest opted for getting the same converted into equity shares as per the terms of issue. Debenture Redemption Reserve Investment realized at market price which was 120% of the face value. (d) To issue shares to employees in pursuance of the ESOP. On 1.4.2019 the company granted 100 options to each of its 1728 employees @ ₹ 60. The face value of equity share is ₹ 10 per share. The vesting date was 31st March,2022 and the exercise date is 1st April,2023. Only 1700 employees exercised their options on 1st April,2023 when the Fair Value of a share issued under ESOP was ₹ 90.

Later on the company made final call on the partly paid equity shares and received the same and the Company decided to issue bonus shares to equity shareholders at the rate of 9 shares for every 10 shares held and for this purpose, it decided that there should be minimum reduction in free reserves.

Required: Pass the necessary Journal Entries relating to part (a), (b), (c), (d) and bonus shares Also state the amount by which Authorised Capital is required to be increased by passing the necessary resolution at general body meeting of the company.

SOLUTION

JOURNAL

[₹ in lakh]

Data	Particulars	Dr. (₹)	Cr. (₹)
1	Bank A/c [₹ 80 lakh × 125%]	100	
	Profit & Loss A/c	60	
	To Investments A/c		160
	(Being the Investments (Face Value of 80 Lakh) of Book value of ₹ 160 lakh sold at 125% of face value		
	Book value = ₹ 400 × ₹ 80/₹ 200 = ₹ 160 lakh		
	Sale Proceeds = ₹ 80 lakh × 125% = ₹ 100 lakh		
2.	Equity Share Capital A/c	20	
	Premium payable on Buy Back A/c	80	
	To Equity Share Buyback/ Equity shareholders A/c		100
	(Being the amount due on Buy Back)		
3.	Equity Shares Buy Back/ Equity shareholders A/c	100	
	To Bank A/c		100
	(Being the payment made on buy-back)		
4	Securities Premium A/c	100	
	To Premium payable on Buy Back A/c		80
	To Capital Redemption Reserve A/c		20
	(Being the adjustment of Premium payable on Buy Back and the t/f of nominal value of Equity Shares bought back out of free reserves to CRR)		
5	10% Red. Preference Share Capital A/c	100	
	Premium on redemption of Preference Shares A/c	10	
	To Preference Shareholders A/c		110
	(Being the amount due to Preference Shareholders)		
6	Preference Shareholders A/c Dr.	110	
	To Bank A/c		110
	(Being the payment made to Preference Shareholders)		
7	General Reserve A/c	110	
	To Premium on Redemption of Pref. Shares A/c		10
	To Capital Redemption Reserve A/c		100
	(Being the adjustment of premium payable on redemption of pref. shares and the t/f of nominal value of pref. shares redeemed out of divisible profits t/f to Capital Redemption Reserve)		
8	12% Debentures A/c	50.0	
	Premium on redemption of Debentures A/c	2.5	
	To Debentureholders A/c		52.5
	(Being the amount due to Debentureholders)		

9	Debentureholders' A/c Dr. To Bank A/c (Being the payment made to Debentureholders)	42	42
10	Debentureholders' A/c Dr. To Equity Share Capital A/c To Securities Premium A/c (Being the issue of 70,000 Equity Shares of ₹ 10 each at ₹ 15 on conversion of Debentures)	10.5	7.0 3.5
11	Bank A/c Dr. Debenture Redemption Reserve A/c Dr To Debenture Redemption Reserve Investment A/c (Being the realisation of Investments & t/f of loss on sale)	18 2	20
12	Debenture Redemption Reserve A/c Dr. To Premium on Redemption of Debentures A/c To General Reserve (Being the adjustment of premium on redemption of Debentures and t/f of Balance of DRR to GR)	23.5	2.5 21
13	Bank A/c (₹ 60 × 170000) Dr Employees Stock Option Outstanding A/c (₹ 30 × 170000) Dr To Equity Share Capital A/c (170000 × ₹ 10) To Securities Premium A/c (170000 × ₹ 80) (Being exercise of 170000 options at an exercise price of ₹ 60 each and a fair value of ₹ 30 each)	102.00 51.00	17.00 136.00
14	Employees Stock Option Outstanding A/c (2800 × ₹ 30) To General Reserve A/c (Being the fair value of options lapsed t/f to General Reserve)	0.84	0.84
15	Equity Share Final Call A/c Dr. To Equity Share Capital A/c (Being the final call due on partly paid equity shares)	10	10
16	Bank A/c Dr. To Equity Share Final Call A/c (Being the final call received)	10	10
17	Capital Redemption Reserve A/c Dr. Securities Premium A/c [130-10-100+136-51] Dr. Capital Reserve A/c Dr. General Reserve A/c Dr. To Bonus to Equity Share holders A/c (Being the utilization of CRR & Securities Premium to issue 9 bonus shares for every 10 shares held) [(26-2+5+0.70+1.70) x 9/10]	121.00 105.00 2.50. 54.10.	282.60

18	Bonus to Equity Shareholders A/c	282.60	
	To Equity Share Capital A/c		282.60
	(Being the issue of 9 bonus shares for every 10 equity shares held)		

Note: Securities Premium on issue of Shares on conversion of Debentures into Shares and on issue of Shares under ESOP to the extent of discount,will not be considered for issue of bonus shares since Securities Premium not realised in cash.

Working Notes:

1. CALCULATION OF PAYMENT TO DEBENTUREHOLDERS IN CASH & SHARES

	Not opted for conversion (30000)	*opted for conversion (20000)*	*Total*
Face Value	30 lakh	20 lakh	50 lakh
Premium on redemption @ 5%	1.50 lakh	1 lakh	2.5 lakh
Total Value	31.5 lakh	21 lakh	52.5 lakh
Cash %	100%	50%	
Cash to be paid	31.5 lakh	10.5 lakh	42 lakh
50% of their value converted into equity shares		10.5 lakh	
No of equity shares to be issued [₹ 10,50,000/₹ 15]		70,000 shares	

Dr. **2. DEBENTURE REDEMPTION RESERVE ACCOUNT** *Cr.*

Particulars	₹	*Particulars*	₹
To DRR Investment A/c (Loss on sale)	2	By Balance b/d	25.5
To Premium on redemption of Deb	2.5		
To General Reserve	21		
	25.5		25.5

3. AUTHORISED SHARE CAPITAL

Particulars	
Nominal Value of Existing Equity Shares(after buy back)[260+50-20]	290.00
Add: Nominal Value of Shares required for conversion of debentures	7.00
Add: Nominal Value of Shares required for ESOPs	17.00
Add: Nominal Value of bonus shares issued to existing equity shareholders	282.60
Total Authorised Share Capital should be	596.60
Total Authorised Share Capital at present[260+50+100]	410.00
Increase in Authorised Share Capital required by passing the necessary resolution at general body meeting of the company	186.60

COMPREHENSIVE ILLUSTRATION 4

The following is the summarized Balance Sheet of R Limited as at 31st March, 2023:

	₹
Liabilities	
Authorized Capital	
1,50,000 Equity shares of ₹ 10 each	15,00,000
30,000 10% Redeemable Preference shares of ₹ 100 each	30,00,000
	45,00,000
Issued, subscribed and paid up	
90,000 Equity shares of ₹ 10 each	9,00,000
15,000 10% Redeemable Preference shares of ₹ 100 each	15,00,000
Reserves & Surplus	
Securities Premium	18,00,000
General Reserve	16,50,000
Profit & Loss A/c	1,20,000
7500, 9% Debentures of ₹ 100 each	7,50,000
Trade Payables	2,12,500
	69,32,500
Assets	
Non-Current Assets	
Property Plant & Equipment	31,60,000
Investments (Market Value, ₹ 17,40,000)	14,70,000
Trade Receivables	17,60,000
Cash & Bank Balance	5,42,500
	69,32,500

In Annual General Meeting held on 15th May, 2023 the company passed the following resolutions:

(i) To redeem 10% preference shares at a premium of 5%.

(ii) To redeem 9% Debentures by making offer to Debenture holders to convert their holding into equity shares at ₹ 40 per share or accept cash on redemption.

(iii) To issue fully paid bonus shares in the ratio of one equity share for every three shares held on 31st March, 2023.

(iv) Redemption of preference shares and debentures will be paid through company's cash & bank balance subject to leaving a minimum cash & bank balance of ₹ 2,00,000.

(v) To issue sufficient number of equity shares @ ₹ 40 per share if required to finance redemption of Preference Shareholders and debenture holders.

On 5th June, 2023 investments were sold for ₹ 16,80,000 and preference shares were redeemed.

30% of Debenture holders exercised their option to accept cash and their claims were settled on 1st August, 2023. The bonus issue was concluded by 10th August, 2023.

You are requested to journalize the above transactions including cash transactions and prepare Balance Sheet as at 30th September, 2023.

SOLUTION

JOURNAL

Date	Particulars		(Dr) ₹	(Cr) ₹
June 5	Cash & Bank A/c	Dr.	16,80,000	
	To Investment A/c			14,70,000
	To Profit & Loss A/c			2,10,000
	(Being investment sold out and profit on sale credited to Profit & Loss A/c)			
June 5	10% Redeemable preference share capital A/c		15,00,000	
	Premium on redemption of pref. share A/c	Dr.	75,000	
	To Preference shareholders A/c			15,75,000
	(Being amount payable to preference shareholders on redemption)			
June 5	Preference shareholders A/c	Dr.	15,75,000	
	To Cash & bank A/c			15,75,000
	(Being amount paid to preference shareholders)			
June 5	General reserve* A/c	Dr.	15,00,000	
	To Capital redemption reserve A/c			15,00,000
	(Being amount equal to nominal value of preference shares transferred to Capital Redemption Reserve A/c on its redemption as per the law)			
Aug. 1	9% Debentures A/c	Dr.	7,50,000	
	Interest on debentures A/c		22,500	
	(₹ 7,50,000 x 9% x 4/12)			
	To Debenture holders A/c			7,72,500
	(Being amount payable to debenture holders along with interest payable)			
Aug. 1	Debenture holders A/c	Dr.	7,72,500	
	To Cash & bank A/c (2,25,000 + 22,500)			2,47,500
	To Equity share capital A/c (13,125 X₹ 10)			1,31,250
	To Securities premium A/c (13,125 x ₹ 30)			3,93,750
	(Being claims of debenture holders satisfied)			
Aug. 10	Capital Redemption Reserve A/c	Dr.	3,00,000	
	To Bonus to shareholders A/c			3,00,000
	(Being balance in capital redemption reserve capitalized to issue bonus shares)			
Aug. 10	Bonus to shareholders A/c	Dr.	3,00,000	
	To Equity share capital A/c			3,00,000
	(Being 30,000 fully paid equity shares of ₹ 10 each issued as bonus in ratio of 1 share for every 3 shares held)			

Sept.30	General Reserve* A/c	Dr.	75,000	
	To Premium on redemption of preference shares A/c			75,000
	(Being premium on preference shares adjusted from general reserve)			
Sept.30	Profit & Loss A/c	Dr.	22,500	
	To Interest on debentures A/c			22,500
	(Being interest on debentures transferred to Profit and Loss Account)			

BALANCE SHEET AS AT 30TH SEPTEMBER, 2023

		Particulars	*Notes*	₹
		Equity and Liabilities		
1		**Shareholders' funds**		
	a	Share capital	1	13,31,250
	b	Reserves and Surplus	2	37,76,250
2		**Current liabilities**		
	a	Trade Payables		2,12,500
			Total	53,20,000
		Assets		
1		**Non-current assets**		
	a	Property, Plant and Equipment		31,60,000
2		**Current assets**		
	a	Trade receivables		17,60,000
	b	Cash and bank balances (W.N.2)		4,00,000
			Total	53,20,000

Notes to accounts:

		₹	₹
1	**Share Capital**		
	Authorized share capital		
	1,50,000 Equity shares of ₹ 10 each	15,00,000	
	30,000 Redeemable Preference shares of ₹ 100 each	30,00,000	
	Issued, subscribed and paid up		
	1,33,125 Equity shares of ₹ 10 each [90,000+13,125+30,000] (Out of which 1,33,125 shares were issued for the consideration other than cash)		13,31,250
2	**Reserves and Surplus**		
	Securities Premium		
	Balance as per balance sheet	18,00,000	

Add: Premium on equity shares issued on conversion of debentures (13,125 x 30)		3,93,750	
Balance			21,93,750
Capital Redemption Reserve (15,00,000 - 3,00,000)			12,00,000
General Reserve			
Opening Balance	16,50,000		
Less Transfer to Capital Redemption Reserve	(15,00,000)		
	1,50,000		
Less: Premium on redemption of preference shares	(75,000)		75,000
Profit & Loss A/c		1,20,000	
Add: Profit on sale of investment		**2,10,000**	
Less: Interest on debentures		(22,500)	3,07,500
Total			37,76,250

Working Notes:

		₹
1.	**Redemption of Debentures**	
	7,500 Debentures of ₹ 100 each	7,50,000
	Less: Cash option exercised by 30% holders	(2,25,000)
	Conversion option exercised by remaining 70%	5,25,000
	Equity shares issued on conversion = 5,25,000/40 = 13,125 shares	
2.	**Cash and Bank Balance**	
	Balance as per balance sheet	5,42,500
	Add: Realization on sale of investment	16,80,000
		22,22,500
	Less: Paid to preference share holders	(15,75,000)
	Paid to Debenture holders (2,25,000 + 22,500)	(2,47,500)
	Balance	4,00,000

Note:

1. There is no need to issue fresh equity shares as the company is having sufficient cash balance.
2. Securities premium has not been utilized for the purpose of premium payable on redemption of preference shares assuming that the company referred in the PROBLEM is governed by Section 133 of the Companies Act, 2013 and comply with the Accounting Standards prescribed for them.

COMPREHENSIVE ILLUSTRATION 5

Balance Sheet of CEE TULSI Ltd (Listed)on 31st March, 2023 was as follows:

Particulars	₹
Authorised Capital 50,000, Equity Shares of ₹ 10 each	5,00,000
Issued and Subscribed Capital 25,000 Equity shares of ₹ 10 each fully paid up	2,50,000
General Reserve	2,75,000
Profit and Loss A/c	1,25,000
Debenture Redemption Reserve	2,50,000
12% Convertible Debentures (5,000 Debentures of ₹.100 each)	5,00,000
Other Secured loans	2,50,000
Current Liabilities	6,00,000
Property,Plant & Equipment and Intangible Assets	8,00,000
Debenture Redemption Fund Investment	2,00,000
Cash balance	2,50,000
Other Current Assets	10,00,000

At the General Meeting it was resolved to:

1. Pay dividend of 10% in cash.
2. Give existing shareholders the option to purchase one share of ₹.10 each at ₹.15 for every five shares held. This option was taken up by all the shareholders.
3. Redeem the debentures at a premium of 5% and also confer option to the debentureholders to convert 50% of their holding into equity shares at a predetermined price of ₹ 15 per share and balance payment to be made in cash.

Holders of 3,000 Debentures opted to get their debentures redeemed in cash only while the rest opted for getting the same converted into equity shares as per the terms of issue. Debenture redemption fund investment realized ₹ 1,80,000 on sales.

Required: Redraft the Balance Sheet after giving effects to the right issue and redemption of debentures. Also show the calculations in respect of number of equity shares issued and cash payment.

SOLUTION

BALANCE SHEET OF CEE TULSI LTD.(LISTED) AS AT 31.3.2023

Particulars	*Note No*	*₹ (lacs)*
I. Equity and Liabilities		
(1) Shareholders' Funds		
(a) Share Capital (₹ 10 each)		3,70,000
(b) Reserves and Surplus	1	6,40,000
(2) Non-Current Liabilities[Secured Loans]		2,50,000
(3) Current Liabilities		6,00,000
Total		18,60,000

II.	Assets		
	(1) Non-Current Assets		
	(a) Property, Plant & Equipment and Intangible Assets		
	Property, Plant & Equipment		8,00,000
	(2) Current Assets		
	(a) Cash and Cash Equivalents		60,000
	(b) Other Current Assets		10,00,000
	Total		18,60,000

Notes To Accounts:

Particulars	₹ *(lacs)*
1. Reserves and Surplus	
General Reserve	4,80,000
Profit & Loss Account [1,25,000 -25,000 (Dividend)]	1,00,000
Securities Premium	60,000
Total	6,40,000

CALCULATION OF NUMBER OF EQUITY SHARES ISSUED

I.	Number of equity shares issued as right issue (25,000 Shares/5)	5,000 shares
II.	Debentureholders who opted for the scheme of conversion into equity shares 2,000 debentureholders opted for the scheme	
	Total value (2,000 debentures × ₹.100)	₹ 2,00,000
	Premium on redemption @ 5%	₹ 10,000
		2,10,000
	50% of their holding converted into equity shares	₹ 1,05,000
	Number of equity shares to be issued to debentureholders (₹ 1,05,000/₹ 15) = [₹ 1,05,000/₹ 15]	7,000 shares
	Total number of equity shares issued = (5,000 + 7,000) shares	12,000 shares

CASH PAYMENT TO DEBENTUREHOLDERS

Particulars		₹
I. 3,000 Debentureholders preferred cash		
Total cash paid to them	3,00,000	
Premium on redemption @ 5%	15,000	3,15,000
II. 2,000 Debentureholders opted for the scheme		
Total Value	2,00,000	
Add: Premium on redemption @ 5%	10,000	
	2,10,000	
50% of their value converted into equity shares	1,05,000	
Balance paid to debentureholders in cash		1,05,000
Total cash paid to debentureholders		4,20,000

Working Notes:

Dr. **(I) DEBENTURE REDEMPTION RESERVE ACCOUNT** Cr.

Particulars	₹	Particulars	₹
To Premium on redemption of debentures (15,000 + 10,000)	25,000	By Balance b/d	2,50,000
To Loss on sale of Debenture Redemption Reserve Investment	20,000		
To General Reserve	2,05,000		
	2,50,000		2,50,000

Dr. **(II) GENERAL RESERVE ACCOUNT** Cr.

Particulars	₹	Particulars	₹
To Balance c/d	4,80,000	By Balance b/d	2,75,000
		By Debenture Redemption Reserve	2,05,000
	4,80,000		4,80,000

(iii) Total of Securities Premium = 12000 shares × ₹ 5 = ₹ 60,000

Dr. **(IV) CASH ACCOUNT** Cr.

Particulars	₹	Particulars	₹
To Balance b/d	2,50,000	By Dividend Payable A/c	25,000
To Equity Shareholders (5,000 × 15)	75,000	By Debentureholders (₹ 1,05,000 + ₹ 3,15,000)	4,20,000
To Sale of Debenture Redemption Reserve Investment	1,80,000	By Balance c/d	60,000
	5,05,000		5,05,000

COMPREHENSIVE ILLUSTRATION 6

CEE AMLA Ltd.(Listed) furnishes the following summarized Balance Sheet as at 31st March, 2023:

Particulars	₹' 000
Authorised Issued and Subscribed 3,00,000, Equity Shares of ₹ 10 each	3,000
20,000, 9% Preference Shares of ₹ 100 each fully paid up Issued two months back for buy back purposes)	2,000
Capital Reserve	10
Revenue Reserve	4,000
Securities Premium	500
Profit and Loss A/c	1,800
10% Convertible Debentures	400
Current Liabilities	40
Property, Plant & Equipment and Intangible Assets	2,750
Non-Current Investments	5,000
Current Assets	4,000

1. The company passed a resolution to buy back 20% of its equity capital @ ₹ 15 per share. For this purpose, it sold its investments of ₹ 30 lakhs for ₹ 25 lakhs.
2. The company redeemed the preference shares at a premium of 10% on 1st April, 2023.
3. Included in its investments were 'Investments in own debentures' costing ₹ 3 lakhs (face value ₹ 3.30 lakhs). These debentures were cancelled on 1st April, 2023.

You are required to pass necessary Journal entries and prepare the Balance Sheet on 01.04.2023.

SOLUTION

JOURNAL *(₹ in '000)*

Date	*Particulars*		*L.F.*	*Dr. (₹)*	*Cr. (₹)*
1.	Bank A/c	Dr.		2,500	
	Profit and Loss A/c	Dr.		500	
	To Investments A/c	Dr.			3,000
	(Being the investments sold for Buy back)				
2.	Equity Share Capital A/c			600	
	Premium payable on Buy Back A/c			300	
	To Equity Share Buyback/ Equity shareholders A/c				900
	(Being the amount due on Buy Back)				
3.	Equity Shares Buy Back/ Equity shareholders A/c			900	
	To Bank A/c				900
	(Being the payment made on buy-back)				
4	Securities Premium A/c			300	
	To Premium payable on Buy Back A/c				300
	(Being the adjustment of Premium payable on Buy Back out of free reserves to CRR)				
5.	9% Redeemable Preference Share Capital A/c	Dr.		2,000	
	Premium on redemption of Preference Shares A/c	Dr.		200	
	To Preference Shareholders A/c				2,200
	(Being the amount due to Preference Shareholders)				
6.	Preference Shareholders A/c	Dr.		2,200	
	To Bank A/c				2,200
	(Being the payment made to Preference Shareholders)				
7.	Revenue Reserve A/c	Dr.		2,200	
	To Capital Redemption Reserve A/c				2,200
	(Being the face value of RPS redeemed out of free reserves t/f to Capital Redemption Reserve & premium on redemption of preference shares adjusted through RR)				

8.	10% Debentures A/c Dr.		330	
	To Investments (Own Debentures) A/c			300
	To Capital Reserve A/c			30
	(Being cancellation of own debentures and T/F of profit on cancellation of debentures)			

BALANCE SHEET OF CEE AMLA LTD. (LISTED) AS AT 01.04.2023

Particulars	*Note No*	*₹ ('000)*
I. Equity and Liabilities		
(1) Shareholders' Funds		
(a) Share Capital	1	2,400
(b) Reserves and Surplus	2	5,340
(2) Non-Current Liabilities[10% Debentures] [400 – 330]		70
(3) Current Liabilities [70 – 5]		40
Total		7,850
II. Assets		
(1) Non-Current Assets		
(a) Property,Plant & Equipment and Intangible Assets		2,750
(b) Non-Current Investments [5,000 – 3,000 – 300]		1,700
(2) Current Assets [4,000 + 2,500 – 2,200 – 900]		3,400
Total		7,850

Notes To Accounts:

Particulars	*₹ ('000)*
1. Share Capital	
Authorised Capital	
2,40,000 Equity Shares of ₹ 10 each	2,400
Issued & Subscribed Capital	
2,40,000 Equity Shares of ₹ 10 each (60,000 Equity Shares bought back)	2,400
2. Reserves and Surplus	
Revenue Reserve [4,000 – 2,000 – 200]	1,800
Capital Reserve [10 + 30]	40
Capital Redemption Reserve	2,000
Securities Premium [500 – 300]	200
Surplus (P & L A/c) [1800 – 500]	1,300
Total	5,340

COMPREHENSIVE ILLUSTRATION 7

CEE ALOE VERA Ltd.(Listed) furnishes you with the following Balance Sheet as on 31st March, 2023:

Particulars	[₹ in lakhs]
Equity Shares of ₹ 10 each fully paid A	100
9% Redeemable Preference Shares of ₹ 100 each fully paid	20
Capital Reserves	6
Revenue Reserves	52
Securities Premium	60
10% Debentures	4
Current liabilities	70
Property, Plant & Equipment and Intangible Assets	50
Investments at cost	120
Current Assets	142

(i) The company redeemed the preference shares at a premium of 10% on 1st April, 2023.

(ii) It also bought back 3 lakhs equity shares of ₹ 10 each at ₹ 30 per share.

The payment for the above were made out of huge bank balances, which appeared as a part of the current assets.

(iii) Included in its investment were "investments in own debentures" costing ₹ 2 lakhs (face value ₹ 2.20 lakhs). These debentures were cancelled on 1st April, 2023.

(iv) The company had 1,00,000 equity stock options outstanding on the above mentioned date, to the employees at ₹ 20 when the market price was ₹ 30. (This was included under current liabilities). On 1.04.2023 employees exercised their options for 50,000 shares.

(v) Pass the journal entries to record the above & Prepare Balance Sheet as at 01.04.2023.

SOLUTION

JOURNAL *(₹ in lakhs)*

Date	Particulars	L.F.	Dr. (₹)	Cr. (₹)
1.	9% Redeemable Preference Share Capital A/c Dr.		20.00	
	Premium on redemption of Preference Shares A/c Dr.		2.00	
	To Preference Shareholders A/c			22.00
	(Being preference Share Capital Transferred to shareholders account)			
2.	Preference Shareholders A/c Dr.		22.00	
	To Bank A/c			22.00
	(Being payment made to shareholders)			
3.	Revenue Reserve A/c (20 + 2) Dr.		22.00	
	To Capital Redemption Reserve A/c			20.00
	To Premium on Redemption of Pref. Shares A/c			2.00
	(Being the face value of RPS redeemed out of free reserves t/f to Capital Redemption Reserve Account and premium on redemption of RPS w/o)			
4.	Equity Share Capital A/c Dr.		30.00	
	Premium payable on Buy Back A/c		60.00	

	To Equity Share Buyback/ Equity shareholders A/c			90.00
	(Being the amount due on Buy Back)			
5.	Equity Shares Buy Back/ Equity shareholders A/c Dr.		90.00	
	To Bank A/c			90.00
	(Being the payment made on buy-back)			
6	Securities Premium A/c Dr.		60.00	
	Revenue Reserve A/c Dr.		30.00	
	To Premium payable on Buy Back A/c			60.00
	To Capital Redemption Reserve A/c			30.00
	(Being the adjustment of Premium payable on Buy Back and the t/f of nominal value of Equity Shares bought back out of free reserves to CRR)			
7.	10% Debentures A/c Dr.		2.20	
	To Investments (Own Debentures) A/c			2.00
	To Capital Reserve A/c			0.20
	(Being cancellation of own debentures costing ₹ 2 lakhs, face value being ₹ 2.20 lakhs and the balance being profit on cancellation of debentures t/f to Capital Reserve Account)			
8.	Bank A/c Dr.		10.00	
	Employees Stock Option Outstanding (Current liabilities) A/c Dr.		5.00	
	To Equity Share Capital A/c			5.00
	To Securities Premium A/c			10.00
	(Being the allotment to employees, of 50,000 shares of ₹ 10 each at a premium of ₹ 20 per share in exercise of stock options by employees)			

BALANCE SHEET OF CEE ALOE VERA LTD. (LISTED) AS AT 01.04.2023

Particulars	***Note No***	***₹ (lacs)***
I. Equity and Liabilities		
(1) Shareholders' Funds		
(a) Share Capital (₹ 10 each) [100 + 5 – 30]		75.00
(b) Reserves and Surplus	1	66.20
(2) Non-Current Liabilities [10% Debentures] [4.00 – 2.20]		1.80
(3) Current Liabilities [70 – 5]		65.00
Total		208.00
II. Assets		
(1) Non-Current Assets		
(a) Property, Plant & Equipment and Intangible Assets		
Property, Plant & Equipment		50.00
(b) Non-Current Investments [120 – 2]		118.00

(2) Current Assets [142 + 10 – 22 – 90]	40.00
Total	208.00

Notes To Accounts:

Particulars	***₹ (lacs)***
1. Reserves and Surplus	
Revenue Reserve [52 – 30 – 22]	0
Capital Reserve [6.00 + 0.20]	6.20
Capital Redemption Reserve	50.00
Securities Premium [60 + 10 – 60]	10.00
Total	66.20

SOLVED PROBLEMS I

PROBLEM 1

Himalayas Ltd.(Listed) had ₹ 10,00,000, 8% Debentures of ₹ 100 each as on 31st March, 2022. The company purchased in the open market following debentures for immediate cancellation:

On 01-07-2022-1,000 Debentures @ ₹ 97 (cum interest), On 29-02-2023-1,800 Debentures @ ₹ 99 (ex interest), Debenture interest due date is 30th September and 31st March.

Give Journal Entries in the books of the company for the year ended 31st March, 2023.

SOLUTION

JOURNAL

Date	*Particulars*		*L.F.*	*Dr. (₹)*	*Cr. (₹)*
01.07.2022	Own Debentures A/c	Dr.		95,000	
	Debenture Interest A/c [1,000 × 100 × 8% × (3/12)]	Dr.		2,000	
	To Bank A/c				97,000
	(Being 1,000 Debentures purchased @ ₹ 97 cum interest for immediate cancellation)				
01.07.2022	8% Debentures A/c	Dr.		1,00,000	
	To Own Debentures A/c				95,000
	To Capital Reserve A/c				5,000
	(Being profit on cancellation of own Debentures t/f)				
30.09.2022	Debenture Interest A/c [9,000 × 100 × 8% × (1/2)]	Dr.		36,000	
	To Debenture holders A/c				36,000
	(Being interest accrued on 9,000 Debentures)				
	Debentureholders A/c	Dr.		36,000	
	To Bank A/c				36,000
	(Being interest amount paid)				
29.02.2023	Own Debentures A/c	Dr.		1,78,200	
	Debenture Interest A/c [1,800 × 100 × 8% × (5/12)]	Dr.		6,000	
	To Bank A/c				1,84,200

	(Being the Purchase of 1,800 Debentures @ ₹ 99 ex interest for immediate cancellation)			
29.02.2023	8% Debentures A/c Dr.		1,80,000	
	To Own Debentures A/c			1,78,200
	To Capital Reserve A/c			1,800
	(Being the Profit on cancellation of own Debentures t/f)			
31.03.2023	Debentures Interest A/c [7,200 × 100 × 8% × (1/2)] Dr.		28,800	
	To Debentureholders A/c			28,800
	(Being interest accrued on 7,200 Debentures)			
31.03.2023	Profit and Loss A/c Dr.		72,800	
	To Debentures Interest A/c			72,800
	(Being interest on debentures for the year transferred)			

PROBLEM 2

On January 2023, CAS Ltd.(Listed), had outstanding in its books 500 Debentures of ₹ 100 each interest at 6% per annum. In accordance with the powers in the deed, the directors acquired in the open market Debentures for immediate cancellation as follows:

March 1 ₹ 5,000 @ ₹ 98.00 (cum interest)

Aug. 1 ₹ 10,000 @ ₹ 100.25 (cum interest)

Dec. 15 ₹ 2,500 @ ₹ 98.50 (ex-interest)

Debenture interest is payable half-yearly, on 30th June and 31st December.

Required: Show ledger account of Debentures, Debenture Interest and Profit *or* Loss on cancellation, ignoring income-tax.

SOLUTION

1st Half Year

Dr. **6% DEBENTURES ACCOUNT** *Cr.*

Date	Particulars	₹	Date	Particulars	₹
2023			2023		
Mar. 01	To Bank A/c		Jan. 01	By Balance b/d	50,000
	Deb. Purchased 4,850				
	P&L on cancellation of				
	Debentures A/c 150	5,000			
June 30	To Balance c/d	45,000			
		50,000			50,000

Dr. **PROFIT & LOSS ON CANCELLATION OF DEBENTURES ACCOUNT** *Cr.*

Date	Particulars	₹	Date	Particulars	₹
2023			2023		
June 30	To Capital Reserve A/c	150	Mar. 01	By 6% Debentures A/c	150

Dr. **DEBENTURE INTEREST ACCOUNT** Cr.

Date	Particulars	₹	Date	Particulars	₹
2023			2023		
Mar. 01	To Bank A/c (Interest for 2 months on ₹ 5,000 Debentures)	50	June 30	By P & L A/c	1,400
June 30	To Debenture-holders A/c (Interest)	1,350			
		1,400			1,400

Dr. **DEBENTURE-HOLDERS' (INTEREST) ACCOUNT** Cr.

Date	Particulars	₹	Date	Particulars	₹
2023			2023		
June 30	To Bank A/c	1,350	June 30	By Deb. Interest A/c (Int. on ₹ 45,000 @ 6% upto 30th June)	1,350
		1,350			1,350

2nd Half Year

Dr. **6% DEBENTURES ACCOUNT** Cr.

Date	Particulars	₹	Date	Particulars	₹
2023			2023		
Aug. 01	To Bank, (Debentures Purchased) 9,975 P&L on Cancellation 25	10,000	July 01	By Balance b/d	45,000
Dec. 15	To Bank A/c Debentures Purchased 2,462.50 P&L on Cancellation of Debentures 37.50	2,500			
Dec. 31	To Balance c/d	32,500			
		45,000			45,000

Dr. **PROFIT & LOSS CANCELLATION OF DEBENTURES ACCOUNT** Cr.

Date	Particulars	₹	Date	Particulars	₹
2023			2023		
Dec. 31	To Capital Reserve	62.50	Aug. 01	By Debenture A/c	25.00
			Dec. 15	By Debenture A/c	37.50
		62.50			62.50

Dr. **DEBENTURE INTEREST ACCOUNT** Cr.

Date	Particulars	₹	Date	Particulars	₹
2023			2023		
Aug. 01	To Bank A/c (Interest for one month on ₹ 10,000)	50.00	Dec. 31	By Profit & Loss A/c	1,093.75
Dec. 15	To Bank A/c	68.75			
Dec. 31	To Deben. holders' A/c	975.00			
		1,093.75			1,093.75

Dr. **DEBENTURE HOLDERS' (INTEREST) ACCOUNT** Cr.

Date	Particulars	₹	Date	Particulars	₹
2023			2023		
Dec. 31	To Bank A/c	975.00	Dec. 31	By Debenture Interest A/c (on ₹ 32,500 @ 6% for 6 months)	975.00
		975.00			975.00

PROBLEM 3

A Company had issued 20,000, 13% Convertible debentures of ₹ 100 each on 1st April, 2016. The debentures are due for redemption on 1st July, 2019. The terms of issue of debentures provided that they were redeemable at a premium of 5% and also conferred option to the debentureholders to convert 20% of their holding into equity shares (Nominal value ₹ 10) at a price of ₹ 15 per share. Debentureholders holding 2,500 debentures did not exercise the option. Calculate the number of equity shares to be allotted to the Debentureholders exercising the option to the maximum.

SOLUTION

(I) CALCULATION OF NUMBER OF EQUITY SHARES TO BE ALLOTTED

Total number of debentures	20,000
Less: Debenture holders not opted for conversion	(2,500)
Debenture holders opted for conversion	17,500
Option for conversion	20%
Number of Debentures to be converted (20% of 17,500)	3,500
Redemption Value of 3,500 debentures at a premium of 5% [3, 500 × (100 + 5)]	₹ 3,67,500
Equity Shares of ₹.10 each issued on conversion [₹ 3,67,500/ ₹.15]	24,500 shares

PROBLEM 4

AB Limited (a listed company) recently made a public issue in respect of which the following information is available:

(i) No. of partly convertible 8% debentures issued 3,00,000; face value and issue price ₹ 100 per debenture.

(ii) Convertible portion per debenture- 60%, date of conversion- on expiry of 7 months from the date of closing of issue.

(iii) Date of closure of subscription lists 1-5-2021, date of allotment 1-6-2021, rate of interest on debenture 8% payable from the date of allotment, market value of equity share as on date of conversion ₹ 60 (Face Value ₹ 10).

(iv) Underwriting Commission 1%

(v) No. of debentures applied for 2,50,000.

(vi) Interest payable on debentures half-yearly on 30th September and 31st March. Write relevant journal entries for all transactions arising out of the above during the year ended 31st March, 2022 (including cash and bank entries).

SOLUTION

JOURNAL [₹ in lakh]

Date	Particulars		Dr. (₹)	Cr. (₹)
1.05.2021	Bank A/c	Dr.	250	
	To Debenture Application A/c			250
	(Being application money received on 2,50,000 debentures @ ₹100/- each)			
1.06.2021	Debenture Application A/c	Dr.	250	
	Underwriters A/c	Dr.	50	
	To 8% Debentures A/c			300
	(Being allotment of 2,50,000 debentures to applicants and 50,000 debentures to underwriters)			
1.06.2021	Underwriting Commission A/c	Dr.	3	
	To Underwriters A/c			3
	(Being commission payable to underwriters @ 1% on ₹ ₹ 300 lakh)			
1.06.2021	Bank A/c	Dr.	47	
	To Underwriters A/c			47
	(Being amount received from underwriters in settlement)			
1.06.2021	Debenture Redemption Investments A/c	Dr.	18	
	To Bank A/c			18
	(3, 00,000 x 100 x 15% x 40% - Being investments for redemption purposes)			
30.09.2021	Debenture Interest A/c	Dr.	8	
	To Bank			8
	(Being interest paid on debentures for 4 months @ 8% on ₹ 300 lakh)			
30.11.2021	8% Debentures A/c	Dr.	180	
	To Equity Share Capital A/c			30

	To Securities Premium A/c		150
	(Being conversion of 60% of the debentures into shares of ₹ 60 each with a face value of ₹10/-)		
31.03.2022	Debenture Interest A/c Dr.	7.20	
	To Bank A/c		7.20
	(Being interest paid on debentures for 6 months @ 8%)		

Working Note: Calculation of Debenture Interest for the half year ended 31st March, 2022 = (₹ 120 lakh x 6/12 x 8%) + (₹ 180 lakh x 2/12 x 8%) = ₹ 7.20 lakh

VERY SHORT ANSWER TYPE QUESTIONS

1. Briefly explain the following:
   (a) Redemption out of Profit
   (b) Redemption out of Capital
2. Enumerate the following:
   (a) Two Methods of Redemption of Debentures
   (b) Two Sources of finance for Redemption of Debentures
   (c) Two advantages of 'Redemption by purchase in the open market
3. Which of the following company(s) is required to transfer adequate amounts out of its profits every year to Debenture Redemption Reserve until such debentures are redeemed:
   (a) Listed Co
   (b) Unlisted Co which is NBFC registered with RBI
   (c) Unlisted Co which is HFC registered with National Housing Bank
   (d) Unlisted Co other than NBFCs registered with RBI, HFCs registered with National Housing Bank
4. Every company required to create/maintain DRR shall before the 30th day of April of each year, deposit or invest (as the case may be) at least .....% of the amount of its debentures maturing during the year ending on the 31st day of March next following in prescribed securities.
5. State the minimum amount of profit required to be transferred to Debenture Redemption Reserve.
6. List any two cases where the creation of Debenture Redemption Reserve is not mandatory as per SEBI Guidelines.
7. In which case Discount on Issue of Debentures Account is credited in case of Redemption of Debentures by Conversion?
8. In which case Discount on Issue of Debentures Account is not credited in case of Redemption of Debentures (which were originally issued at a discount) by Conversion?

SHORT ANSWER TYPE PRACTICAL QUESTIONS

1. X Ltd. redeemed 3,200, 12% Debentures of ₹ 50 each at 20% premium by converting them into equity shares of ₹ 10 each, issued at par. Calculate the number of shares to be issued on conversion. **[Ans.** 19,200]

2. X Ltd. redeemed 3,200, 12% Debentures of ₹ 50 each at 20% premium by converting them into equity shares of ₹ 10 each, issued at a premium of 20%. Calculate the number of shares to be issued on conversion. **[Ans.** 16,000]

3. X Ltd. redeemed 3,200, 12% Debentures of ₹ 50 each issued at a discount of 10% by converting them into equity shares of ₹ 10 each, issued at a premium of 20%. Calculate the number of shares to be issued on conversion before maturity. **[Ans.** 12,000]

4. X Ltd. redeemed 3,200, 12% Debentures of ₹ 50 each issued at a discount of 10% by converting them into 13% Debentures of ₹ 100 each, issued at a premium of 25%. Calculate the number of 13% Debentures to be issued on conversion before maturity. **[Ans.** 1,280]

5. ₹ 95,000, 14% Debentures of ₹ 100 each issued at 5% premium and redeemable at 10% premium were converted into Equity Shares of ₹ 10 each issued at a premium of 25%. Journalise the redemption of debentures. **[Ans.** No of Shares 8,360]

6. ₹ 1,00,000, 14% Debentures of ₹ 100 each issued at a discount of 5% and redeemable at 10% premium after 4 years were converted into 15% Debentures of ₹ 100 each issued at ₹ 80 paid-up before maturity. Journalise the redemption of debentures.

[Ans. No of Debentures 1375]

7. ₹ 1,00,000, 14% Debentures of ₹ 100 each issued at a discount of 5% and redeemable at 10% premium after 4 years were converted into Equity Shares of ₹ 10 each issued at a premium 25% before maturity. Journalise the redemption of debentures.

[Ans. No of Shares 7600]

8. A Company had issued 20,000, 13% Convertible debentures of ₹ 100 each on 1st April, 2021. The debentures are due for redemption on 1st July, 2023. The terms of issue of debentures provided that they were redeemable at a premium of 5% and also conferred option to the debentureholders to convert 20% of their holding into equity shares (Nominal value ₹ 10) at a price of ₹ 15 per share. Debentureholders holding 2,500 debentures did not exercise the option. Calculate the number of equity shares to be allotted to the Debentureholders exercising the option to the maximum. **[Ans.** 24500]

9. On 1st April, 2021, X Ltd. took over assets of ₹ 10,80,000 and liabilities of ₹ 80,000 of Y Ltd. at an agreed value of ₹ 9,60,000 payable as to 25% in cash and the balance by an issue of 12% Debentures of ₹ 100 each at a discount of 10 % redeemable at a premium of 5% by converting into Equity Shares of ₹ 10 each issued at a premium of 25%. Pass the necessary journal entries at the time of Redemption of Debentures.

[Ans. Capital Reserve ₹40,000, No of Shares 57600]

10. A company had issued 40,000, 12% debentures of ₹ 100 each on 1st April, 2018. The debentures are due for redemption on 1st March, 2022. The terms of issue of debentures provided that they were redeemable at a premium of 5% and also conferred option to the debenture holders to convert 20% of their holding into equity shares (nominal value ₹ 10) at a predetermined price of ₹ 15 per share and the payment in cash. 50 debentures holders holding totally 5,000 debentures did not exercise the option. Calculate the number of equity shares to be allotted to the debenture holders and the amount to be paid in cash on redemption.

[Ans. No of Shares 49,000, Amount to be paid into cash ₹ 34,65,000]

11. The 4,420, 15% Debentures of ₹ 100 each issued at par are to be redeemed at a premium of 5% after 4 years. Investments are expected to realise 10% p.a. The table shows that

Re. 0.215470803 invested at the end of each year at 10% compound interest will amount to Re. 1 at the end of 4 years and Re. 1 p.a. at 10% interest amounts to ₹ 4.641 in 4 years. Calculate the amount of profits to be set aside each year. **[Ans.** ₹ 1,00,000]

12. ₹ 1,80,000 being the Debenture Redemption Reserve(represented by ₹ 1,50,000 own Debentures purchased at 80% and ₹ 50,000, 10% Govt. Paper). 10% Govt. Paper realised 110%. Calculate the Profit or Loss on sale of Debenture Redemption Reserve Investments.

[Ans. Loss ₹ 5,000]

13. ₹ 1,80,000 being the Debenture Redemption Reserve(represented by ₹ 2,00,000, 10% Govt. Stock). ₹ 1,50,000, 10% Govt. Stock realised 83% for redemption of a part of debentures. Calculate the Profit or Loss on sale of Debenture Redemption Reserve Investments.

[Ans. Loss ₹ 10,500]

14. On 1.4.2022 the Debentures Redemption Reserve of a company showed a balance of ₹ 1,80,000 represented by ₹ 2,00,000, 10% Govt. Stock. On that date the outstanding 9% debentures of the company were ₹ 2,50,000. The annual contribution to Debenture Redemption Reserve was ₹ 50,000. On 31st March. 2023, the company decided to redeem Debentures of ₹ 1,20,000. For this purpose ₹ 1,50,000 10% Govt. Stock was sold at 83% and debentures were duly redeemed. On 31st March. the bank balance before the receipt of interest on investments was ₹ 70,000. Prepare Debentures Redemption Reserve Account.

[Ans. Loss ₹ 10,500]

15. On 1st April 2023, Tulsian Ltd. had 1,000, 12% Debentures of ₹ 100 each. Interest on debentures is payable half yearly on 30th Sept. and on 31st March. On 1st Aug. 2023, the company purchased 300 Own Debentures at ₹ 93 ex-interest for immediate cancellation. Record the necessary journal entries on Aug. 1.

[Ans. Accrued Interest ₹ 1,200 ,Gain on Cancellation ₹ 2,100]

16. On 1st April 2023, Tulsian Ltd. had 1,000, 12% Debentures of ₹ 100 each. Interest on debentures is payable half yearly on 30th Sept. and on 31st March. On 1st Aug. 2023, the company purchased 300 Own Debentures at ₹ 97 cum-interest for immediate cancellation. Record the necessary journal entries on Aug. 1.

[Ans. Accrued Interest ₹ 1,200 ,Gain on Cancellation ₹ 2,100]

LONG ANSWER TYPE PRACTICAL QUESTIONS

1.0 SINKING FUND METHOD

1.1. A company had 16,000, 12% debentures of 100 each outstanding as on 1st April, 2022, redeemable on 31st March, 2023. On that day, Sinking fund was ₹ 14,98,000 represented by 2,000 own debentures purchased at the average price of ₹ 99 and 9% stocks face value of ₹ 13,20,000. The annual instalment was ₹ 56,800.

On 31st March, 2023 the investments were realized at ₹ 98 and the debentures were redeemed. You are required to write up the following accounts for the year ending 31st March 2023:

(a) 12% Debentures Account

(b) Debenture Redemption Sinking Fund Account.

[Ans. T/f to General Reserve ₹ 16,93,200]

1.2. The following balances appeared in the books of Paradise Ltd on 1-4-2022:

(i) 12% Debentures ₹ 7,50,000

(ii) Balance of Sinking Fund ₹ 6,00,000

(iii) Sinking Fund investment ₹ 6,00,000 represented by 10% ₹ 6,50,000 secured bonds of government of India.

Annual contribution to the Sinking funds was ₹ 1,20,000 made on 31st March each year. On 31-03-2023, balance at bank was ₹ 3,00,000 before receipt of interest. The company sold the investment at 90% for redemption of debentures at a premium of 10% on the above date.

You are required to prepare the following accounts for the year ended 31st March, 2023.

(1) Debentures Account

(2) Sinking Fund Account

(3) Sinking Fund Investment Account

(4) Bank Account

(5) Debenture Holders Account

[**Ans.** T/f to General Reserve ₹ 7,70,000, Loss on Investments sold ₹ 15,000]

1.3. A company had 40,000; 10% debentures of ₹ 100 each outstanding on 1st April, 2021 redeemable on 31st March, 2022. On that day, sinking fund was ₹ 37,45,000 represented by 5,000 own debentures purchased at average price of ₹ 99 and 9% stocks of the face value of ₹ 33,00,000. The annual instalment was ₹ 1,42,000. On 31st March, 2022, the investments were realized at ₹ 98 and the debentures were redeemed.

Draw the following accounts for the year ending 31st March, 2022:

(i) 10% Debentures Accounts.

(ii) Debentures Redemption Sinking Fund Account.

[**Ans.** T/f to General Reserve ₹ 40,00,000, Loss on Investments sold ₹ 16,000]

1.4. The following balances appeared in the books of Heaven Ltd. on 1st April, 2021:

(i) 12% Debentures ₹ 9,50,000;

(ii) Balance of Sinking Fund ₹ 8,00,000

(iii) Sinking Fund Investment ₹ 8,00,000 represented by 10% ₹ 8,50,000 Secured Bonds of Government of India.

Annual contribution to the Sinking Fund was ₹ 1,50,000 made on 31st March every year. On 31st March, 2022, balance at bank was ₹ 4,00,000 before receipt of interest. The company sold the 90% face value of its investments, for redemption of debentures at a premium of 10% on the above date.

You are required to prepare the following accounts for the year ended on 31st March, 2022: (a) Debentures Account; (b) Sinking Fund Account; (c) Sinking Fund Investment Account; (d)Bank Account; and (e) Debenture Holders Account.

[**Ans.** T/f to General Reserve ₹ 9,50,000, T/f to Capital Reserve ₹ 1,30,000, Profit on Investments sold ₹ 0]

2.0 REDEMPTION BY PURCHASE IN THE OPEN MARKET

2.1. Rama Limited issued 8% Debentures of ₹ 3,00,000 in earlier year on which interest is payable half yearly on 31st March and 30th September. The company has power to purchase its own debentures in the open market for immediate cancellation. The following purchases were made during the financial year 2022-2023 for immediate cancellation:

(a) On 1st April, ₹ 50,000 nominal value debentures purchased for ₹ 49,450, ex-interest.

(b) On 1sl September, ₹ 30,000 nominal value debentures purchased for ₹ 30,250 cum interest.

Show the Journal Entries (without narrations) for the transactions held in the year 2022-2023.

2.2. Himalayas Ltd. had ₹ 10,00,000, 8% Debentures of ₹ 100 each as on 31st March, 2022. The company purchased in the open market following debentures for immediate cancellation:

On 01-07-2022-1,000 Debentures @ ₹ 97 (cum interest)

On 29-02-2023-1,800 Debentures @ ₹ 99 (ex interest)

Debenture interest due date is 30th September and 31st March.

Give Journal Entries in the books of the company for the year ended 31st March, 2023.

[**Ans.** Gain on 1st Cancellation ₹ 5,000, Gain on 2nd Cancellation ₹ 1,800]

2.3. On 1.4.2022, Tulsian Ltd. (Listed) had 1,000 12% Debentures of ₹ 100 each and Debentures Redemption Reserve ₹ 20,000. In accordance with the powers in the deed, the following debentures were purchased in the open market during the year ended 31st Mar. 2023 for immediate cancellation:

1st Aug 300 Debentures @ ₹ 97 cum-Interest

1st Nov. ₹ 20,000 nominal purchased for ₹ 19,350 Ex-Interest

Interest on debentures is payable half-yearly on 30th Sept and on 31st Mar.

Required: Pass the necessary journal entries.

[**Ans.** Gain on 1st Cancellation ₹ 2,100, Gain on 2nd Cancellation ₹ 650]

2.4. Gurudev Limited purchases for immediate cancellation 6,000 of its own 12% debentures of ₹100 each on 1st November, 2022. The dates of interest being 31st March, and 30th September. Pass necessary journal entries relating to the cancellation if:

(i) Debentures are purchased at ₹ 98 ex-interest.

(ii) Debentures are purchased at ₹ 98 cum-interest.

[**Ans.** Gain on 1st Cancellation ₹ 12,000, Gain on 2nd Cancellation ₹ 18,000]

3.0 REDEMPTION BY CONVERSION

3.1. On 1st January, 2016 CAMIB Limited issued 10,000 fifteen years debentures of ₹ 100 each bearing interest at 10% p.a. One of the conditions of issue was that the company could redeem the debentures by giving six month notice at any time after 5 years, at a premium of 4%, either by payment in cash or by allotment of preference shares and/or other debentures at the option of the debenture holders.

On 1st April 2021 the Company gave notice to the debenture holders of its intention to redeem the debentures on 1st October, 2021 either by payment in cash or by allotment of 11% preference shares of ₹ 100 each at ₹ 130 per share or 11% Second Debentures of ₹ 100 at ₹ 96 per debenture.

Holders of 4,000 debentures accepted the offer of the preference shares; holders of 4,800 debentures accepted the offer of the 11% second debentures and the rest demanded cash on 1st, October 2021.

Required: Give the journal entries to give effect to the above as of 1st October, 2021. Suggest how discount on issue of debentures can be dealt in the accounts. Ignore Interest.

[**Ans.** New PS 3,200, New Deb. 5,200]

3.2. Given below are the extracts of Balance Sheet of CANHE Limited, as at 30th June 2023:

Particulars	₹
5,00,000 equity shares of ₹ 10 each full paid	50,00,000
General Reserve	75,00,000
Debenture Redemption Reserve	50,00,000
13.5% Convertible Debentures of ₹ 100 each	1,00,00,000
Current Liabilities	1,75,00,000
Fixed Assets	1,60,00,000
Debenture Redemption Fund investments	40,00,000
Current Assets (including Cash and Bank Balance ₹ 50,00,000)	2,00,00,000

The debentures are due for redemption on 1st July, 2023. The terms of issue of debentures provided they were redeemable at a premium of 5% and also conferred option to the debenture-holders to convert 20% of their holding into equity shares at a predetermined price of ₹ 15.75 per share and the payment in cash.

Assuming that:-

(i) except for 100 debenture holders holding totally 25,000 debentures, the rest of them exercised the option for maximum conversion;

(ii) the investments realise ₹ 44 lakhs on sale; and

(iii) all the transactions are put through, without any lag, on 1st July 2023.

Required: Redraft the Balance Sheet of the company as on 1st July, 2023 after giving effect to the redemption. Show your calculations in respect of the number of equity shares to be allotted and the cash payment necessary.

[**Ans.** No. of ES ₹ 1,00,000, Cash paid ₹ 89,25,000,
Cash & Bank Balance ₹ 4,75,000, T/f to DRR ₹ 49,00,000]

3.3. Given below are the extracts of Balance Sheet of Dee Limited on 31st March, 2022 was as follows:

Particulars	₹
Authorised Capital 50,000, Equity Shares of ₹ 10 each	5,00,000
Issued and Subscribed Capital 25,000 Equity shares of ₹ 10 each fully paid up	2,50,000
General Reserve	2,75,000
Profit and Loss A/c	1,25,000
Debenture Redemption Reserve	2,50,000
12% Convertible Debentures (5,000 Debentures of ₹.100 each)	5,00,000
Other Secured loans	2,50,000
Current Liabilities and Provisions	6,00,000
Fixed Assets (at cost *less* depreciation)	8,00,000

Debenture Redemption Fund Investment	2,00,000
Cash balance	2,50,000
Other Current Assets	10,00,000

At the General Meeting it was resolved to:

1. Pay dividend of 10% in cash.
2. Give existing shareholders the option to purchase one share of ₹.10 each at ₹.15 for every five shares held. This option was taken up by all the shareholders.
3. Redeem the debentures at a premium of 5% and also confer option to the debenture holders to convert 50% of their holding into equity shares at a predetermined price of ₹ 15 per share and balance payment to be made in cash.

Holders of 3,000 debentures opted to get their debentures redeemed in cash only while the rest opted for getting the same converted into equity shares as per the terms of issue. Debenture redemption fund investment realized ₹ 1,80,000 on sales.

Required: Redraft the Balance Sheet after giving effects to the right issue and redemption of debentures. Also show the calculations in respect of number of equity shares issued and cash payment.

[**Ans.** No. of Shares Issued 12,000, Cash paid ₹ 4,20,000, Total of B/S ₹ 18,60,000]

4.0 MISCELLANEOUS

4.1. Given below are the extracts of Balance Sheet of Tulsian Ltd. as at 31st March 2022:

Particulars	₹
30,000 Equity shares of ₹ 10 each	3,00,000
5,000 Redeemable 8% Preference shares of ₹ 100 each	5,00,000
Securities Premium	6,00,000
General Reserve	6,50,000
Profit & Loss A/c	40,000
2500, 9% Debentures of ₹ 100 each	2,50,000
Sundry Creditors	1,70,000
Fixed Assets (net)	7,80,000
Investments (Market Value ₹ 6,80,000)	4,90,000
Deferred Tax Assets	3,40,000
Sundry Debtors	6,20,000
Cash & Bank balance	2,80,000

In Annual General Meeting held on 20th June the company passed the following resolutions:

(i) To split equity share ₹ 10 each into 5 equity shares of ₹ 2 each from 1st July.

(ii) To redeem 8% Preference Shares at a premium of 5%.

(iii) To redeem 9% Debentures by making offer to debenture holders to convert their holdings into equity shares at ₹ 10 per share *or* accept cash on redemption.

(iv) To issue fully paid bonus shares in the ratio of one equity share for every 3 shares held on record date.

On 10th July investments were sold for ₹ 5,55,000 and preference shares were redeemed. 40% of Debentureholder exercised their option to accept cash & their claims were settled on 1st Aug.

The company fixed 5th September as record date and bonus issue was concluded by 12th September. You are requested to journalize the above transactions including cash transactions and prepare Balance Sheet as at 30th September.

[**Ans** Profit on sale of Investment ₹ 65,000,T/f to CRR ₹ 5,00,000, equity shares issued to Debentureholders 3000, Bonus Shares 55,000, Cash Paid to Debenture holders ₹1,07,500, Cash & Bank Balance ₹1,07,500]

4.2. The following is the summarized Balance Sheet of R Limited as at 31st March, 2022:

	₹
Liabilities	
Authorized Capital	
1,50,000 Equity shares of ₹ 10 each	15,00,000
30,000 10% Redeemable Preference shares of ₹ 100 each	30,00,000
	45,00,000
Issued, subscribed and paid up	
90,000 Equity shares of ₹ 10 each	9,00,000
15,000 10% Redeemable Preference shares of ₹ 100 each	15,00,000
Reserves & Surplus	
Securities Premium	18,00,000
General Reserve	16,50,000
Profit & Loss A/c	1,20,000
7500, 9% Debentures of ₹ 100 each	7,50,000
Trade Payables	2,12,500
	69,32,500
Assets	
Non-Current Assets	
Property Plant & Equipment	31,60,000
Investments (Market Value, ₹ 17,40,000)	14,70,000
Trade Receivables	17,60,000
Cash & Bank Balance	5,42,500
	69,32,500

In Annual General Meeting held on 15th May, 2022 the company passed the following resolutions:

(i) To redeem 10% preference shares at a premium of 5%.

(ii) To redeem 9% Debentures by making offer to Debenture holders to convert their holding into equity shares at ₹ 40 per share or accept cash on redemption.

(iii) To issue fully paid bonus shares in the ratio of one equity share for every three shares held on 31st March, 2022.

(iv) Redemption of preference shares and debentures will be paid through company's cash & bank balance subject to leaving a minimum cash & bank balance of ₹ 2,00,000.

(v) To issue sufficient number of equity shares @ ₹ 40 per share if required to finance redemption of Preference Shareholders and debenture holders.

On 5th June, 2022 investments were sold for ₹ 16,80,000 and preference shares were redeemed.

30% of Debenture holders exercised their option to accept cash and their claims were settled on 1st August, 2022. The bonus issue was concluded by 10th August, 2022.

You are requested to journalize the above transactions including cash transactions and prepare Balance Sheet as at 30th September, 2022.

[**Ans** Profit on sale of Investment ₹ 2,10,000,T/f to CRR ₹ 15,00,000, equity shares issued to Debentureholders 13125, Bonus Shares 30,000, Cash Paid to Debenture holders ₹ 2,47,500, Cash& Bank Balance ₹4,00,000, Total of B/S ₹ 53,20,000]

6 UNDERWRITING OF SHARES AND DEBENTURES

LEARNING OBJECTIVES

After studying this chapter, you should be able to understand:

- ◇ Meaning of Underwriting Agreement and Underwriting Commission
- ◇ Purpose for which Underwriting Commission may be paid
- ◇ Conditions for Payment of Underwriting Commission
- ◇ Distinction Between Brokerage and Underwriting Commission
- ◇ Terms Used in Underwriting
- ◇ Practical Steps Involved in the Calculation of Net and Total Liability
- ◇ How to Prepare Statement Showing the Net and Total Liability of Underwriters?
- ◇ How to Prepare Statement Showing the Net Amount Due To/From Underwriters
- ◇ Accounting Entries

1.0 MEANING OF UNDERWRITING AGREEMENT AND UNDERWRITING COMMISSION

An underwriting agreement is an agreement between the company and certain party *(known as underwriter)* under which the latter agrees to take up the whole *or* part of the securities which may not be subscribed by the public for an agreed consideration *(known as underwriting commission)*. It is in the nature of an assurance against the risk involved in placing the securities before the public.

Note: An underwriting agreement is enforceable against the executors of deceased underwriter.

[Wasner Engineering Co. v. Benan (1913) 307 L.R. 191]

2.0 PURPOSE FOR WHICH UNDERWRITING COMMISSION MAY BE PAID

A company may pay a commission to any person in consideration of the number of securities underwritten *or* subscribed by underwriter whether absolutely *or* conditionally.

[Rule 13 of Companies (Prospectus and Allotment of Securities) Rules, 2014]

3.0 CONDITIONS FOR PAYMENT OF UNDERWRITING COMMISSION [RULE 13]

A company may pay underwriting commission if the following conditions are fulfilled, namely:

1. **Authorised by Articles:** The payment of the commission must be authorised by the articles.
2. **Source:** The commission may be paid out of proceeds of issue *or* Profits of the Company.

3. **Maximum Rate of Commission:** The commission paid *or* agreed to be paid must not exceed in the case of shares, 5% of the price at which the shares are issued *or* the amount *or* rate authorised by the articles, whichever is *less* and in the case of debentures, 2½% of the price at which the debentures are issued *or* the amount *or* rate authorised by the articles, whichever is less.

4(i). **Disclosure of Amount and Rate:** The amount and rate per cent of the commission paid *or* agreed to be paid must be disclosed in the prospectus *or* in the statement in lieu of prospectus *or* in a statement in the prescribed form signed in a like manner as a statement in lieu of prospectus and filed before the payment of the commission with the Registrar.

4(ii). **Disclosure of No. of Securities Underwritten:** The number of shares *or* debentures underwritten by each of the underwriters must be disclosed in the prospectus *or* statement in lieu of prospectus.

5. **No Commission:** No commission shall be paid to any underwriter on securities which are not offered to the public for subscription.

6. **Delivery of the Contract:** A copy of the contract for the payment of the commission must be delivered to the Register at the time of delivery of the prospectus for registration.

4.0 DISTINCTION BETWEEN BROKERAGE AND UNDERWRITING COMMISSION

Brokerage is paid to brokers for procuring other persons who will take shares *or* debentures where underwriter commission is paid to the underwriters for agreeing to take up the whole *or* part of shares *or* debentures which may not be subscribed by the public.

If broker fails to place any share, he is not personally liable to take them *nor* he is entitled to any brokerage. On the other hand, the underwriter is bound to take up the shares which have not been subscribed by public.

5.0 TERMS USED IN UNDERWRITING

MARKED APPLICATIONS

(a) The application forms bearing the stamp of the underwriter are termed as "Marked Application forms.

(b) The benefit of marked applications is given to the concerned underwriters in whose favour application forms have been marked.

UNMARKED APPLICATIONS

(a) The application forms which do not bear the stamp of the underwriter are termed as 'Unmarked Application forms'.

(b) The benefit of unmarked applications is given first to the company to the extent of issue not underwritten by underwriters (in case any part of the issue is not underwritten).

(c) In case there is surplus, the benefit of surplus unmarked applications will be given to the underwriters in the ratio of their gross liability.

FULL UNDERWRITING

(a) When the entire issue is underwritten such underwriting is termed as 'full underwriting'. For example, X Ltd. decided to make a public issue of 1,00,000 Equity Shares of ₹ 10 each which is entirely underwritten by A, B, C and D in the ratio of 2 : 2 : 1 : 1.

(b) In such a case the benefit of unmarked applications is given to the underwriter in the ratio of their gross liability i.e., 2 : 2 : 1 : 1.

PARTIAL UNDERWRITING

(a) When only a part of issue is underwritten, such underwriting is termed as 'Partial Underwriting.' For example, X Ltd. decided to make a public issue of 1,00,000 Equity Shares of ₹ 10 each out of which 90,000 shares are underwritten by A, B, C and D in the ratio of 2 : 2 : 1 : 1. It means 10,000 shares are underwritten by the company itself.

(b) In such a case, the benefit of unmarked applications will first be given to the company.

(c) In case there is surplus, such surplus will be distributed among other underwriters in the ratio of their gross liability.

SOLE UNDERWRITING

(a) When the issue is underwritten only by one underwriter, such underwriting is termed as 'Sole Underwriting'. For example, if an issue of 1,00,000 shares of ₹ 10 each of X Ltd. is underwritten by A, it is a case of sole underwriting.

(b) In such a case, the distinction between marked and unmarked applications is not of such significance.

JOINT UNDERWRITING

(a) When the issue is underwritten by two *or* more underwriters, such underwriting is termed as 'Joint Underwriting'. For example, if an issue of 1,00,000 shares of ₹ 10 each of X Ltd. is underwritten by A, B, C and D in the ratio of 2 : 2 : 1 : 1, it is a case of joint underwriting.

(b) In such a case the benefit of unmarked applications is given to the underwriters in the ratio of their gross liability.

(c) The benefit of marked applications is given to the concerned underwriters in whose favour applications have been marked.

FIRM UNDERWRITING

(a) **Meaning** Firm underwriting refers to a definite commitment by the underwriter to take up a specified number of securities irrespective of the number of securities subscribed by the public.

For example, the entire issue of X Ltd. is underwritten as follows:

A. 1,60,000 shares (firm underwriting 3,600 shares)

B. 1,60,000 shares (firm underwriting 2,000 shares)

C. 80,000 shares (firm underwriting 1,200 shares)

D. 80,000 shares (firm underwriting 10,000 shares)

In this case only 4,63,200 shares (i.e., 4,80,000 shares: firm underwriting of 16,800 shares) will be offered to public and 16,800 shares will be taken up by the underwriters even if the issue is oversubscribed.

(b) **Treatment** The benefit of firm underwriting should be given to an individual underwriter on the basis of his individual firm underwriting. In other words, firm underwriting shares should be treated at par with 'Marked Applications'.

6.0 PRACTICAL STEPS INVOLVED IN THE CALCULATION OF NET AND TOTAL LIABILITY

Step 1: *Calculate Gross Liability of each underwriter by dividing the number of securities underwritten in the ratio of shares underwritten by underwriters.*

Step 2: *Give credit for Marked Application on actual basis.*

Step 3: *Give credit for 'Unmarked application' in the ratio of their gross liability.*

Note: *In case of partial Underwriting, the credit of unmarked applications will first be given to the company to the extent of securities not underwritten and then to the underwriters.*

Step 4: *Give credit for 'Firm Underwriting' applications to an individual underwriter on the basis of his individual firm underwriting.*

Step 5: *Calculate the balance (i.e., Step 1 – Step 2 – Step 3 – Step 4).*

Step 6: *Give the credit for total negative balance to the underwriter(s) having positive balance(s) in the ratio of their gross liability.*

At the same time, eliminate the negative balance(s) of underwriter(s) of adding an equivalent number.

Step 7: *Calculate the Balance.*

Step 8: *If Balance of any underwriter is still negative, go to Step 6, otherwise go to Step 9.*

Note: *Net Positive Balance represents Net Liability.*

Step 9: *Add liability for firm underwriting to individual underwriter on actual basis.*

Step 10: *Calculate total liability by adding Step 8 and Step 9.*

7.0 HOW TO PREPARE STATEMENT SHOWING THE NET AND TOTAL LIABILITY OF UNDERWRITERS

STATEMENT SHOWING THE NET AND TOTAL LIABILITY OF UNDERWRITERS (NO. OF SHARES)

Particulars	*Basis*	*A*	*B*	*C*	*Total*
A. Gross Liability (No. of Shares)	Ratio of shares underwritten	...	...	...	...
B. *Less:* Marked Applications	Actual	(...)	(...)	(...)	(...)
C. Balance (A – B)		...	...	...	...
D. *Less:* Unmarked Applications [Total Applications – Marked Applications]	Ratio of Gross Liability	(...)	(...)	(...)	(...)
E. Balance (C – D)		...	...	...	...
F. *Less:* Firm Underwriting	Actual Ratio	(...)	(...)	(...)	(...)
G. Net Liability (if no balance is negative) [E – F]		...	...	...	...
H. *Add:* Liability for firm underwriting	Actual	...	...	...	...
I. Total Liability [G + H]		...	...	...	...

8.0 HOW TO PREPARE STATEMENT SHOWING THE NET AMOUNT DUE TO/FROM UNDERWRITERS

STATEMENT SHOWING THE NET AMOUNT DUE TO/FROM UNDERWRITERS

	Particulars	A	B	C
A	Total Liability (including firm underwriting) (No. of Shares)	...	...	...
B	Amount Due on Total Liability	...	...	...
C	*Less:* Amount already paid on Firm Applications	(...)	(...)	(...)
D	Amount Due on Net Liability	...	...	...
E	*Less:* Underwriting Commission	(...)	(...)	(...)
F	Net Amount Due to Underwriters (if D < E)			
	or			
	Net Amount Due from Underwriters (if D > E)			

ILLUSTRATION 1

Tulsian Ltd. made a public issue of 4,80,000 equity shares of ₹ 10 each, ₹ 5 payable on application and the balance on allotment. The entire issue was underwritten by A, B, C and D in the proportion of 2:2:1:1 and respectively at the maximum rate of commission permissible as per law. The total subscription received were for 4,20,000 shares.

Required: Prepare the statement showing the liability of the individual underwriter in each of the following alternative cases:

Case (a) If no other information is given:

Case (b) If marked applications received were as under:

A 60,000, C 68,000, B 1,12,000, D 1,20,000

The credit for unmarked applications is to be given to underwriter, in proportion to their gross liability.

Case (c) If marked applications received were as under:

A 60,000, C 68,000, B, 1,12,000, D 1,20,000

The credit for unmarked applications is to be given in the ratio of liability after giving credit for marked applications.

Case (d) If marked applications received were A, 60,000, C 68,000, B 1,12,000, D 1,20,000

A, B, C, and D also agreed on firm underwriting of 3,600, 2,000, 1,200 and 10,000 shares respectively. The benefit of firm underwriting is to be given to individual underwriter.

Case (e) If marked applications received were A 60,000, C 68,000, B 1,12,000, D 1,20,000.

A, B, C and D also agreed on firm underwriting of 3,600, 2,000, 1,200 and 10,000 shares respectively. The benefit of firm underwriting is not to be given on individual basis.

SOLUTION

CASE (A) STATEMENT SHOWING THE LIABILITY OF UNDERWRITERS FOR SUBSCRIPTION OF SHARES NOT YET SUBSCRIBED FOR

Particulars	*Basis*	*A*	*B*	*C*	*D*	*Total*
A Gross Liability	2 : 2 : 1 : 1	1,60,000	1,60,000	80,000	80,000	4,80,000
B *Less:* Credit for Application received	2 : 2 : 1 : 1	(1,40,000)	(1,40,000)	(70,000)	(70,000)	(4,20,000)
C Net Liability [A – B]		20,000	20,000	10,000	10,000	60,000

Note: *In the absence of any information regarding marked/unmarked applications, it has been assumed that the applications have been received in the proportion of the total number of the shares underwritten and hence the total applications received have been divided in the ratio of gross liability of underwriters.*

CASE: (B) STATEMENT SHOWING THE LIABILITY OF UNDERWRITERS FOR SUBSCRIPTION OF SHARES NOT YET SUBSCRIBED FOR

Particulars	*Basis*	*A*	*B*	*C*	*D*	*Total*
A Gross Liability	2 : 2 : 1 : 1	1,60,000	1,60,000	80,000	80,000	4,80,000
B *Less:* Marked Applications	Actual	(60,000)	(1,12,000)	(68,000)	(1,20,000)	(3,60,000)
C Balance (A – B)		1,00,000	48,000	12,000	–40,000	1,20,000
D *Less:* Unmarked Applications [4,20,000 – 3,60,000]	2:2:1:1	(20,000)	(20,000)	(10,000)	(10,000)	(60,000)
E Balance (C – D)		80,000	28,000	2,000	– 50,000	60,000
F Credit for D 's oversubscription	2:2:1	(20,000)	(20,000)	(10,000)	50,000	—
G Balance [E – F]		60,000	8,000	– 8,000	—	60,000
H Credit for C 's oversubscription	2:2	(4,000)	(4,000)	8,000		—
I Net Liability [G – H]		56,000	4,000	—	—	60,000

CASE: (C) STATEMENT SHOWING THE LIABILITY OF UNDERWRITERS FOR SUBSCRIPTION OF SHARES NOT YET SUBSCRIBED FOR

Particulars	*Basis*	*A*	*B*	*C*	*D*	*Total*
A Gross Liability	2 : 2 : 1 : 1	1,60,000	1,60,000	80,000	80,000	4,80,000
B *Less:* Marked App.	Actual	(60,000)	(1,12,000)	(68,000)	(1,20,000)	(3,60,000)

C Balance (A – B)		1,00,000	48,000	12,000	(40,000)	1,20,000
D *Less:* Unmarked App. [4,20,000 – 3,60,000]	100 : 48 : 12	(37,500)	(18,000)	(4,500)	—	(60,000)
E Balance (C – D)		62,500	30,000	7,500	(40,000)	60,000
F Credit for D 's oversubscription	100 : 48 : 12	(25,000)	(12,000)	(3,000)	40,000	—
G Net Liability (E – F)		37,500	18,000	4,500	—	60,000

CASE: (D) STATEMENT SHOWING THE LIABILITY OF UNDERWRITERS FOR SUBSCRIPTION OF SHARES NOT YET SUBSCRIBED FOR

Particulars	*Basis*	*A*	*B*	*C*	*D*	*Total*
A Gross Liability	2 : 2 : 1 : 1	1,60,000	1,60,000	80,000	80,000	4,80,000
B *Less:* Marked App.	Actual	(60,000)	(1,12,000)	(68,000)	(1,20,000)	(3,60,000)
C Balance (A – B)		1,00,000	48,000	12,000	(40,000)	1,20,000
D *Less:* Unmarked App. [4,20,000 – 3,60,000]	2 : 2 : 1 : 1	(20,000)	(20,000)	(10,000)	(10,000)	(60,000)
E Balance (C – D)		80,000	28,000	2,000	(50,000)	60,000
F *Less:* Firm Underwriting	Actual	(3,600)	(2,000)	(1,200)	(10,000)	(16,800)
G Balance (E – F)		76,400	26,000	800	(60,000)	43,200
H Credit for D's oversubscription	2 : 2 : 1	(24,000)	(24,000)	(12,000)	60,000	—
I Balance (G – H)		52,400	2,000	(11,200)	—	43,200
J Credit for C's oversubscription	2 : 2	(5,600)	(5,600)	11,200	—	—
K Balance (I – J)		46,800	(3,600)	—	—	43,200
L Credit for B 's subscription		(3,600)	3,600	—	—	
M Net Liability excluding firm oversubscription		43,200	—	—	—	43,200

N	*Add:* Firm underwriting	Actual	3,600	2,000	1,200	10,000	16,800
O	Total Liability including firm underwriting		46,800	2,000	1,200	10,000	60,000

CASE: (E) STATEMENT SHOWING THE LIABILITY OF UNDERWRITERS FOR SUBSCRIPTION OF SHARES NOT YET SUBSCRIBED FOR

	Particulars	*Basis*	*A*	*B*	*C*	*D*	*Total*
A	Gross Liability	2 : 2 : 1 : 1	1,60,000	1,60,000	80,000	80,000	4,80,000
B	*Less:* Marked App.	Actual	(60,000)	(1,12,000)	(68,000)	(1,20,000)	(3,60,000)
C	Balance (A – B)		1,00,000	48,000	12,000	(40,000)	1,20,000
D	*Less:* Unmarked App. [4,20,000 – 3,60,000]	2 : 2 : 1 : 1	(20,000)	(20,000)	(10,000)	(10,000)	(60,000)
E	Balance (C – D)		80,000	28,000	2,000	(50,000)	60,000
F	*Less:* Firm Underwriting	2 : 2 : 1 : 1	(5,600)	(5,600)	(2,800)	(2,800)	(16,800)
G	Balance (E – F)		74,400	22,400	(800)	(52,800)	43,200
H	Credit for C ' & D 's oversubscription	2 : 2	(26,800)	(26,800)	800	52,800	—
I	Balance (G – H)		47,600	(4,400)	—	—	43,200
J	Credit for B 's oversubscription		(4,400)	4,400	—		—
K	Net Liability excluding firm underwriting		43,200	—	—	—	43,200
L	*Add:* Firm underwriting	Actual	3,600	2,000	1,200	10,000	16,800
M	Total Liability including firm underwriting		46,800	2,000	1,200	10,000	60,000

9.0 ACCOUNTING ENTRIES

1. On receipt of Application Money from general public and from underwriters (for shares underwritten firm)	
Bank A/c	Dr.
To Share Application A/c	
2. On Adjustment of Application Money	

Share Application A/c	Dr.
To Share Capital A/c	
To Securities Premium A/c *(if any payable on Application)*	
3. On Making Allotment Money due from general public and from Underwriters (for shares underwritten firm)	
Share Allotment A/c [with Allotment money due from Public]	Dr.
Underwriter's A/c[with Allotment money due on firm underwriting]	Dr.
To Share Capital A/c	
To Securities Premium A/c	
4. On Making Application & Allotment Money due on Net liability (i.e. excluding firm underwriting) devolved on underwriters	
Underwriters' A/c	Dr.
To Share Capital A/c	
To Securities Premium A/c	
5. On Receipt of Allotment Money from General Public	
Bank A/c	Dr.
To Share Allotment A/c	
6. On Making Underwriting Commission due	
Underwriting Commission A/c	Dr.
To Underwriters' A/c	
7. On Receipt of amount from Underwriter on final settlement	
Bank A/c	Dr.
To Concerned Underwriter's A/c	
8. On Payment of amount to Underwriter on final settlement	
Concerned Underwriter's A/c	Dr.
To Bank A/c	

Tutorial Note: Subject to agreement, Underwriting Commission may be adjusted against the money due on allotment/call.

ILLUSTRATION 2

TULSIAN (1) Ltd issued 1,50,000 shares of ₹ 10 each at a premium of ₹ 10 payable ₹ 6 (including ₹ 3 premium) application and ₹ 4 (including ₹ 2 premium) on allotment and the balance on call. The entire issue was underwritten as follows:

X – 90,000 shares (Firm underwriting 12,000 shares)

Y – 37,500 shares (Firm underwriting 4,500 shares)

Z – 22,500 shares (Firm underwriting 15,000 shares)

Total applications received by the company (excluding firm underwriting) were 65,000 shares.

The marked applications (excluding firm underwriting) were as follows:

X- 15,000 shares; Y- 30,000 shares: Z- 7,500 shares.

Maximum Commission as per law is payable to underwriters. The underwriting contract provides that credit for unmarked applications be given to the underwriters in proportion to the shares underwritten and benefit of firm underwriting is to be given to individual underwriters.

Required:

(i) Determine the liability of each underwriter (number of shares)

(ii) Compute the amount payable or due to underwriters; and

(iii) Pass necessary journal entries in the books of Co. relating to underwriting.

SOLUTION

CALCULATION OF UNMARKED APPLICATIONS

Shares subscribed excluding firm underwriting but including marked applications	75,000
Less: Marked Applications	52,500
Unmarked Applications	22,500

COMPUTATION OF UNDERWRITERS' LIABILITY (NUMBER OF SHARES)

Particulars	*X*	*Y*	*Z*
A Gross Liability	90,000	37,500	22,500
B *Less:* Marked applications	(15,000)	(30,000)	(7,500)
C *Less:* Unmarked applications in ratio of 12:5:3	(13,500)	(5,625)	3,375
D *Less:* Firm Underwriting	(12,000)	(4,500)	(15,000)
E Balance	49,500	(2,625)	(3,375)
F *Less:* Surplus of Y & Z distributed to X	(6,000)	2,625	3,375
G Net Liability (excluding firm underwriting)	43,500	Nil	Nil
H *Add:* Firm Underwriting	12,000	4,500	15,000
I Total Liability (number of shares)	55,500	4,500	15,000

(B) COMPUTATION OF AMOUNT PAYABLE BY UNDERWRITERS

Particulars	₹	₹	₹
Liability towards shares to be subscribed @ ₹ 10	5,55,000	45,000	1,50,000
Less: Amount paid on Firm Applications @ ₹ 6	(72,000)	(27,000)	(90,000)
Balance due before adjustment of Under. Comm.	4,83,000	18,000	60,000
Less: Underwriting Comm. [1,50,000 × ₹ 20 × 5%]	(90,000)	(37,500)	(22,500)
Net Amount payable/(receivable) by Underwriters	3,93,000	(19,500)	37,500

(C) JOURNAL

Date	Particulars		L.F.	Dr. (₹)	Cr. (₹)
	X	Dr.		48,000	
	Y	Dr.		18,000	
	Z	Dr.		60,000	
	To Share Capital A/c				63,000
	To Securities Premium A/c				63,000
	(Being the Allotment money due on Firm underwritten shares)				
	X	Dr.		4,35,000	
	To Share Capital A/c				2,17,500
	To Securities Premium A/c				2,17,500
	(Being the Application & Allotment money due on shares allotted to Underwriters on account of Net Liability (excluding firm underwriting)devolved)				
	Underwriting Commission A/c	Dr.		1,50,000	
	To X				90,000
	To Y				37,500
	To Z				22,500
	(Being underwriting commission due)				
	Bank A/c	Dr.		4,30,500	
	To X				3,93,000
	To Z				37,500
	(Being the net amount received in final settlement)				
	Y	Dr.		19,500	
	To Bank A/c				19,500
	(Being the net amount paid in final settlement)				

ILLUSTRATION 3

TULSIAN(2) Ltd. decided to issue 12,50,000 Equity Shares of ₹ 10 each at a premium of ₹ 10 payable ₹ 6 (including ₹ 3 premium) on application and ₹ 4 (including ₹ 2 premium) on allotment and the balance on call. Out of which 20% issued to the promoters and the balance offered to the public. 90% of the public issue was underwritten by X, Y, and Z as follows:

X – 4,50,000 shares (Firm underwriting 20,000 shares)

Y – 2,70,000 shares (Firm underwriting 30,000 shares)

Z – 1,80,000 shares (Firm underwriting 50,000 shares)

Applications were received for 6,20,000 shares (excluding Firm underwriting shares), of which marked applications (excluding firm underwriting) were as follows:

X 58,000 Shares, Z 1,76,000 Shares, Y 1,86,000 Shares

The underwriting contract provides that credit for unmarked applications be given to the underwriters in proportion to the shares underwritten and benefit of firm underwriting is to be given to individual underwriters. The commission payable to underwriters is maximum as per The Companies Act,2013.

Required:

(i) Determine the liability of each underwriter (number of shares)

(ii) Compute the amount payable or due to underwriters; and

(iii) Pass necessary journal entries in the books of Co. relating to underwriting.

SOLUTION

COMPUTATION OF UNDERWRITERS' LIABILITY (NUMBER OF SHARES)

Particulars	X	Y	Z
A Gross Liability [Ratio = 45:27:18 or 5 : 3 : 2]	4,50,000	2,70,000	1,80,000
B *Less:* Marked applications	(58,000)	(1,86,000)	(1,76,000)
C *Less:* Unmarked applications in ratio of 5 : 3 : 2			
Total Unmarked App. 6.2 Lac – 4.2Lac = 2 Lac			
Less: Benefit to Company to the extent of issue not underwritten = 1 Lac			
Balance Unmarked Applications = 1 Lac	(50,000)	(30,000)	(20,000)
D *Less:* Firm Underwriting	(20,000)	(30,000)	(50,000)
E Balance[A - B - C]	3,22,000	24,000	(66,000)
F *Less:* Surplus of Z distributed to X & Y	(41,250)	24,750	66,000
G Balance[E - F]	2,80,750	(750)	
H *Less:* Surplus of Y distributed to X	(750)	750	
G Net Liability (excluding firm underwriting)	2,80,000	Nil	Nil
H *Add:* Firm Underwriting	20,000	30,000	50,000
I Total Liability (number of shares)	3,00,000	30,000	50,000

(B) COMPUTATION OF AMOUNT PAYABLE BY UNDERWRITERS

Particulars	₹	₹	₹
A Liability towards shares to be subscribed @ ₹ 10	30,00,000	3,00,000	5,00,000
B Less: Amount paid on Firm Applications @ ₹ 6	(1,20,000)	(1,80,000)	(3,00,000)
C Balance due before adjustment of Under. Comm.	28,80,000	1,20,000	2,00,000
D *Less:* Underwriting Comm. [Gross Liability × ₹ 20 × 5%]	(4,50,000)	(2,70,000)	(1,80,000)
E Net Amount payable/(receivable) by Underwriters	24,30,000	(1,50,000)	20,000

(C) JOURNAL

Date	Particulars		L.F.	Dr. (₹)	Cr. (₹)
	X	Dr.		80,000	
	Y	Dr.		1,20,000	
	Z	Dr.		2,00,000	
	To Share Capital A/c				2,00,000
	To Securities Premium A/c				2,00,000
	(Being the Allotment money due on Firm underwritten shares)				
	X	Dr.		28,00,000	
	To Share Capital A/c				14,00,000
	To Securities Premium A/c				14,00,000
	(Being the Application & Allotment money due on shares allotted to Underwriters on account of Net Liability (excluding firm underwriting)devolved)				
	Underwriting Commission A/c	Dr.		9,00,000	
	To X				4,50,000
	To Y				2,70,000
	To Z				1,80,000
	(Being underwriting commission due)				
	Bank A/c	Dr.		24,50,000	
	To X				24,30,000
	To Z				20,000
	(Being the net amount received in final settlement)				
	Y	Dr.		1,50,000	
	To Bank A/c				1,50,000
	(Being the net amount paid in final settlement)				

ILLUSTRATION 4

CAMHE Ltd. comes out with a public issue of share capital on 1st Jan. of 10,00,000 equity shares of ₹ 10 each at a premium of 5%. ₹ 2.50 is payable on application (on *or* before 31st Jan. and ₹ 3.00 (including premium) on allotment (31st March).

The issue is underwritten by two underwriters-A and B equally. The maximum commission is payable as per law. Each of the underwriters underwrites 20,000 shares firm.

Subscriptions totalled (including firm underwriting) 9,60,000 shares, the distribution of forms being:

A: 5,20,000, B: 3,60,000 and unmarked forms: 80,000.

One of the allottees (using forms marked with the name of A) for 2,000 shares, fails to pay the amount due to allotment, all other money due being received in all including any due from the shares developing upon the underwriters. The shares of defaulter were forfeited and reissued @ ₹ 4 per share on June 30.

Required: Pass journal entries to record the above transactions (including cash).

SOLUTION

JOURNAL

Date	*Particulars*		*L.F.*	*Dr. (₹)*	*Cr. (₹)*
Jan. 31	Bank A/c	Dr.		24,00,000	
	To Equity Share Application A/c				24,00,000
	(Being application money received @ ₹ 2.50 per share)				
Mar. 31	Equity Share Application A/c	Dr.		24,00,000	
	To Equity Share Capital A/c				24,00,000
	(Being the transfer of application money to share capital on 9,60,000 shares vide Board's Resolution)				
Mar. 31	Equity Share Allotment A/c	Dr.		27,60,000	
	A	Dr.		60,000	
	B	Dr.		60,000	
	To Equity Share Capital A/c				24,00,000
	To Securities premium A/c				4,80,000
	(Being allotment money due on 9,20,000 allotted to public, on 20,000 shares allotted to A, 20,000 shares allotted to B under firm underwriting)				
	B	Dr.		2,20,000	
	To Equity Share Capital A/c				2,00,000
	To Securities Premium A/c				20,000
	(Being the application and allotment money due on net liability of underwriter)				
Mar. 31	Bank A/c	Dr.		27,54,000	
	To Equity Share Allotment A/c				27,54,000
	(Being the receipt of money due on allotment except from the allottee for 2,000 shares including premium on 9,18,000 shares)				
Mar. 31	Underwriting Commission A/c	Dr.		5,25,000	
	To A				2,62,500
	To B				2,62,500
	(Being commission @ 5% on issue price of ₹ 10.50 for 10 lakhs shares payable to underwriters)				

	A Dr.		2,02,500	
	To Bank A/c			2,02,500
	(Being amount paid to A in final settlement)			
	Bank A/c Dr.		17,500	
	To B			17,500
	(Being amount received from B in final settlement)			
June 30	Equity Share Capital A/c Dr.		10,000	
	Securities Premium A/c Dr.		1,000	
	To Share Allotment A/c			6,000
	To Forfeited Shares A/c			5,000
	(Being 2,000 shares forfeited vide Board's Resolution)			
June 30	Bank A/c (2000 × ₹ 4) Dr.		8,000	
	Forfeited Shares A/c Dr.		2,000	
	To Equity Share Capital A/c (2000 × ₹ 5)			10,000
	(Being the reissue of 2,000 shares @ ₹4 as ₹5 paid up)			
	Forfeited Shares A/c Dr.		3,000	
	To Capital Reserve A/c			3,000
	(Being the transfer of profit on reissue)			

Working Notes:

(I) STATEMENT SHOWING THE NET AND TOTAL LIABILITY OF UNDERWRITERS

	Particulars	*Basis*	*A*	*B*
A.	Gross Liability [No. of shares]	1 : 1	5,00,000	5,00,000
B.	*Less:* Marked Applications [Net of firm underwriting]		(5,00,000)	(3,40,000)
C.	Balance [A – B]		0	1,60,000
D.	*Less:* Unmarked Applications	1 : 1	(40,000)	(40,000)
E.	Balance [C – D]		(40,000)	1,20,000
F.	*Less:* Firm Underwriting		(20,000)	(20,000)
G.	Balance		(60,000)	1,00,000
H.	Credit for A's Oversubscription		60,000	(60,000)
I.	Net Liability		0	40,000
J.	*Add:* Firm Underwriting		20,000	20,000
K.	Total Liability [No. of Shares]		20,000	60,000

(II) STATEMENT SHOWING NET AMOUNT DUE TO/FROM UNDERWRITERS

Particulars	A	B
A. Total Liability [including firm underwriting]	20,000	60,000
B. Amount due on total liability [Amount payable @₹ 5.50 per share]	1,10,000	3,30,000
C. *Less:* Amount paid already on Firm Applications @2.50 per share	(50,000)	(50,000)
D. Amount on Net Liability [B – C]	60,000	2,80,000
E. *Less:* Underwriting Commission @5%	(2,62,500)	(2,62,500)
F. Net Amount Due to A	2,02,500	
G. Net Amount Due from B		17,500

SOLVED PROBLEMS

PROBLEM 1

CAS Limited issued a prospectus inviting applications for 40,000 equity shares of ₹ 10 each. The whole issue was fully underwritten by A, B and C as follows:

A 20,000 Shares, B 12,000 Shares, C 8,000 Shares

Applications were received for 32,000 shares, of which marked applications were as follows:

A 16,000 Shares, B 5,700 Shares, C 8,300 Shares

Required: Find out the liabilities of individual underwriters.

SOLUTION

STATEMENT OF NET LIABILITY OF UNDERWRITERS (NUMBER OF SHARES)

	Gross Liability	*Marked applications*	*Unmarked applications in the ratio of gross liability*	*Total (2) + (3)*	*Credit for C's Surplus (10 : 6)*	*Total (4) + (5)*	*Net liability (1) – (6)*
	(1)	*(2)*	*(3)*	*(4)*	*(5)*	*(6)*	*(7)*
A	20,000	16,000	1,000	17,000	438	17,438	2,562
B	12,000	5,700	600	6,300	262	6,562	5,438
C	8,000	8,300	400	8,700	(700)	8,000	—
	40,000	30,000	2,000	32,000	—	32,000	8,000

Note: *The applications are for 32,000 shares out of which those for 30,000 are marked. Hence unmarked applications are for 2,000 shares.*

PROBLEM 2

CANHF Ltd. issued 10,000 shares of ₹ 100 each at a premium of ₹ 15 each. Ninety per cent of the issue was underwritten by A at a commission of 1% on the nominal face value. Applications were received for 8,000 shares and allotment was fully made. All the moneys due from allottees was received in one instalment. The accounts with A were settled.

Required: Show the Journal entries to record the transactions.

SOLUTION

JOURNAL

Date	*Particulars*		*L.F.*	*Dr. (₹)*	*Cr. (₹)*
	Bank A/c	Dr.		9,20,000	
	To Share Application and Allotment A/c				9,20,000
	(Moneys received in respect of 8,000 shares at ₹ 115 per share)				
	Share Application and Allotment A/c	Dr.		9,20,000	
	To Share Capital A/c				8,00,000
	To Securities Premium A/c				1,20,000
	(Transfer of moneys received on 8,000 Shares to Capital Account and Securities Premium A/c @ ₹ 100 and ₹ 15 respectively vide Board's Resolution....)				
	A	Dr.		2,07,000	
	To Share Capital A/c				1,80,000
	To Securities Premium A/c				27,000
	(Being the amount due on 1,800 shares taken up in terms of underwriting agreement by A)				
	Underwriting Commission A/c	Dr.		9,000	
	To A				9,000
	(Commission at 1% on 9,000 shares at ₹ 100 each nominal value)				
	Bank A/c	Dr.		1,98,000	
	To A				1,98,000
	(Moneys received from the broker in settlement of the account)				

Working Notes:

(i) It has been assumed that the remaining 10% of the shares are underwritten by the company itself.

In the absence of details of 'marked' application, 'net liability' is worked out on the basis of gross liability as follows:

Particulars	*A* ₹	*CANHF Ltd.* ₹
Gross Liability (Number of shares)	9,000	1,000
Less: Applications received allotted in the ratio of 9 : 1	7,200	800
	1,800	200

PROBLEM 3

CAMHD Ltd. came up with an issue of 20,00,000 equity shares of ₹ 10 each at par. 5,00,000 shares were issued to the promoters and the balance offered to the public was underwritten by three underwriters: A, B and C: equally with firm underwriting of 50,000 shares each. Subscriptions totalled 12,97,000 shares including the marked forms which were:-

A 4,25,000 shares, B 4,50,000 shares, C 3,50,000 shares

The underwriters had applied for the number of shares covered by firm underwriting. The amounts payable on application and allotment were ₹ 2.50 and ₹ 2 respectively. The agreed commission was 5%.

Required: Pass summary journal entries for:

(a) the allotment of shares to the underwriters;

(b) the commission due to each of them; and

(c) the net cash paid and/or received.

Note: *Unmarked applications are to be credited to the underwriters equally.*

SOLUTION

JOURNAL

Date	Particulars		L.F.	Dr. (₹)	Cr. (₹)
	Bank A/c	Dr.		3,75,000	
	To Equity Share Application A/c				3,75,000
	(Application money received on firm applications for, 1,50,000 shares @ ₹ 2.50 per share from underwriters)				
	Equity Share Application A/c	Dr.		3,75,000	
	To Equity Share Capital A/c				3,75,000
	(Being the transfer of share Application money to Share Capital A/c)				
	A	Dr.		1,00,000	
	B	Dr.		1,00,000	
	C	Dr.		3,38,500	
	To Equity Share Capital A/c				5,38,500
	(Allotment of shares to underwriters: 50,000 to A; 50,000 to B and 1,03,000 to C; application money due on 53,000 shares and allotment money due on 2,03,000 shares)				
	Underwriting Commission A/c	Dr.		7,50,000	
	To A				2,50,000
	To B				2,50,000
	To C				2,50,000
	(Amount of underwriting commission payable to underwriters 5% on the amount of shares underwritten)				
	A	Dr.		1,50,000	
	B	Dr.		1,50,000	

	To Bank A/c (Amount paid to A & B in final settlement of underwriting commission due *less* amount payable on shares allotted)			3,00,000
	Bank A/c	Dr.	88,500	
	To C (Amount received from C on shares allotted *less* underwriting commission payable to him)			88,500

Working Notes:

(I) CALCULATION OF THE NET AND TOTAL LIABILITY OF UNDERWRITERS:

	Particulars	A ₹	B ₹	C ₹
A	Gross liability (No. of shares)	5,00,000	5,00,000	5,00,000
B	*Less:* Marked Applications	(4,25,000)	(4,50,000)	(3,50,000)
C	*Less:* Unmarked Applications (equally)	(36,000)	—	(36,000)
D	*Less:* Firm Underwriting	(50,000)	(50,000)	(50,000)
E	Balance	(11,000)	—	64,000
F	Adjustment of A's surplus	11,000	—	(11,000)
G	Net liability (excluding firm underwriting)	—	—	53,000
H	*Add:* Firm underwriting	50,000	50,000	50,000
I	Total liability	50,000	50,000	1,03,000

Note: Since B's firm underwriting (i.e. 50,000 shares) is equal to his gross liability *less* marked applications, no credit for unmarked applications has been given.

(II) CALCULATION OF AMOUNTS PAYABLE BY UNDERWRITERS:

Liability (No. of shares)	50,000 ₹	50,000 ₹	1,03,000 ₹
Amount payable @ ₹ 4.50 per share	2,25,000	2,25,000	4,63,500
Less: Amount paid on Firm Application for 50,000 each @ ₹ 2.50	(1,25,000)	(1,25,000)	(1,25,000)
Balance payable	1,00,000	1,00,000	3,38,500
Underwriting Commission Receivable	(2,50,000)	(2,50,000)	(2,50,000)
Amount Paid	1,50,000	1,50,000	
Amount Received by the Co.	—	—	88,500

*Benefit of unmarked applications has not been given to B as his surplus would have ultimately been credited for A & C.

PROBLEM 4

CANHG Ltd. made a public issue of 1,25,000 equity shares of ₹ 100 each, ₹ 50 payable on application. The entire issue was underwritten by four parties—A, B, C and D in the proportion of 30%, 25%, 25% and 20% respectively. Under the terms agreed upon, a commission of 2% was payable on the amounts underwritten.

A, B, C and D had also agreed on "firm" underwriting of 4,000, 6,000, Nil and 15,000 shares respectively.

The total subscriptions, excluding firm underwriting, including marked applications were for 90,000 shares. Marked applications received were as under:

A 24,000 C 12,000 B 20,000 D 24,000

Required: Ascertain the liability of the individual underwriters.

SOLUTION

Approach I—*If benefit of firm underwriting is given to individual underwriters*

(I) TOTAL MARKED APPLICATIONS

A	B	C	D
24,000	+20,000	+12,000	+24,000 = 80,000

(II) CALCULATION OF UNMARKED APPLICATIONS

Shares subscribed excluding firm underwriting but including marked applications	90,000 shares
Less: Marked Applications	80,000 shares
Unmarked Applications	10,000

(III) STATEMENT SHOWING THE NET AND TOTAL LIABILITY OF UNDERWRITERS

Particulars	*A*	*B*	*C*	*D*	*Total*
Gross liability (30 : 25 : 25 : 20)	37,500	31,250	31,250	25,000	1,25,000
Less: Marked applications	(24,000)	(20,000)	(12,000)	(24,000)	(80,000)
Balance	13,500	11,250	19,250	1,000	45,000
Less: Unmarked (In Gross Ratio)	(3,000)	(2,500)	(2,500)	(2,000)	(10,000)
Balance	10,500	8,750	16,750	(1,000)	35,000
Less: Firm Underwriting	(4,000)	(6,000)	—	(15,000)	(25,000)
Balance	6,500	2,750	16,750	(16,000)	10,000
Surplus of D allocated to A B & C 30 : 25 : 25	(6,000)	(5,000)	(5,000)	16,000	—
Balance	500	(2,250)	11,750		10,000
Surplus of 'B' allocated	(500)	2,250	(1,750)		
Net liability	—	—	10,000	—	10,000
Add: Firm underwriting	4,000	6,000	—	15,000	25,000
Total Liability	4,000	6,000	10,000	15,000	35,000

(IV) STATEMENT SHOWING THE AMOUNT DUE FROM UNDERWRITERS

Particulars	*A*	*B*	*C*	*D*	*Total*
Shares to be subscribed	4,000	6,000	10,000	15,000	35,000
Amount due @ ₹ 50 per share (₹)	2,00,000	3,00,000	5,00,000	7,50,000	17,50,000
Less: Commission due @2% on nominal value of share under written (₹)	(75,000)	(62,500)	(62,500)	(50,000)	(2,50,000)
(₹)	1,25,000	2,37,500	4,37,500	7,00,000	15,00,000

Approach II—*If the benefit of firm underwriting is not given to individual underwriter*

(i) Total marked applications = 80,000

(II) CALCULATION OF UNMARKED APPLICATIONS

Shares subscribed excluding firm underwriting but including marked applications	90,000 shares
Firm underwriting	25,000 shares
Total subscription	1,15,000 shares
Less: Marked Applications	80,000 shares
Unmarked Applications	35,000 shares

(III) STATEMENT SHOWING THE LIABILITY OF UNDERWRITERS

	Particulars	*A*	*B*	*C*	*D*	*Total*
A	Gross liability	37,500	31,250	31,250	25,000	1,25,000
B	*Less:* Marked applications	(24,000)	(20,000)	(12,000)	(24,000)	(80,000)
C	*Less:* Unmarked Applications	(3,000)	(2,500)	(2,500)	(2,000)	(10,000)
D	*Less:* Firm underwriting (in the ratio of 30:25:25:20)	(7,500)	(6,250)	(6,250)	(5,000)	(25,000)
E	Balance	3,000	2,500	10,500	(6,000)	10,000
F	Surplus of D transferred to others in the ratio of 30 : 25 : 25	(2,250)	(1,875)	(1,875)	6,000	—
G	Net Liability	750	625	8,625	—	10,000
H	*Add:* Firm underwriting	4,000	6,000	Nil	15,000	25,000
I	Total Liability	750	625	8,625	—	10,000
		4,750	6,625	8,625	15,000	35,000

(IV) STATEMENT SHOWING THE AMOUNT DUE FROM UNDERWRITERS

Particulars	*A*	*B*	*C*	*D*	*Total*
Shares to be subscribed	4,750	6,625	8,625	15,000	35,000
Amount due @ ₹ 50 shares (₹)	2,37,500	3,31,250	4,31,250	7,50,000	17,50,000
Less: Commission due at 2% on nominal value of shares underwritten (₹)	(75,000)	(62,500)	(62,500)	(50,000)	(2,50,000)
(₹)	1,62,500	2,68,750	3,68,750	7,00,000	15,00,000

(V) VERIFICATION

(a) Taken by public-unmarked application	10,000 shares
(b) Public through underwriters—marked	80,000 shares
(c) By underwriters—under agreement	35,000 shares
	1,25,000 shares

PROBLEM 5

CAMIJ Limited issued to public 1,50,000 equity shares of ₹ 100 each at par. ₹ 60 per shares was payable along with application and the balance on allotment. The issue was underwritten equally by A, B, and C for a commission of 5 per cent. Applications for 1,40,000 shares were received as per details below:

Underwriter	*Firm Applications*	*Marked Applications*	*Total*
A	5,000	40,000	45,000
B	5,000	46,000	51,000
C	3,000	34,000	37,000
Unmarked Applications			7,000
Total			1,40,000

It was agreed to credit the unmarked applications equally to A and C. CAMIJ Ltd. accordingly made the allotment and received the amounts due from the public. The underwriters settled their accounts.

You are required to:

(i) Prepare a statement showing the liability of the underwriters, and

(ii) Journalise the above transactions (including cash) in the books of CAMIJ Ltd.

SOLUTION

CAMIJ LIMITED

(a) If the benefit of firm underwriting is given to individual underwriters.

(I) STATEMENT SHOWING THE NET AND TOTAL LIABILITY OF UNDERWRITERS

Particulars	*A*	*B*	*C*	*Total*
Gross Liability	50,000	50,000	50,000	1,50,000
Less: Marked Applications	(40,000)	(46,000)	(34,000)	(1,20,000)
Balance	10,000	4,000	16,000	30,000
Less: Unmarked Applications	(3,500)	—	(3,500)	(7,000)
Balance	6,500	4,000	12,500	23,000
Less: Firm Underwriting	(5,000)	(5,000)	(3,000)	(13,000)
Balance	1,500	(1,000)	9,500	10,000
Credit for B 's oversubscription to A and C in the ratio 1 : 1	(500)	1,000	(500)	—
Net Liability	1,000	—	9,000	10,000

Add: Firm Underwriting	5,000	5,000	3,000	13,000
Total Liability	6,000	5,000	12,000	23,000

(II) STATEMENT SHOWING THE NET AMOUNT DUE FROM UNDERWRITERS

Particulars		*A*	*B*	*C*	*Total*
Shares to be subscribed		6,000	5,000	12,000	23,000
Amount due @ ₹ 60 per share	(₹)	3,60,000	3,00,000	7,20,000	13,80,000
Less: Commission due @ 5% on nominal value of shares underwritten	(₹)	(2,50,000)	(2,50,000)	(2,50,000)	(7,50,000)
	(₹)	1,10,000	50,000	4,70,000	6,30,000

(B) IF THE BENEFIT OF FIRM UNDERWRITING IS NOT GIVEN TO INDIVIDUAL UNDERWRITERS

(i) Total subscription	1,40,000 Shares
Less: Marked Applications	1,20,000 Shares
Firm and Unmarked Applications	20,000 Shares

(II) STATEMENT SHOWING THE NET AND TOTAL LIABILITY OF UNDERWRITERS

Particulars	*A*	*B*	*C*	*Total*
Gross Liability	50,000	50,000	50,000	1,50,000
Less: Firm and Unmarked applications	(10,000)	—	(10,000)	(20,000)
Balance	40,000	50,000	40,000	1,30,000
Less: Marked applications	(40,000)	(46,000)	(34,000)	(1,20,000)
Net liability	—	4,000	6,000	10,000
Firm underwriting	5,000	5,000	3,000	13,000
	5,000	9,000	9,000	23,000

(III) STATEMENT SHOWING THE AMOUNT DUE FROM UNDERWRITERS

Particulars	*A*	*B*	*C*	*Total*
Shares to be subscribed	5,000	9,000	9,000	23,000
	₹	₹	₹	₹
Amount due @ ₹ 60 per share	3,00,000	5,40,000	5,40,000	13,80,000
Less: Commission due @ 5% on nominal value of shares underwritten	(2,50,000)	(2,50,000)	(2,50,000)	(7,50,000)
	50,000	2,90,000	2,90,000	6,30,000

JOURNAL

Date	*Particulars*		*L.F.*	*Dr. (₹)*	*Cr. (₹)*
	Bank A/c	Dr.		82,50,000	
	Underwriting Commission A/c	Dr.		7,50,000	
	To Equity Share Capital A/c				90,00,000

	(Being amount received @ ₹ 60/- per share on issue of 1,50,000 equity shares and underwriting commission paid @ 5% on nominal value of shares underwritten vide Directors' resolution No.......... dated..........)		
	Bank A/c Dr.	60,00,000	
	To Share Capital A/c		60,00,000
	(Amount of allotment money received on 1,50,000 shares @ ₹ 40 per share credited to share capital vide resolution dated.........)		

PROBLEM 6

CAMID Limited planned to set up a unit for manufacture of bulk drugs. For the purpose of financing the unit the Board of Directors have issued 15,00,000 equity shares of ₹ 10 each. 30% of the issue was reserved for promoters and the balance was offered to the public. A, B and C have come forward to underwrite the public issue in the ratio of 3:1:1 and also agreed for firm undertaking of 30,000; 20,000 and 10,000 shares, respectively. The underwriting commission was fixed at 4%. The amount payable on application was ₹ 2.50 per share. The details of subscriptions (excluding firm underwriting) are:

Marked forms of A	5,50,000 Shares
Marked forms of B	2,00,000 Shares
Marked forms of C	1,50,000 Shares
Unmarked forms	50,000 Shares

(a) You are required to show the allocation of liability among underwriters with workings.

(b) Pass journal entries in the books of CAMID Limited:

(i) For underwriters' net liability and the receipt *or* payment of cash to *or* from underwriters.

(ii) Determining the liability towards the payment of commission to the underwriters.

SOLUTION

(A) STATEMENT SHOWING THE NET AND TOTAL LIABILITY OF UNDERWRITERS

	Particulars	*A (No. of Shares)*	*B (No. of Shares)*	*C (No. of Shares)*	*Total (No. of Shares)*
A	Gross Liability	6,30,000	2,10,000	2,10,000	10,50,000
B	*Less:* Marked Applications	(5,50,000)	(2,00,000)	(1,50,000)	(9,00,000)
C	*Less:* Unmarked Applications (in the ratio of 3 : 1 : 1)	(30,000)	(10,000)	(10,000)	(50,000)
D	*Less:* Firm underwriting	(30,000)	(20,000)	(10,000)	(60,000)
E	Balance	20,000	(20,000)	40,000	40,000
F	Surplus of B distributed between A and C in the ratio of 3 : 1	(15,000)	20,000	(5,000)	—
G	Net liability	5,000		35,000	40,000

H	*Add:* Firm underwriting	30,000	20,000	10,000	60,000
I	Total Liability	35,000	20,000	45,000	1,00,000

JOURNAL

Date	*Particulars*		*L.F.*	*Dr. (₹)*	*Cr. (₹)*
	A	Dr.		12,500	
	C	Dr.		87,500	
	To Equity Share Capital A/c				1,00,000
	(Allotment of shares to underwriters: 5,000 shares to A and 35,000 shares to C)				
	Underwriting Commission A/c	Dr.		4,20,000	
	To A				2,52,000
	To B				84,000
	To C				84,000
	(Underwriting commission payable @ 4% on the amount of shares underwritten)				
	A	Dr.		2,39,500	
	B	Dr.		84,000	
	To Bank A/c				3,23,500
	(Amount paid to A and B in final settlement)				
	Bank A/c	Dr.		3,500	
	To C				3,500
	(Amount received from C on shares allotted *less* underwriting commission)				

Working Notes:

(I) CALCULATION OF AMOUNTS PAYABLE TO/BY UNDERWRITERS

Particulars	*A*	*B*	*C*
Liability (No. of shares)	35,000	20,000	45,000
Less: Firm underwriting (No. of shares)	30,000	20,000	10,000
Net Liability (No. of shares)	5,000	—	35,000

Particulars	₹	₹	₹
Amount payable on application @ ₹ 2.50 per share	12,500	—	87,500
Less: Underwriting commission receivable by underwriters @ 4%	(2,52,000)	(84,000)	(84,000)
Amount payable to underwriters	2,39,500	84,000	—
Amount receivable from underwriters	—	—	3,500

(ii) No Journal entry is shown for firm underwritings by the underwriters on the assumption that the amounts have been already paid by the underwriters at the opening days of the issue. Alternatively, the students may pass entries for firm underwriting on the ground that the allotment of shares will be made by the company at a time.

PROBLEM 7

CAS Ltd. made a public issue of 8,00,000 Equity Shares of ₹ 10 each ₹ 2 payable on application. The entire issue was underwritten by five underwriters as follows: A: 25% B: 25%; C: 25% D: 10% and E: 15%. Under the underwritten terms a commission of 2% was payable on the amounts underwritten. Further, the underwriter was at liberty to apply, during the tenure of public issue, for any number of shares in which case he was entitled to a brokerage equal to 1/2% of the par value of shares so applied for.

Applications received were to be analysed on the basis of Rubber Stamp of the underwriter, who was to be given credit for the number of applications received bearing his rubber stamp. Applications received which did not bear any Rubber Stamp were considered as "Direct applications" to be credited to all the underwriters in the ratio of their respective underwriting commitment. If, on such credits being given, a "surplus" result in respect of any underwriter, as compared to his commitment, such surplus was to be distributed amongst the remaining underwriters in the ratio of their respective underwriting commitments.

As a result of the issue the following applications were received;

Bearing rubber stamp of:

A	2,04,000 shares
B	1,90,000 shares
C	1,20,000 shares
D	64,000 shares
E	1,02,000 shares
Not bearing any stamp	20,000 shares
	7,00,000 shares

Included in the number of applications mentioned against D in the above table was an application made by D himself for 20,000 shares. The underwriters were informed of the amounts due to *or* from them and the amounts were duly received *or* paid.

Required: Show, with the aid of necessary workings, the entries to record the amounts so received *or* paid.

SOLUTION

JOURNAL

Date	*Particulars*	*L.F.*	*Dr. (₹)*	*Cr. (₹)*
	B Dr.		4,000	
	C Dr.		1,44,000	
	D Dr.		25,600	
	E Dr.		26,400	
	To Equity Share Capital A/c			2,00,000
	(Being the amount due from underwriters on Net Liability)			

	Particulars		Dr. (₹)	Cr. (₹)
	Underwriting Commission A/c	Dr.	1,60,000	
	To A			40,000
	To B			40,000
	To C			40,000
	To D			16,000
	To E			24,000
	(Being the underwriting commission due)			
	Brokerage A/c	Dr.	1,000	
	To D			1,000
	(Being the brokerage due to D)			
	Bank A/c	Dr.	1,15,000	
	To C			1,04,000
	To D			8,600
	To E			2,400
	(Being the net amount received from C, D and E)			
	A	Dr.	40,000	
	B	Dr.	36,000	
	To Bank A/c			76,000
	(Being the net amount paid to A and B)			

Workings:

Name	Commit-ment No. of Shares	Market Appli-cations	Additional Pro-pertinent No. of direct Applications	Total (2) + (3) of	Allo-cation of Surplus	Total (4) + (5)	Final Deficit (1) − (6)	Amount Re-ceivable @ ₹ 2/- per share ₹	Under-writing commission due @ on nominal value ₹	Brokerage Due @ % ₹	Due from Under-writers ₹	Due to Under-writers ₹
	(1)	(2)	(3)	(4)	(5)	(6)	(7)	(8)	(9)	(10)	(11)	(12)
A	2,00,000	2,04,000	5,000	2,09,000	− 9,000	2,00,000	—	—	40,000	—	—	40,000
B	2,00,000	1,90,000	5,000	1,95,000	3,000	1,98,000	2,000	4,000	40,000			36,000
C	2,00,000	1,20,000	5,000	1,25,000	3,000	1,28,000	72,000	1,44,000	40,000		1,04,000	
D	80,000	64,000	2,000	66,000	1,200	67,200	12,800	25,600	16,000	1,000	8,600	
E	1,20,000	1,02,000	3,000	1,05,000	1,800	1,06,800	13,200	26,400	24,000		2,400	
	8,00,000	6,80,000	20,000	7,00,000	—	7,00,000	1,00,000	2,00,000	1,60,000	1,000	1,15,000	76,000

PROBLEM 8

ABC Ltd. came up with public issue of 3,00,000 Equity Shares of ₹ 10 each ₹ 15 per share. P, Q and R took underwriting of the issue in ratio of 3 : 2 : 1 with the provisions of firm underwriting of 20,000, 14,000 and 10,000 shares respectively.

Applications were received for 2,40,000 shares excluding firm underwriting. The marked applications from public were received as under:

P-60,000; Q-50,000; R-60,000

Compute the liability of each underwriter as regards the number of shares to be taken up assuming that the benefit of firm underwriting is not given to individual underwriters.

SOLUTION

CALCULATION OF LIABILITY OF EACH UNDERWRITER (IN NO. OF SHARES)

Particulars	*P*	*Q*	*R*	*Total*
Gross Liability	1,50,000	1,00,000	50,000	3,00,000
Less: Marked Applications (excluding firm underwriting)	(60,000)	(50,000)	(60,000)	(1,70,000)
Balance	90,000	50,000	(10,000)	1,30,000
Less: Surplus of R allocated to P and Q in the ratio of 3.2	(6,000)	(4,000)	10,000	
Balance	84,000	46,000		1,30,000
Less: Unmarked applications including firm underwriting (Refer W.N.)	(57,000)	(38,000)	(19,000)	(1,14,000)
Net Liability	27,000	8,000	(19,000)	16,000
Less: Surplus of R allocated to P and Q in the ratio of 3 : 2	(11,400)	(7,600)	19,000	
	15,600	400	–	16,000
Add: Firm underwriting	20,000	14,000	10,000	44,000
Total Liability	35,600	14,400	10,000	60,000

Working Note:

A.	Applications received from public	2,40,000
B.	*Add:* Shares underwritten firm (20,000 + 14,000 + 10,000)	44,000
C.	Total Applications [A + B]	2,84,000
D.	*Less:* Marked applications (60,000 + 50,000 + 60,000)	(1,70,000)
E.	Unmarked applications including firm underwriting [C – D]	1,14,000

VERY SHORT ANSWER TYPE QUESTIONS

1. Briefly explain the following:
   (a) Underwriting Agreement
   (b) Underwriting Commission
   (c) Purpose for which Underwriting Commission may be paid
   (d) Maximum Rates of Underwriting Commission
   (e) Marked Application forms
   (f) Unmarked Application forms
   (g) Full Underwriting
   (h) Partial Underwriting
   (i) Sole Underwriting
   (j) Joint Underwriting

(k) Firm Underwriting

(l) Gross Liability of each underwriter

2. Write the basic difference between Brokerage and Underwriting Commission.
3. Write the Conditions for Payment of Underwriting Commission.

SHORT ANSWER TYPE PRACTICAL QUESTIONS

1. CEED Ltd. incorporated on 1st January, 2018 issued a prospectus inviting application for 40,000 Equity Shares of ₹ 10 each. The whole issue was fully underwritten by X, Y and Zas follows:

X 20,000 shares, Y 12,000 shares, Z 8,000 shares.

Applications were received for 32,000 shares, of which marked applications were as follows:

X 16,000 shares, Y 5,700 shares, Z 8,300 shares.

You are required to find out the liabilities of individual underwriters

[**Ans** Total Liability (number of shares):X 2562,Y 5438,Z 0]

2. CEEP Limited issues 2,00,000 equity shares of ₹ 10 each at par. The entire issue is underwritten as follows :

Underwriter	*No. of shares Underwritten*	*Firm Underwritten*	*Marked Applications, Including firm Underwriting*
A	1,20,000	16,000	36,000
B	50,000	6,000	46,000
C	30,000	20,000	30,000

Total number of shares applied for were 1,42,000. Ascertain the liability of underwriters in number of Shares.

(i) If Firm Underwriting treated as Marked.

(ii) If Firm Underwriting treated as Unmarked.

[**Ans** (i) Total Liability (number of shares): A74000, B 6000, C 20000,
(ii) Total Liability (number of shares): A 66400, B 6000, C 27600]

3. CEEB Limited issued to public 1,50,000 equity shares of ₹ 100 each. ₹ 60 per share was payable along with application and the balance on allotment. The issue was underwritten equally by A, B and C for a commission of 5%. Application for 1,40,000 shares were received including firm underwriting.

Underwriter	*Firm Underwriting*	*Marked Applications[excluding firm underwriting]*
A	5,000 Shares	40,000 Shares
B	5,000 Shares	46,000 Shares
C	3,000 Shares	34,000 Shares

Unmarked Application 7,000 shares

It was agreed to credit the unmarked application equally to A and C. The Company accordingly made the allotment and received the amount due from public. The underwriters settled their accounts. (Treat application of shares in Firm Underwriting as Marked Applications)

You are required to prepare a statement showing the liability of the underwriters in shares as well as in amount.

[**Ans** (i) Total Liability (number of shares): A 6000, B 5000, C 12000, Net Amount payable/(receivable) by Underwriters A ₹ 50,000, B (₹ 50,000), C ₹ 7,70,000]

LONG ANSWER TYPE PRACTICAL QUESTIONS

1. CEER Ltd., issued 3,00,000 shares of ₹ 10 each at a premium of ₹ 5. The entire issue was underwritten by P, Q and R in the ratio of 3:2:1. Their firm underwriting was as follows:

P - 35,000 shares, Q - 20,000 shares, R - 22,500 shares

The total subscriptions, excluding firm underwriting, including marked applications were for 1,60,000 shares. Marked applications received were as follows:

P - 45,000 shares, Q - 22,500 shares, R - 17,500 shares

The underwriting contract provided that credit for unmarked applications be given to the underwriters in proportion to the shares underwritten and benefit of firm underwriting is to be given to individual underwriters. The underwriters were entitled to commission @ 5%.

You are required to:

(i) Compute the underwriter's liability in number of shares.

(ii) Compute the amount payable to or due from underwriters.

(iii) Pass Journal entries in the books of the company relating to underwriting assuming that the net amount was settled.

[**Ans** Total Liability (number of shares): P 66,000, Q 51,500, R 22,500, Net Amount payable/(receivable) by Underwriters P ₹ 8,77,500,Q (₹ 6,97,500), R ₹ 3,00,000]

2. CEEA Ltd. made a public issue of 11,00,000 equity shares of ₹ 10 each at a premium of ₹ 10, the amounts payable on application were ₹ 4 along with the full amount of premium and ₹ 6 at allotment. Out of the above 1,00,000 equity shares were issued to promoters and the balance was offered to the public which was underwritten by three underwriters X, Y and Z as follows: ·

X - 4,00,000 shares including firm underwriting 80,000 shares

Y - 3,00,000 shares including firm underwriting 30,000 shares

Z - 3,00,000 shares including firm underwriting 1,10,000 shares

Total subscriptions received by the company were 1,50,000 shares (excluding firm underwriting and marked applications)

The marked applications (excluding firm underwriting) were:

X 97,500 shares, Y 1,95,000 shares and Z 1,48,500 shares.

Underwriters are entitled to maximum commission permissible by law on the issue price of shares. The underwriting contract provides that benefit of firm underwriting is to be given to individual underwriters. You are required to :

(i) Determine the liability of each underwriter in number of shares;

(ii) Compute the amounts payable to or due from underwriters; and

(iii) Pass Journal Entries in the books of the company relating to underwriting.

[**Ans** Total Liability (number of shares):X 2,40,500,Y 58,500,Z 1,10,000,Net Amount payable/(receivable) by Underwriters X ₹ 32,90,000,Y ₹ 4,50,000,Z ₹ 3,60,000]

3. Jay Ltd. offered 45 Lakhs equity shares of ₹ 10 each at par to the public. The issue was underwritten equally by three underwriters A, B and C. The firm underwriting by the underwriters was for 1,50,000 shares each. Total subscriptions were for 38,91,000 shares out of which marked forms were as follows:

A: 12,75,000 Shares, B: 13,50,000 Shares, C: 10,50,000 Shares.

Benefit of firm underwriting was given to underwriters and unmarked applications were credited to the underwriters equally. The underwriters applied for number of shares covered by firm underwriting.

The amount payable on application was ₹ 4 and on allotment ₹ 3 per share. The underwriting commission payable to underwriters was agreed at 3%.

You are required to give Journal Entries in the books of Jay Ltd. for allotment of shares to underwriters, commission due to each of the underwriters and the net cash paid to or received from the underwriters.

[**Ans** (i) Total Liability (number of shares): A 150000,B 150000, C 309000, Net Amount payable by Underwriters C ₹ 11,13,000]

4. A Company issued 2,00,000 shares of ₹ 10 each at a premium of ₹ 15.

The other details in this regard are as follows:

Underwriter	*No. of shares Underwritten*	*Firm underwriting*	*No. of marked applications*
P	1,20,000	15,000	25,000
Q	50,000	10,500	32,000
R	30,000	20,000	9,500

Other Information:

(i) The marked application are excluding firm underwriting.

(ii) Total subscriptions received by the company (excluding firm underwriting and marked applications) were 32,500 shares.

(iii) Maximum Commission is payable to underwriters as per law.

(iv) The underwriting contract provides that credit for unmarked applications will be given to the underwriters in proportion to the shares underwritten and benefit of firm underwriting is to be given to individual underwrites.

Based on the above information, determine the liability of each underwriter (number of shares), compute the amounts payable to or due from underwriters and Pass Journal Entries in the books of the company relating to underwriting.

[**Ans** Total Liability (number of shares): P 70,500,Q 10,500, R 20,000, Net Amount payable/(receivable) by Underwriters P ₹ 16,12,500, Q ₹ 2,00,000, R ₹ 4,62,500]

5. A company issued 1,50,000 shares of ₹ 10 each at a premium of ₹ 10. The entire issue was underwritten as follows:

X – 90,000 shares (Firm underwriting 12,000 shares)

Y – 37,500 shares (Firm underwriting 4,500 shares)

Z – 22,500 shares (Firm underwriting 15,000 shares)

Total applications received by the company (excluding firm underwriting and marked applications) were 22,500 shares.

The marked applications (excluding firm underwriting) were as follows:

X- 15,000 shares; Y- 30,000 shares: Z- 7,500 shares.

Commission payable to underwriters is at 5% of the issue price. The underwriting contract provides that credit for unmarked applications be given to the underwriters in proportion to the shares underwritten and benefit of firm underwriting is to be given to individual underwriters. The amount payable on application and allotment were ₹ 6 (including ₹ 3 premium) & ₹ 4 (including ₹ 2 premium) respectively and the balance on call.

(i) Determine the liability of each underwriter (number of shares)

(ii) Compute the amount payable or due to underwriters; and

(iii) Pass necessary journal entries in the books of co. relating to underwriting.

[**Ans** Total Liability (number of shares): X 55,500, Y 4,500, Z 15,000, Net Amount payable/(receivable) by Underwriters X ₹ 3,93,000, Y (₹ 19,500), Z ₹ 37,500]

7 ACCOUNTING FOR EMPLOYEE STOCK OPTION PLAN

LEARNING OBJECTIVES

After studying this chapter, you should be able to understand:

- ◇ What is Included in the term 'Employee' for the purpose of Employee Share–based Payments?
- ◇ What are the various forms of Employee Share–based Payments?
- ◇ What is Objective and Importance of Employee Share–based Payments?
- ◇ What are the various Transfers that are Treated as Employee Share–based Payments?
- ◇ Which Transactions are not treated as Employee share–based Payments?
- ◇ Accounting Treatment of Employee Share – Based Plans in Financial Statements of an Enterprise
- ◇ Fair Value Method
- ◇ Intrinsic Value Method

1.0 WHAT IS INCLUDED IN THE TERM 'EMPLOYEE' FOR THE PURPOSE OF EMPLOYEE SHARE–BASED PAYMENTS?

The term 'employee' includes a director of the enterprise(whether whole time *or* not) for the purpose of Employee Share – based Payments

2.0 WHAT ARE THE VARIOUS FORMS OF EMPLOYEE SHARE – BASED PAYMENTS?

Employee share–based payments generally take the following three forms:

1. Employee Stock Option Plan [ESOP]	It is a plan under which the enterprise grants employee stock option. Employee Stock Option is a contract that gives the employees of the enterprise the right, but not the obligation, for a specified period of time to purchase *or* subscribe to the shares of the enterprise at a fixed *or* determinable price.
2. Employee Stock Purchase Plan [ESPP]	It is a plan under which the enterprise grants rights to its employees to purchase its shares at a stated price at the time of public issue *or* otherwise.
3. Stock Appreciation Rights [SARs]	It is a right that entitles the employees to receive cash *or* shares for an amount equivalent to any excess of the market value of a stated number of enterprise's shares over a stated price. The form of payment may be specified when the rights are granted *or* may be determined when they are exercised. However, in some plans, the employee may choose the form of payment.

3.0 WHAT IS OBJECTIVE AND IMPORTANCE OF EMPLOYEE SHARE – BASED PAYMENTS?

1. Objective	The objective of Employee Share–based payments is to encourage employees to have a higher participation in the company.
2. Importance	1. Stock options provide an opportunity to employees to share in the growth of the company. 2. Stock options create long–term wealth in the hands of the employees. 3. Stock options create a common sense of ownership between the company and its employees paving the way for a unified approach to the common objective of enhancing overall shareholder value. 4. Stock options are important means to attract, retain and motivate the best available talent for the company.

4.0 LEGAL POSITION [SECTION 62 (1)(B)]

Where at any time, a company having a share capital proposes to increase its subscribed capital by the issue of further shares, such shares shall be offered to employees under a scheme of employees' stock option, subject to special resolution passed by company and subject to such conditions as may be prescribed.

Explanation: For the purposes of section 62 (1)(b) and this rule "Employee" means.

(a) a permanent employee of the company who has been working in India *or* outside India*; or*

(b) a director of the company, whether a whole time director *or* not but excluding an independent director*; or*

(c) an employee as defined in clauses (a) *or* (b) of a subsidiary, in India *or* outside India, *or* of a holding company of the company *or* of an associate company but does not include–

(i) an employee who is a promoter *or* a person belonging to the promoter group*; or*

(ii) a director who either himself *or* through his relative *or* through any body corporate, directly *or* indirectly, holds more than 10% of the outstanding equity shares of the company.

5.0 TERMS USED WITH REFERENCE TO ESOS

1. Grant	Grant means the issue of option to the employee under ESOS.
2. Grant Date **[say, 1.7.2019]**	Grant Date is the date at which the enterprise grants rights to its employees to receive cash *or* shares of the enterprise, on satisfaction of specified vesting conditions under an employee share–based payment plan.
3. Vesting	Vesting means the process by which the employee is given the right to apply for the shares of the company against the option granted to him under the ESOS.
4. Vesting Date **[say, 31.03.2022]**	Date on which all the specified vesting conditions of an employee share–based payment plan are to be satisfied. **Note:** Vesting Conditions are the conditions that must be satisfied for the employee to become entitled to receive cash, *or* shares of the enterprise, pursuant to an employee share–based payment plan. Vesting conditions include service conditions, which require the employee to complete a specified period of service, and performance

	conditions, which require specified performance targets to be met (such as a specified increase in the enterprise's share price over a specified period of time).
5. Vesting Period [33 months]	Vesting Period is the period between the Grant Date and Vesting Date.
6. Minimum Gap	There must be a minimum period of **1 year** between Grant Date and Vesting Date.
7. Exercise	Exercise means making of an application by an employee to the company for issue of shares against option vested in him under the ESOS.
8. Exercise Date [say, 31.03.2023]	Date by which an employee should exercise his right to apply for the shares vested in him under the ESOS.
9. Exercise Period [12 months]	Exercise Period is the period between the Vesting Date and Exercise Date.

6.0 WHAT ARE THE VARIOUS TRANSFERS THAT ARE TREATED AS EMPLOYEE SHARE–BASED PAYMENTS?

The following transfers are treated as employee share – based payments:

1. A transfer of shares *or* stock options of an enterprise by its shareholders to its employees, unless the transfer is clearly for a purpose other than payment for services rendered to the enterprise.
2. A transfer of shares *or* stock options of the parent of the enterprise.
3. A transfer of shares *or* stock options of another enterprise in the same group as the enterprise, to the employees of the enterprise.
   Note: A 'Group' is a parent and all its subsidiaries.

7.0 WHICH TRANSACTIONS ARE NOT TREATED AS EMPLOYEE SHARE – BASED PAYMENTS?

The following transactions are not treated as employee share – based payments:

TRANSACTION IN THE CAPACITY OF SHAREHOLDER

A transaction with an employee in his/her capacity as a holder of shares of the enterprise. ***For Example***, if an enterprise grants all holders of a particular class of its shares the right to acquire additional shares *or* stock options of the enterprise at a price that is *less* than the fair value of those shares *or* stock options, and an employee receives such a right because he/she is a holder of shares *or* stock options of that particular class, the granting *or* exercise of that right is not an employee share – based payment.

RIGHT TO ACQUIRE SHARES ON THE SAME TERMS AS APPLICABLE TO INVESTORS

A grant of shares to the employees at the time of public issue if the price and other terms at which the shares are offered to employees are the same *or* similar to those at which the shares have been offered to general investors. ***For Example***, in a public issue an enterprise grants shares to its employees as a preferential allotment while the price and other terms remain the same as those to other investors.

8.0 ACCOUNTING TREATMENT OF EMPLOYEE SHARE – BASED PLANS IN FINANCIAL STATEMENTS OF AN ENTERPRISE

WHAT ARE THE VARIOUS CATEGORIES OF EMPLOYEE SHARE – BASED PLAN FOR THE PURPOSE OF THE REPORTING IN THE FINANCIAL STATEMENTS OF AN ENTERPRISE?

The various categories of employee share – based plan for the purpose of the reporting in the financial statements of an enterprise are as follows:

1. Equity–settled plans	Under these plans, the employees **receive shares.**
2. Cash–settled plans	Under these plans, the employees **receive cash** based on the price (or value) of the enterprise's shares.
3. Equity/cash–settled plans	Under these plans, either the enterprise *or* the employee has a choice of whether the enterprise settles the payment in **cash or by issue of shares.**

HOW SHOULD THESE CATEGORIES BE ACCOUNTED FOR IN THE FINANCIAL STATEMENTS OF THE ENTERPRISE?

These categories may be accounted for in the financial statements of the enterprise by any of the following two methods:

1. Fair Value Method	A fair value is the amount for which stock option granted *or* a share offered for purchase could be exchanged between knowledgeable, willing parties in an arm's length transaction.
2. Intrinsic Value Method	An Intrinsic Value is the amount by which the quoted market price of the underlying share in case of a listed enterprise *or* the value of the underlying share determined by an independent valuer in case of an unlisted enterprise exceeds the exercise price of an option. This method may be followed as alternative but with fair value disclosure.

9.0 FAIR VALUE METHOD

TOTAL FAIR VALUE OF OPTIONS

Total No. of Options expected to vest at the end of the Vesting Period × Fair value of each Option

HOW TO MEASURE FAIR VALUE

(a) If Market Prices are available	On the basis of market prices as on grant date and the terms and conditions upon which those shares *or* stock options were granted.
(b) If Market Prices are not available	The enterprise should estimate the fair value of the instruments granted using a valuation technique to estimate what the price of those instruments would have been on the grant date in an arm's length transaction between knowledgeable, willing parties. The valuation technique should be consistent with generally accepted valuation methodologies for pricing financial instruments (e.g., use of an option pricing model for valuing stock options) and should incorporate all factors and assumptions that knowledgeable, willing market participants would consider in setting the price.

SHOULD MARKET CONDITIONS BE TAKEN INTO ACCOUNT WHILE ESTIMATING THE FAIR VALUE OF SHARES OR STOCK OPTIONS?

Yes, market conditions should be taken into account while estimating the fair value of shares *or* stock options.

Note: Market Condition is a condition that is related to the market price of the shares of the enterprise, upon which the exercise price, vesting *or* exercise ability of a share *or* a stock option depends, such as attaining a specified share price *or* a specified amount of intrinsic value of a stock option, *or* achieving a specified target that is based on the market price of the shares of the enterprise relative to an index of market prices of shares of other enterprises.

SHOULD VESTING CONDITIONS OTHER THAN MARKET CONDITIONS BE TAKEN INTO ACCOUNT WHILE ESTIMATING THE FAIR VALUE OF SHARES OR STOCK OPTIONS?

No, vesting conditions other than market conditions should not be taken into account when estimating the fair value of the shares *or* stock options at the grant date.

WHAT ARE THE FACTORS TO BE TAKEN INTO ACCOUNT WHILE ESTIMATING THE FAIR VALUE OF THE SHARES?

The fair value of the shares granted are measured at the market price of the share at the grant date *or* an estimated value by an independent valuer. However, the following factors are to be considered while estimating the fair value of the shares:

1. Dividend	If the employee is not entitled to receive dividends during the vesting period then the present value of such dividend should be deducted from fair value of the shares. However, if employee is entitled to receive dividends during the vesting period then no adjustment is required.
2. Restriction on transfer	If the shares are subject to restrictions on transfer after vesting date, that factor should be taken into account, but only to the extent that the post–vesting restrictions affect the price that a knowledgeable, willing market participant would pay for that share. ***For Example***, if the shares are actively traded in a deep and liquid market, post–vesting transfer restrictions may have little, if any, effect on the price that a knowledgeable, willing market participant would pay for those shares. Restrictions on transfer *or* other restrictions that exist during the vesting period should not be taken into account while estimating the fair value of the shares granted at grant date, because those restrictions stem from the existence of vesting conditions.

WHAT ARE THE FACTORS TO BE TAKEN INTO ACCOUNT WHILE ESTIMATING THE FAIR VALUE OF THE STOCK OPTION?

In many cases of stock option granted to employees market prices are not available, because the options granted are subject to terms and conditions that do not apply to traded options. If traded options with similar terms and conditions do not exist, the fair value of the options granted should be estimated by applying an option pricing model. An Option Pricing Model, as a minimum, should consider the following factors:

(a) **Exercise Price of the Option:** It is the price payable by the employee for exercising the option granted to him in pursuance of the Employee Stock Option Plan.

(b) **Expected Life of the Option:** It is the period of time from grant date to the date on which an option is expected to be exercised.

(c) Current price of the underlying shares

(d) **Expected Volatility of the Share Price:** It is a measure of the amount by which a price has fluctuated (historical volatility) *or* is expected to fluctuate (expected volatility) during a period. The volatility of a share price is the standard deviation of the continuously compounded rates of return on the share over a specified period.

(e) Dividends expected on the shares (if appropriate)

(f) Risk–free interest rate for the life of the option

(g) Other factors that knowledgeable, willing market participants would consider in setting the price should also be taken into account

Note: There is difference between exercise period and expected life of the option. Exercise period means the time period after vesting period within which the employee should exercise his right to apply for shares against the option vested in him in pursuance of the Employee Stock Option Plan whereas the expected life of the option is the total period of time from grant date to the date on which an option is expected to be exercised.

HOW SHOULD EXPECTED NUMBER OF SHARES OR STOCK OPTIONS EXPECTED TO VEST BE MEASURED?

The enterprise should estimate the expected number of shares *or* stock options expected to vest during the vesting period based on the best available estimate and should revise that estimate, if necessary, if subsequent information indicates that the number of shares *or* stock options expected to vest differs from previous estimates on vesting date, the enterprise should revise the estimate to equal the number of shares *or* stock options that ultimately vest.

Note: In case of grants of shares *or* stock options with market conditions, the enterprise should recognize the services received from an employee who satisfies all other vesting conditions other than market condition (e.g., services received from an employee who remains in service for the specified period of service), irrespective of the fact whether that market condition is satisfied *or* not since market conditions are incorporated into measurement of fair value.

11.0 HOW TO COMPUTE EXPECTED NO. OF EMPLOYEES AS AT VESTING DATE?

Expected No. of Employees as at Vesting Date = No. of Employees as at the beginning of current year – No. of Employees actually left during current year – No. of Employees expected to leave during the future till Vesting Date

ILLUSTRATION 1 [HOW TO COMPUTE EXPECTED NO. OF EMPLOYEES AS AT VESTING DATE?]

As at 31.03.2020,X Ltd. desires to know the expected No. of Employees as at Vesting Date i.e. 31.03.2022 and provides you the following information:

Number of Employees as at April 1,2019	2100
Number of Employees actually left during 2019 – 2020	100
No. of Employees expected to leave during 2020 – 2021	10%
No. of Employees expected to leave during 2021– 2022	10%
No. of Employees expected as at 31.03.2022	?

SOLUTION

CALCULATION OF EXPECTED NO. OF EMPLOYEES AS AT VESTING DATE

A. No. of Employees as at April 1,2019	2100
B. No. of Employees actually left during 2019–2020	100

C. No. of Employees expected to leave during 2020–2021 [10% of (2100 – 100)]	200
D. No. of Employees expected to leave during 2021–2022 [10% of (2100 – 100 –200)]	180
E. Expected No. of Employees as at 31.03.2022[2100–100–200–180] **or [(2100–100) x 90% x 90%]**	1620

ILLUSTRATION 2 [HOW TO COMPUTE EXPECTED NO. OF EMPLOYEES AS AT VESTING DATE?]

As at 31.03.2021,X Ltd. desires to know the expected No. of Employees as at Vesting Date i.e. 31.03.2022 and provides you the following information:

Number of Employees as at April 1,2019	2100
Number of Employees actually left during 2019–2020	100
Number of Employees actually left during 2020–2021	80
No. of Employees expected to leave during 2021–2022	5%
Expected No. of Employees as at 31.03.2022	?

SOLUTION

CALCULATION OF EXPECTED NO. OF EMPLOYEES AS AT VESTING DATE

A. N0. of Employees as at April 1,2019	2100
B. No. of Employees actually left during 2019–2020	100
C. Number of Employees actually left during 2020–2021	80
D. No. of Employees expected to leave during 2021–2022 [5% of (2100 – 100 –80)]	96
E. Expected No. of Employees as at 31.03.2022[2100–100–80–96] **or [(2100–100 –80) x 95%]**	1824

ILLUSTRATION 3

As at 31.03.2022,X Ltd. desires to know the No. of Employees as at Vesting Date i.e. 31.03.2022 and provides you the following information:

Number of Employees as at April 1,2019	2100
Number of Employees actually left during 2019–2020	100
Number of Employees actually left during 2020–2021	80
Number of Employees actually left during 2021–2022	192
No. of Employees as at 31.03.2022	?

SOLUTION

CALCULATION OF NO. OF EMPLOYEES AS AT VESTING DATE

A. No. of Employees as at April 1,2019	2100
B. No. of Employees actually left during 2019–2020	100
C. Number of Employees actually left during 2020–2021	80

D. No. of Employees actually left during 2021–2022	192
E. No. of Employees as at 31.03.2022[2100–100–80–192]	1728

12.0 HOW TO COMPUTE TOTAL NO OF OPTIONS EXPECTED TO VEST?

Total Number of Options expected to vest = (No. of Employees entitled to Option* No. of Options per Employee) – Unvested Options Lapsed

ILLUSTRATION 4 [HOW TO COMPUTE TOTAL NO OF OPTIONS EXPECTED TO VEST?]

On 1.4.2019 AMLA (1) Ltd grants 100 options to each of its 2100 employees at ₹ 60 when the Market price is ₹ 90. The face value of equity share is ₹ 10 per share. The vesting date is 31st March, 2022 and the exercise date is 31st March, 2023. At the end of year 1, the company found that 100 employees had left and estimated the expected annual forfeitures rate at 10%. At the end of year 2,the company found that 80 employees had left and re–estimated the expected annual forfeitures rate at 5%. At the end of year 3,the company found that 192 employees had left. Compute Total Number of Options expected to vest each year.

SOLUTION

CALCULATION OF TOTAL NUMBER OF OPTIONS EXPECTED TO VEST

Particulars	Year 1	Year 2	Year 3
A. No. of Employees entitled to Option	(2100–100) =2000*90%*90% =1620	(2000–80) =1920*95%=1824	(1920–192)=1728
B. No. of Options per Employee	100	100	100
C. Total Number of Options [A*B]	1,62,000	1,82,400	1,72,800

ILLUSTRATION 5 [HOW TO COMPUTE TOTAL NO OF OPTIONS EXPECTED TO VEST WHEN UNVESTED OPTIONS LAPSED?]

On 1.4.2019 AMLA (2) Ltd grants 100 options to each of its 2100 employees at ₹ 60 (Face Value ₹ 10)depending upon the employment of the employees at the time of vesting of options. The Market Price is ₹ 90. The vesting date is 31st March, 2022 and the exercise date is 31st March,2023. 48,000 unvested options lapsed on 31st March, 2020. 27,600 unvested options lapsed on 31st March, 2021 and lastly 37,200 unvested options lapsed on 31st March, 2022. Compute Total Number of Options expected to vest each year.

SOLUTION

CALCULATION OF TOTAL NUMBER OF OPTIONS EXPECTED TO VEST

Particulars	31.03.2020	31.03.2021	31.03.2022
A. No. of Employees	2100	2100	2100
B. No. of Options per Employee	100	100	100
C. Total Number of Options [A*B]	210000	210000	210000
D. Unvested Options lapsed	48000	27600	37200
D. Total Number of Options expected to vest [C – D]	162000	182400	172800

13.0 HOW TO COMPUTE TOTAL FAIR VALUE OF OPTIONS AT THE END OF EACH YEAR?]

Fair Value of Option per Share = *Fair Value of Shares issued under ESOP – Exercise Price per Share

*If Fair Value of Shares issued under ESOP is not given, then Market Price per share may be used.

ILLUSTRATION 6 [HOW TO COMPUTE TOTAL FAIR VALUE OF OPTIONS AT THE END OF EACH YEAR?]

On 1.4.2019 GILOY (1) Ltd grants 100 options to each of its 2100 employees at ₹ 60 when the Market price is ₹ 90. The face value of equity share is ₹ 10 per share. The vesting date is 31st March,2022 and the exercise date is 31st March, 2023.

	31.03.2020	31.03.2021	31.03.2022
Expected No. of Employees as at 31.03.2022	1620	1824	1728
Market Price per share (₹)	100	90	80
Fair Value of a share issued under ESOP (₹)	90	80	70

Required: Compute Total Fair Value of Options at the end of each year.

SOLUTION

CALCULATION OF FAIR VALUE OF OPTION PER SHARE AT THE END OF EACH YEAR

Particulars	31.03.2020	31.03.2021	31.03.2022
A. Fair Value of a share issued under ESOP	90	80	70
B. Exercise Price per Share	60	60	60
C. Fair Value of Option per Share(A – B)	30	20	10

CALCULATION OF TOTAL FAIR VALUE OF OPTION AT THE END OF EACH YEAR

	Particulars	31.03.2020	31.03.2021	31.03.2022
A.	Expected No. of Employees as at	1620	1824	1728
B.	No. of Options per Employee	100	100	100
C.	Fair Value of Option per Share	30	20	10
D.	Total Fair Value of Option [A*B*C]	48,60,000	36,48,000	17,28,000

ILLUSTRATION 7 [HOW TO COMPUTE TOTAL FAIR VALUE OF OPTIONS AT THE END OF EACH YEAR?]

On 1.4.2019 GILOY (2) Ltd grants 100 options to each of its 2100 employees at ₹ 60 when the Market price is ₹ 90. The face value of equity share is ₹ 10 per share. The vesting date is 31st March,2022 and the exercise date is 31st March,2023.

	31.03.2020	31.03.2021	31.03.2022
Expected No. of Employees as at 31.03.2022	1620	1824	1728
Market Price per share (₹)	100	90	80
Fair Value of an Option under ESOP (₹)	30	20	10

Required: Compute Total Fair Value of Options at the end of each year.

SOLUTION

CALCULATION OF TOTAL FAIR VALUE OF OPTION AT THE END OF EACH YEAR

Particulars	*31.03.2020*	*31.03.2021*	*31.03.2022*
A. Expected No. of Employees as at	1620	1824	1728
B. No. of Options per Employee	100	100	100
C. Fair Value of Option per Share	30	20	10
D. Total Fair Value of Option [A*B*C]	48,60,000	36,48,000	17,28,000

14.0 HOW TO CALCULATE EMPLOYEES COMPENSATION EXPENSE TO BE RECOGNIZED?

$$= [\text{Total Fair Value of Options expected to vest estimated at the end of each accounting period} \times \frac{\text{Vesting Period Expired}}{\text{Total Vesting Period}} - [\text{Expense already recognized during previous years.}]$$

STATEMENT SHOWING THE EXPENSE TO BE RECOGNISED IN EACH YEAR

Particulars	*Year 1*	*Year 2*	*Year 3*
A. No. of Employees entitled to Option			
B. No. of Options per Employee			
C. Fair Value of Option per Share			
D. Total Fair Value of Option [A*B*C]			
E. Total Expense till date [Total Fair Value* Expired Vesting Period/ Total Vesting Period]			
F. Expenses already recognized during previous year(s)			
G. Expenses to be recognized(de–recognized) [E – F]			

ILLUSTRATION 8 [HOW TO COMPUTE EMPLOYEE COMPENSATION EXPENSE TO BE RECOGNIZED EACH YEAR ?]

TULSI Ltd.(1) provides the following information:

Total Fair Value of Options as at 31.03.2020	₹ 48,11,400
Total Fair Value of Options as at 31.03.2021	₹ 36,08,550
Total Fair Value of Options as at 31.03.2022	₹ 17,28,000
Vesting Date	March 31, 2022
Exercise Date	March 31, 2023

Required: Compute Expenses to be recognised at the end of each year by Fair Value Method if Grant Date is (i) 1.4.2019 (ii) 1.7.2019 (iii) 1.10.2019 (iv) 1.1.2020

SOLUTION

(i) Vesting Period =from 1.4.2019 to 31.3.2022 = 36 months

EXPENSE TO BE RECOGNISED EACH YEAR IF GRANT DATE IS 1.4.2019

Particulars	31.03.2020	31.03.2021	31.03.2022
A. Total Fair Value of Option	48,11,400	36,08,550	17,28,000
B. Total Expense till date [Total Fair Value* Expired Vesting Period/ Total Vesting Period]	= 48,11,400× 12/36 = 16,03,800	= (36,08,550 × 24/36) = 24,05,700	= 17,28,000
C. Expenses already recognized during previous year(s)	0	= 16,03,800	= 24,05,700
D. Expenses to be recognized(de recognized) [B – C]	= 16,03,800	= 8,01,900	(6,77,700)

(ii) Vesting Period =from 1.7.2019 to 31.3.2022 = 33 months

EXPENSE TO BE RECOGNISED EACH YEAR IF GRANT DATE IS 1.7.2019

Particulars	31.03.2020	31.03.2021	31.03.2022
A. Total Fair Value of Option	48,11,400	36,08,550	17,28,000
B. Total Expense till date [Total Fair Value* Expired Vesting Period/ Total Vesting Period]	= 48,11,400 × 9/33 = 13,12,200	= (36,08,550 × 21/33) = 22,96,350	= 17,28,000
C. Expenses already recognized during previous year(s)	0	= 13,12,200	= 22,96,350
D. Expenses to be recognized(de recognized) [B – C]	= 13,12,200	= 9,84,150	(5,68,350)

(iii) Vesting Period =from 1.10.2019 to 31.3.2022 = 30 months

EXPENSE TO BE RECOGNISED EACH YEAR IF GRANT DATE IS 1.10.2019

Particulars	31.03.2020	31.03.2021	31.03.2022
A. Total Fair Value of Option	48,11,400	36,08,550	17,28,000
B. Total Expense till date [Total Fair Value* Expired Vesting Period/ Total Vesting Period]	= 48,11,400× 6/30 = 9,62,280	= (36,08,550 × 18/30) = 21,65,130	= 17,28,000
C. Expenses already recognized during previous year(s)	0	= 9,62,280	= 21,65,130
D. Expenses to be recognized(de recognized) [B – C]	= 9,62,280	= 12,02,850	(4,37,130)

(iv) Vesting Period =from 1.1.2020 to 31.3.2022 = 27 months

EXPENSE TO BE RECOGNISED EACH YEAR IF GRANT DATE IS 1.1.2020

Particulars	31.03.2020	31.03.2021	31.03.2022
A. Total Fair Value of Option	48,11,400	36,08,550	17,28,000
B. Total Expense till date [Total Fair Value* Expired Vesting Period/ Total Vesting Period]	= 48,11,400× 3/27 = 5,34,600	= (36,08,550 × 15/27) = 20,04,750	= 17,28,000

C. Expenses already recognized during previous year(s)	0	= 5,34,600	= 20,04,750
D. Expenses to be recognized(de recognized) [B –C]	= 5,34,600	= 14,70,150	(2,76,750)

15.0 HOW TO COMPUTE VALUE OF OPTIONS FORFEITED?

Value of Options Forfeited = Options not exercised till the end of exercise period × Fair Value of Option per Share

ILLUSTRATION 9 [HOW TO COMPUTE VALUE OF OPTIONS FORFEITED?]

No of Employees covered 2100, No of Options granted per Employee 100, Exercise Date March 31, 2023. Fair Value of Option per Share as at 31st March,2023: ₹ 10. No. of Employees as at 31.03.2022:1728. Only 1700 employees exercised their options on 31st March,2023. Compute the Value of Options Forfeited.

SOLUTION

Value of Options Forfeited = [(1728 – 1700) × 100 × ₹ 10] = ₹ 28,000

ILLUSTRATION 10

On 1.4.2019 TULSI Ltd.(2) Ltd grants 100 options to each of its 2100 employees at ₹ 60 when the market price is ₹ 100 . The vesting date is 31st March,2022 and the exercise date is 31st March,2023. At the end of year 1,the company found that 100 employees had left and estimated the expected annual forfeitures rate at 10%. Fair Value of a share issued under ESOP was ₹ 90. At the end of year 2,the company found that 80 employees had left and re–estimated the expected annual forfeitures rate at 5%. Fair Value of a share issued under ESOP was ₹ 80. At the end of year 3,the company found that 192 employees had left. Fair Value of a share issued under ESOP was ₹ 70. Only 1700 employees exercised their options on 31st March,2023. The face value of equity share is ₹ 10 per share. Determine the compensation expense to be recognised each year and Value of Options Forfeited.

SOLUTION

CALCULATION OF FAIR VALUE OF OPTION PER SHARE

Particulars	*Year 1 end*	*Year 2 end*	*Year 3 end*
A. Fair Value of a share issued under ESOP	90	80	70
B. Exercise Price per Share	60	60	60
C. Fair Value of Option per Share(A x B)	30	20	10

STATEMENT SHOWING THE EXPENSE TO BE RECOGNISED IN EACH YEAR

Particulars	*Year 1*	*Year 2*	*Year 3*
A. No.of Employees entitled to Option	(2100–100) = 2000*90%*90% = 1620	(2000–80) = 1920*95%=1824	(1920–192) = 1728
B. No.of Options per Employee	100	100	100
C. Fair Value of Option per Share	30	20	10

D. Total Fair Value of Option [A*B*C]	48,60,000	36,48,000	17,28,000
E. Total Expense till date [Total Fair Value* Expired Vesting Period/ Total Vesting Period]	= 48,60,000/3 = 16,20,000	= (36,48,000 × 2/3) = 24,32,000	= 17,28,000
F. Expenses already recognized during previous year(s)	0	= 16,20,000	= 24,32,000
G. Expenses to be recognized(reversed) [E – F]	= 16,20,000	= 8,12,000	(7,04,000)

Value of Options Forfeited = [(1728 – 1700) × 100 × ₹ 10] = ₹ 28,000

ILLUSTRATION 11

On 1.4.2019 TULSI Ltd.(3) Ltd grants 100 options to each of its 2100 employees at ₹ 60 (Face Value ₹ 10) depending upon the employment of the employees at the time of vesting of options. The Market Price is ₹ 100. The vesting date is 31st March,2022 and the exercise date is 31st March,2023. 48,000 unvested options lapsed on 31st March, 2020 when Fair Value of a share issued under ESOP was ₹ 90. 27,600 unvested options lapsed on 31st March, 2021 when Fair Value of a share issued under ESOP was ₹ 80. and lastly 37,200 unvested options lapsed on 31st March, 2022 when Fair Value of a share issued under ESOP was ₹ 70. Determine the compensation expense to be recognised each year.

SOLUTION

CALCULATION OF FAIR VALUE OF OPTION PER SHARE

Particulars	*Year 1 end*	*Year 2 end*	*Year 3 end*
A. Fair Value of a share issued under ESOP	90	80	70
B. Exercise Price per Share	60	60	60
C. Fair Value of Option per Share(A x B)	30	20	10

STATEMENT SHOWING THE EXPENSE TO BE RECOGNISED IN EACH YEAR

Particulars	*31.03.2020*	*31.03.2021*	*31.03.2022*
A. No. of Employees	2100	1620	1344
B. No. of Options per Employee	100	100	100
C. Total Number of Options [A*B]	210000	162000	134400
D. Unvested Options lapsed	48000	27600	37200
E. Total Number of Options expected to vest [C – D]	162000	134400	97200
F. Fair Value of Option per Share	30	20	10
G. Total Fair Value of Option [A*B*C]	48,60,000	26,88,000	9,72,000
H. Total Expense till date [Total Fair Value* Expired Vesting Period/ Total Vesting Period]	= 48,60,000/3 = 16,20,000	= (26,88,000 × 2/3) = 17,92,000	9,72,000
I. Expenses already recognized during previous year(s)	0	= 16,20,000	= 17,92,000
J. Expenses to be recognized(reversed) [H –I]	= 16,20,000	= 1,72,000	(8,20,000)

16.0 HOW SHOULD AN ENTERPRISE RECOGNIZE THE LIABILITY IN RESPECT OF EQUITY SETTLED SHARE –BASED PAYMENT TO EMPLOYEES?

(a) In Case of Shares or Stock Options that vest immediately	An enterprise should immediately recognize as an expense (except where service received qualifies to be included as a part of the cost of an asset) the services received in full with a corresponding credit to an appropriate equity account, i.e. 'Stock Options Outstanding Account'.
(b) In Case of Shares or Stock Options that do not vest immediately	The enterprise should account for those services as they are rendered by the employee during the vesting period on time proportion basis with a corresponding credit to the Equity Account. If the shares *or* stock options granted do not vest until the employee completes a specified period of service, the enterprise should presume that the services to be rendered by the employee as consideration for those instruments will be received in the future, during the vesting period.

Notes:

(i) A grant of shares *or* stock options to an employee is typically conditional on the employee remaining in the employment of the enterprise for a specified period of time. Thus, if an employee is granted stock options conditional upon completing three years' service, then the enterprise should presume that the services to be rendered by the employee as consideration for the stock options will be received in the future, over that three–year vesting period.

(ii) There might be performance conditions that must be satisfied, such as the enterprise achieving a specified growth in profit *or* a specified increase in the share price of the enterprise. Thus, if an employee is granted stock options conditional upon the achievement of a performance condition and remaining in the employment of the enterprise until that performance condition is satisfied, and the length of the vesting period varies depending on when that performance condition is satisfied, the enterprise should presume that the services to be rendered by the employee as consideration for the stock options will be received in the future, over the expected vesting period. The enterprise should estimate the length of the expected vesting period at grant date, based on the most likely outcome of the performance condition.

(iii) If the performance condition is a market condition, the estimate of the length of the expected vesting period should be consistent with the assumptions used in estimating the fair value of the options granted, and should not be subsequently revised since fair market value which has been calculated has already taken into consideration the market conditions.

(iv) If the performance condition is not a market condition, the enterprise should revise its estimate of the length of the vesting period, if necessary, if subsequent information indicates that the length of the vesting period differs from previous estimates.

17.0 WHAT SHOULD BE THE CONSIDERATION FOR SHARES ISSUED BY THE ENTERPRISE ON EXERCISE OF THE RIGHT TO OBTAIN SHARES *or* STOCK OPTIONS?

The shares issued by the enterprise on exercise of the right to obtain shares *or* stock options should be considered to have been issued at the consideration comprising the Exercise Price and the corresponding amount standing to the credit of the relevant equity account (i.e. Employee Stock Options Outstanding Account)

Note: Where the right to obtain shares *or* stock option expires unexercised, the balance standing to the credit of the relevant equity account should be t/f to General Reserve.

18.0 ACCOUNTING TREATMENT OF ESOPS

The following journal entries are required to be passed to account for Employee Share Based Payments:

1. To recognize an appropriate proportion of the Total Fair Value of Options expected to vest as an expense at the end of each accounting period during the vesting period.

Employees Compensation Expense A/c		Dr.
To Employee Stock Option Outstanding A/c		
(Being expense in respect of ESOP recognized during the year)		

Note: Expense to be recognized:

$$= [\text{Total Fair Value of Options expected to vest estimated at the end of each accounting period} \times \frac{\text{Vesting Period Expired}}{\text{Total Vesting Period}}] - [\text{Expense already recognized during previous years.}]$$

2. To transfer Employees Compensation Expense Account to Profit & Loss Account at the end of each accounting period during the vesting period.

Profit & Loss A/c		Dr.
To Employees Compensation Expense A/c		
(Being the transfer of Employees Compensation Expense A/c. to P&L A/c.)		

3. To record the issue of shares when the options are exercised during exercise period.

Bank A/c	Dr.	[No. of options × Exercise Price]
Employee Stock Option Outstanding A/c	Dr.	[No. of options × Fair Value of option]
To Share Capital A/c		[No. of options × Face Value]
To Securities Premium A/c		[No. of options × (Exercise Price + Fair Value of option – Face Value)]
(Being ...... options exercised during ..... period)		

4. To cancel Fair Value of options lapsed at the end of exercise period.

Employee Stock Option Outstanding A/c	Dr.	[No. of options lapsed × Fair Value of each option]
To General Reserve		
(Being the fair value of options lapsed t/f to General Reserve)		

Disclosure: Stock Options Outstanding Account will continue to appear on the liabilities side of the Balance Sheet under the head **'Reserves & Surplus'** until all the options are exercised/ lapsed.

ILLUSTRATION 12

On 1.4.2019 AMLA, GILOY & TULSI (1) Ltd grants 100 options to each of its 2100 employees at ₹ 60 when the Market price is ₹ 100. The vesting date is 31st March, 2022 and the exercise date is 31st March, 2023. At the end of year 1, the company found that 100 employees had left. At the end of year 2,the company found that 80 employees had left. At the end of year 3, the company found that 192 employees had left. Only 1700 employees exercised their options on 31st March,

2023. The face value of equity share is ₹ 10 per share. Pass the necessary journal entries in the books of the company upto 31st March,2023 (Assume that the Fair Value of a share issued under ESOP is ₹ 90 at 31st March of each year).

SOLUTION

STATEMENT SHOWING THE EXPENSE TO BE RECOGNISED IN EACH YEAR

Particulars	Year 1	Year 2	Year 3
A. No. of Employees entitled to Option	(2100 – 100) = 2000	(2000 – 80) = 1920	(1920 – 192) = 1728
B. No. of Options per Employee	100	100	100
C. Fair Value of Option per Share	30	30	30
D. Total Fair Value of Option [A*B*C]	60,00,000	57,60,000	51,84,000
E. Total Expense till date [Total Fair Value* Expired Vesting Period/ Total Vesting Period]	= 60,00,0000/3 = 20,00,000	= (57,60,000 × 2/3) = 38,40,000	= 51,84,000
F. Expenses already recognized during previous year(s)	0	= 20,00,000	= 38,40,000
G. Expenses to be recognized [E – F]	= 20,00,000	= 18,40,000	= 13,44,000

Value of Options Forfeited = [(1728 – 1700) × 100 × ₹ 30] = ₹ 84,000

JOURNAL [₹ in lakh]

Date	Particulars	Dr. (₹)	Cr. (₹)
31.3.2020	Employees Compensation Expense A/c Dr.	20.00	
	To Employees Stock Option Outstanding A/c		20.00
	(Being Employees Compensation Expense recognized)		
	Profit and Loss A/c Dr.	20.00	
	To Employees Compensation Expense A/c		20.00
	(Being Employees Compensation Expense t/f to P&L A/c)		
31.3.2021	Employees Compensation Expense A/c Dr.	18.40	
	To Employees Stock Option Outstanding A/c		18.40
	(Being Employees Compensation Expense recognized)		
	Profit and Loss A/c Dr.	18.40	
	To Employees Compensation Expense A/c		18.40
	(Being Employees Compensation Expense t/f to P&L A/c)		
31.3.2022	Employees Compensation Expense A/c Dr.	13.44	
	To Employees Stock Option Outstanding A/c		13.44
	(Being Employees Compensation Expense recognized)		
	Profit and Loss A/c Dr.	13.44	
	To Employees Compensation Expense A/c		13.44
	(Being Employees Compensation Expense of the year t/f to P&L A/c)		

31.03.2023	Bank A/c (₹ 60 × 170000) Dr.	102.00	
	Employees Stock Option Outstanding A/c (₹ 30 × 170000) Dr.	51.00	
	To Equity Share Capital A/c (170000 × ₹ 10)		17.00
	To Securities Premium A/c (170000 × ₹ 80)		136.00
	(Being exercise of 170000 options at an exercise price of ₹ 60 each and an accounting value of ₹ 30 each)		
31.03.2023	Employees Stock Option Outstanding A/c (2800 × ₹ 30) Dr.	0.84	
	To General Reserve A/c		0.84
	(Being the fair value of options lapsed t/f to General Reserve)		

ILLUSTRATION 13

On 1.4.2019 AMLA, GILOY & TULSI (2) Ltd grants 100 options to each of its 2100 employees at ₹ 60 when the Market price is ₹ 100. The face value of equity share is ₹ 10 per share. The vesting date is 31st March, 2022 and the exercise date is 31st March, 2023. At the end of year 1, the company found that 100 employees had left and estimated the expected annual forfeitures rate at 10%. At the end of year 2, the company found that 80 employees had left and re–estimated the expected annual forfeitures rate at 5%. At the end of year 3, the company found that 192 employees had left. Only 1700 employees exercised their options on 31st March, 2023. Pass the necessary journal entries in the books of the company upto 31st March, 2023 (Assume that the Fair Value of a share issued under ESOP is ₹ 90 at 31st March of each year).

SOLUTION

STATEMENT SHOWING THE EXPENSE TO BE RECOGNISED IN EACH YEAR

Particulars	*Year 1*	*Year 2*	*Year 3*
A. No. of Employees entitled to Option	(2100 – 100) = 2000*90%*90% = 1620	(2000 – 80) = 1920*95% = 1824	(1920 – 192) = 1728
B. No. of Options per Employee	100	100	100
C. Fair Value of Option per Share	30	30	30
D. Total Fair Value of Option [A*B*C]	48,60,000	54,72,000	51,84,000
E. Total Expense till date [Total Fair Value* Expired Vesting Period/ Total Vesting Period]	= 48,60,000/3 = 16,20,000	= (54,72,000 × 2/3) = 36,48,000	= 51,84,000
F. Expenses already recognized during previous year(s)	0	= 16,20,000	= 36,48,000
G. Expenses to be recognized [E – F]	= 16,20,000	= 20,28,000	= 15,36,000

Value of Options Forfeited = [(1728 – 1700) × 100 × ₹ 30] = ₹ 84,000

JOURNAL [₹ in lakh]

Date	Particulars		Dr. (₹)	Cr. (₹)
31.3.2020	Employees Compensation Expense A/c	Dr.	16.20	
	To Employees Stock Option Outstanding A/c			16.20
	(Being Employees Compensation Expense recognized)			
	Profit and Loss A/c	Dr.	16.20	
	To Employees Compensation Expense A/c			16.20
	(Being Employees Compensation Expense t/f to P&L A/c)			
31.3.2021	Employees Compensation Expense A/c	Dr.	20.28	
	To Employees Stock Option Outstanding A/c			20.28
	(Being Employees Compensation Expense recognized)			
	Profit and Loss A/c	Dr.	20.28	
	To Employees Compensation Expense A/c			20.28
	(Being Employees Compensation Expense t/f to P&L A/c)			
31.3.2022	Employees Compensation Expense A/c	Dr.	15.36	
	To Employees Stock Option Outstanding A/c			15.36
	(Being Employees Compensation Expense recognized)			
	Profit and Loss A/c	Dr.	15.36	
	To Employees Compensation Expense A/c			15.36
	(Being Employees Compensation Expense of the year t/f to P&L A/c)			
31.03.2023	Bank A/c (₹ 60 × 170000)	Dr.	102.00	
	Employees Stock Option Outstanding A/c (₹ 30 × 170000)	Dr.	51.00	
	To Equity Share Capital A/c (170000 × ₹ 10)			17.00
	To Securities Premium A/c (170000 × ₹ 80)			136.00
	(Being exercise of 170000 options at an exercise price of ₹ 60 each and an accounting value of ₹ 30 each)			
31.03.2023	Employees Stock Option Outstanding A/c (2800 × ₹ 30)	Dr.	0.84	
	To General Reserve A/c			0.84
	(Being the fair value of options lapsed t/f to General Reserve)			

ILLUSTRATION 14

On 1.4.2019 AMLA, GILOY & TULSI (3) Ltd grants 100 options to each of its 2100 employees at ₹ 60 when the market price is ₹ 100 . The vesting date is 31st March,2022 and the exercise date is 31st March,2023. At the end of year 1,the company found that 100 employees had left and estimated the expected annual forfeitures rate at 10%. Fair Value of a share issued under ESOP was ₹ 90. At the end of year 2,the company found that 80 employees had left and re-estimated the expected annual forfeitures rate at 5%. Fair Value of a share issued under ESOP was ₹ 80. At the end of year 3,the company found that 192 employees had left. Fair Value of a share issued under ESOP was ₹ 70. Only 1700 employees exercised their options on 31st March,2023. The face value of equity share is ₹ 10 per share. Pass the necessary journal entries in the books of the company upto 31st March,2023.

SOLUTION

CALCULATION OF FAIR VALUE OF OPTION PER SHARE

Particulars	*Year 1 end*	*Year 2 end*	*Year 3 end*
A. Fair Value of a share issued under ESOP	90	80	70
B. Exercise Price per Share	60	60	60
C. Fair Value of Option per Share(A – B)	30	20	10

STATEMENT SHOWING THE EXPENSE TO BE RECOGNISED IN EACH YEAR

Particulars	*Year 1*	*Year 2*	*Year 3*
A. No. of Employees entitled to Option	(2100 – 100) = 2000*90%*90% = 1620	(2000 – 80) = 1920*95% = 1824	(1920 – 192) = 1728
B. No.of Options per Employee	100	100	100
C. Fair Value of Option per Share	30	20	10
D. Total Fair Value of Option [A*B*C]	48,60,000	36,48,000	17,28,000
E. Total Expense till date [Total Fair Value* Expired Vesting Period/ Total Vesting Period]	= 48,60,000/3 = 16,20,000	= (36,48,000 × 2/3) = 24,32,000	= 17,28,000
F. Expenses already recognized during previous year(s)	0	= 16,20,000	= 24,32,000
G. Expenses to be recognized(reversed) [E –F]	= 16,20,000	= 8,12,000	(7,04,000)

Value of Options Forfeited = [(1728 – 1700) × 100 × ₹ 10] = ₹ 28,000

JOURNAL [₹ in lakh]

Date	*Particulars*	*Dr. (₹)*	*Cr. (₹)*
31.3.2020	Employees Compensation Expense A/c Dr.	16.20	
	To Employees Stock Option Outstanding A/c		16.20
	(Being Employees Compensation Expense recognized)		
	Profit and Loss A/c Dr.	16.20	
	To Employees Compensation Expense A/c		16.20
	(Being Employees Compensation Expense t/f to P&L A/c)		
31.3.2021	Employees Compensation Expense A/c Dr.	8.12	
	To Employees Stock Option Outstanding A/c		8.12
	(Being Employees Compensation Expense recognized)		
	Profit and Loss A/c Dr.	8.12	
	To Employees Compensation Expense A/c		8.12

	(Being Employees Compensation Expense t/f to P&L A/c)		
31.03.2022	Employees Stock Option Outstanding A/c Dr.	7.04	
	To General Reserve A/c		7.04
	(Being Employees Compensation Expense de-recognized)		
31.03.2023	Bank A/c (₹ 60 × 170000) Dr.	102.00	
	Employees Stock Option Outstanding A/c (₹ 10 × 170000) Dr.	17.00	
	To Equity Share Capital A/c (170000 × ₹ 10)		17.00
	To Securities Premium A/c (170000 × ₹ 60)		102.00
	(Being exercise of 170000 options at an exercise price of ₹ 60 each and an accounting value of ₹ 10 each)		
31.03.2023	Employees Stock Option Outstanding A/c (2800 × ₹ 10) Dr.	0.28	
	To General Reserve A/c		0.28
	(Being the fair value of options lapsed t/f to General Reserve)		

ILLUSTRATION 15A

On 1.7.2019 AMLA, GILOY & TULSI (4) Ltd grants 100 options to each of its 2100 employees at ₹ 60 when the market price is ₹ 200. The vesting date is 31st March,2022 and the exercise date is 31st March, 2023. At the end of year 1,the company found that 100 employees had left. Fair Value of a share issued under ESOP was ₹ 93. At the end of year 2,the company found that 80 employees had left. Fair Value of a share issued under ESOP was ₹ 104. At the end of year 3, the company found that 192 employees had left. Fair Value of a share issued under ESOP was ₹ 80. Only 1700 employees exercised their options on 31st March, 2023. The face value of equity share is ₹ 10 per share. Calculate the compensation expense to be recognised each year and Value of Options Forfeited.

SOLUTION

CALCULATION OF FAIR VALUE OF OPTION PER SHARE

Particulars	*Year 1 end*	*Year 2 end*	*Year 3 end*
A. Fair Value of a share issued under ESOP	93	104	80
B. Exercise Price per Share	60	60	60
C. Fair Value of Option per Share(A – B)	33	44	20

STATEMENT SHOWING THE EXPENSE TO BE RECOGNISED IN EACH YEAR

Particulars	*Year 1*	*Year 2*	*Year 3*
A. No. of Employees entitled to Option	(2100–100)=2000	(2000–80)=1920	(1920–192)=1728
B. No. of Options per Employee	100	100	100
C. Fair Value of Option per Share	33	44	20
D. Total Fair Value of Option [A*B*C]	66,00,000	84,48,000	34,56,000

E. Total Expense till date [Total Fair Value* Expired Vesting Period/ Total Vesting Period]	= 66,00,000*9/33 = 18,00,000	= 84,48,000*21/33 = 53,76,000	34,56,000
F. Expenses already recognized during previous year(s)	0	= 18,00,000	= 53,76,000
G. Expenses to be recognized (reversed) [E – F]	= 18,00,000	= 35,76,000	(19,20,000)

Value of Options Forfeited = [(1728 – 1700) × 100 × ₹ 20] = ₹ 56,000

ILLUSTRATION 15B

On 1.7.2019 AMLA, GILOY & TULSI (4) Ltd grants 100 options to each of its 2100 employees at ₹ 60 when the market price is ₹ 200. The vesting date is 31st March, 2022 and the exercise date is 31st March, 2023. At the end of year 1, the company found that 100 employees had left and estimated the expected annual forfeitures rate at 10%. Fair Value of a share issued under ESOP was ₹ 93. At the end of year 2, the company found that 80 employees had left and re–estimated the expected annual forfeitures rate at 5%. Fair Value of a share issued under ESOP was ₹ 104. At the end of year 3, the company found that 192 employees had left. Fair Value of a share issued under ESOP was ₹ 80. Only 1700 employees exercised their options on 31st March, 2023. The face value of equity share is ₹ 10 per share. Pass the necessary journal entries in the books of the company upto 31st March, 2023.

SOLUTION

CALCULATION OF FAIR VALUE OF OPTION PER SHARE

Particulars	*Year 1 end*	*Year 2 end*	*Year 3 end*
A. Fair Value of a share issued under ESOP	93	104	80
B. Exercise Price per Share	60	60	60
C. Fair Value of Option per Share (A – B)	33	44	20

STATEMENT SHOWING THE EXPENSE TO BE RECOGNISED IN EACH YEAR

Particulars	*Year 1*	*Year 2*	*Year 3*
A. No. of Employees entitled to Option	(2100 – 100) = 2000*90%*90% = 1620	(2000 – 80) = 1920*95% = 1824	(1920 – 192) = 1728
B. No. of Options per Employee	100	100	100
C. Fair Value of Option per Share	33	44	20
D. Total Fair Value of Option [A*B*C]	53,46,000	80,25,600	34,56,000
E. Total Expense till date [Total Fair Value* Expired Vesting Period/Total Vesting Period]	= 53,46,000*9/33 = 14,58,000	= 80,25,600*21/33 = 51,07,200	34,56,000
F. Expenses already recognized during previous year(s)	0	= 14,58,000	= 51,07,200
G. Expenses to be recognized (reversed) [E –F]	= 14,58,000	= 36,49,200	(16,51,200)

Value of Options Forfeited = [(1728 – 1700) × 100 × ₹ 20] = ₹ 56,000

JOURNAL [₹ in lakh]

Date	Particulars		Dr. (₹)	Cr. (₹)
31.3.2020	Employees Compensation Expense A/c	Dr.	14.58	
	To Employees Stock Option Outstanding A/c			14.58
	(Being Employees Compensation Expense recognized)			
	Profit and Loss A/c	Dr.	14.58	
	To Employees Compensation Expense A/c			14.58
	(Being Employees Compensation Expense t/f to P&L A/c)			
31.3.2021	Employees Compensation Expense A/c	Dr.	36.492	
	To Employees Stock Option Outstanding A/c			36.492
	(Being Employees Compensation Expense recognized)			
	Profit and Loss A/c	Dr.	36.492	
	To Employees Compensation Expense A/c			36.492
	(Being Employees Compensation Expense t/f to P&L A/c)			
31.03.2022	Employees Stock Option Outstanding A/c	Dr.	16.512	
	To General Reserve A/c			16.512
	(Being Employees Compensation Expense de-recognized)			
31.03.2023	Bank A/c (₹ 60 × 170000)	Dr.	102.00	
	Employees Stock Option Outstanding A/c (₹ 20 × 170000)	Dr.	34.00	
	To Equity Share Capital A/c (170000 × ₹ 10)			17.00
	To Securities Premium A/c (170000 × ₹ 60)			119.00
	(Being exercise of 170000 options at an exercise price of ₹ 60 each and an accounting value of ₹ 20 each)			
31.03.2023	Employees Stock Option Outstanding A/c (2800 × ₹ 20)	Dr.	0.56	
	To General Reserve A/c			0.56
	(Being the fair value of options lapsed t/f to General Reserve)			

ILLUSTRATION 16

On 1st April 2019, CEE AMLA Limited granted 100 Stock Options to each of its 1000 employees @₹ 40 depending upon the employees at the time of vesting of options. Options would be exercisable within a year it is vested. The Fair Value of a share issued under ESOP was ₹ 60. These options will vest at the end of Year 1, if the earning of Virtual Limited is more than 15% *or* it will vest at the end of the year 2, if the average earnings of two years is more than 12% *or* lastly it will vest at the end of third year, if the average earnings of 3 years will be 9% *or* more. 6000 unvested options lapsed on 31st March 2020. 5,500 unvested options lapsed on 31st

March 2021 and finally 3,000 unvested options lapsed on 31st March 2022. The earnings of the company for the three years ended on 31st March, 2020; 2021 and 2022 are 13%, 9% and 7% respectively.

850 employees exercised their vested options within a year and remaining options were unexercised at the end of the contractual life. Pass the necessary journal entries.

SOLUTION

JOURNAL

Date	*Particulars*		*Dr. (₹)*	*Cr. (₹)*
31.3.2020	Employees Compensation Expenses A/c	Dr.	9,40,000	
	To ESOS Outstanding A/c			9,40,000
	(Being Compensation Expenses recognized in respect of Employee Stock Option, i.e. 94,000 options at a discount of ₹ 20 each)			
	P & L A/c	Dr.	9,40,000	
	To Employees Compensation Expense A/c			9,40,000
	(Being the t/f of ECE A/c)			
31.3.2021	Employees Compensation Expenses A/c	Dr.	2,40,000	
	To ESOS Outstanding A/c			2,40,000
	(Being Compensation Expenses recognized in ESOP A/c)			
	P & L A/c	Dr.	2,40,000	
	To Employees Compensation Expense A/c			2,40,000
	(Being the t/f of ECE A/c)			
31.3.2022	Employees Compensation Expenses A/c	Dr.	5,30,000	
	To ESOS Outstanding A/c			5,30,000
	(Being Compensation Expenses recognized in ESOP)			
	P & L A/c	Dr.	5,30,000	
	To Employees Compensation Expense A/c			5,30,000
	(Being the t/f of ECE A/c)			
2022–2023	Bank A/c [85,000 × ₹ 40]	Dr.	34,00,000	
	ESOS Outstanding A/c [85,000 × ₹ 20]	Dr.	17,00,000	
	To Equity Share Capital A/c [85,000 × ₹ 10]			8,50,000
	To Securities Premium A/c [85,000 × ₹ 50]			42,50,000
	(Being 85,000 Options exercised)			
31.03.2023	ESOS Outstanding A/c [500 × ₹ 20]	Dr.	10,000	
	To General Reserve A/c			10,000
	(Being ESOP outstanding A/c on lapse of 500 options t/f to General Reserve)			

Working Notes:

EXPENSE TO BE RECOGNISED EACH YEAR

Particulars	*Year 1*	*Year 2*	*Year 3*
Length of the expected vesting period (at the end of the year)	2 years	3 years	3 years
A. No. of Employees	1000	940	885
B. No. of Options per Employee	100	100	100
C. Total Number of Options [A*B]	100000	94000	88500
D. Unvested Options lapsed	6000	5500	3000
E. No. of Options expected to vest	94,000	88,500	85,500
F. Fair Value of An option	₹ 20	₹ 20	₹ 20
G. Total Fair Value of Option [E × F]	18,80,000	17,70,000	17,10,000
H. Total Expense accrued at the end of year (₹)	9,40,000 (C/2)	11,80,000 (C × 2/3)	17,10,000 (C × 3/3)
I. Expense recognised till the end of previous year (₹)	Nil	9,40,000	11,80,000
J. Expense to be recognized for the year (₹) [H – I]	9,40,000	2,40,000	5,30,000

19.0 ACCOUNTING TREATMENT OF EMPLOYEES' STOCK PURCHASE PLANS (ESPP)

Meaning	Under Employees' Stock Purchase Plans (ESPP), employees are given an option to subscribe to shares of employer in a public issue *or* otherwise. The exercise price is set at a specified rate of discount on the issue price/ market price on the date of exercise. ***For Example***, a company may offer specified number of shares to its employees at 25% discount on market price on grant date. **Note:** ESPP with option features is treated as ESOP. ***For Example***, If employees have the option to pay either 75% of market price of shares on grant date *or* on date of purchase, the plan is treated as ESOP rather than ESPP.
Accounting	**Step 1:** *Compute the Total Fair Value of ESPP as follows:* *= No. of Shares issued × (Fair Value of a Share – Issue Price)* **Step 2:** *Recognise Expense over the vesting period in the same way as ESOP.* **Note:** *The Fair Value of ESPP can be less than the discount due to post–vesting restrictions on transfers and similar other factors.*
Journal Entry to Record the Issue of Shares	Bank A/c Dr. [No. of Shares issued × Issue Price] Employees' Compensation Exp. A/c Dr.[No. of Shares issued × (Fair Value of Share – Issue Price] To Equity Share Capital A/c [No. of Shares issued × Nominal Value] To Securities Premium A/c [No. of Shares issued × (Fair Value of Share – Nominal Value]

ILLUSTRATION 17

On April 1, 2023, Tulsian [ESPP] Ltd. offered 100 shares to each of its 500 employees at 20% discount on market price on grant date. The employees are given a month to decide whether *or* not to accept the offer. The shares issued under the plan shall be subject to lock–in on transfers for three years from grant date. The market price of shares of the company on the grant date is ₹ 250 per share. Due to post–vesting restrictions on transfer, the fair value of shares issued under the plan is estimated at ₹ 240 per share.

On April 30, 2023, 400 employees accepted the offer and paid ₹ 200 per share purchased. Nominal value of each share is ₹ 10.

Required: Record the issue of shares in book of the company under the aforesaid plan.

SOLUTION

Fair value of ESPP = (400 × 100) × (₹ 240 – ₹ 200) = ₹ 16,00,000

Vesting period = One month, Expense recognised in 2023–2022 = ₹ 16,00,000

Date	*Particulars*	*L.F.*	*Dr. (₹)*	*Cr. (₹)*
30.04.2023	Bank A/c [40,000 × ₹ 200] Dr.		80,00,000	
	Employees' Compensation Exp. A/c [40,000 × ₹ 40] Dr.		16,00,000	
	To Share Capital A/c [40,000 × ₹ 10]			4,00,000
	To Securities Premium A/c [40,000 × ₹ 230]			92,00,000

20.0 INTRINSIC VALUE METHOD

Intrinsic Value (in case of a Listed Enterprise) is the difference between Quoted Market Price on Grant Date and Exercise Price of an option. Intrinsic Value (in case of an Unlisted Enterprise) is the difference between Value determined by an Independent Valuer on Grant Date and Exercise Price of an option . Under Intrinsic Value Method Employee Share–Based Payment Plans are accounted for in the same manner as under Fair Value Method with the following differences:

1. Intrinsic Value is used in place of Fair Value.
2. Securities Premium is = Market Price on Grant Date – Nominal Value

ILLUSTRATION 18

Tulsian (ESOP) Ltd provides you the following particulars in respect of stock options granted:

Grant Date	April 1,2019
Number of Employees covered	1050
Number of Options granted per Employee	50
Vesting Condition: Continuous employment for 3 years	
Nominal Value per share (₹)	100
Exercise Price per share (₹)	125
Market Price per share e (₹)	149
Vesting Date	March 31, 2022
Exercise Date	March 31, 2023
Fair Value of Option per share (₹)	30

Position on	31.03.2020	31.03.2021	31.03.2022
Estimated Annual Rate of Departure	2%	3%	
Number of Employees left	30	20	16

On 31st March, 2023 ,only 960 Employees exercised the option.

Required: Compute Expenses to be recognised in each year by (i) Fair Value Method (ii) Intrinsic Value Method and Prepare Employees Compensation Expense Account and ESOP Outstanding Account in books of the company by both of the Methods.

SOLUTION

(i) Fair Value Method

EXPENSE TO BE RECOGNISED IN EACH YEAR

Particulars	2019–2020	2020–2021	2021–2022
A. No. of Employees entitled to Option	= (1050 – 30)*0.98* 0.98 = 980 App	= (1050 – 30 – 20)* 0.97 =970	= (1050 – 30 – 20 – 16) = 984
B. No. of Options per Employee	50	50	50
C. Fair Value of Option per Share	30	30	30
D. Total Fair Value of Option [A*B*C]	14,70,000	14,55,000	14,76,000
E. Expense to be recognized [Total Fair Value* No. of years expired/ Vesting Period] – [Expenses already recognized during previous years]	= 14,70,000/3 = 4,90,000	= [14,55,000* 2/3] – [4,90,000] = 4,80,000	= 14,76,000 – 4,90,000 – 4,80,000 = 5,06,000

Value of Options Forfeited = [(984 – 960) × 50 × ₹ 30] = ₹ 36,000

Dr. **EMPLOYEES' COMPENSATION EXPENSE ACCOUNT** *Cr.*

Year	Particulars	₹	Year	Particulars	₹
31.03.2020	To ESOP Outstanding A/c	4,90,000	31.03.2020	By Profit & Loss A/c	4,90,000
31.03.2021	To ESOP Outstanding A/c	4,80,000	31.03.2021	By Profit & Loss A/c	4,80,000
31.03.2022	To ESOP Outstanding A/c	5,06,000	31.03.2022	By Profit & Loss A/c	5,06,000

Dr. **ESOP OUTSTANDING ACCOUNT** *Cr.*

Year	Particulars	₹	Year	Particulars	₹
31.03.2020	To Balance c/d	4,90,000	31.03.2020	By Employees' Compensation Exp. A/c	4,90,000
31.03.2021	To Balance c/d	9,70,000	01.04.2020	By Balance b/d	4,90,000
			31.03.2021	By Employees' Compensation Exp. A/c	4,80,000

		9,70,000			9,70,000
31.03.2022	To Balance c/d	14,76,000	01.04.2021	By Balance b/d	9,70,000
			31.03.2022	By Employees' Compensation Exp. A/c	5,06,000
		14,76,000			14,76,000
31.03.2023	To General Reserve (1,200 × 30)	36,000	01.04.2022	By Balance b/d (49,200 × 30)	14,76,000
	To Share Capital (48,000 × 100)	48,00,000	31.03.2023	By Bank (48,000 × 125)	60,00,000
	To Securities Premium (48,000 × 55)	26,40,000			
		74,76,000			74,76,000

Note: Securities Premium = (Exercise Price + Fair Value) – Nominal Value = (125 + 30) – 100 = 55

(ii) Intrinsic Value Method

EXPENSE TO BE RECOGNISED IN EACH YEAR

Particulars	*2019–2020*	*2020–2021*	*2021–2022*
A. No.of Employees entitled to Option	= (1050 – 30)*0.98* 0.98 = 980 App	= (1050 – 30 – 20)*0.97 =970	= (1050 – 30 – 20 – 16) = 984
B. No.of Options per Employee	50	50	50
C. Intrinsic Value of Option per Share	24	24	24
D. Total Intrinsic Value of Option [A*B*C]	11,76,000	11,64,000	11,80,800
E. Expense to be recognized [Total Intrinsic Value * No. of years expired/ Vesting Period] – [Expenses already recognized during previous years]	= 11,76,000/3 = 3,92,000	= [11,64,000* 2/3] – [3,92,000] = 3,84,000	= 11,80,800 – 3,92,000 – 3,84,000 = 4,04,800

Value of Options Forfeited = [(984 – 960) × 50 × ₹ 24] = ₹ .28,800

Dr. **EMPLOYEES' COMPENSATION EXPENSE ACCOUNT** *Cr.*

Year	*Particulars*	₹	*Year*	*Particulars*	₹
31.03.2020	To ESOP Outstanding A/c	3,92,000	31.03.2020	By Profit & Loss A/c	3,92,000
31.03.2021	To ESOP Outstanding A/c	3,84,000	31.03.2021	By Profit & Loss A/c	3,84,000
31.03.2022	To ESOP Outstanding A/c	4,04,800	31.03.2022	By Profit & Loss A/c	4,04,800

ESOP OUTSTANDING ACCOUNT

Dr. | | | | | Cr.

Year	Particulars	₹	Year	Particulars	₹
31.03.2020	To Balance c/d	3,92,000	31.03.2020	By Employees' Compensation Exp. A/c	3,92,000
		3,92,000			3,92,000
31.03.2021	To Balance c/d	7,76,000	01.04.2020	By Balance b/d	3,92,000
			31.03.2021	By Employees' Compensation Exp. A/c	3,84,000
		7,76,000			7,76,000
31.03.2022	To Balance c/d	11,80,800	01.04.2021	By Balance b/d	7,76,000
			31.03.2022	By Employees' Compensation Exp. A/c	4,04,800
		11,80,800			11,80,800
31.03.2023	To General Reserve (1,200 × 24)	28,800	01.04.2022	By Balance b/d (49,200 × 24)	11,80,800
	To Share Capital (48,000 × 100)	48,00,000	31.03.2023	By Bank A/c (48,000 × 125)	60,00,000
	To Securities Premium (48,000 × 49)	23,52,000			
		71,80,800			71,80,800

Working Note: *Calculation of Intrinsic Value and Securities Premium*

A. Intrinsic Value=Market Price on Grant Date – Exercise Price = ₹ 149 – ₹ 125 = 24

B. Securities Premium = Market Price on Grant Date – Nominal Value = ₹ 149 – ₹ 100 = ₹ 49

SOLVED PROBLEMS

PROBLEM 1

On 1.4.2019 TUSHAR(1) Ltd grants 100 options to each of its 2100 employees at ₹ 60 when the Market price is ₹ 10 . The vesting date is 31st March,2022 and the exercise date is 31st March,2023. Only 1700 employees exercised their options on 31st March,2023. The face value of equity share is ₹ 10 per share. Compute Expenses to be recognised in each year by Fair Value Method and the Value of Options Forfeited (Assume that the Fair Value of a share issued under ESOP is ₹ 90 at 31st March of each year).

SOLUTION

STATEMENT SHOWING THE EXPENSE TO BE RECOGNISED IN EACH YEAR

Particulars	Year 1	Year 2	Year 3
A. No. of Employees entitled to Option	2100	2100	2100

B. No. of Options per Employee	100	100	100
C. Fair Value of Option per Share	30	30	30
D. Total Fair Value of Option [A*B*C]	63,00,000	63,00,000	63,00,000
E. Total Expense till date [Total Fair Value* Expired Vesting Period/ Total Vesting Period]	= 63,00,0000/3 = 21,00,000	= (63,00,000 × 2/3) = 42,00,000	= 63,00,000
F. Expenses already recognized during previous year(s)	0	= 21,00,000	= 42,00,000
G. Expenses to be recognized[E–F]	= 21,00,000	= 21,00,000	= 21,00,000

Value of Options Forfeited = [(2100 – 1700) × 100 × ₹ 30] = ₹ 1,20,000

PROBLEM 2

On 1.4.2019 TUSHAR (2) Ltd grants 100 options to each of its 2100 employees at ₹ 60 when the Market price is ₹ 100 . The vesting date is 31st March,2022 and the exercise date is 31st March,2023. At the end of year 1,the company found that 100 employees had left. At the end of year 2,the company found that 80 employees had left. At the end of year 3,the company found that 192 employees had left. Only 1700 employees exercised their options on 31st March,2023. The face value of equity share is ₹ 10 per share. Compute Expenses to be recognised in each year by Fair Value Method and the Value of Options Forfeited (Assume that the Fair Value of a share issued under ESOP is ₹ 90 at 31st March of each year).

SOLUTION

STATEMENT SHOWING THE EXPENSE TO BE RECOGNISED IN EACH YEAR

Particulars	*Year 1*	*Year 2*	*Year 3*
A. No. of Employees entitled to Option	(2100 – 100) = 2000	(2000 – 80) = 1920	(1920 – 192) = 1728
B. No. of Options per Employee	100	100	100
C. Fair Value of Option per Share	30	30	30
D. Total Fair Value of Option [A*B*C]	60,00,000	57,60,000	51,84,000
E. Total Expense till date [Total Fair Value* Expired Vesting Period/ Total Vesting Period]	= 60,00,0000/3 = 20,00,000	= (57,60,000 × 2/3) = 38,40,000	= 51,84,000
F. Expenses already recognized during previous year(s)	0	= 20,00,000	= 38,40,000
G. Expenses to be recognized [E – F]	= 20,00,000	= 18,40,000	= 13,44,000

Value of Options Forfeited = [(1728 – 1700) × 100 × ₹ 30] = ₹ 84,000

PROBLEM 3

On 1.4.2019 TUSHAR (3) Ltd grants 100 options to each of its 2100 employees at ₹ 60 when the Market price is ₹ 100. The vesting date is 31st March, 2022 and the exercise date is 31st March, 2023. At the end of year 1,the company found that 100 employees had left and estimated the expected annual forfeitures rate at 10%. At the end of year 2,the company found that 80 employees had left and re–estimated the expected annual forfeitures rate at 5%. At the end of year 3, the company found that 192 employees had left. Only 1700 employees exercised their options on 31st March, 2023. The face value of equity share is ₹ 10 per share. Compute the Expenses to be recognised in each year by Fair Value Method and the Value of Options Forfeited (Assume that the Fair Value of a share issued under ESOP is ₹ 90 at 31st March of each year).

SOLUTION

STATEMENT SHOWING THE EXPENSE TO BE RECOGNISED IN EACH YEAR

Particulars	Year 1	Year 2	Year 3
A. No. of Employees entitled to Option	(2100 – 100) = 2000*90%* 90% = 1620	(2000 – 80) = 1920*95% = 1824	(1920 – 192) = 1728
B. No. of Options per Employee	100	100	100
C. Fair Value of Option per Share	30	30	30
D. Total Fair Value of Option [A*B*C]	48,60,000	54,72,000	51,84,000
E. Total Expense till date [Total Fair Value* Expired Vesting Period/ Total Vesting Period]	= 48,60,000/3 = 16,20,000	= (54,72,000 × 2/3) = 36,48,000	= 51,84,000
F. Expenses already recognized during previous year(s)	0	= 16,20,000	= 36,48,000
G. Expenses to be recognized [E – F]	= 16,20,000	= 20,28,000	= 15,36,000

Value of Options Forfeited = [(1728 – 1700) × 100 × ₹ 30] = ₹ 84,000

PROBLEM 4

On 1.4.2019 TUSHAR (4) Ltd grants 100 options to each of its 2100 employees at ₹ 60 when the Market price is ₹ 90. The face value of equity share is ₹ 10 per share. The vesting date is 31st March, 2022 and the exercise date is 31st March, 2023. At the end of year 1, the company found that 100 employees had left and estimated the expected annual forfeitures rate at 10%. At the end of year 2,the company found that the actual annual forfeitures rate was at 4% and re–estimated the expected annual forfeitures rate at 5%. At the end of year 3,the company found that the actual annual forfeitures rate was at 10%. Only 1700 employees exercised their options on 31st March, 2023. Compute the Expenses to be recognised in each year by Fair Value Method and the Value of Options Forfeited (Assume that the Fair Value of a share issued under ESOP is ₹ 90 at 31st March of each year).

SOLUTION

STATEMENT SHOWING THE EXPENSE TO BE RECOGNISED IN EACH YEAR

Particulars	Year 1	Year 2	Year 3
A. No. of Employees entitled to Option	(2100–100) =2000*90%*90% =1620	(2000–4%) =1920*95%=1824	(1920–10%) =1728
B. No. of Options per Employee	100	100	100
C. Fair Value of Option per Share	30	30	30

D. Total Fair Value of Option [A*B*C]	48,60,000	54,72,000	51,84,000
E. Total Expense till date [Total Fair Value* Expired Vesting Period/ Total Vesting Period]	= 48,60,000/3 = 16,20,000	= (54,72,000 × 2/3) = 36,48,000	= 51,84,000
F. Expenses already recognized during previous year(s)	0	= 16,20,000	= 36,48,000
G. Expenses to be recognized [E –F]	= 16,20,000	= 20,28,000	= 15,36,000

Value of Options Forfeited = [(1728 – 1700) × 100 × ₹ 30] = ₹ 84,000

PROBLEM 5

On 1.4.2019 TUSHAR(5) Ltd grants 100 options to each of its 2100 employees at ₹ 60 when the Market price is ₹ 100. The face value of equity share is ₹ 10 per share. The vesting date is 31st March, 2022 and the exercise date is 31st March, 2023. At the end of year 1, the company found that 100 employees had left and estimated the expected annual forfeitures rate at 10%. Earning per Share and Price–Earning Ratio were ₹ 18 and 5 respectively. At the end of year 2, the company found that the actual annual forfeitures rate was at 4% and re–estimated the expected annual forfeitures rate at 5%. Earning per Share and Price –Earning Ratio were ₹ 20 and 4 respectively. At the end of year 3, the company found that the actual annual forfeitures rate was at 10%. Earning per Share and Price –Earning Ratio were ₹ 14 and 5 respectively. Only 1700 employees exercised their options on 31st March, 2023. Determine the compensation expense to be recognised each year and Value of Options Forfeited.

SOLUTION

CALCULATION OF FAIR VALUE OF OPTION PER SHARE

Particulars	*Year 1 end*	*Year 2 end*	*Year 3 end*
A. Earning per Share	18	20	14
B. Price –Earning Ratio	5	4	5
C. Market Price per Share(A x B)	90	80	70
D. Exercise Price per Share	60	60	60
E. Fair Value of Option per Share(C – D)	30	20	10

STATEMENT SHOWING THE EXPENSE TO BE RECOGNISED IN EACH YEAR

Particulars	*Year 1*	*Year 2*	*Year 3*
A. No. of Employees entitled to Option	(2100–100) =2000*90%*90% =1620	(2000–4%) =1920*95%=1824	(1920–10%) =1728
B. No. of Options per Employee	100	100	100
C. Fair Value of Option per Share	30	20	10
D. Total Fair Value of Option [A*B*C]	48,60,000	36,48,000	17,28,000
E. Total Expense till date [Total Fair Value* Expired Vesting Period/ Total Vesting Period]	= 48,60,000/3 = 16,20,000	= (36,48,000 × 2/3) = 24,32,000	= 17,28,000

F. Expenses already recognized during previous year(s)	0	= 16,20,000	= 24,32,000
G. Expenses to be recognized(reversed) [E –F]	= 16,20,000	= 8,12,000	(7,04,000)

Value of Options Forfeited = [(1728 – 1700) × 100 × ₹ 10] = ₹ 28,000

PROBLEM 6

On 1.4.2020 Sheena Ltd grants 2 options to each of its 500 employees at ₹ 60 when the Market price is ₹ 90. The vesting period is two and a half years. The maximum exercise period is one year. Only 450 employees exercised their options on 30.9.2023. The face value of equity share is ₹ 10 per share. Pass the necessary journal entries in the books of the company upto 30th Sept, 2023.

SOLUTION

JOURNAL OF SHEENA LTD.

Date	*Particulars*		*Dr. (₹)*	*Cr. (₹)*
31.3.2021	Employees Compensation Expense A/c	Dr.	12,000	
	To Employees Stock Option Outstanding A/c			12,000
	(Being compensation expense recognized in respect of 1,000 options granted to employees at discount of ₹ 30 each, amortized on straight line basis over 2½ years)			
	Profit and Loss A/c	Dr.	12,000	
	To Employees Compensation Expense A/c			12,000
	(Being employees compensation expense of the year t/f to P&L A/c)			
31.3.2022	Employees Compensation Expense A/c	Dr.	12,000	
	To Employees Stock Option Outstanding A/c			12,000
	(Being compensation expense recognized in respect of 1,000 options granted to employees at discount of ₹ 30 each, amortized on straight line basis over 2½ years)			
	Profit and Loss A/c	Dr.	12,000	
	To Employees Compensation Expense Account			12,000
	(Being employees compensation expense of the year t/f to P&L A/c)			
31.3.2023	Employees Compensation Expense A/c	Dr.	6,000	
	To Employees Stock Option Outstanding A/c			6,000
	(Being balance of compensation expense amortized ₹ 30,000 *less* ₹ 24,000)			
	Profit and Loss A/c	Dr.	6,000	
	To Employees Compensation Expense A/c			6,000
	(Being employees compensation expense of the year t/f to P&L A/c)			

30.09.2023	Bank A/c (₹ 60 × 900)	Dr.	54,000	
	Employees Stock Option Outstanding A/c (₹ 30 × 900)	Dr.	27,000	
	To Equity Share Capital A/c (900 × ₹ 10)			9,000
	To Securities Premium A/c (900 × ₹ 80)			72,000
	(Being exercise of 900 options at an exercise price of ₹ 60 each and an accounting value of ₹ .30 each)			
30.09.2023	Employees Stock Option Outstanding A/c (100 × ₹ 30)	Dr.	3,000	
	To General Reserve A/c			3,000
	(Being the fair value of options lapsed t/f to General Reserve)			

Working Notes:

(i) Total Employees Compensation Expense = 500 × 2 (₹ 90 – ₹ 60) = ₹ 30,000

(ii) Employees Compensation Expense has been written off during 2½ years on straight line basis as under:

I year = ₹ 30,000 × 1/2.5 = ₹ 12,000

II year = (₹ 30,000 × 2/2.5) – ₹ 12,000 = ₹ 12,000

III year = (₹ 30,000 – ₹ 24,000) = ₹ 6,000

PROBLEM 7

On 1st April 2023, a company offered 100 shares to each of its 500 employees at ₹ 50 per share. The employees are given a month to decide whether *or* not to accept the offer. The shares issued under the plan (ESPP) shall be subject to lock in one transfers for three years from grant date. The market price of shares of the company on the grant date is ₹ 60 per share. Due to post–vesting restrictions on transfer, the fair value of shares issued under the plan is estimated at ₹ 56 per share.

On 30th April, 2023, 400 employees accepted the offer and paid ₹ 50 per share purchased. Nominal value of each share is ₹ 10.

Required: Record the issue of shares in the books of the company under the aforesaid plan.

SOLUTION

Fair value of an ESPP = ₹ 56 – ₹ 50 = ₹ 6

Number of shares issued = 400 employees × 100 shares per employee = 40,000 shares

Fair value of ESPP with be recognized as expenses in the year 2023–2022

= 40,000 shares × ₹ 6 = ₹ 2,40,000.

Vesting period = 1 month

Expenses recognized in 31.03.2022 = ₹ 2,40,000

JOURNAL

Date	Particulars		L.F.	Dr. (₹)	Cr. (₹)
30.04.2023	Bank [40,000 shares × ₹ 50]	Dr.		20,00,000	
	Employees' Compensation Expenses A/c	Dr.		2,40,000	
	To Share Capital A/c (40,000 shares × ₹ 10)				4,00,000
	To Securities Premium A/c (40,000 shares × ₹ 46)				18,40,000
	(Being shares issued under ESPP @ ₹ 50)				

VERY SHORT ANSWER TYPE QUESTIONS

1. Briefly explain the following: [1/2 Mark each]
   (a) Employee Stock Option Plan [ESOP]
   (b) Employee Stock Purchase Plan [ESPP]
   (c) Stock Appreciation Rights [SARs]
   (d) Grant,Vesting, Exercise
   (e) Grant Date, Vesting Date, Exercise Date
   (f) Vesting Period, Exercise Period
   (g) Minimum Gap
2. How are the following computed?
   (a) Expected No. of Employees as at vesting Date
   (b) Total Number of Options expected to vest
   (c) Fair Value of Option per Share
   (d) Total Fair Value of Options
   (e) Employees Compensation Expense to be recognized
   (f) Value of Options Forfeited
3. What are the various forms of Employee Share–based Payments?
4. What is Objective and Importance of Employee Share–based Payments?

VERY SHORT ANSWER TYPE PRACTICAL QUESTIONS

1. As at 31.03.2020,X Ltd. desires to know the expected No. of Employees as at Vesting Date i.e. 31.03.2022 and provides you the following information:

Number of Employees as at April 1,2019	4200
Number of Employees actually left during 2019 – 2020	200
No. of Employees expected to leave during 2020 – 2021	10%
No. of Employees expected to leave during 2021– 2022	10%
No. of Employees expected as at 31.03.2022	?

[**Ans** 3240]

2. As at 31.03.2021,X Ltd. desires to know the expected No. of Employees as at Vesting Date i.e. 31.03.2022 and provides you the following information:

Number of Employees as at April 1,2019	4200
Number of Employees actually left during 2019–2020	200
Number of Employees actually left during 2020–2021	160
No. of Employees expected to leave during 2021–2022	5%
Expected No. of Employees as at 31.03.2022	?

[Ans 3648]

3. As at 31.03.2022,X Ltd. desires to know the No. of Employees as at Vesting Date i.e. 31.03.2022 and provides you the following information:

Number of Employees as at April 1,2019	4200
Number of Employees actually left during 2019–2020	200
Number of Employees actually left during 2020–2021	160
Number of Employees actually left during 2021–2022	384
No. of Employees as at 31.03.2022	?

[Ans 3456]

4. On 1.4.2019 AMLA (1) Ltd grants 100 options to each of its 4200 employees at ₹ 60 when the Market price is ₹ 90. The face value of equity share is ₹ 10 per share. The vesting date is 31st March,2022 and the exercise date is 31st March,2023. At the end of year 1,the company found that 200 employees had left and estimated the expected annual forfeitures rate at 10%. At the end of year 2,the company found that 160 employees had left and re–estimated the expected annual forfeitures rate at 5%. At the end of year 3,the company found that 384 employees had left. Compute Total Number of Options expected to vest each year.

[Ans 3,24,000,3,64,800,3,45,600]

5. On 1.4.2019 AMLA (2) Ltd grants 100 options to each of its 4200 employees at ₹ 60 (Face Value ₹ 10)depending upon the employment of the employees at the time of vesting of options. The Market Price is ₹ 90. The vesting date is 31st March,2022 and the exercise date is 31st March,2023. 96,000 unvested options lapsed on 31st March, 2020. 55,200 unvested options lapsed on 31st March, 2021 and lastly 74,400 unvested options lapsed on 31st March, 2022. Compute Total Number of Options expected to vest each year.

[Ans 3,24,000,2,68,800,1,94,400]

6A. On 1.4.2019 GILOY (1) Ltd grants 100 options to each of its 4200 employees at ₹ 60 when the Market price is ₹ 90. The face value of equity share is ₹ 10 per share. The vesting date is 31st March, 2022 and the exercise date is 31st March,2023.

	31.03.2020	*31.03.2021*	*31.03.2022*
Expected No. of Employees as at 31.03.2022	3240	3648	3456
Market Price per share (₹)	100	90	80
Fair Value of a share issued under ESOP (₹)	90	80	70

Required: Compute Total Fair Value of Options at the end of each year.

[Ans ₹ 97,20,000,₹ 72,96,000,₹ 34,56,000]

6B. On 1.4.2019 GILOY (2) Ltd grants 100 options to each of its 4200 employees at ₹ 60 when the Market price is ₹ 90. The face value of equity share is ₹ 10 per share. The vesting date is 31st March,2022 and the exercise date is 31st March,2023.

	31.03.2020	31.03.2021	31.03.2022
Expected No. of Employees as at 31.03.2022	3240	3648	3456
Market Price per share (₹)	100	90	80
Fair Value of an Option under ESOP (₹)	30	20	10

Required: Compute Total Fair Value of Options at the end of each year.

[**Ans** ₹ 97,20,000,₹ 72,96,000,₹ 34,56,000]

7. On 1.4.2019 GILOY (1) Ltd grants 100 options to each of its 4200 employees at ₹ 60 when the Market price is ₹ 90. The face value of equity share is ₹ 10 per share. The vesting date is 31st March,2022 and the exercise date is 31st March,2023.

	31.03.2020	31.03.2021	31.03.2022
Expected No. of Employees as at 31.03.2022	3240	3648	3456
Earning per Share	18	20	14
Price –Earning Ratio	5	4	5

Required: Compute Total Fair Value of Options at the end of each year.

[**Ans** ₹ 97,20,000,₹ 72,96,000,₹ 34,56,000]

8. TULSI Ltd.(1) provides the following information:

Total Fair Value of Options as at 31.03.2020	₹ 96,22,800
Total Fair Value of Options as at 31.03.2021	₹ 72,17,100
Total Fair Value of Options as at 31.03.2022	₹ 34,56,000
Vesting Date	March 31, 2022
Exercise Date	March 31, 2023

Required: Compute Expenses to be recognised at the end of each year by Fair Value Method if Grant Date is (i) 1.4.2019 (ii) 1.7.2019 (iii) 1.10.2019 (iv) 1.1.2020
[**Ans** (i) ₹ 32,07,600,₹ 16,03,800, (₹ 13,55,400), (ii) ₹ 26,24,400, ₹ 19,68,300,(₹ 11,36,700)(iii)₹ 19,24,560,₹ 24,05,700, (₹ 8,74,260), (iv)₹ 10,69,200,₹ 29,40,300,(₹ 5,53,500)]

9. No of Employees covered 4200, No of Options granted per Employee 100, Exercise Date March 31, 2023. Fair Value of Option per Share as at 31st March,2023: ₹ 10. No. of Employees as at 31.03.2022:3456. Only 3400 employees exercised their options on 31st March,2023. Compute the Value of Options Forfeited.

[**Ans** ₹ 56,000]

10. CEE AMLA Ltd. provides the following information:

Grant Date	April 1, 2019
Total Fair Value of Options as at 31.03.2020	₹ 37,60,000
Total Fair Value of Options as at 31.03.2021	₹ 35,40,000
Total Fair Value of Options as at 31.03.2022	₹ 34,20,000
These options will vest at the end of Year 1, if the earning is more than 15% *or* it will vest at the end of the year 2, if the average earnings of two years is more than 12% *or* lastly it will vest at the end of third year, if the average earnings of 3 years will be 9% *or* more. The earnings of the company for the three years ended on 31st March, 2020; 2021 and 2022 are 13%, 9% and 7% respectively.	

Required: Compute Expenses to be recognised at the end of each year by Fair Value Method.

[Ans ₹ 18,80,000, ₹ 4,80,000, ₹ 10,60,000]

LONG ANSWER TYPE PRACTICAL QUESTIONS

1. On 1.4.2019 TULSI Ltd. (2) Ltd grants 100 options to each of its 4200 employees at ₹ 60 when the market price is ₹ 100. The vesting date is 31st March, 2022 and the exercise date is 31st March,2023. At the end of year 1, the company found that 200 employees had left and estimated the expected annual forfeitures rate at 10%. Fair Value of a share issued under ESOP was ₹ 90. At the end of year 2,the company found that 160 employees had left and re–estimated the expected annual forfeitures rate at 5%. Fair Value of a share issued under ESOP was ₹ 80. At the end of year 3,the company found that 384 employees had left. Fair Value of a share issued under ESOP was ₹ 70. Only 3400 employees exercised their options on 31st March,2023. The face value of equity share is ₹ 10 per share. Determine the compensation expense to be recognised each year and Value of Options Forfeited.

   [Ans ₹ 32,40,000,₹ 16,24,000,(₹ 14,08,000), Forfeited ₹ 56,000]

2. On 1.4.2019 TULSI Ltd. (3) Ltd grants 100 options to each of its 4200 employees at ₹ 60 (Face Value ₹ 10) depending upon the employment of the employees at the time of vesting of options. The Market Price is ₹ 100. The vesting date is 31st March, 2022 and the exercise date is 31st March,2023. 96,000 unvested options lapsed on 31st March, 2020 when Fair Value of a share issued under ESOP was ₹ 90. 55,200 unvested options lapsed on 31st March, 2021 when Fair Value of a share issued under ESOP was ₹ 80. and lastly 74,400 unvested options lapsed on 31st March, 2022 when Fair Value of a share issued under ESOP was ₹ 70. Determine the compensation expense to be recognised each year.

   [Ans ₹ 32,40,000,₹ 3,44,000, (₹ 16,40,000)]

3. On 1.4.2019 AMLA, GILOY & TULSI (1) Ltd grants 100 options to each of its 4200 employees at ₹ 60 when the Market price is ₹ 100. The vesting date is 31st March, 2022 and the exercise date is 31st March, 2023. At the end of year 1, the company found that 200 employees had left. At the end of year 2, the company found that 160 employees had left. At the end of year 3, the company found that 384 employees had left. Only 3400 employees exercised their options on 31st March, 2023. The face value of equity share is ₹ 10 per share. Pass the necessary journal entries in the books of the company upto 31st March, 2023 (Assume that the Fair Value of a share issued under ESOP is ₹ 90 at 31st March of each year).

   [Ans ₹ 40,00,000,₹ 36,80,000,₹ 26,88,000 Forfeited ₹ 1,68,000]

4. On 1.4.2019 AMLA, GILOY & TULSI (2) Ltd grants 100 options to each of its 4200 employees at ₹ 60 when the Market price is ₹ 100. The face value of equity share is ₹ 10 per share. The vesting date is 31st March, 2022 and the exercise date is 31st March, 2023. At the end of year 1, the company found that 200 employees had left and estimated the expected annual forfeitures rate at 10%. At the end of year 2, the company found that 160 employees had left and re–estimated the expected annual forfeitures rate at 5%. At the end of year 3, the company found that 384 employees had left. Only 3400 employees exercised their options on 31st March,2023. Pass the necessary journal entries in the books of the company upto 31st March, 2023 (Assume that the Fair Value of a share issued under ESOP is ₹ 90 at 31st March of each year).

   [Ans ₹ 32,40,000,₹ 40,56,000,₹ 30,72,000 Forfeited ₹ 1,68,000]

5. On 1.4.2019 AMLA, GILOY & TULSI (3) Ltd grants 100 options to each of its 4200 employees at ₹ 60 when the market price is ₹ 100 . The vesting date is 31st March, 2022

and the exercise date is 31st March,2023. At the end of year 1,the company found that 200 employees had left and estimated the expected annual forfeitures rate at 10%. Fair Value of a share issued under ESOP was ₹ 90. At the end of year 2, the company found that 80 employees had left and re–estimated the expected annual forfeitures rate at 5%. Fair Value of a share issued under ESOP was ₹ 80. At the end of year 3, the company found that 384 employees had left. Fair Value of a share issued under ESOP was ₹ 70. Only 3400 employees exercised their options on 31st March, 2023. The face value of equity share is ₹ 10 per share. Pass the necessary journal entries in the books of the company upto 31st March, 2023.

[**Ans** ₹ 32,40,000,₹ 16,24,000, (₹ 14,08,000), Forfeited ₹ 56,000]

6A. On 1.7.2019 AMLA, GILOY & TULSI (4) Ltd grants 100 options to each of its 4200 employees at ₹ 60 when the market price is ₹ 200. The vesting date is 31st March, 2022 and the exercise date is 31st March, 2023. At the end of year 1, the company found that 200 employees had left. Fair Value of a share issued under ESOP was ₹ 93. At the end of year 2, the company found that 160 employees had left. Fair Value of a share issued under ESOP was ₹ 104. At the end of year 3, the company found that 384 employees had left. Fair Value of a share issued under ESOP was ₹ 80. Only 3400 employees exercised their options on 31st March, 2023. The face value of equity share is ₹ 10 per share. Calculate the compensation expense to be recognised each year and Value of Options Forfeited.

[**Ans** ₹ 36,00,000, ₹ 71,52,000, (₹ 38,40,000), Forfeited ₹ 1,12,000]

6B. On 1.7.2019 AMLA, GILOY & TULSI (4) Ltd grants 100 options to each of its 4200 employees at ₹ 60 when the market price is ₹ 200. The vesting date is 31st March, 2022 and the exercise date is 31st March, 2023. At the end of year 1, the company found that 200 employees had left and estimated the expected annual forfeitures rate at 10%. Fair Value of a share issued under ESOP was ₹ 93. At the end of year 2, the company found that 160 employees had left and re–estimated the expected annual forfeitures rate at 5%. Fair Value of a share issued under ESOP was ₹ 104. At the end of year 3, the company found that 384 employees had left. Fair Value of a share issued under ESOP was ₹ 80. Only 3400 employees exercised their options on 31st March, 2023. The face value of equity share is ₹ 10 per share. Pass the necessary journal entries in the books of the company upto 31st March, 2023.

[**Ans** ₹ 29,16,000, ₹ 72,98,400, (₹ 33,02,400), Forfeited ₹ 1,12,000]

7. On 1st April 2019, CEE AMLA Limited granted 100 Stock Options to each of its 2000 employees @₹ 40 depending upon the employees at the time of vesting of options. Options would be exercisable within a year it is vested. The Fair Value of a share issued under ESOP was ₹ 60. These options will vest at the end of Year 1, if the earning is more than 15% *or* it will vest at the end of the year 2, if the average earnings of two years is more than 12% *or* lastly it will vest at the end of third year, if the average earnings of 3 years will be 9% *or* more. 12000 unvested options lapsed on 31st March 2020. 11,000 unvested options lapsed on 31st March 2021 and finally 6,000 unvested options lapsed on 31st March 2022. The earnings of the company for the three years ended on 31st March, 2020; 2021 and 2022 are 13%, 9% and 7% respectively.

1700 employees exercised their vested options within a year and remaining options were unexercised at the end of the contractual life. Pass the necessary journal entries.

[**Ans** ₹ 18,80,000, ₹ 4,80,000, ₹ 10,60,000, Forfeited ₹ 20,000]

8. On April 1, 2023, Tulsian [ESPP] Ltd. offered 100 shares to each of its 1000 employees at 20% discount on market price on grant date. The employees are given a month to decide whether *or* not to accept the offer. The shares issued under the plan shall be subject to lock–in on transfers for three years from grant date. The market price of shares of the company on the grant date is ₹ 250 per share. Due to post–vesting restrictions on transfer, the fair value of shares issued under the plan is estimated at ₹ 240 per share.

On April 30, 2023, 800 employees accepted the offer and paid ₹ 200 per share purchased. Nominal value of each share is ₹ 10.

Required: Record the issue of shares in book of the company under the aforesaid plan.

[**Ans** Expense recognised in 2023–2024 ₹ 32,00,000]

9. Tulsian (ESOP) Ltd provides you the following particulars in respect of stock options granted:

Grant Date	April 1,2019
Number of Employees covered	2100
Number of Options granted per Employee	50
Vesting Condition: Continuous employment for 3 years	
Nominal Value per share (₹)	100
Exercise Price per share (₹)	125
Market Price per share e (₹)	149
Vesting Date	March 31, 2022
Exercise Date	March 31, 2023
Fair Value of Option per share (₹)	30

Position on	***31.03.2020***	***31.03.2021***	***31.03.2022***
Estimated Annual Rate of Departure	2%	3%	
Number of Employees left	59	41	32

On 31st March, 2023 ,only 1920 Employees exercised the option.

Required: Compute Expenses to be recognised in each year by Fair Value Method and Prepare Employees Compensation Expense Account and ESOP Outstanding Account in books of the company.

[**Ans** ₹ 9,80,000, ₹ 9,60,000, ₹ 10,12,000, Forfeited ₹ 72,000]

10. On 1.4.2020 Sheena Ltd grants 2 options to each of its 1000 employees at ₹ 60 when the Market price is ₹ 90. The vesting period is two and a half years. The maximum exercise period is one year. Only 900 employees exercised their options on 30.9.2023. The face value of equity share is ₹ 10 per share. Pass the necessary journal entries in the books of the company upto 30th Sept, 2023.

[**Ans** ₹ 24,000, ₹ 24,000, ₹ 12,000, Forfeited ₹ 6,000]

11. On 1st April 2023, a company offered 100 shares to each of its 1000 employees at ₹ 50 per share. The employees are given a month to decide whether *or* not to accept the offer. The shares issued under the plan (ESPP) shall be subject to lock in one transfers for three years from grant date. The market price of shares of the company on the grant date is ₹ 60 per share. Due to post–vesting restrictions on transfer, the fair value of shares issued under the plan is estimated at ₹ 56 per share.

On 30th April, 2023, 800 employees accepted the offer and paid ₹ 50 per share purchased. Nominal value of each share is ₹ 10.

Required: Record the issue of shares in the books of the company under the aforesaid plan.

[Ans Expense recognised in 2023–2024 ₹ 4,80,000]

8 FINANCIAL STATEMENTS OF A COMPANY

LEARNING OBJECTIVES

After studying this chapter, you should be able to understand:

◇ Meaning of Financial Statements
◇ Legal Requirements
◇ Contents and Forms
◇ Form of Preparing a Statement of Profit and Loss of a Company
◇ Accounting Treatment of Provision for Tax
◇ Dividend
◇ Option to Transfer to Reserves
◇ Declaration of Dividend out of Reserves
◇ Capital Reserve
◇ Interim Dividend
◇ Final Dividend
◇ Payment of Dividend
◇ Unpaid/Unclaimed Dividend
◇ Right to dividend, rights shares and bonus shares to be held in abeyance pending registration of transfer of shares
◇ Punishment for failure to distribute dividends
◇ Payment of Dividend on Partly Paidup Shares
◇ Dividend on Preference Shares
◇ Capitalisation of Profits
◇ Accounting Treatment of Dividend, Transfer to Reserves, Bonus, Etc.
◇ Form of Preparing a Balance Sheet of a Company
◇ Vertical Form of Summarised Balance Sheet of a Company
◇ Vertical Form of Detailed Balance Sheet of a Company
◇ Distinction Between a Company's Balance Sheet and Firm's Balance Sheet
◇ Statement of Changes in Equity

1.0 MEANING OF FINANCIAL STATEMENTS AND FINANCIAL YEAR

GENERAL MEANING OF FINANCIAL STATEMENTS

The financial statements are historical documents which show the organised summaries of detailed information about the financial performance of an accounting entity for an accounting period and financial position at the end of an accounting period.

There are two basic financial statements, viz., Income statement and Balance Sheet.

1. **An Income Statement** is a Statement of Revenue from Operations, Other Incomes and Expenses during a given accounting period. It indicates the Financial Performance of an enterprise for an accounting period.
2. **A Balance Sheet** is a Statement of Assets (Current and Non-Current), Liabilities (Current and Non-Current) and Equity (i.e., Shareholders' Funds) indicating the Financial Position of an enterprise at a given date.

LEGAL MEANING OF FINANCIAL STATEMENTS

As per Section 2(40) of the Companies Act, 2013, Financial Statements include-

(i) a Balance Sheet as at the end of the financial year;

(ii) a Profit and Loss Account, *or* in the case of a company carrying on any activity not for profit, an Income and Expenditure Account for the financial year;

(iii) Cash Flow Statement for the financial year;

(iv) a Statement of Changes in Equity, if applicable; and

(v) any explanatory note annexed to, *or* forming part of, any document referred to in sub-clause (i) to (iv):

Provided that the Financial Statements, with respect to One Person Company(OPC), Small Company and Dormant Company, may not include the Cash Flow Statement.

LEGAL MEANING OF FINANCIAL YEAR

As per Section 2(41) of the Companies Act, 2013, Financial Year in relation to any company or body corporate, means the period ending on the 31st day of March every year, and where it has been incorporated on or after the 1st day of January of a year, the period ending on the 31st day of March of the following year, in respect whereof financial statement of the company or body corporate is made up: **Examples:**

(i) The financial year of X Ltd incorporated on 31st December 2022 will end on 31st March,2022.

(ii) The financial year of X Ltd incorporated on 1st January 2022 will end on 31st March,2023.

2.0 LEGAL REQUIREMENTS

1. **Company's Duty to prepare Books of Account, etc., [Sec 128 (1)]**

   Every company must prepare and keep at its registered office books of account and other relevant books and papers and financial statement for every financial year which give a true and fair view of the state of the affairs of the company, including that of its branch office *or* offices, if any, and explain the transactions effected both at the registered office and its branches.
2. **On Accrual Basis:** Such books must be kept on accrual basis and according to the double entry system of accounting [Sec 128(1)].
3. **At Place other than Registered Office:** All *or* any of the books of account aforesaid and other relevant papers may be kept at such other place in India as the Board of Directors

may decide and where such a decision is taken, the company must, within 7 days thereof, file with the Registrar a notice in writing giving the full address of that other place [Proviso to Sec 128(1)].

4. **In Electronic Mode:** The company may keep such books of account *or* other relevant papers in electronic mode in such manner as may be prescribed. [Proviso to Sec 128(1)]

5. **In case of Branch Books of Account:** Where a company has a branch office in India *or* outside India, it shall be deemed to have complied with the provisions of the Act, if proper books of account relating to the transactions effected at the branch office are kept at that office and proper summarized returns periodically are sent by the branch office to the company at its registered office *or* such other place where accounts are kept. [Sec 128 (2)]

6. **Director's Right to Inspect:** The books of account and other books and papers maintained by the company within India shall be open for inspection at the registered office of the company *or* at such other place in India by any director during business hours, and in the case of financial information, if any, maintained outside the country, copies of such financial information shall be maintained and produced for inspection by any director subject to such conditions as may be prescribed.

   However, the inspection in respect of any subsidiary of the company shall be done only by the person authorised in this behalf by a resolution of the Board of Directors. [Sec 128 (3)]

   Employees' Duty to give Assistance: Where an inspection is made by any director, the officers and other employees of the company must give to the person making such inspection all assistance in connection with the inspection which the company may reasonably be expected to give. [Sec 128 (4)]

7. **Preservation of Books etc:** The books of account of every company relating to a period of atleast 8 financial years immediately preceding a financial year, *or* where the company had been in existence for a period *less* than 8 years, in respect of all the preceding years together with the vouchers relevant to any entry in such books of account shall be kept in good order.

   However, where an investigation has been ordered in respect of the company under Chapter XIV, the Central Government may direct that the books of account may be kept for such longer period as it may deem fit [Sec 128 (5)].

8. **Penalty:** In case of contravention of Sec 128, Managing Director, Whole-time Director in charge of finance, Chief Financial Officer *or* any other person charged by the Board with the duty of complying with the provisions of Sec. 128, shall be punishable with imprisonment for a term which may extend to 1 year *or* with fine which shall be at least ₹ 50,000 but which may extend to ₹ 5,00,000 *or* with both [Sec 128 (6)].

9. **Compliance with AS and in Forms as per Schedule III:** The Financial Statements must give a true and fair view of the state of affairs of the company *or* companies, comply with the accounting standards notified under Sec 133 and must be in the form *or* forms as may be provided for different class *or* classes of companies in Schedule III [Sec 129 (1)]:

10. **BOD's Responsibility to lay:** At every annual general meeting of a company, the Board of Directors of the company must lay before such meeting Financial Statements for the financial year [Sec 129 (2)].

11. **Consolidated Financial Statements:** Where a company has one *or* more subsidiaries, it must, in addition to financial statements, prepare a consolidated financial statement of the company and of all the subsidiaries in the same form and manner as that of its own which must also be laid before the annual general meeting of the company along with the laying of its Financial Statements.

Provided that the company must also attach along with its financial statement, a separate statement containing the salient features of the financial statement of its subsidiary *or* subsidiaries in Form AOC-1.

Provided further that the Central Government may provide for the consolidation of accounts of companies in such manner as may be prescribed.

Explanation. For the purposes of this sub-section, the word "subsidiary" shall include Associate Company and Joint Venture [Sec 129 (3)].

Note: The provisions of this Act applicable to the preparation, adoption and audit of the financial statements of a holding company shall, *mutatis mutandis*, apply to the consolidated financial statements [Sec 129 (4)].

12. **Reasons for Deviation from AS:** Where the financial statements of a company do not comply with the accounting standards the company must disclose in its financial statements, the deviation from the accounting standards, the reasons for such deviation and the financial effects, if any, arising out of such deviation [Sec 129 (5)].

13. **Penalty:** If a company contravenes the provisions of Sec. 129, the Managing Director, the Whole-time Director in charge of finance, the Chief Financial Officer *or* any other person charged by the Board with the duty of complying with the requirements of this section and in the absence of any of the officers mentioned above, all the directors shall be punishable with imprisonment for a term which may extend to 1 year *or* with fine which shall be atleast ₹ 50,000 but which may extend to ₹ 5,00,000, *or* with both. [Sec 129(7)]

    Explanation: For the purposes of this section, except where the context otherwise requires, any reference to the financial statement must include any notes annexed to *or* forming part of such financial statement, giving information required to be given and allowed to be given in the form of such notes under this Act.

14. **Voluntary Revision of Financial Statements** *or* **Board's Report:** If it appears to the directors of a company that:

    (a) the financial statement of the company; *or*

    (b) the report of the Board,

    do not comply with the provisions of Sec. 129 *or* 134, they may prepare revised financial statement *or* a revised report in respect of any of the 3 preceding financial years after obtaining approval of the Tribunal on an application made by the company in such form and manner as may be prescribed and a copy of the order passed by the Tribunal shall be filed with the Registrar. [Sec 131(1)]

Notes:

(i) Tribunal shall give notice to the Central Government and the Income tax authorities and shall take into consideration the representations, if any, made by that Government *or* the authorities before passing any order under this section:

(ii) Such revised Financial Statement *or* Report shall not be prepared *or* filed more than once in a financial year:

(iii) The detailed reasons for revision of such financial statement *or* report shall also be disclosed in the Board's report in the relevant financial year in which such revision is being made.

Scope of Revision: Where copies of the previous financial statement *or* report have been sent out to members *or* delivered to the Registrar *or* laid before the company in general meeting, the revisions must be confined to:

(a) the correction in respect of which the previous Financial Statement *or* Report do not comply with the provisions of section 129 *or* 134; and

(b) the making of any necessary consequential alternation. [Sec 131(2)]

15. Approval of and Signature on Financial Statement: The financial statement, including consolidated financial statement, if any, must be approved by the Board of Directors before they are signed on behalf of the Board at least by the chairperson of the company where he is authorised by the Board *or* by two directors out of which one shall be Managing Director and the Chief Executive Officer, if he is a director in the company, the Chief Financial Officer and the Company Secretary of the company, wherever they are appointed, *or* in the case of a One Person Company, only by one director, for submission to the Auditor for his Report thereon [Sec 134 (1)].

16. Auditor's Report to be attached: The Auditors' Report shall be attached to every financial statement [Sec 134 (2)].

17. BOD's Report to be attached: The Board's Report must be attached to statements laid before a company in general meeting.

18. Contents of BOD's Report: BOD Report must include:

(a) the extract of the Annual Return as provided u/s 92 (3);

(b) Number of Meetings of the Board;

(c) Directors' Responsibility Statement;

(d) a Statement on Declaration given by Independent Directors u/s 149 (6);

(e) in case of a company covered u/s 178 (1), company's policy on directors' appointment and remuneration including criteria for determining qualifications, positive attributes, independence of a director and other matters provided u/s 178 (3);

(f) explanations *or* comments by the Board on every qualification, reservation *or* adverse remark *or* disclaimer made:

(i) by the auditor in his report; and

(ii) by the company secretary in practice in his secretarial audit report;

(g) particulars of loans, guarantees *or* investments under section 186;

(h) particulars of contracts *or* arrangements with related parties referred to in sub-section (1) of section 188 in the prescribed **Form AOC-2;**

(i) the state of the company's affairs;

(j) the amounts, if any, which it proposes to carry to any reserves;

(k) the amount, if any, which it recommends should be paid by way of dividend;

(l) material changes and commitments, if any, affecting the financial position of the company which have occurred between the end of the financial year of the company to which the financial statements relate and the date of the report;

(m) the conservation of energy, technology absorption, foreign exchange earnings and outgo, in such manner as may be prescribed;

(n) a statement indicating development and implementation of a risk management policy for the company including identification therein of elements of risk, if any, which in the opinion of the Board may threaten the existence of the company;

(o) the details about the policy developed and implemented by the company on corporate social responsibility initiatives taken during the year;

(p) in case of a listed company and every other public company having such paid-up share capital as may be prescribed, a statement indicating the manner in which formal annual evaluation has been made by the Board of its own performance and that of its committees and individual directors;

(q) such other matters as may be prescribed under Rule 8 of the Companies (Account) Rules, 2022.

19. Signature on BOD's Report: The Board's Report and any annexure must be signed by its chairperson of the company if he is authorised by the Board and where he is not so authorised, must be signed by at least two directors, one of whom shall be a managing director, *or* by the director where there is one director. [Sec 134 (6)]

20. BOD's Report in case One Person Company [Sec 134 (4)]: The BOD's Report of in case of a One Person Company, means a report containing explanations *or* comments by the Board on every qualification, reservation *or* adverse remark *or* disclaimer made by the Auditor in his Report.

21. Contents of Directors' Responsibility Statement [Sec 134 (5)]:

The Directors' Responsibility Statement must state that:

(a) **Compliance with AS:** in the preparation of the annual accounts, the applicable accounting standards had been followed along with proper explanation relating to material departures;

(b) **Accounting Policies:** the directors had selected such accounting policies and applied them consistently and made judgments and estimates that are reasonable and prudent so as to give a true and fair view of the state of affairs of the company at the end of the financial year and of the profit and loss of the company for that period;

(c) **Maintenance of Adequate Accounting Records:** the directors had taken proper and sufficient care for the maintenance of adequate accounting records in accordance with the provisions of this Act for safeguarding the assets of the company and for preventing and detecting fraud and other irregularities;

(d) **Accounts on a Going Concern Basis:** the directors had prepared the annual accounts on a going concern basis; and

(e) **Internal Financial Controls:** the directors, in the case of a listed company, had laid down internal financial controls to be followed by the company and that such internal financial controls are adequate and were operating effectively.

Explanation: For the purposes of this clause, the term "Internal Financial Controls" mean the policies and procedures adopted by the company for ensuring the orderly and efficient conduct of its business, including adherence to company's policies, the safeguarding of its assets, the prevention and detection of frauds and errors, the accuracy and completeness of the accounting records, and the timely preparation of reliable financial information;

(f) **Proper Systems to ensure compliance with Law:** the directors had devised proper systems to ensure compliance with the provisions of all applicable laws and that such systems were adequate and operating effectively.

22. Circulation: A signed copy of every financial statement, including consolidated financial statement, if any, must be issued, circulated *or* published along with a copy each of:

(a) any notes annexed to *or* forming part of such financial statement;

(b) the auditor's report; and

(c) the Board's report [Sec 134 (7)].

23. Penalty: If a company contravenes the provisions of Sec 134, the company shall be punishable with fine which shall be atleast ₹ 50,000 but which may extend to ₹ 25,00,000 and every officer of the company who is in default shall be punishable with imprisonment for a term which may extend to 3 years *or* with fine which shall be atleast ₹ 50,000 but which may extend to ₹ 5,00,000 *or* with both.

24. Corporate Social Responsibility (CSR):

1. Every company having **Net Worth of atleast ₹ 500 crore** *or* **Turnover of atleast ₹ 1,000 crore** *or* **a Net Profit of atleast ₹ 5 crores** during any financial year must constitute a Corporate Social Responsibility Committee of the Board consisting of atleast 3 directors, out of which at least one director shall be an Independent Director [Sec 135 (1)].

Example: State whether X Ltd is required to constitute a Corporate Social Responsibility Committee in the following cases:

	2019-2020 (crore)	*2020-2021 (crore)*	*2021-2022 (crore)*	*2022-2023 (crore)*
Net Worth	₹ 499	₹ 499	₹ 499	₹ 500
Turnover	₹ 999	₹ 999	₹ 1000	₹ 999
Net Profit	₹ 4.99	₹ 5	₹ 4.99	₹ 4.99

Answer: X Ltd is required to constitute a Corporate Social Responsibility Committee since 2020-2021 when one of the 3 criteria was satisfied for the first time.

2. The Board's Report must disclose the composition of the Corporate Social Responsibility Committee [Sec 135 (2)].

3. **The Corporate Social Responsibility Committee is required:**
   (a) To Formulate and recommend to the Board, a Corporate Social Responsibility Policy which shall indicate the activities to be undertaken by the company as specified in Schedule VII;
   (b) To Recommend the amount of expenditure to be incurred on the activities referred to in clause (a); and
   (c) To Monitor the Corporate Social Responsibility Policy of the company from time to time. [Sec 135(3)]

4. **The Board of every company is required:**
   (a) after taking into account the recommendations made by the Corporate Social Responsibility Committee, approve the Corporate Social Responsibility Policy for the company and disclose contents of such Policy in its report and also place it on the company's website, if any, in such manner as may be prescribed; and
   (b) ensure that the activities as are included in Corporate Social Responsibility Policy of the company are undertaken by the company. [Sec 135(4)]

5. **Spending of 2% of Average Net Profits on CSR:** The Board of every company must ensure that the company spends, in every financial year, **at least 2%. of the Average Net Profits (as per Sec 198)** of the company made **during 3 immediately preceding financial years**, in pursuance of its Corporate Social Responsibility Policy. [Sec 135(5)]

Notes:

(i) The company must give preference to the local area and areas around it where it operates, for spending the amount earmarked for Corporate Social Responsibility activities. [Proviso to Sec 135(5)]

(ii) If the company fails to spend such amount, the Board must, in its report made u/s 134, specify the reasons for not spending the amount. [Proviso to Sec 135(5)]

(ii) As per Rule 2(1)(e) of the Companies (CSR Policy) Rules, 2022, "CSR Policy" relates to the activities to be undertaken by the company as specified in Schedule VII to the Act and the expenditure thereon, excluding activities undertaken in pursuance of normal course of business of a company.

(iv) As per Rule 2(1)(f) "Net Profit" means the Net Profit of a company as per its financial statement prepared in accordance with the applicable provisions of the Act, but shall not include the following, namely:

(a) any profit arising from any overseas branch *or* branches of the company, whether operated as a separate company *or* otherwise; and

(b) any dividend received from other companies in India, which are covered under and complying with the provisions of Sec 135.

(v) As per Rule 4(5), the CSR projects *or* programs *or* activities that benefit only the employees of the company and their families shall not be considered as CSR activities in accordance with Sec 135.

EXAMPLE: Net Profits of JIV AATMA Ltd. for the years 2022-2023,2021-2022,2020-2021,2019-2020,2018-2019 are ₹ 25 crore,₹ 20 crore,₹ 15 crore,₹ 10 crore and ₹ 5 crore respectively. During 2022-2023,the company incurred only ₹ 7,00,000 and ₹ 3,00,000 on free education and medical treatment of the employees of the company and their families respectively under CSR projects.

***Required:* State the Amount of Short Fall of Expenditure on Corporate Social Responsibility during 2022-2023 as per The Companies Act,2013.**

SOLUTION

Minimum expenditure on CSR required as per Sec 135(5) = 2% of[(₹ 20 crore + ₹ 15 crore + ₹ 10 crore)/3] = ₹ 0.30 crore

Free education and medical treatment of the employees of the company and their families shall not be considered as CSR activities in accordance with Sec 135. Hence, **Short fall of expenditure on CSR as per Sec 135** = ₹ 0.30 crore

25. Right of member to copies of Audited Financial Statement [Sec 136]: Without prejudice to the provisions of Sec 101, a copy of the financial statements, including consolidated financial statements, if any, Auditor's Report and every other document required by law to be annexed *or* attached to the financial statements, which are to be laid before a company in its general meeting, must be sent to every member of the company, to every trustee for the debenture-holder of any debentures issued by the company, and to all persons other than such member *or* trustee, being the person so entitled, atleast 21 days before the date of the meeting. [Sec 136(1)]

However, in the case of a listed company, the provisions of Sec 136(1) shall be deemed to be complied with, if the copies of the documents are made available for inspection at its registered office during working hours for a period of 21 days before the date of the meeting and a statement containing the salient features of such documents in Form AOC-3 *or* copies of the documents, as the company may deem fit, is sent to every member of the company and to every trustee for the holders of any debentures issued by the company atleast 21 days before the date of the meeting unless the shareholders ask for full financial statements. [Provisio to Sec 136(1)]

However, that the Central Government may prescribe the manner of circulation of financial statements of companies having such Net Worth and Turnover as may be Prescribed. [Provisio to Sec 136(1)]

26. Manner of Circulation of Financial Statements in certain cases (Rule 11 of the Companies (Account) Rules, 2022): In case of all listed companies and such public companies which have a **Net Worth of more than ₹ 1 crore** and **Turnover of more than ₹ 10 crore,** the financial statements may be sent:

(a) by electronic mode to such members whose shareholding is in dematerialised format and whose email Ids are registered with Depository for communication purposes;

(b) where Shareholding is held otherwise than by dematerialised format, to such members who have positively consented in writing for receiving by electronic mode; and

(c) by despatch of physical copies through any recognised mode of delivery as specified u/s 20 of the Act, in all other cases.

27. Duty to File with Registrar [Sec 137]:

1. Where Financial Statements adopted	At AGM, a copy of the financial statements, including consolidated financial statement, if any, along with all the documents which are required to be *or* attached to such financial statements under this Act, duly adopted at the AGM of the company, must be filed with the Registrar **within 30 days of the date of AGM** in such manner, with such fees *or* additional fees as may be prescribed within the time specified u/s 403.
2. Where Financial Statements Not adopted at AGM	Where the financial statements are not adopted at AGM *or* Adjourned AGM, such unadopted financial statements along with the required documents must be filed with the Registrar **within 30 days of the date of AGM** and the Registrar shall take them in his records as provisional till the Financial Statements are filed with him after their adoption in the Adjourned AGM for that purpose:
3. Where Financial Statement adopted at Adjourned AGM	Financial Statements adopted in the Adjourned AGM must be filed with the Registrar **within 30 days of the date of such Adjourned AGM** with such fees *or* such additional fees as may be prescribed within the time specified u/s 403:
4. In case of One Person Company	A One Person Company must file a copy of the financial statements duly adopted by its member, along with all the documents which are required to be attached to such financial statements, **within 180 days from the closure of the financial year**.
5. In case of Subsidiary/ Subsidiaries	A company must, along with its financial statements to be filed with the Registrar, attach the accounts of its subsidiary *or* subsidiaries which have been incorporated outside India and which have not established their place of business in India.
6. Where AGM not held	Where the AGM of a company for any year has not been held, the financial statements along with the documents required to be attached duly signed along **with the Statement of Facts and Reasons for not holding the AGM** must be filed with the Registrar **within 30 days of the last date before which the AGM** should have been held and in such manner, with such fees *or* additional fees as may be prescribed within the time specified, u/s 403.

Penalty for Failure to File: If a company fails to file the copy of the financial statements before the expiry of the specified period the company shall be punishable with fine of ₹ 1,000 for every day during which the failure continues but which shall not be more than ₹ 10,00,000, and the Managing Director and the Chief Financial Officer of the company, if any, and, in the absence of the Managing Director and the Chief Financial Officer, any other director who is charged by the Board with the responsibility of complying with the provisions of this section, and, in the absence of any such director, all the directors of the company, shall be punishable with imprisonment for a term which may extend to 6 months *or* with fine which shall be atleast ₹ 1,00,000 but which may extend to ₹ 5,00,000, *or* with both.

28. Internal Audit [Sec 138]: Such class *or* classes of companies as may be prescribed shall be required to appoint an internal auditor, who shall either be a Chartered Accountant *or* a

Cost Accountant, *or* such other professional as may be decided by the Board to conduct internal audit of the functions and activities of the company.

Note: The Central Government may, by rules, prescribe the manner and the intervals in which the internal audit shall be conducted and reported to the Board.

3.0 CONTENTS AND FORMS [SECTION 129]

(a) The Balance Sheet is required to give a true and fair view of the state of affairs of the company as at the end of the financial year and is to be in the form set out in Part I of Schedule III.

(b) The Statement of Profit and Loss is required to give a true and fair view of the profit *or* loss of the company for the financial year and is to be in the form set out in Part II of Schedule III.

4.0 FORM OF PREPARING A STATEMENT OF PROFIT AND LOSS

1. **Vertical form** has been prescribed under The Companies Act, 2013 for Statement of Profit and Loss of a company.
2. A format of Statement of Profit and Loss has been given on next page:

SPECIMEN OF STATEMENT OF PROFIT & LOSS

NAME OF THE COMPANY........................

STATEMENT OF PROFIT AND LOSS FOR THE YEAR ENDED ....

	Particulars	*Note No.*	*Figures for the Current Reporting Period*	*Figures for the Previous Reporting Period*
			₹	₹
I.	Revenue from Operations	1	xxx	xxx
II.	Other Income	2	xxx	xxx
III.	**Total Income [I + II]**		xxx	xxx
IV.	**Expenses:**			
	Cost of Materials consumed	3	xxx	xxx
	Purchases of Stock-in-Trade		xxx	xxx
	Changes in Inventories	4	xxx	xxx
	Employee Benefits Expense	5	xxx	xxx
	Finance Costs	6	xxx	xxx
	Depreciation and Amortization Expense	7	xxx	xxx
	Other Expenses	8	xxx	xxx
	Total Expenses		xxx	xxx
V.	**Profit before Tax(III–IV)**		xxx	xxx
VI.	**Exceptional Items**		xxx	xxx

VII. Profit Before Extraordinary Items and Tax (V – VI)		xxx	xxx
VIII. Extraordinary Items		xxx	xxx
IX. Profit before tax (VII – VIII)		xxx	xxx
X. Tax Expense:			
(1) Current Tax		xxx	xxx
(2) Deferred Tax		xxx	xxx
		xxx	xxx
XI. Profit (Loss) for the period		xxx	xxx
XII. Earnings per Equity Share:			
(1) Basic		xxx	xxx
(2) Diluted		xxx	xxx

Notes to Accounts:

NOTE 1: REVENUE FROM OPERATIONS

(a) From Sale of Products	xxx	xxx
(b) From Sale of Services	xxx	xxx
(ba) Grants or Donations received (relevant in case of Sec 8 Companies only)	xxx	xxx
(c) From Other Operating Revenues [Trading Commission]	xxx	xxx
(d) *Less:* Excise Duty	(xxx)	(xxx)
	xxx	xxx

NOTE 2: OTHER INCOME

(a) Interest Income (in case of a company other than a finance company)	xxx	xxx
(b) Dividends From Subsidiary Companies	xxx	xxx
(c) Dividend Income From Companies other than Subsidiary Companies	xxx	xxx
(d) Net Gain/Loss on Sale of Investments [Gain – Loss)]	xxx	xxx
(e) Other Non-Operating Income (Net of Expenses directly attributable to such income) [Income – Expenses)]	xxx	xxx
(f) Net Gain on Foreign Currency Transaction of Translation (other than considered as Finance Cost)	xxx	xxx
	xxx	xxx

NOTE 3: COST OF MATERIALS CONSUMED

(a) Opening Stock of Materials	xxx	xxx
(b) *Add:* Purchases of Materials	xxx	xxx
(c) *Less:* Closing Stock of Materials	(xxx)	(xxx)
Cost of Materials consumed	xxx	xxx

NOTE 4: CHANGES IN INVENTORIES

Particulars	*Work-in-Progress* (₹)	*Finished Goods* (₹)	*Total*
Closing Stock	xxx	xxx	xxx
Less: Opening Stock	(xxx)	(xxx)	(xxx)
	xxx	xxx	xxx

NOTE 5: EMPLOYEE BENEFITS EXPENSE

Salaries and Wages	xxx	xxx
Contribution To Provident and Other Funds	xxx	xxx
Expense On Employee Stock Option Scheme (ESOP) and Employee Stock Purchase Plan (ESPP)	xxx	xxx
Staff Welfare Expenses	xxx	xxx
	xxx	xxx

NOTE 6: FINANCE COSTS

(a) Interest Expense	xxx	xxx
(b) Other Borrowing Costs	xxx	xxx
(c) Applicable Net Gain/Loss on Foreign Currency Transactions and Translation	xxx	xxx
	xxx	xxx

NOTE 7: DEPRECIATION AND AMORTIZATION EXPENSE

Buildings	xxx	xxx
Plant and Equipment	xxx	xxx
Vehicles	xxx	xxx
Office Equipment	xxx	xxx
Brands	xxx	xxx
Computer Software	xxx	xxx
	xxx	xxx

NOTE 8: OTHER EXPENSES

(a) Consumption of Stores and Spare Parts	xxx	xxx
(b) Power and Fuel	xxx	xxx
(c) Rent.	xxx	xxx
(d) Repairs to Buildings	xxx	xxx
(e) Repairs to Machinery	xxx	xxx
(f) Insurance	xxx	xxx
(g) Rates and Taxes [Excluding Taxes on Income]	xxx	xxx
(h) Miscellaneous Expenses	xxx	xxx
(i) Provisions for Losses of Subsidiary Companies	xxx	xxx

(j) Provisions, if material	xxx	xxx
(k) Withdrawal from Provisions, if material	xxx	xxx
(l) Expenditure on Corporate Social Responsibility (CSR)	xxx	xxx
(m) Payments to the Auditor as:		
(a) Auditor	xxx	xxx
(b) For Taxation Matters	xxx	xxx
(c) For Company Law Matters	xxx	xxx
(d) For Management Services	xxx	xxx
(e) For Other Services	xxx	xxx
(f) For Reimbursement of Expenses	xxx	xxx
	xxx	xxx

NOTE: SURPLUS I.E. BALANCE IN THE STATEMENT OF P&L TO BE TAKEN TO BALANCE SHEET

Opening Balance	xxx	xxx
Add: Profit for the period	xxx	xxx
Less: Transfer to Reserve	(xxx)	(xxx)
Less: Interim Dividend	(xxx)	(xxx)
Less: Preference Dividend	(xxx)	(xxx)
Less: Equity Dividend	(xxx)	(xxx)
Closing Balance	xxx	xxx

Notes:

1. Any item of Income *or* Expenditure which exceeds **1% of the Revenue from Operations *or* ₹ 1,00,000, *whichever is higher*** is to be disclosed separately.
2. The Statement of Profit and Loss shall also contain by way of a note the following information, namely:

(a) **Value of imports calculated on C.I.F. basis** by the company during the financial year in respect of:

I. Raw Materials; II. Components and spare parts; III. Capital Goods;

(b) **Expenditure in Foreign Currency** during the financial year on account of royalty, know-how, professional and consultation fees, interest, and other matters;

(c) **Total Value of all imported raw materials, spare parts and components** consumed during the financial year and the total value of all indigenous raw materials, spare parts and components similarly consumed and the percentage of each to the total consumption;

(d) **The amount remitted during the year in Foreign Currencies** on account of dividends with a specific mention of the total number of Non-Resident Shareholders, the total number of shares held by them on which the dividends were due and the year to which the dividends related.

(e) **Earnings in Foreign Exchange** classified under the following heads, namely:

I. Export of Goods calculated on F.O.B. basis;

II. Royalty, know-how, professional and consultation fees;

III. Interest and Dividend;

IV. Other Income, indicating the nature thereof.

(f) Where the company is covered under section 135 of the companies act,the following shall be disclosed with regard to CSR activities:

(i) amount required to be spent by the company during the year,

(ii) amount of expenditure incurred,

(iii) shortfall at the end of the year,

(iv) total of previous years shortfall,

(v) reason for shortfall,

(vi) nature of CSR activities,

(vii) details of related party transactions, e.g., contribution to a trust controlled by the company in relation to CSR expenditure as per relevant Accounting Standard,

(viii) where a provision is made with respect to a liability incurred by entering into a contractual obligation, the movements in the provision during the year should be shown separately.

(g) Where the Company has traded or invested in Crypto currency or Virtual Currency during the financial year, the following shall be disclosed:

(i) profit or loss on transactions involving Crypto currency or Virtual Currency

(ii) amount of currency held as at the reporting date,

(iii) deposits or advances from any person for the purpose of trading or investing in Crypto Currency/ virtual currency

(h) The figures appearing in the Financial Statements are compulsorily required to be rounded off to the nearest lakhs, millions or crores or decimal thereof if TOTAL INCOME is at least ₹ 100 crore.

(i) The figures appearing in the Financial Statements are compulsorily required to be rounded off to the nearest hundreds, thousands, lakhs, millions or decimal thereof if TOTAL INCOME is less than ₹ 100 crore.

ILLUSTRATION 1

From the following information, prepare Statement of Profit and Loss for the year ended 31st March, 2023:

Particulars	*(₹ in lacs)*
Revenue from Operations	2605
Other Income	40
Cost of Materials consumed	1000
Changes in Inventories	(275)
Employee Benefits Expense	850
Finance Costs	20
Depreciation and Amortization Expense	150
Other Expenses	100
Tax Rate @ 30%	
60 lacs Equity Shares of ₹ 10 each fully paid up, 50 lacs Equity Shares of ₹ 10 each, ₹ 8 paid up, 14%, 1,00,000 Preference Shares of ₹ 100 each fully paid up	

SOLUTION

TULSIAN LTD.
STATEMENT OF PROFIT AND LOSS FOR THE YEAR ENDED 31ST MARCH, 2023

Particulars	*Note No.*	*(₹ in lacs)*
I. Revenue from Operations		2605
II. Other Income		40
III. Total Revenue [I + II]		2645
IV. Expenses:		
Cost of Materials consumed		1000
Changes in Inventories		(275)
Employee Benefits Expense		850
Finance Costs		20
Depreciation and Amortization Expense		150
Other Expenses		100
Total Expenses		1845
V. Profit before Tax (III – IV)		800
VI. Tax Expense@30%		(240)
VII. Profit for the period		560
Basic Earnings per Equity Share: = (560 – 14)/(40+60) = ₹ 5.46		

ILLUSTRATION 2

From the following information, prepare the relevant Notes to Accounts:

Particulars	*(₹ in lacs)*
Sales of Products	2700
Sales of Services	30
Trading Commission	60
Excise Duty	185
Interest Income	20
Dividends From Companies	10
Net Loss on Sale of Investments	4
Rental Income	15
Rental Collection Expenses	1

SOLUTION

1. REVENUE FROM OPERATIONS

Particulars	*(₹ in lacs)*
(a) From Sale of Products	2700
(b) From Sale of Services	30

(c) From Other Operating Revenues [Trading Commission]	60
(d) *Less:* Excise Duty	(185)
	2605

2. OTHER INCOME

Particulars	(₹ in lacs)
(a) Interest Income	20
(b) Dividends From Companies	10
(c) Net Loss on Sale of Investments	(4)
(d) Rental Income (15 lacs – 1 lac Collection Expenses)	14
	40

ILLUSTRATION 3

From the following information, prepare the relevant Notes to Accounts:

Particulars	(₹ in lacs)
Opening Stock of Materials	84.6
Purchases of Materials	955.2
Closing Stock of Materials	39.8
Opening Stock of WIP	150
Closing Stock of WIP	200
Opening Stock of Finished Goods	175
Closing Stock of Finished Goods	400

SOLUTION

3. COST OF MATERIALS CONSUMED

Particulars	(₹ in lacs)
(a) Opening Stock of Materials	84.6
(b) *Add:* Purchases of Materials	955.2
(c) *Less:* Closing Stock of Materials	(39.8)
Cost of Materials consumed	1000

4. CHANGES IN INVENTORIES

Particulars	Work-in-Progress (₹ in lacs)	Finished Goods (₹ in lacs)	Total (₹ in lacs)
Opening Stock	150	175	325
Less: Closing Stock	200	400	600
	(50)	(225)	(275)

ILLUSTRATION 4

From the following information, prepare the relevant Notes to Accounts:

Particulars	*(₹ in lacs)*
Salaries and Wages	600
Contribution To Provident and Other Funds	72
Expense on Employee Stock Option Scheme (ESOP) and Employee Stock Purchase Plan (ESPP)	28
Staff Welfare Expenses	150
Interest Expense	24
Other Borrowing Costs(Brokerage)	4
Gain on Foreign Currency Transactions and Translation	8

SOLUTION

5. EMPLOYEE BENEFITS EXPENSE

Particulars	*(₹ in lacs)*
Salaries and Wages	600
Contribution To Provident and Other Funds	72
Expense on Employee Stock Option Scheme (ESOP) and Employee Stock Purchase Plan (ESPP)	28
Staff Welfare Expenses	150
	850

6. FINANCE COSTS

Particulars	*(₹ in lacs)*
(a) Interest Expense	24
(b) Other Borrowing Costs(Brokerage)	4
(c) Gain on Foreign Currency Transactions and Translation	(8)
	20

ILLUSTRATION 5

From the following information, prepare the relevant Notes to Accounts:

Particulars	*(₹ in lacs)*	*Particulars*	*(₹ in lacs)*
Buildings	400	Provision for Doubtful Debts	2
Plant and Equipment	200	Consumption of Stores and Spare Parts	14
Vehicles	50	Power and Fuel	16
Furniture and Fixtures	60	Rent	10
Brands	200	Repairs to Buildings	8
Computer Software	90	Repairs to Machinery	6

Insurance	4	Rates and Taxes	2
Sundry Debtors	80	Expenditure on CSR Activities	2
Payments to the Auditor	32		

(a) Depreciate Buildings @ 5%, Plant and Equipment @ 20%, Vehicles @ 20%, Furniture and Fixtures @ 10% and Brands@ 10%,Computer Software@60%.

(b) Maintain a Provision for Doubtful Debts @ 10%

SOLUTION

7. DEPRECIATION AND AMORTIZATION EXPENSE

Particulars	*(₹ in lacs)*
Buildings [5% of ₹ 400 lacs]	20
Plant and Equipment [20% of ₹ 200 lacs]	40
Vehicles [20% of ₹ 50 lacs]	10
Furniture & Fixtures [10% of ₹ 60 lacs]	6
Brands [10 % of ₹ 200 lacs]	20
Computer Software [60% of ₹ 90 lacs]	54
	150

8. OTHER EXPENSES

Particulars	*(₹ in lacs)*
(a) Consumption of Stores and Spare Parts	14
(b) Power and Fuel	16
(c) Rent.	10
(d) Repairs to Buildings	8
(e) Repairs to Machinery	6
(f) Insurance	4
(g) Rates and Taxes	2
(h) Expenditure on CSR Activities	2
(i) Provision for Doubtful Debts [(10% of ₹ 80 lacs) – ₹ 2 lac]	6
(j) Payments to the Auditor	32
	100

ILLUSTRATION 6

From the following information, prepare the relevant Notes to Accounts:

Particulars	*(₹ in lacs)*
Opening Balance of Profit and Loss Statement	452
Profit for the period	560
Transfer to Reserve @ 5%	
Interim Dividend	100

Preference Dividend	140
Final Equity Dividend	285
Transfer to Debenture Redemption Reserve	100

SOLUTION

9. SURPLUS IN THE STATEMENT OF P & L TO BE TAKEN TO BALANCE SHEET

Particulars	***(₹ in lacs)***
Opening Balance	452
Add: Profit for the period	560
Less: Transfer to Reserve @ 5%	(28)
Less: Interim Dividend	(100)
Less: Preference Dividend	(140)
Less: Final Equity Dividend	(285)
Less: Debenture Redemption Reserve	(100)
Closing Balance	359

ILLUSTRATION 7

The following items appear in the Trial Balance of Bharat Ltd. as at 31st March, 2023:

Particulars	₹
1. Revenue from Operations	48,00,000
2. Other Income	2,00,000
3. Expenses other than Interest	7,60,000

4. 12%, 20,000 Debentures of ₹ 100 each fully paid up
5. Opening Balance of Profit and Loss Statement ₹ 6,56,000.
6. Transfer to Reserve @ 5%.
7. Interim Dividend paid ₹ 1,60,000, Final Equity Dividend paid ₹ 80,000, Preference Dividend paid ₹ 1,40,000,
8. 6 lacs Equity Shares of ₹ 10 each fully paid up, 5 lacs Equity Shares of ₹ 10 each, ₹ 8 paid up, 14%, 10,000 Preference Shares of ₹ 100 each fully paid up
9. The recommendation of the company's Board of Directors include Transfer to Debenture Redemption Reserve @ 25% of Debentures.
10. Corporate Tax 30%.

Required: Show the above items in Statement of Profit and Loss and calculate Surplus i.e. Balance in Statement of Profit & Loss.

SOLUTION

BHARAT LTD.
STATEMENT OF PROFIT AND LOSS FOR THE YEAR ENDED 31ST MARCH, 2023

Particulars	***Note No.***	***(₹ in lacs)***
I. Revenue from Operations		48
II. Other Income		2
III. Total Revenue [I + II]		50

IV. Expenses:		
Finance Costs		2.4
Other Expenses		7.6
Total Expenses		10.0
V. Profit before Tax(III – IV)		40
VI. Tax Expense [30% of ₹ 40 lacs]		(12)
VII. Profit for the period		28
Basic Earnings per Equity Share: = (28 – 1.4)/(4+6) = ₹ 2.66		

SURPLUS I.E. BALANCE IN STATEMENT OF PROFIT & LOSS

Opening Balance	6.56
Add: Profit for the period	28.00
Less: Transfer to Reserve @ 5%	(1.4)
Less: Interim Dividend	(1.6)
Less: Preference Dividend	(1.4)
Less: Final Equity Dividend	(0.8)
Less: Debenture Redemption Reserve [25% of ₹ 20 lacs]	(5)
	24.36

ILLUSTRATION 8

TULSIAN Ltd. provides the following information for the year ended 31st March, 2023:

Particulars	₹	*Particulars*	₹
Excise Duty paid	92.5	Sale of Products	1350
Net Loss on Sale of Investments	2	Sale of Services	15
Rental Collection Expenses	0.5	Trading Commission received	30
Opening Stock of Materials	42.3	Interest Income	10
Opening Stock of WIP	75	Dividends From Companies	5
Opening Stock of Finished Goods	87.5	Rental Income	7.5
Purchases of Materials	477.6	Gain on Foreign Currency	
Salaries and Wages	300	Transactions and Translation	4
Contribution To Provident and Other Funds	36	50 lacs Equity Shares of ₹ 10 each, ₹ 8 paid up	400
Expense on Employee Stock Option		60 lacs Equity Shares of ₹ 10 each	600
Scheme (ESOP) & Emp. Stock		Profit and Loss Account [01.04.2022]	226
Purchase Plan (ESPP)	14	10%, 70 lacs Pref. Shares of ₹ 10 each	700
Staff Welfare Expenses	75	General Reserve	80
Interest Expense	12	12% Debentures	100
Other Borrowing Costs(Brokerage)	2	Provision for Doubtful Debts	1
Buildings	200	Consum. of Stores and Spare Parts	7

Plant and Equipment	100	Power and Fuel	8
Vehicles	25	Rent	5
Furniture and Fixtures	30	Repairs to Buildings	4
Brands	100	Repairs to Machinery	3
Computer Software	45	Insurance	2
Prepaid Expenses	1	Rates and Taxes	1
Interim Dividend paid	150	Expenditure on CSR Activities	1
Sundry Debtors	40	Pref. Dividend paid	70
Payments to the Auditor	16		

Additional Information:

(a) Closing Stocks: Materials ₹ 19.9 lacs, WIP ₹ 100,Finished Goods ₹ 200 lacs

(b) Depreciate Buildings @ 5%, Plant and Equipment @ 20%, Vehicles @ 20%, Furniture and Fixtures @ 10% and Brands@ 10%,Computer Software@60%.

(c) Payments to the Auditor include as Auditor ₹ 5 lacs,For Taxation Matters ₹ 4 lacs, For Company Law Matters ₹ 3 lacs, For Management Services ₹ 2 lacs, For Other Services ₹ 1 lac, For Other Services ₹ 1 lac

(d) Make a Provision for Doubtful Debts @ 10%

(e) The director's recommended:(i) to transfer to Debenture Redemption Reserve @ 25% of Debentures. (ii) to transfer to General Reserve @ 5%.

(f) Income Tax Rate 30%.

Required: Prepare Statement of Profit and Loss for the year ended 31st March, 2023 and a Note showing the computation of Surplus in the Statement of Profit and Loss to be taken to the Balance Sheet (as per Schedule III to The Companies Act, 2013) as on that date.

SOLUTION

TULSIAN LTD.

STATEMENT OF PROFIT AND LOSS FOR THE YEAR ENDED 31ST MARCH, 2023

	Particulars	***Note No.***	***(₹ in lacs)***
I.	Revenue from Operations	1	1302.5
II.	Other Income	2	20.0
III.	**Total Revenue [I + II]**		1322.5
IV.	**Expenses:**		
	Cost of Materials consumed	3	500
	Changes in Inventories	4	(137.5)
	Employee Benefits Expense	5	425
	Finance Costs	6	10
	Depreciation and Amortization Expense	7	75
	Other Expenses	8	50
	Total Expenses		922.5
V.	**Profit before Tax(III – IV)**		400

VI. Tax Expense@30%		(120)
VII. Profit for the period		280
Basic Earnings per Equity Share: = (280 – 70)/(40+60) = ₹ 2.10		

Notes to Accounts: [₹ in lacs]

1. REVENUE FROM OPERATIONS

(a) From Sale of Products	1350
(b) From Sale of Services	15
(c) From Other Operating Revenues [Trading Commission]	30
(d) *Less:* Excise Duty	(92.5)
	1302.5

2. OTHER INCOME

(a) Interest Income	10
(b) Dividends From Companies	5
(c) Net Loss on Sale of Investments	(2)
(d) Rental Income (7. 5 lacs – 0.5 lac Collection Expenses)	7
	20

3. COST OF MATERIALS CONSUMED

(a) Opening Stock of Materials	42.3
(b) *Add:* Purchases of Materials	477.6
(c) *Less:* Closing Stock of Materials	(19.9)
Cost of Materials consumed	500

4. CHANGES IN INVENTORIES

Particulars	***Work-in-Progress (₹ in lacs)***	***Finished Goods (₹ in lacs)***	***Total (₹ in lacs)***
Opening Stock	75	87.5	162.5
Less: Closing Stock	100	200	300
	(25)	(112.5)	(137.5)

5. EMPLOYEE BENEFITS EXPENSE

Salaries and Wages	300
Contribution To Provident and Other Funds	36
Expense on Employee Stock Option Scheme (ESOP) and Employee Stock Purchase Plan (ESPP)	14
Staff Welfare Expenses	75
	425

6. FINANCE COSTS

(a) Interest Expense	12
(b) Other Borrowing Costs(Brokerage)	2
(c) Gain on Foreign Currency Transactions and Translation	(4)
	10

7. DEPRECIATION AND AMORTIZATION EXPENSE

Buildings [5% of ₹ 200 lacs]	10
Plant and Equipment [20% of ₹ 100 lacs]	20
Vehicles [20% of ₹ 25 lacs]	5
Furniture & Fixtures [10% of ₹ 30 lacs]	3
Brands [10 % of ₹ 100 lacs]	10
Computer Software [60% of ₹ 45 lacs]	27
	75

8. OTHER EXPENSES

(a) Consumption of Stores and Spare Parts	7
(b) Power and Fuel	8
(c) Rent.	5
(d) Repairs to Buildings	4
(e) Repairs to Machinery	3
(f) Insurance	2
(g) Rates and Taxes	1
(h) Expenditure on CSR Activities	1
(i) Provision for Doubtful Debts [(10% of ₹ 40 lacs) – ₹1 lac]	3
(j) Payments to the Auditor as:	
(a) Auditor	5
(b) For Taxation Matters	4
(c) For Company Law Matters	3
(d) For Management Services	2
(e) For Other Services	1
(f) For Other Services	1
	50

9. SURPLUS IN THE STATEMENT OF P & L TO BE TAKEN TO BALANCE SHEET

Opening Balance	226
Add: Profit for the period	280
Less: Transfer to General Reserve @ 5%	(14)
Less: Interim Dividend	(150)
Less: Preference Dividend [10% of ₹ 700 lacs]	(70)
Less: Debenture Redemption Reserve [25% of ₹ 100 lacs]	(25)
Closing Balance	247

5.0 ACCOUNTING TREATMENT OF PROVISION FOR TAX

The worth noting points in this regard are as follows:

1. Provision for tax for Current Year	It is shown in Statement of Profit and Loss Statement.
2. Advance Payment of Tax	It is shown under the head **'Current Assets'** and sub-head **'Short-term Loans and Advances'** in the Balance Sheet.
3. Tax Deducted at source (T.D.S.) from Incomes received from Others	It is shown under the head **'Current Assets'** and sub-head **'Short term Loans and Advances'** in the Balance Sheet.
4. Advance Tax and T.D.S. (Dr. Balance)	These are usually adjusted against the Income Tax liability at the time of settlement of liability for income tax.

The accounting entries to be passed in this regard are summarised on next page:

JOURNAL ENTRIES

1. On Making Provision for Tax for current year

Profit & Loss A/c Dr.
  To Provision for Tax A/c

2. On Converting Provision into Liability on Settlement

Provision for Tax A/c Dr.
  To Income Tax payable A/c

3. On Adjustment of Advance tax and T.D.S. (Dr. Balance)

Income Tax Payable A/c Dr. [with Actual Settled Liability]
Income Tax Refund Due A/c Dr. [with Refund, *if any* Due]
  To Advance Tax A/c
  To T.D.S. A/c (Debit Balance)

4. On Payment of Balance of tax payable (if any)

Income Tax Payable A/c Dr.
  To Bank A/c

5. On Receipt of Income tax Refund Due (if any)

Bank A/c Dr.
  To Income Tax Refund due A/c

ILLUSTRATION 9

The following items appear in the Trial Balance of Tulsian Ltd. as at 31st March 2023:

Particulars	***Dr. (₹)***	***Cr. (₹)***
Advance Payment of Tax (2021–2022)	4,50,000	—
Advance Payment of Tax (2022–2023)	6,00,000	
Provision for Tax (2021–2022)		5,00,000
Net Profit subject to Tax @ 35%		20,00,000

Required: Prepare Journal, Statement of Profit & Loss and Balance Sheet if the actual tax liability for 2021–2022 was settled and paid for ₹ 5,00,000 on 31.3.2023 but no accounting effect has yet been given.

SOLUTION

JOURNAL OF TULSIAN LTD.

Date	Particulars	L.F.	Dr. (₹)	Cr. (₹)
31.3.2023	Profit & Loss A/c Dr. To Provision for Income Tax A/c (Being the provision for I.T. for current year made)		7,00,000	7,00,000
31.3.2023	Provision for Income Tax A/c Dr. To Income Tax Payable A/c (Being the tax for previous year finally settled)		5,00,000	5,00,000
31.3.2023	Income Tax Payable A/c Dr. To Advance Tax A/c To Bank A/c (Being the advance tax for 2020–2022 adjusted against tax payable and Balance paid)		5,00,000	4,50,000 50,000

AN EXTRACT OF STATEMENT OF PROFIT & LOSS FOR THE YEAR ENDED 31.3.2023

Particulars	₹
Net Profit before Tax	20,00,000
Tax Expense	(7,00,000)
Profit for the period	13,00,000

AN EXTRACT OF BALANCE SHEET AS AT 31ST MARCH, 2023

Particulars	₹
Reserves & Surplus (Balance in Statement of Profit & Loss)	13,00,000
Current Liabilities [Short-term Provisions (Provisions for Tax)]	7,00,000
Current Assets [Short-term Loans & Advances (Advance Payment of Tax)]	6,00,000

6.0 DIVIDEND

MEANING OF DIVIDEND

(a) Dividend ordinarily means that portion of divisible profits *or* reserves which is distributed among the shareholders of a company which is a going concern.

(b) In case of a liquidating company, dividend means a division of the realised assets among the creditors and contributories according to their respective rights.

[CIT v. *Girdhar Dass & Co. (P) Ltd.* Supreme Court]

(c) The Institute of Chartered Accountants of India has defined 'dividend' as a "a distribution to shareholders out of profits *or* reserves available for this purpose."

[Guidance Note on terms used in Financial Statements]

(d) As per Sec 2(35), the term 'Dividend' includes Interim Dividend also.

CAN A COMPANY DECLARE AND DISTRIBUTE DIVIDEND IF THE MEMORANDUM AND ARTICLES ARE SILENT?

Yes, a company can declare and distribute dividend even if its Memorandum and Articles are silent because it has an inherent power to declare and distribute dividend. Such power need not expressly be given by the Memorandum *or* Articles though the Articles may regulate the manner in which dividends are to be distributed.

LEGAL PROVISIONS RELATING TO DIVIDEND

1. Sources from which Dividends can be Declared *or* Paid [Section 123(1)]

Section 123(1) of The Companies Act, 2013 specifies the following 4 sources from which dividends can be declared *or* paid:

(i) out of Profits of Current Financial Year;
(ii) out of Undistributed Profits of the Previous Financial Year *or* Years;
(iii) out of both above;
(iv) out of Moneys provided by the Central Government *or* State Government for payment of dividend in pursuance of a guarantee given by that government.

2. Provision for Depreciation [Section 123(2)]

Before declaring any dividend, the company must provide for:

(i) depreciation for current financial year, and
(ii) arrears of depreciation for previous financial year *or* years.

3. Extent of Depreciation [Section 123(2)]

Depreciation must be provided to the extent specified in Schedule II. Further, when the asset is sold, discarded, demolished *or* destroyed in any financial year, the Excess of the Written Down Value over its Sale Proceeds as scrap, if any should be written off in the same financial year.

Note: A company need not provide for depreciation if it does not want to declare dividends. In such a case, the fact that depreciation has not been provided for *or* written off, together with the quantum of arrears of depreciation must be disclosed in the Financial Statements.

4. Provision relation to Past Losses and Arrears of Depreciation [Rule 3(5)]

Before declaring any dividend, the company must provide for Past Losses and Arrears of Depreciation relating to previous year(s).

5. Out of Free Reserves only: No dividend shall be declared *or* paid by company from its reserves other than free reserves.

Note: Meaning of Free Reserves: As per Sec 2(43) of the Companies Act, 2013, "Free Reserves" mean such reserves which, as per the latest audited balance sheet of a company, are available for distribution as dividend.

ILLUSTRATION 10

Particulars	*₹ (in lakh)*		
	2020-2021	*2021-2022*	*2022-2023*
1. Profit (Loss) before charging Depreciation	(5)	6	16
2. Depreciation Chargeable u/s 123 (2)	3	7	6
3. Profit (Loss) after charging depreciation	(8)	(1)	10

Required: Calculate the Divisible Profits for the year 2022-2023

SOLUTION

COMPUTATION OF DIVISIBLE PROFIT FOR THE YEAR 2022-2023

Particulars	*₹ in (lakh)*
A. Profits for the Current Year	16
B. *Less:*	
(a) Depreciation for Current Year	(6)

(b) Past Loss for 2020-2021	(8)
(c) Past Loss for 2021-2022	(1)
C. Divisible Profits for the Current Year	1

7.0 OPTION TO TRANSFER OF PROFITS TO RESERVES

According to Proviso to Sec 123(1), a company may transfer an appropriate % of Current Profits to Reserve before declaring a dividend.

8.0 CAPITAL RESERVE

MEANING OF CAPITAL RESERVE

Capital Reserve is the reserve which does not include any amount regarded as free for distribution through the Statement of Profit and Loss. Only profits *or* a surplus of a capital nature are credited to such a reserve.

EXAMPLES OF PROFITS OR SURPLUSES WHICH ARE CREDITED TO CAPITAL RESERVE

1. Profit on Re-issue of Forfeited Shares.
2. Profit prior to incorporation.
3. The excess of the value of Net Assets over the price paid for the acquisition of a business.
4. Profit on Redemption/Cancellation of Debentures.
5. The credit balance in the Capital Reduction/Reconstruction Account, where there has been a reduction of capital with the consent of the Tribunal.

ITEMS NOT CREDITED TO CAPITAL RESERVE

1. Securities Premium as per Sec 52
2. Capital Redemption Reserve as per Sec. 55 & Sec 69

These accounts are to be kept separately.

9.0 INTERIM DIVIDEND

MEANING OF INTERIM DIVIDEND

Interim dividend is the dividend which is declared between two AGMs. It is declared during the current year for the current year.

NO LIMIT ON NUMBER OF INTERIM DIVIDEND [REGULATION 83 OF TABLE F]

The Board may from time to time pay to the members such interim dividends as appear to it to be justified by the profits of the company. Thus, there is no limit on the number of interim dividends a company may declare in a year.

LEGAL PROVISIONS AS TO INTERIM DIVIDEND

1. As per Sec 123(3) the Board of Directors of a company may declare interim dividend during any financial year out of the Surplus in the Profit and Loss Account and out of profits of the financial year in which such interim dividend is sought to be declared: However, in case the company has incurred loss during the current financial year up to the end of the quarter immediately preceding the date of declaration of interim dividend, such interim dividend shall not be declared at a rate

higher than the average dividends declared by the company during the immediately preceding 3 financial years.

2. The term 'Dividend' includes Interim Dividend also [Section 2(35)].

3. All provisions of the Companies Act which apply to dividends have now become applicable to interim dividends also.

LEADING CASE LAWS AS TO INTERIM DIVIDEND

1. It is declared by the Board of directors. It does not require approval of members at General Meeting. *[Scott v. Scott, (1943)]*

2. Before declaring an interim dividend, the directors must satisfy themselves that the financial position of the company warrants the payment of such dividend out of its distributable profits because "the declaration of interim dividends depends much more upon estimates and opinions than the declaration of final dividend which is made upon the information contained in a formal balance sheet." *[Lucas v. Fitzgarald (1903)]*

10.0 FINAL DIVIDEND

WHO TAKES DIVIDEND DECISION?

The dividend decision is taken by the Board of Directors and is then recommended to the shareholders for their final approval at AGM (i.e., Annual General Meeting) of the company. The shareholders can reduce the amount of dividend even to zero but can not increase the amount of dividend as recommended by the Board of Directors. If the directors decide not to declare and dividend, the shareholders in general meeting cannot themselves declare it. *[Regulation 80 of Table F]*

DECLARATION OF FINAL DIVIDEND AT AGM/EGM [REGULATION 80 OF TABLE F]

1. A company usually declares dividend at its Annual General Meeting. But it may declare dividend at any other general meeting unless the articles provide otherwise.
2. A company cannot declare a further dividend after having declared a final dividend at its annual general meeting.
3. It may also be noted that there can be no declaration of dividend for past years in respect of which the accounts have already been closed at previous annual general meetings.

11.0 LEGAL PROVISIONS AS TO PAYMENT OF DIVIDEND [SEC 123(4) & (5)]

1. The amount of dividend including interim dividend must be deposited in a separate bank account within 5 days of the declaration of such dividend and the same shall be used for payment of dividend.
2. No dividend shall be paid by a company in respect of any share therein except to the registered shareholder of such share *or* to his order *or* to his banker and shall not be payable except in cash.
3. Any dividend payable in cash may be paid by cheque *or* warrant *or* in any electronic mode to the shareholder entitled to the payment of the dividend.

12.0 UNPAID/UNCLAIMED DIVIDEND [SEC 124 & 125]

DUTY OF COMPANY TO TRANSFER TO SPECIAL DIVIDEND ACCOUNT [SEC 124(1)]

The company must transfer the total amount of dividend which remains unpaid/unclaimed within 30 days of its declaration, to a special account 'Unpaid Dividend Account of ... Company limited/

Company (Private) Limited, within 7 days of the expiry of aforesaid 30 days. This account is to be opened in a Scheduled Bank.

DUTY OF COMPANY TO PREPARE A STATEMENT OF SHAREHOLDERS TO WHOM UNPAID DIVIDEND RELATES [SEC 124(2)]

The company must, within a period of 90 days of making any transfer of an amount to the Unpaid Dividend Account, prepare a statement containing the names, their last known addresses and the unpaid dividend to be paid to each person and place it on the website of the company, if any, and also on any other website approved by the Central Government for this purpose, in such form, manner and other particulars as may be prescribed.

PENALTY FOR DEFAULT IN TRANSFER [SEC 124(3)]

If unpaid/unclaimed dividend is not transferred to Unpaid Dividend Account within the stipulated period of 7 days, the company shall be liable to pay interest @ 12% p.a. The interest accruing on such an amount must ensure to the benefit to the members of the company, in proportion to the amount remaining unpaid to them.

PAYMENT OF UNCLAIMED/UNPAID DIVIDEND [SEC 124(4)]

Any person claiming to be entitled to any money transferred to the Unpaid/Unclaimed Dividend Account may make an application to the Company within 7 years from the date of transfer for payment of money claimed.

TRANSFER OF UNCLAIMED/UNPAID DIVIDEND AFTER 7 YEARS[SEC 124(5)]

If any amount transferred to Unpaid Dividend Account remains unclaimed/unpaid for 7 years, it must be transferred by the company to the 'Investor Education and Protection Fund' along with Interest Accrued.

TRANSFER OF SHARES [SEC 124(6)]

All shares in respect of which unpaid *or* unclaimed dividend has been transferred to Investor Education and Protection Fund must also be transferred by the company in the name of Investor Education and Protection Fund along with a statement containing such details as may be prescribed.

However, any claimant of shares transferred above shall be entitled to claim the transfer of shares and unclaimed dividend from Investor Education and Protection Fund in accordance with such procedure and on submission of such documents as may be prescribed.

INVESTOR EDUCATION AND PROTECTION FUND [SEC 125]

Objective of the Fund	The Fund shall be used for promotion of investors' awareness and protection of interests of investors in accordance with such rules as may be prescribed.
Amount to be Credited to Fund	The following amounts shall be credited to the fund: (a) Unpaid dividends (b) Matured deposits with companies other than Banking Companies (c) Refund of application money (d) Matured debentures with the companies (e) Interest accrued on the amounts referred to in Clauses (a) to (d) above.

	(f) Grants and donations given to the fund by the Central Government, State Government, Companies *or* any other institution. (g) The interest *or* other income received out of instruments made from the fund. (h) Sale proceeds of fractional shares arising out of issuance of bonus shares, merger and amalgamation for 7 *or* more years; (i) Redemption amount of preference shares remaining unpaid *or* unclaimed for 7 *or* more years; and
Utilization of Fund	The Fund shall be utilised for: 1. Refund of Unclaimed Dividends, 2. Refund of Matured Deposits, 3. Refund of Matured Debentures, 4. Refund of the Application Money due for refund and Interest thereon; 5. Promotion of Investors' Education, Awareness and Protection; 6. Reimbursement of Legal Expenses, 7. Any other purpose as per Rules
Power of Central Government to Constitute Committee	The Central Government shall by notification in the Official Gazette, constitute a committee to administer the Fund, and maintain separate accounts and other relevant records in relation to the Fund in such form as may be prescribed in consultation with the Comptroller and Auditor General of India (CAG).
Power of Committee to Spend	The committee shall be entitled to spend money out of the fund for carrying out the objectives of the fund.

13.0 RIGHT TO DIVIDEND, RIGHTS SHARES AND BONUS SHARES TO BE HELD IN ABEYANCE PENDING REGISTRATION OF TRANSFER OF SHARES [SEC 126]

Where any instrument of transfer of shares has been delivered to any company for registration and the transfer of such shares has not been registered by the company, it must, irrespective of anything contained in any other provision of this Act,:

(a) transfer the dividend in relation to such shares to the Unpaid Dividend Account unless the company is authorised by the registered holder of such shares in writing to pay such dividend to the transferee specified in such instrument of transfer; and

(b) keep in abeyance in relation to such shares, any offer of rights shares and any issue of fully paid-up bonus shares.

14.0 PUNISHMENT FOR FAILURE TO DISTRIBUTE DIVIDENDS [SEC 127]

Where a dividend has been declared by a company but has not been paid *or* the warrant in respect thereof has not been posted within 30 days from the date of declaration to any shareholder entitled to the payment of the dividend, every director of the company shall, if he is knowingly a party to the default, be punishable with imprisonment which may extend to 2 years and with fine which shall be atleast ₹ 1,000 for every day during which such default continues and the company shall be liable to pay simple interest at the rate of 18% p.a. during the period for which such default continues:

Circumstances under which No Offence (Proviso to Sec 127): No offence under this section shall be deemed to have been committed:

(a) where the dividend could not be paid by reason of the operation of any law;

(b) where a shareholder has given directions to the company regarding the payment of the dividend and those directions cannot be complied with and the same has been communicated to him;

(c) where there is a dispute regarding the right to receive the dividend;

(d) where the dividend has been lawfully adjusted by the company against any sum due to it from the shareholder; *or*

(e) where, for any other reason, the failure to pay the dividend *or* to post the warrant within the period under this section was not due to any default on the part of the company.

15.0 PAYMENT OF DIVIDEND ON PARTLY PAIDUP SHARES [SEC 51 AND REGULATION 83]

As per Sec 51 a company may, if so authorised by its articles, pay dividends in proportion to the amount paid up on each share where a larger amount is paid up on some shares than on others.

Note: If the articles do not contain any such provision, dividend will have to be paid only in proportion to the nominal value of shares. *[Oak Bank Oil Co. v. Crum, (1882)]*

Note: In the case of fresh issue of capital, the holders thereof, unless precluded by the terms of issue, are entitled to receive dividend pari passu with the shares already issued. *[Regulation 83 of Table F]*

LEGAL POSITION AS TO DIVIDEND ON PARTLY PAID UP SHARES

Case	*Dividend on Partly paid shares*
1. Where the Articles specify provision in this regard	Dividend is payable on the nominal/called up/ paid up amount of shares as per Articles.
2. Where the Articles are silent In this regard and Table F has not been excluded.	
(a) If some amount has been paid on any of the shares of the company.	Dividend must be declared and paid on the amount paid up (excluding calls-in-advance) on shares.
(b) If nothing has been paid on any of the shares of the company.	Dividend may be declared and paid according to the nominal amounts of the shares.
3. Where the Articles are silent in this regard and Table F has been excluded.	Dividend must be declared and paid on nominal amount of shares.

ILLUSTRATION 11

X Ltd. provides you the following information:

10,000 Equity Shares of ₹ 10 each, ₹ 6 per share called up	₹ 60,000
Less: Calls-in-arrears on 1,000 shares @ ₹ 2 per share	₹ 2,000
Add: Calls-in advance on 500 shares @ ₹ 3 per share	₹ 1,500
	₹ 59,500

The Board of Directors recommend a dividend @ 10%.

Required: Calculate the amount of Dividend in each of the following alternative cases:

Case (a) If no other information is given.

Case (b) If the Articles prescribe the payment of dividend on the nominal amount of shares.

Case (c) If the Articles prescribe the payment of dividend on the called up amount of shares.

Case (d) If the Articles prescribe the payment of dividend on the paid up amount of shares.

Case (e) If the Articles are silent and Table F has been excluded.

SOLUTION

Case (a) 10% of ₹ 58,000 = ₹ 5,800 [As per Regulation 83 of Table F]

Case (b) 10% of ₹ 1,00,000 = ₹ 10,000 [As per Articles]

Case (c) 10% of ₹ 60,000 = ₹ 6,000 [As per Articles]

Case (d) 10% of ₹ 58,000 = ₹ 5,800 [As per Articles]

Case (e) 10% of ₹ 1,00,000 = ₹ 10,000 [Oak Bank Oil Co. v. Crum, (1882)]

ILLUSTRATION 12

X Ltd. was registered with an authorised capital of ₹ 40,00,000 divided into 10,000 12% Preference Shares of ₹ 100 each and 3,00,000 Equity Shares of ₹ 10 each. On 1st April 2022, all the preference shares and 2,00,000 equity shares had been issued and were fully paid with the exception of 40,000 of equity shares on which only ₹ 5 per share had been called up. On 1st Nov. 2022 the director made the final call of ₹ 5 per share on the partly paid equity shares and the call was dully paid except by a shareholders-holding 2,000 shares. The recommendation of directors include the dividend on equity shares @ 15% p.a.

Required: Calculate the amount of dividend in each of the following alternative cases:

Case (a) If no other information is given;

Case (b) If the shares on which calls were in arrears were duly forfeited before the end of the accounting year.

Case (c) If the shares on which calls were in arrears were duly forfeited and were reissued @ ₹ 9 per share before the end of the accounting year.

SOLUTION

Case (a)

I	On 12% Preference Shares (12% on ₹ 10,00,000)		1,20,000
II	On Equity shares		
	On 1,60,000 Equity Shares (1,60,000 × ₹ 10 × 15/100)	2,40,000	
	On 40,000 Equity Shares (40,000 × ₹ 5 × 15/100)	30,000	
	On 38,000 Equity Shares (38,000 × ₹ 5 × 15/100 × 5/12)	11,875	2,81,875
III	Total Dividend [I + II]		4,01,875

Case (b)

I	On 12% Preference Shares (12% on ₹ 10,00,000)		1,20,000
II	On Equity shares		
	On 1,60,000 Equity Shares (1,60,000 × ₹ 10 × 15/100)	2,40,000	
	On 38,000 Equity Shares (38,000 × ₹ 5 × 15/100)	28,500	

	On 38,000 Equity Shares (38,000 × ₹ 5 × 15/100 × 5/12)	11,875	2,80,375
III	Total Dividend [I + II]		4,00,375

Case (c)

I	On 12% Preference Shares (12% on ₹ 10,00,000)		1,20,000
II	On Equity Shares		
	On 1,60,000 Equity Shares (1,60,000 × ₹ 10 × 15/100)	2,40,000	
	On 40,000 Equity Shares (40,000 × ₹ 5 × 15/100)	30,000	
	On 40,000 Equity Shares (40,000 × ₹ 5 × 15/100 × 5/12)	12,500	2,82,500
III	Total Dividend [I + II]		4,02,500

16.0 DIVIDEND ON PREFERENCE SHARES

RIGHT TO RECEIVE PREFERENCE DIVIDEND

Holders of preference shares are entitled to receive a dividend at a fixed rate before any dividend is declared on equity shares. They can exercise this right only when there are sufficient divisible profits and a dividend is declared as per the provisions of the Act.

ARREARS OF DIVIDEND IN CASE OF CUMULATIVE PREFERENCE SHARES

(a) If the company is a going concern	Holders of Cumulative Preference Shares are entitled to receive the arrears of dividend out of the profits of subsequent years before any dividend is paid on equity shares.
(b) If the company goes into liquidation	
(i) ***Where Articles contain an express provision to that effect.***	(i) Arrears of dividend are payable alongwith return of preference share capital before return of equity capital.
(ii) ***Where Articles are silent***	
(a) *If such dividends have been declared.*	(a) Arrears of dividend are payable alongwith return of preference share capital before return of equity capital.
(b) *If such dividends have not been declared*	(b) Arrears of undeclared dividends are payable out of any surplus if any left after the return of full preference and equity share capital.

Note: In India Unless otherwise stated, all Preference Shares are assumed to be Cumulative.

DIVIDEND IN CASE OF NON-CUMULATIVE PREFERENCE SHARES

Holders of non-cumulative preference shares are not entitled to receive the arrears of dividend out of the profits of subsequent years if no divided is declared in a particular year *or* years. In other words, they are entitled to receive the dividend only for the year in which the dividend is declared.

DIVIDEND IN CASE OF PARTICIPATING PREFERENCE SHARES

Holders of Participants Preference shares are entitled to receive their fixed dividend before any dividend is paid on the equity shares *plus* a fixed percentage of surplus profits remaining after a certain percentage of equity dividend has been paid to equity shareholders.

ILLUSTRATION 13

ATMA Ltd provides you the following information:

50,000,9% Participating Pref. Shares of ₹ 100 each		₹ 50 lakhs
1,00,000,10% Preference Shares of ₹ 100 each		₹100 lakhs
1,50,000,11% Non-Cumulative Preference Shares of ₹ 100 each		₹150 lakhs
20,00,000,Equity Shares of ₹ 10 each, ₹ 7 per share called up & paid up	₹ 140 lakhs	
Add: Calls-in advance on 1,00,000 shares @ ₹ 4 per share	₹4 lakhs	₹144 lakhs
DVRs (entitled to 5% more dividend than Equity) ₹ 10 lakhs		₹10 lakhs
		₹ 454 lakhs

Current Year's Tax @ 25% amounted to ₹ 34.5 lakhs. Participating Pref. Shareholders are entitled to participate to the extent of 20% of Surplus Profits as per Articles. Last year no dividend could be paid on any share due to absence of profits. At the end of current year, the Board decided and paid dividend on Equity Shares @ 20%.

***Required:* Calculate the Total Amount of Dividend paid by the company.**

SOLUTION

On 9% Participating Pref. Share Capital [₹ 4.50 lakhs (arrears) + ₹ 4.50 lakhs (current) + ₹ 5.50 lakhs*]	₹ 14.50 lakhs
On 10% Preference Share Capital [₹ 10 lakhs (arrears) + ₹ 10 lakhs (current)]	₹ 20.00 lakhs
On 11% Non-Cumulative Preference Share Capital [₹ 11% of 150 lakhs (current)]	₹ 16.50 lakhs
On Equity Share Capital [20% of ₹140 lakhs]	₹ 28.00 lakhs
On DVRs [25% of ₹10 lakhs]	₹ 2.50 lakhs
Total Amount of Dividend	₹ 81.50 lakhs

Current Year's Profits after Tax =₹ 34.50 lakhs x 75%/25% = ₹ 103.50 lakhs

* Surplus Profit = Profits available – Dividend

= ₹ 103.50 lakhs – [₹ 9 lakhs (on Participating) + ₹ 20 lakhs (on 10% Pref. Shares) + ₹ 16.50 lakhs (on 11% Pref. Shares) + ₹ 28 lakhs (on Equity) +₹ 2.50 lakhs (on DVRs)] = ₹ 27.50 lakhs

20% share of participating pref. shareholders = 20% of ₹ 27.5 lakhs = ₹ 5.50 lakhs

Note: In India unless otherwise stated, all Preference Shares are assumed to be Cumulative and Non-participating.

17.0 DECLARATION OF DIVIDEND OUT OF RESERVES [PROVISO TO SEC 123(1)]

According to The Companies *(Declaration and Payment of Dividend out of Reserves)* Rules, 2014, in the event of inadequacy *or* absence of profit in any financial year, dividend may be declared by a company for that year out of free reserves subject to fulfilment of the following 4 conditions:

1. Maximum Withdrawal of Reserve	The total amount so drawn from the reserves must not exceed 10% of the sum of its Paid up Capital and Free Reserves as appearing in latest Audited Financial Statement.
2. Minimum Balance after Withdrawal	The balance of Reserves after such drawn must be at least 15% of its Paid up share capital as appearing in latest Audited Financial Statement.

3. First Set-off Losses	The amount so drawn shall first be utilised to set off the losses incurred in the financial year before any dividend in respect of equity shares is declared; and
4. Maximum Rate of Dividend	The rate of the dividend declared must not exceed the Average Rate of Dividend declared in 3 years immediately preceding that year.

Note: *In the event of inadequacy or absence of profit in any financial year, if dividend is declared by a company for that year out of Surplus,then 4 conditions as per The Companies (Declaration and Payment of Dividend out of Reserves) Rules, 2014 need not be fulfilled.*

ILLUSTRATION 14

Tushar Ltd. provides you the following information:

Equity Shares of ₹ 10 Each	₹ 100 lakh
General Reserves	₹ 20 lakh
Revaluation Reserves	₹ 5 lakh
Loss for the year ending: 31.3.2022 ₹ 2 lakh, 31.3.2023 ₹ 1 lakh	
Rates of Equity Dividend : 9 % in 2019-2020,10% in 2020-2021,11% in 2021-2022,	

The management recommends a dividend of 8% on equity share capital. As an expert comment upon the management's decision.

SOLUTION

As per the Companies Act, 2013 dividend out of reserves may be declared in accordance with the Companies (Declaration and Payment of Dividend out of Reserves) Rules, 2018. These rules provide the following four conditions to be fulfilled:

Step 1 Maximum withdrawal of Reserve if condition (i) is satisfied
= 10% of Paid up Capital and free reserves = 10% of (₹ 100 lakh + 20 lakh) = 12 lakh

Step 2: Maximum withdrawal of Reserve if condition (ii) is satisfied

A.	Opening Balance of Reserves in the beginning of the year	20,00,000
B.	*Less:* Closing Balance of Reserve being 15% of paid up share capital	15,00,000
C.	Reserve available (A – B)	5,00,000

Step 3 Permissible withdrawal of Reserve if conditions (i) and (ii) are satisfied
= ₹ 5,00,000 (being lower of limits as per Step 1 and Step 2)

Step 4 Maximum Permissible Divisible Profits

A.	Permissible withdrawal of Reserve (as per Step 3)	5,00,000
B.	*Less:* Loss	1,00,000
C.	Maximum Permissible Divisible profit [A – B]	4,00,000

Step 5 Actual Permissible Rate of Dividend

A. Maximum Permissible Rate of Dividend $\frac{₹ 4 \text{ lakh}}{₹ 100 \text{ lakh}} \times 100 = 4\%$

B. Average Rate of Dividend based on 3 years [(11% + 10% + 9%)/3] = 10%

C. Actual Permissible Rate of Dividend being lowest of two i.e. 4%

Comment: The management can declare dividend only upto a rate of 4%. Hence, the management's dividend decision of 8% is not as per Rules.

ILLUSTRATION 15

PARAM ATMA Ltd. provides you the following information:

Equity Shares of ₹ 10 Each	₹ 100 lakh
8% Preference shares of ₹ 100 each, fully paid up	₹ 20 lakh
General Reserves	₹ 30 lakh
Revaluation Reserves	₹ 5 lakh
Loss for the year ending: 31.3.2022 ₹ 2 lakh, 31.3.2023 ₹ 1 lakh	
Rates of Equity Dividend : 0 % in 2019-2020,16% in 2020-2021,17% in 2021-2022,	

PARAM ATMA Ltd. desires to declare dividend @ 10% for the year 2022-2023. As an expert comment upon the management's decision.

Required: **Can PARAM ATMA Ltd.do so? State giving reason as per law.**

SOLUTION

As per the Companies Act, 2013 dividend out of reserves may be declared in accordance with the Companies (Declaration and Payment of Dividend out of Reserves) Rules, 2018. These rules provide the following four conditions to be fulfilled:

Step 1 Maximum withdrawal of Reserve if condition (i) is satisfied = 10% of Paid up Capital and free reserves = 10% of (₹ 100 lakh + ₹ 20 lakh + ₹ 30 lakh) = ₹ 15 lakh

Step 2: Maximum withdrawal of Reserve if condition (ii) is satisfied= Opening Reserves -Closing Reserves(being 15% of paid up share capital = ₹ 30 lakh - [(15% of (₹ 100 lakh + ₹ 20 lakh)] = ₹ 12 lakh

Step 3 Permissible withdrawal of Reserve if conditions (i) and (ii) are satisfied = ₹ 12 lakh (being lower of limits as per Step 1 and Step 2)

Step 4 Maximum Permissible Divisible Profits for Equity Shareholders = Permissible withdrawal of Reserve (as per Step 3) – Current Year's Loss – Preference Dividend = ₹ 12 lakh – ₹ 1 lakh – ₹ 1.60 lakh = ₹ 9.40 lakh

Step 5 Maximum Permissible Rate of Dividend = Maximum Permissible Divisible Profits for Equity Shareholders /Equity Share Capital = ₹ 9.40 lakh /₹ 100 lakh =9.40%

Step 6 Actual Permissible Rate of Dividend = Lower of Maximum Permissible Rate of Dividend and Average Rate of Dividend based on 3 years = 9.40% or [(0% + 16% + 17%)/3] = 11% Actual Permissible Rate of Dividend being lowest of two i.e. 9.4%

Comment: NO. The management can declare dividend only upto a rate of 9.4%.

ILLUSTRATION 16

Due to inadequacy of profits during the year ended 31st March, 2023, PQR Ltd. proposes to declare 8.5% dividend out of general reserves. From the following particulars, ascertain the amount that can be utilized from general reserves for this purpose, according to the Companies (Declaration of Dividend out of Reserves) Rules, 2014.

8% Preference shares of ₹ 100 each, fully paid up	₹ 15,00,000
Equity shares of ₹ 10 each, fully paid up	₹ 1,10,00,000
General Reserves as on 1.4.2022	₹ 25,00,000
Capital Reserves as on 1.4.2022	₹ 10,00,000
Revaluation Reserves as on 1.4.2022	₹ 15,00,000
Net Profit for the year ended 31st March, 2023	₹ 4,85,000

Average rate of dividend during the last three years has been 12%.

SOLUTION

As per the Companies Act, 2013 dividend out of reserves may be declared in accordance with the Companies (Declaration and Payment of Dividend out of Reserves) Rules, 2014. These rules provide the following four conditions to be fulfilled:

Step 1 Maximum withdrawal of Reserve if condition (i) is satisfied

= 10% of Paid up Capital and free reserves

= 10% of (₹ 15 lakh + 110 lakh + 25 lakh) = 15 lakh

Step 2 Maximum withdrawal of Reserve if condition (ii) is satisfied

A. Opening Balance of Reserves in the beginning of the year	25,00,000
B. *Less:* Closing Balance of Reserve being 15% of paid up share capital	18,75,000
C. Reserve available (A – B)	6,25,000

Step 3 Permissible withdrawal of Reserve if conditions (i) and (ii) are satisfied

= ₹ 6,25,000 (being lower of limits as per Step 1 and Step 2)

Step 4 Maximum Permissible Divisible Profits

A. Permissible withdrawal of Reserve (as per Step 3)	6,25,000
B. *Add:* Profit [₹ 4,85,000 – ₹ 1,20,000 (Preference Dividend)]	3,65,000
C. Maximum Permissible Divisible profit [A – B]	9,90,000

Step 5 Actual Permissible Rate of Dividend

A. Maximum Permissible Rate of Dividend $\left(\frac{₹\,9,90,000}{₹\,110,00,000} \times 100\right) = 9\%$

B. Average Rate of Dividend based on 3 years =12%

C. Actual Permissible Rate of Dividend being lowest of two i.e. 9%

Comment: The management can declare dividend only upto a rate of 9%. To declare dividend @ 8.5% the Company can utilize ₹ 5,70,000 (i.e. ₹ 9,35,000 – ₹ 3,65,000) out of General Reserves.

18.0 ACCOUNTING TREATMENT OF DIVIDEND, TRANSFER TO RESERVES, BONUS, ETC.

1. On Transfer of Profits to General Reserve (Board's Option)

Profit & Loss (Appropriation) A/c Dr.

*To General Reserve

2. On Declaration of Final Dividend for the previous year at Annual General Meeting

Profit & Loss (Appropriation) A/c Dr.

*To Pref. Dividend Payable A/c

*To Equity Dividend Payable A/c

3.	**On Transfer of the amount of Dividend Payable to a Separate Bank Account**	
	Dividend Bank A/c	Dr.
	To Bank A/c	
4.	**On Payment of a Dividend Payable out of Dividend Bank**	
	Pref. Dividend Payable A/c	Dr.
	Equity Dividend Payable A/c	Dr.
	To Dividend Bank A/c	

*These Appropriations shall be shown by way of deduction while computing, 'Surplus' in the Statement of Profit & Loss, in the Note as to 'Reserves and Surplus'.

ILLUSTRATION 17

An Extract of the Balance Sheet of Tulsian Ltd. as at 31st March, 2022 is as follows:

Share Capital:	
Authorised:	
1,40,000 Equity Shares of ₹ 10 Each	14,00,000
10% 7,000 Preference Shares of ₹ 100 each	7,00,000
Issued & Subscribed:	
10% 7,000 Preference Shares of ₹ 100 each	7,00,000
110,000 Equity Shares of ₹ 10 each fully paid	11,00,000
Reserves & Surplus:	
Capital Redemption Reserve	60,000
Revaluation Reserve	60,000
Securities Premium Account	40,000
General Reserve	3,00,000
Profit & Loss A/c (including Net Profit after tax for the year 2021-2022 ₹ 4,00,000)	5,78,000
Cash at Bank	6,00,000

At the Annual General Meeting held on 30th Sept 2022, it was resolved:

(a) To transfer Profits to General Reserve @5% and to declare and pay the dividend on Equity Shares @15%.

(b) To issue fully paid bonus shares to the holders of fully paid equity shares in the ratio of 1:4.

(c) To give existing shareholders the option to subscribe one ₹ 10 Right share at ₹ 15 for every four shares held after the bonus distribution.

The aforesaid right shares were subscribed by all the shareholders. The bonus shares and right shares were fully allotted on 1st Jan. 2023.

Required: Pass the necessary journal entries on 30th Sept., 2022 and 1st Jan 2023.

SOLUTION

JOURNAL OF TULSIAN LTD.

Particulars		*L.F.*	*Dr. (₹)*	*Cr. (₹)*
Profit & Loss (Appropriation) A/c	Dr.		20,000	
To General Reserve				20,000

(Being the t/f of 5% of current Profits ₹ 4,00,000 to reserve)			
Profit & Loss (Appropriation) A/c Dr.		2,35,000	
To Pref. Dividend Payable A/c			70,000
To Equity Dividend Payable A/c			1,65,000
(Being final pref. dividend & equity dividend declared at AGM).			
Dividend Bank A/c Dr.		2,35,000	
To Bank A/c			2,35,000
(Being the amount of dividend payable t/f to separate Bank A/c)			
Pref. Dividend Payable A/c Dr.		70,000	
Equity Dividend Payable A/c Dr.		1,65,000	
To Dividend Bank A/c			2,35,000
(Being the payment of dividend)			
Capital Redemption Reserve A/c Dr.		60,000	
Securities Premium A/c Dr.		40,000	
General Reserve A/c Dr.		1,75,000	
To Bonus to Shareholders A/c			2,75,000
(Being the bonus declared for issuing fully paid bonus shares at the rate of 1 share for every 4 shares held as per General Body's resolution dated 30th Sept. 2022)			
Bonus to Shareholders A/c Dr.		2,75,000	
To Equity Share Capital A/c			2,75,000
(Being the issue of 27,500 equity shares of ₹10 each by way of bonus shares in the ratio of 1 for every 4 held)			
Bank A/c Dr.		5,15,625	
To Equity Share Application & Allotment A/c			5,15,625
(Being application money received on 34,375 @ ₹ 15 per share to be issued as right shares in the ratio of 1 : 4)			
Equity Share Application & Allotment A/c Dr.		5,15,625	
To Equity Share Capital A/c			3,43,750
To Securities Premium A/c			1,71,875
(Being application money on 34,375 shares @ ₹ 10 per share transferred to Share Capital Account and ₹ 5 per share to Securities Premium Account)			

19.0 FORM OF PREPARING A BALANCE SHEET OF A COMPANY

VERTICAL FORM OF BALANCE SHEET

Part I of Schedule III to The Companies Act, 2013 prescribes only vertical form of Balance Sheet.

GENERAL INSTRUCTIONS FOR PREPARATION OF BALANCE SHEET

1. Current Assets	An asset shall be classified as current when it satisfies any of the following **criteria**: (a) it is expected to be realized in, *or* is intended for sale *or* consumption in, the company's normal operating cycle; (b) it is held primarily for the purpose of being traded; *or* (c) it is expected to be realized within 12 months after the reporting date; *or* (d) it is cash *or* cash equivalent unless it is restricted from being exchanged *or* used to settle a liability for at least 12 months after the reporting date.
2. Non-Current Assets	All other assets shall be classified as non-current.
3. An Operating Cycle	An operating cycle is the time between the acquisition of assets for processing and their realization in cash *or* cash equivalents. Where the normal operating cycle cannot be identified, it is assumed to have a duration of 12 months.
3. Current Liabilities	A liability shall be classified as current when it satisfies **any of the following criteria:** (a) it is expected to be settled in the company's normal operating cycle; (b) it is held primarily for the purpose of being traded; (c) it is due to be settled within 12 months after the reporting date; *or* (d) the company does not have an unconditional right to defer settlement of the liability for at least twelve months after the reporting date. Terms of a liability that could, at the option of the counterparty, result in its settlement by the issue of equity instruments do not affect its classification.
4. Non-Current Liabilities	All other liabilities shall be classified as non-current.
5. Trade Receivable	A receivable shall be classified as a 'Trade Receivable' if it is in respect of the amount due on account of goods sold *or* services rendered in the normal course of business.
6. Trade Payable	A payable shall be classified as a 'Trade Payable' if it is in respect of the amount due on account of goods purchased *or* services received in the normal course of business.
7. Use of Prefix 'At' instead of 'On'	It may be noted that the prescribed form of Balance Sheet prefixes 'At' instead of 'On'. For example, if a Balance Sheet of X Ltd. is prepared on 31st march, then the date of the balance-sheet will be stated as 'At 31st March, 2023' and not as 'On 31st March, 2023. The word 'On' refers to the entire duration (which consists of 24 hours) of the day whereas the word 'At' refers to a specific point of time. Since the balance-sheet is prepared to represent the financial position of the concern at a particular point of time (viz. at the end of the day's business hours), it is **appropriate to use the word 'At' instead of 'On'.**

20.0 VERTICAL FORM OF SUMMARISED BALANCE SHEET [WITH MAJOR HEADINGS ONLY]

...NAME OF THE COMPANY...
BALANCE SHEET AS AT... *(Rupees in...)*

Particulars	*Note No.*	*Figures for the Current Reporting Period*	*Figures for the Previous Reporting Period*
I. EQUITY AND LIABILITIES			
(1) Shareholders' Funds		xxx	xxx
(2) Share Application Money pending Allotment		xxx	xxx
(3) Non-Current Liabilities		xxx	xxx
(4) Current Liabilities		xxx	xxx
Total		xxx	xxx
II. ASSETS			
(1) Non-Current Assets		xxx	xxx
(2) Current Assets		xxx	xxx
Total		xxx	xxx

11.0 VERTICAL FORM OF DETAILED BALANCE SHEET

...NAME OF THE COMPANY...
BALANCE SHEET AS AT... *(Rupees in...)*

Particulars	*Note No.*	*Figures for the Current Reporting Period*	*Figures for the Previous Reporting Period*
I. EQUITY AND LIABILITIES			
(1) Shareholders' Funds			
(a) Share Capital	1	………	………
(b) Reserves and Surplus [e.g. Debit Balance of Profit & Loss A/c as negative figure, Amalgamation Adjustment A/c as a negative figure)]	2	………	………
(c) Money received against Share Warrants		………	………
(2) Share Application Money pending Allotment		………	………
(3) Non-Current Liabilities			
(a) Long-term Borrowings [e.g. Bonds/ Debentures/Loans repayable after 12 months]	3	………	………

(b) Deferred Tax Liabilities (Net)		....	....
(c) Other Long term Liabilities [e.g. Trade Payables to be settled after 12 months]		....	....
(d) Long-term Provisions [e.g. Provision for Employee Benefits to be settled after 12 months]		....	....
(4) Current Liabilities			
(a) Short-Term Borrowings [e.g. Loans repayable on demand *or* within 12 months]	4	....	....
(b) Trade Payables [e.g. Trade Creditors,Bills Payables to be settled within 12 months]	5	....	....
(c) Other Current Liabilities [e.g. Bank Overdraft,Unpaid Dividend/ matured Deposits/ matured Debentures, That portion of Long-term Borrowings repayable within 12 months, Interest accrued(whether due *or* not) on borrowings,Calls-in-Advance,Outstanding Expenses, Tax Payable]	6	....	....
(d) Short-Term Provisions [e.g. Provision for Tax, Proposed Dividend, Provision for Employee Benefits to be settled within 12 months]	7	....	....
Total		....	....
II. ASSETS			
(1) Non-Current Assets			
(a) **Property, Plant and Equipment and Intangible assets**			
(i) Property, Plant and Equipment [e.g. Land, Buildings, Plant & Equipment]	8	....	....
(ii) Intangible Assets [e.g. Goodwill Purchased, Goodwill on Consolidation, Brands/ Trademarks]	9	....	....
(iii) Capital Work-in-Progress [e.g. Building under construction]		....	....
(iv) Intangible Assets under Development [e.g. Computer Software under Development]		....	....
(b) Non-Current Investments [e.g. Investment in Property/Partnership Firms]	10	....	....
(c) Deferred Tax Assets (Net)		....	....

(d) Long-Term Loans and Advances [e.g. Capital Advances, Loans & Advances receivable after 12 months]	11	....	....
(e) Other Non-Current Assets [e.g. , Security Deposits]	12	....	....
(2) Current Assets			
(a) Current Investments	13	....	....
(b) Inventories [e.g. Raw- Materials, Work-in-Progress, Finished Goods,Loose Tools,Stores & Spares]	14	....	....
(c) Trade Receivables [e.g. Trade Debtors,Bills Receivables to be realized within 12 months, Provision for Doubtful Debts by way of deduction]	15	....	....
(d) Cash and Cash Equivalents [e.g. Cheques/Drafts on hand, Bank Deposits with more than 12 months maturity]	16	....	....
(e) Short-term Loans and Advances [e.g. Loans & Advances receivable within 12 months]	17	....	....
(f) Other Current Assets [e.g. Prepaid Expenses]	18	....	....
Total		....	....

Notes To Accounts:

NOTE 1: SHARE CAPITAL

Particulars	₹	₹
Authorised Capital		
..... Shares of ₹... each	xxx	xxx
Issued Capital		
..... Shares of ₹... each	xxx	xxx
Subscribed Capital and fully paid		
..... Shares of ₹... each ₹... per share paid up	xxx	xxx
*Subscribed Capital but not fully paid		
..... Shares of ₹... each ₹... per share paid up	xxx	xxx
Less: Calls unpaid:		
(a) by Directors & Officers	(xxx)	(xxx)
(b) by Others	(xxx)	(xxx)
Add: Forfeited Shares	xxx	xxx
	xxx	xxx

Notes:

1. For the period of 5 years immediately preceding the date as at which the Balance Sheet is prepared
   - (a) Aggregate Number and Class of **Shares** allotted as fully paid up pursuant to a contract **without payments being received in cash**
   - (b) Aggregate Number and Class of **Shares** allotted as fully paid up by way of **Bonus Shares**
   - (c) Aggregate Number and Class of Shares bought back
2. Shares in the company held by each shareholder holding more than 5% shares specifying the number of shares
3. Shares Reserved for issue under options and contracts/commitments for the sale of shares/disinvestment, including the terms and amounts
4. Shares held by Holding Company/Ultimate Holding Company/Subsidiaries/Associates of Holding Company/Ultimate Holding Company.
5. A company shall disclose Shareholding of Promoters* as below:

S.N.	*Promoter's Name*	*No. of Shares at the end of the year*	*% of total shares*	*% Change during the year*
1.				
2.				
3.				
4.				

6. **Reconciliation** of the No of shares outstanding at the beginning and at the end of the reporting period

Particulars	*Figures for the Current Reporting Period*	*Figures for the Previous Reporting Period*
A. Shares at the beginning of the year		
B. *Add:* Shares allotted as fully paid up pursuant to a contract without payments being received in cash		
C. *Add:* Shares issued on Right/Preferential/Private Placement basis		
D. *Add:* Shares allotted as fully paid up by way of Bonus Shares		
E. *Add:* Shares Issued on exercise of Employee Stock Options		
F. *Add:* Shares Issued on conversion/surrender of Debentures/Bonds/Term Loan.		
G. *Less:* Shares cancelled on buy back of Shares		
H. *Less:* Shares Forfeited but not issued during the current year		
I. Shares at the end of the year		

***Note:** *Subscribed and Paid up Share Capital will include Unpaid Amount on Shares subscribed by Subscribers to Memorandum of Association and such Unpaid Amount will be disclosed under the head* **'Current Assets' and sub-head 'Other Current Assets'.**

NOTE 2: RESERVES AND SURPLUS

Particulars	₹	₹
Capital Reserve		
Capital Redemption Reserve		
Securities Premium Reserve		
Debenture Redemption Reserve		
Revaluation Reserve		
Share Options Outstanding Account		
Other Reserves – (specify the nature and purpose of each reserve and the amount in respect thereof)		
General Reserve, Dividend Equalisation Reserve, Reserve for Contingent Liabilities, Reserve for bad debts, Tonnage Tax Reserve created under the Income-tax Act, 1961.		
Amalgamation Adjustment A/c (shown as a negative figure)		( )
Surplus i.e. Balance in Statement of Profit & Loss		
Opening Balance		
Add: Profit for the period		
Less: Transfer to Reserve		
Less: Used for Bonus Shares		
Less: Interim Dividend		
Less: Preference Dividend		
Less: Equity Dividend		
Closing Balance		

Notes:

1. Debit Balance of Profit & Loss A/c is to be shown as negative figure.
2. Similarly Debit Balance of Reserve & Surplus is shown as negative figure.
3. 'Fund' is to be used if Reserve is earmarked for specific purpose.

NOTE 3: LONG-TERM BORROWINGS

Particulars	₹	₹
Bonds/Debentures		
Term Loans from Banks		
Term Loans from Other Parties		
Deferred Payment Liabilities		
Deposits		
Loans and Advances from Related Parties		
Long term Maturities of Finance Lease Obligations		
Other Loans and Advances (specify nature)		

Notes:

1. Aggregate Amount of Secured Borrowings along with Nature of security.
2. Aggregate Amount of Unsecured Borrowings
3. Aggregate Amount of Loans guaranteed by Directors *or* Others under each head
4. Bonds/debentures (along with the Rate of Interest and particulars of redemption *or* conversion, as the case may be) in descending order of maturity *or* conversion, starting from farthest redemption *or* conversion date, as the case may be. Where bonds/debentures are redeemable by installments, the date of maturity for this purpose must be reckoned as the date on which the first installment becomes due.
5. Particulars of any Redeemed Bonds/Debentures which the company has power to reissue shall be disclosed.
6. Terms of Repayment of Term Loans and Other Loans
7. Period and amount of continuing default as on the Balance Sheet Date in repayment of Loans and Interest

NOTE 4: OTHER LONG TERM LIABILITIES

(a) Trade payables

(b) Others

NOTE 5: LONG-TERM PROVISIONS

(a) Provision for employee benefits.

(b) Others (specify nature).

NOTE 6: SHORT-TERM BORROWINGS

Particulars	₹	₹
Loans repayable on demand from Banks		
Loans repayable on demand from Other Parties		
Loans and Advances from Related Parties		
Deposits		
Current maturities of Long-term Borrowings		
Other Loans and Advances (specify nature)		

Notes:

1. Aggregate Amount of Secured Borrowings along with Nature of security and Unsecured Borrowings.
2. Aggregate Amount of Unsecured Borrowings
3. Aggregate Amount of Loans guaranteed by Directors *or* Others under each head
4. Period and amount of continuing default as on the Balance Sheet Date in repayment of Loans and Interest

NOTE 7: TRADE PAYABLES

Particulars	₹	₹
Sundry Creditors		
Bills Payables		

Note: TRADE PAYABLES AGEING SCHEDULE IS TO GIVEN.

Particulars	***Outstanding for following periods from due date of payment***				***Total***
	Less than 1 year	***1-2 years***	***2-3 years***	***More than 3 years***	
(i) MSME					
(ii) Others					
(iii) Disputed dues MSME					
(iv) Disputed dues Others					

NOTE 8: OTHER CURRENT LIABILITIES

Particulars	₹	₹
Current maturities of Finance Lease Obligations		
Interest accrued but not due on Borrowings		
Interest accrued and due on Borrowings		
Income received in advance		
Unpaid Dividends		
Application Money received for allotment of securities and due for refund and interest accrued thereon.		
Unpaid matured Deposits and Interest accrued thereon		
Unpaid matured Debentures and Interest accrued thereon		
Other Payables (specify nature e.g.)		
Bank Overdraft		
Outstanding Expenses		
Calls-in-Advance		

NOTE 7: SHORT-TERM PROVISIONS

Particulars	₹	₹
Provision for Employees' Benefit		
Provision for Income Tax		
Provision for Dividend Distribution Tax		

NOTE 8: PROPERTY, PLANT & EQUIPMENT

Asset	*Original Cost in the beg*	*Additions*	*Disposal*	*Original Cost at the end*	*Total Depreciation in the beg*	*Depreciation for Current year*	*Depreciation on Asset Disposed off*	*Total Depreciation at the end*	*W.D.V at the end*
A	*B*	*C*	*D*	*E = B + C − D*	*F*	*G*	*H*	*I = F + G − H*	*J = E − I*
Land									
Building									
Plant & Equipment									
Furniture and Fixtures									
Vehicles									

Office Equipment									
Others (specify nature)									
Assets under Lease									

Notes:

1. Impairment Losses/Reversals
2. Every Balance Sheet subsequent to date of Capital Reduction/Revaluation must show the reduced *or* increased figures and must by way of a note also show the amount of the reduction *or* increase together with the date thereof for the first 5 years subsequent to the date of such reduction *or* increase.

NOTE 9: INTANGIBLE ASSETS

Asset	*Original Cost in the beg*	*Additions*	*Disposal*	*Original Cost at the end*	*Total Depreciation in the beg*	*Depreciation for Current year*	*Depreciation on Asset Disposed off*	*Total Depre-ciation at the end*	*W.D.V at the end*
A	*B*	*C*	*D*	*E = B + C − D*	*F*	*G*	*H*	*I = F + G − H*	*J = E − I*
Goodwill									
Brands									
Trademarks									
Computer Software									
Mastheads and Publishing Titles.									
Mining Rights.									
Copyrights, and Patents and Other Intellectual Property Rights, Services & Operating Rights.									
Recipes, Formulae, Models, Designs and Prototypes.									
Licenses and Franchise.									
Others (Specify Nature).									

Notes: Same as for Property, Plant & Equipment

NOTE 10: NON-CURRENT INVESTMENTS

Particulars	₹	₹
Trade Investments		
Investment in Property		
Investments In Equity Instruments		
Investments In Preference Shares		
Investments In Government *or* Trust Securities		
Investments In Debentures *or* Bonds		
Investments In Mutual Funds		
Investments In Partnership Firms		
Other Non-Current Investments (Specify Nature)		

Notes:

1. Basis for Valuation in case of Investments carried at other than at cost
2. Aggregate amount of Quoted Investments and Market Value thereof;
3. Aggregate amount of Unquoted Investments;
4. Aggregate Provision for Diminution in Value of Investments

NOTE 11: LONG-TERM LOANS AND ADVANCES

Particulars	₹	₹
Capital Advances		
Loans and Advances to Related Parties		
Other Loans and Advances (specify nature)		

Notes:

1. Amount of Secured Loans & Advances considered good
2. Amount of Unsecured Loans & Advances considered good
3. Amount of Loans & Advances considered Doubtful
4. Allowance for Bad and Doubtful on Loans and Advances
5. Loans and advances due by directors *or* other officers of the company *or* any of them either severally *or* jointly with any other persons *or* amounts due by firms *or* private companies respectively in which any director is a partner *or* a director *or* a member

NOTE 12: OTHER NON-CURRENT ASSETS

Particulars	₹	₹
Long Term Trade Receivables (including trade receivables on deferred credit terms)		
Security Deposits		
Others (specify nature e.g.)		
Discount/Loss on Issue of Debentures		

Notes: Same as for Long-term Loans and Advances

NOTE 13: CURRENT INVESTMENTS

Particulars	₹	₹
Investments In Equity Instruments		
Investments In Preference Shares		
Investments In Government *or* Trust Securities		
Investments In Debentures *or* Bonds		
Investments In Mutual Funds		
Investments In Partnership Firms		
Other Current Investments (Specify Nature)		

Notes: Same as for Non-Current Investments

NOTE 14: INVENTORIES

Particulars	₹	₹
Raw- Materials		
Work-in-Progress		
Finished Goods		
Stock-in-Trade		
Stores & Spares		
Loose Tools		
Others (specify nature)		

Notes:

1. Goods-in-transit under relevant sub-head
2. Mode of Valuation

NOTE 15: TRADE RECEIVABLES

Particulars	₹	₹
Sundry Debtors		
Less: Provision for Doubtful Debts		
Bills Receivables		

Notes:

1. Aggregate amount of Trade Receivables outstanding for a period exceeding six months from the date they are due for payment
2. Other Notes Same as for Long-term Loans and Advances

3. TRADE RECEIVABLES AGEING SCHEDULE IS TO GIVEN.

Particulars	*Outstanding for following periods from due date of payment*					*Total*
	Less than 6 months	*1/2-1 year*	*1-2 years*	*2-3 years*	*More than 3 years*	
(i) Undisputed Trade receivables – considered good						

(ii) Undisputed Trade Receivables – considered doubtful						
(iii) Disputed Trade receivables – considered good						
(iv) Disputed Trade Receivables – considered doubtful						

NOTE 16: CASH AND CASH EQUIVALENTS

Particulars	₹	₹
Bank Balance		
Cheques/Drafts on hand		
Cash Balance		
Others (specify nature)		

Notes:

1. Earmarked balances with banks (***For Example*** for unpaid dividend)
2. Balances with banks to the extent held as margin money *or* security against the borrowings, guarantees, other commitments
3. Repatriation restrictions, if any, in respect of cash and bank balances
4. Bank deposits with more than 12 months maturity

NOTE 17: SHORT-TERM LOANS AND ADVANCES

Particulars	₹	₹
Loans and Advances to Related Parties		
Other Loans and Advances (specify nature)		

Notes: Same as for Long-term Loans and Advances

NOTE 18: OTHER CURRENT ASSETS (SPECIFY NATURE E.G.)

Particulars	₹	₹
Prepaid Expenses		
Unpaid Amount on Shares subscribed by Subscribers to Memorandum of Association		

NOTE 19: CONTINGENT LIABILITIES AND COMMITMENTS (TO THE EXTENT NOT PROVIDED FOR)

Particulars	₹	₹
(i) CONTINGENT LIABILITIES		
(a) Claims against the company not acknowledged as debt (e.g., Towards Excise, Customs, GST, Service Tax, Income Tax, Suppliers, Customers)		
(b) Guarantees (e.g. to Banks on behalf of others)		
(c) Other money for which the company is contingently liable (e.g. Bills Discounted but not yet matured)		

(ii) COMMITMENTS		
(a) Estimated amount of contracts remaining to be executed on Capital Account and not provided for;		
(b) Uncalled Liability on Shares and Other Investments (e.g. Debentures) partly paid		
(c) Other Commitments (e.g. Arrears of Fixed Cumulative Dividends on Preference Shares)		

NOTE 20: Following Ratios are to be disclosed:

1. Current Ratio,	7. Trade Payables turnover ratio,
2. Debt-Equity Ratio,	8. Net Capital Turnover Ratio,
3. Debt Service Coverage Ratio,	9. Net Profit Ratio,
4. Return on Equity Ratio,	10 Return on Capital employed,
5. Inventory Turnover Ratio,	11. Return on Investment.
6. Trade Receivables turnover ratio,	

The company shall explain the items included in numerator and denominator for computing the above ratios. Further explanation shall be provided for any change in the ratio by more than 25% as compared to the preceding year.

1. LIQUIDITY RATIOS

1. CURRENT RATIO

$$\text{Current Ratio} = \frac{\text{Current Assets}}{\text{Current Liabilities}}$$

Notes:

1. **Current Assets** = Current Investments + Inventories + Trade Receivables + Cash and Cash Equivalents + Short-term Loans and Advances + Other Current Assets (e.g., Prepaid Expenses, Accrued Incomes, Advance Tax) **- Non-Current Assets classified as held for sale**
2. **Current Liabilities** = Short-Term Borrowings + Trade Payables + Other Current Liabilities + Short-Term Provisions **- Current Maturities of long-term debt - Interest accrued on borrowings**
3. **Working Capital** = Current Assets – Current Liabilities
4. **Interpretation:** Current Ratio indicates rupees of current assets available for each rupee of current liability. Higher the ratio, greater the margin of safety for short-term creditors and vice versa.

Traditionally, a Current Ratio of 2 : 1 is considered to be a satisfactory ratio. On the basis of this traditional rule, if the Current Ratio is 2 *or* more, it means the firm is adequately liquid and has the ability to meet its current obligations but if the Current Ratio is *less* than 2, it means the firm has difficulty in meeting its current obligations. The logic behind this rule is that even if the value of current assets becomes half, the firm can still meet its short-term obligations.

A too high Current Ratio may be the result of excessive investment in current assets which may result in idle funds which further results in low profitability since idle funds earn nothing. On the other hand, a too low Current Ratio may be the result of inadequate investment in current assets which may result in low liquidity and may threaten the solvency of the enterprise. Higher liquidity means lower profitability and vice versa.

2.SOLVENCY RATIOS

2. DEBT-EQUITY RATIO

$$\text{Debt-Equity Ratio} = \frac{\text{Total Debt}}{\text{Total Equity}}$$

Notes:

1. **Total Debt** = Long-term Borrowings + Short-term Borrowings
2. **Total Equity [i.e.** Funds belonging to all the Shareholders (whether Equity *or* Preference)].
   = Equity Share Capital + Pref. Share Capital + Reserves & Surplus
3. **Interpretation:** Debt-Equity Ratio indicates the margin of safety to Lenders. A low debt-equity ratio implies the use of more equity than debt which means a larger safety margin for Lenders since owner's equity is treated as a margin of safety by Lenders and vice versa. Traditionally, a Debt Equity Ratio of 2 : 1 is considered to be satisfactory which means debt could be twice the equity.

3. DEBT SERVICE COVERAGE RATIO

Approach 1: When Principal Repayment is not adjusted for tax effects

$$\text{Debt-Service coverage Ratio} = \frac{\text{Net Profit before Interest,Tax and Exceptional Items}}{\text{Interest on Borrowings + Principal Repayment}}$$

Approach 2: When Principal Repayment is adjusted for tax effects

$$\text{Debt-Service coverage Ratio} = \frac{\text{Net Profit before Interest Tax and Exceptional Items}}{\text{Interest + [Principal portion of Instalment /(1-tax rate)]}}$$

Note: *The principal portion of instalment is adjusted for tax effects since such payment is not deductible from net profit for tax purposes.*

Approach 3 When Cash from operations is used instead of Net Profit

Some Accountants who are interested in determining the firm's Cash Operating capacity to pay off both interest and principal, prefer to calculate the Debt Service Coverage Ratio as follows:

$$= \frac{\text{Cash from operations before Interest,Tax and Exceptional Items}}{\text{Interest + (Principal portion of Instalment /(1-tax rate)}}$$

Interpretation: Debt-Service Coverage Ratio shows the number of times the amount of interest on long-term debts and the principal portion of instalment is covered by the profits out of which that will be paid. It indicates the limit beyond which the ability of the firm to service its debt would be adversely affected. *For instance*, a Debt Service Ratio of five times would imply that even if the firm's Net Profits before Interest and Tax decrease by 80% of the present level, the firm will still be able to pay interest and instalment out of profits. Higher the ratio, greater the firm's ability to pay current interest and instalment but very high ratio may imply lesser use of debt and very efficient operations.

3. ACTIVITY (OR TURNOVER) RATIOS

4. Net Capital Turnover Ratio

$$\text{Net Capital Turnover Ratio} = \frac{\text{Net Revenue from Operations}}{\text{Net Working Capital}} = \ldots \text{Times}$$

Notes:

1. **Net Working Capital** = Current Assets – Current Liabilities
2. **Interpretation:** It indicates the firm's ability to generate Revenue from Operations/ Sales per rupee of Working Capital. In general, higher the ratio, the more efficient the management and utilisation of Working Capital. A too high ratio may indicate the situation of over-trading (or under-capitalisation) if current ratio is lower than that required reasonably and vice versa.

Thus, an enterprise should have *neither* a very high *nor* a very low ratio, it should have a satisfactory ratio. To judge whether the ratio is satisfactory or not, it should be compared with its own past ratios or with the ratio of similar enterprises in the same industry or with the industry average.

5. Inventory Turnover Ratio

$$\textbf{Inventory Turnover Ratio} = \frac{\textbf{Cost of Revenue from Operations}}{\textbf{Average Inventory}} = \textbf{... Times}$$

Notes:

1. **Cost of Revenue from Operations**

= Cost of Materials Consumed + Purchases of Stock-in-Trade + Changes in Inventories of Finished Goods + Direct Expenses

2. **Average Inventory** = (Opening Inventory + Closing Inventory)/2

Note: Inventory includes Raw materials and components, Work-in-progress, Finished goods, Stores and spare parts, Consumable tools and Goods-in-transit.

3. **Interpretation:** Inventory turnover indicates the speed with which the Inventory is converted into Revenue from Operations. In general, a high ratio indicates efficient performance since an improvement in the ratio shows that *either* the same volume of Revenue from Operations has been maintained with a lower investment in Inventory, *or* the volume of Revenue from Operations has increased without any increase in the amount of Inventory. However, too high ratio and too low ratio call for further investigation. A too high ratio may be the result of a very low inventory levels which may result in frequent Inventory-outs and thus the firm may incur high Inventory-out costs. On the other hand, a too low ratio may be the result of excessive inventory levels, slow-moving *or* obsolete inventory and thus, the firm may incur high carrying costs. Thus, a firm should have *neither* a very high *nor* a very low Inventory Turnover Ratio, it should have a satisfactory level.

6. Trade Receivables Turnover Ratio

$$\textbf{Debtors Turnover Ratio} = \frac{\textbf{Credit Revenue from Operations}}{\textbf{Average Trade Receivables}} = \textbf{. . . Times}$$

Notes:

1. Credit Revenue from Operations

= Revenue from Operations – Cash Revenue from Operations

2. Average Trade Receivables = (Opening Trade Receivables + Closing Trade Receivables)/ 2

Note: Trade Receivables = Trade Debtors + Bills Receivable

3. Interpretation: Debtors Turnover Ratio indicates both the quality of Trade Receivables and the credit collection efforts of the enterprise. It indicates the speed with which the debtors are converted into cash each year. In general, a high ratio indicates the shorter collection period which implies prompt payments by Trade Receivables, and a low ratio indicates a longer collection period which implies delayed payments by Trade Receivables. However, too high ratio and too low ratio calls for further investigation. A too high ratio may be the result of a restrictive credit and collection policy which may curtail the Revenue from Operations and consequently profits. On the other hand, a too low ratio may be the result of liberal and inefficient credit and collection policy which may involve the risk of bad debts and burden of high interest cost involved in maintaining a higher level of Trade Receivables. Thus, a firm should *neither* have a very high *nor* a very low Debtors Turnover Ratio, but should have a satisfactory level.

7. Trade Payables Turnover Ratio

$$\textbf{Trade Payables Turnover Ratio} = \frac{\textbf{Cost of Materials Consumed}}{\textbf{Average Trade Payables}} = \ldots \text{ Times}$$

Notes:

1.Cost of Materials Consumed = Cost of Materials Consumed + Purchases of Stock-in-Trade + Other Operating Expenses

2.Average Trade Payables = (Opening Trade Payables + Closing Trade Payables)/2

Note: Trade Payables = Trade Creditors + Bills Payable

3. Interpretation: Creditors Turnover indicates the speed with which the Creditors turn over on an average each year. In general, a high ratio indicates the shorter payment period which implies *either* the availability of *less* credit *or* earlier payments and a low ratio indicates a larger payment period which implies *either* the availability of more credit *or* delayed payments.

4. PROFITABILITY RATIOS

8. Net Profit Ratio

1. $$\text{Net Profit Ratio} = \frac{\text{Net Profit Before Tax}}{\text{Revenue from Operations}} \times 100 = \ldots \%$$

or,

$$\text{Net Profit Ratio} = \frac{\text{Net Profit After Tax}}{\text{Revenue from Operations}} \times 100 = \ldots \%$$

Notes:

1. Net Profit = Revenue from Operations – Cost of Revenue from Operations – Operating Expenses – Non-Operating Expenses + Non-Operating Incomes

or, **= Revenue from Operations – Operating Cost – Non-Operating Expenses + Non-Operating Incomes**

or, **= Operating Profit – Non-Operating Expenses + Non-Operating Incomes**

2. Revenue from Operations = Credit Revenue from Operations + Cash Revenue from Operations

3. Interpretation: Net Profit Ratio indicates (a) an average Net Margin earned on a Revenue from Operations of ₹ 100 (b) what portion of Revenue from Operations is left to pay dividend and to create reserves, and (c) firm's capacity to withstand adverse economic conditions when selling price is declining, cost of production is rising and the demand for the product is falling. In general, Higher the ratio, greater is the capacity of the firm to withstand adverse economic conditions and vice versa.

9. Return on Capital Employed

$$\text{Return on Capital Employed (Pre-tax)} = \frac{\text{Net Profit before Interest and Tax}}{\text{Average Capital Employed}} \times 100 = .. \%$$

Return on Capital Employed(Post-tax)=

$$\frac{\text{Net Profit after Interest and Tax + Interest + Deferred Tax Expense/(Income) + Finance Cost - Other Income}}{\text{Average Capital Employed}} \times 100$$

= ..... %

Notes:

1. Average Capital Employed =[Opening Capital Employed+ Closing Capital Employed]/2
2. Capital Employed = Shareholders' Funds + Borrowings+ Deferred Tax Liabilities+ Creditors for Capital Expenditure – Non-Trade Investments– Capital WIP– Intangible Assets under Development– Advances for Purchase of Non-Current Assets – Cash and Cash Equivalents
3. Income from Non-Operating Assets should also be excluded from the Net Profit.
4. **Interpretation:** Return on Capital Employed Ratio indicates the firm's ability of generating profit per rupee of Capital Employed. Higher the Ratio, the more efficient the management and utilisation of Capital Employed.

An enterprise should have a satisfactory ratio. To judge whether the ratio is satisfactory *or* not, it should be compared with its own past ratios *or* with the ratio of similar enterprises in the same industry *or* with the industry average.

10. Return on Investment [ROI]

$$\text{Return on Investments} = \frac{\text{Other Income (Excluding Dividend)}}{\text{Average Investments}} \times 100 = .. \%$$

Notes:

1. Average Investments =[Opening Investments + Closing Investments]/2

2. Investments = Cash, Cash Equivalents + Other Marketable Securities

3. Interpretation: **Return on Investments** Ratio indicates the firm's ability of generating profit per rupee of **Investments**. Higher the Ratio, the more efficient the management and utilisation of **Invested Capital** .An enterprise should have a satisfactory ratio. To judge whether the ratio is satisfactory or not, it should be compared with its own past ratios or with the ratio of similar enterprises in the same industry or with the industry average.

11. Return on Equity

$$\textbf{Return on Equity} = \frac{\textbf{Net Profit after Interest and Tax}}{\textbf{Average Shareholders' Funds}} \textbf{ x 100 = . . . \%}$$

Notes:

1. Average Shareholders' Funds. =[Opening Shareholders' Funds.+ Closing Shareholders' Funds]/2

2. Shareholders' Funds = Funds supplied by the Shareholders = Equity Share Capital + Pref. Share Capital + Reserves & Surplus

3. Interpretation: Return on Equity Ratio indicates the firm's ability of generating profit per rupee of Shareholders' Funds. Higher the ratio, the more efficient the management and utilization of Shareholders' Funds.

An enterprise should have a satisfactory ratio. To judge whether the ratio is satisfactory *or* not, it should be compared with its own past ratios *or* with the ratio of similar enterprises in the same industry *or* with the industry average.

ILLUSTRATION 20

TULSI, AMLA, GILOY Ltd provides the following information:

Particulars	₹	*Particulars*	₹
Equity Share Capital (₹ 10 each)	1,50,000	Tangible Fixed Assets	9,00,000
18% Pref. Share capital	1,00,000	Intangible Fixed Assets	1,50,000
Reserves & Surplus	1,50,000	Non-Current Investments [Trade]	50,000
15% Long-term Borrowings (payable in annual instalments of ₹ 90,000)	8,00,000	Inventories	1,00,000
Current Liabilities (including Trade Payables ₹ 1,00,000,Short-term Borrowings nil)	4,00,000	Trade Receivables	1,00,000
Revenue from Operations (on credit)	24,00,000	Cash & Cash equivalents	3,00,000
Purchases (on credit)	12,00,000	Tax Rate 25%	
Net Profit before Interest & Tax	6,00,000	Gross Profit Ratio 50%	

Required: Calculate the 11 ratios required as per Schedule III to The Companies Act,2013.

SOLUTION:

$$\textbf{1. Current Ratio} = \frac{\text{Current Assets}}{\text{Current Liabilities}} = \frac{₹\,5{,}00{,}000}{₹\,4{,}00{,}000} = 1.25 : 1$$

Note: Current Assets = ₹ 1,00,000 + ₹ 1,00,000 + ₹ 3,00,000= ₹ 5,00,000

$$\textbf{2. Debt-Equity Ratio} = \frac{\text{Total Debts}}{\text{Shareholders' Funds}} = \frac{₹\,8{,}00{,}000}{₹\,4{,}00{,}000} = 2 : 1$$

Note: Shareholders' Funds = Equity Share Capital + Pref. Share Capital + Reserves & Surplus

= ₹ 1,50,000 + ₹ 1,00,000 + ₹ 1,50,000 = ₹ 4,00,000

3. Debt-Service Coverage Ratio

Approach 1: When Principal Repayment is not adjusted for tax effects

$$\textbf{Debt-Service Coverage Ratio} = \frac{\textbf{Net Profit before Interest, Tax and Exceptional Items}}{\textbf{Interest on Borrowings + Principal Repayment}}$$

$$= \frac{₹\,6{,}00{,}000}{₹\,1{,}20{,}000 + ₹\,90{,}000} = \textbf{2.857 times}$$

Approach 2: When Principal Repayment is adjusted for tax effects

$$\textbf{Debt-Service coverage Ratio} = \frac{\textbf{Net Profit before Interest Tax and Exceptional Items}}{\textbf{Interest + [Principal portion of Instalment /(1-tax rate)]}}$$

$$= \frac{₹\ 6,00,000}{₹\ 1,20,000 + [₹\ 90,000/(1-0.25)]} = \textbf{2.5 times}$$

$$\textbf{4. Capital Turnover Ratio} = \frac{\text{Revenue from Operations}}{\text{Average Working Capital}} = \frac{₹\ 24,00,000}{₹\ 1,00,000} = 24 \text{ times}$$

Note: Net Working Capital = Current Assets – Current Liabilities

= ₹ 5,00,000 – ₹ 4,00,000 = ₹ 1,00,000

$$\textbf{5. Inventory Turnover Ratio} = \frac{\text{Cost of Revenue from Operations}}{\text{Average Inventory}}$$

$$= \frac{₹\ 12,00,000}{₹\ 1,00,000} = 12 \text{ Times}$$

Note: Cost of Revenue from Operations = Revenue from Operations – Gross Profit

= (₹ 24,00,000) – (50% of ₹ 24,00,000) = ₹ 12,00,000

$$\textbf{6. Debtors Turnover Ratio} = \frac{\text{Credit Revenue from Operations}}{\text{Average Trade Receivables}} = ₹\ 24,00,000/₹\ 1,00,000 = 24 \text{ times}$$

$$\textbf{7. Creditors Turnover Ratio} = \frac{\text{Net Credit Purchases}}{\text{Average Trade Payables}} = ₹\ 12,00,000/₹\ 1,00,000 = 12 \text{ Times}$$

NET PROFIT AFTER INTEREST & TAX

Particulars	₹
A. Net Profit before Interest & Tax	6,00,000
B. *Less:* Interest on Long-term Borrowings [₹ 8,00,000 x 15/100]	(1,20,000)
C. Net Profit before tax	4,80,000
D. *Less:* Tax @25%	(1,20,000)
E. Net Profit after Interest & Tax	3,60,000

$$\textbf{8. Net Profit Ratio} = \frac{\text{Net Profit Before Tax}}{\text{Revenue from Operations}} \times 100 = (₹4,80,000/₹24,00,000) \times 100 = 20\%$$

$$\textit{or,}\textbf{Net Profit Ratio} = \frac{\text{Net Profit After Tax}}{\text{Revenue from Operations}} \times 100 = (₹3,60,000/₹24,00,000) \times 100 = 15\%$$

$$\textbf{9. Return on Capital Employed (Pre-tax)} = \frac{\text{Net Profit before Interest and Tax}}{\text{Average Capital Employed}} \times 100$$

$$= \frac{₹\ 6,00,000}{₹\ 9,00,000} \times 100 = 66.67\%$$

$$\textbf{Return on Capital Employed (Post-tax)} = \frac{\text{Net Profit after Interest and Tax + Interest}}{\text{Average Capital Employed}} \times 100$$

$$= \frac{₹\ 3,60,000 + ₹\ 1,20,000}{₹\ 9,00,000} \times 100 = 53.33\%$$

Note: Capital Employed = Shareholders' Funds + Borrowings+ Deferred Tax Liabilities+ Creditors for Capital Expenditure – Non-Trade Investments– Capital WIP– Intangible Assets under Development– Advances for Purchase of Non-Current Assets – Cash and Cash Equivalents

= ₹ 1,50,000 + ₹ 1,00,000, + ₹ 1,50,000 + ₹ 8,00,000– ₹ 3,00,000= ₹ 9,00,000

10. Return on Invested Capital = $\frac{\text{Other Income}}{\text{Average Investments}} \times 100$

$= \frac{₹\ 0}{₹\ 3,00,000} \times 100 = 0\%$

Note: Investments = Cash, Cash Equivalents + Other Marketable Securities= ₹ 3,00,000

11. Return on Equity = $\frac{\text{Net Profit after Interest and Tax}}{\text{Average Shareholders' Funds}} \times 100$

$= \frac{₹\ 3,60,000}{₹\ 4,00,000} \times 100 = 90\%$

Note: Shareholders' Funds = Equity Share Capital + Pref. Share Capital + Reserves & Surplus

= ₹ 1,50,000 + ₹ 1,00,000, + ₹ 1,50,000 = ₹ 4,00,000

Note: Since 'Average Figures' cannot be ascertained due to non-availability of information, 'Closing Figures' have been used.

ILLUSTRATION 21

How will you disclose the following items while preparing the Balance Sheet of a TULSIAN Ltd (having operating cycle of 14 months) as at 31st March,2023, as per the Schedule III to The Companies Act, 2013? (Name the Head, Sub-Head and Sub-Sub-Head,if any)

SOLUTION

DISCLOSURE AS PER SCHEDULE III TO THE COMPANIES ACT, 2013

Item	*Major Head*	*Sub- Head*	*Sub- Sub- Head*
1. Current Maturities of Long-term Debt	Current Liabilities	Short-Term Borrowings	
2. Security Deposit	Non-Current Assets	Other Non-Current Assets	
3. Debit Balance of Profit & Loss A/c	Shareholders' Funds	Reserves and Surplus (As a negative figure)	
4. Computer Software under Development	Non-Current Assets	Property,Plant, Equipment & Intangible Assets	Intangible Assets under Development
5. Building under construction	Non-Current Assets	Property,Plant, Equipment & Intangible Assets	Capital Work-in-Progress
6. Uncalled Liability on partly paid Debentures held as Investments	Notes to Accounts	Contingent Liabilities and Commitments	Commitments
7. Employees' earned leave payable on retirement	Non-Current Liabilities	Long-term Provisions	

8. Share application money received in excess of issued share capital	Other Current Liabilities		
9. Share option outstanding account	Reserves & Surplus		
10. Unpaid matured debentures and interest accrued thereon	Other Current Liabilities		
11. Uncalled liability on shares and other partly paid investments	Notes to Accounts	Contingent Liabilities and Commitments	Commitments
12. Calls-in-Advance	Current Liabilities	Other Current Liabilities	
13. Investment in Bonds of Reliance Ltd. (Redeemable within 1 year)	Current Assets	Current Investments	
14. Interest accrued on Bonds of Reliance Ltd.	Current Assets	Other Current Assets	
15. Tonnage Tax Reserve	Shareholders' Funds	Reserves and Surplus	Other Reserves
16. Arrears of Fixed Cumulative Dividends on Preference Shares	Notes to Accounts	Contingent Liabilities and Commitments	Commitments
17. Crypto Currency or Virtual Currency	Non-Current Assets	Property,Plant, Equipment & Intangible Assets	Intangible Assets
18. Crypto Currency or Virtual Currency held for sale in ordinary course of business	Current Assets	Inventories	
19. Leasehold Land	Non-Current Assets	Property,Plant, Equipment & Intangible Assets	Property,Plant & Equipment
20. Licenses & Franchise	Non-Current Assets	Property,Plant, Equipment & Intangible Assets	Intangible Assets
21. *X*, a customer whose expected realisation date is 30th June, 2024	Non-Current Assets	Other Long-term Assets	Long-term Trade Receivables

22. Unpaid matured debenture and interest accrued thereon.	Current Liabilities	Other Current Liabilities	
23. Amalgamation Adjustment A/c	Shareholders' Funds	Reserves & Surplus(shown as a negative figure)	
24. Bank deposits with more than 12 months maturity	Current Assets	Cash and Cash Equivalents	Balances with Bank with more than 12 months maturity

ILLUSTRATION 22 [DISCLOSURE OF SHARE CAPITAL]

Tulsian Ltd. was formed with a capital of ₹ 1,00,000 divided into 10,000 Equity Shares of ₹ 10 each. Out of these 2,000 Equity Shares were issued to the Vendors as fully paid as purchase consideration for a fixed asset acquired. 6,000 Equity Shares were offered to the public and the issue was fully subscribed. The directors called ₹ 6 per share and received the entire amount except a call of ₹ 2 per share on 500 shares out of which 200 shares were forfeited.

Required: How would you show the relevant items in the Balance Sheet of Tulsian Ltd., as per Schedule III to The Companies Act, 2013.

SOLUTION

AN EXTRACT OF BALANCE SHEET OF TULSIAN LTD AS AT ....

Particulars	*Note No*	*Current Year* ₹	*Previous Year* ₹
Equity & Liabilities			
I. Shareholders' Funds			
Share Capital	1	55,000	

Notes To Accounts:

NOTE 1: SHARE CAPITAL

Particulars	₹	₹
Authorised Capital:		
10,000 Equity Shares of ₹ 10 each		1,00,000
Issued Capital:		
8,000 Equity Shares of ₹ 10 each		80,000
Subscribed Capital and fully paid		
2,000 Equity Shares of ₹ 10 each (allotted as fully paid up pursuant to a contract without payments being received in cash)		20,000
Subscribed Capital but not fully paid		
5,800 Equity Shares of ₹ 10 each ₹ 6 paid up		34,800
Less: Calls unpaid (300 × ₹ 2)		(600)
Add: Forfeited Shares (200 × ₹ 4)		800
		55,000

ILLUSTRATION 23

Prepare Reconciliation of the No of Shares outstanding at the beginning and at the end of the reporting period from the following information:

Shares at the beginning of the year	90,00,000
Shares allotted as fully paid up pursuant to a contract without	
payments being received in cash	50,00,000
Shares allotted as fully paid up by way of Bonus Shares	45,00,000
Shares Issued on exercise of Employee Stock Options	5,00,000
Shares Issued on conversion/surrender of Debentures,Bonds and Term Loan.	10,00,000
Shares cancelled on buy back of Shares	20,00,000

SOLUTION

RECONCILIATION OF NO OF SHARES

	Particulars	***2022-2023***	***2020-2022***
A.	Shares at the beginning of the year	90,00,000	
B.	*Add:* Shares allotted as fully paid up pursuant to a contract without payments being received in cash	50,00,000	
C.	*Add:* Shares allotted as fully paid up by way of Bonus Shares	45,00,000	
D.	*Add:* Shares Issued on exercise of Employee Stock Options	5,00,000	
E.	*Add:* Shares Issued on conversion/surrender of Debentures, Bonds &Term Loan.	10,00,000	
F.	*Less:* Shares cancelled on buy back of Shares	(20,00,000)	
G.	Shares at the end of the year	1,80,00,000	

ILLUSTRATION 24

X Ltd. provides you the following information:

1. Raw material stock holding period: 3 months
2. Work-in-progress holding period: 1 month
3. Finished goods holding period: 4 months
4. Debtors collection period: 6 months

You are required to compute the operating cycle

ANSWER:

As per Schedule III "An operating cycle is the time between the acquisition of assets for processing and their realization in cash *or* cash equivalents".

Operating Cycle = Raw material stock holding period + Work-in-progress holding period + Finished goods holding period + Debtors collection period = 3 + 1 + 4 + 6 = 14 months.

ILLUSTRATION 25

State giving reason whether the Trade Receivables are Current Assets *or* Non-Current Assets as per Schedule III in the following cases:

Case	Operating Cycle Period	Expected Realisation Period
1.	11 Months	10 Months
2.	11 Months	12 Months
3.	11 Months	13 Months
4.	14 Months	13 Months
5.	14 Months	15 Months

ANSWER:

Case	Current Assets or Non-Current Assets	Reason
1.	Current Assets	Expected Realisation Period — is *less* than the Operating Cycle Period and — is within 12 Months.
2.	Current Assets	Expected Realisation Period is within 12 Months although it is more than the Operating Cycle Period.
3.	Non-Current Assets	Expected Realisation Period is more than the Operating Cycle Period and 12 Months Period.
4.	Current Assets	Expected Realisation Period is *less* than the Operating Cycle Period although it is more than the 12 Months Period.
5.	Non-Current Assets	Expected Realisation Period is more than the Operating Cycle Period and the 12 Months Period.

ILLUSTRATION 26

State giving reason whether the Trade Payables are Current Liabilities *or* Non-Current Liabilities as per Schedule III in the following cases:

Case	Operating Cycle Period	Expected Payment Period
1.	11 Months	10 Months
2.	11 Months	12 Months
3.	11 Months	13 Months
4.	14 Months	13 Months
5.	14 Months	15 Months

ANSWER:

Case	Current Assets or Non-Current Assets	Reason
1.	Current Assets	Expected Payment Period — is *less* than the Operating Cycle Period and — is within 12 Months.
2.	Current Assets	Expected Payment Period is within 12 Months although it is more than the Operating Cycle Period.

3.	Non-Current Assets	Expected Payment Period is more than the Operating Cycle Period and 12 Months Period.
4.	Current Assets	Expected Payment Period is *less* than the Operating Cycle Period although it is more than the 12 Months Period.
5.	Non-Current Assets	Expected Payment Period is more than the Operating Cycle Period and the 12 Months Period.

ILLUSTRATION 27

PCT Ltd. is in the process of finalizing its accounts for year ended 31st March, 2023 and furnishes the following information:

(i) Finished goods normally are held for 1 month before sale.

(ii) Sales realization from Debtors usually takes 2 months from date of credit invoice.

(iii) Raw materials are held in stock to cover 1 month's production requirements.

(iv) Packing materials, being specifically made for the company and having lead time of 3 months is held in stock for 3 months.

(v) The holding period in respect of unfinished goods is 1 month.

(vi) Being a monopoly KAY Ltd. enjoys a credit period of 12.5 months from its suppliers who sometimes at the end of their credit period opt for conversion of their dues into long term debt of KAY Ltd.

You are required to compute the operating cycle of PCT Ltd. as per Schedule III of The Companies Act, 2013. As the suppliers of the company are paid off after a credit period of 12.5 months should this be part of Current Liability? Would your answer be the same if the creditors are settled in 330 days?

ANSWER:

Operating Cycle = 1 + 1 + 3 + 1 + 2 = 8 months

Classification of liability to suppliers: Schedule III provides that:

"A liability shall be classified as current when it satisfies any of the following criteria:

(i) it is expected to be settled in the company's normal operating cycle;

(ii) it is held primarily for the purpose of being traded;

(iii) it is due to be settled within 12 months after the reporting date*; or*

(iv) the company does not have an unconditional right to defer settlement of the liability for at least 12 months after the reporting date. Terms of a liability that could, at the option of the counterparty, result in its settlement by the issue of equity instruments and do not affect its classification."

(a) **When credit period is 12.5 months:** It will be treated as non-current liability since it is not due to be settled within 12 months after the reporting date.

(b) **When credit period is 330 days (i.e. 11 months approx.):** It will be treated as current liability since it is due to be settled within 12 months after the reporting date.

ILLUSTRATION 28

The management of X Ltd. contends that the work in process is not valued since it is difficult to ascertain the same in view of the multiple processes involved. They opined that the value of opening and closing work in process would be more or *less* the same. Accordingly, the management had not separately disclosed work in process in its financial statements. Comment in line with Schedule III.

ANSWER

Schedule III to the Companies Act, 2013 requires the disclosure of opening and closing WIP under broad heads by way of additional information [General Instructions 5 (iii)]. In addition, AS-2 also requires the valuation of WIP. Therefore, the non-disclosure in the financial statements by the company amounts to violation of Schedule III.

ILLUSTRATION 29

TULSIAN Ltd is having the following Fixed Deposit Receipts:

Bank	*Date of FDR*	*Maturity Date*	*Amount*
Yes Bank Limited	01–Jan–2023	2–Jan–2024	30,00,000
Bank of Baroda	01–Jan–2023	31–Mar–2024	20,00,000
State Bank of India	28–Feb–2023	30–May–2023	10,00,000
ICICI Bank	1–Jan–2022	1–Apr–2024	40,00,000

Prepare Notes to Accounts showing the above Deposits in accordance with the requirements of Schedule III as at the Balance Sheet date i.e. 31st March, 2023.

ANSWER:

NOTE 'X': CASH & BANK BALANCES AS AT 31.03.2023 (BALANCE SHEET DATE)

Particulars	₹
A. Cash in Hand	xxx
B. Balances with Bank	
(i) Less than *or* equal to 12 Months Maturity.	
– Cash Equivalent as per AS–3 (less than 3 Months Maturity) [SBI]	10,00,000
– Other Bank Balances [30,00,000 + 20,00,000]	50,00,000
(ii) More than 12 Months Maturity [ICICI]	40,00,000
	100,00,000

ILLUSTRATION 30

Is non-disclosure of source from which Bonus shares have been issued, a violation of Schedule III to the Companies Act, 2013?

ANSWER

No since Schedule III does not require such disclosure. Schedule III merely requires the disclosure of aggregate number and class of shares allotted as fully paid up bonus shares for a period of 5 years immediately preceding the Balance Sheet date in the Notes to Accounts.

ILLUSTRATION 31

X Ltd. paid ₹ 25 lakhs as advance to Y Ltd. towards the purchase of printing machinery on 15-01-2023 with delivery instruction to deliver the same in the last week of June, 2023. Further on 15-02-2023 X Ltd. purchased two diesel generator sets from Y Ltd. for ₹ 30 lakhs on 90 days Credit term. In the accounts for 2022-2023, X Ltd. intends to adjust the advance paid against Credit purchase and show the net amount of ₹ 5 lakhs as due from them. As the statutory auditor, how would you deal with this?

ANSWER

Since X Ltd. has paid advance amount to the supplier of machinery to be used in the project, such advance amount should be grouped under the main heading 'Non-Current Assets' with the sub-head as Property,Plant,Equipment & Intangible Assets with a sub-classification as 'Capital Work-in-Progress.' This is as per requirement of Schedule III to The Companies Act, 2013 and the existing accounting practice.

If the advance is for purchase of other machinery, it should be grouped under a separate head – 'Long Term Loan and Advance' with a sub-classification as 'Capital advance' under the main heading 'Non-current Assets'. In view of the above, the proposal of X Ltd., to show the net balance in the personal account of Y Ltd. is not correct. Such proposal will conceal the two material items in the balance sheet – one, expenditure towards capital asset and the other current liability for purchase of the generator set.

Hence, the auditor should advice X Ltd., to show these two items separately. If X Ltd. does not accept the advice, the auditor should qualify his report with suitable quantification of amount involved.

ILLUSTRATION 33

The Balance Sheet of G Ltd is as under: Comment on the presentation in terms of Schedule III and Accounting Standards issued by NACAS.

BALANCE SHEET AS AT ... *(Rupees in ...)*

Particulars	*Note No.*	*31.03.2023*	*31.03.2022*
I. EQUITY AND LIABILITIES			
Share Capital	1	xxx	xxx
Reserves & Surplus	2	0	0
Employee stock option outstanding	3	xxx	xxx
Share application money	4	xxx	xxx
Non-Current Liabilities			
Deferred tax liability (Arising from Indian Income Tax)	5	xxx	xxx
Current Liabilities			
Trade Payables	6	xxx	xxx
Total		xxx	xxx
II. ASSETS			
Non-Current Assets			
Property,Plant,Equipment & Intangible Assets	7	xxx	xxx
Property,Plant & Equipment			
CWIP (including capital advances)	8	xxx	xxx
Current Assets			
Trade Receivables	9	xxx	xxx
Deferred Tax Asset (Arising from Indian Income Tax)	10	xxx	xxx
P & L Debit balance			
Total		xxx	xxx

ANSWER

Following Errors are noticed in presentation as per Schedule III:

(i) Share Capital & Reserve & Surplus are to be reflected under the heading "Shareholders' funds", which is not shown while preparing the balance sheet. Although it is a part of Equity and Liabilities yet it must be shown under head "shareholders' funds". The heading "Shareholders' funds" is missing in the balance sheet given in the question.

(ii) Reserve & Surplus is showing zero balance, which is not correct in the given case. Debit balance of statement of profit & Loss should be shown as a negative figure under the head 'Surplus'. The balance of 'Reserves and Surplus', after adjusting negative balance of surplus shall be shown under the head 'Reserves and Surplus' even if the resulting figure is in the negative.

(iii) Schedule III requires that Employee Stock Option outstanding should be disclosed under the heading "Reserves and Surplus"

(iv) Share application money refundable shall be shown under the sub-heading "Other Current Liabilities". As this is refundable and not pending for allotment, hence it is not a part of equity.

(v) Deferred Tax Liability has been correctly shown under Non-Current Liabilities. But Deferred tax assets and deferred tax liabilities, both, cannot be shown in balance sheet because only the net balance of Deferred Tax Liability *or* Asset is to be shown

(vi) Under the main heading of Non-Current Assets, Property,Plant,Equipment & Intangible Assets are further classified as under:

(i) Property,Plant & Equipment

(ii) Intangible assets

(iii) Capital work in Progress

(iv) Intangible assets under development.

Keeping in view the above, the CWIP shall be shown under Property, Plant,Equipment & Intangible Assets as Capital Work in Progress. The amount of Capital advances included in CWIP shall be disclosed under the sub-heading "Long term loans and advances" under the heading Non-Current Assets.

(vii) Deferred Tax Asset shall be shown under Non-Current Asset. It should be the net balance of Deferred Tax Asset after adjusting the balance of deferred tax

ILLUSTRATION 34

From the following information extracted from the books of XY Ltd., prepare a Balance Sheet of the company as at 31st March, 2023 as per Schedule III of the Companies Act. 2013:

Particulars	***(₹ in "000)***
Long term borrowings	500
Share Capital	390
Property,Plant & Equipment	600
Trade Receivables	80
Share Application Money pending Allotment	10
Trade Payables	20
Reserve and Surplus	90
Inventories	20

Cash and Cash Equivalents	120
Non-Current Investments	200
Proposed Dividend	10

SOLUTION

XY LTD.

BALANCE SHEET AS AT 31ST MARCH, 2023

Particulars	*Note No*	*2022-2023 (₹ in "000)*	*2021-2022 (₹ in "000)*
I. EQUITY AND LIABILITIES			
(1) Shareholders' Funds			
(a) Share Capital		390	
(b) Reserves and Surplus		90	
(2) Share Application Money pending Allotment		10	
(3) Non-Current Liabilities			
(a) Long term Borrowings		500	
(4) Current Liabilities			
(a) Trade Payables		20	
(b) Short-term Provisions		-	
Total		1010	
II. ASSETS			
1. Non-Current Assets			
(a) Property,Plant,Equipment & Intangible Assets			
(i) Property,Plant & Equipment		600	
(b) Non-Current Investments		200	
2. Current Assets			
(a) Inventories		20	
(b) Trade Receivables		80	
(c) Cash and Cash Equivalents		120	
Total		1010	

ILLUSTRATION 35

From the following information, prepare the relevant Notes to Accounts:

Capital Reserve	20
Capital Redemption Reserve	40
Securities Premium	60
General Reserve	160
Statutory Reserves	20
Amalgamation Adjustment Account	20

Opening Balance of Profit and Loss Statement	452
Profit for the period	560
Transfer to General Reserve @ 5%	
Interim Dividend	100

SOLUTION

2. RESERVES AND SURPLUS

Capital Reserve		20
Capital Redemption Reserve		40
Securities Premium		60
General Reserve [160 + 28]		188
Statutory Reserves		20
Amalgamation Adjustment Account		(20)
Profit & Loss Account:		
Opening Balance	452	
Add: Profit for the period	560	
Less: Transfer to General Reserve @ 5%	(28)	
Less: Interim Dividend	(100)	884
		1192

ILLUSTRATION 36

From the following information, prepare the relevant Notes to Accounts:

Sundry Creditors	40
Bills Payables	20
Bank Overdraft	10
Unpaid Dividend	2
Outstanding Expenses	4
Calls-in-Advance	2
Interest accrued on Borrowings	24
Current Maturity of 12% Debentures	40
Provision for Tax	240

SOLUTION

2. SHORT-TERM BORROWINGS

Current Maturity of 12% Debentures	40
Bank Overdraft	10
	50

3. TRADE PAYABLES

Sundry Creditors	40
Bills Payables	20
	60

4. OTHER CURRENT LIABILITIES

Unpaid Dividend	2
Outstanding Expenses	4
Calls-in-Advance	2
Interest accrued on Borrowings	24
	32

5. SHORT-TERM PROVISIONS

Provision for Tax	240
	240

ILLUSTRATION 37

From the following information, prepare the relevant Notes to Accounts:

Particulars	*Cost*	*Provision for Depreciation/ Amortization*
Buildings	400	20
Plant and Equipment	200	40
Vehicles	50	10
Furniture and Fixtures	60	6
Brands	200	20
Computer Software	90	54

SOLUTION

6. PROPERTY,PLANT & EQUIPMENT

Particulars	*Cost*	*Provision for Depreciation*	*Closing WDV*
Buildings	400	20	380
Plant and Equipment	200	40	160
Vehicles	50	10	40
Furniture and Fixtures	60	6	54
	710	76	634

7. INTANGIBLE ASSETS

Particulars	*Cost*	*Provision for Amortization*	*Closing WDV*
Brands	200	20	180
Computer Software	90	54	36
	290	74	216

ILLUSTRATION 38

From the following information, prepare the relevant Notes to Accounts:

Trade Investments	
300 lacs Shares of X Ltd of ₹ 10 each,₹ 8 paid up	2400
6 lacs,14% Debentures of ₹ 100 each,₹ 80 paid up	480
Other Investments	26
Security Deposits	2

SOLUTION

8. NON-CURRENT INVESTMENTS

Trade Investments		
300 lacs Shares of X Ltd of ₹ 10 each,₹ 8 paid up	2400	
6 lacs,14% Debentures of ₹ 100 each,₹ 80 paid up	480	2880
Other Investments		26
		2906

9. OTHER NON-CURRENT ASSETS

Security Deposits	2
	2

ILLUSTRATION 39

From the following information, prepare the relevant Notes to Accounts:

Closing Stock of Materials	39.8
Closing Stock of WIP	200.00
Closing Stock of Finished Goods	400.00
Loose Tools	12.00
Stores & Spares	8.00
Sundry Debtors	80
Provision for Doubtful Debts	8
Bills Receivables	20
Cash Balance	4
Bank Balance	16
Cheques/Drafts on hand	4
Prepaid Expenses	2
Interest accrued on Investments	2

SOLUTION

10. INVENTORIES

Closing Stock of Materials	39.80
Closing Stock of WIP	200.00
Closing Stock of Finished Goods	400.00

Loose Tools	12.00
Stores & Spares	8.00
	659.8

11. TRADE RECEIVABLES

Sundry Debtors	80
Less: Provision for Doubtful Debts	(8)
Bills Receivables	20
	92

12. CASH AND CASH EQUIVALENTS

Cash Balance	4
Bank Balance	16
Cheques/Drafts on hand	4
	24

13. OTHER CURRENT ASSETS

Prepaid Expenses	2
Interest accrued on Investments	2
	4

ILLUSTRATION 40

From the following information, prepare the relevant Notes to Accounts:

1. Bills Discounted but not yet matured 2 lacs
2. 300 lacs Shares of X Ltd of ₹ 10 each,₹ 8 paid up held as Investments
3. 6 lacs,14% Debentures of ₹ 100 each, ₹ 80 paid up held as Investments

SOLUTION

14. CONTINGENT LIABILITIES AND COMMITMENTS (TO THE EXTENT NOT PROVIDED FOR)

(i) Contingent Liabilities	
Bills Discounted but not yet matured	₹ 2 lacs
(ii) Commitments	
(a) Uncalled Liability on partly paid Shares [300 lacs Shares of X Ltd of ₹ 10 each,₹ 8 paid up]	₹ 600 lacs
(b) Uncalled Liability on partly paid Debentures held as Investments [6 lacs,14% Debentures of ₹ 100 each, ₹ 80 paid up]	₹ 120 lacs

ILLUSTRATION 41

From the details given below prepare Balance Sheet of TULSIAN Ltd. as at 31st March, 2023, as per the Schedule III to The Companies Act 2013:

	(₹ in crores)
P & L A/c (Dr.)	210
Stock Options Outstanding Account	10
Amalgamation Adjustment Account	20
Statutory Reserves	20
12% Debentures [20% Redeemable within 1 year]	200
Provision for Tax	20
Equity Share Capital (₹ 10 each)	500
Cash in Hand	40
Cheques & Drafts on hand	7
Fixed Deposits with Banks as per Details given	1
15% Pref. Share Capital (₹ 100 each)	400
Prepaid Expenses	50
Bank Overdraft	45
Interest accrued on Debentures of Tata Steels	12
Building under construction	115
2,500,12% Tata Steel Deb. of ₹ 100 each, ₹ 80 paid up	200
Premium on Red. of Debentures	20
Application Money pending allotment	40
Bills Payables	75
Calls-in Advance	5
Employees' earned leave payable on Retirement	45
Stores & Spares	50
Securities Deposit	5
Crypto Currency(Not for sale in the ordinary course of business)	10
Brands	100
Computer Software under development	20
Bills Receivables	120
Plant & Machinery	120
12% Debentures of Reliance Ltd. [20% Redeemable within 1 year]	100
Investment in Land & Building	200

1. Details of Fixed Deposits with Banks

Bank	*Date of FDR*	*Maturity Date*	*Amount*
Yes Bank Limited	01–Jan–2023	2–Jan–2024	30,00,000
Bank of Baroda	01–Jan–2023	31–Mar–2024	20,00,000
State Bank of India	28–Feb–2023	30–May–2023	10,00,000
ICICI Bank	1–Jan–2022	1–Apr–2024	40,00,000

Note: Bills Discounted but not yet matured ₹ 1 crore, Dividends on Preference Shares are in arrears for 2 years

SOLUTION

TULSIAN LTD.
BALANCE SHEET AS AT 31ST MARCH, 2023

Particulars	*Note No*	*2022-2023 (₹ in crores)*	*2021-2022 (₹ in crores)*
I. EQUITY AND LIABILITIES			
(1) Shareholders' Funds			
(a) Share Capital	1	900	
(b) Reserves and Surplus	2	(200)	
(2) Share Application Money pending Allotment		40	
(3) Non - Current Liabilities			
(a) Long term Borrowings [12% Debentures]		160	
(b) Other Long term Liabilities			
(Premium on Red. of Debentures)		16	
(c) Long term Provisions (Earned Leave)		45	
(4) Current Liabilities			
(a) Short term Borrowings (Current Maturities including Premium + Bank Overdraft)		89	
(b) Trade Payables (B/P)		75	
(c) Other Current Liabilities		5	
(d) Short term Provisions (Provision for Tax)		20	
Total		1150	
II. ASSETS			
(1) Non-Current Assets			
(a) Property,Plant,Equipment & Intangible Assets			
(i) Property,Plant & Equipment (Plant & Machinery)		120	
(ii) Intangible Assets (Brands + Crypto Currency)		110	
(iii) Capital Work in progress (Building)		115	
(iv) Intangible Assets under development		20	
(b) Non-Current Investments	4	480	
(c) Long-term Loans & Advances			
(d) Other Non-Current Assets (Security Deposits)		5	
(2) Current Assets			
(a) Current Investments (Deb. of Reliance Ltd.)		20	
(b) Inventories (Stores & Spares)		50	
(c) Trade Receivables (B/R)		120	
(d) Cash and Cash Equivalents (Ch. & DD+ Bank deposits)		48	
(e) Other Current Assets	5	62	
Total		1150	

Notes to Accounts:

NOTE 1: SHARE CAPITAL

Particulars	*2022-2023 (₹ in crores)*	*2021-2022 (₹ in crores)*
50,000 Equity Shares of ₹10 each	500	
4,000, 15% Pref. Shares of ₹100 each	400	
	900	

NOTE 2: RESERVES AND SURPLUS

Particulars	*2022-2023 (₹ in crores)*	*2021-2022 (₹ in crores)*
Stock Options Outstanding Account	10	
Statutory Reserves	20	
Amalgamation Adjustment Account	(20)	
P & L A/c (Dr.)	(210)	
	(200)	

NOTE 3: OTHER CURRENT LIABILITIES

Particulars	*2022-2023 (₹ in crores)*	*2021-2022 (₹ in crores)*
Calls-in-advance	5	
	5	

NOTE 4: NON-CURRENT INVESTMENTS

Particulars	*2022-2023 (₹ in crores)*	*2021-2022 (₹ in crores)*
2,500,12% Tata Steel Deb. of ₹100 each, ₹80 paid up	200	
12% Debentures of Reliance Ltd. [100 – 20]	80	
Investment in Land & Building	200	
	480	

NOTE 5: OTHER CURRENT ASSETS

Particulars	*2022-2023 (₹ in crores)*	*2021-2022 (₹ in crores)*
Prepaid Expenses	50	
Interest accrued on Debentures of Tata Steels	12	
	62	

NOTE 6: CASH & BANK BALANCES

Particulars	*(₹ in crores)*	*(₹ in crores)*
A. Cash in Hand		40.00
B. Cheques & Drafts on hand		7.00
C. Balances with Bank		
(i) Less than *or* equal to 12 Months Maturity.		
– Cash Equivalent as per AS–3 (less than 3 Months Maturity) [SBI]	0.10	
– Other Bank Balances [30,00,000 + 20,00,000]	0.50	
(ii) More than 12 Months Maturity [ICICI]	0.40	1.00
		48.00

NOTE 7: CONTINGENT LIABILITIES & COMMITMENTS

Particulars	*2022-2023 (₹ in crores)*	*2021-2022 (₹ in crores)*
(i) Contingent Liabilities		
Bills Discounted but not yet matured	1	
(ii) Commitments		
(a) Uncalled Liability on partly paid Debentures held as Investments [2,500,12% Tata Steel Debentures of ₹ 100 each, ₹ 80 paid up] [2,500 × ₹ 20]	50	
(b) Arrears of Fixed Cumulative Dividends on Preference Shares [₹ 4,00,000 × 15/100 × 2]	120	

ILLUSTRATION 42

The following items appear in the Trial Balance of Bharat Ltd. as at 31st March, 2023:

Particulars	₹
1. Revenue from Operations	24,00,000
2. Other Income	1,00,000
3. Expenses other than Interest	3,80,000
4. General Reserve (as on 1st April, 2022)	1,30,000
5. Profit and Loss Account (as on 1.4.2022)	2,70,000
6. 12%, 10,000 Debentures of ₹ 100 each fully paid up	
7. 16%, 5,000 Preference Shares of ₹ 100 each fully paid up	
8. 6,000 Equity Shares of ₹ 100 each	
9. 8,000 Equity Shares ₹ 100 each, ₹ 25 paid up	

On 31.03.2023,dividends (including Equity Dividend @15%) were paid for which no accounting effect has yet been given. The recommendations of the company's Board of Directors include transfer to General Reserve @ 5%. (Assume Corporate Tax 25%).

Required: Show the relevant items in Statement of Profit and Loss and Balance Sheet.

SOLUTION

BHARAT LTD.
STATEMENT OF PROFIT AND LOSS FOR THE YEAR ENDED 31ST MARCH, 2023

	Particulars	*Note No.*	*(₹ in lacs)*
I.	**Revenue from Operations**		24
II.	**Other Income**		1
III.	**Total Income [I + II]**		25
IV.	**Expenses:**		
	Finance Costs		1.2
	Other Expenses		3.8
	Total Expenses		5.0
V.	**Profit before Tax(III – IV)**		20
VI.	**Tax Expense [25% of ₹ 20 lacs]**		(5)
VII.	**Profit for the period**		15
	Basic Earnings per Equity Share:		
	= [Profit for the period – Pref. Dividend] /*No. of Equity Shares		
	= (15 – 0.80)/*(6000+2000) = ₹ 177.50		

AN EXTRACT OF BALANCE SHEET OF BHARAT LTD. AS AT 31ST MARCH, 2023

Particulars	*Note No.*	*(₹ in lacs)*
I. EQUITY AND LIABILITIES		
(1) Shareholders' Funds		
(a) Share Capital	1	13.00
(b) Reserves and Surplus	2	17.00
(2) Non-Current Liabilities		
(a) Long-term Borrowings [10% Debentures]		10.00
(3) Current Liabilities		
(a) Other Current Liabilities [Interest accrued on Debentures]	4	1.20
(b) Short-Term Provisions (Provision for Tax)	5	5.00
Total		46.20

Notes To Accounts:

1. SHARE CAPITAL

Authorised Capital	?
Issued Capital	
14,000 Equity Shares of ₹ 100 each	14.00
5,000, 16% Pref. Shares of ₹ 100 each	5.00
	19.00

Subscribed Capital and fully paid	
6,000,Equity Shares of ₹ 100 each	6
16%,5,000 Pref. Shares of ₹ 100 each	5
Subscribed Capital but not fully paid	
8,000, Equity Shares of ₹ 100 each,₹ 25 paid up	2
	13

2. RESERVES AND SURPLUS

General Reserve [1.30 + 0.75]		2.05
Surplus:		
Opening Balance	2.70	
Add: Profit for the period	15.00	
Less: Transfer to General Reserve @ 5%	(0.75)	
Less: Preference Dividend	(0.8)	
Less: Equity Dividend [15% of(6 lacs + 2 lacs)]	(1.2)	14.95
		17.00

3. SHORT-TERM PROVISIONS

Provision for Tax	5.00

ILLUSTRATION 43

The following are the extracts of the Trial Balance of AMLA & GILOY Ltd.(Listed Co) as at 31st March, 2023:

Particulars	*(₹ in lakh)*
Revenue from Operations	480
3.75 lakh,10% Tata Steel Debentures of ₹ 100 each, ₹ 80 paid up	300
Net Loss on Sale of Investments	14
Rent received	15
Expenses other than Interest (including Rent Collection Expenses ₹ 1 lakh)	87
40 lakh Equity Shares of ₹10 each fully paid up	400
10 lakh Equity Shares of ₹ 10 each,₹ 7.50 paid up	75
4 lakh 10% Pref. Shares of ₹ 100 each fully paid up	400
12%, 2,00,000 Debentures of ₹ 100 each fully paid up (issued on 01.04.2022)	200
General Reserve (as at 01.04.2022)	15
P & L A/c (Dr.)(as at 01.04.2022)	1
Employees Stock Option Outstanding A/c	10

As on 01.04.2022, Dividends on Preference Shares were in arrears for 2 years for 2021-2022 and 2020-2021. On 31.03.2023,dividends(including Equity Dividend @20%) were paid for which no accounting effect has yet been given. The recommendations of the company's Board of Directors include transfer to General Reserve @ 5%.Assume Corporate Tax 25%.

Required: Calculate Profit for the period and Basic Earnings per Equity Share as per Statement of Profit and Loss for the year ended 31st March,2023 and also Show the calculation of Reserves and Surplus.

SOLUTION

AMLA & GILOY Ltd.

STATEMENT OF PROFIT AND LOSS FOR THE YEAR ENDED 31ST MARCH, 2023

Particulars	*Note No.*	*(₹ in lakh)*
I. Revenue from Operations		480
II. Other Income		30
III. Total Revenue [I + II]		510
IV. Expenses:		
Finance Costs[12% of ₹ 200 lakh]		24
Other Expenses(₹ 87 lakh – ₹ 1 lakh)		86
Total Expenses		110
V. Profit before Tax(III – IV)		400
VI. Tax Expense [25% of ₹ 400 lakh]		(100)
VII. Profit for the period		300
Basic Earnings per Equity Share:		
= [Profit for the period – Pref. Dividend] /No.of Equity Shares		
= (₹300 lakh – ₹ 40 lakh*)/47.5** = ₹ 5.4737		

* Only current year's Pref. Dividend **[(75/7.5)x7.5/10]+ 40 = 47.5 lakh Equity Shares

Notes to Accounts:

1. OTHER INCOME

Particulars	*(₹ in lakh)*
(a) Interest Income [10% of ₹ 300 lakh]	30
(b) Net Loss on Sale of Investments	(14)
(c) Rental Income (₹15 lakh – ₹ 1 lakh Collection Expenses)	14
	30

2. RESERVES AND SURPLUS

General Reserve [15 + 15]		30
Employees Stock Option Outstanding A/c		10
Surplus i.e. Balance in Statement of Profit & Loss:		
Opening Balance	(1)	
Add: Profit for the period	300	
Less: Transfer to General Reserve [5% of ₹ 300 lakh]	(15)	
Less: Preference Dividend [400 x 10% x 3]	(120)	
Less: Equity Dividend[20% of(400 lakh + 75 lakh)]	(95)	69
		109

ILLUSTRATION 44

Fine Products Ltd. was registered with a nominal capital of ₹ 5,00,000 divided into shares of ₹ 100 each. The following Trial Balance is extracted from the books on 31st March, 2023:

Dr. *Cr.*

Particulars	₹	Particulars		₹
Buildings	2,90,000	Sales		5,20,000
Machinery	1,00,000	Outstanding Expenses		2,000
Closing Stock	90,000	Provision for Doubtful Debt (1-4-2022)		3,000
Purchases (adjusted)	2,10,000	Equity Share Capital		2,00,000
Salaries	60,000	General Reserve		90,000
Directors Fees	10,000	Profit and Loss A/c (1-4-2022)		25,000
Rent	26,000	Creditors		92,000
Depreciation	20,000	Provision for depreciation:		
Bad Debts	6,000	on Building	50,000	
Interest accrued on Investment	2,000	on Machinery	55,000	1,05,000
12,000 shares of X Ltd. of		14% Debentures		2,00,000
₹ 10 each ₹ 8 paid up	1,20,000	Interest on Debentures		
Debenture Interest	28,000	accrued but not due		14,000
Loose Tools	23,000	Interest on Investments		12,000
Advance Tax	60,000	Unclaimed dividend		5,000
Sundry expenses	18,000	(Bills Discounted but not yet		
Debtors	1,25,000	matured ₹ 10,000)		
Bank	80,000			
	12,68,000			12,68,000

You are required to prepare Statement of Profit and Loss for the year ending 31st March, 2023 and Balance Sheet as at that date after taking into consideration the following information:

(a) Closing stock is more than opening stock by ₹ 80,000; (b) Provide for doubtful debts @ 4% on Debtors: (c) Make a provision for income tax @ 30%; (d) Depreciation expense includes depreciation of ₹ 8,000 on Buildings and that of ₹ 12,000 on Machinery; (e) The directors decided to pay an interim dividend @ 25% immediately and to transfer to General Reserve @ 10%.

SOLUTION

FINE PRODUCTS
PROFIT AND LOSS STATEMENT FOR THE YEAR ENDED 31ST MARCH, 2023

Particulars	Note No.	(₹ in lacs)
I. Revenue from Operations		5,20,000
II. Other Income		12,000
III. Total Revenue [I + II]		5,32,000
IV. Expenses:		
Cost of Purchases [2,10,000 + 80,000]		2,90,000
Changes in Inventories [10,000 – 90,000]		(80,000)

	Employee Benefits Expense		60,000
	Finance Costs		28,000
	Depreciation and Amortization Expense		20,000
	Other Expenses	1	62,000
	Total Expenses		3,80,000
V.	**Profit before Tax (III – IV)**		1,52,000
VI.	**Tax Expense@30%**		(45,600)
VII.	**Profit for the period**		1,06,400
	Basic Earnings per Equity Share: = 1,06,400/20,000 = ₹ 5.32		

Notes to Accounts:

1.	**Other Expenses**	
	Rent.	26,000
	Miscellaneous Expenses	18,000
	Directors' Fees	10,000
	Bad Debts	6,000
	Provision for Doubtful Debts[(4% of ₹ 1,25,000) – ₹ 3,000]	2,000
		62,000

BALANCE SHEET OF FINE PRODUCTS LTD. AS AT 31ST MARCH, 2023

Particulars	**Note No.**	***(₹ in lacs)***
I. EQUITY AND LIABILITIES		
(1) Shareholders' Funds		
(a) Share Capital	1	2,00,000
(b) Reserves and Surplus	2	1,71,400
(2) Non-Current Liabilities		
(a) Long-term Borrowings [Debentures]		2,00,000
(3) Current Liabilities		
(a) Trade Payables [Sundry Creditors]		92,000
(b) Other Current Liabilities	3	21,000
(c) Short-Term Provisions	4	45,600
Total		7,30,000
II. ASSETS		
(1) Non-Current Assets		
(a) Property,Plant,Equipment & Intangible Assets		
(i) Property,Plant & Equipment	5	2,85,000
(b) Non-Current Investments [12,000 Shares of X Ltd of ₹ 10 each, ₹ 8 paid up]		1,20,000
(2) Current Assets		
(a) Inventories	6	1,13,000

(b) Trade Receivables	7	1,20,000
(c) Cash and Cash Equivalents [80,000 - 50,000]		30,000
(d) Short-term Loans and Advances [Advance Payment of Tax]		60,000
(f) Other Current Assets(Interest accrued on Investments)		2,000
Total		7,30,000

Notes To Accounts:

1. SHARE CAPITAL

Authorised Capital	
5,000 Equity Shares of ₹ 100 each	5,00,000
Issued Capital	
2,000 Equity Shares of ₹ 100 each	2,00,000
Subscribed Capital and fully paid	
2,000 Equity Shares of ₹ 100 each	2,00,000
	2,00,000

2. RESERVES AND SURPLUS

General Reserve [90,000 + 10,640]		1,00,640
Balance of Statement of Profit & Loss Account:		
Opening Balance	25,000	
Add: Profit for the period	1,06,400	
Less: Transfer to General Reserve @ 10%	(10,640)	
Less: Equity Dividend [25% of 2,00,000]	(50,000)	70,760
		1,71,400

3. OTHER CURRENT LIABILITIES

Unclaimed Dividend	5,000
Outstanding Expenses	2,000
Interest accrued on Borrowings	14,000
	21,000

4. SHORT-TERM PROVISIONS

Provision for Tax	45,600

5. PROPERTY, PLANT & EQUIPMENT

Particulars	***Cost***	***Provision for Depreciation***	***Closing WDV***
Buildings	2,90,000	50,000	2,40,000
Plant and Equipment	1,00,000	55,000	45,000
	3,90,000	1,05,000	2,85,000

6. INVENTORIES

Closing Stock of Finished Goods	90,000
Loose Tools	23,000
	1,13,000

7. TRADE RECEIVABLES

Sundry Debtors	1,25,000
Less: Provision for Doubtful Debts	(5,000)
	1,20,000

8. CONTINGENT LIABILITIES AND COMMITMENTS (TO THE EXTENT NOT PROVIDED FOR)

(i) Contingent Liabilities	
Bills Discounted but not yet matured	10,000
(ii) Commitments	
(a) Uncalled Liability on partly paid Shares [12,000 Shares of X Ltd of ₹ 10 each,₹ 8 paid up]	24,000

ILLUSTRATION 45

TULSIAN Ltd. provides the following information for the year ended 31st March, 2023:

Particulars	***₹ lacs***
Buildings	200
Plant and Equipment	100
Vehicles	25
Furniture and Fixtures	30
Brands	100
Computer Software	45
Buildings under construction	100
Computer Software under Development	40
Trade Investments	
150 lacs Shares of X Ltd of ₹ 10 each, ₹ 8 paid up	1200
3 lacs,14% Debentures of ₹ 100 each, ₹ 80 paid up	240
Other Investments	13
Long-Term Loans and Advances (Dr)	17.6
Discount/Loss on Issue of Debentures	1
Amalgamation Adjustment A/c	2
Current Investments	100
Closing Stock of Materials	19.9
Closing Stock of WIP	100
Closing Stock of Finished Goods	200

Loose Tools	6
Stores & Spares	4
Sundry Debtors	40
Bills Receivables	10
Cash Balance	222
Bank Balance	8
Cheques/Drafts on hand	2
Advance Payment of Tax	50
Prepaid Expenses	1
Interest accrued on Investments	1
60 lacs Equity Shares of ₹ 10 each	600
50 lacs Equity Shares of ₹ 10 each, ₹ 8 paid up	400
10%, 70 lacs Pref. Shares of ₹ 10 each	700
Profit and Loss Statement (Opening Balance)	396
Profit before Interest & tax for the year 2022-2023	412
General Reserve	80
Capital Reserve	8
Statutory Reserves	2
Capital Redemption Reserve	20
Securities Premium	30
12% Debentures (20% Redeemable within 1 year)	100
Long term Loans and Advances (Cr)	3
Provision for Gratuity & Provident Fund	8.5
Sundry Creditors	20
Bills Payables	10
Outstanding Expenses	8
Calls-in-Advance	1
Provision for Doubtful Debts	4
Provision for Depreciation:	
Buildings	10
Plant and Equipment	20
Vehicles	5
Furniture and Fixtures	3
Provision for Amortization:	
Brands	10
Computer Software	27

Additional Information:

(a) On 31.03.2023, dividends (including Equity Dividend @15%) were paid for which no accounting effect has yet been given. Transfer to Reserve @ 5% is to be made. Assume Corporate Tax 25%

(b) Bills Discounted but not yet matured ₹ 1 lac

Required: Prepare the Balance Sheet (as per Schedule III to The Companies Act, 2013) as at 31st March, 2023.

SOLUTION

TULSIAN LTD.
BALANCE SHEET AS AT 31ST MARCH, 2023

Particulars	*Note No.*	*(₹ in lacs)*
I. EQUITY AND LIABILITIES		
(1) Shareholders' Funds		
(a) Share Capital	1	1,700.00
(b) Reserves and Surplus	2	613.00
(2) Non-Current Liabilities		
(a) Long-term Borrowings [Debentures]		80.00
(b) Deferred Tax Liabilities (Net)		
(c) Other Long term Liabilities (Long-term Loans & Adv.)		3.00
(d) Long-term Provisions [Provision for Gratuity & Provident Fund]		8.50
(3) Current Liabilities		
(a) Short-Term Borrowings (Current Maturity of 12% Debentures)		20.00
(b) Trade Payables	3	30.00
(c) Other Current Liabilities	4	21.00
(d) Short-Term Provisions	5	100.00
Total		2,575.50
II. ASSETS		
(1) Non-Current Assets		
(a) Property,Plant,Equipment & Intangible Assets		
(i) Property,Plant & Equipment	6	317.00
(ii) Intangible Assets	7	108.00
(iii) Capital Work-in-Progress [Buildings under construction]		100.00
(iv) Intangible Assets under Development		40.00
(b) Non-Current Investments	8	1,453.00
(c) Deferred Tax Assets (Net)		
(d) Long-Term Loans and Advances		17.60
(e) Other Non-Current Assets		
(2) Current Assets		
(a) Current Investments		100.00
(b) Inventories	9	329.90

(c) Trade Receivables	10	46.00
(d) Cash and Cash Equivalents	11	12.00
(e) Short-term Loans and Advances [Advance Payment of Tax]		50.00
(f) Other Current Assets	12	2.00
Total		2,575.50

Notes To Accounts:

1. SHARE CAPITAL

Authorised Capital	
250 lacs shares of ₹ 10 each	2,500
Issued Capital	
110 lacs Equity Shares of ₹ 10 each	1,100
70 lacs, 10% Pref. Shares of ₹ 10 each	700
	1,800
Subscribed Capital and Fully paid up	
60 lacs Equity Shares of ₹ 10 each	600
70 lacs 10%, Pref. Shares of ₹ 10 each	700
Subscribed Capital but not fully paid up	
50 lacs Equity Shares of ₹ 10 each,₹ 8 paid up	400
	1,700

2. RESERVES AND SURPLUS

Capital Reserve		8
Capital Redemption Reserve		20
Securities Premium		30
General Reserve [80 + 15]		95
Statutory Reserves		2
Amalgamation Adjustment A/c		(2)
Profit & Loss Statement:		
Opening Balance	396	
Add: Profit for the period [(412 – 12) × (1 – 0.25)]	300	
Less: Transfer to Reserve @ 5%	(15)	
Less: Preference Dividend	(70)	
Less: Equity Dividend [15% of(600 lacs + 400 lacs)]	(150)	
Discount/Loss on Issue of Debentures	(1)	460
		613

3. TRADE PAYABLES

Sundry Creditors	20
Bills Payables	10
	30

4. OTHER CURRENT LIABILITIES

Outstanding Expenses	8
Calls-in-Advance	1
Interest accrued on Borrowings [12% of ₹ 100 lacs (12% Debentures)]	12
	21

5. SHORT-TERM PROVISIONS

Provision for Tax [(412 – 12) × (0.25)]	100

6. PROPERTY, PLANT & EQUIPMENT

Particulars	*Cost*	*Provision for Depreciation*	*Closing WDV*
Buildings	200	10	190
Plant and Equipment	100	20	80
Vehicles	25	5	20
Furniture and Fixtures	30	3	27
	355	38	317

7. INTANGIBLE ASSETS

Particulars	*Cost*	*Provision for Amortization*	*Closing WDV*
Brands	100	10	90
Computer Software	45	27	18
	145	37	108

8. NON-CURRENT INVESTMENTS

Trade Investments		
150 lacs Shares of X Ltd of ₹ 10 each,₹ 8 paid up	1,200	
3 lacs,14% Debentures of ₹ 100 each,₹ 80 paid up	240	1440
Other Investments		13
		1453

9. INVENTORIES

Closing Stock of Materials	19.90
Closing Stock of WIP	100.00
Closing Stock of Finished Goods	200.00
Loose Tools	6.00
Stores & Spares	4.00
	329.90

10. TRADE RECEIVABLES

Sundry Debtors	40
Less: Provision for Doubtful Debts	(4)
Bills Receivables	10
	46

11. CASH AND CASH EQUIVALENTS

Cash Balance	2
Bank Balance	8
Cheques/Drafts on hand	2
	12

12. OTHER CURRENT ASSETS

Prepaid Expenses	1
Interest accrued on Investments	1
	2

14. CONTINGENT LIABILITIES AND COMMITMENTS (TO THE EXTENT NOT PROVIDED FOR)

(i) Contingent Liabilities	
Bills Discounted but not yet matured	1
(ii) Commitments	
(a) Uncalled Liability on partly paid Shares [150 lacs Shares of X Ltd of ₹ 10 each,₹ 8 paid up]	300
(b) Uncalled Liability on partly paid Debentures held as Investments [3 lacs,14% Debentures of ₹ 100 each, ₹ 80 paid up]	60

ILLUSTRATION 46

The following is the Trial Balance of H Ltd., as on 31st March, 2023:

	Dr.	*Cr.*
Equity Capital (Shares of ₹ 100 each)		8,05,000
5,000, 6% Preference Shares of ₹ 100 each		5,00,000
9% Debentures		4,00,000
General Reserve		40,00,000
Profit & Loss A/c (of previous year)		72,000
Sales		60,00,000
Trade Payables		10,40,000
Provision for Depreciation on Plant & Machinery		1,72,000
Suspense Account		40,000
Land at cost	24,00,000	

Plant & Machinery at cost	7,70,000	
Trade Receivables	19,60,000	
Inventories (31-03-2023)	9,50,000	
Bank	2,30,900	
Adjusted Purchases	22,32,100	
Factory Expenses	15,00,000	
Administration Expenses	3,00,000	
Selling Expenses	14,00,000	
Debenture Interest	36,000	
Goodwill	12,50,000	
	1,30,29,000	1,30,29,000

Additional Information:

(i) The authorised share capital of the company is : ₹

5,000, 6% preference shares of ₹ 100 each 5,00,000
10,000, equity shares of ₹ 100 each 10,00,000

Issued equity capital as on 1st April 2022 stood at ₹ 7,20,000, that is 6,000 shares fully paid and 2,000 shares of ₹ 60 paid. The directors made a call of ₹ 40 per share on 1st October 2022. A shareholder could not pay the call on 100 shares and his shares were then forfeited and reissued @ ₹ 90 per share as fully paid.

(ii) On 31st March 2023, the Directors declared a dividend of 5% on equity shares, transferring any amount that may be required from General Reserve. Ignore Taxation.

(iii) The company on the advice of independent valuer wishes to revalue the land at ₹ 36,00,000.

(iv) Suspense account of ₹ 40,000 represents amount received for the sale of some of the machinery on 1-4-2022. The cost of the machinery was ₹ 1,00,000 and the accumulated depreciation thereon being ₹ 30,000.

(v) Depreciation is to be provided on plant and machinery at 10% on cost.

(vi) Amortize 1/5th of Goodwill.

You are required to prepare H Limited's Balance Sheet as on 31-3-2023 and Statement of Profit and Loss with notes to accounts for the year ended 31-3-2023 as per Schedule III of the Companies Act, 2013. Ignore previous years' figures & taxation.

SOLUTION

H LTD

BALANCE SHEET AS AT 31ST MARCH 2023

Particulars	Note No	Amount in ₹
Equity and Liabilities		
I. Shareholders' Funds		
a. Share Capital	1	13,00,000
b. Reserves and Surplus	2	53,91,900
II. Non-Current Liabilities		
a. Long Term Borrowings	3	4,00,000

III. Current Liabilities		
a. Trade Payables	4	10,40,000
b. Other Current Liabilities	5	70,000
Total		82,01,900
Assets		
I. Non-Current Assets		
a. Property, Plant and Equipment	6	40,61,000
b. Intangible Assets	7	10,00,000
II. Current Assets		
a. Inventories		9,50,000
b. Trade Receivables		19,60,000
c. Cash and Cash equivalents		2,30,900
Total		82,01,900

STATEMENT OF PROFIT AND LOSS FOR THE YEAR ENDED 31ST MARCH 2023

Particulars	*Note No*	*Amount in ₹*
I. Revenue from operations		60,00,000
Total Revenue		60,00,000
II. Expenses		
Purchases (adjusted)		22,32,100
Finance Costs	8	36,000
Depreciation and Amortization	9	3,17,000
Other Expenses	10	32,30,000
Total Expenses		58,15,100
III. Profit/(Loss) for the period		1,84,900

Notes to Accounts **(Amount in ₹)**

1	**Share Capital**		
	a. *Authorized Capital*		
	5,000, 6% Preference shares of ₹ 100/- each		5,00,000
	10,000 Equity Shares of ₹100/- each		10,00,000
			15,00,000
	b. *Issued & Subscribed Capital*		
	5,000, 6% Preference shares of ₹100/- each	5,00,000	
	8,000, Equity shares of ₹100/- each	8,00,000	
	Total	13,00,000	
2	**Reserves & Surplus**		
	Capital Reserve (100 x (90-40))	5,000	
	Revaluation Reserve (36,00,000-24,00,000)	12,00,000	
	General Reserve	40,00,000	

	Surplus	1,84,900	
	Add: Balance from previous year	72,000	
	Less: Dividends declared	(70,000)	
	Profit/(Loss) carried forward to Balance Sheet		1,86,900
	Total		53,91,900
3	**Long-Term Borrowings**		
	Secured		
	9% Debentures		4,00,000
4	**Trade Payables**		10,40,000
5	**Other Current Liabilities**		
	Dividend Payable		
	Preference Dividend		30,000
	Equity Dividend		40,000
	Total		70,000
6	**Property, Plant and Equipment**		
	Land		
	Opening balance	24,00,000	
	Add: Revaluation Adjustment	12,00,000	
	Closing Balance		36,00,000
	Plant and Machinery		
	Opening Balance	7,70,000	
	Less: Disposed off	(1,00,000)	
	Depreciation	(2,09,000)	
	Closing Balance		4,61,000
	Total		40,61,000
7	**Intangible Assets**		
	Goodwill		12,50,000
	Less: Amortized (1/5th)		(2,50,000)
	Total		10,00,000
8	**Finance Costs**		
	Debenture Interest		36,000
9	**Depreciation and Amortization**		
	Plant and Machinery		67,000
	Goodwill		2,50,000
	Total		3,17,000
10	**Other Expenses**		
	Factory Expenses		15,00,000
	Selling Expenses		14,00,000
	Administrative Expenses		3,00,000

	Loss on sale of Plant and Machinery Book Value (1,00,000-30,000) *Less:* Sale Value	70,000 (40,000)	30,000
	Total		32,30,000

Notes:

1. The inventories (31.3.20) amounting ₹ 9,50,000 (given in the trial balance of the Illustration) should have been as closing inventory i.e. as on 31.3.21. In the above solution, this inventory has been considered as closing inventory i.e. for 31.3.21. If this is considered as inventory of 31.3.20, the closing inventory (as on 31.3.21) will not be available for the balance sheet as on 31.3.21 and in that case, the balance sheet will not tally without using suspense account amounting ₹ 9,50,000.
2. The financial statements given in the above Solution include adjustment for dividend declared on 31st March, 2023, strictly, as per the information given in the Illustration. However, practically dividends are declared in the annual general meetings which take place after the reporting date.

ILLUSTRATION 47

An Extract of the Balance Sheet of a CAMHC Ltd.(Listed)as at 31st March 2023 is as follows:

Particulars	₹
Share Capital:	
Authorised:	
30,000 Equity Shares of ₹ 10 each	3,00,000
Issued and Subscribed:	
20,000 Equity Shares of ₹ 10 each fully paid	2,00,000
Profit and Loss Account	1,16,000
12% Debentures	1,20,000
Creditors	1,15,000
Property,Plant & Equipment [Freehold Property]	1,15,000
Inventories	1,35,000
Trade Receivables	75,000
Cash at Bank	2,51,000

At the Annual General Meeting it was resolved:

(a) To increase the authorised capital to ₹ 4,00,000.

(b) To pay the dividend @ 10% in cash.

(c) To issue one bonus share for every four shares held

(d) To give existing shareholders the option to purchase one ₹ 10 share, at ₹ 15 for every four shares held prior to the bonus distribution, this option being taken up by all the shareholders.

(e) To repay the debentures at a premium of 3 per cent.

Required: Pass the necessary Journal Entries.

SOLUTION

JOURNAL

Date	Particulars		L.F.	Dr. (₹)	Cr. (₹)
1	Profit & Loss A/c	Dr.		20,000	
	To Dividend Payable A/c				20,000
	(Being dividend declared)				
2	Dividend Bank A/c	Dr.		20,000	
	To Bank A/c				20,000
	(Being the t/f of Balance to Dividend Bank A/c)				
3	Dividend Payable A/c	Dr.		20,000	
	To Dividend Bank A/c				20,000
	(Being payment of dividend)				
4	Bank A/c	Dr.		75,000	
	To Equity Share Application & Allotment A/c				75,000
	(Being the Application money received on 5,000 shares @ ₹ 15 per share to be issued as rights shares in the ratio of 1 : 4)				
5	Equity Share Application & Allotment A/c	Dr.		75,000	
	To Equity Share Capital A/c				50,000
	To Securities Premium A/c				25,000
	(Share application money on 5,000 shares @ ₹ 10 per share transferred to Share Capital Account and ₹ 5 per share to Securities Premium Account, vide Board's Resolution dated....)				
6	Securities Premium A/c	Dr.		25,000	
	Profit & Loss A/c	Dr.		37,500	
	To Bonus to Shareholders A/c				62,500
	(Amount transferred for issue of bonus shares to existing shareholders in the ratio of 1 : 4 vide General Body's Resolution dated....)				
7	Bonus to Shareholders A/c	Dr.		62,500	
	To Equity Share Capital A/c				62,500
	(Issue of bonus shares in the ratio of 1 for 4)				
8	12% Debentures A/c	Dr.		1,20,000	
	Premium Payable on Redemption A/c	Dr.		3,600	
	To Debenture holders A/c				1,23,600
	(Amount due to Debentures on redemption, at a premium of 3%, transferred to Debentures A/c)				
9	Debenture holders A/c	Dr.		1,23,600	
	To Bank A/c				1,23,600
	(Amount paid to debentures holders)				

10	Profit & Loss A/c	Dr.		3,600	
	To Premium Payable on Redemption A/c				3,600
	(Premium payable on redemption charged to P&L A/c)				
11	Debenture Redemption Reserve A/c	Dr.		30,000	
	To General Reserve A/c				30,000
	(Being the Transfer of DRR to General Reserves)				

ILLUSTRATION 48

The following is the Balance Sheet of Bumbum Ltd.(Listed) as at 31st March, 2023:

Particulars	₹
Sources of Funds:	
Authorized capital:	
50,000 Equity Shares of ₹ 10 each	5,00,000
10,000 Preference Shares of ₹ 100 each	10,00,000
	15,00,000
Issued subscribed and paid up	
30,000 Equity shares of ₹ 10 each	3,00,000
5,000 Redeemable 8% Preference shares of ₹ 100 each	5,00,000
Reserves & Surplus	
Securities Premium	6,00,000
General Reserve	6,50,000
Profit & Loss A/c	40,000
2500, 9% Debentures of ₹ 100 each	2,50,000
Sundry Creditors	1,70,000
	25,10,000
Application of Funds:	
Property,Plant,Equipment & Intangible Assets (net)	7,80,000
Investments (Market Value ₹ 6,80,000)	4,90,000
Deferred Tax Assets	3,40,000
Sundry Debtors	6,20,000
Cash & Bank balance	2,80,000
	25,10,000

In Annual General Meeting held on 20th June the company passed the following resolutions:

(i) To split equity share ₹ 10 each into 5 equity shares of ₹ 2 each from 1st July.

(ii) To redeem 8% Preference Shares at a premium of 5%.

(iii) To redeem 9% Debentures by making offer to debenture holders to convert their holdings into equity shares at ₹ 10 per share *or* accept cash on redemption.

(iv) To issue fully paid bonus shares in the ratio of one equity share for every 3 shares held on record date.

On 10th July investments were sold for ₹ 5,55,000 and preference shares were redeemed. 40% of Debentureholder exercised their option to accept cash & their claims were settled on 1st Aug. The company fixed 5th September as record date and bonus issue was concluded by 12th September. You are requested to journalize the above transactions including cash transactions and prepare Balance Sheet as at 30th September.

SOLUTION

JOURNAL OF BUMBUM LIMITED

Date	*Particulars*		*L.F.*	*Dr. (₹)*	*Cr. (₹)*
July 01	Equity Share Capital A/c (10 each)	Dr.		3,00,000	
	To Equity share Capital A/c (2 each)				3,00,000
	(Being equity shares of ₹ 10 each splitted into 5 equity shares of ₹ 2 each)				
July 10	Cash & Bank A/c	Dr.		5,55,000	
	To Investment A/c				4,90,000
	To Profits Loss A/c				65,000
	(Being investment sold out and profit on sale credited to Profit & Loss A/c)				
July 10	8% Redeemable Preference Share Capital A/c	Dr.		5,00,000	
	Premium on redemption of Preference Share A/c	Dr.		25,000	
	To Preference shareholders A/c				5,25,000
	(Being amount payable to preference share holders on redemption)				
July 10	Preference Shareholders A/c	Dr.		5,25,000	
	To Cash & bank A/c				5,25,000
	(Being amount paid to preference shareholders)				
July 10	General Reserve A/c	Dr.		5,25,000	
	To Capital Redemption Reserve A/c				5,00,000
	To Premium on redemption of Preference Share A/c				25,000
	(Being amount equal to nominal value of preference shares transferred to Capital Redemption Reserve A/c & premium on preference shares adjusted as per the law)				
Aug 1	9% Debentures A/c	Dr.		2,50,000	
	Interest on debentures A/c	Dr.		7,500	
	To Debentureholders A/c				2,57,500
	(Being amount payable to debentureholders along with interest payable)				
Aug. 1	Debentureholders A/c	Dr.		2,57,500	
	To Cash & Bank A/c (1,00,000 + 7,500)				1,07,500
	To Equity share capital A/c				30,000
	To Securities premium A/c				1,20,000
	(Being claims of debenture holders satisfied)				

Sept. 5	Capital Redemption Reserve A/c Dr. To Bonus to shareholders A/c (Being CRR capitalized to issue bonus shares)		1,10,000	1,10,000
Sept. 12	Bonus to Shareholders A/c Dr. To Equity Share Capital A/c (Being 55,000 fully paid equity shares of ₹ 2 each issued as bonus in ratio of 1 share for every 3 shares held)		1,10,000	1,10,000
Sept. 30	Profit & Loss A/c Dr. To Interest on Debentures A/c (Being interest on debentures transferred to Profit and Loss Account)		7,500	7,500

Note: For capitalisation of Bonus shares and transfer to Capital Redemption Reserve Account any other free reserves given in the Balance Sheet may also be used.

BALANCE SHEET AT 30TH SEPTEMBER, 2023

Particulars	*Note*	₹
I. Equity & Liabilities		
1. Share Capital	1	4,40,000
2. Reserves & Surplus	2	13,32,500
3. Current Liabilities [Sundry Creditors]		1,70,000
Total		19,42,500
II. Assets		
1. Non-Current Assets		
Property,Plant,Equipment & Intangible Assets (Net)		7,80,000
Deferred Tax Assets		3,40,000
2. Current Assets		
Trade Receivables [Sundry Debtors]		6,20,000
Cash & Cash Equivalents		2,02,500
Total		19,42,500

Notes to Accounts:

1. Share Capital	₹
Authorized Share capital	
2,50,000 Equity Shares of 2 each	5,00,000
10,000 Preference Shares of 100 each	10,00,000
	15,00,000
Issued, Share Capital	
2,20,000 Equity Shares of ₹ 2 each	4,40,000

	Subscribed and fully paid up 2,20,000 Equity Shares of 2 each	4,40,000
2.	**Reserves & Surplus**	
	Securities Premium	7,20,000
	Capital Redemption Reserve	3,90,000
	General Reserve	1,25,000
	Profit & Loss A/c (40,000 + 65,000 – 7,500)	97,500
		13,32,500

Working Notes:

1. Amount payable to Preference Shareholders = ₹ 5,00,000 + 5% = ₹ 5, 25,000
2. Equity shares issued on conversion = (2,50,000 – 1,00,000)/10 = 15,000 shares
3. Bonus shares to be issued = (150000 + 15000)/3 = 55,000 shares

4. SECURITIES PREMIUM A/C

Balance as per Balance Sheet	6,00,000
Add: Premium on equity shares issued on conversion of debentures (15,000 × 8)	1,20,000
Balance	7,20,000

5. CASH AND BANK BALANCE

Balance as per balance sheet	2,80,000
Add: Realization on sale of investment	5,55,000
Less: Paid to preference share holders	5,25,000
Paid to Debenture holders (7,500 + 1,00,000)	1,07,500
Balance	2,02,500

6. Interest of ₹ 7,500 paid to debenture holders have been debited to Profit & Loss Account.

MEANING OF STATEMENT OF CHANGES IN EQUITY

Equity represents owners' stake in the entity which is the residual interest in the Assets of the entity after deducting all of its external liabilities.

A Statement of Changes in Equity is a Financial Statement which shows:

1. the Opening Balances of various Equity Accounts such as Share Capital, Retained Earnings, Securities Premium, Capital Redemption Reserve, Revaluation Reserve
2. the Increase/Decrease in various Equity Accounts
3. the Closing Balances of various Equity Accounts

A Statement of Changes in Shareholders' Equity is a Financial Statement which reconciles the opening balances of Equity Accounts with their closing balances by showing a summary of the changes in Shareholders' Equity Accounts over the reporting period.

The Change in Shareholders' Equity over the reporting period usually occurs due to the following:

1. **Corrections of Prior Period errors and Changes in Accounting Policy**
2. **Changes in Net Income for the period,**

3. **Effect of Revaluation of Property,Plant,Equipment & Intangible Assets, Changes on re- measuring of Financial Assets held as Available for Sale, Effect of Foreign Exchange Translation (if not included in Net Income Determination), Effective Portion of Change in Fair Value of Hedging Instruments in Cash Flow Hedges and Actuarial Gains & Losses on Defined Benefit Plans**
4. **Transactions with Shareholders such as Issue/ Buy back of Shares, Payment of Dividends, Issue of Bonus Shares etc.**
5. **Changes in Ownership Interests in Subsidiaries that do not result in a loss of control**

Note: The Consolidated Statement of Changes in Equity (of a group that includes one *or* more partly-owned subsidiaries) also provides information about the share of equity attributable to the owners of the parent and that attributable to the non-controlling interests and information about changes in such interests.

FORMAT OF STATEMENT OF CHANGES IN EQUITY

STATEMENT OF CHANGES IN EQUITY

For the period ended 31st March, 20...

Particulars	*Share Capital*	*Reserves & Surplus*					*Total Equity*
		Retained Earnings	*Securities Premium*	*Capital Reserve*	*Capital Red. Reserve*	*Revaluation Reserve*	
A. Balance in the beg.	XXX	XXX	XXX	XXX	XXX	XXX	XXX
B. Corrections of Prior Period errors		XXX					XXX
C. Changes in Accounting Policy		XXX					XXX
D. Re–stated Balance in the beg. (A + B + C)	XXX	XXX	XXX	XXX	XXX	XXX	XXX
E. Net Income for the period		XXX					XXX
F. Effect of Revaluation							
(i) Revaluation of Property,Plant,Equipment & Intangible Assets						XXX	XXX
(ii) Change on re measuring of Financial Assets held as Available for Sale						XXX	XXX
(iii) Effective Portion of Change in Fair Value of Hedging Instruments in Cash Flow Hedges						XXX	XXX
(iv) Effect of Foreign Exchange Translation (if not included in net income determination)						XXX	XXX
(v) Actuarial Gains and Losses on Defined Benefit Plans						XXX	XXX
TOTAL (F)	-	-	-	-	-	XXX	XXX
G. Transactions with Shareholders							
(i) Dividends		(XXX)					(XXX)
(ii) Issue of New Shares	XXX		XXX				XXX

(iii) Buy back of Shares	(XXX)	(XXX)	(XXX)		XXX		(XXX)
(iv) Issue of Bonus Shares	XXX		(XXX)		(XXX)		
TOTAL (G)	XXX	(XXX)	XXX		XXX	-	XXX
H. Balance at the end [D + E + F + G]	XXX	XXX	XXX	XXX	XXX	XXX	XXX

ILLUSTRATION 49

From the following Information, Prepare Statement of Changes in Equity of TULSIAN LTD For the period ended 31st March,2023:

Equity Share Capital of ₹ 10 each in the beg.	₹ 50 crores
5% Preference Share Capital of ₹ 100 each in the beg.	₹ 10 crores
Retained Earnings in the beg.	₹ 100 crores
Securities Premium in the beg.	₹ 50 crores
Capital Redemption Reserve in the beg.	₹ 50 crores
Revaluation Reserve in the beg.	₹ 50 crores
Corrections of Prior Period errors resulting in increase in Profits	₹ 5 crores
Changes in Accounting Policy resulting in increase in Profits	₹ 10 crores
Net Income for the period (incl. ₹ 4 crores Net Gains on Foreign Exchange Translation)	₹ 20 crores
Revaluation Gain on Property, Plant, Equipment & Intangible Assets	₹ 10 crores
Dividends paid during the year	₹ 5 crores
Issue of 50 lacs New Shares of ₹ 10 each at ₹ 100 each during the year	
Buy back of 20 lacs Shares of ₹ 10 each at ₹ 50 each out of Securities Premium during the year	
Issue of Bonus Shares out of Capital Redemption Reserve during the year	₹ 45 crores

SOLUTION

STATEMENT OF CHANGES IN EQUITY OF TULSIAN LTD
For the period ended 31st March, 2023

Particulars	*Share Capital*	*Reserves & Surplus*				*Total Equity*
		Retained Earnings	*Securities Premium*	*Capital Red. Reserve*	*Revaluation Reserve*	
A. Balance in the beg.	60	100	50	50	50	310
B. Corrections of Prior Period errors		5				5
C. Changes in Accounting Policy		10				10
D. Re-stated Balance in the beg. (A + B + C)	60	115	50	50	50	325
E. Net Income for the period		20				20
F. Effect of Revaluation of Property,Plant,Equipment & Intangible Assets					10	10

G. Transactions with Shareholders						
(i) Dividends		(5)				(5)
(ii) Issue of New Shares	5		45			50
(iii) Buy back of Shares	(2)		(10)	2		(10)
(iv) Issue of Bonus Shares	45			(45)		0
TOTAL (G)	**48**	**(5)**	**35**	**(43)**	**0**	**35**
H. Balance at the end [D + E + F + G]	**108**	**130**	**85**	**7**	**60**	**390**

ILLUSTRATION 50

From the following information, prepare Statement of Equity of XYZ Ltd.:

Particulars	***31.03.2023*** ₹	***31.03.2022*** ₹
Equity Share Capital of ₹ 10 each	8,25,000	6,00,000
5% Preference Share Capital of ₹ 100 each	2,00,000	4,00,000
Retained Earnings	6,82,000	3,12,000
Securities Premium	35,000	20,000
Capital Redemption Reserve	—	5,000
Revaluation Reserve	—	15,000

An Interim Dividend @ 35% was paid on equity shares of ₹ 6,00,000 on 31.12.2022.

SOLUTION

STATEMENT OF CHANGES IN EQUITY OF XYZ LTD

For the period ended 31st March, 2023

Particulars	***Share Capital***	***Reserves & Surplus***				***Total Equity***
		Retained Earnings	***Securities Premium***	***Capital Red. Reserve***	***Revaluation Reserve***	
A. Balance in the beg.	10,00,000	3,12,000	20,000	5,000	15,000	13,52,000
B. Net Income for the period		5,80,000				5,80,000
C. Revaluation of Property, Plant, Equipment & Intangible Assets					(15,000)	(15,000)
D. Transactions with Shareholders						
(i) Dividend		(2,10,000)				(2,10,000)
(ii) Issue of New Shares	2,20,000		15000			2,35,000
(iii) Redemption of Pref. Shares	(2,00,000)					(2,00,000)
(iv) Issue of Bonus Shares	5,000			(5,000)		0
TOTAL (D)	25,000	(2,10,000)	15000	(5,000)		(85,000)
E. Balance at the end [A + B + C + D]	10,25,000	6,82,000	35000	0	0	17,42,000

Notes:

1. Net Profit for the year = Balance of Retained Earnings at 31 March 2023 + Dividend for the year 2022 - 2023 – (Balance of Retained Earnings at 31 March 2022) = ₹ 6,82,000 + ₹ 2,10,000 – ₹ 3,12,000 = ₹ 5,80,000

2. Issue of Bonus Share is equal to ₹ 5,000 since Balance of Capital Redemption Reserve in beginning was ₹ 5,000 and it can only be utilized to issue fully paid bonus shares.

ILLUSTRATION 51

From the following information, prepare Statement of Equity of IPC (2) Ltd.:

Particulars	*31.03.2023* ₹	*31.03.2022* ₹
Equity Share Capital of ₹ 10 each	8,25,000	6,00,000
5% Preference Share Capital of ₹ 100 each (redeemable at a premium of 5%)	2,00,000	4,00,000
Retained Earnings	6,82,000	3,12,000
Securities Premium	45,000	20,000
Capital Redemption Reserve	—	5,000
Revaluation Reserve		15,000

Additional Information: On 1.4.2022 an Interim Dividend @ 35% was paid on equity shares. During the year 12,000 New Equity Shares of ₹ 10 each were issued. The company reversed upward revaluation of Property,Plant & Equipment by ₹ 16,000.

SOLUTION

STATEMENT OF CHANGES IN EQUITY OF XYZ LTD

For the period ended 31st March,2023

Particulars	*Share Capital*	*Reserves & Surplus*				*Total Equity*
		Retained Earnings	*Securities Premium*	*Capital Red. Reserve*	*Revaluation Reserve*	
A. Balance in the beg.	10,00,000	3,12,000	20,000	5000	15,000	13,52,000
B. Net Income for the period		6,91,000				6,91,000
C. Revaluation of Non-Current Fixed Assets		(1,000)			(15,000)	(16,000)
D. Transactions with Shareholders						
(i) Dividend		(2,10,000)				(2,10,000)
(ii) Issue of New Shares	1,20,000		25,000			1,45,000
(iii) Redemption of Pref. Shares	(2,00,000)	(1,10,000)		1,00,000		(2,10,000)
(iv) Issue of Bonus Shares	1,05,000			(1,05,000)		0
TOTAL (D)	25,000	(3,20,000)	25,000	(5,000)		(2,75,000)
E. Balance at the end [A + B + C + D]	10,25,000	6,82,000	45,000	0	0	17,52,000

Working Notes:

1. Redemption of Preference Shares of ₹ 2,00,000 has been made out of Issue of new shares to the extent of ₹ 1,00,000 and the balance of ₹ 1,00,000 out of Retained earnings by transfer to Capital Redemption Reserve.
2. Net Income for the period = Balance of Retained Earnings at 31 March 2023 +Transfer to Capital Redemption Reserve+ Interim Dividend for the year 2022 - 2023+Premium on Redemption of RPS– Revaluation of Non-Current Fixed Assets –(Balance of Retained Earnings at 31 March 2022) = ₹ 6,82,000 + ₹ 1,00,000 (CRR) + ₹ 2,10,000+ ₹ 10,000+₹ 1,000 – ₹ 3,12,000 = ₹ 6,91,000.

3. Total Revaluation loss amounts to ₹ 16,000. Revaluation loss is first provided from Revaluation Reserve to the extent available i.e. ₹ 15,000 and the remaining balance of ₹ 1,000 is provided from Profit & Loss A/c.

ILLUSTRATION 52

From the following information, prepare Statement of Equity of IPC (2) Ltd.:

Particulars	*31.03.2023* ₹	*31.03.2022* ₹
Equity Share Capital of ₹ 10 each	8,25,000	6,00,000
5% Preference Share Capital of ₹ 100 each(redeemable at a premium of 5%)	2,00,000	4,00,000
Retained Earnings	6,82,000	3,12,000
Securities Premium	45,000	20,000
Capital Redemption Reserve	—	5,000
Revaluation Reserve	—	15,000
Property,Plant & Equipment (Net)	12,70,000	10,20,000

Additional Information:

(a) During the year a machine costing ₹ 1,40,000 (depreciation provided thereon ₹ 60,000) was sold for ₹ 50,000. Depreciation charged was ₹ 1,40,000. A machine was purchased by issue of Equity Shares of ₹ 10 each at a premium of 25%. Some Machines were purchased during the year by a cheque of ₹ 4,61,000. Some Machines were revalued at year end.

(b) An Interim Dividend @ 35% was paid on equity shares on 1.4.2022.

(c) 10,000 New Equity Shares of ₹ 10 each were issued on 01.01.2023.

SOLUTION

STATEMENT OF CHANGES IN EQUITY OF XYZ LTD

For the period ended 31st March,2023

Particulars	*Share Capital*	*Reserves & Surplus*				*Total Equity*
		Retained Earnings	*Securities Premium*	*Capital Red. Reserve*	*Revaluation Reserve*	
A.Balance in the beg.	10,00,000	3,12,000	20,000	5000	15,000	13,52,000
B.Net Income for the period		6,91,000				6,91,000
C.Revaluation of Non-Current Fixed Assets		(1,000)			(15,000)	(16,000)
D.Transactions with Shareholders						
(i) Dividend		(2,10,000)				(2,10,000)
(ii) Issue of New Shares	1,20,000		25,000			1,45,000
(iii) Redemption of Pref. Shares	(2,00,000)	(1,10,000)		1,00,000		(2,10,000)
(iv) Issue of Bonus Shares	1,05,000			(1,05,000)		0
TOTAL (D)	25,000	(3,20,000)	25,000	(5,000)		(2,75,000)
E.Balance at the end [A + B + C + D]	10,25,000	6,82,000	45,000	0	0	17,52,000

Working Notes:

1. Redemption of Preference Shares of ₹ 2,00,000 has been made out of Issue of new shares to the extent of ₹ 1,00,000 and the balance of ₹ 1,00,000 out of Retained earnings by transfer to Capital Redemption Reserve.

2. Net Income for the period = Balance of Retained Earnings at 31 March 2023 +Transfer to Capital Redemption Reserve+ Interim Dividend for the year 2022 - 2023+Premium on Redemption of RPS– Revaluation of Non-Current Fixed Assets –(Balance of Retained Earnings at 31 March 2022) = ₹ 6,82,000 + ₹ 1,00,000 (CRR) + ₹ 2,10,000+ ₹ 10,000+₹ 1,000 – ₹3,12,000 = ₹ 6,91,000.

Dr. 4. CAPITAL REDEMPTION RESERVE ACCOUNT Cr.

Particulars	₹	Particulars	₹
To Bonus to Shareholders A/c [b.f.]	1,05,000	By Balance b/d	5,000
		By Profit and Loss A/c	1,00,000
	1,05,000		1,05,000

Dr. 5. EQUITY SHARE CAPITAL ACCOUNT Cr.

Particulars	₹	Particulars	₹
To Balance c/d	8,25,000	By Balance b/d	6,00,000
		By Vendor of PPE A/c (b.f.)	20,000
		By Bank A/c (new shares)	1,00,000
		By Bonus to Shareholders A/c	1,05,000
	8,25,000		8,25,000

Dr. 6. SECURITIES PREMIUM ACCOUNT Cr.

Particulars	₹	Particulars	₹
To Balance c/d	45,000	By Balance b/d	20,000
		By Vendor of PPE A/c	5,000
		By Bank A/c (new shares) (b.f.)	20,000
	45,000		45,000

Dr. 7. PPE ACCOUNT Cr.

Particulars	₹	Particulars	₹
To Balance b/d	10,20,000	By Bank A/c (Sale)	50,000
To Bank A/c (Purchases)	4,61,000	By P&L A/c (Loss)	30,000
To Vendor of PPE A/c	25,000	By Depreciation A/c	1,40,000
		By Revaluation Reserve A/c (b.f.)	15,000
		By P & L A/c (b.f.)	1,000
		By Balance c/d	12,70,000
	15,06,000		15,06,000

Note: Total Revaluation loss amounts to ₹ 16,000. Revaluation loss is first provided from Revaluation Reserve to the extent available i.e. ₹ 15,000 and the remaining balance of ₹ 1,000 is provided from Profit & Loss A/c.

ILLUSTRATION 53

CEO of XYZ Ltd. has asked you to prepare a statement of changes in equity for the year ended 31st March 2023.

The components of the company's shareholders equity as at 1 April 2022 was as follows:

Particulars	*₹ (in crores)*
Authorized Share Capital 40 crores, Issued 10 crores shares of ₹ 10 each	100
Securities Premium	240
Capital Reserve	60
Retained earnings	180
Revaluation Reserve	30

Additional Information:

(a) On 31 July 2022, the company declared and issued 10% bonus shares. Market Price per share at the date was ₹ 40.

(b) On 30 June 2022, the company issued 2 crore new shares for total consideration of ₹ 90 crores.

(c) Profit for the financial year ended 31 March 2023 amounted to ₹100 crores and the company paid dividends totaling ₹ 32 crores.

(d) The company set aside 10% of net income for the period for transfer to capital reserve

(e) 1 crore shares were bought back on 30 December 2022 at ₹ 40 per share.

(f) The company reversed upward revaluation of an asset by ₹ 10 crores. The revaluation surplus already includes ₹ 14 crores of such initial upward revaluation.

SOLUTION

STATEMENT OF CHANGES IN EQUITY OF XYZ LTD

For the period ended 31st March,2023

Particulars	*Share Capital*	*Reserves & Surplus*					*Total Equity*
		Retained Earnings	*Securities Premium*	*Capital Reserve*	*Capital Red. Reserve*	*Revaluation Reserve*	
A.Balance in the beg.	100	180	240	60	0	30	610
B.Corrections of Prior Period errors						0	
C.Changes in Accounting Policy						0	
D.Re-stated Balance in the beg. (A + B + C)	100	180	240	60	0	30	610
E.Net Income for the period		100					100
F.Revaluation Property,Plant,Equipment & Intangible Assets						(10)	(10)
G.Transactions with Shareholders							
(i) Issue of Bonus Shares	10		(10)				0

(ii) Issue of New Shares	20		70				90
(iii) Dividend		(32)					(32)
(iii) Transfer to Capital Reserve		(10)		10			0
(iv) Buy back of Shares	(10)	(10)	(30)		10		(40)
TOTAL (G)	**20**	**(52)**	**30**	**10**	**10**	**0**	**18**
H.Balance at the end [D + E + F + G]	**120**	**228**	**270**	**70**	**10**	**20**	**718**

ILLUSTRATION 54

From the following Information, Prepare Statement of Changes in Equity of TULSIAN FINAL LTD For the period ended 31st March, 2023:

Share Capital in the beg.	₹ 100 crores
Retained Earning in the beg.	₹ 200 crores
Securities Premium in the beg.	₹ 100 crores
Capital Redemption Reserve in the beg.	₹ 100 crores
Revaluation Reserve in the beg.	₹ 100 crores
Corrections of Prior Period errors resulting in increase in Profits	₹ 10 crores
Changes in Accounting Policy resulting in increase in Profits	₹ 20 crores
Net Income for the period (incl. ₹ 4 crores Net Gains on Foreign Exchange Translation)	₹ 40 crores
Revaluation Gain on Property,Plant,Equipment & Intangible Assets	₹ 20 crores
Profit on re-measuring of Financial Assets held as Available for Sale	₹ 40 crores
Effective Portion of Upward Change in Fair Value of Hedging Instruments in Cash Flow Hedges	₹ 10 crores
Actuarial Gain on Defined Benefit Plans	₹ 10 crores
Dividends	₹ 10 crores
Issue of 1 crore New Shares of ₹ 10 each at ₹ 100 each	
Buy back of 40 lacs Shares of ₹ 10 each at ₹ 50 each out of Securities Premium	
Issue of Bonus Shares out of Capital Red. Reserve	₹ 90 crores

SOLUTION

STATEMENT OF CHANGES IN EQUITY OF TULSIAN FINAL LTD

For the period ended 31st March, 2023

Particulars	*Share Capital*	*Reserves & Surplus*				*Total Equity*
		Retained Earnings	*Securities Premium*	*Capital Red. Reserve*	*Revaluation Reserve*	
A. Balance in the beg.	100	200	100	100	100	600
B. Corrections of Prior Period errors		10				10
C. Changes in Accounting Policy		20				20

D. Re-stated Balance in the beg. (A + B + C)	100	230	100	100	100	630
E. Net Income for the period		40				40
F. Effect of Revaluation						
(i) Revaluation Property, Plant, Equipment & Intangible Assets					20	20
(ii) Change on re measuring of Financial Assets held as Available for Sale					40	40
(iii) Effective Portion of Change in Fair Value of Hedging Instruments in Cash Flow Hedges					10	10
(iv) Actuarial Gains and Losses on Defined Benefit Plans					10	10
TOTAL (F)	**0**	**0**	**0**	**0**	**80**	**80**
G. Transactions with Shareholders						
(i) Dividends		(10)				(10)
(ii) Issue of New Shares	10		90			100
(iii) Buy back of Shares	(4)	(4)	(16)	4		(20)
(iv) Issue of Bonus Shares	90			(90)		0
TOTAL (G)	**96**	**(14)**	**74**	**(86)**	**0**	**70**
H. Balance at the end [D + E + F + G]	**196**	**256**	**174**	**14**	**180**	**820**

MULTIPLE CHOICE QUESTIONS [MCQ]

1. The financial year of X Ltd incorporated on 1st January 2022 will end on
   (a) 31st March,2022.
   (b) 31st Dec,2022
   (c) 31st March,2023
   (d) 31st March,2024

2. Which of the following is not true?
   (a) Financial Statements of a company include a Balance Sheet, a Profit and Loss Account, Cash Flow Statement, a Statement of Changes in Equity and an explanatory note(s).
   (b) Cash Flow Statement is not required to be prepared by One Person Company, Small Company and Dormant Company.
   (c) While preparing Balance Sheet of OM TAT SAT Ltd (of which operating cycle is 14 months) as at 31st March,2022, ₹ 60 lakh due from Y, a customer on 30th April, 2023 will be classified as Current Asset.
   (d) The financial year of X Ltd incorporated on 1st January 2022 will end on 31st March,2022.

3. Net Profits of AATMA Ltd. for the years 2021-2022,2020-2021,2019-2020,2018-2019,2017-2018 are ₹ 25 crore, ₹ 20 crore, ₹ 15 crore, ₹ 10 crore and ₹ 5 crore respectively. During 2021-2022,the company incurred ₹ 7,00,000 and ₹ 3,00,000 on free education and medical treatment of the employees of the company and their families respectively under CSR projects. State the short fall of expenditure on Corporate Social Responsibility as per The Companies Act,2013.

(a) ₹ 40,00,000

(b) ₹ 30,00,000

(c) ₹ 20,00,000

(d) ₹ 10,00,000

4. The figures appearing in the Financial Statements SHALL be rounded off to the nearest crores only if Total Income is

(a) less than ₹ 100 crore

(b) ₹ 100 crore or more

(c) more than ₹ 100 crore

(d) more than ₹ 500 crore

5. An item of Income or Expenditure is to be disclosed separately as per The Companies Act, 2013 if its amount exceeds

(a) 1% of the revenue from operations or ₹ 1,00,000, whichever is higher;

(b) 1% of the revenue from operations or ₹ 1,00,000, whichever is lower;

(c) 1% of the revenue from operations or ₹ 10,00,000, whichever is higher;

(d) 1% of the revenue from operations or ₹ 10,00,000, whichever is lower;

6. Which of the following is not true?

(a) The name of 3rd main Item in Statement of Profit/Loss is 'TOTAL INCOME'.

(b) The figures appearing in the Financial Statements are compulsorily required to be rounded off to the nearest crores if TOTAL INCOME is at least ₹ 100 crore.

(c) 2% of Average Net Profits of the company made during 3 immediately preceding financial years is required to be spent on Corporate Social Responsibility activities.

(d) An item of Income or Expenditure is to be disclosed separately in Statement of Profit/ Loss of a Company if it exceeds 1% of the Revenue from Operations or ₹ 10,00,000, whichever is higher.

7. Which of the following is not true?

(a) Expenditure on Corporate Social Responsibility (CSR) is disclosed as a separate item under the head "Other Expenses" in the Statement of Profit/Loss of a Company.

(b) Eleven Ratios are required to be calculated and disclosed while preparing Financial Statements of a Company.

(c) 'Bank deposits with more than 12 months maturity' appear under the Sub-head "Cash and Cash Equivalents" of Balance Sheet of a Company.

(d) While preparing Balance Sheet of a Company Trade Receivables/ Payables Ageing Schedule are not required to be prepared.

8. Which of the following is not true?

(a) Amalgamation Adjustment Account is disclosed as a negative figure item under the head "Reserves & Surplus" of Balance Sheet of a Company.

(b) 'Current Maturities of Long-Term Borrowings' appear under the Sub-head "Short-Term Borrowings" of Balance Sheet of a Company.

(c) 'Security Deposits' appears under the Sub-head "Other Non-Current Assets" of Balance Sheet of a Company.

(d) Building appears under the Sub-head "Tangible Assets" of Balance Sheet of a Company.

9. 'Bank deposits with 15 months maturity appear under the Sub-head........... of Balance Sheet of a Company.

(a) Non-Current Assets-Non-Current Investments

(b) Current Assets-Current Investments

(c) Current Assets-Cash and Cash Equivalents

(d) Current Assets - Other Current Assets

10. In the Balance Sheet of a company, Reserve Capital

(a) is required to be disclosed under Authorised Capital.

(b) is required to be disclosed under Issued Capital.

(c) is required to be disclosed under Subscribed Capital.

(d) is not required to be disclosed.

11. Five Years Ago X Ltd. had Issued 12% Debentures of ₹ 30 Lakhs (Redeemable in 6 Equal Annual Instalments). Now, these Debentures will be shown In the Balance Sheet of a Company under the heading

(a) Shareholders' Funds

(b) Non-Current Liabilities-Long-Term Borrowings

(c) Current Liabilities-Short-Term Borrowings

(d) Current Liabilities-Other Current Liabilities

12. Profit of NEEM & TULSI Ltd for the year ended 31st March,2022 ₹ 114 lakh, Equity Share Capital (Shares of ₹ 10 each) fully paid up ₹ 200 lakh, Equity Share Capital (Shares of ₹ 10 each) ₹ 6 called up & paid up ₹ 60 lakh,10% Pref. Share Capital (Shares of ₹ 10 each) fully paid up ₹ 100 lakh, On 31.03.2022, dividends (including Equity Dividend @25%) were paid for which no accounting effect has yet been given. Calculate the Basic Earnings per Share(Basic EPS).

(a) ₹ 3.8

(b) ₹ 3.47

(c) ₹ 4

(d) ₹ 4.47

13. If the Articles are silent, as per Table F the minimum rate of interest to be allowed on calls-in advance is-

(a) 12% p.m.

(b) 12% p.a.

(c) 10% p.a.

(d) No Rate specified

14. If the Articles are silent, as per Table F the minimum rate of interest to be allowed on calls-in arrears is-

(a) 10% p.m.

(b) 10% p.a.

(c) 12% p.a.

(d) No Rate specified

15. Which of the following is not true?

(a) A Company can not pay dividend on calls-in-advance.

(b) A Company can declare and distribute Final Dividend in the event of loss in any financial year.

(c) In the event of inadequacy or absence of profit in any financial year, if dividend is declared by a company for that year out of Surplus, then 4 conditions as per The Companies (Declaration and Payment of Dividend out of Reserves) Rules, 2014 need not be fulfilled.

(d) A Company can declare and distribute Interim Dividend in the event of loss in any financial year.

VERY SHORT ANSWER TYPE QUESTIONS

1. **Briefly explain the following:**

   (a) Financial Statements as per Sec 2(40) of the Companies Act, 2013

   (b) Financial Year as per Sec 2(41) of the Companies Act, 2013

   (c) An Operating Cycle

   (d) Current Asset

   (e) Current Liability

   (f) Trade Receivable

   (g) Trade Payable

   (h) **Spending on** Corporate Social Responsibility as per Sec 135(5) of the Companies Act, 2013

   (i) Statement of Changes in Equity

2. **Enumerate the following:**

   (a) Companies not required to prepare Cash Flow Statement

   (b) Major headings into which the Liabilities side of a company's Balance Sheet is organised and presented, as per the Schedule III to The Companies Act 2013.

   (c) Major headings into which the Assets side of a company's Balance Sheet is organised and presented, as per the Schedule III to The Companies Act 2013.

   (d) Companies required to constitute a Corporate Social Responsibility Committee as per Sec 135(1) of the Companies Act, 2013

3. Prepare the format of the following as per Schedule III to The Companies Act 2013:

   (a) Trade Payables Ageing Schedule

   (b) Trade Receivables Ageing Schedule

   (c) Statement of Changes in Equity

4. (a) Name the 11 Ratios which are required to be disclosed in the Financial Statements as per Schedule III to The Companies Act 2013.

   (b) When is an explanation required to be provided for any change in these ratios ?

5. Prepare the format of the Balance Sheet of a Company (with main headings only), as per the Schedule III to The Companies Act 2013.

6. Prepare a layout of information required to be given under sub-heading 'Share Capital' of the company's Balance Sheet, as per the Schedule III to The Companies Act 2013.

7. List any four items which are included under the head 'Reserves and Surplus' of the company's Balance Sheet, as per the Schedule III to The Companies Act 2013.

8. List any four items which are included in 'Other Reserves' under the head 'Reserves and Surplus' of the company's Balance Sheet, as per the Schedule III to The Companies Act 2013.

9. List any four items which are included under the head 'Non-Current Liabilities' of the company's Balance Sheet, as per the Schedule III to The Companies Act 2013.

10. List any four items which are included under the head 'Current Liabilities' of the company's Balance Sheet, as per the Schedule III to The Companies Act 2013.

11. List any four items which are included under the head 'Non-Current Assets' of the company's Balance Sheet, as per the Schedule III to The Companies Act 2013.

12. List any four items which are included under the head 'Fixed Assets' of the company's Balance Sheet, as per the Schedule III to The Companies Act 2013.

13. Prepare "Notes to Accounts" giving details of "Tangible Fixed Assets" with imaginary figures, as per the Schedule III to The Companies Act 2013.

14. List any four items which are included under the head 'Current Assets' of the company's Balance Sheet, as per the Schedule III to The Companies Act 2013.

15. Prepare "Notes to Accounts" giving details of "Inventories" with imaginary figures, as per the Schedule III to The Companies Act 2013.

16. Give two examples each of Contingent Liabilities and Commitments as per the Schedule III to The Companies Act 2013.

17. Under which head and sub-head the following items will appear in the Balance Sheet of a company as per Schedule III to The Companies Act 2013:

1. Bank Overdraft
2. Preliminary Expenses
3. Brands
4. Proposed Dividend
5. Debit Balance of Profit & Loss A/c
6. Computer Software
7. Live Stock
8. Mining Rights
9. Security Deposit for Telephone
10. Provision for Warranties
11. Cheques/Drafts on hand
12. Calls-in-Advance & Interest thereon
13. Unpaid Dividend
14. Investment in Land & Building
15. Premium on Redemption of Debentures
16. Employees' earned leave payable on retirement
17. Investment in Bonds of Reliance Ltd. (Redeemable within 1 year)
18. Interest accrued on Bonds of Reliance Ltd.
19. Interest accrued & due on Long-term Borrowings
20. Provision for Employees Benefits to be settled within 12 months

18. How will you disclose the following items while preparing the Balance Sheet of a TULSIAN Ltd(having operating cycle of 14 months) as at 31st March,2023, as per the Schedule III to The Companies Act, 2013?(Name the Head,Sub-Head and Sub-Sub-Head,if any)

1. Current Maturities of Long-term Debt
2. Security Deposit
3. Debit Balance of Profit & Loss A/c
4. Computer Software under Development
5. Building under construction
6. Uncalled Liability on partly paid Debentures held as Investments

7. Employees' earned leave payable on retirement
8. Share application money received in excess of issued share capital
9. Share option outstanding account
10. Unpaid matured debentures and interest accrued thereon
11. Uncalled liability on shares and other partly paid investments
12. Calls-in-Advance
13. Investment in Bonds of Reliance Ltd. (Redeemable within 1 year)
14. Interest accrued on Bonds of Reliance Ltd.
15. Tonnage Tax Reserve
16. Arrears of Fixed Cumulative Dividends on Preference Shares
17. Crypto Currency or Virtual Currency
18. Crypto Currency or Virtual Currency held for sale in ordinary course of business
18. Leasehold Land
19. Licenses & Franchise
20. *X*,a customer whose *expected realisation date is* 30th June, 2024
21. Unpaid matured debenture and interest accrued thereon.
22. Amalgamation Adjustment A/c
23. Bank deposits with more than 12 months maturity

SHORT ANSWER TYPE PRACTICAL QUESTIONS

1. Compute the Operating Cycle from the following information:

1. Raw material stock holding period: 3 months
2. Work-in-progress holding period: 1 month
3. Finished goods holding period: 4 months
4. Debtors collection period: 6 months

2. Operating Cycle Period of MODI Ltd is 14 Months but Expected Realisation Period of Trade Receivables is 13 Months from the date of Balance Sheet. State giving reason whether its Trade Receivables are Current Assets or Non-Current Assets as per Schedule III to The Companies Act, 2013

3. Operating Cycle Period of SHAH Ltd is 11 Months but Expected Payment Period of Trade Payables is 12 Months from the date of Balance Sheet. State giving reason whether its Trade Payables are Current Liabilities or Non-Current Liabilities as per Schedule III to The Companies Act, 2013.

4. PCT Ltd. is in the process of finalizing its accounts for year ended 31st March, 2022 and furnishes the following information:

(i) Finished goods normally are held for 1 month before sale.

(ii) Sales realization from Debtors usually takes 2 months from date of credit invoice.

(iii) Raw materials are held in stock to cover 1 month's production requirements.

(iv) Packing materials, being specifically made for the company and having lead time of 3 months is held in stock for 3 months.

(v) The holding period in respect of unfinished goods is 1 month.

(vi) Being a monopoly KAY Ltd. enjoys a credit period of 12.5 months from its suppliers who sometimes at the end of their credit period opt for conversion of their dues into long term debt of KAY Ltd.

You are required to compute the operating cycle of PCT Ltd. as per Schedule III of The Companies Act, 2013. As the suppliers of the company are paid off after a credit period of 12.5 months should this be part of Current Liability? Would your answer be the same if the creditors are settled in 330 days?

[**Ans** Operating Cycle 8 months, When credit period is 12.5 months: Non-current liability When credit period is 330 days : Current liability]

5. TULSIAN Ltd is having the following Fixed Deposit Receipts:

Bank	*Date of FDR*	*Maturity Date*	*Amount*
Yes Bank Limited	01–Jan–2022	2–Jan–2023	₹30,00,000
Bank of Baroda	01–Jan–2022	31–Mar–2023	₹ 20,00,000
State Bank of India	28–Feb–2022	30–May–2022	₹ 10,00,000
ICICI Bank	1–Jan–2021	1–Apr–2023	₹ 40,00,000

Prepare Notes to Accounts showing the above Deposits in accordance with the requirements of Schedule III as at the Balance Sheet date i.e. 31st March, 2022.

[**Ans** Cash Equivalent ₹ 10,00,000 as per AS–3 (less than 3 Months Maturity) [SBI],Other Bank Balances [₹ 30,00,000 + ₹ 20,00,000], More than 12 Months Maturity [ICICI] ₹40,00,000]

6. It is found from the books, that a loan of ₹ 50,00,000 was advanced on 30.09.2021 @ 14% p.a. Interest payable half yearly; but the loan was outstanding as on 31.3.2022 without any payment recorded in the meantime, either towards principal or towards interest. The security for the loan was 1,00,000 fully paid shares of ₹ 100 each (the market value was ₹ 98 per share as per the Stock Exchange information as on 30th September 2021.) But due to fluctuations, the price fell to ₹ 45 per share in January, 2022. On 31-3-2022, the price as per Stock Exchange rate was ₹ 85 per share. State how would you classify the loan as secured/unsecured in the Balance Sheet of the Company.

[**Ans** good and fully secured]

7. State whether X Ltd is required to constitute a Corporate Social Responsibility Committee in the following case:

	2019-2020 (₹ crore)	*2020-2021 (₹ crore)*	*2021-2022 (₹ crore)*	*2022-2023 (₹ crore)*
Net Worth	₹ 499	₹ 499	₹ 499	₹ 500
Turnover	₹ 999	₹ 999	₹ 1000	₹ 999
Net Profit	₹ 4.99	₹ 5	₹ 4.99	₹ 4.99

[**Ans Yes since** 2020-2021]

8. Net Profits of JIV AATMA Ltd. for the years 2022-2023,2021-2022,2020-2021,2019-2020,2018-2019 are ₹ 50 crore,₹ 40 crore,₹ 30 crore,₹ 20 crore and ₹ 10 crore respectively. During 2022-2023,the company incurred only ₹ 14,00,000 and ₹ 6,00,000 on free education and medical treatment of the employees of the company and their families respectively under CSR projects.

Required: State the Amount of Short Fall of Expenditure on Corporate Social Responsibility during 2022-2023 as per The Companies Act,2013.

[**Ans** ₹ 0.60 crore]

9. From the following information, prepare the relevant Notes to Accounts:

Particulars	***(₹ in lacs)***
Opening Balance of Profit and Loss Statement	904
Profit for the period	1120
Transfer to Reserve @ 5%	
Interim Dividend	200
Preference Dividend	280
Final Equity Dividend	570
Transfer to Debenture Redemption Reserve	200

[**Ans**. Surplus ₹ 718 lacs]

10. From the following information, prepare the relevant Notes to Accounts:

Capital Reserve	40
Capital Redemption Reserve	80
Securities Premium	120
General Reserve	320
Statutory Reserves	40
Amalgamation Adjustment Account	40
Opening Balance of Profit and Loss Statement	904
Profit for the period	1120
Transfer to General Reserve @ 5%	
Interim Dividend	200

[**Ans** Surplus ₹ 1768 lacs, Reserves and Surplus ₹ 2384 lacs]

11. Tulsian Ltd. was formed with a capital of ₹ 2,00,000 divided into 10,000 Equity Shares of ₹ 10 each. Out of these 4,000 Equity Shares were issued to the Vendors as fully paid as purchase consideration for a fixed asset acquired. 12,000 Equity Shares were offered to the public and the issue was fully subscribed. The directors called ₹ 6 per share and received the entire amount except a call of ₹ 2 per share on 1000 shares out of which 400 shares were forfeited.

Required: How would you show the relevant items in the Balance Sheet of Tulsian Ltd., as per Schedule III to The Companies Act, 2013.

[**Ans** Authorised Capital ₹ 2,00,000, Issued Capital ₹ 1,60,000, Subscribed Capital ₹ 110,000]

12. From the following information, prepare the relevant Notes to Accounts:

1. Bills Discounted but not yet matured 2 lacs
2. 600 lacs Shares of X Ltd of ₹ 10 each,₹ 8 paid up held as Investments
3. 12 lacs,14% Debentures of ₹ 100 each, ₹ 80 paid up held as Investments

[**Ans** Contingent Liabilities ₹ 4 lacs, Commitments ₹ 1440 lacs]

13. X Ltd provides the following information:

Particulars	***₹ (in lakh)***		
	2020-2021	***2021-2022***	***2022-2023***
1. Profit (Loss) before charging Depreciation	(10)	12	32
2. Depreciation Chargeable u/s 123 (2)	6	14	12
3. Profit (Loss) after charging depreciation	(16)	(2)	20

Required: Calculate the Divisible Profits for the year 2022-2023

[**Ans.** Divisible Profits ₹ 2 lacs]

14. Tushar Ltd. provides you the following information:

Equity Shares of ₹ 10 Each	₹ 200 lakh
General Reserves	₹ 40 lakh
Revaluation Reserves	₹ 10 lakh
Loss for the year ending: 31.3.2022 ₹ 4 lakh, 31.3.2023 ₹ 2 lakh	
Rates of Equity Dividend : 9 % in 2019-2020,10% in 2020-2021,11% in 2021-2022,	

The management recommends a dividend of 8% on equity share capital. As an expert comment upon the management's decision.

[**Ans.** The management can declare dividend only upto a rate of 4%. Hence, the management's dividend decision of 8% is not as per Rules]

15. PARAM ATMA Ltd. provides you the following information:

Equity Shares of ₹ 10 Each	₹ 200 lakh
8% Preference shares of ₹ 100 each, fully paid up	₹ 40 lakh
General Reserves	₹ 60 lakh
Revaluation Reserves	₹ 10 lakh
Loss for the year ending: 31.3.2022 ₹ 4 lakh, 31.3.2023 ₹ 2 lakh	
Rates of Equity Dividend : 0 % in 2019-2020,16% in 2020-2021,17% in 2021-2022,	

PARAM ATMA Ltd. desires to declare dividend @ 10% for the year 2022-2023. As an expert comment upon the management's decision.

[**Ans.** The management can declare dividend only upto a rate of 9.4%. Hence, the management's dividend decision of 10% is not as per Rules]

16. Due to inadequacy of profits during the year ended 31st March, 2023, PQR Ltd. proposes to declare 8.5% dividend out of general reserves. From the following particulars, ascertain the amount that can be utilized from general reserves for this purpose, according to the Companies (Declaration of Dividend out of Reserves) Rules, 2014.

8% Preference shares of ₹ 100 each, fully paid up	₹ 30,00,000
Equity shares of ₹ 10 each, fully paid up	₹ 2,20,00,000
General Reserves as on 1.4.2022	₹ 50,00,000
Capital Reserves as on 1.4.2022	₹ 20,00,000
Revaluation Reserves as on 1.4.2022	₹ 30,00,000
Net Profit for the year ended 31st March, 2023	₹ 9,70,000

Average rate of dividend during the last three years has been 12%.

[**Ans.** The management can declare dividend only upto a rate of 9%. To declare dividend @ 8.5% the Company can utilize ₹ 11,40,000 (i.e. ₹ 18,70,000 – ₹ 7,30,000) out of General Reserves.]

17. X Ltd. provides you the following information:

20,000 Equity Shares of ₹ 10 each, ₹ 6 per share called up	₹ 1,20,000
Less: Calls-in-arrears on 2,000 shares @ ₹ 2 per share	₹ 4,000
Add: Calls-in advance on 1000 shares @ ₹ 3 per share	₹ 3,000
	₹1,19,000

The Board of Directors recommend a dividend @ 10%.

Required: Calculate the amount of Dividend in each of the following alternative cases:

Case (a) If no other information is given.

Case (b) If the Articles prescribe the payment of dividend on the nominal amount of shares.

Case (c) If the Articles prescribe the payment of dividend on the called up amount of shares.

Case (d) If the Articles prescribe the payment of dividend on the paid up amount of shares.

Case (e) If the Articles are silent and Table F has been excluded.

[**Ans** (a) ₹ 11,600,(b) ₹ 20,000, (c) ₹ 12,000,(d) ₹ 11,600,(e) ₹ 20,000]

18. X Ltd. was registered with an authorised capital of ₹ 80,00,000 divided into 20,000 12% Preference Shares of ₹ 100 each and 6,00,000 Equity Shares of ₹ 10 each. On 1st April 2022, all the preference shares and 4,00,000 equity shares had been issued and were fully paid with the exception of 80,000 of equity shares on which only ₹ 5 per share had been called up. On 1st Nov. 2022 the director made the final call of ₹ 5 per share on the partly paid equity shares and the call was dully paid except by a shareholders-holding 4,000 shares. The recommendation of directors include the dividend on equity shares @ 15% p.a.

Required: Calculate the amount of dividend in each of the following alternative cases:

Case (a) If no other information is given;

Case (b) If the shares on which calls were in arrears were duly forfeited before the end of the accounting year.

Case (c) If the shares on which calls were in arrears were duly forfeited and were reissued @ ₹ 9 per share before the end of the accounting year.

[**Ans** (a) ₹ 8,03,750,(b) ₹ 8,00,750, (c) ₹ 8,05,000]

19. ATMA Ltd provides you the following information:

100,000,9% Participating Pref. Shares of ₹ 100 each		₹ 100 lakhs
2,00,000,10% Preference Shares of ₹ 100 each		₹ 200 lakhs
3,00,000,11% Non-Cumulative Preference Shares of ₹ 100 each		₹ 300 lakhs
40,00,000,Equity Shares of ₹ 10 each, ₹ 7 per share called up & paid up	₹ 280 lakhs	
Add: Calls-in advance on 2,00,000 shares @ ₹ 4 per share	₹ 2 lakhs	₹ 288 lakhs
DVRs (entitled to 5% more dividend than Equity) ₹ 20 lakhs		₹ 20 lakhs
		₹ 908 lakhs

Current Year's Tax @ 25% amounted to ₹ 69 lakhs. Participating Pref. Shareholders are entitled to participate to the extent of 20% of Surplus Profits as per Articles. Last year no dividend could be paid on any share due to absence of profits. At the end of current year, the Board decided and paid dividend on Equity Shares @ 20%.

Required: Calculate the Total Amount of Dividend paid by the company.

[**Ans** Surplus Profit = ₹ 55 lakhs, Total Dividend ₹ 163 lakhs]

20. The Balance Sheet of G Ltd is as under: Comment on the presentation in terms of Schedule III.

BALANCE SHEET AS AT... *(Rupees in ...)*

Particulars	*Note No.*	*31.03.2023*	*31.03.2022*
I. **EQUITY AND LIABILITIES**			
Share Capital	1	xxx	xxx
Reserves & Surplus	2	0	0

Employee stock option outstanding	3	xxx	xxx
Share application money	4	xxx	xxx
Non-Current Liabilities			
Deferred tax liability (Arising from Indian Income Tax)	5	xxx	xxx
Current Liabilities			
Trade Payables	6	xxx	xxx
Total		xxx	xxx
II. ASSETS			
Non-Current Assets			
Fixed Assets-Tangible	7	xxx	xxx
CWIP (including capital advances)	8	xxx	xxx
Current Assets			
Trade Receivables	9	xxx	xxx
Deferred Tax Asset (Arising from Indian Income Tax)	10	xxx	xxx
P & L Debit balance			
Total		xxx	xxx

LONG ANSWER TYPE PRACTICAL QUESTIONS

1. From the following information, prepare Statement of Profit and Loss for the year ended 31st March, 2023:

Particulars	*(₹ in lacs)*
Revenue from Operations	5210
Other Income	80
Cost of Materials consumed	2000
Changes in Inventories	(550)
Employee Benefits Expense	1700
Finance Costs	40
Depreciation and Amortization Expense	300
Other Expenses	200
Tax Rate @ 30%	
120 lacs Equity Shares of ₹ 10 each fully paid up, 100 lacs Equity Shares of ₹ 10 each, ₹ 8 paid up, 14%, 2,00,000 Preference Shares of ₹ 100 each fully paid up	

[**Ans.** Profit ₹ 1120 lacs, Basic EPS ₹ 10.92]

2. The following items appear in the Trial Balance of Bharat Ltd. as at 31st March, 2023:

Particulars	₹
1. Revenue from Operations	96,00,000
2. Other Income	4,00,000
3. Expenses other than Interest	15,20,000

4. 12%, 40,000 Debentures of ₹ 100 each fully paid up
5. Opening Balance of Profit and Loss Statement ₹ 13,12,000.
6. Transfer to Reserve @ 5%

7. Interim Dividend paid ₹ 3,20,000,Final Equity Dividend paid ₹ 1,60,000, Preference Dividend paid ₹ 2,80,000,
8. 12 lacs Equity Shares of ₹ 10 each fully paid up, 10 lacs Equity Shares of ₹ 10 each, ₹ 8 paid up, 14%, 20,000 Preference Shares of ₹ 100 each fully paid up
9. The recommendation of the company's Board of Directors include Transfer to Debenture Redemption Reserve @ 25% of Debentures.
10. Corporate Tax 30%.

Required: Show the above items in Statement of Profit and Loss and calculate Surplus i.e. Balance in Statement of Profit & Loss.

[**Ans**. Profit ₹ 56 lacs, Basic EPS ₹ 5.32, Surplus ₹ 48.72 lacs]

3. The following items appear in the Trial Balance of Bharat Ltd. as at 31st March, 2023:

Particulars	₹
1. Revenue from Operations	48,00,000
2. Other Income	2,00,000
3. Expenses other than Interest	7,60,000
4. General Reserve (as on 1st April, 2022)	2,60,000
5. Profit and Loss Account (as on 1.4.2022)	5,40,000
6. 12%, 20,000 Debentures of ₹ 100 each fully paid up	
7. 16%, 10,000 Preference Shares of ₹ 100 each fully paid up	
8. 126,000 Equity Shares of ₹ 100 each	
9. 16,000 Equity Shares ₹ 100 each, ₹ 25 paid up	

On 31.03.2023,dividends (including Equity Dividend @15%) were paid for which no accounting effect has yet been given. The recommendations of the company's Board of Directors include transfer to General Reserve @ 5%. (Assume Corporate Tax 25%).

Required: Show the relevant items in Statement of Profit and Loss and Balance Sheet.

[**Ans**. Profit ₹ 30 lacs, Basic EPS ₹ 355, Surplus ₹ 29.90 lacs]

4. The following are the extracts of the Trial Balance of AMLA & GILOY Ltd.(Listed Co) as at 31st March, 2023:

Particulars	***(₹ in lakh)***
Revenue from Operations	960
7.5 lakh,10% Tata Steel Debentures of ₹ 100 each, ₹ 80 paid up	600
Net Loss on Sale of Investments	28
Rent received	30
Expenses other than Interest (including Rent Collection Expenses ₹ 1 lakh)	174
80 lakh Equity Shares of ₹10 each fully paid up	800
20 lakh Equity Shares of ₹ 10 each,₹ 7.50 paid up	150
8 lakh 10% Pref. Shares of ₹ 100 each fully paid up	800
12%, 4,00,000 Debentures of ₹ 100 each fully paid up (issued on 01.04.2022)	400
General Reserve (as at 01.04.2022)	30
P & L A/c (Dr.)(as at 01.04.2022)	2
Employees Stock Option Outstanding A/c	20

As on 01.04.2022, Dividends on Preference Shares were in arrears for 2 years for 2021-2022 and 2020-2021. On 31.03.2023,dividends (including Equity Dividend @20%) were paid for which no accounting effect has yet been given. The recommendations of the company's Board of Directors include transfer to General Reserve @ 5%.Assume Corporate Tax 25%.

Required: Calculate Profit for the period and Basic Earnings per Equity Share as per Statement of Profit and Loss for the year ended 31st March, 2023 and also Show the calculation of Reserves and Surplus.

[**Ans**. Profit ₹ 600 lacs, Basic EPS ₹ 10.9474, Surplus ₹ 138 lacs, Reserves and Surplus ₹ 218 lacs]

5. An Extract of the Balance Sheet of a CAMHC Ltd.(Listed)as at 31st March 2023 is as follows:

Particulars	₹
Share Capital:	
Authorised:	
30,000 Equity Shares of ₹ 10 each	3,00,000
Issued and Subscribed:	
20,000 Equity Shares of ₹ 10 each fully paid	2,00,000
Profit and Loss Account	1,16,000
12% Debentures	1,20,000
Creditors	1,15,000
Property,Plant & Equipment [Freehold Property]	1,15,000
Inventories	1,35,000
Trade Receivables	75,000
Cash at Bank	2,51,000

At the Annual General Meeting it was resolved:

(a) To increase the authorised capital to ₹ 4,00,000.

(b) To pay the dividend @ 10% in cash.

(c) To issue one bonus share for every four shares held

(d) To give existing shareholders the option to purchase one ₹ 10 share, at ₹ 15 for every four shares held prior to the bonus distribution, this option being taken up by all the shareholders.

(e) To repay the debentures at a premium of 3 per cent.

Required: Pass the necessary Journal Entries.

[**Ans.** Dividend ₹ 20,000,Bonus Shares 6250, Right Shares 5000]

6. An Extract of the Balance Sheet of Tulsian Ltd. as at 31st March, 2022 is as follows:

Share Capital:	
Authorised:	
2,80,000 Equity Shares of ₹ 10 Each	28,00,000
10% 14,000 Preference Shares of ₹ 100 each	14,00,000
Issued & Subscribed:	
10% 14,000 Preference Shares of ₹ 100 each	14,00,000
220,000 Equity Shares of ₹ 10 each fully paid	22,00,000

Reserves & Surplus:	
Capital Redemption Reserve	1,20,000
Revaluation Reserve	1,20,000
Securities Premium Account	80,000
General Reserve	6,00,000
Profit & Loss A/c (including Net Profit after tax for the year 2021-2022 ₹ 8,00,000)	11,56,000
Cash at Bank	12,00,000

At the Annual General Meeting held on 30th Sept 2022, it was resolved:

(a) To transfer Profits to General Reserve @5% and to declare and pay the dividend on Equity Shares @15%.

(b) To issue fully paid bonus shares to the holders of fully paid equity shares in the ratio of 1:4.

(c) To give existing shareholders the option to subscribe one ₹ 10 Right share at ₹ 15 for every four shares held after the bonus distribution.

The aforesaid right shares were subscribed by all the shareholders. The bonus shares and right shares were fully allotted on 1st Jan. 2023.

Required: Pass the necessary journal entries on 30th Sept., 2022 and 1st Jan 2023.

[**Ans** T/f to Reserve ₹ 40,000, Dividend ₹ 4,70,000, Bonus Shares 55,000, Right Shares 68750]

7. TULSIAN Ltd. provides the following information for the year ended 31st March, 2023:

Particulars	₹	***Particulars***	₹
Excise Duty paid	185	Sale of Products	2700
Net Loss on Sale of Investments	4	Sale of Services	30
Rental Collection Expenses	1	Trading Commission received	60
Opening Stock of Materials	84.6	Interest Income	20
Opening Stock of WIP	150	Dividends From Companies	10
Opening Stock of Finished Goods	175	Rental Income	15
Purchases of Materials	955.2	Gain on Foreign Currency	0
Salaries and Wages	600	Transactions and Translation	8
Contribution To Provident and Other Funds	72	50 lacs Equity Shares of ₹ 10 each, ₹ 8 paid up	800
Expense on Employee Stock Option	0	60 lacs Equity Shares of ₹ 10 each	1200
Scheme (ESOP) & Emp. Stock	0	Profit and Loss Account [01.04.2022]	452
Purchase Plan (ESPP)	28	10%, 70 lacs Pref. Shares of ₹ 10 each	1400
Staff Welfare Expenses	150	General Reserve	160
Interest Expense	24	12% Debentures	200
Other Borrowing Costs(Brokerage)	4	Provision for Doubtful Debts	2
Buildings	400	Consum. of Stores and Spare Parts	14
Plant and Equipment	200	Power and Fuel	16
Vehicles	50	Rent	10

Furniture and Fixtures	60	Repairs to Buildings	8
Brands	200	Repairs to Machinery	6
Computer Software	90	Insurance	4
Prepaid Expenses	2	Rates and Taxes	2
Interim Dividend paid	300	Expenditure on CSR Activities	2
Sundry Debtors	80	Pref. Dividend paid	140
Payments to the Auditor	32		

Additional Information:

(a) Closing Stocks: Materials ₹ 39.80 lacs, WIP ₹ 200,Finished Goods ₹ 400 lacs

(b) Depreciate Buildings @ 5%, Plant and Equipment @ 20%, Vehicles @ 20%, Furniture and Fixtures @ 10% and Brands@ 10%,Computer Software@60%.

(c) Payments to the Auditor include as Auditor ₹ 10 lacs,For Taxation Matters ₹ 8 lacs, For Company Law Matters ₹ 6 lacs, For Management Services ₹ 4 lacs, For Other Services ₹ 2 lac, For Other Services ₹ 2 lac

(d) Make a Provision for Doubtful Debts @ 10%

(e) The director's recommended:(i) to transfer to Debenture Redemption Reserve @ 25% of Debentures. (ii) to transfer to General Reserve @ 5%.

(f) Income Tax Rate 30%.

Required: Prepare Statement of Profit and Loss for the year ended 31st March, 2023 and a Note showing the computation of Surplus in the Statement of Profit and Loss to be taken to the Balance Sheet (as per Schedule III to The Companies Act, 2013) as on that date.

[**Ans**. Profit ₹ 560 lacs, Basic EPS ₹ 4.20, Surplus ₹ 494 lacs]

8. From the details given below prepare Balance Sheet of TULSIAN Ltd. as at 31st March, 2023, as per the Schedule III to The Companies Act 2013:

	(₹ in crores)
P & L A/c (Dr.)	420
Stock Options Outstanding Account	20
Amalgamation Adjustment Account	40
Statutory Reserves	40
12% Debentures [20% Redeemable within 1 year]	400
Provision for Tax	40
Equity Share Capital (₹ 10 each)	1000
Cash in Hand	80
Cheques & Drafts on hand	14
Fixed Deposits with Banks as per Details given	2
15% Pref. Share Capital (₹ 100 each)	800
Prepaid Expenses	100
Bank Overdraft	90
Interest accrued on Debentures of Tata Steels	24
Building under construction	230

5,000,12% Tata Steel Deb. of ₹ 100 each, ₹ 80 paid up	400
Premium on Red. of Debentures	40
Application Money pending allotment	80
Bills Payables	150
Calls-in Advance	10
Employees' earned leave payable on Retirement	90
Stores & Spares	100
Securities Deposit	10
Crypto Currency (Not for sale in the ordinary course of business)	20
Brands	200
Computer Software under development	40
Bills Receivables	240
Plant & Machinery	240
12% Debentures of Reliance Ltd. [20% Redeemable within 1 year]	200
Investment in Land & Building	400

1. Details of Fixed Deposits with Banks

Bank	*Date of FDR*	*Maturity Date*	*Amount*
Yes Bank Limited	01–Jan–2023	2–Jan–2024	₹ 60,00,000
Bank of Baroda	01–Jan–2023	31–Mar–2024	₹ 40,00,000
State Bank of India	28–Feb–2023	30–May–2023	₹ 20,00,000
ICICI Bank	1–Jan–2022	1–Apr–2024	₹ 80,00,000

Note: Bills Discounted but not yet matured ₹ 1 crore, Dividends on Preference Shares are in arrears for 2 years.

[**Ans** Total of B/S ₹ 2300 crores]

9. Fine Products Ltd. was registered with a nominal capital of ₹ 10,00,000 divided into shares of ₹ 100 each. The following Trial Balance is extracted from the books on 31st March, 2023:

Dr. *Cr.*

Particulars	₹	*Particulars*		₹
Buildings	5,80,000	Sales		10,40,000
Machinery	2,00,000	Outstanding Expenses		4,000
Closing Stock	1,80,000	Provision for Doubtful Debt (1-4-2022)		6,000
Purchases (adjusted)	4,20,000	Equity Share Capital		4,00,000
Salaries	1,20,000	General Reserve		1,80,000
Directors Fees	20,000	Profit and Loss A/c (1-4-2022)		50,000
Rent	52,000	Creditors		1,84,000
Depreciation	40,000	Provision for depreciation:		
Bad Debts	12,000	on Building	1,00,000	
Interest accrued on Investment	4,000	on Machinery	1,10,000	2,10,000
24,000 shares of X Ltd. of		14% Debentures		4,00,000

₹ 10 each ₹ 8 paid up	2,40,000	Interest on Debentures	
Debenture Interest	56,000	accrued but not due	28,000
Loose Tools	46,000	Interest on Investments	24,000
Advance Tax	1,20,000	Unclaimed dividend	10,000
Sundry expenses	36,000	(Bills Discounted but not yet	
Debtors	2,50,000	matured ₹ 20,000)	
Bank	1,60,000		
	25,36,000		25,36,000

You are required to prepare Statement of Profit and Loss for the year ending 31st March, 2023 and Balance Sheet as at that date after taking into consideration the following information:

(a) Closing stock is more than opening stock by ₹ 1,60,000; (b) Provide for doubtful debts @ 4% on Debtors: (c) Make a provision for income tax @ 30%; (d) Depreciation expense includes depreciation of ₹ 8,000 on Buildings and that of ₹ 24,000 on Machinery; (e) The directors decided to pay an interim dividend @ 25% immediately and to transfer to General Reserve @ 10%.

[**Ans** Profit ₹ 2,12,800, Basic EPS ₹ 10.64, Surplus ₹ 1,41,520, Reserves and Surplus ₹ 3,42,800,] Total of B/S ₹ 14,60,000]

10. The following is the Balance Sheet of Bumbum Ltd.(Listed) as at 31st March, 2023:

Particulars	₹
Sources of Funds:	
Authorized capital:	
50,000 Equity Shares of ₹ 10 each	5,00,000
10,000 Preference Shares of ₹ 100 each	10,00,000
	15,00,000
Issued subscribed and paid up	
30,000 Equity shares of ₹ 10 each	3,00,000
5,000 Redeemable 8% Preference shares of ₹ 100 each	5,00,000
Reserves & Surplus	
Securities Premium	6,00,000
General Reserve	6,50,000
Profit & Loss A/c	40,000
2500, 9% of ₹ 100 each	2,50,000
Sundry Creditors	1,70,000
	25,10,000
Application of Funds:	
Property,Plant,Equipment & Intangible Assets (net)	7,80,000
Investments (Market Value ₹ 6,80,000)	4,90,000
Deferred Tax Assets	3,40,000
Sundry Debtors	6,20,000
Cash & Bank balance	2,80,000
	25,10,000

In Annual General Meeting held on 20th June the company passed the following resolutions:

(i) To split equity share ₹ 10 each into 5 equity shares of ₹ 2 each from 1st July.

(ii) To redeem 8% Preference Shares at a premium of 5%.

(iii) To redeem 9% Debentures by making offer to debenture holders to convert their holdings into equity shares at ₹ 10 per share *or* accept cash on redemption.

(iv) To issue fully paid bonus shares in the ratio of one equity share for every 3 shares held on record date.

On 10th July investments were sold for ₹ 5,55,000 and preference shares were redeemed. 40% of Debentureholder exercised their option to accept cash & their claims were settled on 1st Aug. The company fixed 5th September as record date and bonus issue was concluded by 12th September. You are requested to journalize the above transactions including cash transactions and prepare Balance Sheet as at 30th September.

[**Ans** Profit on sale of Investments ₹ 65,000,T/f to CRR ₹ 5,00,000,Bonus Shares 11,000, Cash to Debentureholders ₹ 1,07,500, Shares to Debentureholders 3000,Total of B/S ₹ 19,42,500]

11. On 31st March, 2023 X and Y Ltd. provides to you the following ledger balances after preparing its Profit and Loss Account for the year ended 31st March, 2023:

Credit Balances:

Particulars	₹
Equity Share Capital, fully paid shares of ₹ 10 each	70,00,000
General Reserve	15,49,100
Loan from State Finance Corporation	10,50,000
Secured by hypothecation of Plant & Machinery	
(Repayable within one year ₹ 2,00,000)	
Loans: Unsecured (Long term)	8,47,000
Sundry Creditors for goods & expenses (Payable within 6 months)	14,00,000
Profit & Loss Account	11,91,400
Provision for Taxation	3,25,500
	1,33,63,000

Debit Balances:

Particulars	₹
Calls in arrears	7,000
Land	14,00,000
Buildings	20,50,000
Plant and Machinery	36,75,000
Furniture & Fixture	3,50,000
Stocks: Finished goods	14,00,000
Raw Materials	3,50,000
Sundry Debtors	14,00,000
Advances: Short-term	2,98,900
Cash in hand	2,10,000
Balances with banks	17,29,000
Preliminary Expenses	93,100
Patents & Trade marks	4,00,000
	1,33,63,000

The following additional information is also provided:

(i) 4,20,000 fully paid equity shares were allotted as consideration for land & buildings.

(ii) Cost of Building ₹ 28,00,000

Cost of Plant & Machinery ₹ 49,00,000

Cost of Furniture & Fixture ₹ 4,37,500

(iii) Sundry Debtors for ₹ 3,80,000 are due for more than 6 months.

(iv) The amount of Balances with Bank includes ₹ 18,000 with a bank which is not a scheduled Bank and the deposits of ₹ 5 lakhs are for a period of 9 months.

(v) Unsecured loan includes ₹ 2,00,000 from a Bank and ₹ 1,00,000 from related parties.

Required: Prepare the Balance Sheet of the Company as at 31st March, 2023 as required under Schedule III to the Companies Act, 2013.

[**Ans.** Total of B/S ₹ 1,32,62,900, Surplus ₹ 6,06,900]

12. From the following particulars furnished by the CEEP Ltd., prepare the Balance Sheet as at 31st March, 2023 as required by Schedule III of the Companies Act, 2013 :

Particulars	*Debit (₹)*	*Credit (₹)*
Equity share capital (face value of ₹ 10 each)		15,00,000
Calls-in-arrears	5,000	
Land	5,50,000	
Building	4,85,000	
Plant & machinery	5,60,000	
General reserve		2,70,000
Loan from State Financial Corporation		2,10,000
Inventories	3,15,000	
Provision for taxation		72,000
Trade receivables	2,95,000	
Short-term loans & advances	58,500	
Profit & loss account		1,06,800
Cash in hand	37,300	
Cash at bank	2,85,000	
Unsecured loans		1,65,000
Trade payables		2,67,000
Total	25,90,800	25,90,800

The following additional information is also provided :

(1) 10,000 equity shares were issued for consideration other than cash.

(2) Trade receivables of ₹ 55,000 are due for more than six months.

(3) The cost of building and plant & machinery is ₹ 5,50,000 and ₹ 6,25,000 respectively.

(4) The loan from State Financial Corporation is secured by hypothecation of plant & machinery. The balance of ₹ 2,10,000 in this account is inclusive of ₹ 10,000 for interest accrued but not due.

(5) Balance at Bank included ₹ 15,000 with Aakash Bank Ltd., which is not a scheduled bank.

[**Ans.** Total of B/S ₹ 25,85,800]

13. The following is the Trial Balance of H Ltd., as on 31st March, 2023:

	Dr.	Cr.
Equity Capital (Shares of ₹ 100 each)		8,05,000
5,000, 6% preference shares of ₹ 100 each		5,00,000
9% Debentures		4,00,000
General Reserve		40,00,000
Profit & Loss A/c (of previous year)		72,000
Sales		60,00,000
Trade Payables		10,40,000
Provision for Depreciation on Plant & Machinery		1,72,000
Suspense Account		40,000
Land at cost	24,00,000	
Plant & Machinery at cost	7,70,000	
Trade Receivables	19,60,000	
Inventories (31-03-2023)	9,50,000	
Bank	2,30,900	
Adjusted Purchases	22,32,100	
Factory Expenses	15,00,000	
Administration Expenses	3,00,000	
Selling Expenses	14,00,000	
Debenture Interest	36,000	
Goodwill	12,50,000	
	1,30,29,000	1,30,29,000

Additional Information:

(i) The authorised share capital of the company is :

	₹
5,000, 6% preference shares of ₹ 100 each	5,00,000
10,000, equity shares of ₹ 100 each	10,00,000

Issued equity capital as on 1st April 2022 stood at ₹ 7,20,000, that is 6,000 shares fully paid and 2,000 shares of ₹ 60 paid. The directors made a call of ₹ 40 per share on 1st October 2022. A shareholder could not pay the call on 100 shares and his shares were then forfeited and reissued @ ₹ 90 per share as fully paid.

(ii) On 31st March 2023, the Directors declared an Interim dividend of 5% on equity shares.

(iii) The company on the advice of independent valuer wishes to revalue the land at ₹ 36,00,000.

(iv) Suspense account of ₹ 40,000 represents amount received for the sale of some of the machinery on 1-4-2022. The cost of the machinery was ₹ 1,00,000 and the accumulated depreciation thereon being ₹ 30,000.

(v) Depreciation is to be provided on plant and machinery at 10% on cost.

(vi) Amortize 1/5th of Goodwill.

You are required to prepare H Limited's Balance Sheet as on 31-3-2023 and Statement of Profit and Loss with notes to accounts for the year ended 31-3-2023 as per Schedule III of the Companies Act, 2013. Ignore previous years' figures & taxation.

[**Ans**. Profit ₹ 1,84,900, Total of B/S ₹ 82,01,900, Surplus ₹ 1,86,900]

14. From the following Information, Prepare Statement of Changes in Equity of TULSIAN LTD For the period ended 31st March,2023:

Equity Share Capital of ₹ 10 each in the beg.	₹ 100 crores
5% Preference Share Capital of ₹ 100 each in the beg.	₹ 20 crores
Retained Earnings in the beg.	₹ 200 crores
Securities Premium in the beg.	₹ 100 crores
Capital Redemption Reserve in the beg.	₹ 100 crores
Revaluation Reserve in the beg.	₹ 100 crores
Corrections of Prior Period errors resulting in increase in Profits	₹ 10 crores
Changes in Accounting Policy resulting in increase in Profits	₹ 20 crores
Net Income for the period (incl. ₹ 8 crores Net Gains on Foreign Exchange Translation)	₹ 40 crores
Revaluation Gain on Property,Plant,Equipment & Intangible Assets	₹ 20 crores
Dividends paid during the year	₹ 10 crores
Issue of 100 lacs New Shares of ₹ 10 each at ₹ 100 each during the year	
Buy back of 40 lacs Shares of ₹ 10 each at ₹ 50 each out of Securities Premium during the year	
Issue of Bonus Shares out of Capital Redemption Reserve during the year	₹ 90 crores

[**Ans**. SC ₹ 216 crores, RE ₹ 260 crores,SP ₹ 170 crores, CRR ₹ 14 crores, RR ₹ 120 crores]

9 AS 20 – EARNINGS PER SHARE

WHAT IS BASIC EARNING PER SHARE [EPS]?

Basic EPS = Net Profit for the year attributable to Equity Shareholders/ Weighted Average Shares O/S during the year

HOW TO CALCULATE BASIC EARNING PER SHARE AS PER AS 20?

The calculation of Basic EPS involves the following STEPS:

STEP 1: Calculation of Net Profit attributable to Equity Shareholders

STEP 2: Calculation of Weighted Average Number of Equity Shares Outstanding during the period

HOW TO CALCULATE NET PROFIT ATTRIBUTABLE TO EQUITY SHAREHOLDERS ?

Net Profit attributable to Equity Shareholders is calculated as follows:

A.	Net Profit before Tax (includes Prior Period and Extraordinary Items)	
B.	*Less:* Current Tax (including tax on Prior Period and Extraordinary Items) + Deferred Tax + Tax Pertaining to Earlier Years.	
C.	Net Profit after Tax [A – B]	
D.	*Less:* Pref. Dividend on Cumulative Preference Shares for Current Period only (whether or not provided in accounts).	
E.	*Less:* Pref. Dividend on Non-Cumulative Preference Shares for Current Period only (only if provided in accounts)	
F.	Net Profit attributable to Equity Shareholders [C – E – F]	

ILLUSTRATION 1

TULSIAN Ltd provides you the following information:

Net Profit for year ended 31-03-2022	₹ 85,00,000
Net Profit for year ended 31-03-2023	₹ 1,10,00,000
10% Cumulative Preference Shares	₹1,00,00,000
12% Non-Cumulative Preference Shares	₹1,00,00,000

Note: No dividend has been paid on Preference Shares for the last 3 years.

Required: Compute the Net Profit for the period attributable to Equity Shareholders for the year 2021-2022 and 2022-2023 in each of the following cases:

(a) If no other information is there.

(b) If Pref. Dividend on Preference Shares has not been provided in the books of accounts.

(c) If Pref. Dividend on Preference Shares has been provided in the books of accounts.

SOLUTION:

(a) If no other information is there.

CALCULATION OF NET PROFIT ATTRIBUTABLE TO EQUITY SHAREHOLDERS

Particulars	*2021-2022 (₹)*	*2022-2023 (₹)*
A. Net Profit after Tax	85,00,000	1,10,00,000
B. *Less:* 10 % Preference dividend on Cumulative Preference Shares	(10,00,000)	(10,00,000)
C. Net Profit for the period attributable to Equity Shareholders	75,00,000	1,00,00,000

(b) If Pref. Dividend on Preference Shares has not been provided in the books of accounts. Same Solution as given in case (a)

(c) If Pref. Dividend on Preference Shares has been provided in the books of accounts.

CALCULATION OF NET PROFIT ATTRIBUTABLE TO EQUITY SHAREHOLDERS

Particulars	*2021-2022 (₹)*	*2022-2023 (₹)*
A. Net Profit after Tax	85,00,000	1,10,00,000
B. *Less:* 10 % Preference dividend on Cum. Pref. Shares	(10,00,000)	(10,00,000)
C. *Less:* 12 % Preference dividend on Non-Cum. Pref. Shares	(12,00,000)	(12,00,000)
D. Net Profit for the period attributable to Equity Shareholders	63,00,000	88,00,000

HOW TO CALCULATE WEIGHTED AVERAGE NUMBER OF EQUITY SHARES OUTSTANDING DURING THE PERIOD?

The weighted average number of equity shares outstanding during the period is the number of equity shares outstanding at the beginning of the period, adjusted by the number of equity shares bought back or issued during the period multiplied by the time-weighting factor [i.e. Number of days/months for which the specific shares are outstanding as a proportion of the total number of days/months in the period]

Note: Partly paid equity shares are treated as a fraction of an equity share to the extent that they were entitled to participate in dividends relative to a fully paid equity share during the reporting period.

DATE FROM WHICH WEIGHT IS TO BE CONSIDERED FOR THE PURPOSE OF CALCULATION OF WEIGHTED AVERAGE NUMBER OF SHARES AS PER AS 20 IN CASE OF ISSUE OF SHARES IN VARIOUS CASES

WHEN EQUITY SHARES ARE ISSUED....	*EFFECTIVE DATE FROM WHICH WEIGHT IS TO BE CONSIDERED*
(a) In exchange for Cash.	Date when cash is receivable.
(b) As a result of conversion of a Debt Instrument to Equity.	Date of conversion.
(c) In lieu of Interest or Principal on other Financial Instruments.	Date when interest ceases to accrue.

(d) In exchange for the settlement of a liability of the Enterprise.	Date when settlement becomes effective.
(e) As consideration for acquisition of an asset other than cash.	Date on which the acquisition is recognised.
(f) For the rendering of services to the enterprise.	Date on which the service are rendered.
(g) In case of an amalgamation in nature of purchase.	Date of the acquisition.
(h) In case of an amalgamation in nature of merger.	From beginning of the reporting period.
(i) As Bonus Shares.	From beginning of the reporting period.
(j) In case of Share Split or Reverse Share Split.	From beginning of the reporting period.

ILLUSTRATION 2

TULSIAN Ltd had issued 6,40,000 Equity shares of ₹ 10 each, ₹ 5 per share was called up on that date which was paid by all the shareholders. The remaining ₹ 5 was called up on 1-6-2022. All the Shareholders (except one having 1,60,000 shares) paid the sum on 30th June,2022. Calculate Weighted Average Number of Equity Shares Outstanding during the year 2022-2023.

SOLUTION:

Date	*No. of Equity Shares*	*Amount paid per share*	*Weighted Average No. of Equity Shares*
1.4.2022	6,40,000	5	6,40,000 × 5/10 × 3/12= 80,000
1.7.2022	4,80,000	10	4,80,000 × 9/12= 3,60,000
1.7.2022	1,60,000	5	1,60,000 × 5/10 × 9/12= 60,000
Weighted Average Number of Shares O/S during the year			5,00,000

ILLUSTRATION 3

TULSIAN Ltd had issued 5,00,000 Equity shares of ₹ 100 each. Calculate Weighted Average Number of Equity Shares Outstanding during the year 2022-2023 in each of the following cases:

(a) If new 1,20,000 Shares are issued for Cash on 01.06.2022.

(b) If 6,000 Shares are issued to Underwriters on 01.07.2022.

(c) If 2,69,250 Shares are Bought - Back on 01.08.2022.

(d) If 30,000 Shares are issued to Vendor against Purchase of Building. (Acquisition is recognized on the same day) on 01.09.2022.

(e) If 15,000 Shares are issued in settlement of liability on 01.10.2022.

(f) If 1,20,000 Shares are issued to Y Ltd. on purchase of Y Ltd. on 01.11.2022.

(g) If Shares are Split up into shares of ₹ 10 each on 01.12.2022.

(h) If Bonus Shares are issued in the ratio of 1 share for every 2 held on 01.01.2023.

SOLUTION:

(A) WEIGHTED AVERAGE NUMBER OF SHARES OUTSTANDING ON 31.03.2023

Date A	No. of Shares B	Period for which Shares were O/S during the period(months) C	Product D = B × C/12
01.04.2022	5,00,000	12	5,00,000
01.06.2022	1,20,000	10	1,00,000
Weighted Average Number of Shares O/S during the year			6,00,000

(B) WEIGHTED AVERAGE NUMBER OF SHARES OUTSTANDING ON 31.03.2023

Date A	No. of Shares B	Period for which Shares were O/S during the period(months) C	Product D = B × C/12
01.04.2022	5,00,000	12	5,00,000
01.07.2022	6,000	9	4,500
Weighted Average Number of Shares O/S during the year			5,04,500

(C) WEIGHTED AVERAGE NUMBER OF SHARES OUTSTANDING ON 31.03.2023

Date A	No. of Shares B	Period for which Shares were O/S during the period(months) C	Product D = B × C/12
01.04.2022	5,00,000	12	5,00,000
01.08.2022	(2,69,250)	8	(1,79,500)
Weighted Average Number of Shares O/S during the year			3,20,500

(D) WEIGHTED AVERAGE NUMBER OF SHARES OUTSTANDING ON 31.03.2023

Date A	No. of Shares B	Period for which Shares were O/S during the period(months) C	Product D = B × C/12
01.04.2022	5,00,000	12	5,00,000
01.09.2022	30,000	7	17,500
Weighted Average Number of Shares O/S during the year			5,17,500

(E) WEIGHTED AVERAGE NUMBER OF SHARES OUTSTANDING ON 31.03.2023

Date A	No. of Shares B	Period for which Shares were O/S during the period(months) C	Product D = B × C/12
01.04.2022	5,00,000	12	5,00,000
01.10.2022	15,000	6	7,500
Weighted Average Number of Shares O/S during the year			5,07,500

(F) WEIGHTED AVERAGE NUMBER OF SHARES OUTSTANDING ON 31.03.2023

Date A	No. of Shares B	Period for which Shares were O/S during the period(months) C	Product D = B × C/12
01.04.2022	5,00,000	12	5,00,000
01.11.2022	1,20,000	5	50,000
Weighted Average Number of Shares O/S during the year			5,50,000

(G) WEIGHTED AVERAGE NUMBER OF SHARES OUTSTANDING ON 31.03.2023

Date A	No. of Shares B	Period for which Shares were O/S during the period(months) C	Product D = B × C/12
01.04.2022	5,00,000	12	5,00,000
01.12.2022	Split of shares [5,00,000 shares × 100 / 10]		50,00,000
Weighted Average Number of Shares O/S during the year			50,00,000

(H) WEIGHTED AVERAGE NUMBER OF SHARES OUTSTANDING ON 31.03.2023

Date A	No. of Shares B	Period for which Shares were O/S during the period(months) C	Product D = B × C/12
01.04.2022	5,00,000	12	5,00,000
01.01.2023	Bonus issue: (5,00,000 × 1/2)		2,50,000
Weighted Average Number of Shares O/S during the year			7,50,000

STEP 3. *Calculate Basic Earning Per Share as follows:*

= Net Profit or loss for the period attributable to Equity Shareholders/Weighted Average No. of Equity Shares O/S during the period

ILLUSTRATION 4

TULSIAN Ltd provides you the following information:

Particulars	Amount
Net Profit for year ended 31-03-2022	₹ 85,00,000
Net Profit for year ended 31-03-2023	₹ 1,10,00,000
10% Cumulative Preference Shares	₹1,00,00,000
12% Non-Cumulative Preference Shares	₹1,00,00,000
No. of fully paid Equity shares of ₹ 100 each issued during 2020	5,00,000
On 01.12.2022 Shares are Split up into shares of ₹ 10 each.	
On 01.01.2023 Bonus Shares are issued in the ratio of 1 share for every 2 held.	

Note: No dividend has been paid on Preference Shares for the last 3 years.

Required: Compute the Basic EPS (Earning Per Share) for the year 2022-2023.

SOLUTION:

Step 1.

CALCULATION OF NET PROFIT ATTRIBUTABLE TO EQUITY SHAREHOLDERS

Particulars	2021-2022 (₹)	2022-2023 (₹)
A. Net Profit after Tax	85,00,000	1,10,00,000
B. *Less:* 10 % Preference dividend on Cumulative Preference Shares	(10,00,000)	(10,00,000)
C. Net Profit for the period attributable to Equity Shareholders	75,00,000	1,00,00,000

Step 2.

WEIGHTED AVERAGE NUMBER OF SHARES OUTSTANDING ON 31.03.2023

Date A	No. of Shares B	Period for which Shares were O/S during the period(months) C	Product D = B × C/12
01.04.2022	5,00,000	12	5,00,000
01.12.2022	Split of shares [5,00,000 shares × 100 / 10]		50,00,000
01.01.2023	Bonus issue: (50,00,000 × 1/2)		25,00,000
Weighted Average Number of Shares O/S during the year			75,00,000

CALCULATION OF BASIC EPS

Particulars	*2022-2023*
A. Net Profit for the Year	100,00,000
B. Weighted Average Shares O/S during the year = No. of Shares O/S for the prior period × Share Split Factor × Bonus Issue Factor [5,00,000 × 10 × 1.5]	75,00,000
C. Basic EPS [A/B]	1.33

WHAT IS RESTATEMENT OF BASIC EPS AS PER AS 20?

When the Basic EPS relating to prior periods presented in current period is adjusted, it is termed as Restatement of Basic EPS.

WHEN IS RESTATEMENT REQUIRED AS PER AS 20?

When the number of equity shares outstanding increases as a result of bonus issue, right issue or share split or decreases as a result of reverse share split.

HOW IS ADJUSTED WEIGHTED AVERAGE NO. OF EQUITY SHARES OUTSTANDING FOR THE PRIOR PERIOD CALCULATED ?

= No. of Shares O/S for the prior period × Bonus Issue Factor × Right Issue Factor × Share Split Factor x Reverse Share Split Factor

HOW IS ADJUSTED EPS FOR THE PREVIOUS YEAR CALCULATED?

Adjusted EPS for the Previous Year = Net Profit for the Previous Year attributable to Equity Shareholders/ Weighted Average No. of Shares O/S during the Current Year

ILLUSTRATION 4B

In Illustration 4A Compute the Basic EPS and Adjusted EPS for the year 2021-2022.

SOLUTION:

CALCULATION OF ADJUSTED EPS

Particulars	*Basic EPS 2021-2022*	*Adjusted EPS 2021-2022*
A. Net Profit for the Year	75,00,000	75,00,000
B. Weighted Average Shares O/S during the year	5,00,000	
C. Basic EPS [A/B]	15	
D. Weighted Average Shares O/S for Adjusted EPS = No. of Shares O/S for the prior period × Share Split Factor × Bonus Issue Factor [5,00,000 × 10 × 1.5]		75,00,000
E. Adjusted EPS for 2021-2022= 75,00,000/ 75,00,000		1

HOW IS ADJUSTED EQUITY SHARES OUTSTANDING CALCULATED IN CASE OF RIGHT ISSUE AS PER AS 20?

CALCULATION OF ADJUSTED EQUITY SHARES OUTSTANDING IN CASE OF RIGHT ISSUE

Step 1:	No. of Outstanding Shares prior to Rights
Step 2:	No. of Right Shares
Step 3:	No. of Outstanding Shares after Rights [Step 1 + Step 2]
Step 4:	Aggregate Fair Value of Shares prior to Rights = No. of Outstanding Shares prior to Rights × Fair Value per Share
Step 5:	Proceeds from Rights = No. of Right Shares × Right Issue Price
Step 6:	Theoretical Ex-Right Fair Value Per Share = (Step 4 + Step 5)/Step 3
Step 7:	Adjustment Factor = Fair Value Per Share prior to Rights/ Theoretical Ex-Right Fair Value Per Share
Step 8:	Adjusted Equity Shares O/s = (No. of O/s Shares Prior to Rights × Adjustment Factor) × Period + (No. of O/s Shares after Rights × Period)

ILLUSTRATION 5

Compute Basic EPS and Restated EPS for the previous year and Basic EPS for the current year from the following information:

Net Profit for the period 2021 - 2022	₹ 22,00,000
Net Profit for the period 2022 - 2023	₹ 47,00,000
No. of Shares outstanding prior to right issue	10,00,000 shares
Right issue	2 New Shares for each 5 Shares outstanding

Right issue price	₹15
Last Date to exercise rights	31st December, 2022
Response to Right Issue	Fully Subscribed
Fair Value of one equity share immediately prior to exercise of rights on 31st December, 2022	₹ 22

SOLUTION:

Step 1	No. of O/S Shares after Rights = [10,00,000 + (10,00,000 × 2/5)] = 14,00,000
Step 2	Aggregate Fair Value of Shares prior to Rights =10,00,000 shares x ₹ 22 = ₹ 2,20,00,000
Step 3	Proceeds from Rights = 4,00,000 × ₹15 = ₹ 60,00,000
Step 4	Theoretical Ex-Right Fair Value Per Share = (2,20,00,000 + 60,00,000)/ 14,00,000=₹ 20
Step 5	Adjustment Factor = ₹ 22 / ₹ 20=1.1
Step 6	Adjusted Equity Shares O/s = (No. of O/s Shares Prior to Rights × Adjustment Factor) × Period + (No. of O/s Shares after Rights × Period) = (10,00,000 shares x 1.10 x 9/12) + (14,00,000 shares x 3/12) = 11,75,000 shares

Adjusted EPS for current year = ₹ 47,00,000 / 11,75,000 shares = ₹ 4 per share

Basic EPS for Previous year=₹ 22,00,000/10,00,000 = ₹ 2.20

Restated Basic EPS for Previous year = ₹ 22,00,000/(10,00,000 × 1.1) = ₹ 2.00

ILLUSTRATION 6

Compute Basic EPS and Restated EPS for the previous year and Basic EPS for the current year from the following information:

Net Profit for the period 2021 - 2022	₹ 34,80,000
Net Profit for the period 2022 - 2023	₹ 36,60,000
No. of Shares outstanding prior to right issue	1,00,000 shares
Right issue	2 New Shares for each 5 Shares outstanding
Right issue price	₹ 30
Last Date to exercise rights	31st December, 2022
Response to Right Issue	Fully Subscribed
Fair Value of one equity share immediately prior to exercise of rights on 31st December, 2022	₹ 58
Bonus issue on 31st March, 2023	1 Equity Share for 5 Equity Shares outstanding on 31st March, 2023.

SOLUTION:

BASIC EARNING PER SHARE FOR THE YEAR 2022 - 2023

Particulars	₹
A. Net Profit after tax for the year 2022 - 2023	36,60,000
B. Weighted Average no. of equity shares outstanding during the period (As per W.N. 3)	1,46,400
C. Basic Earning per share for the year 2022 - 2023 (A / B)	25.00

RESTATEMENT OF BASIC EARNING PER SHARE RELATING TO YEAR 2021 - 2022

Particulars	₹
A. Net Profit after tax for the year 2021–2022	34,80,000
B. Weighted Average no. of equity shares outstanding during the period 2022–2023	1,00,000
C. Adjusted Weighted Average No. of Shares outstanding for the year 2021–2022 (As per W.N. 4)	1,39,200
D. Original Basic Earning Per Share for the year 2021–2022 (A / B)	34.80
E. Restated Basic Earning per share for the year 2021–2022 made in current year i.e. 2022–2023 (A/C)	25.00

Working Notes:

1. Calculation of Right Issue Adjustment Factor	
Step 1	No. of O/S Shares after Rights = [1,00,000 + (1,00,000 × 2/5)] = 1,40,000
Step 2	Aggregate Fair Value of Shares prior to Rights = 1,00,000 shares x ₹ 58 = ₹ 58,00,000
Step 3	Proceeds from Rights = 40,000 × ₹ 30 = ₹ 12,00,000
Step 4	Theoretical Ex-Right Fair Value Per Share = (58,00,000 +12,00,000)/ 1,40,000 = ₹ 50
Step 5	Right Issue Adjustment Factor = ₹ 58 / ₹ 50 = 1.16

2. Calculation of Bonus Issue Adjustment Factor	
Step 1	No. of O/S Shares after Rights = [1,00,000 + (1,00,000 × 2/5)] = 1,40,000
Step 2	No. of O/S Shares after Bonus issue = [1,40,000 + (1,40,000 × 1/5)] = 1,68,000
Step 3	Bonus Issue Adjustment Factor = 1,68,000 / 1,40,000 =1.2

3. Calculation of Weighted Average no. of shares outstanding for the year 2022 - 2023

No. of shares outstanding before right issue	100000
Right Issue Adjustment Factor	1.16
Shares outstanding before right issue [100000 × 1.16 × (9 months /12 months)]	87,000
Shares outstanding after right issue (140000 × 3 months / 12 months)	35,000
Shares outstanding before bonus issue (87000 + 35000)	1,22,000
Bonus Issue Adjustment Factor	1.20
Weighted average no. of equity shares outstanding during the period (122000 × 1.2)	1,46,400

4. Calculation of Adjusted Weighted Average No. of shares outstanding for the year 2021 - 2022

A No. of Shares outstanding during the period 2021 - 2022	100000
B Right Issue Adjustment Factor	1.16
C Bonus element in bonus issue	1.20
D Adjusted weighted average no. of shares outstanding for the year 2021–2022 (A × B × C)	1,39,200

WHAT IS POTENTIAL EQUITY SHARE AS PER AS 20?

As per AS 20 A Potential Equity Share is a Financial Instrument or other contract that entitles, or may entitle, its holder to Equity Shares. Some examples are:

(a) Debt Instruments or Preference Shares that are convertible into Equity Shares,

(b) Share Warrants convertible into equity shares

(c) Options including Employee Stock Option Plans (ESOP) under which Employees of an Enterprise are entitled to receive Equity Shares as part of their remuneration, and other similar plans, and

(d) Contingently Issuable Shares [i.e. Shares which would be issued upon the satisfaction of certain conditions resulting from contractual arrangements such as the acquisition of a business or other assets, or shares issuable under a Loan Contract upon default of payment of principal or interest, if the contract so provides.

WHEN ARE POTENTIAL EQUITY SHARES CONSIDERED AS DILUTIVE AS PER AS 20?

Potential Equity Shares are considered as **dilutive** only when, their conversion to equity shares would **decrease Net Profit Per Share** from continuing ordinary operations.

WHEN ARE POTENTIAL EQUITY SHARES CONSIDERED AS ANTI-DILUTIVE AS PER AS 20?

Potential equity shares are considered as **anti-dilutive** when their conversion to equity shares would i**ncrease Earnings Per Share** from continuing ordinary activities or Decrease Loss Per Share from Continuing Ordinary Activities. The effects of anti-dilutive potential equity shares are ignored in calculating diluted earnings per share.

Note: Share application money that is pending allotment or any advance share application money as at balance sheet date, which is not statutorily required to be kept separately and is being utilized for the purpose of business shall be treated as potential equity shares and considered as dilutive.

Note: The most advantageous conversion rate or exercise price from the standpoint of the holder of the potential equity shares should be used for calculating the number of Equity shares to be issued on the conversion of dilutive potential equity shares

HOW IS DILUTED EARNING PER SHARE CALCULATED AS PER AS 20?

STEP 1: *Calculate Adjusted Net Profit attributable to Equity Shareholder as follows:*

A. Net Profit or Loss for the period attributable to Equity Shareholders for Basic EPS	
B. *Add:* Interest or Other Expenses (after tax) saved on the conversion of the dilutive potential equity shares into equity shares	
C. *Add:* Pref. Dividend saved on the conversion of the dilutive potential equity shares into equity shares	
D. *Less:* Income that will cease to accrue (after tax) on the conversion of the dilutive potential equity shares into equity shares	
E. Adjusted Net Profit or Loss for the period attributable to Equity Shareholders [A + B + C – D]	

STEP 2: *Calculate Adjusted Weighted Average Number of Equity Shares Outstanding during the period as follows:*

= Weighted Average No. of Equity Shares O/S for Basic EPS + Weighted Average No. of equity shares which would be issued on the conversion of potential equity shares into equity shares

STEP 3: *Calculate Diluted Earning Per Share as follows:*
= Adjusted Net Profit or loss for the period attributable to Equity Shareholders/ Adjusted Weighted Average No. of Equity Shares O/S during the period.

ILLUSTRATION 7

TULSIAN Ltd provides you the following information:

Number of equity shares outstanding on 1.4.2022	4,00,000 shares
Net Profit before Interest & Tax for the year 2022-2023, Tax Rate 30%	₹ 81,20,000

Required: Compute Basic EPS & Diluted EPS in each of the following cases:

(a) On 01.04.2021 Issued 32,000, 10% Convertible Debentures of ₹ 50 each. Each debenture is convertible into five equity shares.

(b) On 01.07.2021 Issued 32,000, 10% Convertible Debentures of ₹ 50 each. Each debenture is convertible into five equity shares.

(c) On 01.04.2021 Issued 32,000, 10% Convertible Debentures of ₹ 50 each. Each debenture is convertible into five equity shares. These are converted into equity shares on 31.12.2022.

(d) On 01.04.2021 Issued 32,000, 10% Convertible Pref. Shares of ₹ 50 each. Each Pref. Share is convertible into five equity shares. These are converted into equity shares on 31.12.2022.

(e) Average fair value of one equity share during the year 2022-2023:₹ 25,Weighted Average number of shares under option during the year 2021-2022: 1,00,000 shares,Exercise Price for shares under option during the year 2022-2023:₹15.

SOLUTION:

(a) Interest on Debentures =32,000 x ₹ 50 x 10% x 12/12= ₹ 1,60,000

Net Profit after Interest & Tax = 70% (₹ 81,20,000 – ₹ 1,60,000) = ₹ 55,72,000

Weighted average number of equity shares outstanding for Basic EPS = 4,00,000

Basic EPS = [₹ 55,72,000/4,00,000]=₹ 13.93 per share

Adjusted Net Profit for the current year= ₹ [55,72,000 + 1,60,000(Interest) – 48,000 (Tax on Interest)] = ₹ 56,84,000

Adjusted Weighted average number of equity shares outstanding
= 4,00,000 + (32,000 × 5) = 5,60,000

Diluted EPS = [₹ 56,84,000/5,60,000]=₹ 10.15 per share

(b) Interest on Debentures =32,000 x ₹ 50 x 10% x 9/12= ₹ 1,20,000

Net Profit after Interest & Tax = 70% (₹ 81,20,000 – ₹ 1,20,000) = ₹ 56,00,000

Weighted average number of equity shares outstanding for Basic EPS = 4,00,000

Basic EPS = [₹ 56,00,000/4,00,000]=₹ 14 per share

Adjusted Net Profit for the current year= ₹ [56,00,000 + 1,20,000(Interest) – 36,000(Tax on Interest)]= ₹ 56,84,000

Weighted average number of equity shares outstanding for Basic EPS
= 4,00,000 + (32,000 × 5 × 9/12) = 5,20,000

Diluted EPS = [₹ 56,84,000/5,20,000]=₹ 10.93 per share

(c) Interest on Debentures =32,000 x ₹ 50 x 10% x 9/12= ₹ 1,20,000

Net Profit after Interest & Tax = 70% (₹ 81,20,000 – ₹ 1,20,000) = ₹ 56,00,000

Weighted average number of equity shares outstanding for Basic EPS = 4,00,000 + (32,000 × 5 × 3/12) = 4,40,000

Basic EPS = [₹ 56,00,000/4,40,000] = ₹ 12.73 per share

Adjusted Net Profit for the current year = ₹ [56,00,000 + 1,20,000(Interest) – 36,000(Tax on Interest)] = ₹ 56,84,000

Adjusted Weighted average number of equity shares outstanding

= 4,00,000 + (32,000 × 5 × 3/12) = 4,40,000

Diluted EPS = [₹ 56,84,000/4,40,000] = ₹ 12.92 per share

(d) Pref. Dividend = 32,000 x ₹ 50 x 10% x 9/12 = ₹ 1,20,000

Net Profit after Pref. Dividend = [(70% of ₹ 81,20,000) – (₹ 1,20,000)] = ₹ 55,64,000

Weighted average number of equity shares outstanding for Basic EPS

= 4,00,000 + (32,000 × 5 × 3/12) = 4,40,000

Basic EPS = [₹ 55,64,000/4,40,000] = ₹ 12.65 per share

Adjusted Net Profit for the current year = ₹ [55,64,000 + 1,20,000 (Pref. Dividend)] = ₹ 56,84,000

Adjusted Weighted average number of equity shares outstanding

= 4,00,000 + (32,000 × 5 × 3/12) = 4,40,000

Diluted EPS = [₹ 56,84,000/4,40,000] = ₹ 12.92 per share

(e) Net Profit after Tax = 70% ₹ 81,20,000 = ₹ 56,84,000

Weighted average number of equity shares outstanding for Basic EPS = 4,00,000

Basic EPS = [₹ 56,84,000/4,00,000] = ₹ 14.21 per share

Adjusted Net Profit for the current year = 70% ₹ 81,20,000 = ₹ 56,84,000

Adjusted Weighted average number of equity shares outstanding + No. of shares under option– No. of shares that would have been issued at fair value = 4,00,000 + 1,00,000 – [1,00,000 x 15 / 25] = 4,40,000

Diluted EPS = [₹ 56,84,000/4,40,000] = ₹ 12.92 per share

ILLUSTRATION 8

TULSIAN Ltd provides you the following information:

Number of Equity Shares outstanding on 1.4.2022	4,00,000 shares
Net Profit before Interest & Tax for the year 2022-2023. Tax Rate 30%	₹ 81,20,000
On 01.04.2021 Issued 32,000, 10% Convertible Debentures of ₹ 50 each. Each debenture is convertible into five equity shares. These are converted into equity shares on 31.12.2022.	
On 01.04.2021 Issued 32,000, 10% Convertible Pref. Shares of ₹ 50 each. Each Pref. Share is convertible into five equity shares. These are converted into equity shares on 31.12.2022.	
Average fair value of one equity share during the year 2022-2023:₹ 25,Weighted Average number of shares under option during the year 2021-2022: 1,00,000 shares,Exercise Price for shares under option during the year 2022-2023:₹15.	

Required: Compute Basic EPS & Diluted EPS.

SOLUTION:

NET PROFIT FOR BASIC EPS AND DILUTED EPS

Particulars	₹
Net Profit before Interest & Tax for the current year	81,20,000
Less: Interest [32,000 x ₹ 50 x 10% x 9/12]	1,20,000
Net Profit before & Tax	80,00,000

Less: Tax @ 30%	24,00,000
Net Profit after Interest & Tax	56,00,000
Less: Pref. Dividend	1,20,000
Net Profit after Interest, Tax & Pref. Dividend for Basic EPS	54,80,000
Add: Interest expense for the current year	1,20,000
Less: Tax relating to interest expense (30% of ₹ 1,20,000)	(36,000)
Add: Pref. Dividend	1,20,000
Adjusted Net Profit for the current year for Diluted EPS	56,84,000

COMPUTATION OF WEIGHTED NUMBER OF EQUITY SHARES FOR BASIC & DILUTED EPS

Basic EPS [₹55,00,000/4,40,000]	***₹12.73 per share***
Weighted average number of equity shares outstanding	4,00,000
No. of shares that have been issued on Conversion of Debentures (32,000 × 5 × 3/12)	40,000
No. of shares that have been issued on Conversion of Pref. Shares (32,000 × 5 × 3/12)	40,000
Weighted number of equity shares for Basic EPS (4,00,000 + 40,000 + 40,000)	4,80,000
No. of Shares under option	1,00,000
No. of Potential Shares that would have been issued at fair value [1,00,000 x 15/25]	(60,000)
Weighted number of equity shares for Diluted EPS [(4,80,000 + 1,00,000 – 60,000)]	5,20,000

Basic EPS = 54,80,000/ 4,80,000 = ₹ 11.42

Diluted EPS = 56,84,000/ 5,20,000 = ₹ 10.93

ILLUSTRATION 9

TULSIAN Ltd provides you the following information:

Number of Equity Shares outstanding on 1.4.2022	4,00,000 shares
Net Profit before Interest & Tax for the year 2022-2023. Tax Rate 30%	₹ 81,20,000
On 01.07.2021 Issued 32,000, 10% Convertible Debentures of ₹ 50 each. Each debenture is convertible into five equity shares. 50% of these are converted into equity shares on 31.12.2022.	
On 01.07.2021 Issued 32,000, 10% Convertible Pref. Shares of ₹ 50 each. Each Pref. Share is convertible into five equity shares. 50% of these are converted into equity shares on 31.12.2022.	
Average fair value of one equity share during the year 2022-2023:₹ 25, Weighted Average number of shares under option during the year 2021-2022: 1,00,000 shares, Exercise Price for shares under option during the year 2022-2023:₹15.	

Required: Compute Basic EPS & Diluted EPS.

SOLUTION:

NET PROFIT FOR BASIC EPS AND DILUTED EPS

Particulars	₹
Net Profit before Interest & Tax for the current year	81,20,000
Less: Interest [(16,000 x ₹ 50 x 10% x 6/12) + (16,000 x ₹ 50 x 10% x 9/12)]	1,00,000
Net Profit before & Tax	80,20,000
Less: Tax @ 30%	24,06,000
Net Profit after Interest & Tax	56,14,000
Less: Pref. Dividend [(16,000 x ₹ 50 x 10% x 6/12) + (16,000 x ₹ 50 x 10% x 9/12)]	1,00,000
Net Profit after Interest, Tax & Pref. Dividend for Basic EPS	55,14,000
Add: Interest expense for the current year	40,000
Less: Tax relating to interest expense (30% of ₹ 40,000)	(12,000)
Add: Pref. Dividend	40,000
Adjusted Net Profit for the current year for Diluted EPS	55,82,000

COMPUTATION OF WEIGHTED NUMBER OF EQUITY SHARES FOR BASIC & DILUTED EPS

Particulars	₹
Weighted average number of equity shares outstanding	4,00,000
No. of equity shares that have been issued on Conversion of Debentures (16,000 × 5 × 3/12)	20,000
No. of equity shares that have been issued on Conversion of Pref. Shares (16,000 × 5 × 3/12)	20,000
Weighted number of equity shares for Basic EPS (4,00,000 + 20,000 + 20,000)	4,40,000
No. of equity shares which would be issued on the conversion of potential equity shares into equity shares(16,000 × 5 × 9/12)	60,000
No. of equity shares which would be issued on the conversion of potential equity shares into equity shares(16,000 × 5 × 9/12)	60,000
No. of Shares under option	1,00,000
No. of Potential Shares that would have been issued at fair value under option [1,00,000 x 15/25]	(60,000)
Weighted number of equity shares for Diluted EPS [(4,40,000 + 60,000 + 60,000 +1,00,000 – 60,000)]	6,00,000

Basic EPS = 55,14,000/ 4,40,000 = ₹12.53

Diluted EPS = 55,82,000/ 6,00,000 = ₹ 9.30

HOW IS RANKING FROM MOST DILUTIVE TO LEAST DILUTIVE CALCULATED AS PER AS 20?

In order to maximize the dilution of basic earnings per share, each issue or series of potential equity shares is considered in sequence from the most dilutive to the least dilutive. Where the earnings per incremental share is the least, the potential equity share is considered most dilutive and vice-versa.

STEP 1	*Calculate Increase in earnings for each issue or series of potential equity shares*
STEP 2	*Calculate Increase in number of Equity shares for each issue or series of potential equity shares*
STEP 3	*Calculate Earnings per incremental share for each issue or series of potential equity shares*
STEP 4	*Rank from Most Dilutive to Least Dilutive*

HOW IS MOST DILUTIVE EPS CALCULATED AS PER AS 20?

STEP 1	*Calculate EPS for Most Dilutive Potential Equity Shares & Mark it as Dilutive (if less than Basic EPS) or Anti-dilutive (if more than Basic EPS)*
STEP 2	*Calculate EPS for Next Most Dilutive Potential Equity Shares & so on and Mark it as Dilutive (if less than Basic EPS) or Anti-dilutive (if more than Basic EPS)*
STEP 3	*Select the most dilutive EPS*

WHAT ARE THE DISCLOSURE REQUIREMENTS AS TO BASIC AND DILUTED EPS AS PER AS 20?

1. Present Basic and Diluted EPS on the face of the Statement of Profit and Loss for each class of Equity Shares even if the amounts disclosed are negative.
2. Amounts used as the numerators in calculating basic and diluted EPS, and a reconciliation of those amounts to the net profit or loss for the period;
3. Weighted Average Number of Equity Shares used as the denominator in calculating basic and diluted EPS, and a reconciliation of these denominators to each other; and
4. Nominal Value of Shares along with the earnings per share figures

VERY SHORT ANSWER TYPE QUESTIONS

1. Briefly explain the following:
   (a) Basic Earning Per Share[EPS]
   (b) Net Profit attributable to Equity Shareholders
   (c) Weighted Average Number of Equity Shares Outstanding during the period
   (d) Potential Equity Share as per AS 20

2. Enumerate the following:
   (a) Sources of Funds for Buy-back of shares.
   (b) Sources of providing premium payable on redemption
   (c) Three tests to be satisfied before buy back of shares

3. How is Basic Earning Per Share as per AS 20 calculated?

4. How are Net Profit attributable to Equity Shareholders calculated?

5. How is Weighted Average Number of Equity Shares Outstanding during the period calculated?

6. How are Partly paid equity shares treated while calculating Weighted Average Number of Equity Shares Outstanding during the period

7. State the effective date from which weight is to be considered for the purposes of calculation of weighted average number of shares as per AS 20 when equity shares are issued.

(a) In exchange for Cash.

(b) As a result of conversion of a Debt Instrument to Equity.

(c) In lieu of Interest or Principal on other Financial Instruments.

(d) In exchange for the settlement of a liability of the Enterprise.

(e) As consideration for acquisition of an asset other than cash.

(f) For the rendering of services to the enterprise.

(g) In case of an amalgamation in nature of purchase.

(h) In case of an amalgamation in nature of merger.

(i) As Bonus Shares.

(j) In case of Share Split or Reverse Share Split.

8. What is Restatement of Basic Eps as per AS 20?

9. When is Restatement required as per AS 20?

10. How is Adjusted Weighted Average No. of Equity Shares Outstanding for the prior period calculated ?

11. How is Adjusted EPS for the previous year calculated?

12. How is Adjusted Equity Shares Outstanding calculated in case of right issue as per AS 20?

13. How is Theoretical Ex-Right Fair Value Per Share calculated in case of right issue as per AS 20?

14. How is Right Issue Adjustment Factor calculated as per AS 20?

15. How is Bonus Issue Adjustment Factor calculated as per AS 20?

16. How is Adjusted Equity Shares Outstanding calculated in case of right and bonus issue as per AS 20?

17. When are Potential Equity Shares considered as dilutive as per AS 20?

18. When are Potential Equity Shares considered as anti-dilutive as per AS 20?

19. How is Diluted Earning Per Share calculated as per AS 20?

20. How is Ranking from Most Dilutive to Least Dilutive calculated as per AS 20?

21. How is most dilutive EPS calculated as per AS 20?

22. What are the Disclosure Requirements as to Basic and Diluted EPS as per AS 20?

SHORT ANSWER TYPE PRACTICAL QUESTIONS

1. A Ltd provides you the following information:

Net Profit for year ended 31-03-2023	₹ 2,67,50,000
10% Cumulative Preference Shares	₹ 2,00,00,000
12% Non-Cumulative Preference Shares	₹ 2,00,00,000
The company had issued 6,40,000 Equity shares of ₹ 10 each, ₹ 5 per share was called up on that date which was paid by all the shareholders. The remaining ₹ 5 was called up on 1-6-2022. All the Shareholders (except one having 1,60,000 shares) paid the sum on 30th June,2022.	

Note: No dividend has been paid on Preference Shares for the last 3 years.

Required: Compute the Basic EPS (Earning Per Share) for the year 2022-2023.

[**Ans** Net Profit ₹ 2,47,50,000, Weighted Average Number of Equity Shares o/s 5,00,000, Basic EPS ₹ 49.50]

2. B Ltd provides you the following information:

Net Profit for year ended 31-03-2023	₹ 2,67,50,000
10% Cumulative Preference Shares	₹ 2,00,00,000
12% Non-Cumulative Preference Shares	₹ 2,00,00,000
No. of fully paid Equity shares of ₹ 10 each issued during 2020	5,00,000
On 01.06.2022, new 1,20,000 Equity Shares of ₹ 10 each are issued for Cash.	

Note: No dividend has been paid on Preference Shares for the last 3 years.

Required: Compute the Basic EPS (Earning Per Share) for the year 2022-2023.

[**Ans** Net Profit ₹ 2,47,50,000, Weighted Average Number of Equity Shares o/s 6,00,000, Basic EPS ₹ 41.25]

3. C Ltd provides you the following information:

Net Profit for year ended 31-03-2023	₹ 2,67,50,000
10% Cumulative Preference Shares	₹ 2,00,00,000
12% Non-Cumulative Preference Shares	₹ 2,00,00,000
No. of fully paid Equity shares of ₹ 10 each issued during 2020	5,00,000
On 01.07.2022, new 6,000 Equity Shares of ₹ 10 each are issued to Underwriters.	

Note: No dividend has been paid on Preference Shares for the last 3 years.

Required: Compute the Basic EPS (Earning Per Share) for the year 2022-2023.

[**Ans** Net Profit ₹ 2,47,50,000, Weighted Average Number of Equity Shares o/s 5,04,500, Basic EPS ₹ 49.06]

4. D Ltd provides you the following information:

Net Profit for year ended 31-03-2023	₹ 2,67,50,000
10% Cumulative Preference Shares	₹ 2,00,00,000
12% Non-Cumulative Preference Shares	₹ 2,00,00,000
No. of fully paid Equity shares of ₹ 10 each issued during 2020	5,00,000
On 01.08.2022, 2,69,250 Equity Shares of ₹ 10 each are Bought - Back.	

Note: No dividend has been paid on Preference Shares for the last 3 years.

Required: Compute the Basic EPS (Earning Per Share) for the year 2022-2023.

[**Ans** Net Profit ₹ 2,47,50,000, Weighted Average Number of Equity Shares o/s 3,20,500, Basic EPS ₹ 77.22]

5. E Ltd provides you the following information:

Net Profit for year ended 31-03-2023	₹ 2,67,50,000
10% Cumulative Preference Shares	₹ 2,00,00,000
12% Non-Cumulative Preference Shares	₹ 2,00,00,000
No. of fully paid Equity shares of ₹ 10 each issued during 2020	5,00,000
On 01.09.2022, 30,000 Equity Shares of ₹ 10 each are issued to Vendor against Purchase of Building. (acquisition is recognized on the same day).	

Note: No dividend has been paid on Preference Shares for the last 3 years.

Required: Compute the Basic EPS (Earning Per Share) for the year 2022-2023.

[**Ans** Net Profit ₹ 2,47,50,000, Weighted Average Number of Equity Shares o/s 5,17,500, Basic EPS ₹ 47.83]

6. F Ltd provides you the following information:

Net Profit for year ended 31-03-2023	₹ 2,67,50,000
10% Cumulative Preference Shares	₹ 2,00,00,000
12% Non-Cumulative Preference Shares	₹ 2,00,00,000
No. of fully paid Equity shares of ₹ 10 each issued during 2020	5,00,000
On 01.10.2022, 15,000 Equity Shares of ₹ 10 each are issued in settlement of liability.	

Note: No dividend has been paid on Preference Shares for the last 3 years.

Required: Compute the Basic EPS (Earning Per Share) for the year 2022-2023.

[**Ans** Net Profit ₹ 2,47,50,000, Weighted Average Number of Equity Shares o/s 5,07,500, Basic EPS ₹ 48.77]

7. G Ltd provides you the following information:

Net Profit for year ended 31-03-2023	₹ 2,67,50,000
10% Cumulative Preference Shares	₹ 2,00,00,000
12% Non-Cumulative Preference Shares	₹ 2,00,00,000
No. of fully paid Equity shares of ₹ 10 each issued during 2020	5,00,000
On 01.11.2022, 1,20,000 Equity Shares of ₹ 10 each are issued to Y Ltd. on purchase of Y Ltd.	

Note: No dividend has been paid on Preference Shares for the last 3 years.

Required: Compute the Basic EPS (Earning Per Share) for the year 2022-2023.

[**Ans** Net Profit ₹ 2,47,50,000, Weighted Average Number of Equity Shares o/s 5,50,000, Basic EPS ₹ 45]

8. H Ltd provides you the following information:

Net Profit for year ended 31-03-2023	₹ 2,67,50,000
10% Cumulative Preference Shares	₹ 2,00,00,000
12% Non-Cumulative Preference Shares	₹ 2,00,00,000
No. of fully paid Equity shares of ₹ 100 each issued during 2020	5,00,000
On 01.12.2022, Equity Shares are Split up into shares of ₹ 10 each	

Note: No dividend has been paid on Preference Shares for the last 3 years.

Required: Compute the Basic EPS (Earning Per Share) for the year 2022-2023.

[**Ans** Net Profit ₹ 2,47,50,000, Weighted Average Number of Equity Shares o/s 50,00,000, Basic EPS ₹ 4.95]

9. I Ltd provides you the following information:

Net Profit for year ended 31-03-2023	₹ 2,67,50,000
10% Cumulative Preference Shares	₹ 2,00,00,000
12% Non-Cumulative Preference Shares	₹ 2,00,00,000

No. of fully paid Equity shares of ₹ 10 each issued during 2020	50,00,000
On 01.1.2023, Bonus Shares are issued in the ratio of 1 share for every 2 held.	

Note: No dividend has been paid on Preference Shares for the last 3 years.

Required: Compute the Basic EPS (Earning Per Share) for the year 2022-2023.

[**Ans** Net Profit ₹ 2,47,50,000, Weighted Average Number of Equity Shares o/s 75,00,000, Basic EPS ₹ 3.30]

10. J Ltd provides you the following information:

Number of equity shares outstanding on 1.4.2022	4,00,000 shares
Net Profit before Interest & Tax for the year 2022-2023. Tax Rate 30%	₹ 81,20,000
On 01.04.2021 Issued 32,000, 10% Convertible Debentures of ₹ 50 each. Each debenture is convertible into five equity shares.	

Required: Compute Basic EPS & Diluted EPS.

[**Ans** Net Profit ₹ 55,72,000, Weighted Average No. of Equity Shares o/s 4,00,000, Basic EPS ₹ 13.93, Adjusted Net Profit ₹ 56,84,000, Adjusted Weighted Average No. of Equity Shares o/s 5,60,000, Diluted EPS ₹ 10.15]

11. K Ltd provides you the following information:

Number of equity shares outstanding on 1.4.2022	4,00,000 shares
Net Profit before Interest & Tax for the year 2022-2023. Tax Rate 30%	₹ 81,20,000
On 01.07.2021 Issued 32,000, 10% Convertible Debentures of ₹ 50 each. Each debenture is convertible into five equity shares.	

Required: Compute Basic EPS & Diluted EPS.

[**Ans** Net Profit ₹ 56,00,000, Weighted Average No. of Equity Shares o/s 4,00,000, Basic EPS ₹ 14, Adjusted Net Profit ₹ 56,84,000, Adjusted Weighted Average No. of Equity Shares o/s 5,20,000, Diluted EPS ₹ 10.93]

12. L Ltd provides you the following information:

Number of equity shares outstanding on 1.4.2022	4,00,000 shares
Net Profit before Interest & Tax for the year 2022-2023. Tax Rate 30%	₹ 81,20,000
On 01.04.2021 Issued 32,000, 10% Convertible Debentures of ₹ 50 each. Each debenture is convertible into five equity shares. These are converted into equity shares on 31.12.2022.	

Required: Compute Basic EPS & Diluted EPS.

[**Ans** Net Profit ₹ 56,00,000, Weighted Average No. of Equity Shares o/s 4,40,000, Basic EPS ₹ 12.73, Adjusted Net Profit ₹ 56,84,000, Adjusted Weighted Average No. of Equity Shares o/s 4,40,000, Diluted EPS ₹ 12.92]

13. M Ltd provides you the following information:

Number of equity shares outstanding on 1.4.2022	4,00,000 shares
Net Profit before Interest & Tax for the year 2022-2023. Tax Rate 30%	₹ 81,20,000
On 01.04.2021 Issued 32,000, 10% Convertible Pref. Shares of ₹ 50 each. Each Pref. Share is convertible into five equity shares. These are converted into equity shares on 31.12.2022.	

Required: Compute Basic EPS & Diluted EPS.

[**Ans** Net Profit ₹ 55,64,000, Weighted Average No. of Equity Shares o/s 4,40,000, Basic EPS ₹ 12.65, Adjusted Net Profit ₹ 56,84,000, Adjusted Weighted Average No. of Equity Shares o/s 4,40,000, Diluted EPS ₹ 12.92]

14. N Ltd provides you the following information:

Number of equity shares outstanding on 1.4.2022	4,00,000 shares
Net Profit before Interest & Tax for the year 2022-2023. Tax Rate 30%	₹ 81,20,000
Average fair value of one equity share during the year 2022-2023:₹ 25,Weighted Average number of shares under option during the year 2021-2022: 1,00,000 shares,Exercise Price for shares under option during the year 2022-2023:₹15.	

[**Ans** Net Profit ₹ 56,84,000, Weighted Average No. of Equity Shares o/s 4,00,000, Basic EPS ₹ 14.21, Adjusted Net Profit ₹ 56,84,000, Adjusted Weighted Average No. of Equity Shares o/s 4,40,000, Diluted EPS ₹ 12.92]

15. From the following information relating to Y Ltd. Calculate Earnings Per Share (EPS):

	₹ *in crores*
Profit before V.R.S. payments but after depreciation	75.00
Depreciation	10.00
VRS payments	32.10
Provision for taxation	10.00
Fringe benefit tax	5.00
Paid up share capital (shares of ₹ 10 each fully paid)	93.00

[**Ans** Net Profit ₹ 27,90,000, Weighted Average Number of Equity Shares o/s 9,30,000, Basic EPS ₹ 3]

16. From the following information compute Diluted Earnings Per Share.

Net Profit for the year	₹12,00,000
Weighted average number of equity shares outstanding	5,00,000 shares
Average fair value of one equity share	₹ 20
Weighted average number of shares under option	1,00,000 shares
Exercise price per share under option	₹15

[**Ans** Net Profit ₹ 12,00,000, Weighted Average Number of Equity Shares o/s 5,00,000, Basic EPS ₹ 2.40, Adjusted Weighted Average Number of Equity Shares o/s 5,25,000, Diluted EPS ₹ 2.29]

LONG ANSWER TYPE PRACTICAL QUESTIONS

1. TULSIAN Ltd provides you the following information:

Net Profit for year ended 31-03-2022	₹ 170,00,000
Net Profit for year ended 31-03-2023	₹ 2,20,00,000
10% Cumulative Preference Shares	₹ 2,00,00,000

12% Non-Cumulative Preference Shares	₹ 2,00,00,000
No. of fully paid Equity shares of ₹ 100 each issued during 2020	10,00,000
On 01.12.2022 Shares are Split up into shares of ₹ 10 each.	
On 01.01.2023 Bonus Shares are issued in the ratio of 1 share for every 2 held.	

Note: No dividend has been paid on Preference Shares for the last 3 years.

Required: Compute the Basic EPS (Earning Per Share) for the year 2022-2023.

[**Ans** Basic EPS ₹ 1.33]

2. In Previous Problem Compute the Basic EPS and Adjusted EPS for the year 2021-2022.

[**Ans** Basic EPS ₹ 15, Adjusted EPS ₹ 1]

3. Compute Basic EPS and Restated EPS for the previous year and Basic EPS for the current year from the following information:

Net Profit for the period 2021 - 2022	₹ 44,00,000
Net Profit for the period 2022 - 2023	₹ 94,00,000
No. of Shares outstanding prior to right issue	20,00,000 shares
Right issue	2 New Shares for each 5 Shares outstanding
Right issue price	₹15
Last Date to exercise rights	31st December, 2022
Response to Right Issue	Fully Subscribed
Fair Value of one equity share immediately prior to exercise of rights on 31st December, 2022	₹ 22

[**Ans PY:** Basic EPS ₹ 2.20, Adjusted EPS ₹ 2,**CY:** Basic EPS ₹ 4]

4. Compute Basic EPS and Restated EPS for the previous year and Basic EPS for the current year from the following information:

Net Profit for the period 2021-2022	₹ 69,60,000
Net Profit for the period 2022-2023	₹ 73,20,000
No. of Shares outstanding prior to right issue	2,00,000 shares
Right issue	2 New Shares for each 5 Shares outstanding
Right issue price	₹ 30
Last Date to exercise rights	31st December, 2022
Response to Right Issue	Fully Subscribed
Fair Value of one equity share immediately prior to exercise of rights on 31st December, 2022	₹ 58
Bonus issue on 31st March, 2023	1 Equity Share for 5 Equity Shares outstanding on 31st March, 2023.

[**Ans PY:** Basic EPS ₹ 34.80, Adjusted EPS ₹ 25,**CY:** Basic EPS ₹ 25]

5. Diluted EPS (1) Ltd provides you the following information:

Number of Equity Shares outstanding on 1.4.2022	4,00,000 shares
Net Profit before Interest & Tax for the year 2022-2023. Tax Rate 30%	₹ 81,20,000
On 01.04.2021 Issued 32,000, 10% Convertible Debentures of ₹ 50 each. Each debenture is convertible into five equity shares. These are converted into equity shares on 31.12.2022.	
On 01.04.2021 Issued 32,000, 10% Convertible Pref. Shares of ₹ 50 each. Each Pref. Share is convertible into five equity shares. These are converted into equity shares on 31.12.2022.	
Average fair value of one equity share during the year 2022-2023:₹ 25,Weighted Average number of shares under option during the year 2021-2022: 1,00,000 shares,Exercise Price for shares under option during the year 2022-2023:₹15.	

Required: Compute Basic EPS & Diluted EPS.

[**Ans** Net Profit ₹ 54,80,000, Weighted Average No. of Equity Shares o/s 4,80,000, Basic EPS ₹ 11.42, Adjusted Net Profit ₹ 56,84,000, Adjusted Weighted Average No. of Equity Shares o/s 5,20,000, Diluted EPS ₹ 10.93]

6. Diluted EPS(2) Ltd provides you the following information:

Number of Equity Shares outstanding on 1.4.2022	4,00,000 shares
Net Profit before Interest & Tax for the year 2022-2023. Tax Rate 30%	₹ 81,20,000
On 01.07.2021 Issued 32,000, 10% Convertible Debentures of ₹ 50 each. Each debenture is convertible into five equity shares. 50% of these are converted into equity shares on 31.12.2022.	
On 01.07.2021 Issued 32,000, 10% Convertible Pref. Shares of ₹ 50 each. Each Pref. Share is convertible into five equity shares. 50% of these are converted into equity shares on 31.12.2022.	
Average fair value of one equity share during the year 2022-2023:₹ 25,Weighted Average number of shares under option during the year 2021-2022: 1,00,000 shares,Exercise Price for shares under option during the year 2022-2023:₹15.	

Required: Compute Basic EPS & Diluted EPS.

[**Ans** Net Profit ₹ 55,14,000, Weighted Average No. of Equity Shares o/s 4,40,000, Basic EPS ₹ 12.53, Adjusted Net Profit ₹ 55,82,000, Adjusted Weighted Average No. of Equity Shares o/s 6,00,000, Diluted EPS ₹ 9.30]

COMPREHENSIVE QUESTIONS

7. Calculate the Basic Earning Per Share of X Ltd. for year 2022-2023 and restatement for the year 2021-2022:

Date	*Particulars*	*No. of Shares*
01.04.2022	No of Shares of ₹ 100 each at the beginning of year	10,000
01.06.2022	Issue of Shares for Cash	2,400
01.07.2022	Issue of Shares to Underwriters	120
01.08.2022	Buy - Back of Shares	5,385

01.09.2022	Issue of Shares against Purchase of Building. (acquisition is recognized on the same day)	600
01.10.2022	Issue of Shares in settlement of liability	300
01.11.2022	X Ltd. purchased Y Ltd. on the basis of intrinsic value of shares of both the companies. The intrinsic value of shares of X Ltd. and Y Ltd. are ₹ 60 and ₹ 15 respectively. Shares outstanding on 1st April, 2022 of Y Ltd. are 9600.	
01.12.2022	Split up of shares into shares of ₹10 each	
31.12.2022	Right Issue: 2 shares @ ₹ 30 for 5 shares outstanding. Right Issue Fully Subscribed on Last date to exercise right i.e. 31st December, 2022. Fair Value of 1 equity share immediately prior to exercise of right on 31st December, 2022:₹ 58 per share.	
31.03.2023	Bonus issue:1 share for every 5 shares held on 31st March, 2023	
	Net Profit after tax for the year 2021-2022:₹ 34,80,000	
	Net Profit after tax for the year 2022-2023:₹ 36,60,000	

[**Ans PY:** Weighted Average No. of equity shares 1,00,000, Basic EPS ₹ 34.80, Adjusted Weighted Average No. of equity shares 1,39,200, Adjusted EPS ₹ 25, **CY:** Weighted Average No. of equity shares 1,46,400, Basic EPS ₹ 25]

8. TULSIAN LTD provides you the following information:

Date	*Particulars*	*No. of Shares*
01.04.2022	No. of fully paid Shares of ₹100 each at the beginning of year	5,00,000
01.06.2022	Issue of Shares for Cash	1,20,000
01.07.2022	Issue of Shares to Underwriters	6,000
01.08.2022	Buy - Back of Shares	2,69,250
01.09.2022	Issue of Shares against Purchase of Building. (Acquisition is recognized on the same day)	30,000
01.10.2022	Issue of Shares in settlement of liability	15,000
01.11.2022	Tulsian Ltd. purchased Y Ltd. on the basis of intrinsic value of shares of both the companies. The intrinsic value of shares of Tulsian Ltd. and Y Ltd. are ₹ 60 and ₹ 15 respectively Shares outstanding on 1st April, 2022 of Y Ltd. are 4,80,000	
01.12.2022	Split up of shares into shares of ₹ 10 each	
01.01.2023	Bonus issue:1 share for every 2 held	
No. of 12% Convertible Debentures of ₹ 100 each		1,00,000
Interest of Debentures		3,00,000
Conversion Ratio of Debentures		10 shares per debenture
Net Profit for year ended 31-03-2022		₹ 85,00,000

Net Profit for year ended 31-03-2023	₹ 1,10,00,000
Tax Rate	30%
10% Cumulative Preference Shares	₹1,00,00,000
12% Non-Cumulative Preference Shares	₹1,00,00,000

Note: No dividend has been paid on Preference Shares for the last 3 years.

Required: Compute the Basic and Diluted EPS (earning per share) for accounting year 2022-2023 and Adjusted EPS for the year 2021-2022.

[**Ans** Net Profit ₹ 100,00,000, Weighted Average No. of Equity Shares o/s 75,00,000, Basic EPS ₹ 1.33, Adjusted Net Profit ₹ 1,02,10,000, Adjusted Weighted Average No. of Equity Shares o/s 77,50,000, Diluted EPS ₹ 1.317]

10 AS 18 – RELATED PARTY DISCLOSURES

WHAT IS THE OBJECTIVE OF AS 18?

The scope and objective of the standard is to establish requirements for disclosure of (a) related party relationship (b) transaction between a reporting enterprise and its related parties.

This disclosure would make the financial statements of the reporting enterprise more transparent and allow the users to compare both intra-enterprise with corresponding earlier accounting period and inter-enterprise as well.

WHAT ARE THE CASES IN WHICH DISCLOSURE AS PER AS 18 IS NOT REQUIRED?

1. if there is statutory bar on the reporting enterprise on confidentiality (banks) in respect of constituents
2. in case of consolidated financial statements in respect of members of the group (holding & subsidiary) with exception for transaction with Associated Enterprise accounted for under equity method
3. in the financial statements of State/Central controlled enterprises with other State/ Central controlled enterprise even when related party relationship exists.

WHEN WOULD THE PARTIES BE CONSIDERED AS RELATED AS PER AS 18?

Both parties would be considered as related if at any time during the reporting period one party has the ability:

(a) to control the other party

(b) to exercise significant influence over the other party in making financial and/or operating decisions

Meaning of Control:

(i) ownership directly or indirectly, of more than 50% of the voting power of an enterprise

(ii) the composition of the board of directors (in case of a company) or the Governing Body (in case of other enterprise)

(iii) a substantial interest(i.e. at least 20% interest in voting power) in voting power and the power to direct by Statute or by agreement, the financial/operating policies of the enterprise.

Meaning of Significant Influence:

(i) refers to participation in the financial and/or operating policy decisions of an enterprise but not control of those policies.

(ii) may be gained by ownership in share (including investment through intermediaries restricted to mean subsidiaries as defined in AS-21 Consolidated Financial Statement)

WHAT ARE THE RELATED PARTY RELATIONSHIPS TO WHICH RELATED PARTY DISCLOSURES ARE APPLICABLE AS PER AS 18?

1. Enterprises that directly or indirectly through one or more intermediaries control or are controlled by or under common control with the reporting enterprise

2. Associates and joint venturers of the reporting enterprise and the investing party or venturer in respect of which the reporting enterprise is an associate or joint venturer,.
3. Individuals owning directly or indirectly an interest in the voting power of the reporting enterprise that gives them control or significant influence over the enterprise and relatives of any such individual.
4. Key management personnel and relatives of such individuals.
5. Enterprise over which any person in (3) and (4) is able to exercise significant influence (including enterprise owned by directors or major shareholders of the reporting enterprise and enterprise that have a member of key management in common with the reporting enterprise).

Related party transactions involve transfer of resources or obligations between related parties, regardless of whether or not a price is charged, e.g. use of logo/brand name, provision of management services, providing financial guarantee, use of common infrastructure etc.

WHAT ARE THE DISCLOSURE REQUIRED UNDER AS-18?

(a) In case of related party relationship by virtue of significant influence (not control) e.g. those of associates, key management personnel, relatives, there is no need to disclose the related party relationship unless there have been actual transaction during the reporting period with such related parties.

(b) In the event of transaction between related parties during the existence of a related party relationship (control or significant influence) the reporting enterprise should disclose:

   (i) the name of transacting related party
   (ii) description of the relationship between parties
   (iii) description of nature of transaction
   (iv) volume of transaction, either in amount or approximate proportions
   (v) any other element of the related party transactions necessary for understanding of financial statements (e.g. transfer of major asset taken at price different from normal commercial terms i.e. not at fair value)
   (vi) either in amount or proportion of outstanding items and provisions for doubtful debts pertaining to related parties on B/S date.
   (vii) amounts written off/back in the accounting period in respect of debts due from or to related parties.

WHO ARE CONSIDERED AS "RELATED PARTY", WITH REFERENCE TO A COMPANY U/S 2(76)?

As per Sec 2(76) "Related Party", with reference to a company, means:

(i) a director or his relative;
(ii) a key managerial personnel or his relative;
(iii) a firm, in which a director, manager or his relative is a partner;
(iv) a private company in which a director or manager or his relative is a member or director;
(v) a public company in which a director or manager is a director and holds along with his relatives, more than 2% of its paid-up share capital;
(vi) any body corporate whose Board of Directors, managing director or manager is accustomed to act in accordance with the advice, directions or instructions of a director or manager;
(vii) any person on whose advice, directions or instructions a director or manager is accustomed to act:

Provided that nothing in sub-clauses (vi) and (vii) shall apply to the advice, directions or instructions given in a professional capacity;

(viii) any body corporate which is:

(A) a holding, subsidiary or an associate company of such company;

(B) a subsidiary of a holding company to which it is also a subsidiary;or

(C) an investing company or the venturer of a company;

Explanation: For the purpose of this clause, "the investing company or the venturer of a company" means a body corporate whose investment in the company would result in the company becoming an associate company of the body corporate.

(ix) such other person as may be prescribed. Here,a director or key managerial personnel of the holding company or his relative concerning a company shall be considered a related party.

Note: Relative means member of the same HUF, husband, wife, father, stepfather, mother, stepmother, son, stepson, son's wife, daughter, daughter's husband, brother, stepbrother, sister, step-sister)

WHO ARE CONSIDERED RELATED PARTY AS PER SEBI REGULATION 2(1)(ZB)?

1. Related Party u/s 2(76) of the Company Act
2. Related Party under the applicable AS 18 or IND AS 24.
3. Any person or entity belonging to the promoter or promoter group of the listed entity and holding at least 10% (w.e.f. 1st April, 2023) of shareholding in the listed entity.

WHICH TRANSACTIONS ARE CONSIDERED RELATED PARTY TRANSACTIONS?

A transaction covered u/s 188(1)(a) to (g) with a Related Party u/s 2(76) is considered as Related Party Transaction (RTP). Prior Approval of the Board of Directors is required at a duly convened Board's meeting irrespective of the value/consideration of transaction. In addition, Prior Approval of the Members by a special resolution is also required if value/consideration of transaction exceeds the limits prescribed under Rule 15 of The Companies (Meetings of Board and its Powers) Rules, 2014.

Transaction covered u/s 188(1) (a) to (g)	*Limits prescribed under Rule 15*
(a) Sale, Purchase or supply of goods/ materials directly or through an agent	If the value of such transaction is 10% or more of **turnover** of company.
(b) Selling or otherwise disposing of or buying property of any kind directly or through an agent	If the value of such transaction is 10% or more of **net worth** of company .
(c) Leasing of property of any kind directly	If Lease rent is 10% or more of **turnover** of company.
(d) Availing or the rendering services of any kind directly or through an agent	If the consideration is 10% or more of **turnover.**
(e) Appointment of any agent for purchase/ sale of goods, materials, services, or property	Refer to Point (a), (b), (d) as the case may be
(f) Related Party's appointment to any office or place of profit in the company, subsidiary company or associate company.	If the monthly remuneration exceeds 2.5 lacs.
(g) Under writing the subscription of any securities or derivatives of company	If the remuneration exceeds 1% of **net worth** of company

Notes:

1. All the above limits are to be taken on the transactions undertaken on a financial year basis.
2. Turnover or Net Worth shall be based on the audited financial statements of the preceding financial year.
3. Section 188 is not applicable if the transactions are entered into in ordinary course of business and are at Arm Length Price. Burden to establish that the transaction was on arm's length would be on the company. "Arm's Length Transaction" means a transaction between two related parties that is conducted as if they were unrelated, so that there is no conflict of interest. The term 'ordinary course of business' will incorporate the everyday transactions, customs, and practices of a business and a company. The ICAI in its guidance to auditors, has included the following few examples of transactions that are considered outside the entity's ordinary course of business:
   (a) Complex equity transactions – such as corporate restructurings or acquisitions.
   (b) Transactions with foreign entities in areas with weak corporate laws.
   (c) If no consideration is exchanged,
   (d) the leasing of premises or rendering of management services by an entity to another party.
   (e) Sales transactions at abnormally large discounts or huge sales returns.
   (f) Transactions with circular arrangements. For example, sales with a promise to re-purchase.
   (g) Contract transactions whose terms can be changed before expiry.
4. Section 188 is also not applicable if transactions are entered into between holding company and its wholly owned subsidiary whose accounts are consolidated and kept for approval in annual general meeting.

ILLUSTRATION 1

Mr Buffet is a Managing Director of XYZ Ltd. (having **Net Worth** of Rs 800 crore and **Turnover of** Rs 400 crore for the year ended 31st March, 2022). Mr X is son-in-law and Mr Y is brother-in-law of Mr Buffet. Z Ltd is a subsidiary of a W Ltd. which is a holding company of XYZ Ltd. During the year ended 31st March, 2023, the following Transactions took place:

(a) Mr X,supplied Goods for ₹ 15 crore during the 1st quarter ended on 30th June, 2022 and for ₹ 25 crore during the 2nd quarter ended on 30th Sept, 2022.

(b) Mr X,sold a Building for ₹ 15 crore during the 1st quarter ended on 30th June, 2022 and for ₹ 25 crore during the 2nd quarter ended on 30th Sept, 2022.

(c) Mr X,leased a Building at a rent of ₹ 40 crore p.a. on 2nd July,2022.

(d) Mr X rendered some services to XYZ Ltd. for ₹ 15 crore during the 1st quarter ended on 30th June, 2022 and for ₹ 25 crore during the 2nd quarter ended on 30th Sept, 2022.

(e) Mr X is appointed as a Sales Manager at a remuneration of Rs 2.5 lacs p.m. on 1st July,2022.

(f) Z Ltd underwritten the subscription of securities of XYZ Ltd. for a remuneration of Rs 8 crore. on 1st July,2022.

Required: State the legal implications of the above transactions

(a) if Mr Buffet left the company on 1st April, 2023

(b) if Mr Buffet left the company on 1st July, 2022.

(c) if the transactions are entered into in ordinary course of business and are at Arm Length Price.

(d) if the transactions covered in (a) to (e) were entered into by Mr Y and not Mr X and are not at Arm Length Price.

SOLUTION

(a) Legal Implications of the transactions if Mr Buffet left the company on 1st April, 2023

	Whether Related Party Transaction(RTP)	*Is Prior Approval of the Board of Directors required?*	*Is Prior Approval of the Members by a special resolution required?*
(a)	**Yes. Reason:** Transaction is covered u/s 188(1) and Mr X is a related Party u/s 2(76).	**Yes**	**Yes** since the Value of transaction (₹ is ₹ 40 crore i.e. 10% of **turnover** of company.
(b)	**Yes. Reason:** Transaction is covered u/s 188(1) and Mr X is a related Party u/s 2(76).	**Yes**	**No** since the Value of transaction (₹ 40 crore) is less than ₹ 80 crore i.e.10% of **net worth** of company.
(c)	**Yes. Reason:** Transaction is covered u/s 188(1) and Mr X is a related Party u/s 2(76).	**Yes.**	**Yes** since the Value of transaction (₹ is ₹ 40 crore i.e. 10% of **turnover** of company.
(d)	**Yes. Reason:** Transaction is covered u/s 188(1) and Mr X is a related Party u/s 2(76).	**Yes**	**Yes** since the Value of transaction (₹ is ₹ 40 crore i.e. 10% of **turnover** of company.
(e)	**Yes. Reason:** Transaction is covered u/s 188(1) and Mr X is a related Party u/s 2(76).	**Yes**	**No** since the monthly remuneration does not exceed 2.5 lacs.
(f)	**Yes. Reason:** Transaction is covered u/s 188(1) and Z Ltd is a related Party u/s 2(76).	**Yes**	**No** since the Value of transaction (₹ 8 crore) does not exceed ₹ 8 crore i.e. 1% of **net worth** of company.

(b) Legal Implications of the transactions if Mr Buffet left the company on 1st July, 2022

	Whether Related Party Transaction (RTP)	*Is Prior Approval of the Board of Directors required?*	*Is Prior Approval of the Members by a special resolution required?*
(a)	**Yes. Reason:** Transaction is covered u/s 188(1) and Mr X is a related Party u/s 2(76).	**Yes for** Transaction entered into upto 30th June,2022.	**No** since the Value of transaction (₹ 15 crore) is less than ₹ 40 crore i.e. 10% of **turnover** of company.
(b)	**Yes. Reason:** Transaction is covered u/s 188(1) and Mr X is a related Party u/s 2(76).	**Yes for** Transaction entered into upto 30th June,2022.	**No** since the Value of transaction (₹ 15 crore) is less than ₹ 80 crore i.e.10% of **net worth** of company.

(c)	**No. Reason:** Transaction is covered u/s 188(1) but Mr X is not a related Party u/s 2(76).	No	No
(d)	**Yes. Reason:** Transaction is covered u/s 188(1) and Mr X is a related Party u/s 2(76).	**Yes for** Transaction entered into upto 30th June,2022.	**No** since the Value of transaction (₹ 15 crore) is less than ₹ 40 crore i.e. 10% of **turnover** of company.
(e)	**No. Reason:** Transaction is covered u/s 188(1) but Mr X is not a related Party u/s 2(76).	No	No
(f)	**Yes. Reason:** Transaction is covered u/s 188(1) and Z Ltd is a related Party u/s 2(76).	**Yes**	**No** since the Value of transaction (₹ 8 crore) does not exceed ₹ 8 crore i.e.1% of **net worth** of company.

(c) Section 188 is not applicable if the transactions are entered into in ordinary course of business and are at Arm Length Price. Hence, no approval is required.

(d) The transactions covered in (a) to (e) will not be **Related Party Transaction (RTP) since** Mr Y is not a Related Party u/s 2(76). Hence, neither approval nor any disclosure in Notes to Accounts is required.

ILLUSTRATION 2

Mr Buffet is a Managing Director of XYZ Ltd. Miss Massom, his daughter recently qualified CA is appointed as finance officer at a remuneration of ₹ 1,50,000 per month. Mr Anupam, his son supplied Goods for ₹ 50 lakhs and ₹ 100 lakhs during the 1st quarter ended on 30th June, 2022 and the 2nd quarter ended on 30th Sept, 2022 on the same terms of other Suppliers of the company. Mr Buffet left the company on 30th June, 2022. Miss Massom left the service on 30th Sept, 2022. You are required to suggest how these transactions will be treated as at the closing date i.e. on 31st March, 2023 for the purposes of AS 18- Related Party Disclosures.

SOLUTION

As per provision of AS 18, the transactions only for the period in which related party relationships exist need to be reported. Transactions for the period (on 1st July onwards since Mr Buffet left the company on 30th June, 2022) in which related party relationship did not exist need not be reported.

A relative of key management personnel should be identified as related party for disclosure in the financial statements for the year ended 31.3.2023 and hence,

(a) remuneration upto 30th June, 2022 is required to be disclosed as related party transaction.

(b) transaction of sale of goods with the company for first quarter ending 30th June, 2022 for ₹ 50 Lakhs only is required to be disclosed as related party transaction.

ILLUSTRATION 3

XYZ Limited enter into an agreement with Mr. P for running a business for a fixed amount payable to the later every year. The contract states that the day-to-day management of the business will be handled by Mr. P, while all financial and operating policy decisions are taken by the Board of Directors of the Company. Mr. P does not own any voting power in XYZ Limited.

SOLUTION

Mr. P will not be considered as a related party of XYZ Limited in view of provisions of AS 18 "Related Party Disclosures" which states, "individuals owning, directly or indirectly, an interest in the voting power of the reporting enterprise that gives them control or significant influence over the enterprise, and relatives of any such individual are related parties".

In the absence of share ownership, Mr. P would not be considered to exercise significant influence on XYZ Limited, even though there is an agreement giving him the power to manage the company. Further, the fact that Mr. P does not have the ability to direct or instruct the board of directors does not qualify him as a key management personnel.

ILLUSTRATION 4

X Ltd. holds 51% of Y Ltd., Y Ltd holds 51% of W Ltd., Z Ltd holds 49% of W Ltd. Identify the Related Parties as per AS-18.

SOLUTION:

X Ltd.,Y Ltd. & W Ltd. are related to each other. Z Ltd. & W Ltd. are related to each other by virtue of Associate relationship. However, neither X Ltd. nor Y Ltd. is related to Z Ltd. and vice versa

ILLUSTRATION 5

X Ltd. holds 50% of Y Ltd.,Y Ltd holds 40% of W Ltd.,W Ltd holds 50% of Z Ltd. Identify the Related Parties as per AS-18.

SOLUTION:

X Ltd., Y Ltd. & W Ltd. are related to each other. Y Ltd. , Z Ltd. & W Ltd. are related to each other by virtue of Associate relationship. However, X Ltd. is not related to Z Ltd. and vice versa

ILLUSTRATION 6

P Ltd. has 60% voting right in Q Ltd. Q Ltd. has 20% voting right in R Ltd. Also, P Ltd. directly enjoys voting right of 14% in R Ltd. R Ltd. is a listed company and regularly supplies goods to P Ltd.The management of R Ltd. has not disclosed its relationship with P Ltd. How would you assess the situation from the viewpoint of AS 18 on Related Party Disclosures?

SOLUTION:

Provision of AS 18: As per AS 18 Related Party Disclosures', defines related party as one that has at any time during the reporting period, the ability to control the other party or exercise significant influence over the other party in making financial and/or operating decisions. Here, Control is defined as ownership directly or indirectly of more than one-half of the voting power of an enterprise; and Significant Influence is defined as participation in the financial and/or operating policy decisions of an enterprise but not control of those policies.

Advice:

1. P Ltd. has direct economic interest in R Ltd to the extent of 14%, and through Q Ltd. in which it is the majority shareholders, it has further control of 12% in R Ltd. (60% of Q Ltd's 20%). These two taken together (14% + 12%) make the total control of 26%.
2. In the present case, control of P Ltd. in R Ltd. directly and through Q Ltd., does not go beyond 26%. However, as per para 12 of AS 18, significant influence may be exercised as an investing party (P Ltd.) holds, directly or indirectly through intermediaries 20% or more of the voting power of the R Ltd.
3. As R Ltd. is a listed company and regularly supplies goods to P Ltd. therefore, related party disclosure, as per AS 18, is required.

ILLUSTRATION 7

Identify the related parties in the following cases as per AS-18

P Ltd. holds 61 % shares of Q Ltd.

Q Ltd. holds 51 % shares of R Ltd.

S Ltd. holds 49% shares of R Ltd.

Give your SOLUTION- Reporting Entity wise for P Ltd., Q Ltd., S Ltd. and R Ltd.

SOLUTION:

(a) Reporting entity- P Ltd.

- Q Ltd. (subsidiary) is a related party
- R Ltd.(subsidiary) is a related party

(b) Reporting entity- Q Ltd.

- P Ltd. (holding company) is a related party
- R Ltd. (subsidiary) is a related party

(c) Reporting entity- R Ltd.

- P Ltd. (holding company) is a related party
- Q Ltd. (holding company) is a related party
- S Ltd. (investor/ investing party) is a related party

(d) Reporting entity- S Ltd.

- R Ltd. (associate) is a related party

ILLUSTRATION 8

If a majority of directors of X Ltd. constitute the majority of the board of directors of Y Ltd. in their individual capacity as professional (and not by the virtue of their being directors in X Ltd.), can it be considered that the companies are related?

SOLUTION:

Provision of AS 18: As per para 10 of AS 18, 'Related Party Disclosures', control has been defined as

(i) ownership, directly or indirectly, of more than one-half of the voting power of an enterprise, or

(ii) control of the composition of the board of directors in the case of a company or of the composition of the corresponding governing body is case of any other enterprise, or

(iii) a substantial interest in voting power and the power to direct, by statue or agreement, the financial and/or operating policies of the enterprise.

Further, as per para 11 of AS-18, an enterprise is considered to control the composition of the board of directors of company, if it has the power, without the consent of concurrence of any other person, to appoint or removal all or a majority of directors of that company.

Advice: X Ltd. cannot be said to control the composition of the board of directors of the Y Ltd. as the directors have been appointed in their individual capacity and not by virtue of their being directors in the X Ltd.

Further, an evaluation is required to ascertain whether any of the directors has a relationship with both companies [as specified in para 3(c) and (d) of AS-18 which would create a related party relationship between the two companies]. Such relationships would include these directors being key management personnel in both companies, being a key management person one company and owing an interest in another which enables him to exercise significant influence etc.

SOLVED PROBLEMS

PROBLEM 1

XYZ Ltd. sold goods for ₹ 90 lakhs to PQR Ltd. during financial year ended 31-3-2023. The Managing Director of XYZ Ltd. own 100% of PQR Ltd. The sales were made to PQR Ltd. at normal selling prices followed by XYZ Ltd. The Chief accountant of XYZ Ltd contends that these sales need not require a different treatment from the other sales made by the company and hence no disclosure is necessary as per the accounting standard. Is the Chief Accountant correct?

SOLUTION:

Provision of AS 18: As per AS 18 'Related Party Disclosures', Enterprises over which a key management personnel is able to exercise significant influence are related parties. This includes enterprises owned by directors or major shareholders of the reporting enterprise that have a member of key management in common with the reporting enterprise.

Advice: XYZ Ltd. and PQR Ltd are related parties and hence disclosure of transaction between them is required irrespective of whether the transaction was done at normal selling price. Hence the contention of Chief Accountant of XYZ Ltd is wrong.

PROBLEM 2

A Firm of father and a son is receiving ₹ 2 lakhs towards job work done for XYZ Ltd. during the year ended on 31-03.2023. The total job Work Charges paid by XYZ Ltd. during the year are over ₹ 50 lakhs. The father is a Managing Director of XYZ Ltd. having 20% holding. The Managing Director told the Auditor that since he is not involved in the activities of the Firm and since the amount paid to son is insignificant, there is no need to disclose the transaction. He further contended that such a payment made in the last year was not disclosed. Is Managing Director right in his approach?

SOLUTION:

As per AS 18, the Firm is Related Party since significant influence may be exercised by M.D Disclosures are applicable in the case. The arguments put forth by the MD 'No involvement of MD in the Firm's Activities, Non-disclosure in last financial year etc.) are not relevant at all.

PROBLEM 3

(i) Mr. X is Managing Director of A Ltd. and also holds 51% capital of B Ltd.

(ii) Mr. Y a relative of Managing Director, received remuneration of ₹ 2,10,000 for his services in the company for the period from 1st April, 2022 to 30th June, 2022. He left the service on 1st July, 2022. Should the relative be identified as a related party as on closing date i.e. on 31-3-2023 for the purpose of AS-18.

(iii) PQR Limited enter into an agreement with Mr. Zenny for running a business for a fixed amount payable to the later every year. The contract states that the day-to-day management of the business will be handled by Mr. Zenny, while all financial and operating policy decisions are taken by the Board of Directors of the Company. Mr. Zenny does not own any voting power in PQR Limited.

You are required to suggest how the above transactions will be treated as at the closing date i.e. on 31st March, 2023 for the purposes of AS 18- Related Party Disclosures.

SOLUTION

(i) Mr. X is Key management personnel as he has the authority for planning, directing and controlling the activities of A Ltd. He also holds substantial interest in B Ltd. as he holds

51% capital of B Ltd. Thus, Mr. X is related party for both A Ltd. and B Ltd. Moreover, as per the definition of related party relationship described in para 3 of AS 18, enterprises over which Mr. X is able to exercise significant influence are also related parties. Thus, A Ltd. and B Ltd. will also be construed as related to each other.

(ii) According to AS 18 'Related Party Disclosures', parties are considered to be related if at any time during the reporting period, one party has the ability to control the other party or exercise significant influence over the other party in making financial and/or operating decisions.

Hence, Mr. Y a relative of key management personnel should be identified as related party as at the closing date i.e. on 31.3.2023 as he received remuneration for his services in the company from 1st April,2022 to 30th June, 2022 and this period comes under the reporting period.

(iii) Mr. Zenny will not be considered as a related party of PQR Limited in view of provisions of AS 18 "Related Party Disclosures" which states, "individuals owning, directly or indirectly, an interest in the voting power of the reporting enterprise that gives them control or significant influence over the enterprise, and relatives of any such individual are related parties".

In the given case, in the absence of share ownership, Mr. Zenny would not be considered to exercise significant influence on PQR Limited, even though there is an agreement giving him the power to manage the company. Further, the fact that Mr. Zenny does not have the ability to direct or instruct the board of directors does not qualify him as a key management personnel.

PROBLEM 4

Following transactions are disclosed as on 31st March, 2023:

Goods sold amounting to ₹ 50 lakhs to associate company during the 1st quarter ended on 30th June, 2022. After that related party relationship ceased to exist. However, goods were supplied as was supplied to any other ordinary customer.

Decide whether transactions of the entire year have to be disclosed as related party transactions.

SOLUTION

As per provision of AS 18, the transactions only for the period in which related party relationships exist need to be reported.

Hence, transactions of the entity with its associate company for the first quarter ending 30.06.2022 only are required to be disclosed as related party transactions. Transactions of the entire year need not be disclosed as related party transactions and transactions for the period (after 1st July) in which related party relationship did not exist need not be reported.

Hence transaction of sale of goods with the associate company for first quarter ending 30th June, 2022 for ₹ 50 Lakhs only are required to be disclosed as related party transaction on 31.3.2023.

VERY SHORT ANSWER TYPE QUESTIONS

1. **Briefly explain the following:**
   (a) Objective of AS 18
   (b) Meaning of Control as per AS 18
   (c) Significant Influence as per AS 18
2. **Enumerate the following:**
   (a) the cases in which disclosure as per AS 18 is not required.

(b) Related party relationships to which Related party disclosures are applicable as per AS 18

(c) disclosure required under AS-18

3. When would the parties be considered as related as per AS 18?

SHORT ANSWER TYPE PRACTICAL QUESTIONS

1. Mr Buffet is a Managing Director of XYZ Ltd. Miss Massom, his daughter recently qualified CA is appointed as finance officer at a remuneration of ₹ 3,00,000 per month. Mr Anupam,his son supplied Goods for ₹ 150 lakhs and ₹ 200 lakhs during the 1st quarter ended on 30th June, 2022 and the 2nd quarter ended on 30th Sept, 2022 on the same terms of other Suppliers of the company. Mr Buffet left the company on 30th June, 2022. Miss Massom left the service on 30th Sept, 2022. You are required to suggest how these transactions will be treated as at the closing date i.e. on 31st March, 2023 for the purposes of AS 18- Related Party Disclosures.

[**Ans** As per provision of AS 18, the transactions only for the period in which related party relationships exist need to be reported. Transactions for the period (on 1st July onwards since Mr Buffet left the company on 30th June, 2022) in which related party relationship did not exist need not be reported.]

2. XYZ Limited enter into an agreement with Mr. P for running a business for a fixed amount payable to the later every year. The contract states that the day-to-day management of the business will be handled by Mr. P, while all financial and operating policy decisions are taken by the Board of Directors of the Company. Mr. P does not own any voting power in XYZ Limited.

[**Ans** Mr. P will not be considered as a related party]

3. X Ltd. holds 51% of Y Ltd.,Y Ltd holds 51% of W Ltd.,Z Ltd holds 49% of W Ltd. Identify the Related Parties as per AS-18.

[**Ans** X Ltd., Y Ltd. & W Ltd. are related to each other. Z Ltd. & W Ltd. are related to each other by virtue of Associate relationship. However, neither X Ltd. nor Y Ltd. is related to Z Ltd. and vice versa]

4. X Ltd. holds 50% of Y Ltd.,Y Ltd holds 40% of W Ltd., W Ltd holds 50% of Z Ltd. Identify the Related Parties as per AS-18.

[**Ans** X Ltd., Y Ltd. & W Ltd. are related to each other. Y Ltd. , Z Ltd. & W Ltd. are related to each other by virtue of Associate relationship. However, X Ltd. is not related to Z Ltd. and vice versa]

5. P Ltd. has 60% voting right in Q Ltd. Q Ltd. has 20% voting right in R Ltd. Also, P Ltd. directly enjoys voting right of 8% in R Ltd. R Ltd. is a listed company and regularly supplies goods to P Ltd.The management of R Ltd. has not disclosed its relationship with P Ltd. How would you assess the situation from the viewpoint of AS 18 on Related Party Disclosures?

[**Ans** control of P Ltd. in R Ltd. directly and through Q Ltd., is 20%.As R Ltd. is a listed company and regularly supplies goods to P Ltd. therefore, related party disclosure, as per AS 18, is required.]

6. Identify the related parties in the following cases as per AS-18

X Ltd. holds 61 % shares of Y Ltd.

Y Ltd. holds 51 % shares of Z Ltd.

W Ltd. holds 49% shares of Z Ltd.

Give your SOLUTION- Reporting Entity wise for X Ltd., Y Ltd., W Ltd. and Z Ltd.

[**Ans** (a)Reporting entity- X Ltd.: Y Ltd. (subsidiary) and Z Ltd.(subsidiary) are related parties. (b) Reporting entity- Y Ltd.:• X Ltd. (holding company) and Z Ltd.(subsidiary) are related parties.(c) Reporting entity- Z Ltd.:• X Ltd. (holding company) , Y Ltd. (holding company) and W

Ltd. (investor/ investing party) are related parties. (d) Reporting entity- W Ltd.:Z Ltd. (associate) is a related party]

7. If a majority of directors of X Ltd. constitute the majority of the board of directors of Y Ltd. in their individual capacity as professional (and not by the virtue of their being directors in X Ltd.), can it be considered that the companies are related? **[Ans** No]

8. XYZ Ltd. sold goods for ₹ 90 lakhs to PQR Ltd. during financial year ended 31-3-2023. The Managing Director of XYZ Ltd. own 100% of PQR Ltd. The sales were made to PQR Ltd. at normal selling prices followed by XYZ Ltd. The Chief accountant of XYZ Ltd contends that these sales need not require a different treatment from the other sales made by the company and hence no disclosure is necessary as per the accounting standard. Is the Chief Accountant correct?

[Ans XYZ Ltd. and PQR Ltd are related parties]

9. A Firm of father and a son is receiving ₹ 2 lakhs towards job work done for XYZ Ltd. during the year ended on 31-03.2023. The total job Work Charges paid by XYZ Ltd. during the year are over ₹ 50 lakhs. The father is a Managing Director of XYZ Ltd. having 20% holding. The Managing Director told the Auditor that since he is not involved in the activities of the Firm and since the amount paid to son is insignificant, there is no need to disclose the transaction. He further contended that such a payment made in the last year was not disclosed. Is Managing Director right in his approach?

[Ans No]

10. (i) Mr. X is Managing Director of A Ltd. and also holds 51% capital of B Ltd.

(ii) Mr. Y a relative of Managing Director, received remuneration of ₹ 2,10,000 for his services in the company for the period from 1st April, 2022 to 30th June, 2022. He left the service on 1st July, 2022. Should the relative be identified as a related party as on closing date i.e. on 31-3-2023 for the purpose of AS-18.

(iii) PQR Limited enter into an agreement with Mr. Zenny for running a business for a fixed amount payable to the later every year. The contract states that the day-to-day management of the business will be handled by Mr. Zenny, while all financial and operating policy decisions are taken by the Board of Directors of the Company. Mr. Zenny does not own any voting power in PQR Limited.

You are required to suggest how the above transactions will be treated as at the closing date i.e. on 31st March, 2023 for the purposes of AS 18- Related Party Disclosures.

[Ans (i) Mr. X is related party for both A Ltd. and B Ltd. (ii) Mr. Y a relative of key management personnel should be identified as related party (iii) Mr. Zenny will not be considered as a related party]

11. Following transactions are disclosed as on 31st March, 2023:

Goods sold amounting to ₹ 50 lakhs to associate company during the 1st quarter ended on 30th June, 2022. After that related party relationship ceased to exist. However, goods were supplied as was supplied to any other ordinary customer.

Decide whether transactions of the entire year have to be disclosed as related party transactions.

[Ans As per provision of AS 18, the transactions only for the period in which related party relationships exist need to be reported. Transactions for the period in which related party relationship did not exist need not be reported.]

11 CASH FLOW STATEMENT

LEARNING OBJECTIVES

After studying this chapter, you should be able to understand:

- Meaning of Cash Flow Statement
- Objectives of Cash Flow Statement
- Uses/Advantages of Cash Flow Statement
- Limitations of Cash Flow Statement
- What is meant by the term 'Cash Flows'?
- Cash and Cash Equivalents
- Operating Activities
- Investing Activities
- Financial Activities
- Practical Steps involved in the Preparation of Cash Flow Statement

1.0 MEANING OF CASH FLOW STATEMENT

The Cash Flow Statement means the Statement of Changes in Cash and Cash equivalents during a particular accounting period. It shows:

1. Net Cash flows from Operating Activities;
2. Net Cash flows from Investing Activities;
3. Net Cash flows from Financing Activities;
4. Net Change in Cash and Cash Equivalents.

Notes:

1. *Cash Flow Statement is **not a substitute for Income Statement** because it does not disclose the calculation of Profit or Loss.*
2. *Cash Flow Statement is **not a substitute for Position Statement(Balance Sheet)** because it does not disclose the Total Financial Position [i.e. Total Equity,Non-Current Liabilities, Current Liabilities, Non-Current Assets and Current Assets].*
3. *Cash Flow Statement is historical in nature because it is prepared on the basis of Historical Financial Statements.*

2.0 OBJECTIVES OF CASH FLOW STATEMENT

The objectives of Cash Flow Statement are as follows:

1. **To ascertain Net Cash Flows from Operating, Investing and Financing Activities of an enterprise**

2. **To ascertain the Net Change in Cash & Cash Equivalents** indicating the aggregate of Net Cash Flows from Operating, Investing and Financing Activities of an enterprise between the dates of two consecutive Balance Sheets.

3.0 USES/ADVANTAGES OF CASH FLOW STATEMENT

The various uses of Cash Flow Statement are as follows:

1. **Facilitates to ascertain Net Cash flows:** Cash Flow Statement facilitates to ascertain Net Cash Flows from Operating, Investing and Financing Activities and Net Change in Cash and Cash Equivalents.
2. **Facilitates to evaluate Cash Financial Performance:** It facilitates to evaluate Cash Financial Performance by providing information on Net Cash flows from Operating Activities.
3. **Facilitates to evaluate Cash Financial Position:** It facilitates to evaluate Cash Financial Position by providing information on Net Cash flows from investing Activities and Financing Activities.
4. **Facilitates Efficient Cash Management.:** The management can know the situation of shortage *or* surplus cash and can plan for the effective use of surplus cash *or* can make the necessary arrangement in case of an shortage of cash.
5. **Facilitates Comparison:** It facilitates the comparative study of the operating performance of different enterprises because it eliminates the effects of using different accounting treatments for the same transactions and events.
6. **Facilitates Capital Budgeting Decisions:** It facilitates Capital Budgeting Decisions by providing information on Net Cash flows from Investing Activities .
7. **Facilitates Capital Structure Decisions:** It facilitates Capital Structure Decisions by providing information on Net Cash flows from Financing Activities.
8. **Facilitates Planning:** The Projected Cash Flow Statement enables the management to plan its future investments, operating and financial activities such as the repayment of long-term loans and interest thereon, modernisation *or* expansion of plant, payment of cash dividend etc.
9. **Answers to some of the important financial questions:** As a tool of historical analysis, it provides an answer to some of the important financial questions such as:
   (i) How was it possible to distribute dividend in excess of current earnings *or* in the presence of a net loss for the period?
   (ii) Why has the cash decreased although the net income for the period has gone up?
   (iii) Why has the cash increased even though there has been a net loss for the period?
   (iv) What happened to the proceeds of the sale of land and equipments?
   (v) Why did the firm resort to long-term borrowings inspite of large profits?
   (vi) Why did the firm issue new equity *or* preference shares?
   (vii) How was the retirement of long-term debts *or* redemption of redeemable preference shares accomplished?

4.0 LIMITATIONS OF CASH FLOW STATEMENT

The major limitations of Cash Flow Statement are as follows:

1. Ignores Non-cash transactions	It ignores the non-cash transactions. In other words, it does not take into consideration those transactions which do not affect the cash ***For Example***, Issue of Shares against the purchase of Fixed Assets *or* Stock-in-trade, Conversion of Debentures into Shares.

2. Secondary Data Based Statement	It is a secondary data based statement. It merely rearranges the primary data already appearing in other statements viz., Income Statement and Balance Sheet.
3. Historical Statement	It is basically historical in nature because it is prepared on the basis of Historical Financial Statements.
4. Ignores Accrual Concept	It ignores the Fundamental Assumption of Accrual.

5.0 WHAT IS MEANT BY THE TERM 'CASH FLOWS'?

MEANING OF CASH FLOWS

Cash Flows are inflows and outflows of Cash and Cash equivalents.

MEANING OF CASH INFLOWS

Cash Inflow arises when the net effect of transaction is increase in the amount of **Cash *or* Cash Equivalents.**

MEANING OF CASH OUTFLOWS

Cash Outflow arises when the net effect of transaction is decrease in the amount of **Cash *or* Cash Equivalents.**

EXAMPLES OF CASH FLOWS

Cash Inflows	***Cash Outflows***
1. Cash Sales of Goods	1. Cash Purchases of Goods
2. Cash received from Trade Debtors	2. Cash paid to Trade Creditors
3. Cash received from commission & Royalty	3. Operating Expenses paid (e.g. Salaries & Wages, Administration Exp. Selling Exp.)
4. Sale of Fixed Assets for Cash	4. Income Tax paid
5. Sale of Investments (whether Current *or* Non-Current) for Cash	5. Cash Purchase of Fixed Assets
6. Loans & Advances repayment received (whether Short term *or* Long term)	6. Cash Purchase of Investments (whether Short term *or* Long term)
7. Income received on Investments (whether Current *or* Non-Current)	7. Loans & Advances granted (whether Short term *or* Long term)
8. Issue of Equity Shares for Cash	8. Buy-back of Equity Shares for Cash
9. Issue of Preference Shares for Cash	9. Redemption of Preference Shares for Cash
10. Issue of Debentures for Cash	10. Redemption of Debentures for Cash
11. Loans taken (whether Short term *or* Long term)	11. Loans repaid (whether Short term *or* Long term)
	12. Interest on Debentures & Loans paid. (whether Short term *or* Long term)
	13. Final Dividend on Equity Shares paid.
	14. Dividend on Preference Shares paid.
	15. Interim Dividend on Equity Shares paid.

6.0 CASH AND CASH EQUIVALENTS

THE TERM 'CASH'

Meaning	Cash comprises Cash on hand and Demand Deposits with banks.
Examples	Cash in hand, Cash at Bank

THE TERM 'CASH EQUIVALENTS'

Meaning	Cash Equivalents are short term, highly liquid investments that are readily convertible into known amounts of cash and which are subject to an insignificant risk of changes in value.
Purpose	Cash Equivalents are held for the purpose of meeting short-term cash commitments rather than for Investment *or* other purposes.
Two Conditions for an Investment to qualify as a Cash Equivalent	1. It must be readily convertible to a known amount of cash. 2. It must be subject to an insignificant risk of changes in value. Therefore, an investment normally qualifies as a cash equivalent only when it has a **short maturity of, say, 3 months *or* less from the date of acquisition.**
Examples	Treasury Bills, Commercial Papers, Commercial Bills, Call Money, Certificate of Deposit

7.0 TRANSACTIONS NOT CONSIDERED AS CASH FLOWS

Meaning	Transactions which represent movements between items of Cash *or* Cash Equivalents are not considered as Cash Flows.
Reason	These components are part of the cash management of an enterprise rather than part of its Operating, Investing and Financing Activities.
Examples	1. Cash deposited into Bank; 2. Cash withdrawn from Bank; 3. Purchase/Sale of Short-term Marketable Securities (neither held as Current Investments nor held as Non-current Investments).

8.0 NON-CASH TRANSACTIONS

Meaning	Non-Cash transactions are those transactions which do not involve Cash.
Examples [Verification by Journal Entry]	**1. Issue of Equity Shares *or* Debentures against the purchase of an Asset** **JOURNAL ENTRY** Asset A/c Dr To Equity Share Capital A/c/Debentures A/c **2. Issue of Equity Shares on conversion of Convertible Debentures** **JOURNAL ENTRY** Convertible Debentures A/c Dr To Equity Share Capital A/c

	3. Charging of Depreciation on a Fixed Tangible Asset **JOURNAL ENTRY** Depreciation A/c Dr To Fixed Tangible Asset A/c **4. Amortization of a Fixed Intangible Asset** **JOURNAL ENTRY** Profit & Loss A/c Dr To Intangible Asset A/c **5. Written off of an old Fixed Tangible Asset** **JOURNAL ENTRY** Profit & Loss A/c Dr To Fixed Tangible Asset A/c **6. Declaration of Final Dividend on Shares** **JOURNAL ENTRY:** Proposed Dividend A/c Dr To Dividend Payable A/c
Why ignored in CFS?	Non-Cash transactions are ignored while preparing Cash Flow Statement because these do not involve Cash.

9.0 OPERATING ACTIVITIES

MEANING OF OPERATING ACTIVITIES

Operating Activities are the principal revenue-producing activities of the enterprise and other activities that are not investing *or* financing activities.

EXAMPLES OF CASH FLOWS FROM OPERATING ACTIVITIES

Cash Inflows	*Cash Outflows*
1. Cash Sales of Goods	1. Cash Purchases of Goods
2. Cash received from Trade Debtors	2. Cash paid to Trade Creditors
3. Cash received from Trading Commission & Royalty	3. Operating Expenses paid (e.g. Salaries & Wages, Administration Exp. Selling Exp.)
	4. Income Tax (related to Operating Activities only) paid.

TUTORIAL NOTE

In case of Financial Enterprises the following activities are classified as Operating Activities since they relate to the main revenue-producing activity of that enterprise:

1. *Purchases and Sales of Shares & Debentures of other companies for Cash*
2. *Dividend received on Shares of other companies*
3. *Interest received on Debentures of other companies*
4. *Loans & Advances granted*
5. *Interest received on Loans & Advances granted*

DISTINCTION BETWEEN NET PROFIT AND CASH FROM OPERATING ACTIVITIES

Basis of Distinction	*Net Profit*	*Cash from Operating Activities*
1. Meaning	It indicates the net result of Operating & non-operating activities carried out during an accounting year.	It indicates the Cash Flow as a result of operating activities.
2. Non-Cash Operating Item (Depreciation)	It is calculated **after taking into account the effect of non-cash operating items.**	It is calculated **excluding the effect of non-cash operating items** since these items merely represent the book entries.
3. Non-Operating Items	It is calculated **after taking into account the effect of non-operating items.**	It is calculated **excluding the effect of non-operating items** since these items do not relate to operating activities.

10.0 INVESTING ACTIVITIES

MEANING OF INVESTING ACTIVITIES

Investing Activities are the acquisition and disposal of Long-term Assets and other Investments not included in Cash Equivalents.

EXAMPLES OF INVESTING ACTIVITIES

Cash Inflows	*Cash Outflows*
1. Cash Sale of Fixed Assets	1. Cash Purchase of Fixed Assets
2. Cash Sale of Investments (whether Current *or* Non-Current)	2. Cash Purchase of Investments (whether Short term *or* Long term)
3. Loans & Advances repayment received (whether Short term *or* Long term)	3. Loans & Advances granted (whether Short term *or* Long term)
4. Income received on Investments (whether Current *or* Non-Current)	4. Brokerage paid on Purchase of Investments (whether Short term *or* Long term)

11.0 FINANCING ACTIVITIES

MEANING OF FINANCING ACTIVITIES

Financing Activities are activities that result in changes in the size and composition of the Owners' Capital (including Preference Share Capital in the case of a company) and Borrowings (whether Short term *or* Long term) of the enterprise.

EXAMPLES OF FINANCING ACTIVITIES

Cash Inflows	*Cash Outflows*
1. Issue of Equity Shares for Cash	1. Buy-back of Equity Shares for Cash.
2. Issue of Preference Shares for Cash	2. Redemption of Preference Shares for Cash.
3. Issue of Debentures for Cash	3. Redemption of Debentures for Cash
4. Loans taken (whether for short-term *or* long-term)	4. Loans repaid (whether Short term *or* Long term)

5. Interest received on Calls-in-arrears. (whether Short term *or* Long term).	5. Interest on Debentures & Loans paid 6. Final Dividend on Equity Shares paid 7. Dividend on Preference Shares paid 8. Interim Dividend on Equity Shares paid 9. Brokerage & Underwriting commission paid on Issue of Shares & Debentures.

ILLUSTRATION 1

Classify the following activities as (i) Operating Activities; (ii) Investing Activities; (iii) Financing Activities:

(i)	Purchase of Machinery	(vi)	Receipt of Dividend
(ii)	Sale of Land	(vii)	Payment of Interest on Debenture
(iii)	Payment of Income Tax	(viii)	Receipt of Interest on Debenture
(iv)	Refund of Income Tax	(ix)	Issue of Debentures
(v)	Payment of Dividend	(x)	Buy-back of Equity Shares

SOLUTION

(i)	Investing Activity,	(ii)	Investing Activity
(iii)	Operating Activity,	(iv)	Operating Activity
(v)	Financing Activity,	(vi)	Investing Activity
(vii)	Financing Activity,	(viii)	Investing Activity
(ix)	Financial Activity,	(x)	Financing Activity

ILLUSTRATION 2

Classify the following activities as (a) Operating Activities, (b) Investing Activities, (c) Financing Activities, (d) Cash *or* Cash Equivalents.

1. Purchase of Machinery	21. Dividend received on Shares
2. Issue of Equity Share Capital	22. Rent received on property
3. Cash Sales	23. Selling & Distribution Exp paid
4. Interest on Short-term Borrowings	24. Income Tax paid
5. Sale of Machinery	25. Dividend paid on Pref. Shares
6. Cash receipts from Debtors	26. Underwriting Commission paid
7. Commission and Royalty received	27. Rent paid
8. Purchase of Current Investments	28. Brokerage paid on issue of shares
9. Redemption of Preference shares	29. Brokerage paid on purchase of Investments
10. Cash Purchases of Goods	30. Bank Overdraft
11. Sale of Investments	31. Cash Credit
12. Purchase of Goodwill	32. Short-term Deposits having maturity of 3 months
13. Cash paid to suppliers of Goods.	
14. Interim Dividend paid on Equity Shares	33. Marketable Securities having maturity of 3 months
15. Wages & Salaries paid	

16. Sale of Patents	34. Refund of Income Tax received
17. Interest received on Debentures held as Investments	35. Discount allowed to customers
	36. Discount received from Suppliers
18. Interest paid on borrowings	37. Purchase of Marketable Securities having maturity of 6 months
19. Office & Adm. Expenses paid	
20. Manufacturing Overheads paid	

SOLUTION

CLASSIFICATION OF ACTIVITIES

(a) Operating Activities	3, 6, 7, 10, 13, 15, 19, 20, 23, 24, 27, 34, 35, 36
(b) Investing Activities	1, 5, 8, 11, 12, 16, 17, 21, 22, 29, 37
(c) Financing Activities	2, 4, 9, 14, 18, 25, 26, 28, 30, 31
(d) Cash *or* Cash Equivalents	32, 33

ILLUSTRATION 3

Classify the following activities as (i) Operating Activities; (ii) Investing Activities; (iii) Financing Activities in case of (a) a Manufacturing Enterprise; (b) a Financial Enterprise.

1. Purchase of Shares of other companies.
2. Proceeds from Sale of Shares of other companies.
3. Brokerage paid on purchase & sale of Shares.
4. Interest received on Debentures.
5. Dividend received on shares.
6. Loans & Advances made to third parties.
7. Receipts from the repayments of loans & advances made to third parties.
8. Receipt of Interest on loans & advances made to third parties.

SOLUTION

(a) In case of a **Manufacturing Enterprise**, all the given activities are **Investing Activities** since they relate to acquisition and disposal of long-term assets.

(b) In case of a **Financial Enterprise**, all the given activities are **Operating Activities** since they relate to the main revenue-producing activity of the enterprise.

ILLUSTRATION 4

Classify the following activities as (i) Operating Activities; (ii) Investing Activities; (iii) Financing Activities in case of (a) Manufacturing Enterprise; (b) a Real Estate Enterprise.

1. Purchase of Land.
2. Purchase of Building.
3. Sale of Land.
4. Sale of Building.
5. Brokerage paid on purchase and sale of Land & Building.
6. Rent received from a Building.
7. Payment of Construction Cost of a Building.

SOLUTION

(a) In case of a **Manufacturing Enterprise**, all the given activities are **Investing Activities** since they relate to acquisition and disposal of long-term assets.

(b) In case of a **Real Estate Enterprise**, all the given activities are **Operating Activities** since they relate to the main revenue-producing activity of the enterprise.

ILLUSTRATION 5

When is Dividend received considered as Operating Activity?

SOLUTION

Dividend received by a Financial Enterprise is considered as Operating Activity.

ILLUSTRATION 6

Classify the following into Operating, Investing and Financing Activities:

(a) Refund of Income Tax

(b) Sale of Shares & Debentures of other companies by a Finance Co

(c) Dividend on Shares and Interest on Debentures paid by a Mutual Fund Company

(d) Dividend on Shares and Interest on Debentures received by a Bank.

(e) Payment of Brokerage on Purchase of Shares of a Finance Company.

SOLUTION

(a) Operating Activity (b) Operating Activity (c) Financing Activity

(d) Investing Activity (e) Investing Activity

ILLUSTRATION 7

If you want neither Inflow nor Outflow of Cash, which of the following transactions will you select?

(a) A Long-term Loan from Bank

(b) Goodwill written off

(c) Issue of Equity Shares *or* Debentures against the purchase of a Fixed Asset

(d) Issue of Equity shares on conversion of Debentures

(e) Cash deposited into Bank

(f) Cash withdrawn from Bank

(g) Charging Depreciation on Furniture

(h) Declaration of Final Dividend

(i) Purchase of Stock-in-trade on credit

SOLUTION

(b) to (i)

ILLUSTRATION 8

Mention the net amount of 'Source' *or* 'Use' of Cash in the following cases:

1. When Fixed asset (having book value of ₹ 15,000) is sold at a loss of ₹ 5,000.

2. When Goods costing ₹ 10,000 are sold for ₹ 15,000.
3. When ₹ 19,000 received from a debtor and allowed ₹ 1,000 as discount.
4. When Discount of ₹ 1,000 is received on making payment to a creditor of ₹ 10,000.
5. When Issue of shares for ₹ 7,00,000 against purchase of business comprising of fixed assets ₹ 6,00,000; current assets ₹ 2,00,000 and took over current liabilities ₹ 1,00,000.
6. When Old Furniture (Book value ₹ 1,000) written off.
7. When Deferred Revenue Expenditure (₹ 1,000) charged to Profit.

SOLUTION

1. Source ₹10,000,
2. Source ₹ 15,000,
3. Source ₹19,000,
4. Use ₹ 9,000,
5. Nil because this transaction does not involve Cash.
6. Nil because this transaction does not involve Cash.
7. Nil because this transaction does not involve Cash.

12.0 HOW TO COMPUTE CASH FROM OPERATING ACTIVITIES

The amount of cash from operating activities may be computed by following either the Direct Method *or* the Indirect Method.

HOW TO COMPUTE NET CASH FLOW FROM OPERATING ACTIVITIES (UNDER DIRECT METHOD)

	Particulars	₹	₹
A.	***Operating Receipts in Cash (e.g.)***		
	Cash Sales	XXX	
	Cash receipts from Debtors	XXX	
	Trading Commission received	XXX	XXX
B.	***Operating Payments in Cash (e.g.)***		
	Cash Purchases	XXX	
	Cash paid to Suppliers	XXX	
	Wages & Salaries paid	XXX	
	Office and Administration Expenses paid	XXX	
	Manufacturing Overheads paid	XXX	
	Selling and Distribution Expenses paid	XXX	XXX
C.	Cash generated from Operations before taxes (A – B)		XXX
D.	Income Tax paid (Net of Refund of Tax)		XXX
E.	Cash flow before extraordinary item (C – D)		XXX
F.	Extraordinary item		XXX
G.	Net Cash from (used in) Operating Activities		XXX

ILLUSTRATION 9

From the following particulars, Calculate Cash Flows from Operating Activities:

Particulars	₹	*Particulars*	₹
Cash Sales	2,00,000	Manufacturing Overheads paid	30,000
Cash Purchases	50,000	Office & Administration Exp. paid	20,000
Cash receipts from customers	4,00,000	Selling & Distribution Expenses paid	10,000
Cash paid to suppliers	1,00,000	Income Taxes paid	1,18,000
Trading Commission received	1,00,000	Insurance proceeds from earthquake	
Trading Commission Paid	25,000	disaster settlement	1,00,000
Wages & Salaries paid	40,000	Income Tax Refund received	3,000
Rent paid	10,000		

SOLUTION **CASH FLOW FROM OPERATING ACTIVITIES**

Particulars	₹
A. Operating Receipts in Cash:	
Cash Sales	2,00,000
Cash receipts from customers	4,00,000
Trading Commission received	1,00,000
	7,00,000
B. Operating Payments in Cash:	
Cash Purchases	50,000
Cash paid to suppliers	1,00,000
Trading Commission paid	25,000
Wages & Salaries paid	40,000
Rent paid	10,000
Manufacturing Overheads paid	30,000
Office & Administrative Expenses paid	20,000
Selling & Distribution Expenses paid	10,000
	2,85,000
C. Cash generated from Operations before taxes [A – B]	4,15,000
D. Income Tax paid (Net of refund) [₹ 1,18,000 – ₹ 3,000]	1,15,000
E. Cash flow before extraordinary items	3,00,000
F. Insurance proceeds from earthquake disaster settlement	1,00,000
G. Net Cash from Operating Activities	4,00,000

HOW TO COMPUTE NET CASH FLOW FROM OPERATING ACTIVITIES (UNDER INDIRECT METHOD)

Particulars	₹	₹
Step 1: ***Calculate Net Profit before Taxation and Extraordinary Item as follows:***		
A. Closing Balance of P & L A/c		xxx
Less: Opening Balance of P&L A/c [or *Add:* Opening Bal. of P & L A/c (Dr.)]		xxx
Add: Final Dividend declared during the current year		xxx

Add: Interim Dividend paid during the current year		xxx
Add: Transfer to Reserve [or *Less:* Transfer from Reserve]		xxx
Add: Provision for Tax made during the Current Year		xxx
Less: Refund of Tax credited to P&L A/c		(xxx)
Less: Extraordinary item, if any, credited to P&L A/c (e.g., Insurance proceeds from earthquake disaster settlement)		(xxx)
Add: Extraordinary Debit Items (e.g., Loss due to earthquake)		xxx
B. Net Profit before Taxation and Extraordinary Item		xxx
Step 2: *Calculate Operating Profit before Working Capital Changes as follows:*		
A. Net Profit before Taxation and Extraordinary Item		xxx
B. Adjustments for Non-Cash and Non-Operating Items : (***For Example***)		
Depreciation	xxx	
Interest on Debentures & Loans (whether Short term *or* Long term)	xxx	
Preliminary Expenses/Underwriting Commission/Discount on	xxx	
Issue of Debentures/Shares written off	xxx	
Goodwill/Patents/Trade Marks/Copyright amortised	xxx	
Loss on Sale of Investments (whether Current *or* Non-Current).	xxx	
Premium payable on redemption of Preference shares/Debentures	xxx	
Interest Income from Investments (whether Current *or* Non-Current)	(xxx)	
Dividend Income	(xxx)	
Rental Income	(xxx)	
Profit on Sale of Investments (whether Current *or* Non-Current)	(xxx)	xxx
C. Operating Profit before Working Capital Changes		xxx
Step 3: *Calculate Cash from Operations before Tax & Extraordinary Item as follows:*		
A. Operating Profit before Working Capital Changes		xxx
B. Add: Changes in Operating Current Assets (Excluding Cash and Cash Equivalents) & Operating Current Liabilities (Excluding Bank Overdraft & Cash Credit):		
Decrease in Inventories, Trade Receivables etc.	xxx	
Increase in Trade Payables, O/s Exp. etc.	xxx	
Increase in Inventories, Trade Receivables etc.	(xxx)	
Decrease in Trade Payables, O/s Exp. etc.	(xxx)	xxx
C. Cash generated from Operations		xxx
Step 4: Calculate Cash generated from Operations after Tax but before Extraordinary Item as follows:		
A. Cash generated from Operations		xxx
B. *Less:* Income taxes paid (Including Advance Tax but Excluding Refund of Tax)		(xxx)
[**Note:** Income Tax should be related to Operating Activities only]		
C. Cash Flow before Extraordinary Item		xxx

Step 5: *Calculate Net Cash from (used in) Operating Activities as follows:*	
A. Cash Flow before Extraordinary Items	xxx
B. *Add:* Extraordinary Credit Items (e.g., Insurance proceeds from earthquake disaster settlement, Govt. Grant)	xxx
C. *Less:* Extraordinary Debit Items (e.g., Loss due to earthquake)	(xxx)
D. Net Cash Flow from (used in) Operating Activities	xxx

Note: *Negative items which are to be deducted have been shown in brackets.*

ILLUSTRATION 10

From the following information, calculate Net Profit before Taxation and Extraordinary Item:

Particulars	***Closing*** ₹	***Opening*** ₹
Profit & Loss Account	3,36,000	1,00,000
Reserve	2,22,000	1,10,000

Final Dividend paid during the year	60,000
Interim Dividend paid during the year	90,000
Provision for Tax made during the current year	1,50,000
Refund of Tax	3,000
Loss due to Earthquake	2,00,000
Insurance Proceeds from earthquake disaster settlement	1,00,000

SOLUTION

CALCULATION OF NET PROFIT BEFORE TAXATION AND EXTRAORDINARY ITEM

Particulars	₹
A. Net Profit as per Profit & Loss A/c [₹ 3,36,000 – ₹ 1,00,000]	2,36,000
Add: Final Dividend declared during the year	60,000
Add: Interim Dividend paid during the year	90,000
Add: Transfer to Reserve	1,12,000
Add: Provision for Tax made during the Current Year	1,50,000
Less: Refund of Tax	(3,000)
Add: Extraordinary Item (Loss due to Earthquake)	2,00,000
Less: Extraordinary items (i.e., Insurance proceeds from earthquake disaster settlement)	(1,00,000)
B. Net Profit before Taxation and Extraordinary Item	7,45,000

ILLUSTRATION 11

From the following information, calculate Net Cash Flow from Operating Activities:

Particulars	₹
Net Profit before Taxation and Extraordinary Item	7,45,000
Depreciation	1,40,000
Loss on Sale of Machinery	30,000
Interest on Debentures	24,850
Interest on Bank Loan	6,650
Goodwill amortised	9,000
Preliminary Expenses written off	2,000
Premium on Redemption of Preference Shares	10,000
Interest Income on Non-Current Investments	6,000
Interest Income on Current Investments	2,000
Profit on Sale of Current Investments	5,000
Loss on Sale of Non-Current Investments	10,000
Tax paid during the Current Year	1,18,000
Refund of Tax	3,000
Loss due to Earthquake	2,00,000
Insurance Proceeds from earthquake disaster settlement	1,00,000

POSITION OF CURRENT ASSETS & CURRENT LIABILITIES

Particulars	*Closing (₹)*	*Opening (₹)*
Current Assets:		
Inventories	1,00,000	1,06,000
Trade Receivables	6,70,000	10,000
Current Investments	1,20,000	1,00,000
Accrued Interest on Investments	4,000	3,000
Cash & Cash Equivalents	49,000	30,000
Current Liabilities:	6,70,000	10,000
Trade Payables	1,80,000	25,000
Outstanding Expenses	10,000	14,000
Provision for Taxation	62,000	30,000
Short-term Borrowings	1,00,000	1,20,000
Interest outstanding on Short-term Borrowings	3,000	4,000

SOLUTION

CALCULATION OF OPERATING PROFIT BEFORE WORKING CAPITAL CHANGES

Particulars		₹
A. Net Profit before Taxation and Extraordinary Item		7,45,000
B. *Adjustments for Non-Cash and Non-Operating Items:*		
Depreciation	1,40,000	

	Loss on Sale of Machinery	30,000	
	Interest on Debentures	24,850	
	Interest on Bank Loan	6,650	
	Goodwill amortised	9,000	
	Preliminary Expenses written off	2,000	
	Premium on Redemption of Preference Shares	10,000	
	Interest Income on Non-Current Investments	(6,000)	
	Interest Income on Current Investments	(2,000)	
	Profit on Sale of Current Investments	(5,000)	
	Loss on Sale of Non-Current Investments	10,000	2,19,500
C.	**Operating Profit before Working Capital Changes**		9,64,500
D.	**Changes in Current Assets & Current Liabilities:**		
	Decrease in Inventories	6,000	
	Increase in Trade Payables	1,55,000	
	Increase in Trade Receivables	(6,60,000)	
	Decrease in Outstanding Expenses	(4,000)	(5,03,000)
E.	**Cash generated from operations before Taxes**		4,61,500
F.	*Less:* Income taxes paid (Net of Refund) [₹ 1,18,000 – ₹ 3,000]		(1,15,000)
G.	**Cash Flow before Extraordinary Items**		3,46,500
	Add: Extraordinary items (i.e., Insurance proceeds from earthquake disaster settlement)		1,00,000
	Less: Extraordinary items (i.e., Loss due to earthquake)		(2,00,000)
H.	**Net Cash Inflow from Operating Activities**		2,46,500

ILLUSTRATION 12

From the following particulars, calculate the Net Cash Flow from Operating Activities:

(i) Profit made during the year was ₹ 1,00,000 after considering the following items:

Particulars	₹
(a) Depreciation on fixed assets	4,000
(b) Amortization of goodwill	2,000
(c) Transfer to Reserve	2,800
(d) Profit on Sale of Land	1,700
(e) Loss on Sale of Furniture	500
(f) Provision for Taxation	80,000

(ii) The following is the position of Current Assets and Current Liabilities

Particulars	*Closing (₹)*	*Opening (₹)*
Trade Receivables	6,000	4,800
Trade Payables	4,000	6,000
Inventories	3,200	4,000

Outstanding Expenses	2,400	1,600
Provision for Taxation	80,000	70,000

SOLUTION

CALCULATION OF NET CASH FLOW FROM OPERATING ACTIVITIES

Particulars		₹
Net Profit before Tax		1,82,800
Adjustments for Non-Cash and Non-Operating Items:		
Depreciation	4,000	
Goodwill amortized	2,000	
Loss on sale of Furniture	500	
Profit on sale of Land	(1,700)	4,800
Operating Profit before Working Capital Changes		1,87,600
Changes in Current Assets & Current Liabilities:		
Decrease in Inventories	800	
Increase in Outstanding Expenses	800	
Increase in Trade Receivables	(1,200)	
Decrease in Trade Payables	(2,000)	(1,600)
Cash generated from operations		1,86,000
Less: Income taxes paid (Net of Refund)		(70,000)
Net Cash Inflow from Operating Activities		1,16,000

Working Note:

CALCULATION OF NET PROFIT BEFORE TAX

Net Profit as per Profit & Loss A/c	1,00,000
Add: Transfer to Reserve	2,800
Add: Provision for Tax	80,000
Net Profit before Tax	1,82,800

TREATMENT OF SPECIAL ITEMS WHILE CALCULATING NET PROFIT BEFORE TAX

Item	*Treatment and Reason*	*Remarks*
Increase in General Reserve	**Add back** to Balance of P & L A/c to find out **Net Profit Before Tax** **Reason:** It represents an appropriation out of Current year's profits.	
Decrease in General Reserve	**Subtract** from Balance of P&L A/c to find out **Net Profit Before Tax** **Reason:** It represents utilization of past reserves and not of Current year's profits.	

Provision for Tax for Current Year	**Add back Tax provided** to Balance of P & L A/c to find out **Net Profit Before Tax** **Reason:** It is merely a book entry and does not involve any Cash outflow.	1. If only Opening & Closing amounts of Provision for Tax are given,Take Provision for Tax for Current Year as Tax provided during the current year. 2. **If Tax Paid is also given,** Prepare Provision for Tax Account to ascertain the amount of Tax provided during the current year.
Provision for Tax for Previous Year	**Subtract Tax paid** from Cash from Operating Activities before tax **Reason:** It involves Cash outflow.	1. If only Opening & Closing amounts of Provision for Tax are given, Take Provision for Tax for previous year as Tax paid during the current year. 2. **If Tax provided is also given,** Prepare Provision for Tax Account to ascertain the amount of Tax paid during the current year.
Final Dividend declared during the Current Year	**Add back** to Balance of P & L A/c to find out **Net Profit Before Tax** **Reason:** It represents an appropriation out of Profits.	
Interim Dividend Board of [An Interim Dividend is that dividend which is declared by the Directors for the current year during the current year.]	**Add back** to Balance of P & L A/c to find out **Net Profit Before Tax** **Reason:** It represents an appropriation out of Profits.	
Dividend on Pref. Shares	**Add back** to Balance of P & L A/c to find out **Net Profit Before Tax** **Reason:** It represents an appropriation out of profits.	If the date of Fresh issue / Redemption of Pref. Shares is not given, Calculate Dividend on opening balance of Pref. Shares.

TREATMENT OF SPECIAL ITEMS WHILE CALCULATING CASH FROM OPERATING ACTIVITIES

Item	*Treatment and Reason*	*Remarks*
Depreciation for the Current year	**Add back** to Current year's profits in order to find out Cash from Operating Activities. **Reason:** It does not involve any Cash outflow.	In case of Missing Figure, Prepare Fixed Asset A/c (on WDV Basis) OR Provision for Depreciation A/c to ascertain the amount of Depreciation.
Loss on Sale of Fixed Asset / Investments	**Add back** to Current year's profits in order to find out Cash from Operating Activities. **Reason:** It does not represent an operating cost.	In case of Missing Figure, Prepare Fixed Asset A/c / Investments A/c to ascertain the amount of Loss on Sale.

1. Profit on Sale of Fixed Assets/ Investments **2. Income from Investments (whether Current *or* Non-Current)**	**Subtract** from Current year's profits in order to find out Cash from Operating Activities. **Reason:** It does not represent an operating income.	In case of Missing Figure, Prepare Fixed Asset A/c Investments A/c to ascertain the amount of Profit on Sale.
Goodwill/Patents Amortized	**Add back** to Current year's profits in order to find out Cash from Operating Activities. **Reason:** It merely represents a book entry and does not involve any Cash flow.	
Preliminary Expenses/Discount on issue of Debentures written off	**Add back** to Current year's profits in order to find out Cash from Operating Activities. **Reason:** It merely represents a book entry and does not involve any Cash flow.	
Interest on Debentures/Loans (whether disclosed as Current *or* Non-Current)	**Add back** to Current year's profits in order to find out Cash from Operating Activities. **Reason:** It does not represent an operating cost.	If the date of Fresh issue/ Redemption of Debentures is not given, Calculate Interest on opening balance of Debentures.
Premium on Redemption of Debentures/ Pref. Shares	**Add back** to Current year's profits in order to find out Cash from Operating Activities. **Reason:** It does not represent an operating cost.	
Increase in Provision for Doubtful Debts	**Add like** an Increase in Current Liability	
Decrease in Provision for Doubtful Debts	**Subtract like** a Decrease in Current Liability	
Increase in Inventories, Trade Receivables/ Payables against issue of Shares/ Debentures	Exclude from Respective Closing Balances **Reason:** These do not involve any cash flow.	

ILLUSTRATION 13

From the following particulars, Calculate the Net Cash Flow from Operating Activities:

Particulars	*Closing* ₹	*Opening* ₹
Profit and Loss A/c	7,000	1,000
General Reserve	40,000	31,000

Provision for Taxation	25,000	15,000
10% Debentures	25,000	21,000
Trade Payables	1,17,500	8,500
Machinery	44,000	50,000
Goodwill	8,000	10,000
Discount on issue of Debentures	—	200
Current Investments	8,000	3,000
Inventories	24,500	6,000
Trade Receivables	1,12,300	7,300
Cash & Cash Equivalents	17,700	0

Income tax paid during the year ₹ 20,000. Dividend paid during the year ₹ 21,000.

SOLUTION

CALCULATION OF NET CASH FLOW FROM OPERATING ACTIVITIES

Particulars	₹	₹
Net Profit before Tax		66,000
Adjustments for Non-Cash and Non-Operating Items :		
Depreciation	6,000	
Discount on issue of Debentures	200	
Goodwill Amortised	2,000	
Interest on Debentures [₹ 21,000 × 10%]	2,100	10,300
Operating Profit before Working Capital Changes		76,300
Changes in Current Assets & Current Liabilities:		
Increase in Trade Payables	1,09,000	
Increase in Inventories	(18,500)	
Increase in Trade Receivables	(1,05,000)	(14,500)
Cash generated from operations		61,800
Less: Income taxes paid		(20,000)
Net Cash Inflow from Operating Activities		41,800

Working Notes:

1. CALCULATION OF NET PROFIT BEFORE TAX

A. Closing balance as per Profit & Loss A/c:	7,000
Less: Opening Balance as per Profit & Loss A/c	1,000
Add: Dividend declared	21,000
Add: Transfer to Reserve	9,000
Add: Provision for Tax for current year	30,000
B. Net Profit before Tax	66,000

2. *It has been assumed that new Debentures have been issued at the end of current accounting year*

Dr. **3. PROVISION FOR TAX ACCOUNT** Cr.

Particulars	₹	Particulars	₹
To Bank A/c	20,000	By Balance b/d	15,000
To Balance c/d	25,000	By P & L A/c (balancing figure)	30,000
	45,000		45,000

ILLUSTRATION 14

From the following particulars, Calculate the Net Cash Flow from Operating Activities:

Particulars	Closing ₹	Opening ₹
Profit & Loss A/c	7,000	1,000 (Dr)
General Reserve	35,000	36,000
Provision for Taxation	25,000	15,000
15% Debentures	34,000	22,000
Trade Payables	22,000	24,000
Fixed Assets (Gross)	74,000	74,000
Accumulated Depreciation	30,000	24,000
10% Current Investments	20,000	10,000
Trade Receivables (Gross)	48,400	15,000
Provision for Doubtful Debts	10,000	5,000
Inventories	15,000	25,000
Cash & Cash Equivalents	5,600	1,000

Income tax provided during the year ₹ 30,000. Dividend paid during the year ₹ 21,000.

SOLUTION

CALCULATION OF NET CASH FLOW FROM OPERATING ACTIVITIES

Particulars	₹	₹
Net Profit before Tax		58,000
Adjustments for Non-Cash and Non-Operating Items :		
Depreciation [₹ 30,000 – ₹ 24,000]		6,000
Interest on Debentures [₹ 22,000 × 15/100]		3,300
Interest Income on Current Investments		(1,000)
Operating Profit before Working Capital Changes		53,800
Changes in Current Assets & in Current Liabilities:		
Decrease in Inventories	10,000	
Increase in Trade Receivables (Gross)	(33,400)	
Increase in Provision for Doubtful Debts	5,000	
Decrease in Trade Payables	(2,000)	(20,400)

Cash generated from operations before tax	33,400
Less: Income taxes paid	(20,000)
Net Cash Inflow from Operating Activities	13,400

Working Notes:

1. CALCULATION OF NET PROFIT BEFORE TAX

Particulars	₹
A. Closing Balance as per Profit & Loss A/c	7,000
Add: Opening Balance as per Profit & Loss A/c (Dr)	1,000
Add: Dividend declared	21,000
Less: Transfer to Reserve	(1,000)
Add: Provision for Tax	30,000
B. Net Profit before Tax	58,000

Dr. **2. PROVISION FOR TAX ACCOUNT** *Cr.*

Particulars	₹	***Particulars***	₹
To Bank A/c (balancing figure)	20,000	By Balance b/d	15,000
To Balance c/d	25,000	By P & L A/c	30,000
	45,000		45,000

3. *It has been assumed that new Debentures have been issued at the end of current accounting year.*

4. *It has been assumed that new Current Investments have been acquired at the end of current accounting year.*

ILLUSTRATION 15

From the following information, calculate the Net Cash Flow from Operating Activities:

Particulars	***Closing*** ₹	***Opening*** ₹
Equity Share Capital	4,00,000	3,00,000
15% Preference Share Capital	1,00,000	1,50,000
General Reserve	1,20,000	82,000
Profit and Loss A/c	48,000	30,000
Provision for Tax	50,000	40,000
Trade Payables	1,22,000	88,000
Property,Plant & Equipment	3,70,000	2,80,000
Intangible Assets [Goodwill]	90,000	1,15,000
Trade Receivables & Inventories	3,39,000	2,57,000

During the year a machine costing ₹ 50,000 (depreciation provided thereon ₹ 30,000) was sold for ₹ 10,000. A machine was purchased for ₹ 1,30,000. Interim Dividend paid, ₹ 20,000, Income-tax, ₹ 35,000 paid. Dividend paid during the year ₹ 42,000.

SOLUTION

CALCULATION OF NET CASH FLOW FROM OPERATING ACTIVITIES

Particulars	₹	₹
I. Cash Flow from Operating Activities		
A. Net Profit before tax		1,63,000
B. *Adjustments for Non-Cash and Non-Operating Items :*		
Depreciation	20,000	
Loss on Sale of Machinery	10,000	
Goodwill amortised	25,000	55,000
C. Operating Profit before Working Capital Changes		2,18,000
D. Changes in Current Assets & Current Liabilities:		
Increase in Trade Payables	34,000	
Increase in Trade Receivables & Inventories	(82,000)	(48,000)
E. Net Cash Flow from Operating Activities before Tax		1,70,000
F. *Less:* Tax paid		(35,000)
G. Net Cash Inflow from Operating Activities after Tax		1,35,000

Working Notes:

1. CALCULATION OF NET PROFIT BEFORE TAX

Particulars	₹
Closing Balance of P&L A/c	48,000
Less: Opening Balance of P&L A/c	(30,000)
Add: Transfer to Reserve	38,000
Add: Dividend declared	42,000
Add: Interim Dividend on Equity Shares	20,000
Add: Tax	45,000
Net Profit before Tax	1,63,000

Dr. **2. PROPERTY, PLANT & EQUIPMENT ACCOUNT** *Cr.*

Particulars	₹	Particulars	₹
To Balance b/d	2,80,000	By Depreciation A/c (b.f.)	20,000
To Bank A/c (Purchases)	1,30,000	By Bank A/c (Sale)	10,000
		By P&L A/c (Loss) [₹20,000 - ₹10,000]	10,000
		By Balance c/d	3,70,000
	4,10,000		4,10,000

Dr. **3. PROVISION FOR TAX ACCOUNT** *Cr.*

Particulars	₹	Particulars	₹
To Bank A/c	35,000	By Balance b/d	40,000
To Balance c/d	50,000	By P & L A/c (balancing figure)	45,000
	85,000		85,000

ILLUSTRATION 16

From the following information, calculate the Net Cash Flow from Operating Activities:

Particulars	*Closing* ₹	*Opening* ₹
Equity Share Capital	5,50,000	4,50,000
5% Preference Share Capital	2,00,000	3,00,000
General Reserve	1,50,000	1,20,000
Profit and Loss A/c	1,50,000	(1,40,000)
Securities Premium	10,000	—
Provision for Tax	50,000	40,000
Non-Current Liabilities [8% Debentures]	2,60,000	1,50,000
Short-term Borrowings (8% Bank Loan)	40,000	50,000
Trade Payables	1,05,000	1,00,000
Property,Plant & Equipment	8,60,000	6,20,000
Intangible Assets [Goodwill]	15,000	20,000
Trade Receivables & Inventories	3,95,000	3,00,000
Other Non-Current Assets [Preliminary Exp.]	—	20,000

During the year a machinery costing ₹ 60,000 on which depreciation charged was ₹ 20,000 was sold for ₹ 20,000. Depreciation provided on Fixed Assets ₹ 60,000. Additional Debentures were issued at par on 1st October and Bank Loan was repaid on the same date. Dividend on equity shares @ 8% was paid on opening balance. Income Tax ₹ 45,000 has been provided during the year. Preference Shares were redeemed at a premium of 5% at the end of the year.

SOLUTION

CALCULATION OF NET CASH FLOW FROM OPERATING ACTIVITIES

Particulars	₹	₹
Net Profit before tax		4,16,000
Adjustment for Non-Cash and Non-Operating Items :		
Depreciation on Fixed Assets	60,000	
Loss on Sale of Machinery	20,000	
Interest on Debentures [(₹ 1,50,000 × 8/100) + (₹ 1,10,000 × 8/100 × 6/12)]	16,400	
Interest on Bank Loan [(₹ 50,000 × 8/100 × 6/12) + (₹ 40,000 × 8/100 × 6/12)	3,600	
Goodwill Amortised	5,000	
Preliminary Expenses Written off	20,000	
Premium on Redemption of Preference Shares	5,000	1,30,000
Operating Profit before Working Capital Changes		5,46,000

Changes in Current Assets & Current Liabilities:		
Increase in Trade Receivables & Inventories	(95,000)	
Increase in Trade Payables	5,000	(90,000)
Net Cash Flow from Operating Activities before Tax		4,56,000
Less: **Tax paid**		(35,000)
Net Cash Inflow from Operating Activities after Tax		4,21,000

Working Notes:

1. CALCULATION OF NET PROFIT BEFORE TAX

Particulars	₹
Closing Balance of P&L A/c	1,50,000
Add: Opening Balance of P&L A/c (Debit)	1,40,000
Add: Provision for tax	45,000
Add: Transfer to Reserve	30,000
Add: Dividend on Equity Shares	36,000
Add: Dividend on Preference Shares	15,000
Net Profit before Tax	4,16,000

Dr. **2. PROPERTY, PLANT & EQUIPMENT ACCOUNT** *Cr.*

Particulars	₹	*Particulars*	₹
To Balance b/d	6,20,000	By Depreciation A/c	60,000
To Bank A/c (Purchases) (b.f.)	3,40,000	By Bank A/c (Sale)	20,000
		By P&L A/c (Loss)	20,000
		By Balance c/d	8,60,000
	9,60,000		9,60,000

Dr. **3. PROVISION FOR TAX ACCOUNT** *Cr.*

Particulars	₹	*Particulars*	₹
To Bank A/c (balancing figure)	35,000	By Balance b/d	40,000
To Balance c/d	50,000	By P & L A/c	45,000
	85,000		85,000

ILLUSTRATION 17

From the following information calculate Cash Flow from Operating Activities:

Particulars	*Closing* ₹	*Opening* ₹
Trade Payables	1,65,000	40,000
Intangible Assets [Goodwill]	21,000	10,000
Inventories	1,69,000	54,000
Trade Receivables	3,76,000	4,06,000

During the year, the business of Y Ltd. was purchased for ₹60,000 payable in fully paid equity shares of ₹10 each at 20% premium. The assets included Inventories ₹15,000. Trade Receivables ₹10,000 and machine ₹30,000. Trade Payables of ₹15,000 were also taken over. Net Profit before tax for the year was ₹ 7,98,000. Tax paid during the year ₹ 10,000.

SOLUTION

CALCULATION OF CASH FLOW FROM OPERATING ACTIVITIES

Particulars		₹
A. Net Profit before tax		7,98,000
B. *Add:* Goodwill amortised		9,000
C. Operating Profit before Working Capital Changes		8,07,000
D. Changes in Current Assets & Current Liabilities:		
Increase in Inventories [(1,69,000 – 15,000) – 54,000]	(1,00,000)	
Decrease in Trade Receivables [(3,76,000 – 10,000) – 4,06,000]	40,000	
Increase in Trade Payables [(1,65,000 – 15,000) – 40,000]	1,10,000	50,000
E. Net Cash Flow from Operating Activities before Tax		8,57,000
F. *Less:* Tax paid		(10,000)
G. Net Cash Inflow From Operating Activities After Tax		8,47,000

Note: Goodwill Amortised

= Goodwill Purchased + Opening Goodwill – Closing Goodwill

= [₹ 60,000 – (₹ 15,000 + ₹ 10,000 + ₹ 30,000 – ₹ 15,000] + ₹ 10,000 – ₹ 21,000 = ₹ 9,000

13.0 HOW TO COMPUTE CASH FLOW FROM INVESTING ACTIVITIES

TREATMENT OF SPECIAL ITEMS WHILE COMPUTING CASH FLOW FROM INVESTING ACTIVITIES

Item	*Treatment*	*Reason*
1. Sale of Fixed Assets *or* Investments*	Cash Inflow from Investing Activities.	It involves Cash Inflow.
2. Purchase of Fixed Assets *or* Investments*	Cash Outflow in Investing Activities.	It involves Cash Outflow.
3. Interest *or* Dividend on Investments* *or* Rent from Property	Cash Inflow from Investing Activities.	It represents the receipt of Non-Operating Income. **Note:** If the date of Fresh Purchase /Sale of Investments is not given, Calculate Interest on Opening Bal. of Investments.
4. Increase in Accrued Interest on Investments*	**Subtract** from the Total Interest on Investments to ascertain the Net Amount of interest received.	It represents the amount of Interest not yet received.

**whether Current or Non-Current*

CALCULATION OF CASH FLOW FROM INVESTING ACTIVITIES

Particulars	₹
A. Cash Inflow from Investing Activities:	
Sale of Property,Plant & Equipment (e.g. Machinery) for cash	xxx
Sale of Intangible Assets (e.g. Goodwill/Patents/Trademark/Copyright) for cash	xxx
Sale of Investments(whether Current *or* Non-Current) for cash	xxx
Loans & Advances repayments received (whether Short term *or* Long term)	xxx
Incomes from Investments (whether Current *or* Non-Current):(***For Example***)	xxx
Dividend received on Shares held as Investments	xxx
Interest received on Debentures held as Investments	xxx
Rent received from Immovable Property held as Investments	xxx
	xxx
B. Cash used in Investing Activities:	
Purchase of Property, Plant & Equipment (e.g. Machinery) for cash	(xxx)
Purchase of Intangible Assets (e.g. Goodwill/Patents/Trademark/Copyright) for cash	(xxx)
Purchase of Investments (whether Current *or* Non-Current) for cash	(xxx)
Loans & Advances granted (whether Short term *or* Long term)	(xxx)
	(xxx)
C. Net Cash Inflow from Investing Activities [if A > B]	xxx
or	***or***
Net Cash used in Investing Activities [If A < B]	(xxx)

ILLUSTRATION 18

From the following particulars, Calculate Net Cash Flow from Investing Activities:

Particulars	*Closing* ₹	*Opening* ₹
Goodwill	90,000	1,10,000
Patents	1,15,000	90,000
Land	90,000	1,00,000
Plant & Machinery (Net)	1,60,000	1,80,000
Furniture (Gross)	4,25,000	2,00,000
Provision for Depreciation on Furniture	42,500	20,000
10% Non-Current Investments	1,10,000	1,50,000
10% Current Investments	60,000	50,000

SOLUTION

CALCULATION OF NET CASH FLOW FROM INVESTING ACTIVITIES

Particulars	₹
Purchase of Patents [₹ 1,15,000 – ₹ 90,000]	(25,000)
Sale of Land [₹ 1,00,000 – ₹ 90,000]	10,000
Purchase of Furniture [₹ 4,25,000 – ₹ 2,00,000]	(2,25,000)
Sale of Non-Current Investments [₹ 1,50,000 – ₹ 1,10,000]	40,000
Purchase of Current Investments [₹ 60,000 – ₹ 50,000]	(10,000)
Interest on 10% Non-Current Investments [₹ 1,50,000 × 10/100]	15,000
Interest on 10% Current Investments [₹ 50,000 × 10/100]	5,000
Net Cash used in Investing Activities	(1,90,000)

Notes:

1. *It has been assumed that Investments have been sold & purchased at the end of current accounting year.*
2. *Decrease in Goodwill represents Goodwill Amortised.*
3. *Decrease in Plant & Machinery (Net) represents Depreciation.*

HOW TO ASCERTAIN MISSING FIGURES (E.G. SALES, PURCHASES AND PROFIT/LOSS ON SALE) RELATED TO INVESTMENTS

To ascertain Missing Figures (e.g. Sales, Purchases and Profit/Loss on Sale) related to Investments, prepare Investments Account as follows:

Dr. **INVESTMENTS ACCOUNT** *Cr.*

Particulars	₹	Particulars	₹
To Balance b/d	....	By Bank A/c (Sale Proceeds)	....
To Bank A/c (Purchases)	....	By P&L A/c (Loss on Sale)	....
To P&L (Profit)	....	By Balance c/d	....
	....		....

ILLUSTRATION 19

Particulars	Closing ₹	Opening ₹
10% Non-Current Investments	1,60,000	60,000
10% Current Investments	60,000	20,000

At the end of the year Some Non-Current Investments costing ₹ 40,000 were sold at a loss of 1/3rd on sale and Some Current Investments costing ₹ 20,000 were sold at a profit of 25%. Net Profit before Tax ₹ 1,00,000. How will you disclose these items while preparing Cash Flow Statement as per AS–3 issued by ICAI?

SOLUTION

Dr. **1. NON-CURRENT INVESTMENTS ACCOUNT** *Cr.*

Particulars	₹	*Particulars*	₹
To Balance b/d	60,000	By Bank A/c [₹ 40,000 – ₹ 10,000]	30,000
To Bank A/c (Purchases) (b.f.)	1,40,000	By P&L A/c (Loss)	10,000
		By Balance c/d	1,60,000
	2,00,000		2,00,000

Dr. **2. CURRENT INVESTMENTS ACCOUNT** *Cr.*

Particulars	₹	*Particulars*	₹
To Balance b/d	20,000,	By Bank A/c	25,000
To Bank A/c (Purchase)	60,000	By Balance c/d	60,000
To P&L A/c (Profit) [25% of ₹ 20,000]	5,000		
	85,000		85,000

CASH FLOW STATEMENT FOR THE YEAR ENDED ...

	Particulars	₹
A	**Cash Flow from Operating Activities**	
	Net Profit before Tax	1,00,000
	Add: Loss on Sale of Non-Current Investments	10,000
	Less: Profit on Sale of Current Investments	(5,000)
	Less: Interest Income on Non-Current Investments	(6,000)
	Less: Interest Income on Current Investments	(2,000)
	Operating Profit before Working Capital changes	97,000
B	**Cash Flow from Investing Activities**	
	Purchase of Non-Current Investments	(1,40,000)
	Purchase of Current Investments	(60,000)
	Interest Income on Non-Current Investments	6,000
	Interest Income on Current Investments	2,000
	Sale of Non-Current Investments	30,000
	Sale of Current Investments	25,000
	Cash used in Investing Activities	(1,37,000)

ILLUSTRATION 20

Particulars	*Closing* ₹	*Opening* ₹
10% Non-Current Investments	1,60,000	60,000
10% Current Investments	60,000	20,000

At the end of the year Some Non-Current Investments costing ₹ 40,000 were sold at a loss of 1/3rd on sale and Some Current Investments costing ₹ 20,000 were sold at a profit of 25%.

Profit / Loss on Investments was adjusted against the Capital Reserve. Net Profit before Tax ₹ 1,00,000. How will you disclose these items while preparing Cash Flow Statement as per AS–3 issued by ICAI?

SOLUTION

Dr. **1. NON-CURRENT INVESTMENTS ACCOUNT** *Cr.*

Particulars	₹	Particulars	₹
To Balance b/d	60,000	By Bank A/c [₹ 40,000 – ₹ 10,000]	30,000
To Bank A/c (Purchases) (b.f.)	1,40,000	By Capital Reserve A/c (Loss)	10,000
		By Balance c/d	1,60,000
	2,00,000		2,00,000

Dr. **2. CURRENT INVESTMENTS ACCOUNT** *Cr.*

Particulars	₹	Particulars	₹
To Balance b/d	20,000,	By Bank A/c	25,000
To Bank A/c (Purchase)	60,000	By Balance c/d	60,000
To Capital Reserve A/c (Profit) [25% of ₹ 20,000]	5,000		
	85,000		85,000

CASH FLOW STATEMENT OF TULSIAN LTD FOR THE YEAR ENDED .....

		₹
A	**Cash Flow from Operating Activities**	
	Net Profit before Tax	1,00,000
	Less: Interest Income on Non-Current Investments	(6,000)
	Less: Interest Income on Current Investments	(2,000)
	Operating Profit before Working Capital changes	92,000
B	**Cash Flow from Investing Activities**	
	Purchase of Non-Current Investments	(1,40,000)
	Purchase of Current Investments	(60,000)
	Interest Income on Non-Current Investments	6,000
	Interest Income on Current Investments	2,000
	Sale of Non-Current Investments	30,000
	Sale of Current Investments	25,000
	Cash used in Investing Activities	(1,37,000)

HOW TO ASCERTAIN MISSING FIGURES (E.G. SALES, PURCHASES AND PROFIT/LOSS ON SALE) RELATED TO DEPRECIABLE FIXED ASSETS

To ascertain Missing Figures (e.g. Sales, Purchases and Profit/Loss on Sale) related to Depreciable Fixed Assets, prepare PROPERTY, PLANT & EQUIPMENT ACCOUNT as follows:

Dr. **PROPERTY, PLANT & EQUIPMENT ACCOUNT** *Cr.*

Particulars	₹	*Particulars*	₹
To Balance b/d	....	By Depreciation A/c	....
To Bank A/c (Purchases)	....	By Bank A/c (Sale)	....
To Profit & Loss A/c (Profit)	....	By P&L A/c (loss)	....
To Equity Share Capital A/c (Purch.)	....	By Balance c/d	....
	....		....

ILLUSTRATION 21

Property, Plant & Equipment (Net): Closing ₹ 8,60,000, Opening ₹ 6,20,000. During the year a machine costing ₹ 60,000 (depreciation provided thereon ₹ 20,000) was sold at a loss of ₹ 10,000. Depreciation charged was ₹ 60,000. Net Profit before Tax ₹ 1,00,000. How will you disclose these items while preparing Cash Flow Statement as per AS–3 issued by ICAI?

SOLUTION

Dr. **PROPERTY, PLANT & EQUIPMENT ACCOUNT** Cr.

Particulars	₹	*Particulars*	₹
To Balance b/d	6,20,000	By Depreciation A/c	60,000
To Bank A/c (Purchases) (b.f.)	3,40,000	By Bank A/c (Sale)	30,000
		By P&L A/c (Loss)	10,000
		By Balance c/d	8,60,000
	9,60,000		9,60,000

CASH FLOW STATEMENT FOR THE YEAR ENDED ...

		₹
A	**Cash Flow from Operating Activities**	
	Net Profit before Tax	1,00,000
	Add: Depreciation	60,000
	Add: Loss on Sale	10,000
	Operating Profit before Working Capital changes	1,70,000
B	**Cash Flow from Investing Activities**	
	Purchase of Machinery	(3,40,000)
	Sale of Machinery	30,000
	Cash used in Investing Activities	(3,10,000)

ILLUSTRATION 22

Property, Plant & Equipment (Net): Closing ₹ 12,70,000, Opening ₹ 10,20,000. During the year a machine costing ₹ 1,40,000 (depreciation provided thereon ₹ 60,000) was sold for ₹ 50,000. Depreciation charged was ₹ 1,40,000. A machine costing ₹ 30,000 was purchased by issue of Equity Shares of ₹ 10 each at a premium of 20%. Net Profit before Tax ₹ 1,00,000. How will you disclose these items while preparing Cash Flow Statement as per AS–3 issued by ICAI?

SOLUTION

Dr. **PROPERTY, PLANT & EQUIPMENT ACCOUNT** Cr.

Particulars	₹	Particulars	₹
To Balance b/d	10,20,000	By Bank A/c (Sale)	50,000
To Bank A/c (Purchases) (b.f.)	4,40,000	By P&L A/c (Loss on Sale)	30,000
To Equity Share Capital A/c	25,000	By Depreciation A/c	1,40,000
To Securities Premium	5,000	By Balance c/d	12,70,000
	14,90,000		14,90,000

CASH FLOW STATEMENT FOR THE YEAR ENDED ...

		₹
A	**Cash Flow from Operating Activities**	
	Net Profit before Tax	1,00,000
	Add: Depreciation	1,40,000
	Add: Loss on Sale	30,000
	Operating Profit before Working Capital changes	2,70,000
B	**Cash Flow from Investing Activities**	
	Purchase of Machinery	(4,40,000)
	Sale of Machinery	50,000
	Cash used in Investing Activities	(3,90,000)

HOW TO ASCERTAIN MISSING FIGURES (E.G. SALES, PURCHASES AND PROFIT/LOSS ON SALE) RELATED TO DEPRECIABLE FIXED ASSETS WHEN PROVISION FOR DEPRECIATION ACCOUNT IS MAINTAINED.

To ascertain Missing Figures (e.g. Sales, Purchases and Profit/Loss on Sale) related to Depreciable Fixed Assets when Provision for Depreciation Account is maintained, prepare the following three accounts as follows:

Dr. **1. PROPERTY, PLANT & EQUIPMENT ACCOUNT (AT COST)** *Cr.*

Particulars	₹	Particulars	₹
To Balance b/d	....	By PPE DISPOSAL A/C	....
To Bank A/c (Purchases)	....	[T/f of Cost of Machine sold]	
To Equity Share Capital A/c (Purch.)	....	By Balance c/d	....
	....		....

Dr. **2. PROVISION FOR DEPRECIATION ACCOUNT** *Cr.*

Particulars	₹	Particulars	₹
To PPE Disposal A/c	....	By Balance b/d	....
[T/f of Accumulated Dep. on Machine sold]		By P&L A/c	

To Balance c/d	....	(Dep. Provided during the current year)	....
	....		....

Dr. **3. MACHINERY DISPOSAL ACCOUNT** Cr.

Particulars	₹	Particulars	₹
To Plant & Machinery A/c (Cost)	....	By Provision for Depreciation A/c	....
To Profit & Loss A/c (Profit)	....	By Bank A/c (Sale proceeds)	....
		By Profit & Loss A/c (Loss on sale)	....
	....		....

ILLUSTRATION 23

Particulars	Closing (₹)	Opening (₹)
Property,Plant & Equipment	16,20,000	13,20,000
Accumulated Depreciation	3,80,000	3,00,000

During the year a machine having book value of ₹ 80,000 (depreciation provided thereon ₹ 60,000) was sold at a loss of ₹ 30,000. Net Profit before Tax ₹ 1,00,000. How will you disclose these items while preparing Cash Flow Statement as per AS–3 issued by ICAI?

SOLUTION

Dr. **1. PROPERTY, PLANT & EQUIPMENT ACCOUNT (AT COST)** Cr.

Particulars	₹	Particulars	₹
To Balance b/d	13,20,000	By PPE DISPOSAL A/C	1,40,000
To Bank A/c (Purchases)	4,40,000	By Balance c/d	16,20,000
	17,60,000		17,60,000

Dr. **2. PROVISION FOR DEPRECIATION ACCOUNT** Cr.

Particulars	₹	Particulars	₹
To PPE Disposal A/c	60,000	By Balance b/d	3,00,000
To Balance c/d	3,80,000	By P&L A/c (Depreciation for current year) (Balancing figure)	1,40,000
	4,40,000		4,40,000

Dr. **3. MACHINERY DISPOSAL ACCOUNT** Cr.

Particulars	₹	Particulars	₹
To PPE A/c	1,40,000	By Provision for Depreciation A/c	60,000
		By Bank A/c (b.f.)	50,000
		By Profit and Loss A/c (Loss)	30,000
	1,40,000		1,40,000

CASH FLOW STATEMENT FOR THE YEAR ENDED ...

		₹
A	**Cash Flow from Operating Activities**	
	Net Profit before Tax	1,00,000
	Add: Depreciation	1,40,000
	Add: Loss on Sale	30,000
	Operating Profit before Working Capital changes	2,70,000
B	**Cash Flow from Investing Activities**	
	Purchase of Machinery	(4,40,000)
	Sale of Machinery	50,000
	Cash used in Investing Activities	(3,90,000)

ILLUSTRATION 24

Particulars	*Closing* ₹	*Opening* ₹
Property,Plant & Equipment	16,50,000	13,20,000
Accumulated Depreciation	3,80,000	3,00,000

During the year a machine having book value of ₹ 80,000 (depreciation provided thereon ₹ 60,000) was sold at a loss of 37.5%. A machine costing ₹ 30,000 was purchased by issue of Equity Shares of ₹ 10 each at a premium of 20%. Net Profit before Tax ₹ 1,00,000. How will you disclose these items while preparing Cash Flow Statement as per AS–3 issued by ICAI?

SOLUTION

Dr. **1. PROPERTY, PLANT & EQUIPMENT ACCOUNT (AT COST)** *Cr.*

Particulars	₹	*Particulars*	₹
To Balance b/d	13,20,000	By PPE DISPOSAL A/C	1,40,000
To Bank A/c (Purchases)	4,40,000	By Balance c/d	16,50,000
To Equity Share Capital A/c	25,000		
To Securities Premium	5,000		
	17,90,000		17,90,000

Dr. **2. PROVISION FOR DEPRECIATION ACCOUNT** *Cr.*

Particulars	₹	*Particulars*	₹
To PPE Disposal A/c	60,000	By Balance b/d	3,00,000
To Bank c/d	3,80,000	By P&L A/c (Depreciation for current year) (Balancing figure)	1,40,000
	4,40,000		4,40,000

Dr. **3. MACHINERY DISPOSAL ACCOUNT** Cr.

Particulars	₹	Particulars	₹
To PPE A/c	1,40,000	By Provision for Depreciation A/c	60,000
		By Bank A/c (b.f.)	50,000
		By Profit and Loss A/c (Loss)	30,000
	1,40,000		1,40,000

CASH FLOW STATEMENT FOR THE YEAR ENDED ...

		₹
A	**Cash Flow from Operating Activities**	
	Net Profit before Tax	1,00,000
	Add: Depreciation	1,40,000
	Add: Loss on Sale	30,000
	Operating Profit before Working Capital changes	2,70,000
B	**Cash Flow from Investing Activities**	
	Purchase of Machinery	(4,40,000)
	Sale of Machinery	50,000
	Cash used in Investing Activities	(3,90,000)

ILLUSTRATION 25

Particulars	Closing ₹	Opening ₹
Property, Plant & Equipment	16,50,000	13,20,000
Accumulated Depreciation	3,80,000	3,00,000

During the year a machine costing ₹ 1,40,000 was sold at a loss of 37.5%. Depreciation of ₹ 1,40,000 was provided during the current year. A machine costing ₹ 30,000 was purchased by issue of Equity Shares of ₹ 10 each at a premium of 20%. Net Profit before Tax ₹ 1,00,000. How will you disclose these items while preparing Cash Flow Statement as per AS–3 issued by ICAI?

SOLUTION

Same as in case of Previous ILLUSTRATION.

ILLUSTRATION 26

From the following information, Calculate Net Cash Flow from Operating Activities and Investing Activities:

Particulars	Closing ₹	Opening ₹
Profit and Loss A/c	3,92,000	(1,08,000)
General Reserve	2,90,000	4,40,000
Provision for Tax	40,000	20,000
Trade Payables	2,00,000	1,00,000

Property,Plant & Equipment (Net)	12,40,000	10,20,000
Intangible Assets [Goodwill]	1,000	10,000
10% Non-Current Investments	1,60,000	60,000
10% Current Investments	60,000	20,000
Trade Receivables & Inventories	5,20,000	4,60,000

During the year a machine costing ₹ 1,40,000 (depreciation provided thereon ₹ 60,000) was sold for ₹ 50,000. Depreciation charged was ₹ 1,40,000. Tax paid was ₹ 10,000. At the end of the year some Non-Current Investments costing ₹ 40,000 were sold at a profit of 25%. Dividend paid during the year ₹ 1,20,000.

SOLUTION

CALCULATION OF NET CASH FLOW FROM OPERATING ACTIVITIES AND INVESTING ACTIVITIES

Particulars	₹	₹
I. Cash Flow from Operating Activities:		
A. Net Profit before tax		5,00,000
B. Adjustments for Non-Cash and Non-Operating Items:		
Depreciation	1,40,000	
Loss on Sale of Machinery	30,000	
Goodwill amortised	9,000	
Profit on Sale of Non-Current Investments	(10,000)	
Interest Income on Non-Current Investments	(6,000)	
Interest Income on Current Investments	(2,000)	1,61,000
C. Operating Profit before Working Capital Changes		6,61,000
D. Changes in Current Assets & Current Liabilities:		
Increase in Trade Payables	1,00,000	
Increase in Trade Receivables & Inventories	(60,000)	40,000
E. Net Cash Flow from Operating Activities before Tax		7,01,000
F. *Less:* **Tax paid**		(10,000)
G. Net Cash Inflow from Operating Activities after Tax		6,91,000
II. Cash Flow from Investing Activities:		
Sale of Machinery		50,000
Purchases of Fixed Assets		(4,40,000)
Purchases of Non-Current Investments		(1,40,000)
Purchases of Current Investments		(40,000)
Sale of Non-Current Investments		50,000
Interest received on Non-Current Investments		6,000
Interest received on Current Investments		2,000
Net Cash used in Investing Activities		(5,12,000)

Working Notes:

1. CALCULATION OF NET PROFIT BEFORE TAX

Particulars	₹
Closing Balance of P&L A/c	3,92,000
Add: Opening Balance of P&L A/c (Debit)	1,08,000
Less: Transfer from Reserve	(1,50,000)
Add: Dividend declared	1,20,000
Add: Tax	30,000
Net Profit before Tax	5,00,000

2. PROPERTY, PLANT & EQUIPMENT ACCOUNT

Dr. | Cr.

Particulars	₹	*Particulars*	₹
To Balance b/d	10,20,000	By Bank A/c (Sale)	50,000
To Bank A/c (Purchases) (b.f.)	4,40,000	By P&L A/c (Loss)	30,000
		By Depreciation A/c	1,40,000
		By Balance c/d	12,40,000
	14,60,000		14,60,000

3. NON-CURRENT INVESTMENTS ACCOUNT

Dr. | Cr.

Particulars	₹	*Particulars*	₹
To Balance b/d	60,000	By Bank A/c [₹ 40,000 + ₹ 10,000]	50,000
To Bank A/c (Purchases) (b.f.)	1,40,000	By Balance c/d	1,60,000
To Profit and Loss A/c (Profit) [₹ 40,000 × 25/100]	10,000		
	2,10,000		2,10,000

4. PROVISION FOR TAX ACCOUNT

Dr. | Cr.

Particulars	₹	*Particulars*	₹
To Bank A/c [Tax paid]	10,000	By Balance b/d	20,000
To Balance c/d	40,000	By Profit and Loss A/c (b.f.) [Provision made]	30,000
	50,000		50,000

14.0 HOW TO COMPUTE CASH FLOW FROM FINANCING ACTIVITIES

TREATMENT OF SPECIAL ITEMS WHILE CALCULATING CASH FROM FINANCING ACTIVITIES

Item	*Treatment*	*Reason*
1. Increase in Equity Share Capital/Pref. Share Capital/ Debentures/Loans*	Cash Inflow from Financing Activities.	It represents the issue of New Shares/Debentures.
2. Decrease in Equity Share Capital/Pref. Share Capital/ Debentures/Loans*	Cash Outflow in Financing Activities.	It represents the buy-back of Equity Shares *or* Redemption of Pref. Share Capital/Debentures.

3. **Increase in Securities Premium**	Cash Inflow from Financing Activities.	It represents the issue of New Shares/Debentures at premium.
4. **Increase in Discount on Issue of Debentures/ Shares**	**Subtract** from the increase in amount of Share Capital/ Debentures to ascertain the Net amount of issue.	It represents the issue of New shares/Debentures at discount.
5. **Increase in Underwriting Commission**	Cash Outflow in Financing Activities.	It represents the payment of underwriting commission in raising Share Capital/ Debentures.
6. **Interest on Debentures/ Loans***	Cash Outflow in Financing Activities.	It represents the payment of interest on Debentures. **Note:** *If the date of Fresh issue /Redemption of Debentures is not given, Calculate Interest on Opening Balance of Debentures.*
7. **Increase in Unpaid Interest on Debentures/Loans***	Subtract from the Total Interest on Debentures to ascertain the Net amount of Interest paid.	It represents the amount of Interest not yet paid.
8. **Final Dividend paid during the current year**	Cash Outflow in Financing Activities.	It represents the payment of Dividend.
9. **Increase in Unclaimed Dividend**	Subtract from the amount of Dividend to ascertain the Net amount of dividend paid.	It represents the amount of Dividend not yet paid.
10. **Interim Dividend [An Interim Dividend is that dividend which is declared by the Board of Directors for the current year during the current year.]**	Cash Outflow in Financing Activities.	It represents the payment of Dividend.
11. **Dividend on Pref. Shares**	Cash Outflow in Financing Activities.	It represents the payment of Pref. Dividend. **Note:** *If the date of Fresh issue/ Redemption of Pref. Shares is not given, Calculate Dividend on Opening Balance of Pref. Share.*

**whether Short-term or Long-term*

CALCULATION OF NET CASH FLOW FROM FINANCING ACTIVITIES

Particulars	₹
A. Cash Inflows from Financing Activities:	
Issue of Equity Share Capital for cash [including Premium but excl. Discount]	xxx
Issue of Pref. Share Capital for cash [including Premium but excl. Discount]	xxx

Issue of Debentures for cash [including Premium but excl. Discount]	xxx
Loans raised (whether Short term *or* Long term)	xxx
	xxx
B. Cash used in Financing Activities:	
Buy back of Equity Shares [including Premium]	(xxx)
Redemption of Preference Shares for cash [including Premium]	(xxx)
Redemption of Debentures for cash [including Premium]	(xxx)
Repayment of Loans (whether Short term *or* Long term)	(xxx)
Interim Dividend paid on Equity Shares	(xxx)
Final Dividend paid on Equity Shares	(xxx)
Final Dividend paid on Preference Shares	(xxx)
Interest paid on Debentures & Loans (whether Short term *or* Long term)	(xxx)
	(xxx)
C. Net Cash Inflow from Financing Activities [If A > B]	xxx
or	***or***
Net Cash Flow used in Financing Activities [If A < B]	(xxx)

ILLUSTRATION 27

From the following particulars, Calculate Net Cash Flow from Financing Activities:

Particulars	***Closing*** ₹	***Opening*** ₹
Equity Share Capital	4,00,000	3,00,000
Pref. Share Capital	1,00,000	1,50,000
Securities Premium	15,000	5,000
10% Debentures	4,00,000	3,00,000

Dividend paid on Equity ₹ 30,000. Dividend paid on Pref. Shares ₹ 15,000

SOLUTION

CALCULATION OF NET CASH FLOW FROM FINANCING ACTIVITIES

Particulars	₹
Proceeds from Issue of Equity Share Capital [(₹ 4,00,000 – ₹ 3,00,000) + ₹ 10,000 Premium]	1,10,000
Proceeds from Issue of Debentures [₹ 4,00,000 – ₹ 3,00,000]	1,00,000
Redemption of Preference Shares [₹ 1,50,000 – ₹ 1,00,000]	(50,000)
Interest on Debentures paid [₹ 3,00,000 × 10/100]	(30,000)
Dividend on Equity. Shares	(30,000)
Dividend on Pref. Shares	(15,000)
Net Cash Inflow from Financing Activities	85,000

Notes:

1. *It has been assumed that the new Debentures have been issued at par at the end of current accounting year.*
2. *It has been assumed that Preference Shares have been redeemed at the end of current accounting year.*

ILLUSTRATION 28

From the following particulars of BT Ltd., calculate Net Cash Flow from Financing Activities:

Particulars	*Closing* ₹	*Opening* ₹
Equity Share Capital	9,00,000	6,00,000
18% Pref. Share Capital	1,00,000	4,00,000
Securities Premium	1,30,000	1,00,000
14% Debentures	3,00,000	2,00,000

Additional Information: During the year Preference Dividend on preference shares and an Interim Dividend on equity shares @ 15% were paid on 30th Sept. New Shares and Debentures were issued on 1st Oct. Preference shares were redeemed at the end of the year at a premium of 5%. Such premium has been provided out of profits.

SOLUTION

CALCULATION OF NET CASH FLOW FROM FINANCING ACTIVITIES

Particulars	₹
Issue of Equity Share Capital [₹ 9,00,000 – ₹ 6,00,000 + ₹ 30,000 (Premium)]	3,30,000
Issue of Debentures [₹ 3,00,000 – ₹ 2,00,000]	1,00,000
Redemption of Preference Shares [₹ 3,00,000 + ₹ 15,000]	(3,15,000)
Interest paid on Debentures [(₹ 2,00,000 × 14/100) + ₹ 1,00,000 × 14/100 × 6/12)]	(35,000)
Interim Dividend paid on Equity Shares [₹ 6,00,000 × 15/100]	(90,000)
Dividend paid on Pref. Shares [₹ 4,00,000 × 18/100]	(72,000)
Net Cash used in Financing Activities	(82,000)

ILLUSTRATION 29

Particulars	*31.03.2023* ₹	*31.03.2022* ₹
14% Debentures	2,60,000	1,50,000
14% Short-term Bank Loan	40,000	50,000

New Debentures were issued on 01.01.2023 and Bank Loan was repaid on the same date. Unpaid Interest on Debentures on 31.03.2023 ₹ 10,000. Net Profit before Tax ₹ 1,00,000 How will you disclose these items while preparing Cash Flow Statement as per AS–3 issued by ICAI?

SOLUTION

CASH FLOW STATEMENT FOR THE YEAR ENDED 31ST MARCH, 2023

		₹
A	**Cash Flow from Operating Activities**	
	Net Profit before Tax	1,00,000
	Add: Interest on Debentures [(1,50,000 x 14%) + (1,10,000 x 14% x 3/12]	24,850
	Add: Interest on Bank Loan [(50,000 x 14% x 9/12) + (40,000 x 14% x 3/12]	6,650
	Operating Profit before Working Capital changes	1,31,500
B	**Cash Flow from Financing activities**	
	Issue of Debentures	1,10,000
	Bank Loan repaid	(10,000)
	Interest on Debentures [24,850 – 10,000]	(14,850)
	Interest on Bank Loan	(6,650)
	Cash Flow from Financing activities	(78,500)

ILLUSTRATION 30

From the following information, Calculate Net Cash Flow from Operating Activities & Financing Activities:

Particulars	*31.03.2023* ₹	*31.03.2022* ₹
Equity Share Capital	5,50,000	4,50,000
5% Preference Share Capital	2,00,000	3,00,000
General Reserve	1,50,000	1,20,000
Profit and Loss A/c	1,50,000	(1,40,000)
Securities Premium	10,000	—
Provision for Tax	50,000	40,000
Non-Current Liabilities [8% Debentures]	2,60,000	1,50,000
Short-term Borrowings (8% Bank Loan)	40,000	50,000
Increase in Trade Payables	2,00,000	1,00,000
Increase in Trade Receivables & Inventories	5,20,000	4,60,000

Additional Information: During the year Additional Debentures were issued at par on 1st October, and Bank Loan was repaid on the same date. Dividend on equity shares @ 8% was paid on opening balance. Income Tax ₹ 45,000 has been provided during the year. Preference Shares were redeemed at a premium of 5% at the end of the year.

SOLUTION

CALCULATION OF CASH FLOW FROM OPERATING ACTIVITIES AND FINANCING ACTIVITIES

Particulars	₹	₹
I. Cash Flow from Operating Activities:		
Net Profit before tax		4,16,000
Adjustment for Non-Cash and Non-Operating Items:		

	Particulars	₹	₹
	Interest on Debentures [(₹ 1,50,000 × 8/100) + (₹ 1,10,000 × 8/100 × 6/12)]		16,400
	Interest on Bank Loan [(₹ 50,000 × 8/100 × 6/12) + (₹ 40,000 × 8/100 × 6/12)		3,600
	Premium on Redemption of Preference Shares		5,000
	Operating Profit before Working Capital Changes		4,41,000
	Changes in Current Assets & Current Liabilities:		0
	Increase in Trade Payables	1,00,000	
	Increase in Trade Receivables & Inventories	(60,000)	40,000
	Net Cash Flow from Operating Activities before Tax		4,81,000
	Less: **Tax paid**		(35,000)
	Net Cash Inflow from Operating Activities after Tax		4,46,000
II.	**Cash Flow from Financing Activities:**		
	Issue of Share Capital [₹ 1,00,000 + ₹ 10,000 (Premium)]		1,10,000
	Issue of Debentures		1,10,000
	Interest on Debentures		(16,400)
	Interest on Bank Loan		(3,600)
	Dividend on Equity Shares [₹4,50,000 × 8/100]		(36,000)
	Dividend on Preference Shares [₹3,00,000 × 5/100]		(15,000)
	Redemption of Preference Shares[₹ 1,00,000 + ₹ 5,000]		(1,05,000)
	Bank Loan Repaid [₹ 50,000 – ₹ 40,000]		(10,000)
	Net Cash from in Financing Activities		34,000

Working Notes:

1. CALCULATION OF NET PROFIT BEFORE TAX

Particulars	₹
Closing Balance of P&L A/c	1,50,000
Add: Opening Balance of P&L A/c (Debit)	1,40,000
Add: Provision for tax	45,000
Add: Transfer to Reserve	30,000
Add: Dividend on Equity Shares	36,000
Add: Dividend on Preference Shares	15,000
Net Profit before Tax	4,16,000

Dr. **2. PROVISION FOR TAX ACCOUNT** *Cr.*

Particulars	₹	***Particulars***	₹
To Bank A/c (balancing figure)	35,000	By Balance b/d	40,000
To Balance c/d	50,000	By P & L A/c	45,000
	85,000		85,000

15.0 PRACTICAL STEPS INVOLVED IN THE PREPARATION OF CASH FLOW STATEMENT

The various steps involved in the preparation of Cash Flow Statement are given below:

PRACTICAL STEPS INVOLVED IN THE PREPARATION OF CASH FLOW STATEMENT

Step 1: ***Calculate the Cash Flow from Operating Activities.***

Step 2: ***Calculate the Cash Flow from Investing Activities.***

Step 3: ***Calculate the Cash Flow from Financing Activities.***

Step 4: ***Calculate the Net Increase (Decrease) in Cash and Cash Equivalents***

Step 4 = Step 1 + Step 2 + Step 3

Step 5: ***Calculate the Cash and Cash Equivalents at the Beginning of Period***

Step 6: ***Calculate the Cash and Cash Equivalents at the End of Period***

Step 6 = Step 4 + Step 5

IMPORTANT INSTRUCTIONS FOR WORKING NOTES

1. Net Profit before Tax	Calculate Net Profit before Tax *[Refer to Working Note No. 1 under Para 16.0]*.
2. PROPERTY,PLANT & EQUIPMENT ACCOUNT	Prepare PROPERTY,PLANT & EQUIPMENT ACCOUNT to ascertain Missing Figures (e.g. Sales, Purchases and Profit/Loss on Sale) related to Depreciable Fixed Assets *[Refer to Working Note No. 2 under Para 16.0]*.
3. Investments Account	Prepare Investments Account to ascertain Missing Figures (e.g. Sales, Purchases and Profit/Loss on Sale) related to Investments *[Refer to Working Note No. 3 under Para 16.0]*.
4. Provision for Tax Account	Prepare Provision for Tax Account to ascertain Missing Figure (e.g. Tax provided *or* Tax paid) *[Refer to Working Note No. 4 under Para 16.0]*.
5. Interest on Debentures/ Loans (whether Current *or* Non-Current)	Calculate Interest on Opening Balance of Debentures/Loan if the date of Fresh issue/Redemption of Debentures/Loan is not given.
6. Dividend on Pref. Shares	Calculate Dividend on Opening Balance of Pref. Shares if the date of Fresh issue /Redemption of Pref. Shares is not given.
7. Premium on Redemption of Pref. Share Capital/ Debentures	Calculate Premium on Redemption of Pref. Share Capital/ Debentures on Pref. Share Capital/Debentures redeemed during the year.
8. Interest on Investments (whether Current *or* Non-Current)	Calculate Interest at given % on Opening Balance of Investments if the date of Fresh Purchase/Sale of Investments is not given.
9. Provision for Tax for Previous Year	Unless otherwise stated, it presumed that the' Provision for Tax for Previous Year' has been paid subsequently during the current year.
10. Transactions which do not appear in CFS	1. Issue of Shares/Debentures on conversion of Debentures 2. Purchase of an Asset against the issue of Shares/Debentures **Reason:** These transactions do not involve any inflow/ outflow of cash.

PRECAUTIONS WHILE PREPARING CASH FLOW STATEMENT

1. *Check whether Current Year's Figures are given first or Previous Year's Figures are given first*
2. *Check whether Balance of Profit & Loss Account is Debit or Credit. If Balance of Profit & Loss Account is Debit, Add or Less very carefully.*
3. *Check whether Balance of General Reserve during current year has increased or decreased. If Balance of General Reserve during current year has decreased, Subtract Transfer from General Reserve from Closing Balance of Profit & Loss Account.*
4. *Check whether Interest % on Investments is given or not. If Interest % on Investments is given, Do not forget to make adjustment for Interest on Investments (whether Current or Non-Current) while computing Cash from Operating Activities and Investing Activities.*
5. *Do not forget to make adjustment for Interest on Borrowings (whether Short term or Long term) while computing Cash from Operating Activities and Financing Activities.*
6. *Exclude Increase in Inventories, Trade Receivables/ Payables against issue of Shares / Debentures from Respective Closing Balances. Reason: These do not involve any cash flow.*

16.0 FORMAT OF CASH FLOW STATEMENT

A Format of Cash Flow Statement is given below:

CASH FLOW STATEMENT OF M/S ....

for the year ended 31st March,...

Particulars	₹	₹
I. Cash Flow from Operating Activities:		
A. *Net Profit before taxation, and extraordinary item*		xxx
B. *Adjustment for Non-Cash and Non-Operating Items:* ***(For Example)***		
Depreciation	xxx	
Interest on Debentures & Loans (whether Short term *or* Long term)	xxx	
Preliminary Expenses/Underwriting Commission/Discount on	xxx	
Issue of Debentures/Shares written of	xxx	
Goodwill/Patents/Trade Marks/Copyright amortised	xxx	
Loss on Sale of Investments (whether Current *or* Non-Current)	xxx	
Premium payable on redemption of Preference shares/Debentures		
Profit on Sale of Investments (whether Current *or* Non-Current)	(xxx)	
Income from Investments (whether Current *or* Non-Current)	(xxx)	xxx
C. *Operating Profit before Working Capital Changes*		xxx
D. *Changes in Operating Current Assets (Excluding Cash and Cash Equivalents) & Operating Current Liabilities: (Excluding Bank over Draft & Cash Credit) other than due to issue of Shares / Debentures*		
Decrease in Inventories	xxx	
Decrease in Trade Receivables	xxx	
Decrease in Prepaid expenses	xxx	

Decrease in Accrued Commission	xxx	
Increase in Trade Payables	xxx	
Increase in Outstanding expenses	xxx	
Increase in Commission received in advance	xxx	
Increase in Provision for Doubtful Debts *or* Discount on Debtors	xxx	
Increase in Inventories	(xxx)	
Increase in Trade Receivables	(xxx)	
Increase in Prepaid Expenses	(xxx)	
Increase in Accrued Commission	(xxx)	
Decrease in Trade Payables	(xxx)	
Decrease in Outstanding expenses	(xxx)	
Decrease in Commission received in advance	(xxx)	
Decrease in Provision for Doubtful Debts/Discount on Debtors	(xxx)	xxx
E. *Net Cash Flow from Operating Activities before Tax*	xxx	
F. *Less: Income taxes paid (Net of Refund)*	(xxx)	
G. *Net Cash Flow from Operating Activities before extraordinary item*	xxx	
H. *Extraordinary items*		xxx
I. *Net Cash Flow from (used in) Operating Activities*		xxx
II. Cash Flow from Investing Activities:		
Sale of Machinery/Land & Building for cash		xxx
Sale of Investments (whether Current *or* Non-Current) for cash		xxx
Sale of Patents/Trademarks/Copyrights for cash		xxx
Income received from Investments (whether Current *or* Non-Current)	xxx	
Purchase of Machinery/Land & Building for cash		(xxx)
Purchase of Investments (whether Current *or* Non-Current) for cash		(xxx)
Purchase of Patents/Trademarks/Copyrights/Goodwill for cash		(xxx)
Net Cash Flow from (used in) Investing Activities		xxx
III. Cash Flow from Financing Activities:		
Issue of Share Capital for cash		xxx
Issue of Debentures for cash		xxx
Loans raised (whether Short term *or* Long term)		xxx
Redemption of Preference Shares/Buy - back of Equity shares		(xxx)
Redemption of Debentures for cash		(xxx)
Loans repaid (whether Short term *or* Long term)		(xxx)
Interest paid on Debentures/Loans(whether Short term *or* Long term)	(xxx)	
Interim Dividend paid (Excluding Unpaid/Unclaimed)		(xxx)
Final Dividend paid (Excluding Unpaid/Unclaimed)		(xxx)
Net Cash Flow from (used in) Financing Activities		xxx
IV. Net Increase (Decrease) in Cash and Cash Equivalents [I + II + III]	xxx	

V. Cash and Cash Equivalents at the Beginning of Period		
Cash in hand	xxx	
Cash at bank	xxx	
Cash Equivalents (Investments having maturity of 3 months *or* less)	xxx	xxx
VI. Cash and Cash Equivalents at End of Period [IV + V]		
Cash in hand	xxx	
Cash at bank	xxx	
Cash Equivalents (Investments having maturity of 3 months *or* less)	xxx	xxx

Working Notes:

1. CALCULATION OF NET PROFIT BEFORE TAX

Particulars	₹
Closing Balance of P&L A/c	xxx
Less: Opening Balance of P&L A/c (Cr.) [*Add:* Opening Balance of P&L A/c (Dr.)]	xxx
Add: Final Dividend paid during the Current year	xxx
Add: Interim Dividend paid during the Current year	xxx
Add: Transfer to Reserve [*Less:* Transfer from Reserve]	xxx
Add: Provision for Tax made during the Current Year	xxx
Less: Refund of Tax credited to P&L A/c	xxx
Net Profit before Tax	xxx

Dr. **2. PROPERTY, PLANT & EQUIPMENT ACCOUNT** *Cr.*

Particulars	₹	***Particulars***	₹
To Balance b/d	....	By Bank A/c (Sale)	....
To Bank A/c (Purchases)	....	By P&L A/c (Loss)	....
To P & L A/c (Profit)		By Depreciation A/c	....
To Equity Share Capital A/c (Purch.)	....	By Balance c/d	....
	....		....

Dr. **3. INVESTMENTS ACCOUNT** *Cr.*

Particulars	₹	***Particulars***	₹
To Balance b/d	....	By Bank A/c (Sale Proceeds)	....
To Bank A/c (Purchases)	....	By P&L A/c (Loss on Sale)	....
To P&L (Profit)	....	By Balance c/d	....
	....		....

Dr. **4. PROVISION FOR TAX ACCOUNT** *Cr.*

Particulars	₹	***Particulars***	₹
To Bank A/c	....	By Balance b/d	....
To Balance c/d	....	By P & L A/c	....
	....		....

ILLUSTRATION 31

From the following information, prepare a Cash Flow Statement:

Particulars	*Note*	*31.03.2023* ₹	*31.03.2022* ₹
Equity Share Capital		4,00,000	3,00,000
15% Preference Share Capital		1,00,000	1,50,000
General Reserve		1,20,000	82,000
Profit and Loss A/c		48,000	30,000
Securities Premium		10,000	–
Trade Payables		99,000	75,000
Short-term Provisions (Provision for Tax)		50,000	40,000
Property,Plant & Equipment		3,70,000	2,80,000
Intangible Assets [Goodwill]		90,000	1,15,000
Current Investments		10,000	15,000
Cash & Cash Equivalents		18,000	10,000
Other Current Assets		3,39,000	2,57,000

Additional Information: A machine costing ₹ 50,000 (depreciation provided thereon ₹ 30,000) was sold for ₹ 10,000. Depreciation charged during the year was ₹ 20,000. Interim Dividend paid ₹ 62,000, Income-tax ₹ 35,000 paid.

SOLUTION

CASH FLOW STATEMENT
for the year ended 31st March, 2023

Particulars	₹	₹
I. Cash Flow from Operating Activities		
A. Net Profit before tax		1,63,000
B. Adjustments for Non-Cash and Non-Operating Items :		
Depreciation	20,000	
Loss on Sale of Machinery	10,000	
Goodwill amortised	25,000	55,000
C. Operating Profit before Working Capital Changes		2,18,000
D. Changes in Current Assets & Current Liabilities:		
Increase in Trade Payables	24,000	
Increase in Other Current Assets	(82,000)	(58,000)
E. Net Cash Flow from Operating Activities before Tax		1,60,000
F. *Less:* Tax paid		(35,000)
G. Net Cash Inflow from Operating Activities after Tax		1,25,000

II. Cash Flow from Investing Activities:		
Sale of Machinery		10,000
Purchases of Fixed Assets		(1,30,000)
Sale of Current Investments		5,000
Net Cash used in Investing Activities		(1,15,000)
III. Cash Flow from Financing Activities:		
Issue of Share Capital [₹ 1,00,000 + ₹ 10,000]		1,10,000
Dividend paid		(62,000)
Redemption of Preference Shares		(50,000)
Net Cash used in Financing Activities		(2,000)
IV. Net Increase in Cash and Cash Equivalents [I + II + III]		8,000
V. Opening Cash and Cash Equivalents		10,000
VI. Closing Cash and Cash Equivalents		18,000

Working Notes:

1. CALCULATION OF NET PROFIT BEFORE TAX

Particulars	₹
Closing Balance of P&L A/c	48,000
Less: Opening Balance of P&L A/c	(30,000)
Add: Transfer to Reserve	38,000
Add: Dividend	62,000
Add: Tax	45,000
Net Profit before Tax	1,63,000

Dr. **2. PROPERTY, PLANT & EQUIPMENT ACCOUNT** *Cr.*

Particulars	₹	*Particulars*	₹
To Balance b/d	2,80,000	By Depreciation A/c	20,000
To Bank A/c (Purchases) (b.f.)	**1,30,000**	By Bank A/c (Sale)	10,000
		By P&L A/c (Loss)	10,000
		By Balance c/d	3,70,000
	4,10,000		4,10,000

Dr. **3. PROVISION FOR TAX ACCOUNT** *Cr.*

Particulars	₹	*Particulars*	₹
To Bank A/c	35,000	By Balance b/d	40,000
To Balance c/d	50,000	By P & L A/c (balancing figure)	**45,000**
	85,000		85,000

ILLUSTRATION 32

Following are the extracts of Balance Sheets of Tulsian Ltd :

Particulars	*31.03.2023* ₹	*31.03.2022* ₹
Equity Share Capital	5,50,000	4,50,000
5% Preference Share Capital	2,00,000	3,00,000
General Reserve	1,10,000	1,20,000
Profit and Loss A/c	1,90,000	(1,40,000)
Securities Premium	10,000	—
Provision for Tax	50,000	40,000
Short–term Borrowings (10% Bank Loan)	3,00,000	2,00,000
Trade Payables	1,20,000	1,10,000
Land and Buildings	2,00,000	2,20,000
Machinery	10,00,000	7,00,000
Accumulated Depreciation on Machinery	(3,40,000)	(3,00,000)
Intangible Assets [Goodwill]	15,000	40,000
10% Current Investments	70,000	30,000
Trade Receivables & Inventories	3,95,000	3,00,000
Cash and Cash Equivalents	1,90,000	90,000

During the year Machinery costing ₹ 60,000 was sold at a loss of ₹ 20,000. Depreciation provided on Machinery ₹ 60,000. On 1st October,2022, Additional Bank Loan was raised and Current Investments were purchased. Dividend on equity shares @ 8% was paid on opening balance. Income Tax ₹ 45,000 has been provided during the year. Preference Shares were redeemed at a premium of 5% at the end of the year.

SOLUTION

CASH FLOW STATEMENT
for the year ended 31st March, 2023

Particulars	₹	₹
I. Cash Flow from Operating Activities:		
Net Profit before tax		4,21,000
Adjustment for Non–Cash and Non–Operating Items :		
Depreciation on Machinery	60,000	
Depreciation on Land and Buildings	**20,000**	
Loss on Sale of Machinery	20,000	
Interest on Bank Loan [(₹ 2,00,000 × 10/100 × 6/12) + (₹ 3,00,000 × 10/100 × 6/12)	25,000	
Interest on Current Investments [(₹ 30,000 × 10/100 × 6/12) + (₹ 70,000 × 10/100 × 6/12)]	(5,000)	
Goodwill Amortised	25,000	1,45,000
Operating Profit before Working Capital Changes		5,66,000
Changes in Current Assets & Current Liabilities:		
Increase in Inventories & Trade Receivables	(95,000)	

	Increase in Trade Payables	10,000	(85,000)
	Net Cash Flow from Operating Activities before Tax		4,81,000
	Less: **Tax paid**		(35,000)
	Net Cash Inflow from Operating Activities after Tax		4,46,000
II.	**Cash Flow from Investing Activities:**		
	Sale of Machinery		20,000
	Purchase of Fixed Assets		(3,60,000)
	Purchase of Current Investments		(40,000)
	Interest on Current Investments [(₹ 30,000 × 10/100 × 6/12) + (₹ 70,000 × 10/100 × 6/12)]		5,000
	Net Cash used in Investing Activities		(3,75,000)
III.	**Cash Flow from Financing Activities:**		
	Issue of Share Capital [₹ 1,00,000 + ₹ 10,000 (Premium)]		1,10,000
	Redemption of Preference Shares[₹ 1,00,000 + ₹ 5,000]		(1,05,000)
	Bank Loan Raised		1,00,000
	Interest on Bank Loan		(25,000)
	Dividend on Equity Shares		(36,000)
	Dividend on Preference Shares		(15,000)
	Net Cash flow from Financing Activities		29,000
IV.	**Net Increase Cash and Cash Equivalents [I + II + III]**		1,00,000
V.	**Opening Cash and Cash Equivalents**		90,000
VI.	**Closing Cash and Cash Equivalents**		1,90,000

Working Notes:

1. CALCULATION OF NET PROFIT BEFORE TAX

Particulars	₹
Closing Balance of P&L A/c	1,90,000
Add: Opening Balance of P&L A/c (Debit)	1,40,000
Add: Provision for tax	45,000
Less: Transfer from Reserve	(10,000)
Add: Dividend on Equity Shares	36,000
Add: Dividend on Preference Shares	15,000
Add: Premium on Redemption of Preference Shares	5,000
Net Profit before Tax	4,21,000

2. PROPERTY, PLANT & EQUIPMENT ACCOUNT

Particulars	*(₹)*	*Particulars*	*(₹)*
To Balance b/d	7,00,000	By PPE DISPOSAL A/C	60,000
To Bank A/c	3,60,000	By Balance c/d	10,00,000
	10,60,000		10,60,000

3. ACCUMULATED DEPRECIATION ACCOUNT

Particulars	*(₹)*	*Particulars*	*(₹)*
To Machinery Disposal A/c	20,000	By Balance b/d	3,00,000
To Balance c/d	3,40,000	By Profit & Loss A/c	60,000
	1,65,000		3,60,000

4. MACHINERY DISPOSAL ACCOUNT

Particulars	*(₹)*	*Particulars*	*(₹)*
To Machinery A/c	60,000	By Bank A/c	20,000
		By Accumulated Depreciation A/c	20,000
		By Profit & Loss A/c	20,000
	60,000		60,000

Dr. **5. PROVISION FOR TAX ACCOUNT** *Cr.*

Particulars	₹	*Particulars*	₹
To Bank A/c (balancing figure)	35,000	By Balance c/d	40,000
To Balance c/d	50,000	By P & L A/c	45,000
	85,000		85,000

ILLUSTRATION 33

From the following information, prepare a Cash Flow Statement:

Particulars	*31.03.2023* ₹	*31.03.2022* ₹
Share Capital	7,87,500	6,75,000
General Reserve	3,19,500	2,58,750
Profit and Loss A/c	2,13,750	95,625
Capital Reserve	11,250	—
Non-Current Liabilities [15% Debentures]	2,25,000	3,37,500
Trade Payables	2,94,750	1,91,250
Short-term Provisions (Provision for Tax)	85,500	78,750
Property,Plant & Equipment	13,50,000	11,25,000
Accumulated Depreciation	(2,81,250)	(2,25,000)
Non-Current Investments	2,02,500	2,02,500
Inventories	3,03,750	2,25,000
Trade Receivables	4,05,000	3,43,125
Provision for Doubtful debts	(56,250)	(45,000)
Other Current Assets (Prepaid Expenses)	13,500	11,250

Additional Information:

(i) During the year Fixed assets with a net book value of ₹ 11,250 (accumulated depreciation, ₹ 33,750) were sold for ₹ 9,000.

(ii) During the year Investments costing ₹ 90,000 were sold, and also Investments costing ₹ 90,000 were purchased. Profit on Sale was credited to Capital Reserve.

(iii) Debentures were retired at a Premium of 10%

(iv) Tax of ₹ 61,875 was paid during the year. Dividend paid during the year ₹ 33,750.

(v) During the year, bad debts of ₹ 15,750 were written off against the provision for Doubtful Debt account

SOLUTION

CASH FLOW STATEMENT FOR THE YEAR ENDED 31ST MARCH, 2023

Particulars	₹	₹
I. Cash Flows from Operating Activities:		
A. Balance as per Profit and Loss Account		2,13,750
Less: Opening Balance as per Profit and Loss Account		(95,625)
Add: Dividend declared		33,750
Add: Transfer to reserve		60,750
Add: Provision for Tax during the current year		68,625
B. Net Profit before Taxation and Extraordinary item		2,81,250
C. *Add:* Items to be added		
Depreciation	90,000	
Interest on Debentures	50,625	
Loss on sale of Fixed Assets	2,250	
Premium payable on redemption of Debentures	11,250	1,54,125
D. Operating Profit before Working Capital Changes		4,35,375
E. *Add:* Decrease in Current Assets and Increase in Current Liabilities		
Increase in Trade Payables	1,03,500	
F. *Less:* Increase in Current Assets & Decrease in Current Liabilities		
Increase in Inventories	78,750	
Increase in Trade Receivables	50,625	
Increase in Prepaid Expenses	2,250	(28125)
G. Cash generated from operations		4,07,250
H. *Less:* Income taxes paid		(61,875)
I. Net Cash from Operating Activities		3,45,375
II. Cash Flows from financing Activities:		
Proceeds from sale Assets		9,000
Proceeds from sale of Investments [₹ 90,000 + ₹ 11,250]		1,01,250
Purchase of Fixed Assets		(2,70,000)
Purchase of Investments		(90,000)
Net Cash used in Investing Activities		(2,49,750)
III. Cash Flow from Financing Activities:		
Proceeds from issuance of share capital		1,12,500
Repayment of Debentures		(1,23,750)

	Interest paid on Debentures		(50,625)
	Final Dividend paid		(33,750)
	Net cash from Financing Activities		(95,625)
IV.	**Net Increase in cash and cash Equivalents [I + II + III]**		0
V.	**Cash and cash Equivalents at beginning of period**		0
VI.	**Cash and cash Equivalents at End of period [IV + V]**		0

Working Notes:

Dr. **1. PROPERTY, PLANT & EQUIPMENT ACCOUNT** Cr.

Particulars	₹	*Particulars*	₹
To Balance b/d	11,25,000	By PPE Disposal A/c	45,000
To Bank (purchases) (Bal fig.)	2,70,000	By Balance c/d	13,50,000
	13,95,000		13,95,000

Dr. **2. ACCUMULATED DEPRECIATION ACCOUNT** Cr.

Particulars	₹	*Particulars*	₹
To PPE Disposal A/c	33,750	By Balance b/d	2,25,000
To Balance c/d	2,81,250	By Profit and Loss A/c (Provision for dep.) (Bal.fig.)	90,000
	3,15,000		3,15,000

Dr. **3. PROPERTY,PLANT & EQUIPMENT DISPOSAL ACCOUNT** Cr.

Particulars	₹	*Particulars*	₹
To PPE A/c	45,000	By Accumulated Dep, A/c	33,750
		By Bank A/c	9,000
		By Profit & Loss A/c (Loss)	2,250
	45,000		45,000

Dr. **4. PROVISION FOR TAX ACCOUNT** Cr.

Particulars	₹	*Particulars*	₹
To Bank A/c (Tax paid)	61,875	By Balance b/d	78,750
To Balance c/d	85,500	By P&L A/c (Prov.) (Bal. fig.)	68,625
	1,47,375		1,47,375

ILLUSTRATION 34

From the following information, prepare a Cash Flow Statement:

Particulars	*31.03.2023* ₹	*31.03.2022* ₹
Share Capital	4,00,000	3,00,000
General Reserve	1,40,000	1,10,000

Profit and Loss A/c	45,000	22,000
Non-Current Liabilities [10% Debentures]	1,00,000	1,50,000
Trade Payables	70,000	90,000
Other Current Liabilities (Dividend Payable)	4,000	—
Short-term Provisions (Provision for Tax)	40,000	50,000
Property, Plant & Equipment	4,29,250	2,98,000
Intangible Assets [Goodwill]	90,000	1,00,000
Non-Current Investments	60,000	1,00,000
Inventories	80,000	50,000
Trade Receivables	1,10,000	1,60,000
Cash & Cash Equivalents	24,000	10,000
Other Current Assets (Prepaid Expenses)	5,750	4,000

Additional Information:

1. 15% depreciation has been charged in the accounts on plant and machinery.
2. Old machines costing ₹ 50,000 (WDV. ₹ 20,000) have been sold for ₹ 35,000.
3. A machine costing ₹ 10,000 (WDV. ₹ 3,000) has been discarded.
4. ₹ 10,000 profit has been earned by sale of investments.
5. Debentures have been redeemed at 5% premium at the end.
6. ₹ 45,000 income tax has been paid and adjusted against Income Tax Provision Account.
7. Dividend paid during the year ₹ 26,000.

SOLUTION

CASH FLOW STATEMENT FOR THE YEAR ENDING 31.03.2023

		Particulars	₹	₹
I.	**Cash Flows from Operating Activities**			
	A.	Closing balance as per Profit and Loss Account		45,000
		Less: Opening Balance as per Profit and Loss Account		(22,000)
		Add: Dividend declared [26,000 + 4,000]		30,000
		Add: Transfer to Reserve		30,000
		Add: Provision for Tax		35,000
		Add: Premium on Redemption of Debentures		2,500
	B.	Net Profit before taxation and extraordinary item		1,20,500
	C.	*Add:* Items to be added		
		Depreciation	75,750	
		Interest on Debentures	15,000	
		Goodwill written off	10,000	
		Loss on Machinery	3,000	1,03,750
	D.	*Less:* Items to be deducted		
		Profit on sale of Machinery	(15,000)	
		Profit on sale of Investments	(10,000)	(25,000)

E.	Operating Profit before working capital changes [B + C – D]		1,99,250
F.	Decrease in Trade Receivables		50,000
G.	*Less:* Increase in Current Assets & Decrease in Current Liabilities		
	Increase in Inventories	(30,000)	
	Increase in Prepaid Expenses	(1,750)	
	Decrease in Trade Payables	(20,000)	(51,750)
H.	Cash generated from operations [E + F – G]		1,97,500
I.	*Less:* Income taxes paid (Net of Refund)		(45,000)
J.	Net Cash from Operating Activities		1,52,500
II.	**Cash Flows from Investing Activities**		
	Purchase of Machinery		(2,30,000)
	Proceeds for sale of Machinery		35,000
	Proceeds from sale of Investments		50,000
	Net Cash used in investing activities		(1,45,000)
II.	**Cash Flows from Financing Activities**		
	Proceeds from issuance of share capital		1,00,000
	Redemption of Debentures		(52,500)
	Interest on Debentures		(15,000)
	Final dividend paid [₹ 30,000 – ₹ 4,000]		(26,000)
	Net Cash from financing activities		6,500
IV.	**Net Increase in Cash and Cash Equivalents [I + II + III]**		14,000
V.	**Cash and Cash Equivalents at beginning of Period**		10,000
VI.	**Cash and Cash Equivalents at end of Period [IV + V]**		24,000

Working Notes:

Dr. **1. PROPERTY, PLANT & EQUIPMENT ACCOUNT** *Cr.*

Particulars	₹	*Particulars*	₹
To Balance b/d	2,98,000	By Bank A/c (Sale)	35,000
To Bank A/c (Balancing figure)	2,30,000	By Profit and Loss A/c (written off)	3,000
To Profit and Loss A/c (Profit)	15,000	By Depreciation A/c (4,29,250 × 15/85)	75,750
		By Balance c/d	4,29,250
	5,43,000		5,43,000

Dr. **2. PROVISION FOR TAX ACCOUNT** *Cr.*

Particulars	₹	*Particulars*	₹
To Bank A/c	45,000	By Balance b/d	50,000
To Balance c/d	40,000	By P&L A/c (b.f.)	35,000
	85,000		85,000

ILLUSTRATION 35

From the following information, prepare a Cash Flow Statement of TULSI AMLA GILOY Ltd.:

Particulars	*31.03.2023* ₹	*31.03.2022* ₹
Equity Share Capital of ₹ 10 each	10,50,000	7,50,000
5% Preference Share Capital of ₹ 100 each	2,00,000	4,00,000
General Reserve	1,40,000	4,40,000
Profit and Loss A/c	7,27,000	37,000
Securities Premium	55,000	20,000
14% Debentures	2,60,000	1,50,000
Current Liabilities:		
Short-term Borrowings (14% Bank Loan)	40,000	50,000
Trade Payables	1,65,000	40,000
Unclaimed Dividend on Equity Shares	20,000	–
Outstanding Interest on Debentures	10,000	–
Outstanding Underwriting Commission	5,000	–
Provision for Tax	40,000	20,000
Non-Current Assets:		
Property,Plant & Equipment	16,50,000	13,20,000
Accumulated Depreciation	(3,80,000)	(3,00,000)
Intangible Assets [Goodwill]	21,000	10,000
Current Assets:		
10% Current Investments	2,20,000	80,000
Interest Accrued on Current Investments	2,000	–
8% Fixed Deposit (Date of FD 1st Mar., 2023 maturing on 31st May, 2023)	2,84,000	–
Cash at Bank	1,33,000	1,00,000
Inventories	1,69,000	54,000
Trade Receivables	6,13,000	6,43,000

Additional Information:

(a) Dividends (including an Interim Dividend @ 28%) were paid on 1st April,2022.

(b) During the year a machine (having accumulated Depreciation being one third of cost) was sold for ₹ 50,000 at a loss of 37.5%.A fully depreciated machine was also discarded. Machinery costing ₹ 4,40,000 was purchased for cash.

(c) On 1st Jan.,2023, Some Current Investments costing ₹ 2,00,000 were purchased and Some Current Investments were sold at a profit of 20% on sale. New Debentures were issued and Bank Loan was repaid on the same date.

(d) On 1st May,2022 Preference Shares were redeemed at a premium of 5%.

(e) On 30th April,2022, the Business of Y Ltd. was purchased for ₹ 60,000 payable in fully paid equity shares of ₹ 10 each at 20% premium. The assets included Inventories ₹ 15,000. Trade Receivables ₹ 10,000 and Machine ₹ 30,000. Trade Payables of ₹ 15,000 were also taken over.

(f) Tax provided during the year was ₹ 30,000. Being a prudent accountant,ensure minimum reduction in free reserves.

SOLUTION

CASH FLOW STATEMENT

for the year ended 31st March, 2023

Particulars	₹	₹
I. Cash Flow from Operating Activities:		
A. Net Profit before tax [Refer WN 1]		6,60,000
B. Adjustments for Non-Cash and Non-Operating Items :		
Depreciation [Refer WN 3]	1,40,000	
Loss on Sale of Machinery [Refer WN 4]	30,000	
Interest on Debentures [(150000*14%) + (110000*14%*3/12)]	24,850	
Interest on Bank Loan [(50000*14%*9/12) + (40000*14%*3/12)]	6,650	
Goodwill amortised[10000 + 20000* -21000]	9,000	
*[60000 -(₹ 15,000+ ₹ 10,000 + ₹ 30,000 – ₹ 15,000)]		
Interest Income on Current Investments[(80000*10%*9/12) + (220000*10%*3/12)]	(11,500)	
Profit on sale of Current Investments [Refer WN 6]	(15,000)	
Underwriting Commission	5,000	1,89,000
C. Operating Profit before Working Capital Changes		8,49,000
D. Changes in Current Assets & Current Liabilities:		
Increase in Inventories [(1,69,000 – 15,000) – 54,000]	(1,00,000)	
Decrease in Trade Receivables [(6,13,000 – 10,000) – 6,43,000]	40,000	
Increase in Trade Payables [(1,65,000 – 15,000) – 40,000]	1,10,000	50,000
E. Net Cash Flow from Operating Activities before Tax		8,99,000
F. *Less:* Tax paid		(10,000)
G. Net Cash Inflow from Operating Activities after Tax		8,89,000
II. Cash Flow from Investing Activities:		
Sale of Machinery		50,000
Purchases of Fixed Assets		(4,40,000)
Purchases of Current Investments		(2,00,000)
Sale of Current Investments		75,000
Interest received on Current Investments [11,500 – 2,000]		9,500
Net Cash used in Investing Activities		(5,05,500)
III. Cash Flow from Financing Activities:		
Issue of Share Capital [₹ 2,50,000 + ₹ 25,000 (Premium in cash)]		2,75,000

Issue of Debentures		1,10,000
Interest paid on Debentures [24,850 – 10,000]		(14,850)
Interest paid on Bank Loan		(6,650)
Interim Dividend paid on Equity Shares [2,10,000 – 20,000]		(1,90,000)
Pref. Dividend paid		(20,000)
Redemption of Preference Shares [₹ 2,00,000 + 5%]		(2,10,000)
Bank Loan repaid		(10,000)
Underwriting Commission paid		0
Net Cash used in Financing Activities		(66,500)
Net Increase in Cash and Cash Equivalents		3,17,000
Cash and Cash Equivalents in the beginning		1,00,000
Cash and Cash Equivalents at the end		4,17,000

Working Notes:

1. CALCULATION OF NET PROFIT BEFORE TAX

Particulars	₹
Closing Balance of P&L A/c	7,27,000
Less: Opening Balance of P&L A/c	(37,000)
Less: Transfer from Reserve [440000 - 140000]	(3,00,000)
Add: Interim Dividend on Equity Shares [750000*28%]	2,10,000
Add: Pref. Dividend	20,000
Add: Premium on Red of Pref. Shares	10,000
Add: Tax	30,000
Net Profit before Tax	6,60,000

Dr.

2. PROPERTY, PLANT & EQUIPMENT ACCOUNT

Cr.

Particulars	₹	*Particulars*	₹
To Balance b/d	13,20,000	By Asset Sold A/c [80,000 x 3/2]	1,20,000
To Bank A/c (Purchases)	4,40,000	By Asset Discarded A/c	20,000
To Business Purchase A/c	30,000	By Balance c/d	16,50,000
	17,90,000		17,90,000

Dr.

3. PROVISION FOR DEPRECIATION ACCOUNT

Cr.

Particulars	₹	*Particulars*	₹
To PPE Disposal A/c	40,000	By Balance b/d	3,00,000
To PPE Disposal A/c	20,000	By P& L A/c (Depreciation for current year) (Balancing figure)	1,40,000
To Balance c/d	3,80,000		
	4,40,000		4,40,000

Dr. **4. PROPERTY,PLANT & EQUIPMENT SOLD ACCOUNT** Cr.

Particulars	₹	Particulars	₹
To PPE A/c	1,20,000	By Provision for Depreciation A/c	40,000
To PPE A/c	20,000	By Provision for Depreciation A/c	20,000
		By Bank A/c	50,000
		By Profit & Loss A/c (Loss)	30,000
	1,40,000		1,40,000

Dr. **5. NON-CURRENT INVESTMENTS ACCOUNT** Cr.

Particulars	₹	Particulars	₹
To Balance b/d	60,000	By Bank A/c [₹ 40,000 – ₹ 10,000]	30,000
To Bank A/c (Purchases) (b.f.)	1,40,000	By Capital Reserve A/c (Loss)	10,000
		By Balance c/d	1,60,000
	2,00,000		2,00,000

Dr. **6. CURRENT INVESTMENTS ACCOUNT** Cr.

Particulars	₹	Particulars	₹
To Balance b/d	80,000	By Bank A/c [60,000 + 25%]	75,000
To Bank A/c (Purchases)	2,00,000	By Balance c/d	2,20,000
To Profit & Loss A/c (Profit) [25% of ₹ 60,000]	15,000		
	2,95,000		2,95,000

Dr. **7. PROVISION FOR TAX ACCOUNT** Cr.

Particulars	₹	Particulars	₹
To Bank A/c [Tax paid]	10,000	By Balance b/d	20,000
To Balance c/d	40,000	By Profit and Loss A/c (b.f.) [Provision made]	30,000
	50,000		50,000

8. Increase in Inventories (₹ 15,000), Trade Receivables (₹ 10,000), Trade Payables (₹ 15,000) and Machine(₹ 30,000) against the Issue of Equity Shares are non-cash transactions. Hence, these items will not appear in the Cash Flow Statement.

9. 8% Fixed Deposit is Cash Equivalents and hence,its income is operating income. Therefore,no further adjustment is required.

Dr. **10. EQUITY SHARE CAPITAL ACCOUNT** Cr.

Particulars	₹	Particulars	₹
To Balance c/d	10,50,000	By Balance b/d	7,50,000
		By Bank A/c	2,50,000
		By Vendor's A/c	50,000
	10,00,000		10,00,000

Dr. **11. SECURITIES PREMIUM ACCOUNT** Cr.

Particulars	₹	Particulars	₹
To Balance c/d	55,000	By Balance b/d	20,000
		By Bank A/c (b.f.)	25,000
		By Vendor's A/c	10,000
	55,000		55,000

ILLUSTRATION 36

10% Investments: Opening ₹ 1,00,000, Closing ₹ 80,000, Accrued Interest on Investments: Opening ₹ 2,000, Closing ₹ 3,000. How will you disclose these items while preparing Cash Flow Statement as per AS–3 issued by ICAI?

SOLUTION

		₹
A.	**Cash Flow from Operating Activities**	
	Net Profit as per Profit & Loss A/c	
	Less: Interest on 10% Investments	(10,000)
B.	**Cash Flow from Investing Activities**	
	Sale of 10% Investments [1,00,000 – 80,000]	20,000
	Interest on Investments [10,000 – (3,000 – 2,000)]	9,000

ILLUSTRATION 37

10% Debentures: Opening ₹ 2,00,000, Closing ₹ 1,40,000, Unpaid interest on Debentures: Opening ₹ 500, Closing ₹ 2,000. Debentures were redeemed at 5% premium at the end of the year. How will you disclose these items while preparing Cash Flow Statement as per AS–3 issued by ICAI?

SOLUTION

A.	**Cash Flow from Operating Activities**	
	Net Profit as per Profit & Loss A/c	
	Add: Premium on Redemption of Debentures	3,000
	Less: Interest on 10% Debentures	(20,000)
B.	**Cash Flow from Financing activities**	
	Interest on Debentures paid [20,000 – (2,000 – 500)]	(18,500)
	Redemption of Debentures [(2,00,000 – 1,40,000) + 5% premium]	(63,000)

ILLUSTRATION 38

Investment in Shares: Opening ₹ 10,000, Closing ₹ 35,000, Dividend received amounted to ₹ 2,100 which included pre acquisition dividend of ₹ 600. How will you disclose these items while preparing Cash Flow Statement as per AS–3 issued by ICAI?

SOLUTION

A.	Cash Flow from Operating Activities	₹
	Net Profit as per Profit & Loss A/c	
	Less: Dividend (₹ 2,100 – ₹ 600)	(1,500)
B.	**Cash Flow from Investing Activities**	
	Purchase of investment in shares [(35,000 + 600) – 10,000]	(25,600)
	Dividend Income	2,100

ILLUSTRATION 39

Compensation received in a suit filed by the company ₹ 90,000. How will you disclose this item while preparing Cash Flow Statement as per AS–3 issued by ICAI?

SOLUTION

A.	Cash Flow from Operating Activities	₹
	Net Profit as per Profit & Loss A/c	
	Less: Compensation received	(90,000)
B.	**Operating Profit before extraordinary items**	
	Add: Compensation received	90,000

ILLUSTRATION 40

Capital Grant: Opening ₹ Nil, Closing ₹ 8,00,000. Grant of ₹ 10,00,000 amortised in P&L A/c. How will you disclose these items while preparing Cash Flow Statement as per AS–3 issued by ICAI?

SOLUTION

A.	Cash Flow from Operating Activities	₹
	Net Profit as per Profit & Loss A/c	
	Less: Capital Grant amortised	(10,00,000)
B.	**Cash Flow from Financing activities**	
	Grant Received	18,00,000

ILLUSTRATION 41

Voluntary Separation Payments : Opening ₹ 65,000, Closing ₹ 1,25,000. Voluntary Separation Payments ₹ 50,000 adjusted against General Reserve. How will you disclose these items while preparing Cash Flow Statement as per AS–3 issued by ICAI?

SOLUTION

A.	Cash Flow from Operating Activities	₹
	Operating Profit before extraordinary items	
	Less: Voluntary Separation Payments [(125,000+50,000) – 65,000]	(1,10,000)

ILLUSTRATION 42

Debtors of ₹ 2,30,000 were written off against the Provision for Doubtful Debts A/c during the year. Short-term Investments (held for 2 months) costing ₹ 10,000 were sold for ₹ 12,000. How will you disclose these items while preparing Cash Flow Statement as per AS–3 issued by ICAI?

SOLUTION

Profit on sale of short term investments and debtors written off against provision for doubtful debts do not require any further adjustment in **Cash Flow Statement.**

ILLUSTRATION 43

Following are the Extracts of Balance Sheets of Tulsian Ltd.:

Particulars	*31.3.2023 (₹)*	*31.3.2022 (₹)*
Equity Share Capital	9,10,000	5,00,000
General Reserve	2,10,000	2,50,000
Profit & Loss A/c	9,50,000	(40,000)
Securities Premium	50,000	—
Capital Redemption Reserve	—	1,00,000
Capital Grant	8,00,000	Nil
Convertible Debentures (into equity shares at 25% premium)	—	2,00,000
Trade Payables	1,00,000	1,05,000
Goodwill	15,000	—
Plant & Machinery	7,65,000	5,00,000
Inventories	95,640	54,000
Trade Receivables	7,50,000	6,25,000
Less: Provision for Doubtful Debts	(1,90,000)	(1,50,000)
Voluntary Separation Payments	1,25,000	65,000

Additional Information:

(a) Depreciation on Plant & Machinery written off @ 15%.

(b) It was decided to value Inventories at cost whereas previously the practice was to value Inventories at cost less 10%. However the closing stock on 31.03.2023 was correctly valued at cost.

(c) On 31st March 2023, the business of Y Ltd. was purchased for ₹ 60,000 payable in fully paid equity shares of ₹ 10 each at a premium of 20%. The assets included Inventories ₹ 26,640, Trade Receivables ₹ 10,000, and Machine ₹ 18,360. In addition Trade Payables of ₹ 15,000 were taken over.

(d) Debtors of ₹ 2,30,000 were written off against the Provision for Doubtful Debts A/c during the year. Grant of ₹ 10,00,000 amortised in P&L A/c. Compensation received in a suit filed by the company ₹ 90,000. Voluntary Separation Payments ₹ 50,000 adjusted against General Reserve.

Required: How will you disclose these items while preparing Cash Flow Statement as per AS–3 issued by ICAI.

SOLUTION

CASH FLOW STATEMENT OF TULSIAN LTD FOR THE YEAR ENDED 31ST MARCH, 2023

			₹
A	**Cash Flow from Operating Activities**		
	Net Profit [9,50,000 – (40,000) + 10,000 (t/f to Reserve)]		10,00,000
	Add: Depreciation [(7,65,000 x 15/85)] *Add:* Goodwill amortised		1,35,000 5,000
	[60,000 – (26,640 + 10,000 + 18,360 – 15,000)]–15,000		
	Less: Under valuation of Opening stock (54,000 × 10/90) *Less:* Compensation received *Less:* Capital Grant amortised		(6,000) (90,000) (10,00,000)
	Operating Profit before Working Capital changes		44,000
	Add: Increase in Provision for doubtful debts	40,000	
	Less: Increase in Inventories [(95,640 – 26,640) – (54,000 + 6,000)]	(9,000)	
	Increase in Trade Receivables [(7,50,000 – 10,000) – 6,25,000]	(1,15,000)	
	Decrease in Trade Payables [(1,05,000 – 15,000) – 1,00,000]	(10,000)	(94,000)
	Operating Profit before extraordinary items *Add:* Compensation received *Less:* Voluntary Separation Payments [(125,000+50,000) – 65,000] **Cash used in Operating Activities**		(50,000) 90,000 (1,10,000) (70,000)
B	**Cash Flow from Investing Activities**		
	Purchase of Machinery		(3,81,640)
	[(7,65,000+1,35,000) – 5,00,000 – 18,360]		
C	**Cash Flow from Financing Activities**		
	Issue of Equity Share Capital [(9,10,000 – 50,000 – 1,00,000 –1,60,000) – 5,00,000] Grant Received		1,00,000 18,00,000

Note: Debtors written off against provision for doubtful debts do not require any further adjustment in **Cash Flow Statement.**

COMPREHENSIVE ILLUSTRATIONS

COMPREHENSIVE ILLUSTRATION 1

From the following extracts of the Balance Sheets of SATYUG Ltd., **Prepare** Cash Flow Statement as per AS–3 issued by ICAI.

Particulars	*31.03.2023* ₹	*31.03.2022* ₹
Equity Share Capital of ₹ 10 each	10,00,000	6,00,000
5% Preference Share Capital of ₹ 100 each	2,00,000	4,00,000

General Reserve	1,40,000	4,40,000
Profit and Loss A/c	6,42,000	(13,000)
Securities Premium	55,000	20,000
Capital Redemption Reserve	50,000	1,50,000
Employees Stock Option Outstanding A/c	85,000	50,000
14% Debentures	2,60,000	1,50,000
Short-term Borrowings (14% Bank Loan)	40,000	50,000
Trade Payables	1,65,000	40,000
Provision for Tax	40,000	20,000
Property,Plant & Equipment	16,50,000	13,20,000
Accumulated Depreciation	(3,80,000)	(3,00,000)
Intangible Assets [Goodwill]	21,000	10,000
10% Current Investments	2,20,000	80,000
8% Fixed Deposit (Date of FD 1st Mar., 2023 maturing on 31st May, 2023)	2,84,000	-
Cash at Bank	1,00,000	1,00,000
Inventories	1,69,000	54,000
Trade Receivables	6,13,000	6,43,000

Additional Information:

(a) Dividends (including an Equity Dividend @ 35%) were paid on 1st April, 2022.

(b) During the year a machine (having accumulated Depreciation being one third of cost) was sold for ₹ 50,000 at a loss of 37.5%.A fully depreciated machine was also discarded. Machinery costing ₹ 4,40,000 was purchased for cash.

(c) On 1st Jan.,2023, Some Current Investments costing ₹ 2,00,000 were purchased and Some Current Investments were sold at a profit of 20% on sale. New Debentures were issued and Bank Loan was repaid on the same date.

(d) On 1st May,2022 Preference Shares were redeemed at a premium of 5%.

(e) On 01.01.2023, the Business of Y Ltd. was purchased for ₹ 60,000 payable in fully paid equity shares of ₹ 10 each at 20% premium. The assets included Inventories ₹ 15,000. Trade Receivables ₹ 10,000 and Machine ₹ 30,000. Trade Payables of ₹ 15,000 were also taken over.

(f) Tax provided during the year was ₹ 30,000. Being a prudent accountant,ensure minimum reduction in free reserves.

SOLUTION

CASH FLOW STATEMENT

for the year ended 31st March, 2023

Particulars	₹	₹
I. Cash Flow from Operating Activities:		
A. Net Profit before tax [Refer WN 1]		6,25,000
B. Adjustments for Non-Cash and Non-Operating Items :		
Depreciation [Refer WN 3]	1,40,000	

Loss on Sale of Machinery [Refer WN 4]	30,000	
Interest on Debentures [(150000*14%)+(110000*14%*3/12)]	24,850	
Interest on Bank Loan [(50000*14%*9/12)+(40000*14%*3/12)]	6,650	
Goodwill amortised[10000 + 20000* -21000] *[60000 -(₹ 15,000+ ₹ 10,000 + ₹ 30,000 – ₹ 15,000)]	9,000	
Interest Income on Current Investments[(80000*10%*9/12) + (220000*10%*3/12)]	(11,500)	
Profit on sale of Current Investments [Refer WN 6]	(15,000)	
Employees Stock Option Outstanding A/c [₹1,50,000 – ₹ 50,000]	35,000	2,19,000
C. Operating Profit before Working Capital Changes		8,44,000
D. Changes in Current Assets & Current Liabilities:		
Increase in Inventories [(1,69,000 – 15,000) – 54,000]	(1,00,000)	
Decrease in Trade Receivables [(6,13,000 – 10,000) – 6,43,000]	40,000	
Increase in Trade Payables [(1,65,000 – 15,000) – 40,000]	1,10,000	50,000
E. Net Cash Flow from Operating Activities before Tax		8,94,000
F.*Less:* Tax paid [Refer WN 7]		(10,000)
G. Net Cash Inflow from Operating Activities after Tax		8,84,000
II. Cash Flow from Investing Activities:		
Sale of Machinery		50,000
Purchases of Fixed Assets		(4,40,000)
Purchases of Current Investments		(2,00,000)
Sale of Current Investments		75,000
Interest received on Current Investments		11,500
Net Cash used in Investing Activities		(5,03,500)
III. Cash Flow from Financing Activities:		
Issue of Share Capital [₹ 2,50,000 + ₹ 25,000 (Premium in cash)]		2,75,000
Issue of Debentures		1,10,000
Interest paid on Debentures		(24,850)
Interest paid on Bank Loan		(6,650)
Equity Dividend paid		(2,10,000)
Pref. Dividend paid		(20,000)
Redemption of Preference Shares [₹ 2,00,000 + 5%]		(2,10,000)
Bank Loan repaid		(10,000)
Net Cash used in Financing Activities		(96,500)
Net Increase in Cash and Cash Equivalents		2,84,000
Cash and Cash Equivalents in the beginning		1,00,000
Cash and Cash Equivalents at the end		3,84,000

Working Notes:

1. CALCULATION OF NET PROFIT BEFORE TAX

Particulars	₹
Closing Balance of P&L A/c	6,42,000
Add: Opening Balance of P&L A/c (Debit)	13,000
Less: Transfer from Reserve[440000 - 140000]	(3,00,000)
Add: Equity Dividend on Equity Shares [600000*35%]	2,10,000
Add: Pref. Dividend	20,000
Add: Premium on Red of Pref. Shares	10,000
Add: Tax	30,000
Net Profit before Tax	6,25,000

Dr. **2. PROPERTY, PLANT & EQUIPMENT ACCOUNT (AT COST)** *Cr.*

Particulars	₹	*Particulars*	₹
To Balance b/d	13,20,000	By Asset Sold A/c [80,000 x 3/2]	1,20,000
To Bank A/c (Purchases)	4,40,000	By Asset Discarded A/c	20,000
To Business Purchase A/c	30,000	By Balance c/d	16,50,000
	17,90,000		17,90,000

Dr. **3. PROVISION FOR DEPRECIATION ACCOUNT** *Cr.*

Particulars	₹	*Particulars*	₹
To PPE Disposal A/c	40,000	By Balance b/d	3,00,000
To PPE Disposal A/c	20,000	By P& L A/c (Depreciation for current year) (Balancing figure)	1,40,000
To Balance c/d	3,80,000		
	4,40,000		4,40,000

Dr. **4. PPE DISPOSAL A/C** *Cr.*

Particulars	₹	*Particulars*	₹
To PPE A/c	1,20,000	By Provision for Depreciation A/c	40,000
To PPE A/c	20,000	By Provision for Depreciation A/c	20,000
		By Bank A/c	50,000
		By Profit & Loss A/c (Loss)	30,000
	1,40,000		1,40,000

Dr. **5. ASSET DISCARDED ACCOUNT** *Cr.*

Particulars	₹	*Particulars*	₹
To PPE A/c	20,000	By Provision for Depreciation A/c	20,000
	20,000		20,000

Dr. **6. CURRENT INVESTMENTS ACCOUNT** Cr.

Particulars	₹	Particulars	₹
To Balance b/d	80,000	By Bank A/c [60,000 +25%]	75,000
To Bank A/c (Purchases)	2,00,000	By Balance c/d	2,20,000
To Profit & Loss A/c (Profit) [25% of ₹ 60,000]	15,000		
	2,95,000		2,95,000

Dr. **7. PROVISION FOR TAX ACCOUNT** Cr.

Particulars	₹	Particulars	₹
To Bank A/c [Tax paid] (b.f.)	10,000	By Balance b/d	20,000
To Balance c/d	40,000	By Profit & Loss A/c [Provision made]	30,000
	50,000		50,000

8. Increase in Inventories (₹ 15,000), Trade Receivables (₹ 10,000), Trade Payables (₹ 15,000) and Machine(₹ 30,000) against the Issue of Equity Shares are non- cash transactions. Hence, these items will not appear in the Cash Flow Statement.
9. 8% Fixed Deposit is Cash Equivalents and hence,its income is operating income. Therefore,no further adjustment is required.

Dr. **10. EQUITY SHARE CAPITAL A/C** Cr.

Particulars	₹	Particulars	₹
To Balance c/d	10,00,000	By Balance b/d	6,00,000
		By Bank A/c	2,50,000
		By Capital Redemption Reserve A/c (Bonus Shares)	1,00,000
		By Vendor's A/c	50,000
	10,00,000		10,00,000

Dr. **11. SECURITIES PREMIUM A/C** Cr.

Particulars	₹	Particulars	₹
To Balance c/d	55,000	By Balance b/d	20,000
		By Bank A/c(b.f.)	25,000
		By Vendor's A/c	10,000
	55,000		55,000

COMPREHENSIVE ILLUSTRATION 2

From the following extracts of the Balance Sheets of TRETAYUG Ltd. ,**Prepare** Cash Flow Statement as per AS–3 issued by ICAI.

Particulars	*31.03.2023* ₹	*31.03.2022* ₹
Equity Share Capital of ₹ 10 each	10,00,000	6,00,000
5% Preference Share Capital of ₹ 100 each	2,00,000	4,00,000
General Reserve	1,40,000	4,40,000
Profit and Loss A/c	6,42,000	(13,000)
Securities Premium	55,000	20,000
Capital Redemption Reserve	50,000	1,50,000
Employees Stock Option Outstanding A/c	85,000	50,000
14% Debentures	2,60,000	1,50,000
Short-term Borrowings (14% Bank Loan)	40,000	50,000
Trade Payables	1,65,000	40,000
Unclaimed Dividend on Equity Shares	20,000	–
Outstanding Interest on Debentures	10,000	–
Outstanding Underwriting Commission	5,000	
Provision for Tax	40,000	20,000
Property,Plant & Equipment	16,50,000	13,20,000
Accumulated Depreciation	(3,80,000)	(3,00,000)
Intangible Assets [Goodwill]	21,000	10,000
10% Current Investments	2,20,000	80,000
Interest Accrued on Current Investments	2,000	
8% Fixed Deposit (Date of FD 1st Mar., 2023 maturing on 31st May, 2023)	2,84,000	–
Cash at Bank	1,33,000	1,00,000
Inventories	1,69,000	54,000
Trade Receivables	6,13,000	6,43,000

Additional Information:

(a) Dividends (including an Equity Dividend @ 35%) were paid on 1st April,2022.

(b) During the year a machine (having accumulated Depreciation being one third of cost) was sold for ₹ 50,000 at a loss of 37.5%.A fully depreciated machine was also discarded. Machinery costing ₹ 4,40,000 was purchased for cash.

(c) On 1st Jan.,2023, Some Current Investments costing ₹ 2,00,000 were purchased and Some Current Investments were sold at a profit of 20% on sale. New Debentures were issued and Bank Loan was repaid on the same date.

(d) On 1st May,2022 Preference Shares were redeemed at a premium of 5%.Underwriters were entitled to commission @ 5% on issue price of shares.

(e) On 01.01.2023, the Business of Y Ltd. was purchased for ₹ 60,000 payable in fully paid equity shares of ₹ 10 each at 20% premium. The assets included Inventories ₹ 15,000. Trade Receivables ₹ 10,000 and Machine ₹ 30,000. Trade Payables of ₹ 15,000 were also taken over.

(f) Tax provided during the year was ₹ 32,250 (Including tax@15% on short-term capital gain on Investments). Being a prudent accountant,ensure minimum reduction in free reserves.

SOLUTION

CASH FLOW STATEMENT

for the year ended 31st March, 2023

Particulars	₹	₹
I.Cash Flow from Operating Activities:		
A. Net Profit before tax [Refer WN 1]		6,27,250
B. Adjustments for Non-Cash and Non-Operating Items :		
Depreciation [Refer WN 3]	1,40,000	
Loss on Sale of Machinery [Refer WN 4]	30,000	
Interest on Debentures [(150000*14%)+(110000*14%*3/12)]	24,850	
Interest on Bank Loan [(50000*14%*9/12)+(40000*14%*3/12)]	6,650	
Goodwill amortised[10000 + 20000* – 21000]	9,000	
*[60000 – (₹ 15,000+ ₹ 10,000 + ₹ 30,000 – ₹ 15,000)]		
Interest Income on Current Investments[(80000*10%*9/12) + (220000*10%*3/12)]	(11,500)	
Profit on sale of Current Investments [Refer WN 6]	(15,000)	
Employees Stock Option Outstanding A/c [₹1,50,000 – ₹ 50,000]	35,000	
Underwriting Commission [5% on 2,75,000]	13,750	2,32,750
C. Operating Profit before Working Capital Changes		8,60,000
D. Changes in Current Assets & Current Liabilities:		
Increase in Inventories [(1,69,000 – 15,000) – 54,000]	(1,00,000)	
Decrease in Trade Receivables [(6,13,000 – 10,000) – 6,43,000]	40,000	
Increase in Trade Payables [(1,65,000 – 15,000) – 40,000]	1,10,000	50,000
E. Net Cash Flow from Operating Activities before Tax		9,10,000
F. ***Less:*** **Tax paid** [Refer WN 7] [12,250 – (15% of 15,000)]		(10,000)
G. Net Cash Inflow from Operating Activities after Tax		9,00,000
II.Cash Flow from Investing Activities:		
Sale of Machinery		50,000
Purchases of Fixed Assets		(4,40,000)
Purchases of Current Investments		(2,00,000)
Sale of Current Investments		75,000
Interest received on Current Investments [11,500 – 2,000]		9,500
Tax on short-term capital gain on Investments [15% of 15,000]		(2,250)
Net Cash used in Investing Activities		(5,07,750)
III.Cash Flow from Financing Activities:		
Issue of Share Capital [₹ 2,50,000 + ₹ 25,000 (Premium in cash)]		2,75,000
Issue of Debentures		1,10,000
Interest paid on Debentures [24,850 – 10,000]		(14,850)

Interest paid on Bank Loan		(6,650)
Equity Dividend paid [2,10,000 – 20,000]		(1,90,000)
Pref. Dividend paid		(20,000)
Redemption of Preference Shares [₹ 2,00,000 + 5%]		(2,10,000)
Bank Loan repaid		(10,000)
Underwriting Commission paid [(5% on 2,75,000) – 5,000]		(8,750)
Net Cash used in Financing Activities		(75,250)
Net Increase in Cash and Cash Equivalents		3,17,000
Cash and Cash Equivalents in the beginning		1,00,000
Cash and Cash Equivalents at the end		4,17,000

Working Notes:

1. CALCULATION OF NET PROFIT BEFORE TAX

Particulars	₹
Closing Balance of P&L A/c	6,42,000
Add: Opening Balance of P&L A/c (Debit)	13,000
Less: Transfer from Reserve [440000 - 140000]	(3,00,000)
Add: Equity Dividend [600000*35%]	2,10,000
Add: Pref. Dividend	20,000
Add: Premium on Red of Pref. Shares	10,000
Add: Tax	32,250
Net Profit before Tax	6,27,250

Dr. **2. PROPERTY,PLANT & EQUIPMENT ACCOUNT (AT COST)** *Cr.*

Particulars	₹	*Particulars*	₹
To Balance b/d	13,20,000	By Asset Sold A/c [80,000 x 3/2]	1,20,000
To Bank A/c (Purchases)	4,40,000	By Asset Discarded A/c	20,000
To Business Purchase A/c	30,000	By Balance c/d	16,50,000
	17,90,000		17,90,000

Dr. **3. PROVISION FOR DEPRECIATION ACCOUNT** *Cr.*

Particulars	₹	*Particulars*	₹
To PPE Disposal A/c	40,000	By Balance b/d	3,00,000
To PPE Disposal A/c	20,000	By P& L A/c (Depreciation for current year) (Balancing figure)	1,40,000
To Balance c/d	3,80,000		
	4,40,000		4,40,000

Dr. **4. PPE DISPOSAL A/C** *Cr.*

Particulars	₹	*Particulars*	₹
To PPE A/c	1,20,000	By Provision for Depreciation A/c	40,000
To PPE A/c	20,000	By Provision for Depreciation A/c	20,000
		By Bank A/c	50,000

		By Profit & Loss A/c (Loss)	30,000
	1,40,000		1,40,000

5. ASSET DISCARDED ACCOUNT Cr.

Particulars	₹	Particulars	₹
To PPE A/c	20,000	By Provision for Depreciation A/c	20,000
	20,000		20,000

Dr. **6. CURRENT INVESTMENTS ACCOUNT** Cr.

Particulars	₹	Particulars	₹
To Balance b/d	80,000	By Bank A/c [60,000 +25%]	75,000
To Bank A/c (Purchases)	2,00,000	By Balance c/d	2,20,000
To Profit & Loss A/c (Profit) [25% of ₹ 60,000]	15,000		
	2,95,000		2,95,000

Dr. **7. PROVISION FOR TAX ACCOUNT** Cr.

Particulars	₹	Particulars	₹
To Bank A/c [Tax paid] (b.f.)	12,250	By Balance b/d	20,000
To Balance c/d	40,000	By Profit & Loss A/c [Provision made]	32,250
	52,250		52,250

8. Increase in Inventories (₹ 15,000), Trade Receivables (₹ 10,000), Trade Payables (₹ 15,000) and Machine (₹ 30,000) against the Issue of Equity Shares are non-cash transactions. Hence, these items will not appear in the Cash Flow Statement.

9. 8% Fixed Deposit is Cash Equivalents and hence, its income is operating income. Therefore, no further adjustment is required.

Dr. **10. EQUITY SHARE CAPITAL ACCOUNT** Cr.

Particulars	₹	Particulars	₹
To Balance c/d	10,00,000	By Balance b/d	6,00,000
		By Bank A/c	2,50,000
		By Capital Redemption Reserve A/c (Bonus Shares)	1,00,000
		By Vendor's A/c	50,000
	10,00,000		10,00,000

Dr. **11. SECURITIES PREMIUM ACCOUNT** Cr.

Particulars	₹	Particulars	₹
To Pre. Shareholders A/c (Premium)	10,000	By Balance b/d	20,000
To Balance c/d	45,000	By Bank A/c(b.f.)	25,000

		By Vendor's A/c	10,000
	55,000		55,000

COMPREHENSIVE ILLUSTRATION 3

From the following extracts of the Balance Sheets of DWAPARYUG Ltd. ,**Prepare** Cash Flow Statement as per AS–3 issued by ICAI.

Particulars	*31.03.2023* ₹	*31.03.2022* ₹
Equity Share Capital of ₹ 10 each	9,50,000	6,00,000
5% Preference Share Capital of ₹ 100 each	2,00,000	4,00,000
General Reserve	1,40,000	4,40,000
Profit and Loss A/c	6,47,000	(13,000)
Securities Premium	-	20,000
Capital Redemption Reserve	50,000	1,50,000
Employees Stock Option Outstanding A/c	85,000	50,000
14% Debentures	2,60,000	1,50,000
Short-term Borrowings (14% Bank Loan)	40,000	50,000
Trade Payables	1,65,000	40,000
Unclaimed Dividend on Equity Shares	20,000	–
Outstanding Interest on Debentures	10,000	–
Outstanding Underwriting Commission	5,000	
Provision for Tax	40,000	20,000
Property, Plant & Equipment	16,50,000	13,20,000
Accumulated Depreciation	(3,80,000)	(3,00,000)
Intangible Assets [Goodwill]	21,000	10,000
10% Current Investments	2,20,000	80,000
Interest Accrued on Current Investments	2,000	
8% Fixed Deposit (Date of FD 1st Mar., 2023 maturing on 31st May, 2023)	2,84,000	-
Cash at Bank	33,000	1,00,000
Inventories	1,69,000	54,000
Trade Receivables	6,13,000	6,43,000

Additional Information:

(a) Dividends (including an Equity Dividend @ 35%) were paid on 1st April, 2022.

(b) During the year a machine (having accumulated Depreciation being one third of cost) was sold for ₹ 50,000 at a loss of 37.5%. A fully depreciated machine was also discarded. Machinery costing ₹ 4,40,000 was purchased for cash.

(c) On 1st Jan., 2023, Some Current Investments costing ₹ 2,00,000 were purchased and Some Current Investments were sold at a profit of 20% on sale. New Debentures were issued and Bank Loan was repaid on the same date.

(d) On 1st May, 2022, 20000 Equity Shares of ₹ 10 each were issued @ ₹ 15 to redeem Pref. Shares at a premium of 5%,. On 1st Oct., 2022, 1000 Pref. Shares of Rs 100 each were issued @ ₹ 150 to buy back 20000 equity shares @ ₹ 15. Underwriters were entitled to commission @ 5% on issue price of shares.

(e) On 30.04.2022, the Business of Y Ltd. was purchased for ₹ 60,000 payable in fully paid equity shares of ₹ 10 each at 20% premium. The assets included Inventories ₹ 15,000. Trade Receivables ₹ 10,000 and Machine ₹ 30,000. Trade Payables of ₹ 15,000 were also taken over.

(f) Tax provided during the year was ₹ 32,250 (Including tax@15% on short-term capital gain on Investments). Being a prudent accountant,ensure minimum reduction in free reserves.

SOLUTION

CASH FLOW STATEMENT

for the year ended 31st March, 2023

Particulars	₹	₹
I. Cash Flow from Operating Activities:		
A. Net Profit before tax [Refer WN 1]		7,57,250
B. Adjustments for Non-Cash and Non-Operating Items :		
Depreciation [Refer WN 3]	1,40,000	
Loss on Sale of Machinery [Refer WN 4]	30,000	
Interest on Debentures [(150000*14%) + (110000*14%*3/12)]	24,850	
Interest on Bank Loan [(50000*14%*9/12) + (40000*14%*3/12)]	6,650	
Goodwill amortised [10000 + 20000* – 21000]	9,000	
*[60000 -(₹ 15,000 + ₹ 10,000 + ₹ 30,000 – ₹ 15,000)]		
Interest Income on Current Investments [(80000*10%*9/12) + (220000*10%*3/12)]	(11,500)	
Profit on sale of Current Investments [Refer WN 6]	(15,000)	
Employees Stock Option Outstanding A/c [₹ 85,000 – ₹ 50,000]	35,000	
Underwriting Commission [5% on 4,50,000]	22,500	2,41,500
C. Operating Profit before Working Capital Changes		9,98,750
D. Changes in Current Assets & Current Liabilities:		
Increase in Inventories [(1,69,000 – 15,000) – 54,000]	(1,00,000)	
Decrease in Trade Receivables [(6,13,000 – 10,000) – 6,43,000]	40,000	
Increase in Trade Payables [(1,65,000 – 15,000) – 40,000]	1,10,000	50,000
E. Net Cash Flow from Operating Activities before Tax		10,48,750
F. *Less:* Tax paid [Refer WN 7] [12,250 – (15% of 15,000)]		(10,000)
G. Net Cash Inflow from Operating Activities after Tax		10,38,750
II. Cash Flow from Investing Activities:		
Sale of Machinery		50,000
Purchases of Fixed Assets		(4,40,000)
Purchases of Current Investments		(2,00,000)

Sale of Current Investments		75,000
Interest received on Current Investments [11,500 – 2,000]		9,500
Tax on short-term capital gain on Investments [15% of 15,000]		(2,250)
Net Cash used in Investing Activities		(5,07,750)
III. Cash Flow from Financing Activities:		
Issue of Equity Share Capital		3,00,000
Issue of Pref. Share Capital [1,00,000 + 50,000]		1,50,000
Issue of Debentures		1,10,000
Interest paid on Debentures [24,850 – 10,000]		(14,850)
Interest paid on Bank Loan		(6,650)
Equity Dividend paid [2,10,000 – 20,000]		(1,90,000)
Pref. Dividend paid		(20,000)
Redemption of Preference Shares [₹ 3,00,000 + 5%]		(3,15,000)
Buy back of Equity Shares [2,00,000 + 1,00,000]		(3,00,000)
Bank Loan repaid		(10,000)
Underwriting Commission paid [(5% on 4,50,000) – 5,000]		(17,500)
Net Cash used in Financing Activities		(3,14,000)
Net Increase in Cash and Cash Equivalents		2,17,000
Cash and Cash Equivalents in the beginning		1,00,000
Cash and Cash Equivalents at the end		3,17,000

Working Notes:

1. CALCULATION OF NET PROFIT BEFORE TAX

Particulars	₹
Closing Balance of P&L A/c	6,47,000
Add: Opening Balance of P&L A/c (Debit)	13,000
Less: Transfer from Reserve	(1,65,000)
Add: Equity Dividend [600000*35%]	2,10,000
Add: Pref. Dividend	20,000
Add: Tax	32,250
Net Profit before Tax	7,57,250

Dr. **2. PROPERTY, PLANT & EQUIPMENT ACCOUNT (AT COST)** *Cr.*

Particulars	₹	***Particulars***	₹
To Balance b/d	13,20,000	By Asset Sold A/c [80,000 x 3/2]	1,20,000
To Bank A/c (Purchases)	4,40,000	By Asset Discarded A/c	20,000
To Business Purchase A/c	30,000	By Balance c/d	16,50,000
	17,90,000		17,90,000

Dr. **3. PROVISION FOR DEPRECIATION ACCOUNT** Cr.

Particulars	₹	Particulars	₹
To PPE Disposal A/c	40,000	By Balance b/d	3,00,000
To PPE Disposal A/c	20,000	By P& L A/c (Depreciation for	1,40,000
To Balance c/d	3,80,000	current year) (Balancing figure)	
	4,40,000		4,40,000

Dr. **4. PPE DISPOSAL A/C** Cr.

Particulars	₹	Particulars	₹
To PPE A/c	1,20,000	By Provision for Depreciation A/c	40,000
To PPE A/c	20,000	By Provision for Depreciation A/c	20,000
		By Bank A/c	50,000
		By Profit & Loss A/c (Loss)	30,000
	1,40,000		1,40,000

Dr. **5. ASSET DISCARDED ACCOUNT** Cr.

Particulars	₹	Particulars	₹
To PPE A/c	20,000	By Provision for Depreciation A/c	20,000
	20,000		20,000

Dr. **6. CURRENT INVESTMENTS ACCOUNT** Cr.

Particulars	₹	Particulars	₹
To Balance b/d	80,000	By Bank A/c [60,000 +25%]	75,000
To Bank A/c (Purchases)	2,00,000	By Balance c/d	2,20,000
To Profit & Loss A/c (Profit) [25% of ₹ 60,000]	15,000		
	2,95,000		2,95,000

Dr. **7. PROVISION FOR TAX ACCOUNT** Cr.

Particulars	₹	Particulars	₹
To Bank A/c [Tax paid] (b.f.)	12,250	By Balance b/d	20,000
To Balance c/d	40,000	By Profit & Loss A/c [Provision made]	32,250
	52,250		52,250

8. Increase in Inventories (₹ 15,000), Trade Receivables (₹ 10,000), Trade Payables (₹ 15,000) and Machine(₹ 30,000) against the Issue of Equity Shares are non- cash transactions. Hence, these items will not appear in the Cash Flow Statement.

9. 8% Fixed Deposit is Cash Equivalents and hence,its income is operating income. Therefore,no further adjustment is required.

Dr. **10. EQUITY SHARE CAPITAL ACCOUNT** Cr.

Particulars	₹	Particulars	₹
To Equity Buy back A/c	2,00,000	By Balance b/d	6,00,000
To Balance c/d	9,50,000	By Bank A/c	2,00,000
		By Capital Redemption Reserve A/c (Bonus Shares)	3,00,000
		By Vendor's A/c	50,000
	11,50,000		11,50,000

Dr. **11. SECURITIES PREMIUM ACCOUNT** Cr.

Particulars	₹	Particulars	₹
		By Balance b/d	20,000
To Equity Buy back A/c (Premium)	1,00,000	By Bank A/c (Premium on Equity Shares)	1,00,000
To Capital Redemption Reserve A/c	80,000	By Bank A/c (Premium on Pref. Shares)	50,000
To Balance c/d	0	By Vendor's A/c	10,000
	1,80,000		1,80,000

Dr. **12. CAPITAL REDEMPTION RESERVE ACCOUNT** Cr.

Particulars	₹	Particulars	₹
To Equity Share Capital A/c	3,00,000	By Balance b/d	1,50,000
To Balance c/d	50,000	By Securities Premium A/c	80,000
		By General Reserve A/c	20,000
		By General Reserve A/c	1,00,000
	3,50,000		3,50,000

Dr. **13. GENERAL RESERVE ACCOUNT** Cr.

Particulars	₹	Particulars	₹
To Capital Redemption Reserve A/c	20,000	By Balance b/d	4,40,000
To Capital Redemption Reserve A/c	1,00,000		
To P & L A/c	1,65,000		
To Pre. Shareholders A/c (Premium)	15,000		
To Balance c/d	1,40,000		
	4,40,000		4,40,000

COMPREHENSIVE ILLUSTRATION 4

From the following information of KALYUG Ltd., **prepare the Cash Flow Statement as per AS–3 issued by ICAI**:

Particulars	31.3.2023 (₹)	31.3.2022 (₹)
Equity Share Capital	9,10,000	5,00,000
General Reserve	2,10,000	2,50,000
Profit & Loss A/c	6,61,500	(1,40,000)
Employees Stock Option Outstanding A/c	3,00,000	1,00,000
Securities Premium	50,000	—
Capital Redemption Reserve	—	1,00,000
Capital Grant	8,00,000	Nil
Convertible Debentures (into equity shares at 25% premium)	—	2,00,000
Trade Payables	1,05,000	1,00,000
Goodwill	15,000	—
Plant & Machinery	7,65,000	5,00,000
Non-Current Investments	35,000	50,000
Inventories	95,640	54,000
Trade Receivables	7,10,000	5,85,000
Less: Provision for Doubtful Debts	(1,90,000)	(1,50,000)
Voluntary Separation Payments	1,25,000	65,000
Cash and Cash Equivalents	14,69,360	6,000
Advance Tax (including ₹ 1,500 being 15% tax on gain on sale of Investments)	11,500	

Additional Information:

(a) Depreciation on Plant & Machinery written off @ 15%.A fully depreciated machine costing ₹ 1,00,000 was also discarded.

(b) It was decided to value Inventories at cost whereas previously the practice was to value Inventories at cost less 10%. However the closing stock on 31.03.2023 was correctly valued at cost.

(c) On 31st March 2023, the business of Y Ltd. was purchased for ₹ 60,000 payable in fully paid equity shares of ₹ 10 each at a premium of 20%. The assets included Inventories ₹ 26,640, Trade Receivables ₹ 10,000, and Machine ₹ 18,360. In addition Trade Payables of ₹ 15,000 were taken over.

(d) Debtors of ₹ 2,30,000 were written off against the Provision for Doubtful Debts A/c during the year. Grant of ₹ 10,00,000 amortised in P&L A/c. Compensation received in a suit filed by the company ₹ 90,000. Voluntary Separation Payments ₹ 50,000 adjusted against General Reserve.

(e) Dividend received amounted to ₹ 2,100 which included pre acquisition dividend of ₹ 600. Some Investments were sold at profit of 25% on cost.

SOLUTION

CASH FLOW STATEMENT FOR THE YEAR ENDED 31ST MARCH, 2023

			₹
A	**Cash Flow from Operating Activities**		
	Net Profit [6,61,500 – (1,40,000) + 10,000 (t/f to Reserve)]		**8,11,500**

	Add: Employees Stock Option Outstanding A/c [3,00,000 – 1,00,000]		2,00,000
	Add: Depreciation [(7,65,000 x 15/85)]		1,35,000
	Add: Goodwill amortised		5,000
	[60,000 – (26,640 + 10,000 + 18,360 – 15,000)]–15,000		
	Less: Profit on sale of Investments		(10,000)
	Less: Under valuation of Opening stock (54,000 × 10/90)		(6,000)
	Less: Compensation received		(90,000)
	Less: Capital Grant amortised		(10,00,000)
	Less: Dividend Income [2,100 – 600]		(1,500)
	Operating Profit before Working Capital changes		44,000
	Add: Increase in Provision for doubtful debts	40,000	
	Less: Increase in Inventories [(95,640 – 26,640) – (54,000 + 6,000)]	(9,000)	
	Increase in Trade Receivables [(7,10,000 – 10,000) – 5,85,000]	(1,15,000)	
	Decrease in Trade Payables [(1,05,000 – 15,000) – 1,00,000]	(10,000)	(94,000)
	Operating Profit before extraordinary items		(50,000)
	Add: Compensation received		90,000
	Less: Voluntary Separation Payments [(125,000+50,000) – 65,000]		(1,10,000)
	Cash used in Operations		(70,000)
	Less: Income taxes paid [11,500 – 1,500]		(10,000)
	Cash used in Operating Activities		**(80,000)**
B	**Cash Flow from Investing Activities**		
	Purchase of Machinery		(3,81,640)
	Purchase of Investments		(25,600)
	Dividend Received		2,100
	Sale of Investments		50,000
	Capital Gain Tax on Sale of Investments		(1,500)
	Net Cash used in Investing Activities		**(3,56,640)**
C	**Cash Flow from Financing Activities**		
	Issue of Equity Share Capital		1,00,000
	Grant Received		18,00,000
	Cash Flow from Financing Activities		**19,00,000**
	Net increase in Cash and Cash Equivalents		14,63,360
	Cash and Cash Equivalents in the beginning		6,000
	Cash and Cash Equivalents at the end		14,69,360

Note: Debtors written off against provision for doubtful debts do not require any further adjustment in Cash Flow Statement.

Working Notes:

Cr. **1. PROPERTY, PLANT & EQUIPMENT ACCOUNT** *Dr.*

Particulars	₹	*Particulars*	₹
To Balance b/d	5,00,000	By Depreciation A/c	1,35,000
To Business Purchase A/c	18,360	By Balance c/d	7,65,000
To Bank A/c (Purchase) (b.f.)	**3,81,640**		
	9,00,000		9,00,000

Dr. **2. INVESTMENTS ACCOUNT** *Cr.*

Particulars	₹	*Particulars*	₹
To Balance b/d	50,000	By Bank A/c (Dividend received)	600
To Profit & Loss A/c (Profit)	10,000	By Bank A/c (Sale Proceeds)	50,000
To Bank A/c (Purchases) (b.f.)	**25,600**	By Balance c/d	35,000
	85,600		85,600

Dr. **3. EQUITY SHARE CAPITAL ACCOUNT** *Cr.*

Particulars	₹	*Particulars*	₹
To Balance c/d	9,10,000	By Balance b/d	5,00,000
		By Capital Redemption Reserve [Bonus]	1,00,000
		By Debenture holders A/c	1,60,000
		By Y Ltd	50,000
		By Bank A/c (for cash) (b.f.)	**1,00,000**
	9,10,000		9,10,000

COMPREHENSIVE ILLUSTRATION 5

From the following information of TUSHAR LTD, prepare a Cash Flow Statement:

Particulars	*31.03.2023* ₹	*31.03.2022* ₹
Equity Share Capital	6,60,000	5,00,000
Preference Share Capital	—	2,00,000
General Reserve	1,36,000	2,80,000
Profit and Loss A/c	18,300	48,000
Securities Premium	—	8,000
Capital Grant	8,00,000	—
Capital Redemption Reserve	1,00,000	—
10% Debentures	1,40,000	2,00,000
Trade Payables	1,05,000	1,00,000
Unpaid Dividend	4,000	1,000
Unpaid Interest on Debentures	2,000	500
Provision for Tax	8,100	6,000
Property,Plant & Equipment	7,65,000	5,00,000

Intangible Assets [Goodwill]	15,000	—
10% Investments	80,000	1,00,000
Investments in Shares	35,000	10,000
Voluntary Separation Payments	1,25,000	65,000
Current Investments	21,500	31,500
Inventories	95,640	54,000
Trade Receivables	7,50,000	6,25,000
Provision for Doubtful debts	(1,90,000)	(1,50,000)
Cash & Cash Equivalents	2,73,260	1,06,000
Accrued Interest on Investments	3,000	2,000

Additional Information:

(a) Depreciation on Plant & Machinery written off @ 15%.

(b) Dividend received amounted to ₹ 2,100 which included pre acquisition dividend of ₹ 600

(c) Debentures and Preference Shares were redeemed at 5% premium at the end.

(d) Compensation received in a suit filed by the company ₹ 90,000.

(e) Grant of ₹ 10,00,000 amortised in P&L A/c.

(f) It was decided to value Inventories at cost whereas previously the practice was to value Inventories at cost *less* 10%. However the closing Inventories were correctly valued at cost.

(g) Trade Receivables of ₹ 2,30,000 were written off against the Provision for Doubtful Debts A/c during the year.

(h) Current Investments costing ₹ 10,000 were sold for ₹ 12,000.

(i) Voluntary Separation payment ₹ 50000 adjusted against General Reserve.

(j) At the end of the year the business of Y Ltd. was purchased for ₹ 60,000 payable in fully paid equity shares. The assets included Inventories ₹ 26,640, Trade Receivables ₹ 10,000, and Machine ₹ 18,360. In addition Trade Payables of ₹ 15,000 were taken over.

(k) Final Dividend paid during the year ₹ 27,000.

SOLUTION

CASH FLOW STATEMENT OF TULSIAN LTD FOR THE YEAR ENDED 31ST MARCH, 2023

	Particulars	₹	₹
A	Cash Flow from Operating Activities		
	Difference between Closing and Opening balance of P & L A/c		(29,700)
	Transfer to general reserve	6,000	
	Add: Dividend declared [27,000-1,000 + 4,000]	30,000	
	Provision for tax:	7,100	
	Depreciation	1,35,000	
	Premium on redemption of debentures	3,000	
	Premium on redemption of Preference		
	Shares (₹ 10,000 – ₹ 8,000)	2,000	
	Interest on Debentures	20,000	

	Goodwill amortised	5,000	2,08,100
	Less: Capital Grant amortised	10,00,000	
	Under valuation of Opening Inventories (54,000 × 10/90)	6,000	
	Compensation received	90,000	
	Interest on 10% Investment	10,000	
	Dividend (₹ 2,100 – ₹ 600)	1,500	
	Profit on Sale of Current Investments	2,000	(11,09,500)
	Operating profit before working capital changes		(9,31,100)
	Add: Increase in Provision for doubtful debts		40,000
	Less: Increase in Inventories [(95,640 – 26,640) – (54,000 + 6,000)]	9,000	
	Increase in Trade Receivables [(7,50,000–10,000) – 6,25,000]	1,15,000	
	Decrease in Trade Payables [(1,05,000 – 15,000) – 1,00,000]	10,000	(1,34,000)
	Operating Profit before extraordinary items		(10,25,100)
	Add: Compensation received		90,000
	Less: Voluntary Separation Payment		(1,10,000)
	Operating Profit before Income tax		(10,45,100)
	Less: Income Tax paid		(5,000)
	Net Cash Flow from Operating activities		(10,50,100)
B	**Cash Flow from Investing Activities**		
	Purchase of machinery		(3,81,640)
	Sale of 10% investment		20,000
	Interest on investments[10,000 - (3,000 - 2,000)]		9,000
	Purchase of investment in shares		(25,600)
	Dividend income		2,100
	Sale of Current Investments		12,000
	Net Cash Flow from Investing activities		(3,64,140)
C	**Cash flow from Financing activities**		
	Grant Received		18,00,000
	Dividend paid [30,000 – (4,000 – 1,000)]		(27,000)
	Interest on debentures paid [20,000 – (2,000 – 500)]		(18,500)
	Issue of Equity Share Capital [(6,60,000 – 60,000) – 5,00,000]		1,00,000
	Redemption of Red. Preference Shares [2,00,000 + 5% premium]		(2,10,000)
	Redemption of Debentures [60,000 + 5% premium]		(63,000)
	Net Cash Flow from Financing Activities		15,81,500
D	**Net Decrease in Cash & cash equivalents [A + B + C]**		1,67,260
E	**Opening Balance of Cash & Cash Equivalents (1,96,000 – 90,000)**		1,06,000
F	**Closing Balance of Cash & Cash Equivalents (3,73,260 – 1,00,000)**		2,73,260

Working Notes:

Dr. **1. PROVISION FOR TAX ACCOUNT** Cr.

Particulars	₹	Particulars	₹
To Bank A/c (bal. fig.)	5,000	By Balance b/d	6,000
To Balance c/d	8,100	By P & L A/c (Current year Provision)	7,100
	13,100		13,100

Dr. **2. PROPERTY, PLANT & EQUIPMENT ACCOUNT** Cr.

Particulars	₹	Particulars	₹
To Balance b/d	5,00,000	By P & L - Dep. (7,65,000 × 15/85)	1,35,000
To Business Purchase A/c	18,360	By Balance c/d	7,65,000
To Bank A/c (bal. fig.)	3,81,640		
	9,00,000		9,00,000

Dr. **3. GOODWILL ACCOUNT** Cr.

Particulars	₹	Particulars	₹
To Balance b/d	-	By P & L A/c (Amortised)	5,000
To Business Purchase [60,000 – (26,640 + 10,000 + 18,360 – 15,000)]	20,000	By Balance c/d	15,000
	20,000		20,000

Dr. **4. VOLUNTARY SEPARATION PAYMENTS ACCOUNT** Cr.

Particulars	₹	Particulars	₹
To Balance b/d	65,000	By General Reserve	50,000
To Bank A/c (bal. fig.)	1,10,000	By Balance c/d	1,25,000
	1,75,000		1,75,000

Dr. **5. 10% INVESTMENTS ACCOUNT** Cr.

Particulars	₹	Particulars	₹
To Balance b/d	1,00,000	By Bank A/c (Sale) (b.f)	20,000
		By Balance c/d	80,000
	1,00,000		100,000

Dr. **6. INVESTMENT IN SHARES ACCOUNT** Cr.

Particulars	₹	Particulars	₹
To Balance b/d	10,000	By Bank A/c [Pre-acquisition Div.]	600
To Bank A/c (bal. fig.)	25,600	By Balance c/d	35,000
	35,600		35,600

Dr. **7. GENERAL RESERVE ACCOUNT** Cr.

Particulars	₹	Particulars	₹
To Voluntary separation A/c	50,000	By Balance b/d	2,80,000
To Capital Redemption Reserve	1,00,000	By P & L A/c	6,000
To Balance c/d	1,36,000		
	2,86,000		2,86,000

8. Trade Receivables written off against provision for doubtful debts do not require any further adjustment.

SOLVED PROBLEMS

PROBLEM 1

Intelligent Ltd., a non financial company has the following entries in its Bank Account. It has sought your advice on the treatment of the same for preparing Cash Flow Statement.

1. Loans and Advances given to the following and interest earned on them:
   (a) to suppliers
   (b) to employees
   (c) to its subsidiaries companies
2. Investment made in subsidiary Smart Ltd. and dividend received
3. Dividend paid for the year
4. TDS on interest income earned on investments made
5. TDS on interest earned on advance given to suppliers
6. TDS on interest allowed on advance received from customers
7. TDS on interest allowed on Debentures
8. Insurance claim received against loss of fixed asset by fire
9. Insurance claim received against loss of Inventory by fire
10. Compensation paid in a suit filed by a customer
11. Deposit with bank for a term of 3 months
12. Deposit with bank for a term of 12 months
13. Deposit with bank for a term of two years
14. Bad debts written off
15. Purchase of Business for ₹ 20 lakhs payable by issue of Equity Shares of ₹ 11 lakhs,12% Debentures of ₹ 4 lakhs and the balance through RTGS
16. Redemption of 12% Debentures of ₹ 10 lakhs by issue of Equity Shares of ₹ 4 lakhs and the balance through RTGS
17. Pre-acquisition dividend received on investment made
18. Purchased Debentures of X ltd., on. 1st Dec, which are redeemable within 3 months

Discuss in the context of AS 3 Cash Flow Statement.

SOLUTION

1. Loans and advances given and interest earned	
(a) to suppliers	Operating Cash flow
(b) to employees	Operating Cash flow
(c) to its subsidiary companies	Investing Cash flow
2. Investment made in subsidiary company and dividend received	Investing Cash Outflow and Investing Cash Inflow
3. Dividend paid for the year	Financing Cash Outflow
4. TDS on interest income earned on investments made	Investing Cash Outflow
5. TDS on interest earned on advance given to suppliers	Operating Cash Outflow
6. TDS on interest allowed on advance received from customers	Operating Cash Outflow
7. TDS on interest allowed on Debentures	Financing Cash Outflow
8. Insurance claim received against loss of fixed asset by fire	Extraordinary item to be shown under a separate heading as 'Cash inflow from Investing activities'.
9. Insurance claim received against loss of Inventory by fire	Extraordinary item to be shown under a separate heading as 'Cash inflow from Operating activities'.
10. Compensation paid in a suit filed by a customer	Extraordinary item to be shown under a separate heading as 'Cash flow from Operating activities'
11. Deposit with bank for a term of 3 months	Cash Equivalents
12. Deposit with bank for a term of 12 months	Cash and Cash Equivalents
13. Deposit with bank for a term of two years	Cash and Cash Equivalents
14. Bad debts written off	It is a non-cash item which is adjusted from net profit/loss under indirect method, to arrive at net cash flow from operating activity.
15. Purchase of Business for ₹ 20 lakhs payable by issue of Equity Shares of ₹ 11 lakhs, 12% Debentures of ₹ 4 lakhs and the balance through RTGS	Investing Cash Outflow ₹ 5 lakhs Issue of Equity Shares and Debentures shall not be reported since these do not result in cash flow.
16. Redemption of 12% Debentures of ₹ 10 lakhs by issue of Equity Shares of ₹ 4 lakhs and the balance through RTGS	Financing Cash Outflow ₹ 6 lakhs. Issue of Equity Shares shall not be reported since it does not result in cash flow.
17. Pre-acquisition dividend received on investment made	Investing Cash Inflow
18. Purchased Debentures of X Ltd., on. 1st Feb, which are redeemable within 3 months	The investments made in debentures are for short-term, it will be treated as 'cash equivalent' and will not be considered as outflow in cash flow statement.

PROBLEM 2

Classify the following activities as per AS-3 Cash Flow Statement:

(i) Interest paid by financial enterprise

(ii) Dividend paid

(iii) Tax deducted at source on interest received from subsidiary company

(iv) Deposit with bank for a term of two years

(v) Insurance claim received towards loss of machinery by fire

(vi) Bad debts written off

Which activity does the purchase of business falls under and whether netting off of aggregate cash flows from disposal and acquisition of business units is possible?

SOLUTION

(i) Interest paid by financial enterprise	Cash flows from operating activities
(ii) Dividend paid	Cash flows from financing activities
(iii) TDS on interest received from subsidiary company	Cash flows from investing activities
(iv) Deposit with bank for a term of two years	Cash flows from investing activities
(v) Insurance claim received against loss of fixed asset by fire	Extraordinary item to be shown as a separate heading under, 'Cash flow from investing activities'
(vi) Bad debts written off	It is a non-cash item which is adjusted from net profit/loss under indirect method, to arrive at net cash flow from operating activity.

Purchase of Business falls under Investing Activities as per AS 3 "Cash Flow Statement". The aggregate cash flows arising from acquisitions and from disposals of other business units should be presented separately and classified as investing activities. Thus, netting of aggregate cash flows from disposal and acquisition of business units is not possible.

PROBLEM 3

From the following relevant extracts of the Balance Sheets of GINGER TULSI Ltd.,**Calculate Cash Flow from Operating Activities to be** disclosed in the Cash Flow Statement as per AS–3 issued by ICAI.

Particulars	***31.03.2023*** ₹	***31.03.2022*** ₹
General Reserve	1,40,000	4,40,000
Profit and Loss A/c	6,52,000	(13,000)
Capital Grant	2,00,000	Nil
Current Liabilities:		
Trade Payables	1,65,000	40,000
Unclaimed Dividend on Equity Shares	20,000	–
Outstanding Interest on Short-term Borrowings	10,000	–
Outstanding Underwriting Commission	5,000	
Provision for Tax	40,000	20,000

Current Assets:		
Interest Accrued on Current Investments	2,000	
8% Fixed Deposit (Date of FD 1st Mar., 2023 maturing on 31st May, 2023) FD carries payment of interest on monthly basis.	2,84,000	–
Inventories	1,69,000	54,000
Trade Receivables	6,13,000	6,43,000
Less: Provision for Doubtful Debts	(1,90,000)	(1,50,000)
Cash at Bank	1,33,000	1,00,000

Additional Information:

(a) During the year Depreciation provided ₹ 1,40,000, Interest paid on Short-term Borrowings ₹ 14,850, Dividend paid on Equity Shares ₹ 1,90,000, Underwriting Commission paid ₹ 3,250, Interest received on Current Investments ₹ 9,500. Tax provided ₹ 32,250 (including tax@15% on short-term capital gain). Tax paid includes tax@15% on short-term capital gain on Current Investments. Short-term capital gain on Current Investments ₹ 15,000. Capital Grant received ₹ 5,00,000. Compensation received in a suit filed by the company ₹ 90,000. Debtors of ₹ 2,30,000 were written off against the Provision for Doubtful Debts A/c.

(b) On 31.03.2023, the Business of Y Ltd. was purchased for ₹ 60,000 payable in fully paid equity shares of ₹ 10 each at 20% premium. The assets included Inventories ₹ 15,000. Trade Receivables ₹ 10,000 and Machine ₹ 50,000. Trade Payables of ₹ 15,000 were also taken over.

(c) It was decided to value Inventories at cost whereas previously the practice was to value Inventories at cost *less* 10%. However the closing stock on 31.03.2023 was correctly valued at cost.

SOLUTION

STEP 1: CALCULATION OF NET PROFIT BEFORE TAX

Particulars	₹
Closing Balance of P&L A/c	6,52,000
Add: Opening Balance of P&L A/c (Debit)	13,000
Less: Transfer from Reserve	(3,00,000)
Add: Dividend on Equity Shares [1,90,000 + 20,000]	2,10,000
Add: Tax	32,250
Net Profit before Tax	6,07,250

Cash Flow from Operating Activities:

		₹	₹
A.	Net Profit before tax		6,07,250
B.	Adjustments for Non-Cash and Non-Operating Items :		
	Depreciation	1,40,000	
	Interest on Short-term Borrowings [14,850 + 10,000]	24,850	
	Interest Income on Current Investments [9,500 + 2,000]	(11,500)	
Short-term capital gain on sale of Current Investments		(15,000)	
Underwriting Commission [3,250 + 5,000]		8,250	

Less: Under valuation of Opening stock (54,000 × 10/90)	(6,000)	
Less: Compensation received	(90,000)	
Less: Grant amortised	(3,00,000)	(2,49,400)
Operating Profit before Working Capital changes		3,57,850
Changes in Current Assets & Current Liabilities:		
Increase in Inventories [(1,69,000 – 15,000) – (54,000 + 6,000)]	(94,000)	
Decrease in Trade Receivables [(6,13,000 – 10,000) – 6,43,000]	40,000	
Increase in Trade Payables [(1,65,000 – 15,000) – 40,000]	1,10,000	
Increase in Provision for doubtful debts (1,90,000 – 1,50,000)	40,000	96,000
Operating Profit before extraordinary items		4,53,850
Add: Compensation received		90,000
Net Cash Flow from Operating Activities before Tax		5,43,850
***Less:* Tax paid** [12,250 – (15% of 15,000)]		(10,000)
Net Cash Inflow from Operating Activities after Tax		5,33,850

Dr. **PROVISION FOR TAX ACCOUNT** Cr.

Particulars	₹	*Particulars*	₹
To Bank A/c [Tax paid] (b.f.)	12,250	By Balance b/d	20,000
To Balance c/d	40,000	By Profit and Loss A/c [Provision made]	32,250
	52,250		52,250

PROBLEM 4

From the following relevant extracts of the Balance Sheets of HONEY TULSI Ltd., **Calculate Cash Flow from Financing Activities** to be disclosed in the Cash Flow Statement as per AS–3 issued by ICAI.

Particulars	*31.03.2023* ₹	*31.03.2022* ₹
Equity Share Capital (Shares of ₹ 10 each)	10,55,000	6,00,000
5% Pref Share Capital (Shares of ₹ 100 each)	2,00,000	4,00,000
General Reserve	1,40,000	4,40,000
Profit and Loss A/c	6,42,000	(13,000)
Securities Premium	52,500	20,000
Capital Redemption Reserve	-	1,50,000
Non-Current Liabilities(12% Debentures)	2,75,000	1,50,000
Current Liabilities:		
Outstanding Interest on Debentures	10,000	--
Outstanding Underwriting Commission	5,000	--
Unclaimed Dividend on Equity Shares	20,000	--
Non-Current Assets(Machine)	30,000	-

Additional Information:

(a) On 1st April, 2022, Dividends (including an Equity Dividend @ 35%) were paid.

(b) On 1st May,2022, 20000 Equity Shares of ₹ 10 each were issued to public @ ₹ 15 to redeem Pref. Shares at 5% premium.

(c) On 1st Oct., 2022,1000 Pref. Shares of ₹ 100 each were issued to public @ ₹ 150 to buy back 15000 equity shares @ ₹ 15. On the same date, 50% of Debentures were redeemed at 10% premium by converting into Equity Shares of ₹ 10 each @ ₹ 15 each and some New Debentures of ₹ 100 each were issued to public.

(d) Underwriters were entitled to Commission on all public issues of securities at maximum rate as per The Companies Act, 2013.

(e) On 31st Mar., 2023, a Machine costing ₹ 30,000 was purchased by issue of Equity Shares of ₹ 10 each at a premium of 20%.

SOLUTION

CALCULATION OF NET CASH FLOW FROM FINANCING ACTIVITIES

Particulars	₹
Issue of Equity Shares for cash [₹ 2,00,000 + ₹ 1,00,000 Premium]	3,00,000
Buy-back of Equity Shares [₹ 1,50,000 + ₹ 75,000 Premium]	(2,25,000)
Issue of Pref. Shares [₹1,00,000 + ₹ 50,000 Premium]	1,50,000
Redemption of Pref. Shares [₹ 3,00,000 + ₹ 15,000 Prem]	(3,15,000)
Issue of Debentures [₹ 2,00,000]	2,00,000
Interest on Debentures paid [(₹1,50,000 × 6%) + [(₹ 2,75,000 × 6%) – ₹ 10,000]	(15,500)
Dividend on Equity Shares paid [(₹ 6,00,000 × 35%) – ₹ 20,000]	(1,90,000)
Dividend on Pref. Shares paid [(₹ 4,00,000 × 5%)]	(20,000)
Underwriting Commission paid [(₹ 3,00,000 + ₹ 1,50,000) × 5%)] + [₹ ₹ 2,00,000× 2.5%] – ₹ 5,000	(22,500)
Net Cash used in Financing Activities	(1,38,000)

PROBLEM 5

From the following information, prepare a Cash Flow Statement:

Particulars	*31.03.2023* ₹	*31.03.2022* ₹
Equity Share Capital	16,00,000	12,00,000
10% Preference Share Capital	2,80,000	4,00,000
General Reserve	9,44,000	8,00,000
Profit and Loss A/c	2,60,000	1,60,000
Capital Reserve	40,000	—
9% Debentures	2,80,000	4,00,000
Trade Payables	5,20,000	4,80,000
Unpaid Dividend	16,000	—
Provision for Tax	3,40,000	3,60,000
Property,Plant & Equipment	38,00,000	32,00,000

Accumulated Depreciation	(11,60,000)	(9,20,000)
Non-Current Investments	3,20,000	4,00,000
Cash & Cash Equivalents	10,000	10,000
Other Current Assets	13,10,000	11,10,000

Additional Information:

(i) The company sold one fixed asset for ₹ 1,00,000, the cost of which was ₹ 2,00,000 and the depreciation provided on it was ₹ 80,000. The company also decided to write off another fixed asset costing ₹ 56,000 on which depreciation amounting to ₹ 40,000 has been provided. Depreciation on fixed assets provided ₹ 3,60,000.

(ii) Sold some investment at a profit of ₹ 40,000, which was credited to capital reserve.

(iii) Debentures and preference share capital redeemed at 5% premium.

(iv) Company decided to value Inventories at cost, whereas previously the practice was to value Inventories at cost *less* 10%. The opening Inventories was ₹ 2,16,000. The Closing Inventories was correctly valued at ₹ 3,00,000.

(v) Dividend paid during the year ₹ 1,04,000.

SOLUTION

CASH FLOW STATEMENT FOR THE YEAR ENDED 31ST MARCH, 2023

	Particulars	₹	₹
I.	**Cash Flow from operating activities**		
	Profit after appropriation		
	Increase in Profit and Loss Account after inventory adjustment [₹ 2,60,000 – (₹ 1,60,000 + ₹ 24,000)]	76,000	
	Transfer to general reserve	1,44,000	
	Add: Dividend declared [1,04,000+16,000]	1,20,000	
	Provision for tax	3,40,000	
	Net profit before taxation and extraordinary item	6,80,000	
	Adjustments for:		
	Depreciation	3,60,000	
	Loss on sale of fixed assets	20,000	
	Interest on Debentures	36,000	
	Decrease in value of fixed assets	16,000	
	Premium on redemption of preference share' capital	6,000	
	Premium on redemption of debentures	6,000	
	Operating profit before working capital changes	11,24,000	
	Increase in Trade Payables (₹ 5,20,000 – ₹ 4,80,000)	40,000	
	Increase in other current assets [₹ 13,10,000 – (₹ 11,10,000 + ₹ 24,000))	(1,76,000)	
	Cash generated from operations	9,88,000	
	Income taxes paid	(3,60,000)	
	Net Cash from operating activities		6,28,000

II.	**Cash Flow from investing activities**		
	Purchase of fixed assets	(8,56,000)	
	Proceeds from sale of fixed assets	1,00,000	
	Proceeds from sale of investments	1,20,000	
	Net Cash from investing activities		(6,36,000)
III.	**Cash Flow from financing activities**		
	Proceeds from issuance of Share Capital		4,00,000
	Redemption of Preference Share Capital (₹ 1,20,000 + ₹ 6,000)		(1,26,000)
	Redemption of Debentures (₹ 1,20,000 + ₹ 6,000)		(1,26,000)
	Dividend paid (₹ 1,20,000 – ₹ 16,000)		(1,04,000)
	Interest on Debentures		(36,000)
	Net Cash from financing activities		8,000
	Net increase/decrease in cash and cash equivalent during the year		Nil
	Cash and Cash equivalent at the beginning of the year		10,000
	Cash and Cash equivalent at the end of the year		10,000

Working Notes:

(1) Revaluation of Inventories will increase opening Inventories by ₹ 24,000 (i.e. 2,16,000 × 10/90)

Opening of other current assets ₹ 11,10,000 + ₹ 24,000 = ₹ 11,34,000

Due to under valuation of Inventories, the opening balance of Profit and Loss Account be increase by ₹ 24,000.

The opening balance Profit and Loss Account after revaluation of Inventories will be ₹ 1,60,000 + ₹ 24,000 = ₹ 1,84,000

Dr. **2. INVESTMENTS ACCOUNT** *Cr.*

Particulars	₹	*Particulars*	₹
To Balance b/d	4,00,000	By Bank A/c (Balancing figure	1,20,000
To Capital Reserve Account	40,000	being investment sold)	
(Profit on sale of investment)		Balance c/d	3,20,000
	4,40,000		4,40,000

Dr. **3. PROPERTY,PLANT & EQUIPMENT ACCOUNT** *Cr.*

Particulars	₹	*Particulars*	₹
To Balance b/d	32,00,000	By Bank A/c (sale of Assets)	1,00,000
To Bank A/c (Bal. figure	8,56,000	By Accumulated depreciation A/c	80,000
being assets purchased)		By Profit and Loss A/c	20,000
		(Loss on sale of assets)	
		By Accumulated Depreciation A/c	40,000
		By Profit and Loss A/c	16,000

			(Assets written off)	
			By Balance c/d	38,00,000
		40,56,000		40,56,000

Dr. **4. ACCUMULATED DEPRECIATION ACCOUNT** Cr.

Particulars	₹	Particulars	₹
To PPE A/c	80,000	By Balance b/d	9,20,000
To PPE A/c	40,000	By Profit and Loss A/c	3,60,000
To Balance c/d	11,60,000	(Depreciation for the period)	
	12,80,000		12,80,000

PROBLEM 6

From the following information, prepare a Cash Flow Statement:

Particulars	31.03.2023 ₹	31.03.2022 ₹
Equity Share Capital	6,00,000	5,00,000
10% Preference Share Capital	—	2,00,000
General Reserve	1,90,000	3,10,000
Profit and Loss A/c	60,000	25,000
Capital Reserve	1,00,000	—
Capital Redemption Reserve	1,00,000	—
9% Debentures(issued in the beginning)	2,00,000	—
Trade Payables	1,15,000	1,10,000
Other Current Liabilities	30,000	20,000
Provision for Tax	95,000	60,000
Land & Building	1,50,000	2,00,000
Machinery	7,65,000	5,00,000
Non-Current Investments	50,000	80,000
Voluntary Separation Payments	1,25,000	65,000
Inventories	95,000	90,000
Trade Receivables	2,40,000	2,00,000
Cash & Cash Equivalents	65,000	90,000

Additional Information:

(i) A piece of land has been sold out for ₹ 1,50,000 (Cost: ₹ 1,20,000) and the balance land was revalued. Capital Reserve consisted of profit on sale and profit on revaluation.

(ii) During the year on 1st April, 2022 a plant was sold for ₹ 90,000 (Original Cost: ₹ 70,000 and W.D.V.: ₹ 50,000) and Debentures worth ₹ 1 lakhs was issued at par as part consideration for plant of ₹ 4.5 lakhs acquired. Depreciation @ 15% has been written off from Plant account but no depreciation has been charged on Land and Building.

(iii) Part of the investments (Cost ₹ 50,000) was sold for ₹ 70,000.

(iv) Income tax liability for the current year was estimated at ₹ 1,35,000.

(v) Pre-acquisition dividend received ₹ 5,000 was adjusted against cost of investment.

(vi) Voluntary separation cost of ₹ 50,000 was adjusted against General Reserve.

SOLUTION

CASH FLOW STATEMENT FOR THE YEAR ENDED 31ST MARCH, 2023

Particulars	₹
Net Profit before taxation	2,60,000
Adjustment for:	
Depreciation	1,35,000
Profit on sale of plant	(40,000)
Profit on sale of investments	(20,000)
Interest on debentures	18,000
Operating profit before working capital changes	3,53,000
Increase in Inventories	(5,000)
Increase in Trade Receivables	(40,000)
Increase in Trade Payables	5,000
Increase in other current liabilities	10,000
Cash generated from operations	3,23,000
Income taxes paid	(1,00,000)
	2,23,000
Voluntary separation payments	(1,10,000)
Net Cash from operating activities	1,13,000
Cash Flow from investing activities	
Proceeds from sale of land	1,50,000
Proceeds from sale of plant	90,000
Proceeds from sale of investments	70,000
Purchase of plant	(3,50,000)
Purchase of investments	(25,000)
Pre-acquisition dividend received	5,000
Net cash used in investing activities	(60,000)
Cash Flow from financing activities	
Proceeds from issue of equity shares	1,00,000
Proceeds from issue of debentures	1,00,000
Redemption of preference shares	(2,00,000)
Dividends paid	(60,000)
Interest paid on debentures	(18,000)
Net cash used in financing activities	(78,000)
Net decrease in cash and cash equivalents	(25,000)
Cash and cash equivalents at the beginning of the year	90,000
Cash and Cash equivalents at the end of the year	65,000

Working Notes:

1. NET PROFIT BEFORE TAXATION

Particulars	₹
Retained profit	60,000
Less: Opening Balance	(25,000)
Transfer to general reserve	30,000
Add: Dividend declared	60,000
Provision for taxation	1,35,000
	2,60,000

Dr. **2. LAND AND BUILDING ACCOUNT** *Cr.*

Particulars	₹	*Particulars*	₹
To Balance b/d	2,00,000	By Cash (Sale)	1,50,000
To Capital Reserve (Profit on sale)	30,000	By Balance c/d	1,50,000
To Capital Reserve (Revalua. Profit)	70,000		
	3,00,000		3,00,000

Dr. **3. PROPERTY,PLANT & EQUIPMENT ACCOUNT** *Cr.*

Particulars	₹	*Particulars*	₹
To Balance b/d	5,00,000	By Cash (Sale)	90,000
To Profit and Loss A/c	40,000	By Depreciation A/c (b.f.)	1,35,000
To Debentures	1,00,000	By Balance c/d	7,65,000
To Bank A/c	3,50,000		
	9,90,000		9,90,000

Dr. **4. INVESTMENTS ACCOUNT** *Cr.*

Particulars	₹	*Particulars*	₹
To Balance b/d	80,000	By Cash (Sale)	70,000
To Profit and Loss A/c	20,000	By Dividend (Pre-acquisition)	5,000
To Bank A/c (Balancing figure)	25,000	By Balance c/d	50,000
	1,25,000		1,25,000

Dr. **5. PROVISION FOR TAXATION ACCOUNT** *Cr.*

Particulars	₹	*Particulars*	₹
To Bank (Balancing figure)	1,00,000	By Balance b/d	60,000
To Balance c/d	95,000	By Profit and Loss A/c	1,35,000
	1,95,000		1,95,000

Dr. **6. CAPITAL RESERVE ACCOUNT** *Cr.*

Particulars	₹	*Particulars*	₹
To Balance c/d	1,00,000	By Profit on Sale of Land	30,000
		By Profit on Reval. of Land	70,000
	1,00,000		1,00,000

Dr. **7. GENERAL RESERVE ACCOUNT** Cr.

Particulars	₹	Particulars	₹
To Voluntary separation cost	50,000	By Balance b/d	3,10,000
To Capital redemption reserve	1,00,000	By Profit and Loss A/c	30,000
To Balance c/d	1,90,000		
	3,40,000		3,40,000

Dr. **8. VOLUNTARY SEPARATION PAYMENTS ACCOUNT** Cr.

Particulars	₹	Particulars	₹
To balance b/d	65,000	By General Reserve	50,000
To Bank (Balancing figure)	1,10,000	By Balance c/d	1,25,000
	1,75,000		1,75,000

PROBLEM 7

From the following information, prepare a Cash Flow Statement:

Particulars	31.03.2023 ₹	31.03.2022 ₹
Equity Share Capital	2,50,000	1,50,000
8% Preference Share Capital	1,00,000	1,50,000
General Reserve	63,000	47,000
Profit and Loss A/c	27,000	18,000
Capital Reserve	25,000	—
Trade Payables	65,000	44,000
Dividend Payable	4,000	—
Provision for Tax	32,000	28,000
Land & Building	75,000	1,00,000
Machinery	1,91,000	90,000
Intangible Assets [Goodwill]	47,000	60,000
Non-Current Investments	35,000	10,000
Inventories	78,000	85,000
Trade Receivables	1,08,000	75,000
Cash & Cash Equivalents	32,000	17,000

Addition Information:

(i) ₹ 18,000 depreciation has been written off Plant and Machinery and no depreciation has been charged on Land and Building.

(ii) A piece of land has been sold out and the balance has been revalued, profit on such sale and revaluation being transferred to Capital Reserve. There is no other entry in Capital Reserve Account.

(iii) A plant was sold for ₹ 12,000 (WDV being ₹ 15,000).

(iv) Dividend received amounted to ₹ 2,100 which included pre acquisition dividend of ₹ 600.

(v) An interim dividend of ₹ 10,000 has been paid. Final Dividend paid during the year ₹ 23,000.

SOLUTION

CASH FLOW STATEMENT FOR THE YEAR ENDING 31ST MARCH, 2023

	Particulars	₹	₹
I.	**Cash Flows from Operating Activities**		
	A. Closing balance as per Profit and Loss Account		27,000
	Less: Opening balance as per Profit and Loss Account		(18,000)
	Add: Dividend declared [23,000+4,000]		27,000
	Add: Interim dividend paid during the year		10,000
	Add: Transfer to reserve		16,000
	Add: Provision for Tax		32,000
	B. Net profit before taxation, and extra ordinary item		94,000
	C. *Add:* Items to be added		
	Depreciation	18,000	
	Loss on sale of Plant	3,000	
	Goodwill w/o	13,000	34,000
	D. *Less:* Dividend Income		(1,500)
	E. Operating profit before working capital changes [B + C – D]		1,26,500
	F. *Add:* Decrease in Current Assets and Increase in current Liabilities		
	Decrease in Inventories	7,000	
	Increase in Trade Payables	21,000	28,000
	G. *Less:* Increase in Trade Receivables (Gross)		(33,000)
	H. Cash generated from operations [E + F – G]		1,21,500
	I. *Less:* Income taxes paid		(28,000)
	J. Net Cash from (used in) operating activities		93,500
II.	**Cash Flows from Investing Activities:**		
	Purchase of Plant		(1,34,000)
	Sale of Land		50,000
	Sale of Plant		12,000
	Purchase of Investments		(25,600)
	Dividend Received		2,100
	Net Cash used in investing activities		(95,500)
III.	**Cash Flows from Financing Activities:**		
	Proceeds from issuance of share capital		1,00,000
	Redemption of preference shares		(50,000)
	Interim Dividend paid		(10,000)

Final Dividend paid [₹ 27,000 – ₹ 4,000]		(23,000)
Net Cash from Financing Activities		17,000
IV. Net Increase in Cash and Cash Equivalents [I + II + III]		15,000
V. Cash and Cash Equivalents at beginning of Period		17,000
VI. Cash and Cash Equivalents at end of Period [IV + V]		32,000

Working Notes:

Dr. **1. LAND AND BUILDING ACCOUNT** *Cr.*

Particulars	₹	*Particulars*	₹
To Balance b/d	1,00,000	By Bank A/c (sale)	50,000
To Capital Reserve A/c (Profit on sale and revaluation)	25,000	By Balance c/d	75,000
	1,25,000		1,25,000

Cr. **2. PROPERTY, PLANT & EQUIPMENT ACCOUNT** *Dr.*

Particulars	₹	*Particulars*	₹
To Balance b/d	90,000	By Depreciation A/c	18,000
To Bank A/c (Purchase)	1,34,000	By Bank A/c (Sale)	12,000
		By Profit and Loss A/c	
		By (Loss on sale)	3,000
		By Balance c/d	1,91,000
	2,24,000		2,24,000

Dr. **3. INVESTMENTS ACCOUNT** *Cr.*

Particulars	₹	*Particulars*	₹
To Balance b/d	10,000	By Bank A/c (Div. received)	600
To Bank A/c (Purchases)	25,600	By Balance c/d	35,000
	35,600		35,600

4. It has been assumed that proposed dividend includes preference dividend also.

PROBLEM 8

From the following information, prepare a Cash Flow Statement:

Particulars	*31.03.2023* ₹ *'000*	*31.03.2022* ₹ *'000*
Share Capital	1500	1250
Reserves and Surplus	3410	1380
Long Term Debt	1110	1040
Trade Payables	150	1890

Interest Payable	230	100
Income Tax Payable	400	1000
Property,Plant & Equipment	2180	1910
Accumulated Depreciation	(1450)	(1060)
Non-Current Investments	2500	2500
Inventories	900	1950
Trade Receivables	1700	1200
Cash & Cash Equivalents	870	160
Interest Receivable	100	—

STATEMENT OF PROFIT OR LOSS FOR THE YEAR ENDED 31.3.2023

Particulars	*₹ '000*
Sales	30,650
Cost of sales	(26,000)
Gross profit	4,650
Depreciation	(450)
Administrative and selling expenses	(910)
Interest expenses	(400)
Interest income	300
Dividend income	200
Net profit before taxation and extraordinary items	3,390
Extraordinary items:	
Insurance proceeds from earthquake disaster settlement	140
Net Profit after extraordinary items	3,530
Income tax	(300)
	3,230

Additional Information:

(i) An amount of ₹ 250 was raised from the issue of share capital and a further ₹250 was raised from long-term borrowings.

(ii) Interest expense was ₹ 400 of which ₹ 170 was paid during the period ₹ 100 relating to interest expense of the prior period was also paid during the period.

(iii) Dividends paid were ₹ 1,200.

(iv) Tax deducted at source on dividends received (including in the tax expense of ₹ 300 for the year) amounted to ₹ 40.

(v) During the period the enterprise acquired fixed assets for ₹ 350. The payment was made in cash.

(vi) Plant with original cost of ₹ 80 and accumulated depreciation of ₹ 60 was sold for ₹ 20.

(vii) Trade Receivables and Trade Payables include amounts relating to credit sales and credit purchase only.

SOLUTION

CASH FLOW STATEMENT (DIRECT METHOD)

Particulars	₹ '000
Cash flows from Operating Activities	
Cash receipts from customers (30,650 + 1,200 – 1,700)	30,150
Cash paid to suppliers (24,950 + 1,890 – 150)	(26,690)
Cash paid to employees and for expenses	(910)
Cash generated from operations	2,550
Income tax paid (300 + 1000 – 400 – 40)	(860)
Cash flow before extraordinary item:	1,690
Proceeds from earthquake disaster settlement	140
Net cash from operating activities	1,830
Cash flows from Investing Activities	
Purchase of fixed assets	(350)
Proceeds from sale of equipment	20
Interest received (300 – 100)	200
Dividends received (200 – 40)	160
Net cash from investing activities	30
Cash flows from Financing Activities	
Proceeds from issuance of share capital	250
Proceeds from long term borrowings	250
Repayment of long term borrowings (1,040 + 250 – 1,110)	(180)
Interest paid (400 + 100 – 230)	(270)
Dividends paid	(1,200)
Net Cash used in financial activities	1,150
Net increase in cash and cash equivalents	710
Cash and Cash Equivalents at beginning of the period	160
Cash and Cash Equivalents at end of the period	870

Working Note:

CASH PAID TO SUPPLIERS, EMPLOYEES AND FOR EXPENSES

Particulars	₹ '000
Cost of sales	26,000
Add: Closing Inventories	900
Less: Opening Inventories	(1,950)
Credit Purchases	24,950

PROBLEM 9

The following figures have been extracted from the Books of X Ltd. for the year ended on 31.3.2023. You are required to prepare a cash flow statement.

(i) Net profit before taking into account Income Tax and Income from law suits but after taking into Account the following items was ₹ 20 lakhs:

(a) Depreciation on Fixed Assets ₹ 5 lakhs.

(b) Discount on issue of Debentures written off ₹ 30,000.

(c) Interest on Debentures paid ₹ 3,50,000.

(d) Books value of investments ₹ 3 lakhs (Sale of Investments for ₹ 3,20,000).

(e) Interest received on investments ₹ 60,000.

(ii) Compensation received ₹ 90,000 by the company in a suit filed.

(iii) Income tax paid during the year ₹ 10,50,000.

(iv) 15,000, 10% preference shares of ₹ 100 each were redeemed at the end at a premium of 5%. Further the company issued 50,000 equity shares of ₹ 10 each at a premium of 20%. Dividend on preference shares were paid at the time of redemption.

(v) Final Dividends paid ₹ 5 lakhs and Interim dividend paid ₹ 3 lakhs.

(vi) Land was purchased for ₹ 2,40,000 for which the company issued 20,000 equity shares of ₹ 10 each at a premium of 20% to the land owner as consideration.

(vii) Current assets and Current liabilities in the beginning and at the end of the years were as detailed below:

Particulars	*Opening* ₹	*Closing* ₹
Inventories	12,00,000	13,18,000
Trade Receivables	2,58,000	2,53,100
Cash in hand	1,96,300	35,300
Trade Payables	2,11,000	2,11,300
Outstanding expenses	75,000	81,800

SOLUTION

CASH FLOW STATEMENT FOR THE YEAR ENDED 31ST MARCH, 2023

Particulars	₹
Net Profit before income tax and extraordinary items:	20,00,000
Adjustments for:	
Depreciation on Fixed Assets	5,00,000
Discount on issue of Debentures	30,000
Interest on Debentures paid	3,50,000
Interest on Investments received	(60,000)
Profit on Sale of Investments	(20,000)
Operating profit before working capital changes	28,00,000
Adjustments for:	
Increase in Inventories	(1,18,000)
Decrease in Trade Receivables	4,900
Increase in Trade Payables	300

Increase in outstanding expenses	6,800
Cash flow from operation	26,94,000
Income Tax paid	(10,50,000)
	16,44,000
Cash flow from extraordinary items:	
Compensation received in a suit filed	90,000
Net Cash flow from operating activities	17,34,000
Cash flow from investing activities:	
Sale proceeds of investments	3,20,000
Interest received on investment	60,000
Net cash flow from investing activities	3,80,000
Cash flow from financing activities:	
Proceeds by issue of equity shares at a premium	6,00,000
Redemption of preference shares at a premium	(15,75,000)
Preference Dividend paid	(1,50,000)
Interest on debentures paid	(3,50,000)
Dividend paid (5,00,000 + 3,00,000)	(8,00,000)
	(22,75,000)
Net Decrease in Cash and Cash Equivalents	(1,61,000)
Cash & Cash Equivalents at the beginning of the year	1,96,300
Cash & Cash Equivalents at the end of the year	35,300

PROBLEM 10

From the following information, calculate Cash Flow from Operating Activities:

Cash Sales one fourth of Net Credit Sales

Net Credit purchases are four times the Cash Purchases

Discount allowed to customers..	₹ 6,000
Discount received from Suppliers..	₹ 3,000
Returns Inward..	₹ 10,000
Returns Outward..	₹ 5,000
Office & Selling Expenses	₹ 51,000
Depreciation..	₹ 19,000
Provision for Tax..	₹ 40,000
Trading Commission earned	₹ 1,02,000
Total Sales (Net of Returns)	₹ 2,00,000
Total Purchases (Net of Returns)	₹ 1,00,000
Bad Debts	₹ 4,000

Particulars	Opening	Closing
Trade Receivables	₹ 1,00,000	₹ 2,00,000
Trade Payables	₹ 1,00,000	₹ 50,000
Outstanding Office & Selling Expenses	₹ 500	₹ 1,000
Prepaid Office & Selling Expenses	₹ 1,000	₹ 500
Accrued Trading Commission	₹ 1,000	₹ 2,000
Advance Trading Commission	₹ 2,000	₹ 1,000
Provision for Tax	₹ 50,000	₹ 60,000

SOLUTION

STATEMENT SHOWING THE COMPUTATION OF CASH FLOW FROM OPERATING ACTIVITIES

Particulars	₹
A. Operating Receipts in Cash:	
(a) Cash Sales	40,000
(b) Collection from Trade Receivables	50,000
(c) Trading Commission received	1,00,000
	1,90,000
B. Operating Payments in Cash:	
(a) Cash Purchases	20,000
(b) Payments made to Trade Payables	1,27,000
(c) Office & Selling Expenses paid	50,000
	1,97,000
C. Cash used in Operations before taxes	7,000
D. Income Tax paid	30,000
E. Net Cash used in Operating Activities	37,000

Working Notes:

1. *Calculation of Cash Sales, Net Credit Sales and Gross Credit Sales*

Total Sales = Net Credit Sales + Cash Sales

Let Net Credit Sales be X

₹ 2,00,000 = X + ¼X

Multiplying the above equation by 4

₹ 8,00,000 = 4 X + X

X = ₹ 8,00,000/5 = ₹ 1,60,000

Cash Sales = ¼ × ₹ 1,60,000 = ₹ 40,000

Gross Credit Sales = Net Credit Sales + Returns Inwards = ₹ 1,60,000 + ₹ 10,000 = ₹ 1,70,000

2. *Calculation of Cash Purchases, Net Credit Purchases and Gross Credit Purchases*

Total Purchases = Net Credit Purchases + Cash Purchases

Let Cash Purchases be X

₹ 1,00,000 = 4X + X

X = ₹ 1,00,000/5 = ₹ 20,000

Net Credit Purchases = 4 × ₹ 20,000 = ₹ 80,000

Gross Credit Purchases = Net Credit Purchases + Returns Outward

= ₹ 80,000 + ₹ 5,000 = ₹ 85,000

Dr. **3. TOTAL TRADE RECEIVABLES ACCOUNT** Cr.

Particulars	₹	Particulars	₹
To Balance b/d	1,00,000	By Sales Returns	10,000
To Credit Sales	1,70,000	By Discount Allowed	6,000
		By Bad Debts	4,000
		By Cash Received (b.f.)	50,000
		By Balance c/d	2,00,000
	2,70,000		2,70,000

Dr. **4. TOTAL TRADE PAYABLES ACCOUNT** Cr.

Particulars	₹	Particulars	₹
To Purchases Returns	5,000	By Balance b/d	1,00,000
To Discount Received	3,000	By Credit Purchases	85,000
To Cash paid [Balancing Figure]	1,27,000		
To Balance c/d	50,000		
	1,85,000		1,85,000

Dr. **5. OFFICE & SELLING EXPENSES ACCOUNT** Cr.

Particulars	₹	Particulars	₹
To Prepaid Expenses A/c (in the beginning)	1,000	By Outstanding Expenses A/c (in the beginning)	500
To Bank A/c (Balancing figure)	50,000	By P & L A/c	51,000
To Outstanding Expenses A/c (at the end)	1,000	By Prepaid Expenses A/c (at the end)	500
	52,000		52,000

Dr. **6. TRADING COMMISSION ACCOUNT** Cr.

Particulars	₹	Particulars	₹
To Accrued Commission A/c (in the beginning)	1,000	By Advance Commission A/c	2,000
To P&L A/c	1,02,000	By Cash/Bank A/c (Balancing figure)	1,00,000
To Advance Commission A/c (at the end)	1,000	By Accrued Commission A/c (at the end)	2,000
	1,04,000		1,04,000

Dr. **7. PROVISION FOR TAX ACCOUNT** Cr.

Particulars	₹	Particulars	₹
To Bank A/c (Tax Paid) (Balancing figure)	30,000	By Balance b/d	50,000
		By P&L A/c (Provision made)	40,000
To Balance c/d	60,000		
	90,000		90,000

THEORETICAL QUESTIONS

1.0 INTRODUCTION

1.1. What is meant by Cash Flow Statement?

1.2. Why is Cash Flow Statement prepared?

1.3 List any two objectives of preparing Cash Flow Statement.

1.4. Enumerate any two uses/advantages of Cash Flow Statement.

1.5. Enumerate any two limitations of Cash Flow Statement.

1.6. What is meant by the term 'Cash Flows'?

1.7. When does the flow of Cash take place?

1.8. What is meant by the term 'Cash Inflows'?

1.9. What is meant by the term 'Cash Outflows'?

1.10. Which Transactions are not considered as Cash Flows?

1.11. List any two examples of Transactions which are not considered as Cash Flows.

1.12. Give one Transaction which may result into Cash Outflow and one which may result into no Cash flow.

1.13. What is meant by the term 'Cash' as per AS 3? Also state any two examples.

1.14. What is meant by the term 'Cash Equivalents' as per AS 3?

1.15. State the Purpose of the term 'Cash Equivalents' as per AS 3.

1.16. List any two examples of Cash Equivalents.

1.17. State the Conditions for an Investment to qualify as a Cash Equivalent as per AS 3.

1.18. What is meant by Operating Activities?

1.19. List any two Operating Activities which result into Inflow of Cash.

1.20. List any two Operating Activities which result into Outflow of Cash.

1.21. What is meant by Investing Activities?

1.22. List any two Investing Activities which result into Inflow of Cash.

1.23. List any two Investing Activities which result into Outflow of Cash.

1.24. What is meant by Financing Activities?

1.25. List any two Financing Activities which result into Inflow of Cash.

1.26. List any two Financing Activities which result into Outflow of Cash.

1.27. List any one difference between Operating Activity and Investing Activity.

1.28. List any one difference between Operating Activity and Financing Activity.

1.29. List any one difference between Investing Activity and Financing Activity.

2.0 STATE WITH REASON WHETHER......... WOULD RESULT IN INFLOW, OUTFLOW OR NO FLOW OF CASH OR CASH EQUIVALENTS.

2.1. State with reason whether Cash deposited into Bank would result in Inflow,Outflow or No Flow of Cash or Cash Equivalents.

2.2. State with reason whether Cash withdrawn from Bank for office use would result in Inflow, Outflow or No Flow of Cash or Cash Equivalents.

2.3. State with reason whether Sale of Marketable Securities at par would result in Inflow, Outflow or No Flow of Cash or Cash Equivalents.

2.4. State with reason whether Purchase of Treasury Bills would result in Inflow, Outflow or No Flow of Cash or Cash Equivalents.

2.5. State with reason whether Short-term Deposits with Banks would result in Inflow, Outflow or No Flow of Cash or Cash Equivalents.

2.6. State with reason whether Redemption of Debentures for cash would result in Inflow, Outflow or No Flow of Cash or Cash Equivalents.

2.7. State with reason whether Buy-back of Equity Shares for cash would result in Inflow, Outflow or No Flow of Cash or Cash Equivalents.

2.8. State with reason whether Purchase of Patents for cash would result in Inflow, Outflow or No Flow of Cash or Cash Equivalents.

2.9. State with reason whether Cash paid as Salaries to Workers would result in Inflow, Outflow or No Flow of Cash or Cash Equivalents.

2.10. State with reason whether Cash paid to Trade Payables would result in Inflow,Outflow or No Flow of Cash or Cash Equivalents.

2.11. State with reason whether Interest paid on Debentures would result in Inflow,Outflow or No Flow of Cash or Cash Equivalents.

2.12. State with reason whether Interest received on Debentures would result in Inflow,Outflow or No Flow of Cash or Cash Equivalents.

2.13. State with reason whether Issue of Equity Shares against the purchase of a machine would result in Inflow,Outflow or No Flow of Cash or Cash Equivalents.

2.14. State with reason whether Issue of Equity Shares on conversion of Debentures would result in Inflow,Outflow or No Flow of Cash or Cash Equivalents.

2.15. State with reason whether Declaration of Final Dividend would result in Inflow,Outflow or No Flow of Cash or Cash Equivalents.

2.16. State with reason whether Purchase of Stock-in-trade on credit would result in Inflow,Outflow or No Flow of Cash or Cash Equivalents.

2.17. State with reason whether Charging of Depreciation on Furniture would result in Inflow,Outflow or No Flow of Cash or Cash Equivalents.

2.18. State with reason whether Old furniture written-off would result in Inflow,Outflow or No Flow of Cash or Cash Equivalents.

2.19. State with reason whether Purchase of a Fixed Asset on deferred payment would result in Inflow,Outflow or No Flow of Cash or Cash Equivalents.

2.20. State with reason whether Discount received on making payment to Suppliers would result in Inflow,Outflow or No Flow of Cash or Cash Equivalents.

2.21. State with reason whether Discount allowed on receiving payment from Customers would result in Inflow,Outflow or No Flow of Cash or Cash Equivalents.

3.0 .... IS CLASSIFIED UNDER WHICH KIND OF ACTIVITY WHILE PREPARING A CASH FLOW STATEMENT?

3.1. Dividend received by a Finance Company is classified under which kind of activity while preparing a Cash Flow Statement?

3.2. Dividend received by a Manufacturing Company is classified under which kind of activity while preparing a Cash Flow Statement?

3.3. Dividend paid by a Finance Company is classified under which kind of activity while preparing a Cash Flow Statement?

3.4. Dividend paid by a Manufacturing Company is classified under which kind of activity while preparing a Cash Flow Statement?

3.5. Interest received by a Finance Company is classified under which kind of activity while preparing a Cash Flow Statement?

3.6. Interest received by a Manufacturing Company is classified under which kind of activity while preparing a Cash Flow Statement?

3.7. Interest paid by an Investment Company is classified under which kind of activity while preparing a Cash Flow Statement?

3.8. Interest paid by a Manufacturing Company is classified under which kind of activity while preparing a Cash Flow Statement?

3.9. Purchase of Shares/ Debentures of other companies for Cash by a Trading Company is classified under which kind of activity while preparing a Cash Flow Statement?

3.10. Purchase of Shares/ Debentures of other companies for Cash by an Investment Company is classified under which kind of activity while preparing a Cash Flow Statement?

3.11. Sale of Shares/ Debentures of other companies for Cash by a Manufacturing Company is classified under which kind of activity while preparing a Cash Flow Statement?

3.12. Sale of Shares/ Debentures of other companies for Cash by a Finance Company is classified under which kind of activity while preparing a Cash Flow Statement?

3.13. Cash received from Trade Receivables is classified under which kind of activity while preparing a Cash Flow Statement?

3.14. Proceeds from sale of Machinery is classified under which kind of activity while preparing a Cash Flow Statement?

3.15. Rent of a Building received by a Manufacturing Company is classified under which kind of activity while preparing a Cash Flow Statement?

3.16. Rent of a Building received by a Real Estate Enterprise is classified under which kind of activity while preparing a Cash Flow Statement?

3.17. Payment of Income Tax is classified under which kind of activity while preparing a Cash Flow Statement?

3.18. Refund of Income Tax received is classified under which kind of activity while preparing a Cash Flow Statement?

3.19. Payment of Preliminary Expenses is classified under which kind of activity while preparing a Cash Flow Statement?

3.20. Payment of Underwriting Commission & Brokerage is classified under which kind of activity while preparing a Cash Flow Statement?

3.21. Purchase of Goodwill by a Finance Company is classified under which kind of activity while preparing a Cash Flow Statement?

3.22. Brokerage paid on issue of shares paid by ICICI Bank is classified under which kind of activity while preparing a Cash Flow Statement?

3.23. Brokerage paid on purchase of Shares or Debentures of other companies by UTI Mutual Fund Company is classified under which kind of activity while preparing a Cash Flow Statement?

3.24. Classify the following as Cash or Cash Equivalents:

1. Bank Overdraft,
2. Cash Credit,
3. Short-term Deposits,
4. Marketable Securities

3.25. Classify the following activities as (i) Operating Activities, (ii) Investing activities, (iii) Financial activities and (iv) Cash Equivalents:

(1) Cash receipts from Trade Receivables

(2) Marketable Securities

(3) Purchase of investment

(4) Proceeds from long term borrowings

(5) Wages and Salaries paid

(6) Bank overdraft

(7) Purchase of Goodwill

(8) Interim dividend paid on equity shares

(9) Short term Deposits

(10) Underwriting commission paid

[**Ans** (a) Operating Activities: Items 1 and 5, (b) Investing Activities: Items 3, 7 and 9 (c) Financing Activities: Items 4, 6, 8 and 10, (d) Cash Equivalent: 2]

3.26. Classify the following into Operating, Investing and Financing Activities:

(a) Refund of Income Tax

(b) Sale of Shares & Debentures of other companies by a Finance Company

(c) Dividend on Shares and Interest on Debentures paid by a Mutual Fund Company

(d) Dividend on Shares and Interest on Debentures received by a Bank.

(e) Payment of Preliminary Expenses

(f) Interest paid on Short-term Borrowings.

(g) Income received from Current Investments.

(h) Commission & Royalty received

3.27. Classify the following into Operating, Investing and Financing Activities in case of a Financial Enterprise:

(a) Proceeds from Sale of Investments

(b) Income received on Debentures held as Investments

4.0 MENTION THE NET AMOUNT OF 'SOURCE' OR USE OF CASH WHEN...

4.1. Mention the net amount of 'Source' or 'Use' of Cash when Fixed asset (having book value of ₹ 15,000) is sold at a loss of ₹ 5,000.

4.2. Mention the net amount of 'Source' or 'Use' of Cash when Goods costing ₹ 10,000 are sold for ₹ 15,000.

4.3. Mention the net amount of 'Source' or 'Use' of Cash when ₹ 19,000 received from a debtor and allowed ₹ 1,000 as discount.

4.4. Mention the net amount of 'Source' or 'Use' of Cash when Discount of ₹ 1,000 is received on making payment to a creditor of ₹ 10,000.

4.5. Mention the net amount of 'Source' or 'Use' of Cash when Issue of shares for ₹ 7,00,000 against purchase of business comprising of fixed assets ₹ 6,00,000; current assets ₹ 2,00,000 and took over current liabilities ₹ 1,00,000.

4.6. Mention the net amount of 'Source' or 'Use' of Cash when Old Furniture (Book value ₹ 1,000) written off.

4.7. Mention the net amount of 'Source' or 'Use' of Cash when Deferred Revenue Expenditure (₹ 1,000) charged to Profit.

5.0 ANALYTICAL QUESTIONS

5.1. State why Cash Flow Statement is not a substitute for Income Statement.

5.2. State how Cash Flow Statement is historical in nature.

5.3. State why Non-Cash transactions are ignored while preparing Cash Flow Statement.

5.4. List any two examples of significant Non-Cash transactions.

5.5. When is Interest received considered as Financing Activity?

5.6. When is Dividend received considered as Operating Activity?

5.7. Give one example of an activity which is classified as Operating Activity in case of all enterprises;

5.8. Give one example of an activity which is classified as Investing Activity in case of all enterprises.

5.9. Give one example of an activity which is classified as financing activity in case of all enterprises.

5.10. State with reason two examples of activities which are classified as Operating in case of one enterprise and Investing in case of another enterprise.

5.11. If you want neither Inflow nor Outflow of Cash, which of the following transactions will you select?

(a) A Long-term Loan from Bank

(b) Goodwill written off

(c) Issue of Equity Shares or Debentures against the purchase of a Fixed Asset

(d) Issue of Equity shares on conversion of debentures

(e) Cash deposited into Bank

(f) Cash withdrawn from Bank

(g) Charging Depreciation on Furniture

(h) Declaration of Final Dividend

(i) Purchase of Stock-in-trade on credit

5.12. What is meant by the term 'Cash Equivalents' as per AS 3?

5.13. State the Purpose of the term 'Cash Equivalents' as per AS 3.

5.14. List any two examples of Cash Equivalents.

5.15. State the Conditions for an Investment to qualify as a Cash Equivalent.

5.16. State any one example of extraordinary income under operating activities.

5.17. State any one example of extraordinary loss under operating activities.

5.18. State the nature and amount of cash flow on purchase of building of ₹ 10,00,000 paying 25% down payment and executing a bond for the balance.

5.19. Capital gain tax paid by a manufacturing company is classified under which kind of activity while preparing cash flow statement?

5.20. Dividend distribution tax paid by a manufacturing company is classified under which kind of activity while preparing cash flow statement?

SHORT ANSWER PRACTICAL QUESTIONS

1. Property,Plant & Equipment (Net): Closing ₹ 12,70,000, Opening ₹ 10,20,000. During the year a machine costing ₹ 1,40,000 (depreciation provided thereon ₹ 60,000) was sold for ₹ 50,000. Depreciation charged was ₹ 1,40,000. A machine costing ₹ 30,000 was purchased by issue of Equity Shares of ₹ 10 each at a premium of 20%.Net Profit before Tax ₹ 1,00,000. How will you disclose these items while preparing Cash Flow Statement as per AS–3 issued by ICAI?

[**Ans.** CF from Operating Activities ₹ 2,70,000, Cash used in Investing Activities ₹ 3,90,000]

2. Property,Plant & Equipment (Net): Closing ₹ 16,50,000, Opening ₹ 13,20,000. Accumulated Depreciation: Closing ₹ 3,80,000, Opening ₹ 3,00,000. During the year a machine having book value of ₹ 80,000 (depreciation provided thereon ₹ 60,000) was sold at a loss of 37.5%. A machine costing ₹ 30,000 was purchased by issue of Equity Shares of ₹ 10 each at a premium of 20%. Net Profit before Tax ₹ 1,00,000. How will you disclose these items while preparing Cash Flow Statement as per AS–3 issued by ICAI?

[**Ans.** CF from Operating Activities ₹ 2,70,000, Cash used in Investing Activities ₹ 3,90,000]

3. 10% Non-Current Investments: Closing ₹ 1,60,000, Opening ₹ 60,000. 10% Current Investments: Closing ₹ 60,000, Opening ₹ 20,000. At the end of the year Some Non-Current Investments costing ₹ 40,000 were sold at a loss of 1/3rd on sale and Some Current Investments costing ₹ 20,000 were sold at a profit of 25%. Net Profit before Tax ₹ 1,00,000. How will you disclose these items while preparing Cash Flow Statement as per AS–3 issued by ICAI?

[**Ans.** CF from Operating Activities ₹ 87,000, Cash used in Investing Activities ₹ 1,37,000]

4. 10% Non-Current Investments: Closing ₹ 1,60,000, Opening ₹ 60,000. 10% Current Investments: Closing ₹ 60,000, Opening ₹ 20,000. At the end of the year Some Non-Current Investments costing ₹ 40,000 were sold at a loss of 1/3rd on sale and Some Current Investments costing ₹ 20,000 were sold at a profit of 25%. Profit / Loss on Investments was adjusted against the Capital Reserve. Net Profit before Tax ₹ 1,00,000. How will you disclose these items while preparing Cash Flow Statement as per AS–3 issued by ICAI?

[**Ans.** CF from Operating Activities ₹ 92,000, Cash used in Investing Activities ₹ 1,37,000]

5. 14% Debentures: 31.03.2023 ₹ 2,60,000, 31.03.2022 ₹ 1,50,000. 14% Short-term Bank Loan : 31.03.2023 ₹ 40,000, 31.03.2022 ₹ 50,000. New Debentures were issued on 01.01.2023 and Bank Loan was repaid on the same date. Unpaid Interest on Debentures on 31.03.2023 ₹ 10,000. Net Profit before Tax ₹ 1,00,000 How will you disclose these items while preparing Cash Flow Statement as per AS–3 issued by ICAI?

[**Ans.** CF from Operating Activities ₹ 1,31,500, CF from Financing Activities ₹ 78,500]

6. From the following information calculate Cash Flow from Operating Activities:

Particulars	31.03.2023 (₹)	31.03.2022 (₹)
Trade Payables	1,65,000	40,000
Intangible Assets [Goodwill]	21,000	10,000
Inventories	1,69,000	54,000
Trade Receivables	3,76,000	4,06,000

On 01.01.2023, the business of Y Ltd. was purchased for ₹60,000 payable in fully paid equity shares of ₹10 each at 20% premium. The assets included Inventories ₹15,000. Trade Receivables ₹10,000 and machine ₹30,000. Trade Payables of ₹15,000 were also taken over. Net Profit before tax for the year 2022-2023 ₹ 7,98,000. Tax paid ₹ 10,000.

[**Ans.** CF from Operating Activities ₹ 8,47,000]

7. Investment in Shares: Opening ₹ 10,000,Closing ₹ 35,000, Dividend received amounted to ₹ 2,100 which included pre acquisition dividend of ₹ 600. How will you disclose these items while preparing Cash Flow Statement as per AS–3 issued by ICAI?

[**Ans.** CF used in Operating Activities ₹ 1,500, Cash used in Investing Activities ₹ 23,500]

8. Compensation received in a suit filed by the company ₹ 90,000 .How will you disclose this item while preparing Cash Flow Statement as per AS–3 issued by ICAI?

9. Capital Grant :Opening ₹ Nil, Closing ₹ 8,00,000. Grant of ₹ 10,00,000 amortised in P&L A/c. How will you disclose these items while preparing Cash Flow Statement as per AS–3 issued by ICAI?

[**Ans.** CF used in Operating Activities ₹ 10,00,000, CF from Financing Activities ₹ 18,00,000]

10. Voluntary Separation Payments: Opening ₹ 65,000, Closing ₹ 1,25,000. Voluntary Separation Payments ₹ 50,000 adjusted against General Reserve. How will you disclose these items while preparing Cash Flow Statement as per AS–3 issued by ICAI?

[**Ans.** CF used in Operating Activities ₹ 1,10,000]

11. 10% Investments: Opening ₹ 1,00,000, Closing ₹ 80,000, Accrued Interest on Investments: Opening ₹ 2,000, Closing ₹ 3,000. How will you disclose these items while preparing Cash Flow Statement as per AS–3 issued by ICAI?

[**Ans.** CF used in Operating Activities ₹ 10,000, Cash from Investing Activities ₹ 29,000]

12. 10% Debentures: Opening ₹ 2,00,000, Closing ₹ 1,40,000, Unpaid interest on Debentures: Opening ₹ 500, Closing ₹ 2,000. Debentures were redeemed at 5% premium at the end of the year. How will you disclose these items while preparing Cash Flow Statement as per AS–3 issued by ICAI?

[**Ans.** CF used in Operating Activities ₹ 17,000, CF used in Financing Activities ₹ 81,500]

13. Debtors of ₹ 2,30,000 were written off against the Provision for Doubtful Debts A/c during the year.Short-term Investments (held for 2 months) costing ₹ 10,000 were sold for ₹ 12,000. How will you disclose these items while preparing Cash Flow Statement as per AS–3 issued by ICAI?

[**Ans.** No Adjustment required]

14. From the following information,calculate Cash flow from Operating Activities as per AS 3 for year ended 31.3.2023:

1. Operating Profit before Working Capital Changes	₹ 9,64,500
2. Income tax provided during the year	₹ 1,50,000

3. POSITION OF CURRENT ASSETS & CURRENT LIABILITIES

Particulars	*Closing (₹)*	*Opening (₹)*
Current Assets:		
Inventories	1,06,000	1,00,000
Trade Receivables	10,000	6,70,000
Current Investments	1,00,000	1,20,000
Accrued Interest on Investments	3,000	4,000
Cash & Cash Equivalents	30,000	49,000
Current Liabilities:	10,000	6,70,000
Trade Payables	25,000	1,80,000
Outstanding Expenses	14,000	10,000
Provision for Taxation	62,000	30,000
Short-term Borrowings	1,20,000	1,00,000
Interest outstanding on Short-term Borrowings	4,000	3,000

[Ans Cash from Operating Activities ₹ 3,43,500]

15. From the following information, calculate Cash flow from Investing Activities as per AS 3 for year ended 31.3.2023:

Particulars	*31.03.2023* ₹	*31.03.2022* ₹
Property,Plant & Equipment	16,50,000	13,20,000
Accumulated Depreciation	(3,80,000)	(3,00,000)
Intangible Assets [Goodwill]	21,000	10,000
10% Current Investments	2,20,000	80,000
Interest Accrued on Current Investments	2,000	
8% Fixed Deposit (Date of FD 1st Mar., 2023 maturing on 31st May, 2023)	2,84,000	-

Additional Information:

(a) During the year a machine (having accumulated Depreciation being one third of cost) was sold for ₹ 50,000 at a loss of 37.5%. A fully depreciated machine was also discarded. Machinery costing ₹ 4,40,000 was purchased for cash.

(b) On 1st Jan., 2023, Some Current Investments costing ₹ 2,00,000 were purchased and Some Current Investments were sold at a profit of 20% on sale. New Debentures were issued and Bank Loan was repaid on the same date.

(c) On 01.01.2023, the Business of Y Ltd. was purchased for ₹ 60,000 payable in fully paid equity shares of ₹ 10 each at 20% premium. The assets included Inventories ₹ 15,000. Trade Receivables ₹ 10,000 and Machine ₹ 30,000. Trade Payables of ₹ 15,000 were also taken over.

[Ans C used in IA ₹ 5,05,500]

16. From the following information,calculate Cash flow from Financing Activities as per AS 3 for year ended 31.3.2023:

Particulars	*31.03.2023* ₹	*31.03.2022* ₹
Equity Share Capital of ₹ 10 each	10,00,000	6,00,000
5% Preference Share Capital of ₹ 100 each	2,00,000	4,00,000
Securities Premium	45,000	20,000
Capital Redemption Reserve	50,000	1,50,000
14% Debentures	2,60,000	1,50,000
Short-term Borrowings (14% Bank Loan)	40,000	50,000
Unclaimed Dividend on Equity Shares	20,000	–
Outstanding Interest on Debentures	10,000	–

Additional Information:

(a) Dividends (including an Equity Dividend @ 35%) were paid on 1st April, 2022.

(b) On 1st Jan., 2023, New Debentures were issued and Bank Loan was repaid on the same date.

(c) On 1st May, 2022 Preference Shares were redeemed at a premium of 5%.

(d) On 01.01.2023, the Business of Y Ltd. was purchased for ₹ 60,000 payable in fully paid equity shares of ₹ 10 each at 20% premium. The assets included Inventories ₹ 15,000. Trade Receivables ₹ 10,000 and Machine ₹ 30,000. Trade Payables of ₹ 15,000 were also taken over.

(e) Being a prudent accountant, ensure minimum reduction in free reserves.

[Ans Cash used in FA ₹ 2,15,000]

17. From the following information, calculate Cash flow from Investing Activities as per AS 3 for year ended 31.3.2023:

Particulars	(₹)
Machinery acquired by issue of shares at face value	2,00,000
Claim received for loss of machinery in earthquake	55,000
Unsecured loans given to associates	5,00,000
Interest on loan received from associate company	70,000
Pre-acquisition dividend received on investment made	52,600
Debenture interest paid	1,45,200
Term loan repaid	4,50,000
Interest received on investment (TDS of ₹ 8,200 was deducted on the above interest)	73,800
Purchased debentures of X Ltd., on. 1st December, 2022 which are redeemable within 3 months	3,00,000
Book value of plant & machinery sold (loss incurred ₹ 9,600)	90,000

[Ans Cash used in Investing Activities ₹1,68,200]

18. Following are the extracts from the Balance Sheet of ABC Ltd.

Liabilities	***31.3.2022 (₹)***	***31.3.2023 (₹)***
Equity Share Capital	25,00,0000	35,60,000
10% Preference Share Capital	7,00,000	6,00,000
Securities Premium Account	5,00,000	5,50,000
Profit & Loss A/c	20,00,000	28,00,000

Equity Share Capital for the year ended 31st March, 2023 includes ₹ 60,000 of equity shares issued to Grey Ltd. at par for supply of Machinery of ₹ 60,000.

Profit & Loss account on 31st March, 2023 includes ₹ 50,000 of dividend received on Equity shares invested in X Ltd.

Show how the related items will appear in the Cash Flow Statement of ABC Ltd. as per AS-3 (Revised)

[Ans CFO 7,50,000, CIA 50,000, CFA 9,50,000]

19. PRITHVI & JAL Ltd purchased a Machine on 1.10.2021 for ₹ 20,80,000 payable as to 25% by a cheque and 50% of the balance by an issue of 14% Preference Shares of ₹ 500 each at a premium of ₹ 20 per Share and the remaining by an issue of 12% Debentures of ₹ 500 each at a premium of 4%. Unpaid interest on these debentures and Unpaid Preference Dividend on 31st March, 2022 amounted to ₹ 5,000 and ₹ 2,500 respectively. Calculate Cash flow from Investing and Financing Activities for Cash Flow Statement as per AS–3.

20. PRITHVI & JAL Ltd purchased a Machine on 1.10.2021 for ₹ 20,80,000 payable as to 25% by an issue of 14% Preference Shares of ₹ 500 each at a premium of ₹ 20 per Share and 50% of the balance by an issue of 12% Debentures of ₹ 500 each at a premium of 4%. and the remaining by a cheque. Unpaid interest on these debentures and Unpaid Preference Dividend on 31st March, 2022 amounted to ₹ 5,000 and ₹ 2,500 respectively. Calculate Cash flow from Investing and Financing Activities for Cash Flow Statement as per AS–3.

LONG ANSWER PRACTICAL QUESTIONS

1. Prepare cash flow statement of CEEGEE Limited for the year ended 31st March, 2023 in accordance with AS-3 (Revised) from the following cash account summary :

CASH SUMMARY ACCOUNT

Inflows	***₹ ('000)***	***Outflows***	***₹ ('000)***
Opening Balance	945	*Payment to suppliers*	54,918
Receipts from Customers	74,682	*Purchase of Investments*	351
Sale of Investments (Cost ₹ 4,05,000)	459	*Property, plant and equipment acquired*	6,210
Issue of Shares	8,100	*Wages and salaries*	1,863
Sale of Property, Plant and equipment	3,456	*Payment of overheads*	3,105
		Taxation	6,561
		Dividends	2,160

		Repayment of Bank Overdraft	6,750
		Interest paid on Bank Overdraft	1,350
		Closing Balance	4,374
	87,642		87,642

[Ans CFO ₹ 8,235, Cash used in IA ₹ 2,646,Cash used in FA ₹ 2,160]

2. The following figures have been extracted from the books of CEEM Limited for the year ended on 31.3.2023. You are required to prepare the Cash Flow statement as per AS 3 using indirect method.

(i) Net profit before taking into account income tax and income from law suits but after taking into account the following items was ₹ 30 lakhs :

(a) Depreciation on Property, Plant & Equipment ₹ 7.50 lakhs.

(b) Discount on issue of Debentures written off ₹ 45,000.

(c) Interest on Debentures paid ₹ 5,25,000.

(d) Book value of investments ₹ 4.50 lakhs (Sale of Investments for ₹ 4,80,000).

(e) Interest received on investments ₹ 90,000.

(ii) Compensation received ₹1,35,000 by the company in a suit filed.

(iii) Income tax paid during the year ₹ 15,75,000.

(iv) 22,500, 10% preference shares of ₹ 100 each were redeemed on 02-04-2022 at a premium of 5%.

(v) Further the company issued 75,000 equity shares of ₹10 each at a premium of 20% on 30.3.2023 (Out of 75,000 equity shares, 25,000 equity shares were issued to a supplier of machinery)

(vi) Dividend for FY 2021-2022 on preference shares were paid at the time of redemption.

(vii) Dividend on Equity shares paid on 31.01.2023 for the year 2021-2022 ₹ 7.50 lakhs and interim dividend paid ₹ 2.50 lakhs for the year 2022-2023.

(viii) Land was purchased on 02.4.2022 for ₹ 3,00,000 for which the company issued 22,000 equity shares of ₹ 10 each at a premium of 20% to the land owner and balance in cash as consideration.

(ix) Current assets and current liabilities in the beginning and at the end of the years were as detailed below :

	As on 01.04.2022 ₹	*As on 31.3.2023 ₹*
Inventory	18,00,000	19,77,000
Trade receivables	3,87,000	3,79,650
Cash in hand	3,94,450	16,950
Trade payables	3,16,500	3,16,950
Outstanding expenses	1,12,500	1,22,700

[Ans CFO ₹ 26,01,000,C IA ₹ 5,34,000,Cash used in FA ₹ 35,12,500]

3. Following information was extracted from the books of S Ltd. for the year ended 31st March, 2023 :

1. Net profit before taking into account income tax and after taking into account the following items was ₹ 30 lakhs;

(i) Depreciation on Property, Plant & Equipment ₹ 7,00,000

(ii) Discount on issue of debentures written off ₹ 45,000.

(iii) Interest on debentures paid ₹ 4,35,000

(iv) Investment of Book value ₹ 3,50,000 sold for ₹3,75,000.

(v) Interest received on Investments ₹ 70,000

2. Income tax paid during the year ₹ 12,80,000

3. Company issued 60,000 Equity Shares of ₹10 each at a premium of 20% on 10th April,2022.

4. 20,000,9% Preference Shares of ₹100 each were redeemed on 31st March, 2023 at a premium of 5%

5. Dividend paid during the year amounted to ₹11 Lakhs.

6. A new Plant costing ₹7 Lakhs was purchased in part exchange of an old plant on 1st January,2023. The book value of the old plant was ₹8 Lakhs but the vendor took over the old plant at a value of ₹6 Lakhs only. The balance amount was paid to vendor through cheque on 30th March,2023.

7. Company decided to value inventory at cost, whereas previously the practice was to value inventory at cost less 10%. The inventory according to books on 31.03.2023 was ₹ 14,76,000.

The inventory on 31.03.2022 was correctly valued at ₹ 13,50,000.

8. Current Assets and Current Liabilities in the beginning and at the end of year 2022-2023 were as:

	As on 1st April, 2022 (₹)	*As on 31st March, 2023 (₹)*
Inventory	13,50,000	14,76,000
Trade Receivables	3,27,000	3,13,200
Cash &Bank Balances	2,40,700	3,70,500
Trade Payables	2,84,700	2,87,300
Outstanding Expenses	97,000	1,01,400

You are required to prepare a Cash Flow Statement for the year ended 31st March, 2023 as per AS 3 (revised) using the indirect method.

[Ans CFO ₹ 26,99,800, CIA ₹ 3,45,000,Cash used in FA ₹ 29,15,000**]**

4. Prepare Cash Flow Statement. for the year ended 31st March, 2023 with the help of the following information:

(i) Company sold goods for cash only.

(ii) Gross Profit Ratio was 30% for the year, gross profit amounts to ₹ 3,82,500.

(iii) Opening inventory was lesser than closing inventory by ₹ 35,000.

(iv) Wages paid during the year ₹ 4,92,500.

(v) Office and selling expenses paid during the year ₹ 75,000.

(vi) Dividend paid during the year ₹ 3,000 (including dividend distribution tax.)

(vii) Bank loan repaid during the year ₹ 2,15,000 (included interest ₹ 15,000).

(viii) Trade payables on 31st March, 2022 exceed the balance on 31st March, 2023 by ₹ 25,000.

(ix) Amount paid to trade payables during the year ₹ 4,60,000.

(x) Tax paid during the year amounts to ₹ 65,000 (Provision for taxation as on 31.03.2023 ₹ 45,000).

(xi) Investments of ₹ 7,00,000 sold during the year at a profit of ₹ 20,000.

(xii) Depreciation on fixed assets amounts to ₹ 85,000.

(xiii) Plant and machinery purchased on 15th November, 2022 for ₹ 2,50,000.

(xiv) Cash and Cash Equivalents on 31st March, 2022 ₹ 2,00,000.

(xv) Cash and Cash Equivalents on 31st March, 2023 ₹ 6,07,500.

[Ans CFO ₹ 1,82,500, C used in IA ₹ 4,70,000, Cash used in FA ₹ 2,45,000]

5. Following are the extracts of Balance Sheets of Tulsian Ltd :

Particulars	*31.03.2023* ₹	*31.03.2022* ₹
Equity Share Capital	5,50,000	4,50,000
5% Preference Share Capital	2,00,000	3,00,000
General Reserve	1,10,000	1,20,000
Profit and Loss A/c	1,90,000	(1,40,000)
Securities Premium	10,000	—
Provision for Tax	50,000	40,000
Short–term Borrowings (10% Bank Loan)	3,00,000	2,00,000
Trade Payables	1,20,000	1,10,000
Land and Buildings	2,00,000	2,20,000
Machinery	10,00,000	7,00,000
Accumulated Depreciation on Machinery	(3,40,000)	(3,00,000)
Intangible Assets [Goodwill]	15,000	40,000
10% Current Investments	70,000	30,000
Trade Receivables & Inventories	3,95,000	3,00,000
Cash and Cash Equivalents	1,90,000	90,000

During the year Machinery costing ₹ 60,000 was sold at a loss of ₹ 20,000. Depreciation provided on Machinery ₹ 60,000. On 1st October, 2022, Additional Bank Loan was raised and Current Investments were purchased. Dividend on equity shares @ 8% was paid on opening balance. Income Tax ₹ 45,000 has been provided during the year. Preference Shares were redeemed at a premium of 5% at the end of the year.

[Ans CFO ₹ 4,46,000, C used in IA ₹ 3,75,000, Cash FA ₹ 29,000]

6. From the following information, prepare a Cash Flow Statement of X 33 Ltd:

Particulars	*Note*	*31.03.2023* ₹	*31.03.2022* ₹
Share Capital		7,87,500	6,75,000
General Reserve		3,19,500	2,58,750
Profit and Loss A/c		2,13,750	95,625
Capital Reserve		11,250	
Non-Current Liabilities [15% Debentures]		2,25,000	3,37,500
Trade Payables		2,94,750	1,91,250
Short-term Provisions (Provision for Tax)	2	85,500	78,750

Property,Plant & Equipment	13,50,000	11,25,000
Accumulated Depreciation	(2,81,250)	(2,25,000)
Non-Current Investments	2,02,500	2,02,500
Inventories	3,03,750	2,25,000
Trade Receivables	4,05,000	3,43,125
Provision for Doubtful debts	(56,250)	(45,000)
Other Current Assets (Prepaid Expenses)	13,500	11,250

Additional Information:

(i) During the year Fixed assets with a net book value of ₹ 11,250 (accumulated depreciation, ₹ 33,750) were sold for ₹ 9,000.

(ii) During the year Investments costing ₹ 90,000 were sold, and also Investments costing ₹ 90,000 were purchased. Profit on Sale was credited to Capital Reserve.

(iii) Debentures were retired at a Premium of 10%

(iv) Tax of ₹ 61,875 was paid during the year. Dividend paid during the year ₹ 33,750.

(v) During the year, bad debts of ₹ 15,750 were written off against the provision for Doubtful Debt account

[**Ans** CFO ₹ 3,45,375,C used in IA ₹ 2,49,750,Cash used in FA ₹ 95,625]

7. From the following information, prepare a Cash Flow Statement of X 34 Ltd:

Particulars	***Note***	***31.03.2023*** ₹	***31.03.2022*** ₹
Share Capital		4,00,000	3,00,000
General Reserve		1,40,000	1,10,000
Profit and Loss A/c		45,000	22,000
Non-Current Liabilities [10% Debentures]		1,00,000	1,50,000
Trade Payables		70,000	90,000
Other Current Liabilities (Dividend Payable)		4,000	—
Short-term Provisions (Provision for Tax)	2	40,000	50,000
Property, Plant & Equipment		4,29,250	2,98,000
Intangible Assets [Goodwill]		90,000	1,00,000
Non-Current Investments		60,000	1,00,000
Inventories		80,000	50,000
Trade Receivables		1,10,000	1,60,000
Cash & Cash Equivalents		24,000	10,000
Other Current Assets (Prepaid Expenses)		5,750	4,000

Additional Information:

1. 15% depreciation has been charged in the accounts on plant and machinery.
2. Old machines costing ₹ 50,000 (WDV. ₹ 20,000) have been sold for ₹ 35,000.
3. A machine costing ₹ 10,000 (WDV. ₹ 3,000) has been discarded.

4. ₹ 10,000 profit has been earned by sale of investments.
5. Debentures have been redeemed at 5% premium at the end.
6. ₹ 45,000 income tax has been paid and adjusted against Income Tax Provision Account.
7. Dividend paid during the year ₹ 26,000.

[**Ans** CFO ₹ 1,52,500, C used in IA ₹ 1,45,000, Cash FA ₹ 6,500]

8. From the following information, prepare a Cash Flow Statement of TULSI AMLA GILOY Ltd.:

Particulars	***31.03.2023*** ₹	***31.03.2022*** ₹
Equity Share Capital of ₹ 10 each	10,50,000	7,50,000
5% Preference Share Capital of ₹ 100 each	2,00,000	4,00,000
General Reserve	1,40,000	4,40,000
Profit and Loss A/c	7,27,000	37,000
Securities Premium	55,000	20,000
14% Debentures	2,60,000	1,50,000
Current Liabilities:		
Short-term Borrowings (14% Bank Loan)	40,000	50,000
Trade Payables	1,65,000	40,000
Unclaimed Dividend on Equity Shares	20,000	–
Outstanding Interest on Debentures	10,000	–
Outstanding Underwriting Commission	5,000	–
Provision for Tax	40,000	20,000
Non-Current Assets:		
Property,Plant & Equipment	16,50,000	13,20,000
Accumulated Depreciation	(3,80,000)	(3,00,000)
Intangible Assets [Goodwill]	21,000	10,000
Current Assets:		
10% Current Investments	2,20,000	80,000
Interest Accrued on Current Investments	2,000	–
8% Fixed Deposit (Date of FD 1st Mar.,2023 maturing on 31st May,2023)	2,84,000	-
Cash at Bank	1,33,000	1,00,000
Inventories	1,69,000	54,000
Trade Receivables	6,13,000	6,43,000

Additional Information:

(a) Dividends (including an Interim Dividend @ 28%) were paid on 1st April, 2022.

(b) During the year a machine (having accumulated Depreciation being one third of cost) was sold for ₹ 50,000 at a loss of 37.5%.A fully depreciated machine was also discarded. Machinery costing ₹ 4,40,000 was purchased for cash.

(c) On 1st Jan.,2023, Some Current Investments costing ₹ 2,00,000 were purchased and Some Current Investments were sold at a profit of 20% on sale. New Debentures were issued and Bank Loan was repaid on the same date.

(d) On 1st May, 2022 Preference Shares were redeemed at a premium of 5%.

(e) On 30th April, 2022, the Business of Y Ltd. was purchased for ₹ 60,000 payable in fully paid equity shares of ₹ 10 each at 20% premium. The assets included Inventories ₹ 15,000. Trade Receivables ₹ 10,000 and Machine ₹ 30,000. Trade Payables of ₹ 15,000 were also taken over.

(f) Tax provided during the year was ₹ 30,000. Being a prudent accountant,ensure minimum reduction in free reserves.

[Ans CFO ₹ 8,89,000, C used in IA ₹ 5,05,500, Cash used in FA ₹ 66,500]

9. From the following extracts of the Balance Sheets of SATYUG Ltd., Prepare Cash Flow Statement as per AS–3 issued by ICAI.

Particulars	***31.03.2023*** ₹	***31.03.2022*** ₹
Equity Share Capital of ₹ 10 each	10,00,000	6,00,000
5% Preference Share Capital of ₹ 100 each	2,00,000	4,00,000
General Reserve	1,40,000	4,40,000
Profit and Loss A/c	6,42,000	(13,000)
Securities Premium	55,000	20,000
Capital Redemption Reserve	50,000	1,50,000
Employees Stock Option Outstanding A/c	85,000	50,000
14% Debentures	2,60,000	1,50,000
Short-term Borrowings (14% Bank Loan)	40,000	50,000
Trade Payables	1,65,000	40,000
Provision for Tax	40,000	20,000
Property, Plant & Equipment	16,50,000	13,20,000
Accumulated Depreciation	(3,80,000)	(3,00,000)
Intangible Assets [Goodwill]	21,000	10,000
10% Current Investments	2,20,000	80,000
8% Fixed Deposit (Date of FD 1st Mar.,2023 maturing on 31st May, 2023)	2,84,000	-
Cash at Bank	1,00,000	1,00,000
Inventories	1,69,000	54,000
Trade Receivables	6,13,000	6,43,000

Additional Information:

(a) Dividends (including an Equity Dividend @ 35%) were paid on 1st April,2022.

(b) During the year a machine (having accumulated Depreciation being one third of cost) was sold for ₹ 50,000 at a loss of 37.5%.A fully depreciated machine was also discarded. Machinery costing ₹ 4,40,000 was purchased for cash.

(c) On 1st Jan., 2023, Some Current Investments costing ₹ 2,00,000 were purchased and Some Current Investments were sold at a profit of 20% on sale. New Debentures were issued and Bank Loan was repaid on the same date.

(d) On 1st May, 2022 Preference Shares were redeemed at a premium of 5%.

(e) On 01.01.2023, the Business of Y Ltd. was purchased for ₹ 60,000 payable in fully paid equity shares of ₹ 10 each at 20% premium. The assets included Inventories ₹ 15,000. Trade Receivables ₹ 10,000 and Machine ₹ 30,000. Trade Payables of ₹ 15,000 were also taken over.

(f) Tax provided during the year was ₹ 30,000. Being a prudent accountant,ensure minimum reduction in free reserves.

[Ans CFO ₹ 8,84,000,C used in IA ₹ 5,03,500,Cash used in FA ₹ 96,500]

12 VALUATION OF GOODWILL

LEARNING OBJECTIVES

After studying this chapter, you should be able to understand:

◇ Meaning of Goodwill
◇ Nature of Goodwill
◇ Characteristics of Goodwill
◇ Types of Goodwill
◇ Factors Affecting Goodwill
◇ Methods of Valuation of Goodwill
◇ How to calculate Goodwill under Average Profits Method
◇ How to calculate Goodwill under Super Profits Method
◇ How to calculate Goodwill under Annuity Method
◇ How to calculate Goodwill under Capitalisation of Super Profits Method
◇ How to calculate Goodwill under Capitalisation of Average Profits Method

1.0 WHAT IS THE MEANING OF GOODWILL?

Goodwill is the value of reputation of a firm in respect of the profits expected in future over and above the normal profits earned by other similar firms belonging to the same industry. Such excess of future profits over the normal profits is known as super profits. Thus, goodwill exists only when the firm earns super profits. Any firm that earns only normal profits *or* is incurring losses has no goodwill. If time value of money is considered, goodwill can be defined as the present value of anticipated super profits.

OTHER DEFINITIONS

1. *"Goodwill is the difference between the value of a business as a whole and the aggregate of the fair values of its separable Net Assets".* ***Separable Net Assets*** are those assets which can be identified and sold (or discharged) separately without necessarily disposing off the business as a whole. This includes the identifiable intangibles. ***Fair value*** is the amount for which an asset (or liability) could be exchanged in an arm's length transaction.

2. "Goodwill is a thing very easy to describe, very difficult to define. It is the benefit and advantage of the good name, reputation and connection of a business. It is the attractive force which brings in customers. It is one thing which distinguishes an old established business from a new business at its first start... Goodwill is composed of a variety of elements. It differs in its composition in different trades and in different businesses in the same trade. One element may preponderate here and another there."

—Lord Macnaughton In IRC Vs. Muller (1901).

3. From the accountant's point of view, goodwill is said to be that element arising from reputation, connection *or* other advantages possessed by a business which enables it to earn greater profits than the return normally to be expected on the capital represented by net assets employed in the business. In considering the return normally to be expected, regard must be had to the nature of the business, the risk involved, fair management remuneration and other relevant circumstances.

2.0 WHAT IS THE NATURE OF GOODWILL?

Goodwill is regarded as an intangible asset and not a fictitious asset, but like other tangible assets it contributes to the profit earning capacity of the business. Goodwill is a valuable asset if the firm is earning profits and is a valueless asset if the firm is incurring losses.

However, in the periods of temporary recession, the goodwill of the firm which is incurring least losses as compared to other similar firms, may be a valuable asset.

3.0 WHAT ARE THE CHARACTERISTICS OF GOODWILL?

1. Goodwill is an unidentifiable intangible asset.
2. Goodwill can not be sold like other identifiable and separable assets, without disposing off the business as a whole.
3. Individual intangible factors which may contribute to goodwill cannot be valued.
4. The value of goodwill may fluctuate widely according to internal and external factors over relatively short periods of time.
5. Subjectivity is involved in the assessment of the value of goodwill.
6. The value of goodwill has no reliable *or* predictable relationship to any costs which may have been incurred.

4.0 WHAT ARE THE TYPES OF GOODWILL?

1. **Purchased Goodwill** Purchased goodwill is the goodwill acquired while purchasing any business. Purchased Goodwill can be defined as being the excess of fair value of the purchase consideration over the fair value of the separable net assets acquired. The value of purchased goodwill is not necessarily equal to the inherent goodwill of the business acquired as the purchase price may reflect the future prospects of the entity as a whole. **As per AS–26 only purchased goodwill should be recognised in the accounts.**
2. **Non–Purchased Goodwill/Inherent Goodwill** Non–purchased goodwill is any goodwill other than purchased goodwill.

5.0 WHAT ARE THE FACTORS AFFECTING GOODWILL?

The factors giving rise to goodwill are as follows:

1. Producing/providing customers satisfying products.
2. Outstanding Quality of Products.
3. After Sales Service.
4. Outstanding Human Resources like Outstanding Marketing Manager/Production Manager/Customer Relation Manager/Suppliers Relation Manager/Labour Relation Manager.
5. Good relations with, (a) Govt. (b) Labour (c) Customers and (d) Suppliers.
6. Economies of Scale (production, advertising, distribution, research, management).
7. Cost Savings (employing technology, transaction costs, co–ordinating activities, Inventories–holding savings).

8. Cost of Financing (reduction in cost of borrowings and lender's risk).
9. Financial Resources.
10. Fiscal Incentives
11. **Efficiency of Management** A well–managed firm usually enjoys the advantages of high productivity and cost efficiency. This leads to higher profits and so the value of goodwill will also be high.
12. **Special Advantages** The firm that enjoys special advantages like import licences, patents, trade marks, low rate and assured supply of electricity, long–term contracts for supply of materials, well–known collaborators etc. enjoy higher value of goodwill.
13. **Favourable Location** When the business is centrally located *or* is at a place having heavy customer traffic, the goodwill tends to be high.
14. **Nature of Business** A firm which produces high value added products *or* having a stable demand is able to earn more profits and therefore has more goodwill.
15. **Market situation** The monopoly condition *or* limited competition enables the concern to earn high profits which leads to higher value of goodwill.
16. Management's attitude towards fulfillment of commitments (e.g. Timely delivery of goods to customers, timely payment to creditors, delivery of goods to customers at committed prices inspite of increase in market prices).
17. Technical know how.
18. Weakness in the management of Competitors.

6.0 WHAT ARE THE METHODS OF VALUATION OF GOODWILL?

The various methods of valuing the goodwill are as follows:

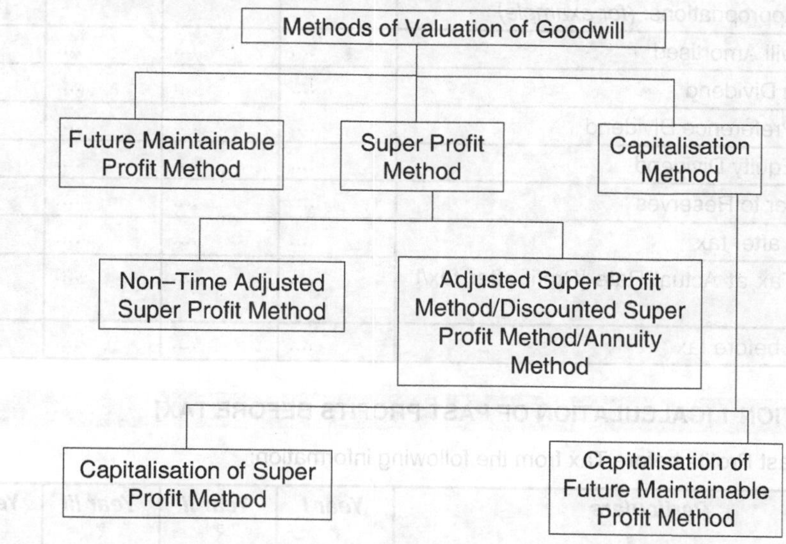

7.0 AVERAGE PROFIT METHOD

MEANING OF AVERAGE PROFIT METHOD

The Goodwill under this method is ascertained by multiplying the Average Future Maintainable Profit by a certain number of years' purchases. It is based on the assumption that a new business will not be able to earn profits during the first few years of its operations. Hence the person who purchases an existing business has to pay in the form of Goodwill a sum equal to Average Future Maintainable Profits multiplied by the number of years during which he is likely to receive the profits for the first few years. While calculating past profits any abnormal gain is excluded by deducting from and any abnormal loss is excluded by adding to the past profits.

HOW TO CALCULATE GOODWILL UNDER AVERAGE PROFIT METHOD

The various steps involved under this method are given below:

Step 1: *Calculate Past Profits before tax.*

Step 2: *Calculate Past Adjusted Profits before tax after making* ***past adjustments*** *(if any).*

Step 3: *Calculate Average Past Adjusted Profits before tax. [Note: Take Weighted Average if Past Adjusted Profits show rising or declining trend]*

Step 4: *Calculate Future Maintainable Profits after tax after making* ***future adjustments*** *(if any).*

Step 5: *Calculate Goodwill as follows:*

Goodwill = Future Maintainable Profits after Tax × No. of years' purchase.

HOW TO CALCULATE PAST PROFITS BEFORE TAX

Particulars	*Year I* ₹	*Year II* ₹	*Year III* ₹	*Year IV* ₹
A. Closing Cr. Balance of Profits and Loss A/c	....	....	....	....
B. *Less:* Opening Cr. Balance of Profit and Loss A/c	(....)	(....)	(....)	(....)
C. *Add:* Appropriations: *(for example)*				
Goodwill Amortised	....	....	....	....
Interim Dividend	....	....	....	....
Final Preference Dividend	....	....	....	....
Final Equity Dividend	....	....	....	....
Transfer to Reserves	....	....	....	....
D. Profits after tax	....	....	....	....
E. *Add:* Tax at Actual Rate [Profit after tax/t* (1 – t)]	....	....	....	....
F. Profits before tax	....	....	....	....

ILLUSTRATION 1 [CALCULATION OF PAST PROFITS BEFORE TAX]

Calculate Past Profits before Tax from the following information:

Particulars	*Year I* ₹	*Year II* ₹	*Year III* ₹	*Year IV* ₹
Closing Balance of Profit and Loss A/c	1,03,100	1,68,250	2,48,225	3,28,825
Opening Balance of Profit and Loss A/c	50,500			
Opening Balance of Goodwill A/c	40,000			
6% Preference Share Capital	1,00,000	1,00,000	1,00,000	1,00,000
Equity Share Capital	2,00,000	2,00,000	2,00,000	2,00,000

Rate of Equity Dividend	12.50%	15%	20%	21%
Transfer to Reserves (% of Profit after Tax)	2.5%	5%	7.5%	10%
Tax Rate	40%	35%	30%	30%

Goodwill was purchased during the year I which has been amortised over a period of 4 years.

SOLUTION

COMPUTATION OF PAST PROFITS BEFORE TAX

Particulars	*Year I* ₹	*Year II* ₹	*Year III* ₹	*Year IV* ₹
A. Closing Balance of Profit and Loss A/c	1,03,100	1,68,250	2,48,225	3,28,825
B. *Less:* Opening Balance of Profits and Loss A/c	(50,500)	(1,03,100)	(1,68,250)	(2,48,225)
C. *Add:* Appropriations				
Goodwill written off [₹ 40,000/4]	10,000	10,000	10,000	10,000
Preference Dividend	6,000	6,000	6,000	6,000
Equity Dividend	25,000	30,000	40,000	42,000
D. Profits after Transfer to Reserves [A – B + C]	93,600	1,11,150	1,35,975	1,38,600
E. % of Profit T/F to Reserves	2.5	5	7.5	10
F. Profits after Transfer to Reserves (in %)	97.5	95	92.5	90
G. Profits before T/f to Reserves [D/F]	96,000	1,17,000	1,47,000	1,54,000
H. *Add:* Tax at Actual Rate [Profits after tax * t/(1 – t)]	64,000	63,000	63,000	66,000
I. Profits before tax	1,60,000	1,80,000	2,10,000	2,20,000

HOW TO CALCULATE ADJUSTED PAST PROFITS

Adjusted Past Profits for the purpose of valuation of Goodwill are calculated after rectifying errors(if any, committed in past),excluding Abnormal Profits /Losses and Income from Non–Trade Investments.

Particulars	*Year I* ₹	*Year II* ₹	*Year III* ₹	*Year IV* ₹
A. Profits before Adjustments	....	....	....	....
B. *Add:* Abnormal Losses (e.g. Loss on Sale of Fixed Assets)	....	....	....	....
C. *Less:* Abnormal Profits (e.g. Profit on Sale of Fixed Assets)	(............)	(............)	(............)	(............)
D. *Less:* Income from Non–Trade Investments	(............)	(............)	(............)	(............)
E. *Add:* Capital Expenditure charged to Revenue (e.g. Purchase of Machinery wrongly charged to P&L A/c)	....	....	....	....
F. *Less:* Depreciation on above Fixed Asset	(............)	(............)	(............)	(............)

G. *Less:* Capital Receipt credited to Revenue (e.g. Sale Proceeds of Machinery wrongly credited to P&L A/c)	(............)	(............)	(............)	(............)
H. *Add:* Depreciation on above Fixed Asset	....	....	....	....
I. *Add:* Over Valuation of Opening Inventories	....	....	....	....
J. *Less:* Over Valuation of Closing Inventories	(............)	(............)	(............)	(............)
K. *Add:* Revenue Incomes relating to previous years not yet credited	....	....	....	....
L. *Less:* Revenue Expenses relating to previous years not yet provided	(............)	(............)	(............)	(............)
M. Adjusted Past Profits	....	....	....	....

ILLUSTRATION 2 [CALCULATION OF ADJUSTED PAST PROFITS]

The result of operations during the years I, II, III and IV were: Profit ₹ 1,00,000, Profit ₹ 2,00,000 (including an insurance claim received of ₹ 2,50,000),Loss ₹ 3,00,000 (after charging Loss on sale of a fixed asset of ₹ 4,00,000), Profit ₹ 3,25,000 (excluding ₹ 15,000 payable for the insurance of Assets) respectively. Calculate Adjusted Past Profits of last three years.

SOLUTION

CALCULATION OF ADJUSTED PAST PROFITS

Particulars	***Year II*** ₹	***Year III*** ₹	***Year IV*** ₹
Profits(Loss)	2,00,000	(3,00,000)	3,25,000
Less: Insurance claim received	(2,50,000)		
Add: Loss on sale of a fixed asset		4,00,000	
Less: Insurance Premium payable			(15,000)
Adjusted Past Profits (Loss)	(50,000)	1,00,000	3,10,000

ILLUSTRATION 3 [CALCULATION OF ADJUSTED PAST PROFITS]

The result of operations during the years I, II, III and IV were: I Profit ₹ 12,00,000, II Profit ₹ 13,50,000 , III Profit ₹ 18,00,000, IV Profit ₹ 22,50,000 respectively. Incomes from non–trade investments: year II ₹ 36,000,year III ₹ 72,000, year IV ₹ 72,000. Calculate Adjusted Past Profits of last three years.

SOLUTION

CALCULATION OF ADJUSTED PAST PROFITS

Particulars	***Year II*** ₹	***Year III*** ₹	***Year IV*** ₹
Profits	13,50,000	18,00,000	22,50,000
Less: Incomes from Non–trade Investments	(36,000)	(72,000)	(72,000)
Adjusted Past Profits	13,14,000	17,28,000	21,78,000

ILLUSTRATION 4 [CALCULATION OF ADJUSTED PAST PROFITS]

The result of operations during the years I, II, III and IV were: I Profit ₹ 12,00,000, II Profit ₹ 13,50,000 , III Profit ₹ 18,00,000, IV Profit ₹ 22,50,000 respectively.Closing Inventories were over–valued by ₹ 9,00,000 in *Year II*, by ₹ 8,10,000 in *Year III*, by ₹ 7,29,000 in *Year IV*.Calculate Adjusted Past Profits of last three years.

SOLUTION

CALCULATION OF ADJUSTED PAST PROFITS

Particulars	*Year II* ₹	*Year III* ₹	*Year IV* ₹
Profits	13,50,000	18,00,000	22,50,000
Less: Over Valuation of Closing Inventories	(9,00,000)	(8,10,000)	(7,29,000)
Add: Over Valuation of Opening Inventories		9,00,000	8,10,000
Adjusted Past Profits	4,50,000	18,90,000	23,31,000

ILLUSTRATION 5 [CALCULATION OF ADJUSTED PAST PROFITS]

The result of operations during the years I, II, III and IV were: I Profit ₹ 12,00,000, II Profit ₹ 13,50,000 , III Profit ₹ 18,00,000, IV Profit ₹ 22,50,000 respectively. Closing Inventories were under–valued by ₹ 9,00,000 in *Year II*, by ₹ 8,10,000 in *Year III*, by ₹ 7,29,000 in *Year IV*. Calculate Adjusted Past Profits of last three years.

SOLUTION

CALCULATION OF ADJUSTED PAST PROFITS

Particulars	*Year II* ₹	*Year III* ₹	*Year IV* ₹
Profits	13,50,000	18,00,000	22,50,000
Add: Under Valuation of Closing Inventories	9,00,000	8,10,000	7,29,000
Less: Under Valuation of Opening Inventories		(9,00,000)	(8,10,000)
Adjusted Past Profits	22,50,000	17,10,000	21,69,000

ILLUSTRATION 6 [CALCULATION OF ADJUSTED PAST PROFITS]

The result of operations during the years I, II, III and IV were: I Profit ₹ 12,00,000, II Profit ₹ 13,50,000 , III Profit ₹ 18,00,000, IV Profit ₹ 22,50,000 respectively. Closing Inventories were over–valued by ₹ 9,00,000 in *Year II*, under–valued by ₹ 8,10,000 in *Year III*, over–valued by ₹ 7,29,000 in *Year IV*. Calculate Adjusted Past Profits of last three years.

SOLUTION

CALCULATION OF ADJUSTED PAST PROFITS

Particulars	*Year II* ₹	*Year III* ₹	*Year IV* ₹
Profits	13,50,000	18,00,000	22,50,000
Less: Over Valuation of Closing Inventories	(9,00,000)		(7,29,000)
Add: Over Valuation of Opening Inventories		9,00,000	
Add: Under Valuation of Closing Inventories		8,10,000	
Less: Under Valuation of Opening Inventories			(8,10,000)
Adjusted Past Profits	4,50,000	35,10,000	7,11,000

ILLUSTRATION 7 [CALCULATION OF ADJUSTED PAST PROFITS]

The result of operations during the years I, II, III and IV were: I Profit ₹ 12,00,000, II Profit ₹ 13,50,000 , III Profit ₹ 18,00,000, IV Profit ₹ 22,50,000 respectively. In the beginning of *Year II* a new machine costing ₹ 10,00,000 was purchased but wrongly charged to revenue. (No effect has yet been given for rectifying the same).Depreciation is charged on machine @ 10% on reducing balance method. Calculate Adjusted Past Profits of last three years.

SOLUTION

CALCULATION OF ADJUSTED PAST PROFITS

Particulars	*Year II* ₹	*Year III* ₹	*Year IV* ₹
Profits	13,50,000	18,00,000	22,50,000
Add: Purchase of Machinery charged to P&L A/c	10,00,000		
Less: Depreciation on above machinery	(1,00,000)	(90,000)	(81,000)
Adjusted Past Profits	22,50,000	17,10,000	21,69,000

ILLUSTRATION 8 [CALCULATION OF ADJUSTED PAST PROFITS]

The result of operations during the years I, II, III and IV were: I Profit ₹ 12,00,000, II Profit ₹ 13,50,000, III Profit ₹ 18,00,000, IV Profit ₹ 22,50,000 respectively. In the beginning of *Year II* a machine having a book value of ₹ 10,00,000 was sold for ₹ 13,00,000 but the proceeds were wrongly credited to Profit and Loss Account. (No effect has yet been given for rectifying the same). Depreciation is charged on machine @ 10% on reducing balance method. Calculate Adjusted Past Profits of last three years.

SOLUTION

CALCULATION OF ADJUSTED PAST PROFITS

Particulars	*Year II* ₹	*Year III* ₹	*Year IV* ₹
Profits	13,50,000	18,00,000	22,50,000
Less: Sale of Machinery Cr to P&L A/c	(13,00,000)		
Add: Depreciation on above machinery	1,00,000	90,000	81,000
Adjusted Past Profits	1,50,000	18,90,000	23,31,000

ILLUSTRATION 9 [CALCULATION OF ADJUSTED PAST PROFITS]

The result of operations during the years I, II, III and IV were: I Profit ₹ 12,00,000, II Profit ₹ 13,50,000 , III Profit ₹ 18,00,000, IV Profit ₹ 22,50,000 respectively. 10% Investments (Face Value ₹ 8,00,000) appear in the balance sheet as at *Year IV* at ₹ 10,00,000. Of the Investments 10% is trade and the balance non–trade. 50% of the non–trade Investments were acquired on in the beginning of *Year III* and the rest in the beginning of *Year II.* Calculate Adjusted Past Profits of last three years.

SOLUTION

CALCULATION OF ADJUSTED PAST PROFITS

Particulars	*Year II* ₹	*Year III* ₹	*Year IV* ₹
Profits	13,50,000	18,00,000	22,50,000
Less: Incomes from Non–trade Investments	(36,000)	(72,000)	(72,000)
Adjusted Past Profits	13,14,000	17,28,000	21,78,000

ILLUSTRATION 10 [CALCULATION OF ADJUSTED PAST PROFITS]

From the following information,Calculate Adjusted Past Profits of last three years:

(a) The result of operations during the years I, II, III and IV were: I Profit ₹ 12,00,000, II Profit ₹ 13,50,000 , III Profit ₹ 18,00,000, IV Profit ₹ 22,50,000 respectively.

(b) 10% Investments (Face Value ₹ 8,00,000) appear in the balance sheet as at *Year IV* at ₹ 10,00,000. Of the Investments 10% is trade and the balance non–trade. 50% of the non–trade Investments were acquired on in the beginning of *Year III* and the rest in the beginning of *Year II*.

(c) In the beginning of *Year II* a new machine costing ₹ 10,00,000 was purchased but wrongly charged to revenue. (No effect has yet been given for rectifying the same).Depreciation is charged on machine @ 10% on reducing balance method.

(d) In the beginning of *Year II* a machine having a book value of ₹ 10,00,000 was sold for ₹ 13,00,000 but the proceeds were wrongly credited to Profit and Loss Account. (No effect has yet been given for rectifying the same). Depreciation is charged on machine @ 10% on reducing balance method.

(e) Closing Inventories were over–valued by ₹ 9,00,000 in *Year II*, under–valued by ₹ 8,10,000 in *Year III*, over–valued by ₹ 7,29,000 in *Year IV*.

SOLUTION

CALCULATION OF ADJUSTED PAST PROFITS

Particulars	*Year II* ₹	*Year III* ₹	*Year IV* ₹
Profits	13,50,000	18,00,000	22,50,000
Less: Incomes from Non–trade Investments	(36,000)	(72,000)	(72,000)
Add: Purchase of Machinery charged to P&L A/c	10,00,000		
Less: Depreciation on above machinery	(1,00,000)	(90,000)	(81,000)
Less: Sale of Machinery Cr to P&L A/c	(13,00,000)		
Add: Depreciation on above machinery	1,00,000	90,000	81,000
Less: Over Valuation of Closing Inventories	(9,00,000)		(7,29,000)
Add: Over Valuation of Opening Inventories		9,00,000	
Add: Under Valuation of Closing Inventories		8,10,000	
Less: Under Valuation of Opening Inventories			(8,10,000)
Adjusted Past Profits	1,14,000	34,38,000	6,39,000

ILLUSTRATION 11 [CALCULATION OF ADJUSTED PAST PROFITS]

Calculate Adjusted Past Profits Before Tax from the following information:

(a) Past Profits Before Tax are as under:
2019–2020, ₹ 1,60,000, 2020–2021, ₹ 1,80,000, 2021–2022, ₹ 2,10,000, 2022–2023, ₹ 2,20,000

(b) In 2021–2022, some old furniture having a Book Value of ₹ 5,000 was disposed off for ₹ 3,000. In 2022–2023, Profit on sale of furniture credited to Profit and Loss A/c ₹ 5,420 and in 2020–2021 Loss on sale of furniture debited to Profit and Loss A/c ₹ 21,000.

(c) 8% Investments (Face Value ₹ 1,00,000) appear in the Balance Sheet as on 31.03.2023 at ₹ 80,000. Of the investment, 10% is Trade and balance non–trade. 50% of the non–trade investments were acquired on 1.4.2021 and the rest on 1.4.2020.

(d) A Bad Debt of ₹ 500 was omitted to be written off in 2022–2023.

(e) An expense of ₹ 500 was omitted to be provided in 2022–2023.

(f) Closing Inventories were over–valued as : 2020–2021, ₹ 2,000, 2021–2022, ₹ 3,800, 2022–2023, ₹ 5,000.

(g) In 2020 – 2021, a new machinery costing ₹ 10,000 was purchased but wrongly charged to revenue and a machine having a Book Value of ₹ 20,000 was sold for ₹ 21,000 but the proceeds were wrongly credited to Profit and Loss A/c. Depreciation is charged on machinery @ 10% on reducing system. (No rectification has yet been made).

SOLUTION

CALCULATION OF ADJUSTED PAST PROFITS

Particulars	*2019–2020*	*2020–2021*	*2021–2022*	*2022–2023*
A. Profits before tax	1,60,000	1,80,000	2,10,000	2,20,000
B. *Add:* Loss on sale of Furniture	—	21,000	2,000	—
C. *Less:* Profit on Sale of Furniture			—	(5,420)
D. *Less:* Income from non–trade investments		(3,600)	(7,200)	(7,200)
E. *Add:* Purchase of Machinery charged to Profit and Loss A/c)		10,000		
F. *Less:* Depreciation on above Machinery		(1,000)	(900)	(810)
E. *Less:* Bad Debt not provided				(500)
F. *Less:* Expenses not provided				(500)
G. *Add:* Over Valuation of Opening Inventories			2,000	3,800
H. *Less:* Over Valuation of Closing Inventories		(2,000)	(3,800)	(5,000)
I. *Less:* Sale proceeds of Machinery wrongly credited		(21,000)		
J. *Add:* Depreciation on above Machinery		2,000	1,800	1,620
K. Past Adjusted Profits	1,60,000	1,85,400	2,03,900	2,05,990

HOW TO CALCULATE AVERAGE PAST ADJUSTED PROFITS BEFORE TAX

Take Weighted Average if Past Adjusted Profits show rising *or* declining trend by assigning the appropriate weights (*say 1, 2, 3, 4, ..., in case of rising profits, 4, 3, 2, 1 in case of declining profits*), otherwise take Simple Average.

Tutorial Note: *If the loss during a particular accounting year has occurred due to any abnormal factor(s) (say prolonged strike, fire, earthquake, floods) such loss to the extent of abnormal factor should be ignored while taking average.*

ILLUSTRATION 12 [CALCULATION OF AVERAGE PROFITS]

From the following information, Calculate the Average Profits of last three years :

	Year I	*Year II*	*Year III*	*Year IV*
	Profits	Profits	Profits	Profits
Case I	₹ 10,00,000	₹ 18,00,000	₹ 30,00,000	₹ 24,00,000
Case II	₹ 10,00,000	₹ 18,00,000	₹ 24,00,000	₹ 30,00,000

SOLUTION

Case I : Average Profits = (₹ 18,00,000 + ₹ 30,00,000 + ₹ 24,00,000)/3 = ₹ 24,00,000

Case II : Weighted Average of Past Adjusted Profits SINCE PROFITS SHOW RISING TREND

CALCULATION OF WEIGHTED AVERAGE PROFITS

Year A	*Profits* B	*Weights* C	*Weighted Profits* D = B * C
II	₹ 18,00,000	1	₹ 18,00,000
III	₹ 24,00,000	2	₹ 48,00,000
IV	₹ 30,00,000	3	₹ 90,00,000
Total		6	₹ 156,00,000

Weighted Average of Past Adjusted Profits = Total Weighted Profits/Total of Weights

= ₹ 156,00,000/6 = ₹ 26,00,000

ILLUSTRATION 13 [CALCULATION OF AVERAGE ADJUSTED PAST PROFITS]

Calculate the Average Past Adjusted Profits from the following information:

Year I	*Year II*	*Year III*	*Year IV*	*Year V*
Losses	Profits	Profits	Profits	Profits
₹ 1,00,000	₹ 60,000	₹ 1,85,400	₹ 2,03,900	₹ 2,05,990

The loss during the year I occurred due to a prolonged strike. During year II a loss due to fire occurred to the extent of ₹ 1,00,000.

SOLUTION

CALCULATION OF AVERAGE PAST ADJUSTED PROFITS [WEIGHTED AVERAGE SINCE PAST ADJUSTED PROFITS SHOW RISING TREND]

Year A	*Profits* B	*Weights* C	*Weighted Profits* D = B * C
II	1,60,000	1	1,60,000
III	1,85,400	2	3,70,800
IV	2,03,900	3	6,11,700

V	2,05,990	4	8,23,960
Total		10	19,66,460

Weighted Average of Past Adjusted Profits = Total Weighted Profits/Total of Weights

= 19,66,460/10 = 1,96,646

Note: The loss during the year I occurred due to a prolonged strike and hence the year I being abnormal year has been ignored while computing average.

HOW TO CALCULATE FUTURE MAINTAINABLE PROFITS (FMP) AFTER TAX

Future Maintainable Profits after Tax for the purpose of valuation of Goodwill are calculated after excluding Incomes earned in the past but not likely to be earned in the future and Expenses incurred in the past but not likely to be incurred in the future but including Incomes not earned in the past but likely to be earned in the future and Expenses not incurred in the past but likely to be incurred in the future.

	Particulars	₹
A.	Average Past Adjusted Profits	....
B.	*Add:* Incomes not earned in the past but likely to be earned in the future (e.g. Advantage from any future contract)	....
C.	*Less:* Incomes earned in the past but not likely to be earned in the future (e.g. Discontinuance of Advantage from any past contract)	(...........)
D.	*Add:* Expenses incurred in the past but not likely to be incurred in the future (e.g. Rent of a Rented Building after the purchase of owned Building)	....
E.	*Less:* Expenses not incurred in the past but likely to be incurred in the future (e.g. Increase in managerial remuneration, Additional Depreciation on increase in value of Fixed Assets)	(...........)
F.	Future Maintainable Profits before Tax (FMPBT)	....
G.	*Less:* Tax at likely Future Rate on(FMPBT + Additional Depreciation)	(...........)
H.	Future Maintainable Profits after Tax	....

Note: Additional depreciation on increase in value of fixed assets is not deductible u/s 32 for Tax purposes.

ILLUSTRATION 14 [CALCULATION OF FUTURE MAINTAINABLE PROFITS (FMP) AFTER TAX]

Calculate Future Maintainable Profits after Tax (as on 1.4.2023) from the following information:

(a) Average Adjusted Past Profits before Tax ₹ 23,00,000.

(b) Additional Revenue Expenditure with effect from 1st April, 2023. ₹ 1,00,000 p.a.

(c) Profits till 2022–2023 have been ascertained after debiting ₹ 10,00,000 as remuneration to the managing director. The Government has approved a remuneration of ₹ 12,00,000 with effect from 1st April, 2023.

(d) The company has been able to secure a contract for supply on materials at advantageous prices. The advantage has been valued at ₹ 4,00,000 p.a. for the next five years.

(e) The income tax rate is likely to be 25% from 1st April, 2023 onwards.

SOLUTION

CALCULATION OF FUTURE MAINTAINABLE PROFITS AFTER TAX

Particulars	₹
A. Average Past Adjusted Profits	23,00,000
B. *Less:* Additional Revenue Expenditure	(1,00,000)
C. *Less:* Increase in M.D remuneration	(2,00,000)
D. *Add:* Advantage from contract	4,00,000
E. Future Maintainable Profits before Tax	24,00,000
F. *Less:* Tax (18,00,000 * 25%)	(6,00,000)
G. Future Maintainable Profits after Tax	18,00,000

ILLUSTRATION 15

Bharat Tulsian Ltd. provides you the following information:

1. Profits/Losses after tax @ 40%:

2018–2019 Losses	*2019–2020 Profits*	*2020–2021 Profits*	*2021–2022 Profits*	*2022–2023 Profits*
5,50,000	9,04,320	12,04,320	15,04,320	18,04,320

   The loss in 2018–2019 occurred due to a prolonged strike.

2. Incomes from non–trade investments ₹ 7,200 p.a.
3. In 2020–2021 a machine having a book value of ₹ 10,000 was sold for ₹ 11,000 but the proceeds were wrongly credited to Profit and Loss Account. (No effect has yet been given for rectifying the same). Depreciation is charged on machine @ 10% on reducing balance method.
4. Closing Inventories were under–valued by ₹ 10,000 in 2020–2021, by ₹ 9,100 in 2021–2022, by ₹ 8,290 in 2022–2023.
5. With effect from 1st April, 2023, there will be increase in manager's remuneration of ₹ 2,00,000 p.a. and Advantage from new contract for supply of goods of ₹ 4,00,000 p.a.
6. Rate of Income Tax 30% with effect from 1st April, 2023.

Required: Calculate the Value of Goodwill at 3 years' purchase of average profits.

SOLUTION

Note: The year 2018–2019 has been treated as abnormal year and hence ignored.

STEP 1: CALCULATION OF PAST ADJUSTED PROFIT BEFORE TAX

Particulars	*2019–2020* ₹	*2020–2021* ₹	*2021–2022* ₹	*2022–2023* ₹
Profits after tax	9,04,320	12,04,320	15,04,320	18,04,320
Profits before tax [A/60%]	15,07,200	20,07,200	25,07,200	30,07,200
Less: Income from non-trade investments	(7,200)	(7,200)	(7,200)	(7,200)

Less: Sale proceeds of machinery wrongly credited	—	(11,000)	—	—
Add: Depreciation on above machinery	—	1,000	900	810
Add: Under valuation of Closing Inventories	—	10,000	9,100	8,290
Less: Under valuation of Opening Inventories	—	—	(10,000)	(9,100)
Past Adjusted Profit	15,00,000	20,00,000	25,00,000	30,00,000

STEP 2: CALCULATION OF AVERAGE PAST ADJUSTED PROFITS [WEIGHTED AVERAGE SINCE PAST ADJUSTED PROFITS SHOW RISING TREND]

Year A	*Profits* B	*Weights* C	*Weighted Profits* D = B * C
2019–2020	15,00,000	1	15,00,000
2020–2021	20,00,000	2	40,00,000
2021–2022	25,00,000	3	75,00,000
2022–2023	30,00,000	4	1,20,00,000
Total		10	2,50,00,000

Weighted average of Past adjusted profits

= Total Weighted Profits/Total of Weights = 2,50,00,000/10 = ₹ 25,00,000

STEP 3: CALCULATION OF FUTURE MAINTAINABLE PROFITS AFTER TAX

Particulars	₹
A. Average Past Adjusted Profits	25,00,000
B. *Less:* Increase in manager's remuneration p.a.	(2,00,000)
C. *Add:* Advantage from contract p.a.	4,00,000
D. Future Maintainable Profits before Tax	27,00,000
E. *Less:* Tax @ 30%	(8,10,000)
F. Future Maintainable Profits after Tax	18,90,000

Step 4: Goodwill = Future Maintainable Profits × No. of years' purchase

= ₹ 18,90,000 * 3 = ₹ 56,70,000

ILLUSTRATION 16

Mr. X purchased a building for ₹ 10,00,000 and let out to Mr. Y on a rent of ₹ 10,500 p.m for business the profits of which are as follows:

Year	*Profit after tax @ 40 %*
I	3,60,000 (excluding ₹ 2,00,000 payable for the insurance of Plant and Machinery)
II	6,00,000 (including profit of ₹ 1,50,000 on sale of fixed asset)
III	3,00,000 (after charging loss of ₹ 2,00,000 on sale of a fixed asset)

The building is subject to SLM deprecation @ 5% p.a. Mr. X pays ₹ 500 for the insurance of building.

Required: Calculate the value of goodwill on the basis of four years' purchase of the average profits for the last three years if Landlord wants to purchase the business of tenant. Assuming income tax rate is likely to be 30% from year IV onwards.

SOLUTION

STEP 1: CALCULATE PAST PROFITS BEFORE TAX.

Particulars	*Year I* ₹	*Year II* ₹	*Year III* ₹
A. Profits after tax	3,60,000	6,00,000	3,00,000
B. *Add:* Tax (profits after tax × 40%/60%)	2,40,000	4,00,000	2,00,000
C. Profits before Tax	6,00,000	10,00,000	5,00,000

STEP 2: PAST ADJUSTED PROFITS BEFORE TAX

Year	*Profit*	
I	(6,00,000 – 2,00,000) =	4,00,000
II	(10,00,000 – 1,50,000) =	8,50,000
III	(5,00,000 + 2,00,000) =	7,00,000
Total		19,50,000

Step 3: Average Past Adjusted Profits = ₹ 19,50,000/3 = ₹ 6,50,000

Step 4: Future Maintainable Profits

Future Maintainable Profits = ₹ 6,50,000 + ₹ 1,26,000 (Rent) – ₹ 50,000 (Dep.) – ₹ 6,000 (Ins.)	₹ 7,20,000
Less: Tax @ 30%	₹ 2,16,000
Future Maintainable Profits after tax	₹ 5,04,000

Step 5: Goodwill at 4 years' purchase of Average Profit = ₹ 5,04,000 × 4 = ₹ 20,16,000

Note: Rent is no longer payable and depreciation & insurance are likely to be claimed.

ILLUSTRATION 17

Tushar Tulsian Ltd. provides you the following information:

1. Profits and Losses after tax @ 40%:

2018–2019 Losses	*2019–2020 Profits*	*2020–2021 Profits*	*2021–2022 Profits*	*2022–2023 Profits*
5,50,000	9,00,000	12,02,160	15,04,320	18,04,320

The loss in 2018–2019 occurred due to a prolonged strike.

2. 8% Investments (Face value ₹ 1,00,000) appear in the balance sheet as at 31.12.2022 at ₹ 80,000 Of the Investments 10% is trade and the balance non–trade. 50% of the non–trade Investments were acquired on 1.4.2021 and the rest on 1.4.2020. All trade Investments are to be valued at 10% below cost.
3. In 2020–2021 a new machine costing ₹ 1,00,000 was purchased but wrongly charged to revenue. (No effect has yet been given for rectifying the same) Depreciation is charged on machine @ 10% on reducing balance method.

4. Closing Inventories were over–valued by ₹ 90,000 in 2020–2021, by ₹ 81,000 in 2021–2022, by ₹ 72,900 in 2022–2023.
5. Disputed Bonus claim of ₹ 1,00,000 not yet provided in the accounts for 2022–2023 is expected to be settled.
6. In 2022–2023 some old Furniture having a book value of ₹ 2,50,000 was sold for ₹ 1,50,000.
7. With effect from 1st April, 2023, there will be increase in manager's remuneration of ₹ 2,00,000 p.a.,Advantage from new contract for supply of goods of ₹ 4,00,000 p.a. and Additional Revenue Expenditure of ₹ 1,50,000 p.a.
8. Rate of Income Tax 30% with effect from 1st April, 2023.

Required: Calculate the Value of Goodwill at 3 years' purchase of average profits.

SOLUTION

Note: The year 2018–2019 has been treated as abnormal year and hence ignored.

STEP 1: CALCULATION OF PAST ADJUSTED PROFIT BEFORE TAX

Particulars	*2019–2020* ₹	*2020–2021* ₹	*2021–2022* ₹	*2022–2023* ₹
Profits after tax	9,00,000	12,02,160	15,04,320	18,04,320
Profits before tax [A/60%]	15,00,000	20,03,600	25,07,200	30,07,200
Less: Incomes from non–trade investments	—	(3,600)	(7,200)	(7,200)
Add: Purchase of machinery charged to P&L A/c	—	1,00,000	—	—
Less: Depreciation on above machinery	—	(10,000)	(9,000)	(8,100)
Less: Over valuation of Closing Inventories	—	(90,000)	(81,000)	(72,900)
Add: Over valuation of Opening Inventories	—	—	90,000	81,000
Add: Loss on sale of Furniture	—	—	—	1,00,000
Less: Bonus	—	—	—	(1,00,000)
Past Adjusted Profit	15,00,000	20,00,000	25,00,000	30,00,000

STEP 2: AVERAGE PAST ADJUSTED PROFITS [WEIGHTED AVERAGE SINCE PAST ADJUSTED PROFITS SHOW RISING TREND]

Year A	*Profits* B	*Weights* C	*Weighted Profits* D = B * C
2019–2020	15,00,000	1	15,00,000
2020–2021	20,00,000	2	40,00,000
2021–2022	25,00,000	3	75,00,000
2022–2023	30,00,000	4	1,20,00,000
Total		10	2,50,00,000

Weighted Average of Past adjusted profits = Total Weighted Profits/Total of Weights
= 2,50,00,000/10 = ₹ 25,00,000

STEP 3: CALCULATION OF FUTURE MAINTAINABLE PROFITS AFTER TAX

Particulars	₹
A. Average Past Adjusted Profits	25,00,000
B. *Less:* Increase in manager remuneration p.a.	(2,00,000)
C. *Add:* Advantage from contract p.a.	4,50,000
D. *Less:* Additional Revenue Expenditure p.a.	(1,50,000)
E. Future Maintainable Profits before Tax	26,00,000
F. *Less:* Tax [@ 30%	(7,80,000)
G. Future Maintainable Profits after Tax	18,20,000

Step 4: Goodwill = Future Maintainable Profits × No. of years' purchase
= ₹ 18,20,000 * 3 = ₹ 54,60,000

ILLUSTRATION 18 [GOODWILL IN THE BASIS OF PROJECTED FMP]

Y is interested in purchasing the business of X for which he is willing to pay a goodwill amount equal to four years' purchase of maintainable profits for the next four years.

The Revenues Statement for the past four years were under:

REVENUE STATEMENTS

Particulars	*Year I* ₹	*Year II* ₹	*Year III* ₹	*Year IV* ₹
Sales	5,00,000	7,00,000	9,00,000	11,00,000
Less: Cost of Goods Gold	(3,50,000)	(4,90,000)	(6,30,000)	(7,70,000)
Gross Profit	1,50,000	2,10,000	2,70,000	3,30,000
Less: Overheads	(1,00,000)	(1,40,000)	(1,80,000)	(2,20,000)
Net Profit	50,000	70,000	90,000	1,10,000

The following further information is given:

(a) Sales will increase by 25% each year over the increased figure of the earlier years.

(b) Cost of Goods sold will decline by 10% each year as compared to the earlier years.

(c) Overheads each year will increase by 2% as compared to the earlier years.

Required: Find out the value of goodwill. Income–tax may be ignored.

SOLUTION

STEP 1: CALCULATION OF FUTURE MAINTAINABLE PROFITS

Particulars	*Year V*	*Year VI* ₹	*Year VII* ₹	*Year VIII* ₹
A. Sales	13,75,000	17,18,750	21,48,438	26,85,547
B. *Less:* Cost of Goods Sold	(8,66,250)	(9,74,531)	(10,96,348)	(12,33,391)

C. Gross Profit	5,08,750	7,44,219	10,52,090	14,52,156
D. *Less:* Overheads	(2,80,500)	(3,57,638)	(4,55,988)	(5,81,384)
E. Net Profit	2,28,250	3,86,581	5,96,102	8,70,772

Step 2: Goodwill = ₹ 2,28,250 + ₹ 3,86,581 + ₹ 5,96,102 + ₹ 8,70,772 = ₹ 20,81,705

Working Notes:

(i) Projected Sales	
Year V	11,00,000 × 1.25 = 13,75,000
Year VI	13,75,000 × 1.25 = 17,18,750
Year VII	17,18,750 × 1.25 = 21,48,438
Year VIII	21,48,438 × 1.25 = 26,85,547
(ii) Projected Cost of Goods Sold	
Year V	7,70,000 × 1.25 × 0.9 = 8,66,250
Year VI	8,66,250 × 1.25 × 0.9 = 9,74,531
Year VII	9,74,531 × 1.25 × 0.9 = 10,96,348
Year VIII	10,96,348 × 1.25 × 0.9 = 12,33,391
(iii) Projected Overheads	
Year V	2,20,000 × 1.25 × 1.02 = 2,80,500
Year VI	2,80,500 × 1.25 × 1.02 = 3,57,638
Year VII	3,57,638 × 1.25 × 1.02 = 4,55,988
Year VIII	4,55,988 × 1.25 × 1.02 = 5,81,384

8.0 SUPER PROFIT METHOD

MEANING OF SUPER PROFIT METHOD

The Goodwill under this method is ascertained by multiplying the Super Profits by certain number of year's purchase. It is based on the assumption that a new business will not be able to earn excess profits (though it may earn normal profits) during the first few years of its operations. Hence, the person who purchases an existing business has to pay in the form of Goodwill a sum equal to Super Profits multiplied by the number of years during which buyer is likely to receive excess profits for the first few years.

HOW TO CALCULATE GOODWILL UNDER SUPER PROFITS METHOD

The various steps involved in valuing the Goodwill according to Super Profits method are given below:

Step 1: *Calculate Capital Employed as follows:*
Capital Employed = All assets (other than Goodwill, Fictitious Assets and Non–Trade Investments) ***at Current Values*** *less Outsiders' Liabilities* ***at Current Amounts.***
Step 2: *Calculate Average Capital Employed as follows:*
I WHERE TWO YEARS' ASSETS AND LIABILITIES ARE GIVEN
Average Capital Employed =(Opening Capital Employed+ Closing Capital Employed)/2

II WHERE ONLY ONE YEAR'S ASSETS AND LIABILITIES ARE GIVEN	
A. Closing Capital Employed [A + B]	XXX
B. *Less:* Half of [(Current Year's Adjusted Profits before Tax + Income from Non–Trade Investments) – Tax]	(XXX)
C. Average Capital Employed [A – B]	XXX

Step 3: *Calculate Normal Profits as follows:*

Normal Profit = Average Capital Employed × Normal Rate of Return.

Note: Normal Rate of Return refers to the rate of return normally earned by an average firm belonging to the same industry.

Step 4: *Calculate Average Future Maintainable Profits (according to steps given under Average Profits Method)*

Step 5: *Calculate Super Profits as follows:*

Super Profits = Average Future Maintainable Profits – Normal Profits

Step 6: *Goodwill = Super Profits × No. of years' Purchase.*

HOW TO CALCULATE CAPITAL EMPLOYED ON THE BASIS OF SHAREHOLDERS' FUNDS APPROACH

(A) COMPUTATION OF CLOSING CAPITAL EMPLOYED FROM ASSETS SIDE

Particulars	₹
A. Total Assets at their Current Values:	
Non–Current Assets ***[excluding*** *Goodwill, Non–trade Investments, Capital work in progress and other Non–Operating Assets]*	XXX
Current Assets	XXX
Total	XXX
B. *Less:* **Outsiders' Liabilities at Current Amounts:**	
Non–Current Liabilities	XXX
Current Liabilities ***[including*** *Provision for Tax]*	XXX
Total	XXX
C. Closing Capital Employed [A – B]	XXX

(B) COMPUTATION OF CLOSING CAPITAL EMPLOYED FROM LIABILITIES SIDE

Particulars	₹
A. Equity Share Capital	XXX
B. *Add:* Reserves & Surplus	XXX
C. *Add:* Preference Share Capital	XXX
D. *Add:* Net Profit on Revaluation of Assets & Liabilities	XXX
Or	
Less: Net Loss on Revaluation of Assets & Liabilities	(XXX)
E. *Less:* Book Value of Goodwill	(XXX)

F. *Less:* Non–Trading Assets (e.g.)	(XXX)
(a) Non–Trade Investments	
(b) Capital Work–in–progress	
(c) Advance for the Purchase of a Fixed Asset	
G. Closing Capital Employed	XXX

HOW TO CALCULATE AVERAGE CAPITAL EMPLOYED ON THE BASIS OF SHAREHOLDERS' FUNDS APPROACH

CASE I WHERE ONLY ONE YEAR'S ASSETS AND LIABILITIES ARE GIVEN

Particulars	₹
A. Closing Capital Employed	XXX
B. *Add:* Dividend paid at the end of current year	XXX
C. Adjusted Closing Capital Employed [A + B]	XXX
D. *Less:* Half of [(Current Year's Adjusted Profits before Tax + Income from Non–Trade Investments) – Tax]	(XXX)
E. Average Capital Employed [C – D]	XXX

CASE II WHERE MORE THAN ONE YEAR'S ASSETS AND LIABILITIES ARE GIVEN

Particulars	₹
A. Closing Capital Employed	XXX
B. *Add:* Dividend paid at the end of current year	XXX
C. Adjusted Closing Capital Employed (A + B)	XXX
D. Opening Capital Employed.	XXX
E. Average Capital Employed [(C+D)/2]	XXX

LLUSTRATION 19 [Calculation of Capital Employed and Average Capital Employed When only one year's Assets and Liabilities are given]

Given below are the extracts from the Balance Sheets of TULSIAN Ltd. as at 31st March, 2023:

Particulars	₹
Equity Share Capital (Shares of ₹ 10 each)	40,00,000
12% Preference Share Capital (Shares of ₹ 100 each)	10,00,000
Reserves and Surplus	20,00,000
10% Debentures[60% Debentures are to be redeemed prior to valuation of Goodwill]	20,00,000
Current Liabilities	10,00,000
Goodwill	4,00,000
Property,Plant & Equipment	60,00,000
10% Trade Investments [Face Value ₹ 8,00,000]	10,00,000
Current Assets	26,00,000

Additional Information: Profits after tax @ 40% for 2022–2023:₹ 15,00,000. All trade Investments are to be valued at 150% of Face Value.

Required: Calculate the Closing Capital Employed and Average Capital Employed for valuation of goodwill:

(a) If no Dividend was paid during the year

(b) If Dividend of ₹ 7,20,000 was paid at the end of the year

SOLUTION

(A) IF NO DIVIDEND WAS PAID DURING THE YEAR

		₹
A.	Total Assets at their current values:	
	Property, Plant & Equipment	60,00,000
	Trade Investments [150% of ₹ 8,00,000]	12,00,000
	Current Assets [₹ 26,00,000 – ₹ 12,00,000 (60% Debentures)]	14,00,000
	Total Assets	86,00,000
B.	*Less:* Outsiders' Liabilities at their current amounts:	
	10% Debentures [₹ 20,00,000 – ₹ 12,00,000]	8,00,000
	Current Liabilities	10,00,000
	Total	18,00,000
C.	Closing Capital Employed (A – B)	68,00,000
D.	*Less:* Half of Current Years' Adjusted Profits after Tax [50% ₹ 15,00,000]	(7,50,000)
E.	Average Capital Employed (C – D)	60,50,000

(B) IF DIVIDEND OF ₹ 7,20,000 WAS PAID AT THE END OF THE YEAR

		₹
A.	Total Assets at their current values	
	Property, Plant & Equipment	60,00,000
	Trade Investments [150% of ₹ 8,00,000]	12,00,000
	Current Assets [₹ 26,00,000 – ₹ 12,00,000 (60% Debentures)]	14,00,000
	Total Assets	86,00,000
B.	*Less:* Outsiders' Liabilities at their current amounts:	
	10% Debentures [₹ 20,00,000 – ₹ 12,00,000]	8,00,000
	Current Liabilities	10,00,000
	Total	18,00,000
C.	Closing Capital Employed (A – B)	68,00,000
D.	*Add:* Dividend paid at the end of the year	7,20,000
E.	Adjusted Closing Capital Employed (C + D)	75,20,000
F.	*Less:* Half of Current Years' Adjusted Profits after Tax [50% ₹ 15,00,000]	(7,50,000)
G.	Average Capital Employed (E – F)	67,70,000

ILLUSTRATION 20 [Calculation of Capital Employed and Average Capital Employed from Liabilities side]

Given below are the extracts from the Balance Sheets of TULSIAN Ltd. as at 31st March, 2023:

Particulars	₹
Equity Share Capital (Shares of ₹ 10 each)	40,00,000
12% Preference Share Capital (Shares of ₹ 100 each)	10,00,000
Reserves and Surplus	20,00,000
10% Debentures[60% Debentures are to be redeemed prior to valuation of Goodwill]	20,00,000
Current Liabilities	10,00,000
Goodwill	4,00,000
10% Trade Investments [Face Value ₹ 8,00,000]	10,00,000

Additional Information: Profits after tax @ 40% for 2022–2023: ₹ 15,00,000. All trade Investments are to be valued at 150% of Face Value.

Required: Calculate the Closing Capital Employed and Average Capital Employed for valuation of goodwill:

(a) If no Dividend was paid during the year

(b) If Dividend of ₹ 7,20,000 was paid at the end of the year

SOLUTION

(A) IF NO DIVIDEND WAS PAID DURING THE YEAR

Particulars	₹
A Equity Share Capital (Shares of ₹ 10 each)	40,00,000
B 12% Preference Share Capital (Shares of ₹ 100 each)	10,00,000
C Reserves and Surplus	20,00,000
D Add: Net Profit on Revaluation of Trade Investments [(₹ 8,00,000 * 150%) – ₹ 10,00,000]	**2,00,000**
E Less: Book Value of Goodwill	**(4,00,000)**
F Closing Capital Employed (A + B+ C + D – E)	68,00,000
G *Less:* Half of Current Years' Adjusted Profits after Tax [50% ₹ 15,00,000]	(7,50,000)
H Average Capital Employed (F–G)	60,50,000

(B) IF DIVIDEND OF ₹ 7,20,000 WAS PAID AT THE END OF THE YEAR

Particulars	₹
A Equity Share Capital (Shares of ₹ 10 each)	40,00,000
B 12% Preference Share Capital (Shares of ₹ 100 each)	10,00,000
C Reserves and Surplus	20,00,000
D Add: Net Profit on Revaluation of Trade Investments [(₹ 8,00,000 * 150%) – ₹ 10,00,000]	**2,00,000**
E Less: Book Value of Goodwill	**(4,00,000)**
F Closing Capital Employed (A + B+ C + D – E)	68,00,000

G *Add:* Dividend paid at the end of the year	7,20,000
H Adjusted Closing Capital Employed (F +G)	75,20,000
I *Less:* Half of Current Years' Adjusted Profits after Tax [50% ₹ 15,00,000]	(7,50,000)
J Average Capital Employed (H – I)	67,70,000

ILLUSTRATION 21 [Calculation of Capital Employed and Average Capital Employed When more than one year's assets and liabilities are given]

Given below are the extracts from the Balance Sheets of TULSIAN Ltd. as at 31st March of year I, II, III:

[Figures in lacs]

Particulars	*I*	*II*	*III*
Profit and Loss A/c	0.8	0.9	1.2
General Reserves	4.5	5.5	6.5
Equity Share Capital (Shares of ₹ 10 each fully paid)	10	10	10
Current Liabilities	3.5	4.5	5.5
Goodwill	4	3	2
Property,Plant & Equipment	9	10	10
10% Trade Investments: [Face Value ₹ 80,000]	1	1	1
Current Assets	4.8	6.9	10.2

Additional Information:

Particulars	*I* ₹	*II* ₹	*III* ₹
1. Assets were valued as follows:			
Property,Plant & Equipment	10	11	12.5
Current Assets	6	8	12.2
2. The Book Value of Goodwill was ₹ 4 lacs			
3. Capital Employed at the beginning of the year I was ₹ 19.30 lacs including Goodwill.			

Required: Calculate Average Capital Employed for each of the three years for the purposes of Valuation of Goodwill.

SOLUTION

CALCULATION OF AVERAGE CAPITAL EMPLOYED

Particulars	*I* ₹	*II* ₹	*III* ₹
A. Total Assets at their Current Values:			
Property,Plant & Equipment	10	11	12.5
10% Trade Investments	1	1	1.0
Current Assets	6	8	12.2
Total Assets	17	20	25.7

B. *Less:* Outsiders' Liabilities	(3.5)	(4.5)	(5.5)
C. Closing Capital Employed (A – B)	13.5	15.5	20.2
D. Opening Capital employed	15.3	13.5	15.5
E. Average Capital Employed [(C + D)/2]	14.4	14.5	17.85

HOW TO CALCULATE NORMAL RATE OF RETURN/EXPECTATION

The following points are worth noting in this regard:

1. Normal Rate of Return comprises—
   (i) the risk–free rate, i.e., the pure interest rate prevailing in the concerned economy; (the rate of return on long term government securities *or* fixed deposit in bank may be taken as risk–free rate), and
   (ii) the premium for business risks appropriate for the industry to which the firm/company belongs.
2. In practice, Normal Rate of Return refers to that average rate at which the similar enterprises of the same industry to which the enterprise valuing the goodwill/share belongs, are earning profits. Thus, for practical purposes industry average return is taken as normal rate of return.
3. Normal Rate of Return/Expectation for the enterprise valuing goodwill/share need not necessarily be the same as that of an Industry to which the enterprise belongs because of its individual factors affecting the Normal Rate of Return. For example in case of a company having fluctuations in the payment of dividends, some additional risk premium may be added to Normal Rate of Return of the Industry as compared to the case of a company having stability in the payment of dividends.
4. **High Risk Cases**—In the following cases the risk of the equity investors is high:
   (a) If Fixed Interest and Fixed dividend Coverage Ratio is **less than** the prescribed ratio.
   (b) If Net Asset backing (or Cover) is **less than** the prescribed ratio.
   (c) If Capital Gearing Ratio is **higher than** the prescribed ratio.
   Hence, an additional risk **premium should be added to** industry's Normal Rate of Return.
5. **Low Risk Cases**—In the following cases, the risk of the equity investors is low:
   (a) If Fixed Interest and Fixed dividend Coverage Ratio is **more than** the prescribed ratio.
   (b) If Net Asset backing (or Cover) is **more than** prescribed ratio.
   (c) If Capital Gearing Ratio is **lower than** the prescribed ratio.
   Hence, the Industry's Normal Rate of Return should be **reduced** on account of lower risk premium.

6. CALCULATION OF NORMAL RATE OF RETURN/EXPECTATION FOR THE COMPANY

	Particulars	*X Ltd*	*Y Ltd.*	*Z Ltd.*
A.	Normal Rate of Expectation in the Industry	13%	13%	13%
B.	*Less:* Low Risk Premium: for high Fixed Interest and Fixed Dividend Coverage (say)	(0.5%)	(0.5%)	(0.5%)
	for low Capital Gearing Ratio (say)	(0.5%)	(0.5%)	(0.5%)
	for high Net Asset Backing (say)	(0.5%)	(0.5%)	(0.5%)

for stability in payment of Dividends (say)	(0.5%)	(0.5%)	(0.5%)
C. *Add:* Additional Risk Premium for low Fixed Interest and Fixed Dividend Coverage (say)	0.5%	0.5%	0.5%
for high Capital Gearing Ratio (say)	0.5%	0.5%	0.5%
for low Net Asset Backing (say)	0.5%	0.5%	0.5%
for fluctuations in payment of Dividends (say)	0.5%	0.5%	0.5%
D. Normal Rate of Expectation for the company [A – B + C]			

Tutorial Note: *Normal Rate of Return for Equity is to be taken after tax. Unless otherwise stated, it is presumed that the given Normal Rate of Return is after tax.*

ILLUSTRATION 22 [Calculation of Normal Rate of Return/Expectation]

Calculate the Normal Rate of Return/Expectation in each of the following cases:

Case (a) If Normal Rate of Return before tax is 12.5% and Tax Rate is 20%.

Case (b) If Average Rate of Dividend in industry is 12.5% and the Market Price of similar company's share is ₹ 125.

Case (c) If dividends were distributed at the rate of 10% in year I and year II and at the rate of 15% in year III and year IV. Market Price of company's share is ₹ 125.

SOLUTION

Case (a) Normal Rate of Return after tax= Normal Rate of Return before tax * (1–tax rate)

$= 12.5\% \times (1 - 0.20) = 10\%$

Case (b) Normal Rate of Return= Average Rate of Dividend/Market price = 12.5%/125 = 10%

Case (c) Average Rate of Dividend declared during past 4 years = (10 + 10 + 15 + 15)/4 = 12.5

Normal Rate of Return = Average Rate of Dividend/Market Price = 12.5/125 = 10%.

ILLUSTRATION 23 [Calculation of Normal Rate of Return/Expectation]

Particulars	*X Ltd.*	*Y Ltd.*	*Z Ltd.*
Fixed Interest and Fixed Dividends coverage	3	4.8	2.0
Capital Gearing Ratio	3	1.0	5.67

Normal Rate of Return in the industry to which the companies belongs is 12% provided:

(a) Fixed Interest and Fixed Dividends coverage is at least 3 times.

(b) Capital Gearing Ratio is 3 times.

Required: Calculate Normal rate of Return/Expectation for the above companies.

SOLUTION

CALCULATION OF NORMAL RATE OF RETURN/EXPECTATION FOR THE COMPANY

Particulars	*X Ltd.*	*Y Ltd.*	*Z Ltd.*
A. Normal Rate of Expectation in the Industry	12	12	12
B. *Less:* Low Risk Premium:			
for high Fixed Interest and Fixed Dividend Coverage (say)	—	(0.5)	—

for low Capital Gearing Ratio (say)		(0.5)	—
C. *Add:* Additional Risk Premium:			
for low Fixed Interest and Fixed Dividend Coverage (say)	—	—	0.5
for high Capital Gearing Ratio (say)			0.5
D. Normal Rate of Expectation for the company	12	11	13

ILLUSTRATION 24 [Calculation of Normal Rate of Return/Expectation]

[₹ in lacs]

Particulars	*X Ltd.*	*Y Ltd.*	*Z Ltd.*
Equity Shares of ₹ 10 each fully paid	10	20	10
Reserves	10	20	2
12.5% Preference Shares of ₹ 100 each fully paid	40	20	40
10% Debentures	20	20	28
Profits before Interest and Tax	30	30	20.8
Tax Rate @ 30%			

Normal Rate of Return in the industry to which the companies belongs is 12% provided:

(a) Fixed Interest and Fixed Dividends coverage is at least 3 times.

(b) Capital Gearing Ratio is 3 times.

Required: Calculate Normal Rate of Return/Expectation for the above companies.

SOLUTION

STEP 1: PROFITS BEFORE INTEREST BUT AFTER TAX

Particulars	*X Ltd.*	*Y Ltd.*	*Z Ltd.*
Profits before Interest and Tax	30	30	20.8
Less: Interest	(2)	(2)	(2.8)
Profits after Interest but before Tax	28	28	18
Less: Tax	(8.4)	(8.4)	(5.4)
Profits after Interest and Tax	19.6	19.6	12.6
Add: Interest	2	2	2.8
Profits before Interest but after Tax	21.6	21.6	15.4

STEP 2: FIXED INTEREST AND FIXED DIVIDENDS COVERAGE

Particulars	*X Ltd.*	*Y Ltd.*	*Z Ltd.*
Interest	2	2	2.8
Preference Dividend	5	2.5	5
Fixed Interest and Fixed Dividends	7	4.5	7.8
Fixed Interest and Fixed Dividends Coverage $= \frac{\text{Profits before Interest but after Tax}}{\text{Fixed Interest and Fixed Dividends}}$	3.085714	4.8	1.97436

STEP 3: CAPITAL GEARING RATIO			
$= \frac{\text{Preference Share Capital + Debentures}}{\text{Equity Share Capital + Net Reserves \& Surplus}}$	3	1	5.7

STEP 4: NORMAL RATE OF RETURN/EXPECTATION

	Particulars	*X Ltd.*	*Y Ltd.*	*Z Ltd.*
A.	Normal Rate of Expectation in Industry	12	12	12
B.	*Less:* Low Risk Premium:			
	for high Fixed Interest and Fixed Dividend Coverage (say)	—	(0.5)	—
	for low Capital Gearing Ratio (say)	—	(0.5)	—
C.	*Add:* Additional Risk Premium			
	for low Fixed Interest and Fixed Dividend Coverage (say)	—	—	0.5
	for high Capital Gearing Ratio (say)	—	—	0.5
D.	Normal Rate of Expectation for companies	12	11	13

ILLUSTRATION 25A

Given below are the extracts from the Balance Sheet of BHARAT Ltd. as at 31st March, 2023:

Particulars	₹
Equity Share Capital (Shares of ₹ 10 each)	40,00,000
12% Preference Share Capital (Shares of ₹ 100 each)	10,00,000
Reserves and Surplus	20,00,000
10% Debentures [60% Debentures are to be redeemed prior to valuation of Goodwill]	20,00,000
Current Liabilities	10,00,000
Goodwill	4,00,000
Property,Plant & Equipment	60,00,000
10% Trade Investments [Face Value ₹ 8,00,000]	10,00,000
Current Assets	26,00,000

Additional Information: Profits after tax @ 40%: 2020–2021 :₹ 12,00,000, 2021–2022: ₹ 18,00,000, 2022–2023: ₹ 15,00,000.Trade Investments are to be valued at 150% of Face Value.Rate of Income Tax — 30% with effect from 1st April, 2023.

Required: Calculate the Value of Goodwill at 3 years' purchase of Super Profits:

(a) If Normal Rate of Return on Net Assets is 10%.

(b) If Normal Rate of Return on Net Assets for Equity Shareholders is 10%.

(c) If Normal Rate of Return on Average Capital Employed is 10%.

SOLUTION

Part (a) If Normal Rate of Return on Net Assets is 10%

STEP 1: PAST ADJUSTED PROFIT BEFORE TAX

Particulars	2020–2021 ₹	2021–2022 ₹	2022–2023 ₹
A. Profits after tax	12,00,000	18,00,000	15,00,000
B. Past Adjusted Profits before tax (A/60%)	20,00,000	30,00,000	25,00,000

Step 2: Average Past Adjusted Profits [Simple Average since Past adjusted profits are fluctuating]

= [(₹ 20,00,000 + ₹ 30,00,000 + ₹ 25,00,000)/3] = ₹ 25,00,000

STEP 3: FUTURE MAINTAINABLE PROFITS AFTER TAX

Particulars	₹
A. Average Past Adjusted Profits	25,00,000
B. *Add:* Interest on Debentures [(60% of ₹ 20,00,000)*10%] [no longer payable]	1,20,000
C. Future Maintainable Profits before Tax	26,20,000
D. *Less:* Tax @ 30%	(7,86,000)
E. Future Maintainable Profits after Tax for Shareholders	18,34,000

STEP 4: NET ASSETS

	₹
A. Total Assets at their current values:	
Property,Plant & Equipment	60,00,000
Trade Investments [150% of ₹ 8,00,000]	12,00,000
Current Assets [₹ 26,00,000 – ₹ 12,00,000 (60% Debentures)]	14,00,000
Total Assets	86,00,000
B. *Less:* Outsiders' Liabilities at their current amounts:	
10% Debentures [₹ 20,00,000 – ₹ 12,00,000]	8,00,000
Current Liabilities	10,00,000
Total	18,00,000
C. **Net Assets** (A – B)	68,00,000

Step 5: Normal Profit = Net Assets* Normal Rate of Return = ₹ 68,00,000 * 10% = ₹ 6,80,000

Step 6: Super Profits = Future Maintainable Profits after tax – Normal Profits

= ₹ 18,34,000 – ₹ 6,80,000 = ₹ 11,54,000

Step 7: Goodwill = Super Profits * No. of years' purchase

= ₹ 11,54,000 * 3 = ₹ 34,62,000

Part (b) If Normal Rate of Return on Net Assets for Equity shareholders is 10%

STEP 1: PAST ADJUSTED PROFIT BEFORE TAX

Particulars	2020–2021 ₹	2021–2022 ₹	2022–2023 ₹
A. Profits after tax	12,00,000	18,00,000	15,00,000
B. Past Adjusted Profits before tax (A/60%)	20,00,000	30,00,000	25,00,000

Step 2: Average Past Adjusted Profits [Simple Average since Past adjusted profits are fluctuating]

= [(20,00,000 + 30,00,000 + 25,00,000)/3]= ₹ 25,00,000

STEP 3: FUTURE MAINTAINABLE PROFITS AFTER TAX

Particulars	₹
A. Average Past Adjusted Profits	25,00,000
B. *Add:* Interest on Debentures [(60% of ₹ 20,00,000)*10%][no longer payable]	1,20,000
C. Future Maintainable Profits before Tax	26,20,000
D. *Less:* Tax @ 30%	(7,86,000)
E. Future Maintainable Profits after Tax for Shareholders	18,34,000
F. Less: Pref. Dividend [10,00,000 * 12%]	**(1,20,000)**
G. Future Maintainable Profits after Tax for Equity Shareholders [E–F]	17,14,000

STEP 4: NET ASSETS FOR EQUITY SHAREHOLDERS

A. Total Assets at their current values:	₹
Property,Plant & Equipment	60,00,000
Trade Investments [150% of ₹ 8,00,000]	12,00,000
Current Assets [₹ 26,00,000 – ₹ 12,00,000 (60% Debentures)]	14,00,000
Total Assets	86,00,000
B. *Less:* Outsiders' Liabilities at their current amounts:	
10% Debentures [₹ 20,00,000 – ₹ 12,00,000]	8,00,000
Current Liabilities	10,00,000
Total	18,00,000
C. **Net Assets for Shareholders** (A – B)	68,00,000
D. *Less:* Pref. Share Capital	10,00,000
E. **Net Assets for Equity shareholders** (A – B)	58,00,000

Step 5: Normal Profit = Net Assets for Equity shareholders* Normal Rate of Return

= ₹ 58,00,000 * 10% = ₹ 5,80,000

Step 6: Super Profits = FMP after tax for Equity shareholders – Normal Profits

= ₹ 17,14,000 – ₹ 5,80,000 = ₹ 11,34,000

Step 7: Goodwill = Super Profits * No. of years' purchase

= ₹ 11,34,000 * 3 = ₹ 34,02,000

Part (c) If Normal Rate of Return on Average Capital Employed is 10%

STEP 1: PAST ADJUSTED PROFIT BEFORE TAX

Particulars	*2020–2021* ₹	*2021–2022* ₹	*2022–2023* ₹
A.Profits after tax	12,00,000	18,00,000	15,00,000
B.Past Adjusted Profits before tax (A/60%)	20,00,000	30,00,000	25,00,000

Step 2: Average Past Adjusted Profits [Simple Average since Past adjusted profits are fluctuating]

= [(20,00,000 + 30,00,000 + 25,00,000)/3] = ₹ 25,00,000

STEP 3: FUTURE MAINTAINABLE PROFITS AFTER TAX

Particulars	₹
A. Average Past Adjusted Profits	25,00,000
B. *Add:* Interest on Debentures [(60% of ₹ 20,00,000)*10%] [no longer payable]	1,20,000
C. Future Maintainable Profits before Tax	26,20,000
D. *Less:* Tax @ 30%	(7,86,000)
E. Future Maintainable Profits after Tax for Shareholders	18,34,000

STEP 4: AVERAGE CAPITAL EMPLOYED:

	₹
A. Total Assets at their current values:	
Property,Plant & Equipment	60,00,000
Trade Investments [150% of ₹ 8,00,000]	12,00,000
Current Assets [₹ 26,00,000 – ₹ 12,00,000 (60% Debentures)]	14,00,000
Total Assets	86,00,000
B. *Less:* Outsiders' Liabilities at their current amounts:	
10% Debentures [₹ 20,00,000 – ₹ 12,00,000]	8,00,000
Current Liabilities	10,00,000
Total	18,00,000
C. **Closing Capital Employed** (A – B)	68,00,000
D. *Less:* Half of Current Years' Adjusted Profits after Tax [50% ₹ 15,00,000]	(7,50,000)
E. **Average Capital Employed** (C–D)	60,50,000

Step 5: Normal Profit = Average Capital Employed * Normal Rate of Return
= ₹ 60,50,000 * 10% = ₹ 6,05,000

Step 6: Super Profits = Future Maintainable Profits after tax – Normal Profits
= ₹ 18,34,000 – ₹ 6,05,000 = ₹ 12,29,000

Step 7: Goodwill = Super Profits * No. of years' purchase
= ₹ 12,29,000 * 3 = ₹ 36,87,000

ILLUSTRATION 25B

Given below are the extracts from the Balance Sheet of BHARAT & SHEENA Ltd. as at 31st March, 2023:

Particulars	₹
Equity Share Capital (Shares of ₹ 10 each)	40,00,000
12% Preference Share Capital (Shares of ₹ 100 each)	10,00,000
Reserves and Surplus	20,00,000
10% Debentures [60% Debentures are to be redeemed prior to valuation of Goodwill]	20,00,000

Current Liabilities	10,00,000
Goodwill	4,00,000
10% Trade Investments [Face Value ₹ 8,00,000]	10,00,000

Additional Information: Profits after tax @ 40%: 2020–2021 :₹ 12,00,000, 2021–2022: ₹ 18,00,000, 2022–2023: ₹ 15,00,000. Trade Investments are to be valued at 150% of Face Value. Rate of Income Tax — 30% with effect from 1st April, 2023.

Required: Calculate the Value of Goodwill at 3 years' purchase of Super Profits:

(a) If Normal Rate of Return on Net Assets is 10%.

(b) If Normal Rate of Return on Net Assets for Equity Shareholders is 10%.

(c) If Normal Rate of Return on Average Capital Employed is 10%.

SOLUTION

Calculation of Net Assets for Shareholders and Net Assets for Equity Shareholders

Particulars	₹
Equity Share Capital (Shares of ₹ 10 each)	40,00,000
12% Preference Share Capital (Shares of ₹ 100 each)	10,00,000
Reserves and Surplus	20,00,000
Less: Goodwill	4,00,000
Add: Profit on Revaluation of Trade Investments [₹ 12,00,000 – ₹ 10,00,000]	2,00,000
Net Assets for Shareholders	68,00,000
Less: Pref. Share Capital	10,00,000
Net Assets for Equity Shareholders	58,00,000

Calculation of Average Capital Employed

Particulars	₹
Equity Share Capital (Shares of ₹ 10 each)	40,00,000
12% Preference Share Capital (Shares of ₹ 100 each)	10,00,000
Reserves and Surplus	20,00,000
Less: Goodwill	4,00,000
Add: Profit on Revaluation of Trade Investments [₹ 12,00,000 – ₹ 10,00,000]	2,00,000
Closing Capital Employed	68,00,000
Less: Half of Current Years' Adjusted Profits after Tax [50% ₹ 15,00,000]	(7,50,000)
Average Capital Employed	60,50,000

Remaining solution is same as in previous Illustration.

ILLUSTRATION 26

From the following information, calculate the Value of Goodwill at 5 years' purchase of Super Profits of TUSHAR & TASHIKA Ltd:

4,00,000 Equity Shares of ₹ 10 each,₹ 8 paid up
7,00,000 Equity Shares of ₹ 5 each fully called up (Calls–in–arrears @₹ 2 on 2,00,000 shares)

10,000 9% Preference Shares of ₹100 each fully paid up
Reserves & Surplus ₹ 74,66,000
Property,Plant & Equipments ₹ 3,00,000. 50% of Total Property,Plant & Equipments are found undervalued by 50% of market value and 50% of the remaining are found overvalued by 50% of market value.
10% Investments: [Face Value₹ 80,000] ₹ 1,00,000. Of the Investments 10% is trade and the balance non–trade. All trade Investments are to be valued at 10% below cost.
External Liabilities ₹ 10,00,000
Expected Future Maintainable Profits before tax ₹ 25,59,000
Rate of Tax—30%, Normal Rate of Earnings for Equity Shareholders — 10%

SOLUTION

STEP 1:NET ASSETS FOR EQUITY SHAREHOLDERS

4,00,000 Equity Shares of ₹ 10 each,₹ 8 paid up	32,00,000
7,00,000 Equity Shares of ₹ 5 each fully called up (Calls–in–arrears @₹ 2 on 2,00,000 shares)	31,00,000
Reserves & Surplus	74,66,000
Profit on Revaluation of PPE [3,00,000 x 50% x 100%]	1,50,000
Loss on Revaluation of PPE [3,00,000 x 50% x 50% x 1/3]	(25,000)
Loss on Revaluation of Trade Investments[1,00,000 x 10% x 10%]	(1,000)
Less: Non–Trade Investments	(90,000)
Net Assets for Equity Shareholders	138,00,000

STEP 2:EXPECTED FMP FOR EQUITY SHAREHOLDERS

	₹
A. Expected Future Maintainable Profits before tax	25,59,000
B. *Less:* Tax @ 30%	(7,67,700)
C. Expected FMP after tax (A–B)	17,91,300
D. *Less:* Preference Dividend @ 9%	(90,000)
E. Expected FMP for Equity Shareholders	17,01,300

Step 3: Normal Profit = Net Assets for Equity Shareholders * Normal Rate of Return for Equity

= ₹ 138,00,000 * 10% = ₹ 13,80,000

Step 4: Super Profits = FMP after tax for Equity Shareholders – Normal Profits

= ₹ 17,01,300 – ₹ 13,80,000 = ₹ 3,21,300

Step 5: Goodwill = Super Profits * No. of years' purchase

= ₹ 3,21,300 * 5 = ₹ 16,06,500

ILLUSTRATION 27

Given below are the extracts from the Balance Sheet of BSTT Ltd. as at 31st March, 2023:

Liabilities	₹
Equity Share Capital (Shares of ₹ 10 each)	40,00,000
9% Preference Share Capital (Shares of ₹ 100 each)	10,24,000
Reserves and Surplus	21,56,000
Non–Current Liabilities	10,00,000
Current Liabilities	34,80,000
Goodwill	4,00,000
Property,Plant & Equipment	49,27,100
10% Investments: [Face Value ₹ 80,000]	1,00,000
Current Assets	62,32,900

Additional Information:

1. Profits and Losses after tax @ 40%:

2018–2019 Losses	*2019–2020 Profits*	*2020–2021 Profits*	*2021–2022 Profits*	*2022–2023 Profits*
5,50,000	9,00,000	12,02,160	15,04,320	18,04,320

The loss in 2018–2019 occurred due to a prolonged strike.

2. Of the Investments 10% is trade and the balance non–trade. 50% of the non–trade Investments were acquired on 1.4.2021 and the rest on 1.4.2020. All trade Investments are to be valued at 10% below cost.
3. In 2020–2021 a new machine costing ₹ 1,00,000 was purchased but wrongly charged to revenue. (No effect has yet been given for rectifying the same) Depreciation is charged on machine @ 10% on reducing balance method.
4. Closing Inventories were over–valued by ₹ 90,000 in 2020–2021, by ₹ 81,000 in 2021–2022, by ₹ 72,900 in 2022–2023.
5. Disputed Bonus claim of ₹ 1,50,000 not yet provided in the accounts for 2022–2023 is settled at ₹ 1,00,000.
6. In 2022–2023 some old Furniture having a book value of ₹ 2,50,000 was sold for ₹ 1,50,000.
7. With effect from 1st April, 2023, there will be increase in manager's remuneration of ₹ 2,00,000 p.a.,Advantage from new contract for supply of goods of ₹ 4,50,000 p.a. and Additional Revenue Expenditure of ₹ 50,000 p.a.
8. Property,Plant & Equipment are worth 20% above their actual book value.
9. Rate of Income Tax—30% with effect from 1st April, 2023.
10. Normal Rate of Return is 10% on Average Capital Employed.

Required: Calculate the Value of Goodwill at 3 years' purchase of Super Profits.

SOLUTION

STEP 1: CALCULATION OF PAST ADJUSTED PROFIT BEFORE TAX

Particulars	*2019–2020* ₹	*2020–2021* ₹	*2021–2022* ₹	*2022–2023* ₹
Profits after tax	9,00,000	12,02,160	15,04,320	18,04,320
Profits before tax [A/60%]	15,00,000	20,03,600	25,07,200	30,07,200
Less: Incomes from Non–trade Investments		(3,600)	(7,200)	(7,200)
Add: Purchase of Machinery charged to P&L A/c		1,00,000		
Less: Depreciation on above machinery		(10,000)	(9,000)	(8,100)
Less: Over Valuation of Closing Inventories		(90,000)	(81,000)	(72,900)
Add: Over Valuation of Opening Inventories			90,000	81,000
Add: Loss on Sale of Furniture				1,00,000
Less: Bonus				(1,00,000)
Past Adjusted Profit	15,00,000	20,00,000	25,00,000	30,00,000

STEP 2: CALCULATION OF AVERAGE PAST ADJUSTED PROFITS [WEIGHTED AVERAGE SINCE PAST ADJUSTED PROFITS SHOW RISING TREND]

Year A	*Profits* B	*Weights* C	*Weighted Profits* D = B * C
2019–2020	15,00,000	1	15,00,000
2020–2021	20,00,000	2	40,00,000
2021–2022	25,00,000	3	75,00,000
2022–2023	30,00,000	4	1,20,00,000
Total		10	2,50,00,000

Weighted average of Past adjusted profits = 2,50,00,000/10 = ₹ 25,00,000

STEP 3: CALCULATION OF FUTURE MAINTAINABLE PROFITS AFTER TAX

Particulars	₹
A. Average Past Adjusted Profits	25,00,000
B. *Less:* Increase in manager remuneration p.a.	(2,00,000)
C. *Add:* Advantage from contract p.a.	4,50,000
D. *Less:* Additional Revenue Expenditure p.a.	(50,000)
E. *Less:* Additional Depreciation on increase in value of Fixed Assets	(1,00,000)
F. Future Maintainable Profits before Tax	26,00,000
G. *Less:* Tax [@ 30% on (₹ 26,00,000 + ₹ 1,00,000]	(8,10,000)
H. Future Maintainable Profits after Tax	17,90,000

Note: *Additional Depreciation on Increase in value of Fixed Assets is not deductible for tax purposes.*

STEP 4: CALCULATION OF AVERAGE CAPITAL EMPLOYED

		₹
A.	Total Assets at their current values:	₹
	Property,Plant & Equipment	60,00,000
	Trade Investments [90% of ₹ 10,000]	9,000
	Current Assets [₹ 62,32,900 – ₹ 72,900 + ₹ 81,000]	62,41,000
	Total Assets	1,22,50,000
B.	*Less:* Outsiders' Liabilities at current amounts:	
	Non–Current Liabilities	10,00,000
	Current Liabilities	34,80,000
	Unrecorded Liability (Bonus)	1,00,000
	Total	45,80,000
C.	Closing Capital Employed (A – B)	76,70,000
D.	*Less:* Half of [(Current Years' Adjusted Profits before Tax + Incomes from Non–Trade Investments) – Tax] 50% [(₹ 30,00,000 + 7,200) – 40%]	(9,02,160)
F.	Average Capital Employed	67,67,840

Step 5: Normal Profit = Average Capital Employed * Normal Rate of Return

= ₹ 67,67,840 * 0.1 = ₹ 6,76,784

Step 6: Super Profits = Future Maintainable Profits – Normal Profits

= ₹ 17,90,000 – ₹ 6,76,784 = ₹ 11,13,216

Step 7: Goodwill = Super Profits * No. of years' purchase

= ₹ 11,13,216 * 3 = ₹ 33,39,648

Working Note:

CALCULATION OF INCREASE IN VALUE OF FIXED ASSETS AND ADDITIONAL DEPRECIATION THEREON

	Particulars	₹
A.	Book value before rectification	49,27,100
B.	*Add:* Purchase of Machinery wrongly charged to P&L A/c	1,00,000
C.	*Less:* Depreciation on above machinery [₹ 10,000 + ₹ 9,000 + ₹ 8,100]	(27,100)
D.	Book value after rectification	50,00,000
E.	Increase in value of Fixed Assets @20% on ₹ 50,00,000	10,00,000
F.	Current value after rectification	60,00,000

ILLUSTRATION 28

Given below are the extracts from the Balance Sheet of BHARAT TULSIAN Ltd. as at 31st March, 2023:

Particulars	₹
5,000, Equity Shares of ₹ 100 each fully paid up	5,00,000
3,000, 12% Cum Preference Shares of ₹ 100 each, fully paid up	3,00,000

General Reserve		2,40,000
Profit and Loss A/c:		
Balance on 1.4.2022	1,20,000	
Profit including Investment Income of current year	4,80,000	
Less: Provision for Tax	(1,20,000)	4,80,000
Trade Creditors		2,10,000
Provision for Tax		1,20,000
Property, Plant & Equipment:		7,80,000
6% Government Securities at cost (Face value ₹ 2,00,000)		1,60,000
Trade Debtors		3,80,000
Inventories (Taken at 90% of market value)		4,50,000
Cash and Bank Balances		80,000

Additional information:

(a) The Property, Plant & Equipment are understated by ₹ 2,80,000. Ignore additional Depreciation on an increase in Property, Plant & Equipment.

(b) Companies doing similar business as that of Glory Ltd. show a market return of 15% on Average Capital Employed.

(c) Profits after tax over the prior 3 years period have been increasing at the rate of ₹ 60,000 per annum.

Required: Calculate the value of goodwill at 3 years' purchase of super profits.

SOLUTION

Tax Rate = ₹ 1,20,000/ ₹ 4,80,000 = 0.25 or 25%

STEP 1: PAST ADJUSTED PROFIT BEFORE TAX

Particulars	*2020–2021* ₹	*2021–2022* ₹	*2022–2023* ₹
Profits after tax(PAT)	2,40,000 (3,00,000 – 60,000)	3,00,000 (3,60,000 – 60,000)	3,60,000
Profits before tax(PAT/75%)	3,20,000	4,00,000	4,80,000
Less: Incomes from non–trade investment	(12,000)	(12,000)	(12,000)
Past Adjusted Profits before tax	3,08,000	3,88,000	4,68,000

STEP 2: AVERAGE PAST ADJUSTED PROFITS [WEIGHTED AVERAGE SINCE PAST ADJUSTED PROFITS SHOW RISING TREND]

Year A	*Profits* B	*Weights* C	*Weighted Profits* D = B * C
2020–2021	3,08,000	1	3,08,000
2021–2022	3,88,000	2	7,76,000

2022–2023	4,68,000	3	14,04,000
Total		6	24,88,000

Weighted Average of Past Adjusted Profits = Total Weighted Profits/Total of Weights

= ₹ 24,88,000/6 = ₹ 4,14,666.7

Step 3: Future Maintainable Profits after tax = Average Past Adjusted Profits – Tax

= ₹ 4,14,666.7 – 1,03,666.7 = ₹ 3,11,000

STEP 4: AVERAGE CAPITAL EMPLOYED

		₹
A.	Total Assets at their current values:	
	Property,Plant & Equipment [₹ 7,80,000 + ₹ 2,80,000]	10,60,000
	Inventories [₹ 4,50,000 + ₹ 50,000]	5,00,000
	Trade Debtors	3,80,000
	Cash and Bank Balances	80,000
	Total Assets	20,20,000
B.	*Less:* Outsiders' Liabilities:	
	Trade Creditors	2,10,000
	Provision for tax	1,20,000
	Total	3,30,000
C.	Closing Capital Employed (A – B)	16,90,000
D.	*Less:* Half of the current year's past adjusted profits after tax (including after tax Incomes from Non–trade Investment) [50% of [(₹ 4,68,000 + ₹ 12,000) – 25%]	1,80,000
E.	Average Capital Employed	15,10,000

Step 5: Normal Profit = Average Capital Employed * Normal Rate of Return

= ₹ 15,10,000 * 0.15 = ₹ 2,26,500

Step 6: Super Profits = Future Maintainable Profits – Normal Profit

= ₹ 3,11,000 – ₹ 2,26,500 = ₹ 84,500

Step 7: Goodwill =₹ 84,500 × 3 = ₹ 2,53,500

ILLUSTRATION 29

Given below are the extracts from the Balance Sheet of TULSIAN Ltd. for the year ended on 31st March, 2021, 2022 and 2023:

Particulars	*2020 –2021* ₹	*2021 –2022* ₹	*2022 –2023* ₹
Equity Share Capital (Shares of ₹ 10 each)	32,00,000	32,00,000	32,00,000
General Reserve	24,00,000	28,00,000	32,00,000
Profit & Loss A/c	2,80,000	3,20,000	4,80,000
Current Liabilities	12,00,000	16,00,000	20,00,000
Goodwill	20,00,000	16,00,000	12,00,000
Tangible Fixed Assets	28,00,000	32,00,000	32,00,000

Inventories	20,00,000	24,00,000	28,00,000
Trade Debtors	40,000	3,20,000	8,80,000
Bank balance	2,40,000	4,00,000	8,00,000

Additional Information:

	2020 –2021 ₹	*2021 –2022* ₹	*2022 –2023* ₹
Current Valuation of Property,Plant & Equipment [Ignore additional Depreciation on an increase in Property,Plant & Equipment]	36,00,000	40,00,000	44,00,000
Current Valuation of Inventories	24,00,000	28,00,000	32,00,000
Net Profit (including opening balance after writing off depreciation, goodwill, tax provision and transfer to General Reserve)	8,40,000	12,40,000	16,40,000

(b) Capital employed in the business at market value at the beginning of 2020–2021 was ₹ 73,20,000 which included the cost of goodwill. The normal annual return on average capital employed in this line of business is 12½%.

(c) The balance in the General Reserve on 1st April, 2020 was ₹ 20 lakhs.

(d) The goodwill shown on 31.3.2021 was purchased on 1.4.2020 for ₹ 20 lakhs on which date the balance in the Profit & Loss account was ₹ 2,40,000.

(e) Goodwill is to be valued at 4 years' purchase of Simple Average Super Profit.

Required: Find out the average capital employed in each year. Find out the Value of Goodwill.

SOLUTION

1. AVERAGE CAPITAL EMPLOYED AT THE END OF EACH YEAR

Particulars	*2020 –2021* ₹	*2021 –2022* ₹	*2022 –2023* ₹
A. Total Assets at their Current Values:			
*Goodwill	20,00,000	16,00,000	12,00,000
Property,Plant & Equipment	36,00,000	40,00,000	44,00,000
Inventories	24,00,000	28,00,000	32,00,000
Trade Receivable	40,000	3,20,000	8,80,000
Bank Balance	2,40,000	4,00,000	8,00,000
Total Assets	82,80,000	91,20,000	104,80,000
B. *Less:* Outsiders' Liabilities	(12,00,000)	(16,00,000)	(20,00,000)
C. Closing Capital Employed (A – B)	70,80,000	75,20,000	84,80,000
D. Opening Capital employed	73,20,000	70,80,000	75,20,000
G. Average Capital Employed [(C + D)/2]	72,00,000	73,00,000	80,00,000

* Since the goodwill has been purchased, it is taken as a part of capital employed.

2. FUTURE MAINTAINABLE PROFIT & SUPER PROFIT

Particulars	*2020 –2021* ₹	*2021 –2022* ₹	*2022 –2023* ₹
Net Profit (Including Opening Balance)	8,40,000	12,40,000	16,40,000
Less: Opening Balance	(2,40,000)	(2,80,000)	(3,20,000)
Transfer to General Reserve	4,00,000	4,00,000	4,00,000
Add: Under Valuation of Closing Stock	4,00,000	4,00,000	4,00,000
Less: Under Valuation of Opening Stock	—	(4,00,000)	(4,00,000)
Add: Goodwill written off	—	4,00,000	4,00,000
Future Maintainable Profit	14,00,000	17,60,000	21,20,000
Less: 12.50% Normal Return of average capital	(9,00,000)	(9,12,500)	(10,00,000)
Super Profit	5,00,000	8,47,500	11,20,000

3. **Average Super Profit** =(₹ 5,00,000 + ₹ 8,47,500 + ₹ 11,20,000) / 3 = ₹ 8,22,500
4. **Goodwill at four years' Purchase** = ₹ 8,22,500 × 4 = ₹ 32,90,000

9.0 PRESENT VALUE OF SUPER PROFIT METHOD *OR* DISCOUNTED SUPER PROFITS METHOD *OR* ANNUITY METHOD

MEANING OF ANNUITY METHOD

Under Annuity Method, time value of money is considered. Time value of money is the difference between value of money at t_0 (i.e., present date) and value of money at t_1 (i.e., future date). Suppose it is expected that the super profits would be available to the firm for 5 years. In this case, the value of super profits to be received in different 5 years would be different depending upon the rate of interest. Since there is a time gap between the payment for goodwill at present date and the receipt of super profits at some future date, this method suggests to calculate the present value of future super profits as follows:

Present value of Super Profit = Super Profit to be received at the end of 1st year × $[1/(1 + r)^1]$ + Super Profit to be received at the end of 2nd year × $[1/(1 + r)^2]$ + ...

Where, r = Rate of Interest or Rate of Discount.

HOW TO CALCULATE GOODWILL UNDER ANNUITY METHOD

Step 1:	*Calculate the Future Super Profits.*
Step 2:	*Select the appropriate Rate of Interest/Discount.*
Step 3:	*Calculate the Present Value Factors for different years as follows:*
	P.V. Factor for 1st year = $[1/(1 + r)^1]$
	P.V. Factor for 2nd year = $[1/(1 + r)^2]$ *and so on.*
Step 4:	*Calculate Present Value of Super Profits of each year by multiplying the amount of future Super Profits with the present value factor.*
Step 5:	*Calculate the value of Goodwill by taking aggregate of Present Value of Super Profits calculated as per Step 4.*

ILLUSTRATION 30 [Annuity Method]

The expected profits of a firm for the next 5 years are as follows:

Year	I	II	III	IV	V
Profits (₹)	1,00,000	2,00,000	3,00,000	4,00,000	5,00,000

The total assets of the firm are ₹ 20,00,000 and outside liabilities are ₹ 11,00,000. The normal expectation in the industry is 10% on Closing Capital Employed. The present value factor at 10% are as follows:

Year	I	II	III	IV	V
PVF	0.9091	0.8264	0.7513	0.6830	0.6209

Required: Calculate the Value of Goodwill on the basis of Present Value of Super Profits for 5 years.

SOLUTION

Particulars	I	I	III	IV	V
A. Average Profits (₹)	1,00,000	2,00,000	3,00,000	4,00,000	5,00,000
B. Normal Profit [10% of (₹ 20 lacs – ₹ 11 lacs)	90,000	90,000	90,000	90,000	90,000
C. Super Profit [A – B]	10,000	1,10,000	2,10,000	3,10,000	4,10,000
D. PVF @ 10%	0.9091	0.8264	0.7513	0.6830	0.6209
E. Present Value of Super Profits	9091	90,904	1,57,773	2,11,730	2,54,569

Thus, Value of Goodwill = ₹9,091 + ₹ 90,904 + ₹ 1,57,773 + ₹ 2,11,730 + ₹ 2,54,569 = ₹ 7,24,067

10.0 CAPITALISATION OF SUPER PROFIT METHOD

MEANING OF CAPITALISATION OF SUPER PROFIT METHOD

The goodwill under this method is ascertained by capitalising the Super Profits on the basis of Normal Rate of Return.

HOW TO CALCULATE GOODWILL UNDER CAPITALISATION OF SUPER PROFIT METHOD

The various steps involved in valuing the goodwill according to this method are given below:

Step 1:	*Calculate Super Profits (according to steps given under Super Profits Method).*
Step 2:	*Goodwill = Super Profits /Normal Rate of Return*

Tutorial Note: Capitalisation of Super Profits Method is used if the question so directs *or* number of year's purchase of Super Profits is not given.

ILLUSTRATION 31

Calculate the Value of goodwill according to capitalisation of Super Profits Method from the following information:

1. Future Maintainable Profits after tax ₹ 5,00,000
2. Net Assets Employed ₹ 10,00,000
3. Normal Rate of Return 10%.

SOLUTION

Step 1: Super Profit = Future Maintainable Profits after tax – Normal Profits

= ₹ 5,00,000 – (10% of ₹ 10,00,000) = ₹ 5,00,000 – ₹ 1,00,000

= ₹ 4,00,000

Step 2: Goodwill = Super Profits /Normal Rate of Return

= ₹ 4,00,000 /10% = ₹ 40,00,000

11.0 CAPITALIZATION OF AVERAGE PROFITS METHOD

MEANING OF CAPITALISATION OF AVERAGE PROFIT METHOD

The goodwill under this method is ascertained by deducting the actual capital employed i.e., Net Assets (excluding Goodwill) as on the Date of Valuation in business from the Capitalised Value of the Average Profits on the basis of Normal Rate of Return.

HOW TO CALCULATE GOODWILL UNDER CAPITALISATION OF AVERAGE PROFITS METHOD

The various steps involved in valuing the goodwill according to this method are given below:

Step 1: *Calculate Average Future Maintainable Profits (according to steps given under Average Profits Method).*

Step 2: *Calculate the Capitalised Value of Average Profits as under:*

Capitalised Value = Average Future Maintainable Profits/Normal Rate of Return

Step 3: *Calculate the value of Net Assets as on the date of valuation of goodwill as under: Net Assets = All Assets (other than goodwill, fictitious assets and non–trade investments) at their current values less Outsiders' Liabilities.*

Step 4: *Goodwill = Capitalised Value – Net Assets*

Tutorial Note: Capitalisation of Super Profits Method is used if the question so directs *or* number of year's purchase of profits is not given.

ILLUSTRATION 32

Calculate the value of Goodwill according to Capitalization of Average Profits Method in the previous Illustration.

SOLUTION

Step 1: Future Maintainable Profits after tax = ₹ 5,00,000

Step 2: Capitalised Value of Average Profits

=Average Future Maintainable Profits/Normal Rate of Return

= ₹ 5,00,000/10% = ₹ 50,00,000

Step 3: Net Assets as on date of valuation of Goodwill = ₹ 10,00,000

Step 4: Goodwill = Capitalised Value – Net Assets

= ₹ 50,00,000 – ₹ 10,00,000 = ₹ 40,00,000

COMPREHENSIVE ILLUSTRATIONS

ILLUSTRATION 33

Given below are the extracts from the Balance Sheet of Rajasthali Ltd. as at 31st March, 2023:

Particulars	₹
Equity Share Capital (Shares of ₹ 10 each)	4,40,000
15% Preference Share Capital (Shares of ₹ 100 each)	96,000
General Reserve	50,000
Profit & Loss A/c	1,82,340
Long–term Borrowings	1,00,000
Short–term Borrowings	88,960
Goodwill	90,000
Property,Plant & Equipment	2,10,000
Patents & Trade Marks	2,00,000
10% Investments: [Face Value ₹ 80,000]	1,00,000
Current Assets	3,57,300

Additional Information *(Ignore tax)* :

(a) Net Profit for the year 2022–2023 ₹ 4,40,000.

(b) Expected Normal Rate of Return is 10% on Closing Capital Employed.

(c) Of the Investments 10% is trade and the balance non–trade. All trade Investments are to be valued at 10% below cost. Disputed Bonus claim of ₹ 29,000 not yet provided in the accounts for 2022–2023 is settled at ₹ 19,000.

(d) On 01.04.2022, new machines costing ₹ 1,00,000 were purchased but wrongly charged to revenue. New Machines and other Property,Plant & Equipment are subject to Depreciation @ 10% (No rectification has yet been made). 50% of Total Property,Plant & Equipment are found undervalued by 50% of market value and 50% of the remaining are found overvalued by 50% of market value.

(e) With effect from 01.04.2023 the Managing Director's remuneration will be ₹ 14,17,966 instead of ₹ 12,00,000.

Required: Calculate the Value of Goodwill (a) at 3 years' purchase of Future Maintainable Profits (b) at 3 years' purchase of Super Profit (c) as per Annuity Method (Annuity Factor @ 10% for 3 years is 2.486) (d) as per Capitalization of Super Profit Method. (e) as per Capitalisation of Future Maintainable Profit Method. (f) If it is considered reasonable to increase the Value of Goodwill by an amount equal to average of the book value and a valuation made at 3 years' purchase of Average Super Profit.

SOLUTION

(a) **Goodwill as per Average Profits Method** = Future Maintainable Profits × 3

= ₹ 2,73,334 × 3 = ₹ 8,20,002

(b) **Goodwill as per Super Profit Method**= Super Profit × 3 = ₹ 1,95,000 × 3 = ₹ 5,85,000

(c) **Goodwill as per Annuity Method** = Super Profit × Annuity factor

= ₹ 1,95,000 × 2.486 = ₹ 4,84,770

(d) **Goodwill as per Capitalization of Super Profit Method**

= Super Profit /Normal Rate of Return = ₹ 1,95,000/10% = ₹ 19,50,000

(e) **Goodwill as per Capitalisation of Future Maintainable Profit Method**

A. Capitalised Value of Future Maintainable Profit

= Future Maintainable Profit /Normal Rate of Return

= ₹ 2,73,334 /10% = ₹ 27,33,340

B. *Less:* Net Assets as on date of Valuation = ₹ 7,83,340

C. Goodwill (A – B) = ₹ 19,50,000

(f) Increase in Value of Goodwill= ½(Book Value + 3 years' Super Profit)

= ½[90,000 + (1,95,000 × 3)] = ₹ 3,37,500

Value of Goodwill = Book Value + Increase in Value of Goodwill

= ₹ 90,000 + ₹ 3,37,500 = ₹ 4,27,500

Working Notes:

1. CALCULATION OF FUTURE MAINTAINABLE PROFITS

Particulars	₹
C. Net Profit for the year	4,40,000
D. Past Adjustments:	
Less: Income from Non–Trade Investments [10% of ₹ 72,000]	(7,200)
Add: Purchase of Machinery charged to P&L A/c	1,00,000
Less: Depreciation on above Machinery	(10,000)
Less: Unrecorded Bonus	(19,000)
E. Past Adjusted Profits	5,03,800
F. Future Adjustments:	
Less: Additional Depreciation on Net Increase in Total Property,Plant & Equipment [1,25,000 × 10%]	(12,500)
Less: Increase in MD Remuneration	(2,17,966)
G. Future Maintainable Profit	2,73,334

2. CALCULATION OF CLOSING CAPITAL EMPLOYED

Particulars	₹
A. Total Assets at their current values:	
Property,Plant & Equipment [50% of (2,10,000 + 90,000) + 100% of 1,50,000] + [50% of 1,50,000 – 1/3 of ₹ 75,000] + [50% of ₹ 1,50,000]	4,25,000
Patents & Trade Marks	2,00,000
Trade Investments [(10% of 1,00,000) – (10% of 10,000)]	9,000
Current Assets	3,57,300
Total Assets	9,91,300
B. *Less:* Outsiders' Liabilities:	
Long–term Borrowings	1,00,000
Short–term Borrowings	88,960

Unrecorded Liability (Bonus)	19,000
	2,07,960
C. Closing Capital Employed [A – B]	7,83,340

3. Super Profit = FMP – Normal Profit = ₹ 2,73,334 – (10% of ₹ 7,83,340) = ₹ 1,95,000

ILLUSTRATION 34

Given below are the extracts from the Balance Sheet of BHARAT & TUSHAR Ltd. as at 31st March, 2023:

Particulars	₹
Equity Share Capital (Shares of ₹ 10 each)	4,40,000
15% Preference Share Capital (Shares of ₹ 100 each)	96,000
General Reserve	50,000
Profit & Loss A/c	1,82,340
Long–term Borrowings	1,00,000
Short–term Borrowings	88,960
Property,Plant & Equipment	2,10,000
Goodwill	90,000
10% Investments: [Face Value ₹ 80,000]	1,00,000

Additional Information *(Ignore tax)* :

(a) Net Profit for the year 2022–2023 ₹ 4,40,000.

(b) Expected Normal Rate of Return is 10% on Closing Capital Employed.

(c) Of the Investments 10% is trade and the balance non–trade. All trade Investments are to be valued at 10% below cost. Disputed Bonus claim of ₹ 29,000 not yet provided in the accounts for 2022–2023 is settled at ₹ 19,000.

(d) On 01.04.2022, a new machinery costing ₹ 1,00,000 was purchased but wrongly charged to revenue. Machinery and other Property,Plant & Equipment are subject to Depreciation @ 10% (No rectification has yet been made). 50% of Total Property,Plant & Equipment are found undervalued by 50% of market value and 50% of the remaining are found overvalued by 50% of market value.

(e) With effect from 01.04.2023 the Managing Director's remuneration will be ₹ 14,17,966 instead of ₹ 12,00,000.

Required: Calculate the Value of Goodwill (a) at 3 years' purchase of Future Maintainable Profits (b) at 3 years' purchase of Super Profit (c) as per Annuity Method (Annuity Factor @ 10% for 3 years is 2.486) (d) as per Capitalization of Super Profit Method. (e) as per Capitalisation of Future Maintainable Profit Method. (f) If it is considered reasonable to increase the Value of Goodwill by an amount equal to average of the book value and a valuation made at 3 years' purchase of Average Super Profit.

SOLUTION

1. CALCULATION OF CLOSING CAPITAL EMPLOYED

Particulars	₹
Equity Shares of ₹ 10 each	4,40,000
15% Preference Shares of ₹ 100 each	96,000

General Reserve	50,000
Profit & Loss A/c	1,82,340
Less: Book Value of Goodwill	90,000
Less: Non–Trade Investments	90,000
Less: Loss on Revaluation of Trade Investments	1,000
Add: Book Value of new machines wrongly charged to revenue [₹ 1,00,000 – ₹ 10,000]	90,000
Add: Profit on Revaluation of Property,Plant & Equipment [100% of 50% of (₹ 2,10,000 + ₹ 90,000)]	1,50,000
Less: Loss on Revaluation of Property,Plant & Equipment [1/3 of 50% of ₹ 1,50,000]	25,000
Less: Unrecorded Liability (Bonus)	19,000
Closing Capital Employed	7,83,340

Remaining solution is same as in previous Illustration.

SOLVED PROBLEMS

PROBLEM 1

Given below are the extracts from the Balance Sheets of A Ltd. and B Ltd. as on 31–03–2023:

Particulars	***A Ltd.*** ₹	***B Ltd.*** ₹
Equity Share Capital (Shares of ₹ 10 each)	15,00,000	10,00,000
Reserves	3,00,000	2,00,000
10% Debentures	6,00,000	4,00,000
Trade Creditors	3,00,000	5,00,000
Goodwill	2,00,000	1,00,000
Net Tangible Block	17,00,000	14,00,000
Current Assets	8,00,000	6,00,000

Additional information:

(a) Assets to be revalued as follows

Particulars	***A Ltd.***(₹)	***B Ltd.***(₹)
Revaluation of Tangible Block	21,00,000	12,00,000
Revaluation of Current Assets	10,00,000	4,00,000

(b) Average annual profit for three years before charging debenture interest A Ltd. 4,50,000, B Ltd. 3,10,000

(c) Goodwill is to be valued at four year's purchase of average super profits for three years. Average is to be calculated after adjustment of depreciation at 10% on the amount of increase/decrease on revaluation of fixed assets. In the case of B Ltd. a claim of ₹ 10,000, which was omitted, is to be adjusted against its average profit. Income tax is to be ignored.

(d) Normal Profit on closing capital employed is to be taken at 15%.

Required: Ascertain the Value of Goodwill of A Ltd. and B Ltd.

SOLUTION

STEP 1: CALCULATION OF CLOSING CAPITAL EMPLOYED

Particulars	*A Ltd.*(₹)	*B Ltd.*(₹)
A. Total Assets at Current Values:		
Property,Plant & Equipment (Revalued)	21,00,000	12,00,000
Current Assets (Revalued)	10,00,000	4,00,000
	31,00,000	16,00,000
B. *Less:* **Outside Liabilities:**		
Debentures	(6,00,000)	(4,00,000)
Creditors	(3,00,000)	(5,00,000)
Claim	–	(10,000)
	9,00,000	9,10,000
C. Closing Capital Employed [A – B]	22,00,000	6,90,000

STEP 2:EXCESS/SHORT DEPRECIATION

Particulars	*A Ltd.*(₹)	*B Ltd.*(₹)
Revalued Assets	21,00,000	10,00,000
Less: Property,Plant & Equipment as per the Balance Sheet	(17,00,000)	(12,00,000)
Upward/(Downward) Revaluation	4,00,000	(2,00,000)
(Increase)/decrease in Depreciation @ 10%	(40,000)	20,000

STEP 3: VALUATION OF GOODWILL

Particulars	*A Ltd.*(₹)	*B Ltd.*(₹)
Average Annual Profit	4,50,000	3,10,000
Less: Debenture Interest	(60,000)	(40,000)
Less: Depreciation on amount increased on revaluation	(40,000)	–
Add: Depreciation on amount reduced on revaluation	–	20,000
Less: Omission of claim	–	(10,000)
A. Average Profit	3,50,000	2,80,000
B. *Less:* Normal Profit @ 15% on closing capital employed	(3,30,000)	(1,03,500)
C. Super Profit [A – B]	20,000	1,76,500
D. Goodwill valued at 4 years' purchase of Super Profits [C × 4]	80,000	7,06,000

PROBLEM 2

Given below are the extracts from the Balance Sheet of X Ltd. as at 31.3.2023.

Particulars	₹
Equity Share Capital (Shares of ₹ 10 each)	8,00,000
13% Preference Share Capital (Shares of ₹ 100 each)	2,00,000
Reserve and Surplus	4,00,000

12% Debentures	2,00,000
Trade Creditors	1,00,000
Goodwill	1,00,000
Property,Plant & Equipment	11,00,000
Non–Trade Investments	1,00,000
Current Assets	4,00,000

Additional Information:

(a) Profit before tax for 2022–2023 amounted to ₹ 6,00,000 including ₹ 10,000 as interest on investment. Income tax rate may be taken at 25%.

(b) An additional amount of ₹ 50,000 p.a. shall be required to be spent for smooth running of the business. Market values of Property,Plant & Equipment are estimated at ₹ 19,00,000. Further depreciation to the extent of ₹ 40,000 should be taken into consideration.

(c) Return on Average Trading Capital employed at the rate of 20% before tax may be considered normal for this business.

Required: Calculate the Value of Goodwill at 4 years' purchase of super profits.

SOLUTION

STEP 1: FUTURE MAINTAINABLE PROFITS

Particulars	₹
A. Profits before tax	6,00,000
B. *Less:* Incomes from Non–Trade Investments	(10,000)
C. Past Adjusted Profit	5,90,000
D. *Less:* Additional Depreciation	(40,000)
E. *Less:* Additional Expenditure	(50,000)
F. Future Maintainable Profit	5,00,000
G. *Less:* *Tax [25% of (₹ 5,00,000 + ₹ 40,000)]	(1,35,000)
H. Future Maintainable Profit after tax	3,65,000

Note: **Additional Depreciation on Increase in value of Property,Plant & Equipment is not deductible for Tax purposes.*

STEP 2: AVERAGE CAPITAL EMPLOYED:

A. Total Assets at their Current Values:	₹
Property,Plant & Equipment	19,00,000
Current Assets	4,00,000
Total Assets	23,00,000
B. *Less:* Outsiders' Liabilities:	
12% Debentures	2,00,000
Trade Creditors	1,00,000
Total	3,00,000
C. Closing Capital Employed (A – B)	20,00,000

D. *Less:* Half of the Current year's Adjusted Profits after tax 50% of [(₹ 5,90,000 + 10,000) – Tax @25%]	75,000
E. Average Capital Employed	19,25,000

Step 3: Normal Profits = Average Capital Employed * Normal Rate of Return (after tax)
= ₹ 19,25,000 * 0.10 = ₹ 1,92,500

Step 4: Super Profits = Future Maintainable Profits – Normal Profits
= ₹ 3,65,000 – ₹ 1,92,500 = ₹ 1,72,500

Step 5: Goodwill = Super Profits * No. of years' purchase = ₹ 1,72,500 * 4 = ₹ 6,90,000

PROBLEM 3

Given below are the extracts from the Balance Sheet of ND Ltd. as at 31st March, 2023:

Particulars	***(₹ in lakhs)***
Equity Share Capital (Shares of ₹ 10 each)	50.00
9% Preference Share Capital (Shares of ₹ 100 each)	10.00
General Reserve	11.50
Profit and Loss A/c	30.90
16% Debentures	23.00
Trade Creditors	22.40
Property,Plant & Equipment	115.75
Investments	10.00
Current Assets	22.05

10% Non–trade investments(purchased on 31.03.2023) were 20% of the total investments. On 1.4.2022 Profit and Loss account ₹ 8.70 lakhs, General Reserve ₹ 6 lakhs. Companies doing similar business as that of ND Ltd. show a market return of 20% on Average capital employed.

Required: Calculate the value of goodwill at 3 years' purchase of super profits.

SOLUTION

Step 1: Profit Earned

Closing Balance of Profit & Loss A/c	₹ 30.90 lakhs
Less: Opening Balance of Profit & Loss A/c	₹ 8.70 lakhs
Add: Transfer to General Reserve [₹ 11.5 lakhs – ₹ 6 lakhs]	₹ 5.50 lakhs
Profit Earned	₹ 27.70 lakhs

Step 2: Average Capital Employed *()*

A. Total Assets at Current Values:	*₹ in Lakhs*
Total Assets as per Balance Sheet	147.80
Less: Non–trade Investments (20% of ₹ 10 lakhs)	(2.00)
	145.80

B. *Less:* Outside Liabilities:	
16% Debentures	23.00
Trade Creditors	22.40
	45.40
C. Capital Employed [A – B]	100.40
D. *Less:* 1/2 of Profit Earned [50% of ₹ 27.70 lakhs]	(13.85)
E. Average Capital Employed [C – D]	86.55

Step 3: Normal Profit = ₹ 86,55,000 * 0.20 = ₹ 17,31,000

Step 4: Super Profits = ₹ 27,70,000 – ₹ 17,31,000 = ₹ 10,39,000

Step 5: Goodwill = ₹ 10,39,000 × 3 = ₹ 31,17,000

PROBLEM 4

On the basis of the following information, calculate the value of goodwill of CEE AMLA Ltd. at three years' purchase of Super Profits, if any, earned by the company in the previous four completed accounting years. Given below are the extracts from the Balance Sheet of CEE AMLA Ltd. as at 31.3.2023:

Particulars	*₹ in lakhs*
5 crore Equity Shares of ₹ 10 each, fully paid up	5,000
Reserves & Surplus	4,010
Trade Creditors	568
Provision for Taxation (net)	22
Goodwill	310
Property,Plant & Equipment	6,625
Patents and Trade Marks	32
9% Non–trading Investments	600
Current Assets	2,033

(a) The profits before tax of the four years have been as follows:

Year ended 31st March	*2019*	*2020*	*2021*	*2022*
Profit before tax in lakhs of Rupees	3,190	2,500	3,108	2,900

(b) The rate of income tax 25%.

(c) In the accounting year 2018–2019, the company earned an extraordinary income of ₹ 1 crore due to a special foreign contract. In August, 2019 there was an earthquake due to which the company lost property worth ₹ 50 lakhs and the insurance policy did not cover the loss due to earthquake *or* riots.

(d) 9% Non–trading investments appearing in the above mentioned Balance Sheet were purchased at par by the company on 1st April, 2020.

(e) The normal rate of return for the industry in which the company is engaged is 20%. Also note that the company's shareholders, in their general meeting have passed a resolution sanctioning the directors an additional remuneration of ₹ 50 lakhs every year beginning from the accounting year 2022–2023.

SOLUTION

STEP 1 : CAPITAL EMPLOYED

A. Total Assets at Current Values:	*₹ in lakhs*
Property,Plant & Equipment	6,625
Patents and Trade Marks	32
Current Assets	2,033
	8,690
B. *Less:* **Outside Liabilities**	
Trade Creditors	568
Provision for Taxation (Net)	22
	590
C. Capital Employed [A – B]	8,100

STEP 2 : FUTURE MAINTAINABLE PROFIT (*₹ in lakhs*)

Particulars	*2018–2019* ₹	*2019–2020* ₹	*2020–2021* ₹	*2021–2022* ₹
A. Profit before tax	3,190	2,500	3,108	2,900
B. *Less:* Extra–ordinary income due to foreign contract	100			
C. *Add:* Loss due to earthquake		50		
D. *Less:* Income from non–trading investments			54	54
	3,090	2,550	3,054	2,846

As there is no trend, Simple Average Profits will be considered for calculation of goodwill.

Total Adjusted Trading Profits for the last four years = ₹ (3,090 + 2,550 + 3,054 + 2,846)
= ₹ 11, 540 lakhs

₹ in lakhs

Average Trading Profit before tax = (₹ 11,540 lakhs/4)	2,885
Less: Additional remuneration to directors	(50)
Less: Income tax @ 25%	(708.75)
FMP after Tax	2126.25

STEP 3 : VALUATION OF GOODWILL ON SUPER PROFITS BASIS

A. Future Maintainable Profits	2126.25
B. *Less:* Normal Profits (20% of ₹ 8,100 lakhs)	1,620
C. Super Profits	506.25
D. Goodwill at 3 years' purchase of Super Profits = 3 × ₹ 506.25 lakhs = ₹ 1518.75 lakhs	

Note: *Since the current year's profit has not been given in the question, goodwill has been calculated on the basis of capital closing employed and not on the basis of Average Capital Employed.*

PROBLEM 5

The following information has been provided by CEE AMLA Limited:[₹ *in lakhs]*

Particulars	*2020–2021*	*2021–2022*	*2022–2023*
12000, Equity Share Capital (Shares of ₹100 each)	12.00	12.00	12.00
General Reserve	6.85	7.75	9.00
Profit and Loss Account	2.64	5.95	8.25
Current Liabilities	6.80	5.45	3.85
Property,Plant & Equipment	12.00	13.00	14.00
Intangible Assets(Goodwill)	6.30	5.30	4.30
Inventories	6.28	7.34	8.51
Other Current Assets	3.71	5.51	6.29

(i) The valuation of the Property,Plant & Equipment has been done by a Professional Valuer and increase of 10% in the year 2020–2021, 2021–2022 and 2022–2023 is estimated over the given book value. The Company has been charging depreciation @ 10% p.a.

(ii) The inventories have been valued at ₹ 6.32 Lakhs as on 31st March 2021, ₹ 8.47 Lakhs as on 31st March 2022 and ₹ 10.68 Lakhs as on 31st March 2023.

(iii) The balance of P & L Account and General Reserve on 1st April 2020 was ₹ 2.18 Lakhs and ₹ 4.25 Lakhs respectively.

(iv) Tax Rate was 30% in all the years. The normal expectation in the industry is 10%.

(v) The Goodwill shall be revalued based on 4 years purchase of average super profits of last three years.

Required: Calculate the Value of Goodwill.

SOLUTION

STEP 1: AVERAGE CAPITAL EMPLOYED [₹ IN LAKHS]

Particulars	*2020–2021* ₹	*2021–2022* ₹	*2022–2023* ₹
Property,Plant & Equipment [Book Value]	12.00	13.00	14.00
Add: Increase @ [10%/10%/12.5%]	1.20	1.30	1.40
Less: Depreciation on increase	0.12	0.13	0.14
Property,Plant & Equipment at Current Value	13.08	14.17	15.26
Inventories	6.32	8.47	10.68
Other Current Assets	3.71	5.51	6.29
	23.11	28.15	32.23
Less: Current Liabilities	6.80	5.45	3.85
A. Closing Capital Employed	16.31	22.70	28.38
B. Opening Capital Employed	18.43*	16.31	22.70
C. Total	34.74	39.01	51.08
D. Average Capital Employed (Total/2)	17.37	19.51	25.54

*Equity Share Capital + P & L Account + General Reserve = 12,00,000 + 2,18,000 + 4,25,000 = 18,43,000

STEP 2: FUTURE MAINTAINABLE PROFITS

Particulars	*2020–2021* ₹	*2021–2022* ₹	*2022–2023* ₹
Closing balance of P & L A/c	2.64	5.95	8.25
Add: Transfer to General reserve	2.60	0.90	1.25
Less: Opening Balance of P & L A/c	2.18	2.64	5.95
Profit after tax	3.06	4.21	3.55
Add: Tax @ 30%	1.31	1.80	1.52
Profit before tax	4.37	6.01	5.07
Add: Amortisation of goodwill	–	1.00	1.00
Less: Additional depreciation on Increase	0.12	0.13	0.14
Add: Under valuation of closing inventories	0.04	1.13	2.17
Less: Under valuation of opening inventories	–	0.04	1.13
FMP before Tax	4.29	7.97	6.97
Less: Tax @ 30%	1.29	2.39	2.09
FMP after Tax	3.00	5.58	4.88

STEP 3: VALUATION OF GOODWILL

Future Maintainable Profit	3.00	5.58	4.88
Normal Profit @ 10% on Average Capital Employed	1.74	1.95	2.55
Super Profits	1.26	3.63	2.33
Average Super Profits [(1.26 + 3.63 + 2.33)/3]	2,40,667		
Goodwill at 4 years' purchase	9,62,667		

MULTIPLE CHOICE QUESTIONS [MCQ]

1. Following are the factors affecting goodwill except:
   (a) Nature of business (b) Efficiency of management
   (c) Technical Know-how (d) Location of the customers
2. Under average profit basis goodwill is calculated by:
   (a) No. of years purchased multiplied with average profits.
   (b) No. of years purchased multiplied with super profits.
   (c) Super Profit multiplied with Annuity Factor.
   (d) Super profit divided with expected rate of return.
3. Under super profit method goodwill is calculated by:
   (a) No. of years purchased multiplied with average profits.
   (b) No. of years purchased multiplied with super profits.
   (c) Super Profit multiplied with Annuity Factor.
   (d) Super Profit divided with expected rate of return.

4. Under capitalisation basis goodwill is calculated by:
   (a) No. of years purchased multiplied with average profits.
   (b) No. of years purchased multiplied with super profits
   (c) Super Profit multiplied with Annuity Factor.
   (d) Super profit divided with expected rate of return.
5. Normal Rate of Return relates to:
   (a) Net Assets for Shareholders only.
   (b) Net Assets for Equity Shareholders only.
   (c) Long –term Funds only
   (d) Any of these
6. Weighted average method of calculating goodwill should be followed when:
   (a) Profits are uneven (b) Profits has increasing trend
   (c) Profits has decreasing trend (d) Either 'b' or 'c'
7. The profits of last five years are ₹ 1,70,000; ₹ 1,80,000; ₹ 1,40,000; ₹ 2,00,000 and ₹ 1,60,000. Find the value of goodwill, if it is calculated on average profits of last five year on the basis of three year's purchase.
   (a) ₹ 1,70,000 (b) ₹ 5,10,000 (c) ₹ 5,30,000 (d) ₹ 5,70,000
8. The result of operations during the years I, II, III and IV were: Losses ₹ 10,000; Losses ₹ 12,000; Profits ₹ 1,50,000 & Profits ₹ 1,20,000 respectively. The value of goodwill on the basis of 5 years' purchase of average profit of the business is:
   (a) ₹ 2,50,000 (b) ₹ 3,10,000 (c) ₹ 20,000 (d) ₹ 3,40,000
9. The result of operations during the years I, II, III and IV were: Losses ₹ 20,000; Losses ₹ 5,000; Profits ₹ 1,96,000 & Profits ₹ 1,52,000 respectively. The average capital employed in the business is ₹ 6,00,000. The rate of interest expected from capital invested is 12%. The value of goodwill on the basis of two years' purchase of super profits based on the average of four years is:
   (a) ₹ 18,000 (b) ₹ 17,500 (c) ₹ 17,000 (d) ₹ 16,500
10. The result of operations during the last three years were: Profits ₹ 40,000; Profits ₹ 60,000 and Profits ₹ 66,500 respectively. The total liabilities of the firm are ₹ 10,00,000 of which outsiders liabilities is ₹ 5,42,500. The rate of interest expected from capital invested is 10%. The value of goodwill on capitalisation basis is:
   (a) ₹ 97,000 (b) ₹ 97,250 (c) ₹ 97,500 (d) ₹ 97,750
11. The result of operations during the years I, II, III and IV were : Losses ₹ 20,000; Losses ₹ 5,000; Profits ₹ 1,96,000 & Profits ₹ 1,52,000 respectively. The average capital employed in the business is ₹ 6,00,000. The rate of interest expected from capital invested is 12%. The value of goodwill on the basis of four years purchase of super profits based on annuity of the four years. (Take annuity factor at discounting rate of 10% as 3.169.) is:
   (a) ₹ 27,000 (b) ₹ 27,136 (c) ₹ 27,336 (d) ₹ 27,729
12. The profits for Year I are ₹ 4,000; for Year II is ₹ 52,200 and for Year III is ₹ 62,400. Closing stock for Year II and Year III includes the defective items of ₹ 4,400 and ₹ 12,400 respectively which were considered as having market value NIL. The value of goodwill on average profit method is:
   (a) ₹ 47,400 (b) ₹ 35,400 (c) ₹ 27,400 (d) ₹ 34,600
13. Total Capital Employed in the firm ₹ 16,00,000, Reasonable Rate of Return 15%, Profits for the year ₹ 24,00,000. The value of goodwill using capitalisation method is:
   (a) ₹ 1,64,00,000 (b) ₹ 24,00,000 (c) ₹ 1,44,00,000 (d) ₹ 84,00,000

ANSWERS TO MCQ

1.	(d)	2.	(a)	3.	(b)	4.	(d)	5.	(d)	6.	(d)	7.	(b)	8.	(b)
9.	(b)	10.	(c)	11.	(d)	12.	(b)	13.	(c)						

VERY SHORT ANSWER TYPE QUESTIONS

1. Briefly explain the following: [1/2 Mark each]
   (a) Goodwill
   (b) Nature of Goodwill
   (c) Number of years' purchase
   (d) Closing Capital Employed and Average Capital Employed
   (e) Normal Rate of Return
   (f) Normal Profit
   (g) Super Profits
   (g) Future Maintainable Profits

2. Enumerate the following: [1 Mark each]
   (a) Two factors affecting goodwill.
   (b) Two circumstances when there is a need to revalue goodwill.
   (c) Three methods of valuation of goodwill.
   (d) Steps involved in valuing the Goodwill according to Average Profits Method.
   (e) Steps involved in valuing the Goodwill according to Super Profits Method.
   (f) Steps involved in valuing the Goodwill according to Capitalisation of Super Profits Method.
   (g) Steps involved in valuing the Goodwill according to Capitalisation of Average Profits Method.

3. The result of operations during the years I, II, III and IV were: Profit ₹ 2,00,000, Profit ₹ 4,10,000,Loss ₹ 2,20,000 and Profit ₹ 4,70,000 respectively. Calculate goodwill based on four years' purchase of average profits of last three years.

   [Ans ₹ 8,80,000]

4. Average Profits ₹ 1,20,000, Capital Employed ₹ 4,00,000, Normal Rate of Return 15%. Calculate the value of goodwill on the basis of two years' purchase of Super Profits.

   [Ans ₹ 1,20,000]

5. Average Profits ₹ 1,20,000, Capital Employed ₹ 4,00,000, Normal Rate of Return 15%. Calculate the value of goodwill on the basis of Capitalisation of Super Profits.

   [Ans ₹ 4,00,000]

6. Average Profits ₹ 1,20,000, Capital Employed ₹ 4,00,000, Normal Rate of Return 15%. Calculate the value of goodwill on the basis of Capitalisation of Average Profits.

   [Ans ₹ 4,00,000]

7. Average Profits ₹ 1,50,000, Normal Rate of Return 10%. Opening Capital Employed ₹ 8,00,000. Closing Capital Employed ₹ 12,00,000. Calculate the value of goodwill on the basis of Capitalisation of Super Profits.

   [Ans ₹ 5,00,000]

8. Goodwill on the basis of Capitalisation of Super Profits ` 5,00,000. Normal Rate of return 10%. Capital Employed ₹ 25,00,000. Calculate Goodwill of the firm at 3 years' purchase of Average Profits of the firm.

[**Ans** ₹ 9,00,000]

9. Goodwill of the firm at 3 years' purchase of Average Profits ` 6,00,000. Normal Rate of return 15%. Capital Employed ₹ 10,00,000. Calculate Goodwill of the firm at 3 years' purchase of Super Profits of the firm.

[**Ans** ₹ 1,50,000]

SHORT ANSWER TYPE PRACTICAL QUESTIONS

Goodwill on the basis of Average Profits

1. The result of operations during the years I, II, III and IV were: Profit ₹ 2,00,000, Profit ₹ 4,00,000 (including an insurance claim received of ₹ 5,00,000), Profit ₹ 6,50,000 (excluding ₹ 30,000 payable for the insurance of Assets),Loss ₹ 6,00,000 (after charging Loss on sale of a fixed asset of ₹ 8,00,000) respectively. With effect from year V, there will be increase in manager's remuneration of ₹ 2,00,000 p.a. and Advantage from new contract for supply of goods of ₹ 2,60,000 p.a. Calculate the value of goodwill on the basis of four years' purchase of average profits of last three years.

[**Ans** Average Profits ₹ 2,40,000, FMP ₹ 3,00,000,Goodwill ₹ 12,00,000]

2. The result of operations during the years I, II, III and IV were: I Profit ₹ 24,00,000, II Profit ₹ 27,00,000, III Profit ₹ 45,00,000, IV Profit ₹ 36,00,000 respectively. Incomes from non–trade investments: year II ₹ 72,000,year III ₹ 1,44,000, year IV ₹ 1,44,000. With effect from year V, there will be increase in manager's remuneration of ₹ 2,00,000 p.a. and Advantage from new contract for supply of goods of ₹ 3,20,000 p.a. Calculate the value of goodwill on the basis of four years' purchase of average profits of last three years.

[**Ans** Average Profits ₹ 34,80,000, FMP ₹ 36,00,000, Goodwill ₹ 144,00,000]

3. The result of operations during the years I, II, III and IV were: I Profit ₹ 24,00,000, II Profit ₹ 27,00,000 , III Profit ₹ 36,00,000, IV Profit ₹ 45,00,000 respectively. Closing Inventories were over–valued by ₹ 18,00,000 in Year II, by ₹ 16,20,000 in Year III, by ₹ 14,58,000 in Year IV. With effect from year V, there will be increase in manager's remuneration of ₹ 3,14,000 p.a. and Advantage from new contract for supply of goods of ₹ 2,00,000 p.a. Calculate the value of goodwill on the basis of four years' purchase of average profits of last three years.

[**Ans** Average Profits ₹ 31,14,000,FMP ₹ 30,00,000,Goodwill ₹ 120,00,000]

4. The result of operations during the years I, II, III and IV were: I Profit ₹ 24,00,000, II Profit ₹ 27,00,000 , III Profit ₹ 36,00,000, IV Profit ₹ 45,00,000 respectively. Closing Inventories were under–valued by ₹ 18,00,000 in Year II, by ₹16,20,000 in Year III, by ₹ 14,58,000 in Year IV.

With effect from year V, there will be increase in manager's remuneration of ₹ 2,00,000 p.a. and Advantage from new contract for supply of goods of ₹ 3,14,000 p.a. Calculate the value of goodwill on the basis of four years' purchase of average profits of last three years.

[**Ans** Average Profits ₹ 40,86,000,FMP ₹ 42,00,000,Goodwill ₹ 168,00,000]

5. The result of operations during the years I, II, III and IV were: I Profit ₹ 24,00,000, II Profit ₹ 27,00,000 , III Profit ₹ 45,00,000, IV Profit ₹ 36,00,000 respectively. Closing Inventories were over–valued by ₹ 18,00,000 in Year II, under–valued by ₹ 16,20,000 in Year III, over–valued by ₹ 14,58,000 in Year IV. With effect from year V, there will be increase in manager's remuneration of ₹ 3,14,000 p.a. and Advantage from new contract for supply of goods of ₹ 2,00,000 p.a. Calculate the value of goodwill on the basis of four years' purchase of average profits of last three years.

[**Ans** Average Profits ₹ 31,14,000,FMP ₹ 30,00,000,Goodwill ₹ 120,00,000]

6. The result of operations during the years I, II, III and IV were: I Profit ₹ 24,00,000, II Profit ₹ 27,00,000 , III Profit ₹ 36,00,000, IV Profit ₹ 45,00,000 respectively. In the beginning of Year II a new machine costing ₹ 20,00,000 was purchased but wrongly charged to revenue. (No effect has yet been given for rectifying the same).Depreciation is charged on machine @ 10% on reducing balance method. With effect from year V, there will be increase in manager's remuneration of ₹ 2,00,000 p.a. and Advantage from new contract for supply of goods of ₹ 3,14,000 p.a. Calculate the value of goodwill on the basis of four years' purchase of average profits of last three years.

[**Ans** Average Profits ₹ 40,86,000,FMP ₹ 42,00,000,Goodwill ₹ 168,00,000]

7. The result of operations during the years I, II, III and IV were: I Profit ₹ 24,00,000, II Profit ₹ 27,00,000 , III Profit ₹ 45,00,000, IV Profit ₹ 36,00,000 respectively. In the beginning of Year II a machine having a book value of ₹ 20,00,000 was sold for ₹ 26,00,000 but the proceeds were wrongly credited to Profit and Loss Account. (No effect has yet been given for rectifying the same). Depreciation is charged on machine @ 10% on reducing balance method. With effect from year V, there will be increase in manager's remuneration of ₹ 2,00,000 p.a. and Advantage from new contract for supply of goods of ₹ 2,86,000 p.a. **Calculate the** value of goodwill on the basis of four years' purchase of average profits of last three years.

[**Ans** Average Profits ₹ 29,14,000,FMP ₹ 30,00,000,Goodwill ₹ 120,00,000]

8. The result of operations during the years I, II, III and IV were: I Profit ₹ 24,00,000, II Profit ₹ 27,00,000 , III Profit ₹ 45,00,000, IV Profit ₹ 36,00,000 respectively. 10% Investments (Face Value ₹ 16,00,000) appear in the balance sheet as at the end of year IV at ₹ 20,00,000. Of the Investments 10% is trade and the balance non–trade. 50% of the non–trade Investments were acquired in the beginning of year III and the rest in the beginning of year II. With effect from year V, there will be increase in manager's remuneration of ₹ 2,00,000 p.a. and Advantage from new contract for supply of goods of ₹ 3,20,000 p.a. Calculate the value of goodwill on the basis of four years' purchase of average profits of last three years.

[**Ans** Average Profits ₹ 34,80,000,FMP ₹ 36,00,000,Goodwill ₹ 144,00,000]

Goodwill on the basis of Super Profits

9. In Questions 2 to 8, Calculate the value of goodwill on the basis of four years' purchase of super profits based on the average of last three years if Capital Employed is ₹ 80,00,000 and Normal Rate of Return is 15%.

[**Ans** Goodwill **2.** ₹ 96,00,000, **3.** ₹ 72,00,000, **4.** ₹ 120,00,000, **5.** ₹ 72,00,000, **6.** ₹120,00,000, **7.** ₹ 72,00,000, **8.** ₹ 96,00,000]

Goodwill on the basis of Capitalisation of Super Profits

10. In Questions 2 to 8, Calculate the value of goodwill on the basis of Capitalisation of super profits based on the average of last three years if Capital Employed is ₹ 80,00,000 and Normal Rate of Return is 15%.

[**Ans** Goodwill **2.** ₹ 160,00,000, **3.** ₹ 120,00,000, **4.** ₹ 200,00,000, **5.** ₹ 120,00,000, **6.** ₹ 200,00,000, **7.** ₹ 120,00,000, **8.** ₹ 160,00,000]

Goodwill on the basis of Capitalisation of Average Profits

11. In Questions 2 to 8, Calculate the value of goodwill on the basis of Capitalisation of average profits based on the average of last three years if Capital Employed is ₹ 80,00,000 and Normal Rate of Return is 15%.

[**Ans** Goodwill **2.** ₹ 160,00,000, **3.** ₹ 120,00,000, **4.** ₹ 200,00,000, **5.** ₹ 120,00,000, **6.** ₹ 200,00,000, **7.** ₹ 120,00,000, **8.** ₹ 160,00,000]

12. Capital Employed ₹ 4,00,000. Value of goodwill on the basis of Capitalisation of Super Profits ₹ 3,00,000. Calculate the value of goodwill on the basis of Capitalisation of Average Profits.

[**Ans** ₹ 3,00,000]

13. Goodwill on the basis of Capitalisation of Super Profits ₹ 5,00,000. Goodwill on the basis of Capitalisation of Average Profits ₹ 3,00,000. Goodwill on the basis of four years' purchase of Super Profits ₹ 2,00,000. Opening Capital Employed is 2/3rd of Closing Capital Employed. Calculate **Goodwill of the firm at 3 years' purchase of Average Profits of the firm.**

14. Given below are the extracts from the Balance Sheet of TULSIAN Ltd. as at 31st March, 2023:

Particulars	₹
Equity Share Capital (Shares of ₹ 10 each)	63,00,000
9% Preference Share Capital (Shares of ₹ 100 each)	10,00,000
10% Debentures	8,00,000
Current Liabilities	2,00,000
Property,Plant & Equipment	60,00,000
10% Trade Investments [Face Value ₹ 8,00,000]	10,00,000
Current Assets	64,00,000

Additional Information: 50% of Total Property,Plant & Equipment are found undervalued by 50% of market value and 50% of the remaining are found overvalued by 50% of market value. All trade Investments are to be valued at 10% below cost. Current Year' Adjusted Profits after Tax ₹ 16,00,000 Expected Future Maintainable Profits after Interest & Tax ₹ 17,80,000.

Required: Calculate(a) Net Assets (b) Net Assets for Equity Shareholders (c) Closing Capital Employed (d) Average Capital Employed.

[**Ans** (a) Net Assets ₹ 148,00,000, (b) Net Assets for Equity Shareholders ₹ 138,00,000, (c) Closing Capital Employed ₹ 148,00,000 (d) Average Capital Employed ₹ 130,00,000]

15A. Given below are the extracts from the Balance Sheet of TULSIAN Ltd. as at 31st March, 2023:

Particulars	₹
Equity Share Capital (Shares of ₹ 10 each)	63,00,000
9% Preference Share Capital (Shares of ₹ 100 each)	10,00,000
Reserves and Surplus	51,00,000
10% Debentures	8,00,000
Current Liabilities	2,00,000
Property,Plant & Equipment	60,00,000
10% Trade Investments [Face Value ₹ 8,00,000]	10,00,000

Additional Information: 50% of Total Property,Plant & Equipment are found undervalued by 50% of market value and 50% of the remaining are found overvalued by 50% of market value. All trade Investments are to be valued at 10% below cost. Current Year' Adjusted Profits after Tax ₹ 16,00,000 Expected Future Maintainable Profits after Interest & Tax ₹ 17,80,000.

Required: Calculate(a) Net Assets (b) Net Assets for Equity Shareholders (c) Closing Capital Employed (d) Average Capital Employed.

[**Ans** (a) Net Assets ₹ 148,00,000, (b) Net Assets for Equity Shareholders ₹ 138,00,000, (c) Closing Capital Employed ₹ 148,00,000 (d) Average Capital Employed ₹ 130,00,000]

15B. In the previous Question Calculate the Value of Goodwill at 3 years' purchase of Super Profits:

(a) If Normal Rate of Return on Net Assets is10%.

(b) If Normal Rate of Return on Net Assets for Equity Shareholders is 10%.

(c) If Normal Rate of Return on Closing Capital Employed is 10%.

(d) If Normal Rate of Return on Average Capital Employed is 10%.

[**Ans** (a) Net Assets ₹ 148,00,000, SP ₹ 3,00,000,Goodwill ₹ 9,00,000, (b) Net Assets for Equity Shareholders ₹ 138,00,000, SP ₹ 4,00,000 ,Goodwill ₹ 12,00,000, (c) Closing Capital Employed ₹ 148,00,000,SP ₹ 3,00,000,Goodwill ₹ 9,00,000 (d) Average Capital Employed ₹ 140,00,000,SP ₹ 3,80,000,Goodwill ₹ 11,40,000]

LONG ANSWER TYPE PRACTICAL QUESTIONS

16. Tulsian(15) Ltd. provides you the following information:

1. Profits/Losses after tax @ 40%:

2018–2019 *Losses*	*2019–2020* *Profits*	*2020–2021* *Profits*	*2021–2022* *Profits*	*2022–2023* *Profits*
15,50,000	18,08,640	24,08,640	30,08,640	36,08,640

The loss in 2018–2019 occurred due to a prolonged strike.

2. Incomes from non–trade investments ₹ 14,400 p.a.
3. In 2020–2021 a machine having a book value of ₹ 20,000 was sold for ₹ 22,000 but the proceeds were wrongly credited to Profit and Loss Account. (No effect has yet been given for rectifying the same). Depreciation is charged on machine @ 10% on reducing balance method.
4. Closing Inventories were under–valued by ₹ 20,000 in 2020–2021, by ₹ 18,200 in 2021–2022, by ₹ 16,580 in 2022–2023.
5. With effect from 1st April, 2023, there will be increase in manager's remuneration of ₹ 4,00,000 p.a. and Advantage from new contract for supply of goods of ₹ 8,00,000 p.a.
6. Rate of Income Tax 30% with effect from 1st April, 2023.

Required: Calculate the Value of Goodwill at 3 years' purchase of average profits.

[**Ans** Average Profits ₹ 50,00,000, FMP ₹ 37,80,000,Goodwill ₹ 113,40,000]

17. Tulsian(17) Ltd. provides you the following information:

1. Profits and Losses after tax @ 40%:

2018–2019 *Losses*	*2019–2020* *Profits*	*2020–2021* *Profits*	*2021–2022* *Profits*	*2022–2023* *Profits*
15,00,000	18,00,000	24,04,320	30,08,640	36,08,640

The loss in 2018–2019 occurred due to a prolonged strike.

2. 8% Investments (Face value ₹ 2,00,000) appear in the balance sheet as at 31.03.2023 at ₹ 1,60,000 Of the Investments 10% is trade and the balance non–trade. 50% of the non–trade Investments were acquired on 1.4.2021 and the rest on 1.4.2020. All trade Investments are to be valued at 10% below cost.
3. In 2020–2021 a new machine costing ₹ 2,00,000 was purchased but wrongly charged to revenue. (No effect has yet been given for rectifying the same) Depreciation is charged on machine @ 10% on reducing balance method.

4. Closing Inventories were over–valued by ₹ 1,80,000 in 2020–2021, by ₹ 1,62,000 in 2021–2022, by ₹ 1,45,800 in 2022–2023.
5. Disputed Bonus claim of ₹ 2,00,000 not yet provided in the accounts for 2022–2023 is expected to be settled.
6. In 2022–2023 some old Furniture having a book value of ₹ 5,00,000 was sold for ₹ 3,00,000.
7. With effect from 1st April, 2023, there will be increase in manager's remuneration of ₹ 4,00,000 p.a.,Advantage from new contract for supply of goods of ₹ 8,00,000 p.a. and Additional Revenue Expenditure of ₹ 3,00,000 p.a.
8. Rate of Income Tax 30% with effect from 1st April, 2023.

Required: Calculate the Value of Goodwill at 3 years' purchase of average profits.

[**Ans** Average Profits ₹ 50,00,000,FMP ₹ 36,40,000,Goodwill ₹ 109,20,000]

18. Given below are the extracts from the Balance Sheet of TULSIAN Ltd. as at 31st March, 2023:

Particulars	₹
Equity Share Capital (Shares of ₹ 10 each)	40,00,000
12% Preference Share Capital (Shares of ₹ 100 each)	10,00,000
Reserves and Surplus	20,00,000
10% Debentures	8,00,000
Current Liabilities	10,00,000
Goodwill	4,00,000
Property,Plant & Equipment	60,00,000
10% Trade Investments [Face Value ₹ 8,00,000]	10,00,000
Current Assets	14,00,000

Additional Information: Average Profits after tax @ 40%:₹ 15,00,000. Trade Investments are to be valued at 150% of Face Value. Rate of Income Tax—30% with effect from 1st April, 2023. Normal Rate of Return — 20% on Closing Capital Employed.

Required: Calculate the Value of Goodwill at 5 years' purchase of Super Profits.

[**Ans.** Closing Capital Employed ₹ 68,00,000, FMP ₹ 17,50,000,Goodwill ₹ 19,50,000]

19. TULSIAN Ltd. provides you the following information:

Particulars	₹
Equity Share Capital	30,00,000
Reserves and Surplus	10,70,000
12% Preference Share Capital	20,00,000
10% Debentures	20,00,000
Current Liabilities	1,00,000
Goodwill	50,000
Non–Trade Investments	20,000
Future Maintainable Profits before Interest and Tax	30,00,000
Tax rate 30%	
Normal Rate of Return: 14% on Closing Capital Employed.	

Required: Calculate the Value of Goodwill at 5 years' purchase of Super Profits.

[**Ans.** Closing Capital Employed ₹ 60,00,000, FMP ₹ 19,60,000,Goodwill ₹ 56,00,000]

20. Given below are the extracts from the Balance Sheet of TULSIAN(25A) Ltd. as at 31st March, 2023:

Particulars	₹
Equity Share Capital (Shares of ₹ 10 each)	20,00,000
12% Preference Share Capital (Shares of ₹ 100 each)	5,00,000
Reserves and Surplus	10,00,000
10% Debentures [60% Debentures are to be redeemed prior to valuation of Goodwill]	10,00,000
Current Liabilities	5,00,000
Goodwill	2,00,000
Property,Plant & Equipment	30,00,000
10% Trade Investments [Face Value ₹ 4,00,000]	5,00,000
Current Assets	13,00,000

Additional Information: Profits after tax @ 40%: 2020–2021 :₹ 6,00,000, 2021–2022: ₹ 9,00,000, 2022–2023: ₹ 7,50,000.Trade Investments are to be valued at 150% of Face Value. Rate of Income Tax — 30% with effect from 1st April, 2023.

Required: Calculate the Value of Goodwill at 3 years' purchase of Super Profits:

(a) If Normal Rate of Return on Net Assets is10%.

(b) If Normal Rate of Return on Net Assets for Equity Shareholders is 10%.

(c) If Normal Rate of Return on Average Capital Employed is 10%.

[**Ans** (a) Net Assets ₹ 34,00,000, FMP ₹ 9,17,000,Goodwill ₹ 17,31,000, (b) Net Assets for Equity Shareholders ₹ 29,00,000, FMP ₹ 8,57,000 ,Goodwill ₹ 17,01,000, (c) Average Capital Employed ₹ 30,25,000, FMP ₹ 9,17,000,Goodwill ₹ 18,43,500]

21. Given below are the extracts from the Balance Sheet of TULSIAN (25B) Ltd. as at 31st March, 2023:

Particulars	₹
Equity Share Capital (Shares of ₹ 10 each)	20,00,000
12% Preference Share Capital (Shares of ₹ 100 each)	5,00,000
Reserves and Surplus	10,00,000
10% Debentures [60% Debentures are to be redeemed prior to valuation of Goodwill]	10,00,000
Current Liabilities	5,00,000
Goodwill	2,00,000
10% Trade Investments [Face Value ₹ 4,00,000]	5,00,000

Additional Information: Profits after tax @ 40%: 2020–2021 :₹ 6,00,000, 2021–2022: ₹ 9,00,000, 2022–2023: ₹ 7,50,000. Trade Investments are to be valued at 150% of Face Value. Rate of Income Tax — 30% with effect from 1st April, 2023.

Required: Calculate the Value of Goodwill at 3 years' purchase of Super Profits:

(a) If Normal Rate of Return on Net Assets is 10%.

(b) If Normal Rate of Return on Net Assets for Equity Shareholders is 10%.

(c) If Normal Rate of Return on Average Capital Employed is 10%.

[**Ans** (a) Net Assets ₹ 34,00,000, FMP ₹ 9,17,000,Goodwill ₹ 17,31,000, (b) Net Assets for Equity Shareholders ₹ 29,00,000, FMP ₹ 8,57,000 ,Goodwill ₹ 17,01,000, (c) Average Capital Employed ₹ 30,25,000, FMP ₹ 9,17,000,Goodwill ₹ 18,43,500]

22. From the following information, calculate the Value of Goodwill at 5 years' purchase of Super Profits of TULSIAN(26) Ltd:

8,00,000 Equity Shares of ₹ 10 each,₹ 8 paid up
14,00,000 Equity Shares of ₹ 5 each fully called up (Calls–in–arrears @₹ 2 on 4,00,000 shares)
20,000 9% Preference Shares of ₹100 each fully paid up
Reserves & Surplus ₹ 149,32,000
Property,Plant & Equipment ₹ 6,00,000. 50% of Total Property,Plant & Equipment are found undervalued by 50% of market value and 50% of the remaining are found overvalued by 50% of market value.
10% Investments: [Face Value₹ 1,60,000] ₹ 2,00,000. Of the Investments 10% is trade and the balance non–trade. All trade Investments are to be valued at 10% below cost.
External Liabilities ₹ 20,00,000
Expected Future Maintainable Profits before tax ₹ 51,18,000
Rate of Tax—30%, Normal Rate of Earnings for Equity Shareholders — 10%

[**Ans** Net Assets for Equity Shareholders ₹ 276,00,000, FMP ₹ 34,02,600 ,Goodwill ₹ 32,13,000]

23. Given below are the extracts from the Balance Sheet of TULSIAN(27) Ltd. as at 31st March, 2023:

Liabilities	₹
Equity Share Capital (Shares of ₹ 10 each)	80,00,000
9% Preference Share Capital (Shares of ₹ 100 each)	20,48,000
Reserves and Surplus	43,12,000
Non–Current Liabilities	20,00,000
Current Liabilities	69,60,000
Goodwill	8,00,000
Property,Plant & Equipment	98,54,200
10% Investments: [Face Value ₹ 1,60,000]	2,00,000
Current Assets	124,65,800

Additional Information:

1. Profits and Losses after tax @ 40%:

2018–2019 Losses	***2019–2020 Profits***	***2020–2021 Profits***	***2021–2022 Profits***	***2022–2023 Profits***
15,00,000	18,00,000	24,04,320	30,08,640	36,08,640

The loss in 2018–2019 occurred due to a prolonged strike.

2. Of the Investments 10% is trade and the balance non–trade. 50% of the non–trade Investments were acquired on 1.4.2021 and the rest on 1.4.2020. All trade Investments are to be valued at 10% below cost.
3. In 2020–2021 a new machine costing ₹ 2,00,000 was purchased but wrongly charged to revenue. (No effect has yet been given for rectifying the same) Depreciation is charged on machine @ 10% on reducing balance method.
4. Closing Inventories were over–valued by ₹ 1,80,000 in 2020–2021, by ₹ 1,62,000 in 2021–2022, by ₹ 1,45,800 in 2022–2023.

5. Disputed Bonus claim of ₹ 3,00,000 not yet provided in the accounts for 2022–2023 is settled at ₹ 2,00,000.
6. In 2022–2023 some old Furniture having a book value of ₹ 5,00,000 was sold for ₹ 3,00,000.
7. With effect from 1st April, 2023, there will be increase in manager's remuneration of ₹ 4,00,000 p.a., Advantage from new contract for supply of goods of ₹ 9,00,000 p.a. and Additional Revenue Expenditure of ₹ 1,00,000 p.a.
8. Property,Plant & Equipment are worth 20% above their actual book value.
9. Rate of Income Tax—30% with effect from 1st April, 2023.
10. Normal Rate of Return is 10% on Average Capital Employed.

Required: Calculate the Value of Goodwill at 3 years' purchase of Super Profits.

[**Ans** Average Capital Employed ₹ 135,35,680, FMP ₹ 35,80,000,Goodwill ₹ 66,79,296]

24. Given below are the extracts from the Balance Sheet of TULSIAN(28) Ltd. Ltd. as at 31st March, 2023:

Particulars		₹
20,000 Equity Shares of ₹ 100 each fully paid up		20,00,000
12,000 12% Cum Preference Shares of ₹ 100 each, fully paid up		12,00,000
General Reserve		9,60,000
Profit and Loss A/c:		
Balance on 1.4.2022	4,80,000	
Profit including Investment Income of current year	19,20,000	
Less: Provision for Tax	(4,80,000)	19,20,000
Trade Creditors		8,40,000
Provision for Tax		4,80,000
Property,Plant & Equipment:		31,20,000
6% Government Securities at cost (Face value ₹ 8,00,000)		6,40,000
Trade Debtors		15,20,000
Inventories (Taken at 90% of market value)		18,00,000
Cash and Bank Balances		3,20,000

Additional information:

(a) The Property,Plant & Equipment are understated by ₹ 11,20,000. Ignore additional Depreciation on an increase in Property,Plant & Equipment.

(b) Companies doing similar business as that of TULSIAN(28) Ltd. Ltd. as at 31st March, 2023: Ltd. show a market return of 15% on Average Capital Employed.

(c) Profits after tax over the prior 3 years period have been increasing at the rate of ₹ 2,40,000 per annum.

Required: Calculate the value of goodwill at 3 years' purchase of super profits.

[**Ans** Average Capital Employed ₹ 60,40,000, FMP ₹ 12,44,000,Goodwill ₹ 10,14,000]

25. Given below are the extracts from the Balance Sheet of TULSIAN(29) Ltd. for the year ended on 31st March, 2021, 2022 and 2023:

Particulars	***2020 –2021*** ₹	***2021 –2022*** ₹	***2022 –2023*** ₹
Equity Share Capital (Shares of ₹ 10 each)	64,00,000	64,00,000	64,00,000
General Reserve	48,00,000	56,00,000	64,00,000

Profit & Loss A/c	5,60,000	6,40,000	9,60,000
Current Liabilities	24,00,000	32,00,000	40,00,000
Goodwill	40,00,000	32,00,000	24,00,000
Tangible Fixed Assets	56,00,000	64,00,000	64,00,000
Inventories	40,00,000	48,00,000	56,00,000
Trade Debtors	80,000	6,40,000	17,60,000
Bank balance	4,80,000	8,00,000	16,00,000

Additional Information:

(a) Actual Valuations were as under:	2020–2021 ₹	2021–2022 ₹	2022–2023 ₹
Property,Plant & Equipment [Ignore additional Depreciation on an increase in Property,Plant & Equipment]	72,00,000	80,00,000	88,00,000
Inventories	48,00,000	56,00,000	64,00,000
Net Profit (including opening balance after writing off depreciation, goodwill, tax provision and transfer to General Reserve)	16,80,000	24,80,000	32,80,000

(b) Capital employed in the business at market value at the beginning of 2020–2021 was ₹ 146,40,000 which included the cost of goodwill. The normal annual return on average capital employed in the line of business engaged by TULSIAN(29) Ltd. is 12.5%.

(c) The balance in the General Reserve on 1st April, 2020 was ₹ 40 lakhs.

(d) The goodwill shown on 31.3.2021 was purchased on 1.4.2020 for ₹ 40 lakhs on which date the balance in the Profit & Loss account was ₹ 4,80,000.

(e) Goodwill is to be valued at 5 years' purchase of Simple Average Super Profit.

Required: Find out the average capital employed in each year. Find out the Value of Goodwill.

[**Ans** Average Capital Employed ₹ 144,00,000,₹ 146,00,000, ₹ 160,00,000, Average Super Profit ₹ 16,45,000,Goodwill ₹ 82,25,000]

26. The expected profits of TULSIAN(30) Ltd. for the next 5 years are as follows:

Year	*I*	*II*	*III*	*IV*	*V*
Profits (₹)	3,00,000	6,00,000	9,00,000	12,00,000	15,00,000

The total assets of the firm are ₹ 60,00,000 and outside liabilities are ₹ 33,00,000. The normal expectation in the industry is 10% on Closing Capital Employed.The present value factor at 10% are as follows:

Year	*I*	*II*	*III*	*IV*	*V*
PVF	0.9091	0.8264	0.7513	0.6830	0.6209

Required: Calculate the Value of Goodwill on the basis of Present Value of Super Profits for 5 years.

[**Ans** Capital Employed ₹ 27,00,000, Goodwill ₹ 21,72,201]

27. Calculate the Value of goodwill according to (a) Capitalisation of Super Profits Method (b) Capitalization of Average Profits Method from the following information:

1. Future Maintainable Profits after tax ₹ 15,00,000
2. Net Assets Employed ₹ 30,00,000
3. Normal Rate of Return 10% on Closing Capital Employed.

[(a) **Ans** ₹ 120,00,000, (b) **Ans** ₹ 120,00,000]

28. Given below are the extracts from the Balance Sheet of TULSIAN(34) Ltd. as at 31st March, 2023:

Particulars	₹
Equity Share Capital (Shares of ₹ 10 each)	22,00,000
15% Preference Share Capital (Shares of ₹ 100 each)	4,80,000
General Reserve	2,50,000
Profit & Loss A/c	9,11,700
Long–term Borrowings	5,00,000
Short–term Borrowings	4,44,800
Property,Plant & Equipment	10,50,000
Goodwill	4,50,000
10% Investments: [Face Value ₹ 4,00,000]	5,00,000

Additional Information*(Ignore tax)*:

(a) Net Profit for the year 2022–2023 ₹ 22,00,000.

(b) Expected Normal Rate of Return is 10% on Closing Capital Employed.

(c) Of the Investments 10% is trade and the balance non–trade. All trade Investments are to be valued at 10% below cost. Disputed Bonus claim of ₹ 1,45,000 not yet provided in the accounts for 2022–2023 is settled at ₹ 95,000.

(d) On 01.04.2022, a new machinery costing ₹ 5,00,000 was purchased but wrongly charged to revenue. Machinery and other Property,Plant & Equipment are subject to Depreciation @ 10% (No rectification has yet been made). 50% of Total Property,Plant & Equipment are found undervalued by 50% of market value and 50% of the remaining are found overvalued by 50% of market value.

(e) With effect from 01.04.2023 the Managing Director's remuneration will be ₹ 70,89,830 instead of ₹ 60,00,000.

Required: Calculate the Value of Goodwill (a) at 3 years' purchase of Future Maintainable Profits (b) at 3 years' purchase of Super Profit (c) as per Annuity Method (Annuity Factor @ 10% for 3 years is 2.486) (d) as per Capitalization of Super Profit Method. (e) as per Capitalisation of Future Maintainable Profit Method. (f) If it is considered reasonable to increase the Value of Goodwill by an amount equal to average of the book value and a valuation made at 3 years' purchase of Average Super Profit.

[**Ans** Average Capital Employed ₹ 39,16,700, FMP ₹ 13,66,670,Goodwill (a) ₹ 41,00,010, (b) ₹ 29,25,000, (c) ₹ 24,23,850, (d) ₹ 97,50,000, (e) ₹ 97,50,000, (f) ₹ 21,37,500]

13 VALUATION OF BRAND

LEARNING OBJECTIVES

After studying this chapter, you should be able to understand:

- ◇ Concept of Brand
- ◇ Identification of Brands as an Asset
- ◇ Objectives of Corporate Branding
- ◇ Corporate Brand Accounting
- ◇ Objectives of Brand Accounting
- ◇ Difficulties in Brand Accounting
- ◇ Variables Affecting the methods of Valuation of Brands
- ◇ Valuation of Purchased/Acquired Brands
- ◇ Valuation of Self-generated Brands
- ◇ Whole Organisation as a Brand
- ◇ Human Resources as a Brand
- ◇ Corporate Brand Strength

In the modern world of complex and competitive business environment the key to success and survival of an Entity is the image of their brands since the brand gives tremendous competitive advantage to Entity. It can be said that rather than product selling itself, it is brand that sells the product. Brands are strategic assets.

1.0 CONCEPT OF BRAND

According to American Marketing Association, *'Brand means a name, term, sign, symbol or design or a combination of these intended to identify the goods or services of one seller or group of sellers and to differentiate them from those of competitors.'*

Brands may be that which is acquired from outside source while acquiring business *or* may also be nurtured internally by a company, which are known as 'Home-grown brands'.

By assigning a brand name to the product, the manufacturer distinguishes it from rival products and helps the customers to identity it while going in for it.

The necessity of branding of products has increased enormously due to influence of various factors like growth of competition, increasing importance of advertising etc.

Power brands make such a lasting impact on the consumers that it is almost impossible to change his preferences even if cheaper and alternative products are available in the market. Brands have major influence on takeover decisions as the premium paid on takeover is almost always in respect of the strong brand portfolio of the acquired company and of its long-term effect on the profits of the acquiring company in the post-acquisition period.

2.0 IDENTIFICATION OF BRANDS AS AN ASSET

Brands are considered as assets since:

1. There exists some specific right to future benefits *or* service potentials.
2. Rights over Brands accrue to a specific individual *or* firm.
3. There is a legally enforceable claim to the rights *or* services over the Brand after getting the brands registered.
4. The Brands are the result of several past transactions and events. Brands are created through marketing efforts over time.

3.0 OBJECTIVES OF CORPORATE BRANDING

The important objectives of corporate branding are as follows:

1. Corporate Identity	Brands help companies in creating and maintaining an identity for them in the market place by brand popularity and the eventual customer loyalty attached to the brands
2. TQM	Brands help companies in adopting and practicing Total Quality Management (TQM).
3. Customer Preference	Brands help **Customers** to identity the product while going in for it.
4. Market Segmentation	Brands enable firms in Segmenting a market to effectively target consumers and to meet the competition through the built-up strong brand values.
5. Strong Market	By building strong brands, firms can enlarge and strengthen their market base. This would also facilitate programmes, designed to achieve maximum market share.

4.0 CORPORATE BRAND ACCOUNTING

1. Corporate brand accounting can be defined as a process of identification, measurement and communication of brand value and brand equity to permit informed judgment and decisions by the users of the information.
2. The term brand accounting refers to "the practice of valuation and reporting of the value of brand of a product *or* service in the financial statements of a corporate entity, the value of a brand being ascertained either as a result of revaluation in the case of home-grown brands *or* as a result of acquisition/ merger in the case of newly acquired brands.
3. It is a system designed to determine the brand value with a view to reflect the brands as assets in the corporate balance sheet. However, brand accounting goes beyond valuation of corporate brand. It is the process of total brand management through accounting information.

5.0 OBJECTIVES OF BRAND ACCOUNTING

The important objectives of Brand Accounting are as follows:

1. To ascertain the Real Economic Value of the company
2. To ascertain the Future Profitability of the company
3. To enhance the market value of the share of the company
4. To put up a powerful defense against potential predators and thereby ward off possible acquisition and take-over bids.

5. To resort to easy & enhanced debt borrowings with the increase in NAV and thereby avail Benefits of Leverage, sound capital structure and an improved Capital Gearing Ratio.
6. To help managers in placing importance on brand promotion and strategic brand positioning which hold the key for corporate marketing success.
7. To enhance the quality of accounting practice since the value added by corporate brands are considered significant in financial statements.
8. To help firms in fulfilling their social obligations by helping especially the shareholders in making an objective evaluation of companies (rating) before investing their money.
9. To help firms in making a perfect estimate of the ability to take on the competitors.

6.0 DIFFICULTIES IN BRAND ACCOUNTING

Some of the difficulties faced by the accountants in brand valuation are as follows:

1. Distinctiveness	Brands need to be valued distinctively as different from other intangibles such as Goodwill etc. In case of Mergers and Amalgamations, the inseparability of brand from other intangible assets makes it difficult to value the brands. In fact, a brand needs to be separately disclosed in the Balance sheet, because of its significant contribution to corporate image and identity. For instance, any attempt to commonly treat brand as a part of Goodwill as is done at present may create serious distortions in accounting position.
2. Disclosure	There is always a problem of making disclosure of brand values in financial statements because there is no standard accounting practice requiring disclosure of brand values in a particular way.
3. Uncertainty	Its possible returns are uncertain, immeasurable and non-current in nature.
4. The Dilemma	**The Dilemma** is whether to amortise *or* capitalise the value of brand. There is no question of amortising brand values as either the economic life of the brand cannot be determined in advance *or* its value depreciates over time. In fact, it is "to be noted that a brand can be purchased *or* generated and maintained, thus enhancing the corporate future income earnings capacity. The challenge could, however, be overcome by categorising the brand expenditure into Maintenance and Investment. Whereas the maintenance expenditure could be charged to Profit and Loss Account and the Capital Expenditures be shown in the Balance Sheet.
5. No Market	Brands can not be revalued according to some accounting standards due to non-existence of an active secondary market for them. In fact, the need for brand accounting arises mainly on account of conditions warranted by acquisition and merger.
6. New Brands	It is often difficult to determine whether a new one is being gradually substituted for an existing brand. This raises the issue as to how to account for it in subsequent years. In such case, the relevant question is: Should the original cost of brand be written-down as it erodes? It may be difficult to determine whether a brand remains the same asset overtime as it is subtly reshaped to meet new market opportunities.

7. Joint Costs	It is very difficult to segregate and account for joint costs that are incurred and the cost of brand developed as a result of general operations of the business.

7.0 VARIABLES AFFECTING THE METHODS OF VALUATION OF BRANDS

The variables affecting the methods of brand valuation are as follows:

1. Exclusive earning power of brand.
2. Product as a brand and hence, product life cycle.
3. Separating a brand from other less important value drivers
4. Cost of acquisition of brand.
5. Expenses incurred on nurturing a home grown brand.
6. Impact of other brands as new entrants to the market.
7. Intrinsic strength of the people and process handling the brand.
8. Accuracy in projecting the super *or* extra earnings offered by a brand and rate of discounting such cash flows.
9. The cost of withdrawing *or* replacing the brand.
10. Internationalisation of a brand and therefore, local earning power of a brand in various countries *or* markets.

8.0 VALUATION OF PURCHASED/ ACQUIRED BRANDS

Meaning	A purchased/ acquired brand is one, which is acquired from other existing concerns.
Valuation	***1. Where the Acquiring Company acquires only the brand name(s)*** Brand Value = Price paid for acquisition ***2. Where the Acquiring Company acquires an existing business concern along with its brands.*** Brand Value = Purchase Consideration − Net Assets taken over However, it is questionable to say that the excess price paid always represents the brand value since the acquiring company may have paid the excess price for location of the factory, long term contracts with suppliers, better employee morale, better manufacturing technology etc. besides for brands. It would be difficult to ascertain what part of the excess price paid is attributable to brands.

9.0 VALUATION OF SELF-GENERATED BRANDS

The important Methods of Valuation of Self-Generated Brands are discussed below:

HISTORICAL COST MODEL

Meaning	1. Brand is valued at actual costs incurred in the creation, maintenance and growth of brand. The Brand Value is computed as follows: Brand Value = Brand Development Cost + Brand Marketing and Distribution Cost + Brand Promotion Costs including Advertising and other costs.

Merits	1. It is based on the actual costs which are objectively verifiable. 2. It facilitates easy computation of brand values.
Demerits	1. The entire advertisement costs cannot be regarded as incurred for brand. 2. Several Heavily advertised brands today show hardly any value *or* presence. 3. It does not explain the impact of brand value on the profitability of a firm.

REPLACEMENT COST MODEL

Meaning	1. Brand is valued at Replacement costs which would be required to recreate the existing brands. It is the opportunity cost of investments made for the replacement of the brand. The Brand Value is computed as follows: Brand Value = Replacement Brand Cost
Assumption	The existing brands can be recreated exactly by new brands.
Merits	It gives an estimation of brand value.
Demerits	1. It is based on the Replacement costs which are subjective ones. 2. It is near impossible to replace the existing brands by new brands.

MARKET PRICE MODEL

Meaning	1. Brand is valued at probable Market Price which a company would get for sale of its brand. The Brand Value is computed as follows: Brand Value = Net Realisable Value
Demerits	1. This value is only an assumed value because there exist no ready-made market for many brands. 2. Brands are created *or* bought by corporate not for sale *or* resale. 3. Value payable by the purchaser depends upon the benefits expected from the purchase of brand. 4. This Method determines the value from the seller's point of view.

CURRENT COST MODEL

Meaning	1. Brand is valued at the Current Value (Current Costs) to the Group, which is reviewed annually and is not subject to amortisation. The Brand Value is computed as follows: Brand Value = Current Value = Current Costs
Demerits	It ignores any possible alternative use of brand, any possible extension to the range of products currently marketed under a brand, any element of hope value and any possible increase in value of a brand due to either a special investment *or* a financial transaction (e.g. licensing) which would leave the Group with different interest from the one being valued.

ILLUSTRATION 1

From the following information determine the possible Value of Brand under the Historical Cost Model, Replacement Cost Model , Market Price Model and Current Cost Model:

Particulars	*Costs incurred in the creation, maintenance and growth of the Existing Brand*	*Costs which would be required to recreate the Existing Brand*
Brand Development Cost [BDC]	₹ 1000 lakhs	₹ 1500 lakhs
Brand Marketing and Distribution Cost [BMDC]	₹ 300 lakhs	₹ 450 lakhs
Brand Promotion Cost [BPC]	₹ 200 lakhs	₹ 300 lakhs

The existing Brand could be purchased for ₹ 2000 lakhs and could be disposed off for ₹ 1600 lakhs

SOLUTION

Brand Value under Historical Cost Model = ₹ 1000 lakhs + ₹ 300 lakhs + ₹ 200 lakhs
= ₹ 1500 lakhs

Brand Value under Replacement Cost Model = ₹ 1500 lakhs + ₹ 450 lakhs + ₹ 300 lakhs
= ₹ 2250 lakhs

Brand Value under Current Cost Model = ₹ 2000 lakhs

Brand Value under Market Price Model = ₹ 1600 lakhs

PRESENT VALUE MODEL/DISCOUNTED CASH FLOW MODEL

Meaning	1. Brand is valued at the present value of future estimated flow of brand revenues for the entire economic life of the brand plus the Residual Value attached to the brand. The residual value is estimated on the basis of a perpetual income, assuming that such revenue is constant *or* increased at a constant rate. A realistic present value of a particular brand having strong loyalty of customers can thus be obtained from summation of discounted values of the expected future incomes from it. The Brand Value is computed as follows: Brand Value = $R_t/(1 + r)^t$ + Residual Value/$(1 + r)^n$ *Where,* R_t = Anticipated revenue in year t, attributable to the brand. r = Discounting Rate =Weighted Average Capital Cost
Demerit	The DCF model for evaluating brand values has got three sources of failure: (i) Anticipation of cash flow, (ii) Choice of period, and (iii) Discounting rate.

ILLUSTRATION 2

TULSIAN LTD. gives the following estimates of cash flows relating to Brand on 01.04.2018.

Year	*I*	*II*	*III*	*IV*	*V*
Cash Flow (₹ In lakhs)	4000	6000	6000	8000	4000

Residual Value at the end of 2022-2023 = ₹ 1000 lakhs

Brand purchased on 01.04.2018 = ₹ 10,000 lakhs

Useful life = 5 years

Weighted Average Capital Cost =15%

Year	*I*	*II*	*III*	*IV*	*V*
PVF@15%	0.870	0.756	0.658	0.572	0.497

Required: Determine the Value of Brand under the Present Value Model.

SOLUTION

CALCULATION OF BRAND VALUE UNDER PRESENT VALUE MODEL

Year	*Cash Flow*	*PV Factor@ 15%*	*Present Value*
I	4000	0.870	3480
II	6000	0.756	4536
III	6000	0.658	3948
IV	8000	0.572	4576
V	4000	0.497	1988
VI	1000	0.497	497
Brand Value under Present Value Model =			19025

POTENTIAL EARNING MODEL

Meaning	1. Brand is valued at the Capitalised Value of Estimated Potential Earnings that would be generated by a brand. The Brand Value is computed as follows: Brand Value = Net Brand Revenue / Capitalisation Rate *Where* Net Brand Revenue = [Brand Units (Unit Brand Price – Unit Brand Cost)] – (Marketing Cost + R & D Cost + Tax Costs). Capitalisation Rate = Appropriate Discount Rate
Demerits	1. It is difficult to ascertain the actual marketing cost incurred for particular brand of a product. 2. It is difficult to select an appropriate capitalisation rate.

ILLUSTRATION 3

From the following information determine the possible Value of Brand under the Potential Earning Model:

Particulars	*₹ in lakhs*
Profit before tax	10000
Tangible Fixed Assets	30000
Identifiable Intangible Assets other than Brand Model	500

Expected Return on Tangible Fixed Assets = Weighted Average Cost (15%) + Normal Spread (5%)*Appropriate capitalization factor for intangibles' is 25%. Tax Rate 25%*

SOLUTION

VALUE OF BRAND UNDER THE POTENTIAL EARNING MODEL

Particulars	*₹ in lakhs*
A. Profit after tax [10000 – (25% of 10000)]	7500
B. *Less:* Profit allocated to Tangible Fixed Assets [30000 × 20%]	6000
C. Profit relating to Identifiable Intangible including brand model [A – B]	1500
D. Capitalisation Factor 25%	
E. Capitalised Value of Intangibles Including Brand[1500/0.25]	6000
F. *Less:* Identifiable Intangible other than brand model	(500)
G. Brand Value [E – F]	5500

ILLUSTRATION 4

From the following information determine the possible Value of Brand under the Potential Earning Model:

Brand Units	10 lakhs
Unit Brand Price	₹ 2000
Unit Brand Cost	₹ 850
Research & Development Cost	₹ 500 lakhs
Marketing & Distribution Cost	₹ 1000 lakhs

Appropriate capitalization factor for intangibles is 25%. Tax Rate 25%

SOLUTION

VALUE OF BRAND UNDER THE POTENTIAL EARNING MODEL

Particulars	*₹ in lakhs*
A. Brand Revenue [10 lakhs units × (₹ 2000 – ₹ 850)]	11500
B. *Less:* Marketing & Distribution Cost	1000
C. *Less:* R & D Cost	500
D. Net Brand Revenue [A – B – C]	10000
E. *Less:* Tax	2500
F. Net Brand Revenue after Tax [D – E]	7500
G. Capitalisation Factor 25%	
H. Brand Value [Net Brand Revenue after Tax/Capitalisation Rate] [7500/0.25]	30000

EARNING MULTIPLE MODEL

Meaning	Brand is valued at the Capitalised Value of Earnings generated by a brand. The Brand Value is computed as follows:
	Brand Value = Brand Earnings / Capitalisation Rate

Practical Steps Involved	The practical steps involved in the calculation of Brand Value are given below: **Step 1:** *Calculate Past EBIT from Branded Product* *= Total EBIT – Other Income – EBIT from Unbranded Products* **Step 2:** *Calculate Indexed EBIT from Branded Product* *Indexed EBIT = EBIT × Current Index/Index of the respective year* **Step 3:** *Calculate Average Indexed EBIT from Branded Product* *Average Indexed EBIT= Total Indexed EBIT/ No. of years* **Step 4:** *Calculate Average Indexed EAT* *Average Indexed EAT= Average Indexed EBIT – Tax* **Step 5:** *Calculate Brand Earnings* *Brand Earnings = Average Indexed EAT – Weighted Average Capital Cost of Funds used in Branded Activities* **Step 6:** *Calculate Brand Value* *Brand Value = Brand Earnings/Capitalisation Rate*

ILLUSTRATION 5

TULSIAN LTD. gives the following information:

Year	*I*	*II*	*III*
Total Earnings before Interest & Tax of an enterprise (₹ In lakhs)	4000	6000	8000
Total Earnings before Interest & Tax of an enterprise from Unbranded Products (₹ In lakhs)	1000	2000	3000
Other Income (₹ In lakhs)	100	150	300
Index	100	110	115

Weighted Average Capital Cost = 15%,Total Funds(out of which ₹ 1000 lakhs used in Branded Activities) ₹ 3000 lakhs,Tax Rate 30%, Appropriate capitalization factor for intangibles' is 25%.

Required: Determine the Value of Brand under the Earning Multiple Model .

SOLUTION

CALCULATION OF BRAND VALUE UNDER EARNING MULTIPLE MODEL

Year	*I*	*II*	*III*
A. Total Earnings before Interest & Tax of an enterprise (₹ In lakhs)	4000	6000	8000
B. Total Earnings before Interest & Tax of an enterprise from Unbranded Products (₹ In lakhs)	1000	2000	3000
C. Other Income (₹ In lakhs)	100	150	300
D. Past EBIT from Branded Product [A – B – C]	2900	3850	4700
E. Index	100	110	115
F. Indexed EBIT [EBIT × Current Index/Index of the respective year]	3335	4025	4700

Average Indexed EBIT = Total Indexed EBIT/ No. of years = (3335 + 4025 + 4700)/3 = 4020

Average Indexed EAT = 4020 – 30% of 4020 = ₹ 2814 lakhs

Brand Earnings = Average Indexed EAT – Weighted Average Capital Cost of Funds used in Branded Activities
= ₹ 2814 lakhs – 15% of ₹ 1000 lakhs = ₹ 2664 lakhs

Brand Value = Brand Earnings/Capitalisation Rate = ₹ 2664 lakhs/0.25
= ₹ 10656 lakhs

SENSITIVITY MODEL

Meaning	1. Brand Value is determined by the sensitivity of three market forces- level of Awareness of Brand (AB), level of Brand Influence (BI) and level of Brand Autonomy (BA) in the market. The Brand Value is computed as follows: Brand Value = (Brand units sold × Unit Brand price) × AB × BI × BA– (BDC + BMDC + BPC) *Where,* AB, BI and BA are sensitivity index of brand values BDC = Brand Development Cost BMDC = Brand Marketing and Distribution Cost BPC = Brand Promotion Cost
Demerit	It gives more importance to subjective variables in the estimation of brand value and this renders the whole exercise less reliable.

ILLUSTRATION 6

From the following information determine the possible Value of Brand under the Sensitivity Model:

Brand Units	10 lakhs
Unit Brand Price	₹ 2000
Brand Development Cost [BDC]	₹ 1000 lakhs
Brand Marketing and Distribution Cost [BMDC]	₹ 300 lakhs
Brand Promotion Cost [BPC]	₹ 200 lakhs

Awareness of Brand (AB) Index 0.9, Brand Influence (BI) Index 0.6 and Brand Autonomy (BA) Index 0.4

SOLUTION

Brand Value = [(Brand units sold × Unit Brand Price) × AB × BI × BA] – (BDC + BMDC + BPC)
= [(10 lakhs × ₹ 2000) × 0.9 × 0.6 × 0.4] – [₹ 1000 lakhs + ₹ 300 lakhs + ₹ 200 lakhs]
= [₹ 4320 lakhs – ₹ 1500 lakhs] = ₹ 2820 lakhs

SUPER PROFITS MODEL

Meaning	Brand is valued at the Present Value of Expected Profit of an enterprise attributable to the use of brand. The Brand Value is computed as follows: Brand Value = Discounting Factor × (Total Profit of an enterprise in 'n' years – Profit of an enterprise without the brand in 'n' years)

Demerits	
	1. It is difficult to decide How many years ('n') profits to be considered? 2. It is difficult to decide What should be the discounting rate? 3. It is difficult to decide the profit of an enterprise without the brand

ILLUSTRATION 7

TULSIAN LTD. gives the following estimates of Profit of an enterprise:

Year	*I*	*II*	*III*	*IV*	*V*
Total Profit of an enterprise (₹ In lakhs)	4000	6000	6000	8000	4000
Total Profit of an enterprise without the Brand (₹ In lakhs)	1000	2000	3000	4000	1000

Useful life of Brand = 5 years
Weighted Average Capital Cost = 15%

Year	*I*	*II*	*III*	*IV*	*V*
PVF@15%	0.870	0.756	0.658	0.572	0.497

Required: *Determine the Value of Brand under the Super Profits Model.*

SOLUTION

CALCULATION OF BRAND VALUE UNDER SUPER PROFITS MODEL

Year	*Total Profit of an enterprise (₹ In lakhs)*	*Total Profit of an enterprise without the Brand (₹ In lakhs)*	*Profit of an enterprise attributable to Brand (₹ In lakhs)*	*PV Factor @ 15%*	*Present Value*
A	*B*	*C*	*D = B – C*	*E*	*F = D × E*
I	4000	1000	3000	0.870	2610
II	6000	2000	4000	0.756	3024
III	6000	3000	3000	0.658	1974
IV	8000	4000	4000	0.572	2288
V	4000	1000	3000	0.497	1491
Value of Brand under the Super Profits Model =					11387

MARKET ORIENTED APPROACH

Meaning	Brand is valued at the Present Value of Expected Profit of an enterprise on its market share in next 10 years. The Brand Value is computed as follows: Brand Value = Discounting Factor × Company's Profitability Ratio × (Cumulative Market's Size in next 10 years – Cumulative Total of Market Share enjoyed by other Branded and Non-Branded Products in next 10 years)
Merits	1. It looks at macro aspects governing the brand's growth *or* shrinkage. 2. It also takes into consideration other branded & non-branded products and their threat to the company's brand.

Demerits	1. It is difficult to decide What should be the discounting rate? 2. It is difficult to project the Company's profitability ratio in next 10 years. 3. It is difficult to project What will be the market's size in next ten years? 4. It is difficult to project What will be the market's size enjoyed by other branded and non-branded products in next 10 years? 5. It requires very good understanding of the market, new entrants, exit of old competitors, market expansion and shrinkage and impact of other macro-level variables on the market.

ILLUSTRATION 8

TULSIAN LTD. gives the following information:

Year	*Company's Profitability Ratio*	*Cumulative Market's Size in next ten years (₹ In lakhs)*	*Cumulative Total market share enjoyed by other branded and non-branded products in next 10 years (₹ In lakhs)*	*PVF @15%*
1	20%	1000	900	0.870
2	20%	1200	800	0.756
3	20%	1500	700	0.658
4	25%	2000	600	0.572
5	25%	2500	500	0.497
6	25%	3000	400	0.432
7	30%	3500	300	0.376
8	30%	4000	300	0.327
9	30%	5000	300	0.284
10	30%	5000	300	0.247

Weighted Average Capital Cost =15%

Required: Determine the Value of Brand under the Market Oriented Approach.

SOLUTION

CALCULATION OF VALUE OF BRAND UNDER THE MARKET ORIENTED APPROACH

Year	*Company's Profitability Ratio*	*Cumulative Market's Size in next ten years (₹ In lakhs)*	*Cumulative Total market share enjoyed by other branded and non-branded products in next 10 years (₹ In lakhs)*	*Expected Profit*	*PVF @ 15%*	*Present Value*
A	B	C	D	E = (C – D) × B	F	G = E × F
1	20%	1000	900	20	0.870	17.40
2	20%	1200	800	80	0.756	60.48
3	20%	1500	700	160	0.658	105.28

4	25%	2000	600	350	0.572	200.20
5	25%	2500	500	500	0.497	248.50
6	25%	3000	400	650	0.432	280.80
7	30%	3500	300	960	0.376	360.96
8	30%	4000	300	1110	0.327	362.97
9	30%	5000	300	1410	0.284	400.44
10	30%	5000	300	1410	0.247	348.27
Value of Brand under the Market Oriented Approach =						2385.30

LIFE CYCLE MODEL

Meaning	The Brand Value is indicated by means of relating the brand dimensions to the brand strength. The model is so called because the various brand dimensions behave in a way over a period of time thus forming the brand value to its life. This results in the formation of S-curve. The model merely gives diagrammatic representation of formation and behaviour of brand strength. The figure depicts the life cycle model of corporate brand strength.
Merit	This model is applicable to home-grown brands, where the brands are generated, nurtured and developed throughout their life which resembles a product life cycle.
Demerit	It is difficult to quantify the various dimension assumed in this approach.

INCREMENTAL MODEL

Meaning	The Brand Value is measured in terms of incremental benefits accruing to a firm on account of additions made to the brand value as a result of acquisition *or* revaluation of brands. The Brand Value is computed as follows: Brand Value = Total Expected Benefits after Acquiring *or* Revaluing Brands – Total Benefits of Brands Owned

10.0 WHOLE ORGANISATION AS A BRAND

All the value drivers bring together and make the enterprise a big integrated brand, the premium enjoyed by such enterprise becomes the value of the brand.

Brand Value = Intrinsic Value of an enterprise – Net Assets Value of an enterprise

This method is useful under the following circumstances:

1. The buyer acquires the whole of the enterprise.
2. A going concern values itself and exhibits such premium enjoyed by it, in its Balance Sheet.
3. One company becomes the brand equity *or* brand name for whole of the group.
4. Valuation of an enterprise as a brand is to be used as a base for computing the brand value of each value driver in the value chain of the enterprise.

This method is a very accurate choice of performance indicators and their weightages which together decide the Intrinsic Value of the enterprise.

11.0 HUMAN RESOURCES AS A BRAND

Top Executives *or* Divisional Heads being the leading value drivers in an organisation could effectively be the brand. For example, many CEOs of most profitable corporations who enjoy the maximum brand value in the market. The valuation of branded employees goes parallel with the intrinsic valuation of the enterprise, for an obvious reason that most of the value addition is done by these employees. The various approaches to valuation may be as follows:

Cost Approach	Branded Employees are valued on the basis of Total Cost incurred on developing these Branded employees. Such cost is capitalised as an 'asset' and shown in the Balance sheet with yearly alternations on account of recurring development costs incurred further.
Compensation Approach	Branded Employees are valued on the basis of Discounted value of the total future compensation payable to the key employees for their remaining tenure with the organization. **Demerit:** Employees of a high profile organisation may be unnecessarily valued at a much higher price. Hence, it may not be a genuine representation of the employees brand-equity enjoyed by the organisation.
Intrinsic Approach	Branded Employees are valued on the basis of Discounted Value of the total future compensation payable to the key employees for their remaining tenure with the organization which is further increased (or decreased) by the 'performance index' of the enterprise. This performance index explains the overall intrinsic value of an enterprise's potentials.
Remainder Approach	Branded Employees are valued on the basis of Present Value of Expected Profit of an enterprise attributable to the use of branded employees. The Brand Value is computed as follows: Brand Value = Discounting Factor × Total Profit of an enterprise in next 10 years – Profit of an enterprise without the branded employees in next 10 years) **Merits:** 1. Entrepreneurial wages can be determined, based on 'brand value'. 2. Strategy of taking over an enterprise with branded employees can be better handled, if such valuation is done. 3. Empowerment for growth and diversification becomes easy, when different benchmarks are available on the valuation of the employees to be empowered. 4. Branded employees and their valuation make the enterprise's Balance sheet distinctive strong and much more transparent. 5. Products, processes and programmes can be distinguished from the important value driven employees, valuation becomes easy. Exclusively of the products and processes from the employees becomes clear, when the branding of employees is done. **Demerits:** 1. It is difficult to decide How many years ('n') profits to be considered? 2. It is difficult to decide What should be the discounting rate? 3. It is difficult to decide the profit of an enterprise without the branded employees 4. This approach would be very notional and subjective, as it depends upon, the computation of 'non-branded employees' in an organization.

Value Chain Approach	Brand Value of the organisation is ascertained on the basis of Discounted Value of Surplus offered by the brand for 10 years *Where,* Surplus offered by the Brand = Total Contribution achieved by the organisation – Contribution associated with every Value Driver *or* Factor of Production Discounted Rate = Rate applicable to average market conditions. **Merit:** The outsourcing approach is used considerably to find out the Cost & Contribution.

ILLUSTRATION 9

TULSIAN LTD. gives the following information:

Year	***Total Profit of an enterprise (₹ In lakhs)***	***Total Profit of an enterprise without Branded Employees (₹ In lakhs)***	***PVF@15%***
A	*B*	*C*	*D*
1	1000	900	0.870
2	1200	800	0.756
3	1500	700	0.658
4	2000	600	0.572
5	2500	500	0.497
6	3000	400	0.432
7	3500	300	0.376
8	4000	300	0.327
9	5000	300	0.284
10	5000	300	0.247

Weighted Average Capital Cost =15%

Required: Determine the Value of Branded Employees under the Remainder Approach

SOLUTION

CALCULATION OF VALUE OF BRANDED EMPLOYEES UNDER THE REMAINDER APPROACH

Year	***Total Profit of an enterprise (₹ In lakhs)***	***Total Profit of an enterprise without Branded Employees (₹ In lakhs)***	***Profit of an enterprise attributable to Branded Employees (₹ In lakhs)***	***PV @ 15%***	***Present Value***
A	***B***	***C***	***D = B – C***	***E***	***F = D × E***
1	1000	900	100	0.870	87.0
2	1200	800	400	0.756	302.4
3	1500	700	800	0.658	526.4
4	2000	600	1400	0.572	800.8

5	2500	500	2000	0.497	994.0
6	3000	400	2600	0.432	1123.2
7	3500	300	3200	0.376	1203.2
8	4000	300	3700	0.327	1209.9
9	5000	300	4700	0.284	1334.8
10	5000	300	4700	0.247	1160.9
Value of Branded Employees under the Remainder Approach =					8742.6

12.0 CORPORATE BRAND STRENGTH

'Brand Strength' is defined as the sum total of all benefits flowing from different dimensions of a brand such as quality of Market Leadership (ML) of the brand, relative Stability of Market (SM) enjoyed by the brand, the extent of Market Share (MS) of the brand, the levels of International Acceptance (IA) of the brand, ability of the brand to meet the changing modern Marketing Trends (MT), the extent of Strategic Support (SS) provided by the brand to the corporate's survival and growth, Competitive Strength (CS) offered by the brand and above all the legal and social Brand Protection (BP).

Thus, the Brand Strength can be stated as follows:

Brand Value = (ML + MS + SM + IA + MT + SS + CS + BP)

SOLVED PROBLEMS

PROBLEM 1

From the following information determine the possible value of brand under the Potential Earning Model:

Particulars	*₹ in lakhs*
Profit after tax	2500
Tangible Fixed Assets	10000
Identifiable Intangible other than brand model	1500

Expected return on tangible fixed assets = weighted Average Cost (14%) + Normal Spread 4%

Appropriate capitalization factor for intangibles' is 25%.

SOLUTION

Particulars	*₹ in lakhs*
A. Profit after tax	2500
B. *Less:* Profit allocated to Tangible Fixed Assets[10000 × 18%]	1800
C. Profit relating to Identifiable Intangible including brand model [A– B]	700
D. Capitalisation Factor 25%	
E. Capitalised value of intangibles including Brand[700/.25]	2800
F. *Less:* Identifiable Intangible other than brand model	(1500)
G. Brand Value [E – F]	1300

PROBLEM 2

From the following information determine the possible value of brand under the potential earning model:

Particulars	*₹ in lakhs*
Profit before tax	13
Income tax	3
Tangible Fixed Assets	20
Identifiable Intangible other than brand model	10
Expected return on tangible fixed assets	6

Appropriate capitalization factor for intangible's is 25%.

SOLUTION

Particulars	*₹ in lakhs*
A. Profit after tax [13 – 3]	10
B. *Less:* Profit allocated to Tangible Fixed Assets	(6)
C. Profit relating to Identifiable Intangible including brand model [A – B]	4
D. Capitalisation Factor 25%	
E. Capitalised value of intangibles including Brand [4/.25]	16
F. *Less:* Identifiable Intangible other than brand model	(10)
G. Brand Value [E – F]	6

PROBLEM 3

ZED Ltd. is an FMCG player in the range of Men's Cosmetics and deals in both Branded and Unbranded products. The Branded products are sold under the Brand of 'ZED' and are fully outsourced from third party manufacturers. The company's unbranded products are manufactured at its own manufacturing units. The earnings for the last three years (lakh ₹) are furnished below:

Particulars	*Year 1*	*Year 2*	*Year 3*
Earnings Before Interest & Tax (EBIT) from sale of products	5,100	7,500	9,900
Other Income-Royalty for partial usage of ZED Brand	90	135	225

The details of Fixed Assets employed at the company's manufacturing units are given below:

Particulars	*Year 1*	*Year 2*	*Year 3*
Tangible Fixed assets employed (₹ Lakhs)	9,000	10,800	13,500
Returns (before interest & tax) on cost of tangible assets	14%	12%	14%
Spread over Return	2%	3%	3%

The average annual funds used in the company's operations is ₹ 5,200 lakhs of which ₹ 2,800 lakh is in respect of the branded business. The company's tax rate is 33.33% and has an average cost of funds of 17% after considering tax shelter on cost of borrowed funds. You are required to determine the value of the Brand ZED considering a capitalization rate of 20%.

SOLUTION

1. CALCULATION OF EBIT ON UNBRANDED PRODUCT (₹ IN LAKHS)

Particulars	*Year 1*	*Year 2*	*Year 3*
Tangible Fixed Assets	9,000	10,800	13,500
Return on cost + spread	16	15	17
Absolute value of the above	1,440	1,620	2,295
EBIT from sale of unbranded products	1,440	1,620	2,295

2. AVERAGE EARNINGS AFTER TAX ON BRANDED PRODUCTS(₹ IN LAKHS)

Particulars	*Year 1*	*Year 2*	*Year 3*
Total EBIT	5,100	7,500	9,900
Less: EBIT in respect of unbranded products	1,440	1,620	2,295
Add: Brand Royalty	90	135	225
EBIT from ZED Branded products	3,750	6,015	7,830
Average EBIT from Branded sold [(3750 + 6015 + 7830)/3]			5,865
Less: Tax @ 33.33%			1,955
Average post tax earnings from Branded Goods (including tax shelter on interest)			3,910

3. NET EARNINGS FROM BRAND (LAKH ₹)

Average post tax earnings from Branded Goods	₹ 3,910
Less: Cost of funds used in Branded operations [2,800 × 17%]	₹ 476
Net earnings from brand	₹ 3,434
Brand Value [Net Earnings from Brand × Capitalisation Rate = 3,434 × 100/20]	₹ 17,170

VERY SHORT ANSWER TYPE QUESTIONS

1. **Briefly explain the following:**
   (a) Concept of Brands
   (b) Whole Organisation as a Brand
   (c) Human Resources as a Brand
   (d) Corporate Brand Strength
   (e) Identification of Brands as an Asset
   (f) Historical Cost Model
   (g) Replacement Cost Model
   (h) Market Price Model
   (i) Current Cost Model
   (j) Present Value Model/Discounted Cash Flow Model
   (k) Potential Earning Model
   (l) Earning Multiple Model
   (j) Present Value Model/Discounted Cash Flow Model
   (k) Sensitivity Model

(l) Super Profits Model
(j) Market Oriented Approach
(k) Incremental Model

2. **Enumerate the following:**
(a) Two Objectives of Corporate Branding
(b) Two Objectives of Brand Accounting
(c) Two Difficulties in Brand Accounting
(d) Two Variables Affecting the methods of Valuation of Brands
(e) Two Methods of Valuation of Self-Generated Brands
(f) Two reasons for identify Brands as an Asset

3. How are Purchased/Acquired Brands valued?

4. How are Self-generated Brands valued?

5. Match the Column A with Column B:

Column A	*Column B*
A. Historical Cost Model	1. Brand Earnings / Capitalisation Rate
B. Replacement Cost Model	2. Net Brand Revenue / Capitalisation Rate
C. Market Price Model	3. $R_t/(1 + r)^t$ + Residual Value/$(1 + r)^n$
D. Current Cost Model	4. Current Value = Current Costs
E. Present Value Model/ Discounted Cash Flow Model	5. Replacement Brand Cost
F. Potential Earning Model	6. Net Realisable Value
G. Earning Multiple Model	7. Brand Value = Brand Development Cost + Brand Marketing and Distribution Cost + Brand Promotion Costs including Advertising and other costs.
H. Sensitivity Model	8. Total Expected Benefits after Acquiring *or* Revaluing Brands – Total Benefits of Brands Owned
I. Super Profits Model	9. S curve
J. Market Oriented Approach	10. Discounting Factor × (Total Profit of an enterprise in 'n' years – Profit of an enterprise without the brand in 'n' years)
K. Life Cycle Model	11. Brand Value = (Brand units sold × Unit Brand price) × AB × BI × BA(–) (BDC + BMDC + BPC)
L. Incremental Model	12. Discounting Factor × Company's Profitability Ratio × (Cumulative Market's Size in next 10 years – Cumulative Total of Market Share enjoyed by other Branded and Non-Branded Products in next 10 years)

[**Ans** A7, B5, C6, D4, E3, F2, G1, H11, I10, J12, K9, L8]

PRACTICAL QUESTIONS

1. From the following information determine the possible Value of Brand under the Historical Cost Model, Replacement Cost Model , Market Price Model and Current Cost Model:

Particulars	*Costs incurred in the creation, maintenance and growth of the Existing Brand*	*Costs which would be required to recreate the Existing Brand*
Brand Development Cost [BDC]	₹ 2000 lakhs	₹ 3000 lakhs
Brand Marketing and Distribution Cost [BMDC]	₹ 600 lakhs	₹ 900 lakhs
Brand Promotion Cost [BPC]	₹ 400 lakhs	₹ 600 lakhs

The existing Brand could be purchased for ₹ 4000 lakhs and could be disposed off for ₹ 3200 lakhs

[**Ans** Historical Cost Model = ₹ 3000 lakhs, Replacement Cost Model = ₹ 4500 lakhs, Current Cost Model = ₹ 4000 lakhs, Market Price Model = ₹ 3200 lakhs]

2. TULSIAN LTD. gives the following estimates of cash flows relating to Brand on 01.04.2018.

Year	*I*	*II*	*III*	*IV*	*V*
Cash Flow (₹ In lakhs)	8000	12000	12000	16000	8000

Residual Value at the end of 2022-2023 = ₹ 2000 lakhs

Brand purchased on 01.04.2018 = ₹ 20,000 lakhs

Useful life = 5 years

Weighted Average Capital Cost =15%

Year	*I*	*II*	*III*	*IV*	*V*
PVF@15%	0.870	0.756	0.658	0.572	0.497

Required: Determine the Value of Brand under the Present Value Model.

[**Ans** ₹ 38050 lakhs]

3. From the following information determine the possible Value of Brand under the Potential Earning Model:

Particulars	*₹ in lakhs*
Profit before tax	20000
Tangible Fixed Assets	60000
Identifiable Intangible Assets other than Brand Model	1000

Expected Return on Tangible Fixed Assets = Weighted Average Cost (15%) + Normal Spread (5%)*Appropriate capitalization factor for intangibles' is 25%. Tax Rate 25%*

[**Ans** ₹ 11000 lakhs]

4. From the following information determine the possible Value of Brand under the Potential Earning Model:

Brand Units	20 lakhs
Unit Brand Price	₹ 2000
Unit Brand Cost	₹ 850
Research & Development Cost	₹ 1000 lakhs
Marketing & Distribution Cost	₹ 2000 lakhs

Appropriate capitalization factor for intangibles is 25%. Tax Rate 25%

[**Ans** ₹ 60000 lakhs]

14 VALUATION OF SHARES

LEARNING OBJECTIVES

After studying this chapter, you should be able to understand:

◇ What are the purposes of Valuation of a Share?

◇ When does the Valuation by a Valuer become necessary?

◇ What is the limitation of Stock Exchange Price as a basis for valuation?

◇ What are the factors affecting the Valuation of Shares?

◇ What are the methods of Valuation of Shares?

◇ What is the suitability of methods of Valuation of Shares?

◇ How to Value Equity Shares on Net Assets Basis?

◇ How to Value Equity Shares on Earning Basis [When Controlling Interest is to be transferred]?

◇ How to Value Equity Shares on Dividend Basis [When only a Few Shares are to be transferred]?

◇ How to Value Equity Shares on Fair Value/Mean Value/Dual Basis?

The considerations governing the share valuation are varied, intricate and numerous of which some are accounting and others non–accounting; some are objective, others are subjective. Valuation calls for judicious assessment of the rights, advantages, interests, expectations, hazards and difficulties of the parties involved in it, having conflicting interests. The valuer's approach is influenced by the purpose for which the valuation is requested.

1.0 WHAT ARE THE PURPOSES OF VALUATION OF A SHARE?

The purposes of valuation of share are:

(i) To Assess under the Wealth Tax Act.

(ii) To Purchase a block of Shares which may or may not give the holder thereof a controlling interest in the company.

(iii) To Purchase Shares by employees of the company where the retention of such shares is limited to the period of their employment.

(iv) To Formulate Schemes of Amalgamation, Absorption, etc.

(v) To Acquire Interest of dissenting shareholders under a scheme of reconstruction.

(vi) To Compensate Shareholders, on the acquisition of their shares, by the Government under a scheme of nationalisation.

(vii) To Convert Shares, say, preference into equity shares.

(viii) To Advance a Loan on the security of shares.

(ix) To Resolve a deadlock in the management of a company on the basis of the controlling block of shares given to either of the parties.

2.0 WHEN DOES THE VALUATION BY A VALUER BECOME NECESSARY?

The valuation, by a valuer becomes necessary in the following circumstances:

(i) Where Statutes so require (like Wealth Tax, Act);

(ii) Where the Court so directs;

(iii) Where Articles of Association or relevant agreements so provide;

(iv) Where Shares are not quoted;

(v) Where a large block of shares is under transfer; and

(vi) Where Shares relate to private limited companies.

3.0 WHAT IS THE LIMITATION OF STOCK EXCHANGE PRICE AS A BASIS FOR VALUATION?

Stock exchange price is mostly determined by bull and bear effects rather than fundamental factors like Net Assets, Earnings, Yield, etc. Stock exchange price is basically determined by the forces of demand and supply and may not reflect a true value of shares.

4.0 WHAT ARE THE FACTORS AFFECTING THE VALUATION OF SHARES?

BASIC FACTORS AFFECTING THE VALUATION OF SHARES

Case	*Factor affecting Valuation of Shares*
1. In case of a **Liquidating Concern**	Net Assets
2. In case of a **Going Concern**	
(a) Carrying on Professional Practice as Lawyers, Architects etc.	Earning Capacity
(b) Carrying on business like Reliance Industries	Earning Capacity and Net Assets Backing

OTHER FACTORS AFFECTING THE VALUATION OF SHARES

I. Industry	1. Nature of industry, its history and risks to which it is subject;
	2. Prospects of the industry in the future;
	3. Yield on shares of companies engaged in the same industry, which are listed on the stock exchanges;
	4. Govt. Policy regarding fiscal Incentives etc.
II. Company—History	5. The company's history—its past performance and its record of past dividends;
	6. The nature of management and chance for its continuation;
III. Company's Capital Structure	7. The number of shareholders;
	8. The basis of valuation of assets of the company and their value;
	9. The ratio of liabilities to capital;
	10. Capital Gearing Ratio;

IV. Company's Product etc.	11. Size, Location and Reputation of the company's products; 12. Composition of purchasers of the products of the company; and
V. Others	13. Size of the Block of Shares offered for sale since, for large blocks, very few buyers would be available and that has a depressing effect on the valuation. Question of control, however, may become important when large blocks are involved.

5.0 WHAT ARE THE METHODS OF VALUATION OF SHARES?

The various methods of valuation of shares are as follows:

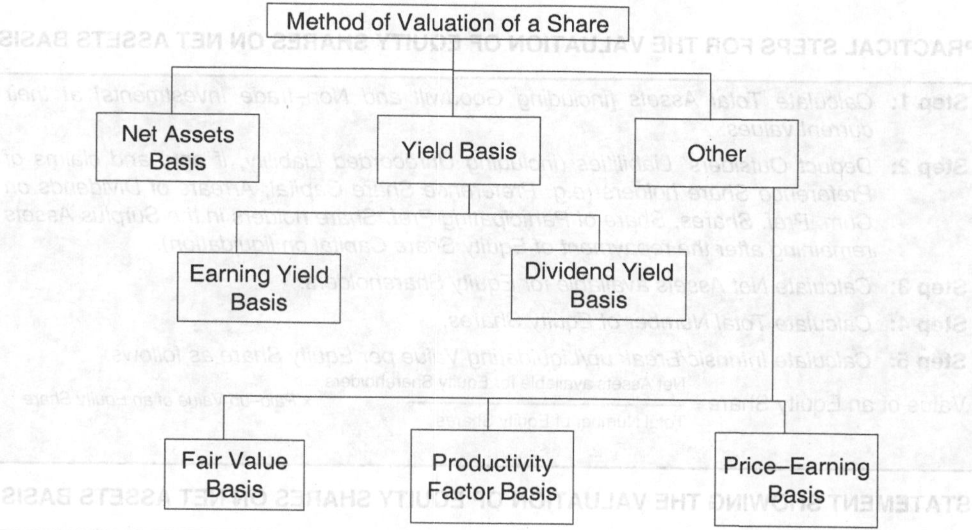

6.0 WHAT IS THE SUITABILITY OF METHODS OF VALUATION OF SHARES?

Method of Valuation of Shares	*Suitable for...*
1. Net Assets Basis	Liquidating companies
2. Yield Basis	Going concern companies
(a) Earning Yield	Where a large block of shares is under transfer
(b) Dividend Yield	Where a small block of shares is under transfer
3. Fair Value Basis	Going concern companies where Assets are also significant & where a Controlling Interest is under transfer.
4. Productivity Factor Basis	Going concern companies where both Capital Employed and Earnings are fluctuating

7.0 HOW TO VALUE EQUITY SHARES ON NET ASSETS BASIS?

Valuation of Equity Shares on Net Assets basis can be better explained with reference to the following situations:

Situation I	Where all Equity Shares are of same Nominal value and are fully paid–up Value.
Situation II	Where all Equity Shares are of same Nominal Value and Called–up Value but there are Calls–in–arrears on some shares.
Situation III	Where all Equity Shares are of same Nominal Value but of different Paid–up Value.
Situation IV	Where Equity Shares are of different Nominal Value and different Paid–up Value.

Let us discuss each of these situations one by one.

SITUATION I—WHERE ALL EQUITY SHARES ARE OF SAME NOMINAL VALUE AND ARE FULLY PAID–UP

PRACTICAL STEPS FOR THE VALUATION OF EQUITY SHARES ON NET ASSETS BASIS

Step 1: *Calculate Total Assets [including Goodwill and Non–trade Investments] at their current values.*

Step 2: *Deduct Outsiders' Liabilities (including Unrecorded Liability, if any) and claims of Preference Share holders (e.g. Preference Share Capital, Arrears of Dividends on Cum. Pref. Shares, Share of Participating Pref. Share holders in the Surplus Assets remaining after the repayment of Equity Share Capital on liquidation).*

Step 3: *Calculate Net Assets available for Equity Shareholders.*

Step 4: *Calculate Total Number of Equity Shares.*

Step 5: *Calculate Intrinsic/Break up/Liquidating Value per Equity Share as follows:*

$$\text{Value of an Equity Share} = \frac{\text{Net Assets available for Equity Shareholders}}{\text{Total Number of Equity Shares}} \times \textit{Paid–up Value of an Equity Share}$$

STATEMENT SHOWING THE VALUATION OF EQUITY SHARES ON NET ASSETS BASIS

Particulars	₹
A. Total Assets [including Goodwill and Non–Trade Investments] at their Current Values:	
Property,Plant & Equipment	...
Goodwill	...
Patents, Copyright & Other Intangible Assets	...
Trade Investments	...
Non–trade Investments	...
Inventories	...
Debtors	...
Cash and Bank Balances	...
Total Assets	...
B. *Less:* **Outsiders' Liabilities (including Unrecorded Liability, if any):**	
Long–term Borrowings	
Short–term Borrowings	
Creditors	...

	Provision for Tax	...
	Unrecorded Liability (e.g. Bonus)	...
	Total	...
C.	Net Assets available for Shareholders [A – B]	...
D.	*Less:* Claims of Preference Share holders (e.g. Preference Share Capital, Arrears of Cum. Pref. Dividend etc.)	(...)
E.	Net Assets available for Equity Shareholders [C – D]	...
F.	Total Number of Equity Shares	...
G.	**Intrinsic/Break up/Liquidating Value per Equity Share [E/F]**	...

ALTERNATIVE METHOD OF CALCULATING NET ASSETS FOR EQUITY SHAREHOLDERS (FROM LIABILITIES SIDE)

	Particulars	₹
A.	Paid up Equity Share Capital	...
B.	*Add:* Reserves & Surplus	...
C.	*Add:* Net Profit on the Revaluation of Assets & Liabilities (or *Less:* Net Loss on Revaluation of Assets & Liabilities)	...
D.	Net Assets for Equity Shareholders [A +B + C]	...

ILLUSTRATION 1 [Where all Equity Shares are of same Nominal Value and are fully Paid–up]

Given below are the extracts from the Balance Sheet of TULSIAN(1) Ltd. as at 31st March, 2023:

Particulars	₹
Equity Shares of ₹ 10 each fully paid	5,00,000
Reserves and Surplus	3,00,000
15% Preference Shares of ₹ 100 each fully paid	1,00,000
Short–term Borrowings	1,00,000
10% Debentures [60% Debentures are to be redeemed prior to valuation of Shares]	1,00,000
Goodwill	90,000
Property,Plant & Equipment	3,00,000
10% Investments: [Face Value ₹ 80,000]	1,00,000
Current Assets	6,10,000

Additional Information:

(a) Goodwill is valued at ₹ 1,70,000 and Property,Plant & Equipment are found undervalued by ₹ 1,50,000. Of the Investments 10% is trade and the balance non–trade. All trade Investments are to be valued at 10% below cost.

(b) Disputed Bonus claim of ₹ 29,000 not yet provided in the accounts for 2022–2023 is settled at ₹ 19,000. Debtors constitute ₹ 10,000 as irrecoverable.

Required: Calculate the Intrinsic Value of Equity Shares *[Ignore Tax]*.

SOLUTION

STATEMENT SHOWING THE VALUATION OF EQUITY SHARES ON NET ASSETS BASIS

	Particulars	₹
A.	Total Assets at their current values:	
	Goodwill	1,70,000
	Property,Plant & Equipment [₹ 3,00,000 + ₹ 1,50,000]	4,50,000
	Trade Investments [(10% of ₹ 1,00,000) – (10% of ₹ 10,000)]	9,000
	Non–trade Investments [90% of ₹ 1,00,000]	90,000
	Current Assets [₹ 6,10,000 – ₹ 10,000(Bad Debts) – ₹ 60,000 (60% Debentures)]	5,40,000
	Total Assets	12,59,000
B.	*Less:* Outsiders' Liabilities:	
	10% Debentures [₹ 1,00,000 – ₹ 60,000 (60% Debentures)]	40,000
	Short–term Borrowings	1,00,000
	Unrecorded Liability (Bonus)	19,000
	Total	1,59,000
C.	Net Assets available for Share holders [A – B]	11,00,000
D.	*Less:* Preference Share Capital	(1,00,000)
E.	Net Assets available for Equity Share holders [C – D]	₹ 10,00,000
F.	Total Number of Equity Shares	50,000
G.	Value per Equity Share of ₹ 10 each fully paid up [E/F]	₹ 20.00

ALTERNATIVE METHOD OF CALCULATING NET ASSETS FOR EQUITY SHAREHOLDERS (FROM LIABILITIES SIDE)

Particulars	₹
Paid up Equity Share Capital	5,00,000
Reserves & Surplus	3,00,000
Profit on Revaluation of Goodwill	80,000
Profit on Revaluation of Property,Plant & Equipment	1,50,000
Loss on Revaluation of Trade Investments [10% of 10,000]	(1,000)
Unrecorded Bonus	(19,000)
Bad Debts	(10,000)
Net Assets for Equity Shareholders	10,00,000

SITUATION II—WHERE ALL EQUITY SHARES ARE OF SAME NOMINAL VALUE AND CALLED–UP VALUE BUT THERE ARE CALLS–IN–ARREARS ON SOME SHARES

If there are calls–in–arrears on some shares, follow the following guidelines:

1. *Add a Notional Unpaid Call (Calls–in–arrears) to the Net Assets.*
2. *Calculate the Value of shares as if partly paid–up shares are notionally fully paid–up.*
3. *Calculate the Value of partly paid–up share as follows:*

   Value of Partly paid–up share = Value of fully paid–up share – Calls–in–arrears

ALTERNATIVE METHOD OF CALCULATING NET ASSETS FOR EQUITY SHAREHOLDERS (FROM LIABILITIES SIDE)

	Particulars	₹
A.	Paid up Equity Share Capital	....
B.	***Add:* Notional Calls–in–arrears**	....
C.	*Add:* Reserves & Surplus	....
D.	Net Profit on the Revaluation of Assets & Liabilities [or *Less:* Loss on Revaluation]	....
E.	Net Assets for Equity Shareholders	....

ILLUSTRATION 2 [Where all Equity Shares are of same Nominal and Called–up Value but there are Calls–in arrears on some shares]

Net Assets for Equity Shareholders at their current values	₹ 98 lacs
Equity Shares of ₹ 10 each fully called–up	₹ 50 lacs
Less: Calls–in–arrears @ ₹ 2	₹ 2 lacs

Required: Calculate the Intrinsic Value of Equity Shares.

SOLUTION

Step 1: Net Assets available for Equity Share holders

A.	Net Assets at their Current Values	₹ 98 lacs
B.	*Add:* Calls–in arrears on Equity Shares [1,00,000 × ₹ 2]	₹ 2 lacs
C.	Net Assets available for Equity Share holders [A + B]	₹ 100 lacs

Step 2: Value of an Equity Share of ₹ 10 each fully paid–up

= (Net Assets)/(Total number of Equity Shares) = ₹ 100 lacs/5 lacs = ₹ 20

Step 3: Value of an Equity Share of ₹ 10 each, ₹ 8 paid–up

= Value of Equity Share of ₹ 10 each fully paid–up – Calls–in arrears

= ₹ 20 – ₹ 2 = ₹ 18

ILLUSTRATION 3 [Where all Equity Shares are of same Nominal and Called–up Value but there are Calls–in arrears on some shares]

Given below are the extracts from the Balance Sheet of TULSIAN Ltd. as at 31st March, 2023:

Particulars	₹
Equity Shares of ₹ 10 each fully called up	5,00,000
Less: Calls–in–arrears @ ₹ 2	(20,000)
15% Preference Shares of ₹ 100 each fully paid	1,00,000
Less: Calls–in–arrears @ ₹ 20	(4,000)
Reserves and Surplus	3,00,000
Short–term Borrowings	1,00,000
10% Debentures [60% Debentures are to be redeemed prior to valuation of Shares]	1,00,000

Goodwill	90,000
Property,Plant & Equipment	3,00,000
10% Investments: [Face Value ₹ 80,000]	1,00,000
Current Assets	5,86,000

Additional Information:

(a) Goodwill is valued at ₹ 1,70,000 and Property,Plant & Equipment are found undervalued by ₹ 1,50,000. Of the Investments 10% is trade and the balance non–trade. All trade Investments are to be valued at 10% below cost.

(b) Disputed Bonus claim of ₹ 29,000 not yet provided in the accounts for 2022–2023 is settled at ₹ 19,000. Debtors constitute ₹ 10,000 as irrecoverable.

Required: Calculate the Intrinsic Value of Equity Shares *[Ignore Tax]*.

SOLUTION

STATEMENT SHOWING THE VALUATION OF EQUITY SHARES ON NET ASSETS BASIS

Particulars	₹
A. **Total Assets at their Current Values:**	
Goodwill	1,70,000
Property,Plant & Equipment [₹ 3,00,000 + ₹ 1,50,000]	4,50,000
Trade Investments [(10% of ₹ 1,00,000) – (10% of ₹ 10,000)]	9,000
Non–trade Investments [90% of ₹ 1,00,000]	90,000
Current Assets [₹ 5,86,000 – ₹ 10,000(Bad Debts) – ₹ 60,000 (60% Debentures)]	5,16,000
Calls–in–arrears on Equity Shares	20,000
Calls–in–arrears on Pref Shares	4,000
Total Assets	12,59,000
B. *Less:* **Outsiders' Liabilities:**	
10% Debentures [₹ 1,00,000 – ₹ 60,000 (60% Debentures)]	40,000
Short–term Borrowings	1,00,000
Unrecorded Liability (Bonus)	19,000
Total	1,59,000
C. Net Assets available for Shareholders [A – B]	11,00,000
D. *Less:* Preference Share Capital	(1,00,000)
E. Net Assets available for Equity Shareholders [C – D]	10,00,000
F. Total Number of Equity Shares	50,000
G. Value per Equity Share of ₹ 10 each fully paid–up [E/F]	20.00
Value per Equity Share of ₹ 10 each, ₹ 8 paid–up = ₹ 20 – ₹ 2	18.00

ALTERNATIVE METHOD OF CALCULATING NET ASSETS FOR EQUITY SHAREHOLDERS (FOR LIABILITIES SIDE)

Particulars	₹
Paid up Equity Share Capital	4,80,000
Add: Notional Calls–in–arrears [10,000 Shares × ₹ 2]	20,000
Reserves & Surplus	3,00,000

Profit on Revaluation of Goodwill	80,000
Profit on Revaluation of Property,Plant & Equipment	1,50,000
Loss on Revaluation of Trade Investments [10% of 10,000]	(1,000)
Unrecorded Bonus	(19,000)
Bad Debts	(10,000)
Net Assets for Equity Shareholders	10,00,000

SITUATION III—WHERE ALL EQUITY SHARES ARE OF SAME NOMINAL VALUE BUT OF DIFFERENT PAID–UP VALUE

If there are uncalled amounts on some shares follow the following guidelines:

1. *Add a notional call equivalent to the uncalled amount to the Net Assets.*
2. *Calculate the value of shares as if partly paid–up shares are notionally fully paid–up.*
3. *Calculate the value of party paid–up share as follows:*

   Value of Partly paid–up share = Value of Fully paid–up share – Uncalled amount.

ILLUSTRATION 4 [Where Shares are of Same Nominal Value but different Paid–up Value]

Net Assets for Equity Shareholders at their current values	₹ 98 lacs
Equity Shares of ₹ 10 each, ₹ 8 paid–up	₹ 8 lacs
Equity Shares of ₹ 10 each fully paid–up	₹ 40 lacs

Required: Calculate the Intrinsic Value of Equity Shares.

SOLUTION

Step 1: Net Assets available for Equity Share holders

A.	Net Assets at their Current Values	₹ 98 lacs
B.	*Add:* Uncalled Amount on Equity Shares [1,00,000 × ₹ 2]	₹ 2 lacs
C.	Net Assets available for Equity Share holders [A + B]	₹ 100 lacs

Step 2: Total Number of Equity Shares = (₹ 8,00,000/₹ 8) + (₹ 40,00,000/₹ 10) = 5,00,000

= (Net Assets)/(Total number of Equity Shares) = ₹ 100 lacs/5 lacs = ₹ 20

Step 3: Value of an Equity Share of ₹ 10 each, ₹ 8 paid–up

= Value of Equity Share of ₹ 10 each fully paid–up – Calls–in arrears

= ₹ 20 – ₹ 2 = ₹ 18

ILLUSTRATION 5 [Where Shares are of same Nominal Value but different Paid–up Value]

Given below are the extracts from the Balance Sheet of TULSIAN Ltd. as at 31st March, 2023:

Particulars	₹
Equity Shares of ₹ 10 each, ₹ 8 paid	80,000
Equity Shares of ₹ 10 each fully paid	4,00,000
15% Preference Shares of ₹ 100 each fully paid	1,00,000
Less: Calls–in–arrears @ ₹ 20	(4,000)
Reserves and Surplus	3,00,000

Short–term Borrowings	1,00,000
10% Debentures [60% Debentures are to be redeemed prior to valuation of Shares]	1,00,000
Goodwill	90,000
Property,Plant & Equipment	3,00,000
10% Investments: [Face Value ₹ 80,000]	1,00,000
Current Assets	5,86,000

Additional Information:

(a) Goodwill is valued at ₹ 1,70,000 and Property,Plant & Equipment are found undervalued by ₹ 1,50,000. Of the Investments 10% is trade and the balance non–trade. All trade Investments are to be valued at 10% below cost.

(b) Disputed Bonus claim of ₹ 29,000 not yet provided in the accounts for 2022–2023 is settled at ₹ 19,000. Debtors constitute ₹ 10,000 as irrecoverable.

Required: Calculate the Intrinsic Value of Equity Shares *[Ignore Tax]*.

SOLUTION

STATEMENT SHOWING THE VALUATION OF EQUITY SHARES ON NET ASSETS BASIS

	Particulars	₹
A.	**Total Assets at their current values:**	
	Goodwill	1,70,000
	Property,Plant & Equipment [₹ 3,00,000 + ₹ 1,50,000]	4,50,000
	Trade Investments [(10% of ₹ 1,00,000) – (10% of ₹ 10,000)]	9,000
	Non–trade Investments [90% of ₹ 1,00,000]	90,000
.	Current Assets [₹ 5,86,000 – ₹ 10,000(Bad Debts) – ₹ 60,000 (60% Debentures)]	5,16,000
	Notional Uncalled Amount on paid–up Shares of ₹ 8 paid–up [10,000 × ₹ 2]	20,000
	Calls–in–arrears on Preference Shares [200 × ₹ 20]	4,000
	Total Assets	12,59,000
B.	*Less:* **Outsiders' Liabilities:**	
	10% Debentures [₹ 1,00,000 – ₹ 60,000 (60% Debentures)]	40,000
	Short–term Borrowings	1,00,000
	Unrecorded Liability (Bonus)	19,000
	Total	1,59,000
C.	Net Assets available for Share holders [A – B]	11,00,000
D.	*Less:* Preference Share Capital	(1,00,000)
E.	Net Assets available for Equity Share holders [C – D]	10,00,000
F.	Total Number of Equity Shares	50,000
G.	Value per Equity Share of ₹ 10 each fully paid–up [E/F]	20.00
	Value per Equity Share of ₹ 10 each, ₹ 8 paid–up = ₹ 20 – ₹ 2	18.00

SITUATION IV—WHERE EQUITY SHARES ARE OF DIFFERENT NOMINAL VALUES AND DIFFERENT PAID–UP VALUES

Where Equity Shares are of different Nominal Value and Paid–up Value, follow the following guidelines:

1. *Calculate Equivalent No. of Shares of a particular Nominal Value (say ₹ 10).*
2. *Calculate the Value per Equivalent Share of that Nominal Value as follows:*

$$= \frac{\text{Net Assets}}{\text{Total Equivalent Number of Equity Shares of Rs 10 each (say)}}$$

3. *Calculate the proportionate value of shares of other nominal values (say ₹ 5, ₹ 1) on the basis of value per equivalent share of given nominal value (say ₹ 10).*

   For example, If value per equivalent share of ₹ 10 each works out to be ₹ 20, then the proportionate value of shares of ₹ 5 each will be ₹ 10 (i.e., ₹ 20 × 5/10).
4. *Calculate the Value of partly paid–up share as follows:*

   Value of Partly Paid–up Share = Value of Fully Paid–up Share—Unpaid/Uncalled Amount

   For example, value of share of ₹ 5 each, ₹ 3 paid–up will be ₹ 8 (i.e., ₹ 10 – ₹ 2).

ILLUSTRATION 6 [Where Equity Shares are of different Nominal Value and Paid–up Value]

Net Assets for Equity Shareholders at their current values	₹ 100 lacs
Equity Shares of ₹ 10 each fully paid–up	₹ 10 lacs
Equity Shares of ₹ 5 each fully paid–up	₹ 40 lacs

Required: Calculate the Intrinsic Value of Equity Shares.

SOLUTION

Step 1: Total Equivalent Number of Equity Shares of ₹ 10 each

= [(₹ 10,00,000/₹ 10) + ₹ 40,00,000/₹ 10)] = 5,00,000

Step 2: Value of an Equity Share of ₹ 10 each

$$= \frac{\text{Net Assets}}{\text{Total Equivalent Number of Equity Shares of Rs 10 each}}$$

= ₹ 100 lacs/5 lacs = ₹ 20 per share equivalent share of ₹ 10 each

Step 3: Value of Equity Share of ₹ 5 each

= Value of an Equity Share of ₹ 10 each × ₹ 5/₹ 10

= ₹ 20 × 5/10 = ₹ 10

ILLUSTRATION 7 [Where Equity Shares are of different Nominal Value and Paid–up Value]

Net Assets for Equity Shareholders at their Current Values		₹ 94,00,000
Equity Shares of ₹ 10 each fully paid–up		₹ 10,00,000
Equity Shares of ₹ 10 each ₹ 8 paid–up		₹ 16,00,000
Equity Shares of ₹ 5 each fully called–up	₹ 15,00,000	
Less: Calls–in–arrears @ ₹ 2	(₹ 2,00,000)	₹ 13,00,000
Equity Shares of ₹ 1 each fully paid–up		₹ 5,00,000
Reserves & Surplus		₹ 50,00,000

Required: Calculate the Intrinsic Value of Equity Shares.

SOLUTION

Step 1: Net Assets available for Shareholders

Net Assets at their current values	₹ 94,00,000
Notional Uncalled Call on Partly–paid–up Shares of ₹ 8 paid up [2,00,000 × ₹ 2]	₹ 4,00,000
Notional Unpaid Call on Equity Shares of ₹ 5 paid up [1,00,000 × ₹ 2]	₹ 2,00,000
Net Assets available for Shareholders	₹ 100,00,000

Step 2: Total Equivalent Number of Equity Shares of ₹ 10 each

= [(₹ 10,00,000/₹ 10) + (₹ 16,00,000/₹ 8) + ₹ 15,00,000/₹ 10) + (₹ 5,00,000/₹ 10)]

= 5,00,000

Step 3: Value of an Equity Share of ₹ 10 each

$$= \frac{\text{Net Assets}}{\text{Total Equivalent Number of Equity Shares of Rs 10 each}}$$

= ₹ 100 lacs/5 lacs = ₹ 20 per share of ₹ 10 each

Step 4: Value of Equity Share of ₹ 10 each, ₹ 8 paid up

= Value of an Equity Share of ₹ 10 each – Uncalled Call

= ₹ 20 – ₹ 2 = ₹ 18

Step 5: Value of Equity Share of ₹ 5 each

= Value of an Equity Share of ₹ 10 each × ₹ 5/₹ 10

= ₹ 20 × 5/10 = ₹ 10

Step 6: Value of Equity Share of ₹ 5 each, ₹ 3 paid–up

= Value of Equity Share of ₹ 5 each – Unpaid Call = ₹ 10 – ₹ 2 = ₹ 8

Step 7: Value of Equity Share of ₹ 1 each

= Value of an Equity Share of ₹ 10 each × ₹ 1/₹ 10

= ₹ 20 × 1/10 = ₹ 2

ALTERNATIVE METHOD OF CALCULATING NET ASSETS FOR EQUITY SHAREHOLDERS (FROM LIABILITIES SIDE)

Particulars	₹
Equity Shares of ₹ 10 each fully paid up	10,00,000
Equity Shares of ₹ 10 each, ₹ 8 paid–up	16,00,000
Equity Shares of ₹ 5 each fully paid up	13,00,000
Equity Shares of ₹ 1 each fully paid up	5,00,000
Notional Uncalled Call on Partly–paid–up Shares of ₹ 10 each, ₹ 8 paid–up [2,00,000 × ₹ 2]	4,00,000
Calls–in–arrears on Equity Shares of ₹ 5 each [1,00,000 × ₹ 2]	2,00,000
Reserves & Surplus	50,00,000
Net Assets for Equity Shareholders	100,00,000

ILLUSTRATION 8 [Where Equity Shares are of different Nominal Value and Paid–up Value]

Given below are the extracts from the Balance Sheet of Rajasthali Ltd. as at 31st March, 2023:

Particulars	₹
Equity Shares of ₹ 10 each fully paid up	1,00,000
Equity Shares of ₹ 10 each, ₹ 8 paid–up	1,60,000
Equity Shares of ₹ 5 each fully paid up	1,50,000
Less: Calls–in–arrears @ ₹ 2	(20,000)
Equity Shares of ₹ 1 each fully paid up	50,000
15% Preference Shares of ₹ 100 each fully paid	1,00,000
Less: Calls–in–arrears @ ₹ 20	(4,000)
Reserves & Surplus	3,00,000
Short–term Borrowings	1,00,000
10% Debentures [60% Debentures are to be redeemed prior to valuation of Shares]	1,00,000
Goodwill	90,000
Property,Plant & Equipment	3,00,000
10% Investments: [Face Value ₹ 80,000]	1,00,000
Current Assets	5,46,000

Additional Information:

(a) Goodwill is valued at ₹ 1,95,000 and Property,Plant & Equipment are found undervalued by ₹ 1,25,000.

(b) Of the Investments 10% is trade and the balance non–trade. All trade Investments are to be valued at 10% below cost. Disputed Bonus claim of ₹ 29,000 not yet provided in the accounts for 2022–2023 is settled at ₹ 19,000. Debtors constitute ₹ 10,000 as irrecoverable.

Required: Calculate the Intrinsic Value of Equity Shares.*[Ignore Tax]*

SOLUTION

STATEMENT SHOWING THE VALUATION OF EQUITY SHARES ON NET ASSETS BASIS

Particulars	₹
A. Total Assets at their current values:	
Goodwill	1,95,000
Property,Plant & Equipment [3,00,000 + 1,25,000]	4,25,000
Trade Investments [(10% of 1,00,000) – (10% of 10,000)]	9,000
Non–trade Investments [90% of 1,00,000]	90,000
Current Assets [₹ 5,46,000 – ₹ 10,000(Bad Debts) – ₹ 60,000 (60% Debentures)]	4,76,000
Notional Uncalled Call on Partly–paid–up Shares ₹ 8 paid–up [20,000 × ₹ 2]	40,000
Calls–in–arrears on Equity Shares of ₹ 5 each [10,000 × ₹ 2]	20,000
Calls–in–arrears on Preference Shares [200 × ₹ 20]	4,000
Total Assets	12,59,000

B. *Less:* **Outsiders' Liabilities:**	
10% Debentures [₹ 1,00,000 – ₹ 60,000 (60% Debentures)]	40,000
Short–term Borrowings	1,00,000
Unrecorded Liability (Bonus)	19,000
Total	1,59,000
C. Net Assets available for Share holders [A – B]	11,00,000
D. *Less:* Preference Share Capital	(1,00,000)
E. Net Assets available for Equity Shareholders [C – D]	10,00,000
F. Total Equivalent Number of Equity Shares of ₹ 10 each [10,000 (₹ 10 each) + 20,000 (₹ 8) + 15,000 (₹ 5) + 5,000 (₹ 1)]	50,000
G. Value per Equity Share of ₹ 10 each fully paid up [E/F]	20
Value per Equity Share of ₹ 10 each, ₹ 8 paid–up = ₹ 20 – ₹ 2	18
Value per Equity Share of ₹ 5 each = ₹ 20 * 5/10	10
Value per Equity Share of ₹ 5 each, ₹ 3 paid–up = ₹ 10 – ₹ 2	8
Value per Equity Share of ₹ 1 each fully paid–up = ₹ 20 * 1/10	2

ALTERNATIVE METHOD OF CALCULATING NET ASSETS FOR EQUITY SHAREHOLDERS (FROM LIABILITIES SIDE)

Particulars	₹
Equity Shares of ₹ 10 each fully paid up	1,00,000
Equity Shares of ₹ 10 each, ₹ 8 paid–up	1,60,000
Equity Shares of ₹ 5 each fully paid up	1,30,000
Equity Shares of ₹ 1 each fully paid up	50,000
Notional Uncalled Call on Partly–paid–up Shares of ₹ 8 paid–up [20,000 × ₹ 2]	40,000
Calls–in–arrears on Equity Shares of ₹ 5 each [10,000 × ₹ 2]	20,000
Reserves & Surplus	3,00,000
Profit on Revaluation of Goodwill	1,05,000
Profit on Revaluation of Property,Plant & Equipment	1,25,000
Loss on Revaluation of Trade Investments [10% of 10,000]	(1,000)
Unrecorded Bonus	(19,000)
Bad Debts	(10,000)
Net Assets for Equity Shareholders	10,00,000

ILLUSTRATION 9A

Given below are the extracts from the Balance Sheet of BHARAT TUSHAR Ltd. as at 31st March, 2023:

Particulars	₹
Equity Shares of ₹ 10 each fully paid up	1,00,000
Equity Shares of ₹ 10 each, ₹ 8 paid–up	1,60,000
Less: Calls–in–arrears @ ₹ 2	(20,000)

Equity Shares of ₹ 5 each fully paid up	1,50,000
Less: Calls–in–arrears @ ₹ 2	(10,000)
Equity Shares of ₹ 1 each fully paid up	50,000
15% Preference Shares of ₹ 100 each fully paid	1,00,000
Less: Calls–in–arrears @ ₹ 20	(4,000)
Reserves & Surplus	60,000
10% Debentures [60% Debentures are to be redeemed prior to valuation of Shares]	1,00,000
Short–term Borrowings	2,50,000
Property,Plant & Equipment	2,10,000
Goodwill	90,000
Patents & Trade Marks	2,00,000
10% Investments: [Face Value ₹ 80,000]	1,00,000
Current Assets	3,36,000

Additional Information:

(a) Goodwill is found undervalued by ₹ 1,05,000.

(b) On 01.04.2022, a new machinery costing ₹ 1,00,000 was purchased but wrongly charged to revenue. Machinery and other Property,Plant & Equipment are subject to Depreciation @ 10% (No rectification has yet been made). 50% of Total Property,Plant & Equipment are found undervalued by 50% of market value and 50% of the remaining are found overvalued by 50% of market value.

(c) Of the Investments 10% is trade and the balance non–trade. All trade Investments are to be valued at 10% below cost. Disputed Bonus claim of ₹ 29,000 not yet provided in the accounts for 2022–2023 is settled at ₹ 19,000. Debtors constitute ₹ 10,000 as irrecoverable.

Required: Calculate the Intrinsic Value of Equity Shares.*(Ignore Tax)*

SOLUTION

STATEMENT SHOWING THE VALUATION OF EQUITY SHARES ON NET ASSETS BASIS

Particulars	₹
A. **Total Assets at their current values:**	
Goodwill [₹ 90,000 + ₹ 1,05,000]	1,95,000
Patents & Trade Marks	2,00,000
Property,Plant & Equipment [50% of (2,10,000 + 90,000) + 100% of 1,50,000] + [50% of 1,50,000 – 1/3 of ₹ 75,000] + [50% of ₹ 1,50,000]	4,25,000
Trade Investments [(10% of 1,00,000) – (10% of 10,000)]	9,000
Non–trade Investments [90% of 1,00,000]	90,000
Current Assets [₹ 3,36,000 – ₹ 10,000(Bad Debts) – ₹ 60,000 (60% Debentures)]	2,66,000
Notional Uncalled Call on Partly–paid–up Shares of ₹ 8 paid–up [20,000 × ₹ 2]	40,000
Calls–in–arrears on Equity Shares of ₹ 8 paid–up [10,000 × ₹ 2]	20,000
Calls–in–arrears on Equity Shares of ₹ 5 paid–up [5,000 × ₹ 2]	10,000

Calls–in–arrears on Preference Shares [200 × ₹ 20]	4,000
Total Assets	12,59,000
B. *Less:* **Outsiders' Liabilities:**	
10% Debentures [₹ 1,00,000 – ₹ 60,000 (60% Debentures)]	40,000
Short–term Borrowings	2,50,000
Unrecorded Liability (Bonus)	19,000
Total	3,09,000
C. Net Assets available for Share holders [A – B]	9,50,000
D. *Less:* Preference Share Capital	(1,00,000)
E. Net Assets available for Equity Share holders [C – D]	8,50,000
F. Total Equivalent Number of Equity Shares of ₹ 10 each [10,000 (₹ 10 each) + 20,000 (₹ 8) + 15,000 (₹ 5) + 5,000 (₹ 1)]	50,000
G. Value per Equity Share of ₹ 10 each fully paid up [E/F]	17.00
Value per Equity Share of ₹ 10 each, ₹ 8 paid–up = ₹ 17 – ₹ 2	15.00
Value per Equity Share of ₹ 10 each, ₹ 6 paid–up = ₹ 15 – ₹ 2	13.00
Value per Equity Share of ₹ 5 each = ₹ 17 * 5/10	8.5
Value per Equity Share of ₹ 5 each, ₹ 3 paid–up = ₹ 8.5 – ₹ 2	6.5
Value per Equity Share of ₹ 1 each fully paid–up = ₹ 17 * 1/10	1.70

ILLUSTRATION 9B

Given below are the extracts from the Balance Sheet of BHARAT TUSHAR Ltd. as at 31st March, 2023:

Particulars	₹
Equity Shares of ₹ 10 each fully paid up	1,00,000
Equity Shares of ₹ 10 each, ₹ 8 paid–up	1,60,000
Less: Calls–in–arrears @ ₹ 2	(20,000)
Equity Shares of ₹ 5 each fully paid up	1,50,000
Less: Calls–in–arrears @ ₹ 2	(10,000)
Equity Shares of ₹ 1 each fully paid up	50,000
15% Preference Shares of ₹ 100 each fully paid	1,00,000
Less: Calls–in–arrears @ ₹ 20	(4,000)
Reserves & Surplus	60,000
10% Debentures [60% Debentures are to be redeemed prior to valuation of Shares]	1,00,000
Property,Plant & Equipment	2,10,000
Goodwill	90,000
10% Investments: [Face Value ₹ 80,000]	1,00,000

Additional Information:

(a) Goodwill is found undervalued by ₹ 1,05,000.

(b) On 01.04.2022, a new machinery costing ₹ 1,00,000 was purchased but wrongly charged to revenue. Machinery and other Property,Plant & Equipment are subject to Depreciation

@ 10% (No rectification has yet been made). 50% of Total Property,Plant & Equipment are found undervalued by 50% of market value and 50% of the remaining are found overvalued by 50% of market value.

(c) Of the Investments 10% is trade and the balance non–trade. All trade Investments are to be valued at 10% below cost. Disputed Bonus claim of ₹ 29,000 not yet provided in the accounts for 2022–2023 is settled at ₹ 19,000. Debtors constitute ₹ 10,000 as irrecoverable.

Required: Calculate the Intrinsic Value of Equity Shares.*(Ignore Tax)*

SOLUTION

STATEMENT SHOWING THE VALUATION OF EQUITY SHARES ON NET ASSETS BASIS

Particulars	₹
Equity Shares of ₹ 10 each fully paid up	1,00,000
Equity Shares of ₹ 10 each, ₹ 8 paid–up	1,40,000
Equity Shares of ₹ 5 each fully paid up	1,40,000
Equity Shares of ₹ 1 each fully paid up	50,000
Notional Uncalled Call on Partly–paid–up Shares of ₹ 8 paid–up [20,000 × ₹ 2]	40,000
Calls–in–arrears on Equity Shares of ₹ 8 paid–up [10,000 × ₹ 2]	20,000
Calls–in–arrears on Equity Shares of ₹ 5 paid–up [5,000 × ₹ 2]	10,000
Reserves & Surplus	60,000
Add: Book Value of new machines wrongly charged to revenue [₹ 1,00,000 – ₹ 10,000]	90,000
Profit on Revaluation of Property,Plant & Equipment	1,25,000
Profit on Revaluation of Goodwill	1,05,000
Loss on Revaluation of Trade Investments [10% of 10,000]	(1,000)
Unrecorded Bonus	(19,000)
Bad Debts	(10,000)
Net Assets for Equity Shareholders	8,50,000

Remaining solution is same as in previous Illustration.

8.0 VALUATION OF EQUITY SHARES ON EARNING BASIS [WHEN CONTROLLING INTEREST IS TO BE TRANSFERRED]

PRACTICAL STEPS FOR THE VALUATION OF EQUITY SHARES ON EARNING BASIS

Step 1: *Calculate Average Earnings **(including Income from Non–Trade Investments)** available for Equity Share holders (Weighted if rising/declining) as follows:*

Year	*Earnings*	*Weight*	*Earnings × Weight*
I	…	…	…
II	…	…	…
III	…	…	…
Total	…	…	…

	Particulars	₹
A.	Average Earnings [Total Weighted Profits/Total Weights]	...
B.	Future Adjustments *[for Example]*	...
	Less: Increase in Managing Director's remuneration p.a.	(...)
	Less: Additional Depreciation on Increase in Value of PPE	(...)
	Add: Advantage from contract p.a.	...
C.	Earnings Before Tax [EBT]	...
D.	*Less:* Tax*on [EBT+ Additional Depreciation on Increase in Value of PPE	(...)
E.	Earnings after Tax [EAT] [C – D]	...
F.	*Less:* Appropriations (e.g. Preference Dividend)	(...)
G.	Earnings available for Equity Shareholders [E – F]	...

***Note:** Additional Depreciation on Increase in value of PPE is not deductible for tax purposes.

Step 2: *Calculate Total Paid–up Value of all Equity Shares.*

Step 3: *Calculate Average Rate of Earning*

$$\textit{Average Rate of Earnings} = \frac{\text{Average Earnings}}{\text{Total Paid–up Value of all Equity Shares}} \times 100$$

Step 4: *Calculate Normal Rate of Expectation* ***for the Company.***

Step 5: *Calculate Yield Value of an Equity Share as follows:*

$$\textit{Yield Value of an Equity Share} = \frac{\text{Average Rate of Earnings}}{\text{Normal Rate of Expectation}} \times \textit{Paid–up Value of an Equity Share}$$

ILLUSTRATION 10

Given below are the extracts from the Balance Sheet of TULSIAN Ltd. as at 31st March, 2023:

Particulars	₹
2,00,000 Equity Shares of ₹ 10 each	20,00,000
6,00,000 Equity Shares of ₹ 5 each fully paid up	30,00,000
Less: Calls–in–arrears on 2,00,000 Shares	(4,00,000)
14.4% Preference Shares of ₹ 100 each	10,00,000
Reserves and Surplus	20,00,000
10% Debentures[60% Debentures are to be redeemed prior to valuation of Shares.]	20,00,000
Current Liabilities	10,00,000
Goodwill	4,00,000
Property,Plant & Equipment	60,00,000
10% Trade Investments [Face Value ₹ 8,00,000]	10,00,000
Current Assets	32,00,000

Additional Information:

1. Profits after tax @ 40%:2020–2021 : ₹ 12,00,000, 2021–2022: ₹ 18,00,000 ,2022–2023: ₹ 15,00,000. With effect from 1st April, 2023. Rate of Income Tax—25% and an increase in manager remuneration p.a. ₹ 2,20,000 p.a.

2. Normal Rate of Return on Net Assets for equity shareholders is 12%

Required: Calculate the Value of an Equity Share on Earning Yield basis.

SOLUTION

STEP 1: PAST ADJUSTED PROFIT BEFORE TAX

Particulars	*2020–2021*	*2021–2022*	*2022–2023*
	₹	₹	₹
A. Profits after tax	12,00,000	18,00,000	15,00,000
B. Past Adjusted Profits before tax [A/60%]	20,00,000	30,00,000	25,00,000

Step 2: Average Past Adjusted Profits [Simple Average since Past adjusted profits are fluctuating]

= [(20,00,000 + 30,00,000 + 25,00,000)/3]= ₹ 25,00,000

STEP 3: FUTURE MAINTAINABLE PROFITS AFTER TAX

Particulars	₹
Average Past Adjusted Profits	25,00,000
Add: Interest on Debentures [(60% of ₹ 20,00,000)*10%]	1,20,000
Less: Increase in manager remuneration p.a.	(2,20,000)
Future Maintainable Profits before Tax	24,00,000
Less: Tax @ 25%	(6,00,000)
Future Maintainable Profits after Tax for Shareholders	18,00,000
Less: Pref. Dividend [10,00,000 * 12%]	(1,44,000)
Future Maintainable Profits after Tax for Equity Shareholders [E– F]	16,56,000

STEP 4: VALUATION OF AN EQUITY SHARE ON EARNING YIELD BASIS

1. Average Rate of Earnings = $\frac{\text{Average Earnings}}{\text{Total Paid–up Value of all Equity Shares}} \times 100$

= (₹16,56,000 /₹ 46,00,000) x 100 = 36%

2. Yield Value of an Equity Share = $\frac{\text{Average Rate of Earnings}}{\text{Normal Rate of Expectation}} \times$ *Paid–up Value of an Equity Share*

Value of an Equity Share of ₹ 10 paid–up = (36%/12%) × ₹ 10 = ₹ 30

Value of an Equity Share of ₹ 5 paid–up = (36%/12%) × ₹ 5 = ₹ 15

Value of an Equity Share of ₹ 3 paid–up = (36%/12%) × ₹ 3 = ₹ 9

ILLUSTRATION 11

Tulsian Ltd. provides you the following information:

1. Profits (after tax @ 40%):

Year	*I*	*II*	*III*	*IV*
Profits	₹ 9,00,000	₹ 12,00,000	₹15,00,000	₹ 18,00,000

2. With effect from the year V there will be an increase in manager remuneration p.a. ₹ 3,00,000, Advantage from a new contract p.a. ₹ 4,50,000,Additional Revenue Expenditure p.a. ₹ 3,40,000,Rate of Tax from the year V—30%.
3. Normal Rate of Expectation in the same industry 12%
4. 10% Non Trade Investments (Face Value ₹ 1,44,000) at cost ₹ 1,80,000.
5. Details of Shares:

10,000, 10.5% Preference Share Capital(Shares of ₹ 100 each fully paid)		₹ 10,00,000
Equity Share Capital (Shares of ₹ 10 each fully paid–up)		₹ 29,00,000
Equity Share Capital (Shares of ₹ 10 each ₹ 8 paid–up)		₹ 16,00,000
Equity Share Capital (Shares of ₹ 5 each fully called–up)	₹ 15,00,000	
Less: Calls–in–arrears @ ₹ 2	₹ 2,00,000	₹ 13,00,000
Equity Share Capital (Shares of ₹ 1 each fully paid–up)		₹ 5,00,000

Required: Calculate the Value of an Equity Share assuming that controlling interest is to be transferred. (Make calculations in the nearest multiple of ₹ 100)

SOLUTION

STEP 1: AVERAGE EARNINGS AVAILABLE FOR EQUITY SHARE HOLDERS (WEIGHTED SINCE PROFITS ARE RISING)

Year ***A***	***Profits*** ***B***	***Weights*** ***C***	***Weighted Profits*** ***D = B * C***
I	15,00,000	1	15,00,000
II	20,00,000	2	40,00,000
III	25,00,000	3	75,00,000
IV	30,00,000	4	1,20,00,000
Total		10	2,50,00,000

	₹
Average Earnings = [250/10]	25,00,000
Less: Increase in manager remuneration p.a.	(3,00,000)
Add: Advantage from contract p.a.	4,50,000
Less: Additional Revenue Expenditure p.a.	(3,40,000)
Earnings Before Tax [EBT]	23,10,000
Less: Tax [@ 30% on ₹ 23,10,000]	9,24,000
Earnings After Tax [EAT]	16,17,000
Less: Preference Dividend	(1,05,000)
Earnings available for Equity Shareholders	₹ 15.12

Note: Income from Non–Trade Investment is part of earnings for Equity Shareholders for the purposes of Valuation of Share and hence is not excluded.

Step 2: Total Paid–up Value of all Equity Shares

= ₹ 29 lacs + ₹ 16 lacs + ₹ 13 lacs + ₹ 5 lacs = ₹ 63 lacs

Step 3: Average Rate of Earnings = $\frac{\text{Average Earnings}}{\text{Total Paid–up Value of all Equity Shares}} \times 100$

= (₹ 15,12,000/₹ 63,00,000) x 100= 24%

Step 4: Normal Rate of Expectation in the same industry = 12%

Step 5: Yield Value of an Equity Share = $\frac{\text{Average Rate of Earnings}}{\text{Normal Rate of Expectation}} \times$ Paid–up Value of an Equity Share

Earnings Yield Value of a Share of ₹ 10 paid–up = 24/12 × ₹ 10 = ₹ 20

Earnings Yield Value of a Share of ₹ 8 paid–up = 24/12 × ₹ 8 = ₹ 16

Earnings Yield Value of a Share of ₹ 5 paid–up = 24/12 × ₹ 5 = ₹ 10

Earnings Yield Value of a Share of ₹ 3 paid–up = 24/12 × ₹ 3 = ₹ 6

Earnings Yield Value of a Share of ₹ 1 paid–up = 24/12 × ₹ 1 = ₹ 2

HOW TO CALCULATE NORMAL RATE OF RETURN/EXPECTATION FOR THE COMPANY

The following points are worth noting in this regard:

1. Normal Rate of Return comprises—
   (i) the risk–free rate, i.e., the pure interest rate prevailing in the concerned economy; (the rate of return on long term government securities *or* fixed deposit in bank may be taken as risk–free rate), and
   (ii) the premium for business risks appropriate for the industry to which the firm/company belongs.
2. In practice, Normal Rate of Return refers to that average rate at which the similar enterprises of the same industry to which the enterprise valuing the goodwill/share belongs, are earning profits. Thus, for practical purposes industry average return is taken as normal rate of return.
3. Normal Rate of Return/Expectation for the enterprise valuing goodwill/share need not necessarily be the same as that of an Industry to which the enterprise belongs because of its individual factors affecting the Normal Rate of Return. For example in case of a company having fluctuations in the payment of dividends, some additional risk premium may be added to Normal Rate of Return of the Industry as compared to the case of a company having stability in the payment of dividends.
4. **High Risk Cases:** In the following cases the risk of the equity investors is high:
   (a) If Fixed Interest and Fixed dividend Coverage Ratio is **less than** the prescribed ratio.
   (b) If Net Asset backing (or Cover) is **less than** the prescribed ratio.
   (c) If Capital Gearing Ratio is **higher than** the prescribed ratio.

   Hence, an additional risk **premium should be added to** industry's Normal Rate of Return.
5. **Low Risk Cases:** In the following cases, the risk of the equity investors is low:
   (a) If Fixed Interest and Fixed dividend Coverage Ratio is **more than** the prescribed ratio.
   (b) If Net Asset backing (or Cover) is **more than** prescribed ratio.
   (c) If Capital Gearing Ratio is **lower than** the prescribed ratio.

   Hence, the Industry's Normal Rate of Return should be **reduced** on account of lower risk premium.

6. CALCULATION OF NORMAL RATE OF RETURN/EXPECTATION FOR THE COMPANY

Particulars	*X Ltd*	*Y Ltd.*	*Z Ltd.*
A. Normal Rate of Expectation in the Industry	13%	13%	13%
B. *Less:* Low Risk Premium:			
for high Fixed Interest and Fixed Dividend Coverage (say)	(0.5%)	(0.5%)	(0.5%)
for low Capital Gearing Ratio (say)	(0.5%)	(0.5%)	(0.5%)
for high Net Asset Backing (say)	(0.5%)	(0.5%)	(0.5%)
for stability in payment of Dividends (say)	(0.5%)	(0.5%)	(0.5%)
C. *Add:* Additional Risk Premium			
for low Fixed Interest and Fixed Dividend Coverage (say)	0.5%	0.5%	0.5%
for high Capital Gearing Ratio (say)	0.5%	0.5%	0.5%
for low Net Asset Backing (say)	0.5%	0.5%	0.5%
for fluctuations in payment of Dividends (say)	0.5%	0.5%	0.5%
D. Normal Rate of Expectation for the company [A – B + C]			

Tutorial Note: *Normal Rate of Return for Equity is to be taken after tax. Unless otherwise stated, it is presumed that the given Normal Rate of Return is after tax.*

ILLUSTRATION 12 [Calculation of Normal Rate of Return/Expectation]

Calculate the Normal Rate of Return/Expectation in each of the following cases:

Case (a) If Normal Rate of Return before tax is 12.5% and Tax Rate is 20%.

Case (b) If Average Rate of Dividend in industry is 12.5% and the Market Price of similar company's share is ₹ 125.

Case (c) If dividends were distributed at the rate of 10% in year I and year II and at the rate of 15% in year III and year IV. Market Price of company's share is ₹125.

SOLUTION

Case (a) Normal Rate of Return after tax= Normal Rate of Return before tax * (1–tax rate)
= 12.5% × (1 – 0.20) = 10%

Case (b) Normal Rate of Return= Average Rate of Dividend/Market price = 12.5%/125 = 10%

Case (c) Average Rate of Dividend declared during past 4 years = (10 + 10 + 15 + 15)/4 = 12.5

Normal Rate of Return = Average Rate of Dividend/Market Price = 12.5/125 = 10%.

ILLUSTRATION 13 [Calculation of Normal Rate of Return/Expectation]

Particulars	*X Ltd.*	*Y Ltd.*	*Z Ltd.*
Fixed Interest and Fixed Dividends coverage	3	4.8	2.0
Capital Gearing Ratio	3	1.0	5.67

Normal Rate of Return in the industry to which the companies belongs is 12% provided:

(a) Fixed Interest and Fixed Dividends coverage is at least 3 times.

(b) Capital Gearing Ratio is 3 times.

Required: Calculate Normal rate of Return/Expectation for the above companies.

SOLUTION

CALCULATION OF NORMAL RATE OF RETURN/EXPECTATION FOR THE COMPANY

Particulars	*X Ltd.*	*Y Ltd.*	*Z Ltd.*
A. Normal Rate of Expectation in the Industry	12	12	12
B. *Less:* Low Risk Premium:			
for high Fixed Interest and Fixed Dividend Coverage (say)	—	(0.5)	—
for low Capital Gearing Ratio (say)	—	(0.5)	—
C. *Add:* Additional Risk Premium:			
for low Fixed Interest and Fixed Dividend Coverage (say)			0.5
for high Capital Gearing Ratio (say)	—	—	0.5
D. Normal Rate of Expectation for the company	12	11	13

ILLUSTRATION 14 [Calculation of Normal Rate of Return/Expectation]

[₹ in lacs]

Particulars	*X Ltd.*	*Y Ltd.*	*Z Ltd.*
Equity Shares of ₹ 10 each fully paid	10	20	10
Reserves & Surplus	10	20	2
12.5% Preference Shares of ₹ 100 each fully paid	40	20	40
10% Debentures	20	20	28
Profits before Interest and Tax	30	30	20.8
Tax Rate @ 30%			

Normal Rate of Return in the industry to which the companies belongs is 12% provided:

(a) Fixed Interest and Fixed Dividends coverage is at least 3 times.

(b) Capital Gearing Ratio is 3 times.

Required: Calculate Normal Rate of Return/Expectation for the above companies.

SOLUTION

STEP 1: PROFITS BEFORE INTEREST BUT AFTER TAX

Particulars	*X Ltd.*	*Y Ltd.*	*Z Ltd.*
Profits before Interest and Tax	30	30	20.8
Less: Interest	(2)	(2)	(2.8)
Profits after Interest but before Tax	28	28	18
Less: Tax	(8.4)	(8.4)	(5.4)
Profits after Interest and Tax	19.6	19.6	12.6
Add: Interest	2	2	2.8
Profits before Interest but after Tax	21.6	21.6	15.4

STEP 2: FIXED INTEREST AND FIXED DIVIDENDS COVERAGE

Particulars	*X Ltd.*	*Y Ltd.*	*Z Ltd.*
Interest	2	2	2.8
Preference Dividend	5	2.5	5
Fixed Interest and Fixed Dividends	7	4.5	7.8
Fixed Interest and Fixed Dividends Coverage $= \frac{\text{Profits before Interest but after Tax}}{\text{Fixed Interest and Fixed Dividends}}$	3.085714	4.8	1.97436
CAPITAL GEARING RATIO $= \frac{\text{Preference Share Capital + Debentures}}{\text{Equity Share Capital + Net Reserves \& Surplus}}$	3	1	5.7

STEP 4: NORMAL RATE OF RETURN/EXPECTATION

Particulars	*X Ltd.*	*Y Ltd.*	*Z Ltd.*
A. Normal Rate of Expectation in Industry	12	12	12
B. *Less:* Low Risk Premium:			
for high Fixed Interest and Fixed Dividend Coverage (say)	—	(0.5)	—
for low Capital Gearing Ratio (say)	—	(0.5)	
C. *Add:* Additional Risk Premium			
for low Fixed Interest and Fixed Dividend Coverage (say)	—		0.5
for high Capital Gearing Ratio (say)	—	—	0.5
D. Normal Rate of Expectation for companies	12	11	13

IILLUSTRATION 15

The capital structure of CANIC Ltd. on 31st March, 2023 was as under:

Equity Share Capital (of ₹ 100 each)	₹ 5,00,000
11% Preference Share Capital	₹ 3,00,000
12% Secured Debentures	₹ 4,00,000
Reserves	₹ 3,00,000

The company, on an average, earns a profit of ₹ 4 lakhs annually before deduction of interest on debentures and income tax (rate 25%).

The normal return on equity shares of companies similarly placed is 15%, provided:

(a) the profit after tax covers the fixed interest and fixed dividends at least four times:

(b) Capital Gearing Ratio is 0.67 times;

(c) yield on shares is calculated at 60% of profits distributed and 5% on undistributed profits.

The company has been paying regularly an equity dividend of 18%.

Required: Ascertain the Value of each Equity Share of the company.

SOLUTION

STEP 1: PROFIT BEFORE INTEREST BUT AFTER TAX

Particulars	₹
A. Average Profit of the Company (before interest and tax)	4,00,000
B. *Less:* Debenture Interest (12% on ₹ 4,00,000)	(48,000)
C. Profit before Tax	3,52,000
D. *Less:* Tax @ 25%	(88,000)
E. Profit after Interest and Tax	2,64,000
F. Add back: Debenture interest	48,000
G. Profit before interest but after tax	3,12,000

STEP 2: CALCULATION OF FIXED INTEREST & DIVIDEND COVERAGE

A. Debenture interest	48,000
B. Preference dividends	33,000
C. Fixed Interest and Dividends:	81,000
D. Fixed Interest and Dividend Coverage = ₹ 3,12,000/₹ 81,000 = 3.85 times	
E. Since Interest and Fixed Dividend Coverage (3.85 times) is less than the prescribed 4 times coverage, the risk of investor is high, an additional risk premium (say 0.50%) should be provided.	

Step 3: Capital Gearing Ratio

$$= \frac{\text{Preference Share Capital + Debentures}}{\text{Equity Share Capital + Net Reserves \& Surplus}}$$

$$= \frac{₹\ 3,00,000 + ₹\ 4,00,000}{₹\ 5,00,000 + ₹\ 3,00,000} = 0.875 \text{ times}$$

Since the company's Ratio 0.875 times is more than the prescribed Industry ratio of 0.67 times, the risk of investors is high and hence an additional risk premium (say (0.50%) should be provided.

STEP 4: YIELD ON EQUITY SHARES

Particulars	₹	₹
A. Average Profit after Interest and Tax		2,64,000
B. *Less:* Dividends:		
Preference	(33,000)	
Equity 18% on ₹ 5,00,000	(90,000)	(1,23,000)
C. Undistributed profit		1,41,000
D. Yield 60% of distributed profit (60% of ₹ 90,000)		54,000
5% of undistributed profit (5% of ₹ 1,41,000)		7,050
Yield on Equity Shares = ₹ 61,050/₹ 5,00,000=12.21		

STEP 5: EXPECTED YIELD OF EQUITY SHARES

Normal Return	15.00%
Add: For low coverage of fixed interest and dividends (3.85 < 4)	0.50 (say)
For high Capital Gearing Ratio (0.875 > 0.67)	0.50 (say)
	16.00

Step 6: Value per Equity Share = 12.21/16 × ₹ 100 = ₹ 76.31

9.0 VALUATION OF EQUITY SHARES ON DIVIDEND BASIS [WHEN ONLY A FEW SHARES ARE TO BE TRANSFERRED]

PRACTICAL STEPS FOR THE VALUATION OF EQUITY SHARES ON DIVIDEND BASIS

Step 1: *Calculate Average Rate of Dividend (Weighted if rising/declining) as follows:*

Year	*Rate of Dividend*	*Weight*	*Weighted Rate of Dividend*
I	...	...	...
II	...	...	...
III	...	...	...
IV	...	...	...
Total		...	...

Average Rate of Dividend = Weighted Rate of Dividend/Total Weight

Step 2: *Calculate Normal Rate of Expectation in the same industry.*

Step 3: *Calculate Value of an Equity Share on Dividend basis as follows:*

$$\text{Value of an Equity Share} = \frac{\text{Average Rate of Dividend}}{\text{Normal Rate of Expectation}} \times \textit{Paid–up Value of an Equity Share}$$

ILLUSTRATION 16

Tulsian (1) Ltd. provides you the following information:

1. Profits (after tax @ 40%) and Equity Dividend:

Year	*Profits*	*Equity Dividend*
I	1,32,000	12%
II	1,92,000	18%
III	1,50,000	15%

2. Share Capital:
   30,000 Equity Shares of ₹ 10 each fully paid
   40,000 Equity Shares of ₹ 10 each, ₹ 5 paid
   1,000 9% Preference Shares of ₹ 100 each fully paid.
3. Normal Rate of Expectation is 12%.

Required: Calculate the Value of an Equity Share assuming that only a few shares are to be transferred.

SOLUTION

VALUATION OF EQUITY SHARES ON DIVIDEND BASIS
[WHEN ONLY A FEW SHARES ARE TO BE TRANSFERRED]

Step 1: Average Rate of Dividend = (12% + 18% + 15%)/3 = 15%

Step 2: Normal Rate of Expectation = 12%

Step 3: *Value of an Equity Share* = $\frac{\text{Average Rate of Dividend}}{\text{Normal Rate of Expectation}}$ x *Paid–up Value of an Equity Share*

Value of ₹ 10 paid–up Equity Share = 15%/12% × ₹10 = ₹ 12.50

Value of ₹ 5 paid–up Equity Share =15%/12% × ₹ 5 = ₹ 6.25

ILLUSTRATION 17

Tulsian (2) Ltd. provides you the following information:

1. Profits (after tax @ 40%) and Equity Dividend:

Year	*Profits*	*Equity Dividend*
I	1,32,000	12%
II	1,50,000	15%
III	1,92,000	18%

2. Share Capital

   30,000 Equity Shares of ₹ 10 each fully paid

   40,000 Equity Shares of ₹ 10 each, ₹ 5 paid

   1,000, 9% Preference Shares of ₹ 100 each fully paid.

3. Fully paid Equity Shares of ₹ 10 each of similar companies in the same industry with an average dividend of 12% are quoted at ₹ 15.

Required: Calculate the Value of an Equity Share assuming that only a few shares are to be transferred.

SOLUTION

Step 1: Calculation of Average Rate of Dividend (Weighted since rising):

Year	*Rate of Dividend*	*Weight*	*Dividend × Weight*
I	12%	1	0.12
II	15%	2	0.30
III	18%	3	0.54
Total		6	0.96

Average Rate of Dividend = 0.96/6 = 16%

Step 2: Normal Rate of Expectation

= Average Dividend of same industry/Market Price × 100 = 1.2/15 × 100 = 8%

Step 3: Value of an Equity Share

= Average Rate of Dividend/Normal Rate of Expectation × Paid–up Value of Equity Share

Value of ₹ 10 paid–up Equity Share = 16%/8% × ₹10 = ₹ 20

Value of ₹ 5 paid–up Equity Share = 16%/8% × ₹ 5 = ₹ 10

ILLUSTRATION 18

From the following figures, calculate the value of the share of ₹ 100 on (i) Earning Basis, and (ii) on Dividend Basis assuming market expectation being 12%.

[Figures being in lacs of ₹]

Year	*Capital Employed* ₹	*Profit earned after tax* ₹	*Equity Share Capital* ₹	*Equity Dividend* ₹
I	5	0.80	4	0.48
II	8	1.60	7	1.05
III	10	2.20	9	1.62
IV	15	3.75	14	2.80

SOLUTION

(I) VALUATION ON EARNING BASIS

Year	*Capital Employed* ₹	*Profit earned after tax* ₹	*Rate of Earning on Capital*
I	5.00	0.80	16%
II	8.00	1.60	20%
III	10.00	2.20	22%
IV	15.00	3.75	25%

Since rate of earnings has been rising, it would be better to take the weighted average.

Year	*Rate of Earning*	*Weight*	*Product*
I	16	1	16
II	20	2	40
III	22	3	66
IV	25	4	100
		10	222

Weighted Average Rate of Earning = 222/10 = 22.2%

Value of a Share = (Average Rate of Earning/Normal Rate of Expectation) × Paid–up Value

= (22.2/12)× 100 = ₹ 185

(II) VALUATION ON DIVIDEND BASIS

Year	*Equity Capital*	*Dividend Distributed To Equity Share holders*	*Rate of Dividend*
I	4.00	0.48	12%
II	7.00	1.05	15%
III	9.00	1.62	18%
IV	14.00	2.80	20%

Since rate of dividend has been rising, it would be better to take weighted average, thus:

Year	*Rate of Dividend*	*Weight*	*Product*
I	12	1	12
II	15	2	30
III	18	3	54
IV	20	4	80
		10	176

Weighted Average Rate of Dividend = 176/10 = 17.6%

Value of a Share = Average Rate of Dividend/Normal Rate of Expectation × Paid–up value

= 17.6/12 × ₹ 100 = ₹ 146.67.

10.0 FAIR VALUE/MEAN VALUE/DUAL METHODS

Fair Value/Mean Value is taken as an average of Net Assets Value and Earning Yield Based Value. Such average is called the Fair Value of share because it incorporates the advantages of both the methods and attempts to minimize the demerits of both the methods. Fail Value Method is generally used when controlling interest is to be transferred.

PRACTICAL STEPS INVOLVED UNDER FAIR VALUE METHOD

Step 1: *Calculate Net Assets Value*

Step 2: *Calculate Earning Yield Based Value*

Step 3: *Calculate Fair Value/Mean Value as Follows:*

Fair Value of a Share = (Net Assets Value + Earning Yield Based Value)/2

ILLUSTRATION 19 [Calculation of Fair Value of an Equity Share]

Tulsian Ltd. provides you the following information:

Net Assets for Equity Shareholders at their current values:	₹ 100 lacs
Average Annual Earnings available for Equity Share holders	₹ 15 lacs
8,00,000 Equity Shares of ₹ 5 each fully paid	₹ 40 lacs
1,00,000 Equity Shares of ₹ 10 each fully paid–up	₹ 10 lacs
Normal Rate of Expectation	12%

Required: Calculate the Fair Value of an Equity Share assuming that controlling interest is to be transferred.

SOLUTION

Net Assets Value

Step 1: Total Equivalent Number of Equity Shares of ₹ 10 each

= [1,00,000 (₹ 10 each) + 4,00,000 (₹ 5 each)] = 5,00,000

Step 2: Value of an Equity Share of ₹ 10 each

= Net Assets/Total Equivalent number of Equity Shares of ₹ 10 each

= ₹ 100 lacs/₹ 5 lacs = ₹ 20

Step 3: Value of Equity Share of ₹ 5 each

= Value of an Equity Share of ₹ 10 each × ₹ 5/₹ 10

= ₹ 20 × 5/10 = ₹ 10

Earning Yield Based Value

Step 1: Average Earnings available for Equity Share holders = ₹ 15 lacs

Step 2: Total Paid–up Value of all Equity Shares = ₹ 50 lacs

Step 3: Average Rate of Earning = (Average Earning/Total Paid–up Value of all Equity Shares) × 100

= 15/50 × 100 = 30%

Step 4: Normal Rate of Expectation in the same industry = 12%

Step 5: Value of a Share

= (Average Rate of Earning/Normal Rate of Expectation)× Paid–up Value of an Equity Share

Value of a Share of ₹ 10 paid–up = ₹ 30/12 × ₹ 10 = ₹ 25

Value of a Share of ₹ 5 paid–up = ₹ 30/12 × ₹ 5 = ₹ 12.5

Fair Value of Share

Fair Value of a Share = (Net Assets Value + Yield Based Value)/2

Fair Value of a Share of ₹ 10 paid–up = (₹ 20 + ₹ 25)/2 = ₹ 22.5

Fair Value of a Share of ₹ 5 paid–up = (₹ 10 + ₹ 12.5)/2 = ₹ 11.25

ILLUSTRATION 20A

Given below are the extracts from the Balance Sheet of TULSIAN Ltd. as at 31st March, 2023:

Particulars	₹
1,00,000 Equity Shares of ₹ 10 each	10,00,000
6,00,000 Equity Shares of ₹ 5 each fully paid up	30,00,000
Less: Calls–in–arrears on 2,00,000 Shares	(4,00,000)
12% Preference Shares of ₹ 100 each	10,00,000
Reserves and Surplus	20,00,000
10% Debentures[60% Debentures are to be redeemed prior to valuation of Shares]	20,00,000
Current Liabilities	10,00,000
Property,Plant & Equipment	60,00,000
Goodwill	4,00,000
10% Trade Investments [Face Value ₹ 8,00,000]	10,00,000
Current Assets	22,00,000

Additional Information: Average Profits before tax : ₹ 25,00,000. With effect from the next year Rate of Income Tax : 25% and an increase in managerial remuneration ₹ 4,44,000 p.a. Normal Rate of Return on net assets for equity shareholders is 8%.Trade Investments are to be valued at 275% of Face Value. Goodwill is found undervalued by ₹ 26,00,000.

Required: Calculate the Fair Value of an Equity Share.

SOLUTION

VALUATION OF AN EQUITY SHARE ON NET ASSETS BASIS

		₹
A.	Total Assets at their current values:	
	Goodwill [₹ 4,00,000 + ₹ 26,00,000]	30,00,000
	Property,Plant & Equipment	60,00,000
	Trade Investments [275% of ₹ 8,00,000]	22,00,000
	Current Assets [₹ 22,00,000 – ₹ 12,00,000 (60% Debentures)]	10,00,000
	Notional Unpaid Call on Equity Shares of ₹ 5 each [2,00,000 x ₹ 2]	4,00,000
	Total	126,00,000
B.	*Less:* Outsiders' Liabilities at their current amounts:	
	10% Debentures [₹ 20,00,000 – ₹ 12,00,000]	8,00,000
	Current Liabilities	10,00,000
	Total	18,00,000
C.	**Net Assets for shareholders** (A – B)	108,00,000
D.	*Less:* Preference Share Capital	10,00,000
E.	**Net Assets for Equity shareholders** (C – D)	98,00,000
F.	Number of Equity Shares	4,00,000
G.	Value of an Equity Share(₹ 10 paid up)[₹ 98,00,000/ 4,00,000]	₹ 24.50
Value of an Equity Share (₹ 5 paid up) [₹ 24.50 × 5/10]		₹ 12.25
Value of an Equity Share (₹ 3 paid up) [₹ 12.25 – ₹ 2]		₹ 10.25

VALUATION OF AN EQUITY SHARE ON EARNING YIELD BASIS

Step 1: Future Maintainable Profits after tax for Equity Shareholders

Particulars	₹
Average Profits	25,00,000
Add: Interest on Debentures [(60% of ₹ 20,00,000)*10%]	1,20,000
Less: Increase in manager remuneration p.a.	(4,44,000)
Future Maintainable Profits before Tax	21,76,000
Less: Tax @ 25%	(5,44,000)
Future Maintainable Profits after Tax for Shareholders	16,32,000
Less: Pref. Dividend [10,00,000 * 12%]	(1,20,000)
Future Maintainable Profits after Tax for Equity Shareholders	15,12,000

Step 2: Average Rate of Earnings = $\frac{\text{Average Earnings}}{\text{Total Paid–up Value of all Equity Shares}} \times 100$

= ₹ 15,12,000/₹ 36,00,000 × 100 = 42%

Step 3: *Value of an Equity Share* = $\frac{\text{Average Rate of Earnings}}{\text{Normal Rate of Expectation}}$ x *Paid–up Value of an Equity Share*

Earning Yield based Value of an equity share (₹ 10 paid up) = 42%/8% × ₹ 10 = ₹ 52.50

Earning Yield based Value of an equity share (₹ 5 paid up) = 42%/8% × ₹ 5 = ₹ 26.25

Earning Yield based Value of an equity share (₹ 3 paid up) = 42%/8% × ₹ 3 = ₹ 15.75

Fair Value of an Equity Share = (Net Assets Value + Yield Based Value)/2

Fair Value of an Equity Share (₹ 10 paid up) = (₹ 24.50 + ₹ 52.50)/2 = ₹ 38.50

Fair Value of an Equity Share (₹ 5 paid up) = (₹ 12.25 + ₹ 26.25)/2 = ₹ 19.25

Fair Value of an Equity Share (₹ 3 paid up) = (₹ 10.25 + ₹ 15.75)/2 = ₹ 13

ILLUSTRATION 20B

Given below are the extracts from the Balance Sheet of TULSIAN Ltd. as at 31st March, 2023:

Particulars	₹
1,00,000 Equity Shares of ₹ 10 each	10,00,000
6,00,000 Equity Shares of ₹ 5 each fully paid up	30,00,000
Less: Calls–in–arrears on 2,00,000 Shares	(4,00,000)
12% Preference Shares of ₹ 100 each	10,00,000
Reserves and Surplus	20,00,000
10% Debentures [60% Debentures are to be redeemed prior to valuation of Goodwill]	20,00,000
Current Liabilities	10,00,000
Goodwill	4,00,000
10% Trade Investments [Face Value ₹ 8,00,000]	10,00,000

Additional Information: Profits after tax @ 40%:2020–2021: ₹12,00,000, 2021–2022: ₹18,00,000, 2022–2023: ₹15,00,000. With effect from the next year Rate of Income Tax : 25% and an increase in manager remuneration ₹ 4,44,000 p.a. Normal Rate of Return on net assets for equity shareholders is 8%.Trade Investments are to be valued at 275% of Face Value. Goodwill is to be valued at 3 years' purchase of Super Profits.

Required: Calculate the Fair Value of an Equity Share.

SOLUTION

VALUATION OF AN EQUITY SHARE ON NET ASSETS BASIS	
A. Value of Net Assets (As computed for Goodwill)	64,00,000
B. Value of Goodwill [See Working Note]	30,00,000
C. Notional Unpaid Call on Equity Shares of ₹ 5 each [2,00,000 x ₹ 2]	4,00,000
D. Net Assets for Equity shareholders(A + B + C)	98,00,000
E. Number of Equity Shares	4,00,000
F. Value of an Equity Share(₹ 10 paid up)[₹ 98,00,000/ 4,00,000]	₹ 24.50
Value of an Equity Share (₹ 5 paid up) [₹ 24.50 × 5/10]	₹ 12.25
Value of an Equity Share (₹ 3 paid up) [₹ 12.25 – ₹ 2]	₹ 10.25

VALUATION OF AN EQUITY SHARE ON EARNING YIELD BASIS

Step 2: Average Rate of Earnings = $\frac{\text{Average Earnings}}{\text{Total Paid–up Value of all Equity Shares}} \times 100$

= ₹ 15,12,000/₹ 36,00,000 × 100 = 42%

Step 3: *Value of an Equity Share* = $\frac{\text{Average Rate of Earnings}}{\text{Normal Rate of Expectation}}$ x *Paid–up Value of an Equity Share*

Earning Yield based Value of an equity share (₹ 10 paid up) = 42%/8% × ₹ 10 = ₹ 52.50

Earning Yield based Value of an equity share (₹ 5 paid up) = 42%/8% × ₹ 5 = ₹ 26.25

Earning Yield based Value of an equity share (₹ 3 paid up) = 42%/8% × ₹ 3 = ₹ 15.75

Fair Value of an Equity Share = (Net Assets Value + Yield Based Value)/2

Fair Value of an Equity Share (₹ 10 paid up) = (₹ 24.50 + ₹ 52.50)/2 = ₹ 38.50

Fair Value of an Equity Share (₹ 5 paid up) = (₹ 12.25 + ₹ 26.25)/2 = ₹ 19.25

Fair Value of an Equity Share (₹ 3 paid up) = (₹ 10.25 + ₹ 15.75)/2 = ₹ 13

Working Note: Calculation of Goodwill

STEP 1: PAST ADJUSTED PROFIT BEFORE TAX

Particulars	*2020–2021* ₹	*2021–2022* ₹	*2022–2023* ₹
A. Profits after tax	12,00,000	18,00,000	15,00,000
B. Past Adjusted Profits before tax [A/60%]	20,00,000	30,00,000	25,00,000

Step 2: Average Past Adjusted Profits [Simple Average since Past adjusted profits are fluctuating]

= [(20,00,000 + 30,00,000 + 25,00,000)/3]= ₹ 25,00,000

STEP 3: FUTURE MAINTAINABLE PROFITS AFTER TAX

Particulars	₹
Average Profits	25,00,000
Add: Interest on Debentures [(60% of ₹ 20,00,000)*10%]	1,20,000
Less: Increase in manager remuneration p.a.	(4,44,000)
Future Maintainable Profits before Tax	21,76,000
Less: Tax @ 25%	(5,44,000)
Future Maintainable Profits after Tax for Shareholders	16,32,000
Less: Pref. Dividend [10,00,000 * 12%]	(1,20,000)
Future Maintainable Profits after Tax for Equity Shareholders	15,12,000

STEP 4: NET ASSETS FOR EQUITY SHAREHOLDERS

Particulars	₹
1,00,000 Equity Shares of ₹ 10 each fully paid up	10,00,000
6,00,000 Equity Shares of ₹ 5 each fully paid up(less Calls–in–arrears)	26,00,000
Reserves and Surplus	20,00,000
Add: Profit on Revaluation of Trade Investments [₹ 22,00,000 – ₹ 10,00,000]	12,00,000
Less: Goodwill	4,00,000
Net Assets for Equity Shareholders	64,00,000

Step 5: Normal Profit = **Net Assets for Equity shareholders* Normal Rate of Return**

= ₹ 64,00,000 * 8% = ₹ 5,12,000

Step 6: Super Profits = Future Maintainable Profits after tax for Equity shareholders – Normal Profits

= ₹ 15,12,000 – ₹ 5,12,000 = ₹ 10,00,000

Step 7: Goodwill = Super Profits * No. of years' purchase

= ₹ 10,00,000 * 3 = ₹ 30,00,000

ILLUSTRATION 21

From the following information, calculate the Fair Value of an Equity Share of TUSHAR & TASHIKA Ltd:

4,00,000 Equity Shares of ₹ 10 each,₹ 8 paid up
7,00,000 Equity Shares of ₹ 5 each fully called up (Calls–in–arrears @₹ 2 on 2,00,000 shares)
10,000, 9.9% Preference Shares of ₹100 each fully paid up
Reserves & Surplus ₹ 73,76,000
Property,Plant & Equipment ₹ 3,00,000. 50% of Total Property,Plant & Equipment are found undervalued by 50% of market value and 50% of the remaining are found overvalued by 50% of market value.
10% Investments: [Face Value ₹ 80,000] ₹ 1,00,000. Of the Investments 10% is trade and the balance non–trade. All trade Investments are to be valued at 10% below cost.
10% Debentures [60% Debentures are to be redeemed prior to valuation of Shares] ₹ 20,00,000
Average Profits before tax : ₹ 25,00,000. With effect from the next year Rate of Income Tax : 25% and an increase in manager remuneration ₹ 2,20,000 p.a.
Normal Rate of Expectation is 9%.

SOLUTION

Fair Value of an Equity Share = (Net Assets Value + Earning Yield Based Value)/2

NET ASSETS VALUE

4,00,000 Equity Shares of ₹ 10 each,₹ 8 paid up	32,00,000
7,00,000 Equity Shares of ₹ 5 each fully called up (Calls–in–arrears @₹ 2 on 2,00,000 shares)	31,00,000
Notional Uncalled Call [4,00,000 x ₹ 2]	8,00,000
Notional Unpaid Call [2,00,000 x ₹ 2]	4,00,000
Reserves & Surplus	73,76,000
Profit on Revaluation of PPE [3,00,000 x 50% x 100%]	1,50,000
Loss on Revaluation of PPE [3,00,000 x 50% x 50% x 1/3]	(25,000)
Loss on Revaluation of Trade Investments[1,00,000 x 10% x 10%]	(1,000)
Net Assets for Equity Shareholders	150,00,000
Total Equivalent No. of Equity Shares of ₹ 10 each [4,00,000 (of ₹ 10 each) + 3,50,000 (of ₹ 5 each)]	7,50,000
Value of an Equivalent Equity Share of ₹ 10 each[150,00,000/ 7,50,000]	₹ 20
Value of an Equity Share (₹ 8 paid up) [₹ 20 – ₹ 2]	₹ 18
Value of an Equity Share (₹ 5 paid up) [₹ 20 × 5/10]	₹ 10
Value of an Equity Share (₹ 3 paid up) [₹ 10 – ₹ 2]	₹ 8

EARNING YIELD BASED VALUE

Particulars	₹
Average Profits	25,00,000
Add: Interest on Debentures [(60% of ₹ 20,00,000)*10%]	1,20,000
Less: Increase in manager remuneration p.a.	(2,20,000)
Future Maintainable Profits before Tax	24,00,000
Less: Tax @ 25%	(6,00,000)
Future Maintainable Profits after Tax for Shareholders	18,00,000
Less: Pref. Dividend [10,00,000 * 9.9%]	(99,000)
Future Maintainable Profits after Tax for Equity Shareholders	17,01,000

Step 3: Average Rate of Earnings = $\frac{\text{Average Earnings}}{\text{Total Paid–up Value of all Equity Shares}}$ x 100

= ₹ 17,01,000/₹ 63,00,000 × 100 = 27%

Step 4: Value of an Equity Share = $\frac{\text{Average Rate of Earnings}}{\text{Normal Rate of Expectation}}$ x *Paid–up Value of an Equity Share*

Value of an equity share (₹ 10 paid up) = 27/9 × ₹ 10 = ₹ 30

Value of an equity share (₹ 8 paid up) = 27/9 × ₹ 8 = ₹ 24

Value of an equity share (₹ 5 paid up) = 27/9 × ₹ 5 = ₹ 15

Value of an equity share (₹ 3 paid up) = 27/9 × ₹ 3 = ₹ 9

Step 5: Fair Value of an Equity Share = (Net Assets Value + Yield Based Value)/2

Fair Value of an Equity Share (₹ 10 paid up) = (₹ 20 + ₹ 30)/2 = ₹ 25

Fair Value of an Equity Share (₹ 8 paid up) = (₹ 18 + ₹ 24)/2 = ₹ 21

Fair Value of an Equity Share (₹ 5 paid up) = (₹ 10 + ₹ 15)/2 = ₹ 12.50

Fair Value of an Equity Share (₹ 3 paid up) = (₹ 8 + ₹ 9)/2 = ₹ 8.50

ILLUSTRATION 22

Given below are the extracts from the Balance Sheet of CAMHH Ltd. as on 31.03.2023:

Particulars	₹
Equity Share Capital (₹ 10 each) ₹ 10 paid–up per share	3,00,000
Equity Share Capital (₹ 10 each) ₹ 5 paid–up per share	2,00,000
15 % Preference Share Capital (₹ 100)	1,00,000
Reserve	3,00.000
Trade Creditors	2,00,000
Property,Plant & Equipment	6,00,000
Current Assets	5,00,000

Profit and dividend in last several years were as under:

Year	***Profit (before Tax)*** ₹	***Equity Dividend Paid*** ₹
2022 –2023	3,20,000	18%

2021 –2022	2,50,000	15%
2020 –2021	2,20,000	12%

Property,Plant & Equipment are worth ₹ 10,00,000. Managerial remuneration is likely to go up by ₹ 60,000 p.a. Income tax may be provided at 25%. Equity shares(₹ 10 each) of companies in the same industry with dividend rate of 45% are quoted at ₹ 30.

Required: Find the most appropriate value of an equity share assuming that:

(a) Controlling interest is to be transferred.

(b) Only a few shares are to be transferred.

Ignore goodwill value, depreciation adjustment for revaluation.

SOLUTION

(a) Valuation of Controlling Interest

Method I: Earning Yield Basis

AVERAGE FUTURE MAINTAINABLE PROFITS FOR EQUITY SHAREHOLDERS

Year	***Profit*** ₹	***Weight***	***Product*** ₹
2022 –2023	3,20,000	3	9,60,000
2021 –2022	2,50,000	2	5,00,000
2020 –2021	2,20,000	1	2,20,000
		6	16,80,000

Average Profit = (16,80,000/6)	₹ 2,80,000
Less: Increase in Managerial remuneration	(60,000)
Profit before tax	2,20,000
Less: Tax @25%	(55,000)
Profit after Tax	1,65,000
Less: Preference Dividend	(15,000)
Future Maintainable Profit for Equity Share holders	1,50,000

Average Earning Rate = (₹ 1,50,000/₹ 5,00,000) × 100 = 30%

Normal Rate =(₹ 4.50/₹ 30) × 100 = 15%

Earning Yield Value = (Average Earning Rate/Normal Rate) × Paid up Value of an Equity Share

Value of ₹ 10 paid up Share = (30%/15%) × ₹10 = ₹ 20

Value of ₹ 5 paid up Share = (30%/15%) × ₹ 5 = ₹ 10

METHOD II: NET ASSET BASIS

Particulars		₹
Property,Plant & Equipment		10,00,000
Current Assets		5,00,000
Notional call on shares		2,00,000
Less: Trade Creditors		(2,00,000)

Less: Pref. Share Capital		(1,00,000)
Net Assets available for Equity Share holders		14,00,000
Equivalent No. of Equity Shares[30000 + 40000]		70,000
Value of Fully paid Share (₹ 14,00,000/70,000)		₹ 20
Value of Partly paid Share (₹ 20 – ₹ 5)		₹ 15

Fair Value of Fully Paid Share = (Net Asset Value + Yield Based Value)/2
= (₹ 20 + ₹ 20)/2 = ₹ 20

Fair Value of Partly Paid Share = (₹ 15 + ₹ 10)/2 = ₹ 12.50

Tutorial Note: The above solution is based upon the assumption that A Ltd. is a going concern and it is likely that it will call the unpaid part of share capital at a distant future and not immediately.

(B) VALUATION OF FEW SHARES

Step 1: Average Rate of Dividend

Year	*Rate of Dividend*	*Weight*	*Product*
2023	18	3	54
2022	15	2	30
2021	12	1	12
		6	96

Average Rate of Dividend = 96/6 = 16%.

Step 2: Dividend Yield Value = (Average Dividend Rate/Normal Rate) × Paid up Value of an Equity Share

Value of ₹ 10 paid–up share = 16%/45% × ₹ 10= ₹ 3.56

Value of ₹ 5 paid–up share = 16%/45% × ₹ 5 = ₹ 1.78

COMPREHENSIVE ILLUSTRATIONS

ILLUSTRATION 23

Given below are the extracts from the Balance Sheet of TULSIAN Ltd. as at 31st March, 2023:

Particulars	₹	₹
Equity Shares of ₹ 10 each fully paid up		10,00,000
Equity Shares of ₹ 10 each,₹ 8 paid up	16,00,000	
Less: Calls–in–arrears @ ₹ 2	(2,00,000)	14,00,000
Equity Shares of ₹ 5 each fully paid up		15,00,000
Equity Shares of ₹ 5 each,₹ 3 paid up	18,00,000	
Less: Calls–in–arrears @ ₹ 2	(1,00,000)	17,00,000
Equity Shares of ₹ 1 each fully paid up		5,00,000
27% Preference Shares of ₹ 100 each fully paid	10,00,000	
Less: Calls–in–arrears @ ₹ 20	(40,000)	9,60,000
Reserves & Surplus		16,00,000
10% Debentures [60% Debentures are to be redeemed prior to valuation of Shares]		10,00,000
Short–term Borrowings		25,00,000

Additional Information:

(a) Goodwill is found undervalued by ₹ 10,50,000. Property,Plant & Equipment are found undervalued by ₹ 15,00,000.Of the Investments (appear at ₹ 10,00,000 in Balance Sheet) 10% is trade and the balance non–trade. All trade Investments are to be valued at 10% below cost. Disputed Bonus claim of ₹ 1,29,000 not yet provided in the accounts for 2022–2023 is settled at ₹ 90,000. Debtors(appear at ₹ 25,00,000 in Balance Sheet) constitute 10% as irrecoverable. Inventories (Taken at 90% of market value) appear at ₹ 18,00,000 in Balance Sheet.

(b) Profits before tax: 2020–2021 : ₹ 24,00,000, 2021–2022: ₹ 34,00,000, 2022–2023: ₹ 30,40,000.

(c) With effect from the year 2023–2024 there will be an increase in manager remuneration p.a. ₹ 1,60,000 and the Rate of Tax will be 25%.

(d) Normal Rate of Expectation in the same industry: 12%.

(e) Ignore additional Depreciation on an increase in Property,Plant & Equipment.

Required: Calculate the Fair Value per share.

SOLUTION

VALUATION OF EQUITY SHARES ON NET ASSETS BASIS

Particulars	₹
Equity Shares of ₹ 10 each fully paid up	10,00,000
Equity Shares of ₹ 10 each, ₹ 8 paid–up	14,00,000
Equity Shares of ₹ 5 each fully paid up	15,00,000
Equity Shares of ₹ 5 each, ₹ 3 paid–up	17,00,000
Equity Shares of ₹ 1 each fully paid up	5,00,000
Notional Uncalled Call on Partly–paid–up Shares of ₹ 8 paid–up [2,00,000 × ₹ 2]	4,00,000
Notional Uncalled Call on Partly–paid–up Shares of ₹ 3 paid–up [6,00,000 × ₹ 2]	12,00,000
Calls–in–arrears on Equity Shares of ₹ 8 paid–up [1,00,000 × ₹ 2]	2,00,000
Calls–in–arrears on Equity Shares of ₹ 3 paid–up [50,000 × ₹ 2]	1,00,000
Reserves & Surplus	16,00,000
Profit on Revaluation of Property,Plant & Equipment	15,00,000
Profit on Revaluation of Goodwill	10,50,000
Loss on Revaluation of Trade Investments [10% of 1,00,000]	(10,000)
Profit on Revaluation of Inventories	2,00,000
Unrecorded Bonus	(90,000)
Bad Debts	(2,50,000)
Net Assets for Equity Shareholders	120,00,000
Total Equivalent Number of Equity Shares of ₹ 10 each [1,00,000 (₹ 10 each) + 2,00,000 (₹ 8 paid up) +1,50,000 (₹ 5) + 3,00,000 (₹ 3 paid up)+ 50,000 (₹ 1)]	8,00,000
Value per Equity Share of ₹ 10 each fully paid up [120,00,000/8,00,000]	15
Value per Equity Share of ₹ 10 each, ₹ 8 paid–up = ₹ 15 – ₹ 2	13

Value per Equity Share of ₹ 10 each, ₹ 6 paid–up = ₹ 13 – ₹ 2	11
Value per Equity Share of ₹ 5 each = ₹ 15 * 5/10	7.50
Value per Equity Share of ₹ 5 each, ₹ 3 paid–up = ₹ 7.50 – ₹ 2	5.50
Value per Equity Share of ₹ 5 each, ₹ 1 paid–up = ₹ 5.50 – ₹ 2	3.50
Value per Equity Share of ₹ 1 each fully paid–up = ₹ 15 * 1/10	1.5

VALUATION OF EQUITY SHARES ON EARNING YIELD BASIS

Step 1: Earnings available for Equity Shareholders

Adjusted Earnings for 2022–2023 = ₹ 30,40,000 + 2,00,000 – 90,000 – 2,50,000 = ₹ 29,00,000

Average Earnings = [(₹ 24,00,000 + ₹ 34,00,000 + ₹ 29,00,000)/3]	₹ 29,00,000
Add: Interest on Debentures [(60% of ₹ 10,00,000)*10%]	60,000
Less: Increase in manager remuneration p.a.	(1,60,000)
Earnings Before Tax [EBT]	28,00,000
Less: Tax @ 25%	7,00,000
Earnings After Tax [EAT]	21,00,000
Less: Preference Dividend	(2,70,000)
Earnings available for Equity Shareholders	₹ 18,30,000

Step 2: Total Paid–up Value of all Equity Shares

= ₹ 10 lacs + ₹ 14 lacs + ₹ 15 lacs + ₹ 17 lacs + ₹ 5 lacs = ₹ 61 lacs

Step 3: Average Rate of Earnings = $\frac{\text{Average Earnings}}{\text{Total Paid–up Value of all Equity Shares}} \times 100$

= (₹ 18,30,000/₹ 61,00,000) x 100= 30%

Step 4: Normal Rate of Expectation in the same industry = 12%

Step 5: Yield Value of an Equity Share = $\frac{\text{Average Rate of Earnings}}{\text{Normal Rate of Expectation}} \times$ *Paid–up Value of an Equity Share*

Value of a Share of ₹ 10 paid–up = 30/12 × ₹ 10 = ₹ 25

Value of a Share of ₹ 8 paid–up = 30/12 × ₹ 8 = ₹ 20

Value of a Share of ₹ 6 paid–up = 30/12 × ₹ 6 = ₹ 15

Value of a Share of ₹ 5 paid–up = 30/12 × ₹ 5 = ₹ 12.50

Value of a Share of ₹ 3 paid–up = 30/12 × ₹ 3 = ₹ 7.50

Value of a Share of ₹ 1 paid–up = 30/12 × ₹ 1 = ₹ 2.50

VALUATION OF EQUITY SHARES ON FAIR VALUE BASIS

Fair Value of an Equity Share = (Net Assets Value + Yield Based Value)/2

Fair Value of an Equity Share (₹ 10 paid up) = (₹ 15 + ₹ 25)/2 = ₹ 20

Fair Value of an Equity Share (₹ 8 paid up) = (₹ 13 + ₹ 20)/2 = ₹ 16.50

Fair Value of an Equity Share (₹ 6 paid up) = (₹ 11 + ₹ 15)/2 = ₹ 13

Fair Value of an Equity Share (₹ 5 paid up) = (₹ 7.50 + ₹ 12.50)/2 = ₹ 10

Fair Value of an Equity Share (₹ 3 paid up) = (₹ 5.50 + ₹ 7.50)/2 = ₹ 6.50

Fair Value of an Equity Share (of ₹ 5 each, ₹ 1 paid up) = (₹ 3.50 + ₹ 2.50)/2 = ₹ 3

Fair Value of an Equity Share (₹ 1 fully paid up) = (₹ 1.50 + ₹ 2.50)/2 = ₹ 2

ILLUSTRATION 24

Given below are the extracts from the Balance Sheet of N Ltd. as at 31st March, 2023:

Particulars	₹
4,00,000 Equity shares of ₹ 10 each fully paid	40,00,000
13.5% Redeemable Preference Shares of ₹ 100 each fully paid	20,00,000
Reserves & Surplus	17,20,000
Non–Current Liabilities	12,00,000
Current Liabilities	37,00,000
Goodwill	4,00,000
Property,Plant & Equipment(including Plant and machinery at ₹ 22,00,000)	74,00,000
Investments	16,00,000
Inventories	11,00,000
Trade Debtors	18,00,000
Bank Balance	3,20,000

Further information:

(a) Return on Capital Employed is 20% in similar businesses.

(b) Property,Plant & Equipment are worth 30% more than book value. Inventories are overvalued by ₹ 1,00, 000, Debtors constitute ₹ 20,000 as irrecoverable.

(c) Trade investments, which constitute 10% of the total investments are to be valued at 10% below cost. Trade investments were purchased on 1.4.2022. 50% of non–Trade Investments were purchased on 1.4.2021 and the rest on 1.4.2020. Non–Trade Investments yielded 15% return on cost. Non–Trade Investments are found undervalued by ₹ 1,95,724.

(d) In 2020–2021 new machinery costing ₹ 2,00,000 was purchased, but wrongly charged to revenue. This amount should be adjusted taking depreciation at 10% on reducing value method.

(e) In 2021–2022 furniture with a book value of ₹ 1,00,000 was sold for ₹ 60,000.

(f) For calculating goodwill two years purchase of super profits based on simple average profits of last four years are to be considered. Profits of last four years are as under: 2019–2020 ₹ 16,00,000, 2020–2021 ₹ 18,00,000, 2021–2022 ₹ 21,00,000, 2022–2023 ₹ 22,00,000.

(g) Depreciation on the increased value of assets (worth 30% more than book value) need not be considered. Depreciation on the additional value of only plant and machinery to be considered taking depreciation at 10% on reducing value method while calculating average adjusted profit.

Required: Calculate the Intrinsic Value of an equity share. *(Ignore Tax)*.

SOLUTION

VALUATION OF AN EQUITY SHARE ON NET ASSETS BASIS	₹
Value of Net Assets (As computed for Goodwill)	81,53,540
Non–trade investments [₹ 14,40,000 + ₹ 1,95,724]	16,35,724

Value of Goodwill [See Working Note]	2,10,736
Less: Preference Share Capital	(20,00,000)
Net Assets for Equity shareholders	80,00,000
Number of Equity Shares	4,00,000
Intrinsic Value of an Equity Share [C/D]	₹20

Working Notes:

(I) CAPITAL EMPLOYED

Particulars	₹	₹
A. Total Assets at Current Values:		
Property,Plant & Equipment		74,00,000
Machinery charged to revenue (₹ 2,00,000 – ₹ 20,000 – ₹ 18,000 – ₹16,200)		1,45,800
		75,45,800
Add: 30% Increase		22,63,740
		98,09,540
Trade Investments (₹ 16,00,000 × 10% × 90%)		1,44,000
Trade Debtors (₹ 18,00,000 – ₹ 20,000)		17,80,000
Inventories (₹ 11,00,000 – ₹ 1,00,000)		10,00,000
Bank balance		3,20,000
		1,30,53,540
B. *Less:* Non–Current Liabilities		12,00,000
Current Liabilities		37,00,000
		49,00,000
C. Capital Employed [A – B]		81,53,540

(II) FUTURE MAINTAINABLE PROFIT

Particulars	*2019–2020* ₹	*2020–2021* ₹	*2021–2022* ₹	*2022–2023* ₹
A. Profit given	16,00,000	18,00,000	21,00,000	22,00,000
B. *Add:* Capital expenditure of Machinery charged to revenue	—	2,00,000	—	—
C. *Add:* Loss on Sale of Furniture	—	—	40,000	—
D. *Less:* Depreciation on Machinery		(20,000)	(18,000)	(16,200)
Income from non–trade investments	—	(1,08,000)	(2,16,000)	(2,16,000)
Reduction in Value of Inventories	—	—	—	(1,00,000)
Bad Debts	—	—		(20,000)
E. Adjusted Profit	16,00,000	18,72,000	19,06,000	18,47,800
F. Total Adjusted Profit for four years				72,25,800
G. Average Profit (₹ 72,25,800/4)				18,06,450

H. *Less:* Depreciation at 10% on additional value of machinery (22,00,000 + 1,45,800) x 30/100 i.e. ₹ 7,03,740	(70,374)
I. Adjusted Average Profit	17,36,076

(iii) Normal Profit = 20% on ₹ 81,53,540 = ₹ 16,30,708

(iv) Super Profit = FMP – Normal Profit = ₹ 17,36,076 – ₹ 16,30,708 = ₹ 1,05,368

(v) Goodwill at 2 years' purchase of Super Profit = ₹ 1,05,368 × 2 = ₹ 2,10,736

ILLUSTRATION 25

Given below are the extracts from the Balance Sheet of BHARAT TULSIAN Ltd. as at 31st March, 2023:

Particulars		₹
5,000, Equity Shares of ₹ 100 each fully paid up		5,00,000
3,000, 13.2% Cum Preference Shares of ₹ 100 each, fully paid up		3,00,000
General Reserve		1,20,000
Profit and Loss A/c:		
Balance on 1.4.2022	1,20,000	
Profit including Investment Income of current year	4,80,000	
Less: Provision for Tax	(1,20,000)	4,80,000
Trade Creditors		2,10,000
Provision for Taxation		2,40,000
Property,Plant & Equipment		7,80,000
6% Government Securities at cost (Face value ₹ 2,00,000)		1,60,000
Trade Debtors		3,80,000
Inventories (Taken at 90% of market value)		4,50,000
Cash and Bank Balances		80,000

Additional information:

(a) The Property,Plant & Equipment are understated by ₹ 4,80,000 and have suffered a further depreciation of ₹ 2,00,000.

(b) Companies doing similar business as that of BHARAT TULSIAN Ltd. show a market return of 15% on Average Capital Employed.

(c) Profits after tax over the prior 3 years period have been increasing at the rate of ₹ 60,000 per annum.

(d) Goodwill is to be valued at 3 years' purchase of super profits.

Required: Calculate the Fair Value of an Equity Share assuming normal yield on net worth attributable to Equity Share holders is also 15%.

SOLUTION

(a) VALUATION OF AN EQUITY SHARE ON NET ASSETS BASIS	
A. Value of Net Assets (As computed for Goodwill)	16,90,000
B. Value of Goodwill [See Working Note]	2,53,500
C. 13.2% Cum Preference Share Capital	3,00,000

D. Net Assets for Equity shareholders(A + B – C)	16,43,500
E. Number of Equity Shares	5000
F. Value of an Equity Share [D/E]	₹ 328.70

(b) VALUATION OF AN EQUITY SHARE ON EARNING YIELD BASIS		
A. Future Maintainable Trading Profit for equity Share holders		₹
(a) Future maintainable Trading Profit (before tax)		4,14,666.7
(b) *Add:* Income from Non–trade Investments		12,000
(c) Future Maintainable Profit before Tax		4,26,666.7
(d) *Less:* Tax		(1,06,666.7)
(e) FMP after tax		3,20,000
(f) *Less:* Preference Dividend @ 13.2% on ₹ 3,00,000		(39,600)
(g) FMP for Equity Shareholders		2,84,000
B. Net Assets for Equity Shareholders		16,43,500
C. Average Rate of Earning = ₹ 2,84,000/₹ 16,43,500 × 100 = 17.28%		
D. Earning Yield based value per share = (17.28%/15%) × ₹ 100 = ₹ 115.20		

(c) Fair Value= (Net Asset Value + Yield based Value)/2 = (₹ 328.70 + ₹115.20)/2 = ₹ 221.95

Working Notes: *Calculation of Goodwill.*

Tax Rate = ₹ 1,20,000/ ₹ 4,80,000 = 0.25 or 25%

STEP 1: PAST ADJUSTED PROFIT BEFORE TAX

Particulars	***2020–2021*** ₹	***2021–2022*** ₹	***2022–2023*** ₹
Profits after tax(PAT)	2,40,000 (3,00,000 – 60,000)	3,00,000 (3,60,000 – 60,000)	3,60,000
Profits before tax(PAT/75%)	3,20,000	4,00,000	4,80,000
Less: Incomes from non–trade investment	(12,000)	(12,000)	(12,000)
Past Adjusted Profits before tax	3,08,000	3,88,000	4,68,000

STEP 2: AVERAGE PAST ADJUSTED PROFITS [WEIGHTED AVERAGE SINCE PAST ADJUSTED PROFITS SHOW RISING TREND]

Year ***A***	***Profits*** ***B***	***Weights*** ***C***	***Weighted Profits*** ***D = B * C***
2020–2021	3,08,000	1	3,08,000
2021–2022	3,88,000	2	7,76,000
2022–2023	4,68,000	3	14,04,000
Total		6	24,88,000

Weighted Average of Past Adjusted Profits = Total Weighted Profits/Total of Weights

= ₹ 24,88,000/6 = ₹ 4,14,666.7

Step 3: Future Maintainable Profits after tax = Average Past Adjusted Profits – Tax

= ₹ 4,14,666.7 – 1,03,666.7 = ₹ 3,11,000

STEP 4: AVERAGE CAPITAL EMPLOYED

		₹
A.	Total Assets at their current values:	
	Property,Plant & Equipment [7,80,000 + 4,80,000 – 2,00,000]	10,60,000
	Inventories [₹ 4,50,000 + 50,000]	5,00,000
	Trade Debtors	3,80,000
	Cash and Bank Balances	80,000
	Total Assets	20,20,000
B.	*Less:* Outsiders' Liabilities:	
	Trade Creditors	2,10,000
	Provision for taxation	1,20,000
	Total	3,30,000
C.	Closing Capital Employed (A – B)	16,90,000
D.	*Less:* Half of the current year's past adjusted profits after tax (including after tax Incomes from Non–trade Investment) [50% of [(₹ 4,68,000 + 12,000) – 25%]	1,80,000
E.	Average Capital Employed	15,10,000

Step 5: Normal Profit = Average Capital Employed * Normal Rate of Return

= ₹ 15,10,000 * 0.15 = ₹ 2,26,500

Step 6: Super Profits = Future Maintainable Profits – Normal Profit

= ₹ 3,11,000 – ₹ 2,26,500 = ₹ 84,500

Step 7: Goodwill =₹ 84,500 × 3 = ₹ 2,53,500

ILLUSTRATION 26

Given below are the extracts from the Balance Sheet of TULSIAN Ltd. for the year ended on 31st March, 2021, 2022 and 2023:

Particulars	*2020 –2021*	*2021 –2022*	*2022 –2023*
	₹	₹	₹
Equity Share Capital (Shares of ₹ 10 each)	32,00,000	32,00,000	32,00,000
General Reserve	24,00,000	28,00,000	32,00,000
Profit & Loss A/c	2,80,000	3,20,000	4,80,000
Current Liabilities	12,00,000	16,00,000	20,00,000
Goodwill	20,00,000	16,00,000	12,00,000
Property,Plant & Equipment	28,00,000	32,00,000	32,00,000
Inventories	20,00,000	24,00,000	28,00,000
Trade Debtors	40,000	3,20,000	8,80,000
Bank balance	2,40,000	4,00,000	8,00,000

Additional Information:

	2020 –2021 ₹	2021 –2022 ₹	2022 –2023 ₹
Current Valuation of Property, Plant & Equipment	36,00,000	40,00,000	44,00,000
Current Valuation of Inventories	24,00,000	28,00,000	32,00,000
Net Profit (including opening balance after writing off depreciation, goodwill, tax provision and transfer to General Reserve)	8,40,000	12,40,000	16,40,000

(b) Capital employed in the business at market value at the beginning of 2020–2021 was ₹ 73,20,000 which included the cost of goodwill. The normal annual return on average capital employed in this line of business is 12.5%.

(c) The balance in the General Reserve on 1st April, 2020 was ₹ 20 lakhs.

(d) The goodwill shown on 31.3.2021 was purchased on 1.4.2020 for ₹ 20 lakhs on which date the balance in the Profit & Loss account was ₹ 2,40,000.

(e) Goodwill is to be valued at 4 years' purchase of Super Profit (Simple Average Method).

Required: Find out the Average Capital Employed in each year. Find out the Fair Value of a Share.

SOLUTION

1. AVERAGE CAPITAL EMPLOYED AT THE END OF EACH YEAR

Particulars	*2020 –2021* ₹	*2021 –2022* ₹	*2022 –2023* ₹
A. Total Assets at their Current Values:			
*Goodwill	20,00,000	16,00,000	12,00,000
Property, Plant & Equipment	36,00,000	40,00,000	44,00,000
Inventories	24,00,000	28,00,000	32,00,000
Trade Receivable	40,000	3,20,000	8,80,000
Bank Balance	2,40,000	4,00,000	8,00,000
Total Assets	82,80,000	91,20,000	104,80,000
B. *Less:* Outsiders' Liabilities	(12,00,000)	(16,00,000)	(20,00,000)
C. Closing Capital Employed (A – B)	70,80,000	75,20,000	84,80,000
D. Opening Capital employed	73,20,000	70,80,000	75,20,000
G. Average Capital Employed [(C + D)/2]	72,00,000	73,00,000	80,00,000

* Since the goodwill has been purchased, it is taken as a part of capital employed.

2. FUTURE MAINTAINABLE PROFIT & SUPER PROFIT

Particulars	*2020 –2021* ₹	*2021 –2022* ₹	*2022 –2023* ₹
Net Profit (Including Opening Balance)	8,40,000	12,40,000	16,40,000
Less: Opening Balance	(2,40,000)	(2,80,000)	(3,20,000)
Transfer to General Reserve	4,00,000	4,00,000	4,00,000
Add: Under Valuation of Closing Stock	4,00,000	4,00,000	4,00,000

Less: Under Valuation of Opening Stock	—	(4,00,000)	(4,00,000)
Add: Goodwill written off	—	4,00,000	4,00,000
Future Maintainable Profit	14,00,000	17,60,000	21,20,000
Less: 12.50% Normal Return of average capital	(9,00,000)	(9,12,500)	(10,00,000)
Super Profit	5,00,000	8,47,500	11,20,000

3. **Average Super Profit** =(₹ 5,00,000 + ₹ 8,47,500 + ₹ 11,20,000) / 3 = ₹ 8,22,500
4. **Goodwill at five years' Purchase** = ₹ 8,22,500 × 4 = ₹ 32,90,000

5. VALUE OF SHARE ON NET ASSETS BASIS

Net Assets excluding Goodwill	₹ 84,80,000
Goodwill	₹ 32,90,000
A. Total Net Assets	₹ 117,70,000
B. Number of Equity Shares	3,20,000
C. Value of an Equity Share	₹ 36.78

6. VALUE OF SHARE ON YIELD BASIS

A. Average Future Maintainable Profits [(14 + 17.6 + 21.2)/3]	₹ 17,60,000
B. *Less:* Transfer to Reserve	₹ 4,00,000
C. Profit available for Equity Share holders	₹ 13,60,000
C. Average Rate of Earning = (₹ 13,60,000/₹ 32,00,000) × 100 = 42.5%	
D. Earning Yield based value per share = (42.5%/12.5%) × ₹ 10 = ₹ 34	

7.**Fair Value of Share** = (Net Asset value + Yield based Value)/2

= (₹ 36.78 + ₹ 34)/2 = ₹ 35.39

SOLVED PROBLEMS

Intrinsic Value of an Equity Share

PROBLEM 1

From the following data, compute the 'Net Assets' Value of each category of equity shares:

10,000 'A' Equity shares of ₹ 100 each, fully paid

10,000 'B' Equity shares of ₹ 100 each, ₹ 80 paid

10,000 'C' Equity shares of ₹ 100 each, ₹ 50 paid

Retained Earnings ₹ 9,00,000

SOLUTION

	₹
Paid up value of 'A' equity shares [10,000 × ₹100]	10,00,000
Paid up value of 'B' equity shares [10,000 x ₹ 80]	8,00,000
Paid up value of 'C' equity shares [10,000 x ₹ 50]	5,00,000

	Retained earnings	9,00,000
	Add: Notional calls (10,000 × ₹ 20 + 10,000 × ₹ 50)	7,00,000
A	Net Assets for Equity shareholders	39,00,000
B	Total Equivalent No. of Equity Shares of ₹ 10 each [10,000 (of ₹ 100 each) + 10,000 (of ₹ 80 each)+ 10,000 (of ₹ 50 each)]	30,000
C	Value of each equity share of ₹ 100 fully paid up [₹ 39,00,000/30,000]	₹ 130
D	Value of 'B' equity shares of ₹ 100 each, ₹ 80 paid up [₹ 130 – ₹ 20]	₹ 110
E	Value of 'C' Equity shares of ₹ 100 each, ₹ 50 paid up [₹ 130 – ₹ 50]	₹ 80

PROBLEM 2

Given below are the extracts from the Balance Sheet of CAS Ltd. as on 31.03.2023:

Particulars	₹
1,50,000 Equity Shares of ₹ 10 each	15,00,000
2,00,000 Equity Shares of ₹ 10 each, ₹ 6 paid–up	12,00,000
15% Cum. Pref. Shares	6,00,000
Profit and Loss A/c	(13,00,000)
18% Term Loan	14,00,000
Trade Creditors	8,00,000
Property,Plant & Equipment	22,00,000
Investments	4,00,000
Inventories	8,00,000
Debtors	4,00,000
Cash and Bank	4,00,000

Other Information: Current Cost of Property, Plant & Equipment ₹ 37,20,000 and Inventories ₹ 10,00,000. Investments could fetch only ₹ 1,00,000. 50% Debtors are doubtful. Preference dividends were in arrear for the last three years.

Required: Calculate the Intrinsic Value per share. *[Ignore Tax]*

SOLUTION

STATEMENT SHOWING THE VALUATION OF EQUITY SHARES

			₹
A.	Total Assets at their current values:		
	Property,Plant & Equipment		37,20,000
	Investments		1,00,000
	Inventories		10,00,000
	Debtors [₹ 4,00,000 –50%]		2,00,000
	Cash and Bank		4,00,000
	Add: Notional Unpaid Amount @ ₹ 4 on 2,00,000 equity shares of ₹ 6 paid up		8,00,000
			62,20,000

B. *Less:* Outside Liabilities		
Trade Creditors	8,00,000	
18% Term Loan	14,00,000	22,00,000
C. Net Assets for Shareholders		40,20,000
D. *Less:* Claims of Preference Shareholders		
15% Cumulative Pref. Shares	6,00,000	
Arrears of Pref. Dividend	2,70,000	8,70,000
E. Total Net Assets available for Equity Shareholders [C – D]		31,50,000
F. Number of Equity Shares		3,50,000
G. Value per fully paid–up Equity Share = ₹ 31,50/₹ 3.50 = ₹ 9		
H. Value per partly paid–up Equity Share = ₹ 9 – ₹ 4 = ₹ 5		

PROBLEM 3

Given below are the extracts from the Balance Sheet of CAMHG Ltd. as at 31st March, 2023:

Particulars	₹
6,000 Equity Shares of ₹ 100 each fully paid–up	6,00,000
Profit and Loss Account	1,10,000
Current and Non–Current Liabilities	1,80,000
Property,Plant & Equipment	3,70,000
Inventories	3,00,000
Trade Debtors	1,60,000
Bank	60,000

The net profits of the company, after deducting usual working expenses but before providing for taxation, were as:2020–2021 ₹ 2,22,000, 2021–2022 ₹ 2,40,000, 2022–2023 ₹ 2,20,000

On 31st March, 2023, Property,Plant & Equipment were found undervalued by ₹ 80,000. Trade Debtors, on the same date, included ₹ 10,000 as irrecoverable. Having regard to nature of the business, a 10% return, on net tangible capital invested, is considered reasonable. Valuation of goodwill may be based on three years' purchase of annual super profits. Depreciation on Property,Plant & Equipment—5%. The income–tax rate is to be assumed at 25%.

Required: Calculate the Value the company's share.

SOLUTION

STEP 1: CAPITAL EMPLOYED

	₹
Assets as per revaluation:	
Property,Plant & Equipment [₹ 3,70,000 + ₹ 80,000]	4,50,000
Inventories	3,00,000
Trade Debtors [₹ 1,60,000 – ₹ 10,000]	1,50,000
Bank	60,000
Less: Current and Non–Current Liabilities	(1,80,000)
	7,80,000

STEP 2: SUPER PROFITS

2020–2021	2,22,000	
2021–2022	2,40,000	
2022–2023 (₹ 2,20,000 – ₹ 10,000)	2,10,000	
Total Profits	6,72,000	
A. Average Profits (₹ 6,72,000/3)		2,24,000
B. *Less:* Depreciation on Increase in value of Fixed Assets		(4,000)
C. FMP Before Tax		2,20,000
D. *Less:** Income tax [@ 25% of (2,20,000 + 4,000)]		(56,000)
E. Future Maintainable Profit after tax		1,64,000
F. Normal Return on Capital employed @ 10% on ₹ 7,80,000		78,000
G. Super Profit [FMP – NP]		86,000

***Note:** Additional Depreciation on Increase in value of PPE is not deductible for tax purposes.

Step 3: Value of Goodwill = Super Profit × 3 = ₹ 86,000 × 3 = ₹ 2,58,000

STEP 4: VALUATION OF SHARES

Particulars	
Valuation of other Net Assets	₹ 7,80,000
Goodwill	2,58,000
A. Net Assets for Equity Share holders	10,38,000
B. No. of Equity Shares	6,000
C. Value per Share (A/B)	173

PROBLEM 4

Given below are the extracts from the Balance Sheet of Bat. Ltd. as at 31st March 2023.

Particulars	₹
3,00,000 Equity Share of ₹ 10 each full paid	30,00,000
12.5% Redeemable Preference Shares of ₹ 100 each fully paid	20,00,000
Reserves & Surplus	17,00,000
Non–Current Liabilities	10,00,000
Current Liabilities	30,00,000
Goodwill	3,00,000
Property,Plant & Equipment(including Plant and machinery at ₹ 22,00,000)	52,00,000
Investments	16,00,000
Inventories	12,00,000
Trade Debtors	20,00,000
Bank Balance	4,00,000

Additional Information:

(a) Property,Plant & Equipment are worth 20% more than value. Inventories is overvalued by ₹ 1,00,000. Debtors constitute ₹ 40,000 as irrecoverable. Trade investments, which constitute 10% of the total investments are to be valued at 10% below cost.

(b) Trade investments were purchased on 1.4.2022. 50% of non–trade investments were purchased on 1.4.2021 and the rest on 1.4.2022. Non–trade investments yield 15% return on cost.

(c) In 2021–2022, Furniture with a book value of ₹ 1,00,000 was sold for ₹ 60,000. This loss should be treated as non–recurring or extraordinary item for the purpose of calculating adjusted average profit.

(d) In 2020–2021, new machinery costing ₹ 2,00,000 was purchased but wrongly charged to revenue. This amount should be adjusted taking depreciation at 10% on reducing value method.

(e) Return on Capital employed is 20% in similar business.

(f) For calculating goodwill two years' purchase of super profits based on simple average profits of last four years are to be considered. Profits of last four years are as under: 2019–2020 ₹ 13,00,000, 2020–2021 ₹ 14,00,000, 2021–2022 ₹ 16,10,000, 2022–2023 ₹ 18,00,000.

(h) Depreciation on the increased value of assets (worth 20% more than book value) need not be considered. Depreciation on the additional value of only plant and machinery to be considered taking depreciation at 10% on reducing value method while calculating average adjusted profit.

Required: Calculate the Intrinsic Value of the equity share.(Ignore Income Tax).

SOLUTION

VALUATION OF AN EQUITY SHARE ON NET ASSETS BASIS	
Value of Net Assets (As computed for Goodwill)	60,18,960
Non–trade investments	14,40,000
Value of Goodwill [See Working Note]	4,14,484
Less: Preference Share Capital	(20,00,000)
Net Assets for Equity shareholders	58,73,444
Number of Equity Shares	3,00,000
Intrinsic Value of an Equity Share [C/D]	₹ 19.59

Working Notes:

(I) CAPITAL EMPLOYED

Particulars	₹
A. Total Assets at Current Values:	
Property,Plant & Equipment	52,00,000
Machinery charged to revenue (₹ 2,00,000 – ₹ 20,000– ₹ 18,000 – ₹16,200)	1,45,800
	53,45,800
Add: 20% Appreciation	10,69,160
Trade Investments (₹ 16,00,000 × 10% × 90%)	1,44,000
Debtors (₹ 20,00,000 – ₹ 40,000)	19,60,000
Inventories (₹ 12,00,000 – ₹ 1,00,000)	11,00,000
Bank Balance	4,00,000
	1,00,18,960

B. *Less:* **Outside Liabilities:**	
Non–Current Liabilities	(10,00,000)
Current Liabilities	(30,00,000)
C. Capital Employed	60,18,960

(ii) Future Maintainable Profit

CALCULATION OF AVERAGE ADJUSTED PROFIT

	Particulars	*2019–2020* ₹	*2020–2021* ₹	*2021–2022* ₹	*2022–2023* ₹
A.	Profit	13,00,000	14,00,000	16,10,000	18,00,000
B.	*Add:* Capital Expenditure of Machinery Charged to revenue	—	2,00,000	—	—
	Loss on sale of furniture	—	—	40,000	—
C.	*Less:* Depreciation on machinery	—	(20,000)	(18,000)	(16,200)
	Income from non–trade investments	—	—	(1,08,000)	(2,16,000)
	Reduction in the value of Inventories	—	—	—	(1,00,000)
	Bad debts	—	—	—	(40,000)
D.	Adjusted Post Profit [A + B – C]	13,00,000	15,80,000	15,24,000	14,27,800
E.	Total adjusted Profit for four years				58,31,800
F.	Average Profit (₹ 58,31,800/4)				14,57,950
	Less: Depreciation at 10% on Additional Value of Machinery (22,00,000 + 1,45,800) × 20% × 10%				(46,916)
H.	Average Adjusted Profit [F – G]				14,11,034

(iii) Normal Profit = 20% of ₹ 60,18,960 = ₹ 12,03,792

(iv) Super Profit = Average Adjusted Profit – Normal Profit

= ₹ 14,11,034 – ₹ 12,03,792 = ₹ 2,07,242

(v) Goodwill = 2 years purchase of super profit = ₹ 2,07,424 × 2 = ₹ 4,14,484

Fair Value of an Equity Share

PROBLEM 5

Given below are the extracts from the Balance Sheet of CEE R Limited as on 31st March, 2023:

Particulars	₹
1,00,000 Equity Shares of ₹ 10 each	10,00,000
10,000, 12% Preference Shares of ₹ 100 each	10,00,000
Reserves & Surplus	7,80,000
15% Debentures	10,00,000
Creditors	8,00,000
Goodwill	5,00,000

Property,Plant & Equipment	25,00,000
10% Non–Trade Investments[[Nominal Value ₹ 5,00,000 and Market Value ₹ 5,20,000]	4,80,000
Current Assets	11,00,000

Additional Information:

(a) Assets are revalued as: Property, Plant & Equipments ₹ 50,00,000,Current Assets ₹ 9,10,000

(b) Average Profits before tax : ₹ 12,00,000 and rate of tax being 25%.

(c) Normal dividend expected on equity shares is 8% while fair return on closing capital employed is 10%.

(d) Goodwill may be valued at three year's purchase of super profits.

Required: Ascertain the Value of each equity share under Fair Value Method.

SOLUTION

STEP 1. CAPITAL EMPLOYED

Property,Plant & Equipment	₹ 50,00,000
Current Assets	9,10,000
Creditors	(8,00,000)
Debentures	(10,00,000)
Capital Employed	41,10,000

Step 2: Actual Profit = Average Profit – Income from Investments – Tax

= 12,00,000 – 50,000 – 2,87,500 = ₹ 8,62,500

Step 3: Normal Profit = 10% of ₹ 41,10,000 = ₹ 4,11,000

Step 4: Super Profit = Actual Profit – Normal Profit = ₹ 8,62,500 – ₹ 4,11,000 = ₹ 4,51,500

Step 5: Goodwill = ₹ 4,51,500 × 3 = ₹ 13,54,500

Step 6: Net Assets for Equity Shareholders = Capital Employed + Goodwill + Investment – Preference Share Capital

= ₹ (41,10,000 + 13,54,500 + 5,20,000 – 10,00,000) = ₹ 49,84,500

Step 7: Intrinsic Value per Share = ₹ 49,84,500/1,00,000 = ₹ 49.845

Step 8. Profit for Equity Shareholders = ₹ 12,00,000 – 25%(Tax) – ₹ 1,20,000(Pref Dividend) = ₹ 7,80,000

Step 9: Earning Yield based Value per Share

Average Earning Rate = (Profit for Equity shareholders /Paid–up Equity Capital) × 100

= (₹ 7,80,000/10,00,000) × 100 = 78%

Earning Yield based Value per Share = (78%/8%) × ₹ 10 = ₹ 97.50

Step 10: Fair Value of Equity Share

(Intrinsic Value + Earning Yield Value)/2 = (₹ 49.845 + ₹ 97.50)/2 = ₹ 73.6725

MULTIPLE CHOICE QUESTIONS

1. Intrinsic Value of an Equity Share can be calculated with the help of:
   (a) Net Assets for valuation of Equity Shares / Number of Equity Shares
   (b) (Average Rate of Earnings / Normal Rate of Earnings) x Paid–up Value of an Equity Share
   (c) (Average Rate of Dividend / Normal Rate of Dividend) x Paid–up Value of an Equity Share
   (d) (Intrinsic Value of an Equity Share + Earning Yield Value of an Equity Share)/2
   (e) Capitalised Value of Future Maintainable Profits / Number of Equity Shares
2. Earning Yield Value of an Equity Share can be calculated with the help of:
   (a) Net Assets for valuation of Equity Shares / Number of Equity Shares
   (b) (Average Rate of Earnings / Normal Rate of Earnings) x Paid–up Value of an Equity Share
   (c) (Average Rate of Dividend / Normal Rate of Dividend) x Paid–up Value of an Equity Share
   (d) (Intrinsic Value of an Equity Share + Earning Yield Value of an Equity Share)/2
   (e) Capitalised Value of Future Maintainable Profits / Number of Equity Shares
   (f) both (b) and (e)
3. Dividend Yield Value of an Equity Share can be calculated with the help of:
   (a) Net Assets for valuation of Equity Shares / Number of Equity Shares
   (b) (Average Rate of Earnings / Normal Rate of Earnings) x Paid–up Value of an Equity Share
   (c) (Average Rate of Dividend / Normal Rate of Dividend) x Paid–up Value of an Equity Share
   (d) (Intrinsic Value of an Equity Share + Earning Yield Value of an Equity Share)/2
   (e) Capitalised Value of Future Maintainable Profits / Number of Equity Shares
   (f) both (c) and (e)
4. Fair Value of an Equity Share can be calculated with the help of:
   (a) Net Assets for valuation of Equity Shares / Number of Equity Shares
   (b) (Average Rate of Earnings / Normal Rate of Earnings) x Paid–up Value of an Equity Share
   (c) (Average Rate of Dividend / Normal Rate of Dividend) x Paid–up Value of an Equity Share
   (d) (Intrinsic Value of an Equity Share + Earning Yield Value of an Equity Share)/2
   (e) Capitalised Value of Future Maintainable Profits / Number of Equity Shares
   (f) (Intrinsic Value of an Equity Share + Dividend Yield Value of an Equity Share)/2
5. Intrinsic Value of an Equity Share is also known as:
   (a) Net Assets Value
   (b) Assets backing Value
   (c) Break-up Value/ Liquidating Value
   (d) All of the above
6. Fair Value of an Equity Share is also known as:
   (a) Average Value
   (b) Mean Value
   (c) Break-up Value/ Liquidating Value
   (d) Both (a) & (b)

VERY SHORT ANSWER TYPE QUESTIONS

1. Briefly explain the following:
   (a) Net Assets Value of Shares
   (b) Earning Yield Value of Shares
   (c) Dividend Yield Value of Shares
   (d) Fair Value of Shares
2. State the type of companies for which each of the following method of valuation of shares is considered most suitable:
   (a) Net Assets Basis of valuation of shares
   (b) Earning Yield Basis of valuation of shares
   (c) Dividend Yield Basis of valuation of shares
   (d) Fair Value Basis of valuation of shares
3. State the method of valuation of shares which is considered most suitable for the following companies:
   (a) Liquidating companies
   (b) Going concern companies where a large block of shares is under transfer
   (c) Going concern companies where a small block of shares is under transfer
   (d) Going concern companies where Assets are also significant & where a Controlling Interest is under transfer.
4. Enumerate the following :
   (a) Two purposes of Valuation of a Share.
   (b) Two circumstances when the Valuation by a Valuer become necessary.
   (c) Two factors affecting the Valuation of Shares.
   (d) Three methods of valuation of Shares.
   (e) Steps involved in valuing the Equity Shares on Net Assets Basis.
   (f) Steps involved in valuing the Equity Shares on Earning Yield Basis.
   (g) Steps involved in valuing the Equity Shares on Dividend Yield Basis.
   (h) Steps involved in valuing the Equity Shares on Fair Value Basis.
5. Write the basic difference between the following : [1 Mark each]
   (a) Net Assets for Shareholders and Net Assets for Equity Shareholders
   (b) Net Assets for valuation of Goodwill and Net Assets for valuation of Equity Shares
   (c) Future Maintainable Profits for valuation of Goodwill and Future Maintainable Profits for Earning Yield valuation of Equity Shares

VERY SHORT ANSWER TYPE PRACTICAL QUESTIONS

1. Net Assets for Equity shareholders ₹ 92,00,000. Number of Equity Shares 4,00,000. Fair Value of an Equity Share ₹ 33. Calculate *Earning* Yield Based Value of an equity share.

[Ans ₹ 43 **]**

2. Capitalised Value of Future Maintainable Profits ₹ 30,00,000. Number of Equity Shares 2,00,000. Fair Value of an Equity Share ₹ 33. Calculate Net Assets for Equity shareholders.

[Ans ₹ 102 lakh**]**

3. 4,00,000 Equity Shares of ₹ 10 each,₹ 8 paid up. 7,00,000 Equity Shares of ₹ 5 each fully called up (Calls–in–arrears @₹ 2 on 2,00,000 shares). 10,000 9% Preference Shares of ₹100 each fully paid up. Normal Rate of Earnings—9%. Fair Value of an Equity Share (₹ 3 paid up) ₹ 8.50. Difference between *Earning Yield* Value and Net Assets Value is ₹ 1. Calculate *Earning Yield Value of an Equity Share*(₹3 paid up) and *Average Rate of Earnings.*

[Ans *Earning Yield Value of an Equity Share* (₹ 3 paid up) ₹ 9, *Average Rate of Earnings* = 27%]

4. 4,00,000 Equity Shares of ₹ 10 each,₹ 8 paid up. 7,00,000 Equity Shares of ₹ 5 each fully called up (Calls–in–arrears @₹ 2 on 2,00,000 shares). 10,000 9% Preference Shares of ₹100 each fully paid up. Normal Rate of Earnings—9%. Fair Value of an Equity Share (₹ 3 paid up) ₹ 8.50. Difference between *Earning Yield* Value and Net Assets Value is ₹ 1. Calculate Net Assets Value *of an Equity Share*(₹3 paid up) and *Average Rate of Earnings.*

[Ans Net Assets Value *of an Equity Share* (₹ 3 paid up) ₹ 8, *Average Rate of Earnings* = 27%]

5. 4,00,000 Equity Shares of ₹ 10 each,₹ 8 paid up. 7,00,000 Equity Shares of ₹ 5 each fully called up (Calls–in–arrears @₹ 2 on 2,00,000 shares). 10,000 9% Preference Shares of ₹100 each fully paid up. Normal Rate of Earnings—9%. Fair Value of an Equity Share (₹ 3 paid up) ₹ 8.50. Difference between *Earning Yield* Value and Net Assets Value is ₹ 1. Calculate Fair Value of an Equity Share *of* ₹ 10 each(₹ 8 paid up).

[Ans Net Assets Value (₹ 8 paid up) ₹ 18, *Average Rate of Earnings* = 27%, *Earning Yield* Value (₹ 8 paid up) ₹ 24, Fair Value (₹ 8 paid up) ₹ 21]

6. 4,00,000 Equity Shares of ₹ 10 each,₹ 8 paid up 7,00,000 Equity Shares of ₹ 5 each fully called up (Calls–in–arrears @₹ 2 on 2,00,000 shares). 10,000 9% Preference Shares of ₹100 each fully paid up. Normal Rate of Earnings—9%. Fair Value of an Equity Share (₹ 3 paid up) ₹ 8.50. Difference between *Earning* Yield Value and Net Assets Value is ₹ 1. Calculate Net Assets for Equity Shareholders and Expected FMP for Equity Shareholders.

[Ans Net Assets Value of an Equity Share *of* ₹ 10 each ₹ 20, Equivalent Number of Equity Shares of ₹ 10 each: 4,00,000 (₹ 10 each) + 3,50,000 (₹ 5) = 7,50,000, Net Assets = ₹ 150 lakh, Paid–up Value of all Equity Shares = ₹ 63,00,000 , *Average Rate of Earnings* = 27%, FMP = ₹ 17.01 lakh]

SHORT ANSWER TYPE PRACTICAL QUESTIONS

Calculation of Equivalent Number of Equity Shares of ₹ 10 each

1. From the following, Calculate the Equivalent Number of Equity Shares of ₹ 10 each:

Equity Shares of ₹ 10 each fully paid up	10,00,000
Equity Shares of ₹ 5 each fully paid up	15,00,000
Equity Shares of ₹ 1 each fully paid up	5,00,000
27% Preference Shares of ₹ 100 each fully paid	10,00,000

[Ans [1,00,000 (₹ 10 each) + 1,50,000 (₹ 5) + 50,000 (₹ 1)= 3,00,000]

2. From the following, Calculate the Equivalent Number of Equity Shares of ₹ 10 each:

Equity Shares of ₹ 10 each fully paid up	10,00,000
Equity Shares of ₹ 10 each,₹ 8 paid up	16,00,000
Equity Shares of ₹ 5 each fully paid up	15,00,000
Equity Shares of ₹ 5 each,₹ 3 paid up	18,00,000
Equity Shares of ₹ 1 each fully paid up	5,00,000
27% Preference Shares of ₹ 100 each fully paid	10,00,000

[Ans [1,00,000 (₹ 10 each) + 2,00,000 (₹ 8 paid up) +1,50,000 (₹ 5) + 3,00,000 (₹ 3 paid up)+ 50,000 (₹ 1)= 8,00,000]

3. From the following, Calculate the Equivalent Number of Equity Shares of ₹ 10 each:

Equity Shares of ₹ 10 each fully paid up		10,00,000
Equity Shares of ₹ 10 each,₹ 8 paid up	16,00,000	
Less: Calls–in–arrears @ ₹ 2	(2,00,000)	14,00,000
Equity Shares of ₹ 5 each fully paid up		15,00,000
Equity Shares of ₹ 5 each,₹ 3 paid up	18,00,000	
Less: Calls–in–arrears @ ₹ 2	(1,00,000)	17,00,000
Equity Shares of ₹ 1 each fully paid up		5,00,000
27% Preference Shares of ₹ 100 each fully paid	10,00,000	
Less: Calls–in–arrears @ ₹ 20	(40,000)	9,60,000

[**Ans** [1,00,000 (₹ 10 each) + 2,00,000 (₹ 8 paid up) +1,50,000 (₹ 5) + 3,00,000 (₹ 3 paid up)+ 50,000 (₹ 1)= 8,00,000]

Calculation of Net Assets for valuation of Equity Shares

4. From the following, Calculate the Net Assets for valuation of Equity Shares:

Particulars		₹
27% Preference Shares of ₹ 100 each fully paid	10,00,000	
Less: Calls–in–arrears @ ₹ 20	(40,000)	9,60,000
10% Debentures [60% Debentures are to be redeemed prior to valuation of Shares]		10,00,000
Short–term Borrowings		25,00,000
Property,Plant & Equipment		30,00,000
Goodwill		9,00,000
10% Investments: [Face Value ₹ 8,00,000]		10,00,000
Trade Debtors		25,00,000
Inventories (Taken at 90% of market value)		18,00,000
Cash and Cash Equivalents		48,60,000

Additional Information: Goodwill is found undervalued by ₹ 10,50,000. Property,Plant & Equipment are found undervalued by ₹ 15,00,000. Of the Investments 10% is trade and the balance non–trade. All trade Investments are to be valued at 10% below cost. Disputed Bonus claim of ₹ 1,29,000 not yet provided in the accounts for 2022–2023 is settled at ₹ 90,000. Debtors constitute 10% as irrecoverable.

[**Ans** Net Assets for valuation of Equity Shares=₹ 120,00,000]

5. From the following, Calculate the Net Assets for valuation of Equity Shares:

Particulars	₹	₹
Equity Shares of ₹ 10 each fully paid up		10,00,000
Equity Shares of ₹ 10 each,₹ 8 paid up	16,00,000	
Less: Calls–in–arrears @ ₹ 2	(2,00,000)	14,00,000
Equity Shares of ₹ 5 each fully paid up		15,00,000
Equity Shares of ₹ 5 each,₹ 3 paid up	18,00,000	
Less: Calls–in–arrears @ ₹ 2	(1,00,000)	17,00,000

Equity Shares of ₹ 1 each fully paid up		5,00,000
Reserves & Surplus		16,00,000
27% Preference Shares of ₹ 100 each fully paid	10,00,000	
Less: Calls–in–arrears @ ₹ 20	(40,000)	9,60,000
10% Debentures [60% Debentures are to be redeemed prior to valuation of Shares]		10,00,000
Short–term Borrowings		25,00,000

Additional Information: Goodwill is found undervalued by ₹ 10,50,000. Property,Plant & Equipment are found undervalued by ₹ 15,00,000. Of the Investments (appear at ₹ 10,00,000 in Balance Sheet) 10% is trade and the balance non–trade. All trade Investments are to be valued at 10% below cost. Disputed Bonus claim of ₹ 1,29,000 not yet provided in the accounts for 2022–2023 is settled at ₹ 90,000. Debtors(appear at ₹ 25,00,000 in Balance Sheet) constitute 10% as irrecoverable. Inventories (Taken at 90% of market value) appear at ₹ 18,00,000 in Balance Sheet.

[**Ans** Net Assets for valuation of Equity Shares= ₹ 104,00,000+ ₹ 4,00,000 (Uncalled Amount on ₹ 8 paid up) + ₹ 12,00,000 (Uncalled Amount on ₹ 3 paid up) + ₹ 1,00,000 (Unpaid Amount on ₹ 3 paid up) = ₹ 120,00,000]

6. From the following, Calculate the Intrinsic Value of each category of Equity Shares:

Equity Shares of ₹ 10 each fully paid up	10,00,000
Equity Shares of ₹ 5 each fully paid up	15,00,000
Equity Shares of ₹ 1 each fully paid up	5,00,000
27% Preference Shares of ₹ 100 each fully paid	10,00,000
Net Assets for Equity Shareholders at their current values	₹ 120,00,000

[**Ans** [Equivalent Number of Equity Shares of ₹ 10 each: 1,00,000 (₹ 10 each) + 1,50,000 (₹ 5) + 50,000 (₹ 1)= 3,00,000, Intrinsic Value: ₹ 40 (₹ 10 each),₹ 20 (₹ 5), ₹ 4 (₹ 1)]

7. From the following, Calculate the Intrinsic Value of each category of Equity Shares:

Equity Shares of ₹ 10 each fully paid up	10,00,000
Equity Shares of ₹ 10 each,₹ 8 paid up	16,00,000
Equity Shares of ₹ 5 each fully paid up	15,00,000
Equity Shares of ₹ 5 each,₹ 3 paid up	18,00,000
Equity Shares of ₹ 1 each fully paid up	5,00,000
27% Preference Shares of ₹ 100 each fully paid	10,00,000
Net Assets for Equity Shareholders at their current values	₹ 104,00,000

[**Ans** [Equivalent Number of Equity Shares of ₹ 10 each: 1,00,000 (₹ 10 each) + 2,00,000 (₹ 8 paid up) + 1,50,000 (₹ 5) + 3,00,000 (₹ 3 paid up) + 50,000 (₹ 1) = 8,00,000, Net Assets for valuation of Equity Shares = ₹ 104,00,000 + ₹ 4,00,000 (Uncalled Amount on ₹ 8 paid up) + ₹ 12,00,000 (Uncalled Amount on ₹ 3 paid up) + ₹ 1,00,000 (Unpaid Amount on ₹ 3 paid up) = ₹ 120,00,000, Intrinsic Value: ₹ 15 (₹ 10 each), ₹ 13 (₹ 8 each), ₹ 7.50 (₹ 5), ₹ 5.50 (₹ 3 each), ₹ 1.50 (₹ 1)]

8. From the following, Calculate the Intrinsic Value of each category of Equity Shares:

Equity Shares of ₹ 10 each fully paid up		10,00,000
Equity Shares of ₹ 10 each,₹ 8 paid up	16,00,000	

Less: Calls–in–arrears @ ₹ 2	(2,00,000)	14,00,000
Equity Shares of ₹ 5 each fully paid up		15,00,000
Equity Shares of ₹ 5 each,₹ 3 paid up	18,00,000	
Less: Calls–in–arrears @ ₹ 2	(1,00,000)	17,00,000
Equity Shares of ₹ 1 each fully paid up		5,00,000
27% Preference Shares of ₹ 100 each fully paid	10,00,000	
Less: Calls–in–arrears @ ₹ 20	(40,000)	9,60,000
Net Assets for Equity Shareholders at their current values		₹ 101,00,000

[**Ans** [Equivalent Number of Equity Shares of ₹ 10 each: 1,00,000 (₹ 10 each) + 2,00,000 (₹ 8 paid up) +1,50,000 (₹ 5) + 3,00,000 (₹ 3 paid up) + 50,000 (₹ 1) = 8,00,000, Net Assets for valuation of Equity Shares = ₹ 101,00,000 + ₹ 4,00,000 (Uncalled Amount on ₹ 8 paid up) + ₹ 2,00,000 (Unpaid Amount on ₹ 8 paid up) + ₹ 12,00,000 (Uncalled Amount on ₹ 3 paid up) + ₹ 1,00,000 (Unpaid Amount on ₹ 3 paid up) = ₹ 120,00,000, Intrinsic Value: ₹ 15 (₹ 10 each), ₹ 13 (₹ 8 each), ₹ 11 (₹ 6 each), ₹ 7.50 (₹ 5 each), ₹ 5.50 (₹ 3 each), ₹ 3.50 (₹ 5 each, ₹ 1 paid up), ₹ 1.50 (₹ 1 fully paid)]

9. From the following, Calculate the Earning Yield Value of each category of Equity Shares:

Equity Shares of ₹ 10 each fully paid up	10,00,000
Equity Shares of ₹ 5 each fully paid up	15,00,000
Rate of Earnings: Year I: 22%,Year II: 28%,Year III: 20% Year IV: 26%	
Normal Rate of Expectation in the same industry 12%	

[**Ans** [Average Rate of *Earnings* = 24%, *Earning Yield Value of an Equity Share:* ₹ 20 (₹ 10 each),₹ 10 (₹ 5 each)]

10. From the following, Calculate the Earning Yield Value of each category of Equity Shares:

Equity Shares of ₹ 10 each fully paid up	10,00,000
Equity Shares of ₹ 5 each fully paid up	15,00,000

Year	*I*	*II*	*III*	*IV*
Earnings after tax for Equity Shareholders	₹ 4,00,000	₹ 5,40,000	₹ 6,60,000	₹ 9,00,000
Equity Shareholders' Funds Employed	₹ 25,00,000	₹ 27,00,000	₹ 30,00,000	₹ 36,00,000

Normal Rate of Expectation in the same industry 12%

[**Ans** [Weighted Average Rate of *Earnings* = 22.2%, *Earning Yield Value of an Equity Share:* ₹ 18.50 (₹ 10 each),₹ 9.25 (₹ 5 each)]

11. From the following, Calculate the Earning Yield Value of each category of Equity Shares:

Equity Shares of ₹ 10 each fully paid up		10,00,000
Equity Shares of ₹ 10 each,₹ 8 paid up	16,00,000	
Less: Calls–in–arrears @ ₹ 2	(2,00,000)	14,00,000
Equity Shares of ₹ 5 each fully paid up		15,00,000
Equity Shares of ₹ 5 each,₹ 3 paid up	18,00,000	
Less: Calls–in–arrears @ ₹ 2	(1,00,000)	17,00,000
Equity Shares of ₹ 1 each fully paid up		5,00,000

27% Preference Shares of ₹ 100 each fully paid		10,00,000
Average Earnings after tax for Shareholders		₹ 21,00,000
Normal Rate of Expectation in the same industry 12%.		

[**Ans** [Earnings for Equity Shareholders = ₹ 21,00,000 – ₹ 2,70,000 (Pref. Divi) = ₹ 18,30,000, Total Paid–up Value of all Equity Shares = ₹ 61,00,000, *Average Rate of Earnings* = 30%, *Earning Yield Value of an Equity Share:* ₹ 25 (₹ 10 each), ₹ 20 (₹ 8 each), ₹ 15 (₹ 6 each), ₹ 12.50 (₹ 5 each), ₹ 7.50 (₹ 3 each), ₹ 2.50 (₹ 5 each, ₹ 1 paid up), ₹ 2.50 (₹ 1 fully paid)]

12. From the following, Calculate the Fair Value of each category of Equity Shares:

	Intrinsic Value	Earning Yield Value
Equity Shares of ₹ 10 each fully paid up	₹ 15	₹ 25
Equity Shares of ₹ 10 each,₹ 8 paid up	₹ 13	₹ 20
Equity Shares of ₹ 10 each,₹ 6 paid up	₹ 11	₹ 15
Equity Shares of ₹ 5 each fully paid up	₹ 7.50	₹ 12.50
Equity Shares of ₹ 5 each,₹ 3 paid up	₹ 5.50	₹ 7.50
Equity Shares of ₹ 5 each,₹ 1 paid up	₹ 3.50	₹ 2.50
Equity Shares of ₹ 1 each fully paid up	₹ 1.50	₹ 2.50

[**Ans** [Fair Value = (Net Assets Value + Earning Yield Value)/2: ₹ 20 (₹ 10 each),₹ 16.50 (₹ 8 each),₹ 13 (₹ 6 each),₹ 10 (₹ 5 each), ₹ 6.50 (₹ 3 each), ₹ 3 (₹ 5 each, ₹ 1 paid up),₹ 2 (₹ 1 fully paid)]

13. From the following, Calculate the Dividend Yield Value of each category of Equity Shares:

Equity Shares of ₹ 10 each fully paid up	10,00,000
Equity Shares of ₹ 5 each fully paid up	15,00,000
Rate of Dividend: Year I 12%,Year II 18%,Year III 15% Year IV 21%	
Normal Rate of Expectation in the same industry 12%	

[**Ans** [Average Rate of Dividend = 16.5%, Dividend *Yield Value of an Equity Share:*₹ 13.75 (₹ 10 each),₹ 6.875 (₹ 5 each)]

14. From the following, Calculate the Dividend Yield Value of each category of Equity Shares:

Equity Shares of ₹ 10 each fully paid up	10,00,000
Equity Shares of ₹ 5 each fully paid up	15,00,000

Year	***I***	***II***	***III***	***IV***
Equity Dividend	₹ 3,00,000	₹ 3,75,000	₹ 4,50,000	₹ 5,25,000
Equity Share Capital	₹ 25,00,000	₹ 25,00,000	₹ 25,00,000	₹ 25,00,000

Normal Rate of Expectation in the same industry 12%.

[**Ans** [Average Rate of Dividend = 18%, Dividend *Yield Value of an Equity Share:*₹ 15 (₹ 10 each),₹ 7.50 (₹ 5 each)]

15. From the following, Calculate the Dividend Yield Value of each category of Equity Shares:

Equity Shares of ₹ 10 each fully paid up		10,00,000
Equity Shares of ₹ 10 each,₹ 8 paid up	16,00,000	
Less: Calls–in–arrears @ ₹ 2	(2,00,000)	14,00,000

Equity Shares of ₹ 5 each fully paid up		15,00,000
Equity Shares of ₹ 5 each,₹ 3 paid up	18,00,000	
Less: Calls–in–arrears @ ₹ 2	(1,00,000)	17,00,000
Equity Shares of ₹ 1 each fully paid up		5,00,000
27% Preference Shares of ₹ 100 each fully paid		10,00,000
Rate of Dividend: Year I 12%,Year II 18%,Year III 15%		
Normal Rate of Expectation in the same industry 12%.		

[**Ans** [Average Rate of Dividend = 15%, Dividend *Yield Value of an Equity Share:* ₹ 12.50 (₹ 10 each), ₹ 10 (₹ 8 each), ₹ 7.50 (₹ 6 each), ₹ 6.25 (₹ 5 each), ₹ 3.75 (₹ 3 each), ₹ 1.25 (₹ 5 each, ₹ 1 paid up), ₹ 1.25 (₹ 1 fully paid)]

16. From the following, Calculate the Dividend Yield Value of each category of Equity Shares:

Equity Shares of ₹ 10 each fully paid up		10,00,000
Equity Shares of ₹ 10 each,₹ 8 paid up	16,00,000	
Less: Calls–in–arrears @ ₹ 2	(2,00,000)	14,00,000
Equity Shares of ₹ 5 each fully paid up		15,00,000
Equity Shares of ₹ 5 each,₹ 3 paid up	18,00,000	
Less: Calls–in–arrears @ ₹ 2	(1,00,000)	17,00,000
Equity Shares of ₹ 1 each fully paid up		5,00,000
27% Preference Shares of ₹ 100 each fully paid		10,00,000
Rate of Dividend: Year I 12%,Year II 15%,Year III 18%		
Normal Rate of Expectation in the same industry 8%.		

[**Ans** [Average Rate of Dividend = 16%, Dividend *Yield Value of an Equity Share:* ₹ 20 (₹ 10 each), ₹ 16 (₹ 8 each), ₹ 12 (₹ 6 each), ₹ 10 (₹ 5 each), ₹ 6 (₹ 3 each), ₹ 2 (₹ 5 each, ₹ 1 paid up), ₹ 2 (₹ 1 fully paid)]

LONG ANSWER TYPE PRACTICAL QUESTIONS

1. Given below are the extracts from the Balance Sheet of Rajasthali (8) Ltd. as at 31st March, 2023:

Particulars	₹
Equity Shares of ₹ 10 each fully paid up	20,00,000
Equity Shares of ₹ 10 each, ₹ 8 paid–up	32,00,000
Equity Shares of ₹ 5 each fully paid up	30,00,000
Less: Calls–in–arrears @ ₹ 2	(4,00,000)
Equity Shares of ₹ 1 each fully paid up	10,00,000
15% Preference Shares of ₹ 100 each fully paid	20,00,000
Less: Calls–in–arrears @ ₹ 20	(80,000)
Reserves & Surplus	60,00,000
Short–term Borrowings	20,00,000
10% Debentures [60% Debentures are to be redeemed prior to valuation of Shares]	20,00,000
Goodwill	18,00,000
Property,Plant & Equipment	60,00,000
10% Investments: [Face Value ₹ 16,00,000]]	20,00,000
Current Assets	10,92,000

Additional Information:

(a) Goodwill is valued at ₹ 39,00,000 and Property,Plant & Equipment are found undervalued by ₹ 25,00,000.

(b) Of the Investments 10% is trade and the balance non–trade. All trade Investments are to be valued at 10% below cost. Disputed Bonus claim of ₹ 5,80,000 not yet provided in the accounts for 2022–2023 is settled at ₹ 3,80,000. Debtors constitute ₹ 2,00,000 as irrecoverable.

Required: Calculate the Intrinsic Value of Equity Shares.*[Ignore Tax]*

[Ans [Equivalent Number of Equity Shares of ₹ 10 each: 2,00,000 (₹ 10 each) + 4,00,000 (₹ 8 paid up) + 3,00,000 (₹ 5) + 1,00,000 (₹ 1) = 10,00,000, Intrinsic Value: ₹ 20 (₹ 10 each), ₹ 18 (₹ 8 each), ₹ 10 (₹ 5), ₹ 8 (₹ 3 each), ₹ 2 (₹ 1)]

2. Given below are the extracts from the Balance Sheet of Rajasthali(8) Ltd. as at 31st March, 2023:

Particulars	₹
Equity Shares of ₹ 10 each fully paid up	20,00,000
Equity Shares of ₹ 10 each, ₹ 8 paid–up	32,00,000
Equity Shares of ₹ 5 each fully paid up	30,00,000
Less: Calls–in–arrears @ ₹ 2	(4,00,000)
Equity Shares of ₹ 1 each fully paid up	10,00,000
15% Preference Shares of ₹ 100 each fully paid	20,00,000
Less: Calls–in–arrears @ ₹ 20	(80,000)
Reserves & Surplus	60,00,000
Short–term Borrowings	20,00,000
10% Debentures [60% Debentures are to be redeemed prior to valuation of Shares]	20,00,000
Goodwill	18,00,000
Property,Plant & Equipment	60,00,000
10% Investments: [Face Value ₹ 16,00,000]]	20,00,000
Current Assets	10,92,000

Additional Information:

(a) Goodwill is valued at ₹ 39,00,000 and 50% of Total Property, Plant & Equipment are found undervalued by 50% of market value and 50% of the remaining are found overvalued by 50% of market value.

(b) Of the Investments 10% is trade and the balance non–trade. All trade Investments are to be valued at 10% below cost. Disputed Bonus claim of ₹ 5,80,000 not yet provided in the accounts for 2022–2023 is settled at ₹ 3,80,000. Debtors constitute ₹ 2,00,000 as irrecoverable.

Required: Calculate the Intrinsic Value of Equity Shares.*[Ignore Tax]*

[Ans [Equivalent Number of Equity Shares of ₹ 10 each: 2,00,000 (₹ 10 each) + 4,00,000 (₹ 8 paid up) + 3,00,000 (₹ 5) + 1,00,000 (₹ 1) = 10,00,000, Intrinsic Value: ₹ 20 (₹ 10 each), ₹ 18 (₹ 8 each), ₹ 10 (₹ 5), ₹ 8 (₹ 3 each), ₹ 2 (₹ 1)]

3. Given below are the extracts from the Balance Sheet of BHARAT TUSHAR (9A)Ltd. as at 31st March, 2023:

Particulars	₹
Equity Shares of ₹ 10 each fully paid up	20,00,000
Equity Shares of ₹ 10 each, ₹ 8 paid–up	32,00,000
Less: Calls–in–arrears @ ₹ 2	(4,00,000)
Equity Shares of ₹ 5 each fully paid up	30,00,000
Less: Calls–in–arrears @ ₹ 2	(2,00,000)
Equity Shares of ₹ 1 each fully paid up	10,00,000
15% Preference Shares of ₹ 100 each fully paid	20,00,000
Less: Calls–in–arrears @ ₹ 20	(80,000)
Reserves & Surplus	12,00,000
10% Debentures [60% Debentures are to be redeemed prior to valuation of Shares]	20,00,000
Short–term Borrowings	50,00,000
Property,Plant & Equipment	42,00,000
Goodwill	18,00,000
Patents & Trade Marks	40,00,000
10% Investments: [Face Value ₹ 16,00,000]	20,00,000
Current Assets	67,20,000

Additional Information:

(a) Goodwill is found undervalued by ₹21,00,000.

(b) On 01.04.2022, a new machinery costing ₹ 20,00,000 was purchased but wrongly charged to revenue. Machinery and other Property,Plant & Equipment are subject to Depreciation @ 10% (No rectification has yet been made). 50% of Total Property,Plant & Equipment are found undervalued by 50% of market value and 50% of the remaining are found overvalued by 50% of market value.

(c) Of the Investments 10% is trade and the balance non–trade. All trade Investments are to be valued at 10% below cost. Disputed Bonus claim of ₹ 5,80,000 not yet provided in the accounts for 2022–2023 is settled at ₹ 3,80,000. Debtors constitute ₹ 2,00,000 as irrecoverable.

Required: Calculate the Intrinsic Value of Equity Shares.*(Ignore Tax)*

[**Ans** [Equivalent Number of Equity Shares of ₹ 10 each: 2,00,000 (₹ 10 each) + 4,00,000 (₹ 8 paid up) + 3,00,000 (₹ 5) + 1,00,000 (₹ 1) = 10,00,000, Intrinsic Value: ₹17 (₹10 each), ₹ 15 (₹ 8 each), ₹ 13 (₹ 6 paid–up), ₹ 8.5 (₹ 5 each), ₹ 6.5 (₹ 3 paid–up), ₹ 1.70 (₹ 1 each)]

4. Given below are the extracts from the Balance Sheet of TULSIAN (10)Ltd. as at 31st March, 2023:

Particulars	₹
2,00,000 Equity Shares of ₹ 10 each	20,00,000
6,00,000 Equity Shares of ₹ 5 each fully paid up	30,00,000
Less: Calls–in–arrears on 2,00,000 Shares	(4,00,000)
14.4% Preference Shares of ₹ 100 each	10,00,000

Additional Information:

1. Profits after tax @ 40%:2020–2021 : ₹ 12,00,000, 2021–2022: ₹ 18,00,000 ,2022–2023: ₹ 15,00,000. With effect from 1st April, 2023. Rate of Income Tax—25% and an increase in manager remuneration p.a. ₹ 1,00,000 p.a.

2. Normal Rate of Expectation is 12%.

Required: Calculate the Value of an Equity Share on Earning Yield basis.

[**Ans** [Earnings for Equity Shareholders = ₹ 18,00,000 – ₹ 1,44,000 (Pref. Divi) = ₹ 16,56,000, Total Paid–up Value of all Equity Shares = ₹ 46,00,000, *Average Rate of Earnings = 36%, Earning Yield Value of an Equity Share:* ₹ 30 (₹ 10 each), ₹ 15 (₹ 5 each), ₹ 9 (₹ 3 each)]

5. Given below are the extracts from the Balance Sheet of TULSIAN Ltd. as at 31st March, 2023:

Particulars	₹
2,00,000 Equity Shares of ₹ 10 each	20,00,000
6,00,000 Equity Shares of ₹ 5 each fully paid up	30,00,000
Less: Calls–in–arrears on 2,00,000 Shares	(4,00,000)

Additional Information:

1. Rates of Equity Dividend:2020–2021 :12%, 2021–2022: 18% ,2022–2023: 15%.
2. Normal Rate of Expectation is 12%.

Required: Calculate the Value of an Equity Share on Dividend Yield basis.

[**Ans** [Average Rate of Dividend = 15%, Dividend Yield Value of an Equity Share:₹ 12.50 (₹ 10 each),₹ 6.25 (₹ 5 each), ₹ 3.75 (₹ 3 each)]

6. Given below are the extracts from the Balance Sheet of TULSIAN Ltd. as at 31st March, 2023:

Particulars	₹
2,00,000 Equity Shares of ₹ 10 each	20,00,000
6,00,000 Equity Shares of ₹ 5 each fully paid up	30,00,000
Less: Calls–in–arrears on 2,00,000 Shares	(4,00,000)

Additional Information:

1. Rates of Dividend:2020–2021 :12%, 2021–2022: 15% ,2022–2023: 18%.
2. Fully paid Equity Shares of ₹ 10 each of similar companies in the same industry with an average dividend of 30% are quoted at ₹ 37.5.

Required: Calculate the Value of an Equity Share on Dividend Yield basis.

[**Ans** [Weighted Average Rate of Dividend = 16%, Normal Rate of Expectation= (30% of ₹ 10)/ ₹ 37.5=8%,Dividend *Yield Value of an Equity Share:*₹ 20 (₹ 10 each),₹ 10 (₹ 5 each), ₹ 6 (₹ 3 each)]

7. Given below are the extracts from the Balance Sheet of TULSIAN(20A) Ltd. as at 31st March, 2023:

Particulars	₹
2,00,000 Equity Shares of ₹ 10 each	20,00,000
6,00,000 Equity Shares of ₹ 5 each fully paid up	30,00,000
Less: Calls–in–arrears on 2,00,000 Shares	(4,00,000)
14.4% Preference Shares of ₹ 100 each	10,00,000
Reserves and Surplus	20,00,000
10% Debentures[60% Debentures are to be redeemed prior to valuation of Shares.]	20,00,000
Current Liabilities	10,00,000
Goodwill	4,00,000

Property,Plant & Equipment	60,00,000
10% Trade Investments [Face Value ₹ 8,00,000]	10,00,000
Current Assets	32,00,000

Additional Information:

1. Profits after tax @ 40%:2020–2021 : ₹ 12,00,000, 2021–2022: ₹ 18,00,000 ,2022–2023: ₹ 15,00,000. With effect from 1st April, 2023. Rate of Income Tax—25% and an increase in manager remuneration ₹ 2,20,000 p.a.
2. Normal Rate of Expectation is 12%.
3. Trade Investments are to be valued at 175% of Face Value. Goodwill is found undervalued by ₹ 26,00,000.

Required: Calculate the Fair Value of an Equity Share.

[**Ans** [Equivalent Number of Equity Shares of ₹ 10 each: 2,00,000 (₹ 10 each) + 3,00,000 (₹ 5) = 5,00,000, Net Assets for valuation of Equity Shares = ₹ 100,00,000, Intrinsic Value: ₹ 20 (₹ 10 each), ₹ 10 (₹ 5 each), ₹ 8 (₹ 3 each), Earnings for Equity Shareholders = ₹ 18,00,000 – ₹ 1,44,000(Pref. Divi) = ₹ 16,56,000, Total Paid–up Value of all Equity Shares = ₹ 46,00,000, *Average Rate of Earnings* = 36%, *Earning Yield Value of an Equity Share:* ₹ 30 (₹ 10 each), ₹ 15 (₹ 5 each), ₹ 9 (₹ 3 each), *Fair Value of an Equity Share:* ₹ 25 (₹ 10 each), ₹ 12.50 (₹ 5 each), ₹ 8.50 (₹ 3 each)]]

8. From the following information, calculate the Fair Value of an Equity Share of TUSHAR & TASHIKA (21)Ltd:

8,00,000 Equity Shares of ₹ 10 each,₹ 8 paid up
14,00,000 Equity Shares of ₹ 5 each fully called up (Calls–in–arrears @₹ 2 on 4,00,000 shares)
20,000, 9.9 % Preference Shares of ₹100 each fully paid up
Reserves & Surplus ₹ 147,52,000
Property,Plant & Equipment ₹ 6,00,000. 50% of Total Property,Plant & Equipment are found undervalued by 50% of market value and 50% of the remaining are found overvalued by 50% of market value.
10% Investments: [Face Value ₹ 1,60,000] ₹ 2,00,000. Of the Investments 10% is trade and the balance non–trade. All trade Investments are to be valued at 10% below cost.
10% Debentures [60% Debentures are to be redeemed prior to valuation of Share] :₹ 40,00,000
Average Profits before tax : ₹ 50,00,000. With effect from the next year Rate of Income Tax : 25% and an increase in manager remuneration ₹ 4,40,000 p.a.
Normal Rate of Expectation is 9%.

[**Ans** [Equivalent Number of Equity Shares of ₹ 10 each: 8,00,000 (₹ 10 each) + 7,00,000 (₹ 5) = 15,00,000, Net Assets for valuation of Equity Shares = ₹ 300,00,000, Intrinsic Value: ₹ 20 (₹ 10 each), ₹ 18 (₹ 8 paid–up), ₹ 10 (₹ 5 each), ₹ 8 (₹ 3 each), Earnings for Equity Shareholders = ₹ 36,00,000 – ₹ 1,98,000 (Pref. Divi) = ₹ 34,02,000, Total Paid–up Value of all Equity Shares = ₹ 126,00,000, *Average Rate of Earnings* = 27%, *Earning Yield Value of an Equity Share:*₹ 30 (₹ 10 each), ₹ 24 (₹ 8 paid–up), ₹ 15 (₹ 5 each), ₹ 9 (₹ 3 each), *Fair Value of an Equity Share:* ₹ 25 (₹ 10 each), ₹ 21 (₹ 8 paid–up), ₹ 12.50 (₹ 5 each), ₹ 8.50 (₹ 3 each)]]

15 VALUE ADDED STATEMENT [INCLUDING ECONOMIC VALUE ADDED, MARKET VALUE ADDED & SHAREHOLDERS' VALUE ADDED]

LEARNING OBJECTIVES

After studying this chapter, you should be able to understand:

- What is Value Added [VA]?
- What is Value Added Statement?
- What is Economic Value Added [EVA]?
- What is Market Value Added [MVA]?
- What is Shareholders' Value Added [SVA]?

1.0 VALUE ADDED

WHAT IS VALUE ADDED (VA)?

VA is the wealth which a reporting entity has been able to create through the collective effort of resources (i.e. Capital, Management and Employees). In economic terms, Value Added is the Market Price of the output of an enterprise less the Price of the goods and services acquired from outside Suppliers. Value Added may be calculated on gross *or* net basis. Value Added arises due to input-output relationship with various Stakeholders (such as Employees, Directors, Govt., Financiers)

Input-Output Relationship with various Stockholders

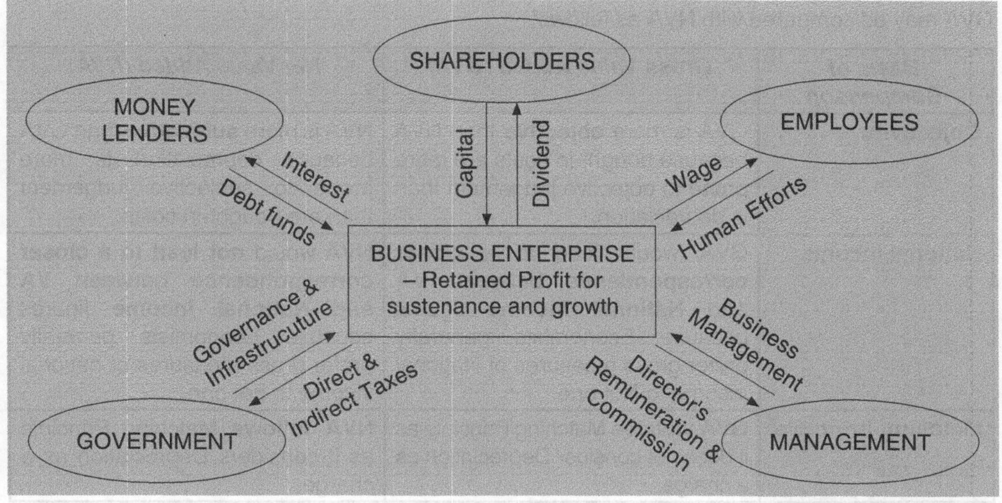

WHAT IS GROSS VALUE ADDED (GVA)?

Gross Value Added of a manufacturing entity is calculated as follows:

HOW TO CALCULATE GROSS VALUE ADDED?

Particulars	₹	₹
Revenue from Operations [including Recoverable Taxes]		xxx
***Add:* Direct Income (e.g. Trading Commission)**		xxx
***Less:* Cost of bought-in Material and Services:**		
Production and Operational Expenses [excluding Wages, Salaries, Bonus, Gratuities and Other Benefits to Administrative Staff, Staff Welfare Expenses, Cess & Local Taxes]	xxx	
Administration Expenses [excluding Remuneration & Sitting Fees to Directors]	xxx	
Interest on Working Capital Loans/ Cash Credit /Bank Overdraft [of Temporary nature]	xxx	
Recoverable Taxes [e.g. Excise Duty, Service Tax, VAT]	xxx	
Other Misc. Charges	xxx	(xxx)
Value Added by Manufacturing and Trading Activities		xxx
***Add:* Other Income**		
Dividend & Interest	xxx	
Misc. Income	xxx	xxx
***Add/Less:* Extraordinary Items**		xxx
(e.g., Surplus on Sale and lease back of properties, Loss of Cash by Theft, Insurance Proceeds from Earthquake Disaster Settlement)		
Gross Value Added		xxx

WHAT IS NET VALUE ADDED (NVA)?

NVA can be defined as GVA less Depreciation.

HOW TO COMPARE GROSS VALUE ADDED WITH NET VALUE ADDED?

GVA may be compared with NVA as follows:

Basis of Comparison	*Gross Value Added (GVA)*	*Net Value Added (NVA)*
Objectivity	GVA is more **objective** than NVA because bought-in costs are more prone to objective judgement than is depreciation.	NVA is more **subjective** than GVA because depreciation is more prone to subjective judgement than are bought-in costs.
National Income	GVA would lead to a **closer correspondence between VA and National Income** figures because Economists generally prefer gross measures of National Income to Net one.	NVA would **not lead to a closer correspondence between VA and National Income** figures because Economists generally prefer gross measures of national income to net one.
Matching Principle	**GVA violates** Matching Principle as it does not consider Depreciation as a charge.	**NVA follows** Matching Principle as it considers Depreciation as a charge.

Wealth Creation	Wealth Creation will be **overstated** because no allowance is made Depreciation.	Wealth Creation will **not** be **overstated** because an allowance is made for Depreciation.
Productivity Bonus	Productivity Bonus will be **overstated** because of overstated VA as no allowance is made for Depreciation.	Productivity Bonus will **not** be **overstated** because it is linked to NVA.

2.0 VALUE ADDED STATEMENT

WHAT IS VALUE ADDED STATEMENT?

Value Added Statement is a Statement of which the first part shows the Computation of Value Added and the second part shows the Application of Value Added to several interest groups (like Employees, Government, Outside Financiers, Shareholders, etc.),

WHAT IS THE OBJECTIVE OF VALUE ADDED STATEMENT?

The objective of Value Added Statement is–

(a) to ascertain total wealth created by Entity during a particular accounting period.

(b) to ascertain who are the participants of such wealth and to what extent.

WHAT ARE THE ADVANTAGES OF VALUE ADDED (VA) STATEMENTS?

Various advantages of preparation of Value Added (VA) Statements are as follows:

Improves Employees' attitude	Reporting on VA improves the attitude of employees towards their employing companies because the VA statement reflects a broader view of the company's objectives and responsibilities.
Productivity Linked bonus	VA Statement makes it easier for the company to introduce a productivity linked bonus scheme for employees based on VA. The employees may be given productivity bonus on the basis of VA / Payroll Ratio.
Diagnostic & Predictive Tools	VA based Ratios (e.g. VA / Payroll, Taxation / VA, VA / Revenue from Operations etc.) are useful diagnostic and predictive tools. Trends in VA ratios, comparisons with other companies and international comparisons may be useful.
Good Measure of Size & Importance	VA provides a very good measure of the size and importance of a company. To use Revenue from Operations figure *or* capital employed figures as a basis for company's rankings can cause distortion. This is because Revenue from Operations may be inflated by large bought-in expenses *or* a capital-intensive company with a few employees may appear to be more important than a highly skilled labour–intensive company.
Linked to National Income	VA Statement links a company's financial accounts to National Income. A company's VA indicates the company's contribution to National Income.
Based on Conceptual Principles	VA Statement is built on the basic conceptual foundations which are currently accepted in Balance Sheets and Income Statements. Concepts such as Going Concern, Matching, Consistency and Substance over Form are equally applicable to VA statement.

WHAT IS THE FORMAT OF VALUE ADDED STATEMENT (VA STATEMENT)?

A General Format of Value Added Statement (VA Statement) is shown below:

VALUE ADDED STATEMENT (VA STATEMENT)
for the year ended 31st March, 2023

Particulars	₹	₹	
Revenue from Operations [including Recoverable Taxes]		xxx	
***Add:* Direct Income (e.g. Trading commission)**		xxx	
***Less:* Cost of bought-in Material and Services:**			
Production and Operational Expenses[excluding Wages, Salaries, Bonus, Gratuities and Other Benefits to Administrative Staff, Staff Welfare Expenses, Cess & Local Taxes]	xxx		
Administration Expenses [excluding Remuneration & Sitting Fees to Directors]	xxx		
Interest on Working Capital Loans/ Cash Credit /Bank Overdraft [of Temporary nature]	xxx		
Recoverable Taxes [e.g., Excise Duty, Service Tax, GST]	xxx		
Other Misc. Charges	xxx	xxx	
Value added by Manufacturing and Trading Activities		xxx	
***Add:* Other Income**			
Dividend & Interest	xxx		
Misc. Income	xxx		
Add/Less: Extraordinary Items			
[e.g. Surplus on Sale and Lease back of Properties,			
Loss of Cash by Theft, Insurance Proceeds from earthquake Disaster settlement)	xxx	xxx	
Gross Value Added		xxx	
Application of Gross Value Added:			%
To Pay Employees:			
Wages, Salaries, Bonus, Gratuities and Other Benefits to Administrative Staff	xxx		
Staff Welfare Expenses [e.g. Leave Travel concession]	xxx	xxx	xxx
To Pay Directors			
Salaries & Commission Sitting Fees		xxx	xxx
To Pay Government			
Cess & Local Taxes	xxx		
Income Tax [excluding Deferred Tax]*	xxx	xxx	xxx
*Including Interest, Penalties, Fine			
To Pay Providers of Capital			
Interest on Debentures/Fixed Loans	xxx		
Interim Dividends paid	xxx	xxx	xxx
To Provide for the Maintenance & Expansion of the company:			
Depreciation	xxx		

Retained Profit [Closing – Opening]	xxx		
General Reserve [excluding any Reserve written back]	xxx		
Fixed Assets Replacement Reserve	xxx		
Debenture Redemption Reserve	xxx		
Deferred Tax	xxx	xxx	xxx
Total		xxx	100

RECONCILIATION BETWEEN GROSS VALUE ADDED AND PROFIT BEFORE TAXATION

A. Profit before Income Tax [Excluding Extra-ordinary Items]		xxx
B. Add back:		
Depreciation	xxx	
Wages, Salaries, Bonus, Gratuities and Other Benefits to Administrative Staff	xxx	
Staff Welfare Expenses	xxx	
Salaries Commission & Sitting Fees To Directors	xxx	
Cess & Local Taxes	xxx	
Interest on Debentures/Fixed Loans	xxx	xxx
C. Gross Value Added		xxx

Notes:

(i) Deferred tax may alternatively be shown as a part of 'To Pay Government'.

(ii) Bank overdraft, being a temporary source of finance, has been considered as the provision of a banking service rather than of capital. Therefore, interest on bank overdraft has been shown as a part of 'Cost of bought in Material and Services'.

WHAT ARE THE LIMITATIONS OF VA?

Risk	The concept of showing value added as applied to several interested groups is being questioned by many academics. They advocate that since the shareholders are the ultimate risk takers, the residual profit remaining after meeting the obligations of outside interest groups should only be shown as value added accruing to the shareholders.
Non-Standardised	VA Statements are non-standardised because there is no clarity as to – (a) whether the **Depreciation** should be included *or* excluded in the calculation of Value Added. (b) whether the **Excise Duty** should be shown as a part of bought-in cost and deducted while calculating Value Added *or* should be shown as an Application of VA. However, this practice of non-standardisation can be effectively eliminated by bringing out an Accounting Standard on Value Added. Therefore, this criticism is a temporary phenomenon. The power of EVA comes from the fact that it marries both the Income Statement and the Balance Sheet and reflects the economic reality after eliminating accounting distortions. The role of EVA in driving a company's ability to create wealth is evident.

ILLUSTRATION 1

Following is the Profit and Loss Account of Tulsian Value Added Ltd.

PROFIT AND LOSS ACCOUNT FOR THE YEAR ENDED 31ST MARCH, 2023

Income	*Notes*	*(₹ in crores)*	*(₹ in crores)*
Revenue from Operations			210
Other Income			10
Total Income			220
Expenditure:			
Cost of Materials consumed		81.00	
Changes in Inventories		31.00	
Consumption of Stores		13.00	
Employee Benefits Expense	(i)	18.00	
Finance Costs	(ii)	8.00	
Other Manufacturing Expenses	(iii)	32.70	
Depreciation and Amortization Expense		5.00	(188.70)
Profit before Tax			31.30
Provision for Tax			(3.30)
Profit after Tax			28.00

SURPLUS TO BE TAKEN TO BALANCE SHEET

Opening Balance	2
Add: Profit for the period	28
Less: Transfer to General Reserve	(20)
Less: Transfer to Fixed Assets Replacement Reserve	(4)
Less: Interim Dividend	(3)
Closing Balance	3

Notes:

(i) Employee Benefits Expense includes ₹ 3.00 crores for Remuneration to Directors and ₹ 12.00 crores for Departments other than Production.

(ii) Finance Costs include ₹ 2 crores for Interest on Working Capital, Loan, Cash Credit & Bank Overdraft.

(iii) Other Manufacturing Expenses include ₹ 7.70 crores for Cess and Local Taxes & Excise Duty.

Required: Prepare a Gross Value Added Statement and show the Reconciliation between Gross Value Added and Profit before Taxation:

(a) If Excise Duty is 4% of Cost of bought-in Material.

(b) If Excise Duty is 3.125% of Cost of bought-in Material and Services.

(c) If Excise Duty is 10% of Value Added by Manufacturing and Trading Activities

SOLUTION

(a) If Excise Duty is 4% of Cost of bought-in Material.

TULSIAN VALUE ADDED LTD

VALUE ADDED STATEMENT (VA STATEMENT)

for the year ended 31st March, 2023 *[₹ in lacs]*

Particulars	₹	₹	%
Revenue from Operations		210	
Less: **Cost of bought-in Material and Services:**			
Cost of Materials consumed	81.00		
Changes in Inventories	31.00		
Consumption of Stores	13.00		
Employee Benefits Expense (₹ 18 crores – ₹ 3 crores – ₹ 12 crores)	3.00		
Finance Costs (Interest on Working Capital, Loan, Cash Credit & Bank Overdraft ₹ 2 crores)	2.00		
Other Manufacturing Expenses (₹ 32.70 crores – ₹ 7.70 crores)	25.00		
Excise Duty [Refer to working Note]	5.00	160	
Value Added by Manufacturing and Trading Activities		50	
Add: **Other Income**		10	
Gross Value Added		**60**	
Application of Value Added:			%
To Pay Employees:			
Employee Benefits Expense (for Departments other than Production)		12.00	20
To Pay Directors			
Salaries & Commission		3.00	5
To Pay Government:			
Cess & Local Taxes(₹ 7.70 crores – ₹ 5crores)	2.70		
Income Tax	3.30	6.00	10
To Pay Providers of Capital:			
Finance Costs (₹ 8 crores – ₹ 2 crores)	6.00		
Interim Dividends paid	3.00	9.00	15
To Provide for the Maintenance & Expansion of the company:			
Depreciation and Amortization Expense	5.00		
Retained Profit (₹ 3 crores – ₹ 2 crores)	1.00		
General Reserve	20.00		
Fixed Assets Replacement Reserve	4.00	30.00	50
Total		**60.00**	100

RECONCILIATION BETWEEN TOTAL VALUE ADDED AND PROFIT BEFORE TAXATION

₹ *[in lacs]*

A. Profit before tax		31.30
B. Add back:		
Depreciation and Amortization Expense	5.00	
Employee Benefits Expense (for Departments other than Production)	12.00	
Salaries & Commission To Directors	3.00	
Cess & Local Taxes(₹ 7.70 crores – ₹ 5 crores)	2.70	
Finance Costs (₹ 8 crores – ₹ 2 crores)	6.00	28.70
C. Total Value Added		60.00

Working Note: *Calculation of Excise Duty*

(i) **Total Cost of bought-in Material** =81 + 31 + 13 = 125

(ii) Excise Duty = 4% of 125 = 5

(b) If Excise Duty is 3.125% of Cost of bought-in Material and Services

Working Note: *Calculation of Excise Duty*

Let Excise Duty = x

Total Cost of bought-in Material and Services = 81 + 31 + 13 + 3 + 2 + 25 + x = 155 +x

Excise Duty = 3.125% of (155 + x)

x = 3.125% of (155 + x) = 5

Now Remaining Solution is same as in Case (a)

(c) If Excise Duty is equal to 10% of Value Added by Manufacturing and Trading Activities

Working Note: *Calculation of Excise Duty*

Let Excise Duty = x

Total Value Added = 210 – (81 + 31 + 13 + 3 + 2 + 25 + x) = 55 – x

x = 10% of (55 – x) = 5

Now Remaining Solution is same as in Case (a)

ILLUSTRATION 2

Total Value Added ₹ 60 crores, Revenue from Operations ₹ 200 crores, Employee Benefits Expense ₹ 12 crores,Number of Employees 800. Calculate the Value Added per Employee, Average Earning per Employee, Revenue from Operations per Employee and Payroll Value Added Ratio .

SOLUTION

(i) Value Added per Employee = $\frac{\text{Value Added}}{\text{No of Employees}}$

= (60 crores/800) = ₹ 7,50,000

(ii) Average Earning per Employee = $\frac{\text{Employees Costs}}{\text{No of Employees}}$

= (12 crores/800) = ₹ 1,50,000

(iii) Revenue from Operations per Employee = $\frac{\text{Revenue from Operations}}{\text{No of Employees}}$

= (200 crores/800) = ₹ 25,00,000

(iv) Payroll Value Added Ratio = $\frac{\text{Employees Costs}}{\text{Value Added}} \times 100$

= (12 crores/60 crores) × 100 = 20%

ILLUSTRATION 3

Total Value Added ₹ 60 crores, Employee Benefits Expense ₹ 12 crores, Calculate the Bonus to be paid to the Employees, if any, for the year 2023 if any actual improvement in the Target Index (i.e., Employees Costs to Value Added) is to be shared by employer and employee in the ratio of 1 : 2 and Target Index is 25%

SOLUTION

Payroll Value Added Ratio = $\frac{\text{Employees Costs}}{\text{Value Added}} \times 100$

= (12 crores/60 crores) × 100 = 20%

Bonus to Employees = (Target Index − Payroll VA Ratio for current year) × Value Added × Share of Employee in Bonus

= [25% − 20%] × ₹ 60 crores × 2/3 = ₹ 2 crores

ILLUSTRATION 4

(a) Under which part of Gross Value Added Statement, will you classify the following items:

1. Surplus on Sale and Lease back of Properties
2. Leave Travel concession to Employees
3. Director's Sitting Fees
4. Interest & Penalties under Income Tax Act
5. Deferred Tax
6. Amount written back from Reserves
7. Depreciation
8. Tax Deducted at source from Employee's' Salary
9. Provision for Doubtful Debts

(b) How will you deal with the above items while preparing the Reconciliation Statement between Gross Value Added and Profit before Taxation?

SOLUTION

(A) TREATMENT OF ITEMS IN GROSS VALUE ADDED STATEMENT

Item	*First Part of VAS*	*Application Part of VAS*
Surplus on Sale and Lease back of Properties	Added As Extra-ordinary Item after Other Income	—
Leave Travel concession to Employees	—	Towards Employees
Director's Sitting Fees	—	Towards Directors

Interest & Penalties under Income Tax Act	—	Towards Government
Deferred Tax	—	Towards Entity
Amount written back from Reserves	—	Towards Entity (Excluded from Reserves)
Depreciation	—	Towards Entity
Tax Deducted at source from Employee's' Salary	—	Towards Employees
Provision for Doubtful Debts	Deducted as Expense	—

(B) TREATMENT OF ITEMS WHILE PREPARING RECONCILIATION STATEMENT

Item	*Treatment*
Surplus on Sale and Lease back of Properties	Not considered at all
Leave Travel concession to Employees	Add back
Directors' Sitting Fees	Add back
Interest & Penalties under Income Tax Act	Not considered at all
Deferred Tax	Not considered at all
Amount written back from Reserves	Not considered at all
Depreciation	Add back
Tax Deducted at source from Employees' Salary	Add back
Provision for Doubtful Debts	Not considered at all

3.0 ECONOMIC VALUE ADDED [EVA]

WHAT IS EVA?

Economic Value Added (EVA) is primarily a benchmark to measure earnings efficiency. EVA as a residual income measure of financial performance is simply the Operating Profit after tax less a Charge for the Operating Capital Employed, used in the business.

HOW TO CALCULATE EVA?

EVA = Net Operating Profit after Tax (NOPAT) – Cost of Operating Capital Employed

Notes:

Calculation of Net Operating Profit after Tax (NOPAT)
= Profit before Interest & Tax × (1– Tax Rate)
or, = (Profit before Tax + Interest) × (1– Tax Rate)
or, = Profit after Interest and Tax + Interest net of Tax
Note: Interest net of Tax =Interest × (1– Tax Rate)
Financial Leverage = Profit before Interest & Tax/(Profit before Interest & Tax – Interest)
While Computing Net Operating Profit after Tax (NOPAT), Income from Non-Trade Investments is excluded.

Calculation of Cost of Operating Capital Employed
= Operating Capital Employed (OCE) × Weighted Average Cost of Capital (WACC)
Operating Capital Employed = Long-term Debt. + Pref. Share Capital + Equity – Non-Trading Assets (e.g. Non-Trade Investments, Advance for Purchase of Fixed Assets, Capital Work-in-progress), Immovable Property held as Investment]
WACC=[(Debt/TCE)x Cost of Debt]+[(PSC/TCE)x Cost of PSC]+[(Equity/TCE)x Cost of Equity] Where, Cost of Debt = k_d = Rate of Interest (1 – Tax Rate), Cost of PSC = k_p = Rate of Pref. Dividend Cost of Equity = k_e = Risk Rate + (Beta) × *(Market Rate – Risk Free Rate) *Market Risk Premium = (Market Rate – Risk Free Rate) TCE = Total Capital Employed

WHAT ARE THE USES OF EVA?

1. To measure Business Performance.
2. To guide Managerial Decision Making.
3. To align Managerial Incentives with the Shareholders' Interests.
4. To improve the Financial and Business literacy throughout the organisation.
5. EVA is better linked to changes in shareholders wealth and is superior to traditional financial measures such as PAT *or* percentage of return measures such as ROCE *or* ROE because EVA includes both profit and loss as well as balance sheet efficiency as well as the opportunity cost of investor capital.
6. EVA, additionally, is a tool for management to focus on the impact of their decisions in increasing shareholders wealth. These include both strategic decisions such as what investments to make, which business to exit, what financing structure is optimal; as well as operational decisions involving trade-offs between profit and asset efficiency such as whether to make inhouse *or* outsource, repair *or* replace an equipment, whether to make short *or* long production runs etc.
7. To better align managers interests with shareholders' - the EVA framework needs to be holistically applied in an integrated approach - simply measuring EVA is not enough; it must also become the basis of key management decisions as well as be linked to senior management's variable compensation.

WHAT ARE THE LIMITATIONS OF EVA?

However, EVA as a strategic tool has the following limitations:

1. It is not easy to use it is too complicated for small businesses.
2. It recommends inexpensive debts in order to reduce the cost of capital.
3. It is a passive tool and measures past performance.

ILLUSTRATION 5

Tulsian EVA (1) Ltd. provides you the following information:

Particulars	*₹ (In Crores)*
Equity Share Capital (₹ 10 each)	250
15% Preference Share Capital (₹ 100 each)	100
Reserves & Surplus	50

12% Debentures	800
Tax Rate: 25%	
Weighted Average Cost of Capital (WACC):12.25%	

Required: Calculate the Economic Value Added :

(a) If Operating Profit after Tax is ₹ 297 crores
(b) If Profit before Tax is ₹ 300 crores
(c) If Profit before Interest and Tax is ₹ 396 crores
(d) If Profit after Interest and Tax is ₹ 225 crores
(e) If Financial Leverage is 1.32 times

SOLUTION

COMPUTATION OF ECONOMIC VALUE ADDED [EVA]

Particulars	*₹ (In Crores)*
Net Operating Profit after Tax [NOPAT]	297
Less: Cost of Operating Capital Employed [12.25% of ₹ 1,200]	(147)
Economic value Added [EVA]	150

Working Note:

Total Capital Employed = [Equity Share Capital + Net Reserves & Surplus + Pref. Share Capital + Debentures]
= [250 + 50 + 100 + 800] = 1,200 crores

Working Notes for Case (b):

Net Operating Profit after Tax = Profit before Tax + Interest – Tax
= 300 + 96 – (25% of 396) = 297

Now, EVA is same as in case (a)

Working Notes for Case (c):

Net Operating Profit after Tax = Profit before Interest & Tax – Tax
= 396 – 25% of 396 = 297

Now EVA is same as in case (a)

Working Notes for Case (d):

Net Operating Profit after Tax = [Profit after Interest & Tax + Tax – Interest on Debt] – Tax
= [225 + (225*25%/75%) + 96] – (396*25%) = 297

Alternatively,

= Profit after Interest and Tax + Interest net of Tax
= 225 + (96 – 25% of 96) = 225 + 72 = 297

Now EVA is same as in case (a)

Working Notes for Case (e):

Financial Leverage = Profit before Interest & Tax/(Profit before Interest & Tax – Interest)
1.32 = Profit before Interest & Tax/(Profit before Interest & Tax – 96)

Profit before Interest & Tax = (96 × 1.32)/0.32 = 396

Net Operating Profit after Tax = Profit before Interest & Tax – Tax

= 396 – 25% of 396 = 297

Now EVA is same as in case (a)

ILLUSTRATION 6

Tulsian EVA(2) Ltd. provides you the following data to calculate the Economic Value Added:

Particulars	₹ *(In Crores)*
Equity Share Capital (₹ 10 each)	250
15% Preference Share Capital (₹ 100 each)	100
Reserves & Surplus	50
12% Debentures	800
Profit after Interest and Tax	225
Tax Rate: 25%	
Beta Factor:1.5	
Market Rate of Return:15.5%	
Risk Free Rate:6.5%	

SOLUTION

COMPUTATION OF ECONOMIC VALUE ADDED [EVA]

Particulars	₹ *(In Crores)*
Net Operating Profit after Tax [NOPAT]	297
Less: Cost of Operating Capital Employed [12.25% of ₹ 1,200]	(147)
Economic value Added [EVA]	150

Working Notes:

1. **Cost of Equity** = Risk Free Rate + Beta Factor × (Market Rate – Risk Free Rate)
   = 6.5% + 1.5 (15.5 – 6.5) = 20%
2. **Cost of Pref. Shares** = 15%
3. **Cost of Debt** = Interest Rate × (1 – Tax Rate) = 12% × (1 – 0.25) = 9 %
4. **Total Capital Employed** = [Equity Shareholders' Funds
   + Pref. Share Capital + Debentures]
   = [(250 + 50) + 100 + 800] = 1,200 crores
5. **Weighted Average Cost of Capital (WACC)**
   [(Debt/TCE)x Cost of Debt]+[(PSC/TCE)x Cost of PSC]+[(Equity/TCE)x Cost of Equity]
   =[(800/1200)x 9%]+[(100/1200)x15%]+[(300/1200)x 20%]
   = 6% + 1.25% + 5% = 12.25%
6. **Net Operating Profit after Tax [NOPAT]**=[Profit after Interest & Tax + Tax – Interest on Debt] – Tax
   = [225 + (225*25%/75%) + 96] – (396*25%) = 297

Alternatively,

= Profit after Interest and Tax + Interest net of Tax

= 225+ (96 – 25% of 96) = 225 + 72 = 297

ILLUSTRATION 7

Tulsian EVA(3) Ltd. provides you the following data to calculate the Economic Value Added:

Particulars	*₹ (In Crores)*
Equity Share Capital (₹ 10 each)	250
15% Preference Share Capital (₹ 100 each)	100
Reserves & Surplus	50
12% Debentures	800
Profit after Interest and Tax	225
Tax Rate: 25%	
Beta Factor:1.5	
Market Rate of Return:15.5%	
Equity Market Risk Premium: 9%	

SOLUTION

1. **Cost of Equity** = Risk Free Rate + (Beta × Equity Market Risk Premium)

   = (15.5% – 9%) + (1.5 × 9) = 20%

Now EVA is same as in Previous Illustration.

*ILLUSTRATION 8

Tulsian EVA(4) Ltd. provides you the following data to calculate the Economic Value Added:

Particulars	*₹ (In Crores)*
Equity Share Capital (₹ 10 each)	?
15% Preference Share Capital (₹ 100 each)	?
Reserves & Surplus	50
12% Debentures	800
Debt-Equity Ratio (Long-term Debt/Shareholders' Funds) = 2:1	
Capital Gearing Ratio (Funds bearing Fixed Payments to Equity Shareholders' Funds) = 3:1	
Financial Leverage = 1.32 times	
Tax Rate: 25%	
Market Rate of Return: 15.5%	
Equity Market Risk Premium: 9%	

Beta for the last 5 years as follows:

Year	*1*	*2*	*3*	*4*	*5*
Beta	1.6	1.7	1.8	1.3	1.1

SOLUTION

COMPUTATION OF ECONOMIC VALUE ADDED [EVA]

Particulars	*₹ (In Crores)*
Net Operating Profit after Tax [NOPAT]	297
Less: Cost of Operating Capital Employed [12.25% of ₹ 1,200]	(147)
Economic value Added [EVA]	150

Working Notes:

1. ***Calculation of Equity Shareholders' Funds***

Debt Equity Ratio = $\frac{\text{Long-term Debts}}{\text{Shareholders' Funds}}$

2 = ₹ 800/Shareholders' Funds

Shareholders' Funds = ₹ 800/2 = ₹ 400

Supposing Pref. Share Capital = x

Equity Shareholders' Funds = ₹ 400 – x

2. ***Calculation of Pref. Share Capital***

Capital Gearing Ratio = $\frac{\text{Funds bearing Fixed Financial payments}}{\text{Equity Shareholders' Funds}}$

3 = (₹ 800 + x)/(₹ 400 – x)

₹ 1,200 – 3x = ₹ 800 + x

x = (1,200 – 800)/4 = 100

Equity Shareholders' Funds = 400 – 100 = 300

3. **Average Beta** = (1.6+1.7+1.8+1.3+1.1)**/5 =1.5**
4. **Cost of Equity** = Risk Free Rate + (Beta × Equity Market Risk Premium)

   = (15.5% – 9%) + (1.5 × 9) = 20%
5. **Cost of Pref. Shares** = 15%
6. **Cost of Debt** = Interest Rate × (1 – Tax Rate) = 12% × (1 – 0.25) = 9 %
7. **Total Capital Employed** = [Equity Shareholders' Funds + Pref. Share Capital + Debentures]

   = [300 + 100 + 800] = 1,200 crores
8. **Weighted Average Cost of Capital (WACC)**

   [(Debt/TCE)x Cost of Debt]+[(PSC/TCE)x Cost of PS]+[(Equity/TCE)x Cost of Equity]
   =[(800/1200)x 9%]+[(100/1200)x15%]+[(300/1200)x 20%]

   = 6% + 1.25% + 5% = 12.25%
9. Financial Leverage = Profit before Interest & Tax/(Profit before Interest & Tax – Interest)

   1.32 = Profit before Interest & Tax/(Profit before Interest & Tax – 96)

   Profit before Interest & Tax = (96 × 1.32)/0.32 = 396

Net Operating Profit after Tax = Profit before Interest & Tax – Tax

= 396 – 25% of 396 = 297

*ILLUSTRATION 9

XYZ Ltd. has division X, Y and Z. The division Z has recently reported an annual operating profit of ₹ 44.40 crores. The Cost of Capital of division Z is 11% and Cost of Debt is 8%.The Net Assets (Invested Capital) of Division Z as per latest Balance Sheet is ₹ 120 crore, but replacement cost of these assets is estimated at ₹ 168 crores. You are required to compute EVA of the Division Z.

SOLUTION

Invested Capital (as per replacement cost) is ₹ 168 crore.

EVA = Operating Profit – (invested Capital × Cost of Capital)

= ₹ 44.40 Crores – (₹ 168 crores × 11%)

= ₹ 44.40 crore – ₹ 18.48 crores = ₹ 25.92 crores

*ILLUSTRATION 10

Prosperous Bank has a criterion that it will give loans to companies that have an "Economic Value Added" greater than zero for the past three years on an average. The bank is considering lending money to a small company that has the economic value characteristics shown below. The data relating to the company is as follows:

(i) Average operating income after tax equals ₹ 25,00,000 per year for the last three years.

(ii) Average total assets over the last three years equals ₹ 75,00,000.

(iii) Weighted average cost of capital appropriate for the company is 10% which is applicable for all three years.

(iv) The company's average current liabilities over the last three years are ₹ 15,00,000.

Does the company meet the bank's criterion for a positive economic value added?

SOLUTION

CALCULATION OF ECONOMIC VALUE ADDED

1. Capital employed = Average Total Assets – Average Current Liabilities

   = 75 – 15 = ₹ 60 crores

2. Cost of Capital = Capital employed × Weighted Average Cost of Capital

   = ₹ 60 lakh × 10% = ₹ 6 crores

3. Economic Value Added = NOPAT – COC = ₹ 25 crores – ₹ 6 crores = ₹ 19 crores

   Economic value added is greater than zero. Therefore, the company qualifies for the loan.

4.0 DISTINCTION BETWEEN VA (VALUE ADDED) AND ECONOMIC VALUE ADDED (EVA) CONCEPTS

VA differ from EVA in the following respects:

Basis of Distinction	*Value Added (VA)*	*Economic Value Added (EVA)*
Meaning	VA is the **wealth** generated after meeting the cost of Bought in materials & services.	EVA is the **surplus** generated by an entity after meeting an equitable charge towards the providers of Capital.
Computation	**VA** = Market Price of a Output – Cost of Bought in materials and services	**EVA** = (Operating Profit after Tax) – (Operating Capital Employed × WACC)

Purpose	VA is a tool to **analyse the performance** and activity of the reporting entity.	EVA is a management tool to help managers **to take decisions** which increase the shareholders' wealth.
Focus	VA focusses on the Entity's performance and contribution towards **various groups.**	EVA focusses on Entity's ability to create surplus above **shareholders' expectations.**
Information	VA uses **internal information** like the P&L Account.	EVA uses **external information** and like Cost of Capital, Beta, Risk Free Rate of Return etc.
Time Value of Money	It **does not recognise** Time Value of Money, since it deals with the wealth created by the Firm during a specified period of time e.g. a financial year.	It **recognises** Time Value of Money EVA through the use of WACC. The Weighted Average Cost of Capital is based on the PV of Future Interest/ Dividend outflows.

5.0 MARKET VALUE ADDED [MVA]

WHAT IS MARKET VALUE ADDED [MVA]?

1. Market Value Added is the Market Value of Capital Employed in the firm less the Book Value of Capital Employed.
2. The Market Value of a firm reflects not only the Expected EVA of Assets in place but also the Expected EVA from Future Projects.
3. MVA of a company is the **Present Value (PV) of all its future EVAs.**

HOW TO CALCULATE MARKET VALUE ADDED [MVA]?

1. Market Value Added = (Market Value of Equity, Preference and Debt) – Paid up Value of Equity and Preference Share Capital, Retained Earnings, and Debts).

2. Market Value Added = **Present Value (PV) of all its future EVAs**

3. Present Value of EVA [If Return of Capital Employed is expected to be sustained in perpetuity]= Operating Profit after Tax/Cost of Capital

WHAT ARE THE USES OF MARKET VALUE ADDED [MVA]?

Market Value Added measures cumulatively the performance of corporate entity.

WHAT IS THE INTERPRETATION OF MARKET VALUE ADDED [MVA]?

A Positive Value Added indicates that the company has added some value to the wealth of shareholders and positive market expectations about the company. On the other hand Negative MVA indicates that the value of management's actions and investments are less than the value of the capital contributed to the company by the capital market and the company has destroyed the value & hence wealth in other words.

WHAT IS THE RELATIONSHIP BETWEEN EVA AND MARKET VALUE ADDED?

1. The relationship between EVA and Market Value Added is more complicated than the one between EVA and Firm Value.
2. The Market Value of a firm reflects not only the Expected EVA of Assets in place but also the Expected EVA from Future Projects
3. To the extent that the Actual Economic Value Added is smaller than the Expected EVA the Market Value can decrease even though the EVA is higher.
4. MVA of a company is the Net Present Value (NPV) of all its future EVAs.

WHAT ARE THE BENEFITS OF MARKET VALUE ADDED?

1. MVA, *or* Market Value Added, has significant implications for companies on how to make strategic decisions and manage performance in their pursuit of shareholder value.
2. MVA of a company is the Present Value (PV) of all its future EVAs. Thus, a company that continues to improve economic value added, year after year will, sooner than later, find favour with investors. EVA tells us how much shareholder wealth the business has created in a given time period (this is usually a year, but companies can and do use shorter time periods to aid the decision- making process) and provides a road- map to creating wealth at a business unit level within a company. Simply defined, EVA is the economic profit that remains after deducting the cost of all the capital employed (both debt and equity). The power of EVA comes from the fact that it marries both the Income Statement and the Balance Sheet and reflects the economic reality after eliminating accounting distortions.
3. MVA is an ideal measure of wealth creation in the long term. But it suffers from the short-term vagaries of stock market sentiments. If the markets are in the midst of a bull run, companies find their MVA zooming up to stratospheric proportions; if they do a sudden flip and enter the bear- mode, companies find their MVA plummeting. That is one reason why companies should focus on improving their fundamental economic performance as measures by EVA over the long- term.

WHAT ARE THE LIMITATIONS OF MARKET VALUE ADDED?

1. MVA does not take into account the opportunity costs of the invested capital.
2. MVA does not consider the interim cash returns to the shareholders.
3. MVA can not be calculated at divisional *or* business unit levels.
4. MVA can not be calculated in case of unlisted enterprises.

ILLUSTRATION 11

Tulsian MVA Ltd. has the following Capital Structure as at 31st March, 2023:

Equity Share Capital (fully paid shares of ₹ 10 each)	₹ 300 crores
15% Pref. Share Capital (fully paid shares of ₹ 100 each)	₹ 100 crores
15% Debentures (fully paid of ₹ 100 each)	₹ 800 crores
Retained Earnings	₹ 300 crores

Additional Information: Currently Quoted Prices in the stock exchange: Equity Shares @ ₹ 60, Preference Shares @ ₹ 90, Debentures @ ₹ 95.

Required: Calculate the Market Value Added and interpret it.

SOLUTION

COMPUTATION OF MARKET VALUE ADDED

Particulars	*₹ (crores)*
A. Market Value of Capital Employed [(30 crores × ₹ 60) + (1 lakh × ₹ 90) + (8 crores × ₹ 95)]	2,650
B. *Less:* Book Value of Capital Employed [300 crores + 100 crores + 800 crores + 300 crores]	(1,500)
C. Market Value Added	1,150

Interpretation: MVA reflects market expectations and is essentially a future oriented and forward looking approach. A positive MVA of ₹ 1,150 crores implies that the management has created wealth to the extent of ₹ 1,150 crores for its equity shareholders. Investors may be willing to pay more than the Net worth.

ILLUSTRATION 12

Bharat Ltd. has existing assets in which it has capital invested amounting to ₹ 1000 crores. At present the Return of Capital Employed is 15% which is expected to be sustained in perpetuity. The company has a cost of capital of 10%.

Estimate the Present Value of Economic Value Added (EVA) to the firm from its assets-in-place. Also explain the reason for the difference between the EVA and the MVA (Market Value Added).

SOLUTION

Present Value of EVA = Operating Profit after Tax/Cost of Capital

= (15% of 1000 crores)/10% = ₹ 1,500 crores.

Reason for the difference between EVA and Market Value Added

1. The Market Value of a firm reflects not only the Expected EVA of Assets in place but also the Expected EVA from Future Projects.
2. MVA of a company is the Net Present Value (NPV) of all its future EVAs.
3. EVA reflects only the current earning efficiency of the company.

ILLUSTRATION 13

The capital structure of W Ltd. whose shares are quoted on the NSE is as under:

Equity Shares of ₹ 100 each fully paid	₹ 505 crores
9% Convertible Pref. Shares of ₹ 10 each	₹ 150 crores
12% Secured Debentures of ₹ 10 each	₹ 50 crores
Reserves	₹ 101 crores
Statutory Fund	₹ 50,50,000

The Statutory Fund is compulsorily required to be invested in Government Securities. The ordinary shares are quoted at a premium of 500%; Preference Shares at ₹ 30 per share and debentures at par value. You are required to ascertain the Market Value added of the company and also give your assessment on the market value added as calculated by you.

SOLUTION

Market Value Added (MVA) is the difference between the current market value of a firm and the capital contributed by investors (both debentureholders and shareholders). In other words, it is the sum of all capital claims held against the company plus market value of debt and equity. If MVA is positive, firm has added value.

Market Value Added = Market Value of firm *less* amount invested in the firm

Particulars		***(₹ in crores)***
Equity Share Capital (market value) (505 crores × 600%)		3030
Preference Share Capital (15,00,000 × 30)		450
Debentures		50
Current market value of firm		3,530
Less: Equity Share Capital	505	
Preference share capital	150	
Reserves	101	

Debentures	50	
Statutory Reserve	50.50	(856.50)
Market Value Added		2,673.50

The significant Market Value addition implies that the management of W Ltd. has created wealth for its shareholders and that market investors are willing to pay a price greater than the historical net worth of the company.

ILLUSTRATION 14

The following data pertains to X Ltd. engaged in software consultancy business as on 31.03.2023:

Particulars	₹ lacs
Income from consultancy	935.00
EBIT	180.00
Less: Interest on Loan	18.00
EBT	162.00
Tax @ 25%	40.50
	121.50

Particulars	₹ lacs
Equity Shares(of ₹ 10 each)	100
Reserves & Surplus	325
Loans	180
Current Liabilities	120

You are required to compute (a) Economic Value Added (b) Market Value Added. Assuming that: (i) WACC is 12% and (ii) The share of company currently quoted at ₹ 50 each.

SOLUTION

CALCULATION OF ECONOMIC VALUE ADDED (EVA)

Particulars	₹ lacs
A. Net Operating Profit after Tax [180 – 25%]	135.00
B. *Less:* Cost of Capital Employed [12% of (100 + 325 + 180)]	(72.60)
C. Economic Value Added [A – B]	62.40

CALCULATION OF MARKET VALUE ADDED (MVA)

Particulars	₹ lacs
A. Market Value of Equity Stock [10 lacs × ₹ 50]	500
B. *Less:* Equity Funds [100 + 325]	(425)
C. Market Value Added (MVA) [A – B]	75

*ILLUSTRATION 15

Life Industries Ltd. (LIL) furnishes the following information from which you are required to calculate the prevailing Economic Value Added of the company and also explain the reason for the difference, if any, between the EVA as calculated by you and the MVA (Market Value Added) of LIL amounting of ₹ 14005 crores.

Equity Shares of Rs 1,000 face value	1,58,200 units
12% Debentures ₹ 10 face value	50,00,000 units
Current tax rate	30%
Financial Leverage	1.1 times
Securities Premium Account (Rupees in crores)	155
Free Reserves (Rupees in crores)	154
Capital Reserve (Rupees in crores)	109

It is a prevailing practice for companies in the industry to which LIL belongs to pay at least a dividend of 15% p.a. to its common shareholders.

SOLUTION

COMPUTATION OF ECONOMIC VALUED ADDED

Particulars	***₹ in crores***
Net Operating Profit after tax [NOPAT]	462
Less: Cost of Operating Capital Employed [(2000 + 500) × 13.68%]	(342)
Economic Value Added	120

Operating MVA of ₹ 14,005 crore: The MVA of ₹ 14,005 crore is the difference between the current Market Value of LIL and the capital contributed by the fund providers. While EVA measure current earning efficiency of the company, MVA takes into consideration the EVA from the not only the assets in place but also from the future projects/activities of the company. The difference between MVA over EVA thus represents the value attributed to the future potential of the company & may change from the to time based on market sentiments. In short the **MVA is the present value of all future EVA's.**

Working Notes:

(i) Calculation of NOPAT

Interest on Debentures = 50,00,000 × 10 × 12% = ₹ 60 crores

Financial Leverage = Profit before Interest & Tax/ Profit before Interest & Tax – Interest

1.1 = Profit before Interest & Tax/ (Profit before Interest & Tax – 60)

PBIT = ₹ 660 crores

NOPAT= ₹ 660 crores – 30% of 660 crores = ₹ 462 crores

(ii) Calculation of Weighted Average cost of Capital (WACC)

1. Cost of Debt = 12% (1 – 0.30) = 8.4%
2. Equity = Equity shares + Securities Premium + Free Reserves + Reserves
   = 1,582 + 155 + 154 + 109 = 2,000
3. Capital Employed = Equity + Debt = 2,000 + 500 = 2,500 crores
4. WACC = $\left(\frac{500}{2,500} \times 8.4\%\right) + \left(\frac{2,000}{2,500} \times 15\%\right)$ = 13.68%

***ILLUSTRATION 16**

The following information is given for 3 companies that are identical except for their capital structure:

Particulars	X Ltd.	Y Ltd.	Z Ltd.
Total Invested Capital	1,00,000	1,00,000	1,00,000
Debt/Assets Ratio	0.8	0.5	0.2
Shares Outstanding	6,100	8,300	10,000
Pre tax Cost of debt	16%	13%	15%
Cost of Equity	26%	22%	20%
Operating Income (EBIT)	25,000	25,000	25,000

The tax rate is uniform 35% in all cases.

(i) Compute the Weighted Average Cost of Capital for each company.

(ii) Compute the Economic Valued Added (EVA) for each company.

(iii) Based on the EVA, which company would be considered for best investment? Give reasons.

(iv) If the industry PE ratio is 11, estimate the price for the share of each company.

(v) Calculate the estimated market capitalisation for each of the companies.

SOLUTION

(i) Weighted Average Cost of Capital

WACC = (Cost of Debt × Debt%) + (Cost of Equity × Equity%)

Cost of Debt after Tax = Cost of Debt before Tax (1 – Tax Rate)

X Ltd. = 16% (1 – .35) = 10.4%,

Y Ltd. = 13% (1 – 0.35) = 8.45%

Z Ltd. = 15% (1 – 0.35) = 9.75%.

WACC

X Ltd. (10.4 × 0.8) + (26 × 0.2) = 13.52%

Y Ltd. (8.45 × 0.5) + (22 × 0.5) = 15.225%

Z Ltd. (9.75 × 0.2) + (20 × 0.8) = 17.95%

(II) ECONOMIC VALUED ADDED (EVA)

Particulars	X Ltd.	Y Ltd.	Z Ltd.
A. EBIT (1 – T)	16,250	16,250	16,250
B. *Less:* WACC of Invested Capital	13,520	15,225	17.950
C. EVA [A – B]	2,730	1,025	–1,700

(iii) X Ltd. would be considered as the best investment since the EVA of the company is highest and its weighted average cost of capital is the lowest

(IV) ESTIMATED PRICE OF EACH COMPANY SHARES

Particulars	X Ltd.	Y Ltd.	Z Ltd.
EBIT	₹ 25,000	₹ 25,000	₹ 25,000
Less: Interest	(₹ 12,800)	(₹ 6,500)	(₹ 3,000)

Taxable Income	₹ 12,200	₹ 18,500	₹ 22,000
Less: Tax @ 35%	(₹ 4,270)	(₹ 6,475)	(₹ 7,700)
Net Income	₹ 7,930	₹ 12,025	₹ 14,300
Shares	6,100	8,300	10,000
EPS	1.3	1.45	1.43
Stock Price (EPS × PE Ratio)	₹ 14.30	₹ 15.94	₹ 15.73

Since the three entities have different capital structures they would be exposed to different degrees of financial risk. The PE ratio should therefore be adjusted for the risk factor.

(V) MARKET CAPITALISATION

Estimated Stock Price (₹)	14.30	15.94	15.73
No. of Shares	6,100	8,300	10,000
Estimated Market Cap (₹)	87,230	1,32,302	1,57,300

6.0 SHAREHOLDERS' VALUE ADDED [SVA]

WHAT IS SHAREHOLDERS' VALUE ADDED [SVA]?

Shareholders' Value Added is a value-based performance measure of a company's worth to shareholders.

SVA = Net Profit after Tax (NPAT) – Cost of Operating Capital Employed by the Shareholders.

Notes:

1. Net Profit after Tax (NPAT) = [(Profit before Interest & Tax) – Interest] × (1– Tax Rate)

2. Calculation of Cost of Operating Capital Employed by the Shareholders
= Operating Shareholders' Funds × Weighted Average Cost of Shareholders' Funds(WACSF)
Operating Shareholders' Funds(OSF) = Pref. Share Capital + Equity – Non-Trading Assets (e.g. Non-Trade Investments, Advance for Purchase of Fixed Assets, Capital Work-in-progress), Immovable Property held as Investment]
WACSF = [(PSC/OSF) x Cost of PSC] + [(Equity/OSF) x Cost of Equity] *Where,* Cost of PSC= k_p = Rate of Pref. Dividend Cost of Equity = k_e = Risk Free Rate + (Beta) × *(Market Rate – Risk Free Rate) *Market Risk Premium = (Market Rate – Risk Free Rate) OSF = Operating Shareholders' Funds

ILLUSTRATION 17

Tulsian MVA(1) Ltd. provides you the following data to calculate the Economic Value Added:

Particulars	*₹ (In Crores)*
Equity Share Capital (₹ 10 each)	250
15% Preference Share Capital (₹ 100 each)	100

Reserves & Surplus	50
12% Debentures	800
Profit after Interest and Tax	225
Tax Rate: 25%	
Beta Factor:1.5	
Market Rate of Return: 15.5%	
Risk Free Rate:6.5%	

SOLUTION

COMPUTATION OF ECONOMIC VALUE ADDED [EVA]

Particulars	₹ *(In Crores)*
Net Profit after Tax (NPAT)	225
Less: Cost of Operating Capital Employed by the Shareholders [18.75% of ₹ 400]	(75)
Economic Value Added [EVA]	150

Working Notes:

1. **Cost of Equity** = Risk Free Rate + Beta Factor × (Market Rate – Risk Free Rate)
   = 6.5% + 1.5 (15.5 – 6.5) = 20%
2. **Cost of Pref. Shares** = 15%
3. **Operating Capital Employed by the Shareholders**= [Equity Shareholders' Funds + Pref. Share Capital] = [(250 + 50) + 100] = 400 crores
4. **Weighted Average Cost of Equity (WACE)**
   =[(PSC/TCE)x Cost of PSC]+[(Equity/TCE)x Cost of Equity]
   =[(100/400)x15%]+[(300/400)x 20%]
   = 3.75% +15% =18.75%

WHAT ARE THE IMPLICATIONS OF SHAREHOLDERS' VALUE ADDED [SVA]?

Shareholders' Value is a term used in many ways:

- To refer to the concept that the primary goal for a company is to enrich its shareholders (owners) by paying dividends and/or causing the stock price to increase
- To refer to the market capitalization of a company (rarely used)
- To refer to the more specific concept that planned actions by management and the returns to shareholders should outperform certain bench-marks such as the cost of capital concept. In essence, the idea that shareholders money should be used to earn a higher return than they could earn themselves by investing in risk free bonds for

The management principle **'Value Based Management'**, states that management should first and foremost consider the interests of shareholders in its business decisions. This concept is usually highlighted in opposition to alleged examples of CEO's and other management actions which enrich themselves at the expense of shareholders. Examples of this include acquisitions which are dilutive to shareholders, that is, they may cause the combined company to have twice the profits but these might have to be split amongst three times the shareholders.

SOLVED PROBLEMS

PROBLEM 1

Value Added Ltd. furnishes the following Profit and Loss A/c:

PROFIT AND LOSS A/C FOR THE YEAR ENDED 31ST MARCH, 2023

Particulars	*Notes*	*₹ (crores)*
Turnover	1	29,872
Other Income		1,042
		30,914
Expenditure		
Operating expenses	2	26,741
Interest on 8% Debenture		987
Interest on Cash Credit	3	151
Excise duty		1,952
		29,831
Profit before depreciation		1,083
Less: Depreciation		(342)
Profit before tax		741
Provision for tax	4	376
Profit after tax		365
Less: Transfer to Fixed Assets Replacement Reserve		(65)
		300
Less: Dividend paid		(125)
Retained Profit		175

Notes:

(1) Turnover is based on invoice value.

(2) Administrative Salaries, wages and other employee benefits amounting to ₹ 14,761 crores are included in operating expenses.

(3) Cash Credit represents a temporary source of finance. It has not been considered as a part of capital.

(4) Transfer of ₹ 54 crores to the credit of deferred tax account is included in provision for tax.

Required: Prepare Value Added Statement for the year ended 31st March, 2023 and reconcile total value added with profit before taxation.

SOLUTION

VALUE ADDED LTD.
VALUE ADDED STATEMENT FOR THE YEAR ENDED 31ST MARCH, 2023

Particulars	*₹ (crores)*	*₹ (crores)*	%
Turnover		29,872	
Less: Cost of bought in materials and services:			
Operating expenses (26,741 –14,761)	11,980		

Excise duty	1,952		
Interest on Cash Credit	151	(14,083)	
Value Added by manufacturing and trading activities		15,789	
Add: Other income		1,042	
Total Value Added		16,831	
Application of Value Added:			
To Pay to employees:			
Salaries, wages and other employee benefits		14,761	87.70
To Pay to Government:			
Corporation tax (376 – 54)		322	1.91
To Pay to providers of capital:			
Interest on 8% Debentures	987		
Dividends	125	1,112	6.61
To Provide for maintenance and expansion of the company:			
Depreciation	342		
Fixed Assets Replacement Reserve	65		
Deferred Tax Account	54		
Retained Profit	175	636	3.78
		16,831	100

Note: Deferred tax account could alternatively be shown as an item 'To pay to government'.

RECONCILIATION BETWEEN TOTAL VALUE ADDED AND PROFIT BEFORE TAXATION

Particulars	*₹ (crores)*	*₹ (crores)*
Profit before tax		741
Add: Depreciation	342	
Wages, Salaries and other benefits	14,761	
Debenture Interest	987	16,090
Total Value Added		16,831

PROBLEM 2

On the basis of the following income statement pertaining to CEEBEE Ltd., you are required to prepare:(a) Gross value added statement; and (b) Statement showing reconciliation of gross value added with Profit Before Taxation.

PROFIT AND LOSS ACCOUNT OF CEEBEE LTD.

for the year ended 31st March, 2023

Particulars	*₹ (crores)*	*₹ (crores)*
Income:		
Revenue from Operations		15,27,956
Other Income		604
(A)		15,28,560

Expenditure:		
Production and operational expenses:		
Decreases in inventory of finished goods	26,054	
Consumption of raw materials	7,40,821	
Power and lighting	1,20,030	
Wages, salaries and bonus (Admin.)	3,81,760	
Staff welfare expenses (Admin.)	26,240	
Excise duty	14,540	
Other manufacturing expenses	32,565	13,42,010
Administrative expenses:		
Directors' remuneration	7,810	
Other administrative expenses (Factory)	32,640	40,450
Interest on:		
9% Mortgage debentures	14,400	
Long-term loan from financial institution	10,000	
Bank overdraft	100	24,500
Depreciation on fixed assets		50,600
(B)		14,57,560
Profit before Taxation, (A) – (B)		71,000
Provision for Income-tax		25,470
Profit after Taxation		45,530
Balance of account as per last Balance Sheet		6,300
		51,830
Transferred to:		
General Reserve		18,212
Interim Dividend paid		22,000
		40,212
Surplus carried to Balance Sheet		11,618

SOLUTION

BRITE LTD.
VALUE ADDED STATEMENT FOR THE YEAR ENDED 31ST MARCH, 2023

Particulars	**₹ *(crores)***	**₹ *(crores)***
Revenue from Operations less returns		15,27,956
Less: Cost of bought in materials and services,		
Decrease in inventory of finished goods	26,054	
Consumption of raw materials	7,40,821	

Power and lighting	1,20,030	
Other manufacturing expenses	32,565	
Administrative Expenses	32,640	
Interest on bank overdraft	100	
Excise Duty	14,540	9,66,750
Value added by manufacturing and trading activities		5,61,206
Add: Other Income		604
Total Value Added		5,61,810

APPLICATION OF VALUED ADDED

Particulars	*₹ (crores)*	*₹ (crores)*	%
To Pay Employees:			
Wages, salaries and bonus	3,81,760		
Staff welfare expenses	26,240	4,08,000	72.62
To Pay Directors:			
Directors' remuneration		7,810	1.39
To Pay Government:			
Income tax		25,470	4.53
To Pay providers of capital:			
Interest on 9% Debentures	14,400		
Interest on long-term loan from financial institution	10,000		
Dividend to shareholders	22,000	46,400	8.26
To Provide for maintenance and expansion of the company:			
Depreciation on Fixed assets	50,600		
Transfer to General reserve	18,212		
Retained profit, ₹(11,618 – 6,300)	5,318	74,130	13.20
		5,61,810	100.00

STATEMENT SHOWING RECONCILIATION OF TOTAL VALUE ADDED WITH PROFIT BEFORE TAXATION

Particulars	*₹ (crores)*	*₹ (crores)*
Profit Before Taxation		71,000
Add back:		
Wages, salaries and bonus	3,81,760	
Staff welfare expenses	26,240	
Directors' remuneration	7,810	
Interest on 9% mortgage debentures	14,400	

Interest on long-term loan from financial institution	10,000	
Depreciation on Fixed Assets	50,600	4,90,810
Total Value Added		5,61,810

PROBLEM 3

The following is the Profit and Loss Account of CEEGEE Ltd. for the year ended 31.03.2023. Prepare a Gross Value Added Statement and show also the reconciliation between Gross Value Added and Profit before taxation.

PROFIT AND LOSS ACCOUNT FOR THE YEAR ENDED 31.03.2023

Particulars	*Notes*	*Amount (₹ in crores)*	
Income:			
Revenue from Operations		–	890
Other Income		–	55
			945
Expenditure:			
Production and operational expenses	(a)	641	–
Administration expenses (Factory)	(b)	33	–
Interest	(c)	29	–
Depreciation		17	(720)
Profit before taxes		–	225
Provision for taxes	(d)	–	(30)
Profit after tax		–	195
Balance as per last Balance Sheet		–	10
			205
Transferred to General Reserve		45	–
Dividend paid		95	–
		140	–
Surplus carried to Balance Sheet		65	–
		205	–

Notes:

(a) Production and Operational expenses	*₹ in crores*
Consumption of raw materials	293
Consumption of stores	59
Salaries, Wages, Gratuities etc. (Admn.)	82
Cess and Local taxes	98
Other manufacturing expenses	109
	641

(b) Administration expenses include salaries, commission to Directors ₹ 9 crores Provision for doubtful debts ₹ 6.30 crores.

Particulars	₹ *in crores*
(c) Interest on loan from ICICI Bank for working capital	9
Interest on loan from ICICI Bank for fixed loan	10
Interest on loan from IFCI for fixed loan	8
Interest on Debentures	2
	29

(d) The charges for taxation include a transfer of ₹ 3.00 crores to the credit of Deferred Tax Account.

(e) Cess and Local taxes include Excise Duty, which is equal to 10% of cost of bought-in material.

SOLUTION

CEEGEE LTD.

GROSS VALUE ADDED STATEMENT FOR THE YEAR ENDED 31ST MARCH, 2023

Particulars	₹ *in crores*	₹ *in crores*
Revenue from Operations		890
Less: Cost of bought in materials and services:		
Production and operational expenses (293 + 59 + 109)	461	
Administration expenses (33 – 9)	24	
Interest on working capital loan	9	
Excise duty [10% of (293 + 59)]	35.2	(529.20)
Value Added by manufacturing and trading activities		360.80
Add: Other income		55
Total Value Added		415.80

APPLICATION OF VALUE ADDED

Particulars	₹*('000)*	₹*('000)*	%
To Employees			
Salaries, Wages, Gratuities etc.		82	19.72%
To Directors			
Salaries and Commission		9	2.16%
To Government			
Cess and local taxes (98 – 35.2)	62.8		
Income tax	27.0	89.8	21.60%
To Providers of Capital			
Interest on Debentures	2		
Interest on Fixed Loan	18		
Dividends	95	115	27.66%
To Provide for maintenance and expansion of the company			
Depreciation	17		

General reserve	45		
Deferred tax	3		
Retained profits (65 – 10)	55	120	28.86%
		415.80	100%

RECONCILIATION BETWEEN GROSS VALUE ADDED WITH PROFITS BEFORE TAXATION

₹ in crores

Profits before taxes		225
Add: Depreciation	17	
Directors' Remuneration	9	
Salaries, Wages & Gratuities etc.	82	
Cess and Local Taxes	62.8	
Interest on Debentures	2	
Interest on Fixed Loan	18	190.8
Total Value Added		415.8

PROBLEM 4

The following is the Profit and Loss Account of CEEGEE Ltd. for the year ended 31.03.2023. Prepare a Gross Value Added Statement of CEEGEE Ltd. and show also the reconciliation between Gross Value Added and Profit before taxation.

PROFIT AND LOSS ACCOUNT FOR THE YEAR ENDED 31.03.2023

Particulars	*Notes*	*Amount (₹ in crores)*	
Income:			
Revenue from Operations		–	890
Other Income		–	55
			945
Expenditure:			
Production and operational expenses	(a)	641	–
Administration expenses (Factory)	(b)	33	–
Interest	(c)	29	–
Depreciation		17	(720)
Profit before taxes		–	225
Provision for taxes	(d)	–	(30)
Profit after tax		–	195
Balance as per last Balance Sheet		–	10
			205
Transferred to General Reserve			45
Dividend paid			95
Surplus carried to Balance Sheet			65
			205

Notes:

	₹ *in crores*
(a) Production and Operational expenses	
Consumption of raw materials	293
Consumption of stores	59
Salaries, Wages, Gratuities etc. (Admn.)	82
Cess and Local taxes	98
Other manufacturing expenses	109
	641

(b) Administration expenses include salaries, commission to Directors ₹ 9 crores Provision for doubtful debts ₹ 6.30 crores.

Particulars	₹ *in crores*
(c) Interest on loan from ICICI Bank for working capital	9
Interest on loan from ICICI Bank for fixed loan	10
Interest on loan from IFCI for fixed loan	8
Interest on Debentures	2
	29

(d) The charges for taxation include a transfer of ₹ 3.00 crores to the credit of Deferred Tax Account.

(e) Cess and Local taxes include Excise Duty, which is equal to 10% of cost of bought-in material and services

SOLUTION

CEEGEE LTD.
GROSS VALUE ADDED STATEMENT FOR THE YEAR ENDED 31ST MARCH, 2023

Particulars	₹ *in crores*	₹ *in crores*
Revenue from Operations		890
Less: Cost of bought in materials and services:		
Production and operational expenses (293 + 59 + 109)	461	
Administration expenses (33 – 9)	24	
Interest on working capital loan	9	
Excise duty (Refer working note)	55	549
Value Added by manufacturing and trading activities		341
Add: Other income		55
Total Value Added		396

APPLICATION OF VALUE ADDED

Particulars	₹('000)	₹('000)	%
To Employees			
Salaries, wages, gratuities etc.		82	20.71%
To Directors			

Salaries and commission		9	2.27%
To Government			
Cess and local taxes (98–55)	43		
Income tax	27	70	17.68%
To Providers of capital			
Interest on debentures	2		
Interest on fixed loan	18		
Dividends	95	115	29.04%
To Provide for maintenance and expansion of the company			
Depreciation	17		
General reserve	45		
Deferred tax	3		
Retained profits (65–10)	55	120	30.30%
		396	100%

RECONCILIATION BETWEEN GROSS VALUE ADDED WITH PROFITS BEFORE TAXATION

₹ in crores

Profits before taxes		225
Add: Depreciation	17	
Directors' Remuneration	9	
Salaries, Wages & Gratuities etc.	82	
Cess and Local Taxes	43	
Interest on Debentures	2	
Interest on Fixed Loan	18	171
Total Value Added		396

Working Note:

CALCULATION OF EXCISE DUTY

Say Cost of bought in materials and services is 'x'

Excise Duty is 10% of x = x/10

x = 461 + 24 + 9 + x/10

x = 494 + x/10 = 549 (approx.)

Excise Duty = 549 – 494 = ₹ 55

PROBLEM 5

From the following data compute the Economic Value Added:

Equity Share Capital	₹ 1,600 crores
Long-term Debt	₹ 320 crores
Interest	₹ 32 crores
Reserve and Surplus	₹ 3200 crores

Profit before Interest and Tax	₹ 1,432 crores
Tax Rate	30%
Beta Factor	1.05
Market Rate of Return	14%
Risk Free Rate	10%

SOLUTION

COMPUTATION OF ECONOMIC VALUE ADDED

Particulars	*₹ in crores*
Net Operating Profit after tax [NOPAT]	1002.40
Less: Cost of Operating Capital Employed [COCE] (13.75% of ₹ 5,120 crores)	704.00
Economic Value Added [EVA]	298.40

Working Notes:

1. Cost of Equity = Risk Free Rate + Beta factor × (Market Rate – Risk Free Rate)
   = 10 + 1.05 (14 – 10) = 14.2%
2. Cost of Debt = Interest(1 – Tax Rate)/Debt = 32(1 – .30)/320 = 7%
3. Capital Employed = Equity Shareholders' Funds+ Long-term Debt
   = (1600 + 3200) + 320 = 5120
4. WACC = (1600/5120) × 14.2% + (320/5120) × 7% = 13.75%
5. Net Operating Profit after Tax = 1432 – 30% of 1432 = 1002.40

PROBLEM 6

The following information is available of a concern; calculate Economic Value Added:

12% Debt Capital	₹ 2,000 crores
Equity Capital	₹ 500 crores
Reserve and Surplus	₹ 7,500 crores
Capital Employed	₹ 10,000 crores
Beta Factor	1.05
Market Rate of Return	19%
Equity (market) Risk Premium	10%
Operating Profit after tax	₹ 2,100 crores
Tax Rate	30%

SOLUTION

COMPUTATION OF ECONOMIC VALUE ADDED

Particulars	*₹ in crores*
Net Operating Profit after tax [NOPAT]	2100
Less: Cost of Operating Capital Employed [COCE] (17.28% of ₹ 10000 crores)	1728
Economic Value Added [EVA]	372

Working Notes:

1. Cost of Equity = Risk Free Rate + Beta × Equity Risk Premium = 9 + 1.05 × 10 = 19.5%
2. Cost of Debt = 12% (1 – 0.30) = 8.4%
3. Capital Employed = Equity Shareholders' Funds+ Long-term Debt
   = (500 + 7500) + 2000 = ₹ 10,000 crores
4. WACC = (8000/10000) × 19.5% + (2000/10000) × 8.4% = 17.28%

PROBLEM 7

CEEPEE Ltd supplies the following information using which you are required to calculate the Economic Value Added:

Financial Leverage	1.4 times
No. of Equity Shares(₹ 1000)	34000
Accumulated Profits	₹.260 crores
No. of 10% Debentures(₹ 10)	80 crores
Dividend Expectations of Equity Shareholders	17.50%
Tax Rate	30%

SOLUTION

COMPUTATION OF ECONOMIC VALUE ADDED

Particulars	*₹ in crores*
Net Operating Profit after tax [NOPAT]	196
Less: Cost of Operating Capital Employed [COCE] (11.5% of ₹ 1400 crores)	161
Economic Value Added [EVA]	35

Working Notes:

1. Cost of Equity = 17.5%
2. Cost of Debt = Interest(1-Tax Rate)/Debt = 80(1 – .30)/800 = 7%
3. Capital Employed = Equity Shareholders' Funds+ Long-term Debt
   = (340 + 260) + 800 = 1400
4. WACC = (600/1400) × 17.5% + (800/1400) × 7% = 11.50%
5. Financial Leverage = Profit before Interest & Tax/ Profit before Interest & Tax – Interest
   1.4 = Profit before Interest & Tax/ (Profit before Interest & Tax – 80)
   Profit before Interest & Tax = (80 × 1.4)/0.4 = 280
6. Net Operating Profit after Tax= Profit before Interest & Tax – Tax = 280 – 30% of 280 = 196

PROBLEM 8

The following information (as at 31-03-2023) is supplied to you by CEEF:

Particulars	*₹ in crores*
Profit after tax (PAT)	205.90
Interest	4.85
Equity Share Capital	40.00

Accumulated surplus	740.00
Loans (Long term)	37.00
Market capitalization	2,892.00

Addition information:

(a) Risk free rate	12.00 percent
(b) Long Term Market Rate (Based on BSE Sensex)	15.50 percent
(c) Effective tax rate for the company	25.00 percent
(d) Beta (b) for last few years	

Year	1	2	3	4	5
Beta	0.48	0.52	0.60	1.10	0.99

Using the above data you are requested to calculate the Economic Value Added of Fox Limited as on 31st March, 2023.

SOLUTION

COMPUTATION OF ECONOMIC VALUE ADDED

Particulars	*₹ in crores*
Net Operating Profit after tax [NOPAT]	209.5375
Less: Cost of Operating Capital Employed [COCE](14.357% of ₹ 777 crores)	111.5539
Economic Value Added[EVA]	97.9836

Working Notes:

Average Beta = (0.48 + 0.52 + 0.60 + 1.10 + 0.99)/5 = 0.738

1. Cost of Equity = 12% + 0.738 × (15.5% – 12%) = 14.583%
2. Cost of Debt = 4.85(1 – 0.25)/37 = 9.831%
3. Capital Employed = 40 + 700 + 37 = ₹ 777 crores
4. WACC = [(740/777) ×14.583%] + [(37/777) × 9.831%]= 13.889 + 0.468 = 14.357%
5. NOPAT = Profit after Interest and Tax + Interest net of Tax

   = 205.90 + (4.85 – 25% of 4.85) = ₹ 209.5375 crores

PROBLEM 9

Gold Ltd. has provided the following data for the Financial Year ending 2023:

	(Fig. in crores)
Share Capital	1,000
Reserve & Surplus	2,000
Long Term Debt	200
Trade Payables	50

Additional information provided is as follows:

Profit before Interest and Tax	₹ 1,000 Crores
Interest on Long Term Debt	₹ 20 Crores

Tax Rate	25%
Risk Free Rate	10%
Market Rate	15%
Beta factor	1.4

Calculate the Economic Value Added by Gold Ltd.

SOLUTION

COMPUTATION OF ECONOMIC VALUE ADDED

Particulars	*(₹ in crores)*
Net Operating Profit after tax [NOPAT] [1000 × (1 – 25%)]	750.00
Less: Cost of Capital [3200 × 16.4%]	(524.80)
Economic Value Added	225.20

Working Notes:

1. **Cost of Equity** = Risk Free Rate + b Factor (Market Rate – Risk Free Rate)
   = 10% + 1.4 (15% – 10%) = 10% + 7% = 17%
2. **Cost of Debt** = Interest on Long-term Debt (1 – t)/Long-term Debts
   = ₹ 20(1 – 0.25)/₹ 200 = 7.5%
3. **Capital Employed** = ₹ 1,000 + ₹ 2,000 + ₹ 200 = ₹ 3,200
4. **WACC** = (3000/3200) × 17% + (200/3200) × 7.5% = 16.4%

PROBLEM 10

X Ltd. has earned a net profit ₹ 15 lacs after tax at 30%. Interest cost charged by financial institutions was ₹ 10 lacs. The invested capital is ₹ 95 lacs of which 55% is debt. The company maintains weighted average cost of capital of 13%.

Required:

(a) Compute the Operating Income.

(b) Compute the Economic Value Added (EVA).

(c) X Ltd. has 6 lac equity shares outstanding. How much dividend can the company pay before the value of the entity starts declining?

SOLUTION

Taxable Income [EBT] = ₹ 15 lac/(1 – 0.30) = ₹ 21,42,857

Operating Income [EBIT] = Taxable Income + Interest = ₹ 21,42,857 + ₹ 10,00,000 = ₹ 31,42,857

EVA = [EBIT (1 – Tax Rate)] – [WACC × Invested Capital]
= [₹ 31,42,857 (1 – 0.30)] – [13% of ₹ 95,00,000]
= ₹ 22,00,000 – ₹ 12,35,000 = ₹ 9,65,000.

EVA Dividend = ₹ 9,65,000/6,00,000 = ₹ 1.6083 per share

PROBLEM 11

Bharat EVA Ltd. provides you the following data:

No. of Equity Shares(₹ 10)	192 crores
No. of 10% Debentures(₹ 100)	?

Free Reserves	₹ 1440 crores
Capital Reserve	₹ 960 crores
Securities Premium	₹ 480 crores
Tax Rate	30%
Beta Factor	1.05
Market Rate of Return	14%
Risk Free Rate	10%
Debt-Equity Ratio	1 : 2

Required: Compute the Economic Value Added:

(a) If Operating Profit after Tax is ₹ 1848 crores

(b) If Profit before Tax is ₹ 2,400 crores

(c) If Profit before Interest and Tax is ₹ 2640 crores

(d) If Profit after Interest and Tax is ₹ 1680 crores

(e) If Financial Leverage is 1.10 times

SOLUTION

COMPUTATION OF ECONOMIC VALUE ADDED

Particulars	***₹ in crores***
Net Operating Profit after tax [NOPAT]	1848.00
Less: Cost of Operating Capital Employed [COCE](11.8% of ₹ 7200 crores)	(849.60)
Economic Value Added[EVA]	998.40

Working Notes:

1. **Cost of Equity** = Risk Free Rate + Beta factor × (Market Rate – Risk Free Rate)
   = 10 + 1.05 (14 – 10)= 14.2%
2. **Debt-Equity Ratio** = Long-term Debt/Equity
   0.5 = Long-term Debt/(1920 + 1440 + 960 + 480)
   Long-term Debt = 4800 × 0.5 = 2400
3. **Cost of Debt** = Interest Rate (1 – Tax Rate) = 10%(1 – .30) = 7%
4. **Capital Employed** = (Equity Share Capital + Net Reserve and Surplus) + Long-term Debt
   = (1920 + 1440 + 960 + 480) + 2400 = 7200
5. **WACC** = [(4,800/7,200) × 14.2%] + [(2,400/7,200) × 7%] = 11.80%

Working Notes for Case (b):

1. Net Operating Profit after Tax = Profit before Tax + Interest – Tax
   = 2,400 + 240 – (30% of 2,640) = 1,848

   Now, EVA is same as in case (a)

Working Notes for Case (c):

1. Net Operating Profit after Tax = Profit before Interest & Tax – Tax
   = 2640 – 30% of 2640 = 1848

   Now EVA is same as in case (a)

Working Notes for Case (d):

1. Net Operating Profit after Tax = Profit after Interest and Tax + Interest net of Tax
=1680 + (240 – 30% of 240) = 1680 + 168 = 1848

Now EVA is same as in case (a)

Working Notes for Case (e):

1. Financial Leverage = Profit before Interest & Tax/(Profit before Interest & Tax – Interest)
1.1 = Profit before Interest & Tax/(Profit before Interest & Tax – 240)

Profit before Interest & Tax = (240 × 1.1)/0.1 = 2640

2. Net Operating Profit after Tax = Profit before Interest & Tax – Tax
= 2640 – 30% of 2640 = 1848

Now EVA is same as in case (a)

VERY SHORT ANSWER TYPE QUESTIONS

1. **Briefly explain the following: [1/2 Mark each]**
   (a) Value Added [VA]
   (b) Gross Value Added (GVA)
   (c) Net Value Added (NVA)
   (d) Value Added Statement
   (e) Objective of Value Added Statement
   (f) Economic Value Added [EVA]
   (g) Market Value Added [MVA]
   (h) Shareholders' Value Added [SVA]
   (i) Relationship between EVA and Market Value Added
2. **Enumerate the following : [1 Mark each]**
   (a) Two differences between Gross Value Added (GVA) and Net Value Added (GVA)
   (b) Two Differences between VA (Value Added) and Economic Value Added (EVA)
   (c) Two Advantages of Value Added (VA) Statements
   (d) Two Uses of Economic Value Added [EVA]
   (e) Two Limitations of Economic Value Added [EVA]
   (f) Two Uses of Market Value Added [MVA]
   (g) Two Limitations of Market Value Added [MVA]
3. **How are the following calculated ? [1 Mark each]**
   (a) Gross Value Added
   (b) Net Value Added
   (c) Economic Value Added [EVA]
   (d) Market Value Added [MVA]
   (e) Shareholders' Value Added [SVA]
4. How is Reconciliation between Gross Value Added and Profit Before Taxation done?
5. (a) Under which part of Gross Value Added Statement, will you classify the following items:
   1. Surplus on Sale and Lease back of Properties
   2. Leave Travel concession to Employees

3. Director's Sitting Fees
4. Interest & Penalties under Income Tax Act
5. Dividend Distribution Tax
6. Deferred Tax
7. Amount written back from Reserves
8. Depreciation
9. Tax Deducted at source from Employee's' Salary
10. Provision for Doubtful Debts

5.(b) How will you deal with the above items while preparing the Reconciliation Statement between Gross Value Added and Profit before Taxation?

PRACTICAL QUESTIONS

1. Following is the Profit and Loss Account of Tulsian Value Added (1) Ltd.

PROFIT AND LOSS ACCOUNT FOR THE YEAR ENDED 31ST MARCH, 2023

Income	*Notes*	*(₹ in crores)*	*(₹ in crores)*
Revenue from Operations			420
Other Income			20
Total Income			440
Expenditure:			
Cost of Materials consumed		162.00	
Changes in Inventories		62.00	
Consumption of Stores		26.00	
Employee Benefits Expense	(i)	36.00	
Finance Costs	(ii)	16.00	
Other Manufacturing Expenses	(iii)	65.40	
Depreciation and Amortization Expense		10.00	(377.40)
Profit before Tax			62.60
Provision for Tax			(6.60)
Profit after Tax			56.00

SURPLUS TO BE TAKEN TO BALANCE SHEET

Opening Balance	4
Add: Profit for the period	56
Less: Transfer to General Reserve	(40)
Less: Transfer to Fixed Assets Replacement Reserve	(8)
Less: Interim Dividend	(6)
Closing Balance	6

Notes:

(i) Employee Benefits Expense includes ₹ 6 crores for Remuneration to Directors and ₹ 24 crores for Departments other than Production.

(ii) Finance Costs include ₹ 4 crores for Interest on Working Capital, Loan, Cash Credit & Bank Overdraft.

(iii) Other Manufacturing Expenses include ₹ 15.40 crores for Cess and Local Taxes & Excise Duty. Excise Duty is 4% of Cost of bought-in Material.

Required: Prepare a Gross Value Added Statement and show the Reconciliation between Gross Value Added and Profit before Taxation:

[**Ans** Value Added by Manufacturing and Trading Activities ₹ 100 crores, GVA ₹ 120 crores, Application of Value Added: Employees: 20%, Directors:5%,Government: 10%, Providers of Capital: 15%, Provide for the Maintenance & Expansion of the company: 50%]

2. Following is the Profit and Loss Account of Tulsian Value Added (1) Ltd.

PROFIT AND LOSS ACCOUNT FOR THE YEAR ENDED 31ST MARCH, 2023

Income	*Notes*	*(₹ in crores)*	*(₹ in crores)*
Revenue from Operations			630
Other Income			210
Total Income			840
Expenditure:			
Cost of Materials consumed		243.00	
Changes in Inventories		93.00	
Consumption of Stores		39.00	
Employee Benefits Expense	(i)	54.00	
Finance Costs	(ii)	24.00	
Other Manufacturing Expenses	(iii)	98.10	
Depreciation and Amortization Expense		15.00	(566.10)
Profit before Tax			273.90
Provision for Tax			(9.90)
Profit after Tax			264.00

SURPLUS TO BE TAKEN TO BALANCE SHEET

Opening Balance	6
Add: Profit for the period	264
Less: Transfer to General Reserve	(60)
Less: Transfer to Fixed Assets Replacement Reserve	(12)
Less: Interim Dividend	(9)
Closing Balance	189

Notes:

(i) Employee Benefits Expense includes ₹ 9 crores for Remuneration to Directors and ₹ 36 crores for Departments other than Production.

(ii) Finance Costs include ₹ 6 crores for Interest on Working Capital, Loan, Cash Credit & Bank Overdraft.

(iii) Other Manufacturing Expenses include ₹ 23.10 crores for Cess and Local Taxes & Excise Duty. Excise Duty is 3.125% of Cost of bought-in Material and Services.

Required: Prepare a Gross Value Added Statement and show the Reconciliation between Gross Value Added and Profit before Taxation:

[**Ans** Value Added by Manufacturing and Trading Activities ₹ 150 crores, GVA ₹ 360 crores, Application of Value Added: Employees: 10%, Directors: 2.5%, Government: 5%, Providers of Capital: 7.5%, Provide for the Maintenance & Expansion of the company: 75%]

3. Following is the Profit and Loss Account of Tulsian Value Added (1) Ltd.

PROFIT AND LOSS ACCOUNT FOR THE YEAR ENDED 31ST MARCH, 2023

Income	*Notes*	*(₹ in crores)*	*(₹ in crores)*
Revenue from Operations			1050
Other Income			350
Total Income			1400
Expenditure:			
Cost of Materials consumed		405.00	
Changes in Inventories		155.00	
Consumption of Stores		65.00	
Employee Benefits Expense	(i)	90.00	
Finance Costs	(ii)	40.00	
Other Manufacturing Expenses	(iii)	163.50	
Depreciation and Amortization Expense		25.00	(943.50)
Profit before Tax			456.50
Provision for Tax			(16.50)
Profit after Tax			440.00

SURPLUS TO BE TAKEN TO BALANCE SHEET

Opening Balance	10
Add: Profit for the period	440
Less: Transfer to General Reserve	(100)
Less: Transfer to Fixed Assets Replacement Reserve	(20)
Less: Interim Dividend	(15)
Closing Balance	315

Notes:

(i) Employee Benefits Expense includes ₹ 15.00 crores for Remuneration to Directors and ₹ 60.00 crores for Departments other than Production.

(ii) Finance Costs include ₹ 10 crores for Interest on Working Capital, Loan, Cash Credit & Bank Overdraft.

(iii) Other Manufacturing Expenses include ₹ 38.50 crores for Cess and Local Taxes & Excise Duty. Excise Duty is 10% of Value Added by Manufacturing and Trading Activities.

Required: Prepare a Gross Value Added Statement and show the Reconciliation between Gross Value Added and Profit before Taxation:

[**Ans** Value Added by Manufacturing and Trading Activities ₹ 250 crores, GVA ₹ 600 crores, Application of Value Added: Employees: 10%, Directors: 5%, Government: 5%, Providers of Capital: 7.5%, Provide for the Maintenance & Expansion of the company: 75%]

4. Tulsian EVA(1) Ltd. provides you the following data to calculate the Economic Value Added:

Particulars	***₹ (In Crores)***
Equity Share Capital (₹ 10 each)	250
15% Preference Share Capital (₹ 100 each)	100
Reserves & Surplus	50
12% Debentures	800
Operating Profit after Tax	225
Tax Rate: 25%	
Weighted Average Cost of Capital (WACC):12.25%	

[**Ans** NOPAT ₹ 225 crores, OCE ₹ 1200 crores, EVA ₹ 78 crores]

5. Tulsian EVA (1) Ltd. provides you the following data to calculate the Economic Value Added:

Particulars	***₹ (In Crores)***
Equity Share Capital (₹ 10 each)	250
15% Preference Share Capital (₹ 100 each)	100
Reserves & Surplus	50
12% Debentures	800
Profit before Tax	225
Tax Rate: 25%	
Weighted Average Cost of Capital (WACC):12.25%	

[**Ans** NOPAT ₹ 240.75 crores, OCE ₹ 1200 crores, EVA ₹ 93.75 crores]

6. Tulsian EVA(1) Ltd. provides you the following data to calculate the Economic Value Added:

Particulars	***₹ (In Crores)***
Equity Share Capital (₹ 10 each)	250
15% Preference Share Capital (₹ 100 each)	100
Reserves & Surplus	50

12% Debentures	800
Profit before Interest and Tax	225
Tax Rate: 25%	
Weighted Average Cost of Capital (WACC): 12.25%	

[**Ans** NOPAT ₹ 168.75 crores, OCE ₹ 1200 crores, EVA ₹ 21.75 crores]

7. Tulsian EVA(1) Ltd. provides you the following data to calculate the Economic Value Added :

Particulars	***₹ (In Crores)***
Equity Share Capital (₹ 10 each)	250
15% Preference Share Capital (₹ 100 each)	100
Reserves & Surplus	50
12% Debentures	800
Profit after Interest and Tax	225
Tax Rate: 25%	
Weighted Average Cost of Capital (WACC): 12.25%	

[**Ans** NOPAT ₹ 297 crores, OCE ₹ 1200 crores, EVA ₹ 150 crores]

8. Tulsian EVA(2) Ltd. provides you the following data to calculate the Economic Value Added:

Particulars	***₹ (In Crores)***
Equity Share Capital (₹ 10 each)	500
15% Preference Share Capital (₹ 100 each)	200
Reserves & Surplus	100
12% Debentures	1600
Profit after Interest and Tax	675
Tax Rate: 25%	
Beta Factor:1.5	
Market Rate of Return:15.5%	
Risk Free Rate:6.5%	

[**Ans** NOPAT ₹ 819 crores, OCE ₹ 2400 crores, Cost of Equity = 20%, Cost of Pref. Shares = 15%, Cost of Debt = 9 %, WACC = 12.25% EVA ₹ 525 crores]

9. Tulsian EVA(3) Ltd. provides you the following data to calculate the Economic Value Added:

Particulars	***₹ (In Crores)***
Equity Share Capital (₹ 10 each)	750
15% Preference Share Capital (₹ 100 each)	300
Reserves & Surplus	150
12% Debentures	2400
Profit after Interest and Tax	675

Tax Rate: 25%	
Beta Factor:1.5	
Market Rate of Return:15.5%	
Equity Market Risk Premium:9%	

[**Ans** NOPAT ₹ 891 crores, OCE ₹ 3600 crores, Cost of Equity = 20%,Cost of Pref. Shares = 15%,Cost of Debt = 9 %, WACC = 12.25% EVA ₹ 450 crores]

10. Bharat EVA Ltd. provides you the following data:

No. of Equity Shares(₹ 10)	384 crores
No. of 10% Debentures(₹ 100)	?
Free Reserves	₹ 2880 crores
Capital Reserve	₹ 1920 crores
Securities Premium	₹ 960 crores
Tax Rate	30%
Beta Factor	1.05
Market Rate of Return	14%
Risk Free Rate	10%
Debt-Equity Ratio	1 :2

Required: Compute the Economic Value Added:

(a) If Operating Profit after Tax is ₹ 3696 crores

(b) If Profit before Tax is ₹ 5,520 crores

(c) If Profit before Interest and Tax is ₹ 7000 crores

(d) If Profit after Interest and Tax is ₹ 5964 crores

(e) If Financial Leverage is 1.1 times

Also explain the reason for the difference between the EVA as calculated by you and the MVA(Market Value Added) of TULSIAN Value Added LTD amounting to ₹ 15,000 Crores

[**Ans** OCE ₹ 14400 crores, Cost of Equity= 14.2%,Cost of Debt = 7 %,WACC = 11.80%, (a) NOPAT ₹ 3696 crores, EVA ₹ 1996.8 crores, (b) NOPAT ₹ 4200 crores, EVA ₹ 2500.8 crores, (c) NOPAT ₹ 4900 crores, EVA ₹ 3200.8 crores, (d) NOPAT ₹ 6300 crores, EVA ₹ 4600.8 crores, (e) NOPAT ₹ 3696 crores, EVA ₹ 1996.8 crores]

11. Tushar EVA Ltd. provides you the following data to calculate Economic Value Added (EVA):

30 crores, Equity Shares of ₹ 10 each fully paid-up

1 crores, 15% Pref. Shares of ₹ 100 each fully paid-up

8 crores, 15% Debentures of ₹ 100 each fully paid-up

Tax Rate	30%
Beta Factor	1.5
Market Rate of Return	15.5%
Equity Market Risk Premium	9%
Financial Leverage	1.5 times

[**Ans** NOPAT ₹ 252 crores, OCE ₹ 1200 crores, Cost of Equity = 20%, Cost of Pref. Shares = 15%, Cost of Debt = 10.5%, WACC = 13.25% EVA ₹ 93 crores]

12. Tulsian MVA Ltd. has the following Capital Structure as at 31st March, 2023:

Particulars	***₹ (In Crores)***
Equity Share Capital (₹ 10 each)	250
15% Preference Share Capital (₹ 100 each)	100
Reserves & Surplus	50
12% Debentures(₹ 100 each)	800

Additional Information: Currently Quoted Prices in the stock exchange: Equity Shares @ ₹ 60, Preference Shares @ ₹ 90, Debentures @ ₹ 95.

Required: Calculate the Market Value Added and interpret it.

[**Ans** MVA ₹ 1150 crores]

13. Tulsian Ltd. has existing assets in which it has capital invested amounting to ₹ 2000 crores. At present the Return of Capital Employed is 18% which is expected to be sustained in perpetuity. The company has a cost of capital of 12%. Estimate Market Value Added (MVA) on the basis of the Present Value of Economic Value Added (EVA) to the firm from its assets-in-place.

[**Ans** MVA ₹ 3000 crores]

14. In Question 4 to 9 Estimate Market Value Added (MVA) on the basis of the Present Value of Economic Value Added (EVA) to the firm from its assets-in-place assuming that Return of Capital Employed is expected to be sustained in perpetuity.

[**Ans** MVA: ₹ 1836.735 crores, ₹ 1965.306 crores, ₹ 1377.551 crores, ₹ 2424.49 crores, ₹ 6685.714 crores, ₹ 7273.47 crores,]

16 AMALGAMATION OF COMPANIES

LEARNING OBJECTIVES

After studying this chapter, you should be able to understand:

- ◇ General Meaning
- ◇ Legal Meaning of Amalgamation
- ◇ Provisions of Accounting Standard (AS) 14 Issued By ICAI
- ◇ Amalgamation in the Nature of Merger
- ◇ Amalgamation in the Nature of Purchase
- ◇ Distinction between Amalgamation in the Nature of Purchase and Amalgamation in the Nature of Merger
- ◇ Purchase Consideration
- ◇ Accounting Treatment in the Books of Transferor Company or Vendor Company
- ◇ Treatment of Difference between the Purchase Consideration and the Net Assets of the Transferor Company arising on Amalgamation in the Nature of Purchase
- ◇ Accounting Treatment in the Books of Transferee Company or Purchasing Company in case of Purchase
- ◇ Treatment of Reserves arising on Amalgamation in the Nature of Merger
- ◇ Accounting Treatment in the Books of Transferee Company or Purchasing Company In case of Merger

1.0 GENERAL MEANING

Amalgamation	Usually, the term 'Amalgamation' is used when two *or* more existing companies go into liquidation and a new company is formed to take over their business. ***For Example****, if a new company XY Ltd. is formed to take over the businesses of two existing companies, X Ltd. and Y Ltd., it is a case of Amalgamation.*
Absorption	The term 'Absorption' is used when one *or* more existing company(s) goes into liquidation and some existing company takes over its business. ***For Example****, if the business of an existing company X Ltd. is taken over by another existing company Y Ltd., it is a case of absorption.*
External Reconstruction	The term 'External Reconstruction' is used when one existing company goes into liquidation and a new company is formed to take-over its business. ***For Example****, if a new company X (New) Ltd. is formed to take over the business of an existing company X Ltd., it is a case of 'External Reconstruction'.*

2.0 PROVISIONS OF ACCOUNTING STANDARD (AS) 14 ISSUED BY ICAI

Effective date	Accounting Standard (AS) 14 on 'Accounting for Amalgamations' came into effect in respect of accounting periods commencing on *or* after 1.4.1995.
Mandatory	AS 14 is mandatory in nature.
Meaning of Amalgamation	Amalgamation means an amalgamation pursuant to the provisions of the Companies Act, 1956 *or* any other statute which may be applicable to companies.
Types of Amalgamations	An amalgamation may be either (a) an amalgamation in the nature of merger *or* (b) and amalgamation in the nature of purchase.

3.0 AMALGAMATION IN THE NATURE OF MERGER

MEANING OF AMALGAMATION IN THE NATURE OF MERGER

Amalgamation in the nature of merger is an amalgamation which satisfies all the following **five** conditions:

1. Transfer of All Assets & Liabilities	All the assets and liabilities of the transferor company (i.e., the company which is amalgamated into another company) become, after amalgamation, the assets and liabilities of the transferee company (i.e., the company into which a transferor company is amalgamated).
2. Same Equity Shareholders Holding 90%	Shareholders holding at least 90% of the face value of the equity shares of the transferor company (other than the equity shares already held therein, immediately before the amalgamation, by the transferee company *or* its subsidiaries *or* their nominees) become equity shareholders of the transferee company by virtue of the amalgamation.
3. Purchase Consideration in Equity Shares	The consideration for the amalgamation receivable by those equity shareholders of the transferor company who agree to become equity shareholders of the transferee company is discharged by the transferee company wholly by the issue of equity shares in the transferee company, except that cash may be paid in respect of any fractional shares.
4. Same Business	The business of the transferor company is intended to be carried on, after the amalgamation, by the transferee company.
5. Recording of Assets & Liabilities at Book Values	No adjustment is intended to be made to the book values of the assets and liabilities of the transferor company when they are incorporated in the financial statements of the transferee company except to ensure uniformity of accounting policies.

METHOD OF ACCOUNTING FOR AMALGAMATION IN THE NATURE OF MERGER

The **'Pooling of Interests Method'** should be used in accounting for amalgamation in the nature of merger. The salient features of this method are as follows:

Recording of Assets and Liabilities	In preparing the transferee company's financial statements, the assets and liabilities of the transferor company should be recorded at their existing carrying amounts and in the same form as at the date of amalgamation.
Recording of Reserves (whether capital or revenue or arising on revaluation)	The reserves should be recorded at their existing carrying amounts and in the same form as at the date of the amalgamation.
Recording of Balance of Profit and Loss A/c	The balance of the Profit and Loss Account of the transferor company should be aggregated with the corresponding balance of the transferee company *or* transferred to the General Reserve, if any.
Difference between the purchase consideration and the amount of share capital of the transferor company	The difference between the amount recorded as share capital issued *plus* any additional consideration in the form of cash *or* other assets and the amount of share capital of the transferor company should be adjusted in reserves.
Uniform Set of Accounting Policies	If, at the time of the amalgamation, the transferor and the transferee companies have conflicting accountant policies, a uniform set of accounting policies should be adopted following the amalgamation. The effects on the financial statements of any changes in accounting policies should be reported in accordance with Accounting Standard (AS) 5, 'Prior Period and Extraordinary items and changes in Accounting Policies'.

4.0 AMALGAMATION IN THE NATURE OF PURCHASE

MEANING OF AMALGAMATION IN THE NATURE OF PURCHASE

Amalgamation in the nature of purchase is an amalgamation which does not satisfy anyone *or* more of the conditions specified for Amalgamation in the nature of merger.

METHOD OF ACCOUNTING FOR AMALGAMATION IN THE NATURE OF PURCHASE

The **'Purchase Method'** should be used in accounting for amalgamation in the nature of purchase. The salient features of this method are as follows:

Recording of Assets and Liabilities	In preparing the transferee company's financial statements, the assets and liabilities of the transferor company should be incorporated **at their existing carrying amounts or, alternatively,** the consideration should be allocated to individual identifiable assets and liabilities on the basis of their **fair values** at the date of amalgamation.

Recording of Statutory Reserves	Where the requirements of the relevant statute for recording the statutory reserves in the books of the transferee company are complied with, statutory reserves of the transferor company should be recorded in the financial statements of the transferee company. The corresponding debit should be given to a suitable account head (e.g., 'Amalgamation Adjustment Account') which should be disclosed as a part of "Miscellaneous Expenditure" *or* other similar category in the Balance Sheet. When the identity of the statutory reserves is no longer required to be maintained, both the reserves and the aforesaid account should be reversed.
Recording of Reserves other than Statutory Reserves	The reserves (whether capital *or* revenue *or* arising on revaluation) of the transferor company, other than the statutory reserves, should *not be included* in the financial statements of the transferee company.
Balance of Profit and Loss A/c	The balance of the Profit and Loss Account of the transferor company whether debit *or* credit *loses its identity.*
Difference between the Purchase Consideration and the Net Assets of the transferor company	Any **excess of** the amount of the **consideration over the value of the net assets** of the transferor company acquired by the transferee company should be recognised in the transferee company's financial statements **as goodwill** arising on amalgamation. If the amount of the consideration is lower than the value of the net assets acquired, the difference should be treated as **Capital Reserve**. The goodwill arising on amalgamation should be amortised to income on a systematic basis over its useful life. The amortisation period should not exceed 5 years unless a somewhat longer period can be justified.

5.0 DISTINCTION BETWEEN AMALGAMATION IN THE NATURE OF PURCHASE AND AMALGAMATION IN THE NATURE OF MERGER

Basis of Distinction	***Amalgamation in nature of Merger***	***Amalgamation in nature of Purchase***
1. Method of Accounting	Pooling of Interest Method	Purchase Method
2. T/f of Assets & Liabilities	There is transfer of all assets & liabilities.	There need not be transfer of all assets & liabilities.
3. Equity Shareholders holding 90%	Equity shareholders holding 90% equity shares in transferee company **become shareholders of transferee company.**	Equity shareholders, need **not become shareholders of transferee company.**
4. Purchase Consideration	Purchase consideration is discharged **wholly by issue of equity shares** (except cash for fractional shares) to those equity shareholders of the transferor company who agree to become equity shareholders of the transferee company.	Purchase consideration **need not** be discharged wholly by issue of equity shares.

5. Same Business	The **same business** of the transferor company is intended to be carried on by the transferee company.	The business of the transferor company **need not** be intended to be carried on by the transferee company.
6. Recording of Assets & Liabilities	The assets & liabilities taken over are recorded **at their existing carrying amounts** except where adjustment is required to ensure uniformity of accounting policies.	The assets & liabilities taken over are recorded at their existing carrying amounts *or* the basis of their **fair values.**
7. Recording of Reserves of Transferor Co.	**All reserves** are recorded at their **existing carrying amounts** and in the same form.	(a) **only statutory reserves** are recorded at their existing carrying amounts as follows: Amalgamation Adjustment A/c Dr. To Statutory Reserve A/c (b) Other reserves are not recorded at all.
8. Recording of Balance of Profit & Loss A/c of Transferor Co.	The balance of P&L A/c should be **aggregated** with the corresponding balance of the transferee co. *or* transferred to the General Reserve.	The balance of P&L A/c losses its identify and is **not recorded** at all.
9. Difference between the Purchase Consideration and Share Capital/Net Assets of transfer co.	The excess of the purchase consideration over the share capital of transferor company is **debited to Reserves** and the excess of share capital over purchase consideration is **credited to reserves.**	The excess of purchase consideration over the net assets is treated as **Goodwill** and the excess of net assets over purchase consideration is treated as **Capital Reserve.**

6.0 PURCHASE CONSIDERATION

MEANING OF PURCHASE CONSIDERATION

Consideration for the amalgamation means the aggregate of the shares and other securities issued and the payment made in the form of cash *or* other assets by the transferee company to the shareholders of the transferor company.

The analysis of the aforesaid definition of 'Purchase Consideration' makes it clear that the payments made by the transferee company to discharge the debentureholders and other outside liabilities and the cost of winding up of transferor company shall not be considered as part of purchase consideration.

METHODS OF CALCULATING PURCHASE CONSIDERATION

(a) Depending upon the availability of information, the purchase consideration may be calculated on 'Net Assets taken over basis', *or* 'Net Payments to shareholders basis'.

(b) The following criteria may be adopted to select the basis of purchase consideration:

Case	*Basis of Purchase Consideration*
I. If all the modes of discharging the Purchase Consideration (e.g. Pref. Shares, Equity Shares or Cash payable to shareholders of transferor company) are given alongwith their individual amount	'Net Payment to Shareholders basis' should be used.
II. In other cases	'Net Assets taken over basis' should be used.

COMPUTATION OF PURCHASE CONSIDERATION (NET ASSETS BASIS)

	Particulars	₹
A.	Total Assets taken over at their agreed values	xxx
B.	*Less:* Total Liabilities taken over at their agreed amounts	xxx
C.	Net Assets taken over at their agreed values *or* Total Purchase Consideration [A – B]	xxx

$$\text{No. of Shares to be issued by Purchasing Co.} = \frac{\text{Amount to be discharged by issue of shares}}{\text{Issue Price of share}}$$

COMPUTATION OF PURCHASE CONSIDERATION (ON NET PAYMENT BASIS)

	Mode of Discharging Purchase Consideration	*No. of Shares*	*Issue Price*	₹
A.	Preference Shares	xxx	xxx	xxx
B.	Cash for Preference Shareholders	—	—	xxx
C.	Equity Shares	xxx	xxx	xxx
D.	Cash for Equity Shareholders	—	—	xxx
E.	Total Purchase Consideration (A + B + C + D)			xxx

Notes:

1. *The payment made by the transferee Company to discharge the debentureholders and other outside liabilities and the cost of winding up of transferor company* ***shall not be considered as part of purchase consideration.***
2. *The shares shall be issued in whole number and not in fraction.* ***For Example,*** *if no. of shares to be issued comes to 28454.55, only 28454 shares will be issued.*
3. *The fraction share shall be valued at market value and shall be paid in cash.* ***For Example,*** *if the market price of a share is ₹ 100 and the fractional share is 0.55, ₹ 55 (i.e., 0.55 × ₹ 100) will be paid in cash.*
4. *When it is decided to make entries relating to issue of shares at par value only, the number of shares to be issued by the purchasing company are calculated in the usual manner but thereafter are multiplied by par value only for the purposes of computing the purchase consideration.*

ILLUSTRATION 1

Given below are the extracts from the Balance Sheet of V Ltd. as at 31st March, 2023:

Particulars	₹
Equity Share Capital of ₹ 10 each	2,00,000
8% Pref. Share Capital of ₹ 100 each	50,000

Reserves & Surplus	41,100
10% Debentures	50,000
Current Liabilities	1,40,000
Property,Plant & Equipment	1,50,000
Current Assets	3,31,100

The business of V Ltd. is taken over by P Ltd. as on that date on the following terms:

(a) The issue of such an amount of fully paid 14% Debentures in P Ltd at 96 per cent as is sufficient to discharge 10% Debentures in V Ltd. at a premium of 20 per cent.

(b) The issue of such an amount of fully paid 10% Pref. Shares in P Ltd. at 125% as is sufficient to discharge 8% Pref. Shares in V Ltd. at a premium of 20%.

(c) One Equity Share of ₹ 10 each, ₹ 8 paid up valued at ₹ 15 per share and Cash ₹ 1.86 for every two Equity Shares held in V Ltd. The market value of an equity share of P Ltd. at present is ₹ 100.

(d) Expenses of liquidation of V Ltd. are to be reimbursed by P Ltd. to the extent of ₹ 10,000. Actual Expenses amounted to ₹ 12,000.

Show the calculation and discharge of Purchase Consideration.

SOLUTION

CALCULATION AND DISCHARGE OF PURCHASE CONSIDERATION

A. 10,000, Equity Shares to be issued [(20,000 × 1/2) × ₹ 15]	1,50,000
B. 480, 9% Pref. Shares to be issued [(50,000 × 120%)/125] × 125	60,000
C. Cash to Equity Shareholders [(20,000 × 1/2) × ₹ 1.86]	18,600
D. Total Purchase Consideration (A + B + C)	2,28,600

Note: *According to AS-14, the amount paid by purchasing Company to discharge the debentures holders and the liquidation expenses of Vendor Company are not considered as part of purchase consideration.*

I ILLUSTRATION 2

Given below are the extracts from the Balance Sheets of B Ltd. as at 31.03.2023:

Particulars	*(₹ in lacs)*
Equity Share Capital of ₹ 100 each	75
12% Pref. Share Capital of ₹ 100 each	20
Reserves & Surplus	33
10% Debentures of ₹ 100 each	3
Current Liabilities	19
Property,Plant & Equipment	70
Current Assets	80

A Ltd. absorbs B Ltd.as on that date on the following terms:

(a) 10% Debentures of the transferor company are to be discharged by transferee company by issuing such number of its 15% Debentures of ₹ 100 each so as to maintain the same amount of interest.

(b) 12% Preference Shares of the transferor company are to be discharged by transferee company by issuing equivalent numbers of 15% preference Shares of ₹ 100 each at ₹ 150 each.

(c) The transferee company shall issue 4 equity shares of ₹ 10 each at ₹ 30 each for each equity share in the transferor company.

(d) The transferee company shall pay the cost of absorption which amounts to ₹ 1,00,000

Show the calculation and discharge of Purchase Consideration.

SOLUTION

CALCULATION OF PURCHASE CONSIDERATION

20,000,12% Preference Shares [(20,00,000/100) × ₹ 150]	30,00,000
3,00,000 Equity Shares [{(75,00,000/100) × 4} × ₹ 30]	90,00,000
	120,00,000

Note: *According to AS-14, the amount paid by purchasing Company to discharge the debentures holders and the liquidation expenses of Vendor Company are not considered as part of purchase consideration.*

ILLUSTRATION 3

Given below are the extracts from the Balance Sheets of Y Ltd. as at 31st March 2023:

Particulars	***(₹ in lacs)***
Equity Share Capital of ₹ 10 each	10.00
8% Pref. Share Capital of ₹ 100 each	2.00
Reserves & Surplus	3.00
12% Debentures of ₹ 100 each	1.00
Current Liabilities	2.20
Non-Current Assets	12.80
Current Assets	5.40

X Ltd. absorbs Y Ltd. as on that date on the following terms:

(a) 12% Debentures of Y Ltd. are to be discharged by X Ltd. by issuing such number of its 15% Debentures of ₹ 100 each so as to maintain the same amount of interest.

(b) The issue of such an amount of fully paid 10% Pref. Shares in X Ltd. at 125% as is sufficient to discharge 8% Pref. Shares in Y Ltd. at a premium of 20%.

(c) The Equity Shareholders of Y Ltd. will receive the requisite number of Equity Shares of X Ltd. The Equity Shares of X Ltd are to be of a nominal value of ₹ 10 each credited as ₹ 8 paid up and valued at ₹ 15 per share.

(d) The transferee company shall pay the cost of absorption which amounts to ₹ 1,00,000

Show the calculation and discharge of Purchase Consideration.

SOLUTION

CALCULATION OF PURCHASE CONSIDERATION

1920,10% Pref. Shares [(2,00,000 + 20%)/125) × ₹ 125]	2,40,000
1,00,000 Equity Shares [1,00,000 × 15]	15,00,000
	17,40,000

Note: *According to AS-14, the amount paid by purchasing Company to discharge the debentures holders and the liquidation expenses of Vendor Company are not considered as part of purchase consideration.*

ILLUSTRATION 4

Given below are the extracts from the Balance Sheet of V Ltd. as at 31st March, 2023:

Particulars	₹
Equity Share Capital of ₹ 10 each	2,00,000
8% Pref. Share Capital of ₹ 100 each	50,000
General Reserve	20,000
Profit & Loss A/c	16,100
Statutory Reserves	5,000
10% Debentures	50,000
Trade Payables	1,40,000
Property,Plant & Equipment	1,50,000
Goodwill	1,19,500
Inventories	55,000
Trade Receivables	65,000
Cash at Bank	91,600

The business of V Ltd. is taken over by P Ltd. as on that date on the following terms:

(a) 50% of Property,Plant & Equipment are taken over at 100% more than the book value and the remaining Property,Plant & Equipment are taken over at 20% less than the book value.

(b) Goodwill of V Ltd. is to be valued at ₹ 52,500.

(c) Inventories are taken over at book value less 10% and Trade Receivables are taken over at book value subject to an allowance of 10% to cover doubtful debts.

(d) Trade Payables are to be taken over subject to a discount of 5% and Unrecorded Loan Liability of ₹ 38,500 to be discharged by P Ltd. at book value.

(e) The purchase consideration payable by P Ltd. was agreed as follows:

(i) The issue of such an amount of fully paid 14% Debentures in P Ltd at 96 per cent as is sufficient to discharge 10% Debentures in V Ltd. at a premium of 20 per cent.

(ii) The issue of such an amount of fully paid 10% Pref. Shares in P Ltd. at 125% as is sufficient to discharge 8% Pref. Shares in V Ltd. at a premium of 20%.

(iii) One Equity Share of ₹ 10 each, ₹ 8 paid up valued at ₹ 15 per share for every two Equity Shares held in V Ltd. and the balance in cash. The market value of an equity share of P Ltd. at present is ₹ 100.

(iv) Expenses of liquidation of V Ltd. are to be reimbursed by P Ltd. to the extent of ₹ 10,000. Actual Expenses amounted to ₹ 12,000.

Show the calculation and discharge of Purchase Consideration.

SOLUTION

1. CALCULATION OF PURCHASE CONSIDERATION

	Particulars	₹
A	Assets taken over at agreed values	
	Property, Plant & Equipment [(₹ 1,50,000 × 50%) + 100%]	1,50,000
	Property, Plant & Equipment [(₹ 1,50,000 × 50%) –20%]	60,000
	Inventories [₹ 55,000 – ₹ 5,500]	49,500
	Trade Receivables [₹ 65,000 – ₹ 6,500]	58,500
	Cash at Bank [91,600 – 2,000 (Expenses)]	89,600
	Goodwill	52,500
		4,60,100
B	*Less:* Liabilities taken over:	
	Trade Payables [₹ 1,40,000 – 5%]	1,33,000
	10% Debentures [₹ 50,000 + 20%]	60,000
	Unrecorded Loan	38,500
		2,31,500
C	Net Assets taken over (A – B)	2,28,600

2. DISCHARGE OF PURCHASE CONSIDERATION

A. 10,000, Equity Shares to be issued [(20,000 × 1/2) × ₹ 15]	1,50,000
B. 480, 10% Pref. Shares to be issued [(500 × 120%)]	60,000
C. Cash to Equity Shareholders [Balancing figure]	**18,600**
D. Total Purchase Consideration (A + B + C)	2,28,600

Note: *According to AS-14, the amount paid by purchasing Company to discharge the debentures holders and the liquidation expenses of Vendor Company are not considered as part of purchase consideration.*

ILLUSTRATION 5

Given below are the extracts from the Balance Sheet of V Ltd. as at 31st March, 2023:

Particulars	₹
Equity Share Capital of ₹ 10 each	2,00,000
8% Pref. Share Capital of ₹ 100 each	50,000
General Reserve	20,000
Profit & Loss A/c	16,100
Statutory Reserves	5,000
10% Debentures	50,000
Trade Payables	1,40,000
Property, Plant & Equipment	1,50,000
Goodwill	1,19,500

Inventories	55,000
Trade Receivables	65,000
Cash at Bank	91,600

The business of V Ltd. is taken over by P Ltd. as on that date on the following terms:

(a) 50% of Property, Plant & Equipment are taken over at 100% more than the book value and the remaining Property, Plant & Equipment are taken over at 20% less than the book value.

(b) Goodwill of V Ltd. is to be valued at ₹ 52,500.

(c) Inventories are taken over at book value less 10% and Trade Receivables are taken over at book value subject to an allowance of 10% to cover doubtful debts.

(d) Trade Payables are to be taken over subject to a discount of 5% and Unrecorded Loan Liability of ₹ 38,500 to be discharged by P Ltd. at book value.

(e) The purchase consideration payable by P Ltd. was agreed as follows:

(i) The purchase consideration is to be discharged to the extent of 20% in cash.

(ii) The issue of such an amount of fully paid 14% Debentures in P Ltd at 96 per cent as is sufficient to discharge 10% Debentures in V Ltd. at a premium of 20 per cent.

(iii) The issue of such an amount of fully paid 10% Pref. Shares in P Ltd. at 125% as is sufficient to discharge 8% Pref. Shares in V Ltd. at a premium of 20%.

(iv) The balance in the form of equity shares of ₹ 10 each, ₹ 8 paid up at a premium of ₹ 7 per share. The market value of an equity share of P Ltd. at present is ₹ 100.

(v) Expenses of liquidation of V Ltd. are to be reimbursed by P Ltd. to the extent of ₹ 10,000. Actual Expenses amounted to ₹ 12,000.

Show the calculation and discharge of Purchase Consideration.

SOLUTION

1. CALCULATION OF PURCHASE CONSIDERATION

Particulars	**₹**
A. Assets taken over at agreed values	
Property, Plant & Equipment [(₹ 1,50,000 × 50%) + 100%]	1,50,000
Property, Plant & Equipment [(₹ 1,50,000 × 50%) –20%]	60,000
Inventories [₹ 55,000 – ₹ 5,500]	49,500
Trade Receivables [₹ 65,000 – ₹ 6,500]	58,500
Cash at Bank [91,600 – 2,000(Expenses)]	89,600
Goodwill	52,500
	4,60,100
B. *Less:* Liabilities taken over:	
Trade Payables [₹ 1,40,000 – 5%]	1,33,000
10% Debentures [₹ 50,000 + 20%]	60,000
Unrecorded Loan	38,500
	2,31,500
C. Net Assets taken over (A – B)	2,28,600

2. DISCHARGE OF PURCHASE CONSIDERATION

A. Cash to Equity Shareholders [2,28,600 × 20%]	45,720
B. 480, 10% Pref. Shares to be issued [(500 × 120%)]	60,000
C. 8,192, Equity Shares to be issued [(2,28,600 – 45,720 – 60,000)/ ₹ 15] × ₹ 15	**1,22,880**
D. Total Purchase Consideration (A + B + C)	2,28,600

Note: *According to AS-14, the amount paid by purchasing Company to discharge the debentures holders and the liquidation expenses of Vendor Company are not considered as part of purchase consideration.*

ILLUSTRATION 6

Given below are the extracts from the Balance Sheet of V Ltd. as at 31st March, 2023:

Particulars	*₹ lakh*
Equity Share Capital of ₹ 10 each lakh	200.00
8% Pref. Share Capital of ₹ 100 each	50.00
General Reserve	20.00
Profit & Loss A/c	16.10
Statutory Reserves	5.00
10% Debentures	50.00
Trade Payables	140.00
Property,Plant & Equipment	150.00
Goodwill	119.50
Inventories	55.00
Trade Receivables	65.00
Cash at Bank	91.60

Prior to absorption, V Ltd. decides to declare and pay equity dividend @ 5%.The business of V Ltd. is taken over by P Ltd. as on that date on the following terms:

(a) 50% of Property,Plant & Equipment are taken over at 100% more than the book value and the remaining Property,Plant & Equipment are taken over at 20% less than the book value.

(b) Goodwill of V Ltd. is to be valued at ₹ 52.50 lakh.

(c) Inventories are taken over at book value less 10% and Trade Receivables are taken over at book value subject to an allowance of 10% to cover doubtful debts.

(d) Trade Payables are to be taken over subject to a discount of 5% and Unrecorded Loan Liability of ₹ 38.50 lakh to be discharged by P Ltd. at book value.

(e) The purchase consideration payable by P Ltd. was agreed as follows:

(i) The issue of such an amount of fully paid 14% Debentures in P Ltd at 96 per cent as is sufficient to discharge 10% Debentures in V Ltd. at a premium of 20 per cent.

(ii) The issue of such an amount of fully paid 10% Pref. Shares in P Ltd. at 125% as is sufficient to discharge 8% Pref. Shares in V Ltd. at a premium of 20%.

(iii) One Equity Share of ₹ 10 each, ₹ 8 paid up valued at ₹ 15 per share for every two Equity Shares held in V Ltd. and the balance in cash. The market value of an equity share of P Ltd. at present is ₹ 100.

(iv) Expenses of liquidation of V Ltd. are to be reimbursed by P Ltd. to the extent of ₹ 10.00 lakh. Actual Expenses amounted to ₹ 14.10 lakh.

Show the calculation and discharge of Purchase Consideration.

SOLUTION

1. CALCULATION OF PURCHASE CONSIDERATION

	Particulars	*₹ lakh*
A.	Assets taken over at agreed values	
	Property, Plant & Equipment [(₹ 150 lakh × 50%) + 100%]	150.00
	Property, Plant & Equipment [(₹ 150 lakh × 50%) –20%]	60.00
	Inventories [₹ 55 lakh – ₹ 5.5 lakh]	49.50
	Trade Receivables [₹ 65 lakh – ₹ 6.5 lakh]	58.50
	Cash at Bank [91.60 lakh – 10 lakh(ED) – 4 lakh (PD) – 4.1 lakh (Exp.)]	73.50
	Goodwill	52.50
		444.00
B.	*Less:* Liabilities taken over:	
	Trade Payables [₹ 140 lakh – 5%]	133.00
	10% Debentures [₹ 50 lakh + 20%]	60.00
	Unrecorded Loan	38.50
		231.50
C.	Net Assets taken over (A – B)	212.50

2. DISCHARGE OF PURCHASE CONSIDERATION

	₹ lakh
A. 10 lakh, Equity Shares to be issued [(20 lakh × 1/2) × ₹ 15]	150.00
B. 48 lakh, 10% Pref. Shares to be issued [(50 lakh × 120%)]	60.00
C. Cash to Equity Shareholders [Balancing figure]	**2.50**
D. Total Purchase Consideration (A + B + C)	212.50

Note: *According to AS-14, the amount paid by purchasing Company to discharge the debentures holders and the liquidation expenses of Vendor Company are not considered as part of purchase consideration.*

ILLUSTRATION 7

X Ltd. takes over Y Ltd. Given below are the extracts from the Balance Sheets of these companies at 31.03.2023:

Particulars	*X Ltd. (₹)*	*Y Ltd. (₹)*
Equity Share Capital of ₹ 10 each	30,00,000	12,00,000
Reserves & Surplus		10,00,000
15% Debentures	—	8,00,000

Current Liabilities	3,00,000	1,00,000
Tangible Block	24,00,000	18,00,000
Goodwill	—	1,50,000
Non-Current Investments (₹ 1,00,000, 6% tax free G.P. Notes)	1,00,000	—
Inventories	1,90,000	2,20,000
Other Current Assets	6,10,000	9,30,000

Additional Information:

	X Ltd.	*Y Ltd.*
Tangible Block	Valued at 25% more than the book value	Valued at 20% less than the book value
Goodwill	₹ 17,90,000	₹ 1,30,000
Inventories	Undervalued by ₹10,000	Overvalued by ₹ 20,000

X Ltd. to issue shares to share-holders of Y Ltd., on the basis of the intrinsic value of shares on the date of take-over. Calculate Purchase Consideration and show the discharge thereof.

SOLUTION

CALCULATION OF PURCHASE CONSIDERATION

Particulars	*X Ltd.* ₹	*Y Ltd.* ₹
Tangible Block	24,00,000	18,00,000
Add: Undervaluation (24,00,000 × 25%)	6,00,000	
Less: Overvaluation (18,00,000 × 20%]		(3,60,000)
Net Tangible Block at Revalued figure	30,00,000	14,40,000
Goodwill	17,90,000	1,30,000
Non-Current Investments (₹ 1,00,000, 6% tax free G.P. Notes)	1,00,000	—
Inventories	1,90,000	2,20,000
Add: Undervaluation of Cl. Inventory	10,000	
Less: Overvaluation of Cl. Inventory		(20,000)
Other Current Assets	6,10,000	9,30,000
	57,00,000	27,00,000
Less: 15% Debentures	—	(8,00,000)
Less: Current Liabilities	(3,00,000)	(1,00,000)
Net Assets	54,00,000	18,00,000
No. of Shares	3,00,000	1,20,000
Intrinsic Value	18	15
No. of Equity Shares to be issued (1,20,000 × 15/18)		1,00,000
Share Capital [1,00,000 × ₹ 10]		10,00,000
Securities Premium [1,00,000 × ₹ 8]		8,00,000
Purchase Consideration		18,00,000

ILLUSTRATION 8A

X Ltd. takes over Y Ltd. Given below are the extracts from the Balance Sheets of these companies at 31.03.2023:

Particulars	X Ltd. (₹)	Y Ltd. (₹)
Equity Share Capital of ₹ 10 each	30,00,000	12,00,000
Reserves & Surplus		10,00,000
15% Debentures	—	8,00,000
Current Liabilities	3,00,000	1,00,000
Tangible Block	24,00,000	18,00,000
Goodwill	—	1,50,000
Non-Current Investments (₹ 1,00,000, 6% tax free G.P. Notes)	1,00,000	—
Inventories	1,90,000	2,20,000
Other Current Assets	6,10,000	9,30,000

Additional Information:

	X Ltd.	Y Ltd.
Tangible Block	Understated by 20%	Overstated by 20%
Goodwill	17,90,000	70,000
Inventories	Understated by 5%	Overstated by 10%

X Ltd. to issue shares to share-holders of Y Ltd. at a price of ₹1 above the intrinsic value of its shares on the date of take-over. The market value of an equity share of X Ltd. at present is ₹ 100. The scheme of amalgamation was not supported by 100 shareholders of Y Ltd., and had to be paid ₹ 10 per share above their intrinsic value as consideration. The amount of the dissenting shareholders was borne by X Ltd.,Calculate Purchase Consideration and show the discharge thereof.

SOLUTION

CALCULATION OF PURCHASE CONSIDERATION

Particulars	X Ltd. ₹	Y Ltd. ₹
Tangible Block	24,00,000	18,00,000
Add: Undervaluation (24,00,000 × 20/80)	6,00,000	
Less: Overvaluation (18,00,000 × 20/120)		(3,00,000)
Net Tangible Block at Revalued figure	30,00,000	15,00,000
Goodwill	17,90,000	70,000
Non-Current Investments (₹ 1,00,000, 6% tax free G.P. Notes)	1,00,000	—
Inventories	1,90,000	2,20,000
Add: Undervaluation of Cl. Inventory (1,90,000 × 5/95)	10,000	
Less: Overvaluation of Cl. Inventory (2,20,000 × 10/110)		(20,000)
Other Current Assets	6,10,000	9,30,000
	57,00,000	27,00,000

Less: 15% Debentures	—	(8,00,000)
Less: Current Liabilities	(3,00,000)	(1,00,000)
Net Assets	54,00,000	18,00,000
No. of Shares	3,00,000	1,20,000
Intrinsic Value	18	15
Issue Price [₹18 + ₹1]	19	
No. of Equity Shares to be issued [(1,20,000 – 100) × 15/19]		94,657.89
Share Capital [94,657 × ₹ 10]		9,46,570
Securities Premium [94,657 × ₹ 9]		8,51,913
Cash for fraction [0.89 × ₹ 100]		89
Payment to dissenting shareholders[100 × (₹15 + ₹ 10)]		2,500
Purchase Consideration		18,01,072

ILLUSTRATION 8B

IN THE PREVIOUS ILLUSTRATION Calculate Purchase Consideration and show the discharge thereof if it is also decided to make the entries relating to the issue of shares at par value only.

SOLUTION

No. of Equity Shares to be issued [(1,20,000 – 100) × 15/19]	94,657.89
Share Capital [94,657 × ₹ 10]	9,46,570
Cash for fraction [0.89 × ₹ 100]	89
Payment to dissenting shareholders [100 × (₹15 + ₹ 10)]	2,500
Purchase Consideration	9,49,159

ILLUSTRATION 9

Given below are the extracts from the Balance Sheet of B Ltd. on at 31st March 2023:

Particulars	₹
80,000 Equity shares of ₹ 10 each fully paid up	8,00,000
Reserves & Surplus	1,00,000
Current Liabilities	1,00,000
Non-Current Assets	7,00,000
Current Assets	3,00,000

The consideration was agreed to be paid as follows:

(a) A payment in cash of ₹ 5 per share in B Ltd., and

(b) The issue of shares of ₹ 10 each in A Ltd. on the basis of 2 equity shares (valued at ₹ 15) and one 10% Cumulative Preference shares (valued at ₹ 10) for every five shares held in B Ltd.

The whole of the share capital consists of shareholdings in exact multiple of five except the followings holdings:

A	116
B	76
C	72

D	28
Other individual	8 (each member holding one share each)
	300

It was agreed that A Ltd. will pay in cash for fractional shares equivalent at agreed value of shares in B Ltd.

Required: Prepare a Statement showing the purchase consideration receivable in shares and cash.

SOLUTION

STATEMENT SHOWING THE COMPUTATION OF PURCHASE CONSIDERATION

Particulars	₹
31,994 Equity Shares @ ₹ 15 each	4,79,910
15,997 Preference Shares @ ₹ 10 each	1,59,970
Cash [(80,000 – 15) × ₹ 5]	3,99,925
	10,39,805
Add: Cash for fractional shares [15 × ₹ 13]	195
	10,40,000

Working Notes:

(I) SCHEDULE SHOWING FRACTIONAL SHARES

Share holder	*Holding of Shares*	*Exchangeable in multiple of five*	*Non Exchangeable Shares*
A	116	115	1
B	76	75	1
C	72	70	2
D	28	25	3
Others	8	–	8
	300	285	15

(ii) Equity Shares to be issued by A Ltd. = [(80,000 – 15) × 2/5] = 31,994

(iii) Preference Shares to be issued by A Ltd. = [(80,000 – 15) × 1/5] = 15,997

(IV) VALUATION OF FRACTIONAL SHARES

Cash for 5 equity shares [5 × ₹ 5]	₹ 25
2 equity shares for 5 equity shares [2 × ₹15]	₹ 30
1 Pref. share for 5 equity shares [1 × ₹ 10]	₹ 10
Total	₹ 65
Value for 1 equity share [₹65/5]	₹13
No. of fractional shares	15
Cash for fractional shares [15 × ₹ 13]	195

7.0 ACCOUNTING TREATMENT IN THE BOOKS OF TRANSFEROR COMPANY OR VENDOR COMPANY

Step 1: Open a Realisation Account and transfer all the recorded assets [including intangible assets like goodwill at their respective book values (i.e., the values at which they are appearing in the books of vendor company) irrespective of the fact whether the purchasing company has taken over *or* not. However, Cash and Bank Balances are transferred to Realisation Account only to the extent it is taken over by the purchasing company.

JOURNAL ENTRY

Realisation A/c	Dr.	*(with the total)*
To Sundry Assets (individually)		*(with their individual book values)*

Notes:

(i) An asset against which a provision or reserve has been created should be transferred at its gross figure and not at its net figure e.g., debtors.

(ii) Provision/Reserve against a liability is a separate account and thus, it should be transferred to Realisation Account separately like other assets e.g., reserve for discount on creditors.

(iii) The cash and bank balances should not be transferred to Realisation account if these are not taken over by the purchasing company.

Step 2: Transfer all third parties liabilities which are taken over by the purchasing company, at their respective book figures.

JOURNAL ENTRY

Sundry Assets (individually)	Dr.	*(with their individual book values)*
To Realisation A/c		*(with the total)*

Notes:

(i) A liability against which a provision or reserve has been created should be transferred at its gross figure and not at its net figure, e.g., creditors.

(ii) Items in the nature of 'Provisions' (e.g., Provision for taxation, Employees Provident Fund, Pension Fund, Provision for Doubtful Debt, Provision for Depreciation) should be transferred to Realisation Account.

(iii) Items in the nature of "Reserve" (e.g., credit balance of Profit and Loss Account, General Reserve, Dividend Equalisation Fund, Workmen Compensation Fund) should not be transferred to Realisation Account but that portion of any reserve/fund which represents a liability expected to arise in future should be transferred to Realisation Account (e.g., Estimated Workmen Compensation Claim out of Workmen Compensation Reserve).

Step 3: Make due the Purchase Consideration from the Purchasing Company.

JOURNAL ENTRY

Purchasing Company's A/c	Dr.	*(with the Purchase Consideration Due)*
To Realisation A/c		

Step 4: Receive the Purchase Consideration from the Purchasing Company.

Cash/Bank A/c	Dr.	*(with Cash Received)*
Preference Shares in Purchasing Company	Dr.	*(with Issue Price of Pref. Shares)*
Equity Shares in Purchasing Company	Dr.	*(with Issue Price of Equity Shares)*
To Purchasing Company		*(With the total)*

Step 5: Do the Treatment of Liquidation/Realisation expenses.

Case	*JOURNAL ENTRY*
(a) If these expenses are to be borne and paid by the Vendor Company	Realisation A/c To Bank A/c
(b) If these expenses are to be reimbursed by the purchasing company	
(i) *On Payment by Vendor Company*	Purchasing Company Dr. *(with agreed amount)* Realisation A/c Dr. *(with excess)* To Bank A/c (with the total)
(ii) *On reimbursement*	Bank A/c To Purchasing Company

Step 6: Realise those assets which have not been taken over by the purchasing company.

JOURNAL ENTRY

Bank A/c	Dr.	*(with the amount realised)*
To Realisation A/c		

Step 7: Discharge the Claims of Preference Shareholders and transfer the difference between the amount actually payable and the book figure to the Realisation Account.

(A) JOURNAL ENTRY ON MAKING DUE

Preference Share Capital A/c	Dr.	*(with book figure)*
Realisation A/c	Dr.	*(with the loss)*
To Preference Shareholders' A/c's		*(with the amount actually payable)*
To Realisation A/c		*(with the profit)*

(B) JOURNAL ENTRY ON MAKING PAYMENT

Preference Shareholders' A/cs	Dr.
To Bank A/c	
To Preference Shares in purchasing Co.	

Step 8: Ascertain the Profit *or* Loss on Realisation and transfer the same to the Equity Shareholders' A/c.

(a) In case of Profit on Realisation	Realisation A/c Dr. To Equity Shareholders' A/c

(b) In case of Loss on Realisation	Equity Shareholders' A/c Dr. To Realisation A/c

Step 9: Transfer the Equity Share Capital A/c, Accumulated Profits, Reserve and losses to the Equity Shareholders' A/cs.

(a) For Transfer of Equity Share Capital, Accumulated Profits and Reserves [after making adjustment for Dividend, Dividend Tax etc.]	Equity Share Capital A/c Dr. Profit and Loss A/c Dr. General Reserve A/c Dr. Dividend Equalisation Reserve Dr. Workmen Compensation reserve Dr. Capital Reserve A/c Dr. Securities Premium A/c Dr. Debenture redemption Reserve Dr. Capital Redemption Reserve Dr. Statutory Reserves Dr. To Equity Shareholders' A/c
(b) For Transfer of Accumulated Losses	Equity Shareholders' A/c Dr. To Profit and Loss A/c (Dr. Balance)

Step 10: Make Final Payment to Equity Shareholders:

Equity Shareholders' A/c Dr. *(with the total)* To Equity Shares in Purchasing Co. To Cash/Bank A/c

Note: *The net amount payable to the equity shareholders must be equal to the amount of shares in Purchasing Co. and Cash and Bank Balance left after the discharge of all outsiders' liabilities and claims of Preference Shareholders.*

8.0 TREATMENT OF DIFFERENCE BETWEEN THE PURCHASE CONSIDERATION AND THE NET ASSETS OF THE TRANSFEROR COMPANY ARISING ON AMALGAMATION IN THE NATURE OF PURCHASE

Case	*Accounting Treatment*
If Purchase Consideration > Net Assets	The excess of Purchase Consideration over the value of Net Assets acquired should be Treated as **Goodwill arising on amalgamation.** Such goodwill should be amortised on a systematic basis over a period not exceeding 5 years unless longer period can be justified.
If Net Assets > Purchase Consideration	The excess of net assets acquired over the Purchase Consideration should be treated as **Capital Reserve arising on Amalgamation.**

ILLUSTRATION 10

[Treatment of Reserves arising on Amalgamation in the nature of Purchase]

(₹ in lacs)

Particulars	Case I ₹	Case II ₹	Case III ₹
Share Capital issued by Transferee Co.	9.50	9.50	9.50
Cash for fractional Share paid by Transferee Co.	.50	.50	.50
Assets acquired by Transferee Co.	11.20	11.00	10.80
Liabilities undertaken by Transferee Co.	1.00	1.00	1.00

SOLUTION

CALCULATION OF CAPITAL RESERVE/GOODWILL

Particulars	Case I ₹	Case II ₹	Case III ₹
A. Purchase Consideration (9.50 + 0.50)	10.00	10.00	10.00
B. Net Assets acquired (Assets – Liabilities)	10.20	10.00	9.80
C. Goodwill			.20
or			
Capital Reserve	0.20	—	—

9.0 ACCOUNTING TREATMENT IN THE BOOKS OF TRANSFEREE COMPANY *or* PURCHASING COMPANY IN CASE OF PURCHASE

Step 1: Record the Acquisition of business from the Vendor Company.

JOURNAL ENTRY

Business Purchase A/c	Dr.	*(with purchase consideration)*
To Liquidator of the Vendor Co.		

Step 2A: In case of Amalgamation in the nature of Purchase.

"Record the Assets and Liabilities taken over at their respective agreed values (i.e., not their book values) and debit the Goodwill Account with the excess of Purchase Consideration over the Net Assets taken over (if any) *or* credit the Capital Reserve Account with the excess of Net Assets over the Purchase Consideration (if any)".

JOURNAL ENTRY

Assets (Individually)	Dr.	*(with their respective agreed values of the assets taken over)*
Goodwill A/c	Dr.	*(with excess of Purchase Consideration over the Net Assets)*
To Liabilities (Individually)		*(with the respective agreed amount of the liabilities taken over)*
To Business Purchase A/c		*(with the Purchase consideration)*
To Capital Reserve A/c		*(with excess of Net Assets over the Purchase Consideration)*

Step 2B: In case of Amalgamation in the nature of Purchase.

"Record the Statutory Reserves of the Transferor Company"

JOURNAL ENTRY

Amalgamation Adjustment A/c	Dr.	*(with the total)*
To Statutory Reserves A/c (Individually)		*(with their respective book balances)*

Note: *Amalgamation Adjustment Account is disclosed as a negative figure item under the head "Reserves & Surplus" of Balance Sheet of a Company.*

Step 3: Make Payment to Vendor Company.

JOURNAL ENTRY

Liquidator of Vendor Co.'s A/c	Dr.	*(with the total)*
To Equity Share Capital A/c		*(with the paid up value of Equity Shares issued)*
To Preference Share Capital A/c		*(with the paid up value of Pref. Shares issued)*
To Securities Premium A/c		*(with the Securities Premium)*
To Cash A/c/Bank A/c		*(with the Cash Payment)*

Note: *The Shares issued by way of purchase consideration must be recorded at their paid up values (i.e., not at their issued prices) after giving due credit to Securities Premium Account (in case the shares have been issued at premium).*

Step 4: Record the Issue of Debentures (if any) to discharge the existing Debentureholders of vendor company.

JOURNAL ENTRY

Debentures in Vendor Company	Dr.	*(with the amount of debentures)*
Discount on Issue of Debentures in Purchasing Company	Dr.	*(with the Debentures Discount)*
To Debentures in Purchasing Company		*(with the Nominal Value)*
To Securities Premium A/c		*(with the Debenture Premium)*

Step 5: Record the Reimbursement of the Liquidation Expenses of the Vendor Company.

JOURNAL ENTRY

Goodwill A/c (in case of Purchase)	Dr.
To Bank A/c	

Step 6: Eliminate the unrealised profit included in the unsold stock.

(a) Where the Unsold Inventories of the purchasing company includes the goods purchased from the vendor company

Goodwill A/c (in case of Purchase)	Dr.
To Inventories A/c	

(b) Where the Unsold Inventories of the vendor company includes goods purchased from the purchasing company, only the amount of stock is reduced to its cost while passing the entries on acquisition. (i.e., Entry in Step 2).

Note: *In case of sale of goods at loss, no adjustment is required*

Step 7: Eliminate the Inter Company Owings

(a) To eliminate the Debts owed by Vendor Company	Trade Payables of Vendor Co Dr. To Trade Receivables
(b) To eliminate the Debts owed by Purchasing Company	Trade Payables Dr. To Trade Receivables of Vendor Co.
(c) To eliminate the Bills drawn and retained by Vendor Co. upon Purchasing Company	Bills Payable A/c Dr. To Bills Receivable of Vendor Co.
(d) To eliminate the Bills drawn and retained by Purchasing Company upon Vendor Co.	Bills Payable of Vendor Co. Dr. To Bills Receivable A/c
(e) To eliminate the Debentures held by Vendor Co. in Purchasing Co.	Debentures A/c Dr. [Face value] Goodwill A/c Dr. [If FV < BV] To Investment in Debentures A/c (Vendor Co.) [Book Value] To Capital Reserve A/c [If FV > BV]
(f) To eliminate the Debentures held by Purchasing Co. in Vendor Co.	Debentures in Vendor Co. Dr. [Face Value] Goodwill A/c Dr. [If FV < BV] To Investment in Debentures A/c [Book value] To Capital Reserve A/c [If FV > BV]

Notes:

(i) Bills drawn by one company upon the other company and discounted with the bank should not be eliminated because these bills represent owing between the bank and the company and not the inter-company owings.

(ii) Where the debtors of a company include a sum due from another company but the creditors of another company include a lesser sum due to the former company. The difference should be treated as Cash-in-transit.

(iii) The entry (f) in Step 7 should be merged with entry in Step 4 so that the new debentures will be issued to discharge those debentures of vendor company which are held by outsiders (i.e., holders other than the purchasing company).

(iv) In case of entries (e) and (f), the loss should be debited to Goodwill A/c (in case of purchase) and the profit should be credited to Capital Reserve A/c.

Step 8: Set off Goodwill against Capital Reserve

JOURNAL ENTRY

Capital Reserve A/c	Dr.
To Goodwill A/c	

Note: *The objective of passing the aforesaid journal entry is to disclose only one item (i.e., out of Capital Reserve and Goodwill) which is net of other item.*

ILLUSTRATION 11A

Given below are the extracts from the Balance Sheet of V Ltd. as at 31st March, 2023:

Particulars	₹
Equity Share Capital of ₹ 10 each	2,00,000
8% Pref. Share Capital of ₹ 100 each	50,000
General Reserve	20,000
Profit & Loss A/c	16,100
Statutory Reserves	5,000
10% Debentures	50,000
Trade Payables	1,40,000
Property,Plant & Equipment	1,50,000
Goodwill	1,19,500
Inventories	55,000
Trade Receivables	65,000
Cash at Bank	91,600

The business of V Ltd. is taken over by P Ltd. as on that date on the following terms:

(a) 50% of Property,Plant & Equipment are taken over at 100% more than the book value and the remaining Property,Plant & Equipment are taken over at 20% less than the book value.

(b) Goodwill of V Ltd. is to be valued at ₹ 52,500.

(c) Inventories are taken over at book value less 10% and Trade Receivables are taken over at book value subject to an allowance of 10% to cover doubtful debts.

(d) Trade Payables are to be taken over subject to a discount of 5% and Unrecorded Loan Liability of ₹ 38,500 to be discharged by P Ltd. at book value.

(e) The purchase consideration payable by P Ltd. was agreed as follows:

(i) The issue of such an amount of fully paid 14% Debentures in P Ltd at 96 per cent as is sufficient to discharge 10% Debentures in V Ltd. at a premium of 20 per cent.

(ii) The issue of such an amount of fully paid 10% Pref. Shares in P Ltd. at 125% as is sufficient to discharge 8% Pref. Shares in V Ltd. at a premium of 20%.

(iii) One Equity Share of ₹ 10 each, ₹ 8 paid up valued at ₹ 15 per share for every two Equity Shares held in V Ltd. and the balance in cash. The market value of an equity share of P Ltd. at present is ₹ 100.

(iv) Expenses of liquidation of V Ltd. are to be reimbursed by P Ltd. to the extent of ₹ 10,000. Actual Expenses amounted to ₹ 12,000.

(g) Statutory Reserves are to be maintained for 2 more years.

Required: *Pass Journal Entries in the books of V Ltd and P Ltd.*

SOLUTION

JOURNAL OF V LTD.

Date	Particulars		L.F.	Dr. (₹)	Cr. (₹)
1	Realisation A/c	Dr.		4,79,100	
	To Goodwill				1,19,500
	To Property,Plant & Equipment				1,50,000

	To Inventories			55,000
	To Trade Receivables			65,000
	To Cash at Bank [91,600 – 2,000 Exp.]			89,600
	(Being the transfer of various assets to Realisation A/c)			
2	10% Debentures Dr.		50,000	
	Trade Payables Dr.		1,40,000	
	To Realisation A/c			1,90,000
	(Being the transfer of various liabilities to Realisation A/c)			
3	P Ltd Dr.		2,28,600	
	To Realisation A/c			2,28,600
	(Being the purchase consideration due)			
4	Equity Shares in P Ltd. Dr.		1,50,000	
	10% Pref. Shares in P Ltd. Dr.		60,000	
	Cash at Bank Dr.		18,600	
	To P Ltd.			2,28,600
	(Being the receipt of purchase consideration)			
5	P Ltd. Dr.		10,000	
	Realisation A/c Dr.		2,000	
	To Bank A/c			12,000
	(Being liquidation expenses paid out of which ₹ 10,000 are to be reimbursed by purchasing company)			
6	Bank A/c Dr.		10,000	
	To P Ltd.			10,000
	(Being liquidation expenses reimbursed by purchasing company)			
7	8% Pref. Share Capital A/c Dr.		50,000	
	Realisation A/c Dr.		10,000	
	To Pref. Shareholders' A/c			60,000
	(Being the transfer of Pref. Share Capital to Pref. shareholders' A/c & loss on discharge to Realisation A/c)			
8	Pref. Shareholders' A/c Dr.		60,000	
	To 10% Pref. Shares in P Ltd.			60,000
	(Being the claims of Pref. share holders discharged)			
9	Equity Shareholders' A/c Dr.		72,500	
	To Realisation A/c			72,500
	(Being the transfer of loss on Realisation)			
10	Equity Share Capital A/c Dr.		2,00,000	

	General Reserve Dr.		20,000	
	Profit & Loss A/c Dr.		16,100	
	Statutory Reserves A/c Dr.		5,000	
	To Equity Shareholders' A/c			2,41,100
	(Being the transfer of Share Capital & balance of P&L A/c & Reserves to Equity Shareholders' Account)			
11	Equity Shareholders' A/c Dr.		1,68,600	
	To Equity Shares in P Ltd.			1,50,000
	To Bank A/c			18,600
	(Being the claims of Equity Shareholders discharged)			

JOURNAL OF P LTD.

Date	Particulars	L.F.	Dr. (₹)	Cr. (₹)
1	Business Purchase A/c Dr.		2,28,600	
	To Liquidators of V Ltd.			2,28,600
	(Being the purchase of the business)			
2	Goodwill Dr.		52,500	
	Property, Plant & Equipment [₹ 1,50,000 + ₹ 60,000] Dr.		2,10,000	
	Inventories Dr.		49,500	
	Trade Receivables Dr.		65,000	
	Bank Dr.		89,600	
	Reserve for Discount on Trade Payables [5% of ₹ 1,40 000] Dr.		7,000	
	To Provision for Doubtful Debts [10% of ₹ 65,000]			6,500
	To Trade Payables			1,40,000
	To 10% Debentures [₹ 50,000 + 20%]			60,000
	To Unrecorded Loan			38,500
	To Business Purchase A/c			2,28,600
	(Being the Assets and Liabilities taken over)			
3	Liquidators of V Ltd. Dr.		2,28,600	
	To Equity Share Capital A/c [10,000 × ₹ 8]			80,000
	To 10% Pref. Share Capital A/c [480 × ₹ 100]			48,000
	To Securities Premium A/c [(10,000 × ₹ 7) + (480 × ₹ 25)]			82,000
	To Bank A/c			18,600
	(Being the purchase consideration discharged)			
4	Goodwill A/c Dr.		10,000	
	To Bank A/c			10,000

	(Being the payment of Liquidation Expenses of Vendor co.)			
5	10% Debentures of V Ltd. Dr.		60,000	
	Discount on Issue of 14% Debentures A/c Dr.		2,500	
	To 14% Debentures A/c			62,500
	(Being 10% Debentures of Vendor co. redeemed by issue of 625, 14% Debentures of ₹ 100 each at a discount of 4%)			
	[Face Value of Debentures = ₹ 60,000/96% = ₹ 62,500]			
6	Unrecorded Loan A/c Dr.		38,500	
	To Bank A/c			38,500
	(Being the liabilities of Vendor co. discharged)			
7	Amalgamation Adjustment A/c Dr.		5,000	
	To Statutory Reserves			5,000
	(Being the identity of Statutory Reserves retained)			

Working Notes:

1. CALCULATION OF PURCHASE CONSIDERATION

	Particulars	₹
A	Assets taken over at agreed values	
	Property, Plant & Equipment [(₹ 1,50,000 × 50%) + 100%]	1,50,000
	Property, Plant & Equipment [(₹ 1,50,000 × 50%) –20%]	60,000
	Inventories [₹ 55,000 – ₹ 5,500]	49,500
	Trade Receivables [₹ 65,000 – ₹ 6,500]	58,500
	Cash at Bank [91,600 – 2,000(Expenses)]	89,600
	Goodwill	52,500
		4,60,100
B	*Less:* Liabilities taken over:	
	Trade Payables [₹ 1,40,000 – 5%]	1,33,000
	10% Debentures [₹ 50,000 + 20%]	60,000
	Unrecorded Loan	38,500
		2,31,500
C	Net Assets taken over (A – B)	2,28,600

2. DISCHARGE OF PURCHASE CONSIDERATION

A. 10,000, Equity Shares to be issued [(20,000 × 1/2) × ₹ 15]	1,50,000
B. 480, 10% Pref. Shares to be issued [(500 × 120%)]	60,000
C. Cash to Equity Shareholders [Balancing figure]	18,600
D. Total Purchase Consideration (A + B + C)	2,28,600

Note: *According to AS-14, the amount paid by purchasing Company to discharge the debentures holders and the liquidation expenses of Vendor Company are not considered as part of purchase consideration.*

ILLUSTRATION 11B

What shall be the change in the solution of Previous Illustration 11A if the following information is also provided:

"V Ltd. owed P Ltd. ₹ 60,000 for the purchases of stock from P Ltd. which made a profit of 20% on cost. Four fifth of such stock were sold till 31.3.2023."

SOLUTION

1. There will be no change in the Journal Entries of V Ltd.

JOURNAL OF P LTD.

Date	Particulars		L.F.	Dr. (₹)	Cr. (₹)
1	Business Purchase A/c	Dr.		2,28,600	
	To Liquidators of V Ltd.				2,28,600
	(Being the purchase of the business)				
2	**Goodwill (Balancing figure)**	**Dr.**		**55,500**	
	Property,Plant & Equipment	Dr.		2,10,000	
	Inventories	Dr.		49,500	
	Trade Receivables	Dr.		65,000	
	Bank	Dr.		89,600	
	Reserve for Discount on Trade Payables [5% of ₹(1,40 000 – 60,000)]	**Dr.**		**4,000**	
	To Provision for Doubtful Debts [10% of ₹ 65,000]				6,500
	To Trade Payables				1,40,000
	To 10% Debentures [₹ 50,000 + 20%]				60,000
	To Unrecorded Loan				38,500
	To Business Purchase A/c				2,28,600
	(Being the Assets and Liabilities taken over)				
3	Liquidators of V Ltd.	Dr.		2,28,600	
	To Equity Share Capital A/c [10,000 × ₹ 8]				80,000
	To 9% Pref. Share Capital A/c [480 × ₹ 100]				48,000
	To Securities Premium A/c [(10,000 × ₹ 7) + (480 × ₹ 25)]				82,000
	To Bank A/c				18,600
	(Being the purchase consideration discharged)				
4	Goodwill A/c	Dr.		10,000	
	To Bank A/c				10,000
	(Being the payment of Liquidation Expenses of Vendor co.)				

5	10% Debentures of V Ltd. Dr. Discount on Issue of 14% Debentures A/c Dr. To 14% Debentures A/c (Being 10% Debentures of Vendor co. redeemed by issue of 625, 14% Debentures of ₹ 100 each at a discount of 4%) [Face Value of Debentures = ₹ 60,000/96% = ₹ 62,500]		60,000 2,500	62,500
6	Unrecorded Loan A/c Dr. To Bank A/c (Being the liabilities of Vendor co. discharged)		38,500	38,500
7	Amalgamation Adjustment A/c Dr. To Statutory Reserves (Being the identity of statutory Reserves retained)		5,000	5,000
8	**Goodwill A/c Dr.** **To Inventories** **(Being the elimination of unrealized profit included in goods purchased by V Ltd.)[(20% of ₹ 60,000 × 1/6) –(10% of ₹ 12,000)]**		**800**	**800**
9	**Trade Payables (V Ltd.) A/c Dr.** **To Trade Receivables A/c** **(Being the cancellation of Inter Co. Owing)**		**60,000**	**60,000**

ILLUSTRATION 11C

What shall be the change in the solution of Illustration 11A if the following information is also provided:

"Prior to 31st March 2023 V Ltd. sold goods costing ₹ 30,000 to P Ltd. for ₹ 40,000. ₹ 25,000 worth of goods were still in stock of P Ltd. Trade Receivables include ₹ 20,000 still due from P Ltd."

SOLUTION

1. There will be no change in the Journal Entries of V Ltd.

JOURNAL OF P LTD.

Date	*Particulars*	*L.F.*	*Dr. (₹)*	*Cr. (₹)*
1	Business Purchase A/c Dr. To Liquidators of V Ltd. (Being the purchase of the business)		2,28,600	2,28,600
2	**Goodwill (balancing figure) Dr.** Property, Plant & Equipment Dr. Inventories Dr. Trade Receivables Dr.		**50,500** 2,10,000 49,500 65,000	

	Bank	Dr.	89,600	
	Reserve for Discount on Trade Payables [5% of ₹ 1,40 000]	Dr.	7,000	
	To Pro. for Doubtful Debts [10% of ₹ (65,000 – 20,000)]			**4,500**
	To Trade Payables			1,40,000
	To 10% Debentures [₹ 50,000 + 20%]			60,000
	To Unrecorded Loan			38,500
	To Business Purchase A/c			2,28,600
	(Being the Assets and Liabilities taken over)			
3	Liquidators of V Ltd.	Dr.	2,28,600	
	To Equity Share Capital A/c [10,000 × ₹ 8]			80,000
	To 9% Pref. Share Capital A/c [480 × ₹ 100]			48,000
	To Securities Premium A/c [(10,000 × ₹ 7) + (480 × ₹ 25)]			82,000
	To Bank A/c			18,600
	(Being the purchase consideration discharged)			
4	Goodwill A/c	Dr.	10,000	
	To Bank A/c			10,000
	(Being the payment of Liquidation Expenses of Vendor co.)			
5	10% Debentures of V Ltd.	Dr.	60,000	
	Discount on Issue of 14% Debentures A/c	Dr.	2,500	
	To 14% Debentures A/c			62,500
	(Being 10% Debentures of Vendor co. redeemed by issue of 625, 14% Debentures of ₹ 100 each at a discount of 4%) [Face Value of Debentures = ₹ 60,000/96% = ₹ 62,500]			
6	Unrecorded Loan A/c	Dr.	38,500	
	To Bank A/c			38,500
	(Being the liabilities of Vendor co. discharged)			
7	Amalgamation Adjustment A/c	Dr.	5,000	
	To Statutory Reserves			5,000
	(Being the identity of statutory Reserves retained)			
8	**Goodwill**	**Dr.**	**6,250**	
	To Inventories A/c			**6,250**
	(Being the Elimination of unrealized profit on unsold goods worth ₹ 25,000 bought from V Ltd. still unsold (25,000 × 10,000/40,000)			

9	Trade Payables A/c Dr. To Trade Receivables (V Ltd.) A/c (Being Elimination of the amount owed by P to V Ltd.)			20,000	20,000

ILLUSTRATION 12

Given below are the extracts from the Balance Sheet of PRARTHANA Ltd. as at 31st March, 2023:

Particulars	₹
Share Capital [Equity Shares of ₹ 10 fully paid]	6,00,000
Statutory Reserves	1,70,000
General Reserve	10,000
Profit & Loss A/c	1,00,000
12% Debentures	1,00,000
Trade Payables	20,000
Property,Plant & Equipment	6,00,000
Intangible Assets [Goodwill]	1,00,000
Inventories	2,08,000
Trade Receivables	36,000
Cash at Bank	56,000

PIYUSH Ltd. agreed to absorb the business of PRARTHANA Ltd. with effect from 1st Apr. 2023. The purchase consideration payable by Piyush Ltd. was agreed as follows:

(a) A cash payment equivalent to ₹ 2.50 for every ₹ 10 share in PRARTHANA Ltd.

(b) The issue of 90,000 Equity Shares of ₹ 10 each fully paid in PIYUSH Ltd. having an agreed value of ₹ 15 per share.

(c) The issue of such an amount of fully paid 14% Debentures in PIYUSH Ltd. at 96 per cent as is sufficient to discharge 12% Debentures in PRARTHANA Ltd. at a premium of 20 per cent.

While computing purchase consideration, PIYUSH Ltd. valued Property,Plant & Equipment at 100% more than the book value, Inventories at ₹ 1,42,000 and Trade Receivables at their face value subject to a provision of 5 per cent for doubtful debts. The actual cost of liquidation of PRARTHANA Ltd. was ₹ 15,000. Liquidation cost of PRARTHANA Ltd. is to be reimbursed by PIYUSH Ltd. to the extent of ₹ 10,000. Statutory Reserves are to be maintained for 2 more years.

Required: (i) Close the books of PRARTHANA Ltd. by preparing Realisation Account, Piyush Ltd Account, Shareholders' Account and Debentures Account; and

(ii) Pass Journal Entries in the books of PIYUSH Ltd. regarding acquisition of business.

SOLUTION

BOOKS OF PRARTHANA LTD.

REALISATION ACCOUNT

Dr. *Cr.*

Particulars	₹	*Particulars*	₹
To Goodwill	1,00,000	By Trade Payables	20,000
To Property, Plant & Equipment	6,00,000	By PIYUSH Ltd.	15,00,000

To Inventories	2,08,000	By 12% Debentures	1,00,000
To Trade Receivables	36,000		
To Cash & Bank [₹ 56,000 – ₹ 5,000]	51,000		
To Cash & Bank (Expenses)	5,000		
To Profit on Realisation	6,20,000		
	16,20,000		16,20,000

Dr. **PIYUSH LTD. ACCOUNT** *Cr.*

Particulars	₹	*Particulars*	₹
To Realisation A/c	15,00,000	By Bank A/c	1,50,000
To Bank A/c	10,000	By Equity Shares in PIYUSH Ltd.	13,50,000
		By Bank A/c	10,000
	15,10,000		15,10,000

Dr. **EQUITY SHAREHOLDERS' ACCOUNT** *Cr.*

Particulars	₹	*Particulars*	₹
To Cash A/c	1,50,000	By Share Capital	6,00,000
To Equity Shares in PIYUSH Ltd.	13,50,000	By Statutory Reserves	1,70,000
		By General Reserve	10,000
		By Profit & Loss A/c	1,00,000
		By Realisation A/c	6,20,000
	15,00,000		15,00,000

Dr. **12% DEBENTURES ACCOUNT** *Cr.*

Particulars	₹	*Particulars*	₹
To Realisation A/c	1,00,000	By Balance b/d	1,00,000

Dr. **CASH & BANK ACCOUNT** *Cr.*

Particulars	₹	*Particulars*	₹
To Balance b/d	56,000	By Realisation A/c (transfer)	51,000
To PIYUSH Ltd.	1,50,000	By Realisation A/c (Expenses)	5,000
To PIYUSH Ltd.	10,000	By PIYUSH Ltd.	10,000
		By Equity Shareholders' A/c	1,50,000
	2,16,000		2,16,000

JOURNAL OF PIYUSH LTD.

Particulars		*L.F.*	*Dr. (₹)*	*Cr. (₹)*
Business Purchase A/c	Dr.		15,00,000	
To Liquidators of PRARTHANA Ltd.				15,00,000
(Being the Purchase of the business of PRARTHANA Ltd. as per agreement dated ...)				

Goodwill A/c (Balancing Figure)	Dr.		2,12,800	
Property,Plant & Equipment	Dr.		12,00,000	
Inventories	Dr.		1,42,000	
Trade Receivables	Dr.		36,000	
Cash & Bank	Dr.		51,000	
To Trade Payables				20,000
To 12% Debentures in PRARTHANA Ltd.				1,20,000
To Provision for Doubtful Debts A/c				1,800
To Business Purchase A/c				15,00,000
(Being the assets & liabilities taken over recorded, Goodwill being the balancing figure)				
Liquidators of PRARTHANA Ltd.	Dr.		15,00,000	
To Equity Share Capital A/c				9,00,000
To Securities Premium A/c				4,50,000
To Bank A/c				1,50,000
(Being the purchase consideration discharged)				
12% Debentures in PRARTHANA Ltd. A/c	Dr.		1,20,000	
Discount on Issue of Debentures A/c	Dr.		5,000	
To 14% Debentures A/c				1,25,000
(Being the Issue of 14% Debentures to 12% Debenture holders of PRARTHANA Ltd. at a discount of 4%) [Face Value of Debentures ₹ 1,20,000/. 96 = ₹ 1,25,000]				
Amalgamation Adjustment A/c	Dr.		1,70,000	
To Statutory Reserves A/c				1,70,000
(Being the identity of Statutory Reserves retained)				
Goodwill A/c	Dr.		10,000	
To Bank A/c				10,000
(Being the payment of Liquidation Exp. of Vendor Co.)				

Working Notes:

(I) CALCULATION OF PURCHASE CONSIDERATION

Particulars	₹
Cash [₹ 2.50 × 60,000]	1,50,000
Equity Shares [90,000 × 15]	13,50,000
	15,00,000

(ii) It is assumed that PRARTHANA Ltd. will retain the required cash for expenses.

ILLUSTRATION 13

Ajanta Limited agreed to acquire the business of Elora Limited as on 31st March 2023. Given below are the extracts from the Balance Sheet of Elora Ltd. as at 31st March, 2023:

Particulars	₹
20,000 Equity Shares of ₹ 10 each	2,00,000
10,000, 12% Pref. Shares of ₹ 10 each	1,00,000
Statutory Reserves	13,000
General Reserve	2,000
Profit & Loss A/c	30,000
12% Debentures	1,00,000
Trade Payables	1,50,000
Property, Plant & Equipment	2,50,000
Inventories	2,50,000
Trade Receivables	50,000
Cash at Bank	45,000

The consideration payable by Ajanta Limited was agreed as under:

(a) The Preference Shareholders of Elora Limited were to be allotted 8% Preference Shares of ₹ 1,10,000.

(b) Equity Shareholders to be allotted six Equity Shares of ₹ 10 each issued at a premium of 10% and ₹ 3 cash against every five shares held.

(c) 12% Debenture holders of Elora Limited to be paid @ 8% premium by issue of 14% Debentures at 10% discount.

While arriving at the agreed consideration, the directors of Ajanta Limited valued Property, Plant & Equipment at 40% more than the book value. Inventories at 12% less than book value, and Trade Receivables at their book value subject to an allowance of 5% to cover doubtful debts. Trade Receivables of Elora Limited included ₹ 10,000 due from Ajanta Limited. It was agreed that before acquisition, Elora Limited will pay dividend at 10% on Equity Shares. Actual Liquidation expenses are ₹ 15,000. Liquidation Expenses are to be reimbursed by Ajanta Ltd. to the extent of ₹ 10,000. Ignore Corporate Dividend Tax.

Required: Pass Journal entries necessary to close the books of Elora Limited and to record acquisition in the books of Ajanta Limited.

SOLUTION

JOURNAL OF ELORA LTD.

Particulars		L.F.	Dr. (₹)	Cr. (₹)
Profit & Loss A/c	Dr.		30,000	
Reserve A/c	Dr.		2,000	
To Dividend Payable A/c				32,000
(Being the Dividend @ 10% on equity shares & @ 12% as Pref. shares declared)				
Dividend Payable A/c	Dr.		32,000	
To Bank A/c				32,000
(Being the payment of Divided)				
Realisation A/c	Dr.		5,58,000	

To Property,Plant & Equipment			2,50,000
To Inventories			2,50,000
To Trade Receivables			50,000
To Cash At Bank [₹ 45,000 – ₹ 32,000 (Div)– ₹ 5,000 (Exp)]			8,000
(Being the transfer of Sundry assets to realisation account)			
12% Debentures A/c	Dr.	1,00,000	
Trade Payables A/c	Dr.	1,50,000	
To Realisation A/c			2,50,000
(Being the transfer of various liabilities taken over)			
Ajanta Limited A/c	Dr.	3,86,000	
To Realisation A/c			3,86,000
(Being the purchase consideration due from purchasing company)			
8% Preference Shares in Ajanta Ltd. A/c	Dr.	1,10,000	
Equity Shares in Ajanta Limited A/c	Dr.	2,64,000	
Bank A/c	Dr.	12,000	
To Ajanta Limited			3,86,000
(Being the receipt of purchase consideration)			
Realisation A/c	Dr.	5,000	
Ajanta Ltd.	Dr.	10,000	
To Bank A/c			15,000
(Being the payment of realisation expenses)			
Bank A/c	Dr.	10,000	
To Ajanta Ltd.			10,000
(Being the receipt of reimbursement of Exp.)			
12% Preference Share Capital A/c	Dr.	1,00,000	
Realisation A/c	Dr.	10,000	
To Preference Shareholders' A/c			1,10,000
(Being the transfer of Pref. share capital to Pref. shareholders' A/c and provision made for redemption of shareholders)			
Realisation A/c	Dr.	63,000	
To Equity Shareholders' A/c			63,000
(Being the transfer of Profit on realisation)			
Preference Shareholders' A/c	Dr.	1,10,000	
To 8% Preference Shares in Ajanta Ltd.			1,10,000
(Being the payment made to pref. shareholders)			
Equity Share Capital A/c	Dr.	2,00,000	
Statutory Reserves A/c	Dr.	13,000	
To Equity Shareholders' A/c			2,13,000

(Being the transfer of equity share capital and Reserve)			
Equity Shareholders' A/c Dr. To Equity Shares in Ajanta Ltd. To Bank A/c (Being the final Payment made to equity shareholders)		2,76,000	 2,64,000 12,000

JOURNAL OF AJANTA LIMITED

Particulars	*L.F.*	*Dr. (₹)*	*Cr. (₹)*
Business Purchase A/c Dr. To Liquidators of Elora Limited (Being the purchase of business as per agreement dated...)		3,86,000	 3,86,000
Goodwill A/c (Balancing figure) Dr. Property,Plant & Equipment Dr. Inventories A/c Dr. Trade Receivables A/c Dr. Cash at Bank A/c Dr. To Trade Payables A/c To 12% Debentures in Elora Ltd. To Provision for Doubtful Debts A/c [5% of ₹ (50,000 – 10,000)] To Business Purchase A/c (Being the assets & liabilities taken over recorded)		18,000 3,50,000 2,20,000 50,000 8,000	 1,50,000 1,08,000 2,000 3,86,000
Liquidators of Elora Ltd. Dr. To 8% Preference Share Capital A/c To Equity Share Capital A/c To Securities Premium A/c To Bank A/c (Being the purchase consideration discharged)		3,86,000	 1,10,000 2,40,000 24,000 12,000
12% Debentures in Elora Ltd. A/c Dr. Discount on Issue of Debentures A/c Dr. To 14% Debentures A/c (Being the Issue of 14% Debentures of Debentureholders of Elora Ltd.) [face value of Debentures = ₹ 1,08,000 / .90 = ₹ 1,20,000]		1,08,000 12,000	 1,20,000
Ajanta Ltd.'s Trade Payables A/c Dr. To Elora Ltd.'s Trade Receivables A/c (Being the inter-company's debt's cancelled)		10,000	 10,000
Amalgamation Adjustment A/c Dr. To Statutory Reserves A/c (Being the identity of Statutory Reserves retained)		13,000	 13,000

Goodwill A/c	Dr.	10,000	
To Bank A/c			10,000
(Being the liquidation expenses reimbursed)			

Working Notes:

(I) CALCULATION OF PURCHASE CONSIDERATION

Particulars	₹	₹
8% Preference Shares		1,10,000
Equity Shares (20,000 × × ₹ 10)	2,40,000	
Securities Premium	24,000	2,64,000
Cash (3/5 × 20,000)		12,000
		3,86,000

(ii) It has been assured that Elora Ltd. will retain the adequate cash for liquidation expenses.

ILLUSTRATION 14

Given below are the extracts from the Balance Sheet of V Ltd. as at 31st March, 2023:

Particulars	₹ *lakh*
Equity Share Capital (Shares of ₹ 10 each)	200.00
8% Pref. Share Capital (Shares of ₹ 100 each)	50.00
General Reserve	20.00
Profit & Loss A/c	16.10
Statutory Reserves	5.00
10% Debentures	50.00
Trade Payables	140.00
Property,Plant,Equipment	150.00
Intangible Assets	119.50
Inventories	55.00
Trade Receivables	65.00
Cash at Bank	91.60

Prior to absorption, V Ltd. decides to declare and pay equity dividend @ 5%.The business of V Ltd. is taken over by P Ltd. as on that date on the following terms:

(a) 50% of Property,Plant,Equipment are taken over at 100% more than the book value and the remaining Property,Plant,Equipment are taken over at 20% less than the book value.

(b) Intangible Assets are to be valued at ₹ 52.50 lakh.

(c) Inventories are taken over at book value less 10% and Trade Receivables are taken over at book value subject to an allowance of 10% to cover doubtful debts.

(d) Trade Payables are to be taken over subject to a discount of 5% and Unrecorded Loan Liability of ₹ 38.50 lakh to be discharged by P Ltd. at book value.

(e) The purchase consideration payable by P Ltd. was agreed as follows:

(i) The issue of such an amount of fully paid 14% Debentures in P Ltd. at 96 per cent as is sufficient to discharge 10% Debentures in V Ltd. at a premium of 20 per cent.

(ii) The issue of such an amount of fully paid 10% Pref. Shares in P Ltd. at 125% as is sufficient to discharge 8% Pref. Shares in V Ltd. at a premium of 20%.

(iii) One Equity Share of ₹ 10 each, ₹ 8 paid up valued at ₹ 15 per share for every two Equity Shares held in V Ltd. and the balance in cash. The market value of an equity share of P Ltd. at present is ₹ 100.

(iv) Expenses of liquidation of V Ltd. are to be reimbursed by P Ltd. to the extent of ₹ 10.00 lakh. Actual Expenses amounted to ₹ 14.10 lakh.

Required: Show the calculation and discharge of Purchase Consideration and Pass Journal Entries in the books of *P* Ltd. and *V* Ltd.

SOLUTION

1. CALCULATION OF PURCHASE CONSIDERATION

	Particulars	*₹ lakh*
A	Assets taken over at agreed values	
	Property, Plant,Equipment [(₹ 150 lakh × 50%) + 100%]	150.00
	Property, Plant,Equipment [(₹ 150 lakh × 50%) –20%]	60.00
	Intangible Assets	52.50
	Inventories [₹ 55 lakh – ₹ 5.5 lakh]	49.50
	Trade Receivables [₹ 65 lakh – ₹ 6.5 lakh]	58.50
	Cash at Bank [91.60 lakh – 10 lakh(ED) – 4 lakh (PD) – 4.1 lakh (Exp.)]	73.50
		444.00
B	*Less:* Liabilities taken over:	
	Trade Payables [₹ 1.40 lakh – 5%]	133.00
	10% Debentures [₹ 50 lakh + 20%]	60.00
	Unrecorded Loan	38.50
		231.50
C	Net Assets taken over (A – B)	212.50

2. DISCHARGE OF PURCHASE CONSIDERATION

	₹ lakh
A. 10 lakh, Equity Shares to be issued [(20 lakh × 1/2) × ₹ 15]	150.00
B. 48 lakh, 10% Pref. Shares to be issued [(50 lakh × 120%)]	60.00
C. Cash to Equity Shareholders [Balancing figure]	**2.50**
D. Total Purchase Consideration (A + B + C)	212.50

Note: *According to AS-14, the amount paid by purchasing Company to discharge the debentures holders and the liquidation expenses of Vendor Company are not considered as part of purchase consideration.*

JOURNAL OF V LTD.

Date	*Particulars*	*L.F.*	*Dr. (₹)*	*Cr. (₹)*
1.	Profit & Loss A/c Dr.		14.00	
	To Pref Dividend Payable A/c			10.00
	To Equity Dividend Payable A/c			4.00
	(Being the Dividend declared)			

2.	Pref Dividend Payable A/c Dr.	10.00	
	Equity Dividend Payable A/c Dr.	4.00	
	To Bank A/c		14.00
	(Being the Dividend paid)		
3	Realisation A/c Dr.	463.00	
	To Goodwill		119.50
	To Property, Plant & Equipment		150.00
	To Inventories		55.00
	To Trade Receivables		65.00
	To Cash at Bank [91.60 lakh – 10 lakh(ED) – 4 lakh (PD) – 4.1 lakh (Exp.)]		73.50
	(Being the transfer of various assets to Realisation A/c)		
4	10% Debentures Dr.	50.00	
	Trade Payables Dr.	140.00	
	To Realisation A/c		190.00
	(Being the transfer of various liabilities to Realisation A/c)		
5	P Ltd Dr.	212.500	
	To Realisation A/c		212.500
	(Being the purchase consideration due)		
6	Equity Shares in P Ltd. Dr.	150.00	
	10% Pref. Shares in P Ltd. Dr.	60.00	
	Cash at Bank Dr.	2.50	
	To P Ltd.		212.500
	(Being the receipt of purchase consideration)		
7	P Ltd. Dr.	10.00	
	Realisation A/c Dr.	4.10	
	To Bank A/c		14.10
	(Being liquidation expenses paid out of which ₹ 10 lakh are to be reimbursed by purchasing company)		
8	Bank A/c Dr.	10.00	
	To P Ltd.		10.00
	(Being liquidation expenses reimbursed by purchasing company)		
9	8% Pref. Share Capital A/c Dr.	50.00	
	Realisation A/c Dr.	10.00	
	To Pref. Shareholders' A/c		60.00
	(Being the transfer of Pref. Share Capital to Pref. shareholders' A/c & loss on discharge to Realisation A/c)		

Date	Particulars	L.F.	Dr. (₹)	Cr. (₹)
10	Pref. Shareholders' A/c Dr. To 10% Pref. Shares in P Ltd. (Being the claims of Pref. share holders discharged)		60.00	 60.00
11	Equity Shareholders' A/c Dr. To Realisation A/c (Being the transfer of loss on Realisation)		74.60	 74.60
12	Equity Share Capital A/c Dr. General Reserve Dr. Profit & Loss A/c Dr. Statutory Reserves A/c Dr. To Equity Shareholders'A/c (Being the transfer of Share Capital & balance of P&L A/c & Reserves to Equity Shareholders' Account)		200.00 20.00 2.10 5.00	 227.10
13	Equity Shareholders' A/c Dr. To Equity Shares in P Ltd. To Bank A/c (Being the claims of Equity Shareholders discharged)		152.50	 150.00 2.50

JOURNAL OF P LTD.

Date	Particulars	L.F.	Dr. (₹)	Cr. (₹)
1	Business Purchase A/c Dr. To Liquidators of V Ltd. (Being the purchase of the business)		212.50	 212.50
2	Goodwill Dr. Property,Plant & Equipment Dr. Inventories Dr. Trade Receivables Dr. Bank Dr. Reserve for Discount on Trade Payables [5% of ₹ 140 lakh] Dr. To Provision for Doubtful Debts To Trade Payables To 10% Debentures To Unrecorded Loan To Business Purchase A/c (Being the Assets and Liabilities taken over)		52.50 210.00 49.50 65.00 73.50 7.00	 6.500 140.00 60.00 38.50 212.50
3	Liquidators of V Ltd. Dr. To Equity Share Capital A/c [10.00 × ₹ 8]		212.50	 80.00

	To 10% Pref. Share Capital A/c [0.48 lakh × ₹ 100]			48.00
	To Securities Premium A/c [(10 × ₹ 7) + (0.480 × ₹ 25)]			82.00
	To Bank A/c			2.50
	(Being the purchase consideration discharged)			
4	Goodwill A/c	Dr.	10.00	
	To Bank A/c			10.00
	(Being the payment of Liquidation Expenses of Vendor co.)			
5	10% Debentures of V Ltd.	Dr.	60.00	
	Discount on Issue of 14% Debentures A/c	Dr.	2.50	
	To 14% Debentures A/c			62.50
	(Being 10% Debentures of Vendor co. redeemed by issue of 0.625, 14% Debentures of ₹ 100 each at a discount of 4%)			
	[Face Value of Debentures = ₹ 60/96% = ₹ 62.50]			
6	Unrecorded Loan A/c	Dr.	38.50	
	To Bank A/c			38.50
	(Being the liabilities of Vendor co. discharged)			
7	Amalgamation Adjustment A/c	Dr.	5.00	
	To Statutory Reserves			5.00
	(Being the identity of Statutory Reserves retained)			

ILLUSTRATION 15

Given below are the extracts from the Balance Sheets of P Ltd. and V Ltd. as at 31st March, 2023:

Particulars	*P Ltd. (₹)*	*V Ltd. (₹)*
Equity Share Capital of ₹ 10 each	6,00,000	2,00,000
General Reserve	1,50,000	20,000
Profit & Loss A/c	1,77,000	10,000
Statutory Reserves	—	5,000
10% Debentures of ₹ 100 each	—	50,000
Trade Payables	37,500	1,40,000
Goodwill	—	1,19,500
Property,Plant & Equipment	4,75,000	1,50,000
Non-Current Investments (including 100 Debentures of V Ltd. purchased @ of ₹ 90)	1,09,000	—
Inventories	95,000	55,000
Trade Receivables	1,40,000	65,000
Cash at Bank	1,45,500	35,500

The business of V Ltd. is taken over by P Ltd. as on that date on the following terms:

(a) Prior to absorption, V Ltd and P Ltd decide to declare and pay equity dividend @ 5%.

(b) 50% of Property,Plant & Equipment are taken over at 100% more than the book value and the remaining Property,Plant & Equipment are taken over at 20% less than the book value.

(c) Goodwill of V Ltd. is to be valued at ₹ 52,500.

(d) Inventories are taken over at book value less 10% and Trade Receivables are taken over at book value subject to an allowance of 10% to cover doubtful debts.

(e) Trade Payables are to be taken over subject to a discount of 5% and Unrecorded Loan Liability of ₹ 38,500 to be discharged by P Ltd. at book value.

(f) The purchase consideration is to be discharged to the extent of 20% in cash and the balance in the form of equity shares of ₹ 10 each, ₹ 8 paid up at a premium of ₹ 7 per share, The market value of an equity share of P Ltd. at present is ₹ 100.

(g) The issue of such an amount of fully paid 14% Debentures in P Ltd at 96 per cent as is sufficient to discharge 10% Debentures in V Ltd. at a premium of 20 per cent.

(h) Expenses of liquidation of V Ltd. are to be reimbursed by P Ltd. to the extent of ₹ 10,000. Actual Expenses amounted to ₹ 12,000.

(i) Statutory Reserves are to be maintained for 2 more years.

Prior to 31st March 2023 V Ltd. sold goods costing ₹ 30,000 to P Ltd. for ₹ 40,000. ₹ 25,000 worth of goods were still in stock of P Ltd. Trade Receivables include ₹ 20,000 still due from P Ltd. On the date of absorption, V Ltd. owed P Ltd. ₹ 60,000 for the purchases of stock from P Ltd. which made a profit of 20% on cost. Four fifth of such stock were sold till 31.3.2023. Investments of P Ltd. include ₹ 9,000 representing the cost of 10% Debentures of V Ltd.

Required: *(a) Prepare Realisation Account, Bank Account, Equity Shareholders Account and Shares in P Ltd. Account in the books of V Ltd. (b) Pass Journal Entries in the books of P Ltd. and prepare Balance Sheet.*

SOLUTION

IN THE BOOKS OF V LTD.

REALISATION ACCOUNT

Dr. *Cr.*

Particulars	₹	*Particulars*	₹
To Goodwill	1,19,500	By 10% Debentures	50,000
To Property,Plant & Equipment	1,50,000	By Trade Payables	1,40,000
To Inventories	55,000	By P Ltd. (Purchase Consideration)	1,62,557
To Trade Receivables	65,000	By Equity Shareholders' A/c (Loss)	62,443
To Bank [35,500 – 10,000 (Div.) – 2,000 (Exp.)]	23,500		
To Bank A/c (Expenses)	2,000		
	4,15,000		4,15,000

Dr. **BANK ACCOUNT** Cr.

Particulars	₹	Particulars	₹
To Balance b/d	35,500	By Dividend Payable A/c	10,000
To P Ltd. (Expenses)	10,000	By Realisation A/c (Takeover)	23,500
To P Ltd. (Consideration)	32,567	By Realisation A/c (Expenses)	2,000
		By P Ltd. (Expenses)	10,000
		By Equity Shareholders A/c	32,567
	78,067		78,067

Dr. **EQUITY SHAREHOLDERS' ACCOUNT** Cr.

Particulars	₹	Particulars	₹
To Realisation A/c (Loss)	62,443	By Share Capital	2,00,000
To Bank A/c	32,567	By General Reserve	20,000
To Shares in P Ltd.	1,29,990	By Statutory Reserves	5,000
	2,25,000		2,25,000

Dr. **SHARES IN P LTD. ACCOUNT** Cr.

Particulars	₹	Particulars	₹
To P Ltd.	1,29,990	By Sundry Shareholders (transfer)	1,29,990

JOURNAL OF P LTD.

Particulars		L.F.	Dr. (₹)	Cr. (₹)
Profit & Loss A/c	Dr.		30,000	
To Dividend Payable a/c				30,000
(Being the Dividend declared @ 5%)				
Dividend Payable A/c	Dr.		30,000	
To Bank A/c				30,000
(Being the Dividend paid)				
Business Purchase A/c	Dr.		1,62,557	
To Liquidators of V Ltd.				1,62,557
(Being the purchase price agreed to be paid for the business of V Ltd.)				
Goodwill (Balancing figure)	Dr.		53,557	
Property,Plant & Equipment	Dr.		2,10,000	
Inventories	Dr.		49,500	
Trade Receivables	Dr.		65,000	
Bank	Dr.		23,500	
Reserve for Discount on Trade Payables [5% of ₹(1,40 000 – 60,000)]	Dr.		4,000	

Particulars	L.F.	Dr. (₹)	Cr. (₹)
To Provision for Doubtful Debts [10% of ₹ (65,000 – 20,000)]			4,500
To Trade Payables			1,40,000
To 10% Debentures [₹ 50,000 + 20%]			60,000
To Unrecorded Loan			38,500
To Business Purchase A/c			1,62,557
(Being the assets and liabilities taken over from V Ltd.)			
Liquidators of V Ltd. Dr.		1,62,557	
To Bank A/c			32,567
To Equity Share Capital A/c			69,328
To Securities Premium A/c			60,662
(Being the issue of Shares and payment in cash in satisfaction of purchase consideration)			
Goodwill A/c Dr.		10,000	
To Bank A/c			10,000
(Being the payment of Realization Expenses of V Ltd.)			
Goodwill Dr.		6,250	
To Inventories A/c			6,250
(Being the Elimination of unrealized profit on unsold goods worth ₹ 25,000 bought from V Ltd. still unsold (25,000 × 10,000/40,000)			
Trade Payables A/c Dr.		20,000	
To Trade Receivables (V Ltd.) A/c			20,000
(Being Elimination of the amount owed by us to V Ltd.)			
Goodwill A/c Dr.		800	
To Inventories			800
(Being the elimination of unrealized profit included in goods purchased by V Ltd.)[(20% of ₹ 60,000 x1/6) –(10% of ₹ 12,000)]			
Trade Payables (V Ltd.) A/c Dr.		60,000	
To Trade Receivables A/c			60,000
(Being the cancellation of Inter Co. Owing)			
10% Debentures of V Ltd. Dr.		60,000	
Discount on Issue of 14% Debentures A/c Dr.		2,000	
To Investments in 10% Debentures of V Ltd.			9,000
To 14% Debentures A/c			50,000
To Capital Reserve A/c			3,000
(Being the Investment in 10% Debentures of V Ltd. cancelled and the remaining debentures redeemed by issue of 500, 14% Debentures of ₹ 100 each at a discount of 4%)			
[Face Value of Debentures= ₹ 48,000/96% = ₹ 50,000]			
Unrecorded Loan A/c Dr.		38,500	
To Bank A/c			38,500

(Being the liabilities of V Ltd. discharged)			
Amalgamation Adjustment A/c	Dr.	5,000	
To Statutory Reserves			5,000
(Being the identity of statutory Reserves retained)			
Capital Reserve A/c	Dr.	3,000	
To Goodwill A/c			3,000
(Being the goodwill adjusted against Capital Reserve)			

BALANCE SHEET OF P LTD. AS AT 31.03.2023

Particulars	*Note No*	X Ltd. (₹)
I. Equity and Liabilities		
(1) Shareholders' Funds		
(a) Share Capital	1	6,69,328
(b) Reserves and Surplus	2	3,55,662
(2) Non–Current Liabilities		
(a) Long–term Borrowings (14% Debentures)		50,000
(3) Current Liabilities		
(a) Trade Payables [(37,500 – 20,000) + (1,40,000 – 4,000 – 60,000)]		93,500
Total		11,68,490
II. Assets		
(1) Non–Current Assets		
(a) Fixed Assets		
Property, Plant & Equipment [4,75,000 + 2,10,000]		6,85,000
Intangible Assets [Goodwill] [53,557 + 10,000 + 6,250 + 800 – 3,000]		67,607
(b) Non–Current Investments [1,09,000 –9,000]		1,00,000
(2) Current Assets		
(a) Inventories [(95,000 – 6,250)+(49,500 – 800)]		1,37,450
(b) Trade Receivables [(1,40,000 – 60,000)+(65,000 – 4,500 – 20,000)]		1,20,500
(c) Cash and Cash Equivalents [Cash at Bank] [(1,45,500 –30,000 – 10,000 – 32,567 – 38,500) + (23,500)]		57,933
Total		11,68,490

Notes To Accounts:

Particulars	*X Ltd. (₹)*
1. Share Capital	
Equity Shares of ₹ 10 each	6,00,000
Equity Shares of ₹ 10 each,₹ 8 paid up	69,328
	6,69,328

2. **Reserves and Surplus**	
General Reserve	1,50,000
Profit & Loss A/c[1,77,000 – 30,000]	1,47,000
Less: Discount on Issue of 14% Debentures A/c	(2,000)
Statutory Reserves	5,000
Securities Premium	60,662
Amalgamation Adjustment A/c	(5,000)
	3,55,662

Working Notes:

1. CALCULATION OF PURCHASE CONSIDERATION

Particulars		₹
A Assets taken over at agreed values		
Property,Plant & Equipment [(₹ 1,50,000 × 50%) + 100%]		1,50,000
Property,Plant & Equipment [(₹ 1,50,000 × 50%) –20%]		60,000
Inventories [₹ 55,000 – ₹ 5,500]		49,500
Trade Receivables [₹ 65,000 – ₹ 6,500]		58,500
Cash at Bank [35,500 – 10,000 – 2,000]		23,500
Goodwill		52,500
		3,94,000
B *Less:* Liabilities taken over:		
Trade Payables	1,40,000	
Less: Reserve for Discount @ 5%	7,000	1,33,000
10% Debentures[₹ 50,000 + 20%]		60,000
Unrecorded Loan		38,500
		2,31,500
C Net Assets taken over (A – B)		1,62,500

(III) DISCHARGE OF PURCHASE CONSIDERATION

Particulars	₹
Cash (20% of ₹ 1,62,500)	32,500
No of Equity Shares=[(80% of ₹ 1,62,500)/₹15]=8666.67	
8,666 shares of ₹ 10 each, ₹ 8 paid up valued at ₹ 15 per share	1,29,990
Cash for Fractional Share(.67 × ₹ 100)	67
	1,62,557

ILLUSTRATION 16

Given below are the extracts from the Balance Sheet of V Ltd. as at 31st March, 2023:

Particulars	*P Ltd* ₹	*V Ltd* ₹
Equity Share Capital of ₹ 10 each	6,00,000	2,00,000
8% Pref. Share Capital of ₹ 100 each	1,00,000	50,000
General Reserve	1,50,000	20,000
Profit & Loss A/c	1,75,200	14,000
Statutory Reserves	—	5,000
10% Debentures	—	50,000
Trade Payables	37,500	1,40,000
Property,Plant & Equipment	4,75,000	1,50,000
Goodwill	—	1,19,500
Non-Current Investments (including 100 Debentures of V Ltd. purchased @ of ₹ 90)	1,09,000	—
Inventories	95,000	55,000
Trade Receivables	1,40,000	65,000
Cash at Bank	2,43,700	89,500

Prior to absorption, both the companies decide to declare and pay equity dividend @ 5%. The business of V Ltd. is taken over by P Ltd. as on that date on the following terms:

(a) 50% of Property,Plant & Equipment are taken over at 100% more than the book value and the remaining Property,Plant & Equipment are taken over at 20% less than the book value.

(b) Goodwill of V Ltd. is to be valued at ₹ 52,500.

(c) Inventories are taken over at book value less 10% and Trade Receivables are taken over at book value subject to an allowance of 10% to cover doubtful debts.

(d) Trade Payables are to be taken over subject to a discount of 5% and Unrecorded Loan Liability of ₹ 38,500 to be discharged by P Ltd. at book value.

(e) The purchase consideration payable by P Ltd. was agreed as follows:

  (i) The purchase consideration is to be discharged to the extent of 20% in cash.

  (ii) The issue of such an amount of fully paid 14% Debentures in P Ltd at 96 per cent as is sufficient to discharge 10% Debentures in V Ltd. at a premium of 20 per cent.

  (iii) The issue of such an amount of fully paid 10% Pref. Shares in P Ltd. at 125% as is sufficient to discharge 8% Pref. Shares in V Ltd. at a premium of 20%.

  (iv) The balance in the form of equity shares of ₹ 10 each, ₹ 8 paid up at a premium of ₹ 7 per share. The market value of an equity share of P Ltd. at present is ₹ 100.

  (v) Expenses of liquidation of V Ltd. are to be reimbursed by P Ltd. to the extent of ₹ 10,000. Actual Expenses amounted to ₹ 12,000.

Show the calculation & discharge of Purchase Consideration & prepare the Balance Sheet of P Ltd.

SOLUTION

1. CALCULATION OF PURCHASE CONSIDERATION

	Particulars	₹
A	Assets taken over at agreed values	
	Property,Plant & Equipment [(₹ 1,50,000 × 50%) + 100%]	1,50,000
	Property,Plant & Equipment [(₹ 1,50,000 × 50%) –20%]	60,000
	Inventories [₹ 55,000 – ₹ 5,500]	49,500
	Trade Receivables [₹ 65,000 – ₹ 6,500]	58,500
	Cash at Bank [89,500 – 10,000(ED) – 4,000(PD) – 2,000(Exp.)]	73,500
	Goodwill	52,500
		4,44,000
B	*Less:* Liabilities taken over:	
	Trade Payables [₹ 1,40,000 – 5%]	1,33,000
	10% Debentures [₹ 50,000 + 20%]	60,000
	Unrecorded Loan	38,500
		2,31,500
C	Net Assets taken over (A – B)	2,12,500

2. DISCHARGE OF PURCHASE CONSIDERATION

Particulars	₹
A. Cash to Equity Shareholders [2,12,500 × 20%]	42,500
B. 480, 10% Pref. Shares to be issued [(500 × 120%)]	60,000
C. 7,333, Equity Shares to be issued [(2,12,500 – 42,500 60,000)/ ₹ 15]	1,09,995
D. Cash for Fractional Share(.33 × ₹ 100)	33
E. Total Purchase Consideration (A + B + C + D)	2,12,528

Note: *According to AS-14, the amount paid by purchasing Company to discharge the debentures holders and the liquidation expenses of Vendor Company are not considered as part of purchase consideration.*

BALANCE SHEET OF P LTD. AS AT 31.03.2023

Particulars	Note No	X Ltd. (₹)
I. Equity and Liabilities		
(1) Shareholders' Funds		
(a) Share Capital	1	8,06,664
(b) Reserves and Surplus	2	3,48,531
(2) Non–Current Liabilities		
(a) Long–term Borrowings (14% Debentures)		50,000
(3) Current Liabilities		
(a) Trade Payables [(37,500 – 20,000) + (1,40,000 – 4,000 – 60,000)]		93,500
Total		12,98,695

II. Assets		
(1) Non–Current Assets		
(a) Fixed Assets		
Property,Plant & Equipment [4,75,000 + 2,10,000]		6,85,000
Intangible Assets [Goodwill] [53,528 + 10,000 + 6,250 + 800 – 3,000]		67,578
(b) Non–Current Investments[1,09,000 – 9,000]		1,00,000
(2) Current Assets		
(a) Inventories [(95,000 – 6,250) + (49,500 – 800)]		1,37,450
(b) Trade Receivables [(1,40,000 – 60,000) + (65,000 – 4,500 – 20,000)]		1,20,500
(c) Cash and Cash Equivalents [Cash at Bank] [(2,43,700 – 30,000 – 8,000 – 10,000 – 42,533 – 38,500) + (73,500)]		1,88,167
Total		12,98,695

Notes To Accounts:

Particulars	₹
1. Share Capital	
60,000, Equity Shares of ₹ 10 each	6,00,000
7,333, Equity Shares of ₹ 10 each,₹ 8 paid up	58,664
1,000, 8% Pref. Shares of ₹ 100 each	1,00,000
480, 10% Pref. Shares of ₹ 100 each	48,000
	8,06,664
2. Reserves and Surplus	
General Reserve	1,50,000
Profit & Loss A/c [1,75,200 – 30,000 – 8,000]	1,37,200
Less: Discount on Issue of 14% Debentures A/c	(2,000)
Statutory Reserves	5,000
Securities Premium [51,331 + 12,000]	63,331
Amalgamation Adjustment A/c	(5,000)
	3,48,531

ILLUSTRATION 17 [Take-over on a date other than Balance Sheet Date]

Given below are the extracts from the Balance Sheets of CANHA Ltd. and Krishna Ltd., as at 31st March, 2023:

Particulars	*CAHANA Ltd.* ₹	*Krishna Ltd.* ₹
Equity Share Capital of ₹ 10 each	6,00,000	4,00,000
General Reserve	1,40,000	42,500
Statutory Reserves	—	60,000

Profit & Loss A/c	69,000	56,000
Trade Payables	37,500	30,000
Property,Plant & Equipment	5,00,000	3,50,000
Inventories	95,000	82,500
Trade Receivables	1,40,000	1,00,000
Cash at Bank	1,11,500	56,000

CANHA Ltd., took over and absorbed Krishna Ltd., as on 1st Oct. 2023. No Balance Sheet of Krishna Ltd. was prepared on the date of take-over. But the following information is made available to you:

(a) For the six months ended 30th Sept. 2023, CANHA Ltd and Krishna Ltd., made net profits of ₹ 1,51,000 and ₹ 64,000 after providing for depreciation at 10% per annum on fixed assets;

(b) .Both the companies had distributed dividends @ 10% on 1st July 2023.

(c) Goodwill of Krishna Ltd. on the date of take-over was estimated at ₹ 25,000 and it was agreed that the Inventories of Krishna Ltd., subject to an abnormal item of ₹ 7,500 to be fully written off, would be appreciated by 20% for the purpose of take-over:

(d) CANHA Ltd. to issue shares to share-holders of Krishna Ltd., on the basis of the intrinsic value of shares on the date of take-over.

Required: Draft the Balance Sheet of CANHA Ltd., after absorption. (Ignore Corporate Dividend Tax Rate).

SOLUTION

BALANCE SHEET OF CANHA LTD. AS AT 1.10.2023

Particulars	*Note No*	*₹ (lacs)*
I. Equity and Liabilities		
(1) Shareholders' Funds		
(a) Share Capital	1	10.100
(b) Reserves and Surplus	2	5.05
(2) Non-Current Liabilities		
(3) Current Liabilities Trade Payables [0.375 + 0.30]		0.675
Total		15.825
II. Assets		
(1) Non-Current Assets		
(a) Fixed Assets Property,Plant & Equipment [5 + 3.325 – 0.25]		8.075
Intangible Assets		0.250
(2) Current Assets		
(a) Inventories [0.95 + (82,500 – 7,500) + 20%]		1.850
(b) Trade Receivables [1.40 + 1.00]		2.400
(c) Cash and Cash Equivalents	(i)	3.250
Total		15.825

Notes To Accounts:

	Particulars	₹ *(lacs)*
1.	**Share Capital**	
	101,000 Equity Shares of ₹ 10 each	10.10
	(Of the above 41,000 Shares were issued for consideration otherwise than cash)	
2.	**Reserves and Surplus**	
	Securities Premium [41,000 x ₹ 5]	2.05
	General Reserve	1.40
	Statutory Reserves	0.60
	Profit & Loss Account [0.69 + 1.51 – 0.60]*	1.60
	Amalgamation Adjustment A/c	(0.60)
		5.05

Working Notes:

(I) CALCULATION OF CLOSING CASH & BANK BALANCE

	Particulars	*CAHANA Ltd.* ₹	*Krishna Ltd.* ₹
A	Opening Balance	1,11,500	56,000
B	Add Net Profit	1,51,000	64,000
C	*Add:* Depreciation	25,000	17,500
		2,87,500	1,37,500
D	*Less:* Dividend	60,000	40,000
E	Closing Cash & Bank Balance (A + B + C – D)	2,27,500	97,500

(II) CALCULATION OF INTRINSIC VALUE OF SHARES

	Particulars	*CAHANA Ltd.* ₹	*Krishna Ltd.* ₹
A	Total Assets at current values		
	Goodwill	—	25,000
	Fixed Assets	4,75,000	3,32,500
	Trade Receivables	1,40,000	1,00,000
	Inventories *[(82,500 -7,500) + 20%]	95,000	90,000*
	Cash & Bank [Refer to Working Note (i)]	2,27,500	97,500
		9,37,500	6,45,000
B	*Less:* Liabilities	(37,500)	(30,000)
C	Net Assets at current values [A – B]	9,00,000	6,15,000
D	No. of shares	60,000	40,000
E	Intrinsic value per share (C/D)	15	15.375

(III) CALCULATION OF NO. OF SHARES TO BE ISSUED BY PURCHASING COMPANY

A	Net assets of vendor company take over	6,15,000
B	Intrinsic value of an equity share of Purchasing company	15
C	No of shares to be issued by Purchasing company (A/B)	41,000

Note: *In the absence of information about changes in other assets, it is assumed that the profit has resulted in cash only.*

10.0 TREATMENT OF RESERVES ARISING ON AMALGAMATION IN THE NATURE OF MERGER

1. **Provision as per AS-14 [Paragraph 35]**

   The difference between the amount recorded as share capital issued (*plus any additional consideration in the form of cash and other assets*) and the amount of the share capital of the transferor company should be adjusted in reserves.

2. **Opinion of the Expert Advisory Committee of ICAI [Published in 22nd Volume]**

   (a) The difference between the share capital of the transferor companies and share capital issued by company on amalgamation should be treated as **Capital Reserve** for the purpose of paragraph 35 of AS-14.

   (b) Reserve created on amalgamation is not available for the purpose of distribution to shareholders as dividend and/or bonus shares.

3. **Author's Opinion**

   (a) The excess of share capital of the transferor company over the purchase consideration should be treated as **Capital Reserve** which shall not be available for distribution as dividend *or* bonus.

   (b) The excess of purchase consideration over the share capital of the transferor company should be treated as Capital loss and should be adjusted:

   (i) first against the Capital Reserves

   (ii) then against the Revenue Reserves (if capital reserves are insufficient)

Note: *If Revenue Reserves are also insufficient, the necessary required amount should be transferred to Revenue Reserves by debiting Profit & Loss Account. After such transfer if Profit & Loss Account shows debit balance it will be shown as a negative item under Reserves and Surplus.*

ILLUSTRATION 18 [Treatment of Reserves arising on Amalgamation in the nature of Merger]

X Ltd. took over all the assets & liabilities of Y Ltd. and discharged the consideration by issue of equity shares and cash for fractional shares. Calculate the balances of Reserves and Profit & Loss Account which are to appear in the Balance Sheet of X Ltd. in each of the following cases:

(₹ in lacs)

Particulars	*Case I* ₹	*Case II* ₹	*Case III* ₹	*Case IV* ₹	*Case V* ₹
Share Capital issued by X Ltd.	9.50	9.50	9.50	9.50	9.50
Cash for Fractional Shares paid by X Ltd.	.50	.50	.50	.50	.50
Share Capital of Y Ltd.	9.65	9.45	9.15	9.00	8.80

Capital Reserves of Y Ltd.	.40	.40	.40	.40	.40
Revenue Reserves of Y Ltd.	.30	.30	.30	.30	.30
Statutory Reserves of Y Ltd.	.20	.20	.20	.20	.20
Profit & Loss A/c of Y Ltd.	.10	.10	.10	.10	.10
Capital Reserve of X Ltd.	.10	.10	.10	.10	.10
Revenue Reserve of X Ltd.	.20	.20	.20	.20	.20
Profit & Loss Account of X Ltd.	.05	.05	.05	.05	.05

SOLUTION

CALCULATION OF BALANCES OF RESERVES AND PROFIT & LOSS ACCOUNT [₹ *in lacs*]

Particulars	₹	₹	₹	₹	₹
A. Purchase Consideration					
Share Capital Issued:	9.50	9.50	9.50	9.50	9.50
Cash for Fractional Shares paid	.50	.50	.50	.50	.50
	10.00	10.00	10.00	10.00	10.00
B. *Less:* Share Capital of Transferor Co.	9.65	9.45	9.15	9.00	8.80
C. Difference to be adjusted (A–B)	0.35	0.55	0.85	1.00	1.20
D. Debited to:					
Capital Reserves (of Both Co.)	0.35	.50	.50	.50	.50
Revenue Reserves (of Both Co.)	—	.05	.35	.50	.50
Profit & Loss A/c (of Both Co.)	—	—	—	—	.20
	.35	.55	.85	1.00	1.20
Balances of Reserves & P&L A/c:					
Capital Reserves	.15	—	—	—	—
Revenue Reserves	.50	.45	.15	—	—
Statutory Reserves	.20	.20	.20	.20	.20
Profit & Loss A/c (Credit)	.15	.15	.15	.15	—
Profit & Loss A/c (Debit)	—	—	—	—	0.05

12.0 ACCOUNTING TREATMENT IN THE BOOKS OF TRANSFEREE COMPANY *or* PURCHASING COMPANY IN CASE OF MERGER

Step 1: Record the Acquisition of business from the vendor company.

JOURNAL ENTRY

Business Merger A/c	Dr.	*(with Purchase Consideration)*
To Liquidator of the Vendor Co.		

Step 2: In case of Amalgamation in the nature of Merger

"Record the Assets, Liabilities and Reserves (whether Statutory Reserves *or* not) at their respective book values".

JOURNAL ENTRY

Assets (Individually)	Dr.	*[with their respective book values]*
To Liabilities (Individually)		*[with their respective book values]*
To Provision for Doubtful Debts		*[with the book balance]*
To Provision for Depreciation etc.		*[with the book balance]*
To Reserves (other than Revenue Reserves)		*[with their respective book balances]*
To General Reserve		*[Balancing figure]*
To Business Merger A/c		*[with Purchase Consideration]*

Step 3: Make Payment to Vendor Company.

JOURNAL ENTRY

Liquidator of Vendor Co.'s A/c	Dr.	*(with the total)*
To Equity Share Capital A/c		*(with the paid up value of Equity Shares issued)*
To Preference Share Capital A/c		*(with the paid up value of Pref. Shares issued)*
To Securities Premium A/c		*(with the Securities Premium)*
To Cash A/c Bank A/c		*(with the Cash Payment)*

Note: *The Shares issued by way of purchase consideration must be recorded at their paid up values (i.e., not at their issued prices) after giving due credit to Securities Premium Account (in case the shares have been issued at premium).*

Step 4: Record the Issue of Debentures (*if any*) to discharge the existing debentureholders of Vendor Company.

JOURNAL ENTRY

Debentures in Vendor Company	Dr.	*(with the amount of debentures)*
Discount on Issue of Debentures in Purchasing Company	Dr.	*(with the debentures discount)*
To Debentures in Purchasing Company		*(with the nominal value)*
To Securities Premium A/c		*(with the debenture premium)*

Step 5: Record the Reimbursement of the Liquidation Expenses of the vendor company.

JOURNAL ENTRY

Profit & Loss A/c (in case of Merger)	Dr.
To Bank A/c	

Step 6: Eliminate the Unrealised Profit included in the Unsold Inventories.

(a) ***Where the Unsold Inventories of the purchasing company includes the goods purchased from the vendor company***

P&L A/c (in Case of Merger)	Dr.
To Inventories A/c	

(b) ***Where the Unsold Inventories of the vendor company includes goods purchased from the purchasing company, only the amount of stock is reduced to its cost while passing the entries on acquisition. (i.e., Entry in Step 2).***

Note: *In case of sale of goods at loss, no adjustment is required.*

Step 7: Eliminate the Inter Company Owings

(a) To eliminate the Debts owed by Vendor Company	Trade Payables of Vendor Co	Dr.
	To Trade Receivables	
(b) To eliminate the Debts owed by Purchasing Company	Trade Payables	Dr.
	To Trade Receivables of Vendor Co.	
(c) To eliminate the Bills drawn and retained by Vendor Co. upon Purchasing Company	Bills Payable A/c	Dr.
	To Bills Receivable of Vendor Co.	
(d) To eliminate the Bills drawn and retained by Purchasing Company upon Vendor Co.	Bills Payable of Vendor Co.	Dr.
	To Bills Receivable A/c	
(e) To eliminate the Debentures held by Vendor Co. in Purchasing Co.	Debentures A/c	Dr. [Face value]
	Profit & Loss A/c	Dr. [If FV < BV]
	To Investment in Debentures A/c (*Vendor Co.*)	[Book Value]
	To Capital Reserve A/c	[If FV > BV]
(f) To eliminate the Debentures held by Purchasing Co. in Vendor Co.	Debentures in Vendor Co.	Dr. [Face Value]
	Profit & Loss A/c	Dr. [If FV < BV]
	To Investment in Debentures A/c	Dr. [Book value]
	To Capital Reserve A/c	[If FV > BV]

Notes:

(i) *Bills drawn by one company upon the other company and discounted with the bank should not be eliminated because these bills represent owing between the bank and the company and not the inter-company owings.*

(ii) *Where the debtors of a company include a sum due from another company but the creditors of another company include a lesser sum due to the former company. The difference should be treated as cash-in-transit.*

(iii) *The entry (f) in* ***Step 7*** *should be merged with entry in* ***Step 4*** *so that the new debentures will be issued to discharge those debentures of vendor company which are held by outsiders (i.e., holders other than the purchasing company).*

(iv) *In case of entries (e) and (f), the loss should be debited to P & L A/c (in case of merger) and the profit should be credited to Capital Reserve A/c.*

ILLUSTRATION 19

V Ltd has Equity Share Capital of ₹ 95,00,000, Property,Plant & Equipment of ₹ 65,00,000 and Current Assets of ₹ 85,00,000 , Statutory Reserves of ₹ 5,00,000 and General Reserve of ₹ 28,00,000 , Current Liabilities of ₹ 19,00,000, Non-Current Liabilities of ₹ 3,00,000 as at 31.3.2023. Statutory Reserves are to be maintained for 2 more years. The business of V Ltd. is taken over by P Ltd. by issue of 1,00,000 equity shares of ₹ 100 each at 20% premium. Journalise in the books of P Ltd.

SOLUTION

JOURNAL OF P LTD.

Date	*Particulars*	*L.F.*	*Dr. (₹)*	*Cr. (₹)*
	Business Merger A/c. Dr.		120,00,000	
	To Liquidator of V Ltd. A/c.			120,00,000
	(Being the Business taken over)			
	Property,Plant & Equipment Dr.		65,00,000	
	Current Assets Dr.		85,00,000	
	To Non-Current Liabilities			3,00,000
	To Current Liabilities			19,00,000
	To Business Merger A/c			120,00,000
	To General Reserve *(balancing figure)*			**3,00,000**
	To Statutory Reserves			5,00,000
	(Being the assets, liabilities and reserves taken over recorded)			
	Liquidator of V Ltd. Dr.		120,00,000	
	To Equity Share Capital A/c.			100,00,000
	To Securities Premium A/c.			20,00,000
	(Being the purchase consideration discharged)			

Note: Closing Balance of General Reserve = Given Balance of General Reserve – Difference between purchase consideration and the amount of Share capital of the transferor company

= ₹ 28,00,000 – (₹ 120,00,000 – ₹ 95,00,000)

= ₹ 3,00,000

ILLUSTRATION 20

Given below are the extracts from the Balance Sheets of A Ltd. and B Ltd. as at 31.03.2023:

Particulars	*A Ltd. (₹ in lacs)*	*B Ltd. (₹ in lacs)*
Equity Share Capital of ₹ 100 each	80	75
12% Pref. Share Capital of ₹ 100 each	30	20
Capital Reserve	1	1
Capital Redemption Reserve	3	3
Statutory Reserves	5	5
General Reserve	31	22
Profit & Loss A/c	2	2

10% Debentures of ₹ 100 each	6	3
Current Liabilities	42	19
Property,Plant & Equipment	90	65
Non-Current Investments	15	5
Current Assets	95	80

Additional Information:

(a) 10% Debentures of the transferor company are to be discharged by transferee company by issuing such number of its 15% Debentures of ₹ 100 each so as to maintain the same amount of interest.

(b) 12% Preference shares of the transferor company are to be discharged by transferee company by issuing equivalent numbers of 15% preference Shares of ₹ 100 each at ₹ 150 each.

(c) The transferee company shall issue 4 equity shares of ₹ 10 each at ₹ 30 each for each equity share in the transferor company.

(d) The Statutory Reserves are to be maintained for 2 more years.

(e) The transferee company shall pay the cost of absorption which amount to ₹ 1,00,000

Required: (a) Prepare Journal of transferor company (b) Prepare the Journal and Balance Sheet of Transferee Company in each of the following alternative cases:

Case I If A Ltd. absorbs B Ltd. and the amalgamation is in the nature of a purchase.

Case II If A Ltd. absorbs B Ltd., and the amalgamation is in the nature of a merger.

SOLUTION

JOURNAL OF B LTD. *(₹ in lacs)*

Particulars		***L.F.***	***Dr. (₹)***	***Cr. (₹)***
Realisation A/c	Dr.		150	
To Property,Plant & Equipment				65
To Investments				5
To Current Assets				80
(Being the transfer of various assets)				
10% Debentures A/c	Dr.		3	
Current Liabilities	Dr.		19	
To Realisation A/c				22
(Being the t/f of various liabilities taken over by the Purchasing Co.)				
A Ltd.	Dr.		120	
To Realisation A/c				120
(Being the purchase Consideration due from A Ltd.)				
15% Pref. Shares in A Ltd.	Dr.		30	
Equity Shares in A Ltd.	Dr.		90	
To A Ltd.				120
(Being the receipt of purchase consideration)				

12% Preference Share Capital A/c Dr.		20	
Realisation A/c Dr.		10	
To 12% Preference Shareholders' A/c			30
(Being the amount due to 12% Pref. shareholders)			
12% Preference Shareholders' A/c Dr.		30	
To 15% Pref. Shares in A Ltd.			30
(Being the payment made to pref. shareholders)			
Equity Shareholders' A/c Dr.		18	
To Realisation A/c			18
(Being the transfer of loss on realisation)			
Equity Share Capital A/c Dr.		75	
Capital Reserve Dr.		1	
Capital Redemption Reserve Dr.		3	
Statutory Reserves Dr.		5	
General Reserve Dr.		22	
Profit & Loss A/c Dr.		2	
To Equity Shareholders' A/cs			108
(Being the transfer of Equity Share capital, Reserves and accumulated profits)			
Equity Shareholders' A/cs Dr.		90	
To Equity Shares in A Ltd.			90
(Being the final payment made to Equity shareholders)			

CASE I: IF THE AMALGAMATION IN THE NATURE OF PURCHASE

JOURNAL OF A LTD.

[₹ in lacs]

Particulars	*L.F.*	*Dr. (₹)*	*Cr. (₹)*
Business Purchase A/c Dr.		120	
To Liquidator of B Ltd.			120
(Being the purchase of business as per agreement dated...)			
Property,Plant & Equipment Dr.		65	
Investments Dr.		5	
Current Assets Dr.		80	
To 10% Debentures A/c			2
To Current Liabilities			19
To Business Purchase A/c			120
To Capital Reserve A/c			9
(Being the assets & liabilities taken over recorded)			
Amalgamation Adjustment A/c Dr.		5	
To Statutory Reserves A/c			5
(Being the identity of statutory Reserves retained)			

Liquidator of B Ltd. Dr.		120	
To Equity Share Capital A/c			30
To 15% Pref. Share Capital A/c			20
To Securities Premium A/c [60 + 10]			70
(Being the purchase consideration discharged)			
Goodwill A/c Dr.		1	
To Bank A/c			1
(Being the cost of absorption of B Ltd. paid)			
10% Debentures A/c Dr.		2	
To 15% Debentures A/c			2
(Being the issue of 15% Debentures to 10% Debentureholders of B Ltd.) [No. of 15% Debentures = ₹ 30,000/15 = 2,000]			
Capital Reserve A/c Dr.		1	
To Goodwill A/c			1
(Being the goodwill adjusted against Capital Reserve)			

BALANCE SHEET OF A LTD. AS AT 31.3.2023

Particulars	*Note No*	*₹ (lacs)*
I. Equity and Liabilities		
(1) Shareholders' Funds		
(a) Share Capital	1	160
(b) Reserves and Surplus	2	120
(2) Non-Current Liabilities		
(a) Long-term Borrowings	3	8
(3) Current Liabilities [42 + 19]		61
Total		349
II. Assets		
(1) Non-Current Assets		
(a) Fixed Assets		
Property,Plant & Equipment [90 + 65]		155
(b) Non-Current Investments [15 + 5]		20
(2) Current Assets [95 + 80 – 1]		174
Total		349

Notes To Accounts:

Particulars	*₹ (lacs)*
1. Share Capital	
80,000 Equity Shares of ₹ 100 each	80
3,00,000 Equity Shares of ₹ 10 each	30

30,000 Pref. Shares of ₹ 100 each	30
20,000, 15% Pref. Shares of ₹ 100 each	20
(Of the above 3 lacs equity Shares were issued for consideration otherwise than cash)	
	160
2. Reserves and Surplus	
Securities Premium [60 + 10]	70
General Reserve	31
Profit & Loss Account	2
Capital Reserve	1
Capital Reserve on Amalgamation	8
Capital Redemption Reserve	3
Statutory Reserves	10
Amalgamation Adjustment A/c	(5)
	120
3. Long-term Borrowings	
10% Debentures of ₹ 100 each	6
15% Debentures of ₹ 100 each	2
	8

Working Notes:

(I) CALCULATION OF PURCHASE CONSIDERATION

for preference Shareholders [(20,00,000/100) × ₹ 150]	30,00,000
for Equity Shareholders [{(75,00,000/100) × 4} × ₹ 150]	90,00,000
	120,00,000

(II) CALCULATION OF NET ASSETS TAKEN OVER AT THEIR AGREED VALUES

A	Total Assets taken over at their agreed values	
	Fixed Assets	65,00,000
	Investments	5,00,000
	Current Assets	80,00,000
		150,00,000
B	*Less:* Liabilities taken over at their agreed amounts	
	10% Debentures	2,00,000
	Current Liabilities	19,00,000
		21,00,000
C	Net Assets taken over (A – B)	129,00,000

(iii) *Calculation of Capital Reserve on amalgamation*

Capital Reserve = Net Assets taken over at their agreed values – Purchase consideration

= ₹ 129,00,000 – ₹ 120,00,000 = ₹ 9,00,000

CASE II: IF AMALGAMATION IS IN THE NATURE OF MERGER

JOURNAL OF A LTD.

(₹ in lacs)

Particulars		*L.F.*	*Dr. (₹)*	*Cr. (₹)*
Business Merger A/c	Dr.		120	
To Liquidator of B Ltd.				120
(Being the purchase of business as per agreement dated....)				
Property,Plant & Equipment	Dr.		65	
Investments	Dr.		5	
Current Assets	Dr.		80	
To 10% Debentures A/c				3
To Current Liabilities				19
To Business Merger A/c				120
To Capital Redemption Reserve				3
To Statutory Reserves				5
(Being the assets, liabilities and reserves taken over recorded)				
Liquidator of B Ltd.	Dr.		120	
To Equity Share Capital A/c				30
To 15% Preference Share Capital A/c				20
To Securities Premium A/c (60 + 10)				70
(Being the purchase consideration discharged)				
Profit & Loss A/c	Dr.		1	
To Bank A/c				1
(Being the cost of absorption of B Ltd. paid)				
10% Debentures A/c	Dr.		3	
To 15% Debentures, A/c				2
To Capital Reserve A/c				1
(Being the issue of 15% Debentures to 10% Debentureholders of B Ltd.) No. of 15% Debentures = ₹ 30,000/.15 = 20,000]				

BALANCE SHEET OF A LTD. AS AT 31.3.2023

Particulars	*Note No*	*₹ (lacs)*
I. Equity and Liabilities		
(1) Shareholders' Funds		
(a) Share Capital	1	160
(b) Reserves and Surplus	2	120
(2) Non-Current Liabilities [Long-term Borrowings]	3	8
(3) Current Liabilities [42 + 19]		61
Total		349

II. Assets		
(1) Non-Current Assets		
(a) Fixed Assets		
Property, Plant & Equipment [90 + 65]		155
(b) Non-Current Investments [15 + 5]		20
(2) Current Assets [95 + 80 – 1]		174
Total		349

Notes To Accounts:

Particulars	₹ (lacs)
1. Share Capital	
80,000 Equity share of ₹ 100 each	80
3,00,000 Equity Shares of ₹ 10 each	30
30,000 Pref. Shares of ₹ 100 each	30
20,000, 15% Pref. Shares of ₹ 100 each	20
(Of the above 3 lacs equity Shares were issued for consideration otherwise than cash)	
	160
2. Reserves and Surplus	
Securities Premium [60 + 10]	70
General Reserve[Refer to WN]	31
Profit & Loss Account [2 + 2 – 1]	3
Capital Redemption Reserve	6
Statutory Reserves	10
	120
3. Long-term Borrowings	
10% Debentures of ₹ 100 each	6
15% Debenture of ₹ 100 each	2
	8

Working Notes:

(I) CALCULATION OF PURCHASE CONSIDERATION

Particulars	No. of Shares	Issue Price	Total
For Preference Shareholders	20,000	₹ 150	30,00,000
For Equity Shareholders (75000 × 4)	3,00,000	₹ 30	90,00,000
			120,00,000

(ii) Calculation of the difference between purchase consideration and the amount of share capital of the transferor company

Difference = ₹ 120,00,000 – ₹ 95,00,000 (Equity + Pref.) = ₹ 25,00,000

(iii) *Calculation of the difference between the amount of Debentures of transferor company taken over and the amount of Debentures of the transferee company issued in exchange*

Difference = ₹ 3,00,000 – ₹ 2,00,000 = ₹, 1,00,000 (Profit)

(IV) ADJUSTMENT OF DIFFERENCE AGAINST THE RESERVES AND ACCUMULATED PROFITS OF TRANSFEREOR CO.

A	Difference between Purchase Consideration & Share Capital	25.00
B	*Less:* Capital Reserves of both Co. (1+1 + 1)	(3.00)
C	Balance to be adjusted against Revenue Reserve	22.00
D	General Reserves of both Co. (31 + 22)	53.00
E	Closing Balance of General Reserves [D–C]	31.00

AMALGAMATION OF TWO OR MORE COMPANIES IN THE NATURE OF PURCHASE WHEN A NEW COMPANY IS FORMED

ILLUSTRATION 21

Sun Ltd. and Moon Ltd. were amalgamated on and from 1st April, 2023. A new company Star Ltd. was formed to take over the business of the existing companies. Given below are the extracts from the Balance Sheets of Sun Ltd. and Moon Ltd. as at 31st March, 2023 :

(₹ in lakhs)

Particulars	***Sun Ltd.***	***Moon Ltd.***
Equity Shares of ₹ 100 each	400	375
12% Preference Shares of ₹100 each	150	100
Reserves & Surplus	210	165
10% Debentures (₹100 each)	30	15
Current Liabilities	210	95
Property,Plant & Equipment	450	275
Non-Current Investments	75	25
Current Assets	575	450

Additional Information:

(a) Star Ltd. will issue 5 equity shares for each equity share of Sun Ltd. and 4 equity shares for each equity share of Moon Ltd. The shares are to be issued @ ₹ 30 each, having a face value of ₹ 10 per share.

(b) Preference shareholders of the two companies are issued equivalent number of 15% preference shares of Star Ltd. at a price of ₹ 150 per share (face value ₹ 100).

(c) 10% Debentureholders of Sun Ltd. and Moon Ltd. are discharged by Star Ltd., issuing such number of its 15% Debentures of ₹100 each so as to maintain the same amount of interest.

(d) Investment allowance reserve is to be maintained for 4 more years.

(e) Liquidation expenses are: Sun Ltd. ₹2,00,000 Moon Ltd. ₹ 1,00,000. It was decided that these expenses would be borne by Star Ltd.

(f) All the assets and liabilities of Sun Ltd. and Moon Ltd. are taken over at book value.

Required: Calculate Purchase Consideration and show the discharge thereof.

SOLUTION

CALCULATION OF PURCHASE CONSIDERATION

Particulars	X Ltd.	Y Ltd.	Total
A. No of Equity Shares	4,00,000	3,75,000	
B. Exchange Ratio	5:1	4:1	
C. No of Equity Shares to be issued by [A × B]	20,00,000	15,00,000	35,00,000
Equity Share Capital @ ₹ 20	400,00,000	300,00,000	700,00,000
Securities Premium@ ₹ 10	200,00,000	150,00,000	350,00,000
D. No of 15% Pref. Shares to be issued	1,50,000	1,00,000	2,50,000
15% Pref. Share Capital @ ₹ 100	150,00,000	100,00,000	250,00,000
Securities Premium@ ₹ 50	75,00,000	50,00,000	125,00,000
Total Purchase Consideration	825,00,000	600,00,000	1425,00,000

Note: *According to AS-14, the amount paid by purchasing Company to discharge the debentures holders and the liquidation expenses of Vendor Company are not considered as part of purchase consideration.*

ILLUSTRATION 22

Given below are the extracts from the Balance Sheets of X Ltd and Y Ltd. as at 31st March 2023:

Particulars	X Ltd. (₹ in lacs)	Y Ltd. (₹ in lacs)
Equity Share Capital of ₹ 10 each	5.00	10.00
8% Pref. Share Capital of ₹ 100 each	1.00	2.00
Reserves & Surplus	21.71	3.00
12% Debentures of ₹ 100 each	2.00	1.00
Current Liabilities	1.00	2.20
Property,Plant & Equipment	19.00	7.60
Non-Current Investments	3.45	5.20
Current Assets	8.26	5.40

The two companies agree to amalgamate as on Ist April, 2023 and form a new company XY Ltd.

Additional Information:

(a) Goodwill of X Ltd. and Y Ltd. on the date of take-over was valued at ₹ 48,000 and ₹ 38,000 respectively and Property,Plant & Equipment of X Ltd. and Y Ltd were valued at 10% above their book values on the date of take-over. Investments of X Ltd. and Y Ltd. are considered worth ₹ 4,16,000 and ₹ 6,26,000 respectively.

(b) 12% Debentures of X Ltd. and Y Ltd. are discharged by XY Ltd. by issuing such number of its 15% Debentures of ₹ 100 each so as to maintain the same amount of interest.

(c) The issue of such an amount of fully paid 10% Pref. Shares in X Y Ltd. at 125% as is sufficient to discharge 9% Pref. Shares in X Ltd. & Y Ltd. at a premium of 20%.

(d) The Equity Shares of XY Ltd are to be of a nominal value of ₹ 10 each credited as ₹ 8 paid up and valued at ₹ 15 per share.

(e) Liquidation expenses are: X Ltd. ₹ 2,000 ,Y Ltd. ₹ 1,000. It was decided that these expenses would be borne by XY Ltd. Expenses on incorporation of XY Ltd. were ₹ 1,000.

Required: Calculate Purchase Consideration and show the discharge thereof.

SOLUTION

(I) COMPUTATION OF VALUE OF NET ASSETS FOR EQUITY SHAREHOLDERS

₹ (LAKHS)

Particulars	*X Ltd.*	*Y Ltd.*
A. Total Assets at their Current Values:		
Goodwill	0.48	0.38
Net Tangible Block	20.90	8.36
Non-Current Investments	4.16	6.26
Current Assets	8.26	5.40
	33.80	**20.40**
B. *Less:* Liabilities at their Current Amounts:		
12% Debentures [Interest/15%]	1.60	0.80
Current Liabilities	1.00	2.20
8% Pref. Share Capital	1.20	2.40
	3.80	**5.40**
C. Net Assets for Equity Shareholders [A – B]	**30.00**	**15.00**

(II) CALCULATION OF NO. OF EQUITY SHARES TO BE ISSUED BY PURCHASING COMPANY

Particulars	*X Ltd.*	*Y Ltd.*	*Total*
A. Total Value (as calculated above)	30,00,000	15,00,000	45,00,000
B. Issue Price of an Equity Share	15	15	15
C. No of Equity Shares to be issued by [A/B]	2,00,000	1,00,000	3,00,000
Equity Share Capital @ ₹ 8	16,00,000	8,00,000	24,00,000
Securities Premium@ ₹ 7	14,00,000	7,00,000	21,00,000

(III) CALCULATION OF PURCHASING CONSIDERATION

Particulars	*X Ltd.*	*Y Ltd.*	*Total*
Equity Shares @ ₹ 15	30,00,000	15,00,000	45,00,000
9% Pref. Shares @ ₹ 125	1,20,000	2,40,000	3,60,000
Total	31,20,000	17,40,000	48,60,000

Note: *According to AS-14, the amount paid by purchasing Company to discharge the debentures holders and the liquidation expenses of Vendor Company are not considered as part of purchase consideration.*

ILLUSTRATION 23

P Ltd. and Q Ltd. were carrying on the business of manufacturing of auto components. both the companies decided to amalgamate and a new company PQ Ltd. is to be formed with an Authorized Capital of ₹ 10,00,000 divided into 1,00,000 equity shares of ₹ 10 each. The Balance Sheet of the companies as on 31.03.2023 were as under:

Particulars	P (₹)	Q (₹)
I. Equity and Liabilities		
1. Shareholder's Fund		
(a) Share Capital	1,40,000	2,50,000
(b) Reserves & Surplus (Profit & Loss A/c)	30,000	1,55,000
2. Non Current Liabilities (8 % Secured Debentures)	1,10,000	—
3. Current Liabilities (Trade Payables)	54,000	1,40,000
Total	3,34,000	5,45,000
II. Assets		
1. Non-current Assets		
(a) Property,Plant & Equipment	1,25,000	2,95,000
2. Current Assets		
(a) Inventories	1,35,000	50,000
(b) Trade Receivables	44,000	1,42,000
(c) Cash at bank	30,000	58,000
Total	3,34,000	5,45,000

The assets and liabilities of the existing companies are to be transferred at book value with the exception of some items detailed below:

(i) Goodwill of P Ltd. was worth ₹ 50,000 and of Q Ltd. was worth ₹ 1,50,000,.

(ii) Property,Plant & Equipment of Q Ltd. was valued at ₹ 3,05,000.

(iii) The Trade Receivables of P Ltd. are realized fully and bank balance of P Ltd. are to be retained by the liquidator and the Trade Payables are to be paid of the proceeds thereof.

(iv) The debentures of P Ltd. are to be discharged by issue of 8% debentures of PQ Ltd. at a premium of 10%.

You are required to:

(i) Compute the basis on which shares in PQ Ltd. will be issued at par to the shareholders of the existing companies.

(ii) Draw up a Balance Sheet of PQ Ltd. as at 1st April, 2023, the date of completion of amalgamation.

(iii) Write up Journal entries including bank entries for closing the books of P Ltd.

SOLUTION

CALCULATION OF PURCHASE CONSIDERATION

Particulars	P Ltd. (₹)	Q Ltd. (₹)
Assets taken over:		
Goodwill	50,000	1,50,000
Property,Plant & Equipment	1,25,000	3,05,000
Inventories	1,35,000	50,000
Trade Receivables	–	1,42,000
Cash at Bank	–	58,000
	3,10,000	7,05,000

Less: Liabilities taken over:		
8% Debentures	(1,21,000)	–
Trade Payables	–	(1,40,000)
Net Assets taken over	1,89,000	5,65,000
To be satisfied by issue of shares of PQ Ltd. of ₹ 10 each at par	18,900	56,500

BALANCE SHEET OF PQ LIMITED AS AT 1ST APRIL, 2023

Particulars	*Note No.*	*(₹)*
I. Equity and Liabilities		
(1) Shareholder's Funds		
(a) Share Capital	1	7,54,000
(b) Reserve & Surplus [Securities Premium]		11,000
(2) Non-Current Liabilities		
(a) Long term borrowings [8% Debentures]		1,10,000
(3) Current Liabilities		
(a) Trade Payables		1,40,000
Total		10,15,000
II. Assets		
(1) Non-Current assets		
(a) Fixed Assets		
Tangible [₹ 1,25,000 + ₹ 3,05,000]		4,30,000
Intangible [₹ 50,000 + ₹ 1,50,000]		2,00,000
(2) Current Assets		
(a) Inventories		1,85,000
(b) Trade Receivables		1,42,000
(c) Cash at Bank		58,000
Total		10,15,000

Notes to Accounts:

Particulars	₹
1. Share Capital	
Authorized	
1,00,000 shares of ₹ 10 each	10,00,000
Issued, Subscribed and Paid up	
75,400 shares of ₹ 10 each (All the above shares are allotted as fully paid up pursuant to scheme of amalgamation without payments being received in cash)	7,54,000

JOURNAL OF P LTD.

Date	*Particulars*	*L.F.*	*Dr. (₹)*	*Cr. (₹)*
1	Realization A/c Dr.		3,04,000	
	To Property,Plant & Equipment			1,25,000

	To Inventories		1,35,000
	To Trade Receivables		44,000
	(Being all assets except cash t/f to Realization A/c)		
2	8% Debentures A/c Dr.	1,10,000	
	Trade Payables Dr.	54,000	
	To Realization A/c		1,64,000
	(Being all liabilities transferred to Realization Account)		
3	Equity Share Capital A/c Dr.	1,40,000	
	Profit & Loss A/c Dr.	30,000	
	To Equity Shareholder's A/c		1,70,000
	(Being Equity transferred to Equity Shareholder's A/c)		
4	PQ Ltd. Dr.	1,89,000	
	To Realization A/c		1,89,000
	(Being Purchase consideration due)		
5	Bank A/c Dr.	44,000	
	To Realization A/c		44,000
	(Being cash received from trade receivables in full)		
6	Realization A/c Dr.	54,000	
	To Bank A/c		54,000
	(Being payment made to Trade Payables)		
7	Share in PQ Ltd. Dr.	1,89,000	
	To PQ Ltd.		1,89,000
	(Being purchase consideration received in the form of Equity Shares of PQ Ltd.)		
8	Realization A/c (balancing figure) Dr.	39,000	
	To Equity Shareholder's A/c		39,000
	(Being profit on realization transferred to Equity Shareholder's A/c)		
9	Equity Shareholder's A/c Dr.	2,09,000	
	To Shares in PQ Ltd.		1,89,000
	To Bank A/c		20,000
	(Being final payment made to shareholders)		

ILLUSTRATION 24

Given below are the extracts of Balance Sheets of M Ltd. and N Ltd. as at 31st March, 2023:

(₹ in lakhs)

Particulars	*M Ltd.*	*N Ltd.*
Equity Shares of ₹10 each	3,600	900
10% Preference Shares of ₹ 10 each	1,200	–

Capital Reserve	600	–
General Reserve	2,100	–
Profit and Loss Account	780	(39)
8% Redeemable Debentures of ₹ 1,000 each	–	300
Trade Payables	3,291	462
Property,Plant & Equipment	6,615	702
Inventories	2,370	444
Trade Receivables	1,044	237
Cash at Bank	1,542	240

A new Company MN Ltd. was incorporated with an authorised capital of ₹ 15,000 lakhs divided into shares of ₹ 10 each. For the purpose of amalgamation in the nature of merger, M Ltd. and N Ltd. were merged into MN Ltd. on the following terms:

(i) Purchase consideration for M Ltd.'s business is to be discharged by issue of 120 lakhs fully paid 11% preference shares and 720 lakhs fully paid equity shares of MN Ltd. to the preference and equity shareholders of M Ltd. respectively in full satisfaction of their claims.

(ii) To discharge purchase consideration for N Ltd. 's business, MN Ltd. to allot 90 lakhs fully paid up equity shares to shareholders of N Ltd. in full satisfaction of their claims.

(iii) Expenses on the liquidation of M Ltd. and N Ltd. amounting to ₹ 6 lakhs are to be borne by MN Ltd.

(iv) 8% Redeemable Debentures of N Ltd. to be converted into 8.5% redeemable debentures of MN Ltd.

(v) Expenses on incorporation of MN Ltd. were ₹15 lakhs.

You are requested to:

(a) Pass necessary Journal Entries in the books of MN Ltd. to record above transactions, and

(b) Prepare Balance Sheet of MN Ltd. after merger.

SOLUTION

JOURNAL OF MN LTD.

(₹ *in lakhs)*

Date	*Particulars*		*L.F.*	*Dr. (₹)*	*Cr. (₹)*
	Business Purchase A/c	Dr.		9,300	
	To Liquidator of M Ltd.				8,400
	To Liquidator of N Ltd.				900
	(Being consideration payable to liquidators of the two companies taken over)				
	Property,Plant & Equipment (6,615 + 702)	Dr.		7,317	
	Inventories A/c (2,370 + 444)	Dr.		2,814	
	Trade Receivables A/c (1,044 + 237)	Dr.		1,281	
	Cash at Bank A/c (1,542 + 240)	Dr.		1,782	
	Profit and Loss A/c (Refer W.N.)	Dr.		159	
	To 8% Redeemable Debentures of N Ltd. A/c				300
	To Trade Payables A/c (3,291 + 462)				3,753

	To Business Purchase A/c (Being incorporation of all the assets and liabilities and the excess of consideration over the share capital being adjusted against reserves and surplus)			9,300
	Liquidator of M Ltd, A/c Dr. Liquidator of N Ltd. A/c Dr. To Equity Share Capital A/c (7,200 + 900) To 11% Preference Share Capital A/c (Being allotment of fully paid shares in discharge of purchase consideration)		8,400 900	 8,100 1,200
	Profit and Loss A/c Dr. To Bank A/c (Being payment of liquidation expenses of M Ltd, and N Ltd.)		6	 6
	Preliminary Expenses A/c Dr. To Bank A/c (Being expenses on incorporation of MN Ltd.)		15	 15
	8% Redeemable Debentures of N Ltd. A/c Dr. To 8.5% Redeemable Debentures A/c (Being conversion of 8% Debentures of N Ltd. into 8.5% Debentures)		300	 300
	Profit & Loss A/c Dr. To Preliminary Expenses A/c (Being the Preliminary Exp. w/o as per Para 56 of AS 26)		15	 15

BALANCE SHEET OF MN LTD AS AT 1ST APRIL, 2023

Particulars	*Note No.*	*₹ (in lacs)*
I. EQUITY AND LIABILITIES		
(1) Shareholders' Funds		
(a) Share Capital	1	9,300
(b) Reserves and Surplus [159 + 6(liquidation exp) + 15 (incorporation exp)]		(180)
(2) Non-Current Liabilities		
Long-term Borrowings [Debentures]		300
(3) Current Liabilities		
Trade Payables [₹ 3,291 + ₹ 462]		3,753
Total		13,173
II. ASSETS		
(1) Non-Current Assets		
(a) Fixed Assets		
(i) Property,Plant & Equipment [₹ 6,615 + ₹ 702]		7,317

(2) Current Assets		
Inventories [₹ 2,370 + ₹ 444]		2,814
Trade Receivables [₹ 1,044 + ₹ 237]		1,281
Cash and Cash Equivalents [₹ 1,542 + ₹ 240 – 21]		1,761
Total		13,173

Notes To Accounts:

Particulars	₹
1. Share Capital	
810 lakhs Equity Shares of ₹ 10 each	8,100
120 lakhs Pref. Shares of ₹ 10 each	1,200
(Of the above all Shares were issued for consideration otherwise than cash)	9,300

Working Note:

BALANCE OF PROFIT LOSS ACCOUNT *(₹ in lakhs)*

Total Consideration = ₹ (8,400 + 900) lakhs		9,300
Less: Share Capital of Companies taken over [₹(3,600 + 1,200 + 900) lacs]		5,700
		3,600
Amount to be adjusted:		
Capital Reserve	600	
General Reserve	2,100	
Profit & Loss A/c	741	3,441
Debit balance of Profit & Loss Account		159

ILLUSTRATION 25

Sun Ltd. and Moon Ltd. were amalgamated on and from 1st April, 2023. A new company Star Ltd. was formed to take over the business of the existing companies. The Balance Sheets of Sun Ltd. and Moon Ltd. as at 31st March, 2023 are given below:

(₹ in lakhs)

Particulars	*Sun Ltd.*	*Moon Ltd.*
Equity Shares of ₹ 100 each	400	375
12% Preference Shares of ₹100 each	150	100
Revaluation Reserve	75	50
General Reserve	85	75
Investment Allowance Reserve	25	25
Profit and Loss Account	25	15
10% Debentures (₹100 each)	30	15
Trade Payables	210	95
Property,Plant & Equipment	450	325

Investments		75	25
Inventories		175	125
Trade Receivables		150	175
Cash and Bank balances		150	100

Additional Information:

(a) Star Ltd. will issue 5 equity shares for each equity share of Sun Ltd. and 4 equity shares for each equity share of Moon Ltd. The shares are to be issued @ ₹ 30 each, having a face value of ₹ 10 per share.

(b) Preference shareholders of the two companies are issued equivalent number of 15% preference shares of Star Ltd. at a price of ₹ 150 per share (face value ₹ 100).

(c) 10% Debentureholders of Sun Ltd. and Moon Ltd. are discharged by Star Ltd., issuing such number of its 15% Debentures of ₹100 each so as to maintain the same amount of interest.

(d) Investment allowance reserve is to be maintained for 4 more years.

(e) Liquidation expenses are: Sun Ltd. ₹2,00,000 Moon Ltd. ₹ 1,00,000. It was decided that these expenses would be borne by Star Ltd.

(f) All the assets and liabilities of Sun Ltd. and Moon Ltd. are taken over at book value.

(g) Authorised equity share capital of Star Ltd. is ₹ 5,00,00,000, divided into equity shares of ₹ 10 each. After issuing required number of shares to the Liquidators of Sun Ltd. and Moon Ltd., Star Ltd. issued balance shares to Public. The issue was fully subscribed.

Required: Prepare the Balance Sheet of Star Ltd. as at 1st April, 2023 after amalgamation has been carried out on the basis of Amalgamation in the nature of purchase.

SOLUTION

BALANCE SHEET OF STAR LTD AS AT 1ST APRIL, 2023

Particulars	*Note No.*	*₹ (in lacs)*
I. EQUITY AND LIABILITIES		
(1) Shareholders' Funds		
(a) Share Capital	1	750
(b) Reserves and Surplus	2	825
(2) Non-Current Liabilities		
Long-term Borrowings [Debentures] [20 + 10]		30
(3) Current Liabilities		
Trade Payables (210 + 95)		305
Total		1,910
II. ASSETS		
(1) Non-Current Assets		
(a) Fixed Assets		
(i) Property,Plant & Equipment [450 + 325]		775
(ii) Intangible Assets [Goodwill] [10 + 2 + 1]		13
(b) Non-Current Investments [75 + 25]		100

(2) Current Assets		
Inventories [175 + 125]		300
Trade Receivables [150 + 175]		325
Cash and Cash Equivalents [150+100 + 150 – 3]		397
Total		1,910

Notes To Accounts:

Particulars	₹
1. Share Capital	
50 lakhs Equity Shares of ₹ 10 each	500
2.5 lakhs Pref. Shares of ₹ 100 each	250
(Of the above all Shares except 15 lakhs Equity Shares were issued for consideration otherwise than cash)	750
2. Reserves and Surplus	
Securities Premium [75 + 50 + 400 + 300]	825
Investment Allowance Reserve [25 + 25]	50
Amalgamation Adjustment A/c	(50)
	825

Working Notes:

1. CALCULATION OF PURCHASE CONSIDERATION

Particulars	*X Ltd.*	*Y Ltd.*	*Total*
A. No of Equity Shares	4,00,000	3,75,000	
B. Exchange Ratio	5:1	4:1	
C. No of Equity Shares to be issued by [A × B]	20,00,000	15,00,000	35,00,000
Equity Share Capital @ ₹ 10	200,00,000	150,00,000	350,00,000
Securities Premium@ ₹ 20	400,00,000	300,00,000	700,00,000
D. No of 15% Pref. Shares to be issued	1,50,000	1,00,000	2,50,000
15% Pref. Share Capital @ ₹ 100	150,00,000	100,00,000	250,00,000
Securities Premium@ ₹ 50	75,00,000	50,00,000	125,00,000
Total Purchase Consideration	825,00,000	600,00,000	1425,00,000

2. CALCULATION OF NUMBER OF DEBENTURES ISSUED *(₹ in lakhs)*

Particulars	*Sun Ltd.*	*Moon Ltd.*
10% Debentures of ₹100 each	30	15
15% Debentures to be issued to maintain same amount of interest:		
Interest = ₹30,00,000 × 10% = ₹3,00,000		
Number of 15% Debentures = (₹ 3,00,000/15) × 100	20	
Interest = ₹15,00,000 × 10%		
Number of 15% Debentures = (₹ 1,15,000/15) × 100		10

3. NET ASSETS TAKEN OVER *(₹ in lakhs)*

	Particulars	Sun Ltd.	Moon Ltd.
A.	Assets taken over		
	Property,Plant & Equipment	450	325
	Investments	75	25
	Inventories	175	125
	Trade Receivable	150	175
	Cash and bank	150	100
		1,000	750
B.	Less: Liabilities taken over		
	Debentures	20	10
	Trade Payable	210	95
		230	105
C.	Net assets taken over	770	645
D.	Purchase consideration	825	600
E.	(Goodwill)/Capital Reserve	(55)	45
F.	Net Goodwill		(10)

4. Liquidation expenses of Sun Ltd. and Moon Ltd., ₹ 2 lakhs and ₹ 1 lakhs respectively will be debited to Goodwill account in the books of Star Ltd.

ILLUSTRATION 26

Given below are the extracts from the Balance Sheets of X Ltd and Y Ltd. as at 31st March 2023:

Particulars	X Ltd. (₹ in lacs)	Y Ltd. (₹ in lacs)
Equity Share Capital of ₹ 10 each	5.00	10.00
8% Pref. Share Capital of ₹ 100 each	1.00	2.00
Reserves	15.46	0.70
Statutory Reserve	2.00	1.00
Profit & Loss A/c	4.25	1.30
12% Debentures of ₹ 100 each	2.00	1.00
Current Liabilities	1.00	2.20
Property,Plant & Equipment	19.00	7.60
Non-Current Investments	3.45	5.20
Current Assets	8.26	5.40

The two companies agree to amalgamate as on Ist April, 2023 and form a new company XY Ltd.

Additional Information:

(a) Goodwill of X Ltd. and Y Ltd. on the date of take-over was valued at ₹ 48,000 and ₹ 38,000 respectively and Property, Plant & Equipment of X Ltd. and Y Ltd were valued at 10% above their book values on the date of take-over. Non-Current Investments of X Ltd. and Y Ltd. are considered worth ₹ 4,16,000 and ₹ 6,26,000 respectively.

(b) 12% Debentures of X Ltd. and Y Ltd. are discharged by XY Ltd. by issuing such number of its 15% Debentures of ₹ 100 each so as to maintain the same amount of interest.

(c) The issue of such an amount of fully paid 10% Pref. Shares in X Y Ltd. at 125% as is sufficient to discharge 8% Pref. Shares in X Ltd. & Y Ltd. at a premium of 20%.

(d) The Equity Shares of XY Ltd are to be of a nominal value of ₹ 10 each credited as ₹ 8 paid up and issued at ₹ 15 per share.

(e) Statutory Reserve is to be maintained for 3 years more for Income Tax purposes.

(f) Liquidation expenses are: X Ltd. ₹ 2,000 ,Y Ltd. ₹ 1,000. It was decided that these expenses would be borne by XY Ltd. Expenses on incorporation of XY Ltd. were ₹ 1,000.

(g) Authorised equity share capital of XY Ltd. is ₹ 50,00,000, divided into equity shares of ₹ 10 each. After issuing required number of shares to the Liquidators of X Ltd. and Y Ltd., XY Ltd. issued balance shares to Public. The issue was fully subscribed.

Required: Draft the Balance Sheet of XY Ltd. after amalgamation.

SOLUTION

BALANCE SHEET OF XY LTD. AS AT 31.3.2023

Particulars	***Note No***	***₹ (lacs)***
I. Equity and Liabilities		
(1) Shareholders' Funds		
(a) Share Capital	1	42.88
(b) Reserves and Surplus	2	35.71
(2) Non-Current Liabilities [Long-term Borrowings]	3	2.40
(3) Current Liabilities		3.20
Total		84.19
II. Assets		
(1) Non-Current Assets		
(a) Fixed Assets		
Property, Plant & Equipment (20.90 + 8.36)		29.26
Intangible Assets (Goodwill) (0.48 + 0.38+0.2+0.1)		0.89
(b) Non-Current Investments		10.42
(2) Current Assets [8.26+5.40-.02-.01-.01+30]		**43.62**
Total		84.19

Notes To Accounts:

Particulars	***₹ (lacs)***
1. Share Capital	
5,00,000 Equity Shares of ₹ 10 each, ₹ 8 paid up	40.00
2,880, 9% Pref. Shares of ₹ 100 each	2.88
(Of the above all Shares except 2 lakh Equity Shares were issued for consideration otherwise than cash)	
	42.88

2. Reserves and Surplus	
Securities Premium [(3,00,000 × ₹ 7) + (2,880 × ₹ 25) +(2,00,000 × ₹ 7)]	35.72
Statutory Reserve	3.00
Amalgamation Adjustment A/c	(3.00)
Profit & loss A/c [Preliminary Expenses [0.**01**]]	(0.01)
	35.71
3. Long-term Borrowings	
15% Debentures (1.60 + 0.80]	2.40

Working Notes:

(I) COMPUTATION OF VALUE OF NET ASSETS FOR EQUITY SHAREHOLDERS ₹ (LAKHS)

Particulars	***X Ltd.***	***Y Ltd.***
A. Total Assets at their Current Values:		
Goodwill	0.48	0.38
Net Tangible Block	20.90	8.36
Non-Current Investments	4.16	6.26
Current Assets	8.26	5.40
	33.80	**20.40**
B. *Less:* Liabilities at their Current Amounts:		
12% Debentures [Interest/15%]	1.60	0.80
Current Liabilities	1.00	2.20
8% Pref. Share Capital	1.20	2.40
	3.80	**5.40**
C. Net Assets for Equity Shareholders [A – B]	**30.00**	**15.00**

(II) CALCULATION OF NO. OF EQUITY SHARES TO BE ISSUED BY PURCHASING COMPANY

Particulars	***X Ltd.***	***Y Ltd.***	***Total***
A. Total Value (as calculated above)	30,00,000	15,00,000	45,00,000
B. Issue Price of an Equity Share	15	15	15
C. No of Equity Shares to be issued by [A/B]	2,00,000	1,00,000	3,00,000
Equity Share Capital @ ₹ 8	16,00,000	8,00,000	24,00,000
Securities Premium@ ₹ 7	14,00,000	7,00,000	21,00,000

(III) CALCULATION OF PURCHASE CONSIDERATION

Particulars	***X Ltd.***	***Y Ltd.***	***Total***
Equity Shares @ ₹ 15	30,00,000	15,00,000	45,00,000
9% Pref. Shares @ ₹ 125	1,20,000	2,40,000	3,60,000
Total	31,20,000	17,40,000	48,60,000

ILLUSTRATION 27

Given below are the extracts from the Balance Sheet of *BHARAT Ltd and SHEENA* Ltd. as at 31st March, 2023:

Particulars	*BHARAT Ltd* ₹	*SHEENA Ltd* ₹
Equity Share Capital of ₹ 10 each	15,00,000	5,00,000
8% Pref. Share Capital of ₹ 100 each	2,50,000	1,25,000
General Reserve	3,75,000	50,000
Profit & Loss A/c	4,38,000	35,000
Statutory Reserves	—	12,500
10% Debentures of ₹ 100 each	—	1,25,000
Trade Payables	93,750	3,50,000
Property, Plant & Equipment	11,87,500	3,75,000
Goodwill	—	2,98,750
Non-Current Investments	2,72,500	—
Inventories	2,37,500	1,37,500
Trade Receivables	3,50,000	1,62,500
Cash at Bank	6,09,250	2,23,750

Prior to absorption, both the companies decide to declare and pay equity dividend @ 5%. The business of *SHEENA* Ltd. is taken over by *BHARAT Ltd* as on that date on the following terms:

(a) 50% of Property, Plant & Equipment are found understated by 50% of market value and the remaining Property,Plant & Equipment are found overstated by 25% of market value. Property, Plant & Equipment are taken over at market value. Goodwill of *SHEENA* Ltd. is to be valued at ₹ 1,31,250. Inventories are taken over at book value less 10% and Trade Receivables are taken over at book value subject to an allowance of 10% to cover doubtful debts. Trade Payables are to be taken over at ₹ 3,32,500. and Unrecorded Loan Liability of ₹ 1,27,500 to be discharged by *BHARAT Ltd* immediately after acquisition of business.

(b) The amount payable by *BHARAT Ltd.* was agreed as follows:

(i) The purchase consideration is to be discharged to the extent of 20% in cash.

(ii) The issue of such an amount of fully paid 14% Debentures of ₹ 100 each in *BHARAT Ltd* at 96% as is sufficient to discharge 10% Debentures in *SHEENA* Ltd. at a premium of 20%.

(iii) The issue of such an amount of fully paid 10% Pref. Shares of ₹ 100 each in *BHARAT Ltd* at 125% as is sufficient to discharge 8% Pref. Shares in *SHEENA* Ltd. at a premium of 20%.

(iv) The balance in the form of equity shares of ₹ 10 each, ₹ 8 paid up at a premium of ₹ 7 per share. The market value of an equity share of *BHARAT Ltd* at present is ₹ 100.

(v) Expenses of liquidation of *SHEENA* Ltd. are to be reimbursed by *BHARAT Ltd* to the extent of ₹ 25,000. Actual Expenses amounted to ₹ 30,000.

(c) Statutory Reserves are to be maintained for 2 more years.

Required: Show the calculation and discharge of Purchase Consideration and Pass Journal Entries in the books of *BHARAT* Ltd.

SOLUTION

1. CALCULATION OF PURCHASE CONSIDERATION

	Particulars	₹
A	Assets taken over at agreed values	
	Property, Plant & Equipment [(₹ 3,75,000 × 50%) + (1,87,500 × 50%/50%)]	3,75,000
	Property, Plant & Equipment [(₹ 3,75,000 × 50%) – (1,87,500 × 25%/125%)]	1,50,000
	Inventories [₹ 1,37,500 – ₹ 13,750]	1,23,750
	Trade Receivables [₹ 1,62,500 – ₹ 16,250]	1,46,250
	Cash at Bank [2,23,750 – 25,000(ED) – 10,000 (PD) – 5,000 (Exp.)]	1,83,750
	Goodwill	1,31,250
		11,10,000
B	*Less:* Liabilities taken over:	
	Trade Payables	3,32,500
	10% Debentures [₹ 1,25,000 + 20%]	1,50,000
	Unrecorded Loan	1,27,500
		6,10,000
C	Net Assets taken over (A – B)	5,00,000

2. DISCHARGE OF PURCHASE CONSIDERATION

A. Cash to Equity Shareholders [5,00,000 × 20%]	1,00,000
B. 1200, 10% Pref. Shares to be issued [(1,25,000 × 120%)]	1,50,000
C. 16666, Equity Shares to be issued [(5,00,000 – 100,000 – 150,000)/ ₹ 15]	2,49,990
D. Cash for Fractional Share(0.666 × ₹ 100)	67
E. Total Purchase Consideration (A + B + C + D)	5,00,057

3. JOURNAL OF BHARAT Ltd

Date	*Particulars*		*L.F.*	*Dr. (₹)*	*Cr. (₹)*
1.	Profit & Loss A/c	Dr.		95,000	
	To Pref Dividend Payable A/c [2,50,000 x 8%]				20,000
	To Equity Dividend Payable A/c [15,00,000 x 5%]				75,000
	(Being the Dividend declared)				
2.	Pref Dividend Payable A/c	Dr.		20,000	
	Equity Dividend Payable A/c	Dr.		75,000	
	To Bank A/c				95,000
	(Being the Dividend paid)				

3.	Business Purchase A/c	Dr.	5,00,057	
	To Liquidators of *SHEENA Ltd.*			5,00,057
	(Being the purchase of the business)			
4.	Goodwill	Dr.	1,31,307	
	Property, Plant & Equipment [₹ 3,75,000 + ₹ 1,50,000]	Dr.	5,25,000	
	Inventories	Dr.	1,23,750	
	Trade Receivables	Dr.	1,62,500	
	Bank	Dr.	1,83,750	
	To Provision for Doubtful Debts [10% of ₹ 1,62,500]			16,250
	To Trade Payables			3,32,500
	To 10% Debentures [₹ 1,25,000 + 20%]			1,50,000
	To Unrecorded Loan			1,27,500
	To Business Purchase A/c			5,00,057
	(Being the Assets and Liabilities taken over)			
5.	Liquidators of *SHEENA Ltd.*	Dr.	5,00,057	
	To Equity Share Capital A/c [16666 × ₹ 8]			1,33,328
	To 9% Pref. Share Capital A/c [1200 × ₹ 100]			1,20,000
	To Securities Premium A/c [(16666 × ₹ 7) + (1200 × ₹ 25)]			1,46,662
	To Bank A/c			100,067
	(Being the purchase consideration discharged)			
6.	Goodwill A/c	Dr.	25,000	
	To Bank A/c			25,000
	(Being the payment of Liquidation Expenses of Vendor co.)			
7.	10% Debentures of *SHEENA Ltd.*	Dr.	1,50,000	
	Discount on Issue of 14% Debentures A/c	Dr.	6,250	
	To 14% Debentures A/c			1,56,200
	To Bank A/c			50
	(Being 10% Debentures of Vendor co. redeemed by issue of 1562, 14% Debentures of ₹ 100 each at a discount of 4% and balance in cash)			
8.	Unrecorded Loan A/c	Dr.	1,27,500	
	To Bank A/c			1,27,500
	(Being the liabilities of Vendor co. discharged)			
9.	Amalgamation Adjustment A/c	Dr.	12,500	
	To Statutory Reserves			12,500
	(Being the identity of Statutory Reserves retained)			

VERY SHORT ANSWER TYPE QUESTIONS

1. **Briefly explain the following:**
   (a) Purchase Consideration as per AS 13.
   (b) Amalgamation is in the nature of Purchase
   (c) Amalgamation is in the nature of Merger
2. Enumerate the Two main methods of accounting for amalgamations.
3. As per Accounting Standard-14, what are the conditions which must be satisfied for an amalgamation in the nature of merger?
4. A Ltd. is amalgamating with B Ltd. They are undecided on the method of accounting to be followed. You are required to advice the management of B Ltd. on the method of accounting that can be adopted under AS-14.
5. How shall Investment Allowance Reserve A/c of a transferor company be recorded in the books of transferee company if the Amalgamation is in the nature of (a) Purchase (b) Merger?
6. How shall the Amalgamation Expenses incurred by transferee company be recorded in case of amalgamation is the nature of (a) Purchase (b) Merger?
7. How shall the profit included in unsold stock (sold by transferor Co.) of Transferee Co. be dealt with in case Amalgamation is in the nature of (a) Purchase (b) Merger?
8. State whether the Debentures issued by the Purchasing Company to Pref. Share Holders form part of purchase consideration.
9. What disclosures should be made in the first financial statements following the amalgamation?
10. Which of the following is case of Amalgamation in the nature of merger as per AS 14 assuming other conditions are satisfied?
    (i) The transferee company issued Equity Shares to the Equity shareholders and paid Cash to the Preference shareholders of the transferor company.
    (ii) The transferee company issued Equity Shares to the Equity shareholders and Preference Shares to the Preference shareholders of the transferor company.
    (iii) The transferee company issued Equity Shares to the Equity shareholders and Debentures to the Preference shareholders of the transferor company.
    (iv) All of these

SHORT ANSWER TYPE PRACTICAL QUESTIONS

Calculation of Purchase Consideration as per AS-14

1. Given below is the Balance Sheet of Y Ltd. as at 31st March 2023 at which date it was taken over by X Ltd.:

Equity Share Capital (of ₹10 each)	₹ 10,00,000
13% Pref. Shares (of ₹100 each)	₹ 5,00,000
Reserves	₹ 4,00,000
12% Debentures	₹ 1,10,000
Trade Payables for Goods	₹ 55,000
Non-Current Assets	₹ 16,00,000
Current Assets	₹ 4,65,000

The market value of an equity share of X Ltd. at present is ₹ 100. Show the calculation and discharge of Purchase Consideration if X Ltd. agrees:

(a) to issue such an amount of fully paid 13% Pref. Shares at 125% as is sufficient to discharge Pref. Shareholders in Y Ltd. at 110%.

(b) to issue 6 equity shares of ₹ 10 each at a premium of 10% and ₹ 3 per share cash against every 5 equity shares in Y Ltd.

(c) to issue such an amount of fully paid 15% Debentures at 96 % as is sufficient to discharge 12% Debentures in Y Ltd. at a premium of 8%.

(c) to reimburse the expenses of liquidation to the extent of ₹ 10,000. Actual Expenses amounted to ₹ 15,000. **[Ans. PC** ₹19,30,000]

2. Given below is the Balance Sheet of Y Ltd. as at 31st March 2023 at which date it was taken over by X Ltd.:

Equity Share Capital (of ₹10 each)	₹10,00,000
Reserves	₹ 4,00,000
12% Debentures	₹ 1,10,000
Trade Payables for Goods	₹ 55,000
Non-Current Assets	₹11,00,000
Current Assets (including Cash at Bank ₹ 1,65,000)	₹ 4,65,000

The market value of an equity share of X Ltd. at present is ₹ 100. Show the calculation and discharge of Purchase Consideration if X Ltd. agrees to take over the business of Y Ltd. and to discharge the purchase consideration to the extent of one quarter in cash and the balance in the form of equity shares of ₹ 10 each at ₹ 55 each. While arriving at the agreed consideration, the directors of X Ltd. valued Non-Current Assets at 40% more than the book value and Current Assets (except Cash at Bank) at 12% *less* than the book value. Liquidation Expenses are to be reimbursed by X Ltd. to the extent of ₹ 15,000. Actual Liquidation expenses are ₹ 25,000.

[**Ans.** PC ₹ 17,94,029 (including ₹ 64 Cash for fractional share)]

3. Given below are the extracts of Balance Sheet of 'A' Ltd. as at 31.3.2023:

Particulars	₹
14,000 Equity shares of ₹ 100 each fully paid	14,00,000
General reserve	10,000
10% Debentures	2,00,000
Trade Payables	2,00,000
Bank overdraft	50,000
Bills payable	40,000
Sundry assets	18,00,000
Discount on issue of debentures	10,000
Preliminary expenses	30,000
P & L A/c	60,000

'R' Ltd agreed to take over the business of 'A' Ltd. Calculate purchase consideration under Net Assets method on the basis of the following:

The market value of 75% of the sundry assets is estimated to be 12% more than the book value and that of the remaining 25% at 8% *less* than the book value. The liabilities are taken over at book values. There is an unrecorded liability of ₹ 25,000. [**Ans.** PC ₹ 14,11,000]

4. The abstract of the Balance Sheet of the AXE Ltd. as at 31st March 2023, are as follows:

Particulars	₹
Equity Share Capital (₹ 100 each)	15,00,000
12% Preference Share Capital (₹ 100 each)	8,00,000
13% Debentures	3,00,000

On 31st March, 2023, BXE Ltd. agreed to take over AXE Ltd on the following terms:

(1) For each preference share in AXE Ltd.. ₹ 10 in cash and one 9% preference share of ₹ 100 in BXE Ltd.

(2) For each equity share AXE Ltd. ₹ 20 in cash and one equity share in BXE Ltd. of ₹ 100 each. It was decided that the share in BXE Ltd. will be issued at market price ₹ 140 per share.

(3) Liquidation expenses of AXE Ltd. are to be reimbursed by BXE Ltd. to the extent of ₹ 10,000. Actual expenses amounted to ₹ 12,500.

You are required to compute the amount of purchase consideration. [**Ans.** PC ₹ 32,80,000]

5. A Ltd. decides to absorb B Ltd. The draft Balance Sheet of B Limited is as follows:

Liabilities	₹
Share Capital:	
5,000 9% Preference shares of ₹ 100 each (Fully paid up)	5,00,000
12,500 Equity Shares of ₹ 100 each (Fully paid up)	12,50,000
Reserves	7,50,000
6% Debentures	5,00,000
Trade Payables	2,50,000
Total	32,50,000
Assets	
Sundry Assets	32,50,000
Total	32,50,000

A Ltd. has agreed:

(i) To pay ₹ 20 per share in cash to equity shareholders of B Ltd. and will issue six equity shares of ₹ 100 each at ₹ 125 in lieu of every five equity shares held in B Ltd.

(ii) To issue 9% Preference shares of ₹ 100 each, in the ratio of 3 shares of A Ltd. for 4 Preference shares in B Ltd.

(iii) To issue 8% debentures at ₹ 96 in lieu of 6% debentures in B Ltd. which are to be redeemed at a premium of 20%.

You are required to calculate the purchase consideration. [**Ans.** ₹ 25,00,000]

6. On 1st April, 2023, Tina Ltd. take over the business of Rina Ltd. and discharged purchase consideration as follows:

(i) Issued 50,000 fully paid Equity shares of ₹ 10 each at a premium of ₹ 5 per share to the equity shareholders of Rina Ltd.

(ii) Cash payment of ₹ 50,000 was made to equity shareholders of Rina Ltd.

(iii) Issued 2,000 fully paid 12% Preference shares of ₹ 100 each at par to discharge the preference shareholders of Rina Ltd.

(iv) Debentures of Rina Ltd. (₹ 1,20,000) will be converted into equal number and amount of 10% debentures of Tina Ltd.

Calculate the amount of Purchase consideration as per AS-14 and pass Journal Entry relating to discharge of purchase consideration in the books of Tina Ltd.

[Ans. ₹ 10,00,000]

7. Moon Limited is absorbed by Sun Limited; the consideration, being the takeover of liabilities, the payment of cost of absorption not exceeding ₹ 10,000 (actual cost ₹ 9000); the payment of 9% Debentures of ₹ 50,000 at a premium of 20% through 8% debentures issued at a premium of 25% of face value; the payment of ₹ 18 per share in cash; allotment of two 11% preference shares of ₹ 10/- each and one equity share of ₹ 10/- each at a premium of 30% fully paid for every three shares in Moon Limited respectively. The number of shares of the vendor company is 1,50,000 of ₹ 10/- each fully paid. Calculate purchase consideration as per AS-14. **[Ans.** ₹ 43,50,000]

Passing of Journal Entry

8. Y Ltd was taken over by X Ltd. Liquidation Expenses of Y Ltd are to be reimbursed by X Ltd. to the extent of ₹ 10,000. Actual Liquidation expenses are ₹ 15,000. Journalise in the books of both the companies.

[Ans. Debit Goodwill A/c(in case of Purchase)/ Profit & Loss A/c(in case of Merger) in the books of purchasing company.]

9. V Ltd has Equity Share Capital of ₹ 2,00,000 and Cash at Bank of ₹ 37,000 as at 31.3.2023. The business of V Ltd. is taken over by P Ltd. as on that date. Prior to absorption, V Ltd decide to declare and pay dividend @ 5%.Expenses of liquidation of V Ltd. are to be reimbursed by P Ltd. to the extent of ₹ 10,000. Actual Expenses amounted to ₹ 12,000. Calculate the amount of Cash at Bank to be transferred to Realisation Account of V Ltd.

[Ans. ₹ 25,000]

10. V Ltd has 9% Pref. Share Capital (of ₹100 each) ₹ 2,00,000 as at 31.3.2023. The business of V Ltd. is taken over by P Ltd. as on that date. P Ltd. agrees to issue of such an amount of fully paid 10% Pref. Shares of ₹100 each in P Ltd. at 125% as is sufficient to discharge 9% Pref. Shares in V Ltd. at a premium of 20%. Journalise in the books of both the companies.

[Ans. Realisation A/c Dr ₹ 40,000, No. of Pref. Shares 1920]

11. V Ltd has 9% Debentures (of ₹100 each) ₹ 2,00,000 as at 31.3.2023. The business of V Ltd. is taken over by P Ltd. as on that date. P Ltd. agrees to issue of such an amount of fully paid 10% Debentures of ₹100 each in P Ltd. at 96% as is sufficient to discharge 9% Debentures in V Ltd. at a premium of 20%. Journalise in the books of both the companies.

[Ans. No. of Debentures 2500]

12. V Ltd has 9% Debentures (of ₹100 each) ₹ 2,00,000 as at 31.3.2023. The business of V Ltd. is taken over by P Ltd. as on that date. P Ltd. agrees to issue of such an amount of fully paid 10% Debentures of ₹100 each in P Ltd. at 96% as is sufficient to discharge 9% Debentures in V Ltd. at a premium of 20%. Investments of P Ltd. include ₹ 9,000 representing the cost of 5% Debentures of V Ltd. Journalise in the books of both the companies.

[Ans. No. of Debentures 2375]

13. V Ltd has Inventories of ₹ 55,000 as at 31.3.2023. The business of V Ltd. is taken over by P Ltd. as on that date. V Ltd purchased goods for ₹ 60,000 from P Ltd. which made a profit of 20% on cost. Four fifth of such goods were sold till 31.3.2023. Journalise in the books of purchasing company. **[Ans.** Debit Goodwill ₹ 2,000]

14. V Ltd has Inventories of ₹ 55,000 as at 31.3.2023. The business of V Ltd. is taken over by P Ltd. as on that date. Inventories are taken over at book value *less* 10%.V Ltd purchased goods for ₹ 60,000 from P Ltd. which made a profit of 20% on cost. Four fifth of such goods were sold till 31.3.2023. Journalise in the books of purchasing company.

[**Ans.** Debit Goodwill ₹ 800]

15. V Ltd has Trade Receivables of ₹ 2,00,000 and Trade Payables of ₹ 1,40,000 as at 31.3.2023. V Ltd owed P Ltd. ₹ 60,000 as at 31.3.2023. The business of V Ltd. is taken over by P Ltd. as on that date. Journalise in the books of purchasing company.

[**Ans.** Cancellation of inter Co. Owings ₹ 60,000]

16. V Ltd has Trade Receivables of ₹ 2,00,000 and Trade Payables of ₹ 1,40,000 as at 31.3.2023. The business of V Ltd. is taken over by P Ltd. as on that date. V Ltd owed P Ltd. ₹ 60,000 as at 31.3.2023. Trade Receivables include ₹ 20,000 still due from P Ltd. Trade Receivables are taken over at book value *less* 10%.Trade Payables are to be taken over subject to a discount of 5% Journalise in the books of purchasing company.

[**Ans.** Cancellation of inter Co. Owings ₹ 20,000]

17. V Ltd has Investment Allowance Reserves of ₹ 2,00,000 and Export Profit Reserve of ₹ 1,40,000 as at 31.3.2023. These are to be maintained for 2 more years. The business of V Ltd. is taken over by P Ltd. as on that date. Journalise in the books of purchasing company assuming the Amalgamation in the nature of Purchase. [**Ans.** Dr. Amalgamation Adjustment A/c ₹ 3,40,000]

18. V Ltd has Equity Share Capital of ₹ 95,00,000, Tangible Fixed Assets of ₹ 65,00,000 and Current Assets of ₹ 85,00,000, Investment Allowance Reserves of ₹ 2,00,000, Export Profit Reserve of ₹ 3,00,000 and General Reserve of ₹ 28,00,000, Current Liabilities of ₹ 19,00,000, Non-Current Liabilities of ₹ 3,00,000 as at 31.3.2023. Statutory Reserves are to be maintained for 2 more years. The business of V Ltd. is taken over by P Ltd. by issue of 1,00,000 equity shares of ₹ 100 each at 20% premium. Journalise in the books of purchasing company assuming the Amalgamation in the nature of merger.

[**Ans.** Cr. General Reserve ₹ 3,00,000]

19. X Co. Ltd. having share capital of ₹50 lakhs divided into equity shares of ₹10 each was taken over by Y Co. Ltd. X Co. Ltd. has General Reserve of ₹ 10,00,000 and Profit and Loss account Cr. ₹ 5,00,000. Y Co. Ltd. issued 11 equity shares of ₹ 10 each for every 10 shares of X Co. Ltd.

How the Journal entry would be passed in the books of Y Co. Ltd. for the shares issued under the 'Pooling of Interest Method' of amalgamation.

[**Ans.** PC ₹ 55,00,000, Cr. General Reserve ₹ 5,00,000]

LONG ANSWER TYPE PRACTICAL QUESTIONS

When an existing company takes over the business of another existing company

1. Given below are the extracts of Balance Sheet of Hari Ltd. & Vayu Ltd. as at 31st March, 2023:

Particulars	*Hari Ltd. (₹)*	*Vayu Ltd. (₹)*
Equity Share Capital of ₹ 10 each	10,00,000	3,00,000
9% Preference Shares of ₹ 100 each	1,00,000	—
10% Preference Shares of ₹ 100 each	—	1,00,000
General Reserve	70,000	70,000
Retirement Gratuity Fund	50,000	20,000
Trade Payables	1,30,000	80,000
Goodwill	50,000	25,000

Tangible Fixed Assets	8,00,000	2,50,000
Inventories	2,50,000	1,75,000
Trade Receivables	2,00,000	1,00,000
Cash at Bank	50,000	20,000

Hari Ltd. absorbs Vayu Ltd. on the following terms:

(a) 10% Preference Shareholders are to be paid at 10% premium by issue of 9% Preference Shares of Hari Ltd.

(b) Goodwill of Vayu Ltd. is valued at ₹ 50,000, Tangible Fixed Assets are valued at ₹ 3,10,000.

(c) Inventories to be taken over at 10% *less* value and Provision for Doubtful Debts to be created @ 7.5%.

(d) Equity shareholders of Vayu Ltd. will be issued Equity Shares @ 5% premium.

Required: Prepare necessary Ledger Accounts to close the books of Vayu Ltd. and show the acquisition entries in the books of Hari Ltd. Also draft the Balance Sheet after absorption as at 31.03.2023.

[**Ans.** PC: ₹ 5,30,000, Profit on Realisation ₹ 50,000, Total of B/S ₹ 19,80,000]

2. Given below are the extracts of Balance Sheet of Exe Limited as at 31st March, 2023:

Particulars	₹
1,20,000 Eq. Shares of ₹10 each	12,00,000
Profit prior to Incorporation	42,000
Contingency Reserve	2,70,000
Profit and Loss A/c	2,52,000
Trade Payables	2,66,000
Provision for Income Tax	2,20,000
Tangible Fixed Assets	9,64,000
Inventories	7,75,000
Trade Receivables (including B/R ₹ 30,000)	1,82,000
Cash at Bank	3,29,000

Wye Limited took over the following assets at values shown as under:

Fixed assets ₹ 12,80,000, Inventories ₹ 7,70,000 and Bills Receivable ₹ 30,000.

Purchase consideration was settled by Wye Limited as under:

₹ 5,10,000 of the consideration was satisfied by the allotment of fully paid 10% Preference shares of ₹ 100 each. The balance was settled by issuing equity shares of ₹ 10 each at ₹ 8 per share paid up.

Trade Receivables realised ₹ 1,50,000. Income tax authorities fixed the taxation liability at ₹ 2,22,000. Trade Payables were finally settled with the cash remaining after meeting liquidation expenses amounting to ₹ 8,000.

You are required to:

(i) Calculate the number of equity shares and preference shares to be allotted by Wye Limited in discharge of purchase consideration.

(ii) Prepare the Realisation account, Cash/Bank account, Equity Shareholders account and Wye Limited account in the books of Exe Limited.

(iii) Pass journal entries in the books of Wye Limited.

[Ans. PC: ₹ 20,80,000, Profit on Realisation ₹ 3,16,000]

3. Given below are the extracts of Balance Sheet of Vasudha Ltd. & Vaishali Ltd. as at 31.03.2023:

Particulars	*Vasudha Ltd.*	*Vaishali Ltd.*
Equity Shares Capital of ₹ 10 each	5,40,000	4,03,300
General Reserves	1,01,000	65,000
Profit & Loss A/c	51,000	33,490
Trade Payables	44,400	58,200
Tangible Fixed Assets	2,10,000	1,60,000
Goodwill	50,000	35,000
Inventories	91,500	82,500
Trade Receivables	2,86,900	1,72,900
Cash at Bank	98,000	1,09,590

Goodwill of the Companies Vasudha Ltd. and Vaishali Ltd. is to be valued at ₹ 75,000 and ₹ 50,000 respectively. Tangible Fixed Assets of Vasudha Ltd are worth ₹ 1,95,000 and Vaishali Ltd. ₹ 1,75,000. Inventories of Vaishali Ltd. Has been shown at 10% above of its cost.

It is decided that Vasudha Ltd will absorb Vaishali Ltd, by taking over its entire business by issue of shares at the intrinsic Value.

Required: To draft the balance sheet of the Vasudha Ltd. after putting through the scheme.

[Ans. PC: ₹ 5,24,290, Total of B/S ₹ 13,18,890]

4. Given below are the extracts of Balance Sheet of Srishti Ltd. as on 31st March, 2022:

Particulars	*(₹)*
Equity Shares of ₹ 10 fully paid	30,00,000
Export Profit Reserves	8,50,000
General Reserves	50,000
Profit and loss Account	5,00,000
9% Debentures	5,00,000
Trade Payables	1,00,000
Goodwill	5,00,000
Tangible Fixed Assets	30,00,000
Inventories	10,40,000
Trade Receivables	1,80,000
Cash & bank	2,80,000

ANU Ltd. agreed to absorb the business of SRISTI Ltd. with effect from 1st April 2022.

(a) The purchase consideration settled by ANU Ltd. as agreed:

(i) 4,50,000 equity Shares of ₹ 10 each issued by ANU Ltd. by valuing its share @ ₹ 15 per share.

(ii) Cash payment equivalent to ₹ 2.50 for every share in SRISHTI Ltd.

(b) The issue of such an amount of fully paid 8% Debentures in ANU Ltd. at 96% as is sufficient to discharge 9% Debentures in SRISHTI Ltd. at a premium of 20%.

(c) ANU Ltd. will take over the Tangible Fixed Assets at 100% more than the book value, Inventories at ₹ 7,10,000 and Trade Receivables at their face value subject to a provision of 5% for doubtful Debts.

(d) The actual cost of liquidation of SRISHTI Ltd. was ₹ 75,000. Liquidation cost of SRISHTI Ltd. is to be reimbursed by ANU Ltd. to the extent of ₹ 50,000.

(e) Statutory Reserves are to be maintained for 1 more year.

You are required to:

(i) Close the books of SRISHTI Ltd. by preparing Realisation Account, ANU Ltd. Account, Shareholders Account and Debenture Account, and

(ii) Pass Journal Entries in the books of ANU Ltd. regarding acquisition of business.

[**Ans.** PC: ₹ 75,00,000, Profit on Realisation ₹ 31,00,000, Goodwill ₹ 10,64,000]

5. Given below are the extracts of Balance Sheet of A Ltd. as at 31st March, 2023:

Particulars	₹
8,000 Equity Shares of ₹ 100 each	8,00,000
General Reserve	80,000
10% Debentures	4,00,000
Loan from A	1,60,000
Trade Payables	3,20,000
Tangible Fixed Assets	9,80,000
Goodwill	1,30,000
Inventories	2,20,000
Trade Receivables	2,60,000
Bank	1,36,000
Misc. Expenses	34,000

B. Ltd. agreed to absorb A Ltd. on the following terms and conditions:

(a) B Ltd. would take over all Assets, except bank balance at their book values *less* 10% Goodwill is to be valued at 4 year's purchase of super profits, assuming that the normal rate of return be 8% on the combined amount of share capital and general reserve.

(b) B Ltd. is to take over Trade Payables at book value.

(c) The purchase consideration is to be paid in cash to the extent of ₹ 6,00,000 and the balance in fully paid equity shares of ₹ 100 each at ₹ 125 per share.

The average profit is ₹ 1,24,400. The liquidation expenses amounted to ₹ 16,000. B Ltd. sold prior to 31st March, 2023 goods costing ₹ 1,20,000 to A Ltd. for 1,60,000. ₹ 1,00.000 worth of goods are still in Inventories of A Ltd. on 31st March, 2023. Trade Payables of A Ltd. include ₹ 40,000 still due to B Ltd.

Required: Show the necessary Ledger Accounts to close the books of A Ltd. and prepare the Balance Sheet of B Ltd. as at 1st April, 2023 after the takeover.

[**Ans.** PC: ₹ 12,10,000, Loss on Realisation ₹ 76,000,Total of B/S ₹ 14,90,000]

6. The following are the summarized Balance Sheet of VT Ltd. and MG Ltd. as on 31st March, 2023:

Particulars	*VT Ltd. (₹)*	*MG Ltd. (₹)*
Equity and Liabilities		
Equity Shares of ₹ 10 each	12,00,000	6,00,000
10% Pref. Shares of ₹ 100 each	4,00,000	2,00,000
Reserve and Surplus	6,00,000	4,00,000
12% Debentures	4,00,000	3,00,000
Trade Payables	5,00,000	3,00,000
Total	31,00,000	18,00,000
Assets		
Fixed Assets	14,00,000	5,00,000
Investment	1,60,000	1,60,000
Inventory	4,80,000	6,40,000
Trade Receivables	8,40,000	4,20,000
Cash at Bank	2,20,000	80,000
Total	31,00,000	18,00,000

Details of Trade receivables and trade payables are as under:

	VT Ltd. (₹)	*MG Ltd. (₹)*
Trade Receivable		
Debtors	7,20,000	3,80,000
Bills Receivable	1,20,000	40,000
	8,40,000	4,20,000
Trade Payables		
Sundry Creditors	4,40,000	2,50,000
Bills Payable	60,000	50,000
	5,00,000	3,00,000

Fixed Assets of both the companies are to be revalued at 15% above book value.

Inventory in Trade and Debtors are taken over at 5% lesser than their book value.

Both the companies are to pay 10% equity dividend, Preference dividend having been already paid. After the above transactions are given effect to, VT Ltd. will absorb MG Ltd. on the following terms:

(i) VT Ltd. will issue 16 Equity Shares of ₹ 10 each at par against 12 Shares of MG Ltd.

(ii) 10% Preference Shareholders of MG Ltd. will be paid at 10% discount by issue of 10% Preference Shares of ₹ 100 each, at par, in VT Ltd.

(iii) 12% Debenture holders of MG Ltd. are to be paid at 8% premium, by 12% Debentures in VT Ltd., issued at a discount of 10%.

(iv) ₹ 60,000 is to be paid by VT Ltd. to MG Ltd. for Liquidation expenses.

(v) Sundry Debtors of MG Ltd. includes ₹ 20,000 due from VT Ltd.

You are required to prepare :

(1) Journal entries in the books of VT Ltd.

(2) Statement of consideration payable by VT Ltd.

[**Ans.** PC: ₹ 9,80,000]

7. The Summarized Balance Sheets of Sun Ltd. and Light Ltd. as on 31st March, 2023 are given below.

	Sun Ltd. ***(₹)***	***Light Ltd.*** ***(₹)***
I. Liabilities		
Equity Share Capital	1,40,00,000	84,00,000
(Divided into Shares of ₹ 5 each fully paid up)		
General Reserve	28,00,000	16,04,000
Trade Payables	42,00,000	25,96,000
Total	2,10,00,000	1,26,00,000
II. Asset		
Sundry Assets	2,10,00,000	1,26,00,000
Total	2,10,00,000	1,26,00,000

The following further information is also given:

(i) Sun Ltd. absorbed Light Ltd. on the basis of intrinsic value of shares of Sun Ltd.

(ii) The Purchase Consideration is discharged in fully paid up shares.

(iii) Sun Ltd. owed a sum of ₹ 7,00,000 to Light Ltd.

(iv) Inventory of Sun Ltd. included ₹ 8,40,000 supplied by Light Ltd. at cost plus 25%.

(v) Sundry Assets of Light Ltd. included Land of ₹ 28,00,000 the market value of which is ₹ 35,00,000.

You are required to:

(a) Give journal entries in the books of both Sun Ltd. and Light Ltd., if journal entries are passed at intrinsic value of shares of Sun Ltd.

(b) Calculate the intrinsic value of shares of Sun Ltd., and

(c) Prepare Balance Sheet of Sun Ltd. after absorption.

[Ans. PC: ₹ 107,04,000, Total of B/S ₹ 334,32,000]

8. Given below are the extracts of Balance Sheets of P Ltd. and V Ltd. as at 31st March 2023:

Particulars	***P Ltd.*** ***(₹ in lakhs)***	***V Ltd.*** ***(₹ in lakhs)***
Equity Share Capital (Fully paid shares of ₹ 10 each)	15,000	6,000
Securities Premium	3,000	—
Foreign Projects Reserve	—	310
General Reserve	9,500	3,150
Profit and Loss Account	2,870	825
12% Debentures	—	1,000
Trade Payables	3,030	1,165
Tangible Fixed Assets	22,304	6,700
Inventories	7,862	4,041
Trade Receivables	2,120	1,100
Cash at Bank	1,114	609
Cost of Issue of Debentures	—	50

All the bills receivable held by V Ltd. were P Ltd.'s acceptances.

On 1st April, 2023 P Ltd. took over V Ltd. in an amalgamation in the nature of merger. It was agreed that in discharge of consideration for the business P Ltd. would allot three fully paid equity shares of ₹ 10 each at par for every two shares held in V Ltd. It was also agreed that 12% debentures in V Ltd. would be converted into 13% debentures in P Ltd. of the same amount and denomination. Expenses of amalgamation amounting to ₹ 1 lakh were borne by P Ltd.

You are required to: (i) Pass journal entries in the books of P Ltd. and (ii) Prepare P Ltd.'s Balance Sheet immediately after the merger.

[**Ans.** PC: ₹ 9000 lacs, Total of B/S ₹ 45769 lacs]

9. Given below are the extracts of Balance Sheet of Gee Ltd. & Pee Ltd. as at 31st March, 2023:

Particulars	*Gee Ltd. (₹)*	*Pee Ltd. (₹)*
Equity Share Capital (₹ 10 per share)	25,00,000	15,00,000
14% Preference Share Capital (₹100 each)	11,00,000	8,50,000
General Reserve	2,50,000	2,50,000
Export Profit Reserve	1,50,000	1,00,000
Investment Allowance Reserve		50,000
Profit and Loss A/c	3,75,000	1,25,000
15% Debentures (₹ 100 each)	2,50,000	1,75,000
Trade Payables	3,25,000	2,50,000
Tangible Fixed Assets	31,62,500	18,00,000
Investments	3,50,000	2,50,000
Inventories	6,25,000	4,75,000
Trade Receivables	4,50,000	5,15,000
Cash at bank	3,62,500	2,60,000

All the bills receivables of Pee Ltd. were having Gee Ltd.'s acceptances.

Gee Ltd. takes over Pee Ltd. on 1st April, 2023. The purchase consideration is discharged as follows:

(i) Issued 1,65,000 Equity Shares of ₹10 each at par to the equity shareholders of Pee Ltd.

(ii) Issued 15% Preference Shares of ₹ 100 each to discharge the preference shareholders of Pee Ltd. at 10% premium.

(iii) The debentures of Pee Ltd. will be converted into equivalent number of debentures of Gee Ltd.

(iv) The statutory reserves of Pee Ltd. are to be maintained for two more years,

(v) Expenses of amalgamation amounting to ₹ 10,000 will be borne by Gee Ltd.

Required: Show the opening Journal entries and the opening balance sheet of Gee Ltd. as at 1st April, 2023 after amalgamation, on the assumption that the amalgamation is in the nature of the merger. [**Ans.** PC: ₹ 25,85,000, Total of B/S ₹ 81,85,000]

10. Given below are the extracts of Balance Sheet of V Ltd. as on 31st March, 2023:

Particulars	*Note No*	*₹ (lacs)*
I. Equity and Liabilities		
(1) Shareholders' Funds		
(a) Share Capital	1	1,150
(b) Reserves and Surplus (Profit and Loss A/c)		(87)
(2) Non-Current Liabilities		
(a) Long-term Liabilities	2	630
(3) Current Liabilities [Trade Payables]		170
Total		1,863
II. Assets		
(1) Non-Current Assets		
(a) Fixed Assets		
Tangible Assets		1,152
(2) Current Assets		
(a) Inventories		380
(b) Trade Receivables		256
(c) Cash and Cash Equivalents		75
Total		1,863

Notes To Accounts:

Particulars	*₹ (lacs)*
1. Share Capital	
80 lakhs Equity Shares of ₹ 10 each	800
35 lakhs 12% Pref. Shares of ₹ 10 each	350
Total	1,150
2. Long-term Borrowings	
10% Debentures	600
Outstanding Debenture Interest	30
Total	630

On 1st April, 2023, P Ltd took over the entire business of V Ltd. on the following terms:

(a) V. Ltd.'s equity shareholders would receive 4 fully paid equity shares of P Ltd. of ₹ 10 each issued at a premium of ₹ 2.50 each for every five shares held by them in V Ltd.

(b) Preference shareholders of V Ltd. would get 35 lakh 13% Cumulative Preference Shares of ₹ 10 each fully paid up in P Ltd., in lieu of their present holding.

(c) All the debentures of V Ltd. would be converted into equal number of 10.5% Secured Cumulative Debentures of ₹ 100 each, fully paid up after the take over by P Ltd., which would also pay outstanding debenture interest in cash.

(d) Expenses of Amalgamation would be borne by P Ltd. Expenses came to be ₹ 2 lakhs. P Ltd. discovered that its Trade Payables included ₹ 7 lakhs due to V Ltd. for goods purchased.

(e) Also P Ltd.'s Inventories included goods of the invoice price of ₹ 5 lakhs earlier purchased from V Ltd., which had charged profit @ 20% of the invoice price.

You are required to: (i) Prepare Realisation A/c in the books of V Ltd. (ii) Pass journal entries in the books of P Ltd. assuming it to be an amalgamation in the nature of merger.

[**Ans.** PC: ₹ 1,150 lacs, Profit on Realisation ₹ 87 lacs]

11. A Limited and B Limited are carrying on business of same nature. On 31st March, 2023 their summarized Balance Sheet was as follows:

	A Ltd.(₹)	*B Ltd. (₹)*
Share Capital		
- Equity Shares 10 each (Fully Paid)	12,00,000	7,20,000
- 10% Preference Shares of ₹ 100 each	6,00,000	-
- 8% Preference Shares of ₹ 100 each	-	5,00,000
General Reserve	3,00,000	2,50,000
Investment Allowance Reserve	-	60,000
Security Premium	2,40,000	-
Export Profit Reserve	1,80,000	1,20,000
Profit & Loss Account	2,16,000	1,92,000
9% Debentures (₹ 10 each)	3,00,000	2,00,000
Secured Loan	-	3,60,000
Sundry Creditors	3,12,000	2,04,000
Bills Payable	75,000	1,00,000
Other Current Liabilities	50,000	75,000
	34,73,000	27,81,000
Land and Building	10,80,000	8,40,000
Plant and Machinery	6,00,000	5,60,000
Office Equipment	3,45,000	2,10,000
Investments	96,000	3,00,000
Stock in Trade	6,30,000	4,20,000
Sundry Debtors	4,90,000	3,20,000
Bills Receivables	60,000	70,000
Cash at Bank	1,72,000	61,000
	34,73,000	27,81,000

A Limited take over B Limited on the above date, both companies agreeing on a scheme of Amalgamation on the following terms:

(a) A Limited will issue 80,000 Equity Shares of ₹ 10 each at par to the Equity Shareholders of B Limited.

(b) A Limited will issue 10% Preference Shares of ₹ 100 each to discharge the Preference Shareholders of B Limited at 15% premium in such a way that the existing dividend quantum of the preference shareholders of B Limited will not get affected.

(c) The Debentures of B Limited will be converted into equivalent number of Debentures of A Limited.

(d) All the Bills Receivable of A Limited were accepted by B Limited.

(e) A contingent liability of B Limited amounting to ₹ 72,000 to be treated as actual liability in trade payables.

(f) Expenses of Amalgamation amounted to ₹ 12,000 were borne by A Limited.

You are required to pass opening Journal Entries in A Limited and prepare the opening Balance Sheet of A Limited as on 1st April, 2023 after amalgamation, assuming that the amalgamation is in the nature of Merger.

[**Ans** ₹ 5,00,000 pref. shares are discharged at ₹ 5,75,000 (5,00,000*115%) by issue of 4,000 preference shares of ₹ 100 each at premium of ₹ 43.75 each. PC: ₹ 13,75,000,Debit General Reserve with ₹ 1,55,000, Total of B/S ₹ 61,82,000]

When a new company is formed to take over the businesses of existing companies

12. P Ltd. and Q Ltd. were carrying on the business of manufacturing of auto components. both the companies decided to amalgamate and a new company PQ Ltd. is to be formed with an Authorized Capital of ₹ 10,00,000 divided into 1,00,000 equity shares of ₹ 10 each. The Balance Sheet of the companies as on 31.03.2022 were as under:

Particulars	*P (₹)*	*Q (₹)*
I. Equity and Liabilities		
1. Shareholder's Fund		
(a) Share Capital	1,40,000	2,50,000
(b) Reserves & Surplus (Profit & Loss A/c)	30,000	1,55,000
2. Non Current Liabilities (8 % Secured Debentures)	1,10,000	—
3. Current Liabilities (Trade Payables)	54,000	1,40,000
Total	3,34,000	5,45,000
II. Assets		
1. Non-current Assets		
(a) Tangible Fixed Assets	1,25,000	2,95,000
2. Current Assets		
(a) Inventories	1,35,000	50,000
(b) Trade Receivables	44,000	1,42,000
(c) Cash at bank	30,000	58,000
Total	3,34,000	5,45,000

The assets and liabilities of the existing companies are to be transferred at book value with the exception of some items detailed below:

(i) Goodwill of P Ltd. was worth ₹ 50,000 and of Q Ltd. was worth ₹ 1,50,000,.

(ii) Tangible Fixed Assets of Q Ltd. was valued at ₹ 3,05,000.

(iii) The Trade Receivables of P Ltd. are realized fully and bank balance of P Ltd. are to be retained by the liquidator and the Trade Payables are to be paid of the proceeds thereof.

(iv) The debentures of P Ltd. are to be discharged by issue of 8% debentures of PQ Ltd. at a premium of 10%.

You are required to:

(i) Compute the basis on which shares in PQ Ltd. will be issued at par to the shareholders of the existing companies.

(ii) Draw up a Balance Sheet of PQ Ltd. as at 1st April, 2022, the date of completion of amalgamation.

(iii) Write up Journal entries including bank entries for closing the books of P Ltd.

[**Ans.** PC: P ₹ 1,89,000, Q ₹ 5,65,000 ,Profit on Realisation ₹ 39,000,Total of B/S ₹10,15,000]

13. Given below are the extracts of Balance Sheets of M Ltd. and N Ltd. as at 31st March, 2023:

(₹ in lakhs)

Particulars	*M Ltd.*	*N Ltd.*
Equity Shares of ₹10 each	3,600	900
10% Preference Shares of ₹ 10 each	1,200	–
Capital Reserve	600	–
General Reserve	2,100	–
Profit and Loss Account	780	(39)
8% Redeemable Debentures of ₹ 1,000 each	–	300
Trade Payables	3,291	462
Tangible Fixed Assets	6,615	702
Inventories	2,370	444
Trade Receivables	1,044	237
Cash at Bank	1,542	240

A new Company MN Ltd. was incorporated with an authorised capital of ₹ 15,000 lakhs divided into shares of ₹ 10 each. For the purpose of amalgamation in the nature of merger, M Ltd. and N Ltd. were merged into MN Ltd. on the following terms:

(i) Purchase consideration for M Ltd.'s business is to be discharged by issue of 120 lakhs fully paid 11% preference shares and 720 lakhs fully paid equity shares of MN Ltd. to the preference and equity shareholders of M Ltd. in full satisfaction of their claims.

(ii) To discharge purchase consideration for N Ltd. 's business, MN Ltd. to allot 90 lakhs fully paid up equity shares to shareholders of N Ltd. in full satisfaction of their claims.

(iii) Expenses on the liquidation of M Ltd. and N Ltd. amounting to ₹ 6 lakhs are to be borne by MN Ltd.

(iv) 8% Redeemable Debentures of N Ltd. to be converted into 8.5% redeemable debentures of MN Ltd.

(v) Expenses on incorporation of MN Ltd. were ₹15 lakhs.

You are requested to:

(a) Pass necessary Journal Entries in the books of MN Ltd. to record above transactions, and

(b) Prepare Balance Sheet of MN Ltd. after merger.

[**Ans.** (i) PC: M ₹ 8,400 lacs, N ₹ 900 lacs, (ii) P & L A/c Dr ₹159 lacs, Total of B/S ₹ 13,173]

14. Sun Ltd. and Moon Ltd. were amalgamated on and from 1st April, 2023. A new company Star Ltd. was formed to take over the business of the existing companies. The Balance Sheets of Sun Ltd. and Moon Ltd. as at 31st March, 2023 are given below:

(₹ in lakhs)

Particulars	Sun Ltd.	Moon Ltd.
Equity Shares of ₹ 100 each	400	375
12% Preference Shares of ₹100 each	150	100
Revaluation Reserve	75	50
General Reserve	85	75
Investment Allowance Reserve	25	25
Profit and Loss Account	25	15
10% Debentures (₹100 each)	30	15
Trade Payables	210	95
Tangible Fixed Assets	450	325
Investments	75	25
Inventories	175	125
Trade Receivables	150	175
Cash and Bank balances	150	100

Additional Information:

(a) Star Ltd. will issue 5 equity shares for each equity share of Sun Ltd. and 4 equity shares for each equity share of Moon Ltd. The shares are to be issued @ ₹ 30 each, having a face value of ₹ 10 per share.

(b) Preference shareholders of the two companies are issued equivalent number of 15% preference shares of Star Ltd. at a price of ₹ 150 per share (face value ₹ 100).

(c) 10% Debentureholders of Sun Ltd. and Moon Ltd. are discharged by Star Ltd., issuing such number of its 15% Debentures of ₹100 each so as to maintain the same amount of interest.

(d) Investment allowance reserve is to be maintained for 4 more years.

(e) Liquidation expenses are: Sun Ltd. ₹2,00,000 Moon Ltd. ₹ 1,00,000. It was decided that these expenses would be borne by Star Ltd.

(f) All the assets and liabilities of Sun Ltd. and Moon Ltd. are taken over at book value.

(g) Authorised equity share capital of Star Ltd. is ₹ 5,00,00,000, divided into equity shares of ₹ 10 each. After issuing required number of shares to the Liquidators of Sun Ltd. and Moon Ltd., Star Ltd. issued balance shares to Public. The issue was fully subscribed.

Required: Prepare the Balance Sheet of Star Ltd. as at 1st April, 2023 after amalgamation has been carried out on the basis of Amalgamation in the nature of purchase.

[**Ans.** (i) PC: Star ₹ 825 lacs,, Sun ₹ 600 lacs, (ii) , Goodwill ₹ 13 lacs, Total of B/S ₹ 1910 lacs]

15. High Ltd. and Low Ltd. were amalgamated on and from, 1st April, 2023. A new company Little Ltd. was formed to take over the business of the existing Companies. The summarized Balance sheets of High Ltd. and Low Ltd. as on 31st March, 2023 are as under:

(₹ in Lakhs)

Liabilities	*High Ltd.*	*Low Ltd.*	*Assets*	*High Ltd.*	*Low Ltd.*
Share Capital:			Property, Plant and Equipment:		
Equity Shares of ₹ 100 each	1000	850	Land & Building	670	385
14% Pref Shares of ₹ 100 each	320	175	Plant & Machinery	475	355
Reserves & Surplus:			Investments	95	80

Revaluation Reserve	225	110	Current Assets:		
General Reserve	360	240	Stock	415	389
Investment Allowance Reserve	80	40	Sundry Debtors	322	213
P & L Account	85	82	Bills Receivables	35	-
Non-Current Liabilities:			Cash & Bank	303	166
Secured Loans:					
13% Debentures (₹ 100 each)	100	56			
Unsecured Loans (Public Deposits)	50	-			
Current Liabilities & Provisions:		-			
Sundry Creditors	65	35			
Bills Payable	30	-			
TOTAL	2315	1588	TOTAL	2315	1588

Other Information:

1. 13% Debenture holders of High Ltd. & Low Ltd. are discharged by Little Ltd. by issuing such number of its 15% Debentures of ₹ 100 each so as to maintain the same amount of interest.
2. Preference Shareholders of the two companies are issued equivalent number of 15% Preference shares of Little Ltd. at a price of ₹ 125 per share (Face Value ₹ 100)
3. Little Ltd. will issue 4 Equity Shares for each Equity Share of High Ltd. & 3 equity shares for each Equity Share of Low Ltd. The shares are to be issued at ₹ 35 each having a face value of ₹ 10 per share.
4. Investment Allowance Reserve is to be maintained for two more years.

Prepare the Balance sheet of Little Ltd. as on 1st April, 2023 after the amalgamation has been carried out in basis of in the nature of Purchase.

[**Ans.** (i) PC: High ₹ 1800 lacs, Low ₹ 1111.25 lacs, (ii) Capital Reserve ₹ 676.55 lacs, Total of B/S ₹ 3,903 lacs]

17 INTERNAL RECONSTRUCTION

LEARNING OBJECTIVES

After studying this chapter, you should be able to understand:

- ◇ Meaning of Internal Reconstruction
- ◇ Alteration of Share capital
- ◇ Reduction of Share Capital
- ◇ Variation of Shareholders' Rights
- ◇ Scheme of Compromise and Arrangement
- ◇ How to deal with Surrender of Shares?
- ◇ Accounting Entries

1.0 MEANING OF INTERNAL RECONSTRUCTION

In case of internal reconstruction, the company's existing financial structure is reorganised without dissolving the existing Company and without forming a new Company. Taking a wider meaning of the term 'Internal Reconstruction'. It includes:

1. Alteration of Share Capital u/s 61.
2. Reduction of Share Capital u/s 66.
3. Variation of Shareholders' Rights u/s 48.
4. Scheme of Compromise/Arrangement u/s 230 and 231.

2.0 DISTINCTION BETWEEN INTERNAL RECONSTRUCTION AND EXTERNAL RECONSTRUCTION

Basis of Distinction	*Internal Reconstruction*	*External Reconstruction*
1. Liquidation of Existing Company	Existing company does not go into liquidation.	Existing company goes into liquidation.
2. Formation of New Company	No new company is formed.	A new company is formed to take over the business of the existing company.
3. Reduction of Share Capital	It involves the reduction of share capital.	It may *or* may not involve reduction of share capital.

3.0 ALTERATION OF SHARE CAPITAL [SECTIONS 61]

LEGAL REQUIREMENTS

The main legal requirements in connection with the alteration of Share Capital are summarized as follows:

Authorized by Articles	A Company may alter the Capital Clause of its memorandum only if it is authorised by its articles of association to do so.
Manner	A Company may alter the Capital Clause in the following manner: (i) by increasing its share capital by issue of new shares; [e.g. from 1 crore to 5 crores]. (ii) by consolidating the existing shares into shares of larger amount than its existing shares: [e.g. Conversion of Shares of ₹ 10 each into shares of ₹ 100 each]. (iii) by sub-dividing the existing shares into shares of smaller amount than its existing shares; [e.g. Conversion of shares of ₹ 100 each into each into shares of ₹ 10 each]. (iv) by converting fully paid shares into stock *or* vice-versa. (v) by cancelling its unissued shares.
Ordinary Resolution	An ordinary resolution must be passed at a general meeting.
Notice	A notice specifying alteration made must be given to the Registrar within 30 days of alteration.

JOURNAL ENTRIES

The accounting entries in each case of alteration of share capital will be as under:

Particulars	*Dr. (₹)*	*Cr. (₹)*
(a) **For increase in Share Capital:** **Example** *X Ltd. issued 10,000 Equity Shares of ₹ 10 each at par.* (i) Bank A/c Dr. To Equity Share Application and Allotment A/c (Being the application money received)	1,00,000	1,00,000
(ii) Equity Share Application and Allotment A/c Dr. To Equity Share Capital A/c (Being 10,000 Equity shares of ₹ 10 each allotted at par)	1,00,000	1,00,000
(b) **For Consolidation of Shares:** **Example** *X Ltd. having 10,000 Equity Shares of ₹ 10 each decides to convert the Share Capital into Equity Shares of ₹ 100 each.* Equity Share Capital (₹ 10) A/c Dr.	1,00,000	
To Equity Share Capital (₹ 100) A/c (Being 10,000 Equity Shares of ₹ 10 each converted into 1,000 shares of ₹ 100 each)		1,00,000

(c) **For Sub-division of Shares:**		
Example *X Ltd. having 1,000 Equity Shares of ₹ 100 each decides to convert the Share Capital into Equity Shares of ₹ 10 each.*		
Equity Share Capital (₹ 100) A/c Dr.	1,00,000	
To Equity Share Capital (₹ 10) A/c		1,00,000
(Being 1,000 Equity Shares of ₹ 100 each converted into 10,000 Shares of ₹ 10 each)		
(d) **For Conversion of Shares into Stock:**		
Example *X Ltd. having 10,000 Equity Shares of ₹ 10 each decides to convert the Share Capital into Equity Stock*		
Equity Share Capital (₹ 10) A/c Dr.	1,00,000	
To Equity Stock A/c		1,00,000
(Being 10,000 Equity Shares of ₹ 10 each converted into equity stock)		
(e) **For Conversion of Stock into Shares:**		
Example *X Ltd. having Equity Stock of ₹ 1,00,000 decides to convert the Equity Stock into Equity Share Capital of ₹ 10 each*		
Equity Stock A/c Dr.	1,00,000	
To Equity Share Capital (₹ 10) A/c		1,00,000
(Being Equity Stock of ₹ 1,00,000 converted into 10,000 Equity Shares of ₹ 10 each)		
(f) **For Cancelling Unissued Shares:**		
No accounting entry is required to be passed. The Authorised Share Capital gets reduced by the amount of unissued shares now cancelled.		

4.0 REDUCTION OF SHARE CAPITAL [SECTION 66]

LEGAL REQUIREMENTS

The main legal requirements for reduction of Share Capital are summarised as follows:

Authorised by Articles	A company limited by shares *or* a company limited by guarantee having a Share Capital may reduce its Share Capital only if it is authorised by its articles of association to do so.
Ways	A company may reduce its Share Capital in any of the following ways: (i) by extinguishing/reducing the liability on any of its shares in respect of uncalled amount on shares; (ii) by cancelling the paid up Share Capital which is lost *or* is not represented by available assets; (iii) by paying off any paid up Share Capital which is in excess of the requirements of the Company.

Special Resolution	A Special Resolution must be passed at a general meeting.
Auditor's Certificate	Auditors Certificate to the affect that the proposed accounting treatment is as per prescribed Accounting Standard, must be filed with the Tribunal.
Tribunal's Order	A Tribunal's order confirming the reduction must be obtained.
Filing with ROC	A certified copy of Tribunal's order and Minutes approved by the Tribunal must be filed with the Registrar.
Notice	A Company must publish notice of registration in such manner as the Tribunal may direct.
Effective Date	A resolution for reducing Capital as confirmed by the order of the Tribunal shall take effect on its registration by the Registrar.

JOURNAL ENTRIES

The Accounting entries in each case of reduction of share capital will be as follows:

Particulars		*Dr. (₹)*	*Cr. (₹)*
(a) **For Reducing the liability in respect of Uncalled Amount** **Example** *X Ltd. having 1,000 Equity Shares of ₹ 100 each ₹ 60 paid up, decides to cancel the liability of member to the extent of ₹ 20 per share and make shares as of ₹ 80 each. ₹ 60 paid up.*			
Equity. Share Capital (₹ 100) A/c	Dr.	60,000	
To Equity Share Capital (₹ 80)			60,000
(Being Shares of ₹ 100 each converted into shares of ₹ 80 each) **Note:** *The Paid up Share Capital of the company will remain unchanged.*			
(b) **For Paying off the surplus paid up Capital** **Example** *A Ltd. having 1,000 Equity Shares of ₹ 100 each fully paid decides to repay to its members ₹ 20 per share and make shares as of ₹ 80 each fully paid up.*			
(i) Equity Share Capital (₹ 100) A/c	Dr.	1,00,000	
To Equity Share Capital (₹ 80) A/c			80,000
To Sundry Members A/c			20,000
(Being shares of ₹ 100 each converted into shares of ₹ 80 each and make ₹ 20 per share due to members)			
(ii) Sundry Members A/c	Dr.	20,000	
To Bank A/c			20,000
(Being the payment made to members)			
(c) **For Writing off the lost paid up Capital** **Example** *Look at the following Balance Sheet of Bad Luck Ltd.:*			

Liabilities	₹	***Assets***	₹
1,000 Shares of ₹ 100 each	1,00,000	Intangible Assets	25,000
Sundry Creditors.	1,00,000	Other Fixed Assets	1,00,000
		Current Assets	25,000
		P&L A/c	50,000
	2,00,000		2,00,000

Assets	***Present Worth (₹)***
Intangible	Nil
Other Fixed Assets	1,05,000
Current Assets	15,000
Thus, the Company has lost ₹ 80,000 if its paid up Capital as under:	
Intangible Assets	₹ 25,000
Current Assets	₹ 10,000
P&L A/c	₹ 50,000
	₹ 85,000
Less: Appreciation in Fixed Assets	5,000
	₹ 80,000

This reduction can be effected in any of the following two ways:

JOURNAL

Particulars	***Dr. (₹)***	***Cr. (₹)***
(i) By reducing the paid-up value (not Nominal Value) of existing shares		
Share Capital (₹ 100) A/c Dr.	80,000	
To Capital Reduction A/c		80,000
(Being the paid-up value of a share reduced from ₹ 100 to ₹ 20)		
(ii) By reducing both the Nominal values and paid up values of Shares		
Share Capital (₹ 100) A/c Dr.	1,00,000	
To Share. Capital (₹ 20) A/c		20,000
To Capital Reduction A/c		80,000
(Being the shares reduced to ₹ 20 per share)		

Note: The Shareholders will not ordinarily be willing for the first alternative since it puts additional burden on them.

5.0 VARIATION OF SHAREHOLDERS' RIGHTS [SECTION 48]

LEGAL REQUIREMENTS

The main legal requirements for variation of shareholders' rights are summarised as under:

Separate Meeting	If the rights attached to the shares of any particulars class of shareholders are to be varied, a separate meeting of that particular class of shareholders must be held.
Consent of atleast 3/4th	The consent of the holder of at least 3/4th of the shares of the class concerned (or a higher proportion if so required by the articles/ memorandum) must be obtained.

Right to Apply to the Tribunal	The holders of at least 10% of the issued shares of the class concerned whose rights are being varied, may apply to the Tribunal to have the variation cancelled within 21 days after the consent is obtained *or* the resolution is passed.
Tribunal's Confirmation	If such appeal is made, the variation will not have effect unless it is confirmed by the Tribunal whose decision is final.
Notice	Notice of the variation must be filed with the Registrar within 30 days of the Tribunal's order.

EXAMPLE 1

X Ltd. has 1,000, 10% Cum Pref. shares of ₹ 100 each. At a class meeting of Cum Pref. Shareholders, it was decided that the rate of dividend be reduced to 9%. In such a case following Journal Entry will be passed.

Particulars		*Dr. (₹)*	*Cr. (₹)*
10% Cum Pref. Share Capital A/c	Dr.	1,00,000	
To 9% Cum Pref. Share Capital A/c			1,00,000

EXAMPLE 2

Y Ltd. has 1,000, 10% Non-Cumulative Pref. Shares of ₹ 100 each. At a meeting of Non-Cum Pref. Shareholders, it was decided that the existing Non-Cumulative Pref Shares be converted into 9% Cumulative-Pref. Shares.

Particulars		*Dr. (₹)*	*Cr. (₹)*
10% Non-Cum Pref. Share Capital A/c	Dr.	1,00,000	
To 9% Cum Pref. Share Capital A/c			1,00,000

6.0 SCHEME OF COMPROMISE AND ARRANGEMENT [SECTIONS 230 TO 2310]

MEANING OF COMPROMISE

Compromise refers to an amicable settlement of differences by mutual concessions by parties to dispute. It may be noted that the compromise presupposes the existence of some dispute because there can be no compromise unless there is some dispute. The need for compromise may arise for the settlement of some dispute between the company and its creditors/members.

MEANING OF ARRANGEMENT

The term 'Arrangement' carries a wider sense than the term 'Compromise'. It implies re-arrangement of rights and/or liabilities of a member/a class of them/a creditor/a class of them without the existence of any dispute. According to Explanation to Section 230(1), of the Companies Act the term 'Arrangement' includes re-organisation of the share capital of the company by the consolidation of shares of different classes *or* by the division of the shares into shares of different classes *or* by both these methods. An arrangement may involve anyone *or* more of the following:

(a) Debenture-holders foregoing their claims in whole *or* in part;

(b) Debentures exchanging their debentures for new debentures/shares;

(c) Creditors foregoing their claims in whole *or* in part;

(d) Creditor agreeing to receive shares/debentures in whole/in part payment of the claims;

(e) Preference shareholders forgoing their claims for arrears of dividend;

(f) Preference shareholders agreeing to accept a reduced rate of dividend in future;

(g) Fresh issue of shares to raise additional working capital;

(h) Writing off lost Paid-up Capital.

Example In the Balance Sheet 10% Debentures 14,70,000, Sundry Creditors 4,50,000

The debenture holders agree to reduce their claims to ₹ 5,00,000 in consideration of their getting 50,000 Equity Shares of ₹ 10 each. Sundry Creditors agree to reduce their claims to 20% and half the balance to be satisfied by the issue of Equity Shares of ₹ 10 each. The following Journal Entries shall be passed to record the aforesaid arrangement:

Particulars		Dr. (₹)	Cr. (₹)
(i) 10% Debentureholders' A/c	Dr.	9,70,000	
To Equity Shares Capital A/c (₹ 10)			5,00,000
To Reconstruction A/c			4,70,000
(ii) Sundry Creditors A/c	Dr.	4,05,000	
To Equity Share Capital A/c (₹ 10)			45,000
To Reconstruction A/c			3,60,000

7.0 HOW TO DEAL WITH SURRENDER OF SHARES?

Under a scheme of reconstruction, the shareholders may be required to surrender a part of their share-holdings. Such surrendered shares may be re-issued to other parties in whole/in part satisfaction of their claims *or* cancelled. The following Journal Entries may be required to be passed in such connection:

(a) On Surrender of Shares	Share Capital A/c	Dr.
	To Shares Surrendered A/c	
(b) On Re-issue of Surrendered Shares	Shares Surrendered A/c	Dr.
	To Share Capital A/c	
(c) On Cancellation of Surrendered Shares	Shares Surrendered A/c	Dr.
	To Reconstruction A/c	

8.0 ACCOUNTING ENTRIES UNDER INTERNAL RECONSTRUCTION

Date	Particulars		Dr. (₹)	Cr. (₹)
1.	**To Reduce Both the Nominal Value and Paid up Value of Shares**			
	Share Capital A/c (₹ 100 each)	Dr.	100	
	To Share Capital A/c (₹ 80 each)			80
	To Reconstruction A/c/Capital Reduction A/c			20
2.	**To Reduce only the Paid up Value of Shares**			
	Share Capital A/c	Dr.	20	
	To Reconstruction A/c/Capital Reduction A/c			20

3.	**(a) To Pay the Arrears of Preference Dividend** Reconstruction A/c Dr. To Bank A/c/Share Capital A/c **(b) To Cancel the Arrears of Preference Dividend** No Journal Entry is required to cancel a Contingent Liability.		
4.	**To Reduce the Claims of Debentureholders** Debentures A/c Dr. Interest on Debentures A/c Dr. To New Debentures A/c/Share Capital A/c/Bank A/c To Reconstruction A/c		
5.	**To Reduce the claims of Trade Creditors** Trade Creditors A/c Dr. To Share Capital A/c/Bank A/c To Reconstruction A/c		
6.	**To Settle the Tax Liability** Provision for Tax A/c Dr. To Bank A/c To Reconstruction A/c		
7.	**To Pay Reconstruction Expenses** Reconstruction A/c Dr. To Bank A/c		
8.	**To Pay for Cancellation of Capital Commitments etc.** Reconstruction A/c Dr. To Bank A/c		
9.	**To Record the Bad Debts and Doubtful Debts** Reconstruction A/c Dr. [With total] To Debtors A/c [With Bad Debts] To Provision for Doubtful Debts A/c [With Doubtful Debts]		
10.	**To Record the Appreciation in Value of Assets** Investments A/c/Land and Building A/c Dr. To Reconstruction A/c		
11.	**To Transfer Capital Reserve for Reconstruction Purpose** Capital Reserve A/c Dr. To Reconstruction A/c		
12.	**To write off the Accumulated Losses, Fictitious Assets and the over valuation of Over Valued Assets** Capital Reduction A/c/Reconstruction A/c Dr. To Profit and Loss A/c		

	To Preliminary Expenses A/c To Underwriting Commission A/c To Discount on Issue of Shares/Debentures A/c To Goodwill A/c (To the extent of over valuation) To Patents A/c (To the extent of over valuation) To Trade Marks A/c (To the extent of over valuation) To Copy Right A/c (To the extent of over valuation) To Other Overvalued Assets (individually)		
13.	**To Transfer the Credit Balance of Reconstruction A/c/** Capital Reduction A/c/Reconstruction A/c Dr. To Capital Reserve A/c		

Tutorial Notes:

(i) *The author recommends the use of 'Reconstruction Account' particularly when the scheme of compromise/arrangement is carried out under the provisions of Sections 230 to 240. The use of 'Capital Reduction Account' is purely justified when the capital reduction scheme is carried out (u/s 66) without invoking the provisions of Sections 230 to 240.*

(ii) *Even if the question is silent as to writing off, the debit balance of Profit & Loss Account and Unamortized Expense Items (like Preliminary Expenses, Underwriting Comm., Discount on Issue of Shares/Debentures) should be written off to the extent of credit balance available in Reconstruction/Capital Reduction Account.*

(iii) *So far as Fixed Assets are concerned, the amount written off under a scheme of reconstruction must be shown in each Balance Sheet for five years.*

ILLUSTRATION 1

Pass journal entries for the following transactions:

(i) Conversion of 2 lakh fully paid equity shares of ₹ 10 each into stock of ₹ 1,00,000 and balance has 12% fully convertible Debenture.

(ii) Consolidation of 40 lakh fully paid equity shares of ₹2.50 each into 10 lakh fully paid equity share of ₹10 each.

(iii) Sub-division of 10 lakh fully paid 11% preference shares of ₹ 50 each into 50 lakh fully paid 11% preference shares of ₹ 10 each.

(iv) Conversion of 12% preference shares of ₹ 5,00,000 into 13% preference shares ₹ 3,00,000 and remaining balance as 14% Non-cumulative preference shares.

SOLUTION

JOURNAL

Date	*Particulars*		*Dr. (₹)*	*Cr. (₹)*
(i)	Equity share Capital A/c	Dr.	20,00,000	
	To Equity Stock			1,00,000
	To 12% Fully Convertible Debentures			19,00,000

	(Being conversion of 2 lakh equity shares of ₹ 10 each into stock of ₹ 1,00,000 and balance as fully convertible debentures as per resolution)		
(ii)	Equity Share Capital A/c (₹ 2.50) Dr.	100,00,000	
	To Equity Share Capital A/c (₹ 10)		100,00,000
	(Being consolidation of 40 lakh shares of ₹ 2.50 each into 10 lakh shares of ₹ 10 each as per resolution)		
(iii)	11% Preference Shares Capital A/c (₹ 50) Dr.	500,00,000	
	To 11% Preference Share Capital A/c (₹10)		500,00,000
	(Being subdivision of 10 lakh preference shares of ₹ 50 each into 50 lakh shares of ₹ 10 each as per resolution)		
(iv)	12% Preference Share Capital A/c Dr.	5,00,000	
	To 13% Preference Share Capital		3,00,000
	To 14% Non-cumulative Pref. Share Capital		2,00,000
	(Being conversion of preference shares as per resolution)		

ILLUSTRATION 2

V Ltd has Equity Share Capital (of ₹ 10 each) of ₹ 500 lacs. All the equity shares be converted into the same number of equity shares of ₹ 5 each, ₹ 2.50 paid up. Journalise

SOLUTION

JOURNAL [₹ in Lacs]

Date	*Particulars*	*L.F.*	*Dr. (₹)*	*Cr. (₹)*
	Equity Share Capital (₹ 10 each) A/c Dr.		500	
	To Equity Share Capital (₹ 5 each) A/c			125
	To Reconstruction A/c			375
	(Being the conversion of all the equity shares into the same number of equity shares of ₹ 5 each, ₹ 2.50 paid up as per scheme of reconstruction)			

ILLUSTRATION 3

V Ltd has 6% Cum-Pref. Shares (of ₹ 100 each) of ₹ 100 lacs. The preference shares are converted from 6% to 15% but revalued in a manner in which the total return on them remains unaffected. Journalise

SOLUTION

JOURNAL [₹ in Lacs]

Date	Particulars		L.F.	Dr. (₹)	Cr. (₹)
	6% Cum-Preference Share Capital (₹ 100) A/c	Dr.		100	
	To 15% Cum-Pref. Share Capital (₹ 100) A/c				40
	To Reconstruction A/c				60
	(Being 40000 15% cum Pref. share of ₹ 100 each issued so as to maintain the same amount of dividend (i.e. ₹ 6 lacs) vide scheme of reconstruction dated.....)				

ILLUSTRATION 4

V Ltd has 6% Cum-Pref. Shares (of ₹100 each) of ₹ 100 lacs. Dividend on Preference Shares are in arrears for three years. Four equity shares of ₹ 5 each, ₹ 2.50 paid up to be issued for each ₹100 of arrears of preference dividend. Journalise

SOLUTION

JOURNAL [₹ in Lacs]

Date	Particulars		L.F.	Dr. (₹)	Cr. (₹)
	Reconstruction A/c	Dr.		1.8	
	To Equity Share Capital (₹ 5 each, ₹ 2.50 paid up) A/c				1.8
	(Being 72000 equity shares of ₹ 5 each, ₹ 2.50 paid up issued to Pref. Shareholders for dividend arrears vide scheme of Reconstruction dated.....)				

ILLUSTRATION 5

V Ltd has 10% first debentures for ₹ 60 lacs, 10% second debentures for ₹ 100 lacs and Interest on Debentures Outstanding ₹ 16 lacs. Mr. A holds 10% first debentures for ₹ 40 lacs and 10% second debentures for ₹ 60 lacs. He is also a creditor for ₹ 10 lacs. Mr. 'A' is to cancel ₹ 60 lacs of his total debt and to pay ₹ 10 lacs to the company and to receive new 12% Debentures for the balance amount. Journalise.

SOLUTION

JOURNAL [₹ in Lacs]

Date	Particulars		L.F.	Dr. (₹)	Cr. (₹)
	10% First Debentures A/c	Dr.		40	
	10% Second Debentures A/c	Dr.		60	
	Trade Creditors A/c	Dr.		10	
	Interest on Debentures Outstanding A/c [16 x 100/160]	Dr.		10	

Date	Particulars		L.F.	Dr. (₹)	Cr. (₹)
	To Mr. A (Being the total amount due to A t/f to his A/c)				120
	Bank A/c	Dr.		10	
	To Mr. A (Being the amount received from Mr. A under the Reconstruction Scheme)				10
	Mr. A A/c	Dr.		130	
	To 12% New Debentures A/c				70
	To Reconstruction A/c (Being ₹ 60 lacs due to A (Including creditors) cancelled and 12% new debentures allotted for balance amount as per scheme of reconstruction)				60

ILLUSTRATION 6

V Ltd has 10% first debentures for ₹ 60 lacs, 10% second debentures for ₹ 100 lacs and Interest on Debentures Outstanding ₹ 16 lacs. Mr. B holds 10% first debentures for ₹ 20 lacs and 10% second debentures for ₹ 40 lacs and is also a creditor for ₹ 5 lacs. Mr. 'B' is to cancel ₹ 30 lacs of his total debt and to accept new 12% Debentures for the balance amount. Journalise

SOLUTION

JOURNAL [₹ in Lacs]

Date	*Particulars*		*L.F.*	*Dr. (₹)*	*Cr. (₹)*
	10% First Debentures A/c	Dr.		20	
	10% Second Debentures A/c	Dr.		40	
	Trade Creditors A/c	Dr.		5	
	Interest on Debentures Outstanding A/c	Dr.		6	
	To Mr. B (Being the total amount due to Mr. B t/f to his A/c)				71
	Mr. B			71	
	To 12% New Debentures A/c				41
	To Reconstruction A/c (Being ₹ 30 lacs due to B (including creditors) cancelled and 12% new debentures allotted for balance amount as per scheme of reconstruction)				30

ILLUSTRATION 7

V Ltd has Trade Creditors for ₹ 165 lacs. Mr. A and Mr. B are creditors for ₹ 10 lacs and ₹ 5 lacs respectively. Trade Creditors (other than A and B) are given the option of either to accept equity shares of ₹ 5, ₹ 2.50 paid up each, for the amount due to them *or* to accept 80% of the amount due in cash. 40% Creditors accepted equity shares whereas the balance accepted cash in full settlement. Journalise

SOLUTION

JOURNAL [₹ in Lacs]

Date	Particulars	L.F.	Dr. (₹)	Cr. (₹)
	Trade Creditors A/c Dr.		150	
	To Equity Share Capital (₹ 5 each, ₹ 2.50 paid up) A/c			60
	To Bank A/c			72
	To Reconstruction a/c			18
	(Being the Trade creditors for ₹ 60 lakhs accepted 24 lakhs shares of ₹ 5 each, ₹ 2.50 paid up for full amount and those for ₹.90 lakhs accepted cash equal to 80% of claim in full settlement)			

ILLUSTRATION 8

There were capital commitments totalling ₹ 300 lacs. These contracts are to be cancelled on payment of 5% of the contract price as a penalty. The Directors refund ₹ 11 lacs of the fees previously received by them. A dissentient shareholder transferred his 100 shares to a director. Journalise

SOLUTION

JOURNAL [₹ in Lacs]

Date	Particulars	L.F.	Dr. (₹)	Cr. (₹)
	Reconstruction A/c Dr.		15	
	To Bank A/c			15
	(Being payment made for cancellation of capital commitments)			
	Bank A/c Dr.		11	
	To Reconstruction A/c			11
	(Being refund of fees by directors credited to Reconstruction A/c)			

Note: *The transfer of 100 Shares by a dissentient shareholder to the director concerned need not be accounted for.*

ILLUSTRATION 9

V Ltd has Provision for Tax for ₹10 lacs. The taxation liability of the company is settled at ₹ 8.88 lacs and the same is paid immediately. Journalise.

SOLUTION

JOURNAL [₹ in Lacs]

Date	Particulars	L.F.	Dr. (₹)	Cr. (₹)
	Provision for Tax A/c Dr.		10	
	To Bank A/c			8.88
	To Reconstruction A/c			1.12
	(Being payment of tax liability in full settlement)			

ILLUSTRATION 10

Following items appear in the Balance Sheet of V Ltd:

Workmen's Compensation Fund:	Pune	₹1 lac
	Bombay	₹ 2 lacs
10% Government Loan Earmarked Against Workmen's Compensation Fund		₹ 3 lacs
Workmen's Compensation Fund (Bombay) disclosed the fact that actually there was a liability of ₹ 1,20,000 only. As a result the relevant fund amount balance was to be brought down to the required amount. Investments were realised at 10% above the book value. Journalise.		

SOLUTION

JOURNAL [₹ in Lacs]

Date	Particulars	L.F.	Dr. (₹)	Cr. (₹)
	Bank A/c Dr.		0.88	
	To Investment in 10% Government Loan A/c			0.80
	To Workmen's Compensation Fund (Bombay) A/c			0.08
	(Being the Sale of Investments for Workmen's Compensation Fund (Bombay) and the profit on the sale of same transferred to Workmen Compensation Fund (Bombay) Account)			
	Workmen's Compensation Fund (Bombay) A/c Dr.		0.88	
	To Reconstruction A/c			0.88
	(Being the Surplus in Workmen Compensation Fund at Bombay transferred to Reconstruction Account)			

ILLUSTRATION 11

V Ltd has Investments of ₹ 32.4 lacs in Shares in Q Ltd. V Ltd. holds 21,600 shares in Q Ltd. This represents 15% of the share capital of that company. Q Ltd. is not a quoted company. The average net profit (after tax) of the company is ₹ 25 lacs. The shares would be valued based on 12% capitalization rate. Journalise.

SOLUTION

JOURNAL [₹ in Lacs]

Date	Particulars	L.F.	Dr. (₹)	Cr. (₹)
	Reconstruction A/c Dr.		1.15	
	To Investments in Shares in Q Ltd. A/c			1.15
	(Being reduction in the value of Investments)			

Working Notes:

(i) Valuation of Investments in Shares of Q Ltd.= (₹ 25 lacs/.12) × 15% = ₹ 31.25 lacs

(ii) Reduction in the Value of Investment in Shares of Q Ltd. = ₹ 32.40 lacs – ₹.31.25 = ₹.1.15 lacs

ILLUSTRATION 12

Following items appear in the Balance Sheet of V Ltd:

Capital Reserve	₹ 6 lacs
Profit and Loss Account	(₹ 15 lacs)
Goodwill	₹ 10 lacs
Patents & Copy Rights	₹ 5 lacs
Plant & Machinery	₹ 719.6 lacs
Land & Building	₹ 60 lacs
Debtors	₹ 10 lacs
Cash at Bank	₹ 104 lacs
Discount on issue of Debentures	₹ 1 lac

Goodwill is considered worthless. Land & Building is to be valued at 114% of book value. 80% of Debtors are considered as Bad and 20% of the balance Debtors are considered as Doubtful. Any surplus after writing off the various losses should be utilized in writing down the value of plant & machinery. The credit Balance available in Reconstruction A/c is ₹ 538.05 lacs. Journalise.

SOLUTION

JOURNAL [₹ in Lacs]

Date	Particulars		L.F.	Dr. (₹)	Cr. (₹)
	Capital Reserve A/c	Dr.		6	
	To Reconstruction A/c				6
	(Being the transfer of Capital Reserve for purpose of reconstruction)				
	Land & Building A/c	Dr.		8.40	
	To Reconstruction A/c				8.40
	(Being the Land & Building revalued)				
	Reconstruction A/c	Dr.		8.40	
	To Debtors				8.00
	To Provision for Doubtful Debts.				0.40
	(Being the Debtors revalued)				
	Reconstruction A/c	Dr.		544.05	
	To Goodwill A/c				10
	To Profit and Loss A/c				15
	To Discount on issue of Debentures A/c				1
	To Plant & Machinery (balancing figure)				**518.05**
	(Being writing off of losses and reduction in the value of assets as per scheme of reconstruction)				

ILLUSTRATION 13

The ledger balances of X Ltd. as on 31st March, 2023 are:

Fixed Assets ₹ 7,00,000, Investments ₹ 10,000, Stock ₹ 3,90,000 Debtors ₹ 4,60,000, Preliminary Expenses ₹ 20,000, Equity Share Capital (60% paid) ₹ 6,00,000, 10% First Debentures ₹ 2,00,000, 12% Second Debentures ₹ 5,00,000, Bank overdraft ₹ 50,000, Trade Creditors (including Y for ₹ 8,50,000) ₹ 11,50,000, Outstanding interest for one year on both types of debentures.

Due to heavy losses, the following scheme of re-construction is agreed:

(a) To make the existing ₹ 100 equity shares fully paid up and then to reduce them to ₹ 20 each.

(b) To settle the claims of first debenture-holders by issuing 2,000, 13.5% debentures of ₹ 100 each,

(c) To discharge the claims of the second debenture-holders by issuing 15% 4,000 debentures of ₹ 100 each,

(d) To pay ₹ 3,00,000 to Mr. Y in full settlement of his account,

(e) To allot 15,000 fresh equity shares of ₹ 20 each to discharge the remaining trade creditors,

(f) Market value of investments is ₹ 20,000, and

(g) To write off the fictitious assets and to reduce the fixed assets.

Required: Pass journal Entries and prepare the post-reconstruction Balance-Sheet.

STEP 1: BALANCE SHEET OF X LTD. (BEFORE RECONSTRUCTION) AS AT 31 MARCH, 2023

Liabilities	₹	***Assets***	₹
Equity Share Capital (60% Paid-up)	6,00,000	Fixed Assets	7,00,000
10% First Debentures	2,00,000	Trade Debtors	4,60,000
12% Second Debentures	5,00,000	Stock	3,90,000
Outstanding Interest on Debentures for one year	80,000	Investments (Market value ₹ 20,000)	10,000
Bank Overdraft	50,000	Preliminary Expenses	20,000
Trade Creditors (including Y for ₹ 8,50,000)	11,50,000	**Profit and Loss Account (Balancing figure)**	**10,00,000**
	25,80,000		25,80,000

JOURNAL

Particulars		***L.F.***	***Dr. (₹)***	***Cr. (₹)***
Share Final Call A/c	Dr.		4,00,000	
To Equity Share Capital A/c				4,00,000
(Final call made for the balance on equity share)				
Bank A/c	Dr.		4,00,000	
To Equity Share Final Call A/c				4,00,000
(Receipt of Final Call money)				
Equity Share Capital (₹ 100 Shares) A/c	Dr.		10,00,000	

To Equity Shares (₹ 20 Shares) A/c To Reconstruction A/c (Reduction of ₹ 100 share capital to ₹ 20 each)			2,00,000 8,00,000
10% First Debentures A/c Debenture Interest (outstanding) A/c To 13.5% Debentures A/c To Reconstruction A/c (Redemption of First Debentures)	Dr. Dr.	2,00,000 20,000	 2,00,000 20,000
12% Second Debentures A/c Debenture Interest (outstanding) A/c To 15% Debentures A/c To Reconstruction A/c (Redemption of Second Debentures)	Dr. Dr.	5,00,000 60,000	 4,00,000 1,60,000
Sundry Creditors A/c To Bank A/c To Equity Share Capital A/c To Reconstruction A/c (Settlement of creditors' account)	Dr.	11,50,000	 3,00,000 3,00,000 5,50,000
Reconstruction A/c To Profit and Loss A/c To Preliminary Expenses A/c To Fixed Assets A/c (Utilisation of reconstruction account for writing of past losses and fixed assets)	Dr.	15,30,000	 10,00,000 20,000 5,10,000

BALANCE SHEET OF CONTINENTAL CONSTRUCTION LTD. (AND REDUCED) AS AT 31.3.2023

Particulars	**Note No**	₹
I. Equity and Liabilities		
(1) Shareholders' Funds		
(a) Share Capital (₹ 20 each)		5,00,000
(2) Non-Current Liabilities		
(a) Long-term Borrowings	1	6,00,000
(3) Current Liabilities		
Total		11,00,000
II. Assets		
(1) Non-Current Assets		
(a) Fixed Assets		
Tangible Assets [7,00,000 – 5,10,000 (Amt. w/o)]		1,90,000
(b) Non-Current Investments [Market Value ₹ 20,000]		10,000

(2) Current Assets		
(a) Inventories		3,90,000
(b) Trade Receivables [Debtors]		4,60,000
(c) Cash and Cash Equivalents		50,000
Total		11,00,000

Notes To Accounts:

1. Long-term Borrowings		
13.5% Debentures	2,00,000	
15% Debentures	4,00,000	6,00,000

ILLUSTRATION 14A

TASHIKA TUSHAR Ltd. provides you the following information as at March 31, 2023:

Particulars	***(₹ in lakhs)***
Equity Shares of ₹ 10 each	500
6% Cum- Pref. Shares of ₹ 100 each	100
Profit and Loss Account (Dr)	15
10% First Debentures	60
10% Second Debentures	100
Debentures Interest outstanding	16
Trade Creditors	165
Plant & Machinery	719.6

Note: Dividend on Preference Shares are in arrears for three years.

The following scheme of internal reconstruction was approved and implemented:

(a) All the equity shares be converted into the same number of equity shares of ₹ 5 each, ₹ 2.50 paid up.

(b) The preference shares are converted from 6% to 15% but revalued in a manner in which the total return on them remains unaffected. Four equity shares of ₹ 5 each, ₹ 2.50 paid up to be issued for each ₹ 100 of arrears of preference dividend.

(c) Mr. A holds 10% first debentures for ₹ 40 lacs and 10% second debentures for ₹ 60 lacs. He is also a creditor for ₹ 10 lacs. Mr. 'A' is to cancel ₹ 60 lacs of his total debt and to pay ₹ 10 lacs to the company and to receive new 12% Debentures for the balance amount. Mr. B holds the remaining 10% first debentures and 10% second debentures and is also a creditor for ₹ 5 lacs. Mr. 'B' is to cancel ₹ 30 lacs of his total debt and to accept new 12% Debentures for the balance amount

(d) Trade Creditors (other than A and B) are given the option of either to accept equity shares of ₹ 5, ₹ 2.50 paid up each, for the amount due to them or to accept 80% of the amount due in cash. 40% Creditors accepted equity shares whereas the balance accepted cash in full settlement.

(e) Any surplus after writing off the various losses should be utilized in writing down the value of plant & machinery.

Required: Pass the Journal Entries and prepare the Reconstruction Account.

SOLUTION

JOURNAL *[₹ in Lacs]*

Date	Particulars	L.F.	Dr. (₹)	Cr. (₹)
(a)	Equity Share Capital (₹ 10 each) A/c Dr.		500	
	To Equity Share Capital (₹ 5 each) A/c			125
	To Reconstruction A/c			375
	(Being the conversion of all the equity shares into the same number of equity shares of ₹ 5 each, ₹ 2.50 paid up as per scheme of reconstruction)			
(b)(i)	6% Cum-Preference Share Capital (₹ 100) A/c Dr.		100	
	To 15% Cum-Pref. Share Capital (₹ 100) A/c			40
	To Reconstruction A/c			60
	(Being 40000 15% cum Pref. share of ₹ 100 each issued so as to maintain the same amount of dividend (i.e. ₹ 6 lacs) vide scheme of reconstruction dated.....)			
(b)(ii)	Reconstruction A/c Dr.		1.8	
	To Equity Share Capital (₹ 5 each, ₹ 2.50 paid up) A/c			1.8
	(Being 72000 equity shares of ₹ 5 each, ₹ 2.50 paid up issued to pref. Shareholders for dividend arrears vide scheme of Reconstruction dated.....)			
(c)(i)	10% First Debentures A/c Dr.		40	
	10% Second Debentures A/c Dr.		60	
	Trade Creditors A/c Dr.		10	
	Interest on Debentures Outstanding A/c Dr.		10	
	To Mr. A			120
	(Being the total amount due to A t/f to his A/c)			
(c)(ii)	Bank A/c Dr.		10	
	To Mr. A			10
	(Being the amount received from Mr. A under the Reconstruction Scheme)			
(c)(iii)	Mr. A A/c Dr.		130	
	To 12% New Debentures A/c			70
	To Reconstruction A/c			60
	(Being ₹ 60 lacs due to A (Including creditors) cancelled and 12% new debentures allotted for balance amount as per scheme of reconstruction)			
(d)(i)	10% First Debentures A/c Dr.		20	
	10% Second Debentures A/c Dr.		40	
	Trade Creditors A/c Dr.		5	
	Interest on Debentures Outstanding A/c Dr.		6	

	To Mr. B (Being the total amount due to Mr. B t/f to his A/c)			71
d(ii)	Mr. B To 12% New Debentures A/c To Reconstruction A/c (Being ₹ 30 lacs due to B (including creditors) cancelled and 12% new debentures allotted for balance amount as per scheme of reconstruction)		71	41 30
(e)	Trade Creditors A/c Dr. To Equity Share Capital (₹ 5 each, ₹ 2.50 paid up) A/c To Bank A/c To Reconstruction A/c (Being the Trade creditors for ₹ 60 lakhs accepted 24 lakhs shares of ₹ 5 each, ₹ 2.50 paid up for full amount and those for ₹ 90 lakhs accepted cash equal to 80% of claim in full settlement)		150	60 72 18
(f)	Reconstruction A/c Dr. To Profit and Loss A/c To Plant & Machinery (balancing figure) (Being writing off of losses and reduction in the value of assets as per scheme of reconstruction)		541.20	15.00 526.20

Dr. **RECONSTRUCTION ACCOUNT** *Cr.*

Particulars	*₹ (lacs)*	*Particulars*	*₹ (lacs)*
To Equity Share Capital A/c (₹ 5 each)	1.80	By Equity Share Capital (₹ 10 each)	375.00
To Profit & Loss A/c	15.00	By 6% Cum. Pref. Share Capital	60.00
To Plant & Machinery A/c	526.20	By Mr. A (Sundries)	60.00
		By Mr. B (Sundries)	30.00
		By Trade Creditors	18.00
	543.00		543.00

ILLUSTRATION 14B

Given below are the extracts from the Balance Sheet of Road Block Ltd. as at March 31, 2023:

Particulars	*(₹ in lakhs)*
Equity Shares of ₹ 10 each	500
6% Cum-Pref. Shares of ₹ 100 each	100
Capital Reserve	6

Workmen's Compensation Fund:		
Pune	2	
Bombay	1	3
10% First Debentures		60
10% Second Debentures		100
Debentures Interest outstanding		16
Trade Creditors		165
Provision for Tax		10
Goodwill		10
Patents & Copy Rights		5
Plant & Machinery		719.6
10% Government Loan Earmarked Against Workmen's Compensation Fund		3
Investments in Shares in Q Ltd.		32.4
Stock		60
Debtors		10
Cash at Bank		104
Profit and Loss Account (Dr)		16

Note: *Dividend on Preference Shares are in arrears for three years.*

The following scheme of internal reconstruction was approved by the Court and implemented:

(a) All the equity shares be converted into the same number of equity shares of ₹ 5 each, ₹ 2.50 paid up.

(b) The preference shares are converted from 6% to 15% but revalued in a manner in which the total return on them remains unaffected. Four equity shares of ₹ 5 each, ₹ 2.50 paid up to be issued for each ₹ 100 of arrears of preference dividend.

(c) Mr. A holds 10% first debentures for ₹ 40 lacs and 10% second debentures for ₹ 60 lacs. He is also a creditor for ₹ 10 lacs. Mr. 'A' is to cancel ₹ 60 lacs of his total debt and to pay ₹ 10 lacs to the company and to receive new 12% Debentures for the balance amount.

(d) Mr. B holds 10% first debentures for ₹ 20 lacs and 10% second debentures for ₹ 40 lacs and is also a creditor for ₹ 5 lacs. Mr. 'B' is to cancel ₹ 30 lacs of his total debt and to accept new 12% Debentures for the balance amount

(e) Trade Creditors (other than A and B) are given the option of either to accept equity shares of ₹ 5, ₹ 2.50 paid up each, for the amount due to them *or* to accept 80% of the amount due in cash. 40% Creditors accepted equity shares whereas the balance accepted cash in full settlement.

(f) There were capital commitments totalling ₹ 300 lacs. These contracts are to be cancelled on payment of 5% of the contract price as a penalty.

(g) The Directors refund ₹ 11 lacs of the fees previously received by them.

(h) Workmen's Compensation Fund (Bombay) disclosed the fact that actually there was a liability of ₹ 20,000 only. As a result the relevant fund amount balance was to be brought down to the required amount. Investments were realised at 10% above the book value.

(i) The taxation liability of the company is settled at ₹ 8.88 lacs and the same is paid immediately.

(j) Road Block Ltd. holds 21,600 shares in Q Ltd. This represents 15% of the share capital of that company. Q Ltd. is not a quoted company. The average net profit (after tax) of the company is ₹ 25 lacs. The shares would be valued based on 12% capitalization rate.

(k) A dissentient shareholder transferred his 100 shares to a director.

(l) Stock is to be valued at 114% of book value. 80% of Debtors are considered as Bad and 20% of the balance Debtors are considered as Doubtful. Any surplus after writing off the various losses(including Goodwill) should be utilized in writing down the value of plant & machinery.

(m) All equity shareholders paid the balance to make the shares fully paid up and then all equity shares were consolidated into the shares of ₹ 10 each.

Required: Pass the Journal Entries and prepare the Reconstruction Account, Bank Account and Balance Sheet after Reconstruction assuming that the Authorised Capital was increased to 500 lacs by complying with the necessary formalities.

SOLUTION

JOURNAL

[₹ in Lacs]

Date	Particulars		L.F.	Dr. (₹)	Cr. (₹)
(a)	Equity Share Capital (₹ 10 each) A/c	Dr.		500	
	To Equity Share Capital (₹ 5 each) A/c				125
	To Reconstruction A/c				375
	(Being the conversion of all the equity shares into the same number of equity shares of ₹ 5 each, ₹ 2.50 paid up as per scheme of reconstruction)				
(b)(i)	6% Cum-Preference Share Capital (₹ 100) A/c	Dr.		100	
	To 15% Cum-Pref. Share Capital (₹ 100) A/c				40
	To Reconstruction A/c				60
	(Being 40000 15% cum Pref. share of ₹ 100 each issued so as to maintain the same amount of dividend (i.e. ₹ 6 lacs) vide scheme of reconstruction dated.....)				
(b)(ii)	Reconstruction A/c	Dr.		1.8	
	To Equity Share Capital (₹ 5 each, ₹ 2.50 paid up) A/c				1.8
	(Being 72000 equity shares of ₹ 5 each, ₹ 2.50 paid up issued to pref. Shareholders for dividend arrears vide scheme of Reconstruction dated.....)				
(c)(i)	10% First Debentures A/c	Dr.		40	
	10% Second Debentures A/c	Dr.		60	
	Trade Creditors A/c	Dr.		10	
	Interest on Debentures Outstanding A/c	Dr.		10	
	To Mr. A				120
	(Being the total amount due to A t/f to his A/c)				
(c)(ii)	Bank A/c	Dr.		10	
	To Mr. A				10
	(Being the amount received from Mr. A under the Reconstruction Scheme)				

(c)(iii)	Mr. A A/c Dr. To 12% New Debentures A/c To Reconstruction A/c (Being ₹ 60 lacs due to A (Including creditors) cancelled and 12% new debentures allotted for balance amount as per scheme of reconstruction)	130	 70 60
(d)(i)	10% First Debentures A/c Dr. 10% Second Debentures A/c Dr. Trade Creditors A/c Dr. Interest on Debentures Outstanding A/c Dr. To Mr. B (Being the total amount due to Mr. B t/f to his A/c)	20 40 5 6	 71
d(ii)	Mr. B To 12% New Debentures A/c To Reconstruction A/c (Being ₹ 30 lacs due to B (including creditors) cancelled and 12% new debentures allotted for balance amount as per scheme of reconstruction)	71	 41 30
(e)	Trade Creditors A/c Dr. To Equity Share Capital (₹ 5 each, ₹ 2.50 paid up) A/c To Bank A/c To Reconstruction a/c (Being the Trade creditors for ₹ 60 lakhs accepted 24 lakhs shares of ₹ 5 each, ₹ 2.50 paid up for full amount and those for ₹.90 lakhs accepted cash equal to 80% of claim in full settlement)	150	 60 72 18
(f)	Reconstruction A/c Dr. To Bank A/c (Being payment made for cancellation of capital comments)	15	 15
(g)	Bank A/c Dr. To Reconstruction A/c (Being refund of fees by directors credited to Reconstruction A/c)	11	 11
(h)(i)	Bank A/c Dr. To Investment in 10% Government Loan A/c To Workmen's Compensation Fund (Bombay) A/c (Being the Sale of Investments for Workmen's Compensation Fund (Bombay) and the profit on the sale of same transferred to Workmen Compensation Fund (Bombay) Account)	0.88	 0.80 0.08

(h)(ii)	Workmen's Compensation Fund (Bombay) A/c Dr. To Reconstruction A/c (Being the Surplus in Workmen Compensation Fund at Bombay transferred to Reconstruction Account)		0.88	0.88
(h)(iii)	Provision for Tax A/c Dr. To Bank A/c To Reconstruction A/c (Being payment of tax liability in full settlement)		10	8.88 1.12
(j)	Reconstruction A/c Dr. To Investments in Shares in Q Ltd. A/c (Being reduction in the value of Investments)		1.15	1.15
(k)	No Journal Equity is to be passed			
(l)(i)	Capital Reserve A/c Dr. To Reconstruction A/c (Being the transfer of Capital Reserve for purpose of reconstruction)		6	6
(l)(ii)	Stock A/c Dr. To Reconstruction A/c (Being the Stock revalued)		8.40	8.40
(l)(iii)	Reconstruction A/c Dr. To Debtors To Provision for Doubtful Debts. (Being the Debtors revalued)		8.40	8.00 0.40
(l)(iv)	Reconstruction A/c Dr. To Goodwill A/c To Profit and Loss A/c To Plant & Machinery (balancing figure) (Being writing off of losses and reduction in the value of assets as per scheme of reconstruction)		544.05	10 16 518.05
(m)(i)	Equity Share First & Final Call A/c Dr. To Equity Share Capital A/c (Being the first & final call due on 74.72 lakhs Share @ ₹ 2.50)		186.80	186.80
(m)(ii)	Bank A/c Dr. To Equity Share First & Final Call A/c (Being the First & Final Call received)		186.80	186.80
(m)(iii)	Equity Share Capital (₹ 5 each) A/c Dr. To Equity Share Capital (₹ 10 each) A/c (Being the consolidation of 74.72 lakhs equity shares of ₹ 5 each into 37.36 lakhs equity shares of ₹ 10 each)		373.60	373.60

Working Notes:

(i) Valuation of Investments in Shares of Q Ltd.= (₹ 25 lacs/.12) × 15% = ₹ 31.25 lacs

(ii) Reduction in the Value of Investment in Shares of Q Ltd.

= ₹ 32.40 lacs – ₹.31.25 = ₹.1.15 lacs

(iii) *The transfer of 100 Shares by a dissentient shareholder to the director concerned and waiver of the right to arrears of pref., dividend need not be accounted for.*

Dr. **RECONSTRUCTION ACCOUNT** *Cr.*

Particulars	***₹ (lacs)***	***Particulars***	***₹ (lacs)***
To Equity Share Capital A/c (₹ 5 each)	1.80	By Equity Share Capital (₹ 10 each)	375.00
To Bank A/c	15.00	By 6% Cum. Pref. Share Capital	60.00
To Investment in Shares in Q Ltd.	1.15	By Mr. A (Sundries)	60.00
To Debtors	8.00	By Mr. B (Sundries)	30.00
To Provision for Doubtful Debts	0.40	By Trade Creditors	18.00
To Goodwill A/c	10.00	By Bank A/c	11.00
To Profit & Loss A/c	16.00	By Workmen's Compensation	
To Plant & Machinery A/c	518.05	Fund (Bombay) A/c	0.88
		By Provision for Tax A/c	1.12
		By Capital Reserve A/c	6.00
		By Stock A/c	8.40
	570.40		570.40

Dr. **BANK ACCOUNT** *Cr.*

Particulars	***₹ (lacs)***	***Particulars***	***₹ (lacs)***
To Balance b/d	104.00	By Trade Creditors	72.00
To Mr. A	10.00	By Reconstruction A/c	15.00
To Reconstruction A/c	11.00	By Provision for Tax	8.88
To Investment in Govt. Loan A/c	0.88	By Balance c/d	216.80
To Equity Share Capital A/c (₹ 5 each)	186.80		
	312.68		312.68

BALANCE SHEET OF ROAD BLOCK LTD. (AND REDUCED) AS AT 31.3.2023

Particulars	***Note No***	***₹ (lacs)***
I. Equity and Liabilities		
(1) Shareholders' Funds		
(a) Share Capital	1	413.60
(b) Reserves and Surplus [Workmen's Compensation Fund] [2.00 + 0.20]		2.20
(2) Non-Current Liabilities [12% Debentures]		111.00
(3) Current Liabilities		
Total		526.80

II. Assets		
(1) Non-Current Assets		
(a) Fixed Assets		
Tangible Assets [719.60 – 518.05 (Amt. w/o)]		201.55
Intangible Assets [Patents & Copy Rights]		5.00
(b) Non-Current Investments	2	33.45
(2) Current Assets		
(a) Inventories		68.40
(b) Trade Receivables [Debtors][2.00 – 0.40]		1.60
(c) Cash and Cash Equivalents		216.80
Total		526.80

Notes To Accounts:

Particulars	**₹ *(lacs)***
1. Share Capital	
37.36 lacs Equity Shares of ₹ 10 each	373.60
40,000,15% Pref. Shares of ₹ 100 each	40.00
	413.60
2. Non-Current Investments	
10% Govt. Loan earmarked against Workmen's Compensation Fund	2.20
Investments in Shares of Q Ltd.	31.25
	33.45

ILLUSTRATION 15

Given below are the extracts from the Balance Sheet of Unfortunate Bad Luck Ltd. as at 31.3.2023:

Particulars	₹
6% Cum-Pref. Shares of ₹ 100 each	1,00,000
Equity Shares of ₹ 100 each	8,00,000
Securities Premium	70,000
Capital Reserve	10,000
10% Debentures	14,00,000
Accrued Interest on Debentures	70,000
Sundry Creditors	4,50,000
Provision for Tax	10,000
Goodwill	1,00,000
Plant & Machinery	10,00,000
Other Fixed Assets	4,30,000

Investments	15,000
Stock	1,00,000
Sundry Debtors	40,000
Cash at Bank	25,000
Other Current Assets	80,000
P & L A/c(Dr)	10,60,000
Preliminary Expenses	30,000
Underwriting Commission	20,000
Discount on Issue of Shares & Debentures	10,000

Notes: (i) *Dividend on Preference shares are in arrears for three years.*

(ii) *There is a Bill receivable for ₹ 10,000 under discount. The bill was received from Z.*

The following scheme of reconstruction is sanctioned:

(a) Equity Shares to be sub-divided into shares of ₹ 10 each.

(b) Equity Shareholders to surrender 90% of their holdings.

(c) The preference shares are converted from 6% to 15% but revalued in a manner in which the total return on them remains unaffected.

(d) Five equity shares out of those surrendered to be issued for each ₹ 100 of arrears of preference dividend.

(e) The debentureholders agree to reduce their total claims to ₹ 5,00,000 in consideration of their getting equity shares of ₹ 5,00,000 out of the surrendered equity shares.

(f) Sundry Creditors agree to reduce their claims to 20% and 80% of the balance shall be satisfied by issue of equity shares out of those surrendered.

(g) The taxation liability was settled (but not discharged) at ₹ 15,000.

(h) Expenses of re-organization amounted to ₹ 10,000

(i) Z proved insolvent and a dividend of 10% was received from his estate.

(j) Shares surrendered and not re-issued to be cancelled.

(k) The balance in Securities Premium a/c and Capital Reserve A/c to be utilized.

(l) Goodwill is considered worthless.

(m) The company expected to earn profit @ ₹ 45,000 p.a. from the current year which would be utilized entirely for reducing the debit balance of profit & loss account for the next three consecutive years. The remaining balance of the said account would be written off at the time of Capital Reduction process.

(n) Plant & Machinery to be written down by 40%.

(o) Other fixed assets to be written down to ₹ 4,10,000.

(p) Stock to the extent of ₹ 10,000 considered to be obsolete.

(q) Debtors to the extent of ₹ 11,000 considered irrecoverable.

(r) Other current assets to be revalued at 75,000.

(s) Any surplus after writing off the various losses & reducing the value of over-valued assets, should be utilized in writing down value of plant & machinery further.

(t) A dissentient shareholder transferred his 100 shares to a director.

Required: Pass the necessary journal entries and prepare the Balance-Sheet reconstruction.

SOLUTION

JOURNAL OF UNFORTUNATE BAD LUCK LTD.

Date	Particulars		Dr. (₹)	Cr. (₹)
(a)	Equity Share Capital (₹ 100) A/c	Dr.	8,00,000	
	To Equity Share Capital (₹ 10) A/c			8,00,000
	(Being equity of ₹ 100 each converted into equity shares of ₹ 10 each vide scheme of reconstruction dated......)			
(b)	Equity Share Capital (₹ 10) A/c	Dr.	7,20,000	
	To Shares Surrendered A/c			7,20,000
	(Being 90% of equity shares surrendered vide scheme of reconstruction dated.....)			
(c)	6% Cum-preference Shares Capital (₹ 100) A/c	Dr.	1,00,000	
	To 15% Cum-Pref. Share capital (₹ 100) A/c			40,000
	To Reconstruction A/c			60,000
	(Being 400 15% cum Pref. share of ₹ 100 each issued so as to maintain the same amount of dividend (i.e. ₹ 6,000) vide scheme of reconstruction dated.....)			
(d)	Shares Surrendered A/c	Dr.	9,000	
	To Equity Share Capital (₹ 10) A/c			9,000
	(Being 900 equity shares out of those surrendered issued to pref. Shareholders on their surrendering a claim for arrears vide scheme of Reconstruction dated.....)			
(e)(i)	10% Debentures A/c	Dr.	9,00,000	
	Accrued Interest on Debentures A/c	Dr.	70,000	
	To Reconstruction A/c			9,70,000
	(Being the amount sacrificed by debentureholders as per reconstruction scheme dated......)			
(e)(ii)	Shares surrendered A/c	Dr.	5,00,000	
	To Equity shares capital (₹ 10) A/c			5,00,000
	(Being 50,000 equity shares out of those surrendered issued to debentureholders on their surrendering a claim of 9,70,000)			
(f)(i)	Shares Surrendered A/c	Dr.	72,000	
	To Equity Share Capital (₹ 10) A/c			72,000
	(Being 7,200 Equity shares out of those surrendered issued to creditors in part satisfaction of their balance claim)			
(f)(ii)	Sundry Creditors A/c	Dr.	4,32,000	
	To Reconstruction A/c			4,32,000
	(Being total reduction in the claim of sundry creditors from 4,50,000 to ₹ 18,000)			
(g)(i)	Reconstruction A/c	Dr.	5,000	

	To Provision for Tax A/c (Being the writing up the provision for tax as per Reconstruction scheme dated.......)			5,000
(g)(ii)	Provision for Tax A/c To Tax Payable A/c (Being the conversion of provision into settled liability)	Dr.	15,000	15,000
(h)	Reconstruction A/c To Bank A/c (Being the reconstruction expenses paid)	Dr.	10,000	10,000
(i)(i)	Z To Bank A/c (Being the discounted B/R dishonoured)	Dr.	10,000	10,000
(i)(ii)	Bank A/c Reconstruction A/c To Z A/c (Being the ₹ 1,000 received from Z in respect of Discounted B/R met)	Dr. Dr.	1,000 9,000	10,000
(j)	Shares Surrendered A/c To Reconstruction A/c (Being shares surrendered but not re-issued cancelled)	Dr.	1,39,000	1,39,000
(k)	Capital Reserve A/c Securities Premium A/c To Reconstruction A/c (Being the transfer of balances of Capital Reserve A/c and Share Premium A/c vide Scheme of reconstruction dated......)	Dr. Dr.	10,000 70,000	80,000
(l to s)	Reconstruction A/c To Goodwill A/c To P & L A/c[10,40,000 -(45,000 x 3)] To Preliminary Expenses A/c To Underwriting Commission A/c To Discount on Issue of Shares/Deb. A/c To Other fixed assets To Stock To Debtors To Other Current Assets To Plant & Machinery (Being the balance of Reconstruction A/c utilized to written off various losses & to reduce the value of various overvalued assets vide Reconstruction scheme dated.....)	Dr.	16,57,000	 1,00,000 9,25,000 30,000 20,000 10,000 20,000 10,000 11,000 5,000 5,26,000

BALANCE SHEET OF UNFOTUNATE BAD LUCK LTD. (AND REDUCED) AS AT 31.3.2023

Particulars	***Note No***	₹
I. Equity and Liabilities		
(1) Shareholders' Funds		
(a) Share Capital	1	7,01,000
(b) Reserves and Surplus [Profit & Loss A/c (Dr.)]		(1,35,000)
(2) Non-Current Liabilities [10%Debentures]		5,00,000
(3) Current Liabilities		
(a) Trade Payables[Creditors]		18,000
(b) Short-term Provisions [Provision for Tax]		15,000
Total		10,99,000
II. Assets		
(1) Non-Current Assets		
(a) Fixed Assets		
Tangible Assets	2	8,84,000
Intangible Assets [Goodwill] [1,00,000 -1,00,000 (Amt. w/o)]		0
(b) Non-Current Investments		15,000
(2) Current Assets		
(a) Inventories		90,000
(b) Trade Receivables [Debtors]		29,000
(c) Cash and Cash Equivalents		6,000
(d) Other Current Assets		75,000
Total		10,99,000

Notes To Accounts:

Particulars		₹
1. Share Capital		
66100 Equity Shares of ₹ 10 each,₹ paid		6,61,000
400,15% Pref. Shares of ₹ 100 each, ₹ paid		40,000
	7,01,000	
2. Tangible Assets		
Plant & Machinery	10,00,000	
Less: Amt. w/o under Reconstruction Scheme	5,26,000	4,74,000
Other Fixed Assets	4,30,000	
Less: Amt. w/o under Reconstruction Scheme	20,000	4,10,000
Total		8,84,000

Note: *The transfer of 100 Shares by a dissentient shareholder to the director concerned and waiver of the right to arrears of pref., dividend need not be accounted for.*

Working Notes:

(i) *Calculation of the amount of Shares Surrendered to be transferred to Reconstruction Account.*

Dr. **SHARES SURRENDERED ACCOUNT** Cr.

Particulars	₹	Particulars	₹
To Equity Shares Capital A/c (Issued to Debentureholders)	5,00,000	By Equity Share Capital A/c (₹ 10)	7,20,000
To Equity Shares Capital A/c (Issued to sundry Creditors)	72,000		
To Equity Share Capital A/c (Issued to Pref. Shareholders)	9,000		
To Reconstruction A/c (b.f.)	1,39,000		
	7,20,000		7,20,000

(ii) *Calculation of Debit Balance of P & L A/c to be written off now*

= ₹ 10,60,000 – (₹ 45,000 × 3) = ₹ 9,25,000.

(iii) *Calculation of the amount by which the value of Plant & Machinery is to be written down*

Dr. **RECONSTRUCTION ACCOUNT** Cr.

Particulars	₹	Particulars	₹
To Provision for tax	5,000	By 6% Cum Pref. Share Capital A/c	60,000
To Bank A/c (Expenses)	10,000	By 10% Debentures A/c	9,00,000
To Bank A/c (Discounted B/R)	9,000	By Accrued Interest	70,000
To Goodwill A/c	1,00,000	By Sundry Creditors	4,32,000
To P & L A/c	9,25,000	By Share Surrendered A/c	1,39,000
To Preliminary Expenses	30,000	By Capital Reserve A/c	10,000
To Underwriting Commission	20,000	By Securities Premium A/c	70,000
To Discount on Issue of Shares/ Deb. A/c	10,000		
To Other Fixed Assets	20,000		
To Stock	10,000		
To Debtors	11,000		
To Other Current Assets	5,000		
To Plant & Machinery (b.f.)	5,26,000		
	16,81,000		16,81,000

SOLVED PROBLEMS

PROBLEM 1

The following is the balance sheet of CSJHB Ltd. as at 31st March, 2023:

Particulars		₹
Share Capital:		
Authorised:		
30,000 Equity Shares of ₹ 10 each		3,00,000
30,000, 13% Pref. Shares of ₹ 10 each		3,00,000
		6,00,000
Subscribed, Issued and Paid-up:		
20,000 Equity Shares of ₹ 10 each fully paid		2,00,000
18,000 13% Pref. Shares of ₹ 10 fully paid		1,80,000
Reserves & Surplus:		
Workmen's compensation fund:		
Pune	20,000	
Bombay	10,000	30,000
Secured loans:		
12% 'A' Debentures secured on Pune Property	30,000	
12% 'B' Debentures secured on Bombay Property	35,000	65,000
Current Liabilities & Provisions:		
(A) Current Liabilities:		
Sundry Creditors		25,000
(B) Provisions:		
Fixed Assets:		
Pune Property		1,60,000
Bombay Property		1,20,000
Plant and Machinery		1,50,000
Investments:		
10% Government loan earmarked against Workmen's compensation Fund		30,000
Miscellaneous expenditure and losses:		
Profit and Loss Account		40,000

The following scheme of reconstruction was duly approved:

(a) Equity shares were to be reduced to ₹ 1 each.

(b) Preference shares were to be reduced by ₹ 2 per share.

(c) Debentureholders were to forgo their unpaid interest ₹ 5,200 which is included in sundry creditors.

(d) 'B' Debentureholders agreed to take over the Bombay property at ₹ 50,000 and paid the balance amount due from them in cash.

(e) Workmen's compensation fund (Bombay) disclosed the fact that actually there was a liability of ₹ 2,000 only. As a result the relevant fund amount balance was to be brought down to the required amount. Investments were realised at 10% above the book value.

(f) The Plant and machinery were to be written down by ₹ 90,000.

(g) Any balance remaining was to be applied as to 75% in writing down Pune property and 25% transferred to capital reserve.

Required: Pass the necessary journal entries and prepare the Balance Sheet after reconstruction.

SOLUTION

JOURNAL

Particulars		L.F.	Dr. (₹)	Cr. (₹)
Equity Share Capital (Old) A/c	Dr.		2,00,000	
Preference Share Capital A/c	Dr.		36,000	
To Equity Share Capital (New) A/c				20,000
To Reconstruction A/c				2,16,000
(Being the reduction of 20,000 equity shares of ₹ 10 each to ₹ 1 and 18,000 13% preference shares by ₹ 2 per share vide special Resolution No..... dated .... confirmed by court vide order dated......)				
Sundry Creditors A/c	Dr.		5,200	
To Reconstruction A/c				5,200
(Being the Cancellation of debenture interest)				
12% 'B ' Debentures A/c	Dr.		35,000	
To 'B ' Debentureholders A/c				35,000
(Being Transfer of 'B ' Debentures to debentureholders)				
₹B' Debentureholders A/c	Dr.		35,000	
Bank A/c	Dr.		15,000	
To Bombay Property				50,000
(Being the Payment to 'B ' debentureholders by transfer of Bombay Property, the balance received from them in cash)				
Bank A/c	Dr.		8,800	
To Investment in 10% Government Loan A/c				8,000
To Workmen's Compensation Fund (Bombay) A/c				800
[Being the Sale of investments for workmen's compensation fund (Bombay) and the profit on the sale of same transferred to workmen compensation fund (Bombay) account]				
Workmen's Compensation Fund (Bombay) A/c	Dr.		8,800	
To Reconstruction A/c				8,800
(Being the Surplus in workmen compensation fund at Bombay transferred to reconstruction account)				
Reconstruction A/c	Dr.		2,30,000	
To Profit and Loss A/c				40,000
To Plant and Machinery A/c				90,000
To Bombay Property				70,000
To Pune Property				22,500
To Capital Reserve A/c				7,500
(Being the utilisation of the amount available in the reconstruction account to write off the debit balance in the profit and loss account and to write down the value of various assets as per scheme of reconstruction)				

BALANCE SHEET OF CSJHB LTD. (AND REDUCED) AS AT 31.03.2023

Particulars	*Note No*	₹
I. Equity and Liabilities		
(1) Shareholders' Funds		
(a) Share Capital (₹ 10 each)	1	1,64,000
(b) Reserves and Surplus	2	29,500
(2) Non-Current Liabilities [10%Debentures]		30,000
(3) Current Liabilities		
(a) Trade Payables[Creditors]		19,800
Total		2,43,300
II. Assets		
(1) Non-Current Assets		
(a) Fixed Assets		
Tangible Assets	3	1,97,500
(b) Non-Current Investments[10% Govt. Loan]		22,000
(2) Current Assets		
(a) Cash and Cash Equivalents		23,800
Total		2,43,300

Notes To Accounts:

Particulars		₹
1. Share Capital		
20000 Equity Shares of ₹ 1 each		20,000
18000,15% Pref. Shares of ₹ 10 each, ₹ 8 paid		1,44,000
		1,64,000
2. Reserves and Surplus		
Capital Reserve		7,500
[Workmen's Compensation Fund] [20,000 + 2,000]		22,000
Total		29,500
3. Tangible Assets		
Pune Property	1,60,000	
Less: Amt. w/o under Reconstruction Scheme	22,500	1,37,500
Plant & Machinery	1,50,000	
Less: Amt. w/o under Reconstruction Scheme	90,000	60,000
Total		1,97,500

PROBLEM 2

Green Limited had decided to reconstruct the Balance Sheet since it has accumulated huge losses. The following is the Balance Sheet of the Company on 31.3.2023 before reconstruction:

BALANCE SHEET OF GREEN LIMITED AS AT 31.3.2023

Particulars	₹
Share Capital:	
Authorised:	
1,50,000 Equity Shares of ₹ 50 each	75,00,000
Subscribed 50,000 Equity Shares of ₹ 50 each	25,00,000
1,00,000 Equity Shares of ₹ 50 each, ₹ 40 per share paid up	40,00,000
Secured Loans:	
12% First Debentures	5,00,000
12% Second Debentures	10,00,000
Current Liabilities:	
Sundry Creditors	5,00,000
Fixed Assets:	
Goodwill	20,00,000
Building	10,00,000
Plant	10,00,000
Computers	25,00,000
Investments	Nil
Current Assets	Nil
Profit and Loss A/c (Loss)	20,00,000

The Following is the interest of Mr. X and Mr. Y in Green Limited:

Particulars	*Mr. X* ₹	*Mr. Y* ₹
12% First Debentures	3,00,000	2,00,000
12% Second Debentures	7,00,000	3,00,000
Sundry Creditors	2,00,000	1,00,000
	12,00,000	6,00,000
Fully paid up ₹ 50 shares	3,00,000	2,00,000
Partly paid shares (₹ 40 paid up)	5,00,000	5,00,000

The following Scheme of Reconstruction is approved by all parties interested and also by the Court:

(a) Uncalled capital is to be called up in full and such shares and the other fully paid up shares be converted into equity shares of ₹ 20 each.

(b) Mr. X is to cancel ₹ 7,00,000 of his total debt (other than share amount) and to pay ₹ 2 lakhs to the company and to receive new 14% First Debentures for the balance amount.

(c) Mr. Y is to cancel ₹ 3,00,000 of his total debt (other than equity shares) and to accept new 14% First Debentures for the balance.

(d) The amount thus rendered available by the scheme shall be utilised in writing off of Goodwill, Profit and Loss A/c Loss and the balance to write off the value of computers.

Required: Pass the Journal Entries and prepare the Balance Sheet of the reconstructed company.

SOLUTION

JOURNAL

Particulars		*L.F.*	*Dr. (₹)*	*Cr. (₹)*
Bank A/c	Dr.		10,00,000	
To Equity Share Capital A/c				10,00,000
(Being the balance of ₹ 10 per share on 1,00,000 equity shares called up as per reconstruction scheme)				
Equity Share Capital A/c (₹ 50)	Dr.		75,00,000	
To Equity Share Capital A/c (₹ 20)				30,00,000
To Capital Reduction A/c				45,00,000
(Being the reduction of equity shares of ₹ 50 each to shares of ₹ 20 each as per reconstruction scheme)				
12% First Debentures A/c	Dr.		3,00,000	
12% Second Debentures A/c	Dr.		7,00,000	
Sundry Creditors A/c	Dr.		2,00,000	
To X				12,00,000
(Being the total amount due to X, transferred to his account)				
Bank A/c	Dr.		2,00,000	
To X				2,00,000
(Being the amount paid by X under the reconstruction scheme)				
12% First Debentures A/c	Dr.		2,00,000	
12% Second Debentures A/c	Dr.		3,00,000	
Sundry Creditors A/c	Dr.		1,00,000	
To Y				6,00,000
(Being the total amount due to Y, transferred to his account)				
X	Dr.		14,00,000	
To 14% First Debentures A/c				7,00,000
To Capital Reduction A/c				7,00,000
(Being the cancellation of ₹ 7,00,000 out of total debt of Mr. X and issue of 14% first debentures for the balance amount as per reconstruction scheme)				
Y	Dr.		6,00,000	
To 14% First Debentures A/c				3,00,000
To Capital Reduction A/c				3,00,000
(Being the cancellation of ₹ 3,00,000 out of total debt of Mr. Y and issue of 14% first debentures for the balance amount as per reconstruction scheme)				
Capital Reduction A/c	Dr.		55,00,000	
To Goodwill A/c				20,00,000
To Profit and Loss A/c				20,00,000
To Computers A/c (balancing figure)				15,00,000
(Being the balance amount of capital reduction account utilised in writing off goodwill, profit and loss account, and computers)				

BALANCE SHEET OF GREEN LTD. (AND REDUCED) AS AT 31.03.2023

Particulars	*Note No*	₹
I. Equity and Liabilities		
(1) Shareholders' Funds		
(a) Share Capital (₹ 10 each)		30,00,000
(2) Non-Current Liabilities[14% Debentures]		10,00,000
(3) Current Liabilities		
(a) Trade Payables[Creditors]		2,00,000
Total		42,00,000
II. Assets		
(1) Non-Current Assets		
(a) Fixed Assets		
Tangible Assets	3	30,00,000
(2) Current Assets		
(a) Cash and Cash Equivalents		12,00,000
Total		42,00,000

Notes To Accounts:

1. Tangible Assets	
Land & Building	10,00,000
Plant & Machinery	10,00,000
Computers	10,00,000
Total	30,00,000

Working Note:

Dr. **CAPITAL REDUCTION ACCOUNT** *Cr.*

Particulars	₹	*Particulars*	₹
To Goodwill A/c	20,00,000	By Equity Share Capital A/c	45,00,000
To P & L A/c	20,00,000	By X	7,00,000
To Computers (Bal. Fig.)	15,00,000	By Y	3,00,000
	55,00,000		55,00,000

PROBLEM 3

The following is the Balance Sheet of Rocky Ltd. as at March 31, 2023:

Particulars	₹ *in lacs*
Fully paid Equity Shares of ₹ 10 each	500
Capital Reserve	6
12% Debentures	400
Debenture Interest Outstanding	48

Trade Creditors	165
Director's Remuneration Outstanding	10
Other Outstanding Expenses	11
Provisions	33
Goodwill	15
Land and Building	184
Plant and Machinery	286
Furniture and Fixtures	41
Stock	142
Debtors	80
Cash at Bank	27
Discount on Issue of Debentures	8
Profits and Loss Account	390

The following scheme of internal reconstruction was framed, approved by the Court, all the concerned parties and implemented:

(i) All the equity shares be converted into the same number of fully-paid equity shares of ₹ 2.50 each.

(ii) Directors agree to forego their outstanding remuneration.

(iii) The debentureholders also agree to forego outstanding interest in return of their 12% debentures being converted into 13% debentures.

(iv) The existing shareholders agree to subscribe for cash, fully paid equity shares of ₹ 2.50 each for ₹ 125 lacs.

(v) Trade creditors are given the option of either to accept fully-paid equity shares of ₹ 2.50 each for the amount due to them *or* to accept 80% of the amount due in cash. Creditors for ₹ 65 lacs accept equity shares whereas those for ₹ 100 lacs accept ₹ 80 lacs in cash in full settlement.

(vi) The Assets are revalued as under:

Particulars	*₹ in lacs*
Land and building	230
Plant and Machinery	220
Stock	120
Debtors	76

Required: Pass Journal Entries and prepare Balance Sheet after reconstruction.

SOLUTION

JOURNAL *[₹ in lacs]*

Particulars	*L.F.*	*Dr. (₹)*	*Cr. (₹)*
Equity Share Capital (₹ 10 each) A/c Dr.		500	
To Equity Share Capital (₹ 2.50 each) A/c			125
To Reconstruction A/c			375
(Being the conversion of all the equity shares into the same number of fully paid equity shares of ₹ 2.50 each as per scheme of reconstruction)			

Particulars		Dr. (₹)	Cr. (₹)
Director's Remuneration Outstanding A/c	Dr.	10	
To Reconstruction A/c			10
(Being the outstanding remuneration foregone by the directors as per scheme of reconstruction)			
12% Debentures A/c	Dr.	400	
Debenture Interest Outstanding A/c	Dr.	48	
To 13% Debentures A/c			400
To Reconstruction A/c			48
(Being the conversion of 12% debentures into 13% debentures, Debentureholders forgoing outstanding debenture interest)			
Bank	Dr.	125	
To Equity Share Application and Allotment A/c			125
(Being the application money received for equity shares)			
Equity Share Application and Allotment A/c	Dr.	125	
To Equity Share Capital (₹ 2.50 each) A/c			125
(Being the application money transferred to share capital)			
Trade Creditors A/c	Dr.	165	
To Equity Share Capital (₹ 2.50 each) A/c			65
To Bank A/c			80
To Reconstruction A/c			20
(Being the Trade creditors for ₹ 65 lakhs accepting shares for full amount and those for ₹ 100 lakhs accepting cash equal to 80% of claim in full settlement)			
Capital Reserve A/c	Dr.	6	
To Reconstruction A/c			6
(Being the Capital Reserve being used for purpose of reconstruction)			
Land and Building	Dr.	46	
To Reconstruction A/c			46
(Being the appreciation made in the value of land and building as per scheme of reconstruction)			
Reconstruction A/c	Dr.	505	
To Goodwill			15
To Plant and Machinery			66
To Stock			22
To Debtors			4
To Discount on issue of Debentures			8
To Profit and Loss A/c			390
(Being the writing off losses and reduction in the values of assets as per scheme of reconstruction)			

BALANCE SHEET OF ROCKY LTD. (AND REDUCED) AS AT 31.03.2023

Particulars	Note No	₹
I. Equity and Liabilities		
(1) Shareholders' Funds		
(a) Share Capital (₹ 10 each)	1	315
(b) Reserves and Surplus		
(2) Non-Current Liabilities [13% Debentures]		400
(3) Current Liabilities		
(a) Trade Payables[Creditors]		
(b) Short-term Provisions		33
(c) Other Current Liabilities [O/S Expenses]		11
Total		759
II. Assets		
(1) Non-Current Assets		
(a) Fixed Assets		
Tangible Assets	2	491
Intangible Assets [Goodwill] [15 – 15]		0
(2) Current Assets		
(a) Inventories		120
(b) Trade Receivables [Debtors – Prov] [80 – 4]		76
(c) Cash and Cash Equivalents		72
Total		759

Notes To Accounts:

Particulars		₹
1. Share Capital		
126000 Equity Shares of ₹ 2.50 each (Of the above 26000 Shares were issued for consideration otherwise than cash)		315
2. Tangible Assets		
Land & Building	184	
Add: Amt. increased under Reconstruction Scheme	46	230
Plant & Machinery	286	
Less: Amt. w/o under Reconstruction Scheme	66	220
Furniture& Fixtures		41
Total		491

Working Notes:

Dr. **(I) REDUCTION ACCOUNT** *(₹ in lacs) Cr.*

Particulars	₹	Particulars	₹
To Goodwill	15	By Equity Share Capital A/c	375
To Plant and Machinery	66	By Director's Remuneration	

To Stock	22	By Outstanding A/c	10
To Debtors	4	By Deben. Interest Outstanding	48
To Discount on issue of Debentures	8	By Trade Creditors	20
To Profit and Loss A/c	390	By Capital Reserve	6
		By Land and Building	46
	505		505

(ii) Equity share capital (after reconstruction)	₹
Equity Share Capital (₹ 2.50 each)	125
Add: Fresh issue	125
Add: Equity share issued to creditors	65
	315
(iii) Cash at bank (after reconstruction)	
Cash at bank (before reconstruction)	27
Add: Proceeds from issue of equity shares	125
	152
Less: Payment made to creditors	80
	72

PROBLEM 4

Following are the extracts of Balance Sheets as at March 31, 2023:

(₹ '000)

Particulars	*K Ltd.*	*W Ltd.*
Share capital:		
Equity Shares of ₹ 100 each	2,000	1,500
10% Preference Shares of ₹ 100 each	700	400
General Reserve	240	170
Profit & Loss A/c	—	15
12% Debentures of ₹ 100 each	600	200
Sundry Creditors	560	315
Goodwill	20	—
Other Fixed Assets	2,400	1,150
Debtors	625	615
Stock	412	680
Cash at bank	38	155
Own debentures [Nominal value ₹ 2,00,000]	192	—
Discount on issue of debentures	2	—
Profit & Loss A/c	411	—

On 1.4.2023, K Ltd. adopted the following scheme of reconstruction:

(a) Each equity share shall be sub-divided into 10 equity shares of ₹ 10 each fully paid up. 50% of the equity share capital would be surrendered to the company.

(b) Preference dividends are in arrear for 3 years. Preference shareholders agreed to waive 80% of the dividend claim and accept payment for the balance.

(c) Own debentures of ₹ 80,000 were sold at ₹ 98 cum-interest and remaining own debentures were cancelled.

(d) Debentureholders of ₹ 3,00,000 agreed to accept one machinery of book value of ₹ 3,20,000 in full settlement.

(e) Creditors, Debtors and Stocks were valued at ₹ 5,00,000, ₹ 6,00,000 and ₹ 4,00,000 respectively. The goodwill, discount on issue of Debentures & Profit and Loss (Dr.) are to be written off.

(f) The Company paid ₹ 20,000 as penalty to avoid capital commitments of ₹ 4,00,000.

On 2.4.2023 a scheme of absorption was adopted. K Ltd. would take over W Ltd. The purchase consideration was fixed as below:

(i) Equity shareholders of W Ltd. will be given 50 equity shares of ₹ 10 each fully paid up, in exchange for every 5 shares held in W Ltd.

(ii) Issue of 10% Preference Shares of ₹ 100 each in the ratio of 4 Preference Shares of K Ltd. for every 5 Preference Shares held in W Ltd.

(iii) Issue of one 12% Debentures of ₹ 100 each of K Ltd. for every 12% Debentures in W Ltd.

Required: Give journal entries in the books of K Ltd. and draw the resultant Balance Sheet as at 2nd April, 2023.

SOLUTION

JOURNAL

Date	Particulars	L.F.	Dr. (₹)	Cr. (₹)
01.04.2023	Equity Share Capital A/c Dr.		20,00,000	
	To Equity Share Capital A/c			20,00,000
	(Being the sub-division of one share of ₹ 100 each into 10 shares of ₹ 10 each)			
	Equity Share Capital A/c Dr.		10,00,000	
	To Reconstruction A/c			10,00,000
	(Being the reduction of capital by 50%)			
	Reconstruction A/c Dr.		42,000	
	To Bank A/c			42,000
	(Being the payment in cash for 20% of arrears of preference dividend)			
	Bank A/c Dr.		78,400	
	To Own Debentures A/c [(1,92,000/2,00,000) × 80,000]			76,800
	To Reconstruction A/c			1,600
	(Being the T/f of profit on sale of own Debentures)			

Date	Particulars		L.F.	Dr. (₹)	Cr. (₹)
	12% Debentures A/c	Dr.		1,20,000	
	To Own debentures A/c [(1,92,000/2,00,000) × 1,20,000]				1,15,200
	To Reconstruction A/c				4,800
	(Being the T/f of profit on cancellation of own Debentures)				
	12.% Debentures A/c	Dr.		3,00,000	
	Reconstruction A/c	Dr.		20,000	
	To Machinery A/c				3,20,000
	(Being the machinery taken up by debentureholders)				
	Reconstruction A/c	Dr.		37,000	
	To Debtors A/c				25,000
	To Stock A/c				12,000
	(Being the Assets revalued)				
	Creditors A/c	Dr.		60,000	
	To Reconstruction A/c				60,000
	(Being the liabilities revalued)				
	Reconstruction A/c	Dr.		4,33,000	
	To Goodwill A/c				20,000
	To Discount on debentures A/c				2,000
	To Profit and Loss A/c				4,11,000
	(Being the losses w/o)				
	Reconstruction A/c	Dr.		20,000	
	To Bank A/c				20,000
	(Being the penalty paid for avoidance of capital commitments)				
	Reconstruction A/c	Dr.		5,14,400	
	To Capital Reserve A/c				5,14,400
	(Being the transfer of Balance to Capital Reserve)				
02.04.2023	Business Purchase A/c	Dr.		18,20,000	
	To Liquidators of W Ltd.				18,20,000
	(Being the purchase of business)				
	Fixed assets A/c	Dr.		11,50,000	
	Stock A/c	Dr.		6,80,000	
	Debtors A/c	Dr.		6,15,000	
	Cash at bank A/c	Dr.		1,55,000	
	To Sundry Creditors A/c				3,15,000
	To 12% Debentures A/c of W Ltd.				2,00,000
	To Profit and loss A/c				15,000

	To General Reserve A/c ₹ (1,70,000 + 80,000*)			2,50,000
	To Business Purchase A/c			18,20,000
	(Being the recording over of all assets and liabilities taken over)			
	Liquidators of W Ltd. A/c Dr.		18,20,000	
	To Equity share capital A/c			15,00,000
	To 10% Preference share capital A/c			3,20,000
	(Being the purchase consideration discharged)			
	12% Debentures of W Ltd. A/c Dr.		2,00,000	
	To 12% Debentures A/c			2,00,000
	(Being the issue of 12% Debentures against Debentures of W Ltd.)			

**₹ 80,000 is the balancing figure adjusted to General Reserve Account as per AS 14 "Accounting for Amalgamation".

BALANCE SHEET OF K LTD. AS AT 02.04.2023

Particulars	***Note No***	₹
I. Equity and Liabilities		
(1) Shareholders' Funds		
(a) Share Capital	1	35,20,000
(b) Reserves and Surplus	2	10,19,400
(2) Non-Current Liabilities [12%Debentures]	3	3,80,000
(3) Current Liabilities		
(a) Trade Payables [Creditors]	4	8,15,000
Total		57,34,400
II. Assets		
(1) Non-Current Assets		
(a) Fixed Assets		
Tangible Assets	5	32,30,000
(2) Current Assets		
(a) Inventories	6	10,80,000
(b) Trade Receivables [Debtors]	7	12,15,000
(c) Cash and Cash Equivalents	8	2,09,400
Total		57,34,400

Notes To Accounts:

Particulars	₹
1. Share Capital	
2,50,000 Equity Shares of ₹ 10 each	25,00,000
10,200,9% Pref. Shares of ₹ 100 each	10,20,000
(Of the above 1,50,000 Equity Shares & 3200,9% Pref. Shares were issued for consideration otherwise than cash)	
Total	35,20,000

2. Reserves and Surplus	
General Reserve (2,40,000 + 2,50,000)	4,90,000
Profit & Loss Account	15,000
Capital Reserve	5,14,400
Total	10,19,400
3. Long-term Borrowings	
12% Debentures	6,00,000
Less: Settled in consideration of machinery	(3,00,000)
Less: Cancelled debentures	(1,20,000)
Add: 12% Debentures issue to W Ltd.	2,00,000
Total	3,80,000
4. Trade Payables	
of K Ltd.	5,60,000
Less: Reduction due to revaluation	(60,000)
Add: Trade Payables of W Ltd.	3,15,000
Total	8,15,000
5. Tangible assets	
Balance of Other Fixed Assets	24,00,000
Less: Machinery taken up by debenture holders	(3,20,000)
Add: Other Fixed Assets of W Ltd.	11,50,000
Total	32,30,000
6. Inventories	
of K Ltd.	4,12,000
Less: Reduction due to revaluation	(12,000)
Add: Inventories of W Ltd.	6,80,000
Total	10,80,000
7. Trade Receivables	
of K Ltd.	6,25,000
Less: Reduction due to revaluation	(25,000)
Add: Trade Receivables of W Ltd.	6,15,000
Total	12,15,000
8. Cash and Cash Equivalents	
of K Ltd.	38,000
Less: Payment of Arrear of Preference dividend	(42,000)
Add: Profit on Sale of own Debentures	78,400
Less: Penalty Paid	(20,000)
Add: Cash and Cash Equivalents of W Ltd.	1,55,000
Total	2,09,400

Working Notes:

	₹
(i) Purchase Consideration:	
Equity share capital [(15,000 × 50/5) × ₹ 10]	15,00,000
9% Preference share capital [(4,000 × 4/5) × ₹ 100]	3,20,000
	18,20,000
(ii) General Reserve:	₹
Share capital of W Ltd. (Equity + Preference)	19,00,000
Less: Share capital issued by K Ltd.	18,20,000
General reserve (resulted due to absorption)	80,000

PROBLEM 5

The summarized Balance Sheet of Bad Luck Ltd. as on 31st March, 2023 was as follows:

Particulars	*Note No*	*₹ (lacs)*
I. Equity and Liabilities		
(1) Shareholders' Funds		
(a) Share Capital	1	7.50
(b) Reserves and Surplus	2	(10.00)
(2) Non-Current Liabilities (Long-term Borrowings)	3	5.00
(3) Current Liabilities		
(a) Short-term Borrowings	4	5.00
(b) Trade Payables [Creditors]		2.50
Total		10.00
II. Assets		
(1) Non-Current Assets		
(a) Fixed Assets		
Tangible Assets	5	5.50
Intangible Assets [Goodwill]	6	1.50
(2) Current Assets		
(a) Inventories		1.50
(b) Trade Receivables		1.25
(c) Deferred revenue expenditure		0.25
Total		10.00

Notes To Accounts:

Particulars	*₹ (lacs)*
1. Share Capital	
5000 Equity Shares of ₹ 100 each	5.00
2500, 8% Pref. Shares of ₹ 100 each	2.50
	7.50

2. Reserves and Surplus (Profit and Loss A/c)	(10.00)
3. Long-term Borrowings (8% Debentures)	5.00
4. Short-term Borrowings	
Loan from Directors	3.00
Bank Overdraft	2.00
	5.00
5. Tangible Assets	
Freehold Property	4.00
Plant & Machinery	1.50
Total	5.50
6. Intangible Assets	
Goodwill	1.00
Trademark	0.50
	1.50

The following scheme of internal reconstruction was framed, approved by the Court, all the concerned parties and implemented:

(i) The preference shares to be written down to ₹ 25 each and the equity shares to ₹ 20 each. Each class of shares then to be converted into shares of ₹ 100 each.

(ii) The debenture holders to take over freehold property (book value ₹ 2,00,000) at a valuation of ₹ 2,50,000 in part repayment of their holdings. Remaining freehold property to be revalued at ₹ 6,00,000.

(iii) Loan from directors to be waived off in full.

(iv) Stock of ₹ 50,000 to be written off, ₹ 12,500 to be provided for bad debts.

(v) Profit and Loss account balance, Trademark, Goodwill and Deferred Revenue Expenditure to be written off.

Pass Journal Entries for all the above mentioned transactions. Also, Prepare Capital Reduction account and company's Balance Sheet immediately after reconstruction.

SOLUTION

JOURNAL OF BAD LUCK LTD.

Date	*Particulars*		*Dr. (₹)*	*Cr. (₹)*
(i)	8% Preference Share Capital A/c (₹ 100)	Dr.	2,50,000	
	To 8% Preference Share Capital A/c (₹ 25)			62,500
	To Capital Reduction A/c			1,87,500
	(Being preference shares of ₹100 each reduced to ₹ 25 each as per the scheme)			
(ii)	Equity Share Capital A/c (₹ 100)	Dr.	5,00,000	
	To Equity Share Capital A/c (₹ 20)			1,00,000
	To Capital Reduction A/c			4,00,000
	(Being equity shares of ₹ 100 each reduced to ₹ 20 each as per the scheme)			

(iii)	8% Preference Share Capital A/c (₹ 25)	Dr.	62,500	
	To 8% Preference Share Capital A/c (₹ 100)			62,500
	(Being the conversion of 2,500 shares of ₹ 25 each into 625 shares of ₹ 100 each as per the scheme)			
(iv)	Equity Share Capital A/c (₹ 20)	Dr.	1,00,000	
	To Equity Share Capital A/c (₹ 100)			1,00,000
	(Being the conversion of 5,000 shares of ₹ 20 each in to 1,000 shares of ₹ 100 each as per the scheme)			
(v)	Freehold Property A/c	Dr.	50,000	
	To Capital Reduction A/c			50,000
	(Being appreciation in the value of property)			
(vi)	8% Debentures A/c	Dr.	2,50,000	
	To Freehold Property A/c			2,50,000
	(Being claim of debentureholders settled in part by transfer of freehold property as per the scheme)			
(vii)	Freehold Property A/c	Dr.	4,00,000	
	To Capital Reduction A/c			4,00,000
	(Being appreciation in the value of remaining property)			
(viii)	Director's Loan A/c	Dr.	3,00,000	
	To Capital Reduction A/c			3,00,000
	(Being Director's loan waived in full)			
(ix)	Capital Reduction A/c	Dr.	13,37,500	
	To Profit and Loss A/c			10,00,000
	To Deferred Revenue Expenditure A/c			25,000
	To Inventories A/c			50,000
	To Provision for Doubtful Debts A/c			12,500
	To Goodwill A/c			1,00,000
	To Trademark			50,000
	To Capital Reserve A/c			1,00,000
	(Being the various assets written off as per the scheme)			

Dr. **CAPITAL REDUCTION ACCOUNT** Cr.

Particulars	₹	Particulars	₹
To Provision for Doubtful Debts A/c	12,500	By Preference Share Capital A/c	1,87,500
To Inventories A/c	50,000	By Freehold Property A/c	4,50,000
To Trademark A/c	50,000	By Equity Share Capital A/c	4,00,000
To Deferred Revenue Exp. A/c	25,000	By Director's loan A/c	3,00,000
To Goodwill A/c	1,00,000		
To Profit and loss A/c	10,00,000		
To Capital reserve A/c	1,00,000		
	13,37,500		13,37,500

BALANCE SHEET OF BAD LUCK LTD. (AND REDUCED) AS AT 31.03.2023

Particulars	*Note No*	₹
I. Equity and Liabilities		
(1) Shareholders' Funds		
(a) Share Capital	1	1,62,500
(b) Reserves and Surplus [Capital Reserve]		1,00,000
(2) Non-Current Liabilities		
Long-term Borrowings [8% Debentures]		2,50,000
(3) Current Liabilities		
(a) Short-term Borrowings [Bank Overdraft]		2,00,000
(b) Trade Payables [Creditors]		2,50,000
Total		9,62,500
II. Assets		
(1) Non-Current Assets		
(a) Fixed Assets		
Tangible Assets	2	7,50,000
(2) Current Assets		
(a) Inventories		1,00,000
(b) Trade Receivables [1,50,000 – 12,500]		1,12,500
Total		9,62,500

Notes To Accounts:

Particulars	₹
1. Share Capital	
1,000 Equity Shares of ₹ 100 each	1,00,000
625,8% Pref. Shares of ₹ 100 each	62,500
	1,62,500
2. Tangible Assets	
Freehold Property	6,00,000
Plant & Machinery	1,50,000
Total	7,50,000

PROBLEM 6

Given below are the extracts from the Balance Sheet of CANIC Limited as at 31st March, 2023:

Particulars	₹
2,00,000 Equity Shares of ₹ 10 each, ₹ 5 paid	10,00,000
6,000, 8% Preference Shares of ₹ 100 each	6,00,000
Profit & Loss Account (Dr.)	(4,08,000)
9% Debentures	6,00,000

Interest accrued on debentures	1,08,000
Bank overdraft	1,50,000
Interest accrued on Bank overdraft	15,000
Creditors	69,000
Fixed Assets	11,40,000
Patents and Copyrights	80,000
Investments at cost (Market value ₹ 55,000)	65,000
Inventories	4,00,000
Debtors	4,39,000
Bank	10,000

Preference dividend is in arrear for one year:

(a) Preference shareholders to give up their claims, inclusive of dividends, to the extent of 30% and desire to be paid off, (b) Debenture-holders agree to give up their claims to interest in consideration of their interest being enhanced to 12%, (c) Bank agrees to give up 50% of its interest outstanding in consideration of its being paid off at once, (d) Creditors would like to grant a discount of 5% if they are paid immediately, (e) Balance of Profit & Loss Account, Patents and Copyright and Debtors of ₹ 30,000 to be written off, (f) Fixed Assets to be written down by ₹ 34,000, (g) Investments are to reflect their market value, (h) To the extent not specifically stated, equity shareholders suffer on reduction of their rights. Cost of reconstruction is ₹ 3,350.

Required: Pass journal entries assuming that the scheme has been put through fully with the equity shareholders bringing in necessary cash to pay off the parties and to leave a Balance of ₹ 30,000 and prepare the Balance Sheet after reconstruction.

SOLUTION

JOURNAL

Particulars		***L.F.***	***Dr. (₹)***	***Cr. (₹)***
8% Preference Share Capital A/c	Dr.		6,00,000	
To Preference Shareholders' A/c				4,20,000
To Reconstruction A/c				1,80,000
(Being 30% of claim given up by preference shareholders as per reconstruction scheme dated....)				
Reconstruction A/c	Dr.		33,600	
To Preference Shareholders A/c				33,600
(Being 70% of arrears preference dividend payable to preference shareholders as per reconstruction scheme)				
9% Debentures A/c	Dr.		6,00,000	
Interest accrued on debentures A/c	Dr.		1,08,000	
To 12% Debentures A/c				6,00,000
To Reconstruction A/c				1,08,000
(Being 9% debentures converted into equivalent number of 12% debentures and the accrued debenture interest sacrificed as per Reconstruction scheme)				

Particulars		Dr. (₹)	Cr. (₹)
Equity Share Capital A/c To Reconstruction A/c (Being equity shareholders rights reduced to a share of ₹ 3.50 vide Board's Resolution No....dated....., the amount of sacrifice credited to Reconstruction Account) (Working Notes i)	Dr.	3,00,000	3,00,000
Bank A/c To Equity Share Capital A/c (Being the amount received on 2,00,000 equity shares @₹ 3.50 per share as per reconstruction scheme) (Working Notes ii)	Dr.	7,00,000	7,00,000
Bank of India A/c Interest Accrued on Bank overdraft A/c To Bank A/c To Reconstruction A/c (Being the Bank overdraft paid off including 50% of accrued interest as per reconstruction scheme, the interest sacrificed credited to Reconstruction A/c)	Dr. Dr.	1,50,000 15,000	1,57,500 7,500
Creditors A/c To Bank A/c To Reconstruction A/c (Being the Creditors claim discharged to the extent of 95% as per reconstruction scheme, the balance of the claim sacrificed)	Dr.	69,000	65,550 3,450
Reconstruction A/c To Bank A/c (Being the Reconstruction expenses paid)	Dr.	3,350	3,350
Preference shareholders' A/c To Bank A/c (Being the Amount due to preference shareholders discharged)	Dr.	4,53,600	4,53,600
Reconstruction A/c To Profit and Loss A/c To Patents & copyright A/c To Debtors A/c To Investment A/c To Fixed Assets A/c (Being the debit balance of profit and loss account, patents & copy rights writing off and the value of debtors, investments and fixed assets written down as per reconstruction scheme)	Dr.	5,62,000	4,08,000 80,000 30,000 10,000 34,000

BALANCE SHEET OF CANIC LTD. (AND REDUCED) AS AT 31.03.2023

Particulars	*Note No*	₹
I. Equity and Liabilities		
(1) Shareholders' Funds		
(a) Share Capital (₹ 10 each, ₹ 7 paid up)		14,00,000
(b) Reserves and Surplus		

(2) Non-Current Liabilities [12%Debentures]	6,00,000
(3) Current Liabilities	
Total	20,00,000
II. Assets	
(1) Non-Current Assets	
(a) Fixed Assets	
Tangible Assets [11,40,000 – 34,000 (Amt. w/o)]	11,06,000
(b) Non-Current Investments [65,000 – 10,000 (Amt. w/o)]	55,000
(2) Current Assets	
(a) Inventories	4,00,000
(b) Trade Receivables [Debtors – Prov] [80 – 4]	4,09,000
(c) Cash and Cash Equivalents	30,000
Total	20,00,000

Working Notes:

(I) STATEMENT SHOWING LIABILITIES AND EQUITY SACRIFICED AND THEIR USES AS PER SCHEME

Liabilities & Equity Sacrificed	₹	***Uses***	₹
Preference shareholders:		Writing off:	
30% of ₹ 6,00,000	1,80,000	Reconstruction expenses	3,350
Debenture holders:		Profit and Loss account balance	4,08,000
Interest on Debentures	1,08,000	Patents and copyrights	80,000
Bank of India: Interest on bank overdraft (50%)	7,500	Pref. dividend Arrears (70% of ₹ 48,000)	33,600
Creditors:		Writing down:	
5% of ₹ 69,000	3,450	Debtors	30,000
Equity Shareholders:		Investment	10,000
Sacrifice @ ₹ 1.50 per share (Balancing figure)	3,00,000	Fixed Assets	34,000
	5,98,950		5,98,950

(II) CASH TO BE BROUGHT IN BY EQUITY SHAREHOLDERS:

Payments to: Preference shareholders (including arrears of preference dividend)	₹
70% of ₹ 6,48,000	4,53,600
Bank of India (including interest on bank overdraft) ₹ [1,50,000 + ₹ 7,500]	1,57,500
Creditors 95% of ₹ 69,000	65,550
Reconstruction expenses	3,350
Additional cash for working capital [₹ 30,000 – ₹ 10,000]	20,000
	7,00,000

Therefore, Contribution per Equity Share = ₹ 7,00,000/2,00,000 = ₹ 3.50

PROBLEM 7

Given below are the extracts from the Balance Sheet of Sickness Ltd. as at 31st March, 2023:

Particulars	₹
Share Capital:	
8,000 equity shares of ₹ 100 each, ₹ 50 per share paid up	4,00,000
4,000 11% Cumulative Preference shares of ₹ 100 each, fully paid up	4,00,000
Securities Premium A/c	40,000
General Reserve	60,000
Current Liabilities	3,10,000
Contingent liability not provided:	
Preference dividends are in arrears for three years including the year ended 31st March, 2023	—
Fixed Assets	
Tangible Fixed Assets	8,50,000
Less: Depreciation	(2,70,000)
Goodwill at cost	40,000
Investments	25,000
Inventories	2,10,000
Trade Debtors	2,55,000
Cash and Bank Balances	1,00,000

The funds of the Company are sufficient to discharge its liabilities including Preference Dividends in arrears. However, the company does not want to deplete its resources. It would also like to reflect the values of some of its assets in a realistic manner. The Board of Directors of the Company decided and proposed the following scheme of rehabilitation/reconstruction to be effective from 1st April, 2023.

(a) The cumulative preference shareholders are to be issued, in exchange of their holdings, 13% Debentures of the face value of ₹ 100 each at a premium of 10% Fractional holdings are to be paid off in cash.

(b) Arrears in preference dividends to be converted into equity shares of ₹ 100, ₹ 50 per share paid up.

(c) After the issue of the equity shares mentioned in (ii) above, the paid up value of all the equity shares is to be reduced to ₹ 25 each.

(d) The face value of all the equity shares to be reduced to ₹ 50 each and the balance of the unpaid portion is to be called up fully.

(e) Goodwill has lost its value and has to be written off. Market value of Tangible Fixed Assets is determined, as at 31st March, 2023 at ₹ 5,00,000.

(f) Investments have no market value and have to be written off.

(g) Inventories is to be valued at 110% of its book value and Trade Debtors are to be discounted by 5%.

The scheme, as approved by the Directors, is duly accepted by all authorities and put into effect.

During the working for the half year ended 30th September, 2023, it is noticed that the trading for the period has resulted in an increase of bank balances by ₹ 55,100, Sundry Debtors by

₹ 40,000, Trade Creditors by ₹ 26,000 and a decrease in stock by ₹ 8,000. Depreciation for the half year on fixed assets at 10% per annum is to be provided. The increase in the bank balances was prior to the company paying the half yearly interest on the debentures and redeeming one half of the debentures on 30th September, 2023.

Required: Prepare Journal, and the Balance Sheet of Sickness Ltd. as at 30th September, 2023.

SOLUTION

JOURNAL

Particulars		L.F.	Dr. (₹)	Cr. (₹)
11% Cumulative Preference Share Capital A/c	Dr.		4,00,000	
To 13% Debentures A/c				3,63,600
To Securities Premium A/c				36,360
To Cash and Bank A/c				40
(Being the issue of 3,636 13% debentures of ₹ 100 each at a premium of ₹ 10 to cancel 4,000 11% cumulative preference shares of ₹ 100 each, fraction ₹ 40 was paid in cash)				
Capital Reduction A/c	Dr.		1,32,000	
To Equity Share Capital A/c				1,32,000
(Being the Issue of 2,640 equity shares of ₹ 100 each ₹ 50 paid-up for arrears preference dividend)				
Equity Share Capital A/c	Dr.		2,66,000	
To Capital Reduction A/c				2,66,000
(Being the Reduction of paid up value of 10,640 equity shares of ₹ 100 each, ₹ 50 paid up to shares of ₹ 50 each, ₹ 25 paid up)				
Equity Share Capital (₹ 100 each) A/c	Dr.		2,66,000	
To Equity Share Capital (₹ 50 each) A/c				2,66,000
(Being the face value of ₹ 100 reduced to ₹ 50 each as per scheme of reconstruction)				
Cash and Bank A/c	Dr.		2,66,000	
To Equity Share Capital A/c				2,66,000
(Being the Call money on 10,640 equity shares @ ₹ 25 to make the equity shares fully paid up)				
Capital Reduction A/c	Dr.		1,57,750	
To Goodwill A/c				40,000
To Investment A/c				25,000
To Fixed Assets A/c (₹ 8,50,000 – ₹ 2,70,000) – ₹ 5,00,000				80,000
To Sundry Debtors A/c				12,750
(Being the Value of Sundry assets written down)				
Stock A/c	Dr.		21,000	

To Capital Reduction A/c			21,000
(Being the Value of Stock written up			
General Reserve A/c	Dr.	2,750	
To Capital Reduction A/c			2,750
(Being the Transfer from General Reserve)			

BALANCE SHEET OF SICKNESS LTD. (AND REDUCED) AS AT 30.09.2023

Particulars	*Note No*	₹
I. Equity and Liabilities		
(1) Shareholders' Funds		
(a) Share Capital [₹ 50 each]		5,32,000
(b) Reserves and Surplus	1	1,46,076
(2) Non-Current Liabilities [13%Debentures]		1,81,800
(3) Current Liabilities		3,36,000
Total		11,95,876
II. Assets		
(1) Non-Current Assets		
(a) Fixed Assets		
Tangible Assets [5,80,000 – 80,000 (Amt. w/o) – 25,000]		4,75,000
Intangible Assets [Goodwill] [40,000–40,000 (Amt. w/o)]		0
(b) Non-Current Investments[25,000 – 25,000(Amt. w/o)]		0
(2) Current Assets		
(a) Inventories		2,23,000
(b) Trade Receivables [Debtors]		2,82,250
(c) Cash and Cash Equivalents		2,15,626
Total		11,95,876

Notes To Accounts:

1. Reserves and Surplus	
General Reserve	57,250
Profit & Loss Account	12,466
Securities Premium	76,360
Total	1,46,076

Working Notes:

Dr. **(I) CAPITAL REDUCTION ACCOUNT** *Cr.*

Particulars	₹	*Particulars*	₹
To Equity Share Capital A/c	1,32,000	By Equity Share Capital A/c	2,66,000
To Sundries	1,57,750	By Stock	21,000
		By General Reserve	2,750
	2,89,750		2,89,750

(II) CASH AND BANK ACCOUNT

Dr. Cr.

Particulars	₹	Particulars	₹
To Balance b/d	1,00,000	By 11% Cumulative Preference Shares A/c	40
To Equity Share Capital A/c	2,66,000	By Balance c/d	3,65,960
	3,66,000		3,66,000

(III) BALANCE SHEET (AFTER INTERNAL RECONSTRUCTION)

Liabilities	₹	Assets		₹
Share Capital:		Fixed Assets:		
10,640 Equity Shares of ₹ 50 each fully paid	5,32,000	Goodwill	40,000	
Reserves and Surplus:		*Less:* Amt w/o under Reconstruction		—
Securities Premium A/c	76,360	Scheme	40,000	
General Reserve	57,250	Other Fixed Assets	5,80,000	
Secured Loans:		*Less:* Amt w/o under Reconstruction		
13% Debentures	3,63,600	Scheme	80,000	5,00,000
Current Liabilities:	3,10,000	Investments	25,000	
		Less: Amt w/o under		
		Reconstruction Scheme	25,000	—
		Current Assets:		
		Stock in Trade		2,31,000
		Sundry Debtors		2,42,250
		Cash and Bank		3,65,960
	13,39,210			13,39,210

Working Notes:

(I) CALCULATION OF HALF-YEARLY PROFIT

Particulars	₹	₹
Increase in bank balances	55,100	
Increase in sundry debtors	40,000	95,100
Less: Decrease in stock	8,000	
Less: Increase in trade creditors	26,000	34,000
Trading Profit before interest and depreciation		61,100
Less: Interest for 1/2 year @13% on ₹ 3,63,600	23,634	
Less: Depreciation for 1/2 year on ₹ 5,00,000 @ 10% p.a	25,000	48,634
Net Profit		12,466

(II) CALCULATION OF CASH AND BANK BALANCE AS ON 30.9.2023

Particulars	₹	₹
Balance as on 31.3.2023		3,65,960
Add: Increase		55,100
Less: Interest	23,634	
Less: Redemption of 1/2 of 13% debentures	1,81,800	2,05,434
		2,15,626

PROBLEM 8

Given below are the extracts from the Balance Sheet of Munna Ltd. on 31st March, 2023:

Particulars	₹
20,000, Equity shares of ₹ 100 each	20,00,000
10,000, 7% preference shares of ₹ 100 each	10,00,000
Profit & Loss Account (Dr.)	(7,00,000)
Sundry Creditors	7,00,000
Bank overdraft	3,00,000
Goodwill	2,00,000
Plant and Machinery	18,00,000
Stock	3,00,000
Debtors	7,50,000
Cash	1,50,000
Preliminary Expenses	1,00,000

Two years' preference dividend are in arrears. The company had been bad time during the last two years and hopes for better business in future, earning profit and paying dividend provided the capital base is reduced.

An internal reconstruction scheme as follows was agreed to by all concerned:

(i) Creditors agreed to forego 50% of the claim.

(ii) Preference shareholders withdrew arrears dividend claim. They also agreed to lower their capital claim by 20% by reducing nominal value in consideration of 9% dividend effective after reorganisation in case equity shareholders' loss exceeded 50% on the application of the scheme.

(iii) Bank agreed to convert overdraft into term loan to the extent required for making current ratio equal to 2 : 1.

(iv) Revalued figure for plant and machinery was accepted as ₹ 15,00,000.

(v) Debtors to the extent of ₹ 4,00,000 were considered good.

(vi) Equity shares shall be exchanged for the same number of equity shares at a revised denomination as required after the reorganisation.

Required:

(a) Total loss to be borne by the equity and preference shareholders for the reorganisation;

(b) Shares of loss to the individual classes of shareholders;

(c) New structure of share capital after reorganisation;

(d) Working capital of the reorganised Co.; and

(e) A proforma balance sheet after reorganisation.

SOLUTION

(A) LOSS TO BE BORNE BY EQUITY AND PREFERENCE SHAREHOLDERS

Particulars	₹
Profit and Loss A/c (debit balance)	7,00,000
Preliminary Expenses	1,00,000
Goodwill	2,00,000
Plant and Machinery (₹ 18,00,000 – ₹ 15,00,000)	3,00,000
Debtors	3,50,000
Amount to be written off	16,50,000
Less: 50% of Sundry Creditors	3,50,000
Loss to be borne by equity and preference shareholders	13,00,000

Note: *Since preference dividend for 2 years which is in arrears is sacrificed by preference shareholders, the same may be ignored in the above calculation or alternatively may be included in the amount to be written off and then reduced therefrom as preference shareholders' sacrifice.*

(B) SHARES OF LOSS TO PREFERENCE SHAREHOLDERS AND EQUITY SHAREHOLDERS

Total loss being more than 50% of equity share capital:	
Preference shareholders' share of loss = 20% of ₹ 10,00,000	₹ 2,00,000
Equity shareholders' share of loss (₹ 13,00,000 – ₹ 2,00,000)	₹ 11,00,000
Total	₹ 13,00,000

(C) NEW STRUCTURE OF CAPITAL

Equity Shares	₹
20,000 shares of ₹ 45 each fully paid [(20,00,000 - 11,00,000)/20000]	9,00,000
Preference Shares	
10,000, 9% shares of ₹ 80 each fully paid	8,00,000
	17,00,000

(D) WORKING CAPITAL OF THE REORGANISED COMPANY

Current Assets	₹	₹
Stock		3,00,000
Debtors		4,00,000
Cash		1,50,000
		8,50,000
Less: Current Liabilities		
Creditors	3,50,000	
Bank overdraft (see Note)	75,000	4,25,000
Working Capital		4,25,000

Note: *Current ratio shall be 2: 1, i.e., total current liabilities shall be 50% of ₹ 8,50,000 = ₹ 4,25,000. Therefore, Bank overdraft = ₹ 4,25,000 – ₹ 3,50,000 = ₹ 75,000.*

BALANCE SHEET OF MUNNA LTD. (AND REDUCED) AS AT 31.3.2023

Particulars	*Note No*	₹
I. Equity and Liabilities		
(1) Shareholders' Funds		
(a) Share Capital	1	17,00,000
(b) Reserves and Surplus		
(2) Non-Current Liabilities [Term Loan with Bank]		2,25,000
(3) Current Liabilities		
(a) Trade Payables [Creditors]		3,50,000
(b) Other Current Liabilities [Bank overdraft]		75,000
Total		23,50,000
II. Assets		
(1) Non-Current Assets		
(a) Fixed Assets		
Tangible Assets [18,00,000 – 3,00,000 (Amt. w/o)]		15,00,000
Intangible Assets [Goodwill] [2,00,000 – 2,00,000 (Amt. w/o)]		0
(2) Current Assets		
(a) Inventories		3,00,000
(b) Trade Receivables [Debtors]		4,00,000
(c) Cash and Cash Equivalents		1,50,000
Total		23,50,000

Notes To Accounts:

Particulars	₹
1. Share Capital	
20000 Equity Shares of ₹ 45 each	9,00,000
10000,9% Pref. Shares of ₹ 80 each	8,00,000
	17,00,000

PROBLEM 9

Given below are the extracts from the Balance Sheet of X Ltd. as at March 31st, 2023.

Particulars	*(₹ in lakhs)*
Equity Shares of ₹ 100 each	600
14% Preference Shares of ₹ 100 each	200
Profit and Loss Account (Dr.)	(525)
13% Debentures	200
Debenture Interest accrued	26
Loan from bank	74

Trade creditors	340
Land and Building	200
Plant and Machinery	300
Furniture and Fixtures	50
Inventory	150
Sundry Debtors	70
Cash at bank	130
Preliminary expenses	10
Cost of issue of debentures	5

The company did not perform well and has suffered sizable losses during the last few years. However, it is that the company could be nursed back to health by proper financial restructuring. Consequently the following scheme of reconstruction has been drawn up.

(a) Equity shares are to be reduced to ₹ 25 per share, fully paid up;

(b) Preference shares are to be reduced (with coupon rate of 10%) to equal number of shares of ₹ 50 each, fully paid up

(c) Debenture holders have agreed to forgo the accrued interest due to them. In the future, the rate of interest on debentures is to be reduced to 9 percent.

(d) Trade creditors will forego 25% of the amount due to them.

(d) The company issued 6 lakh of equity shares at ₹ 25 each and the entire sum was to be paid on application. The entire amount was fully subscribed by promoters.

(f) Land and Building was to be revalued at ₹ 450 lakhs, Plant and Machinery was to be written down by ₹ 120 lakhs and a provision of ₹ 15 lakhs had to be made for doubtful debts.

Required:

(i) Show the impact of financial restructuring on the company's activities.

(ii) Prepare the fresh balance sheet after the reconstructions is completed on the basis of the above proposals.

SOLUTION

(A) IMPACT OF FINANCIAL RESTRUCTURING

(i)	Benefits of X Ltd.		
	A.	**Reduction of Liabilities payable**	₹ in lakhs
		Reduction in equity share capital (6 lakh shares × ₹ 75 per share)	450
		Reduction in preference share capital (2 lakh shares × ₹ 50 per share)	100
		Waiver of outstanding debenture Interest	26
		Waiver from trade creditors (₹ 340 lakhs × 0.25)	85
			661
	B.	**Revaluation of Assets**	
		Appreciation of Land and Building (₹ 450 lakhs – ₹ 200 lakhs)	250
			911

(ii)	Amount of ₹ 911 lakhs utilized to write off losses, fictitious assets and over-valued assets.	
	Writing of Profit and Loss Account	525
	Cost of Issue of Debentures	5
	Preliminary Expenses	10
	Provision for Doubtful Debts	15
	Revaluation of Plant and Machinery (₹ 300 lakhs – ₹ 104 lakhs)	120
		675
	C. Capital Reserve [A – B]	236

(III) BALANCE SHEET OF X LTD. (AFTER RECONSTRUCTION) AS AT 31.3.2023

Particulars	*Note No*	*₹ (lacs)*
I. Equity and Liabilities		
(1) Shareholders' Funds		
(a) Share Capital	1	400
(b) Reserves and Surplus (Capital Reserve)		236
(2) Non-Current Liabilities [9% Debentures + Loan from Bank [200 + 74]		274
(3) Current Liabilities		
(a) Trade Payables [Creditors]		255
Total		1,165
II. Assets		
(1) Non-Current Assets		
(a) Fixed Assets		
Tangible Assets	2	680
(2) Current Assets		
(a) Inventories		150
(b) Trade Receivables [Debtors – Prov] [70 – 15]		55
(c) Cash and Cash Equivalents [balancing figure]		280
Total		1,165

Notes To Accounts:

Particulars		*₹ (lacs)*
1. Share Capital		
12 lacs Equity Shares of ₹ 25 each		300
2 lacs, 10% Pref. Shares of ₹ 50		100
		400
2. Tangible Assets		
Land & Building	200	
Add: Amt. increased under Reconstruction scheme	250	450

Plant & Machinery	300	
Less: Amit. w/o under Reconstruction scheme	(120)	180
Furniture & Fixtures		50
Total		680

PROBLEM 10

The Shareholders of Sunrise Ltd decided on a corporate restructuring exercise necessitated due to economic recession and a slump in business. From the following prepare:

(i) Balance Sheet after the completion of the restructuring exercise,

(ii) The Capital Reduction Amount,

(iii) The Cash Account of the entity.

BALANCE SHEET OF SUNRISE LTD AS ON 31-03-2023

Particulars		₹
Share Capital		
30,000 Equity Shares (₹ 10 each)		3,00,000
40,000 8% Cumulative Preference Shares (₹ 10 each)		4,00,000
Reserves and Surplus		
Securities Premium Account		10,000
Profit & Loss Account		(1,38,400)
Non-Current Liabilities (Debentures)		1,25,400
Current Liabilities		
Creditors		1,20,000
Deferred Vat Payable		50,000
Temporary Bank Overdraft		2,23,100
Fixed Assets		
Trade Marks and Patents		1,10,000
Goodwill at cost		36,100
Freehold Land		1,20,000
Freehold Premises		2,44,000
Plant and Equipment		3,20,000
Investment (Market to Market)		64,000
Current Assets		
Inventories:		
Raw materials and packing		
Materials	60,000	
Finished goods	16,000	76,000
Trade receivable		1,20,000

Note: Preference Dividends are in arrears for 4 years.

The scheme of reconstruction that received the permission of the Court was on the following lines:

1. The Authorized capital of the Company to be re-fixed at ₹ 10 Lakhs (Preference Capital ₹ 3 Lakhs and Equity Capital ₹ 7 Lakhs both ₹ 10/- shared each).
2. The Preference shares are to be reduced to ₹ 5 each and equity share reduced by ₹ 3 per share. Post reduction, both classes of shares to be re-consolidated into ₹ 10 shares.
3. Trade Investments are to be liquidation in open market
4. One fresh equity share of ₹ 10 to be issued for every ₹ 40 of preference dividends in arrears (ignore taxation).
5. The Securities premium is to be fully utilized to meet the reconstruction programme.
6. The debenture holder took over freehold land at ₹ 2,10,000 and settled the balance after adjusting their dues.
7. Unprovided contingent Liabilities were settled at ₹ 54,000 and a pending insurance claim receivable settled at ₹ 12,500 on condition that claim will be immediately settled.
8. The Intangible assets were all the written off along with ₹ 10,000 worth obsolete packing material and 10% of the Receivables.
9. Reconstruction expenses amounted to ₹ 10,000.
10. Remaining cash available as a result of the above transactions is to be utilised to pay off the bank overdraft to that extent.
11. The equity shareholder agree that they bring in cash to liquidate the balance outstanding on the overdraft account and also agree the sufficient funds will be brought in to bring up the net working capital, after completing the re-structuring exercise, to ₹ 2 lakhs. The Equity Shares will be issued at par for this purpose.

SOLUTION

(I) BALANCE SHEET OF SUNRISE LTD. (AND REDUCED) AS AT 31.03.2023

Particulars	*Note No*	₹
I. Equity and Liabilities		
(1) Shareholders' Funds		
(a) Share Capital	1	7,64,000
(b) Reserves and Surplus		—
(2) Non-Current Liabilities		
(3) Current Liabilities		
(a) Trade Payables [Creditors]		1,20,000
(b) Other Current Liabilities [Deferred VAT Payable]		50,000
Total		9,34,000
II. Assets		
(1) Non-Current Assets		
(a) Fixed Assets		
Tangible Assets	2	5,64,000

(2) Current Assets		
(a) Inventories [50,000 + 16,000]		66,000
(b) Trade Receivables [Debtors]		1,08,000
(c) Cash and Equivalents		1,96,000
Total		9,34,000

Notes to Accounts:

Particulars	₹
1. Share Capital	
56,400 Equity Shares of ₹ 10 each	5,64,000
20,000, 8% Pref. Shares of ₹ 10 each, ₹ 10 paid	2,00,000
(of the above 3,200 Equity Shares were issued for consideration otherwise than case)	
	7,64,000
2. Tangible Assets	
Free hold Premises	2,44,000
	3,20,000
	5,64,000

Dr. **(II) CAPITAL REDUCTION ACCOUNT** Cr.

Particulars	₹	*Particulars*	₹
To Equity Share Capital A/c [(4,00,000 × 8% × 4)/₹ 40] × ₹ 10	32,000	By 8% Cumulative Preference Share Capital A/c [40,000 × ₹ 5]	2,00,000
To Trademarks & Patents w/o To Goodwill w/o	1,10,000 36,100	By Equity Share Capital [30,000 × ₹ 3]	90,000
To Bank A/c (Contingent Liability)	54,000	By Securities Premium A/c	10,000
To Bank A/c (Expenses paid)	10,000	By Bank A/c (Insurance Claim)	12,500
To Trade Receivables (1,20,000 × 10%)	12,000	By Freehold Land (Profit on Transfer) [2,10,000 – 1,20,000]	90,000
To P&L A/c (Debit Bal. w/o)	1,38,400		
	4,02,500		4,02,500

Dr. **(III) CASH ACCOUNT** Cr.

Particulars	₹	*Particulars*	₹
To Investments A/c	64,000	By Capital Reduction A/c (Expenses)	10,000
To Capital Reduction (Insurance Claim)	12,500	By Capital Reduction A/c (Unrecorded Liability)	54,000
To Debentures Holders A/c [2,10,000 – 1,25,400]	84,600	By Bank Overdraft A/c (Settlement) (Balancing Figure)	97,100
	1,61,100		1,61,100

Working Notes:

(i) **Shortage of Working Capital** = ₹ 2,00,000 – Existing Working Capital
= ₹ 2,00,000 – [(60,000 – 10,000) + 16,000 + 1,08,000 – (1,20,000 + 50,000)]
= ₹ 1,96,000 (to be maintained by Bank Balance)

(ii) **Additional Equity Share Capital to be issued to have desired Bank Balance of ₹ 1,96,000**

Dr. **BANK ACCOUNT** *Cr.*

Particulars	₹	***Particulars***	₹
To Cash A/c	97,100	By Balance b/d (given)	2,23,100
To Equity Share Capital (b/f)	3,22,000	By Balance c/d (Desired Balance)	1,96,000
	4,19,100		4,19,100

(III) NO. OF SHARES AFTER RECONSTRUCTION

A. No. of Equity Shares After Consolidation into Shares of ₹ 10 Each = [2,10,000/10]	21,000
B. *Add:* Issued for Arrears of Dividend	3,200
C. *Add:* Issued for Cash Consideration [3,22,000/10]	32,200
D. No. of Shares After Reconstruction	56,400

VERY SHORT ANSWER TYPE QUESTIONS

1. Briefly explain Internal Reconstruction.

2. Enumerate the various ways in which Internal Reconstruction can be carried out.

3. Distinguish between:

(a) Alteration of Share Capital and Reduction of Share Capital.

(b) Internal Reconstruction and External Reconstruction.

4. Which of the following is true?

(i) Internal Reconstruction can be done only in case of companies incurring losses.

(ii) Reconstruction A/c/Capital Reduction A/c is either debited or credited when Internal Reconstruction is carried out either by way of Variation of Shareholders' Rights u/s 48 or Alteration of Share Capital u/s 61.

(iii) Reconstruction A/c/Capital Reduction A/c is always credited when Internal Reconstruction is carried out by way of Reduction of Share Capital u/s 66.

(iv) Reconstruction A/c/Capital Reduction A/c is neither debited nor credited when Internal Reconstruction is carried out either by way of Variation of Shareholders' Rights u/s 48 or Alteration of Share Capital u/s 61.

SHORT ANSWER TYPE PRACTICAL QUESTIONS

1. V Ltd has Equity Share Capital (of ₹ 10 each) of ₹ 500 lacs. All the equity shares be converted into the same number of equity shares of ₹ 5 each, ₹ 2.50 paid up. Journalise

[**Ans.** T/f to Reconstruction ₹ 375 lacs]

2. V Ltd has 6% Cum-Pref. Shares (of ₹ 100 each) of ₹ 100 lacs. The preference shares are converted from 6% to 15% but revalued in a manner in which the total return on them remains unaffected. Journalise. **[Ans.** T/f to Reconstruction ₹ 60 lacs]

3. V Ltd has 6% Cum-Pref. Shares (of ₹100 each) of ₹ 100 lacs. Dividend on Preference Shares are in arrears for three years. Four equity shares of ₹ 5 each, ₹ 2.50 paid up to be issued for each ₹100 of arrears of preference dividend. Journalise.

[Ans. T/f to Reconstruction ₹ 1.80 lacs]

4. V Ltd has 10% first debentures for ₹ 60 lacs, 10% second debentures for ₹ 100 lacs and Interest on Debentures Outstanding ₹ 16 lacs. Mr. A holds 10% first debentures for ₹ 40 lacs and 10% second debentures for ₹ 60 lacs. He is also a creditor for ₹ 10 lacs. Mr. 'A' is to cancel ₹ 60 lacs of his total debt and to pay ₹ 10 lacs to the company and to receive new 12% Debentures for the balance amount. Journalise. **[Ans.** T/f to Reconstruction ₹ 60 lacs]

5. V Ltd has 10% first debentures for ₹ 60 lacs, 10% second debentures for ₹ 100 lacs and Interest on Debentures Outstanding ₹ 16 lacs. Mr. B holds 10% first debentures for ₹ 20 lacs and 10% second debentures for ₹ 40 lacs and is also a creditor for ₹ 5 lacs. Mr. 'B' is to cancel ₹ 30 lacs of his total debt and to accept new 12% Debentures for the balance amount. Journalise

[Ans. T/f to Reconstruction ₹ 30 lacs]

6. V Ltd has Trade Creditors for ₹ 165 lacs. Mr. A and Mr. B are creditors for ₹ 10 lacs and ₹ 5 lacs respectively. Trade Creditors (other than A and B) are given the option of *either* to accept equity shares of ₹ 5, ₹ 2.50 paid up each, for the amount due to them *or* to accept 80% of the amount due in cash. 40% Creditors accepted equity shares whereas the balance accepted cash in full settlement. Journalise. **[Ans.** T/f to Reconstruction ₹ 18 lacs]

7. There were capital commitments totalling ₹ 300 lacs. These contracts are to be cancelled on payment of 5% of the contract price as a penalty. The Directors refund ₹ 11 lacs of the fees previously received by them. A dissentient shareholder transferred his 100 shares to a director. Journalise. **[Ans.** T/f to Reconstruction ₹ 4 lacs]

8. V Ltd has Provision for Tax for ₹10 lacs. The taxation liability of the company is settled at ₹ 8.88 lacs and the same is paid immediately. Journalise.

[Ans. T/f to Reconstruction ₹ 1.12 lacs]

9. Following items appear in the Balance Sheet of V Ltd:

Workmen's Compensation Fund:	Pune	₹1 lac
	Bombay	₹ 2 lacs
10% Government Loan Earmarked Against Workmen's Compensation Fund		₹ 3 lacs
Workmen's Compensation Fund (Bombay) disclosed the fact that actually there was a liability of ₹ 1,20,000 only. As a result the relevant fund amount balance was to be brought down to the required amount. Investments were realised at 10% above the book value. Journalise.		

[Ans. T/f to Reconstruction ₹ 0.88 lacs]

10. V Ltd has Investments in Shares in Q Ltd. ₹ 32.4 lacs V Ltd. holds 21,600 shares in Q Ltd. This represents 15% of the share capital of that company. Q Ltd. is not a quoted company. The average net profit (after tax) of the company is ₹ 25 lacs. The shares would be valued based on 12% capitalization rate. Journalise. **[Ans.** T/f to Reconstruction ₹ 1.15 lacs]

11. Following items appear in the Balance Sheet of V Ltd:

Capital Reserve	₹ 6 lacs
Profit and Loss Account	₹ (15) lacs
Goodwill	₹ 10 lacs

Patents & Copy Rights	₹ 5 lacs
Plant & Machinery	₹ 719.6 lacs
Land & Building	₹ 60 lacs
Debtors	₹ 10 lacs
Cash at Bank	₹ 104 lacs
Discount on issue of Debentures	₹ 1 lac

Goodwill is considered worthless. Land & Building is to be valued at 114% of book value. 80% of Debtors are considered as Bad and 20% of the balance Debtors are considered as Doubtful. Any surplus after writing off the various losses should be utilized in writing down the value of plant & machinery. The credit Balance available in Reconstruction A/c is ₹ 538.05 lacs. Journalise.

[**Ans.** Total Losses w/o ₹552.45, Plant & Machinery written down by ₹ 518.05 lacs]

LONG ANSWER TYPE PRACTICAL QUESTIONS

1. Pass journal entries for the following transactions:

(i) Conversion of 2 lakh fully paid equity shares of ₹ 10 each into Inventories of ₹ 1,00,000 and balance has 12% fully convertible Debenture.

(ii) Consolidation of 40 lakh fully paid equity shares of ₹2.50 each into 10 lakh fully paid equity share of ₹10 each.

(iii) Sub-division of 10 lakh fully paid 11% preference shares of ₹ 50 each into 50 lakh fully paid 11% preference shares of ₹ 10 each.

(iv) Conversion of 12% preference shares of ₹ 5,00,000 into 14% preference shares ₹ 3,00,000 and remaining balance as 12% Non-cumulative preference shares.

2. Given are the extracts of Balance Sheet of X Ltd. as at 31st March, 2015:

Particulars	₹
12,000, 10% Preference Shares of ₹ 100 each	12,00,000
24,000, Equity Shares of ₹ 100 each	24,00,000
Profit & Loss Account	(14,00,000)
10% Debentures	6,00,000
Bank Overdraft	6,00,000
Trade Payables	3,00,000
Goodwill	90,000
Land & building	12,00,000
Plant & Machinery	18,00,000
Inventories	2,60,000
Trade Receivables	2,80,000
Cash	30,000
Preliminary Expenses	40,000

On the above date, the company adopted the following scheme of reconstruction:

(a) The equity shares are to be reduced to shares of ₹ 40 each fully paid and the preference shares to be reduced to fully paid shares of ₹ 75 each.

(b) The debentureholders took over Inventories and Trade Receivables in full satisfaction of their claims.

(c) The Land and Building to be appreciated by 30% and Plant and machinery to be depreciated by 30%.

(d) The fictitious and intangible assets are to be eliminated,

(e) Expenses of reconstruction amounted to ₹ 5,000.

Required: Pass Journal Entries and prepare the reconstructed Balance Sheet.

[**Ans.** Total Losses w/o ₹21,60,000, Total of B/S ₹ 28,45,000]

3. Given are the extracts of Balance Sheet of ABC Ltd. as at 31st March, 2015:

Particulars	₹
2,00,000 Equity shares of ₹ 10 each	20,00,000
6,000 8% Preference shares of ₹ 100 each	6,00,000
Profit and Loss A/c	(4,05,000)
9% Debentures	12,00,000
Bank overdraft	1,50,000
Trade Payables	5,92,000
Plant and machinery	9,00,000
Furniture and fixtures	2,50,000
Patents and copyrights	70,000
Investments (at cost) (Market value ₹ 55,000)	68,000
Inventories	14,00,000
Trade Receivables	14,39,000
Cash and bank balance	10,000

The following scheme of reconstruction was finalised:

(a) Preference shareholders would give up 30% of their capital in exchange for allotment of 11% Debentures to them.

(b) Debentureholders having charge on plant and machinery would accept plant and machinery in full settlement of their dues.

(c) Inventories equal to ₹ 5,00,000 in book value will be taken over by Trade Payables in full settlement of their dues.

(d) Investment value to be reduced to market price.

(e) The company would issue 11% Debentures for ₹ 3,00,000 and augment its working capital requirement after settlement of bank overdraft.

Required: Pass necessary Journal Entries and Prepare Reconstruction Account and Balance Sheet of the company after internal reconstruction.

[**Ans.** Total Losses w/o ₹ 4,18,000, Total of B/S ₹ 28,74,000]

4. Given are the extracts of Balance Sheet of XYZ Ltd. as at 31st March, 2015:

Particulars	₹
8,000 – 7½ Preference Shares @ ₹.100 each	8,00,000
1,80,000 Equity Shares @ ₹.10 each	18,00,000
Profit & Loss A/c	(7,18,000)

11% Debentures	10,00,000
Bank overdraft	1,65,000
Loan from director	15,000
Trade Payables	6,20,000
Plant and Machinery	8,50,000
Furniture and Fittings	1,60,000
Patents and Copyright	60,000
Goodwill	35,000
Investments (at cost)	65,000
Trade Receivables	12,00,000
Inventories	13,00,000
Cash in hand	12,000

Due to heavy losses and overvaluation of assets, the following scheme of reconstruction was finalised:

(a) Preference shareholders will surrender their 20% shares and they have been allotted 9% (new) preference shares for the remaining amount.

(b) Debentureholders having charge on plant and machinery would accept plant and machinery in full settlement.

(c) Trade Payables accepted to take over the Inventories upto the value of ₹ 6,20,000.

(d) Equity shareholders are to accept reduction of ₹ 4 per share.

(e) Investments are to be valued at market price i.e., ₹ 60,000.

(f) Trade Receivables and remaining Inventories is to be valued at 90 % of their book value.

(g) Directors have to forgo their loan in full.

(h) Patents and Copyright and Goodwill have no more value.

Required: Pass necessary journal entries in the books of XYZ Ltd. assuming that all the legal formalities have been completed. Prepare Reconstruction Account and Balance Sheet of the company after reduction.

[**Ans.** Total Losses w/o ₹10,06,000, Total of B/S ₹ 19,24,000]

5. Given are the extracts of Balance Sheet of Weak Ltd. as at 31st March, 2015:

Particulars	₹
Equity Shares of ₹ 100 each	1,00,00,000
12% Cumulative Preference Shares of ₹ 100 each	50,00,000
P & L A/c	(4,00,000)
10% Debentures of ₹ 100 each	40,00,000
Trade Payables	50,00,000
Provision for taxation	1,00,000
Tangible Fixed Assets	1,25,00,000
Investments (Market Value ₹ 9,50,000)	10,00,000
Current Assets	1,00,00,000
Preliminary Expenses	2,00,000

The following scheme of reorganization is sanctioned:

(a) All the existing equity shares are reduced to ₹ 40 each.

(b) All preference shares are reduced to ₹ 60 each.

(c) The rate of interest on debentures is increased to 12%. the debentureholders surrender their existing debentures of ₹ 100 each and exchange the same for fresh debentures of ₹ 70 each for every debenture held by them.

(d) One of the Trade Payables of the company to whom the company owes ₹ 20,00,000 decides to forgo 40% of his claim. He is allotted 30,000 equity shares of ₹ 40 each in full satisfaction of his claim.

(e) Fixed assets are to be written down by 30%.

(f) Current assets are to be revalued at ₹ 45,00,000.

(g) The taxation liability of the company is settled at ₹ 1,50,000.

(h) Investments to be brought to their market value.

(i) It is decided to write off the fictitious assets.

Required: Pass Journal entries and show the Balance Sheet of the company after giving effect to the above.

[Ans. Total Losses w/o ₹99,00,000, Total of B/S ₹ 140,50,000]

6. Given are the extracts of Balance Sheet of Bad Luck Ltd. as on 31st March, 2015:

Particulars	*Note No*	*₹ (lacs)*
I. Equity and Liabilities		
(1) Shareholders' Funds		
(a) Share Capital	1	7.50
(b) Reserves and Surplus (Profit and Loss A/c)		(10.00)
(2) Non-Current Liabilities (8% Debentures)		5.00
(3) Current Liabilities		
(a) Short-term Borrowings	2	5.00
(b) Trade Payables [Trade Payables]		2.50
Total		10.00
II. Assets		
(1) Non-Current Assets		
(a) Fixed Assets		
Tangible Assets	3	5.50
Intangible Assets	4	1.50
(2) Current Assets		
(a) Inventories		1.50
(b) Trade Receivables		1.25
(c) Deferred revenue expenditure		0.25
Total		10.00

Notes To Accounts:

Particulars	*₹ (lacs)*
1. Share Capital	
5000 Equity Shares of ₹ 100 each	5.00
2500, 8% Pref. Shares of ₹ 100 each	2.50
	7.50

2.	**Short-term Borrowings**	
	Loan from Directors	3.00
	Bank Overdraft	2.00
		5.00
3.	**Tangible Assets**	
	Freehold Property	4.00
	Plant & Machinery	1.50
	Total	5.50
4.	**Intangible Assets**	
	Goodwill	1.00
	Trademark	0.50
		1.50

The following scheme of internal reconstruction was framed, approved by the Court, all the concerned parties and implemented:

(i) The preference shares to be written down to ₹ 25 each and the equity shares to ₹ 20 each. Each class of shares then to be converted into shares of ₹ 100 each.

(ii) The debenture holders to take over freehold property (book value ₹ 2,00,000) at a valuation of ₹ 2,50,000 in part repayment of their holdings. Remaining freehold property to be revalued at ₹ 6,00,000.

(iii) Loan from directors to be waived off in full.

(iv) Inventories of ₹ 50,000 to be written off, ₹ 12,500 to be provided for bad debts.

(v) Profit and Loss account balance, Trademark, Goodwill and Deferred Revenue Expenditure to be written off.

Pass Journal Entries for all the above mentioned transactions. Also, Prepare Capital Reduction account and company's Balance Sheet immediately after reconstruction.

[**Ans.** Total Losses w/o ₹12,37,500, Total of B/S ₹9,62,500]

7. Given are the extracts of Balance Sheet of M/s. Cube Limited as at 31-03-2.15:

Particulars	*Note No.*	*(₹ in lakh)*
Equity & Liabilities		
Shareholder's Funds		
Share Capital	1	700
Reserves & Surplus (Profit and Loss A/c)	2	(261)
Non-Current Liabilities		
Long-Current Borrowings	3	350
Current Liabilities		
Trade Payables		51
Other Liabilities [Interest Accrued and Due on 6% Debentures]		12
Total		852
Assets		
Non-current Assets		
Fixed Assets		
Tangible Assets	4	375

Current Assets	
Current Investments [Investment in Equity Instruments]	100
Inventories	150
Trade Receivable	225
Cash & Cash Equivalents	2
Total	852

Notes to Accounts:

Particulars	*(₹ in lakh)*
1. Share Capital	
50 lakh Equity Shares of ₹ 10 each, fully paid up	500
2 lakh 8% Preference Shares of ₹ 100 each, fully paid up	200
	700
2. Reserves & Surplus	
Debit balance of Profit & Loss A/c	(261)
3. Long Term Borrowings	
6% Debentures (Secured by Freehold Property)	200
Director's Loan	150
	350
4. Tangible Assets	
Freehold Property	275
Plant & Machinery	100
	375

The Board of Directors of the company decided upon the following scheme of reconstruction with the consent of respective shareholders:

1. Preference Shares are to be written down to ₹ 80 each and Equity Shares to ₹ 2 each.
2. Preference shares Dividend in arrears for 3 years to be waived by 2/3rd and for balance 1/3rd, Equity Shares of ₹ 2 each to be allotted.
3. Debenture Holders agreed to take one Freehold Property at its book value of ₹ 150 lakh in part payment of their holding. Balance Debentures to remain as liability of the company.
4. Interest accrued and due on Debentures to be paid in cash.
5. Remaining Freehold Property to be valued at ₹ 200 lakh.
6. All investments sold out for ₹ 125 lakh.
7. 70% of Directors' loan to be waived and for the balance, Equity Shares of ₹ 2 each to be allowed.
8. 40% of Trade Receivables and 80% of Inventories to be written off.
9. Company's contractual commitments amounting to ₹ 300 lakh have been settled by paying 5% penalty of contract value.

You are required to:

(a) Pass Journal Entries for all the transactions related to internal reconstruction.

(b) Prepare Reconstruction Account and

(c) Prepare notes on Share Capital and Tangible Assets to Balance Sheet, immediately after the implementation of scheme of internal reconstruction.

[**Ans.** Total Losses w/o ₹629,00,000]

8. Crystal Company Limited decided to reconstruct its business as it has accumulated huge losses. Given are the extracts of Balance Sheet of the company as at 31.03.2022 before reconstruction:

Particulars	₹
3,00,000 Equity shares of ₹ 10 each	30,00,000
1,60,000, 6% Preference shares of ₹ 10 each	16,00,000
Profit & loss A/c	(18,50,000)
6% Debentures (Secured against land & building)	15,00,000
Bank overdraft	5,80,000
Trade Payables	12,00,000
Provision for income tax	2, 00, 000
Goodwill	5,20,000
Patents	1,50,000
Land & building	17,00,000
Plant & machinery	2,00,000
Investments (at cost)	2,20,000
Trade Receivables	17,40,000
Inventories	17,00,000

Following scheme of reconstruction has been approved by all interested parties and the Court:

1. All equity shares are reduced to ₹ 3 each and preference shares to ₹ 7 each.
2. Debentureholders agree to take over a part of land and building, book value of which is ₹ 7,00,000, towards their 50% claim. Rate of interest of balance 50% debentures increased to 9%.
3. Goodwill and patent will be written off.
4. 10% of Trade Receivables to be provided for bad debts.
5. Inventories to be written off by ₹ 2,60,000.
6. 50% of balance land & building sold for ₹ 6,00,000 and remaining land & building valued at ₹ 6,00,000.
7. Investments to be sold for ₹ 2,00,000.
8. There are pending contracts amounting to ₹ 70,00,000. These contracts are to be cancelled on payment of penalty @ 5% of pending contract amount.
9. The income tax liability of the company is settled at ₹ 3, 06, 000. Provision for income tax will be raised accordingly.
10. 1/3 of Trade Payables decided to forgo their claim.
11. After making all the above adjustments, balance amount available through scheme, will be utilized to write off the value of plant & machinery to that extent.

Required: Pass the journal entries and draw up Balance Sheet of the company after reconstruction.

[**Ans.** Total Losses w/o ₹ 32,10,000, Total of B/S ₹ 38,76,000]

9. Given are the extracts of Balance Sheet of M Ltd. as at 31st March, 2015:

Particulars	₹
15,000, 10% Preference Shares of ₹ 100 each	15,00,000
35,000 Equity Shares of ₹ 100 each	35,00,000
Profit & Loss A/c	(15,50,000)
Securities Premium account	1,00,000
7% Debentures of ₹ 100 each	5,00,000
Trade Payables	12,50,000
Loan from Director	1,50,000
Land & Buildings	15,00,000
Plant & Machinery	10,00,000
Goodwill	3,50,000
Inventories	6,00,000
Trade Receivables	15,00,000
Cash at bank	1,00,000
Preliminary Expenses	4,00,000

No dividend on Preference shares has been paid for the last 5 years.

The following scheme of reorganization was duly approved by the court:

(a) Each Equity share to be reduced to ₹ 25.

(b) Each existing Preference share to be reduced to ₹ 75 and then exchanged for 1 new 13% Preference share of ₹ 50 each and 1 Equity share of ₹ 25 each.

(c) Preference shareholders have forgone their right for dividend for four years. One year's dividend at the old rate is however, payable to them in fully paid equity Shares of ₹ 25.

(d) The Debentureholders be given the option to *either* accept 90% of their claims in cash *or* to convert their claims in full into new 13% Preference shares of ₹ 50 each issued at par. One half (in value) of the debentureholders accepted Preference shares for their claims. The rest were paid cash.

(e) Contingent liability of ₹ 1,50,000 is payable, which has been created by wrong action of one Director. He has agreed to compensate this loss out of the loan given by the Director to the company.

(f) Goodwill does not have any value in the present. Decrease the value of Plant and Machinery, Inventories and Trade Receivables by ₹ 4,00,000, ₹ 1,00,000 and ₹ 1,50,000 respectively. Increase the value of Land and Buildings to ₹ 18,00,000.

(g) 40,000 new Equity shares of ₹ 25 each are to be issued at par, payable in full on application. The issue was underwritten for a commission of 4%. Shares were fully taken up.

(h) The total expenses incurred by the company in connection with the scheme excluding, underwriting commission amounted to ₹ 15,000.

Required: Pass necessary Journal Entries to record the above transactions.

[**Ans.** Total Losses w/o ₹30,05,000]

10. Given are the extracts of Balance Sheet of Neptune Ltd as at 31.3.2015:

Particulars	₹
80,000, Equity Shares of ₹ 10 each	8,00,000
5,000, 6% Cumulative Preference Shares of ₹ 100 each	5,00,000
Profit and Loss A/c	(3,65,000)
6% Debentures (secured by free hold property)	3,97,500
Trade Payables	17,500
Director's loan	3,00,000
Freehold property	5,00,000
Plant & Machinery	1,80,000
Trade investment (at cost)	1,70,000
Sundry Debtors	4,50,000
Inventories	2,00,000
Deferred Advertisement Expenditure	1,50,000

The Court approved a scheme of re-organisation to take effect on 1.4.2015 and the terms are given below:

(a) Preference shares are to be written down to ₹ 75 each and equity shares to ₹ 2 each.

(b) Preference dividend in arrear for 4 years to be waived by 75% and for the balance equity shares of ₹ 2 each to be allotted.

(c) Arrear of debenture interest to be paid in cash.

(d) Debentureholders agreed to take one freehold property (Book value ₹ 3,00,000) at a valuation of ₹ 3,00,000 in part payment of their holding. Balance debentures to remain as liability of the company.

(e) Deferred advertisement expenditure to be written off.

(f) Inventories value to be written off fully in the books.

(g) 50% of the Trade Receivables to be written off as bad debt.

(h) Remaining freehold property (after take over by debentureholders) to be valued at ₹ 3,50,000.

(i) Investment sold out for ₹ 2,00,000.

(j) 80% of the Director's loan to be waived and for the balance, equity shares of ₹ 2 each to be issued,

(k) Company's contractual commitments amounting to ₹ 5,00,000 to be cancelled by paying penalty at 3% of contract value.

(l) Cost of re-construction scheme is ₹ 20,000.

Required: Show the Journal entries (with narration) to be passed for giving effect to the above transactions and draw Balance Sheet of the company after effecting the scheme.

[**Ans.** Total Losses w/o ₹ 9,40,000, Total of B/S ₹ 8,97,500]

11. Given are the extracts of Balance Sheet of X Ltd, as at 31st March 2015:

Particulars		₹
Equity and Liabilities		
1. Shareholders' Funds		
Share Capital:		
(a) 40,000 Equity Shares of ₹ 100 each fully paid		40,00,000
(b) 20,000, 10% Preference Shares of ₹ 100 each fully paid		20,00,000
Reserves & Surplus:		
(a) Securities Premium Account		1,50,000
(b) Profit & Loss Account		(23,00,000)
2. Non-Current Liabilities: Long Term borrowings –7% Debentures of ₹ 100 each		4,00,000
3. Current Liabilities:		
Other Current Liabilities		
– Trade Payables		10,00,000
– Loan from Director		2,00,000
Total Liabilities		54,50,000
Assets		
1. Non-Current Assets		
Fixed Assets		
(a) Land & Building	20,00,000	
(b) Plant and Machinery	12,00,000	32,00,000
Intangible Assets: Goodwill		4,00,000
2. Current Assets		
(a) Trade Receivables	12,00,000	
(b) Inventories	5,00,000	
(c) Cash at Bank	1,50,000	18,50,000
Total Assets		54,50,000

No Dividend on Preference Shares has been paid for last 5 years.

The following scheme of reorganization was duly approved by the Court:

(a) Each Equity Share be reduced to ₹ 25.

(b) Each existing Preference Share to be reduced to ₹ 75, and then exchanged for one new 13% Preference Share of ₹ 50 each and one Equity Share of ₹ 25 each.

(c) Preference Shareholders have forgone their right for Dividend for four years. One year's Dividend at the old rate is however, payable to them in fully paid Equity Shares of ₹ 25.

(d) The Debenture Holders be given the option to *either* accept 90% of their claims in cash *or* to convert their claims in full into new 13% Preference Shares of ₹ 50 each issued at par. One-fourth (in value) of the Debenture Holders accepted Preference Shares for their claims. The rest were paid in cash.

(e) Contingent Liability of ₹ 2,00,000 is payable which has been created by wrong action of one Director. He has agreed to compensate this loss out of the Loan given by the Director to the Company

(f) Goodwill does not have any value in the present. Decrease the value of Plant & Machinery, Inventories and Trade Receivables by ₹ 3,00,000, ₹ 1,00,000 and ₹ 2,00,000 respectively. Increase the value of Land & Building to ₹ 25,00,000.

(g) 50,000 new Equity Shares of ₹ 25 each are to be issued at par payable in full on application. The issue was underwritten for a Commission of 4%. Shares were fully taken up.

(h) Total Expenses incurred by the Company in connection with the Scheme excluding Underwriting Commission amounted to ₹ 20,000.

Pass necessary Journal Entries to record the above transactions.

[Ans. Total Losses w/o ₹10,00,000]

12. Given are the extracts of Balance Sheet of R Ltd., at 31st March, 2015:

Particulars	₹
Cumulative Preference Shares of ₹ 10 each	6,40,000
64,000 Equity Shares of ₹ 10 each, ₹ 7.5 paid	4,80,000
Profit & Loss Account	(4,40,000)
Loans from directors	60,000
Trade Payables	4,40,000
Bank Overdraft	2,08,000
Intangibles	68,000
Freehold Premises at cost	1,40,000
Plant and Equipment at cost *less* depreciation	2,40,000
Investments in shares in Q Ltd. (at cost)	3,24,000
Inventories	2,48,000
Trade Receivables	3,20,000
Deferred Revenue Expenditure	48,000

Note: The arrears of Preference Dividends amount to ₹ 51,200.

A scheme of reconstruction was duly approved with effect from 1st April, 2015 under the conditions stated below:

(a) The unpaid amount on the equity shares would be called up.

(b) The preference shareholders would forego their arrear dividends. In addition, they would accept a reduction of ₹ 2.5 per share. The dividend rate would be enhanced to 10%.

(c) The equity shareholders would accept a reduction of ₹ 7.5 per share.

(d) R Ltd. holds 21,600 shares in Q Ltd. This represents 15% of the share capital of that company. Q Ltd. is not a quoted company. The average net profit (after tax) of the company is ₹ 2,50,000. The shares would be valued based on 12% capitalization rate.

(e) A bad debt provision at 2% would be created.

(f) The other assets would be valued as under:

Intangibles ₹ 48,000, Plant ₹ 1,40,000, Freehold premises ₹ 3,80,000, Inventories ₹ 2,50,000

(g) The profit and loss account debit balance and the balance standing to the debit of the deferred revenue expenditure account would be eliminated.

(h) The directors would have to take equity shares at the new face value of ₹ 2.5 per share in settlement of their loan.

(i) The equity shareholders, including the directors, who would receive equity shares in settlement of their loans, would take up two new equity shares for every one held.

(j) The preference shareholders would take up one new preference share for every four held.

(k) The authorised share capital would be restated to ₹ 14,00,000.

(l) The new face values of the shares-preference and equity will be maintained at their reduced levels.

Required: Prepare the Necessary ledger accounts and the Balance Sheet of the company after reconstruction. **[Ans.** Total Losses w/o ₹ 6,25,900, Total of B/S ₹19,56,000]

13. Given are the extracts of Balance Sheet of Y Ltd. as at 31st March, 2015:

Particulars	₹
5,00,000 Equity Shares of ₹ 10 each	50,00,000
9% 20,000 Preference Shares of ₹ 100 each	20,00,000
Profit and Loss Account	(15,00,000)
10% First Debentures	6,00,000
10% Second Debentures	10,00,000
Debentures interest outstanding	1,60,000
Trade Payables	5,00,000
Directors' Loan	1,00,000
Bank O/D	1,00,000
Outstanding Liabilities	40,000
Provision for Tax	1,00,000
Goodwill	10,00,000
Patent	5,00,000
Tangible Fixed Assets	45,00,000
Trade Investments	5,00,000
Trade Receivables	5,00,000
Inventories	10,00,000
Discount on issue of Debentures	1,00,000

Note: Preference Dividend is in arrears for last three years.

A holds 10% first debentures for ₹ 4,00,000 and 10% second debentures for ₹ 6,00,000. He is also a creditor for ₹ 1,00,000. B holds 10% first debentures for ₹ 2,00,000 and 10% second debentures for ₹ 4,00,000 and is also a creditor for ₹ 50,000.

The following scheme of reconstruction has been agreed upon and duly approved by the court:

(a) All the equity shares be converted into fully paid equity shares of ₹ 5 each.

(b) The preference shares be reduced to ₹ 50 each and the preference shareholders agree to forego their arrears of preference dividends in consideration of which 9% preference shares are to be converted into 10% preference shares.

(c) Mr. 'A' is to cancel ₹ 6,00,000 of his total debt including interest on debentures and to pay ₹ 1 lakh to the company and to receive new 12% debentures for the Balance Amount.

(d) Mr. 'B' is to cancel ₹ 3,00,000 of his total debt including interest on debentures and to accept new 12% debentures for the balance amount.

(e) Trade Payables (other than A and B) agreed to forego 50% of their claim.

(f) Directors to accept settlement of their loans as to 60% thereof by allotment of equity shares and balance being waived.

(g) There were capital commitments totalling ₹ 3,00,000. These contracts are to be cancelled on payment of 5% of the contract price as a penalty.

(h) The Directors refund ₹ 1,10,000 of the fees previously received by them.

(i) Reconstruction expenses paid ₹ 10,000.

(j) The taxation liability of the company is settled at ₹ 80,000 and the same is paid immediately.

(k) The assets are revalued as under:

Particulars	₹
Tangible Fixed Assets	24,80,000
Inventories	7,00,000
Trade Receivables	3,00,000
Trade Investment	4,00,000

Required: Pass Journal entries for all the above mentioned transactions including amounts to be written off of Goodwill, Patents, Loss in Profit and Loss Account and Discount on issue of debentures. Prepare Bank Account and working of allocation of Interest on Debentures between A and B.

[**Ans.** Total Losses w/o ₹47,20,000]

14. Given are the extracts of Balance Sheet of Max Ltd. and Mini Ltd. as at March 31, 2015:

(₹ '000)

Particulars	*Max Ltd.*	*Mini Ltd.*
Equity Shares Capital of ₹ 100 each	1,500	1,000
9% Preference shares of ₹ 100 each	500	400
General reserve	180	170
Profit and loss account	(411)	15
12% Debentures of ₹ 100 each	600	200
Trade Payables	415	225
Goodwill	20	—
Tangible Fixed Assets	1,500	760
Own debentures [Nominal value ₹ 2,00,000]	192	—
Inventories	393	680
Trade Receivables	651	440
Cash at bank	26	130
Discount on issue of debentures	2	–

On 1.4.2015, Max Ltd. adopted the following scheme of reconstruction:

(a) Each equity share shall be sub-divided into 10 equity shares of ₹ 10 each fully paid up. 50% of the equity share capital would be surrendered to the company.

(b) Preference dividends are in arrear for 3 years. Preference shareholders agreed to waive 90% of the dividend claim and accept payment for the balance.

(c) Own debentures of ₹ 80,000 were sold at ₹ 98 own-interest and remaining own debentures were cancelled.

(d) Debentureholders of ₹ 2,80,000 agreed to accept one machinery of book value of ₹ 3,00,000 in full settlement.

(e) Trade Payables, Trade Receivables and Inventories were valued at ₹ 3,50,000, ₹ 5,90,000 and ₹ 3,60,000 respectively. The goodwill, discount on issue of debentures and profit and loss (Dr.) are to be written off.

(f) The Company paid ₹ 15,000 as penalty to avoid capital commitments of ₹ 3,00,000.

On 2.4.2015 a scheme of absorption was adopted. Max Ltd. would take over Mini Ltd. The purchase consideration was fixed as below:

(i) Equity shareholders of Mini Ltd. will be given 50 equity shares of ₹ 10 each fully paid up, in exchange for every 5 shares held in Mini Ltd.

(ii) Issue of 9% preference shares of ₹ 100 each in the ratio of 4 preference shares of Max Ltd. for every 5 preference shares held in Mini Ltd.

(iii) Issue of one 12% debentures of ₹ 100 each of Max Ltd. for every 12% Debentures in Mini Ltd.

Required: Give journal entries in the books of Max Ltd. and draw the resultant Balance Sheet as at 2nd April, 2015.

[**Ans.** Total Losses w/o ₹4,33,000, Total of B/S ₹42,35,900]

15. M/s Planet Limited has decided to reconstruct the Balance Sheet since it has accumulated huge losses. The following is the balance sheet of the company as on 31st March, 2023 before reconstruction:

Particulars	***Note No.***	***Amount (₹ In lakh)***
Equity & Liabilities		
Shareholders' Funds		
Share Capital	1	2,100
Reserves & Surplus	2	(783)
Non-Current Liabilities		
Long term Borrowings	3	1,050
Current Liabilities		
Trade Payables	4	153
Other Liabilities	5	36
Total		2,556

Assets		
Non-Current Assets:		
Fixed Assets		
Tangible Assets	6	1,125
Current Investments	7	300
Inventories	8	450
Trade Receivables	9	675
Cash & Cash Equivalents	10	6
Total		2,556

Notes to Accounts:

		₹ *In lakh*
1.	Share capital	
	Authorised:	
	300 lakh shares of ₹ 10 each	3,000
	12 lakh, 8% preference Shares of ₹ 100 each	1,200
		4,200
	Issued, Subscribed and Paid up:	
	150 Lakh Equity Shares of ₹ 10 each, fully paid up	1,500
	6 lakh 8% Preference Shares of ₹ 100 each, fully paid up	600
		2,100
2.	Reserves and Surplus	
	Debit balance of Profit & Loss A/c	(783)
3.	Long term borrowings	
	6% Debentures (Secured by freehold property)	600
	Director's Loan	450
		1,050
4.	Trade Payables	
	Trade Payables for Goods	153
5.	Other Liabilities	
	Interest Accrued and Due on 6% Debentures	36
6.	Tangible Assets	
	Freehold Property	825
	Plant & machinery	300
		1,125

7.	Current Investment	
	Investment in Equity Instruments	300
8.	Inventories	
	Finished Goods	450
9.	Trade Receivables	
	Trade receivables for Goods	675
10.	Cash and Cash equivalents	
	Balance with bank	6

The Board of Directors of the company decided upon the following scheme of reconstruction with the consent of respective shareholders:

1. Preference Shares are to be written down to ₹ 75 each and Equity Shares to ₹ 2 each.
2. Preference Shares Dividend in arrears for 3 years to be waived by 2/3rd and for balance 1/3rd, Equity Shares of ₹ 2 each to be allotted.
3. Debenture holders agreed to take one Freehold Property at its book value of ₹ 450 lakh in part payment of their holding. Balance Debentures to remain as liability of the company.
4. Interest accrued and due on Debentures to be paid in cash.
5. Remaining Freehold Property to be valued at ₹ 550 lakh.
6. All investments sold out for ₹ 425 lakh.
7. 70% of Directors' loan to be waived and for the balance, Equity Shares of ₹ 2 each to be allotted.
8. 40% of Trade receivables and 80% of Inventories to be written off.
9. Company's contractual commitments amounting to ₹ 900 lakh have been settled by paying 8% penalty of contract value.

You are required to:

(a) Pass Journal Entries for all the transactions related to internal reconstruction;

(b) Prepare Reconstruction Account, Bank Account; and

(c) Prepare Notes to Accounts on Share Capital and Tangible Assets, immediately after the implementation of internal reconstruction.

[**Ans.** Total of Reconstruction A/c ₹ 1,965 lakh]

16. The summarized balance sheet of Z Limited as on 31st March, 2023 is as under:

Liabilities	***Amount in ₹***
Share Capital:	
5,00,000 Equity shares of ₹ 10 each fully paid up	50,00,000
9%, 20,000 Preference shares of ₹ 100 each fully paid up	20,00,000
Reserves and Surplus:	
Profit and Loss A/c	(14,60,000)

Non-Current Liabilities:	
10% Secured Debentures	16,00,000
Current Liabilities:	
Interest due on Debentures	1,60,000
Trade Payables	5,00,000
Loan from Directors	1,00,000
Bank Overdraft	1,00,000
Provision for Tax	1,00,000
Total	**81,00,000**
Assets:	
Non-Current Assets:	
Fixed Assets:	
(a) Tangible Assets:	
Land & Buildings	30,00,000
Plant & Machinery	12,50,000
Furniture & Fixtures	2,50,000
(b) Intangible Assets:	
Goodwill	10,00,000
Patents	5,00,000
Current Assets:	
Trade Investments	5,00,000
Trade Receivables	5,00,000
Inventory	10,00,000
Discount on issue of debentures	1,00,000
Total	**81,00,000**

Note: Preference dividend is in arrears for last 2 years.

Mr. Y holds 60% of debentures and Mr. Z holds 40% of debentures. Moreover ₹ 1,00,000 and ₹ 60,000 were also payable to Mr. Y and Mr. Z respectively as trade payable.

The following scheme of reconstruction has been agreed upon and duly approved.

(i) All the equity shares to be converted into fully paid equity shares of ₹ 5.00 each.

(ii) The Preference shares be reduced to ₹ 50 each and the preference shareholders agreed to forego their arrears of preference dividends, in consideration of which 9% preference shares are to be converted into 10% preference shares.

(iii) Mr. Y and Mr. Z agreed to cancel 50% each of their respective total debt including interest on debentures. Mr. Y and Mr. Z also agreed to pay ₹ 1,00,000 and ₹ 60,000 respectively in cash and to receive new 12% debentures for the balance amount.

(iv) Persons relating to Trade Payables, other than Mr. Y and Mr. Z also agreed to forgo their 50% claims.

(v) Directors also waived 60% of their loans and accepted equity shares for the balance.

(vi) Capital commitments of ₹ 3.00 lacs were cancelled on payment of ₹ 15,000 as penalty.

(vii) Directors refunded ₹ 1,00,000 of the fees previously received by them.

(viii) Reconstruction expenses paid ₹ 15,000.

(ix) The taxation liability of the company was settled for ₹ 75,000 and was paid immediately.

(x) The Assets were revalued as under:

Land and Building	32,00,000
Plant and Machinery	6,00,000
Inventory	7,50,000
Trade Receivables	4,00,000
Furniture and Fixtures	1,50,000
Trade Investments	4,50,000

You are required to pass journal entries for all the above mentioned transactions including amounts to be written off of Goodwill, Patents, Loss in Profit and Loss A/c arid Discount on issue of debentures. And also prepare Bank A/c and Reconstruction A/c.

[**Ans.** Total of Reconstruction A/c ₹ 50,15,000]

17. The Balance Sheet of M/s Clean Ltd. as on 31st March, 2023 was summarized as follows:

Liabilities	₹	*Assets*	₹
Share Capital:		Land & Building	75,00,000
Equity Shares of ₹ 50 each, fully paid up	60,00,000	Plant and Machinery	22,00,000
9% Preference Shares of ₹ 10 each, fully paid up	40,00,000	Trade Investment	16,50,000
7% Debentures (secured by plant and machinery)	23,00,000	Inventories	9,50,000
8% Debentures	17,00,000	Trade Receivable	18,00,000
Trade Payables	6,00,000	Cash and Bank Balances	3,60,000
Provision for Tax	75,000	Profit & Loss Account	2,15,000
	1,46,75,000		**1,46,75,000**

The Board of Directors of the company decided upon the following scheme of reconstruction duly approved by all concerned parties;

1. The equity shareholders agreed to receive in lieu of their present holding of ₹ 1,20,000 shares of ₹ 50 each as under:

   (a) fully paid equity shares of ₹ 10 each equal to 2/3rd of their holding.

(b) 9% preference shares of ₹ 8 each to the extent of 25% of the above new equity share capital.

(c) ₹ 2,80,000, 10% debentures of ₹ 80 each.

2. The preference shareholders agreed that their ₹ 10 shares should be reduced to ₹ 8 by cancellation ₹ 2 per share. They also agreed to subscribe for two new equity shares of ₹ 10 each for every five preference shares held.
3. The taxation liability of the company is settled at ₹ 66,000 and the same is paid immediately.
4. One of the trade creditors of the company to whom the company owes ₹ 1,00,000 decides to forgo 30% of his claim. He is allotted equity shares of ₹ 10 each in full satisfaction of his balance claim.
5. Other trade creditors of ₹ 5,00,000 are given option of either to accept fully paid 9% preference shares of ₹ 8 each for the amount due to them or to accept 80% of the amount due to them in cash in full settlement of their claim. Trade creditors for ₹ 3,50,000 accepted preference shares option and rest of them opted for cash towards full settlement of their claim.
6. Company's contractual commitments amounting to ₹ 6,50,000 have been settled by paying 4% penalty of contract value.
7. Debenture holders having charge on plant and machinery accepted plant and machinery in full settlement of their dues.
8. The rate of interest on 8% debentures is increased to 10%. The debenture holders surrender their existing debenture of ₹ 50 each and agreed to accept 10% debentures of ₹ 80 each for every two debentures held by them.
9. The land and building to be depreciated by 5%.
10. The debit balance of profit and loss A/cis to be eliminated.
11. 1/4th of trade receivables and 1/5th of inventory to be written off.

Pass Journal Entries and prepare Balance Sheet after completion of the reconstruction scheme in the books of M/s Clean Ltd., as per Schedule III to the Companies Act. 2013.

[**Ans.** Total of Reconstruction A/c ₹ 60,29,000, Total of B/S ₹ 1,26,33,000]

18. Proficient Infosoft Ltd. is in the hands of a Receiver for Debenture Holders who holds a charge on all asset except uncalled capital. The following statement shows the position as regards creditors as on 30th June, 2023:

Liabilities	₹	*Assets*	₹
8000 shares of ₹ 100 each ₹ 60 paid up	–	Property (cost is ₹ 3,80,800) estimated at	1,08,000
First Debentures	3,60,000	Plant & Machinery (Cost is ₹ 2,87,200) estimated at	72,000
Second Debentures	7,80,000	Cash in hands of the receiver	3,24,000
Unsecured Trade Payables	5,40,000		5,04,000
		Uncalled capital	3,20,000

			8,24,000
		Deficiency	8,56,000
	16,80,000		**16,80,000**

A holds the first debentures for ₹ 3,60,000 and second debentures for ₹ 3,60,000. He is also an unsecured trade payable for ₹ 1,08,000. B holds second debentures for ₹ 3,60,000 and is an unsecured trade payable for ₹ 72,000.

The following scheme of reconstruction is proposed.

(i) A is to cancel ₹ 2,52,000 of the total debt owing to him; to bring ₹ 36,000 in cash and to take first debentures (in cancellation of those already issued to him) for ₹ 6,12,000 in satisfaction of all his claims.

(ii) B to accept ₹ 1,08,000 in cash in satisfaction of all claims by him.

(iii) In full settlement of 60% of the claim, unsecured trade payable (other than A and B) agreed to accept three shares of ₹ 25 each, fully paid against their claim for each ₹ 100.

The balance of 40% is to be postponed and to be payable at the end of three years from the date of Court's approval of the scheme. The nominal share capital is to be increased accordingly.

(iv) Uncalled capital is to be called up in full and ₹ 75 per share cancelled, thus making the shares of ₹ 25 each.

Assuming that the scheme is duly approved by all parties interested and by the court, give necessary journal entries.

[Ans. Profit and loss A/c (Debit balance) ₹ 11,68,000]

19. The summarized Balance Sheet of SK Ltd. as on 31st March, 2023 is given below.

(₹ in '000)

Particulars	₹
Liabilities	
Equity Shares of ₹ 10 each	35,000
8%, Cumulative Preference Shares of ₹ 100 each	17,500
6% Debentures of ₹ 100 each	14,000
Sundry Creditors	17,500
Provision for taxation	350
Total	84,350
Assets	
Fixed Assets	43,750
Investments (Market value ₹ 3325 thousand)	3,500
Current Assets (Including Bank Balance)	35,000
Profit and Loss Account	2,100
Total	84,350

The following Scheme of Internal Reconstruction is approved and put into effect on 31st March, 2023.

(i) Investments are to be brought to their market value.

(ii) The Taxation Liability is settled at ₹ 5,25,000 out of current Assets.

(iii) The balance of Profit and Loss Account to be written off.

(iv) All the existing equity shares are reduced to ₹ 4 each.

(v) All preference shares are reduced to ₹ 60 each.

(vi) The rate of interest on debentures is increased to 9%. The Debenture holders surrender their existing debentures of ₹ 100 each and exchange them for fresh debentures of ₹ 80 each. Each old debenture is exchanged for one new debenture.

(vii) Balance of Current Assets left after settlement of taxation liability are revalued at ₹1,57,50,000.

(viii) Fixed Assets are written down to 80%.

(ix) One of the creditors of the Company for ₹ 70,00,000 gives up 50% of his claim. He is allotted 8,75,000 equity shares of ₹ 4 each in full and final settlement of his claim.

Pass journal entries for the above transactions.

[**Ans.** Total of Reconstruction A/c ₹ 343,00,000]

20. Following is the summarized Balance Sheet of Fortunate Ltd. as on 31st March, 2023.

Particulars	(₹)
Liabilities	
Authorized and Issued Share Capital	
(a) 15,000 8% Preference shares of ₹ 50 each	7,50,000
(b) 18,750 Equity shares of ₹ 50 each	9,37,500
Profit and Loss Account	(5,63,750)
Loan	7,16,250
Trade Payables	2,58,750
Other Liabilities	43,750
Total	21,42,500
Assets	
Building at cost less depreciation	5,00,000
Plant at cost less depreciation	3,35,000
Trademarks and goodwill at cost	3,97,500
Inventory	5,00,000
Trade Receivables	4,10,000
Total	21,42,500

Note: Preference shares dividend is in arrear for last five years.

The Company is running with the shortage of working capital and not earnings profits. A scheme of reconstruction has been approved by both the classes of shareholders. The summarized scheme of reconstruction is as follows:

(i) The equity shareholders have agreed that their ₹ 50 shares should be reduced to ₹ 5 by cancellation of ₹ 45.00 per share. They have also agreed to subscribe for three new equity shares of ₹ 5.00 each for each equity share held.

(ii) The preference shareholders have agreed to forego the arrears of dividends and to accept for each ₹ 50 preference share, 4 new 6% preference shares of ₹ 10 each, plus 3 new equity shares of ₹ 5.00 each, all credited as fully paid.

(iii) Lenders to the company for ₹ 1,87,500 have agreed to convert their loan into shares and for this purpose they will be allotted 15,000 new preference shares of ₹ 10 each and 7,500 new equity shares of ₹ 5.00 each.

(iv) The directors have agreed to subscribe in cash for 25,000 new equity shares of ₹ 5.00 each in addition to any shares to be subscribed by them under (i) above.

(v) Of the cash received by the issue of new shares, ₹ 2,50,000 is to be used to reduce the loan due by the company.

(vi) The equity share capital cancelled is to be applied:

(a) To write off the debit balance in the Profit and Loss A/c, and

(b) To write off ₹ 43,750 from the value of plant.

Any balance remaining is to be used to write down the value of trademarks and goodwill. The nominal capital, as reduced, is to be increased to ₹ 8,12,500 for preference share capital and ₹ 9,37,500 for equity share capital.

You are required to pass journal entries to show the effect of above scheme and prepare the Balance Sheet of the Company after reconstruction.

[**Ans.** Total of Reconstruction A/c ₹ 8,43,750, Total of B/S ₹ 20,93,750]

21. Sapra Limited has laid down the following terms upon the sanction of the reconstruction scheme by the court.

(i) The shareholders to receive in lieu of their present holding at 7,50,000 shares of ₹ 10 each, the following:

– New fully paid ₹ 10 Equity Shares equal to 3/5th of their holding.

– Fully paid ₹ 10, 6% Preference Shares to the extent of 2/5th of the above new equity shares.

– 7% Debentures of ₹ 250,000.

(ii) Goodwill which stood at ₹ 2,70,000 is to be completely written off.

(iii) Plant & Machinery to be reduced by ₹ 1,00,000, Furniture to be reduced by ₹ 88,000 and Building to be appreciated by ₹ 1,50,000.

(iv) Investment of ₹ 6,00,000 to be brought down to its existing market price of ₹ 1,80,000.

(v) Write off Profit & Loss Account debit balance of ₹ 2,25,000.

In case of any shortfall, the balance of General Reserve of ₹ 42,000 can be utilized to write off the losses under reconstruction scheme.

You are required to show the necessary Journal Entries in the books of Sapra Limited of the above reconstruction scheme considering that balance in General Reserve is utilized to write off the losses.

[**Ans.** Total of Reconstruction A/c ₹ 11,03,000]

22. The summarized Balance Sheet of ZED Limited as on 31st March, 2023 is as under:

Balance Sheet as at 31st March, 2023

	Particulars		*Amount* ₹
I	**Equity and Liabilities**		
1.	**Shareholders Fund**		
	Share Capital		
	50,000 equity shares of ₹ 100 each fully paid		50,00,000
	25,000, 10 preference shares of ₹ 100 each fully paid		25,00,000
	Reserve & Surplus		
	(a) Securities Premium Account		1,87,500
	(b) Profit & Loss Account		(28,75,000)
2.	**Non-Current Liabilities**		
	Long Term Borrowings		
	7% Debentures of ₹ 100 each		5,00,000
3.	**Current Liabilities**		
	Other Current Liabilities		
	(a) Creditors		12,50,000
	(b) Loan from Director		2,50,000
	Total Liabilities		68,12,500
II	**Assets**		
1.	**Non-Current Assets**		
	Property, Plant and Equipment		
	(a) Land & Building	25,00,000	
	(b) Plant & Machinery	15,00,000	40,00,000
	Intangible Assets		
	Goodwill		5,00,000
2.	**Current Assets**		
	(a) Debtors	15,00,000	
	(b) Stock	6,25,000	
	(c) Cash at Bank	1,87,500	23,12,500
	Total Assets		68,12,500

No Dividend on Preference Shares has been paid for last 3 Years.

The following scheme of reorganization was duly approved by the Tribunal:

(i) Each equity share of ₹ 100 to be reduced to ₹ 25.

(ii) Each existing Preference Share of ₹ 100 to be reduced to ₹ 75 and then exchange for one new 13% Preference Share of ₹ 50 each and one Equity Share of ₹ 25 each.

(iii) The Debenture Holders be given the option to either accept 90% of their claims in cash or to convert, their claims in full into new 13% Preference Shares of ₹ 50 each issued at par. One-fourth (in value) of the Debenture Holders accepted Preference Shares for their claims. The rest were paid in cash.

(iv) Directors have agreed to forgone 20% their claim in respect of loan and agree to have equity shares for rest of the Loan.

(v) 20,000 new Equity Shares of ₹ 25 each are to be issued at par and full amount is payable at the time of application.

(vi) Preference Shareholders have forgone their right for dividend for two years. One year's dividend at the old rate is however payable to them in fully paid equity shares of ₹ 25.

(vii) Total expenses incurred by the Company in connection with the Scheme amounted to ₹ 25,000.

(viii) Goodwill does not have any value in the present and other remaining assets are valued as follows;

Plant & Machinery	:	Decreased by ₹ 3,75,000
Stock	:	Decreased by ₹ 1,25,000
Debtors	:	Decreased by ₹ 2,50,000
Land & Building	:	Increased by ₹ 6,25,000

You are required to :

(a) Pass necessary Journal Entries to record the above transactions.

(b) Prepare the resultant Balance sheet (after reorganization) as on 31st March, 2023.

[**Ans.** Total of Reconstruction A/c ₹ 50,87,500, Total of B/S ₹ 63,25,000]

18 CORPORATE FINANCIAL REPORTING

LEARNING OBJECTIVES

After studying this chapter, you should be able to understand:

- ◇ Meaning, Need ,Objectives and Constituents of Annual Report
- ◇ Difference between Annual Report and Financial Statements;
- ◇ Contents of Report of the Board of Directors
- ◇ CSR Reporting
- ◇ Drafting of Notes to Accounts
- ◇ Segment Reporting as per AS - 17
- ◇ Triple Bottom Line Reporting
- ◇ Sustainability Reporting
- ◇ XBRL Reporting

WHAT IS ANNUAL REPORT?

Annual Report is the most comprehensive means of communication between a company and its shareholders as to the larger picture of the organisation that includes new products, new markets, emerging strategies, and the company's overall future guidance as to Revenue,Margin etc.

WHAT ARE THE OBJECTIVES OF ANNUAL REPORT?

1. To Present information about the company
2. To Provide information about the financial position, performance and changes in financial position of an entity
3. To provide future outlook as to Revenue,Margin etc.
4. To lure Prospective Investors

WHAT ARE THE CONTENTS OF ANNUAL REPORT?

1. A letter from Chairman
2. A letter from CEO to Shareholders
3. Performance highlights for 5-10 years
4. Financial Statements of the preceding year
5. Performance and outlook for future years
6. Board's Report
7. Management's Discussion and Analysis

8. Material changes and commitments affecting financial position between the end of the financial year and date of the report.
9. Awards and Recognition

DIFFERENCE BETWEEN ANNUAL REPORT AND FINANCIAL STATEMENTS

Basis of distinction	*Financial statements*	*Annual report*
1. Objective	is to convey the company's financial position and performance.	to give a larger picture of the organisation that includes new products, new markets, emerging strategies, and the company's overall future guidance.
2. Contents	1. a Balance Sheet as at the end of the financial year; 2. a Profit and Loss Account, *or* in the case of a company carrying on any activity not for profit, an Income and Expenditure Account for the financial year; 3. Cash Flow Statement for the financial year; 4. a Statement of Changes in Equity, if applicable; and 5. any explanatory note annexed to, *or* forming part of, any document referred to above.	1. A letter from Chairman 2. A letter from CEO to Shareholders 3. Performance highlights for 5-10 years 4. Financial Statements of the preceding year 5. Performance and outlook for future years 6. Board's Report 7. Management's discussion and analysis 8. Material changes and commitments affecting financial position between the end of the financial year and date of the report. 9. Awards and recognition
3. COVERAGE	Narrow	Wide in the sense that it covers many other information besides Financial Statements.
4. Past vs Future	relate to past	relate to future as well
5. Presentation	In prescribed formats.	No formal Format prescribed.
6. Length	much shorter than Annual Report.	much longer than financial statement.

WHAT ARE THE CONTENTS OF BOD'S REPORT?

BOD Report must include:

(i)	The extract of the Annual Return as provided u/s 92 (3)
(ii)	Number of Meetings of the Board
(iii)	Directors' Responsibility Statement
(iv)	Details of frauds reported by the Auditor in his Report u/s 143(12), other than frauds reportable to the Central Government

(v)	A Statement on Declaration given by Independent Directors u/s 149 (6)
(vi)	In case of every listed company and other public companies with a paid up capital of at least Rs. 10 Crore or having turnover of at least Rs. 100 Crore or having in aggregate, outstanding loans or borrowing or debentures or deposits exceeding Rs. 50 Crore, company's policy on directors' appointment and remuneration including criteria for determining qualifications, positive attributes, independence of a director and other matters provided u/s 178 (3)
(vii)	explanations *or* comments by the Board on every qualification, reservation *or* adverse remark *or* disclaimer made: (i) by the auditor in his report; and (ii) by the company secretary in practice in his secretarial audit report
(viii)	particulars of loans, guarantees *or* investments under section 186;
(ix)	particulars of contracts *or* arrangements with related parties referred to in sub-section (1) of section 188 in the prescribed **Form AOC-2**
(x)	the state of the company's affairs
(xi)	the amounts, if any, which it proposes to carry to any reserves
(xii)	the amount, if any, which it recommends should be paid by way of dividend
(xiii)	material changes and commitments, if any, affecting the financial position of the company which have occurred between the end of the financial year of the company to which the financial statements relate and the date of the report;
(xiv)	the conservation of energy, technology absorption, foreign exchange earnings and outgo, in such manner as may be prescribed
(xv)	a statement indicating development and implementation of a risk management policy for the company including identification therein of elements of risk, if any, which in the opinion of the Board may threaten the existence of the company
(xvi)	the details about the policy developed and implemented by the company on corporate social responsibility initiatives taken during the year
(xvii)	in case of a listed company and every other public company having paid-up share capital of at least Rs. 25 Crores, a statement indicating the manner in which formal annual evaluation has been made by the Board of its own performance and that of its committees and individual directors
(xviii)	such other matters as may be prescribed under Rule 8 of the Companies (Account) Rules, 2022. Such as: (a) The financial summary or highlights; (b) The change in nature of business, if any; (c) The details of directors or key managerial personnel who were appointed or have resigned during the year; (d) The names of companies which have become or ceased to be its subsidiaries, joint ventures or associate companies during the year; (e) The details relating to deposits; (f) The details of deposits which are not in compliance with the applicable provisions; (g) The details of significant and material orders passed by the regulators or courts or tribunals impacting the going concern status and company's operations in future; (h) The details in respect of adequacy of internal financial controls with reference to the financial statements.

VARIOUS ANNEXURES WHICH USUALLY FORM PART OF BOD'S REPORT

Annexure 1	Statement containing the salient features of the financial statements of subsidiaries / associate companies / joint ventures
Annexure 2	Particulars of contracts / arrangements made with related parties • [Pursuant To Clause (H) Of Sub-Section (3) Of Section 134 Of The Companies Act, 2013, And Rule 8(2) Of The Companies (Accounts) Rules, 2014 – Aoc-2]
Annexure 3	Particulars of Employees
Annexure 4	Independent Auditor's Certificate On Corporate Governance
Annexure 5	Secretarial Audit Report [Form No. Mr-3 (Pursuant To Section 204(1) of The Companies Act, 2013 And Rule 9 of The Companies (Appointment And Remuneration Of Managerial Personnel) Rules, 2014)]
Annexure 6	Annual Report on CSR Activities [Pursuant To Section 135 Of The Companies Act, 2013 Read With Companies (Corporate Social Responsibility Policy) Rules, 2014, As Amended.]
Annexure 7	Conservation of Energy, Research And Development, Technology Absorption, Foreign Exchange Earnings and Outgo [Particulars Pursuant to The Companies (Accounts) Rules, 2014]
Annexure 8	Corporate Policies
Annexure 9	Committees' Reports
Annexure 10	Standalone and Consolidated Result Of Operations
Annexure 11	Standalone and Consolidated Financial Position

WHAT ARE THE CONTENTS OF DIRECTORS' RESPONSIBILITY STATEMENT [SEC 134 (5)]?

The Directors' Responsibility Statement must state that:

(a) **Compliance with AS:** in the preparation of the annual accounts, the applicable accounting standards had been followed along with proper explanation relating to material departures;

(b) **Accounting Policies:** the directors had selected such accounting policies and applied them consistently and made judgments and estimates that are reasonable and prudent so as to give a true and fair view of the state of affairs of the company at the end of the financial year and of the profit and loss of the company for that period;

(c) **Maintenance of Adequate Accounting Records:** the directors had taken proper and sufficient care for the maintenance of adequate accounting records in accordance with the provisions of this Act for safeguarding the assets of the company and for preventing and detecting fraud and other irregularities;

(d) **Accounts on a Going Concern Basis:** the directors had prepared the annual accounts on a going concern basis; and

(e) **Internal Financial Controls:** the directors, in the case of a listed company, had laid down internal financial controls to be followed by the company and that such internal financial controls are adequate and were operating effectively.

Explanation: For the purposes of this clause, the term "Internal Financial Controls" mean the policies and procedures adopted by the company for ensuring the orderly and efficient conduct of its business, including adherence to company's policies, the safeguarding of its assets, the prevention and detection of frauds and errors, the accuracy and completeness of the accounting records, and the timely preparation of reliable financial information;

(f) **Proper Systems to ensure compliance with Law:** the directors had devised proper systems to ensure compliance with the provisions of all applicable laws and that such systems were adequate and operating effectively.

SIGNATURE ON BOD'S REPORT

The Board's Report and any annexures must be signed by its chairperson of the company if he is authorised by the Board and where he is not so authorised, must be signed by at least two directors, one of whom shall be a managing director, *or* by the director where there is one director. [Sec 134 (6)]

BOD'S REPORT IN CASE OF ONE PERSON COMPANY [SEC 134 (4)]

The BOD's Report in case of a One Person Company, means a report containing explanations *or* comments by the Board on every qualification, reservation *or* adverse remark *or* disclaimer made by the Auditor in his Report.

BOD'S REPORT TO BE ATTACHED

The Board's Report must be attached to statements laid before a company in general meeting.

CIRCULATION OF FINANCIAL STATEMENT

A signed copy of every financial statement, including consolidated financial statement, if any, must be issued, circulated *or* published along with a copy each of:

(a) any Notes annexed to *or* forming part of such financial statement;

(b) the Auditor's Report; and

(c) the Board's report [Sec 134 (7)].

PENALTY FOR CONTRAVENTION OF THE PROVISIONS OF SEC 134

If a company contravenes the provisions of Sec 134, the company shall be punishable with fine which shall be atleast ₹ 50,000 but which may extend to ₹ 25,00,000 and every officer of the company who is in default shall be punishable with imprisonment for a term which may extend to 3 years *or* with fine which shall be atleast ₹ 50,000 but which may extend to ₹ 5,00,000 *or* with both.

CORPORATE SOCIAL RESPONSIBILITY (CSR) [SEC 135]

WHICH COMPANY IS REQUIRED TO CONSTITUTE A CORPORATE SOCIAL RESPONSIBILITY COMMITTEE?

Every company having

Net Worth of at least ₹ 500 crore *or*

Turnover of at least ₹ 1,000 crore *or*

a Net Profit of at least ₹ 5 crores

During any financial year must constitute a Corporate Social Responsibility Committee of the Board consisting of atleast 3 directors, out of which at least one director shall be an Independent Director [Sec 135 (1)].

Example: State whether X Ltd is required to constitute a Corporate Social Responsibility Committee in the following cases:

	2019-2020 (crore)	*2020-2021 (crore)*	*2021-2022 (crore)*	*2022-2023 (crore)*
Net Worth	₹ 499	₹ 499	₹ 499	₹ 500
Turnover	₹ 999	₹ 999	₹ 1000	₹ 999
Net Profit	₹ 4.99	₹ 5	₹ 4.99	₹ 4.99

Answer: X Ltd is required to constitute a Corporate Social Responsibility Committee since 2020-2021 when one of the 3 criteria was satisfied for the first time.

2. The Board's Report must disclose the composition of the Corporate Social Responsibility Committee [Sec 135 (2)].
3. **The Corporate Social Responsibility Committee is required:**
   (a) To Formulate and recommend to the Board, a Corporate Social Responsibility Policy which shall indicate the activities to be undertaken by the company as specified in Schedule VII;
   (b) To Recommend the amount of expenditure to be incurred on the activities referred to in clause (a); and
   (c) To Monitor the Corporate Social Responsibility Policy of the company from time to time. [Sec 135(3)]
4. **The Board of every company is required:**
   (a) after taking into account the recommendations made by the Corporate Social Responsibility Committee, approve the Corporate Social Responsibility Policy for the company and disclose contents of such Policy in its report and also place it on the company's website, if any, in such manner as may be prescribed; and
   (b) ensure that the activities as are included in Corporate Social Responsibility Policy of the company are undertaken by the company. [Sec 135(4)]

WHAT IS THE MINIMUM SPENDING REQUIREMENT ON CSR?

The Board of every company must ensure that the company spends, in every financial year, **at least 2%. of the Average Net Profits (as per Sec 198)** of the company made **during 3 immediately preceding financial years**, in pursuance of its Corporate Social Responsibility Policy. [Sec 135(5)]

Notes:

(i) The company must give preference to the local area and areas around it where it operates, for spending the amount earmarked for Corporate Social Responsibility activities. [Proviso to Sec 135(5)]

(ii) If the company fails to spend such amount, the Board must, in its report made u/s 134, specify the reasons for not spending the amount. [Proviso to Sec 135(5)]

(ii) As per Rule 2(1)(e) of the Companies (CSR Policy) Rules, 2022, "CSR Policy" relates to the activities to be undertaken by the company as specified in Schedule VII to the Act and the expenditure thereon, excluding activities undertaken in pursuance of normal course of business of a company.

(iv) As per Rule 2(1)(f) "Net Profit" means the Net Profit of a company as per its financial statement prepared in accordance with the applicable provisions of the Act, but shall not include the following, namely:
   (a) any profit arising from any overseas branch *or* branches of the company, whether operated as a separate company *or* otherwise; and
   (b) any dividend received from other companies in India, which are covered under and complying with the provisions of Sec 135.

(v) As per Rule 4(5), the CSR projects *or* programs *or* activities that benefit only the employees of the company and their families shall not be considered as CSR activities in accordance with Sec 135.

EXAMPLE: Net Profits of JIV AATMA Ltd. for the years 2022-2023, 2021-2022, 2020-2021. 2019-2020, 2018-2019 are ₹ 25 crore, ₹ 20 crore, ₹ 15 crore,₹ 10 crore and ₹ 5 crore respectively. During 2022-2023, the company incurred only ₹ 7,00,000 and ₹ 3,00,000 on free education and medical treatment of the employees of the company and their families respectively under CSR projects.

Required: State the Amount of Short Fall of Expenditure on Corporate Social Responsibility during 2022-2023 as per The Companies Act, 2013.

SOLUTION

Minimum expenditure on CSR required as per Sec 135(5)=2% of[(₹ 20 crore + ₹ 15 crore +₹ 10 crore)/3]= ₹ 0.30 crore

Free education and medical treatment of the employees of the company and their families shall not be considered as CSR activities in accordance with Sec 135. Hence, **Short fall of expenditure on CSR as per Sec 135=** ₹ 0.30 crore

NOTES TO ACCOUNTS

MEANING OF NOTES TO ACCOUNTS

Notes to Accounts provide:

(a) narrative descriptions or disaggregations of items recognised in those statements; and

(b) information about items that do not qualify for recognition in those statements.

While preparing the notes to accounts, a balance must be maintained between providing excessive detail that may not assist users of financial statements and not providing important information as a result of too much aggregation.

Each item on the face of the Balance Sheet and Statement of Profit and Loss must be cross-referenced to any related information in the notes to accounts.

SUBJECT - MATTER OF NOTES TO ACCOUNTS

Usually, Notes to Accounts relate to:

(a) Accounting Policies(including Effect of Changes in Accounting Policies,if any) as to Revenue Recognition,Property,Plant and Equipment,Intangible Assets, Long term Investments, Current Investments,Inventories,Translation of Transactions in Foreign Currencies, Exchange Differences,Impairment, Employee's Retirement Plans and other benefits etc.

(b) Break-up of Sales including Export Sales

(c) Break-up of Purchases including Imports

(d) Break-up of Expenses

(e) Break-up of Other Income

(f) Break-up of Assets

(g) Break-up of Liabilities

(h) Break-up of Prior-period Items and Extraordinary Items

(i) Company's Commitments

(j) Risk management and other disclosures on capital management

(k) Notable future activities that are expected to have a significant impact on the company's future.

The above list is by no means comprehensive and just an example to showcase a few of the footnotes.

IMPORTANCE OF NOTES TO ACCOUNTS

The notes to accounts are essential to understand fully the items to which the notes relate.

The notes to accounts are integral part of a company's external financial statements since not all relevant financial information can be communicated through the amounts shown (or not shown) on the face of the financial statements.

If the Income Statement, Balance Sheet, and Statement of Cash flow are the heart of the financial statements, then the footnotes are the arteries that keep everything connected.

While analyzing the financial statements of a business, a good way is to read financial statements from bottom to up and from back to front so that Notes may not be overlooked. Those who oversee the notes commit a grave blunder as they can be easily misled that way.

EXAMPLES OF NOTES TO ACCOUNTS

1. Corporate Information:

BHARAT Industries Limited is a listed entity incorporated in India.

The registered office of the Company is located at 4th Floor, Maker Chambers IV, 222, Nariman Point, Mumbai - 400 021, India.

The Company is engaged in activities spanning across hydrocarbon exploration and production, Oil to chemicals, retail, digital services and financial services.

2. Significant Accounting Policies:

2.1 Basis of Preparation and Presentation

The Financial Statements have been prepared on the historical cost basis except for following assets and liabilities which have been measured at fair value amount:

(i) Certain Financial Assets and Liabilities (including derivative instruments),

(ii) Defined Benefit Plans – Plan Assets and

(iii) Equity settled Share Based Payments

2.2 Basis of Presentation:

The Financial Statements of the Company have been prepared to comply with the Indian Accounting standards ('Ind AS'), including the rules notified under the relevant provisions of the Companies Act, 2013, (as amended from time to time) and Presentation and disclosure requirements of Division II of Schedule III to the Companies Act, 2013, (Ind AS Compliant Schedule III) as amended from time to time.

The Company's Financial Statements are presented in Indian Rupees (₹), which is also its functional currency and all values are rounded to the nearest crore (₹00,00,000), except when otherwise indicated.

2.3 Property, Plant and Equipment

Depreciation on Property, Plant and Equipment is provided using written down value method on depreciable amount except in case of certain assets of Oil to Chemicals segment which are depreciated using straight line method. Depreciation is provided based on useful life of the assets as prescribed in Schedule II to the Companies Act, 2013 except in respect of the following assets, where useful life is different than those prescribed in Schedule II;

1. Plant and Machinery (useful life: 2 years or more) Over its useful life as technically assessed
2. Plant and Machinery (useful life: up to 2 years) 100% depreciated in the year of addition
3. Plant and Machinery (useful life: 25 to 50 years) Over its useful life as technically assessed

2.4 Leases

The Company measures the lease liability at the present value of the lease payments that are not paid at the commencement date of the lease. The lease payments are discounted using the interest rate implicit in the lease, if that rate can be readily determined. If that rate cannot be readily determined, the Company uses incremental borrowing rate. For short-term and low value leases, the Company recognises the lease payments as an operating expense on a straight-line basis over the lease term.

2.5 Intangible Assets

The Company's intangible assets comprises assets with finite useful life which are amortised on a straight-line basis over the period of their expected useful life. A summary of amortisation/depletion policies applied to the Company's Intangible Assets to the extent of depreciable amount is as follows:

1. Technical Know-How Over the useful life of the underlying assets ranging from 5 years to 35 years.
2. Computer Software Over a period of 5 years.
3. Development Rights Depleted using the unit of production method.

2.6 Research and Development Expenditure

Revenue expenditure pertaining to research is charged to the Statement of Profit and Loss as and when incurred. Development costs are capitalised as an intangible asset if it can be demonstrated that the project is expected to generate future economic benefits, it is probable that those future economic benefits will flow to the entity and the costs of the asset can be measured reliably, else it is charged to the Statement of Profit and Loss.

2.7 Finance Costs

Borrowing costs include exchange differences arising from foreign currency borrowings to the extent they are regarded as an adjustment to the interest cost. Borrowing costs that are directly attributable to the acquisition or construction of qualifying assets are capitalised as part of the cost of such assets. A qualifying asset is one that necessarily takes substantial period of time to get ready for its intended use. Interest income earned on the temporary investment of specific borrowings pending their expenditure on qualifying assets is deducted from the borrowing costs eligible for capitalisation. All other borrowing costs are charged to the Statement of Profit and Loss for the period for which they are incurred.

2.8 Inventories

Items of inventories are measured at lower of cost and net realisable value after providing for obsolescence, if any, except in case of by-products which are valued at net realisable value. Cost of finished goods, work-in-progress, raw materials, chemicals, stores and spares, packing materials, trading and other products are determined on weighted average basis.

2.9 Impairment of Non-Financial Assets - Property, Plant and Equipment and Intangible Assets

The Company assesses at each reporting date as to whether there is any indication that any Property, Plant and Equipment and Intangible Assets or group of Assets, called Cash Generating Units (CGU) may be impaired. If any such indication exists, the recoverable amount of an asset or CGU is estimated to determine the extent of impairment, if any. When it is not possible to estimate the recoverable amount of an individual asset, the Company estimates the recoverable amount of the CGU to which the asset belongs. An impairment loss is recognised in the Statement of Profit and Loss to the extent, asset's carrying amount exceeds its recoverable amount. The recoverable amount is higher of an asset's fair value less cost of disposal and value in use. Value in use is based on the estimated future cash flows, discounted to their present value using pre-tax discount rate that reflects current market assessments of the time value of money and risk specific to the assets. The impairment loss recognised in prior accounting period is reversed if there has been a change in the estimate of recoverable amount.

2.10 Provisions

Provisions are recognised when the Company has a present obligation (legal or constructive) as a result of a past event, it is probable that an outflow of resources embodying economic benefits will be required to settle the obligation and a reliable estimate can be made of the amount of the obligation. If the effect of the time value of money is material, provisions are discounted using a current pre-tax rate that reflects, when appropriate, the risks specific to the liability. When discounting is used, the increase in the provision due to the passage of time is recognised as a finance cost.

2.11 Provision for Decommissioning Liability

The Company records a provision for decommissioning costs towards site restoration activity. Decommissioning costs are provided at the present value of future expenditure using a current pre-tax rate expected to be incurred to fulfil decommissioning obligations and are recognised as part of the cost of the underlying assets. Any change in the present value of the expenditure, other than unwinding of discount on the provision, is reflected as adjustment to the provision and the corresponding asset. The change in the provision due to the unwinding of discount is recognised in the Statement of Profit and Loss.

2.12 Contingent Liabilities

Disclosure of contingent liability is made when there is a possible obligation arising from past events, the existence of which will be confirmed only by the occurrence or non-occurrence of one or more uncertain future events not wholly within the control of the Company or a present obligation that arises from past events where it is either not probable that an outflow of resources embodying economic benefits will be required to settle or a reliable estimate of amount cannot be made.

2.13 Employee Benefits Expense

Short-Term Employee Benefits: The undiscounted amount of short-term employee benefits expected to be paid in exchange for the services rendered by employees are recognised as an expense during the period when the employees render the services.

Post-Employment Benefits: Defined Contribution Plans

The Company recognises contribution payable to the provident fund scheme as an expense, when an employee renders the related service. If the contribution payable to the scheme for service received before the balance sheet date exceeds the contribution already paid, the deficit payable to the scheme is recognised as a liability. If the contribution already paid exceeds the contribution due for services received before the balance sheet date, then excess is recognised as an asset to the extent that the pre-payment will lead to a reduction in future payment or a cash refund.

Post-Employment Benefits: Defined Benefit Plans

The Company pays gratuity to the employees who have completed five years of service with the Company at the time of resignation/superannuation. The gratuity is paid @15 days basic salary for every completed year of service as per the Payment of Gratuity Act, 1972. The gratuity liability amount is contributed to the Approved Gratuity Fund formed exclusively for gratuity payment to the employees. The gratuity fund has been approved by respective Income Tax authorities. The liability in respect of gratuity and other post-employment benefits is calculated using the Projected Unit Credit Method and spread over the period during which the benefit is expected to be derived from employees' services.

Remeasurement gains and losses arising from adjustments and changes in actuarial assumptions are recognised in the period in which they occur in Other Comprehensive Income.

Employee Separation Costs: The Company recognises the employee separation cost when the scheme is announced, and the Company is demonstrably committed to it.

2.14 Tax Expenses

The tax expenses for the period comprises of current tax and deferred income tax. Tax is recognised in Statement of Profit and Loss, except to the extent that it relates to items recognised in the Other Comprehensive Income. In which case, the tax is also recognised in Other Comprehensive Income.

i. Current Tax: Current Tax Assets and Liabilities are measured at the amount expected to be recovered from or paid to the Income Tax authorities, based on tax rates and laws that are enacted at the Balance sheet date.

ii. Deferred Tax: Deferred Tax is recognised on temporary differences between the carrying amounts of assets and liabilities in the Financial Statements and the corresponding tax bases used in the computation of taxable profit. Deferred tax assets are recognised to the extent it is probable that taxable profit will be available against which the deductible temporary differences, and the carry forward of unused tax losses can be utilised. Deferred tax liabilities and assets are measured at the tax rates that are expected to apply in the period in which the liability is settled or the asset realised, based on tax rates (and tax laws) that have been enacted or substantively enacted by the end of the reporting period. The carrying amount of Deferred tax liabilities and assets are reviewed at the end of each reporting period.

2.15 Share Based Payments

Equity-settled share based payments to employees and others providing similar services are measured at the fair value of the equity instruments at the grant date. The fair value determined at the grant date of the equity-settled share based payments is expensed on a straight-line basis over the vesting period, based on the Company's estimate of equity instruments that will eventually vest, with a corresponding increase in equity. At the end of each reporting period, the Company revises its estimate of the number of equity instruments expected to vest. The impact of the revision of the original estimates, if any, is recognised in Statement of Profit and Loss such that the cumulative expenses reflects the revised estimate, with a corresponding adjustment to the Share Based Payments Reserve. The dilutive effect of outstanding options is reflected as additional share dilution in the computation of diluted earnings per share. In case of Group equity-settled share-based payment transactions, where the Company grants stock options to the employees of its subsidiaries, the transactions are accounted by increasing the cost of investment in subsidiary with a corresponding credit in the equity.

2.16 Foreign Currencies Transactions and Translation

Transactions in foreign currencies are recorded at the exchange rate prevailing on the date of transaction.

Monetary Assets and Liabilities denominated in foreign currencies are translated at the functional currency closing rates of exchange at the reporting date. Exchange differences arising on settlement or translation of monetary items are recognised in Statement of Profit and Loss except to the extent of exchange differences which are regarded as an adjustment to interest costs on foreign currency borrowings that are directly attributable to the acquisition or construction of qualifying assets which are capitalised as cost of assets.

Non-Monetary Items that are measured in terms of historical cost in a foreign currency are recorded using the exchange rates at the date of the transaction. Non-monetary items measured at fair value in a foreign currency are translated using the exchange rates at the date when the fair value was measured.

The gain or loss arising on translation of non-monetary items measured at fair value is treated in line with the recognition of the gain or loss on the change in fair value of the item.

2.17 Revenue Recognition

Revenue from contracts with customers is recognised when control of the goods or services are transferred to the customer at an amount that reflects the consideration entitled in exchange for those goods or services.

Revenue from rendering of services is recognised over time by measuring the progress towards complete satisfaction of performance obligations at the reporting period.

Revenue is measured at the amount of consideration which the Company expects to be entitled to in exchange for transferring distinct goods or services to a customer as specified in the contract, excluding amounts collected on behalf of third parties (for example taxes and duties collected on behalf of the government).

If a customer pays consideration before the Company transfers goods or services to the customer, a contract liability is recognised when the payment is made or the payment is due (whichever is earlier). Contract liabilities are recognised as revenue when the Company performs under the contract.

Interest Income: Interest Income from a Financial Assets is recognised using effective interest rate method.

Dividend Income: Dividend Income is recognised when the Company's right to receive the amount has been established.

2.18 Financial Instruments: All financial instruments are initially recognised and subsequently re-measured at fair value as described below:

(a) The fair value of investment in quoted Equity Shares, Bonds, Government Securities, Treasury Bills, Certificate of Deposit and Mutual Funds is measured at quoted price or NAV.

(b) The fair value of Interest Rate Swaps is calculated as the present value of the estimated future cash flows based on observable yield curves.

(c) The fair value of Forward Foreign Exchange contracts and Currency Swaps is determined using observable forward exchange rates and yield curves at the balance sheet date.

(d) The fair value of over-the-counter Foreign Currency Option contracts is determined using the Black Scholes valuation model.

(e) Commodity derivative contracts are valued using available information in markets and quotations from exchange,brokers and price index developers.

(f) The fair value for level 3 instruments is valued using inputs based on information about market participants assumptions and other data that are available.

(g) The fair value of the remaining financial instruments is determined using discounted cash flow analysis.

(h) All foreign currency denominated assets and liabilities are translated using exchange rate at reporting date.

2.19 Non-Current Assets Held for Sale

Non-current assets are classified as held for sale if their carrying amount will be recovered principally through a sale transaction rather than through continuing use and sale is considered highly probable. Non-current assets held for sale are neither depreciated nor amortised. Assets and liabilities classified as held for sale are measured at the lower of their carrying amount and fair value less cost of disposal and are presented separately in the Balance Sheet.

2.20 Investments: Long term Investments are stated at cost less other than temporary diminution in value, if any. Current Investments are stated at lower of cost and fair value. Fair value of investments in mutual funds are determined on a portfolio basis.

2.20 Redemption premium on Non Convertible Debentures (NCD): Premium payable on redemption of NCD as per the terms of issue, is provided fully in the year of issue by adjusting against the Securities Premium Account (SPA)(net of tax).

3.0 Critical Accounting Judgements and Key Sources of Estimation Uncertainty

The preparation of the Company's Financial Statements requires management to make judgement, estimates and assumptions that affect the reported amount of revenue, expenses, assets and liabilities and the accompanying disclosures. Uncertainty about these assumptions and estimates could result in outcomes that require a material adjustment to the carrying amount of assets or liabilities affected in next financial years.

(A) Estimation of Oil and Gas Reserves: The determination of the Company's estimated oil and natural gas reserves requires significant judgements and estimates to be applied and these are regularly reviewed and updated

(B) Decommissioning Liabilities: The liability for decommissioning costs is recognised when the Company has an obligation to perform site restoration activity

(C) Property Plant and Equipment/ Intangible Assets: Estimates are involved in determining the cost attributable to bringing the assets to the location and condition necessary for it to be capable of operating in the manner intended by the management. Property, Plant and Equipment/Intangible Assets are depreciated/ amortised over their estimated useful life, after taking into account estimated residual value.

(D) Recoverability of Trade Receivables: Judgments are required in assessing the recoverability of overdue trade receivables and determining whether a provision against those receivables is required.

(E) Provisions: The timing of recognition and quantification of the liability (including litigations) requires the application of judgement to existing facts and circumstances, which can be subject to change. The carrying amounts of provisions and liabilities are reviewed regularly and revised to take account of changing facts and circumstances.

(F) Impairment of Financial and Non-Financial Assets: The impairment provisions for Financial Assets are based on assumptions about risk of default and expected cash loss rates.

(G) Recognition of Deferred Tax Assets and Liabilities: Deferred tax assets and liabilities are recognised for deductible temporary differences and unused tax losses for which there is probability of utilisation against the future taxable profit. The Company uses judgement to determine the amount of deferred tax that can be recognised, based upon the likely timing and the level of future taxable profits and business developments.

(H) Fair Value Measurement: For estimates relating to fair value of financial instruments refer note 38 of financial statements.

4.0 Fair Value of Option on the grant date

The fair value of Option at grant date is determined using "Black Scholes Model" which takes into account the exercise price, term of the option, share price at grant date and expected price volatility of the underlying shares, expected dividend yield and the risk free interest rate for the term of the option.

5.0 Excise Duty: The Company had recognised liability for excise duty payable on clearance of goods lying in stock as on 31st March, 2021 as per the estimated pattern of dispatches.

6.0 Financial Risk Management

The company's activities expose it to variety of financial risks: market risk, credit risk, interest rate risk and liquidity risk. Within the boundaries of approved Risk Management Policy framework The Company uses derivative instruments to manage the volatility of financial markets and minimize the adverse impact on its financial performance. Company has adopted a structured risk management policy to hedge all these risks within an acceptable risk limit and an approved hedge accounting framework which allows for Fair Value and Cash Flow hedges. Hedging instruments include exchange traded futures and options, over-the-counter swaps, forwards and options as well as non-derivative instruments to achieve this objective.

WHAT IS TRIPLE BOTTOM LINE REPORTING?

TBL reporting refers to providing information on the economic, environmental and social dimensions of the activities carried on by an organisation.

Thus, The Triple Bottom Line is made up of "Social (People), Economic (Profit) and Environmental (Planet)".

In the private sector, a commitment to CSR implies a commitment to some form of TBL reporting.

WHAT ARE COMMERCIAL ADVANTAGES OF TRIPLE BOTTOM LINE REPORTING?

1. enhancement of reputation and brand
2. securing a social licence to operate
3. attraction and retention of high calibre employees
4. improved access to investors
5. reduced risk profile
6. identification of potential cost savings
7. increased scope for innovation
8. aligning stakeholder needs with management focus, and
9. creating sound basis for stakeholder dialogue

WHAT ARE ORGANISATIONAL ADVANTAGES OF TRIPLE BOTTOM LINE REPORTING?

1. **Reputation and brand benefits:** corporate reputation is a function of the way in which a company is perceived by its stakeholders. Effective communication with stakeholders on one or more of the environmental, social, and economic dimensions can play an important role in managing stakeholder perceptions, and, in doing so, protect and enhance corporate reputation.
2. **Securing a 'social licence to operate':** a 'licence to operate' is not a piece of paper, but informal community and stakeholder support for an organisation's operations. Business is increasingly recognising the link between ongoing business success and its 'licence to operate', especially in the resources sector where the concept of a social licence to operate has been central for some years. Communication with stakeholders is often critical to securing and maintaining a 'licence to operate'. Communities and stakeholders generally, are likely to be more supportive of companies that communicate openly and honestly about their management and performance in relation to environmental, social and economic factors.
3. **Attraction and retention of high calibre employees:** existing and prospective employees have expectations about corporate environmental, social and economic behaviour, and include such factors in their decisions. The publication of TBL-related information can play a role in positioning an employer as an 'employer of choice' which can enhance employee loyalty, reduce staff turnover and increase a company's ability to attract high quality employees.
4. **Improved access to the investor market:** a growing number of investors are including environmental and social factors within their decision making processes. The growth in

socially responsible investment and shareholder activism is evidence of this. Responding to investor requirements through the publication of TBL-related information is a way of ensuring that the company is aligning its communication with this stakeholder group, and therefore enhancing its attractiveness to this segment of the investment market.

5. **Establish position as a preferred supplier:** obtaining a differentiated position in the market place is one way to establish the status of preferred supplier. Effectively communicating with stakeholder groups on environmental, social and economic issues is central to obtaining a differentiated position in the market place.
6. **Reduced risk profile:** there is an expanding body of evidence to suggest that performance in respect of economic, social and environmental factors has the capacity to affect the views of market participants about a company's exposure to, and management of, risk. TBL reporting enables a company to demonstrate its commitment to effectively managing such factors and to communicate its performance in these areas. A communication policy that addresses these issues can play an important role in the company's overall risk management strategy.
7. **Cost savings:** TBL reporting often involves the collection, collation and analysis of data on resource and materials usage, and the assessment of business processes. For example, this can enable a company to better identify opportunities for cost savings through more efficient use of resources and materials.
8. **Innovation:** The development of innovative products and services can be facilitated through the alignment of R&D activity with the expectations of stakeholders. The process of publishing TBL reporting provides a medium by which companies can engage with stakeholders and understand their priorities and concerns.
9. **Aligning stakeholder needs with management focus:** External reporting of information focuses management attention on not only the integrity of the data but also the continuous improvement of the indicator being reported.
10. **Creating a sound basis for stakeholder dialogue:** Publication of TBL reporting provides a powerful platform for engaging in dialogue with stakeholders. Understanding stakeholder requirements and alignment of business performance with such requirements is fundamental to business success. TBL reporting demonstrates to stakeholders the company's commitment to managing all of its impacts, and, in doing so, establishes a sound basis for stakeholder dialogue to take place.

HOW IS TBL REPORTING ACCOMPLISHED?

TBL reporting is accomplished through the application the Global Reporting Initiative 2002 or GRI or "a common framework for sustainability reporting"

1. Economic	*2. Social*	*3. Environmental*
Generally Accepted Accounting Principles	Bribery and corruption	Energy
Customers	Political contributions	Water
Suppliers	Child labor	Biodiversity
Employees	Security practices	Emissions, effluents, and waste
	Indigenous rights	
	Training and diversity	

WHAT IS THE GLOBAL REPORTING INITIATIVE'S (GRI) VISION?

1. The Global Reporting Initiative attempts to make the Triple Bottom Line operational.
2. **Vision:** The Global Reporting Initiative's (GRI) vision is that reporting on economic, environmental, and social performance by all organizations becomes as routine and comparable as financial reporting.
3. **Accomplishes:** GRI accomplishes this vision by developing, continually improving, and building capacity around the use of its Sustainability Reporting Framework.

HOW DO ORGANISATIONS STRATEGICALLY MANAGE CSR THROUGH TBL REPORTING?

TBL reporting enables organizations to:

1. Measure and manage their financial and non-financial performance and impacts, or lack thereof
2. Have their performance and impacts verified independently
3. Communicate effectively with consumers,governments, investors, employees, other stakeholders and watchdog groups

WHAT ARE THE QUALITIES AND CHARACTERISTICS OF TBL REPORTS?

To present objective, balanced and credible information, the information in TBL reports must possess the following characteristics:

1. **Reliability:** information should be accurate, and provide a true reflection of the activities and performance of the company.
2. **Usefulness:** the information must be relevant to both internal and external stakeholders, and be relevant to their decision-making processes.
3. **Consistency of presentation:** throughout the report there should be consistency of presentation of data and information. This includes consistency in aspects such as format, timeframes, graphics, and metrics.
4. **Full disclosure:** reported information should provide an open explanation of specific actions undertaken and performance outcomes.
5. **Reproducible:** information is likely to be published on an ongoing basis, and companies must ensure that they have the capacity to reproduce data and information in future reporting periods.
6. **Auditability:** alignment with the trend towards external verification requires that all statements and data within the report be able to be readily substantiated.

WHAT ARE THE MAJOR STEPS INVOLVED IN UNDERTAKING TBL REPORTING PROCESS?

1. **Planning for Reporting**
    a. Understand the national, international and industry sector trends in TBL reporting
    b. Identify key stakeholders
    c. Establish the 'business case' and set high-level objectives for TBL reporting
    d. Secure support from the Board and senior executives
    e. Identify resource requirements and determine budget
2. **Setting the Direction for TBL Reporting**
    a. Engage with stakeholders to understand their requirements
    b. Prioritise stakeholder requirements and concerns

c. Set overall objectives for TBL reporting

d. Review current approach and assess capability to deliver on reporting objectives

e. Identify gaps and barriers associated with current approach, and prioritise risks associated with overall reporting objective

f. Review of associated legal implications

g. Develop TBL reporting strategy

h. Determine performance indicators for inclusion in report

i. Establish appropriate structure and content of the report

3. Implementation of TBL Reporting Strategy

a. Implementation of TBL reporting strategy (including required data collection and review processes)

b. Clarify relationship to statutory financial reporting

4. Publication of TBL Report

a. Prepare draft report

b. Review content and structure of report internally, and modify accordingly

c. Obtain independent assurance - external verification

d. Publish TBL report

e. Seek feedback from stakeholders and incorporate into planning for the next period's reporting.

WHAT IS SUSTAINABILITY REPORTING?

A sustainability report is an organizational report that gives information about economic, environmental, social and governance performance.

For companies and organizations, sustainability – the capacity to endure, or be maintained – is based on performance in these four key areas.

A sustainability report is the key platform for communicating positive and negative sustainability impacts.

To produce a regular sustainability report, organizations set up a reporting cycle – a program of data collection, communication, and responses. This means that their sustainability performance is monitored on an ongoing basis. Data can be provided regularly to senior decision makers to shape company strategy and policy, and improve performance.

Sustainability Reporting is therefore a vital step for managing change towards a sustainable global economy – one that combines long term profitability with social justice and environmental care. Sustainability reporting can be considered as synonymous with other terms for non-financial reporting; triple bottom line reporting, corporate social responsibility (CSR) reporting, and more. It is also an intrinsic element of integrated reporting; a recent development that combines the analysis of financial and non-financial performance.

A sustainability report enables companies and organizations to report sustainability information in a way that is similar to financial reporting. Systematic sustainability reporting gives comparable data, with agreed disclosures and metrics.

WHAT ARE THE MAJOR PROVIDERS OF SUSTAINABILITY REPORTING GUIDANCE?

1. The Global Reporting Initiative (The GRI Sustainability Reporting Framework and Guidelines)

2. Organization for Economic Cooperation and Development (OECD Guidelines for Multinational Enterprises)
3. The United Nations Global Compact (the Communication on Progress) International Organization for Standardization (ISO 26000, International Standard for social responsibility)

WHAT ARE THE BENEFITS OF AN EFFECTIVE SUSTAINABILITY REPORTING CYCLE?

I. Internal benefits for companies and organizations can include:

1. Increased understanding of risks and opportunities
2. Emphasizing the link between financial and non-financial performance
3. Influencing long term management strategy and policy, and business plans
4. Streamlining processes, reducing costs and improving efficiency
5. Benchmarking and assessing sustainability performance with respect to laws, norms, codes, performance standards, and voluntary initiatives
6. Avoiding being implicated in publicized environmental, social and governance failures

Comparing performance internally, and between organizations and sectors

II. External benefits of sustainability reporting can include:

1. Mitigating - or reversing - negative environmental, social and governance impacts
2. Improving reputation and brand loyalty
3. Enabling external stakeholders to understand company's true value, and tangible and intangible assets
4. Demonstrating how the organization influences, and is influenced by, expectations about sustainable development

WHAT IS FINANCIAL CAPITAL, MANUFACTURED CAPITAL, HUMAN CAPITAL, INTELLECTUAL CAPITAL, NATURAL CAPITAL AND SOCIAL AND RELATIONSHIP CAPITAL?

1. Financial Capital	The pool of funds that is: a. available to an organization for use in the production of goods or the provision of services b. obtained through financing, such as debt, equity or grants, or generated through operations or investments.
2. Manufactured Capital	Manufactured physical objects (as distinct from natural physical objects) that are available to an organization for use in the production of goods or the provision of services, including: a. buildings b. equipment c. infrastructure (such as roads, ports, bridges and waste and water treatment plants). Manufactured capital is often created by one or more other organizations, but also includes assets manufactured by the reporting organization when they are retained for its own use.

3. Human Capital	People's competencies, capabilities and experience, and their motivations to innovate, including their: a. alignment with and support of an organization's governance framework and risk management approach, and ethical values such as recognition of human rights b. ability to understand, develop and implement an organization's strategy c. loyalties and motivations for improving processes, goods and services, including their ability to lead, manage and collaborate.
4. Intellectual Capital	Organizational, knowledge-based intangibles, including: a. intellectual property, such as patents, copyrights, software, rights and licences b. "organizational capital" such as tacit knowledge, systems, procedures and protocols c. intangibles associated with the brand and reputation that an organization has developed.
5. Natural Capital	All renewable and non-renewable environmental stocks that provide goods and services that support the current and future prosperity of an organisation. It includes: a. air, water, land, forests and minerals b. biodiversity and ecosystem health.
6. Social and Relationship Capital	The institutions and relationships established within and between each community, group of stakeholders and other networks (and an ability to share information) to enhance individual and collective well-being. Social and relationship capital includes: a. shared norms, and common values and behaviours b. key relationships, and the trust and willingness to engage that an organization has developed and strives to build and protect with customers, suppliers, business partners, and other external stakeholders c. an organization's social licence to operate

WHAT ARE THE APPROACHES OF BUSINESS MODEL REPORTING?

In reviewing the global examples of Business Model Reporting, it became apparent that they could be broadly allocated into five categories. Common approaches to business model reporting based on a survey of current practices.

Approach	*Description*
1. Organizational overview	What the entity does, how it is structured or where it operates
2. Business strategy	Key aspects of the organization's strategy
3. Value chain	Place in the value chain and dependencies on key inputs
4. Financial performance	How the business model drives profitability or revenue generation
5. Value creation	How the organization's inputs, activities and relationships lead to value and desired outcomes

WHAT IS XBRL?

XBRL stands for **E**xtensible **B**usiness **R**eporting **L**anguage. It is one of a family of "XML" languages which is becoming a standard means of communicating information between businesses and on the internet. XBRL provides major benefits in the preparation, analysis and communication of business information and is fast becoming an accepted reporting language globally. It offers major benefits to all those who have to create, transmit, use or analyse such information.

(a) **Extensible:** Means the user can extend the application of a particular business data beyond its original intended purpose and the major advantage is that the extended use can be determined even by the users and not just the ones who merely prepare the business data. This is achieved by adding tags which are both human and machine readable – describing what the data is.

The property of extensibility is very handy in situations when list of items reported for various elements of the financial statements are not the same across firms, industries, and countries. For example, many of item constituting non-current assets in Oil and Gas Industry (items like rigs, exploratory oil and gas wells) may not be applicable to companies in general. In a situation of this kind, XBRL may prepare a taxonomy called a 'Global Common Document' (GCD) for items common to all the firms, industries, and countries, and, any country specific, industry specific and firm-specific variations (extensions / limitations) can, then, be written as independent taxonomies that can be imported and incorporated with the GCD.

(b) **Business:** means relevant to the type of business transaction. XBRL focus is on describing the financial statements for both public and private companies.

(c) **Reporting:** the intention behind promoting use of XBRL is to have all companies report their financial statements in a consolidated manner using the specified formats.

(d) **Language:** XBRL is based on XML, which prescribes the manner in which the data can be "marked-up" or "tagged" to make it more meaningful to human readers as well as to computers-based system.

WHAT ARE THE POTENTIAL APPLICATIONS OF XBRL?

XBRL stands for e**X**tensible **B**usiness **R**eporting **L**anguage. It is one of a family of "XML" languages which is becoming a standard means of communicating information between businesses and on the internet.

POTENTIAL APPLICATIONS OF XBRL

1. **XBRL for Financial Statements:** Financial statements of all sorts used to exchange financial information
2. **XBRL for Taxes:** Specification for tax returns which are filed and information exchanged for items which end up on tax returns
3. **XBRL for Regulatory Filings:** Specifications for the large number of filings required by government and regulatory bodies
4. **XBRL for Accounting and Business Reports:** Management and accounting reporting such as all the reports that are created by your accounting system rendered in XML to make re-using them possible
5. **XBRL for Authoritative Literature:** A standard way for describing accounting related authoritative literature published by the AICPA, FASB, ASB, and others to make using these resources easier, "drill downs" into literature from financials possible

WHICH TWO SIGNIFICANT ISSUES ARE SOLVED BY XBRL?

1. To prepare a financial statement for printing, for a Web site, and for filing today means that a company could typically enter information three times. With XBRL, information will be entered once and the same information will be "rendered" as a printed financial statement, an HTML document for a Web site, an EDGAR (Electronic Data Gathering, Analysis, Retrieval) filing file, a raw XML file, or a specialized reporting format such as periodic banking and other regulatory reports.
2. To extract specified detailed information from a financial statement, even an electronic financial statement prepared using XBRL.

WHAT ARE THE PURPOSES OF XBRLS?

1. XBRLS means XBRL Simple Application Profile
2. In 2008 Charlie Hoffman and Rene van Egmond proposed a simplified, more user-friendly XBRL application profile of XBRL that makes using XBRL easier for most business users, improves the potential for interoperability, and improves the potential for comparability needed by most business users, business communities, regulators and independent software vendors.
3. XBRLS specifies a subset of XBRL that is designed to meet the needs of most business users in most situations, and offers it as a starting point for others. This approach creates an application profile of XBRL (equivalent to a database view but concerned with metadata i.e. text, voice, or image that describes what the audience wants or needs to see or experience).
4. The stated goals of XBRLS are "to maximize XBRL's benefits, reduce costs of implementation, and maximize the functionality and effectiveness of XBRL. XBRL is a general purpose specification, based on the idea that no one is likely to use 100% of the components of XBRL in building any one solution.
5. XBRLS is intended to enable the non-XBRL expert to create both XBRL metadata and XBRL reports in a simple and convenient manner. At the same time, it seeks to improve the usability of XBRL, the interoperability among XBRL-based solutions, the effectiveness of XBRL extensions and to reduce software development costs.

WHAT ARE THE LIMITATIONS OF XBRL?

1. XBRL does not represent a set of accounting standards, which remain the prerogative of the regulatory standards bodies. XBRL is merely a platform on which reporting standards content will reside and be represented.
2. XBRL is not a detailed universal chart of accounts. Formulation of a company's chart of accounts is an exercise conducted by its management with regard to its specific business intricacies. XBRL can facilitate the implementation of such structures through its ability to transport data between disparate software applications that might be used within an organizations operational structures.
3. XBRL is not a GAAP translator. It does not provide a mechanism for facilitating a drilldown of existing GAAP information into lower levels of information that would be necessary for translating financial statements from one GAAP to another. The business-reporting document contains the same GAAP information, be it in an XBRL format or an MS word or PDF format.
4. XBRL is not a proprietary technology. XBRL is freely licensed and available to the public. XBRL is XML-based and therefore is expected to be widely available in software applications.

5. XBRL is not a Transaction Protocol. XBRL is designated to address issues related to generation and usage of information contained within business reports and begin at the accounting classification level. XBRL is about business reporting information, not about data capture at the transaction level.

WHO ARE THE USERS OF XBRL?

1. **Corporations:** Since XBRL was designed to handle corporate financial information, it logically follows that corporations would be one of the primary users. These days most major corporations provide some sort of company financial information via the Internet. Both the corporations providing this information and the investors who are receiving it need an easy way to do so. XBRL provides a method via which financial information can be delivered to end users quickly and easily.

   The main benefit to the corporation is that the information can be entered once and maintained in a standard format. Required forms and documents can then be automatically generated from the XBRL formatted document. This prevents the duplication of financial data and thereby helps prevent errors and inconsistencies.

2. **Investors, Accountants and other users of Corporate Financial Data:** Having a standardized and machine-readable format is invaluable to consumers of corporate financial information. XBRL provides just such a format. Without it, consumers of the data would be stuck trying to negotiate a format for a data feed with each corporation they wished to receive data from or would be forced to manually enter data obtained from a non-machine-readable source. In addition to the lessening the time and expense involved with either of the alternatives, XBRL also helps prevent the errors they can cause. By having a standardized format, developers can share code designed to read XBRL or purchase tools with XBRL support built in. On top of preventing errors, being able to use previously tested XBRL tools also increases productivity and brings the data to those who might otherwise not have the time, money, know-how to retrieve it on their own.

WHAT ARE THE ADVANTAGES OF XBRL?

1. **Automated Data Processing:** XBRL allows very efficient handling of business data by computer software and supports all the standard tasks involved in compiling, storing and using business data. XBRL software also facilitates automatic checking of information and thus makes the entire process of data collection and analysis more reliable and accurate.
2. **Cost Saving:** Adoption of XBRL for data processing reduces the manpower involved and result in considerable amount of cost saving.
3. **Time Saving:** The powerful XBRL software increases the speed of handling the data and completes all aspects of data processing in quick time. This time reduction will allow users to increase their focus on analysis and help in prompt decision making. For example, searches for particular information which might normally take hours can be completed with XBRL in a fraction of a second.
4. **Better Financial Reporting:** XBRL also facilitates preparation of quality and timely reports to suit different needs. Once data is gathered in XBRL, different types of reports using varying subsets of the data can be produced with minimum effort.
5. **Multi Language Capability:** XBRL can read and understand data in different languages and accounting standards and can be flexibly adapted to meet different needs of various users.
6. **Improved Data Analysis:** The XBRL software helps to automatically validate and manipulate data received electronically. XBRL facilitates a deeper and accurate analysis of the automated data to meet the requirements of all types of end users. This thorough

analysis will equip business leaders with greater confidence to make financial decisions that impact their companies,

For example, banks and other financial institutions can analyse loan applications as well as a borrower's financial records more quickly and more accurately which may increase the approval of good loans and significantly lower the acceptance of loans to high risk borrowers.

7. **Advantages to Individual Stakeholders:** All types of organisations can use XBRL to save costs and improve efficiency in handling business and financial information. Due to its flexible nature, XBRL can be adapted to suit a wide variety of requirements of preparers as well as users of financial data.

   The prominent entities that can benefit from use of XBRL are government regulators, stock exchanges, investment analysts, banks, financial companies, accountants, auditors, accountancy software vendors, and information technology companies.

WHAT ARE THE WAYS IN WHICH ORGANISATIONS BENEFIT BY USE OF XBRL?

1. **Regulators and Government Bodies:** By introducing XBRL for reporting, regulators and other government authorities can:
   - Obtain data which can be entered automatically into systems without reformatting or other "translation" effort.
   - Dramatically reduce costs by automating routine tasks.
   - Quickly and automatically identify problems with filings.
   - Analyse and compare data much more quickly, efficiently and reliably. Benefit from the use of software in validation and analysis.
   - Monitor data and activities and reach judgments with far greater speed and confidence.
   - Focus effort on analysis, decision-making and dealing with counterparties rather than on data manipulation.
   - Provide a much faster and focused response to counterparties.
   - Promote efficiencies and cost savings throughout the regulatory filing process.
2. **Stock Exchanges:** Stock Exchanges can use XBRL to
   - Make their process of company data collection more efficient, comprehensive, and reliable.
   - Increase the value and competitiveness of the data products which they offer to institutions and private investors.
   - Strengthen the transparency and robustness of information on their markets.

   Depending on the circumstances, Exchanges may be able to encourage or mandate the filing of information by companies in XBRL or convert company data into XBRL. They can then offer data in XBRL form, benefitting all consumers of investment information. The result is a set of more competitive and valuable exchange data products as well as improved exposure for the Exchange.
3. **Investment Analysts:** By using XBRL, investment analysts and advisers can benefit from:
   - Much greater transparency, clarity and consistency in company financial data.
   - The ability to handle and compare a broader range of companies and deeper set of information.
   - More powerful software tools for analysis, comparison and benchmarking.

- Far more efficient means of finding specific company data.
- The ability to select data from a variety of companies within seconds for comparison and analysis.

  In short, XBRL can help the analyst community provide quicker and better quality investment advice and decisions.

4. **Financial Companies:** Through the adoption of XBRL, companies in the financial information industry will be able to:
   - Obtain company financial data in a standardised and predictable form.
   - Significantly reduce costs by automating many aspects of the gathering and storage of financial data.
   - Switch efforts from routine data gathering to analysis.
   - Provide a faster, clearer, deeper and more accurate view of company financial performance.
   - Produce richer and more usable products containing XBRL data.
5. **Banks:** Through XBRL, loan and credit management departments of banks can:
   - Obtain data quickly and reliably via automated reporting.
   - Reduce costs in processing data.
   - Compare and analyse financial information much more reliably, fully and effectively using automated processes.
   - Track financial performance more quickly and efficiently.
   - Reach decisions more confidently and provide a quicker response to clients.

   In particular, Credit Risk Assessment companies are already working within XBRL International on the introduction of XBRL in this area. XBRL also facilitates Credit Insurance Underwriting decisions through a high-quality assessment of the concerned data.
6. **Accountants:** The development of XBRL software and its implementation all over the world has helped the community of accountants and auditors immensely. Through the use of XBRL in companies, accountants will be able to:
   - Obtain more rapid and reliable data on company financial performance.
   - Greatly reduce effort and costs in gathering and analysing data.
   - Simplify and automate tasks.
   - Focus effort on analysis and value-added work.
   - Make better use of software to improve efficiency and speed.
   - Facilitate paperless financial reporting.
7. **Software, Systems and IT Companies:** XBRL offers software, systems and IT companies a range of opportunities to enhance existing products, develop new ones and expand their business. It enables these companies to:
   - Adopt a data standard for transferring business and financial information, avoiding the commercial conflicts and client aggravation caused by competing proprietary standards.
   - Create software to support the preparation, publication and collection of data in XBRL.
   - Create software to select, compare and analyse financial data in XBRL.

WHAT IS XBRL INTERNATIONAL?

1. XBRL International is a not-for-profit consortium of approximately 550 companies and agencies worldwide working together to build the XBRL language and promote and support its adoption.
2. It is comprised of jurisdictions which represent countries, regions or international bodies and which focus on the progress of XBRL in their area.
3. It operates mainly through the XBRL Steering Committee and has over the years produced a variety of specifications and taxonomies for digitizing financial information in accordance with the accounting rules and other regulations prevailing in different countries. The consortium members meet periodically in international conferences and conduct committee work regularly throughout the week.

WHAT ARE THE OBJECTIVES OF XBRL INDIA?

XBRL India is the provisional jurisdiction of XBRL International and is facilitated by the Institute of Chartered Accountants of India (ICAI). XBRL India is governed by a Steering Committee which is headed by the President, ICAI.

Its objectives are:

- To promote and encourage the adoption of XBRL in India as the standard for electronic business reporting in India
- To facilitate education and marketing of XBRL
- To develop and manage XBRL taxonomies
- To keep the developed XBRL taxonomies updated with regard to international developments
- To represent Indian interests within XBRL International
- To contribute to the international development of XBRL

XBRL India has developed Draft General Purpose Financial Reporting XBRL taxonomy for Commercial and Industrial Companies. This taxonomy covers the financial statements like Balance Sheet, Statement of Profit and Loss, and Cash Flow Statement and related non-financial information. The draft taxonomy has been developed conforming to Indian Accounting Standards and Company Law. XBRL India is currently developing XBRL Taxonomy for the Banking Sector.

Other Organisations in India using XBRL

Members of XBRL India among others include regulators such as Reserve Bank of India (RBI), Insurance Regulatory and Development Authority (IRDA), Securities and Exchange Board of India (SEBI), Ministry of Corporate Affairs (MCA), stock exchanges like Bombay Stock Exchange Limited (BSE) and National Stock Exchange of India Limited (NSE), and some private sector companies.

WHAT ARE THE ADVANTAGES OF XML?

XML stands for eXtensible Markup Language and is a markup language for documents containing structured information. Structured information contains both content and some indication of what role that content plays. Almost all documents have some structure. A markup language is a mechanism to identify structures in a document. The XML specification defines a standard way to add markup to documents.

Evolution of XML

Limitations of HTML gave birth to XML. The Limitations were as follows:

- Limited number of Tags

- Browsers are forgiving.
- Browser developers may be tempted to add new tags that only work with their product.
- Cannot customize layout from client side
- Product comparison.

Advantages of XML over HTML:

- HTML tells how the data should look whereas XML tells what it means.
- XML applies context to the data and separates data content from data presentation.
- XML provides a hierarchical structure. However XML is not designed to replace HTML.

WHAT IS XML FAMILY OF LANGUAGES?

Meaning: XML stands for eXtensible Markup Language and is a markup language for documents containing structured information. Structured information contains both content and some indication of what role that content plays. Almost all documents have some structure. A markup language is a mechanism to identify structures in a document. The XML specification defines a standard way to add markup to documents.

XML Family of Languages:

1. **XML Accessories** are languages which are intended for wide use to extend the capabilities specified in XML. Examples of XML accessories are the XML Schema language extending the definition capability of XML DTDs and the XML Names extending the naming mechanism to allow in a single XML document element and attribute names that are defined for and used by multiple software modules.
2. **XML Transducers** are languages which are intended for transducing some input XML data into some output form. Examples of XML transducers are the style sheet languages CSS and XSL intended to produce an external presentation from some XML data and XSLT intended for transforming XML documents into other XML documents. A transducer language is associated with some kind of processing model which defines the way output is derived from input.
3. **XML Applications** are languages which define constraints for a class of XML data for some special application area, often by means of a DTD. Examples of XML applications are MathML defined for mathematical data or XML-Signature intended for digital signatures. XML accessories and XML transducers are often XML-based languages and thus also XML applications. In this report a language is however classified as an XML application only if it has not been included in the accessories or transducers.

   The languages in the XML applications category can be further divided into four subcategories according to the application

   - Non-textual forms of data like mathematical data or voice.
   - Web publishing, to replace HTML by XML-based representation format.
   - Semantic web.
   - Web communication and services.

WHAT ARE THE DIFFERENCES BETWEEN XML AND XBRL?

While it is true that XBRL is built on XML, and that all XBRL documents must also be XML valid, there are major differences between the two. The most important conceptual distinction is that XBRL provides a way to express and validate semantics. For example, Assets = Equity +

Liabilities can be expressed using XBRL but not using native XML.

XBRL accommodates change better than XML. For example, XBRL separates the schema from the data. XBRL instance (data) documents are simple, containing normalized data immune to their sequence, and without hierarchy. Users can make changes to the XBRL taxonomy, such as changing parent-child relationships or adding new children, without having to reformat instance documents. Similarly, data in the instance document may be reordered without having an impact on the taxonomy. Normalized data also simplifies database storage.

Another unique feature of XBRL is its native support of multidimensional modeling, which is very similar to Microsoft Excel pivot tables. Consider the situation where you want a metadata model to support segmentation of product sales by country and also by product line. Assuming a simple example of product sales by three countries (US, Canada, and India) and two product lines (software and hardware), a pure element-based approach would result in 12 elements:

- sales_US_software
- sales_US_hardware
- sales_US_allProducts
- sales_Canada_software
- sales_Canada_hardware
- sales_Canada_allProducts
- sales_India_software
- sales_India_hardware
- sales_India_allProducts
- sales_allCountries_software
- sales_allCountries_hardware
- sales_allCountries_allProducts

Adding another product to the product line adds another four elements. Add another line item, such as cost of goods sold, and that one additional line item would result in another twelve elements. Such an approach quickly gets out of control, and is extremely frustrating to model and manage.

Using XBRL dimensions, there would be the single element of sales, along with the two dimensions of country and product line.

WHAT IS THE WORKING PRINCIPLE OF XBRL?

XBRL is a member of the family of languages based on **XML, or Extensible Markup Language**, which is a standard for the electronic exchange of data between businesses and on the internet. Under XML, **identifying tags** are applied to items of data so that they can be processed efficiently by computer software.

XBRL, a more powerful and flexible version of XML, has been defined specifically to meet the requirements of business and financial information. It enables **unique identifying tags** to be applied to items of financial data, such as say 'net profit' or say "Asset". For example let us take the item "Asset". It is defined in XBRL as follows:

<Asset>1000</Asset>

The word Asset together with brackets "<" and ">" is called a tag. Opening tags are denoted by <...> while closing tags are denoted by </...>.

However besides the numerical value of the asset, the computer needs to be told about accounting perspective of the term "Asset", its normal balance nature of "Debit" as well its relationship with other financial terms like Equity or Liabilities etc.

This is done by the powerful XBRL tags. Besides being identifiers, these tags provide a range of information about the item, such as whether it is a monetary item, percentage or fraction. XBRL allows labels in any language to be applied to items, as well as accounting references or other subsidiary information.

XBRL can show how items are related to one another and can thus represent how they are calculated. It can also identify whether they fall into particular groupings for organisation or presentation purposes. Most importantly, XBRL is easily extensible, so companies and other organisations can adapt it to meet a variety of special requirements.

The rich and powerful structure of XBRL allows very efficient handling of business data by computer software. It supports all the standard tasks involved in compiling, storing and using business data. Such information can be converted into XBRL by suitable mapping processes or generated in XBRL by software. It can then be searched, selected, exchanged or analysed by computer, or published for ordinary viewing.

Working of XBRL is governed **mainly by two main features namely Specifications and Taxonomies.**

WHAT ARE THE MAIN FEATURES OF XBRL?

1. **Specifications: Specifications** provide the **fundamental technical definition** of how XBRL works. The main, current specification for XBRL is **version 2.1.**

   New specifications are developed from requirements statements. They are initially discussed as Internal Working Drafts within the consortium and then released as **Public Working Drafts**. After a careful process of review, they are then finally released as **official XBRL Recommendations**. A Recommendation represents consensus within the XBRL International community as well as a stamp of approval for its widespread deployment.

2. **Taxonomies:** The word 'taxonomy', according to the Wikipedia, is derived from Greek verb tassein which means to classify and noun nomos that could be translated into English as law or science. Combined and interpreted word for word it would mean classification of some kind of knowledge. Initially, it referred to the science of classifying living things, but later it received wider meaning and is currently applied to either classification of things in general or rules governing this classification.

   Frequently, taxonomies are given hierarchical structures or are built in the form of networks so, as well as the elements, they also represent relationships.

   Virtually everything could be a subject of classification under some taxonomy. The most common example of taxonomy is classification of living creatures. The root element (the most general one) is Organism since all living things are of this group. Its first child is Domain which in turn is a parent of Kingdom whose subgroup is Division that is divided into Classes and so on.

One important characteristic of taxonomies is that children (lower level elements) may have many parents (upper level elements). In some classifications, spiders could be categorised as insects, in others as eight-legged creatures and in another as non-flying organisms.

3. **Instance Document:** An XBRL instance document is a business report in an electronic format created according to the rules of XBRL. It contains facts that are defined by the elements in the taxonomy it refers to, together with their values and an explanation of the context in which they are placed. The instance document assigns a value to an element and provides additional information about the currency in which it is disclosed and defines a period and the entity that it refers to.

4. **Footnote:** Footnotes appear on instance documents and provide additional information for some of the elements.

5. **Taxonomy Extension:** Public taxonomies, such as IFRS, define elements and relationships between them according to particular legislation or standards and allow companies to create financial statements that are valid and compliant with their requirements.

   But in the diverse world of finance, companies are required to include in their business reports additional concepts (usually related to the area of their activity or the reporting purpose). XBRL allows for such extensions of taxonomy without loss of comparability and integrity of data.

6. **DTS (Discoverable Taxonomy Set):** It contains one or more taxonomies i.e. a number of schemas together with linkbases related to them. This term was developed as taxonomies became more complicated and more closely related to each other.

   After describing the above features of XBRL, one can now mention with reference to the earlier example of **<Asset>1000</Asset>** that

   - values between tags (<Asset>1000</Asset>) will be found in instance documents;
   - information on what an Asset is and how a computer should treat it will be provided in schema files;
   - Relationships will be described in linkbases.

   Thus, the above features of XBRL can be best illustrated by the following diagram:

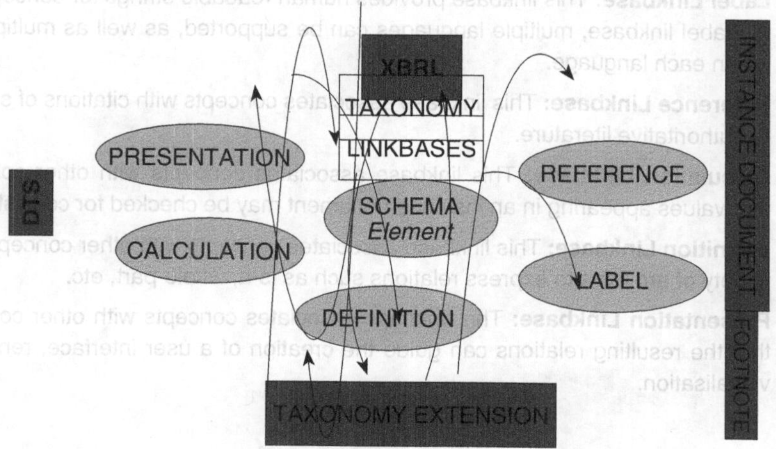

HOW DOES THE TERM TAXONOMIES APPLY TO XBRL?

Taxonomies are the dictionaries used by XBRL. They define the specific tags for individual items of data (such as "Asset"). Different taxonomies will be required for different financial reporting purposes. National jurisdictions may need their own financial reporting taxonomies to reflect their local accounting regulations. Many different organisations, including regulators, specific industries or even companies, may require taxonomies to cover their own business reporting needs. Taxonomy has got the following components:

1. **Schema:** This is the core part of the taxonomy and stores information about taxonomy elements i.e. their names, ids and other characteristics. It can be regarded as a container where an unstructured list of elements and references to linkbase files are described. The main purpose of XBRL schemas is to provide the computer with information on how it should represent and process accounting terms.
2. **Element:** An element (which is a part of the Schema) is a business concept (such as Assets, Liabilities, Income…) presented to a computer in a way that it could learn its main characteristics. Definitions of elements that appear in schemas are constructed according to a specific set of rules.

   For example say in the case of "Asset"

   <element name="Assets" id="Assets" periodType="instant"

   balance="debit" abstract="false" substitutionGroup="item"

   type="monetaryItemType"/>

   The characteristics of "Asset" like its name, type, balance and period type are described from a business perspective by the element to the computer.
3. **Linkbases:** are a collection of Links, which themselves are a collection of locators, arcs, and potentially resources. Locators are elements that essentially reference a concept and provide an arbitrary label for it. In turn, arcs are elements indicating that a concept links to another concept by referencing the labels defined by the locators. Some arcs link concepts to other concepts. Other arcs link concepts to resources, the most common of which are human-readable labels for the concepts. The XBRL 2.1 specification defines five different kinds of linkbases.
   - **Label Linkbase:** This linkbase provides human readable strings for concepts. Using the label linkbase, multiple languages can be supported, as well as multiple strings within each language.
   - **Reference Linkbase:** This linkbase associates concepts with citations of some body of authoritative literature.
   - **Calculation Linkbase:** This linkbase associates concepts with other concepts so that values appearing in an instance document may be checked for consistency.
   - **Definition Linkbase:** This linkbase associates concepts with other concepts using a variety of arc roles to express relations such as is-a, whole-part, etc.
   - **Presentation Linkbase:** This linkbase associates concepts with other concepts so that the resulting relations can guide the creation of a user interface, rendering, or visualisation.

WHAT ARE THE TYPES OF TAXONOMIES OFFICIALLY RECOGNISED BY XBRL INTERNATIONAL?

1. **Financial Reporting Taxonomies:** These have been officially recognised by XBRL International and have two levels of recognition. **Approved Taxonomies** have to comply with the official XBRL guidelines for that type of taxonomy, as well as with the XBRL Specification. Acknowledged Taxonomies just have to comply with the XBRL Specification.

(a) **Approved Taxonomies** must

1. Comply with the FRTA document.
2. Have been used to create a number of instance documents which confirm that it adequately covers the data it purports to represent.
3. Have been through a period of open review following initial Acknowledgement.

(b) **Acknowledged Taxonomies** are recognised by XBRL International as being in compliance with the XBRL Specification. They are acknowledged against a specific version of the Specification. Compliance is confirmed by testing taxonomy in a defined range of XBRL applications which may be upgraded and changed from time to time.

2. **GL Taxonomy:** This is a special taxonomy designed to support collation of data and internal reporting within organisations. It is intended to enable the efficient handling of financial and business information contained within an organisation. Often this is scattered across disparate accounting systems. XBRL allows it to be brought together, analysed and used in a highly cost effective way, overcoming the inefficiencies of different accounting systems or approaches.

The XBRL Global Ledger taxonomy **allows the representation** of anything that is found in a **chart of accounts, journal entries or historical transactions**, financial and non-financial. It does not require a standardised chart of accounts to gather information, but it can be used to tie legacy charts of accounts and accounting detail to a standardised chart of accounts to improve communications within a business.

XBRL Global Ledger is **reporting independent**. It collects general ledger and after-the-fact receivables, payables, inventory and other non-financial facts, and then permits the representation of that information using traditional summaries and through flexible links to XBRL for reporting.

XBRL Global Ledger is **system independent**. Any developer can create import and export routines to convert information to XBRL GL format. This means that accounting software developers need only consider one design for their XML import/export file formats. Application service providers can offer to supply XBRL import and output so end-users can more easily use their own data. Companies developing operational products, such as point of sale systems or job costing, or reporting tools can link with many accounting products without needing specialised links to each one.

XBRL Global Ledger permits **consolidation**. Popular low-end products and mid-market solutions are not designed to facilitate consolidating data from multiple organisations. XBRL GL can help transfer the general ledger from one system to another, be used to combine the operations of multiple organisations, or bring data into tools that will do the consolidation.

XBRL Global Ledger provides **flexibility**, overcoming the limitations of other approaches such as Electronic Data Interchange (EDI). It offers an **extensible, flexible, multinational solution** that can exchange the data required by internal finance, accountants, and creditors.

It complements **XBRL for financial reporting**, linking financial reports to the detail behind them, providing all the specific information required for audit work papers, budget planning, and detailed reporting.

Extensibility

Besides the creation of additional modules, XBRL International supports several methods for continuing expansion of shared XBRL functionality.

- **Link Role Registry:** This registry, hosted at xbrl.org, collects link roles and arc roles to promote reuse across taxonomies.
- **Functions Registry:** This registry collects XPath functions for reuse in formula linkbases.
- **Format Registry:** This registry collects common numeric formats for reuse in online XBRL applications.
- **Best Practice RFCs:** These documents will share common practices among community members to improve interoperability of design.

19 AS 17–SEGMENT REPORTING

TO WHICH ENTERPRISES AS 17 APPLIES?

AS 17 applies to:

1. Enterprises whose equity or debt securities are listed on a recognised stock exchange in India, and enterprises that are in the process of issuing equity or debt securities that will be listed on a recognised stock exchange in India as evidenced by the board of directors' resolution in this regard.
2. All other commercial, industrial and business reporting enterprises, whose turnover for the accounting period exceeds ₹ 50 crores. This standard establishes principles for reporting financial information about different types of products and services an enterprise produces and different geographical areas in which it operates. The information is expected to help users of financial statements, to better understand the performance and assess the risks and returns of the enterprise and make more informed judgements about the enterprise as a whole. The standard is more relevant for assessing risks and returns of a diversified or multilocational enterprise which may not be determinable from the aggregated data.

WHAT IS THE OBJECTIVES OF AS 17?

The objective of this Statement is to establish principles for reporting financial information, about the different types of products and services an enterprise produces and the different geographical areas in which it operates. Such information helps users of financial statements:

(a) Better understand the performance of the enterprise;

(b) Better assess the risks and returns of the enterprise; and

(c) Make more informed judgements about the enterprise as a whole.

WHAT IS THE SCOPE OF AS 17?

An enterprise should comply with the requirements of this Statement fully and not selectively. If a single financial report contains both consolidated financial statements and the separate financial statements of the parent, segment information need be presented only on the basis of the consolidated financial statements

WHAT IS THE MEANING OF A BUSINESS SEGMENT AS PER AS 17?

1. A Business Segment is a distinguishable component of an enterprise that is engaged in providing an individual product or service or a group of related products or services and that is subject to risks and returns that are different from those of other business segments.
2. Factors that should be considered in determining whether products or services are related include:

   a. The nature of the products or services.

   b. The nature of the production processes.

c. The type or class of customers for the products or services;.

d. The methods used to distribute the products or provide the services and

e. If applicable, the nature of the regulatory environment, for example, banking, insurance, or public utilities.

3. A single business segment does not include products and services with significantly differing risks and returns. While there may be dissimilarities with respect to one or several of the factors listed in the definition of business segment, the products and services included in a single business segment are expected to be similar with respect to a majority of the factors.

WHAT IS THE MEANING OF A GEOGRAPHICAL SEGMENT AS PER AS 17?

1. A Geographical Segment is a distinguishable component of an enterprise that is engaged in providing products or services within a particular economic environment and that is subject to risks and returns that are different from those of components operating in other economic environments.
2. Factors that should be considered in identifying geographical segments include:
   a. Similarity of economic and political conditions.
   b. Relationships between operations in different geographical areas.
   c. Proximity of operations.
   d. Special risks associated with operations in a particular area.
   e. Exchange control regulations and
   f. The underlying currency risks.
3. A single geographical segment does not include operations in economic environments with significantly differing risks and returns. A geographical segment may be a single country, a group of two or more countries, or a region within a country. The risks and returns of an enterprise are influenced both by the geographical location of its operations and also by the location of its customers. The definition allows geographical segments to be based on either:
   a. The location of production or service facilities and other assets of an enterprise; or
   b. The location of its customers.

WHAT IS THE MEANING OF A REPORTABLE SEGMENT AS PER AS 17?

1. A Reportable Segment is a business segment or a geographical segment identified on the basis of foregoing definitions for which segment information is required to be disclosed by this Statement.
2. The predominant sources of risks affect how most enterprises are organised and managed.
3. Therefore, the organisational structure of an enterprise and its internal financial reporting system are normally the basis for identifying its segments.

WHAT IS THE MEANING OF SEGMENT REVENUE AS PER AS 17?

A. Inclusions: Segment Revenue is the aggregate of:

1. The portion of enterprise revenue that is directly attributable to a segment,
2. The relevant portion of enterprise revenue that can be allocated on a reasonable basis to a segment, and
3. Revenue from transactions with other segments of the enterprise.

B. Exclusions: Segment Revenue does not include:

1. Extraordinary items as defined in AS 5.
2. Interest or dividend income, including interest earned on advances or loans to other segments unless the operations of the segment are primarily of a financial nature; and
3. Gains on sales of investments or on extinguishment of debt unless the operations of the segment are primarily of a financial nature.

WHAT IS THE MEANING OF SEGMENT EXPENSE AS PER AS 17?

A. Inclusions: Segment Expense is the aggregate of:

1. The expense resulting from the operating activities of a segment that is directly attributable to the segment, and
2. The relevant portion of enterprise expense that can be allocated on a reasonable basis to the segment,
3. Including expense relating to transactions with other segments of the enterprise.

B. Exclusions: Segment Expense does not include:

1. Extraordinary items as defined in AS 5.
2. Interest expense, including interest incurred on advances or loans from other segments, unless the operations of the segment are primarily of a financial nature.
3. Losses on sales of investments or losses on extinguishment of debt unless the operations of the segment are primarily of a financial nature.
4. Income tax expense; and
5. General administrative expenses, head-office expenses, and other expenses that arise at the enterprise level and relate to the enterprise as a whole. However, costs are sometimes incurred at the enterprise level on behalf of a segment. Such costs are part of segment expense if they relate to the operating activities of the segment and if they can be directly attributed or allocated to the segment on a reasonable basis.

WHAT IS THE MEANING OF SEGMENT ASSETS AS PER AS 17?

A. Inclusions:

1. Segment Assets are those operating assets that are employed by a segment in its operating activities and that either are directly attributable to the segment or can be allocated to the segment on a reasonable basis.
2. If the segment result of a segment includes interest or dividend income, its segment assets include the related receivables, loans, investments, or other interest or dividend generating assets.

B. Exclusions: Segment Assets do not include:

1. Income Tax Assets;
2. Assets used for general enterprise or head-office purposes.

Note: Segment assets are determined after deducting related allowances/provisions that are reported as direct offsets in the Balance Sheet of the enterprise.

WHAT IS THE MEANING OF SEGMENT LIABILITIES AS PER AS 17?

A. Inclusions:

1. Segment Liabilities are those operating liabilities that result from the operating activities of a segment and that either are directly attributable to the segment or can be allocated to the segment on a reasonable basis.
2. If the segment result of a segment includes interest expense, its segment liabilities include the related interest-bearing liabilities.
3. Liabilities that relate jointly to two or more segment should be allocated to segments if, and only if, their related revenues and expenses also are allocated to those segments.
4. Examples of segment liabilities include trade and other payables, accrued liabilities, customer advances, product warranty provisions, and other claims relating to the provision of goods and services.

B. Exclusions: Segment Liabilities do not include:

1. Income Tax Liabilities;
2. Borrowings And Other Liabilities that are incurred for financing rather than operating purposes.

WHAT IS THE TREATMENT OF INTEREST FOR DETERMINING SEGMENT EXPENSE AS PER AS 17?

1. The interest expense relating to overdrafts and other operating liabilities identified to a particular segment should not be included as a part of the segment expense unless the operations of the segment are primarily of a financial nature or unless the interest is included as a part of the cost of inventories as per paragraph below.
2. In case interest is included as a part of the cost of inventories where it is so required as per AS 16, read with AS 2, Valuation of Inventories, and those inventories are part of segment assets of a particular segment, such interest should be considered as a segment expense. In this case, the amount of such interest and the fact that the segment result has been arrived at after considering such interest should be disclosed by way of a note to the segment result.

WHAT ARE THE FACTORS, FOR DETERMINING WHICH REPORTING FORMAT IS PRIMARY AND WHICH IS SECONDARY AS PER AS 17?

1. The dominant source and nature of risks and returns of an enterprise should govern whether its primary segment reporting format will be business segments or geographical segments.
2. Internal organisation and management structure of an enterprise and its system of internal financial reporting to the board of directors and the chief executive officer should normally be the basis for identifying the predominant source and nature of risks and differing rates of return facing the enterprise and, therefore, for determining which reporting format is primary and which is secondary, except as provided paragraphs below:
   a. If risks and returns of an enterprise are strongly affected both by differences in the products and services it produces and by differences in the geographical areas in which it operates, as evidenced by a 'matrix approach', then the enterprise should use business segments as its primary segment reporting format and geographical segments as its secondary reporting format; and

b. If internal organisational and management structure of an enterprise are based neither on individual products or services or groups of related products/services nor on geographical areas, it should be determined whether the risks and returns of the enterprise are related more to the products and services it produces or to the geographical areas in which it operates and accordingly, choose segments.

c. If one or more of the segments reported internally to the directors and management is a business segment or a geographical segment based on the factors in the definitions but others are not, paragraph below should be applied only to those internal segments that do not meet the definitions.

HOW WILL YOU DEAL WITH INTERNAL SEGMENTS THAT DO NOT MEET THE DEFINITIONS?

1. For those segments reported internally to the directors and management that do not satisfy the definitions, management of the enterprise should look to the next lower level of internal segmentation that reports information along product and service lines or geographical lines, as appropriate under the definitions and
2. If such an internally reported lower-level segment meets the definition of business segment or geographical segment, the criteria for identifying reportable segments should be applied to that segment.

DOES AS 17 REQUIRE MATRIX PRESENTATION?

A 'matrix presentation',both business segments and geographical segments as primary segment reporting formats with full segment disclosures on each basis, will often provide useful information if risks and returns of an enterprise are strongly affected both by differences in the products and services it produces and by differences in the geographical areas in which it operates. This Statement does not require, but does not prohibit, a 'matrix presentation'.

HOW WILL YOU IDENTIFY REPORTABLE SEGMENTS AS PER AS 17?

A Business Segment or Geographical Segment should be identified as a Reportable Segment if:

1. Its Revenue from Sales to external customers and from transactions with other segments is at least 10% of the Total Revenue, external and internal, of all segments; or
2. Its segment result, whether profit or loss, is at least 10% of:
   (i) The combined result of all segments in profit, or
   (ii) The combined result of all segments in loss,
   (iii) Whichever is greater in absolute amount; or
3. Its Segment Assets are at least 10% of the Total Assets of all segments.

Note: A business segment or a geographical segment which is not a reportable segment as per above paragraph, may be designated as a reportable segment despite its size at the discretion of the management of the enterprise. If that segment is not designated as a reportable segment, it should be included as an unallocated reconciling item.

Additional Segments: If total external revenue attributable to reportable segments constitutes less than 75% of the total enterprise revenue, additional segments should be identified as reportable segments, even if they do not meet the 10 per cent thresholds, until at least 75% of total enterprise revenue is included in reportable segments.

Reportable Segment for Comparative Purposes

1. A segment identified as a reportable segment in the immediately preceding period because it satisfied the relevant 10 % thresholds should continue to be a reportable

segment for the current period notwithstanding that its Revenue, Result, and Assets all no longer meet the 10 % thresholds.

2. If a segment is identified as a reportable segment in the current period because it satisfies the relevant 10 % thresholds, preceding-period segment data that is presented for comparative purposes should, unless it is impracticable to do so, be restated to reflect the newly reportable segment as a separate segment, even if that segment did not satisfy the 10% thresholds in the preceding period.

DOES AS 17 PROHIBIT THE DISCLOSURE OF ADDITIONAL SEGMENT INFORMATION THAT IS PREPARED ON A BASIS OTHER THAN THE ACCOUNTING POLICIES ADOPTED FOR THE ENTERPRISE FINANCIAL STATEMENTS?

1. Segment information should be prepared in conformity with the accounting policies adopted for preparing and presenting the Financial Statements of the enterprise as a whole.
2. This Statement does not prohibit the disclosure of additional segment information that is prepared on a basis other than the accounting policies adopted for the enterprise Financial Statements provided that
   (a) the information is reported internally to the board of directors and the chief executive officer for purposes of making decisions about allocating resources to the segment and assessing its performance and
   (b) the basis of measurement for this additional information is clearly described.
   (c) Assets and liabilities that relate jointly to two or more segments should be allocated to segments if, and only if, their related revenues and expenses also are allocated to those segments.

WHAT ARE THE CONTENTS OF PRIMARY REPORTING FORMAT AS PER AS 17?

An enterprise should disclose the following for each reportable segment:

1. Segment Revenue, classified into segment revenue from sales to external customers and segment revenue from transactions with other segments;
2. Segment Result;
3. Total Carrying Amount of Segment Assets;
4. Total Amount of Segment Liabilities;
5. Total Cost incurred during the period to acquire segment assets that are expected to be used during more than one period (tangible and intangible fixed assets);
6. Total Amount of Expense included in the segment result for depreciation and amortisation in respect of segment assets for the period; and
7. Total Amount of Significant Non-Cash Expenses other than depreciation and amortisation in respect of segment assets, that were included in segment expense and, therefore, deducted in measuring segment result.

Notes: Disclosure of segment cash flow is, therefore, encouraged, though not required. An enterprise that provides segment cash flow disclosures need not disclose depreciation and amortization expense and non-cash expenses.

Reconciliation: An enterprise should present a Reconciliation between the information disclosed for reportable segments and the aggregated information in the enterprise Financial Statements. In presenting the reconciliation, segment revenue should be reconciled to enterprise revenue; segment result should be reconciled to enterprise net profit or loss; segment assets should be reconciled to enterprise assets; and segment liabilities should be reconciled to enterprise liabilities.

WHAT ARE THE CONTENTS OF SECONDARY REPORTING FORMAT AS PER AS 17?

A. If primary format of an enterprise for reporting segment information is Business Segments, it should also report the following information:

1. Segment Revenue from external customers by geographical area based on the geographical location of its customers, for each geographical segment whose revenue from sales to external customers is at least 10% of enterprise revenue;
2. The Total Carrying Amount of Segment Assets by geographical location of assets, for each geographical segment whose segment assets are 10 per cent or more of the total assets of all geographical segments; and
3. The Total Cost incurred during the period to acquire segment assets that are expected to be used during more than one period (tangible and intangible fixed assets) by geographical location of assets, for each geographical segment whose segment assets are 10 per cent or more of the total assets of all geographical segments.

B. If primary format of an enterprise for reporting segment information is Geographical Segments (whether based on location of assets or location of customers), it should also report the following segment information for each business segment whose revenue from sales to external customers is at least 10% of enterprise revenue or whose segment assets are at least 10% of the total assets of all business segments:

1. Segment revenue from external customers;
2. The total carrying amount of segment assets; and
3. The total cost incurred during the period to acquire segment assets that are expected to be used during more than one period (tangible and intangible fixed assets).

C. If primary format of an enterprise for reporting segment information is geographical segments that are based on location of assets, and if the location of its customers is different from the location of its assets, then the enterprise should also report revenue from sales to external customers for each customer-based geographical segment whose revenue from sales to external customers is at least 10% of enterprise revenue.

D. If primary format of an enterprise for reporting segment information is geographical segments that are based on location of customers, and if the assets of the enterprise are located in different geographical areas from its customers, then the enterprise should also report the following segment information for each asset-based geographical segment whose revenue from sales to external customers or segment assets are at least 10% of total enterprise amounts:

1. The total carrying amount of segment assets by geographical location of the assets.
2. The total cost incurred during the period to acquire segment assets that are expected to be used during more than one period (tangible and intangible fixed assets) by location of the assets.

CAN A COMPANY HAVE ITS OWN AN INTER-SEGMENT TRANSFER PRICING?

AS 17 'Segment Reporting' requires that inter-segment transfers should be measured on the basis that the enterprise actually used to price these transfers. The basis of pricing inter-segment transfers and any change therein should be disclosed in the Financial Statements. Hence, the enterprise can have its own policy for pricing inter -segment transfers and hence, inter-segment transfers may be based on cost, below cost or market price. However, whichever policy is followed, the same should be disclosed and applied consistently.

WHAT ARE THE OBJECTIONS TO SEGMENTAL REPORTING?

The possible objections to Segmental Reporting can be enumerated as below:

1. It is generally felt that Segmental Revenues and Expenses are not distinguishable objectively in many cases. Revenues of a weak product line may be derived only because of the existence of a strong product line. Also many joint costs are only separable arbitrarily.
2. Much of segmental results depend on the inter-departmental transfer pricing which are not always logically established.
3. Various segments of an enterprise may use common resources which makes it difficult to arrive at a segment wise performance ratio.
4. Since the users are not in position to know the proper base for cost allocation, the segment results would be less than meaningful.
5. The last objection consists of the competitive implications to the firm. Some academics contend that company secrets will be disclosed while others referred to the competitive hardship suffered by some firms if segmented data is required. Suppose that Company X, a small company, has a segment identical to one in Company Y, a huge conglomerate. Company X would have to disclose the segment while Company Y would not because the segment is not considered material to Y's operations.

However, considering the questions of joint cost allocation, often it is suggested to follow a contribution margin approach for reporting segmental results. By this only identifiable costs are deducted from segment revenues and gross segment margins may only be indicated. But for all practical purposes, this becomes a useless exercise when proportion of identifiable cost is insignificant.

WHAT ARE THE DISCLOSURES REQUIREMENTS AS PER AS 17?

1. The basis of pricing inter-segment transfers and any change therein should be disclosed in the financial statements.
2. Nature of the Changes in accounting policies adopted for segment reporting that have a material effect on Financial Statements and the financial effect of the change if it is reasonably determinable.

   Example could be:
   - changes in identification of segments; and
   - changes in the basis for allocating revenues and expenses to segments.
3. An enterprise should indicate the types of products and services included in each reported business segment and indicate the composition of each reported geographical segment, both primary and secondary, if not otherwise disclosed in the financial statements.

PRACTICAL QUESTIONS FOR PRACTICE

PROBLEM 1

Identify the reportable segment by Revenue test for XYZ Ltd. (₹ in lakhs)

Particulars	*A*	*B*	*C*	*D*	*E*	*F*	*Total*
Segment Revenue	600	1,240	150	120	170	120	2,400

SOLUTION:

As per para 27 of AS 17 'Segment Reporting', a business segment or geographical segment should be identified as a reportable segment if Its revenue from sales to external customers and from other transactions with other segments is **at least 10%** of the total revenue- external and internal of all segments.

(₹ *in lakh*)

Particulars	*A*	*B*	*C*	*D*	*E*	*F*	*Total*
1. Segment Revenue	600	1,240	150	120	170	120	**2,400**
2. % of Total Revenue of all Segments	25%	52%	6%	5%	7%	5%	
Whether Revenue Criteria satisfied	YES	YES	NO	NO	NO	NO	
Reportable Segment	YES	YES	NO	NO	NO	NO	

PROBLEM 2

M/s XYZ Ltd. has three segments namely X, Y, Z. The total assets of the Company are: Segment X ₹ 2.00 crores, Segment Y ₹ 6.00 crores and Segment Z ₹ 12.00 crores. Deferred tax assets included in the assets of each Segments are X- ₹ 1 crore, Y—₹ 0.80 crores and Z—₹ 0.60 crores. The accountant contends that all the three Segments are reportable segments as per AS 17. Comment

SOLUTION:

Provision of AS 17: As per AS 17 "Segment Reporting", A business segment or geographical segment should be identified as a reportable segment if its segment assets are at least 10% of the total assets of all segments. Segment assets do not include Income Tax Assets.

Advice:

1. Revised Total Assets of all segments = 20 crores – (1 + 0.8 + 0.6) = 17.6 crores
2. 10% of Total Assets of all segments = 1.76 crores
3. Segment Assets of X = 2 crore – 1 crore = 1 crore
4. Segment Assets of Y = 6 crore – 0.8 crore = 5.2 crore
5. Segment Assets of Z = 12 crore – 0.6 crore = 11.4 crore

Thus, only Y and Z hold more than 10% of the total assets and hence Only Y and Z are reportable segments.

PROBLEM 3

Identify the reportable segment by profitability test for XYZ Ltd.

Segment	*A*	*B*	*C*	*D*	*E*
Profit (Loss)	450	45	(360)	(30)	(210)

SOLUTION:

As per para 27 of AS 17 'Segment Reporting', on the basis of profitability test a business segment or geographical segment should be identified as a reportable segment if: Its segment result (whether profit or loss) is at least 10% of the combined result of all segments in profit, or the combined result of all segments in loss, whichever is greater in absolute amount;

Segment	*A*	*B*	*C*	*D*	*E*	*Total*
A. Segment Result (Profit)	450	45				**495**
B. Segment Result(Loss)			(360)	(30)	(210)	(600)
C. Combined Segment Result (A *or* B whichever is higher in absolute amount)						600
% Higher Absolute Combined Segment Result i.e. 600	75%	7.5%	60%	5%	35%	
Reportable Segment	Yes	No	Yes	No	Yes	

PROBLEM 4

BHARAT Ltd. gives the following data regarding to its six segments:

(₹ *in lakhs*)

Particulars	*A*	*B*	*C*	*D*	*E*	*F*	*Total*
Segment Assets	90	160	60	30	40	20	400
Segment Results	130	(380)	20	20	(20)	30	(200)
Segment Revenue	600	1,240	150	120	170	120	2,400

Identify the Reportable Segments as per AS 17.

SOLUTION

(₹ *in lakh*)

Particulars	*A*	*B*	*C*	*D*	*E*	*F*	*Total*
1. Segment Revenue	600	1,240	150	120	170	120	**2,400**
2. % of Total Revenue of all Segments	25%	52%	6%	5%	7%	5%	
3A. Segment Result(Profit)	130		20	20		30	**200**
3B. Segment Result(Loss)		380			20		400
3C. Combined Segment Result (3A *or* 3B whichever is higher in absolute amount)							400
4. % Higher Absolute Combined Segment Result i.e. 140	32.5%	95%	5%	5%	5%	7.5%	

5. Segment Assets	90	160	60	30	40	20	400
6. % of Total Assets of all Segments	22.5%	40%	15%	7.5%	10%	5%	
Whether Revenue Criteria satisfied	YES	YES	NO	NO	NO	NO	
Whether Result Criteria satisfied	YES	YES	NO	NO	NO	NO	
Whether Assets Criteria satisfied	YES	YES	YES	NO	YES	NO	
Reportable Segment	YES	YES	YES	NO	YES	NO	

Only segment A, B, C and E are Reportable Segments as per AS 17.

PROBLEM 5

BHARAT Ltd. gives the following data regarding to its six segments: *(₹ in lakhs)*

Particulars	*A*	*B*	*C*	*D*	*E*	*F*	*Total*
Segment Assets	100	168	66	31	48	27	440
Segment Results	130	(380)	20	20	(20)	30	(200)
Segment Revenue	600	1,240	150	120	170	120	2,400

Deferred Tax Assets included in the assets of each Segments are A— ₹ 10 lakh, B— ₹ 8 lakhs, C— ₹ 6 lakhs, D— ₹ 1 lakh, E— ₹ 8 lakhs, F — ₹ 7 lakhs. Identify the Reportable Segments as per AS 17 .

SOLUTION

As per AS 17 "Segment Reporting", A business segment or geographical segment should be identified as a reportable segment if its segment assets are at least 10% of the total assets of all segments. Segment assets do not include Income Tax Assets.

Particulars	*A*	*B*	*C*	*D*	*E*	*F*	*Total*
Segment Assets (including DTA)	100	168	66	31	48	27	440
Deferred Tax Assets	10	8	6	1	8	7	(40)
Segment Assets (excluding DTA)	90	160	60	30	40	20	400

Remaining solution is same as given in previous problem.

PROBLEM 6

Following details are given for RP Ltd. for the year ended 31st March 2023.

Particulars	*(₹ in lakhs)*	*(₹ in lakhs)*
Sales (including inter-segment sales):		
Food Products	10,000	
Plastic and Packaging	1,240	
Health and scientific	690	

Others	364	12,294
Expenses:		
Food Products	7.170	
Plastic and Packaging	800	
Health and Scientific	444	
Others	400	8,814
Other items:		
General corporate expenses		1,096
Income from investments		252
Interest expenses		126
Identifiable Assets:		
Food products	15,096	
Plastic and Packaging	4,000	
Health and Scientific	1,400	
Others	1,364	21,860
General Corporate Assets		1,664

Other information:

Particulars	*(₹ in lakhs)*
(a) Inter-segment sales are as below:	
Food Products	120
Plastic and Packaging	168
Health and Scientific	36
Others	10

(a) Operating Profit includes ₹ ('000) 66 on inter-segment sales.

Required: Identify Reportable Segments.

SOLUTION

Provisions As per AS 17 "Segment Reporting", a business segment or geographical segment should be identified as a reportable segment, if

(i) Its revenue from sales to external customers and from transactions with other segments is 10% or more of the total revenue, external and internal, of all segments; or

(ii) Its segment result whether profit or loss is 10% or more of

(1) The combined result of all segments in profit; or

(2) The combined result of all segments in loss,

(iii) Its segment assets are 10% or more of the total assets of all segments.

Further, if the total external revenue attributable to reportable segments constitutes less than 75% of total enterprise revenue, additional segments should be identified as reportable segments, even if they do not meet the 10% threshold until at least 75% of total enterprise revenue is included in reportable segments.

Particulars	*Sales (₹ in lakhs)*	*Expenses (₹ in lakhs)*	*Segment result (₹ in lakhs)*
Food Products	10,000	7,170	2,830
Plastic & packaging	1,240	800	440
Health & scientific	690	444	246
Other	364	400	(36)

RP Ltd. operates through four segments, namely, 'Food Products', 'Plastic and Packaging', 'Health and Scientific and Other'. The relevant information about these segments is given in the following table:

(*₹ in lakh*)

Particulars	*Food*	*Plastic*	*Health*	*Others*	*Total*
1. Segment Revenue	10,000	1,240	690	364	12,294
2. % of Total Revenue of all Segments	81.34%	10.09%	5.61%	2.96%	
3A. Segment Result(Profit)	2,830	440	246		3,516
3B. Segment Result(Loss)				(36)	(90)
3C. Combined Segment Result (3A *or* 3B whichever is higher in absolute amount)					**3,516**
4. % Higher Absolute Combined Segment Result i.e. 140	80.49%	12.51%	7%	1.02%	
5. Segment Assets	15,096	4,000	1,400	1,364	21,860
6. % of Total Assets of all Segments	69.06%	18.3%	6.4%	6.24%	
Reportable Segment	Yes	Yes	No	No	
Criteria satisfied if any % is >10%	Revenue, Result & Assets	Revenue, Result & Assets			

PROBLEM 7.

M Ltd. Group has three divisions A, B and C. Details of their turnover, results and net assets are given below:

	Head Office ₹ ('000)	*A ₹ ('000)*	*B ₹ ('000)*	*C ₹ ('000)*
Sales to B		3050		
Other Sales (Home)		60		
Export Sales		4090	200	180
Sales to C			30	
Operating Profit or Loss before tax		160	20	(8)

Re-allocated Cost from Head Office		48	24	24
Interest Cost		4	5	1
Fixed Assets	50	200	40	120
Net Current Assets	48	120	40	90
Long-term Liabilities	38	20	10	120

Required: Prepare a Segmental Report for publication in M Ltd. Group.

SOLUTION:

M LTD. SEGMENTAL REPORT

₹ *('000)*

Particulars	*Divisions*			*Inter Segment Eliminations*	*Con-solidated Total*
	A	*B*	*C*		
Segment Revenue					
Sales:					
Domestic	60	–	–	–	60
Export	4,090	200	180	–	4,470
External Sales	4,150	200	180	–	4,530
Inter-segment Sales	3,050	30	–	3,080	–
Total Revenue	7,200	230	180	3,080	4,530
Segment Result (given)	160	20	(8)		172
Head office expenses					(96)
Operating profit					76
Interest expense					(10)
Profit before tax					66
Other information					
Fixed assets	200	40	120		360
Net current assets	120	40	90		250
Segment assets	320	80	210		610
Unallocated corporate assets					98
Segment liabilities	20	10	120		150
Unallocated corporate liabilities					38

SALES REVENUE BY GEOGRAPHICAL MARKET

(₹ *'000)*

Particulars	*Home Sales*	*Export Sales (by division A)*	*Export Sales (by division B)*	*Export Sales (by division C)*	*Consoli-dated Total*
External Sales	60	4,090	200	180	4,530

PROBLEM 8.

From the following information of a company having two primary segments, prepare a statement classifying the same under appropriate heads.

(₹ in lakh)

Segment Revenue	A	27,050
Segment Revenue	B	3,280
Inter Segment Revenue	A	50
Segment Profit	A	4,640
Segment Loss	B	197
Dividend Income		285
Interest Expense		35
Tax Provision		1,675
Capital Expenditure	A	1,300
Capital Expenditure	B	16
Non Cash Expenses (excluding Depreciation):		
Segment	A	114
Segment	B	16
Liabilities	A	3,430
Liabilities	B	770
Other Liabilities		2,200
Assets	A	19,450
Assets	B	2,700
Other Assets		6,550
Depreciation	A	110
Depreciation	B	15

SOLUTION

Particulars	*Segment A*	*Segment B*	*Others*	*Eliminations*	*Total*
I. Revenue:					
(a) External Revenue	27,050	3,280			30,330
(b) Inter segment Revenue	50			50	
Total	27,100	3,280		50	30,330
II. Result:	4,640	–197			4,443
(a) Income from Investment					285
(b) Interest Expenses					(35)
(c) Tax provision					(1,675)
(d) Net profit					3,018

III Assets:					
(a) Segment assets (directly attributable & allocated)	19,450	2,700			22,150
(b) Unallocated assets					6,550
IV Liabilities					
(a) Segment assets (directly attributable & allocated)	3,430	770			4,200
(b) Unallocated liabilities					2,200
V Others:					
(a) Depreciation	110	15			125
(b) Non cash expenses	114	16			130
(c) Capital Expenditure	1,300	16			1,316

PROBLEM 9

Microtech Ltd. produces batteries for scooters, cars, trucks, and specialised batteries for invertors and UPS. How many segments should it have and why?

SOLUTION

In case of Microtech Ltd., the basic product is the batteries, but the risks and returns of the batteries for automobiles (scooters, cars and trucks) and batteries for invertors and UPS are affected by different set of factors. In case of automobile batteries, the risks and returns are affected by the Government policy, road conditions, quality of automobiles, etc. whereas in case of batteries for invertors and UPS, the risks and returns are affected by power condition, standard of living, etc. Therefore, it can be said that Microtech Ltd. has two business segments viz-'Automobile batteries' and 'batteries for Invertors and UPS'.

PROBLEM 10

Manufacturer of traditional electrical and engineering goods such as switchgears, motors, etc. each constituting a separate division has entered into new areas such as telecom, software, etc. Due to significant change in its activity profile, it has changed its internal reporting structure to combine the traditional products such as switchgears, switchboard and motors into one division. According to management the earlier form of segmental reporting is no longer relevant and they plan to switch to reporting the traditional products under one segment. The following questions are relevant:

Can this be done? If no, will we have to reconstruct segment information based on the earlier position?

If yes, would it constitute a change in segment accounting policy? In that case what are the disclosures required?

SOLUTION:

In this regard following factors have to be considered:

Whether the three traditional divisions of the company can be combined into one segment for financial reporting, after they have been merged for internal reporting purposes?

Whether the risks and returns to switchgear, switchboard and motors significantly different from each other?

Can they be for all practical purposes combined into one basket of traditional engineering/ electrical goods?

Factors that should be considered in determining whether products and services are related include:

1. the nature of the products or services,
2. the nature of the production processes,
3. the type or class of customer for the products or services and
4. the methods used to distribute the products or provide the services.

A single business segment does not include products and services with significantly different risks and returns. While there may be dissimilarities with respect to one or several of the above factors, the products and services included in a single business segment are expected to be similar with respect to a majority of the factors.

The predominant sources of risks affect how most enterprises are organized and managed. Therefore, the organizational structure of an enterprise and its internal financial reporting system is normally the basis for identifying its segments. If in the given situation, it can be demonstrated that the traditional products faced the same risks and return situation (i.e., they are not significantly different) and that the internal reporting has actually changed, then it should be possible to combine the three divisions for segment reporting purposes.

Based on the analysis above, the following position would emerge:

(a) Telecom and software development activities cannot be combined with the traditional product line (switch gear etc) and made into one segment.

(b) Subject to fulfillment of definition criteria laid down in AS 17, traditional product lines can be combined into one segment.

(c) Changes in identification of segments would not constitute a change in accounting policy because there is no change in the policy parse, the policy for the current year continues to be to determine segments based on the internal reporting structure and the guidelines set out in AS 17.

PROBLEM 11.

A Company has an inter-segment transfer pricing policy of charging at cost *less* 10%. The market prices are generally 25% above cost. Is the policy adopted by the company correct?

SOLUTION

AS 17 'Segment Reporting' requires that inter-segment transfers should be measured on the basis that the enterprise actually used to price these transfers. The basis of pricing inter-segment transfers and any change therein should be disclosed in the financial statements. Hence, the enterprise can have its own policy for pricing inter -segment transfers and hence, inter-segment transfers may be based on cost, below cost or market price. However, whichever policy is followed, the same should be disclosed and applied consistently. Therefore, in the given case inter-segment transfer pricing policy adopted by the company is correct ,if followed consistently.

SOLVED PROBLEMS

PROBLEM 1

CEE Limited has three segments namely P, Q and R. The assets of the company are ₹15 crores. Segment P has 4 crores, Segment Q has 6 crores and Segment R has 5 crores. Deferred tax assets included in the assets of each segment are P – ₹ 1 crore,Q – ₹ 0.90 crores and R

–₹ 0.80 crores. The accountant contends all these three segments are reportable segments. Comment.

SOLUTION

According to AS 17 "Segment Reporting", segment Assets do not include income tax assets.

Therefore, the revised total assets are 12.3 crores [₹ 15 –(₹1 + 0.9 + 0.8).

Details of Segment wise assets

Segment P holds total assets of ₹ 3 crores (₹ 4 crores – ₹ 1 crores);

Segment Q holds ₹ 5.1 crores (₹ 6 crores – 0.9 crores);

Segment R holds ₹ 4.2 crores (₹ 5 crores – ₹ 0.8 crores).

Thus, all the three segments hold more than 10% of the total assets, all segments are reportable segments.

Hence, the contention of the Accountant that all three segments are reportable segments is correct.

PROBLEM 2

M/s XYZ Ltd. has three segments namely X, Y, Z. The total assets of the Company are ₹ 10.00 crores. Segment X has ₹ 2.00 crores, segment Y has ₹ 3.00 crores and segment Z has ₹ 5.00 crores. Deferred tax assets included in the assets of each segments are X- ₹ 0.50 crores, Y—₹ 0.40 crores and Z—₹ 0.30 crores. The accountant contends that all the three segments are reportable segments. Comment.

SOLUTION:

Provision of AS 17: As per AS 17 "Segment Reporting", A business segment or geographical segment should be identified as a reportable segment if its segment assets are 10% or more of the total assets of all segments. Segment Assets do not include Income Tax Assets.

Advice:

1. Revised Total Assets are 8.8 crores [i.e. 10 crores – (0.5+0.4+0.3)].
2. 10% of Total Assets = 0.88 Crore
3. Segment X holds total assets of 1.5 crores (i.e. 2 crores – 0.5 crores);
4. Segment Y holds 2.6 crores (i.e. 3 crores – 0.4 crores); and
5. Segment Z holds 4.7 crores (i.e. 5 crores – 0.3 crores).

Thus, all the three segments hold more than 10% of the total assets, all segments are reportable segments.

PROBLEM 3

The Chief Accountant of PELF FIN STOCK Ltd. gives the following data regarding its six segments:

₹ In lakhs

Particulars	*M*	*N*	*O*	*P*	*Q*	*R*	*Total*
Segment Assets	50	25	10	5	5	5	100
Segment Results	-50	–140	80	10	–10	10	–100
Segment Revenue	200	320	200	90	90	100	1000
Identify the Reportable Segments as per AS 17.							

SOLUTION

As per para 27 of AS 17 'Segment Reporting', a business segment or geographical segment should be identified as a reportable segment if:

(i) Its revenue from sales to external customers and from other transactions with other segments is 10% or more of the total revenue- external and internal of all segments; or

(ii) Its segment result whether profit or loss is 10% or more of:
The combined result of all segments in profit, (i.e., ₹ 100) or The combined result of all segments in loss, whichever is greater in absolute amount (i.e. ₹ .200 lakhs); or

(iii) Its segment assets are 10% or more of the Total Assets of all segments.

Criteria For Reportable Segment	*Reportable Segment fulfilling Criteria*
1. 10% of Total Revenue (i.e., 100)	M, N, O, R
2. 10% of Total Result (i.e., 20)	M, N, O
3. 10% of Total Assets (i.e., 10)	M, N, O

Hence, Reportable Segments as per AS 17 are M, N, O, R only

PROBLEM 4

Information relating to five segments of V Ltd. is as under: *(₹ in lakhs)*

Segments	A	B	C	D	E	Total
Segment Revenue	100	300	200	100	300	1000
Segment Result	40	(60)	90	10	(30)	50
Segment Assets	45	55	140	20	40	300

As a cost accountant of this company management wishes to know from you which company need to be reported.

SOLUTION

(₹ in lakh)

Particulars	*A*	*B*	*C*	*D*	*E*	*Total*
1. Segment Revenue	100	300	200	100	300	**1,000**
2. % of Total Revenue of all Segments	10%	30%	20%	10%	30%	
3A. Segment Result(Profit)	40		90	10		**140**
3B. Segment Result(Loss)		(60)			(30)	(90)
3C. Combined Segment Result (3A *or* 3B whichever is higher in absolute amount)						140
4. % Higher Absolute Combined Segment Result i.e. 140	28.57%	42.88%	64.29%	7.14%	21.43%	
5. Segment Assets	45	55	140	20	40	**300**
6. % of Total Assets of all Segments	15%	18.33%	46.67%	6.66%	13.33%	

Reportable Segment	Yes	Yes	Yes	Yes	Yes
Criteria satisfied if any % is = >10%	Revenue, Result & Assets	Revenue, Result & Assets	Revenue, Result & Assets	Revenue	Revenue, Result & Assets

PROBLEM 5

The accountant of Parag Limited has furnished you with the following data related to its Business Divisions:

(₹ *in Lacs*)

Division	*A*	*B*	*C*	*D*	*Total*
Segment Revenue	100	300	200	400	1,000
Segment Result	45	-70	80	-10	45
Segment Assets	39	51	48	12	150

You are requested to identify the reportable segments in accordance with the criteria laid down in AS 17. **(Nov 2020)**

SOLUTION

As per AS 17 'Segment Reporting', a business segment or geographical segment should be identified as a reportable segment if:

Its revenue from sales to external customers and from other transactions with other segments is 10% or more of the total revenue- external and internal of all segments; or

Its segment result whether profit or loss is 10% or more of:

- The combined result of all segments in profit; or
- The combined result of all segments in loss,

whichever is greater in absolute amount; or

Its segment assets are 10% or more of the total assets of all segments.

On the basis of revenue criteria, segments A, B, C and D - all are reportable segments.

On the basis of the result criteria, segments A, B and C are reportable segments (since their results in absolute amount is 10% or more of 125 Lakhs).

On the basis of asset criteria, all segments except D are reportable segments.

Since all the segments are covered in at least one of the above criteria, all segments have to be reported upon in accordance with Accounting Standard (AS) 17.

PROBLEM 6

The Senior Accountant of AMF Ltd. gives the following data regarding its five segments:

(₹ *in lakhs*)

Particulars	*P* (₹)	*Q* (₹)	*R* (₹)	*S* (₹)	*T* (₹)	*Total* (₹)
Segment Assets	80	30	20	20	10	160
Segment Results	(190)	10	10	(10)	30	(150)
Segment Revenue	620	80	60	80	60	900

The Senior Accountant is of the opinion that segment "P" alone should be reported. Is he justified in his view? Examine his opinion in the light of provision of AS-17 'Segment Reporting'.

SOLUTION

As per AS 17 'Segment Reporting', a business segment or geographical segment should be identified as a reportable segment if:

(i) Its revenue from sales to external customers and from other transactions with other segments is 10% or more of the total revenue- external and internal of all segments; or

(ii) Its segment result whether profit or loss is 10% or more of:

1. The combined result of all segments in profit; or
2. The combined result of all segments in loss, whichever is greater in absolute amount; or

(iii) Its segment assets are 10% or more of the total assets of all segments.

Accordingly,

(a) On the basis of revenue from sales criteria, segment P is a reportable segment.

(b) On the basis of the result criteria, segments P & T are reportable segments (since their results in absolute amount is 10% or more of ₹ 200 Lakhs).

(c) On the basis of asset criteria, all segments except T are reportable segments.

Since all the segments are covered in at least one of the above criteria, all segments have to be reported upon in accordance with AS 17. Hence, the opinion of chief accountant that only segment 'P' is reportable is wrong.

PROBLEM 7

Mac Ltd. gives the following data regarding to its six segments:

(₹ *in lakhs*)

Particulars	*A*	*B*	*C*	*D*	*E*	*F*	*Total*
Segment assets	80	160	60	40	40	20	400
Segment results	100	(380)	20	20	(20)	60	(200)
Segment revenue	600	1,240	150	120	170	120	2,400

The accountant contends that segments 'A' and 'B' alone are reportable segments. Is he justified in his view? Discuss in the context of AS-17 'Segment Reporting'.

SOLUTION

As per AS 17 'Segment Reporting', a business segment or geographical segment should be identified as a reportable segment if:

(a) Its revenue from sales to external customers and from other transactions with other segments is 10% or more of the total revenue- external and internal of all segments; or

(b) Its segment result whether profit or loss is 10% or more of combined result of all segments in profit; or combined result of all segments in loss, whichever is greater in absolute amount; or

(c) Its segment assets are 10% or more of the total assets of all segments.

If the total external revenue attributable to reportable segments constitutes less than 75% of total enterprise revenue, additional segments should be identified as reportable segments even if they do not meet the 10% thresholds until at least 75% of total enterprise revenue is included in reportable segments.

On the basis of turnover criteria segments A and B are reportable segments.

On the basis of the result criteria, segments A, B and F are reportable segments (since their results in absolute amount is 10% or more of ₹ 400 lakhs).

On the basis of asset criteria, all segments except F are reportable segments.

Since all the segments are covered in at least one of the above criteria all segments have to be reported upon in accordance with Accounting Standard (AS) 17. Hence, the opinion of accountant is wrong.

PROBLEM 8

Prepare a Segmental Report for publication in Diversifiers Ltd. from the following details of the company's three divisions and the head office:

Particulars	*H.O. ₹ ('000)*	*Forging Shop Division ₹ ('000)*	*Bright Bar Division ₹ ('000)*	*Fitting Division ₹ ('000)*
Sales to Bright Bar Division		4575		
Other Sales (Home)		90		
Export Sales		6135	300	270
Sales to Fitting Division			45	
Pre-tax operating result		240	30	(12)
Head office cost reallocated		72	36	36
Interest costs		6	8	2
Fixed assets	75	300	60	180
Net current assets	72	180	60	135
Long-term liabilities	57	30	15	180

SOLUTION:

DIVERSIFIERS LTD. (SEGMENTAL REPORT)

(₹ '000)

Particulars	*Forging shop*	*Bright Bar*	*Fitting*	*Inter Segment Eliminations*	*Consolidated Total*
Segment Revenue					
Sales:					
Domestic	90	–	–	–	90
Export	6,135	300	270	–	6,705
External Sales	6,225	300	270	–	6,795
Inter-segment Sales	4,575	45	–	4,620	–
Total Revenue	10,800	345	270	4,620	6,795

Segment Result (given)	240	30	(12)		258
Head Office Expenses					(144)
Operating Profit					114
Interest Expense					(16)
Profit before tax					98
Information in relation to					
assets and liabilities:					
Fixed Assets	300	60	180	–	540
Net Current Assets	180	60	135	–	375
Segment Assets	480	120	315	–	915
Unallocated Corporate Assets (75 + 72)	–	–	–	–	147
Total Assets					1,062
Segment Liabilities	30	15	180	–	225
Unallocated Corporate Liabilities					57
Total Liabilities					282

SALES REVENUE BY GEOGRAPHICAL MARKET

(₹ '000)

	Home Sales	*Export Sales (by forging shop division)*	*Export Sales (by Bright Bar division)*	*Export Sales (by Fitting division)*	*Consolidated Total*
External sales	90	6,135	300	270	6,795

VERY SHORT ANSWER TYPE QUESTIONS

1. **Briefly explain the following:**

    (a) Enterprises to which AS 17 applies

    (b) Objectives of AS 17

    (c) A Business Segment as per AS 17

    (d) A Geographical Segment as per AS 17

    (e) A Reportable Segment as per AS 17

    (f) Segment Revenue as per AS 17

    (g) Segment Expense as per AS 17

    (h) Segment Assets as per AS 17

    (i) Segment Liabilities as per AS 17

    (j) Additional Segments

2. How will you Identify Reportable Segments as per AS 17?
3. What is the Treatment of Interest for determining Segment Expense as per AS 17?
4. What are the Objections to Segmental Reporting?
5. What are the Disclosures Requirements as per AS 17?
6. Can a Company have its own an inter-segment transfer pricing?

SHORT ANSWER TYPE PRACTICAL QUESTIONS

1. Identify the reportable segment by Revenue test for XYZ Ltd.(₹ in lakhs)

Particulars	*A*	*B*	*C*	*D*	*E*	*F*	*Total*
Segment Revenue	150	120	170	120	600	1,240	2,400

[Ans Reportable Segments E and F only.]

2. M/s XYZ Ltd. has three segments namely X, Y, Z. The total assets of the Company are: Segment X ₹ 6.00 crores, Segment Y ₹ 2.00 crores and Segment Z ₹ 12.00 crores. Deferred tax assets included in the assets of each Segments are X—₹ 0.80 crore, Y—₹ 1 crores and Z—₹ 0.60 crores. The accountant contends that all the three Segments are Reportable Segments as per AS 17. Comment

[Ans Reportable Segments X and Z only.]

3. Identify the reportable segment by profitability test for XYZ Ltd.

Segment	*A*	*B*	*C*	*D*	*E*
Prof it (Loss)	45	450	(30)	(360)	(210)

[Ans Reportable Segments B,D and E only.]

4. BHARAT Ltd. gives the following data regarding to its six segments:(₹ in lakhs)

Particulars	*A*	*B*	*C*	*D*	*E*	*F*	*Total*
Segment Assets	80	160	60	40	40	20	400
Segment Results	100	(380)	20	20	(20)	60	(200)
Segment Revenue	600	1,240	150	120	170	120	2,400

Identify the Reportable Segments as per AS 17.

[Ans Reportable Segments ALL.]

5. BHARAT Ltd. gives the following data regarding to its six segments:(₹ in lakhs)

Particulars	*A*	*B*	*C*	*D*	*E*	*F*	*Total*
Segment Assets	90	168	66	41	48	27	440
Segment Results	100	(380)	20	20	(20)	60	(200)
Segment Revenue	600	1,240	150	120	170	120	2,400

Deferred Tax Assets included in the assets of each Segments are A— ₹ 10 lakh, B—₹ 8 lakhs, C— ₹ 6 lakhs, D— ₹ 1 lakh, E— ₹ 8 lakhs, F — ₹ 7 lakhs. Identify the Reportable Segments as per AS 17.

[Ans Reportable Segments ALL.]

6. The Chief Accountant of TULSIAN STOCK Ltd. gives the following data regarding its six segments: ₹ In lakhs:

Particulars	*M*	*N*	*O*	*P*	*Q*	*R*	*Total*
Segment Assets	50	25	10	5	5	5	100
Segment Results	–50	–140	80	10	–10	10	–100
Segment Revenue	200	320	200	90	90	100	1000
Identify the Reportable Segments as per AS 17.							

[Ans Reportable Segments M, N, O, R only.]

7. Information relating to five segments of V Ltd. is as under: (₹ in lakhs)

Segments	A	B	C	D	E	Total
Segment Revenue	100	300	200	100	300	1000
Segment Result	40	(60)	90	10	(30)	50
Segment Assets	45	55	140	20	40	300

As a cost accountant of this company management wishes to know from you which company need to be reported.

[Ans Reportable Segments ALL.]

8. The accountant of Parag Limited has furnished you with the following data related to its Business Divisions:

(₹ in Lacs)

Division	*A*	*B*	*C*	*D*	*Total*
Segment Revenue	100	300	200	400	1,000
Segment Result	45	-70	80	-10	45
Segment Assets	39	51	48	12	150

You are requested to identify the reportable segments in accordance with the criteria laid down in AS 17.

[Ans Reportable Segments ALL.]

9. The Senior Accountant of AMF Ltd. gives the following data regarding its five segments:

(₹ in lakhs)

Particulars	*P* (₹)	*Q* (₹)	*R* (₹)	*S* (₹)	*T* (₹)	*Total* (₹)
Segment Assets	80	30	20	20	10	160
Segment Results	(190)	10	10	(10)	30	(150)
Segment Revenue	620	80	60	80	60	900

The Senior Accountant is of the opinion that segment "P" alone should be reported. Is he justified in his view? Examine his opinion in the light of provision of AS-17 'Segment Reporting'.

[Ans Reportable Segments ALL.]

10. Mac Ltd. gives the following data regarding to its six segments:

(₹ in lakhs)

Particulars	*A*	*B*	*C*	*D*	*E*	*F*	*Total*
Segment Assets	80	160	60	40	40	20	400
Segment Results	100	(380)	20	20	(20)	60	(200)
Segment Revenue	600	1,240	150	120	170	120	2,400

The accountant contends that segments 'A' and 'B' alone are reportable segments. Is he justified in his view? Discuss in the context of AS-17 'Segment Reporting'.

[Ans Reportable Segments ALL.**]**